EUROPE SINCE 1815

EUROPE
SINCE
1815

GORDON A. CRAIG

STANFORD UNIVERSITY

HOLT, RINEHART AND WINSTON

NEW YORK

To

Susan,

Deborah,

and

Martha.

PREFACE

In the pages that follow I have tried to write a clear and readable account of European history since Waterloo, and one that embodies the results of recent historical scholarship and makes use of the important contributions to historical analysis that have been made by scholars in related disciplines in the humanities and the social sciences.

In going about my work, I have not followed the method, that is sometimes employed, of increasing the scope and detail of the narrative progressively as it approaches the present time. It was my feeling that to do so would be less than respectful to the scholars who have done so much within the last generation to add to our knowledge of the nineteenth century, while it would tend also to confuse students and deprive them of the kind of understanding of the past that would help them understand the problems of their own time. An attempt has been made here, therefore, to maintain a decent balance between the period before 1870, the years that stretch from then until the end of the first World War, and the period since 1918.

Since war and diplomacy bulk so large in our minds today, they are treated somewhat less perfunctorily here than was usual in older accounts of this period. I have tried, however, to indicate the intimate relationship that exists between these and other aspects of history.

Finally, throughout this account, I have been guided by the conviction that men are as important as ideas and have done my best to prevent the human beings in my story from being lost in a welter of tendencies, developments, motive forces, and basic factors.

This book is divided into five sections, each prefaced, for the convenience of the student, with a few pages of general comment upon the principal events and developments that are discussed in the chapters that follow. These "General Observations" are intended, however, as introductions, rather than as summaries.

The enjoyment I have had in writing this book has been exceeded by the pleasure and stimulation derived from talking about it with friends. Without naming names, I should like to express my gratitude to all those who have helped me with their advice and criticism, especially to my colleagues at the Center for Advanced Study in the Behavioral Sciences during the academic year 1956–1957, to the staff and fellows of the Center of International Studies, Princeton University, and, above all, to my colleagues in the Department of History and my graduate and undergraduate students at that university.

Princeton, N. J.   *G. A. C.*
April 15, 1961

CONTENTS

PART ONE: 1815–1850

PART FIVE: Since 1945

PART ONE

1815

1850

GENERAL OBSERVATIONS

Because our own age has been marked by bitter international rivalry and continual preoccupation with war, it is perhaps understandable that whenever we think of the general characteristics of an earlier period, we are apt to turn our attention first to *the state of international politics* during it. Regarded from this point of view, the years that stretch from 1815 to 1848 seem almost, in comparison with our own time, to have formed a golden age of harmony. There was no major conflict between the Great Powers of Europe, indeed, no war of any kind in which Great Powers were ranged against each other as enemies; and fewer Europeans died as a result of international war during these three and a half decades than in any comparable period since 1848.

Why were the European states able in the years after the Congress of Vienna to rise above their conflicting interests and their ideological differences and to resolve their disputes without going to war? Partly, no doubt, because after their long struggle against Napoleon, they were agreed that war was an unpleasant and unprofitable business which should be avoided wherever possible. But this is hardly a complete explanation, for wars are as often the result of blundering as they are of deliberate intent. It is more accurate to say that peace among the Great Powers was the result of a happy combination of determination to avoid war, self-restraint when opportunities for unilateral aggrandizement presented themselves, and skillful diplomacy. With respect to the last of these, the years from 1815 to 1848 were perhaps the last years in the modern period in which the pen was recognizably mightier than the sword; and twentieth-century statesmen could do much worse than to study the methods of the diplomats of this period.

Because Europe was free of wars between the powers, it does not follow that these were entirely peaceful years, for they were not. The political and territorial settlement that had been effected at Vienna in 1814–1815 was not, after all, universally admired. Its most inveterate opponents were those who claimed that it violated what we would today call the principle of national self-determination. Believing that men who shared a common history, language, and culture should be permitted to form independent political units (or nations) under rulers of their own choice, these critics argued that the Vienna settlement denied this right to such peoples as the Belgians, the Germans, the Italians, the Poles, and the Greeks. If they themselves happened to be Belgians or Germans or Italians or Poles or Greeks, they often attempted to correct what they considered to be the deficiencies of the treaties, by means of propaganda, or agitation, or even resort to force.

The *nationalism* that inspired their efforts had little of the narrow arrogance or the frenetic jingoism that was to characterize nationalistic movements in the second half of the century. Early nineteenth century nationalism was animated by an ardent, if idealistic, belief that a Europe based on truly national lines—that is, composed entirely of free nations— would be a healthier and a more peaceful Europe than one in which there were still subject nationalities living under alien rule. Granted the enlightened nature of this philosophy—which was preached by such disparate personalities as Mazzini and Napoleon III—attempts to apply it were usually violent in nature and unhappy in result.

Another and closely related source of turbulence in this period was the continuous struggle between the *conservatism* of the ruling classes of the various European states and the *liberalism* of the educated, professional, and commercial classes. Liberalism, as the word indicates, was a philosophy of freedom, and its adherents—whether in Spain or England, in Austria or France—wished to free the individual from the absolute control of his government and to secure fundamental liberties (like freedom of speech and assembly) for all citizens and a share in political power for a greater number than were permitted to participate in politics under the old regime. To the ruling classes of post-Vienna Europe, whose conservatism was for the most part a completely negative philosophy based on a panicky fear of revolution and an aversion to change of any kind, these liberal objectives were too repellent to admit of compromise. This inflexible opposition to even moderate proposals of reform, and the attempted persecution of the would-be reformers which often accompanied it, had the result of forcing the liberals (as they came to be called) to resort to underground activity, conspiracy, and, ultimately, revolution. Throughout this period, indeed, there was some kind of *coup de main* or insurrection somewhere in Europe every two or three years, while major explosions, affecting several national capitals, occurred in 1820, 1830, and 1848. These uprisings did not always advance the cause of freedom; and they frequently jeopardized the peace that diplomacy was so bent on preserving, since their repercussions could not always be confined within the borders of the countries in which they took place.

Another development which contributed to the agitation of the period was the steady *expansion of machine industry*. The speed with which Europe was conquered by the machine should not, of course, be over-estimated. Throughout the period under review the economy—even of England—remained primarily agrarian, as is demonstrated by the fact that all the economic crises before 1850 had their origins in agricultural disorders of one kind or another. The only sizable industrial area outside England in the two decades after 1815 was in Belgium, where English methods and techniques were introduced into the textile industry and began to transform the extractive and metallurgical industries as well. In France, significant industrial development did not get under way until after 1830, while in countries further east it came even later.

Nevertheless, as the period proceeded, industrial expansion was en-couraged by several factors. With the population of Europe increasing from 187,693,000 in 1800 to 282,893,000 in 1860, industry was provided not only with the labor force it needed but with large numbers of poten-tial customers as well. Currency reforms, the establishment of central banks to control the issue of paper money, and the encouragement of investment by new company and insurance laws made available the capital without which industrial growth would have been impossible. The revolution in transportation effected by the improvement and expansion of highways and canals, the promotion by all European governments of railroad construction, which began on a large scale in the 1840s, and the increasing use of steam transport in rivers and coastal waters and on the high seas improved access to raw materials and markets. Finally, industrial growth benefited from the removal of artificial hindrances to commercial intercourse by such things as the establishment of the Prussian Customs Union and the repeal of the Corn Laws by the British government in 1846. Thanks to these developments, conditions in all European countries —even in Russia, which was still virtually unaffected by the technological progress of the west—were infinitely more favorable for industrial expansion at the end of this period than they had been in 1815.

Moreover, if the scope and magnitude of industrialism was still small by twentieth-century standards, it was sufficiently great to contribute to the unrest of the age. This can be seen even in the sphere of foreign affairs, where industrial development sometimes complicated existing diplomatic problems or created new ones. There is little doubt that both Belgian opposition to Dutch domination in the years leading to 1830 and Lombard opposition to Austrian suzerainty throughout the whole period were rooted in conflicts of interest between the industrialists of the sub-ject and the governing states.

Equally significant were the *changes in social structure* which the expansion of the industrial economy made inevitable. Land, which had

formerly been the basis of social organization in all European states, became less important as industrialism advanced, and capital began slowly
to take its place. Simultaneously, the old division of society into nobility,
clergy, and commons began to break down. The position of the nobles
and their clerical allies was challenged by an emergent and self-confident
bourgeoisie, which made its way in life by the accumulation and manipulation of money and which believed that, to its economic power, political
and social power must be added. The distinction between the upper and
lower bourgeoisie or middle class, which was to assume great significance
later in the century, was not yet obvious and, until the 1840s, the most
striking characteristic of the bourgeoisie was unity of view and purpose.
In politics, they were for the most part militantly liberal; in social
attitude, they were in general agreement that the upper classes—that
is, the older entrenched classes—must be put down. For this very reason,
they were supported by the peasants, the artisans, and the industrial
workers. Economically vulnerable and without direction, these groups
accepted middle-class leadership and participated in all the political
struggles of this period; and it is doubtful whether the July revolution in
France or the fight for the Great Reform Bill in England could have been
successful without their support.

This combination of forces was not destined to last. On the one hand,
the working classes discovered that the victories won by it brought
greater material benefits to the middle class than to themselves, and the
discovery led to disillusionment and resentment. On the other hand, the
bourgeoisie, always uncomfortable with their lower-class allies, grew
alarmed over the increasingly radical nature of the reforms desired by
them. The truth of the matter was, as the revolutions of 1848 were to
show, that there was no real community of interest between the middle
and lower classes. The lower classes were, by instinct, believers in the
kind of *political democracy* that would give the vote to every man,
as well as in a rudimentary *socialism* that held that it was the duty of
the government to improve the lot of the lower classes by economic and
social reform. These ideas were anathema to middle-class liberals who
believed that political power should be restricted to the propertied and
educated classes and that the healthiest societies were those in which
government intervened least in economic and social matters. It was no
accident that classes with such contradictory conviction should have
ceased to be allies.

As this happened, the homogeneity of the middle class itself began to
break down and its wealthiest members—because of their fear of the
working class but also as a result of the social opportunities which their
riches brought them—began to modify their formerly hostile attitude
toward the old aristocracy. By 1848 there were already indications that

the future would bring an alliance, if not a merger, between the older ruling class and the upper bourgeoisie, and that the less wealthy bourgeoisie would find itself as a middle group between the working class and a new aristo-plutocracy. In any case, the stratification of society had, in all countries, become much less simple and clear cut than it was in 1815, while conflict between classes—upon which Karl Marx placed so much emphasis in *The Communist Manifesto* in 1848—had greatly increased in intensity.

Despite all the nationalist risings and liberal agitations and the economic and social dislocations that industrialism brought in its train, these things were not enough to absorb the energy of the peoples of Europe completely. These were rich and exciting years in literature and the arts, for this is the period in which the movement known as *romanticism* reached its height. It would be difficult to find a universally satisfactory definition for this term, which has been used to characterize the work of such different people as Chateaubriand, Coleridge, Berlioz, Pushkin, Manzoni, and Delacroix. It is perhaps better merely to say, as Irving Babbitt once said, that, in literature and the arts, romanticism was a revolt against classicism, which seemed (at least to romantics) to stifle all that was creative and spontaneous in artistic expression, and that, in a more general sense, it was an intellectual reaction against the rationalism and the sometimes barren logic of the eighteenth century. It was marked by a high degree of emotionalism; and, when one considers the great number of romantics who had visions or passed through religious frenzies or saw apparitions or were haunted by *Doppelgänger* or professed satanism, it is easy to understand why conservative critics held that romanticism was a malady similar to sleepwalking or epilepsy. It was characterized also by an exaggerated cult of nature and an excessive veneration of the remote past, as well as by an amazing amount of cloudy talk about solving the riddle of the universe and bridging the gulf between the real and the ideal. With all that, it was a lively and a fertile movement which, as later chapters will attempt to show, produced a lot of good painting and music and poetry and had a healthy influence in other fields beside those of the arts and literature.

There can be little doubt, for instance, that the interest in the past that was awakened by romanticism helped revitalize historical studies. The new appreciation of the organic development of society made men curious about the origins of their own institutions and customs and this promoted research into the past, while simultaneously stimulating archaeology, philology, legal studies, and philosophy as well. It is surely not without significance that the most influential philosopher of this period, Georg Friedrich Hegel, and his most illustrious disciple, Karl

Marx, should have placed such emphasis in their systems upon historical evolution and the laws that guide it.

Because romanticism was so rich and varied a movement, the political views of its adherents were marked by extreme diversity. The movement was one of the most important forces that fed the nationalism of the age, for one of the offshoots of the new interest in the past was national pride and self-consciousness. At the same time, romanticism was a European movement that forged close ties between its followers with little concern for their nationality and thus contributed as much to the spread of internationalism as the reverse. In the same way, although many of the best-known representatives of the movement were conservative and even reactionary in their views in the first years after the Vienna Congress, Stendhal noted in his diary in 1827 that romanticism was becoming the cult of liberal and democratic youth.

The revulsion against the rationalism of the eighteenth century which we find expressed in the romantic movement is seen also in the marked revival, among the intellectuals of this age and the upper classes, of *religion*. Those romantics who were enthusiastic about Gothic cathedrals discovered new enthusiasm for the faith those cathedrals had been built to celebrate. At the same time, an aristocracy whose position had been almost fatally shaken by the French revolution was no longer as tolerant of free thought as it had been in the previous century, but was inclined to regard religious orthodoxy as a valuable—indeed, a necessary—reinforcement of existing institutions.

It is doubtful whether the return to the faith of either of these groups helped the churches in the long run. The romantic intellectuals who were most vocal about their new faith placed more emphasis upon the trappings than upon the essentials of religion; and their enthusiasm was so excessive as to bring ridicule upon its object. More serious was the fact that the religiosity of court and aristocratic circles placed a conservative, if not reactionary, stamp upon the churches which they found hard to shake off at a later date when they were under attack. This was unfortunate because, as a matter of fact, the churches were not one-sidedly conservative in the period before 1848, as the vigorous controversies between liberal and conservative groups inside both the Roman Catholic and the Protestant churches show.

In general, the major religions showed every indication of strength and vigor, and religion was practiced by the great majority of the population. Industrialism and urbanization had not yet advanced so far as to weaken the ties that bound the masses to their traditional faith. As for the bourgeoisie, they were still, for the most part, churchgoers; and even the most doctrinaire liberals among them—who kept up a drumfire of

criticism against religious obscurantism and church influence in education—did not deny that the churches had a legitimate and important role
to play in society.

With respect to *education,* the period was not distinguished by notable
advances. With some exceptions, the governments of Europe neither
made elementary education compulsory nor made it possible for the
children of the poor to attend existing schools. As late as 1835 three
Englishmen in ten could neither read nor write, and the situation was
worse in most parts of the continent. As the years passed, the spread of
industrialism was going to make the extension of popular education
necessary (since machines require literate operators) and possible (by
producing inexpensive books and bringing the masses into urban
centers). But that time was not yet; and when one thinks of the appalling
ignorance of the masses in these years, he finds it easier to understand
why both the aristocracy and the middle classes feared and opposed
democracy.

This dark picture is somewhat alleviated by the flourishing state of
institutions of higher learning in this period. It is perhaps true that
some of the older universities—Oxford and Cambridge, for example, and
the provincial universities of France—seemed content to rest on their
laurels, but the Scottish universities, the newly founded universities in
Berlin and Munich, the Collège de France in Paris, and many others
that might be named were centers of intellectual vitality, inspired
teaching, and enthusiastic scholarship. With respect to scholarship, some
of the fields in which notable advances were made have been mentioned
above. To these several others can be added in which revolutionary work
was accomplished by university savants: mathematics and astronomy,
where the work of Gauss of Göttingen and Leverrier of Paris pushed forward the frontiers of knowledge; physics, where the German Robert
Mayer laid the foundations of thermodynamics, and where the first basic
work in the practical application of electricity was done by the
Scandinavian Oersted, the Frenchman Ampère, and the Englishman
Faraday; chemistry, where Berzelius of Stockholm carried on the work
begun by Lavoisier and Davy and where Justus Liebig began his great
work at Giessen toward the end of this period. In geology and in biology
and its related sciences fewer basic discoveries were made, but here, too,
research activity was systematic and energetic.

A special word concerning *medicine* may be added, for the period of
which we are talking has been described as that in which modern
medicine emerged. This does not seem exaggerated if one remembers
the solid achievements of these years: the progress made toward a
localized pathology, the improvement of diagnostic methods by such
things as the invention of the stethoscope, Pierre Louis' demonstration of

the value of medical statistics, the discovery of the uses of morphine and the isolation of strychnine and quinine, the beginning of serious experimentation with clinical thermometry and anesthesia, and the intensive study of cell structure made possible by the introduction of the achromatic microscope in the 1830s.

These accomplishments of European science and their practical applications were, like other European ideas and institutions, communicated to the outside world and inspired the developments which in the course of the century were to Europeanize the globe. In this connection European ideas were carried to the distant corners of the earth not only by the merchant and by the missionary but also by the *colonial activities* of the governments. This was not, to be sure, a period in which the expansion of European possessions overseas was even remotely comparable to that which was to take place in the fourth quarter of the century; and there was no great enthusiasm for colonial acquisition. But, although these were the years when Spain and Portugal lost their American empires, these setbacks were offset by British and Russian advances in the Middle and Far East and the establishment of the French empire in North Africa.

In his memoirs, the old and disappointed Chateaubriand wrote of his age: "After Napoleon nothing!" Yet this was a period crowded with developments as worthy of note as any of Napoleon's triumphs. Happily free from the ravages of large-scale war, it was characterized by political and intellectual ferment, economic growth, scientific progress, and literary and artistic vitality. It might be more accurate to describe it, as Victor Hugo did, as "a magnificent epoch . . . the virile age of mankind."

1

The Great Powers and the Balance of Power, 1815-1848

THE RECONSTRUCTION OF EUROPE, 1814–1815

The Great Powers and the Postwar Decisions / In March 1814 Austrian cavalry clattered over the cobblestones of Paris, and Prussian grenadiers bivouacked on the heights of Montmartre. An unaccustomed quiet settled over the country. After a brief but spirited struggle at the Clichy Gate, the organized resistance of French armies had collapsed, and Marshals Mortier and Marmont had capitulated to the Allies. At Fontainebleau Napoleon sat, almost alone, still grimly holding on to an imperial title that would have little meaning in the exile to which he was soon to be consigned. The Corsican still had one desperate throw to make but in reality his day was done. After a quarter of a century of almost continuous war, revolutionary and imperialistic France, which had dominated the continent under Napoleon's leadership, had been defeated by Europe.

But what—or rather, who—was Europe? For all practical purposes, Europe meant the four states which, like France, were considered—by virtue of their military, economic, and other resources—to be great powers and which had done most to defeat Napoleon. It is true, of course, that many states and peoples had contributed to the combined efforts that gradually sapped the strength of Bonaparte's armies; one thinks immediately of the Spanish guerrilla bands or those South German patriots who died with Andreas Hofer. But essentially the victory had been won by the Great Powers and by the Grand Alliance that they had finally succeeded in forming in the spring of 1813. And now, in deciding the thorny questions involved in the process of restoring peace to the wartorn continent, those same Great Powers took the initiative and exercised preponderant, if not exclusive, influence.

The First Peace of Paris / From the outset, they recognized that there were two different jobs that had to be done before Europe could return to a peace footing. They had, first, to put a definitive end to hostilities by making some kind of arrangement with the defeated enemy, France. They had, in the second place, to reduce the confusion and disorder and solve the dynastic and territorial problems that had been created all over Europe by the collapse of the Napoleonic empire.

The first of these tasks was the easier and was completed with dispatch. The Allied powers were no longer willing to tolerate Napoleon's continued presence on the throne of France. They had, therefore, to find a successor for him, and they decided—after an inconclusive consideration of such candidates as his son and the Swedish prince Bernadotte, who had won the favor of the tsar of Russia—that the easiest and most logical thing to do was to restore the old dynasty, the House of Bourbon, in the person of Louis XVIII. Once it had been agreed to place this representative of the old Europe on the throne, the Allies had the good sense to see that it would be illogical to saddle him with a punitive peace, which would probably delay the return of the security and repose that they so strongly desired.

The terms of the treaty concluded with Louis XVIII in May 1814—the so-called First Peace of Paris—were, therefore, lenient. France lost its holdings in Italy, Germany, and the Low Countries, as well as such colonial possessions at Tobago, Santa Lucia, and Ile de France, which were ceded to Great Britain, and part of San Domingo, which was handed over to Spain. But these losses were no more than had been expected. On the other hand, France not only was permitted to keep the boundaries that it had had in January 1792 but was allowed to take over certain enclaves that had not formerly belonged to it. Moreover, despite some British interest in the idea of an indemnity to pay the costs of the war and strong Prussian demands that France be forced to restore certain monies extorted from the German states by Napoleon, the new French king let it be known that he was inflexibly opposed to any financial impositions and would submit to arrest rather than pay them. This firmness so impressed the Allies that they dropped the idea of financial reparations. They did not, in the end, even insist that France return the art treasures that Napoleon's agents had systematically looted from the museums of Europe.

The signing of the treaty marked the successful conclusion of the first phase of the reconstruction of Europe. The opening of the second phase, in which a general settlement was to be negotiated, was announced in one of the last paragraphs of the Paris Peace, which read: "All the Powers engaged on either side in the present war shall, within the space of two months, send Plenipotentiaries to Vienna for the purpose of regulating, in General Congress, the arrangements which are to complete the provisions of the present Treaty."

The Congress of Vienna: Organization / The first thing that has to be remembered about the Congress of Vienna is that it never met as a congress or deliberative body at all. Probably the only occasions on which anything like a majority of the delegates of the states represented at Vienna assembled in one place were ceremonial ones—at the innumerable receptions, reviews, fetes, and tournaments held for the entertainment of the notables who poured into Vienna in the last months of 1814. But there was nothing in the nature of a diplomatic assembly at which the great territorial questions and other issues affecting the future of Europe could be debated. If the term Congress of Vienna means anything at all, it refers only to the totality of negotiations that took place in the Austrian capital during the eight months following October 1, 1814.

These negotiations were controlled by the Great Powers. Indeed, if they could have managed it, the four Allied Powers would have settled everything before they ever came to Vienna and would simply have asked the other states to ratify their decisions. But, although there was almost continuous consultation between them during the three months that followed the conclusion of the Paris Peace, they were unable to agree on such thorny questions as the way in which the map was to be redrawn; and, when they arrived in Vienna at the end of September, their real work was just beginning. In the long run, this did not make much difference in the way in which things were done at Vienna. Decisions on the important territorial questions the four Powers reserved to themselves, although they eventually decided to admit France to their inner circle, partly to mediate their own differences of view, partly to prevent the French representative Talleyrand from organizing the lesser states into an anti-Great-Power bloc. To occupy the lesser powers and to ease their susceptibilities, there were ten special committees (on German affairs, on international rivers, and the like), while three of their number

(Spain, Portugal, and Sweden) sat with the great powers on a Committee of Eight. This last body, however, met infrequently and accomplished little.

The delegations of the five Great Powers were strong and included some of the ablest negotiators of the nineteenth century. Chief among them was Clemens Prince Metternich, the Austrian foreign minister, whose carefully timed swing from alliance with Napoleon to union with his enemies had assured the success of the Grand Alliance and, at the same time, made his country its leader. Metternich was an inordinately vain man, who found it impossible to believe that he was capable of mistakes. "I say to myself twenty times a day," he once confessed, "how right I am and how wrong the others are. And yet it is so *easy* to be right." He could also be intolerably dull and pompous, especially when discoursing on his own excellent qualities. Yet he had become minister of foreign affairs in 1809 at the age of 36 and he continued in the post until 1848, a term unequaled by any other European diplomat in the modern period and one which indicates that Metternich possessed uncommon political gifts. Sir Llewellyn Woodward has written that his greatest talent was a "sensitiveness to the existence of general European interests." Far from being a narrow nationalist, he believed that the conflicting interests of national states should be reconciled in the interests of general peace and stability; and he showed genius in producing the formulas that made such reconciliation possible.

Metternich's interest in European stability and in reconciling the interests of the powers was shared by the chief British delegate, Foreign Secretary Viscount Castlereagh. A shy and reserved man, the object of misunderstanding and even persistent denigration in his own country (when he died a suicide in 1822, some of his critics, including the poet Shelley, rejoiced in a wholly indecent manner), Castlereagh was certainly one of the great foreign secretaries of the modern era. It was largely because of his untiring efforts that the Grand Alliance had been able to survive the jealousy and mutual suspicion that had threatened to destroy it before Napoleon was definitively beaten. Now, he wished to restore the kind of balance of power in Europe that would give security and peace to all its members.

Both Metternich and Castlereagh had more freedom of decision than their Russian and Prussian colleagues, for those diplomats had to take account of the desires and prejudices of their sovereigns, who were present and active in Vienna. Thus, the Russian foreign minister, Nesselrode, whose views were "European" in the same sense that Castlereagh's and Metternich's were, had constantly to defer to the whims of his monarch, Tsar Alexander I. Alexander was a neurotic and possibly a schizophrenic. He went through life haunted by a sense of guilt incurred when he was elevated to the throne over the murdered corpse of his father, and his attempts to escape from this by posing alternately as the scourge and the savior of Europe, by indulging in paroxysms of idealistic reform and frenzies of sexual excess, and, finally, by giving his support to experiments in religious mysticism, failed to ease his troubled spirit or to prevent his eventual collapse, ten years after Vienna, into the depths of manic depression. At Vienna Alexander was still a handsome, vigorous, and charming man, but he was also at his most volatile and unpredictable, changing his policies and his close advisors from day to day.

The Prussian delegation was headed by Prince Hardenberg who, because of his advancing years and growing deafness, was assisted by Wilhelm von Humboldt, the former minister of culture who had been chiefly responsible for founding the University of Berlin in 1810. The two men did not get along well, which did not make for efficiency in negotiation. In addition, while Hardenberg was more successful than Nesselrode in influencing the views of his king, the melancholy Frederick William III, he did not succeed in preventing him from following his natural inclination, which was to side with the Russians rather more than was politic. Humboldt, like many German diplomats since his time, proved to be an indefatigable and efficient organizer, whose well-trained staff produced dozens of memoranda that usually turned out to be in support of Prussian claims. As a German historian has written, all

Congress of Vienna, 1814–1815, an engraving from a painting by the French portraitist Jean Baptiste Isabey (1767–1855). Castlereagh is sitting with his legs crossed almost in the center of the picture and is looking toward Metternich, who is standing and pointing to him. In the right foreground sits Talleyrand, with his arm on the table. (THE BETTMANN ARCHIVE)

this energy merely strengthened the impression that the Prussians were both boring and greedy—a conclusion that was not wholly fair.

Finally, hovering on the sidelines at all the levées and balls in Vienna and never absent when great matters were to be decided was the chief of the French delegation, with his badly powdered hair and his club foot, his pendulous lips, and his lusterless but mocking eyes, Talleyrand-Périgord, Prince of Benevento. This was the man who had survived all the perilous storms of the revolution by knowing exactly when it was necessary to change sides, who had served and betrayed Napoleon, who had played a leading part in persuading the Allies to give the succession to the French throne to Louis XVIII, and who was to go on his blithe way for another fifteen years, finally ending a fantastically varied career as Louis Philippe's ambassador in London in 1830. One is never quite certain what Talleyrand's motives were at any given moment; but it would be unfair to him to deny that regard for his country and her national interest was among the strongest of the forces that determined his devious course. Because he believed, further, that France's best interest was to be served by recognizing the legitimate interests of others and by maintaining relations with them on the basis of reciprocal respect, Talleyrand had a point of contact with Metternich and Castlereagh which proved not without importance in the Vienna negotiations.

The Vienna Settlement: Basic Principles / It has been said that the territorial settlement reached at Vienna was based upon three principles: compensation for the victors, legitimacy, and balance of power. Provided too much is not made of these labels, they are useful in illustrating the main features of the Vienna treaties.

Despite their willingness to forego financial reparation from France, the great powers expected some form of *compensation* for their costly efforts against Napoleon, and they thought principally in terms of territorial expansion. Great Britain was no exception. If its representatives seemed to be more disinterested at Vienna than other delegates, this was only because they knew that their country had gotten most of what it wanted before the negotiations began. In the course of the wars, the British had seized such strategic outposts as Helgoland in the North Sea, Malta and the Ionian Islands in the Mediterranean, Cape Colony in South Africa, and Ceylon, Ile de France, Demerara, St. Lucia, Tobago, and Trinidad. These they retained.

The British gains were far exceeded by those of Austria. Metternich took advantage of the general reshuffling of territory that was taking place to disembarrass his country of certain of her former possessions in Belgium and South Germany, which were too far away for efficient administration or military defense; but, in place of them, he won the rich and conveniently situated provinces of Lombardy and Venetia in northern Italy. Austria also regained its Polish possessions and gained territory in the Tyrol and in Illyria, on the eastern coast of the Adriatic. All in all, by the end of the Vienna negotiations, Austria had a population four or five million larger than it had been in 1792.

The process of adjusting the great powers' claims for compensation was not always amicable and sometimes involved bitter quarreling. The territorial ambitions of Prussia and Russia, for instance, caused a very ugly crisis in December 1814.

Russia was already assured of the possession of Finland, which it had conquered from Sweden, and of Bessarabia and other territories which it had taken from the Turks, but Alexander wanted more. He burned to win new renown by standing before Europe as the restorer of the ancient kingdom of Poland (with the understanding, of course, that that kingdom, once restored, would be placed under Russian control), and therefore, demanded that Napoleon's Grand Duchy of Warsaw, which had included the Polish districts formerly belonging to Austria and Prussia, be handed over to him so that he might join them to his own Polish holdings. The Prussians were willing to give up their Polish territory if they were indemnified elsewhere. They proposed that suitable compensation would be the Kingdom of Saxony, a populous and wealthy country that lay immediately south of Prussia. Alexander, remembering that the king of Saxony had remained loyal to Napoleon until after the battle of Leipzig, agreed that Saxony was fair game for the Prussians; and the Russian and Prussian delegations henceforth supported each other's claims.

Neither Austria nor Great Britain was very happy about this. Both powers were concerned over Alexander's Polish project, which would enormously enhance Russian power in central Europe. In addition, Metternich feared that, if he permitted Prussia to annex Saxony, he would be attacked by rivals for his position on the ground that he had increased Prussian influence in the affairs of Germany at the expense of his own country. Castlereagh had no real objection to Prussia's gaining territory, but he preferred to have it do so on the Rhine, where Prussian forces could, if necessary, be employed to prevent new adventures on the part of France. Both Castlereagh and Metternich were irritated by the intimate collaboration between the Russians and the Prussians and by the defiant and even menacing attitude they had adopted toward their allies. As their irritation grew, relations between the two sets of powers became so strained that, by the end of December, armed conflict between them did not seem unlikely.

This situation gave Talleyrand an opportunity to make the most startling coup of the Congress. For the sake of France's future position in Europe, he was anxious to end its isolation in face of the union of the other Powers. He now took advantage of their differences to propose that England and Austria conclude a secret alliance with France, by which the three powers undertook to resist Prusso-Russian pretensions by force of arms if necessary. Perhaps to his surprise, certainly to his delight, Castlereagh and Metternich agreed immediately, and the alliance was concluded in January 1815.

On the part of Metternich, who had no desire to resume hostilities, the promise to do so if necessary was probably bluff; but, if so, it called the bluff of the other side. For Alexander was in no position to go to war either, since his troops were disorganized and disaffected and many of his officers out of sympathy with his European plans. As a result of the secret treaty—the existence and purpose of which were soon known to everyone in Vienna—the crisis between the powers vanished, and an elaborate patching up followed which pleased everybody but the Prussians. The tsar was permitted to take the greater part of the Grand Duchy of Warsaw, but Prussia and Austria retained some of their Polish districts, and Cracow was made a free city. The king of Saxony remained on his throne and kept possession of his two most important cities, Dresden and Leipzig. The Prussians were, it is true, given almost half of Saxony, in addition to Swedish Pomerania and extensive holdings in the Rhineland; but this did not prevent their soldiers from grumbling that the diplomats were giving away all the fruits of victory.

Once the Polish-Saxon crisis was overcome and their own ambitions satisfied, the powers turned their attention to the arrangements that had to be made in the other liberated areas. Here, when it seemed expedient, they observed the principle of *legitimacy*, a term invented by Talleyrand and, in its widest sense, meaning that the rights of the pre-Napoleonic rulers of European states should be respected and their thrones restored to them if they had lost them in the course of the wars. The principle, however, was not applied automatically or consistently. The powers recognized that there was little point in restoring German states that had ceased to exist as far back as 1803, and they ignored legitimacy also in the case of Italian states that had disappeared before 1798. Nor did they allow legitimacy to worry them while they were making their own acquisitions.

They were more consistent in their application of the principle of the *balance of power*, of which Metternich, Castlereagh, and Talleyrand were devoted and eloquent champions. To each of them, balance of power meant what it had generally meant in the eighteenth century: an equilibrium of forces between the Great Powers of such a nature as to discourage unilateral aggression on the part of any of them. Talleyrand was more skeptical than his two associates concerning the possibility of ever attaining more than a precarious equilibrium, and he held that the only true preventive of aggression was a spirit of moderation and justice on the part of the powers. Metternich and Castlereagh, on the other hand, tended to think in almost mathematical terms and to seek an equilibrium of territory, population, and resources that would reduce the danger of war to a minimum.

It was this that determined the course they took in all matters of Great Power compensation—Castlereagh, for instance, holding that, if Russia increased its Polish holdings, both Prussia and Austria must be given equivalent accretions of strength even if this necessitated violations of legitimacy. Their attitude on the German and Italian questions and on that of the Low Countries was inspired by the same desire to construct an equilibrium that would not be easily shaken.

In the Low Countries, the Belgians were united, much against their will, with their northern neighbors and placed under the rule of the House of Orange, largely because it was hoped that this arrangement might serve as an additional barrier against a possibly resurgent France. Germany was left divided among thirty-six separate states, because any other solution would have complicated relations between the powers, whereas it was believed that a disunited block of territory in Central Europe might serve them as a kind of shock absorber. This is what Wilhelm von Humboldt meant when he said that Germany's "true and actual purpose [was] to secure peace, and its whole existence [was] therefore based upon a preservation of balance through an inherent force of gravity." Finally, in Italy, while the king of Piedmont and the pope regained, and even enlarged, their territories, and while it was decided in principle that the Kingdom of the Two Sicilies should be restored to the House of Bourbon, Austria not only was given Lombardy and Venetia but was permitted to extend its influence over the northern duchies of Parma, Modena, Lucca, and Tuscany. Here again the purpose was partly to keep Austrian strength in balance with that of the other powers and partly to place it in a position to make impossible a new French assault on Italy.

It was once the custom to regard the diplomats of the Congress of Vienna as "reactionaries" who wanted to "turn the clock back" and who "flouted the principles of nationalism." Rather than accept these stereotypes, it would be more logical to think of them as men who had an enormously difficult job to do and who accomplished it in a way that satisfied the great majority of the people affected by their decisions. In their work, they were often surprisingly enlightened: in their stipulation that all members of the Germanic Confederation should establish assemblies of estates, for instance, in their guarantee of Switzerland's neutrality and independence, and in their condemnation of the slave trade. In redrawing the map of Europe, they showed that they were not insensible to changes that had taken place since the beginning of the French Revolution; and both the German and Italian settlements prove this. That they did not recognize or try to apply the principle of nationality should not seem strange. They felt that chaos would ensue if attempts were made to free the Italians or unite the Germans in 1815; and they were probably right. Finally, before the Vienna settlement is condemned, it should be noted that it did, in fact, provide a reasonable equilibrium among the Great Powers. It left no power seriously aggrieved and, thus, cannot be said to have contained in its provisions the seeds of a future major war. That in itself was a major accomplishment and deserves recognition.

The Hundred Days and the Second Peace of Paris / While the last details of the settlement were being worked out, the world was electrified by the news that Napoleon had escaped from his exile in Elba, had landed in France, and had seized the throne left vacant by Louis XVIII, who had fled at the first news of his coming. Bonaparte doubtless hoped to split the Allies and defeat them separately, but, if so, he was disappointed. The worst of the differences between the Allies were over before his adventure started; and his return restored the brotherhood in arms that defeated him at Leipzig in 1813. The Corsican, therefore, had only one hundred days of restored power, and their result was the crushing defeat at Waterloo and a new and final exile on St. Helena. For France the consequences were even more serious, for Napoleon's last campaign destroyed most of what Talleyrand had accomplished at Vienna.

There was no longer any disposition on the part of the Allies to spare France the penalties usually imposed on defeated powers; nor were they much concerned about the feelings of Louis XVIII. That monarch was put back on the throne again, but this time over a smaller realm. The Second Peace of Paris (November 20, 1815) deprived France of a number of strategic posts in the north and east and reduced its over-all territory in such a way that it lost about half a million subjects. Moreover, it now had to pay a war indemnity of 700 million francs—by contemporary standards, a heavy burden—and to support an army of occupation for a minimum of three years. Despite all of Talleyrand's efforts at Vienna, his country was now isolated again and regarded with distrust and fear.

The Holy Alliance and the Concert of Europe / At the end of 1815 the powers signed two other engagements that had importance in the future: the Holy Alliance and the Quadruple Alliance.

The Holy Alliance was conceived by Alexander I and, in its original form, seems to have been an attempt to establish a new international order that would be based not on traditional diplomacy but on the principles of Christianity. Castlereagh refused to have anything to do with it. "The fact is," he wrote to his prime minister, "that the Emperor's mind is not completely sound." The Prussians and Austrians were less willing to offend Alexander by turning his project down; and, in the end, they signed, after Metternich had won some amendments in the text. As issued, the Holy Alliance announced that the "sublime truths taught by the eternal religion of God our Saviour" ought to guide not only the relations between nations but their domestic affairs as well. Henceforth, the treaty said, the signatories would consider themselves as delegates of Providence and "thinking of themselves in their relation to their subjects and armies as fathers of families, they will lead them, in the spirit with which they are animated, to protect Religion, Peace and Justice."

These last words were Metternich's addition to the original text. Their meaning was obscure, but their tone was suggestive. Here was an intimation of a kind of paternalism that promised to stifle and suppress freedom within the countries controlled by the three signatory powers and which might seek application outside their boundaries as well.

The second engagement was the treaty of the Quadruple Alliance, signed on November 20, 1815. In this document, the four allied Great Powers undertook to use all their forces to prevent the general tranquility from again being disturbed by France, to keep Napoleon and his family from the French throne, and to preserve France from new revolutionary convulsions. In addition, they agreed to hold periodic meetings "for the purpose of consulting upon their interests, or for the consideration of the measures which, at each of these periods, shall be considered the most salutary for the repose and prosperity of Nations and for the maintenance of the Peace of Europe."

Back in the eighteenth century there had been some discussion among publicists of the idea of a federation or concert of Europe, although no one had taken any steps to realize it. With the signing of the Quadruple Alliance, the Concert of Europe became actual and operative. The Allied Powers—having just concluded a settlement that reconstructed the map of Europe according to the principles of compensation, legitimacy, and balance of power—now established themselves as a continuing European directorate, which would meet whenever necessary to see that their settlement was not endangered.

The only trouble was that there was no agreement among them about what was or was not a danger to their settlement or how far they were committed to take common action when revolutionary situations occurred.

FROM VIENNA TO THE REVOLUTIONS OF 1830

The Conference System / The postwar cooperation of the powers worked best as long as revolutionary France was its object. While the ambassadors of the occupying powers were sitting in Paris, holding weekly meetings to consider such things as projected laws of the French government, the provocative tactics of the Ultra-Royalists, and the contents of speeches made in the Chamber of Deputies, there were no important differences of opinion among them. It was only after 1818, when the occupation of France came to an end, and when other and more dangerous matters came to the fore, that serious disagreement arose, particularly between Great Britain on the one hand and the three signatories of the Holy Alliance on the other.

Signs of this appeared at the first major postwar conference, which was held at Aix-la-Chapelle in the autumn of 1818. This meeting was convened ostensibly to complete the settlement with France, by making a final adjustment of reparations and by authorizing the withdrawal of occupation troops. But the Russians took this opportunity to raise the question of the future of the alliance, now that France had apparently ceased to be a menace to the peace; and Tsar Alexander presented a memorandum to the conference in which he suggested that—given the dangerous temper in certain other areas of Europe—it might be advisable for the powers to clarify the nature of their existing engagements. They should make clear, he urged, that they were "bound in law and in fact" to a general association, the object of which was, first, to maintain the territorial settlement concluded at Vienna and, second, to guarantee all legitimate regimes existing at the present moment of time.

This proposal annoyed and disturbed the British. Castlereagh saw in Alexander's memorandum an attempt to substitute the vague but sweeping principles of the Holy Alliance for the carefully defined obligations of the Quadruple Alliance, and he objected. His government, he pointed out, was not prepared to honor engagements that it had never signed; and Britain's obligations, as laid down clearly in the treaty of the Quadruple Alliance, were simply to help prevent any new French attempt to disturb the peace. Alexander seemed to want to freeze the existing political situation by collecting pledges to support established power everywhere. No British government could give such a pledge except in particular cases and even then only after considering the nature of the regime in question.

This was blunt enough to make Alexander withdraw his proposal; but, if he did so, it was not because he was persuaded that Castlereagh was right. At the beginning of 1820 he came back to his idea and, this time, with more determination. The occasion was a sudden explosion of revolutionary passion in Spain.

To call what happened in Spain in 1820 a "liberal revolution" is to attribute to liberalism a strength which it did not possess in the Iberian peninsula. The revolution that began in January 1820 would more properly be described as a military revolt against a ruler who was stupid enough to neglect what should have been the strongest support of his throne, his army. Ferdinand VII, who had been restored to the throne by the Allies in 1814, was one of the least gifted rulers in Europe, and his only accomplishment since his accession had been to alienate completely the subjects of his American empire, who had declared their independence. The king had organized a large army to win his colonies back again, but he housed it in unspeakable quarters, fed and clothed it abominably, and paid it inadequately and infrequently. The result was a rising in Cadiz, where units were being assembled for shipment overseas. This was supported by riots and demonstrations in Madrid, Barcelona, and Saragossa, and the king—in a desperate attempt to get control of the situation—felt it necessary to proclaim the constitution of 1812 (a document which had been issued by the Cortes during the fight against Napoleon, which was saturated with liberal and even democratic ideas, and which had been revoked in 1814).

This was enough to bring the tsar back into the field; and he now insisted that the Quadruple Alliance must intervene in Spain to check the tide of revolution before it engulfed all Europe. Once more Castlereagh objected. In a now famous memorandum of May 5, 1820, he warned his fellow Allies that the original purpose of their alliance had been to maintain the peace of Europe and the balance of power. Great Britain would always be prepared to cooperate in fulfilling this, but it would neither intervene itself in the domestic affairs of other European states nor view with indifference the intervention of other powers. "The principle," he added tartly, "of one state interfering in the internal affairs of another in order to enforce obedience to the governing authority is always a question of the greatest moral, as well as political, delicacy. . . . To generalize such a principle, to think of reducing it to a system, or to impose it as an obligation, is a scheme utterly impracticable and objectionable."

But Alexander *wanted* to generalize the principle, and everything that was happening around him in 1820 convinced him that he was right. Not only did the Spanish disorders continue, but in July there was a military insurrection in Naples which forced the king to grant a constitution and gave enormous impetus to revolutionary agitation throughout the Italian peninsula, and, in August, a revolt broke out in Portugal as well. Metternich too was alarmed. If he had tried in the past to avoid siding with either Alexander or Castlereagh, he now urged that the powers must concert on measures to meet the European emergency. At the conference at Troppau in October, he presented a memorandum, already approved by the Russians and the Prussians, which laid down the principle that changes brought about by revolutionary action would not be accepted as legal by the powers, and asserted the right of the powers to intervene wherever necessary to put such changes down.

Castlereagh had refused to go to Troppau, and he refused now to adhere to this so-called Troppau Protocol. This did not deter the three eastern powers from adjourning to Laibach where they authorized the Austrian army to intervene in Naples, to restore the witless and treacherous Ferdinand I, and to revoke the constitution that had been imposed on him. The Austrians had no difficulty in executing this assignment or, a few months later, in intervening in Piedmont to put down a revolution that had broken out there in March 1821.

Successful in Italy, the eastern powers were determined to act in the same manner in Spain, and here they received the support of the French government which thought it advantageous to associate with the Holy Alliance in suppressing disorders so close to their own borders. The Spanish affair was regulated at the conference of Verona, which met in October 1822. Castlereagh was now dead, but his arguments were restated by the Duke of Wellington, who staunchly opposed any intervention in Spanish affairs. The conference nevertheless concluded its labors by empowering the French government to restore order in Spain; and, in April 1823, Europe once more saw French armies on the march, as a force of 100,000 men under the Duke of Angoulême crossed the southern frontier. They met no serious resistance; within six months, Ferdinand VII was back on the throne and Spain was in the grip of a wave of savage reaction.

There were no more of the periodic conferences provided for in the treaty of the Quadruple Alliance, for the British, defeated at Verona, decided not to be represented at future meetings of this nature. This did not mean that Britain had seceded from the Concert of Europe. We shall see, later in this chapter, that her governments were willing to meet with the other powers on an *ad hoc* basis, when the peace of Europe was really threatened. But they had no desire to remain a member of what now appeared to have degenerated into a witch-hunting organization.

Moreover, if their wishes were disregarded at Verona, they soon demonstrated that the Holy Alliance could not hope always to have its way. There can be no doubt that Alexander and Metternich would have liked to restore the New World to Spain. But the British, who had important trading connections with the former Spanish-American colonies and poured £22,000,000 of private investments into them between 1821 and 1825, were not anxious to see Spanish control restored. Castlereagh's successor, George Canning, made it clear to all interested parties, therefore, that while Spain doubtless had the right to attempt to reassert its rule, Great Britain would oppose attempts by the other powers to intervene. Since Spain was now impotent to act by itself, this was tantamount to announcing British recognition of Latin America's independence. Canning's attitude was given overwhelming support when the United States government announced, in the so-called Monroe Doctrine (December 1823), that any attempt on the part of the Holy Alliance to extend their system to any portion of the Western Hemisphere would be regarded as "dangerous to our peace and safety" and as "the manifestation of an unfriendly disposition towards the United States."

Against this kind of language there was no effective rejoinder, for the power of the Holy Alliance stopped at the water's edge. Moreover, despite its victories in Spain and Italy, it had other limitations which became apparent in the course of the revolution that had broken out in Greece.

The Greek Rising / The bloody events that took place in Greece during the 1820s marked the opening of a long series of disorders in the Balkans and the Near East that were made inevitable by the internal disintegration of the Ottoman Empire. At the beginning of the nineteenth century that empire still stretched from Asia Minor across Egypt and the southern shores of the Mediterranean to Tunis and Algeria and, to the northwest, across the Dardanelles to the southern borders of the Austrian and Russian empires. In Europe alone the Turks still claimed dominance over about 238,000 square miles of territory with some eight million inhabitants, most of them Christians. But, in many parts of this great empire, the sultan's authority had become more nominal than real. Mehemet Ali in Egypt and Ali Pasha of Janina in Albania, while still recognizing his suzerainty, had become virtually independent; and their examples were emulated by other local governors and military commanders.

This was one of the chief reasons for the troubles that began in the sultan's European provinces. Had Turkish administration been more efficient, the Christian subjects of those provinces would have had little to complain about. Legally they were allowed to observe their own religion and to educate their children without interference; they were permitted a not inconsiderable amount of self-government; and they were exempt from military service. But the decline of the imperial system was accompanied by a cessation of even a pretense at economic improvement and this made the subject peoples restive, while at the same time increasing their opposition to the numerous discriminatory taxes that they had to pay. Even worse, since the government at Constantinople could no longer always control its local governors or its garrison troops—the redoubtable but increasingly undisciplined Janissaries —the subject peoples were often harassed by these officials, who exacted special levies under duress or resorted to pointless outbursts of brutality against Christians and Jews.

It was resentment against the conduct of the Janissary garrison in Belgrade that touched off the first Christian revolt in the Balkans, when the Serbian peasants rose under Kara (Black) George in 1804 and expelled their oppressors. The Turks fought back, and, in 1813, succeeded in driving Kara George into exile and restoring order. But the fight was taken up again two years later under the leadership of Milos Obrenovitch and, although success was jeopardized by the beginning of a feud between the new leader and the old (one that was to last for a century), Serbian freedom was attained within two years. Its nature and limitations were not spelled out until the early 1830s, when Milos was acknowledged by the Turks to be hereditary prince of Serbia and when, in return for an annual tribute and some garrison rights in its fortresses, Serbia was recognized as an autonomous state.

All of this attracted little attention in the west. But when the Greeks followed the Serbian example, the European powers could not be so disinterested.

The Greek revolt, like that of the Serbs, arose in part from exasperation over the maladministration of Turkish officials; but there was an additional factor at work here. The leading spirits in the revolutionary movement were the merchants of the Aegean islands and the so-called *capitani* —commanders of ships or of bands of brigands in the mountains of the Morea. During the period of the French Revolution they had come into touch with French ideas—because of their activities in the carrying trade (Greek ships carried Russian grains to France during the Terror and after) or, later, because Napoleon found it useful to maintain contact with fighting bands in the Balkans—and they had been profoundly influenced by them. As was true in other parts of Europe, French influence stimulated national self-consciousness, which was further inflamed by the writings of propagandists and scholars, like the martyr poet Rhigas, killed by the Turks in 1798, and Koraes, the linguistic reformer who sought to awaken Greek pride in their national heritage, and by the activities of the secret society *Hetairia Philiké*, which worked for the expulsion of the Turks from Europe and which, by the end of 1820, claimed a membership of more than a hundred thousand.

In March 1821 the head of this society, a former general in the Russian army called Prince Alexander Ypsilanti, attempted to start a general rising against the Turks in what is now Rumania. This was a fiasco, but it inspired imitation. A month later, the peasants of the Morea rose and slaughtered the local Turkish troops and officials, thus starting the struggle that was not to stop until Greek independence was won.

The long fight aroused widespread enthusiasm throughout Western Europe. It made an immediate appeal to an age that had a vivid interest in antiquity and which proved all too ready to romanticize the conflict.

Scenes of the Massacres of Chios, painted by the French artist Eugène Delacroix (1799–1863) two years after the event, in 1824. Louvre, Paris.

At a later date, the Russian poet Pushkin wrote bitterly: "This enthusiasm of all cultured nations for Greece is unforgiveable childishness. The Jesuits have told us all that twaddle about Themistocles and Pericles, and so we imagine that the shabby nation of robbers and traders are their legitimate successors." Pushkin was not the only one who, in time, became disillusioned with a struggle that was marked by savagery on both sides. The best-known atrocity of the war was the massacre at Chios in April 1822, where the Turkish governor systematically executed the captured population, which, after the blood-letting, had been reduced from 120,000 to 30,000. But even before this, when the Turks had surrendered at Tripolitsa, 12,000 of them had been hanged, impaled, and roasted alive by their Greek captors, while 200 Jews, also in the town, had been killed, some of them by crucifixion.

The war was of interest to the Great Powers, not only because of its threat to the general peace, but because all of them except Prussia had economic and political interests in the general area of the Near East. But, for most of the powers, the Greek affair was so complicated that they were hesitant to take a firm position with respect to it; and in the end it was the British who took the initiative, when George Canning announced Britain's recognition of Greek belligerency.

If Canning had been thinking only in economic terms, he might well have sided with the Turks. His action seems to have been taken for three reasons. In the first place popular enthusiasm for the Greeks was so strong in England that the government had to do something for them if it wanted to stay in office. In the second place, Canning expected that sooner or later the Russians would have to come to the aid of Greece and that, if they were alone in doing so, Greece might become a Russian satellite. He wished to forestall this. Finally, by acting, the British states-man seems to have wished to embarrass the Holy Alliance and, especially, to annoy Metternich, for whom he had conceived a strong personal dislike.

He certainly succeeded in the last objective. Metternich did not want to see Russia intervene in Greece because this would increase its in-fluence in the Balkans and thus alter the balance of power. Moreover, as he told the tsar, Russian aid to Greece would be a betrayal of the Holy Alliance and a repudiation of the Troppau Protocol and would weaken the security of thrones everywhere, for—whatever one thought of the sultan—he was a legitimate ruler, while the Greeks were undeniably rebels. This argument deterred Alexander from action but had less effect upon his successor Nicholas, who took the throne in December 1825. By that date, it appeared likely that a strong Egyptian-Turkish army under Ibrahim Pasha, which had landed in the Morea in February 1825, might quell the revolt; and this inflamed Russian public opinion, which was pro-Greek for religious and other reasons. Despite Metternich's pleas, Nicholas gradually yielded to the popular temper, detached himself temporarily from the Holy Alliance, joined the British in calling upon the sultan to give the Greeks autonomy, and, when this was refused, con-cluded an alliance with Britain and France (July 6, 1827), with the de-clared object of securing Greek independence. The Turks fought on; but, in October, a joint Anglo-French-Russian fleet under the command of the British admiral Codrington encountered the bulk of the Egyptian navy off Navarino on the west coast of the Morea and destroyed it. The sultan still refused to yield, perhaps deceived by indications of differ-ences among his opponents. This merely encouraged the Russians, sup-ported by the French but not by the English, to open hostilities on the land as well. The war that followed dragged on for two years, with French troops clearing the Morea of Ibrahim's forces while one Russian army invaded Asia Minor and a second crossed the Balkan mountains and, on August 14, 1829, pushed its way into Adrianople. The Turkish government thereupon sued for peace.

Russo-Turkish relations were adjusted by the Treaty of Adrianople of September 14, 1829. The Turks were forced to give up control of the mouths of the Danube, to cede part of the Black Sea coast to Russia, and to pay a large indemnity within a period of ten years. Pending complete payment, the Danubian principalities (covering the area now called Rumania) were to be occupied by Russian troops. Moreover, all Moslems were to be expelled from the principalities and all Turkish fortresses to be destroyed. In effect, these measures spelled the end of Turkish influence in Rumania, which now became practically a Russian protectorate.

The treaty of Adrianople said nothing about Greece, whose fate was determined in February 1830 at a conference in London. Here the independence of the country was declared, and the new kingdom was placed under the guarantee of Great Britain, France, and Russia. The adjustment of Greece's boundaries took longer and, as was perhaps to be expected, the Greeks were not satisfied with them when they were defined. The powers also had difficulty in finding a ruler for the nation, and it was not until 1832 that Greece had a sovereign, when a Bavarian prince ascended the throne as King Otto I.

The liberation of Greece made the first significant change in the map of Europe since the Congress of Vienna. For liberals this was heartening, for it had been accomplished in the face of Metternich's desire to freeze the *status quo*, and it seemed to represent a victory over legitimacy and reaction.

From the standpoint of relations between the Great Powers, the long struggle in Greece had subjected the Holy Alliance to a considerable amount of strain; while Russia's increased strength in Eastern Europe as a result of the treaty of Adrianople aroused misgivings in Vienna, as it did in London, and caused anxious speculation about its effects on the balance of power.

FROM 1830 TO 1848

The Revolution in France and Its Consequences / In the last week of July 1830 civil war broke out in Paris and, at the end of three days of fighting, the Bourbon King Charles X was driven from power and the Duke of Orleans took the throne with the title Louis Philippe, *roi des Francais*.[1] It was rumored that, when the news reached St. Petersburg, Nicholas I said to his aides: "Gentlemen, saddle your horses! Revolution

---

[1] A more detailed account of the background and course of the revolution in France will be found in Chapter 3.

rules again in Paris!" In point of fact, even though what had happened in Paris made a breach in the Vienna settlement and flew in the face of the principle of legitimacy and the Troppau Protocol, no one marched against France. For the revolution in Paris inspired revolutions elsewhere, and soon the members of the Holy Alliance were occupied with troubles closer to their own doorsteps: Russia in Poland, Prussia in the German states, Austria in Italy. Unable to oppose the new French king effectively, therefore, they found it expedient to recognize him, although they did it rather sulkily.

The July revolution destroyed the system of absolutism that Charles X had been seeking to consolidate, and France became a state in which the wealthier bourgeoisie exercised political power. Two years after the events in Paris, a similar development took place in England where the upper-middle class was enfranchised by the passing of the Great Reform Bill.[2] Ideologically, Britain and France were now brought closer together and, at the same time, the difference between them and the members of the Holy Alliance became more pronounced. The result of the events of these years, in short, seemed to be to divide the Great Powers into two tightly organized diplomatic combinations which were firmly opposed to each other. This division impressed contemporary observers, Lord Melbourne, for instance, remarking that "the three and the two think differently and therefore they act differently."

It is important, however, not to make too much of this division, or to regard the two combinations as cohesive and mutually exclusive leagues. In the years between the July revolution and 1848, ideological differences were ignored as often as they were honored; on occasion, Metternich and Nicholas could cooperate with Palmerston as effectively as Metternich and Alexander had cooperated with Castlereagh; and, when dangerous crises arose, the powers demonstrated that the Concert of Europe could still work. This can be illustrated by a brief consideration of their handling of the Belgian revolution.

The Belgian Revolution / The Belgian people had been placed under Dutch rule in 1815 as a matter of international convenience. Their own wishes were not considered, and neither was the fact that there was little community of interest between them and the Dutch. The two countries had had a different historical evolution. They differed in language and in religion—the Belgians being predominantly Roman Catholic, the Dutch militantly Calvinist. Economically, their interests were opposed also, for the Dutch were an agricultural and commercial people, holding to free trade, while Belgium was the home of a flourishing but

[2] For details and analysis, see Chapter 4.

still young industry, with most of the leading industrialists believing in tariff protection. In making the Belgians subjects of the king of the Netherlands, then, the powers succeeded in alienating the liberal intellectuals who took pride in their country's past, the Catholic clergy, and the manufacturers, as well as other groups, including those who would have liked to join the civil service but found all the best positions filled by Dutch officials.

Their resentment grew as the years passed; and, in the late 1820s, they received increasing popular support, for the peasantry were hurt by a series of bad harvests and the industrial workers suffered from a slow rise in the cost of living which was not balanced by any increase in pay. The crisis of overproduction which hit the textile industry at Verviers, Liège, and Tournai in the spring of 1830 probably had the effect of heightening passions further, since all economic troubles were, naturally if unreasonably, blamed on the Dutch. All that was needed now was something to touch off the explosion, and the rising in Paris did that. On August 25, 1830, rioting began in Brussels. Troops were brought into the city but could not restore order and, in September, they were again driven out. By that time, the revolutionary agitation had spread to other towns. The king, William I, who had taken a completely intransigent position at the outset, now tried to make concessions. It was too late. A provisional government had already been formed and, on October 4, it declared Belgium independent.

On October 1, the tsar of Russia had informed his allies that he was prepared to send an army of 60,000 men to extirpate the revolutionary infection and return Belgium to Dutch control; it was known that the king of Prussia had placed his army on a war footing, presumably for the same purpose. This raised the threat of war between the Great Powers. For, as the veteran Talleyrand, who had just been sent to London as ambassador, pointed out to the British government, France would not tolerate any intervention in a country so close to her own borders. The British government was sufficiently alarmed by this communication to urge the Eastern Powers to refrain from any action until representatives of all Great Powers could meet in London to discuss Belgian affairs.

The Eastern Powers accepted the invitation, hoping perhaps to be able to win the British over to their point of view. But the man who was now responsible for British policy was Henry Temple, Viscount Palmerston (1784–1865), who regretted the dissolution of the union of the Low Countries, which he considered "advantageous to the general interests of Europe," but felt that it was too late to restore it. As his long and notable career was to demonstrate, Palmerston had many faults as a diplomat, including an excessive fondness for sensation, an inclination to cocksureness, and a tendency to bully weaker opponents. But these were matched by quick and accurate judgment, rapidity of decision, force of will, an incredible capacity for work, and great skill in negotiation. He displayed these latter qualities now as—disavowing partisan motives, and speaking in the name of peace and the balance of power—he pointed out to the powers that an attempt to restore Belgium to Dutch control would be unrealistic and, from the standpoint of Great Power harmony, dangerous, and that it would be better to admit the fact of Belgian independence under conditions which would, as far as possible, repair the breach in the system of 1815.

Palmerston was aided in his efforts by the sudden rising of the Poles in November 1830 and by disorders in Germany and Italy which began at the end of the year and reduced the ability of any of the Eastern Powers to act in the west. By the end of December 1830, at any rate, all powers had agreed to Belgian independence. There were many other problems that had to be solved before the affair was regulated definitively; and the agitation of annexationist groups in France and the stubborn efforts of the Dutch king to reimpose his will on his former subjects by force of arms caused ugly crises. But the first of these was met by the combination of Palmerston's firmness and Louis Philippe's moderation, while William I's military efforts were finally checked by a French intervention authorized by the powers. The important thing is that, despite frequent flurries of anxiety, the powers held together and made joint decisions.

In the end, by the treaty of November 15, 1831 (ratified in May 1832 but not accepted by the Dutch king until April 1839), Belgium was admitted to the family of nations as an independent state and with a ruler, Leopold of Saxe-Coburg, of its own choosing. In keeping with Palmerston's desire to make good the damage done to the Vienna settlement, the new nation was established as a neutral state. The old barrier fortresses were demolished, and the Great Powers guaranteed that they would all take action against any state that violated Belgian integrity. Whether this arrangement was as effective a means of securing this important strategical area as the continued union of the Low Countries would have been is debatable. It did not, in any case, discourage the aggressor in 1914.

The Italian, German, and Polish Risings / The willingness of the Eastern Powers to agree to Belgian independence was doubtless made easier by the restraint displayed by the British and French governments in the case of the disorders in Southern and Central Europe.

In Italy the suppression of the revolts of 1820–1821 had not put an end to revolutionary agitation. The number of secret societies had increased, and there was greater coordination between them. At the end of 1830 disorders began in central Italy. In a kind of chain reaction, revolution spread from Modena to Parma and to the Papal States, bringing provisional governments and new charters in its train. But the revolutionary movement was not yet so strong that it could defeat the power of Austria without outside help. The rebels expected aid from France, but, in the end, Louis Philippe's government agreed with the English view that it would be dangerous for France either to intervene in Italy or to try to prevent Austria from doing so. The Western Powers, in short, concluded that peace and the balance of power would best be served by allowing Metternich to enforce the 1814 arrangements in Italy, which he proceeded to do.

The radical movement in Germany was suppressed in the same way, without western interference or even much evidence of western interest (see pp. 62–63). As for Poland, in 1831 as on several later occasions, the Poles received the sympathy of the west but no tangible assistance.

Russian Poland had been transformed by Tsar Alexander I into a country with undeniably liberal institutions. Bound to Russia by personal union (the tsar was the king of Poland), it had a constitution that provided for a bicameral parliament, religious toleration, and civil liberties. Polish was the official language, and all official positions had to be filled by Poles. The Poles, in fact, had everything they might reasonably expect except their independence; but it was independence that the politically conscious class wanted more than anything else, and without it, they took no satisfaction in their other privileges. Their Diet began to disregard the tsar's wishes and to criticize the policies of his ministers. They fell increasingly under the influence of western liberal and democratic ideas, which alarmed Alexander and his successor Nicholas and led them to restrict some of the liberties previously granted. By 1830 tempers had been brought to the breaking point; and in November of that year a group of discontented officers and university students started a revolt in Warsaw. It would probably have come to nothing if the Grand Duke Constantine, brother of the tsar and commander of the Polish army, had acted promptly. But Constantine was a man of indecision who was moved, moreover, by sympathy for the Polish cause. He tried to negotiate and this sign of weakness strengthened the rebels and forced Constantine, in the end, to flee the city.

The usual succession of events followed: the calling of a provisional government, attempts at a compromise solution by moderates among the rebels, the ascendancy of the radicals, defiance of the imperial government, a declaration of independence, and counteraction by the imperial power. A Russian army under Diebitch, the conqueror of Adrianople, entered Poland in February 1831. The rebels had expected aid from the Western Powers. But neither Palmerston nor Louis Philippe approved their action or wished Europe to be torn by further complications. The only ally the Poles found was Asiatic cholera, which swept across the whole of Europe in 1831. Cholera killed both Diebitch and Constantine, as well as thousands of soldiers on both sides of the line. It slowed the Russian advance, but it could not check it; and, meanwhile, the rebels fell to fighting among themselves and ruined what chances they might have had. On September 8, Diebitch's successor, the hard-bitten and resolute Paskévitch, was able to send Nicholas the message: "Warsaw is at Your Majesty's feet!"

The Polish revolt of 1830–1831 was a revolt of aristocrats and intellectuals. They had given little thought to the needs and desires of the Polish masses, who in turn had remained apathetic to the revolutionary cause. The result of the ill-considered Warsaw rising was the destruction of the autonomy that Poland had enjoyed since 1815 and the subjection of the country to military rule. While hundreds were put to death or imprisoned, thousands of intellectuals fled to Paris and London, where they lived in poverty and plotted new risings.

With the liquidation of the Polish revolt, calm was restored within the confines of Europe proper, except for the confusion caused by the increasingly complicated political situation in Portugal and Spain, in each of which there were, at the beginning of the 1830s, rival claimants to the throne. All that need be said here of politics in the Iberian peninsula is that the Eastern Powers found it expedient to refrain from inviting trouble with England or France by seeking to meddle there.

Two Egyptian Crises / Some final rays of light may be thrown on the workings of Great Power politics in this period by a brief consideration of two crises in the Near East, each of which was precipitated by the pasha of Egypt, Mehemet Ali.

Mehemet was certainly one of the ablest rulers of this period. Originally an Albanian trader, he had entered Turkish military service at the time of Napoleon's expedition to Egypt and had risen rapidly, being made pasha by the sheiks of Cairo in 1805. In this capacity, he had rebuilt Alexandria and constructed the canal between that city and the Nile; he had carried through an extensive series of agricultural and medical reforms; and, finally, with French assistance, he had modernized the Egyptian army. It is understandable that a man who had risen so high should want to rise higher and that one who had lavished care on a military establishment should wish to test its efficiency. Mehemet Ali had long lusted after the control of Palestine, Syria, and Arabia; in the latter part of 1831 he set out to get them, by manufacturing a dispute with the pasha of Lebanon and sending the redoubtable Ibrahim to invest Acre. Sultan Mahmud II tried to adjudicate the quarrel but, failing, guessed at the Pasha's aims, declared him a rebel, and set out to crush him. Through 1832, however, Turkish forces reeled from one defeat to another and, in December, the Egyptians threatened to overrun all of Asia Minor and to take Constantinople as well.

Metternich recognized the dangers implicit in this situation and tried to bring the Great Powers together to protect the legitimate ruler of Turkey against his rebellious vassal. But the British government was curiously uncertain concerning their interest in the area, and the French sympathized with Mehemet Ali; so Metternich's efforts had no result. The sultan appealed in vain to Britain for help and then, in desperation, turned to the Russians. Nicholas responded at once and dispatched an army and a fleet to the Porte. By May 1833, thanks to this intervention, peace had been restored, on terms that left Syria in Mehemet Ali's hands; and—what was infinitely more important—the Turks and the Russians had signed the treaty of Unkiar Skelessi (July 8, 1833), promising each other mutual assistance in case of attacks by other states, but agreeing (in a secret article) that Turkey need not send military aid to Russia in time of war provided she closed the straits of the Dardanelles to all foreign naval units at the demand of the Russian government.

To both London and Vienna, Unkiar Skelessi came as an unpleasant surprise, for it seemed to give Russia a kind of protectorate over Turkey and, because of this, to upset the balance of power. Yet perhaps the most important thing about this treaty is that the tsar studiously refrained from using it to promote Russian interests.

This became clear in the second Egyptian crisis. In 1839 Mahmud II, warned by the build-up of Egyptian forces that Mehemet Ali was planning a new attack, sought to take the initiative. Attached to the staff of the army he sent against the Egyptians was a young Prussian captain named Helmuth von Moltke, who was to direct the victory of Prussian arms against Austria in 1866 and France in 1870. But the Turkish commanders paid no attention to Moltke's advice, with the result that, when they met Ibrahim Pasha's army at Nezib in June, they were utterly smashed. Once more the Egyptians stood at the gates of Constantinople. The situation of 1833 seemed to be repeated.

This, however, was not true. The British government was no longer as uncertain as it had been in 1833. Since that date successful experiments with steam navigation on the Red Sea and the Euphrates had increased the importance of the overland routes to India in British eyes; and for this reason Palmerston was determined that neither Russia nor Mehemet Ali, whom Palmerston regarded as being under French influence, should be allowed to dominate them. The British foreign secretary wanted action by the Concert of Europe to check Mehemet Ali and to replace Unkiar Skelessi with a general guarantee of Turkish independence.

Metternich agreed with this idea as a matter of course. What is perhaps more surprising is that the tsar did too. But Nicholas seems to have reached the conclusion that Unkiar Skelessi was a burdensome arrangement which, if ever applied, would simply unite the other powers against him. In September he concluded an agreement with the British to make Mehemet Ali give up most of his gains and, once hostilities had ceased, to close both the Bosphorus and the Dardanelles to warships of all powers. To this the Austrians and the Prussians adhered.

After that it was simply a matter of getting the French to go along. This was not easy, for boulevard sentiment was strongly pro-Egyptian and the government in power, which was headed by Adolphe Thiers, dared not run counter to it. The other powers, therefore, acted alone. This touched off an ugly war scare as Paris mobs called for war against England and—rather illogically—against the Germans; but by October, when Thiers fell from office, passions had subsided and the danger had passed. Meanwhile, the powers had sent an ultimatum to Mehemet Ali, and that doughty ruler had decided that discretion was the better part of valor. He had to restore Syria, Crete, and Arabia, which he had conquered, to Turkey; but he was confirmed in his possession of Egypt, at the price of an annual tribute to the Sultan. Finally, in July 1841, the powers signed the famous Straits Convention, which stipulated that the

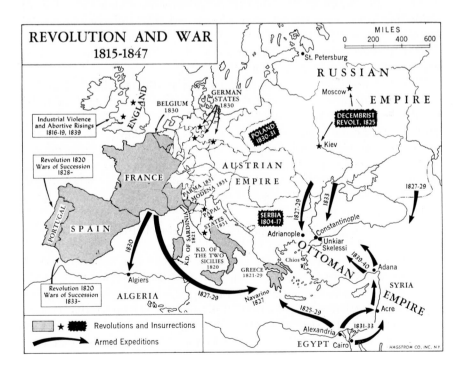

straits of the Bosphorus and the Dardanelles must be closed to foreign warships while Turkey was at peace. This was more to Britain's advantage than to Russia's, but the tsar ratified the treaty; and the long series of Near Eastern troubles came to an end.

The Great Power Consensus / The last years before the explosion of 1848 were relatively free from international complications. From the standpoint of diplomatic history, the most arresting development was a curious tendency toward a reversal of alliances. On the one hand, as a result of political differences in Spain and economic friction everywhere, Britain and France grew less friendly, and Louis Philippe began to draw closer to Austria. Thus, we find his minister Guizot writing to Metternich in May 1847: "France is now disposed to a policy of conservatism." On the other hand, the most conservative of the powers sought the friendship of Britain. After trying in 1840 to induce Britain to become a member of the Holy Alliance (an offer which Palmerston adroitly sidestepped), Tsar Nicholas visited England in 1844 and urged that Russia and Britain pursue a common policy in eastern affairs in the future.

This development should be enough to show that it is unwise to think of the powers as being divided into "liberal" and "conservative" combinations. The ideological differences, while present, were not as important as one might suppose. The diplomatic alignments which existed were fluid; single powers shifted their positions and their influence at crucial moments, when their interests were threatened or war seemed possible. And they were able to do so because, despite all their differences, there was a remarkable consensus among them.

With the possible exception of France, who did not dare admit her uniqueness, all powers accepted the balance of power—that is, the territorial arrangements made at Vienna and the broader principle that no single state should be allowed to increase its possessions except with the consent of the others. And acceptance of this implied certain other things: a high degree of self-restraint on the part of single powers; a willingness to accept the validity of existing treaties; a willingness—when single powers sought unilateral aggrandizement—to participate in concerted action to restrain them.

In their dealings with each other in the period between the Congress of Vienna and the revolutions of 1848, the Great Powers observed these rules. Liberal opinion in France would have welcomed open support of the Poles in 1830 or of Mehemet Ali in 1840; liberal opinion in England would have been enthusiastic if the British government had given aid to the rebels in the Romagna in 1831. But, on those occasions, the governments accepted the risk of losing public support at home in order to avoid embroiling the whole European system. Tsar Nicholas might well have asked a higher price for his aid to Turkey in 1833 and he might have insisted on acting alone in the Near East in 1840. He did not do so because he quite genuinely viewed unilateral action with reprobation.

It may be difficult for us, living as we do in a more lawless age, to believe that the powers were genuine in the respect they paid to treaties. But even in 1914 the world was shocked when a statesman referred to a specific treaty as a scrap of paper; and in the period from 1815 to 1848 it would have been even more so. In these years, at any rate, the powers did not lightly break their pledged word.

Finally, there was a general willingness on the part of the powers to share in the effort to maintain the peace and the balance. This was true even of Great Britain whose geographical position and world-wide interests made her connection with Europe more tenuous than that of other powers. In 1852, Lord John Russell could say with both pride and accuracy: "We are connected, and have been for more than a century, with the general system of Europe, and any territorial increase of one power, any aggrandizement which disturbs the general balance of power in Europe . . . could not be a matter of indifference to this country. . . . "

It was because other powers, too, could not view with indifference changes in the European system that they had established at Vienna in 1815 that the Concert of Europe was a reality in this period and the general peace was maintained.

2

The Eastern Powers: Absolutism and Its Limitations

ABSOLUTISM AND ITS APOLOGISTS

When the exigencies of foreign policy required it, the members of the Holy Alliance could compromise with liberalism and revolution, at least to the extent of cooperating with the liberal powers, Britain and France, and even of accepting revolutionary *faits accomplis,* as in the case of Belgian independence. But within their own national boundaries, or in areas that they effectively controlled, they tolerated no compromise of any kind. The domestic policies of the Russian and Austrian empires and the Kingdom of Prussia were marked by inflexible opposition to revolution; and a good part of the energies of their administrations was devoted to hunting down real or suspected revolutionaries and imprisoning, exiling, or executing them. It was in the eastern empires, for example, that secret police systems attained their fullest development and their greatest influence, with chiefs who stood at the elbows of their sovereigns and participated in the most intimate councils of state.

But fear of revolution went further than persecution of rebels and conspirators. It also involved reverence of existing institutions simply because they existed and reprobation of novelty simply because it was new.

It involved opposition to change because change subverted the established order, to speculation because it led to change, and to learning because it led to speculation. "Too much learning kills character," wrote the reactionary Prussian squire Marwitz. It is responsible for

> the war of the have-nots against property, of industry against agriculture, of the mobile against stability, of crass materialism against God's established order, of [illusory] gain against right, of the present against the past and the future, of the individual against the family, of speculators and counting-desks against fields and trades, of science and puffed-up talent against virtue and honorable character.

Here is the true voice of reaction. Gone were the days when monarchs patronized scholars and a Prussian king was proud to be the friend of so completely subversive a writer as Voltaire. To stand in the good graces of the courts and the ruling classes of the eastern empires, a writer had to compose elaborate justifications of what he saw around him or fulsome panegyrics on the past.

The modern reader will find little stimulation in the works of the men who wrote under these conditions, with the possible exception of those of Joseph de Maistre (1753–1821). This talented writer was a Savoyard who served for fourteen years as Sardinian envoy to the court of St. Petersburg. His essays bear the hallmark of the romantic school in their repudiation of reason, their respect for tradition, and their veneration of established religion. But their most arresting characteristic is the passion that animates them, as de Maistre pours vituperation on the presumption of men who seek to lay impious hands on a civil order that he believes to have been sanctioned by God. To de Maistre opposition to constituted authority was not merely a political crime; it was an act of blasphemy. The high incidence of civil disobedience convinced him that man was too wicked for freedom and absolutism was the only means of holding sinful arrogance in check.

In his own time de Maistre was probably admired less than the Swiss theorist Karl Ludwig von Haller (1768–1854), whose *Restoration of Political Science* became a kind of political Bible in the German courts. This dreary treatise had none of the brilliance or fire that one finds in de Maistre, a fact that probably enhanced its merit in the eyes of its readers. It expressed the political ideas of the eastern courts perfectly by holding up as an ideal a state established on the basis of romantic feudalism and Christian piety, with an absolute king as God's vicegerent ruling over subjects who had no rights except those he gave them of his own free will, a state, moreover, in which nothing new ever happened and nothing old was ever changed.

Haller's perfect society, in short, was authoritarian and completely immobile; and this was the goal of the ruling classes of the eastern empires. But, in the long run, *quieta non movere* is not a very practical principle of politics. Censorship, thought control, and police persecution cannot successfully destroy all new ideas; and, in the period from 1815 to 1848, there were lots of new ideas and new forces at work beneath the surface in Russia, Prussia, and Austria.

THE RUSSIAN EMPIRE TO 1848

The Land and the People / Thanks to the persistent policy of territorial expansion followed by every tsar since the days of Ivan the Terrible the Russian empire in 1815 stretched from Poland, Courland, and Finland in the west to Siberia and the banks of the Amur in the Far East, and from the Arctic Ocean in the north to the shores of the Black, Caspian, and Aral seas in the south. Even if Finland, annexed after the Russo-Swedish war of 1808–1809, and the Kingdom of Poland, as defined at Vienna in 1815, were excluded, this was a vast and potentially powerful realm. Its population, which had remained relatively stable in the first half of the eighteenth century, had begun to grow rapidly thereafter. In 1725, it had stood at about fourteen million; at the turn of the nineteenth century, it had increased to forty million; on the eve of the 1848 revolutions, it was close to seventy million.

Of this population by far the greatest number lived on the land. As late as the middle of the nineteenth century, only 3,500,000 persons were town dwellers. Thus, the Russian economy was primarily agricultural. A thriving export trade was conducted through the Baltic ports, the principal exports being grain, fats, flax, hemp, and furs, and—later in the century—wool and timber; but its scale was not large and, like the import trade, it was carried almost exclusively in foreign bottoms. Moreover, trade was discouraged by the high protective tariffs maintained by the government throughout this whole period. As for industry, according to official statistics, there were 5261 manufacturing enterprises in 1825, with a total of 210,600 workers; but machinery was virtually unknown even in the most important firms, those manufacturing cotton, linen, and woolen cloth; and a large part of what was called industrial production in the official figures went on, not in factories, but in the homes of workers who were also engaged in agriculture.

The great majority of the population, then, was engaged in agriculture and lived on the land; and this majority was divided into two classes: the landholding nobility and the mass of serfs who worked their estates.

0   100   200   300
Miles

EUROPEAN RUSSIA
IN THE
NINETEENTH CENTURY

SWEDEN

GULF OF BOTHNIA

BALTIC SEA

Archangel

N. Dvina R.

Pechora R.

Helsingfors   Vyborg

St. Petersburg

R   U   S   S   I   A

Vyatka R.

Volga R.

Kama R.

Riga

Duna R.

Moscow

EAST PRUSSIA

Vilna

Minsk

Ural

Warsaw

Brest Litovsk

Kiev

Kharkov

Don R.

Dnieper R.

Donets R.

Volga R.

Rostov

RUMANIA   Odessa

CASPIAN SEA

Danube R.

Sebastopol   Yalta

BLACK   SEA

The institution of serfdom dates from the middle of the sixteenth century. Before that time the peasants were free men with the right of transferring their labor from one proprietor to another whenever they wished. After that time, the government began to limit their freedom of movement; and, by the seventeenth century, they were permanently bound to the lords whose lands they occupied. Once this step had been taken, it was not long before they lost other freedoms; serfdom began to be almost indistinguishable from slavery. By the eighteenth century the landholders had received the right to punish their serfs as they saw fit, to exile them to Siberia, even to sell them (although laws at the beginning of the nineteenth century placed limitations on this last right, in order to prevent the division of families by sale).

Serfdom hung like a dead weight over Russian society in the first half of the nineteenth century, stifling its vital energies. If the institution was the mainstay of Russian agriculture, it was also the most important factor in keeping agriculture in a chronic state of inefficiency, for this too plentiful supply of manual labor discouraged efforts to find the capital that might have enabled landowners to buy machinery and introduce scientific farming methods. At the same time, the execrable conditions in which many serfs had to live and the oppressive treatment they received led to sporadic and bloody risings; between 1825 and 1854 there were hundreds of agrarian revolts, all of them violent, and some of them on such a scale that considerable force had to be exerted to suppress them. Fear of a large-scale rising was never far from the minds of the ruling classes of Russia, but only the most enlightened believed that the way to banish this shadow was to emancipate the serfs. The nobility felt that their livelihood depended on serfdom; the government had come to rely on the institution for recruits for the army and for labor for those industries, like the metallurgical and clothing industries, in which, for military reasons, it had an interest. Emancipation seeming impossible, repression appeared to be the only safeguard against revolt; and, thus, the continued existence of serfdom helped fasten a brutal authoritarianism on the country.

The political and social pyramids were identical in Russia. At the apex stood the tsar, his ministers, and his military staff, and, immediately below them, the nobility, which comprised the aristocratic landholders on their estates and all those who had been ennobled for military or civil service. This was the ruling class. It was often divided within itself, for in a country whose history had been marked by frequent palace revolutions there was inevitably tension between the tsar and the great nobles, and the landed nobility was jealous of its traditional privileges and fearful lest they be curtailed. But tsar and nobility generally presented a common front against the classes below them and against dissident aristocrats and intellectuals who wanted to change the existing order.

At the bottom of the triangle was the great mass of the peasantry; and between it and the ruling class was the bourgeoisie, still hardly numerous enough to warrant attention.

Last Years of Alexander I / When Alexander I came to the throne in 1801, there had been some expectation that he would institute liberal political and social changes. These hopes were disappointed. Alexander talked a good deal about reform; he surrounded himself with enlightened advisers; and, in his first years, he actually promulgated laws that seemed to herald the coming of a new age. But, in most cases, nothing came of all these gestures. The constitutional reforms of 1801 and 1809, which were supposed to temper tsarist absolutism, were wholly ineffective; the law of February 1803, which provided for the emancipation of serfs by voluntary agreement with their masters, resulted in the liberation of only 37,000 serfs in the next twenty years; the ambitious educational statute of 1803 broke down because of lack of funds and local interest.

It is of course true that the exertions required by the wars against France made it difficult for Alexander to concentrate on internal policy; but this is only a partial explanation. More important was his volatile nature, which caused him to go haring off after new enthusiasms before his old ones had begun to assume tangible form. By 1815 he was so distracted by his international schemes and his plans for Poland (see p. 16) that he had little time for thoughts of domestic reform. In the years that followed, his concern over the rising tide of revolution in Western Europe made him drift away from the muddled liberalism of his youth. He never broke with it completely—as late as 1820 he was playing again with ideas of constitutional reform—but in general the governmental methods of his last years showed an increasing degree of the kind of arbitrariness he had deprecated earlier. His closest advisors were reactionaries. Arakcheev, the chairman of the department of military affairs in the State Council, a brutal, cynical, dissolute man, whose reprisals against his own serfs at Gruzino when they rebelled and murdered his mistress shocked all Russia, encouraged him to break all contact with progressive circles; and the Archimandrite Photius, a fanatical cleric who was one of Arakcheev's protégés, overcame Alexander's tendency to religious mysticism and brought him back to a narrow and intolerant orthodoxy.

In short, before he fell sick of fever and died at Taganrog in December 1825, Alexander was reverting rapidly to the absolutism of his predecessors. This tendency was to be carried further by the tsar who now came to the throne.

The Decembrist Revolt / Alexander's presumptive successor was his brother, the Grand Duke Constantine, but it had been decided with his permission that he should be passed over and the crown given to the younger brother Nicholas. Alexander's sudden death, however, left the question of succession in confusion, for each of the brothers protested that the other should be tsar. Before the situation had been clarified and Nicholas persuaded to take office, the pathetic incident known as the Decembrist revolt had taken place.

The leaders of this unhappy rising were officers of noble birth, some of them related to the most powerful families in Russia. Many of them had been members of the army that had occupied France after Waterloo and had acquired from the experience political and social ideas somewhat more enlightened than they found in their own country. They were young, romantic, idealistic, and they hated the regime they found when they returned home: the stagnant and corrupt administrative system, the censorship of opinion, the rigid control of the university, the abuses of serfdom, and, worst of all, Arakcheev's "military colonies," instituted after 1815, in which soldiers and their families were ordered to combine soldiering with agricultural labor—men, women, and children wearing uniform and being subjected to brutal discipline. "Is it for this we liberated Europe?", one of them wrote later. "We have bought with our blood the highest place among nations, and at home we are humiliated."

As early as 1816, officers were forming conspiratorial groups. After 1820, there were three principal societies devoted to a change in existing conditions: the Society of the North, led by Prince Troubetzkoy and the poet Ryleev; the Southern Society, led by Serge Mouraviev-Apostol, Bestuzhev-Riumin, and Colonel Paul Pestel; and a smaller group known as the United Slavs. Between these groups there was little coordination; within any one of them there was agreement only on the idea that things must be changed. Some of the members were moved more by religious than political motives; only Pestel had taken the trouble to draw up a detailed program. Pestel was a radical republican who knew what he wanted; most of the others had no clear idea of either their immediate or their ultimate objectives.

Nevertheless, when the succession crisis came, they began feverishly to plan an insurrection and, when the troops were summoned to take the oath of loyalty to the new emperor, the leaders of the Northern Society spread the word among the Moscow garrisons that Nicholas was a usurper and raised the cry, "Long live Constantine! Long live the Constitution!" Some of the men doubtless believed that the Constitution was Constantine's wife; others, the fabricated story that Nicholas had suppressed a decree of Alexander's shortening the term of service. In any case, on December 14, 1825, three thousand troops, including part of the Moscow Regiment, the Life Guards, and the Marines, mutinied and marched to the Senate Square.

It was at this point that the lack of planning made itself felt. For four hours the troops stood shivering in the square, while the leaders harangued them and each other—and did nothing. As darkness fell, government cavalry charged the rebel lines and were thrown back. Four field pieces were then brought into the square and fired point-blank at the mutineers. After the third volley they fled, and the Moscow revolt was over.

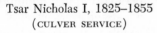

Tsar Nicholas I, 1825–1855   Tsar Alexander I, 1805–1825
(CULVER SERVICE)   (THE BETTMANN ARCHIVE)

The Southern Society had not moved on the 14th, perhaps because Pestel and others had been arrested by General Diebitch the day before. But on December 30, Mouraviev-Apostol and Bestuzhev incited troops of the Tchernigov Regiment to mutiny and—after a ceremony in which they solemnly proclaimed Jesus Christ King of the Universe—advanced on Kiev. This "Christian army," however, was defeated in its first brush with government troops and its officers taken.

After the collapse, most of the leaders of the December revolt surrendered and, in the investigation that followed, they showed an enthusiasm about telling all that reminds one of Russian trials in more recent years. Only Pestel was immune to this epidemic of repentance. The confessions were not answered with clemency. Although the death penalty had not been used in Russia since Catherine's day, Nicholas sentenced five of the ringleaders—Pestel, Ryleev, Mouraviev, Bestuzhev, and Kakhofsky—to death by hanging and handed over a hundred others to penal servitude and exile in Siberia.

The Decembrist revolt created a legend that inspired future revolutionaries. Immediately, however, it encouraged a deepening of government repression.

Repression under Nicholas I / Until his accession to the throne Nicholas I had commanded a brigade of guards and, according to one critic, was hated by them because of "his cold cruelty, his petty fussiness, and his vindictiveness." He was the kind of soldier who put a higher valuation on discipline and drill than on initiative; and, as emperor, he soon showed that his ideal was a disciplined state in which all subjects recognized that their first duty was to obey authority. Like Metternich, Nicholas believed that change was reprehensible in itself; therefore he opposed the reform even of institutions which he personally regarded as evil, like serfdom. He feared the masses; he feared the Russian nobility (so much, indeed, that he preferred to rely on German administrators); he feared intellectuals. His anxieties were constantly heightened—by the Decembrist revolt, by the revolutions in Western Europe, and in 1831 by the rising in his own Kingdom of Poland (see pp. 32–33)—and they gradually narrowed his view and encouraged the dictatorial strain in his character.

The symbol of Nicholas' reign is the secret police—that notorious Third Section of the Imperial Chancery which was directed, from 1826 until 1844, by Count Benckendorff, who, in the words of Alexander Herzen, stood "outside the law and above the law, having a right to meddle in everything." The Third Section operated through a uniformed *gendarmerie* and a vast network of secret agents of every walk of life; its aim was to prevent another 14th of December; its accomplishment was to make a whole generation live in fear of informers and arbitrary police procedure. The intelligentsia of writers, journalists, and teachers were the principal objects of scrutiny by these secret agents, as they were also the targets of government decrees that forbade travel abroad without permission, prohibited the entry of subversive literature or dangerous radicals, and censored newspapers, journals, and university lectures.

The effects of all this were bitterly described by Alexander Herzen, himself an intellectual who suffered five years detention at Perm because of his political views and who finally, in 1848, succeeded in escaping to London. Herzen accused Nicholas of "the moral destruction of a generation" and the "spiritual depraving" of Russian youth, of having frustrated their best impulses and made them "sick, deranged . . . inoculated with a sort of spiritlessness, a sense of impotence, of fatigue before beginning work." Herzen wrote this in his private diary. When P. Y. Chaadaev wrote publicly that "Russia's past is empty, her present insufferable, and there is no future at all; it is a blank sheet, a terrible lesson given to the nations of the plight to which a people can be brought by isolation and slavery," Nicholas ordered the distinguished philosopher to be declared insane and forbidden to write anything else.

Domestic Policy and Territorial Growth / From what has been said above, it follows that Nicholas' reign was barren of domestic reforms.

Indeed, the only notable innovations before 1848 were the successful codification of Russian laws, completed under the supervision of Speransky in 1833, and the stabilization of the currency and the elimination of depreciated paper money by the finance minister Kankrin, a very capable civil servant of Hessian extraction. Both these things had long been needed; unfortunately, Kankrin's achievement was of temporary duration, for, after his retirement in 1844, his successors departed from his cautious policies and encouraged inflation and depreciation by issuing new money whenever they suffered from financial embarrassment.

In other areas there was no sign of reform or improvement. The only change in governmental structure was a steady growth of the executive department (His Majesty's Own Chancery), which, as Nicholas' autocratic tendencies developed, continually absorbed new functions and, by doing so, made the whole government dangerously top-heavy. With respect to serfdom, the tsar deferred to the wishes of the great landowners and studiously avoided anything that resembled reform. In education—another field where improvement was badly needed—conditions worsened, if anything, as a result of the policies of Count S. S. Uvarov, minister of education from 1833 to 1849. Uvarov believed that Russia's educational system must be based on the principles of "orthodoxy, autocracy, and nationality" or, in other words, on piety, respect for the tsar, and patriotism, and that it should serve to freeze the existing social system by discouraging members of the lower classes from seeking advanced education and, in the case of those who refused to be discouraged, by making it impossible for them to acquire it. He was so intent on these objectives that he paid rather too little attention to educational standards, which, especially in the secondary schools, declined sharply.

If Nicholas' domestic accomplishments were unimpressive, he did achieve success in his foreign policy. Russia's international prestige was enhanced by the assistance given to the Greeks, although this was somewhat dimmed by the excesses resorted to in Poland, and by Nicholas' role in the two Egyptian crises of the 1830s. Russia's territorial gains under Nicholas were sufficiently great to indicate that the empire was not yet a sated power. A shortsighted attack on Russia by Persian troops in 1826 led to a brief campaign which left in Russian hands the provinces of Nakhichevan and Erivan in northern Persia, along with naval rights on the Caspian Sea; and, as we have already seen (pp. 27–28), the war against Turkey in 1828 brought more of the Caucasus and the Black Sea coast into Russia's possession, while strengthening its position in Rumania. Attempts to extend Russian influence in Afghanistan were less successful, and an expedition against Khiva in 1839 was a failure.

PRUSSIA TO 1848

The Land and the People / The settlement at Vienna had wrought significant changes in the nature of the Prussian state. When Prussia ceded most of its former Polish possessions to Russia and received compensation in Saxony and in Rhineland-Westphalia, its center of interest shifted from Eastern Europe to Central Europe and its population, hitherto predominantly German, now became overwhelmingly so.

Prussia was destined, before the century was over, to unite all Germany under its control, but few would have guessed that in 1815. Of the eastern powers it was easily the weakest, even in population, which stood at eleven million in 1815 and did not exceed sixteen million in 1848. Moreover, although it had acquired new territories, they did not form a solid mass, for Prussia's Rhenish provinces were separated from the older ones—and from the nation's capital at Berlin—by the independent territories of Hanover, Brunswick, and Hesse-Cassel. The fact that so much of the population was composed of new subjects was also a source of weakness. The inhabitants of the Polish districts had always been recalcitrant and hard to manage. Now, to what remained of them were added many resentful Saxons and thousands of Rhinelanders who differed in religion, historical background, and temperament from their new overlords.

Economically, Prussia was still predominantly agricultural, although not to the same extent as Russia and without Russia's system of servile labor. During the period of basic reform that followed Prussia's defeat by France in 1807, the government abolished serfdom by the emancipation edict of 1807, supplemented by later decrees. The serfs who were affected by these laws had, however, to pay for their liberation by surrendering much of their land to their former masters or by incurring heavy debts in order to acquire ownership. The terms of emancipation helped the owners of the large estates (the so-called *Junkers*) to increase their holdings and transformed the mass of the peasantry into landless agricultural workers who were so dependent on the landlords that their freedom sometimes seemed illusory.

The acquisition of the Rhineland made Prussia potentially the strongest industrial power in Germany, for the rich mineral resources of that area, so happily wedded to coal deposits and water power, were now added to those of Upper Silesia. The importance of this was not widely appreciated in 1815, for industrial enterprise was still hardly existent. Yet notable steps forward were taken in the next thirty years. The efforts of the Westphalian manufacturer Friedrich Harkort to introduce English methods into textile and iron production, to mechanize these industries, and to combine under one control all the processes necessary for the transformation of the raw material into the finished product were the first significant steps in building up German industry. Under Harkort's influence, old small-scale family concerns—like the Stumm iron works and the Hoesch puddling works (famous names in the later history of German industry)—revolutionized their methods and entered the export trade. In the 1820s the Borsig machine works were established, and the Haniel engineering works began to build steamboats for the river trade; in the 1840s the Krupp concern was established at Essen. In the same years the transformation of the textile industry began, with the mechanization of the Mevissen linen mills at Krefeld and the woolen mills of David Hansemann, another notable Rhineland manufacturer. Too much should not be made of these developments, of course. The industrial development of Prussia was still far behind that of her western neighbors; and, despite the richness of the Silesian and Westphalian coal deposits, the coal production of all Germany still lagged behind that of Belgium in 1846. But these developments were pledges of future progress.

Prussian trade was handicapped by the fact that the country had no direct access to the North Sea and did not control the mouths of the Elbe, the Weser, or the Rhine rivers. Moreover, it has been estimated that, until 1818, Prussia had sixty-seven different tariff areas within her borders, a fact which made the transit of goods from one part of the realm to another complicated and costly. In that year, however, in order to make customs duties uniform throughout the kingdom, to discourage smuggling, and to raise a reasonable amount of revenue, the government introduced a new tariff law that abolished all internal tolls, while imposing a moderate tariff on goods coming in from outside. This law was so successful in achieving its purposes that it was emulated by other German states. Moreover, since they wished to avoid having to pay heavy tolls for the privilege of shipping goods across Prussian territory, they began to negotiate economic agreements with the Prussian government. This led to the formation in 1834 of the Prussian Customs Union (*Zollverein*) which included all German states except Hanover, the Hanse towns, Mecklenburg, Oldenburg, Holstein, and Austria. The political importance of this in increasing Prussian influence in Germany is obvious. Economically, the tariff of 1818 and the trade agreements between that date and 1834 enormously stimulated Prussian trade, which was encouraged also in these years by new road building, the beginning of railroad construction (1000 miles of new line were laid on Prussian territory between 1844 and 1848 alone), and a treaty with Holland in 1831 which opened the lower Rhine to Prussian goods.

Prussia's political and social hierarchy was, in its broadest outlines, similar to that of Russia. The tie between the crown and the nobility was perhaps more intimate than in that country; and, since the seventeenth century, Prussian kings had protected the economic privileges of their landed nobles while the nobles had recognized their obligation to send their sons into the service of the state. In the military establishment, although the war against Napoleon had necessitated the commissioning of members of the middle class, their advancement was not encouraged after 1815 and they were isolated, for the most part, in the technical branches of the service. The nobility maintained its virtual monopoly in the officer corps, and its influence was paramount also in the most intimate councils of state.

Because of Prussia's more advanced economic development, the system of social stratification differed from the Russian in two respects. The industrial working class was larger and growing faster than its Russian counterpart and, by the end of the period, was already introducing an element of violence into the Prussian class system. In the second place, the bourgeoisie was more numerous, wealthy, and self-confident than the Russian merchant class. The Mevissens and Hansemanns of the Rhineland, seeking to imitate their models in England and France, looked upon themselves as the progressive force that would make the Germany of the future. They were both contemptuous of the stiff, uncultivated, and sometimes penurious East Elbian squires and resentful of their social and political power. This attitude was strengthened by the political events of the postwar period.

The Return to Reaction / In the melancholy years that followed the Prussian defeat at Jena in 1806, when the country lay under the heel of Napoleon and its status as a Great Power was in question, a remarkable group of new leaders had come to the fore in Prussian politics. These men, among whom Stein, Scharnhorst, Gneisenau, and Humboldt were outstanding, wanted to arouse the patriotic spirit of the nation so that French rule could be thrown off; and they believed that the best way to accomplish this was—in Gneisenau's words—to make all Prussian subjects "free, noble, and independent so that they believe that they are part of the whole." In pursuit of these objects they persuaded the king, between 1807 and 1813, to approve a series of edicts abolishing serfdom, broadening the powers of local government, increasing educational opportunity, opening the officer corps to the bourgeoisie and making merit the test of promotion, reforming the disciplinary code of the army, and making other fundamental changes in the structure of the state and society. By 1815 it appeared that Prussia was on its way to becoming a state with liberal representative institutions; and on May 22, 1815,

Frederick William III promised to repay his subjects for their successful efforts in expelling the French by granting them a written constitution.

All of this, however, was misleading. Frederick William was an honorable man but not a resolute one; timidity and vacillation were the keys to his character, and he distrusted all new ideas. Because of the hard necessities of war, he had allowed himself to be pushed along the road to reform, but he hadn't liked the process or the men who did the pushing. He had never got on with Stein, whom he had once accused of being "refractory, insolent, obstinate, and disobedient"; by 1815 he was grumbling that Gneisenau, Prussia's most gifted military strategist and a passionate advocate of a constitution, was too clever for his own good; and his sympathy for the ideas of other members of the reform group who were still in government service was wearing thin.

The king was influenced in his attitude toward the reformers by the opinions of his fellow monarchs in Eastern Europe and by the criticism of his own nobility. Alexander of Russia, Francis of Austria, and Prince Metternich made no secret of the fact that they believed Frederick William had embarked on a dangerous course when he began to patronize the reformers; and a group of the most influential nobles in Prussia, led by Duke Karl von Mecklenburg and the minister of police, Prince Wittgenstein, used every opportunity to insinuate into the king's mind the idea that Stein and his colleagues had "brought revolution into the country" and that it was only a question of time before the destruction of the monarchy and the war of the propertyless against the propertied got under way.

Under this twofold pressure the king turned against the reformers and their ideas. In 1819 Frederick William dismissed War Minister Boyen because that official had resisted what appeared to be a royal attempt to undo the military reforms. At the same time, he dropped Humboldt and Finance Minister Beyme because they had objected to Prussia's adherence to the Carlsbad Decrees (see pp. 62–63). Since Gneisenau had already gone into retirement, this virtually destroyed the influence of the reform group and left the field free for reaction.

The government functioned effectively enough in the years that followed. In 1817 Frederick William had created a Council of State, composed of princes of the royal house, leaders of the provincial nobility, and high officials; this body improved the government of the dispersed provinces and gradually developed a centralized administration. Ever since the seventeenth century, Prussia had had an efficient bureaucracy, and it worked well now and improved the public services.

Nevertheless, there were many in Prussia after 1819 who felt as the great archaeologist Winckelmann had felt when he fled the rule of Frederick the Great, that it was "better to be a circumcised Turk than a Prussian." All the hopes of the reform era were now disappointed. When the citizens of the Rhineland sent a petition to the king in 1818, reminding him of his promise of a constitution, they were abruptly informed that, by "wantonly casting doubts on the inviolability of the sovereign's word," they were committing the crime of *lèse majesté*. The only concession that the king made to the demand for representative institutions was the reform of the old provincial estates and the establishment, in 1823, of provincial diets. Since these were permitted to meet only infrequently and to possess only advisory powers and since, in addition, they were dominated by the landed aristocracy, there was little danger that they would advocate progressive ideas.

Those reforms that were on the books were seriously watered down in the subsequent period. Every decree designed to supplement the emancipation edict of 1807 seemed to benefit the landlords and hurt the former serfs. The local government ordinance was revised in a conservative direction, and the merit principle was quietly dropped as the test of army promotions. The liberal spirit that had inspired the educational reforms of Humboldt was absent from the administration of Altenstein, minister of education from 1817 to 1838; both universities and schools fell under rigid bureaucratic control.

In Prussian education the influence of Georg Friedrich Hegel (1770–1831) now attained its height. Both Altenstein and his supervisor of secondary schools, Johannes Schulze, were ardent Hegelians; and it was not therefore accidental that so many of Hegel's students began to fill teaching positions in the gymnasia and university chairs in philosophy, education, and political economy. Through their efforts the more extreme Hegelian doctrines—the personification of the state, the insistence that the life of the individual attained meaning only when he was absorbed in the state, the belief that the essence and the justification of the state was its power and that "what is rational is actual, and what is actual is rational"—were drilled into students in the hope of persuading them of the merits of the existing regime. If the system of Haller had been the official philosophy of Prussian authoritarianism in the first years after 1815, it was replaced in Frederick William III's last years by this kind of Hegelianism; and it gave a cast to Prussian political thinking that was to last a long time.

The reaction under Frederick William III had its ludicrous aspects. An incredible amount of effort was expended in keeping members of the reform party under surveillance in the hope of discovering plots against the government. Newspapers were suppressed for reasons that were neither logical nor consistent; and journalists were apt, on the slightest pretext, to be haled into court and charged with disrespect for the royal person, like the hapless publisher who had placed an advertisement for herring too close to the court calendar. But even the incidents that aroused ridicule were depressing when seen in the total context of press and university censorship, thought control, persecution of "demagogues," and what appeared to be an attempt to destroy the independence of the Catholic Church (see pp. 65–66). Prussia, which in the years between 1807 and 1813 had seemed to be in the vanguard of German liberalism, was now apparently what it had always been in the past, an autocratic, militaristic state, whose efficient administration did not redeem the absence of freedom within its borders.

Nor was the picture relieved when the king died in 1840 and was succeeded by his son, under the title Frederick William IV. This ruler was a man of great personal charm and intellectual power, although these gifts were offset by a tendency to abstruse thought and devious methods and a habit of indecision in moments of crisis. But his greatest weakness was his ability to arouse in others mistaken ideas concerning his intentions. Because of this, his first years were filled with misunderstandings.

The new king began his reign with a coronation address in which he talked of the intimate relationship that should exist between a monarch and his subjects. He then issued a series of decrees, freeing political prisoners, moderating the censorship of the press, and restoring former liberals to honor and to office. Not unnaturally, this led to widespread expectation that Prussia, with a liberal monarch on the throne, was now going to receive representative institutions and a written constitution.

But Frederick William was not a liberal; he was a romantic. In the new world of industrialism, he was probably the last sovereign who really believed in the theory of divine right of kings. He expected allegiance from his subjects as a matter of course. He was willing to make certain voluntary concessions to them because he wanted to appear as a wise and magnanimous ruler; but for them to demand something from him was, in his opinion, presumptuous.

The king had no intention of satisfying the hopes of his people. He did, after much hesitation, convoke a joint meeting of the provincial diets in 1847, to discuss financial matters and raise new taxes. But when that body met, he made it clear that this was the limit of his concessions and, at the same time, gave his opinion of constitutions:

> No power on earth will ever force me to transform the natural relationship . . . between prince and people into a conventional constitutional one; neither now nor ever will I permit a written piece of paper to force itself like some second providence, between our Lord God in heaven and this land, to rule us with its paragraphs and, through them, to replace the ancient sacred loyalty.

In the face of this intransigent defence of the authoritarian principle, there was no hope of constitutional progress or social reform; and Prussia remained a center of reaction until the storm of 1848 swept over the land.

THE AUSTRIAN EMPIRE TO 1848

The Land and the People   /   After 1815 the Austrian Empire comprised Austria proper, Bohemia, Galicia, the Kingdom of Hungary, Illyria on the Dalmatian coast, and the northern Italian provinces of Lombardy and Venetia. The Vienna settlement had made it more compact than it had been before the Napoleonic period, but this compactness did not make for internal unity. The thirty million people who inhabited the Habsburg lands differed in racial origins, historical background, language, and customs. The Austrian duchies were peopled for the most part by Germans; but Bohemia was inhabited by Czechs and Slovaks, Galicia by Poles and Ruthenians, Hungary by the Magyars but also by Croats, Ruthenians, Rumanians, and Slovaks, Illyria by Croats, Serbs, and Slovenes, and Lombardy and Venetia by Italians. These peoples had little in common except the bond of the imperial house and the Catholic Church.

Within the empire the Germans were the dominant people. The ruling house was German; German was the official language, the language of commerce, and the language of the towns (not only of Vienna, but also of Budapest and Prague); and Germans filled most of the positions in the imperial bureaucracy. But this position was to be challenged in time by the strongest of the subject nationalities. Even in the first years after 1815 the Magyars were restive, and they did not become any less so as time passed. In general, Austria's greatest problem, which became one of life or death, was one of adjusting and balancing the desires of its diverse peoples in such a way as to preserve the bond of empire.

The Austrian economy was largely agricultural. There were some signs of industrial development in the western towns and in the "hungry forties," this had gone far enough for there to be riots by factory workers in Prague. In Lombardy also factory organization was getting under way at the end of this period in the cotton, silk, and linen industries. But this was still on a very small scale. The government sought to increase export trade by building the port of Trieste as an outlet to the Mediterranean, and it also made some gestures in the direction of railway promotion, although its efforts in this latter respect were neither as consistent nor as successful as those of the Prussian government. This was true also of

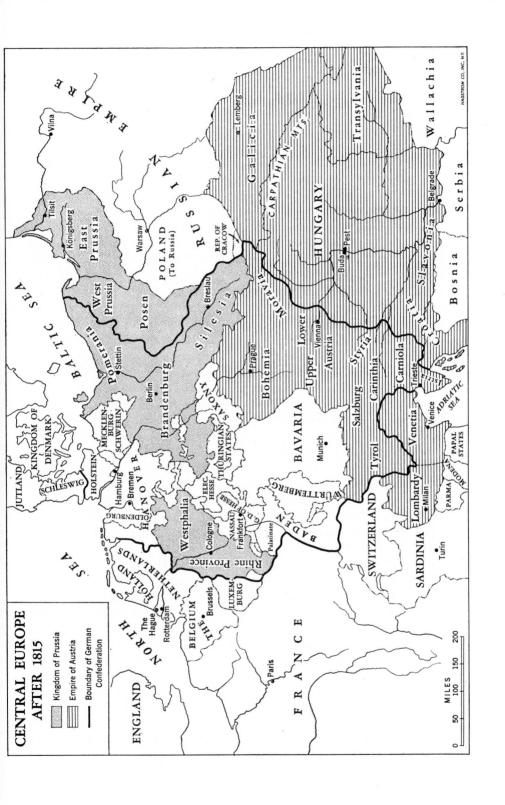

CENTRAL EUROPE
AFTER 1815

Kingdom of Prussia
Empire of Austria
Boundary of German
Confederation

tariff policy, which was certainly less imaginative than the policy that led to the formation of the Prussian *Zollverein,* as is indicated by the continued existence throughout these years of a customs barrier between Austria and Hungary. Austrian trade policy was enlightened only in fits and starts, and there was no appreciable commercial growth. In any event, the backbone of the economy was agriculture in which the great majority of the population were engaged.

As in the case of Russia, the nature of the economy was reflected in the social and political hierarchy. The nobility owned most of the land, dispensed local justice and administered local affairs, and provided the imperial government with officers for its army, diplomats for its foreign service, and department heads for its ministries. Provided their economic rights were protected by the crown, they supported it, although they were jealous of any infringement of their inherited feudal privileges. Within their ranks there were gradations, especially in Hungary, where there was a considerable economic gap between the magnates, who might own estates covering as much as 40,000 acres of land, and the small squires, who often had more pride than possessions. This division had some political importance, but it did not affect the attitude of the nobility, great and small, toward the class that supported it.

The peasants lived in conditions similar to those of the serfs in Russia. They were subject to the legal jurisdiction of the local lord and forced to pay dues and labor services and this burden was heavy. It has been estimated that, in Bohemia, peasants owed half of their time and two thirds of their crops to their lords, and conditions were no different in other parts of the empire. This meant that the great mass of the population was oppressed and miserable and the conditions of their life excluded them from political affairs.

Special mention should perhaps be made of the imperial bureaucracy, which, while not a class in the economic sense, was an important factor in the political and social life of the empire. Although this service included Hungarian and Czech aristocrats and, indeed, men of every nationality, most of its members were Germans, generally of the lesser nobility. They were held together by a tradition inherited from the days of Emperor Joseph II, who had tried to impose German culture and customs on the whole empire; and they believed that their mission was to fight the forces of decentralization, local patriotism, and aristocratic privilege. The labors of the bureaucracy kept the empire functioning but, at the same time, invited conflict with the local magnates and the different national groups.

The Course of Domestic Policy / Until his death in 1835, Austria was ruled by Emperor Francis I. This monarch is sometimes dismissed as childish or frivolous, and Sir Harold Nicolson has written that he was happiest when he was in his workshop stamping seals on sealing wax or making toffee on the stove. But this does not do Francis justice. He may have been indolent, but he was very far from being a cipher in imperial affairs. As Metternich wrote in 1820, the emperor knew exactly what he wanted, and he was autocrat enough to see that he got it. His real weakness was narrowness of view. In an empire held together by bureaucrats, he was the bureaucrat par excellence: fond of red tape and protocol, suspicious of ideas and methods that did not conform to inherited practice and of people who were too obviously brilliant, averse to novelty, and bitterly hostile to reform—a man whose motto might well have been "Govern and change nothing."

Francis succeeded in remaining true to this principle in the face of the dictates of common sense and the arguments of his ministers. There can be little doubt that the imperial administration would have been greatly improved if the welter of redundant chancelleries, courts, directories, and councils which made up the machinery of state could either have been abolished completely or, at least, coordinated by the creation of some kind of council for the whole empire. Metternich, who was certainly no reformer but who was sensible enough to see that even autocracies should be run efficiently, repeatedly suggested such a reorganization. Not only were his proposals never acted upon but after 1826 they were never seriously considered. In that year Count Kolowrat became minister of state, and the Czech aristocrat hated Metternich and succeeded in undermining his position sufficiently so that he had to restrict himself henceforward to foreign affairs. Kolowrat himself was not unaware of the need of administrative reform, but he was not a strong enough man to overcome the emperor's inertia.

The result was that there were no essential changes in any branch of the imperial administration except the army where General Radetzky was able to force through some long needed improvements. Despite the pressing need for financial reform, the imperial debt was allowed to go on mounting; despite the example of effective tariff reform shown by Prussia, the old restrictions on trade remained; and so forth. "I won't have any innovations," Francis said in 1831. "Let the laws be justly applied; they are good and adequate."

People who persisted in advocating change Francis hounded down mercilessly. It is fair to say that in internal affairs Metternich and Kolowrat were both less influential than the man who was minister of police after 1817, Count Sedlnitzky. His agents opened even Metternich's letters, and had little respect for less important persons. Espionage, denunciation, secret trials, and arbitrary punishment were as much a part of life in Austria as they were of Russia in the heyday of Benckendorff. The

Austrian press was censored even more rigorously than the Prussian. Professors and schoolteachers were under constant surveillance, never knowing who in their audiences might not be a police spy; and school authorities were strictly enjoined to report the expression of any sentiments that might be considered subversive. Students were forbidden to study in foreign universities and were forced to content themselves with an educational system in which everything that they and their professors read had to be approved by the government. It is no wonder that so many of them came to regard their country as one large, and very dull, prison.

Francis died in February 1835. He was succeeded by his eldest son, Ferdinand, who was, unfortunately, of such feeble intelligence that it was said that his only sensible remark after his accession was, "I'm the emperor and I want noodles!" However that may be, the direction of the government for the next thirteen years was in the hands of a "council of state" of three men: Archduke Ludwig, the least gifted of the brothers of Francis I, Metternich, and Kolowrat. Ludwig, like his dead brother, wanted nothing changed; Metternich and Kolowrat were engaged in such involved intrigues against each other that they had no time to think of reforms; so the empire lumbered on in its usual way.

Developments in Hungary before 1848 / There were signs of life, however, in Hungary. Despite attempts at Germanization and centralization, the Magyars had preserved their medieval local assemblies, which were sounding boards for the grievances of the nobility. Strong resistance on the part of these bodies to certain tax and recruiting decrees of imperial authorities induced the Vienna government to try to propitiate the Hungarian magnates by convoking a Central Hungarian Diet in 1825. The meeting was so stormy and so critical of the regime that the emperor was forced to agree to raise no taxes in the future without the consent of this body, which was to be reconvened periodically.

It was at the Diet of 1825 that a remarkable leader appeared in the person of Stephan Széchenyi. A former officer and one of the richest men in Hungary, Széchenyi wished to lift his country out of the torpor in which she had lived so long by awakening a sense of responsibility among his fellows in the upper nobility. He dreamed of a Hungary in which the nobility would give up such privileges as its freedom from the land tax and would cooperate in efforts to ameliorate the lot of the peasantry—a Hungary, moreover, in which an economic transformation would be effected by means of technical assistance to improve agriculture, the creation of capital resources to stimulate industry, the improvement of communications, the abolition of the tariff wall separating Hungary from Austria, and the inclusion of Hungary in the Austrian railroad system. Although disappointed in his hopes that he might receive encouragement and assistance from Vienna, Széchenyi was able to induce his fellow magnates, between 1825 and 1832, to carry through some economic improvements, including the construction of a bridge between Buda and Pesth (until now unconnected) and the facilitation of steam navigation on the Danube. Under his influence, the Hungarian Diet of 1832 actually began to consider a reform of the condition of the peasantry.

But Széchenyi could not win the support of the lesser nobility, whose reduced circumstances made them cling to the very privileges that he wanted to abolish; and in 1832 they found a leader in Louis Kossuth. This romantic figure, a journalist by trade, attained tremendous popularity by appealing to the hostility with which the lesser nobles viewed the magnates and by urging, not closer union with Austria, which was the gist of Széchenyi's economic program, but a greater degree of Hungarian independence. Kossuth used the arguments of the German protectionist Friedrich List to urge the necessity of a national economy for Hungary with separate tariff and communications systems and autonomous institutions. The fervor with which he pleaded this case and his increasingly radical views and violent language divided the Hungarian nobility into two camps, while at the same time creating a turbulence that could not help but affect the peasant masses as well. By the late 1840s, Hungary was in a dangerous state of unrest.

The Austrian Mission / One of Metternich's foreign colleagues said on one occasion that Austria was Europe's House of Lords, meaning, no doubt, that her function was to restrain the passions and undo the mistakes of the common run of petty states in Europe. Austria's geographical position made her the logical power to maintain order in central Europe; there is no doubt that Metternich regarded that as the mission of his country after 1815. Some mention has been made above (pp. 23, 32) of the vigilance with which he watched over Italian affairs and the promptness with which he intervened to snuff out revolutionary movements. It is now time to review his activities in Germany.

GERMANY TO 1848

The German States and the Confederation / One of the great services that Napoleon Bonaparte performed for Germany was to simplify its political structure. Before his time the area which we think of as

Germany was a crazy quilt of conflicting sovereignties; it comprised over three hundred separate political units, each with its own laws and regulations. The French emperor had followed a policy of amalgamation and, in the end, had reduced the number to less than fifty. The Congress of Vienna carried Napoleon's work further and, when they were finished, Germany was composed of thirty-eight states, ranging in size and importance from the five kingdoms of Prussia, Hanover, Bavaria, Württemberg, and Saxony to such miniscule states as Lippe and the free cities of the north.

All of these states, plus the German part of the Austrian empire, were members of the Germanic Confederation, which had been created at Vienna. The central body of this organization was the Diet, which met periodically at Frankfurt on the Main and was composed of representatives chosen by the rulers of the various member states. The Diet was not, in other words, an elective assembly or parliament but a diplomatic organization which, in some respects, resembled the United Nations of our time. It had a complicated procedure and a very involved voting system on which it is unnecessary to dilate, except to note that on all matters of importance two thirds of the members had to agree before a decision was taken and on some matters unanimous agreement was required. This made action of any kind difficult. Aside from this, the Congress of Vienna had not defined the competence and jurisdiction of the Diet; and, true to the age-old German tradition of particularism, the member states were not inclined to admit that it had, or should have, any substantial authority.

Article XIII of the Federal Constitution, which was incorporated in the Final Act of the Congress of Vienna, stipulated that all member states should have constitutions that would provide for assemblies of the estates. Such a constitution was granted by the Grand Duke of Saxe-Weimar; he was followed by the rulers of Bavaria, Württemburg, Baden, and Hesse-Darmstadt. But, as we have seen above, Prussia did not follow suit, despite the solemn promise of her king, and other rulers did not even bother to make empty promises. A ruler like the elector of Hesse—who, when he returned to Kassel after seven years of French rule, proceeded to invalidate all laws passed and even all military and bureaucratic promotions made during his absence[1]—was obviously not interested in issuing a charter of liberties to his subjects. As for the ruling groups in the free cities of Hamburg and Lübeck, they outdid the Hessian prince by returning to their charters of 1669 and 1528 respectively. This

---

[1] When it was announced, in 1813, that this prince was returning to his capital, a former servant of his donned his old uniform and went to the residence. As the elector drove up, he shouted proudly, "Here I am, Your Highness! At my post!" The prince replied, "Good heavens, the old chap's been standing there since 1806!"

obviously flouted the sense of Article XIII of the Federal Act, but the Diet proved powerless to do anything about it. Nor was it able to carry out certain other assigned tasks, like the establishment of a competent federal army or of a central court to adjudicate disputes between member states.

It is obvious that if the Confederation could not impose its will on member states in small matters, it would be incapable of giving Germany any real bond of unity. It seemed more likely that—in the words of the Prussian general Clausewitz—"Germany can achieve political unity only in one way, by the sword, by one of its states subjugating all the others." The only states capable of such an act of conquest were Austria and Prussia. The Austrians, who had been invested with the permanent presidency of the Confederation, wanted no change; the Prussians not only agreed with this view but seemed perfectly happy to play second fiddle to the Austrians. The closeness of Austro-Prussian collaboration in these years gave no hint of the future struggle for supremacy between the two great German powers.

Liberalism and Nationalism in Germany / The historian Sybel wrote of the German Confederation that it was "received by the German nation at large partly with cold indifference and partly with patriotic indignation." The first reaction was probably the one felt by most persons. It is always a mistake to think that the majority of any people are interested in politics; and in Germany these years formed the so-called *Biedermeier* period, a time of relative stability and peace in which the ordinary people did not look far beyond their family circle or the affairs of their village and in which they accepted both the political and the social facts of life as they were presented to them.

But there were forces of movement in the German states, and they were to be found in the commercial and industrial towns and in the universities. It was among the latter that the first real movement of protest against the *status quo* got under way. Students who had fought in the war of liberation came back to the universities to found a new kind of organization, unlike the old beer-swilling, dueling corporations, but devoted instead to the moral and political regeneration of Germany and the cause of national unity. These societies were called *Burschenschaften* and, by 1816, they were organized into a national federation with branches in sixteen universities.

In 1817, in celebration of the fourth anniversary of the Battle of Leipzig (symbol of Germany's liberation from tyranny) and also of the three-hundredth anniversary of Martin Luther's defiance of authority, the *Burschenschaft* of the University of Jena convoked a national assembly and held a dramatic meeting at the Wartburg Castle. Here speeches were made about unity and freedom and the disappointment of the high hopes of the liberation period; the princes who had not granted constitutions to their peoples were held up to execration; and a bonfire was kindled into which were thrown such things as a Prussian corporal's cane, Haller's book on political philosophy, some regulations of the Prussian ministry of education, and other symbols of institutions detested by the *Burschen.*

Sporadic agitations of this nature continued for the next two years, to the growing annoyance of the authorities and of Prince Metternich. But in 1819 the protest movement took a turn that played into the hands of the Austrian chancellor. A young student named Karl Sand, of disturbed mind and muddled purpose, stabbed to death a playwright named Kotzebue who was supposed to be a spy in the pay of the tsar of Russia. When he heard of this pointless crime, Metternich struck immediately. He summoned a meeting of the principal German states and, at Carlsbad in August 1819, they drew up a series of decrees—later approved by the Federal Diet—providing for the dissolution of the *Burschenschaften* and the imposition of strict censorship over the press and universities in all German states. Moreover, a commission was to be established at Mainz to study the discontent in Germany and to institute proceedings against subversive individuals and organizations.

Metternich now had the weapons for imposing the same kind of control over Germany that the secret police exercised in the Austrian empire. Yet they failed to prevent new incidents and agitations. When revolution erupted in France in 1830, for instance, it aroused enthusiasm in Germany too; and liberal movements in Brunswick, Hanover, Saxony, and Hesse-Cassel succeeded in forcing constitutional concessions from the rulers of those states. Two years later, at Hambach in Rhenish Bavaria, at least 30,000 people, drawn from every social class, assembled and listened with enthusiasm to a series of speeches extolling national unity and popular freedom. This meeting was even more radical than the Wartburg festival of 1817; one of the speakers not only demanded the destruction of absolutism in Austria and Prussia but called down a "lasting curse upon kings, the betrayers of their peoples and all mankind." This language was alarming enough to make the Diet strike back with more repressive legislation; in June 1832, it passed a series of articles intended to make all existing representative assemblies powerless to limit the sovereignty of their princes or to use whatever financial powers they might possess to exact other concessions. But these attempts to prop up the authority of German princes by decree were no more successful than earlier ones.

Proof of this was given in 1837 when the new king of Hanover dissolved his assembly and absolved all of his civil servants from the oath they had taken to the constitution that his predecessor had granted.

Seven distinguished professors at the University of Göttingen, including the historians Dahlmann and Gervinus and the philologists and folklorists Jakob and Wilhelm Grimm, refused to comply. Jakob Grimm pointed out that the universities were the conscience of the nation and university professors must have a jealous regard for their word, lest students, seeing them waver or compromise on one issue, think them capable of compromising in their teaching. The Göttingen Seven defied their prince and were expelled from Hanover; but they became heroes in the eyes of the middle and intellectual classes of Germany.

But the excitement aroused by these incidents was exceeded by that caused by the sudden war scare of 1840, when it appeared for a time that the French might seek revenge for their isolation in Near Eastern affairs (see pp. 34–35) by striking across the Rhine. The menacing sounds that came from Paris caused a patriotic response so intense that the historian Treitschke wrote later that here, for the first time, the Germans were one, despite the political fragmentation of their country. All over Germany men were singing the new songs brought forth by the crisis: Nikolaus Becker's *Song of the Rhine*, with its challenging opening words

> They shall not have our free German Rhine
> Though they scream after it like greedy ravens;

the now better-known *Watch on the Rhine* by Max Schneckenburger; and, a little later, Hoffmann von Fallersleben's *Deutschland, Deutschland über alles*.

The last of these songs, which was to become the national anthem of the united Germany of the future, has a final verse which calls for

> Unity and Law and Freedom
> For the German Fatherland.

At the time those words were written, there is no doubt that the desired objects went together. The young patriots of 1840, the members of the *Burschenschaften*, the progressive businessmen, the champions of railroad building and tariff reform, in short, all the workers for change and progress saw no reason why they should choose between Unity and Law and Freedom; they took it for granted that attaining one would mean attaining all.

Yet there was already, even among the most sincere believers in constitutional freedom, a tendency to become impatient over the delay in attaining German unity; and impatience led some of them to wonder whether it might not be necessary, temporarily, to give unity the priority over liberal objectives and material considerations priority over high ideals. Even before 1848 German patriots were more conscious of the factor of power than their cloudy rhetoric would seem to indicate. The

Hegelians had done their work well; while it is interesting to note in the writings of that fervent advocate of unity, the economist Friedrich List, how the author, in defining the requirements of nationhood, places increasing emphasis on things like "extensive territory," railroads, protective tariffs, colonies, and "adequate power on land and sea" rather than on matters of law and the spirit.

Nor was this tendency confined to northern Germany. The period before 1848 was the heyday of South German liberalism, for all of the southern states had constitutions and representative assemblies, and their parliamentary orators, like Karl Theodor Welcker and Karl von Rotteck, received a national hearing. Compared with the English and French parliaments of this period, these assemblies had little real power; but the middle classes of South Germany were proud of them and took pleasure in comparing their enlightened institutions with the repressive system of Austria and—more contemptuously—with the reactionary military kingdom of Prussia.

Yet one of the most interesting of the South German political thinkers, Paul Pfizer, believed that, if Germany were ever to be unified, Prussia must lead the way, and he was not put off by his recognition of Prussia's illiberal character:

> Germany is not greatly aided by the mere axioms of civil liberty, however meritorious and necessary their propagation may be. Despite the urge for liberty on the part of individuals, the Germans will always play a sorry role . . . until they desire freedom as a nation. . . . It is, of course, foolish to demand that Germans wholly forget about freedom within until they have secured independence from without; but it is just as wrong, if not more so, to wish to sacrifice the latter to the former.

Pfizer, like List, was not entirely representative of his time; few German intellectuals before 1848 had attained this particular kind of realism. To most of them nationalism and liberalism went hand in hand; and, since they saw Metternich opposing both, they turned all their efforts to the task of undermining the system he was trying to maintain. They were heartened equally by the example of the Göttingen Seven and by the patriotic enthusiasm of 1840; and, as the world neared the great year 1848, they were confident that time was on their side.

RELIGION AND THE ARTS UNDER ABSOLUTISM

Throne and Altar / Whatever disagreements there were between the established churches and the governments of the Eastern Powers, they did not arise from any difference in political attitude. The churches, which had suffered much during the Enlightenment and the French Revolution, were even more inflexible in their opposition to liberal movements than the political authorities; and this supplied a basis for that intimate cooperation between throne and altar that was characteristic of this period.

It should not be assumed, however, that perfect harmony reigned between the two institutions, except perhaps in Russia. In that country the Orthodox Church was completely under governmental control, for its ecclesiastical ruling body, the Holy Synod, had little authority and all real power was in the hands of the chief procurator, who was a government official. Between 1836 and 1855 that office was filled by N. A. Protasov, a colonel of hussars who ran church administration as if he were commanding a cavalry division. This may have been irritating, but there were no essential differences between the government and the religious hierarchy. High church officials gladly cooperated with the state in its opposition to political dissidents, while the government assisted them in the persecution of members of unorthodox religious sects.

The situation in Prussia was more complex. The Protestant majority in that country had been sharply diminished by the acquisition of the predominantly Catholic Rhine provinces, and this fact led Frederick William III into policies that filled his last years with religious controversy. To offset Catholic strength and also, perhaps, to make the Protestant faith a stronger bulwark against liberalism, the king in 1817 ordered the union of the Lutheran and Reformed churches and, after a long dispute and a few concessions on his part, had his way, although his victory was doubtless won at the expense of the independent spirit of the Protestant churches. The king then became involved in a long struggle with the Catholic Church, going so far in 1837 as to imprison the archbishops of Cologne and Posen in order to force them to comply with government decrees in matters of public education and mixed marriages. Here he was less successful, and the quarrel had to be patched up by his successor, after which the government and the Catholic Church, in political matters especially, saw eye to eye.

Frederick William III's attitude toward Catholicism was doubtless influenced by the spread of ultramontanism after 1815. This movement, the religious counterpart to secular absolutism, was designed to enhance the authority of the papacy. It found its most eloquent literary justification in Joseph de Maistre's *Du Pape* (1819), as well as in Lamennais' *Essay on Indifference in Religious Matters* (1817)[2]; it was symbolized also by the return of the Jesuits, those doughty champions of papal au-

---

[2] On Lamennais, see Chapter 3, p. 93.

thority, to Rome in 1814 and to other countries in the course of the next decade. The intensity with which ultramontanism was pushed by some of its advocates alarmed most secular governments, and the Prussians were not alone in their opposition to it. The Austrian government, for instance, showed a decided coolness in its official relations with the Catholic Church, refusing to conclude a concordat with the Vatican or to permit the Jesuit order to re-establish itself in the empire.

On the other hand, Metternich raised no objections to the growth of ultramontanism in southern Germany, where it seemed to him to be a useful counterbalance to liberalism; and he placed no difficulties in the way of the San Fedist Society and other Catholic laymen's societies in Italy, which, with the support of the Jesuits, combated the influence of the liberals. These societies, indeed, helped to supplement the activities of the Austrian secret police and, because they did so, received the chancellor's blessing.

Within both the Catholic and Protestant churches there were some more progressive tendencies than the ones described here; but the men who represented them were less influential than those who shared the reactionary views of the governments.

Literature and the Arts / Enough has been said above about the general nature of the absolutist regimes to indicate that creative artists who tried to say anything about the society in which they lived would encounter difficulties. The heavy hand of the censor hung over everything they did, and their creations were always in danger of disfigurement or complete suppression. That fact that, despite this handicap, this was a remarkably productive period leads one to wonder what might not have been produced if its writers had been completely free.

In Russia, for instance, these were the years in which a truly national literature first came into existence with the appearance of Krylov's fables, Griboedov's fine comedy *The Misfortune of Being Wise* (1823), the lyric and dramatic works of Russia's greatest poet Alexander Pushkin (1799–1837), the poetry and novels of Michael Lermontov (1814–1841), and the novels and dramas of Nicholas Gogol (1809–1852). Yet Griboedov did not live to see a complete version of his satire on Moscow society performed, because parts of it offended the censor. Pushkin, suspected of association with the Decembrists, had to protect himself by taking a position at court and submitting to the patronage of Nicholas and Benckendorff, a situation that he found insupportable and which involved him in emotional problems that led to his early death. Before his death, moreover, the poet seems to have abandoned plans to write a history of Peter the Great and a novel on contemporary life in Russia because he knew that these works would not meet with official approval.

Similarly, Lermontov's great poem, *The Demon* (1829), could not be published during his lifetime, and Gogol was strongly criticized for his satire on impoverished landlords in *Dead Souls* (1842).

Examples of the same kind can be given for the German states. In Austria even the works of the dead Schiller had to be cut before they were performed in the theaters of Vienna; and writers like the German-Hungarian poet Lenau and Anastasius Grün (Count Auersperg), whose *Promenades of a Viennese Poet* openly attacked the Metternich system, were in constant trouble with the censor. The life of Austria's greatest dramatist, Franz Grillparzer (1791–1872), was made a torment by official interference. Although his drama *King Ottokar's Fortune and Death* (1823) was a patriotic tribute to the House of Hapsburg, its production was delayed for two years by the censor; and, in the case of all his subsequent plays, Grillparzer had to fight for the right of publication. After 1838 he buried his future creations in the drawer of his writing table. "Despotism," he said, "has destroyed my literary life."

In Germany the romantic movement reached its height and began its decline in this period. Novalis and Kleist were dead before the end of the wars; the great names of the first years of peace were the brothers Schlegel, Ludwig Tieck, Clemens Brentano, and E. T. A. Hoffmann, a writer of fantastic tales which are still justly admired for their ironical twists and their grotesque humor. They were succeeded by the superb lyricist Eduard Mörike, the Franconian poet Friedrich Rückert, and Joseph von Eichendorff, author of, among other things, the delightful short novel *The Life of a Good-for-nothing* (1826). There was little in the works of these writers to bother the censor, since their themes were generally taken from the remote past or nature or the world of fantasy, or dealt with love and romantic longing.

The reverse was true of the movement known as "Young Germany," which started in the 1830s and whose distinguished representatives were Heinrich Heine (1797–1856), renowned equally for the lyrical passion of his poetry and his satirical genius, and Ludwig Börne, whose *Letters from Paris* (1830–1833) helped stimulate the beginning of critical journalism in Germany. These writers soon dissociated themselves from the movement, whose objectives were confused and whose members spent their time composing impassioned but generally incoherent works about social injustice, the emancipation of women, free love, and other subjects of contemporary interest. It is perhaps a sign of absolutism's fundamental lack of perspective that the works of Young Germany should have been taken so seriously that they were banned by formal decision of the German Confederation in 1835. The persecution of Heine and Börne is more understandable. They were formidable opponents and one is not surprised to learn that they died in exile in Paris.

Painting, sculpture, and music had greater freedom to develop because their subject matter was less obviously political and their message, if they had one, harder to communicate; and for music in particular this was a rich period. In Russia Michael Glinka (1804–1867), the first great Russian composer, wrote his two operas, *A Life for the Tsar* (1836) and *Ruslan and Liudmilla* (1842), and the shorter works, like *Kamarinskaia*, which were to inspire the whole of the later Russian symphonic school. In Germany, Beethoven's last work showed the transition from classicism to romanticism, as did the songs of Schubert and the work of Weber, whose *Der Freischütz* had a sensational première in Berlin in 1821 and marked the birth of modern German opera. Meyerbeer's *Robert the Devil* (1831) and the young Richard Wagner's first operas, *Rienzi* and *The Flying Dutchman* (1841), were also in the romantic manner.

The absolutist regimes, which deformed and crushed so much that lay within their control, left these expressions of the creative spirit, for the most part, alone. One of the king of Saxony's ministers, however, on learning that Weber had composed the music for some songs of the dead soldier poet Theodor Körner, grumbled, "We didn't know that Weber composed that demagogic rubbish or we would never have engaged him to come to Dresden."

3

France: The Restoration and the July Monarchy

THE ECONOMIC AND SOCIAL ORGANIZATION OF THE COUNTRY

The Effects of the Revolution / The period of French history that opened in 1814 is usually called the Restoration; but, as has often been pointed out, very little was in fact restored, except the Bourbon dynasty. France had had twenty-five years of revolutionary change since 1789, and it was so obviously impossible to re-establish the institutions and laws of the old regime that the first French ruler of this period resisted the advice of those councilors who wanted him to turn back the clock. Louis XVIII was wise enough to see that very few people in France had any desire to see the past recaptured.

Thanks to the Revolution and to Napoleon, the feudal customs and the privileges of the nobility had been swept away, the old administrative system with its plethora of provincial agencies and local boundaries had been replaced by a centralized, logical system that really worked, and the ancient judicial system, with its many conflicting sovereignties and law codes, had been replaced by a uniform system of courts and by laws that were codified and binding on all parts of the country. The majority of Frenchmen put too high a valuation on efficiency to want to see out-worn institutions restored merely for the sake of tradition.

There were more persons, perhaps, who were sympathetic to the idea of restoring clerical influence in education; but, even here, the merits of Napoleon's centralization of the whole educational system under the Université de France were too obvious to permit its abolition, and most people were content to argue that neither the state nor the church should be allowed to monopolize education. Finally, in the case of the most profound changes effected by the revolution, those in the economic and social organization of the country, there were too many people who had benefited directly from the transformation of the last twenty-five years to permit efforts to restore the old system.

The changes, then, were permanent; and the economic and social changes in particular made France profoundly different from the countries discussed above, despite occasional superficial similarities.

Economic Organization / In 1815 France had a population of twenty-eight million people, and, by 1850, this had risen to almost thirty-five million. At the latter date there were eight million more Frenchmen than inhabitants of the British Isles, and, among the great powers, France was second only to Russia in number of subjects.

The great majority of Frenchmen still lived on the land. As late as 1850 there were only five French cities with 100,000 inhabitants or more: Paris, with 1,420,000; Marseille, with 195,000; Lyon, with 177,000; Bordeaux, with 131,000; and Rouen, with 100,000. The fact that Paris increased its numbers by 300,000 between 1830 and 1850 indicates that a shift to the cities was getting under way; but this was still on a small scale, and France was a predominantly rural country.

The state of agriculture was potentially healthy. Thanks to the abolition of feudalism, France was now a nation of free farmers, and the division and sale of church properties and of some of the large estates belonging to the nobility had greatly favored the intensive cultivation of the soil. The most important crops were grain, which was protected against foreign competition by an adjustable tariff, grapes, garden products, olives, and—introduced most recently—sugar beets. There was a slow but steady expansion of all crops during this period; and, by 1835, the yield of wine grapes was double what it had been in 1815, while there was generally a surplus of cereals for export.

Both the government and private agricultural societies took an active interest in scientific methods; a Ministry of Agriculture was founded in 1836; and there was widespread dissemination of agricultural studies. The effect of this was diminished, however, by the high degree of illiteracy in the rural districts and the extreme conservatism of the French peasant, who looked with suspicion upon novelty and resisted even such useful innovations as selective breeding and artificial fertilization. The fact that primogeniture had been abolished during the Revolution also has a bearing here, for the distribution of land among all members of the family meant that allotments tended to be small, so that—even when they were used—scientific methods had less striking effects than they might have had on more extensive farms. As a result of this, French agriculture remained highly vulnerable to natural disasters. The effects of poor harvests, for instance, tended to be widespread and, because the peasants were free citizens, to have violent political results.

France's industrial progress was far in advance of that of its eastern neighbors. It had been stimulated by government assistance during the war and by the necessity of producing goods normally imported but now cut off by the blockade. Thus, the cotton industry at Rouen, Lille, and Saint-Quentin was in a flourishing condition when peace was restored. Both it and the linen industry were protected by tariffs and produced for the internal market, rather than the external, where the British were supreme. In both these industries the putting-out system of household production was still the rule, although concentration of manufacture in factories was beginning, especially in the silk industry, which had its center at Lyon. It was in silk also that mechanization was most pronounced, both Jacquard and power looms being widely used in this period.

Aside from textiles, the most important industries were the metallurgical and machine-making industries. France was handicapped by the lack of good coking coal, and, until the mid-forties, most of its pig iron was smelted in small charcoal furnaces. Even so, the beginnings of concentration and mechanization were made, and such firms as Schneider-Creuzot and Wendel were producing iron in modern puddling and rolling mills in the middle 1820s. In this period also, machine industry became firmly established in Alsace, Lille, Marseille, and the vicinity of Paris. Power for manufacturing was still produced by water; but by 1846 France had a total of 5000 steam engines with a combined horsepower of 60,000.

Domestic commerce was encouraged by the improvement of roads and canals and by the creation in 1831 of a special Ministry of Public Works charged with their construction and upkeep. Some measure of French success here can be indicated by the fact that one could travel by highway from Paris to Bordeaux in thirty-six hours in 1848, whereas the same trip had taken eighty-six hours in 1814. In the same period the canal network was tripled in length, and all of France's major rivers were fitted into it. The first regular railway was started at the industrial town of Saint-Etienne on the Loire in 1827 and was extended as far as Lyon by 1832. In 1842, a railroad law was passed, providing for the construction of a national network by private companies with government aid and supervision. By 1848 about 1000 miles of railway were in operation and another 1500 being constructed.

France's foreign commerce had been pretty well ruined by the wars and, at the beginning of this period, the older ports were in decline. Marseille was revived by the conquest of Algeria in 1830 and Bordeaux by the growth of French industry, which also stimulated the rise of the newest and fastest growing port, Le Havre. Probably the greatest barrier to the resuscitation of foreign trade was the generally protectionist character of European tariff policy. After 1846, when Great Britain went in for free trade, there was growing interest in France in the possible advantages of following suit.

Social Organization / The social system of the *ancien régime* had been completely smashed by the revolution. In the new France the king and the court played a much diminished role, and were generally unpopular in Paris, to which they had removed from Versailles. As for the nobility, they found it impossible to regain their former monopoly of political and social power. Even in the first years after their return, their position was contested by the wealthy bourgeoisie and, after 1830, it was captured by the great bankers, merchants, speculators, and industrialists who formed that class. There was a tendency, as time went on, for the nobility and the upper bourgeoisie to cooperate, if not to combine, as there was also for the sons of the bourgeoisie to turn from the business world of their fathers to the professions, government service, and the army. Thus, in Stendhal's penetrating analysis of French society in this period, *Lucien Leuwen*, we find the hero, the son of a great Paris banker, serving first as a lieutenant in a regiment in the provinces and then seeking a post as secretary in one of the ministries.

Beneath the nobility and the upper bourgeoisie was the lower bourgeoisie, that solid, respectable, unadventurous class of urban tradesmen, wealthy peasants, *rentiers*, and pensioners described so well in the pages of Balzac and Flaubert. Their outlook was restricted, for the most part, to the events of their own small world; they were not widely read; and, in politics, they were interested only in actions that affected their financial well-being. But they comprised the class with which any government had to reckon, for their support was necessary if it was to retain power.

At the bottom of the scale were the poorer peasantry and the working class. The majority of French peasants now owned some land of their own, but a large part of what they held was mortgaged and they had to pay ruinous interest rates to the speculators who had sold it to them. Moreover, although their lot was generally far superior to that of their Austrian, Prussian, and Russian counterparts, their standard of living was often not far above the subsistence level, their housing conditions were often wretched, and their lives were lives of unremitting toil. They were mostly illiterate and conservative in their views, although prone to violent action in time of economic distress.

Finally, the working class in the urban centers included craftsmen in small shops, factory workers, construction workers, day laborers, and beggars. Even those who were steadily employed were more vulnerable economically than they would have been under the old guild system, which had now been abolished. They were forbidden to organize and hence had no means of protection against depreciation of wages or abominable working conditions. All the evidence indicates that their existence became steadily more wretched from 1815 to 1848, while they became increasingly rebellious. Although strikes were illegal and were followed by heavy jail sentences for their instigators, they were numerous and violent in these years. The German poet Heine, who visited some of the factories in the Faubourg Saint-Marceau in 1842 and saw the kind of reading matter that was being circulated among the workers and read to them, wrote: "Sooner or later the harvest that will come from this sowing in France threatens to be a republican outbreak."

Thanks to the revolution, then, and to the advance of industry, the old and relatively static division of society had been replaced by one that was much more complicated. It was also more fluid, partly because the revolutionary doctrine of equality was taken seriously by Frenchmen and led them to be less inclined to accept the station into which they were born and readier, when other methods failed, to take violent action to improve it.

THE LAST OF THE BOURBONS, 1814–1830

The King and the Charter / Louis XVIII has generally been treated with respect by French historians, probably because of the sober good sense he showed in the first years of his reign, when it would have been easy to act emotionally. He demonstrated his intelligence at the very outset by admitting that the Allied powers were right in insisting that France be ruled in a constitutional manner; one of his first acts was to grant to his subjects the Constitutional Charter which was to remain in force until the February days of 1848.

This document began with a preamble which sought to justify the divine right of kings in general and to list the great services of the French monarchs of the past, and which then added:

> While We recognized that a free monarchist constitution should fulfill the expectations of an enlightened Europe, We had also to remember that Our first duty toward Our people was, in their own interest, to preserve the rights and prerogatives of the Crown.

It then claimed for the king the right to make treaties, to declare war and make peace, to command the military forces, and to make appointments; and it went on to state that legislative power would be shared between the king and the two houses of parliament, the king alone having the right to introduce or amend laws and the parliament the right to accept or reject them. Parliament was to consist of a Chamber of Peers, composed of hereditary peers and members appointed by the king for life, and a Chamber of Deputies, composed of members elected for a term of five years, unless the king decided to dissolve the Chamber and call for new elections. To be eligible for election as a deputy one had to be at least forty years old and to own enough property to necessitate the annual payment of 1000 francs in direct taxes. To vote in elections one had to be at least thirty years old and to pay taxes amounting to 300 francs a year. What this meant was that only about 100,000 men could vote and only 12,000 stand for election out of a population of twenty-eight million.

The Charter, therefore, did not provide for anything resembling democratic participation in government. On the other hand, it enabled a higher proportion of the population to have some share in politics than was true at this time in countries further to the east. It was relatively enlightened in another way: it declared the equality of all Frenchmen before the law, their eligibility for all civil and military positions, their freedom from arbitrary arrest and from imprisonment without legal process, their freedom to worship as they saw fit and to have a free press. Moreover, in an announcement made a month before the Charter was issued, the king had made it clear that his subjects need have no fear of expropriation in case they had acquired land formerly belonging to the church or the *émigrés*; and he had added:

> The guaranteed government debt, pensions, distinctions, and military honors will be maintained, as well as the old and the new [the Napoleonic] nobility. The Legion of Honor will be preserved, and We will decide upon the nominations.

Taken all together, this was a charter of liberties the like of which was unknown in Eastern Europe. It was, in effect, a recognition of the principal changes wrought by that Revolution that the eastern monarchs regarded with such loathing.

The Charter itself was regarded with aversion by some people in France. Speaking generally, one can distinguish four main political groupings in France in the years from 1814 to 1830, or even in 1848: the Ultra-Royalists, the Doctrinaires, the Liberals, and the Radicals. The first and the last of these groups opposed the constitutional grant and everything it stood for.

In his great novel about Restoration France, *Les Misérables,* Victor Hugo described the attitude of the Ultra-Royalists. He wrote:

> To be Ultra is to quarrel with the stake as to the degree of cooking heretics should undergo; it is to reproach the idol for its want of idolatry; it is to find in the Pope insufficient papism, in the king too little royalty, and too much light in the night.

The Ultras lived in the world of Bouvines and Fontenoy; and, not unnaturally, they regarded the Charter as an abomination. They were, indeed, so completely reactionary that Louis XVIII once grumbled, "If these gentlemen had their way, they would end by purging me."

At the other end of the political spectrum were the Radicals, a confused group of varying views, united only in their desire to destroy the existing regime so that either the empire could be restored or a republic established. They opposed the Charter for obvious reasons, but they had little strength or importance before 1830.

The two middle groups accepted the Charter but differed in their attitude toward it. To the Doctrinaires it seemed as reasonable a balance between government power and individual freedom as could be devised, and should not be tampered with. The Liberals, on the other hand, felt that it was inadequate and should be amended in such a way as to extend civil liberties and strengthen the powers of the Chamber of Deputies by making the king's ministers responsible to it. In other things these groups were in general agreement. Neither favored any real widening of the suffrage; both opposed democracy as steadfastly as they did absolutism; both believed that France should be run by the well-to-do and educated middle class. If they had been able to cooperate in a political system run according to well-defined and mutually satisfactory rules, in which they could have alternated in power, both the Charter and the monarchy might have survived. Instead, as a result of events that could not have been foreseen, the Doctrinaires were driven into the arms of the Ultras, while the Liberals drifted toward the Radical position.

Domestic Politics under Louis XVIII / The political history of this period began with the unedifying spectacle of royalist-inspired riots, plundering forays, and political murders, especially in the southern departments. This White Terror, which the government proved incompetent or disinclined to suppress, had the effect of intimidating liberal-minded electors when the first election of deputies took place in 1815; and the Chamber that resulted from these elections was so reactionary in its complexion that the king called it a *Chambre introuvable*, "a chamber the like of which will never be found again." This body further encouraged rightist excesses by demanding the execution of Marshal Ney and other soldiers who had rallied to the cause of Napoleon during the Hundred Days. A foreign observer was moved by this blood bath to remark: "The French are behaving as if there were no such thing as history or the future." The Chamber's insistence on repressive measures was so patently vindictive that the other great powers became alarmed. The Russian Foreign Minister Nesselrode warned the Count of Artois, the darling of the Ultras, that they were not occupying France in order "to sustain his foolishness," and the Duke of Wellington wrote Louis XVIII that this crude provincial royalism might very well cost him his crown. The king was not opposed to this kind of encouragement. In September 1816 he dissolved the Chamber, forcing new elections which brought a more moderate-minded assembly into existence.

This action ushered in the most constructive period of Louis XVIII's reign. In the next four years the ministers Decazes and Richelieu, supported by a Chamber in which the majority was composed of Doctrinaires and Liberals, passed the laws that were necessary to elaborate the suffrage and press provisions of the Charter. They also restored France's fiscal sovereignty and raised the money needed to pay off the war indemnity, which not only freed French soil of foreign troops but restored France to the family of nations, as was demonstrated by her admission to the consultations at Aix-la-Chapelle in 1818. In the same year, the famous law drafted by Gouvion St. Cyr was passed, providing for the reorganization of the army and laying down the principles—voluntary enlistment, equality of opportunity, promotion by merit—which were to guide military training and recruitment policy until 1868. These and other constructive measures infuriated the Ultras, who found the press law too liberal and the army law prejudicial to the nobility and who accused the king's chief minister, Decazes, of encouraging the growth of liberalism.

Their criticism might have been ineffective if it had not been for an unforeseen calamity. On February 13, 1820, a fanatic named Louvel stabbed and killed the Duke of Berry as he was helping his wife into a carriage at the Opera. The duke was the youngest son of the Count of Artois and he was considered the only member of the Bourbon family likely to have a son who would assure the line of succession. The murderer admitted that his motive was to remove this possibility, although events were to show that his attempt had been belated, the Duchess of Berry being already with child.

The importance of the Berry murder was that it introduced a new period of reaction. As Chateaubriand wrote, "Decazes' foot slipped in the blood and he fell." The ministry that replaced his was Ultra in its views and, in being so, now received the support of many Doctrinaires who seem to have believed that the murder was a sign that their past policies had been too liberal to be safe. As a result the government was able to ram through laws that suspended the liberty of the subject, reconstituted a rigorous censorship of the press, and, finally, rewrote electoral procedure in such a way as to give virtual control of the elections to the Chamber of Deputies to the large landlords and the old nobility. This new law worked so effectively, from the Ultra point of view, that the elections of 1820 reduced the Liberals to a group of 80 in a Chamber of 450 members, leaving the Ultras and their Doctrinaire allies in complete control.

Louis XVIII made little attempt now to resist their demands. He had been genuinely shocked by the Berry assassination, and this inclined him to the Ultras, as did the fact that his new mistress, Mme. du Cayla, was an uncompromising Ultra in her opinions. Moreover, the king's tendency toward indolence had grown with the years, and he was now willing to leave the initiative in most things to his heir, the Count of Artois. Villèle, the minister who came to exercise greatest influence over him after Decazes' fall, was also of the extreme royalist persuasion. It was Villèle who persuaded the hesitant king to authoıize the expedition into Spain in 1823 (see pp. 22–23), which published to all Europe France's apparently inflexible opposition to liberalism. Apart from this, the last years of Louis XVIII were marked, on the one hand, by a deepening of repressive legislation and a growth of religious influence in education and, on the other, by a number of attempts on the part of frustrated liberals and radicals to escape from their impotence by secret conspiracies and *coups de main*. The failure of these further discredited the Left; and, in 1823, there were only fifteen Liberals left in the Chamber.

It is little wonder that, by September 1824, when Louis XVIII died and was succeeded by the Count of Artois, the Ultras felt that the satisfaction of their wildest hopes was at hand.

The Reign of Charles X / The new king was a kindly and charming man, but one with limited intelligence in political matters, a reputation for cowardice, and an ostentatious piety that exasperated his subjects, who were soon repeating the story that he was a Jesuit and bound by the rules of the order. This charge was not true, but it seemed plausible at a time when the government was passing a law punishing certain kinds of sacrilege with death, when the church was conducting a clamant campaign against civil marriage, and when the University of Paris was being submitted to the control of the archbishop of Paris and having certain of its courses suspended by that authority as dangerous to morals.

The favors shown the church were not, however, as unpopular as the persistent attempts to restore the power of the nobility. One of the first actions of Charles X's reign was a clever bit of financial jugglery with the national debt which saved the state a billion francs, which the government promptly handed over to the *émigrés* to indemnify them for their losses during the Revolution. Not only did this seriously hurt the great bankers—the holders of the bonds whose interest rate had been lowered in order to effect the saving—but it infuriated a lot of other people who saw it for what it was: a piece of special legislation for the advantage of a class whose members had not only left France during the Revolution but who had actually fought against their country.

This was followed by an attempt to restore a measure of primogeniture, by allowing fathers to leave a double portion of their estates to their eldest sons—a modest enough proposal on the surface but, quite plainly, a first step in a planned return to the feudal economy. One deputy said indignantly, "This is no law. It is a manifesto against existing society. It is a forerunner of twenty other laws which . . . will break in on us and leave no rest to the society of France. . . . " The bill was passed by the Ultra-dominated Chamber of Deputies but rejected by the Peers, enough of whom still regarded the abolition of primogeniture as one of the great achievements of the Revolution.

But it is really unnecessary to dwell in detail on the events of the reign of Charles X. History is doubtless filled with examples of political folly, but surely there are few that are so unrelieved as the one afforded by the last Bourbon ruler of France. His most marked quality was stubbornness, and it was this that lost him his crown, for it prevented him from learning anything from his defeats. His dogged pursuit of objectives in which only the nobility and the conservative clergy would find any advantage soon united all of the other groups that possessed any political influence against the regime. It alienated the lesser bourgeoisie as well as the great bankers, converted even moderate Liberals into antimonarchists for the time being, and thus effected a fusion between Liberals and Radicals that was ominous for the dynasty. It is significant that the king's successes in the field of foreign affairs—the participation in the Allied fleet action against the Turkish navy at Navarino in 1827 (see p. 27), and, in 1829–1830, the preparation and successful launching of the expedition that was to conquer Algeria and mark the beginning of the establishment of France's new colonial empire—went virtually unnoticed in France, where all attention was focused on the reactionary policies of the king's ministers.

Some kind of crisis was inevitable; and the way for it was prepared at the end of 1829 when Charles reconstructed his ministry, filling it almost completely with extreme royalists, including such men as General Bourmont, who had betrayed Napoleon, and Labourdonnaye, who had been active in the White Terror of 1815. The head of this new combination was Count Polignac, a former *émigré*, an embittered opponent of the Charter, a fanatical churchman who had visions and who claimed to have frequent conversations with the Virgin Mary. Polignac was politically so incompetent that he did not know enough to disguise his real intentions. His object, he admitted openly, was "to reorganize society, to restore to the clergy its former preponderance in the state, to create a powerful aristocracy, and to surround it with privileges."

This was to confirm the worst suspicions of the middle class, and that part of it which possessed political power now met Polignac's challenge. In the elections of 1827, Liberal strength in the Chamber of Deputies had revived markedly, and, in March 1830, it was sufficient to pass an Address to the Throne which, in effect, asked for the dismissal of the ministry. The king responded by dissolving the Chamber and calling for new elections, doubtless expecting the support of the electors. In this he was disappointed, for the voters elected a Chamber that was overwhelmingly antigovernment.

It was apparently at this point that those shrewder reactionaries, Nicholas I and Metternich, advised Charles to yield. But he was too insistent on his royal prerogatives to consider that. He tried, instead, to break the opposition by issuing, on July 26, 1830, four ordinances. These suspended the liberty of the press, dissolved the Chamber again on the grounds that misdemeanors had occurred during the recent elections, altered the electoral law in such a way as to reduce the electorate by about three fourths and to exclude the whole of the bourgeoisie from it, and, finally, set a date for new elections.

Once he had authorized these decrees, Charles went off to Rambouillet to hunt; when he came back, he was no longer king. A protest against the edicts was started by the Liberal editors of Paris, led by Adolphe Thiers (1797–1877) of *Le National*; it was taken up by the printers, unemployed because of the new press law, and by other workers, students, intellectuals, and the like. On July 28 Rouget de Lisle, now seventy years old, burst into a friend's house and quavered, "Things look bad. They are singing *La Marseillaise!*"[1] Outside in the narrow, twisting

---

[1] Rouget de Lisle was the author of *La Marseillaise*.

streets, the great barricades for which Paris was famous began to be erected, barriers fifty to eighty feet high, made of paving stones, boxes, furniture, trees, wagons, and anything else that came to hand.

On the same day General Marmont brought troops into the city and sent them against the barricades, but with indifferent success. The soldiers were neither trained nor properly armed for street fighting; they did not know the unconventional terrain in which they were engaged, whereas the insurgents knew every short cut and alleyway; and their hearts were not in the fight anyway. Marmont was later to claim that he would have had better results if he had been allowed to surround and bombard the city, but this was a favorite excuse of commanders in the mid-century who had the uncomfortable experience of having their troops worsted by untrained students and workers. In any case, after three days of hard fighting, it was clear even to the king that he was not going to be able to put down the revolt. He decided, therefore, to withdraw the edicts, but now it was too late.

Indeed, the only real question now was what was going to take the place of Charles' discredited and defeated regime, and who, if anyone, was to have his throne. The weary and powder-stained fighters on the barricades would probably have voted for a republic; but the initiative was now taken by the Liberal editors and businessmen and deputies, again led by Thiers. After some involved maneuvering, they persuaded a rump Chamber of Deputies to invite Louis Philippe, the Duc d'Orleans, to come to Paris as lieutenant-governor of the kingdom, and when he did so, managed to get Lafayette, the nominal leader of the small republican party, to throw his support to him. Finally, on August 3, 1830, the full Chamber invited Louis Philippe to take the throne, and he accepted.

A week later, Charles X sailed off to melancholy exile in Scotland. He was not destined to return to his country, nor was any of his line ever again to sit upon the throne of France.

THE JULY MONARCHY

Government by the Middle Class / One of the shrewdest political observers of the nineteenth century was Alexis de Tocqueville (1805–1859), who won a European reputation when he published the first part of his *Democracy in America* in 1835. At the time of its publication this book infuriated many Americans because of de Tocqueville's criticism of certain institutions and customs in this country. They would probably have been less annoyed if they had known that de Tocqueville was an infinitely more scathing critic of his own nation. Indeed, it is in his posthumously published memoirs that we find the most trenchant indictment of the regime established after the July revolution.

That revolution, de Tocqueville wrote, marked the definitive conquest of political power by the middle class, and they proceeded now, in exercising it, to exclude the other classes from any share in it.

> The particular spirit of the middle class became the general spirit of the government; it ruled the latter's foreign policy as well as affairs at home: an active, industrious spirit, often dishonorable, generally orderly, occasionally reckless through vanity or egoism, but timid by temperament, moderate in all things except in its love of ease and comfort, and, last but not least, mediocre. It was a spirit which, mingled with that of the people or of the aristocracy, can do wonders; but which, by itself, will never produce more than a government shorn of both virtue and greatness. . . . The middle class, when called upon to assume the government, took it up as an industrial enterprise.

It was not merely aristocratic disdain that prompted these sentiments. De Tocqueville saw clearly what a great many Frenchmen sensed after 1830: the pettiness, the narrowness of view, and what might be called the lack of political style of their new rulers. His charge that the bourgeoisie sought to monopolize power and exercise it in their own interest is a fair one. Before the triumphant Liberals offered the crown to Louis Philippe, they had amended the Charter in such a way as to weaken the position of other classes or institutions that might threaten their own position. They deleted the preamble, thus repudiating the whole idea of divine right of kings (although they substituted no alternative theory to give a logical basis for the institution of monarchy, which they retained). They did away with the paragraph that made Roman Catholicism the official religion of France, thus undermining the position of the clergy. In subsequent years, they greatly weakened the prerogatives of members of the House of Peers and deprived them of their hereditary character. On the other hand, by the law of 1831, they widened the suffrage slightly by reducing the property qualification from 300 to 200 francs in annual taxes and by also giving the vote to professional men, like lawyers, doctors, and professors, who paid at least 100 francs in taxes. This, and the lowering of the voting age to twenty-five years, doubled the electorate; but still only about 200,000 people could vote out of a population that was getting close to thirty-two million; and, if most of the bourgeoisie were now enfranchised, all of the working class was excluded from power. Finally, by a law that is entirely characteristic of the class character of the new regime, the National Guard— the force designed to protect the Charter and maintain law and order—

"The Napoleon of Peace: Louis Philippe"
From an impression by the famous cartoonist, Dicky Doyle, in *Punch*, Oct. 23, 1847.

was reorganized so that service in it was obligatory only for citizens who paid direct taxes and could afford to buy their own uniforms and equipment.

To the bourgeoisie it seemed perfectly reasonable that power should be theirs and theirs alone. The most eloquent spokesman of this class and, in the last stages of the July monarchy, its leading statesman, was François Guizot (1787–1874), university professor, historian of the English revolution, member of the Doctrinaire party. Guizot argued that political power should be exercised by *la classe moyenne* because it alone possessed "not only the necessary fortune [to devote itself to political work] but also the intelligence and the independence without which that work cannot be accomplished." He was not moved by arguments that the middle class was dominated by the commercial and financial oligarchy of the country, although he did not deny that this was true. The political system of the July Monarchy was admirable, he said, because, "at the same time that it sets limits to political rights by a property qualification, it works to remove that limit by allowing men to become wealthy and to extend it."

In general, the new ruling class took a typically middle-class attitude toward government: they regarded it as a necessary evil, whose functions should be kept to the bare minimum. Aside from protecting property from civil disorder, government was not supposed to *do* things. Above all, it was not supposed to become involved in foreign adventures, because nothing was more detrimental to business. Guizot put this in words when he said, "Let us not talk about our country having to conquer territory, to wage great wars, to undertake bold deeds of vengeance. If France is prosperous, if she remains free, rich, peaceful, and wise, we need not complain if we exercise only a small influence in the world abroad."

These attitudes of the bourgeoisie were shared by the new king. Louis Philippe was the son of that Duke of Orleans called Philippe Égalité who had supported, and then been executed by, the Revolution. He himself had fought for his country at Valmy and Jemappes and had gone then into exile, traveling extensively and actually visiting the United States. This romantic background did not alter the fact that he was not a man of wide interests or with a temperament calculated to inspire his people. Fifty-seven years old at the time of his accession to the throne, he showed himself a knowing, garrulous, but cautious man, who distrusted talent unless it had proven itself in the business world and who had a reverence for industry and finance that bordered on the ridiculous. He was personally courageous, as he was to show on numerous occasions during his reign when he was the target of assassins, but his foreign policy especially seemed the reverse of courageous to many Frenchmen. Victor Hugo, who had a high opinion of the king's qualities, wrote in *Les Misérables* that "his great fault was that he was modest in the name of France. . . . [His reign was marked by] excessive timidity, which is offensive to a nation that has July 14 in its civil traditions and Austerlitz in its military annals."

The political principles shared by Louis Philippe and the bourgeoisie could not help but alienate important sections of the population. The supporters of the Bourbons rejected Louis Philippe for obvious reasons; but there was also a marked growth of republicanism in this period and a revival of the democratic spirit of 1793. At the same time, the working classes regarded the existing system as oppressive; the patriots agreed with General Lamarque's bitter description of the July monarchy as a "halt in the mud"; and the intellectuals and the romantically minded youth of the country felt, like Stendhal, that this was a regime of "charlatanism without talent."

Some Insurrections / This opposition took violent forms, and the first years of Louis Philippe's reign were filled with conspiracies, insurrections, and attempts at assassination. The Duchess of Berry, for instance, attempted a legitimist counterrevolution in 1832. This charming, courageous, but giddy-minded woman, scorning the sober doubts of her friends, landed in France in April 1832, with her head a muddle of improbable schemes and unwise expectations. When the city of Marseilles failed to rise in revolution as she had hoped, she made her way by a series of hairbreadth escapes to the Vendée, only to find that her plans had been anticipated by the government. Escaping once more, she went into hiding in Nantes but was betrayed to the police and put in prison, where she astonished both her captors and her supporters by giving birth to a daughter, a fitting end to an episode that resembled sensational fiction rather than fact.

Even before this, there had been disorders in Paris, and in June 1832 there was a bloody republican insurrection in the capital. Since 1830, a radical republican movement had taken form, centered in two societies called *Les amis du peuple* and *La société de l'homme et du citoyen*, the latter of which had branches in the provinces. The 1832 affair, however, was more a spontaneous action by the republican rank and file than a deliberately planned revolt. The occasion for it was the funeral of General Lamarque, a popular and avowedly republican commander. As his funeral procession reached the Place de la Bastille, it was joined by groups of men shouting, "Long live the republic!" The temper of the crowd was inflamed by speeches by several republican notables; cries of "Lamarque to the Pantheon!" began to be heard; some hotheads tried to convert the procession into a column which, with the hearse at its head, would assault the Hôtel de Ville; and dragoons charged the crowd. The disorders spread; barricades were built; and there was open warfare in the streets of Paris for two days before order was restored.

The government struck back by passing a series of measures submitting all political associations to government surveillance and tightening restrictions on the republican press. These, and the prosecution of the ringleaders of the rising, had the effect of discouraging the growth of republicanism for a time; but it is nevertheless true that, in the insurrection of June 1832—so stirringly commemorated in Hugo's *Les Misérables* —French republicanism had found another symbol to hearten future followers.

In addition to these large-scale movements there were several actions against the constituted authorities by individuals, including a number of attempts to assassinate the king. The most shocking of these was the work of a Corsican named Fieschi, who rigged up a kind of machine gun made of linked rifle barrels and fired it off as Louis Philippe, his three sons, and his suite were passing in parade in Paris in July 1835. The king and the princes escaped unhurt, but Fieschi's machine killed eighteen people and wounded many more. The incident inspired a revulsion of feeling in favor of the monarch that lasted for some time.

Workers' Revolts and the Beginnings of Socialism / More serious, and historically more significant, than these incidents were those which gave evidence of an increasingly rebellious temper among the working classes.

In November 1831, the silk weavers of Lyons, who had to work eighteen hours a day for a pittance, rose in desperation and seized the town, controlling it for some days until their revolt was crushed by a military force under Marshal Soult. Three years later the weavers rose again, this time holding on for five days before their resistance was broken; and this time their effort touched off sympathetic disorders among workers in Paris and other cities. The indifference of the bourgeoisie to the plight of the workers and their antagonism to social legislation in these days when industry was expanding rapidly and dislocating the old economic order were forcing the workers to strike out blindly in the hope of securing some kind of relief.

It was in these circumstances that socialism began to grow in France. Among the more progressive bourgeoisie, who were worried by the disaffection of the working class, and among intellectuals in general, serious attention began to be paid to the work of thinkers like Henri de Saint-Simon (1760–1825). This is not the place to elaborate on the various writings of this profound and original thinker, but it can at least be said that Saint-Simon and his followers Bazard and Enfantin demon-

Rue Transnonain, 1834, by Honoré Daumier (1808–1879). This drawing is a biting comment on an incident which occurred during republican disturbances in Paris during April 1834. Government troops, claiming that they had been fired upon from the window of a house on the Rue Transnonain, where workers suspected of being active in the revolt lived, indulged in an indiscriminate massacre of its tenants. (METROPOLITAN MUSEUM OF ART, ROGERS FUND, 1920).

strated to their contemporaries that the age of industrialism could be understood only by analyzing its economic foundations and that the future peace of society would depend on the success with which relations between the different classes were adjusted. Enfantin wrote:

> Charles X thought that a few soldiers would silence inopportune voices, and the bourgeoisie are almost as blind as he; recent events have helped us to show them up. . . . This is the crux of the whole political problem, that it is no longer a question of priests and noblemen as in '89, or even as in 1829, but one of the people and the bourgeoisie or better of workers and nonworkers; one has gone a long way when the question is known, also how it should be put.

The Saint-Simonians hoped that moral reform and education would in the long run promote better understanding between the classes and bring a gradual improvement of the economic conditions of the working class. They were, in short, evolutionary socialists, shunning the use of violent means to attain their objectives. This was true also of Charles Fourier (1772–1837), who believed that the way to regenerate modern society was to decentralize it by encouraging men to organize themselves in small agricultural communities or phalanxes, in which they would live in perfect freedom and harmony. Convinced that the success of only one such utopian experiment would be enough to convince mankind that this was the way of the future, Fourier announced that he would be at home every day at noon in case some benevolent patron might wish to give him the funds for the establishment of a society that would prove the feasibility of his plans. Although he waited for twelve years, no generous stranger ever appeared.

There were also more revolutionary socialists in France in this period. Philippe Buonarroti (1767–1837) had been a member of the Babeuf conspiracy in 1796[2] and now carried on that tradition by preaching the necessity of political revolution as a means of winning social reform. More extreme in his views was Auguste Blanqui (1805–1881), the perpetual conspirator, with his frock coat buttoned up to his chin, his flashing eyes, and that sallow skin that made Herzen think that he must live in the sewers or catacombs. Blanqui talked of "the duel to death between dividends and wages" and called upon the new worker, "the mechanized man," to wage unremitting war against the bourgeoisie, since there could be no community of interest between the classes. In his emphasis on underground activity and on a clear and systematic revolutionary strat-

---

[2] Gracchus Babeuf, sometimes called the first truly class-conscious leader of the European working class, organized a Society of the Pantheon which planned an insurrection against the Directory. Betrayed by informers, he was arrested, tried, and executed in the spring of 1796.

egy, Blanqui was a forerunner of those professional revolutionaries whom Lenin was to consider indispensable for a successful overthrow of bourgeois society. But the enthusiasm with which he supported even the most hopeless of conspiracies and *émeutes* makes one suspect that he believed in violence for the sake of violence and that it would not be illogical to class with him the early anarchists. Anarchist in essence was also the work of Pierre-Joseph Proudhon (1809–1865), whose famous book *What Is Property?* appeared in 1840, with its bold assertion that property was theft and its exposition of the theory that the measure of value is the labor that goes into the product evaluated.

But the most influential of all the French socialists of this period was Louis Blanc (1811–1882). In a sympathetic portrait in her novel *Le Piccinino*, George Sand described Blanc as possessing "great ambition lodged in a small body; a soft, insinuating voice; and a will of iron." Born in poverty, he made his way in life with the aid of these qualities and his great literary gifts. He first attracted attention in 1840, when his *History of Ten Years* gave a striking analysis of the social forces at work in France in the Restoration period. But the effect of this was nothing to that of his book *L'Organisation du Travail*, which appeared in the same year and immediately became one of the most discussed books of the whole period.

This work was a frontal attack upon the competitive system that was held in such reverence by capitalists of the early nineteenth century. Blanc set out to prove that competition was ruinous, not only for the common people but also for the bourgeoisie, since it was always wasteful and was productive of continual crises. All classes, therefore, had an interest in abolishing it; and, in this respect, "there exists a solidarity between all interests, and . . . social reform is for all members of . . . society, without exception, a means of salvation." Blanc wished to replace the competitive system of free enterprise with a national economy. He dreamed of a democratic republic in which the government would organize national workshops, or communal plants, in the most important industries. In each of these organizations the regulation of production and the allocation of function would be decided by the miserable plight of the working class in a country that was slowly adjusting to industrialism, in which unemployment was heavy because of the decline of the older trades, and in which wages were low and working conditions execrable. Both the misery of the workers and the socialist theories it inspired were to have consequences in 1848.

Nationalism and the Revival of Bonapartism / To these opponents of the regime must be added all those who believed that the defeat of 1815 must be avenged and that France must demonstrate to Europe that she was still what she had been under Napoleon. In the cautious foreign policy of Louis Philippe's first decade, these people found little to admire. It is true that French arms were engaged in Algeria, where they were trying to finish the campaign begun by Charles X. But the African fighting gave little cause for national pride, since it was waged against a native people, and one, moreover, for whom the French came to have a good deal of sympathy, especially after Abd-el-Kader, the emir of Mascara, became the leader of the forces opposing France. A handsome and audacious commander, the emir was able to harry French columns and to burn isolated French forts for over ten years; and it was only in the mid-forties, after General Bugeaud had about 100,000 men under his command, that the French were able to win mastery over all of Algeria.

Meanwhile, patriots had been infuriated by the diplomatic defeat imposed on France during the Egyptian crisis of 1840 (pp. 35–36), which seemed to indicate that the other powers believed that she was worth no more consideration than she had been immediately after Waterloo. One of the republican leaders of this period, Edgar Quinet, said in 1840: "We thought that the Revolution was going to pick up her sword again in 1830, but her mighty wounded body could only raise itself on one knee. . . . For five and twenty years we have been bowed beneath the Caudine Forks, endeavoring to put a cheerful face on things and to gild our chain."

It is perhaps not surprising that, in these circumstances, the memory of Napoleon should have occurred to many people and that the glories of his reign should have begun to be contrasted with the drabness of Louis Philippe's regime.

The growth of the Napoleonic cult during the July Monarchy was aided by the work of men like Pierre Jean de Béranger, Victor Hugo, and Adolphe Thiers. Béranger (1780–1857) was a versifier with the common touch, who had tremendous success with songs about the homelier aspects of Napoleon's career and with sentimental tributes like the famous *Memories of the People*, which described the love in which the common people held the emperor. Hugo (1802–1885), an infinitely greater poet, invoked the emperor's memory in his splendid *Ode à la Colonne*, written in 1831, and his *Napoléon II*, written after the death of the emperor's son; while Thiers (1797–1877) wrote a twenty-volume history of the Consulate and the Empire which breathed admiration of Napoleon's political and military genius in every line. It was Thiers also who, as a minister of Louis Philippe, completed the Arc de Triomphe, which had been left incomplete by Napoleon, named streets and bridges after Napoleon's victories, and finally, in a reverent ceremony in 1840, brought the emperor's bones back from St. Helena.

But it would be unwise to give too much credit to individuals for the revival of Bonapartism. It was only natural that, sooner or later, there would be a revulsion of feeling in Napoleon's favor; and even before 1830 there must have been many young men—like Julien Sorel in Stendhal's *The Red and the Black*—who were bored with "the kind of eloquence that had replaced the Empire's rapidity of action," and who made a private cult of the Corsican. The dullness and the timidity of Louis Philippe's government encouraged this cult to spread further, and it is significant that it did so among the common people. It has been said that every popular almanac published between 1840 and 1848 contributed to the apotheosis of Napoleon; it might be added that the tremendous numbers of pipes, handkerchiefs, jam jars, and beer mugs bearing his image, which were sold in village shops or hawked by itinerant pedlars, did the same.

The beneficiary of all this was Louis Napoleon Bonaparte, the son of the emperor's brother Louis and, after the death of the emperor's son, the Bonaparte pretender. He had been educated in Germany (and never, in fact, overcame a slight German accent) and had gone to Italy in 1831. Here he and his older brother had become involved in the secret revolutionary movement known as the *Carbonari* (or Charcoal Burners), and here his brother had died of an illness contracted during flight from the police. Louis Napoleon was a man of energy, ambition, and will; he was determined to win his uncle's throne; and, in 1836, he tried to do so. He appeared with a few companions at the fortress in Strasbourg and called upon the garrison to follow him in an attempt to seize power. He was arrested by an alert commander and taken off to Paris, where the king had to decide what to do with him. Louis Philippe thought it wise in the end to let the prince go and allowed him to sail off to the New World, doubtless hoping he would remain there. But, after a brief visit to the United States, Louis Napoleon returned to Europe and, in August 1840, with sixty companions, he landed at Boulogne, declared the deposition of the House of Orleans, appealed once more for support, and was again arrested.

This time the authorities were not so lenient. The prince was tried before the Chamber of Peers, where he was condemned to imprisonment for life in the fortress of Ham. But he had a chance to make a ringing speech to the Chamber in which he cried: "I represent before you a principle, a cause, a defeat. The principle is the sovereignty of the people; the cause is that of the Empire; the defeat is Waterloo." Eloquence was not the strong suit of the French bourgeoisie, and Louis Napoleon was doubtless dismissed as a crackbrained young man by some of the soberest minds in France. But his words were heard far beyond the walls of the Chamber that condemned him; and that was not unimportant, for although he remained at Ham for some years, writing brochures on such subjects as "The Extinction of Poverty," he eventually tired of this comfortable detention. One morning in the spring of 1846, while a doctor friend, pretending that the prince was ill, hovered around his empty bed, Louis Napoleon, dressed in workman's clothes, put a short pipe in his mouth and a plank on his shoulder and walked out the front gates of the fortress; a day later, he was safe in England. There he remained for two years, happy in the knowledge that his own name was now inextricably tied up with the Napoleonic legend and confident that every failure of Louis Philippe's government brought closer the day when he would be able to restore the Empire in France.

The Guizot System / At the height of the Egyptian crisis the government of France had been headed by Adolphe Thiers, but his inflammatory tactics, his apparent willingness to run the risk of war, and his tendency to pander to the Paris mob led the king to force his resignation. He was replaced by François Guizot, who was to remain in power from 1840 to 1848.

In foreign affairs, the Guizot period was marked by a greater degree of personal intervention by the king. It was largely under his influence that the relationship with England became cooler, and feelers were put out to Vienna, in the hope of encouraging an Austro-French alliance (see pp. 29, 36). On the domestic front, the course followed might aptly be described as one of massive immobility. The advance of the years had strengthened Guizot's conservatism, and he was convinced that neither the Charter nor the basic laws of the realm stood in need of change. He had little understanding of social questions and an excessive fear of offending groups he considered important. Thus, an advantageous conversion of interest rates on government bonds was avoided in order not to alienate the bondholders; a much-needed scaling-down of tariffs because it would be opposed by the big industrialists; the abolition of slavery in the colonies for fear of offending the planters; and so forth. Guizot's direction of policy invited the famous gibe of the poet-politician Lamartine, who said: "If that were all the genius required of a statesman charged with the direction of affairs, there would be no need of statesmen—a post would do as well."

Guizot's greatest failing was self-righteousness, and he was so convinced of the excellence of his policies that he was willing to commit ignoble actions in order to see that they were supported. Thus, he resorted increasingly to bribery and corruption on a large scale. With only a very limited electorate to worry about and with a highly centralized administrative system at his disposal, he was able to use the carrot and the stick in local electoral colleges, so as to secure the election of loyal deputies, and his shrewd distribution of patronage within the Chamber won him the comfortable majorities he desired.

There can be little doubt that his very success with these methods was self-defeating, for it brought discredit upon the regime as a whole. If the Chamber of Deputies was capable of doing only what Guizot commanded, then, people reasoned, something must be wrong with the Chamber. As de Tocqueville wrote later:

> France grew unconsciously accustomed to look upon the debates in the Chamber as exercizes of the intellect rather than as serious discussions and upon all the differences between the various parliamentary parties . . . as domestic quarrels between children of one family trying to trick one another. A few glaring instances of corruption, discovered by accident, led the country to presuppose a number of hidden cases and convinced it that the whole of the governing class was corrupt.

More and more people began to think that radical change in the electoral system was needed; and, by the end of the 1840s, a campaign was under way to effect this.

Meanwhile, France's economic problems were increasing. The harvest of 1846 was a poor one, and agricultural distress was great. An international financial crisis in the same year forced manufacturers to cut back their production by about one third, and this caused a sharp increase in unemployment figures which were already high. As a consequence, about a third of the working population of Paris was starving or being supported by charity in 1847. The government had no machinery for meeting this crisis and was opposed to devising any; and it is not therefore surprising that Louis Blanc's call for a democratic and social republic was heard by an increasing number of the town dwellers. In a speech in the Chamber of Deputies in January 1848, de Tocqueville warned his fellows of the rising discontent of the working class and pointed out that their "passions, instead of being political, [had] become social" and were more and more directed toward the destruction of the whole existing system. "I believe," he said ominously, "we are at this moment sleeping on a volcano. . . . In God's name, change the spirit of the government; for . . . that spirit will lead you to the abyss."

RELIGION AND THE ARTS, 1815–1848

Church, Bourgeoisie, and Working Class / The two most notable religious developments in this period were the reconciliation between the bourgeoisie and the Roman Catholic Church and the parallel decline of the church's influence over the masses.

During the first postwar years, anticlericalism was still strong among the middle classes. Suspicion of the church was encouraged by the activities of the Jesuits, who returned to France after the restoration of the monarchy and whose special missions to the common people assumed the tone of antirevolutionary demonstrations, by the ultramontanism of people like de Maistre (see p. 65), by the growing political influence of the powerful Catholic laymen's society, the *Congrégation*, by the success of the church in infiltrating the commissions of the Université de France, and by the subsequent censorship of university teaching and the dismissal or suspension of liberal professors like the historian Guizot and the philosopher Cousin.

The cumulative effect of these things was to arouse the hostility of the literate classes of society. There was a sudden boom in the books of antireligious writers, and between 1814 and 1824 one and a half million copies of various works by Voltaire were sold. Simultaneously, jokes and songs directed against the clergy circulated, like Béranger's song:

> "Black men, where do you come from?"
> "We come from under the ground.
> Half foxes, half wolves,
> Our discipline is a mystery . . .
> We'll be back, so see that you keep quiet
> And that your children follow our teaching."[3]

This antagonism grew steadily during Villèle's ministry and increased so sharply after Charles X came to the throne that the revolution of 1830 can be considered almost as much an attack against the church as it was against the monarchy.

In the subsequent period, however, there was a change. The new rulers of France, the bourgeoisie, came to regard religion as a useful protection against the social theories of republicanism and the more radical philosophies that threatened their position. All of a sudden it became unfashionable to be irreligious, and the formerly anticlerical bourgeoisie began to troop into the cathedral of Notre Dame where they could

[3] *Hommes noirs, d'où sortez-vous?*
Nous sortons de dessous terre.
Moitié renards, moitié loups,
Notre règle est un mystère . . .
Nous rentrons, songez à vous taire,
Et que vos enfants suivent nos leçons.

Quoted in G. Weill, *La France sous la monarchie constitutionelle* (Paris, 1912), p. 143.

listen to preachers like Lacordaire and Montalembert explaining gravely that property was "one of the fundamental bases of society . . . the guardian of liberty and the dignity of man" and that poverty was the result of the improvidence of the masses. These were comforting doctrines, and the wealthy middle class abandoned its old antagonism to the church as it listened to them.

But the church acquired enemies to replace old-fashioned middle-class anticlericalism. The advance of industrialism, by changing old ways of life, destroying traditional trades, and forcing people to leave their homes and drift toward the towns in search of employment, weakened the hold of the churches on the masses. This had not gone as far as it was to go later in the century; but Proudhon noted in 1844 that some workers in Lyons had lost contact with the church and were no longer baptized, married, or buried by the priest. There was enough evidence of this sort to stimulate attempts to check the religious decline by more missions. When clerics like Félicité Robert de Lamennais (1782–1854) tried to alleviate the misery of the working class by advocating social legislation, however, they received little sympathy from their fellows. Lamennais himself—later described by Saint-Beuve as one of the great cornerstones of French socialism and philanthropy—ended as an outcast from his own church. The church as a whole paid rather too little attention to the ills of the masses; and this was the reason why, among parts of the working class and even of the peasantry, there was, as Lacordaire noted, "an almost total absence of faith . . . and an immense scorn for the priest."

Other Churches / During the early Restoration some of the more fanatical churchmen had hoped for a new crusade against heresy—that is, against Protestantism; but the government discouraged this and protected the rights of the non-Catholic believers. In the first part of this period, the Reformed Church was weakened by internal disorganization and doctrinal disputes; but after 1830, when the *Réveil* or awakening came to France from Geneva, there was a strong movement toward unity, consolidation, and a return to the basic doctrines of the Reformation, and, under this inspiration, membership was greatly strengthened. Within Judaism there were also some doctrinal differences, as modernists sought to modify certain ritual practices; but these had no effect on the orthodoxy of the majority. For the rest, for France's 60,000 Jews, this was a period in which many of the disabilities from which they had formerly suffered disappeared.

A word might be said here of attempts to provide new religions to replace the established ones. The followers of Saint-Simon, for instance, undertook to found a "church" with a dogma, rites, and a priesthood, which was designed to deify science and humanity. A more elaborate attempt of this kind was made by Auguste Comte (1798–1857), who wished to transform modern society into an authoritarian state in which the scientists and the leaders of industry would be priests and rulers alike, and the great benefactors of society would be venerated as saints. Both Saint-Simon and Comte will be remembered for other things than these grandiose schemes—Saint-Simon for his pioneer analysis of industrial society, Comte because he was the father of modern sociology—and it is enough to say here that their churches did not attract many followers.

Literature and the Arts / In literature and the arts this was a period in which romanticism reached its highest flowering and began its decline. The general characteristics of romanticism have been described above (pp. 6–7); but it might be added that, precisely because it was a movement which broke with the standards of the past, it had a verve and a spirit that have rarely been matched since. Its representatives took a belligerent pride in their iconoclasm. A play in the romantic style was not just a play but a kind of military assault on the entrenched positions of classicism; and its presentation was likely to be the scene of stormy altercation and tumultuous demonstration, as was the production of Hugo's *Hernani* in February 1830. Because the movement broke also with the polished urbanity of the eighteenth century and with its cultivated and ironical rationalism, the romantics were apt, on the one hand, to deal with life in the raw—the delights of nature and the adventures of primitive and exotic peoples—and, on the other, to be highly emotional in the content and style of their works. George Sand, probably the most popular romantic novelist, wrote once to Gustave Flaubert, "My style has its ups and downs, its sounding harmonies and its failures. I do not fundamentally much mind, as long as the *emotion* comes through!"

Perhaps the truest representatives of romanticism were François-René de Chateaubriand, (1768–1848), whose popular "epics of nature," *Atala* and *René*, were written before our period begins; Alphonse de Lamartine (1790–1869), whose *Méditations* (1820), with their haunting melodies, their extreme simplicity, and their intense emotion, took France by storm and, incidentally, kept Talleyrand awake all night; the young Hugo, the preface of whose play *Cromwell* (1827) was the manifesto of romanticism in the drama and whose *Hernani* was a kind of July revolution in literature; Alfred de Vigny (1797–1863), whose play *Chatterton* presented the ideal romantic hero, the proud egoist who is "a being apart," and whose somber poetry remains one of the great achievements of this period; Alfred de Musset (1810–1857), who carried emotionalism to the point of morbidity, but whose plays, with their wonderful blend of fantasy and reality, are the most successful products of the romantic

Victor Hugo, 1802–1885   Alexis de Tocqueville, 1805–1859
(FRENCH EMBASSY PRESS & INFORMATION DIVISION)

drama; and, finally, George Sand (1804–1876), who used the novel as a means of expressing her own remarkable individuality and as a vehicle not only for sentiment but also for socialist and humanitarian ideals.

After 1830, romanticism began to lose its vitality, and by 1840 the public was beginning to demand of its writers less sensibility and more realism. In the work of Stendhal (Henri Beyle, 1785–1842), they had realism at its most superb; but, although *The Red and the Black* had appeared in 1831 and *The Charterhouse of Parma* in 1839, these works were not yet widely understood or appreciated, and Stendhal's satirical chronicle of the July Monarchy, *Lucien Leuwen*, was not to be known until years after his death. The other early master of the realistic novel, Honoré de Balzac (1799–1850), was writing his *Comédie humaine* in these years, that vast picture of French society under the Empire, the Restoration, and the July Monarchy. But Balzac's great fame was to come later also, and he can hardly be called a representative writer of this period. Perhaps the man who comes closest to representing the spirit of the last years of the July Monarchy was, as Louise Varèse has suggested, that "spiritual brother of the political and financial go-getters, that old charlatan, Alexandre Dumas, with his factory of ghostwriters, his shameless plagiarism and quite un-romantic love of money—the one-man Hollywood of his day."

Just as romanticism had broken the restrictive mold of the past and breathed new life into literature, so did it perform that service in painting and music. The man who started the revolt against the tyranny of the David school in painting was Géricault, but the man who carried the romantics to victory, and certainly the greatest painter of this period, was Eugène Delacroix. The revolution in sculpture was less violent and the break with classicism less pronounced, as is evident from the works of such men as David d'Angers and Rude. French music, which was inferior to both German and Italian music at this time, had in Hector Berlioz a composer of great originality, mastery of tone and color, and rich emotional appeal; while opera made some significant advances with d'Auber's *Dumb Girl of Portici* (1828), Halévy's *La Juive*, and the operas of Meyerbeer, who found Paris more congenial than Berlin.

The artists of this period were not untouched by the political and social questions of the day, and one of the striking features of the last years of the July Monarchy was the way in which even the most illustrious of them took an active part in the public life of the nation. Victor Hugo turned practically all of his attention to politics for ten years after 1841; and Lamartine, after he had entered the Chamber of Deputies in 1834, became so well-known as a politician that he gave up poetry almost entirely. As for George Sand, by the 1840s she was devoting most of her abundant energies to relieving the misery of the working class, and, in January 1848, it was she who supplied Alexis de Tocqueville with that information about their state of mind with which he tried in vain to impress the Chamber.

4

Great Britain: Social Unrest and Social Compromise, 1815-1848

ECONOMIC AND SOCIAL CONDITIONS AFTER 1815

Tides of Change / Compared with any of the countries discussed so far, Great Britain, in the first half of the nineteenth century, possessed undeniable material advantages. English wealth was a byword on the continent, and English industrial and commercial supremacy was patent to every eye. Foreign visitors to England were often so carried away by the evidences of economic power that they drew hasty and unsound conclusions from them. Thus, in the last stages of the war against Napoleon, one traveler wrote:[1]

> I have found the great mass of the people richer, happier and more respectable than any other with which I am acquainted. I have seen prevailing among all ranks of people that emulation of industry and independence which characterises a state of advancing civilisation properly directed. The manners and the whole deportment of superiors to inferiors are marked with that just regard and circumspection which announce the presence of laws equal for all. By such signs, I know this to be the best government that ever existed.

[1] L. Simond, cited in E. L. Woodward, *The Age of Reform* (Oxford, 1938), p. 28.

One might suppose from this exuberant endorsement that Great Britain was immune to all the agitations and disturbances that infected her continental neighbors. This was far from being true. The very circumstances that led to England's economic growth and her commercial and industrial supremacy gave rise to social and political problems that were incapable of easy solution but which, while unsolved, posed the gravest possible threat to the established order.

At the basis of all social change in Great Britain was the marked demographic growth of this period. Between 1700 and 1801, the population had doubled; it stood at ten and a half million in the latter year; and in the course of the next one hundred years this figure was to increase threefold. This tremendous upsurge was made possible by improved medical services, the first glimmerings of an understanding of public sanitation, and, among other things, certain economic developments that promoted health (the manufacture of cheap washable clothing, for instance). As in the case of other countries where population was rising steeply, the increase had profound and continuing repercussions.

Above all, it doomed the old agricultural system of England—the open-field system of farming, which was characterized by a multiplicity of small holdings and by the possession, by the poorer tenant farmers and the agricultural laborers, of grazing and other rights on waste land and village commons. In the latter half of the eighteenth century, the already significant rise in population increased the demand for food and forced prices upward. High grain prices encouraged landowners to consolidate small individually held plots into large farms capable of meeting the demands of the expanded market; and it induced them also to seek, by legal and other means, to enclose former common lands and turn them into cultivation. These tendencies were heightened during the war against Napoleon, when the need for an increase in the supply of food became so pressing that enclosures seemed almost a patriotic necessity.

The enclosure movement eliminated much of the inefficiency that had been inherent in the old system; it permitted full use of new farming methods; it improved the soil; and it achieved its major purpose by expanding production. But these gains were accompanied by a considerable amount of social dislocation and human suffering. In general, the English agricultural scene came to be dominated by the great landowners and the wealthier tenant farmers (those who held long-term leases on farms of from 100 to 500 acres of land). The less wealthy leaseholders became fewer in number, while the poorest tenants were apt to be squeezed out, either by eviction or by an inability to compete with their more efficient neighbors. This last was true also of many in the so-called yeoman class of small independent proprietors, who were ruined by the erratic harvests and the wild price fluctuations of the war years and were, like the most vulnerable tenant farmers, reduced to the status of agricultural laborers or forced to leave the land.

As long as the war with France continued, there were means of absorbing the shock of these changes. Although it did not keep pace with the increase in rural population, the demand for agricultural labor rose steadily from 1793 to 1815. Most of those who left the soil, moreover, found other occupations. The war years were boom years for England's rapidly expanding industry; its new urban centers—Manchester, Birmingham, Leeds, Sheffield, Bristol—were growing feverishly; and, while English firms were supplying the armies of England, Russia, Prussia, and Sweden with guns and greatcoats and blankets, there were lots of jobs in the foundries and the mills. Even the hordes of Irish immigrants who began to pour into Glasgow and Liverpool in the last years of the war could be absorbed by the expanding economic system.

The Postwar Depression / But all this changed after the wars had ceased, for peace brought with it a general economic slump; and, in the decade that followed—while export trade to Europe and America fell by a third—agriculture, the heavy industries, and textiles alike suffered from severe depression. In 1815, wheat prices fell catastrophically from 126s. 6d. a quarter to 65s. 7d., and, although Parliament immediately passed a Corn Law which imposed heavy duties upon foreign grains, domestic prices recovered very slowly and never completely. In rural areas this brought hardship to all classes and ruin to tenant farmers and yeomen who had overextended their operations. As for the agricultural laborer, deprived by enclosures of the means of having a plot of his own or even of keeping a pig or some geese on the village commons, he now saw his wages forced down implacably and found himself confronted with the choice between misery on the land or flight from it.

Not that the latter course had much to offer. The postwar price slump was general and affected industry as well as agriculture. In the mines and the mills, workers were being dismissed by the thousands after 1815, and those who were kept on were forced to work long hours under appalling conditions for wretched wages. To the prevailing misery, two other factors made a contribution. The first was the disbandment of the militia and the reduction of the regular forces, which added hundreds of thousands of men to an already glutted labor market. The second was the struggle of the old household industries, like handloom weaving and the stocking trades, to hold their own against the advancing factory system—a fight that was doomed to failure and was already throwing many out of employment or subjecting them to the excesses of sweated labor. With the population curve still rising and Irish immigration showing no signs of abatement, the industrial towns of England in the first years of the peace became centers of squalor and want, while the countryside was filled with able-bodied paupers and unemployed handi-craftsmen.

All those who were, directly or indirectly, affected by these conditions looked to the government for measures to correct them. For a number of reasons, the government was ill-prepared to supply them. Dominated as it still was by the landed magnates of the east and south, it had difficulty even in understanding, let alone solving, problems that had their roots in the new industrial society of Manchester and Sheffield. In an age in which statistical information was meager and no civil service existed to collect it, it had, moreover, a very imperfect knowledge of the extent of social misery and was often made aware of it only when it took violent forms.

Years of Violence, 1815–1819 / Writing of the government that ruled England in the first years after Waterloo, the historians J. L. and B. Hammond once asserted that "probably no English government has ever been quite so near, in spirit and licence, to the atmosphere that we used to associate with the tsar's government in Russia."

These are strong words, but, one suspects, singularly inappropriate ones. There was no Alexander or Nicholas, no Arakcheev or Benckendorff in England after 1815. The monarchy was at a low ebb in its fortunes, the king, George III, being sunk in hopeless mania, while his son, the prince regent, was a cypher interested only in painting, architecture, fashion, and women. Effective power lay in the houses of Parliament and was wielded, with their consent, by the cabinet. The prime minister was Lord Liverpool, a patient and phlegmatic man who had been in ministerial posts since 1793. His most important colleagues were the lord chancellor Eldon, the foreign secretary Castlereagh, the home secretary Sidmouth, and the leader of the Tories in the House of Lords, the Duke of Wellington—all men of conservative views. It was said of Liverpool that, if he had been present on the day of creation, he would have said, "Let us conserve chaos!"; while Eldon, a kindly enough man in his personal relationships, was an inflexible supporter of the most severe aspects of the criminal code, apparently on the grounds that social stability depended upon strict observance of the letter of the law. Even so, these men were not heartless tyrants, as they have sometimes been portrayed. They had worked long years to overcome the armies of Napoleon and were, even now, engaged in an effort to establish a Euro-pean system that would prevent new outbursts of revolutionary agitation on the continent. They could not but be sensitive to the possibility of revolution at home. They were responsible to Parliament, which represented the wealthiest classes of society and was prone to panic whenever social misery led to social disorder. Even before 1789, the well-to-do classes of England had learned to fear mob violence—as well they might in an age which possessed no regular police force—and their fears had been enhanced by what had happened in France. After 1815, whenever there were signs of popular unrest, they exaggerated the danger and called for extreme measures to avert it. The government, unfortunately, was usually responsive to their wishes and, all too often, met demands for relief of misery not with reform but with repression.

It should not be supposed, however, that the threat to the established order was imaginary. As the depression deepened, sporadic rioting began in the eastern counties, and there was a considerable amount of machine-breaking in Nottinghamshire. Strikes were widespread, and deputations from the Wolverhampton colliers began to travel about the country to recruit aid. Even more frightening for the wealthy classes was the appearance of a number of popular tribunes and agitators. Some of these were responsible men of moderate opinions who sympathized with the lot of the poor and believed that it could be improved by legal means, usually by a reform that would make Parliament more representative of the country as a whole. These included the indomitable and eloquent William Cobbett, perhaps the most powerful pamphleteer of his time, Sir Francis Burdett, member of Parliament for the borough of Westminster, and the so-called "father of reform," the seventy-five-year-old Major John Cartwright. Some were flamboyant *poseurs*, like the fiery "Orator" Hunt, whose doubtless sincere efforts in behalf of the poor were made ineffective by his personal vanity. Some were harmless fanatics, who advocated primitive communism and other panaceas. But there were also more dangerous agitators, like the perennial conspirator Arthur Thistlewood, who talked of overthrowing the monarchy by force and ruling England by a Committee of Public Safety on the French model.

The extremists, unfortunately, assumed an importance out of proportion to their numbers. In December 1816, for instance, Thistlewood and his associates invaded a reform meeting at Spa Fields in London, led part of the crowd away, broke into a gunshop, and made an attack upon the City of London. This foolish affair—which landed its authors in prison—and a supposed attempt on the regent's life a few days later caused such excitement in ruling circles that the cabinet, after listening to the evidence of hired informers who claimed to have evidence of widespread conspiracy against the government,[2] secured Parliamentary

[2] This evidence came from paid informers and spies upon whom the government had to rely since it had no regular police force. Since these informers were paid only as long as they supplied information, it can be imagined that at least some of the conspiracies they reported were completely imaginary.

approval of the suspension of the Habeas Corpus Act and the banning of seditious meetings. This was not popular in the country and may have encouraged new incidents that increased the uneasiness of the propertied classes: the attempted march of a band of petitioners (the "Blanketeers") from Manchester to London; and, in June 1817 at Pentrich in Derbyshire, a muddled rising of the poor under the leadership of an unemployed stockinger named Jeremiah Brandreth. Against these movements the government struck out quickly and brutally: the Blanketeers' progress was broken up by troops; Brandreth and his associates were arrested, given speedy trial and hanged.

This unhappy state of affairs reached its height in August 1819, when about 50,000 people assembled in St. Peter's Fields, Manchester, to hear Hunt and others talk about the need for government reform. Although some of the banners displayed bore revolutionary slogans, the crowd was an orderly one, made up of respectable artisans and laborers and their families. The local magistrates, however, alarmed by the size of the gathering and perhaps fearing a spontaneous explosion, ordered the Manchester and Salford Yeomanry to advance into the crowd and arrest the speakers. The Yeomanry was a badly trained troop of local notables. In attempting to carry out their orders, they became hopelessly stuck in the middle of the now angry crowd. The magistrates then lost their heads completely and ordered six troops of the 15th Hussars, who were standing by, to extricate the militia; and these professional troops advanced with drawn sabers and cleared the field—killing eleven people and injuring hundreds as they did so.

The 15th had fought last at Waterloo. Their employment against their own countrymen shocked men of all classes and led them to speak bitterly of this incident as the Massacre of Peterloo. But the government was unmoved by this reaction. The prince regent and the home secretary expressed their satisfaction with the behavior of the authorities at Manchester; and, in the fall of 1819, Parliament passed the so-called Six Acts, which, among other things, placed more severe restrictions upon public meetings and upon the circulation of papers and pamphlets.

This sort of thing threatened to drive political dissension underground and to make it to assume secret and conspiratorial forms, as it had on the continent, and, only two months after the passing of the Six Acts, there was some indication that this might be happening. Arthur Thistlewood, once again at liberty, spent the last months of 1819 devising a plot to murder the whole of the cabinet and to establish a Britannic Republic. The plotters were betrayed by a spy and arrested in a loft in Cato Street as they were arming for their effort; but the affair seemed ominous.

Fortunately, the Cato Street conspiracy was not imitated, and the period of violence and counterviolence came to an end. An improvement

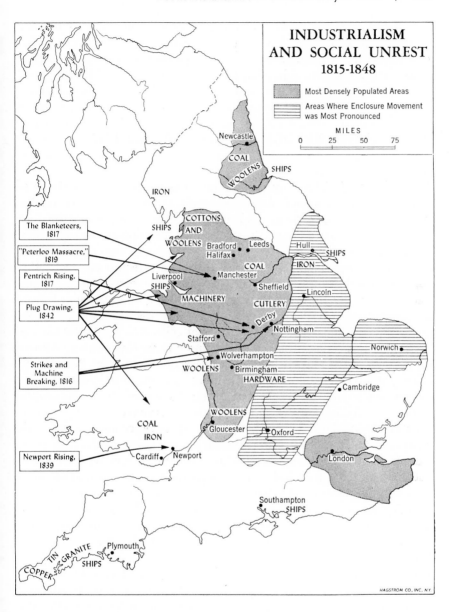

INDUSTRIALISM AND SOCIAL UNREST
1815-1848

Most Densely Populated Areas

Areas Where Enclosure Movement was Most Pronounced

MILES
0   25   50   75

Newcastle

COAL

WOOLENS   SHIPS

IRON

The Blanketeers, 1817

"Peterloo Massacre," 1819

Pentrich Rising, 1817

Plug Drawing, 1842

Strikes and Machine Breaking, 1816

Newport Rising, 1839

SHIPS

COTTONS AND WOOLENS   Bradford   Leeds   Hull   SHIPS
Halifax   IRON
COAL
Liverpool   Manchester
SHIPS   Sheffield   Lincoln
MACHINERY   CUTLERY
Derby
Stafford   Nottingham
Norwich
Wolverhampton
WOOLENS   Birmingham
HARDWARE   Cambridge

WOOLENS
Gloucester   Oxford

COAL
IRON

Cardiff   Newport   London

Southampton
SHIPS

TIN   GRANITE   Plymouth
COPPER   SHIPS

HAGSTROM CO., INC., N.Y.

of economic conditions sensibly modified the misery that had been the principal motive for the machine-breaking, the disorder, and the abortive risings of these years; and Pentrich and Peterloo gradually faded into the past. They had not, however, been without effect. On the one hand, the failure of violence to achieve positive results convinced a great many people that Cobbett and Cartwright were correct in arguing that the best way of achieving improvement of social conditions was by reforming Parliament. On the other hand, the Tory party itself seemed dissatisfied with the policy it had followed since Waterloo and willing to consider remedial and progressive legislation.

THE REFORM MOVEMENT, 1820–1832

Tory Reforms / The Tory party, which commanded the allegiance of most of the great landed families as well as the country gentry, the universities, and the services, had held power almost uninterruptedly since 1793, thanks largely to the persistent disunity of its opponents, the Whigs. Its uninspiring record in the first years of the peace seemed to indicate the onset of that fatal inertia with which long tenure of office often affects political bodies. After 1820, however, the party showed its inherent vitality by throwing up a group of young and energetic leaders to replace those who had directed affairs since the war. Liverpool continued as prime minister, but his principal colleagues were now George Canning at the Foreign Office, F. J. Robinson at the Exchecquer, William Huskisson (1770–1830) at the Board of Trade, and Robert Peel (1788–1850) at the Home Office. While Canning (see pp. 23–24) was investing foreign policy with new vigor, his associates addressed themselves to the problems of the home front with spirit and determination, and, for a few years at least, Tory policy became progressive enough to win the approval even of followers of Jeremy Bentham (1748–1832).

Bentham, the eccentric and inspired analyst of the British political system, had long preached that political and social institutions must constantly be measured by the yardstick of utility, that their continued existence should be approved only if they worked efficiently, and that all antiquated institutions and feudal anomalies must be ruthlessly extirpated. It was very much in accordance with this philosophy that the new Tory group went to work.

All the efforts of Robinson and Huskisson, for example, were animated by the desire to free the country from the restrictions of an outworn fiscal and commercial system. While the former overhauled the tax structure and reformed the national debt, Huskisson attacked the mass of duties and rebates with which English trade was encumbered. Pointing out that the Navigation Acts, which required imports into the country to be carried in British ships or ships of the country of origin, were inviting retaliatory legislation on the part of the United States and other countries, Huskisson succeeded in replacing them by a series of reciprocal trade

Sir Robert Peel, 1788–
1850. From *Illustrated
London News,* Jan. 31,
1846.

agreements which increased British shipping by 50 percent within the
decade. He alleviated the rigidity of the Corn Law of 1815 by placing
grain duties on a sliding scale, and he persuaded Parliament to reduce
duties on a whole range of products from pig iron to raw silk. "National
prosperity," Huskisson said in 1825, "would be most effectually promoted
by an unrestrained competition"; and, although he did not live to see the
coming of free trade, his success in removing commercial regulations that
had outlived their usefulness was the first real step toward the free-trade
economy.

Meanwhile, Huskisson's colleague Peel was attacking the mass of
antiquated procedures and inhuman penalties that passed for criminal
law in England. He drafted a simplified criminal code that abolished the
death penalty in almost 200 cases and simultaneously reduced the number
of offenses punishable by transportation. He reformed judicial procedure
and abolished the use of spies and paid informers in criminal cases; and
he made a beginning to the difficult but necessary job of reforming prison
conditions. Finally, in what is probably his best remembered reform, he
established a trained police force in the national capital. The organization of these "Peelers" or "Bobbies," which was soon copied by other
cities, was an enormously important contribution to the cause of public
order and, by reducing the dependence of local authorities, in time of

popular unrest, upon the militia or the regular army, it prevented the repetition of incidents like Peterloo. Its effectiveness was demonstrated also by the almost immediate reduction of crime, which had hitherto been regarded as an unfortunate but unavoidable feature of society.

Even before this last reform was accomplished, the influence of the reformers in the cabinet had been greatly reduced. After Liverpool's retirement from public life in the spring of 1827, Canning had become prime minister. But his death in August and the failure of Robinson (now Lord Goderich) to fill his place adequately brought the Duke of Wellington to the head of the government, and the mood of the cabinet was immediately less favorable to change of any kind.

Nevertheless, the government was forced against its will to tolerate additional reforms. For one thing, the removal of the disabilities from which nonmembers of the established church had to suffer was long overdue. Whereas Englishmen could worship as they pleased, the Test and Corporation acts prevented them from holding public office unless they were members of the Church of England. In the case of Protestant dissenters, these laws had for years been bypassed by various expedients, but their continued existence was an affront to non-Anglicans; and, in 1828, under opposition pressure, the government agreed to the repeal of the offending acts.

Inevitably, this raised the much more difficult question of Catholic emancipation. The repeal of the Test and Corporation acts opened most public offices to Roman Catholics, but they were still effectively barred from Parliament by an act of 1679, which required all members of Parliament to declare themselves opposed to the doctrine of transsubstantiation and the adoration of the Virgin Mary. This situation was especially anomalous in Ireland where the great bulk of the voting public was Catholic but was forced to vote for Protestants in order to make their votes effective.

The patience of the Irish now seemed to have been exhausted. In 1823 Daniel O'Connell (1775–1847), a Dublin barrister with a talent for leadership and remarkable gifts of oratory, had founded a body known as the Catholic Association in order to fight for the removal of Catholic disabilities. The mass meetings organized by O'Connell inflamed all Ireland and greatly alarmed the government, which tried in vain to obstruct and even to dissolve the association. This alarm increased in 1828, when O'Connell decided to stand as a candidate in a Parliamentary by-election in County Clare and was, in defiance of the existing law, triumphantly elected. It was obvious that, unless something was done, Catholics would be elected for every constituency in Ireland in the next general elections and that attempts to deny them the right to sit in Parliament might, given the country's present temper, lead to something very like civil war.

Wellington and Peel were both opposed to emancipation, but they were realists enough to see that they could not meet O'Connell's challenge. Therefore, they brought in a bill to remove the last restrictions upon the political activities of the Catholics and, in March 1829, it was passed by Parliament.

Its passage marked the end of the long period of Tory political domination. This end had been prepared by the activities of Canning, Huskisson, and their associates, whose zeal for change had worried the majority of the party even while it acquiesced in their reforms. It had been brought closer by the reluctant decision to emancipate the Catholics, which many Tories regarded as a betrayal of principle. And it was made inevitable now by the revival of the agitation for Parliamentary reform, which was much too explosive a question to be handled by a badly split party.

The Great Reform Bill / Perhaps the best way of describing what the reformers wanted to change in the parliamentary system is to quote from a speech made by Lord John Russell during the reform debate:

> A stranger who was told that this country is unparalleled in wealth and industry, that it is a country that prides itself on its freedom and that once in every seven years it elects representatives from its population to act as the guardians and preservers of that freedom, would be anxious and curious to see how . . . the people choose their representatives . . . Such a person would be very much astonished if he were taken to a ruined mound and told that that mound sent two representatives to Parliament; if he were taken to a stone wall and told that three niches in it sent two representatives to Parliament; if he were taken to a park where no houses were to be seen, and told that that park sent two representatives to Parliament. But if he were told all this, and were astonished at hearing it, he would be still more astonished if he were to see large and opulent towns . . . and were then told that these towns sent no representatives to Parliament.

England's system of representative government had simply not changed with the times and with the new social and economic facts of life; and this was painfully obvious when one looked—as Russell was looking—at the way in which men were elected to the House of Commons. That body was composed of some 650 members, of whom 489 came from English constituencies, 100 from Irish, 45 from Scottish, and 24 from Welsh. Those who represented county constituencies (188 of the total) were elected by the so-called forty-shilling freeholders of their county—that is, by the men who owned land which brought them an income of at least forty shillings a year. But, as we have seen, economic developments since the middle of the eighteenth century and especially during the war years had led to a steady reduction of the number of independent proprietors, and this meant that the county electorate was dwindling and that the control of the county seats was falling into the hands of the wealthy few.

The county suffrage was at least uniform. This was far from being the case in the boroughs, which sent 465 members to the House of Commons. In one borough the electorate might comprise all the taxpayers, in another, only the inhabitants of certain houses; in a third, only the mayor and his corporation. In most cases, the number of voters was small enough to be influenced easily by the government or, more generally, by local magnates; and there were some cases, like those described by Russell, in which election was a legal fiction, the members simply being appointed by peers into whose control the borough had fallen. There were members of the House of Lords who controlled as many as nine boroughs at a time and could either fill or sell the seats as they saw fit. In 1827 it was estimated that 276 seats were controlled by landed proprietors and that eight peers alone controlled 51 seats. This was another illustration of the predominantly aristocratic nature of the political system before 1832.

What struck critics as being quite as reprehensible as these features of the system was the obvious inequality of the representation. Scotland, with eight times the population of Cornwall, had fewer members in Parliament than that county. The ten southern counties of England had almost as many members as the thirty others, although their population was only a third as large. The plight of the industrial towns was even more striking. In 1828, when Mr. Pickwick went on his famous but unsuccessful mission to Birmingham to soften the heart of Mr. Winkle's father, he was impressed by the vigor of the town and the way in which

> the sights and sounds of earnest occupation struck . . . forcibly on the senses. The streets were thronged with working-people. The hum of labor resounded from every house, lights gleamed from the long casement windows in the attic stories, and the whirl of wheels and noise of machinery shook the trembling walls. The fires, whose lurid sullen light had been visible for miles, blazed fiercely up, in the great works and factories of the town. The din of hammers, the rushing of steam, and the dead heavy clanking of engines, was the harsh music which arose from every quarter.

Yet this hive of activity had no parliamentary representation whatsoever, and the same was true of Bradford, Halifax, Leeds, Manchester, and Sheffield.

All of these things had been pointed out for years by popular agitators like Cobbett, by followers of Bentham, and by spokesmen for the industrial interest. The defenders of the *status quo* always answered with a variety of arguments: that the existing system enabled men of talent who could not have been elected to Parliament to be appointed to it; that every member of Parliament represented all parts of the country, that this "virtual representation" was preferable to a system in which members regarded themselves as representing individual constituencies, and that, therefore, it was unnecessary and unwise to give representation to all localities; and that any change would destroy the balance of the constitution, diminish the influence of the crown, and give rise to a host of unspecified dangers.

By 1830, however, these last arguments were having a diminishing effect upon the educated classes, who recognized that there were other things in England that needed to be reformed (the spoils system in government, for instance, and the control of municipal government by closed corporations) but which would not be reformed as long as the composition of Parliament remained unchanged. And they had no effect at all upon the common people who seemed to entertain unreasonable expectations concerning reform and were now clamoring for action.

If the passage of the bill for Catholic emancipation had contributed to this agitation, two other events gave it additional impetus: the fall of the Bourbon monarchy in France, which inspired English reformers as much as it frightened their opponents, and the combination of a sudden trade recession and a disastrous crop failure in 1830, which led to a new wave of rioting, machine-breaking, and rick-burning and made a number of people feel that the time had come for political concession. All events, in short, were conspiring in favor of reform, and when the Tory government refused to see this it was swept away. In the fall of 1830, Wellington—whose Parliamentary majority was dangerously slim in any case—had the bad judgment to praise the English government as the acme of perfection and to declare that he was "not only not prepared to bring forward any measure of [parliamentary reform]" but that "as long as he held any station in the Government of the country, he should always feel it his duty to resist such measures when proposed by others." The government was immediately attacked from every quarter, and the duke was compelled to resign.

The new government, which was headed by Lord Grey and was predominantly Whig in composition, although it included some of Canning's former followers, was pledged to reform and got down to it immediately. In March 1831 Lord John Russell introduced a reform bill in the House of Commons. When it was defeated on a technicality, Grey took the issue to the country and, in new elections, won a majority of 100 seats. He then reintroduced the bill; and, after a debate that lasted months and in which the opposition used every possible delaying tactic, it was passed by a majority of 106 votes. This was an illusory victory, for the bill was immediately killed by the House of Lords, then as later a center of hidebound conservatism.

This caused widespread indignation, which was expressed in riots and demonstrations throughout the land. The atmosphere was not unlike that of Paris in July 1830, and this mood deepened when the bill was introduced for a third time and again passed by Commons in March 1832, for it was recognized as virtually certain that the Lords would again thwart the popular desire for reform. This result was, indeed, plainly forecast in May, when Grey became discouraged and handed in his resignation. It was immediately known throughout the country that the king was trying to persuade Wellington to take office; and this brought popular feeling to a whiter heat and increased the dangers of the situation in general.

The constitutional deadlock was, however, overcome. Wellington could not form a cabinet, and his failure may have been due in part to a run on the banks and a tax strike organized by certain middle-class agitators, notably the Benthamite Francis Place. As the price of returning to office, Grey secured a royal promise to create a sufficient number of new peers to secure the passage of the reform bill by the House of Lords. They did not have to be created; the threat was enough to break the resistance of the Lords. On June 4, 1832, the Great Reform Bill passed its final hurdle and became the law of the land.

The bill did not do everything that its supporters had expected, nor did it remove all the abuses that had led to its introduction. There were rotten boroughs after 1832 as before; there were boroughs in which fifty votes could decide the election of a member; and there were still startling inequalities of representation. But there were many fewer abuses of this kind. One hundred and forty-three seats were redistributed in such a way as to take representation away from centers of no population, to add to the representation of the larger counties and of Scotland and Ireland, and to allow the industrial towns to send members to Commons.

At the same time, the suffrage was widened. The county suffrage was no longer restricted to people who owned their land, but was given to long-term tenant farmers whose land yielded ten pounds of value annually and to tenants-at-will whose land was worth fifty pounds a year. In the boroughs, all special franchises were abolished, and the vote was given to all men who owned or rented a building whose annual rental value was ten pounds. Throughout England and Wales one man in five now had the vote; in Scotland, one man in eight; in Ireland, one man in twenty. This was not democracy—a fact that becomes clearer when we recall that members of Parliament still received no pay and that there was a property qualification for election—but it was the first hopeful step in that direction.

In the history of English political organization, the reform campaign has great importance. In it we can discern the first beginnings of the kind of propaganda and pressure tactics that have become commonplace in our own age. At critical junctures in the campaign, the London Radical

Reform Association, in which Francis Place was active, and Joseph Attwood's Birmingham Political Union showed a virtuosity in mobilizing public feeling that would be admired by contemporary professional politicians.

At the same time, the passing of the Reform Act marked the real beginning of modern party organization in England. The Tory and Whig parties of the pre-1832 period were very loose associations of interest, without formal machinery, consultative organs, or internal discipline. After 1832 the transformation of the old groups into the modern Conservative and Liberal parties began. During the reform campaign the Carlton Club was formed with the specific purpose of giving some unity to Tory policy inside and outside Parliament; and a few years later the Reform Club was founded to facilitate unity of view and tactics between the Whigs and their Benthamite allies, the so-called Radicals. These political clubs gave the parties their first machinery, which was developed further as a result of the provisions of the Reform Act itself. For the act made legal enrollment of voters a preliminary condition of voting, and this provision was a stimulus to such things as the formation of party associations in the local constituencies (to promote enrollment in the party interest), the creation of central registration committees, the growth of election agents and party managers, and other features of the modern political party. In a real sense, the present political system of England dates from 1832.

THE POLITICS OF THE PEOPLE

Popular Dissatisfaction with the Reform Act / The passing of the Reform Act had enfranchised virtually the whole of the middle class. It brought fewer obvious advantages to the working class, who had helped secure its passage but had not been granted the vote by it; and the reaction of the articulate sections of the working class was one of disappointment and resentment.

This deepened when the first reformed Parliament met. In the new House of Commons the Whigs and Radicals were in a commanding position. They soon showed, however, by the limited use they made of their power, that they were no real friends of their former working-class supporters and had no intention of doing anything to satisfy their political aspirations. Neither the Whig aristocrats nor the new representatives of the middle class who were allied with them had any sympathy for democracy. In their view—and this was to become doctrine in the Liberal party that emerged from the Whig-Radical fusion—social stability required that the suffrage be restricted to those who had an economic stake in society and were sufficiently educated to use the vote intelligently. The Reform Act represented a limit beyond which they did not wish to go, and Lord John Russell now earned the name "Finality Jack" by making this clear.

The Whigs and the Radicals did not merely rest on their laurels after 1832. They passed some enormously important legislation: the act of 1833 abolishing slavery throughout the British colonies, for instance, and the Municipal Corporations Act of 1835, which removed the government of towns from the hands of self-elected bodies and vested it in corporations elected by all taxpaying residents. But, while they were ready to remove palpable abuses and to take steps to increase efficiency and economy in the government, according to the Benthamite prescription, their attitude toward the economic and social needs of the working class was almost entirely negative. The Factory Act of 1833, which reduced and regulated the labor of children and young people in the textile mills, owed its passage less to them than to the strenuous efforts of Tory reformers like Lord Ashley; and it was opposed by many Whigs and Radicals because it seemed an unwarranted interference with the freedom of trade.

The representatives of the industrial interest were, indeed, all too ready to cite the population studies of Thomas Malthus (1766–1834) and the economic analyses of David Ricardo (1772–1823) to support the view that the mass of the population would always live on the barest subsistence level and that their lot could not be improved by government action but only by self-help, continence, and personal discipline. When they supported legislation in the social field, therefore, it was apt to take severe forms, like the new Poor Law of 1834. This act, which was Benthamite in inspiration, sought to lighten the burden which the relief of poverty imposed upon local taxpayers by ending outdoor relief to the able-bodied and forcing all recipients of relief to enter workhouses, in which they were denied the privilege of living with their families (lest they breed) and were forced to lead the most primitive and degrading kind of existence. The new system was doubtless more economical than the old; but one has only to read Charles Dickens's description of workhouse conditions in *Oliver Twist*, published in 1837, to understand how high the cost was in human suffering.

The spirit and the policies of the post-1832 government alienated the working classes and, at the same time, forced them to realize that improvement of their lot would depend on their own efforts. Out of this realization came two movements: trade unionism and chartism.

The Trade-Union Movement / In the first years after the war the development of a strong union movement had been impossible because of the existence of the Combination Acts of 1799 and 1800 and other legislation that forbade all working-class combinations, except purely benevolent societies, as criminal conspiracies in restraint of trade. In 1824, however, in the period of the Canningite reforms, Parliament had repealed the Combination Acts and permitted the organization of working men for peaceful bargaining about wages and hours, provided such organization did not encourage breach of contract or lead to "molestation" or "obstruction" of employers. The terms of the new act, as amended in 1825, still made it difficult for workers to strike, and the courts were very zealous in finding evidence of obstructionism; but at least trade unions could now pursue their activities openly without disguising themselves as benevolent societies.

Between 1825 and 1832 there was a steady growth of union membership and the beginning of systematic efforts to form national unions out of local ones. In 1829, for example, John Doherty succeeded in forming a single union for the whole cotton trade. Doherty hoped to carry this tendency further and to establish a union of all trades; and, in June 1830, he founded the National Association for the Protection of Labor with this end in view. This organization faded away almost as quickly as it had grown, but in its short existence it did encourage the establishment of new unions among the miners, the colliers, the clothiers, the potters, and other trades.

The disillusionment that affected the working classes after the passing of the Reform Act seems to have encouraged the growth of unionism and added to its militancy. In the latter half of 1832 union membership in general began to grow, strike activity began to increase, and there was a renewal of the earlier effort to unite all the trades. What Doherty had attempted was now tried again with the formation, in October 1833, of the Grand National Consolidated Trades Union which, in a very short space of time, had an estimated membership of half a million skilled and unskilled workers, including agricultural workers, gas workers, miners, tailors, bonnetmakers, bakers, and shearers, and had branches all over England and in Scotland and Ireland as well.

The leading spirit in this movement was Robert Owen (1771–1858). A self-made man, who at the age of twenty was the head of one of Lancashire's greatest cotton mills, Owen was a born social reformer. He had made his New Lanark mills a model establishment in which wages were good and employment regular, and in which sanitary housing and recreational facilities were available to workers and full-time education was provided for their children. His success here encouraged him to think of the possibility of founding model communities in other parts of the world and, in 1824, he actually went to America to try out his gospel there. New Harmony, the Owenite community founded in the United

Child labor in the English mines. These children are being employed as "hurriers." A woodcut from the official report of the Commission on Mines and Manufactures, 1842. (COURTESY JOHN W. DODDS, STANFORD UNIVERSITY)

States, was not a success; but it helped attract the attention of the workers to Owen's schemes and to stimulate what was perhaps the most permanent of his experiments; the establishment of self-governing, nonprofit cooperative shops and producers' societies catering to the needs of the workers. As early as 1830, there were already more than 300 of these cooperative societies in existence.

Owen's thought had progressed from simple philanthropy to a rather unsystematic socialism, and he had come to oppose the whole capitalistic profit system and to support all causes that promised to reduce the exploitation of the workers. It was natural, therefore, that he should be drawn to the trade-union movement. He was heart and soul behind the Grand National and seems to have believed that, within five years, it would enable the organized workers to gain control of the economic machinery of the country, to replace capitalism with a cooperative system, and to supersede both Parliament and all existing bodies of local government. With this dream of a socialist commonwealth before his eyes, Owen threw himself into the effort to spread the principle of unionism and cooperation in the unorganized trades.

The tremendous enthusiasm that attended his efforts made the trade-union movement appear much stronger than it was. In reality, when their strength was tested, the unions collapsed with remarkable celerity. In 1833, alarmed employers began to unite and to refuse employment to union members. Disregarding Owen's advice, the unions responded with strikes, forgetting that it was unwise to attempt to combine expensive cooperative experiments with even more costly strike payments. Before long, they were in serious financial embarrassment. At the same time, the government's attitude toward them hardened. Early in 1834, in the Dorsetshire village of Tolpuddle, six farm laborers were arrested for swearing men into a union which planned to join the Grand National and were subsequently tried and sentenced to seven years' transportation to a penal colony overseas for administering illegal oaths. It was clear from this that the government intended to strain the interpretation of the law if necessary in order to hamper the effectiveness of the union movement; and the fate of the "Tolpuddle martyrs" had a depressing effect upon union organization.

Financial mismanagement, an unwise strike policy, concerted opposition by employers, government persecution, and, finally, personal differences between Owen and his chief collaborators destroyed the militant trade-union movement of the 1830s. By 1835 the Grand National had fallen to pieces, and its member unions were in retreat. Those that survived in the next period were for the most part unions in the highly skilled trades, which resisted all ambitious schemes of organization and concentrated on their own problems and benevolent activities. The extension of union organization among the unskilled came to a halt and made little new progress for the next half century.

The failure of the Owenite union movement had one more positive result, however. It made working-class leaders realize that they could not win measures of social reform unless the workers had the vote. Abandoning the economic weapon, they now turned to political pressure in the hope that they could force the new ruling class to share its power with the workers. This attempt was made in the agitation for the People's Charter.

Chartism / In 1836 a group of working-class leaders in London, headed by William Lovett, a former storekeeper in London's first Owenite cooperative, founded the London Working Men's Association, in order "to draw into one bond of unity the intelligent and influential portion of the working classes in town and country, and to seek by every legal means to place all classes of society in possession of equal political and social rights." To attain this happy state of affairs, six things, it was felt, were necessary, and these were spelled out in the "People's Charter," which was published in May 1838. They were: annual Parliaments, universal male suffrage, equal electoral districts, the removal of the property qualification for membership in Commons, the secret ballot, and payment of members of Parliament. Under the influence of the Birmingham Political

Union, which had played an important part in the reform campaign of 1831–1832 and which was now revived, the Charter was embodied in a national petition and the nation-wide collection of signatures was begun, in the hope that Parliament might be impressed by the number of declared supporters of the program.

The London and Birmingham leaders doubtless wished to carry on this new campaign in a systematic, respectable, and peaceful fashion. But the Charter made a direct appeal to men who were indignant about the provisions of the new Poor Law, who were cast down by the failure of Owen's movement, who were unemployed as a result of the extension of machine industry, or who for more obscure reasons were resentful and disinclined to act moderately. Moreover, the leadership of Lovett and his associates was soon challenged by more violent spirits: the former Wesleyan minister J. R. Stephens, who wanted to establish a new theocracy with the Charter as its Bible and did not hesitate to call for the free employment of the pike and the firebrand to attain that end; G. J. Harney, who thought of himself as the English Marat; James Bronterre O'Brien, an assiduous preacher of class hatred; and Feargus O'Connor, a violent, unprincipled bully who had once been a follower of O'Connell and was now editing a radical newspaper in Leeds called the *Northern Star*.

It was O'Connor and O'Brien who overcame the influence of the moderates at a Convention of the Industrious Classes held in London in February 1839 and persuaded it not only to accept the Charter but to recognize the right of the people to arm themselves and to agree to a general strike in the event that Parliament should reject their claims. This had the effect of arousing a dangerous degree of excitement, and it is not surprising, therefore, that when the petition and the Charter, with 1,200,-000 signatures, were in fact rejected by the House of Commons in July, there were a number of ugly incidents. Although the general strike never materialized, there was actually an attempt at an armed rebellion at Newport in Monmouthshire, in which fourteen men were killed and ten died of wounds. This tragic affair—which was followed by the arrest and imprisonment of a number of Chartist leaders—brought the first phase of Chartism to an end.

The hope of success was never again as bright as it had been in this first period, but Chartism remained alive for another ten years, becoming active in periods of economic hardship, subsiding in better times. It flared up strongly, for instance, in the winter of 1841–1842 when, as a result of bad harvests and a slump in domestic and foreign trade, nearly one tenth of the nation was unemployed and one fifth of the population of Birmingham, to cite one example, was on relief rolls. Under O'Connor's leadership, a new national petition was circulated and in May 1842, bearing 3,317,752 signatures, it was submitted to the House of Commons.

On this occasion the Charter was actually debated, but both political parties opposed the key change proposed by it, universal suffrage, which was described by that epitome of middle-class liberalism, Thomas Babington Macaulay (1800–1859) as "fatal to all the purposes for which government exists and utterly incompatible with the very existence of civilization." The House rejected the petition by 287 to 49. This had the same effect as the earlier rejection: it touched off disorders throughout the country. A strike movement began in Staffordshire and spread rapidly over Lancashire, Yorkshire, Cheshire, Warwickshire, and into Wales and Scotland, the strikers marching from town to town, drawing the plugs from factory boilers in order to stop all work. O'Connor and his associates openly encouraged these disorders, which was a political mistake on their part and made them appear responsible for the eventual, and inevitable, failure of the strike.

By this time it was clear that the supplanting of the moderate Chartist leaders by O'Connor had fatally weakened the movement's hope of success. It was virtually impossible for the Chartists to find any support in Parliament, because even members who sympathized with working-class demands regarded O'Connor—in the words of one of them—as "a foolish, malignant, cowardly demagogue" and wanted nothing to do with a movement that he led. Moreover, under O'Connor's leadership Chartism had become an anti-industrial movement. O'Connor himself hated factories and towns and had a vague dream of restoring England to the small landholder. This creed appealed to thousands who still dreamed of an impossible return to the past, but it was in conflict with all the realities of the age. It gradually destroyed the originally strong following that Chartism had had in the trade unions and, at the same time, made impossible any kind of cooperation with the middle-class movement that might have been an effective ally: namely, the Anti-Corn Law League. For this reason, Chartism declined steadily after 1842, and the objectives that it sought had to be achieved later and by other forces.

THE ROAD TO COMPROMISE

Queen Victoria / During the tumultuous years of trade-union and Chartist agitation, a new sovereign had ascended the throne. William IV, who had become king in the days when Lord Grey was forming his first ministry, died in 1837 and was succeeded by his niece Victoria. A girl of eighteen at the time of her accession, with little knowledge of court ways, the new monarch had energy and determination as well as the intelligence to see that politics is an art that must be learned like anything else. Under the guidance of the Whig leader Melbourne and, after her marriage in 1840, of her husband, Prince Albert of Saxe-Coburg, she became a well-informed and conscientious ruler, aware of the limitations of her constitutional role but insistent upon the proper observance of her prerogatives. Her reign (1837–1901) was to be the longest in English history and, from the standpoint of material prosperity, political power, scientific progress, and cultural attainment, the richest as well.

The first years of Victoria's reign were years of economic distress and social disorder. But they were also years in which a profoundly important political change was completed: the transference of political leadership in the country from the aristocracy to the middle class. This change began, as we have seen, with the passing of the Reform Act, five years before Victoria's accession, but the event that consolidated middle-class predominance was the repeal of the Corn Laws in 1846.

The Repeal of the Corn Laws / The agitation for the repeal of the Corn Laws began during the same years of agricultural and economic depression that saw the rise of Chartism; it received organized form with the establishment of the Anti-Corn Law League in 1839. The leaders of this organization were Richard Cobden (1804–1865) and John Bright (1811–1889), both manufacturers and free traders, sincerely convinced that the existing protective tariff system jeopardized the development of English manufactures, by denying entrance into England of other countries' commodities and hence leading those countries to close their markets to English goods. The Corn Laws were the key to the protective system, and their removal—the free traders believed—would cause the whole system to fall, ushering in a period of unexampled industrial and commercial expansion.

The arguments of the free traders were a curious mixture of economic hardheadedness, social benevolence, cosmopolitan idealism, and class prejudice. Many manufacturers supported the league because they believed that repeal of the Corn Laws would in the long run enable them to decrease wages; but it is probably equally true that just as many sincerely believed that, by lowering the price of bread, repeal would bring direct advantage to the working class and mitigate some of the rigors of industrialism. In some of the speeches for repeal there was evangelistic fervor and a conviction that free trade would bring interdependence of nations and international peace. In others, one can detect a desire to smash the political power of the aristocracy by removing their economic privileges. In 1845, Cobden said: "The sooner the power in this country is transferred from the landed oligarchy, which has so misused it, and is placed absolutely—mind, I say absolutely—in the hands of the intelligent

Richard Cobden, 1804–1865.
From *Illustrated London News*, Feb. 28, 1846.

middle and industrious classes, the better for the condition and destinies of this country." In the heat of public meetings, members of the league were often less temperate in their expression and were wont to refer jeeringly to "bread stealers," "footpad aristocrats," and "titled felons."

The League's arguments could not be lightly disregarded by the government in power. In 1841, the Whigs were replaced by a Tory cabinet under Sir Robert Peel, and that able man of business recognized from the outset that the economic structure of the country was in need of reform. "We must," he wrote to a friend, "make this country a *cheap* country for living." He sought to make it so by reducing import duties in the hope of stimulating trade, making good the loss in revenue by an income tax, by strengthening the monetary system and the credit facilities of the country (by the Bank Charter Act of 1844), and by other financial measures. But Peel was the head of a party that represented the agricultural interest, and this prevented him from touching the Corn Laws.

At least, it would have done so if times had remained good. But, in August 1845 the potato blight appeared in Ireland, and that overpopulated island, dependent almost entirely on that crop, was faced with starvation. The English harvest had been poor, so little help could be expected from that quarter. The Anti-Corn Law League was quick to seize this opportunity to renew its attack upon the protective system; its campaign had been so effective over the years that there was evidence now that the country was behind it; and Peel was courageous enough to face realities and to decide that the Corn Laws must go. In May 1846, after a long and bitter debate, Peel, with opposition aid, carried repeal in Commons, and in June the Duke of Wellington, out of loyalty to Peel, steered it through the Lords.

The immediate economic results of repeal were not as dramatic as had been expected. The nominal price of grain did not fall appreciably and, for the next two decades, it remained stable. Since these were years of rising world prices, on the other hand, it can be argued that there was a real and significant lowering of the price of grain in the English market. To the extent that this was so, repeal contributed to the improvement of the lot of the poor and to the buttressing of social peace.

The agricultural interest suffered no immediate loss. It was not until a quarter of a century later, when improved transportation facilities brought American grains into the domestic market, that British agriculture was seriously threatened. Its vulnerability then, however, can be traced back to the repeal of 1846, the long-range economic effects of which were to weaken agriculture and to transform Great Britain into a country with a predominantly industrial and commercial economy.

By destroying the privileges of the landholding aristocracy, the repeal of the Corn Laws demonstrated the political supremacy of the class that had been enfranchised in 1832. The aristocracy continued to possess great social power, to monopolize the House of Lords, and to control the armed services, diplomacy, and the established church. But at the center of power, the House of Commons, the middle class was in command.

As far as party politics was concerned, the result of repeal was the splitting of the Tory party. Under the lead of Lord George Bentinck and a young and ambitious politician named Benjamin Disraeli, the majority of the party repudiated their greatest statesman, charging him with betrayal. The withdrawal of the Peelites added a new element of confusion to English politics, for, by adding one more to the political groups in the House of Commons, it increased the difficulty of forming a stable majority in that chamber. It was not until the 1860s that this situation was clarified and something like a two-party system was able to emerge.

Toward Social Peace / The laissez-faire philosophy that had animated the drive to repeal the Corn Laws was not, as we have seen, sympathetic to the idea of positive social reform. Measures to ameliorate the conditions of the poor seemed to represent an unwarranted interference with economic laws and one that could have dangerous results. Yet the very men who repeated the shibboleths of Manchesterian liberalism most fervently could not entirely still the voice of their own consciences. In the 1840s a series of reports of royal commissions bared, to all who could read, some of the results of the unregulated extension of industrialism: the deplorable conditions in factory towns, many of which had no sewage systems, no adequate water supply, and no housing for the working classes except the most flimsy and unsanitary hovels; the shameful situation in the mines, where women and children were found working like animals; the wretched state of many of the factories, in which *laissez faire* often meant irresponsibility and callousness on the part of employers.

The effect of these admirable reports was to stimulate a demand for basic reform which cut across party lines and led to effective remedies for the most obvious abuses. The most inveterate Manchesterians held out to the last, but they could not prevent the passage of a series of acts improving the working conditions of the poor: Ashley's Act of 1842, excluding all women, girls, and boys under ten from the mines; Graham's Factory Act of 1844, limiting child labor and providing for inspection to assure the observance of safety measures; and, finally, Fielden's Act of 1847, which established a normal working day of 10½ hours for all women and young people in the factories and, by implication, for the male operatives as well. These acts were important as a first recognition of the responsibility government has for the well-being of its citizens; and they could not help but have the effect of alleviating much of the social resentment that had marked the early part of our period.

To this alleviation the general improvement of economic conditions in the late 1840s also made a contribution. Employment figures were rising steadily; coal production was on the increase, and pig-iron tonnage was three times what it had been in 1832; and the export trade had doubled since that year. These were the years, among other things, of the great development of railways; and, between 1843 and 1849, two hundred thousand laborers, drawn from the depressed classes, laid 5000 miles of track and began the construction of 7000 more. Their labors opened up the interior of the country to heavy as well as light industry, facilitated the transportation of goods and the movement of labor, and had other effects too numerous to mention here. In 1850 there were 6621 miles of railway in operation and they carried seventy-three million travelers before the year was over. In these figures we can sense the social and economic revolution that had taken place since 1815.

The economy, thanks in part to Peel's reforms but also to its own expansion, now possessed a strength and balance that made it less sensitive to crop failures and sudden market fluctuations. It is perhaps for this reason that, although the years 1847 and 1848 were years of some economic unsteadiness and considerable unemployment, there was no serious attempt in England to imitate the risings that were taking place on the continent. The Chartists, who sought to exploit the situation, suffered an ignominious, indeed, a farcical failure; and their movement disappeared completely from the English scene. For the first time since 1815, the social order seemed stable; and Thomas Macaulay, finishing the second volume of his *History of England* in the midst of alarming news from the continent, could write with satisfaction:

> All around us the world is convulsed by the agonies of great nations. Governments which lately seemed likely to stand during ages have been on a sudden shaken and overthrown. . . . Meanwhile, in our island the regular course of government has never been for a day interrupted. . . . We have order in the midst of anarchy.

RELIGION, EDUCATION, AND THE ARTS

The Churches / England was still a churchgoing country, and the churches were powerful bodies with large memberships. The Church of England was supported by the majority of the upper classes and by the mass of the rural population. There was a large minority of Protestant dissenters or Nonconformists, especially in Wales, and in Scotland where there were more Presbyterians than members of the established church. Roman Catholics were, of course, predominant in Ireland and, thanks to immigration, were increasing in towns like Glasgow and Liverpool. In general, as far as England was concerned, the established church, the dissenters, and the Catholics were in the ratio of 120, 80, and 4.

Despite its numerical strength, organized religion was weakened by the tendencies of the time and by the attitude of the churches to social problems. As we have seen in the case of France (see above, pp. 92–93), the advance of industrialism, by drawing rural laborers to the factory towns, often permanently severed their religious connections. The industrial town that is the scene of Dickens' *Hard Times* (written in the early 1850s) is described as having eighteen churches and chapels. But, asks the author

> Who belonged to the eighteen denominations? Whoever did, the labouring people did not. It was very strange to walk through the streets on a Sunday morning and note how few of *them* the barbarous jangling of bells . . . called away from their own quarter, from their own close rooms, from the

corners of their own streets, where they lounged listlessly, gazing at all the church and chapel going as at a thing with which they had no manner of concern.

Factory life was not conducive to religious reflection or observance.

Apart from this, the churches took an almost entirely negative view of the political and social problems that affected the mass of the population. The almost solid resistance of the bishops of the Church of England to Parliamentary reform before 1832 was hardly calculated to inspire popular respect, and the blank indifference of the church to factory abuses tended to alienate the masses. Especially after 1832, the Church of England was the center of vigorous intellectual activity, but none of it seemed to be related to problems of the day. Of the two parties within the church, the evangelicals did much to raise the moral standards of the age by the strict piety of their behavior, but they had no conception of the social responsibility incumbent on a church which was, after all, supported by state funds. The High-Church party, on the other hand, was given over to the kind of absorption in doctrinal speculation that led, in the 1840s, to the Oxford Movement. This movement—perhaps best remembered because it led to the dramatic decision of John Henry Newman (1801–1890) and his followers to join the Roman Catholic church—stimulated internal reform and encouraged, within a body that had not always been scrupulous about its appointments, a deeper conception of the clerical office. But it also had the disadvantage of involving the Church of England in controversy about ritual and dogma at a time when it would have been well advised to give some thought to trade unionism and chartism.

The strongest of the dissenting sects in England was Wesleyanism, which numbered half a million members in 1840. Wesleyanism was less remote from the actualities of contemporary existence. It was usually on the side of authority, but Radicalism and Chartism did not leave its members untouched, and it, in turn, made its contribution to popular movements. Many of the more responsible leaders of the trade unions and other working-class movements, at this time and later in the century, received their first training in administration, government, and public speaking in Wesleyan chapels and the churches of other dissenting sects.

The Schools / Both the established church and the Nonconformists were interested in education, and what primary education there was for the masses was provided by societies established by them: the National Society ("for promoting the education of the poor in the principles of the established church") and the British and Foreign School Society (which was nondenominational). For very low fees, students received training in the Bible and catechism and some acquaintance with the three R's. How slight this acquaintance was likely to be was shown by a survey made in the 1830s which revealed that, of 5000 children in Hull who had been to school, 800 could not read and 1800 could not write, and that, in Leeds, 15,000 children were receiving no schooling whatsoever. It is clear that the general level of education was not high.

The first government grant in aid of education was made in 1833, when a sum of £20,000 was divided between the two voluntary societies mentioned above and was expended for new schools. This sum, which was less than was being currently spent for education in the state of Massachusetts, had little effect in altering the existing state of affairs. One might have imagined that an industrial society, which had a need for educated operatives, clerks, supervisors, and salesmen, would insist upon a more massive effort in the direction of free and compulsory elementary education; and in time, of course, this happened. But in the period under review the suspicion of government intervention in new spheres, which was characteristic of Manchester liberalism, combined with sectarian animosity to block all efforts at large-scale educational reform; and it was not until 1870 that anything constructive was done.

Secondary education was restricted, for obvious reasons, to the upper and middle classes, who sent their sons to private schools of various types. The period before 1848 was one of basic reform in these schools. Between 1828 and 1848, Thomas Arnold, the headmaster at Rugby, modernized and expanded the curriculum and replaced rote learning with a greater degree of free enquiry. These ideas, and others about school government, athletics, and character training, were carried by Arnold's disciples to other schools, with generally beneficial results.

For the universities this was not a distinguished period. Both Oxford and Cambridge were still clerical in character and governed by outworn statutes (dissenters were not yet allowed to graduate) and the reform of studies was badly needed; yet new ideas were blocked by clerical opposition or by the conservative governing boards of the member colleges. It is possible, of course, that this imperviousness to change was not wholly bad. At least, by resisting the tendency to make all learning "useful," the older universities managed to survive as centers of liberal education in an increasingly materialistic society.

In general, university education was expanding. The University of London—radical in origin, secular, and with a wider curriculum than either Oxford or Cambridge—got its start in the late 1820s. The University of Durham was established in 1832; colleges and technical schools were founded in Leeds, Birmingham, and Sheffield in the same decade; and the universities of St. Andrews, Glasgow, Aberdeen, and Edinburgh grew in size. All of this led to an increasing diffusion of university education in the society.

Mention should be made also of the earnest attempts to bring education to adult members of the working class through organizations like the Society for the Diffusion of Useful Knowledge (1827), which published cheap technical handbooks and textbooks on a wide range of subjects, and the mechanics' institutes, which were designed to be libraries and discussion centers for the intelligent and ambitious members of the laboring class.

The Arts / These years of economic expansion and social disorder were also years of remarkable literary activity and achievement. In 1815 the romantics were still at the height of their power, and the great figures in letters were Wordsworth, Coleridge, Keats, Byron, Shelley, Southey, Lamb, Jane Austen, Hazlitt, Landor, Blake, and Scott. By 1832, these had passed away or had written their best work, and a new period opened in which—as perhaps was natural in an age that was becoming more matter of fact—the accent was on prose rather than poetry. It is true that Tennyson and Browning began to write in the 1830s, but they received no very wide following until later. The most respected writers of the post-Reform Act period were prose writers, and by no means all writers of imaginative literature: Dickens, whose *Sketches by Boz* appeared in 1834–1835 and who scored his first great success with *The Posthumous Papers of the Pickwick Club* in 1836–1837; J. H. Newman and Thomas Carlyle; Macaulay, whose *History of England,* the first two volumes of which appeared in 1848, was a runaway best seller; John Stuart Mill, whose *System of Logic* (1843) had a tremendous vogue; and—at the very end of the period—Thackeray and the Brontes, although most of their work was later.

It was a sign of the vitality of English literature that most of even the purely literary figures in these lists concerned themselves with the problems of their time. The liberalism of Byron and Shelley did not, perhaps, produce their best poetry, and Coleridge's political writings are often too Germanic to be intelligible, but it is hard to deny that Blake at the beginning of the period and Dickens at the end were eloquent and persuasive social critics.

This period was enlivened by the development of a vigorous press—in 1815 there were already 252 papers circulating in England—and by a number of excellent critical journals, including the *Edinburgh Review*, of Whig persuasion, the Tory *Quarterly Review*, and the Radical *Westminster Review*, which was founded in 1824 and edited by John Stuart Mill.

Although the theater and the concert hall were popular, England produced no great dramatists or composers in these years. In art, the early part of the period saw the last work of Lawrence, Raeburn, Constable, and Turner. After their passing there was no one to replace them but conventional painters like Landseer and Maclise.

THE EMPIRE

Emigration and Colonial Expansion / The pressure of population and economic misery during the period before 1848 persuaded an increasing number of Englishmen to try their fortunes abroad, in the United States and the Canadian provinces primarily, but in other areas as well. At the beginning of the period only about 30,000 men and women were leaving England annually; by 1832 this figure was in excess of 100,000, and the troubles of the 1840s doubled this number. The practice of using Australia as a dumping ground for convicts was terminated in 1840, and the white population increased rapidly from 130,000 in that year to well over a million twenty years later. To the south, the first English settlers began to move into New Zealand in 1837; and on the other side of the world, in South Africa, there were 5000 English settlers at the Cape as early as 1820.

There was astonishingly little interest in the colonies on the part of the people who stayed home. This was not an age in which Englishmen took pride in their empire; and those who gave any thought to the colonies were likely to regard them as useless encumbrances. This was an article of faith with the followers of Cobden and Bright. Interested in the benefits of trade rather than the problems of overseas adminis-tration, these people could perhaps view with equanimity the high-handed tactics used by Palmerston in his dispute with the Chinese government in 1839–1841, because—at the cost of a small war—they won access for Britain to Shanghai, Canton, and three other ports and acquired the enormously valuable entrepôt of Hong Kong. But they were not disposed to address themselves seriously to the problems of colonial policy. Because they were not, the government was not; and this meant that Great Britain had no colonial policy except what was improvised from day to day by men on the spot. In both South Africa and India, advances were made and commitments taken without the full knowledge or approval of the government. In South Africa, the unremitting pressure of English settlers upon the Dutch farmers already settled there and upon the native tribes was pregnant with future trouble; in India, where British expansion went forward steadily, inconsistency of purpose led to more than one setback, like the humiliating defeat in the Afghan wars of 1842.

The Abolition of Slavery and the Durham Report / Despite the prevailing negativism of British thinking about colonial affairs, two positive and imaginative steps were taken by the British government in this period. The abolition of slavery in the colonies in 1833 has already been mentioned, and all that need be added here is that this action, while setting the world an example that it eventually followed, made it certain that the future colonial empire would be one of free men.

A little later a precedent-making solution was found for difficulties that had arisen in Canada. These were the result of friction that had developed between the elected representative assemblies of the two provinces of Upper and Lower Canada (which controlled legislation and taxation) and their governors (who were responsible to the British crown), and they were complicated further by bad feeling between the British and French populations of the provinces.

In 1838 Lord Durham (1792–1840) and the noted critic of British colonial policy Gibbon Wakefield (1796–1862) went to Canada to study the problem and in the following year they drew up the so-called Durham Report. This urged, first, that Upper and Lower Canada be re-united and, second, that the Canadian executive be made responsible, not to the crown, but to the local parliament. Anything less, they felt, would lead eventually to the violent severance of the ties between Canada and the home country, as had happened in the case of the United States. Responsible government, on the other hand, would forge a tie of imperial unity between them.

The Durham proposals were not immediately accepted. But in 1840 the provinces were united, and, seven years later, when Lord Elgin became governor-general of Canada, the attempt to apply the principle of responsible government began. It succeeded, and its success led to its being copied in New Zealand (1854), Australia (1856), and the Cape Colony (1872). In this way, the British Commonwealth of Nations took form.

5

The Revolutions of 1848

THE TIDE OF REVOLUTION

When the year 1848 opened, significant sections of the populations of all the continental countries lying between the English Channel and the borders of Russia had reasons for dissatisfaction with their governments. With varying degrees of intensity, the middle classes desired either to acquire civil and political rights denied them or to extend rights already acquired; and, in Germany and Italy, these desires were accompanied by a growing fervor for national unity and independence. The vanguard of the middle-class reform movement were merchants and industrialists, professors and journalists, lawyers and intellectuals and university students, all of whom had become alienated from governments that were wedded to the *status quo* and showed no sympathy for their ideas.

At the same time, the mass of the ordinary people of most countries was suffering from economic distress. The period since 1815 had been one of great industrial expansion, but it had been accompanied by the ills attendant upon the replacement of the old handicraft system by new methods of production and also by periodic dislocations caused by overexpansion and unwise speculation. After the prosperity of the early forties, for instance, the seaports and industrial towns of Europe suffered from the repercussions of a sudden and severe economic crash in England, and the subsequent forced retrenchment hurt the old guild trades more severely than it did factory industry and threw thousands of artisans and journeymen out of work. Simultaneously, the failure of the potato crop in 1845 and of both the potato and grain crops in 1846 was felt in all countries from Ireland to Poland and was reflected in a sharp rise in the cost of food—an increase which, in the German states, averaged 50 percent between 1844 and 1847. By the latter year, the linen industry of Belgium was in a pitiable state; the weavers of Silesia were on the verge of starvation; one out of every three families in Solingen in the Rhineland was destitute; and crime, prostitution, and lawlessness was increasing everywhere.

All these conditions were to take a sharp turn for the better in mid-1848, when a new industrial boom got underway. But that could not be foreseen at the beginning of the year. In January and February, economic distress was supplementing political discontent in most continental countries, and the middle-class reformers and the rebellious artisans were drifting together into an uneasy alliance. Conditions in the various countries were so much alike, moreover, that it was likely that a revolutionary explosion in one center would touch off explosions elsewhere.

That is precisely what happened in March.

The Revolution in France / The center from which all the disorders of 1848 spread was Paris; yet revolution succeeded there less because of the strength of the revolutionary forces than because of the weakness and procrastination of the government of the July Monarchy.

We have already noted that, in the late 1840s, there was growing opposition in France to the policies of the Guizot government (see pp. 90–91). In 1847, indeed, the middle-class reforming groups sought to dramatize this and give it greater force by organizing a series of "reform banquets" at which oratory would be the chief item on the bill of fare and antigovernment speeches would be delivered and antigovernment resolutions passed. The government might have drawn the teeth of this movement by some timely reforms. Instead, it did nothing until these windy feasts had attracted widespread attention and then compounded its error by seeking to prevent further banquets. This attitude advertised the movement it was meant to destroy. As excitement mounted, the opposition planned a monster banquet in Paris, to be held on February 22, 1848; and, when the government refused to authorize it, groups of students and workingmen assembled in the streets, there were brushes with the police, and an ugly temper began to reign in the capital. Suddenly alarmed at the pass to which his inactivity had

"Death on the Barricades," a contemporary German woodcut. From Hans Blum, *Die deutsche Revolution*, Leipzig, 1898.

brought him, Louis Philippe turned upon his chief minister, Guizot, who had long been the target of popular hatred, and dismissed him from office.

Taken six months previously this action might have prevented further trouble; now it inspired it. On the evening of February 23 an excited but good-tempered crowd, some of whose members were republican agitators but most of whom were persons drawn together by the excitement in the air, set off to Guizot's official residence, doubtless intending to hold a demonstration in front of it. On the way they ran into a file of soldiers drawn up across a street called the Rue des Capucines and were informed by the commanding officer that they could not pass. The crowd was indignant; there was some shoving and hauling; someone seized a torch and thrust it into the officer's face; a shot was fired—probably by a soldier seeking to protect his commander, possibly by someone in the crowd, perhaps the result of an accidental discharge caused by jostling. It was followed by a volley from the troops which killed some fifty persons—and brought the July Monarchy to an end.

The news of the "massacre" in the Rue des Capucines spread swiftly through the city; before the night was out 1500 barricades had been built in main thoroughfares and across narrow streets, and groups of excited students were attacking police stations to procure arms; and by morning the cry "Long Live the Republic!" could be heard on all sides.

If Louis Philippe wished to save his throne, it was clear that he would have to act now with decision. This was something of which he no longer seemed capable. He shied away from the idea of using all-out force to restore order and actually ordered his regular troops to evacuate the city; and he counted on the support of the National Guard long after it was clear that the citizen force was fraternizing with the rebels. Throughout the morning and afternoon of February 24, the king held interminable conferences with politicians, soldiers, and members of his own family while the situation got increasingly out of hand. Finally, despite the urgent pleas of his wife and daughter-in-law, he signed a note of abdication and fled to England.

Having seen an apparently stable regime overthrown in a matter of hours with a minimum of bloodshed, a stupefied Europe now watched while power in France was assumed by a provisional government whose members were selected in the offices of two radical newspapers (*Le National* and *La Réforme*) and which included a poet (Alphonse Lamartine), an astronomer (Francois Arago), a socialist theorist (Louis Blanc), and a common workingman whose full name no one seemed to remember and who was referred to simply by his given name, Albert. Despite its unorthodox appearance, however, this group got down to work with dispatch. Its first action, taken doubtless to appease the mobs surging in the streets of Paris, was to proclaim the republic. It then announced that elections for a new Parliament would be held in April and, to prepare the way for them, set about restoring order and consolidating the authority of the government. To guard against the possibility of foreign intervention, the armed forces were strengthened and African troops were recalled to France, while within the army and navy long-needed improvements of rations and pay and reforms of the disciplinary code were introduced. To reduce the possibility of new mob violence, service in the National Guard—formerly a middle-class force— was made compulsory for all adult males, and a new mobile guard of 15,000 men was set up in Paris. Strenuous efforts were made to extend the ministry's authority to the provinces by the appointment of commissioners whose first duty was—as the new minister of interior said—"to reassure the public." In Paris itself this process of reassurance included efficient measures to reduce street disorders and crime and to improve the city's food supplies.

The most pressing obstacle to social peace was the continued economic distress. This had worsened as a result of the February rising, which had frightened some employers into leaving the city, had forced some concerns to close by cutting off their sources of credit, and had brought the luxury trades to a virtual standstill. Throughout the early months of 1848, unemployment mounted steadily in Paris, and demands for government relief action increased.

On February 25 the new ministry had proclaimed its belief in the right of all citizens to work. The problem was how to implement this. One man in the ministry, Louis Blanc, had long ago formulated a socialist blueprint for national prosperity; but the majority of the ministry, led by Lamartine, were staunch defenders of property and wanted no part of Blanc's program for the nationalization and decentralization of industry. They could not very well ignore their uncomfortable colleague, but they managed to sidetrack him into a position where his energies were expended on theoretical studies of labor problems and questions of negotiation between labor and management. Meanwhile, they tried to meet the unemployment crisis with what can only be called a caricature of Blanc's old idea of national workshops (see p. 87).

As authorized by the cabinet and administered by a young engineer named Emile Thomas, the national workshops of 1848 were simply semimilitary organizations of unemployed which undertook to find work for their members and to pay them at a rate of two francs a day when employed and one franc a day when not. This assurance of pay was enough to make them popular, and thousands of unemployed workers streamed into Paris to enroll, thus greatly increasing the difficulty of finding jobs for workshop members. The end result was that, while the workshops did some useful work (replanting trees, leveling the Champ de Mars, and other public works), the great majority of their members received wages for doing nothing and gave the impression to the country at large that Paris was filled with idlers living at public expense.

The irritation that this caused among the conservative and frugal peasantry of the country was reflected in the election returns when France went to the polls in April. The National Constituent Assembly that was elected then and assembled in Paris on May 4, was republican in political attitude but predominantly conservative in social philosophy. The election results were received with suspicion on the part of the working classes of Paris and with indignation by the radical clubs of the city, where men like Blanqui were agitating for a more thoroughgoing reform than that carried out so far by Lamartine and his colleagues. It was clear that new disorders were imminent.

The Revolution in the Austrian Empire / While these events were taking place, other parts of the continent were in the throes of revolution. Even before the February rising in Paris, a revolt in Palermo in Sicily had forced the reactionary King Ferdinand II of Naples to grant a constitution to his people. This rising was largely the result of Sicilian particularism and would probably, by itself, have had no further consequences. What started the revolutionary tide rolling in central Europe was the news of Louis Philippe's expulsion from the throne of France.

MILES
0 100 200 300

KINGDOM OF
NORWAY AND
SWEDEN

PRINCIPAL
CENTERS OF
REVOLUTION
1848-1849

UNITED
KINGDOM OF
GREAT BRITAIN
AND
IRELAND

RUSSIAN
EMPIRE

Hanover
★Berlin
Hesse★ Dresden
★Frankfurt ★Prague
Paris★
Baden★ ★Stuttgart
★Munich Vienna★
SWITZ- ★Budapest
ERLAND

Milan★ ★Venice
Parma★ ★Modena OTTOMAN
★Florence

SPAIN

PORTUGAL

Rome★

EMPIRE

Palermo
★

GREECE

HAGSTROM CO., INC., N.Y.

The news of this event reached the city of Vienna on February 29 and aroused great excitement which increased as word came of demonstrations in Stuttgart, Mannheim, and other German cities. Crowds began to gather in the cafés of the Austrian capital to hear the latest news from abroad; nervousness led to a run on the banks; food prices began to rise steeply; and, as they did, criticism of the government became vocal. Then, on March 3, came reports of a speech delivered in Budapest by Kossuth (see p. 59), in which that gifted agitator had denounced the abuses of the absolutist system and called for the immediate introduction of constitutional government in Hungary. This would be impossible, Kossuth admitted, as long as "a corrupting puff of wind that benumbs our senses and paralyzes the flight of our spirit comes to us from the charnel house of the cabinet in Vienna"; therefore, basic reform must be introduced in every branch of the imperial government. Translated immediately into German, this speech was circulated in thousands of copies in the western half of the empire, where its very violence appealed to the middle-class businessmen who felt handicapped by the economic backwardness of the government, the artisans who— despite their lack of employment—had to pay a sales tax on the necessities of life, the peasants who were still bound by the federal restrictions of an outworn agricultural system, and the intellectuals who had long chafed at police supervision of all literary and artistic activity. Petitions began to circulate demanding administrative reform, enlargement of the system of estates and immediate convocation of a diet, abolition of censorship, and economic reform.

In face of this ground swell of opposition, the government in Vienna showed a remarkable lack of imagination, rejecting all petitions and refusing all concessions. This standpat attitude proved to be the immediate cause of an all-out revolution against the regime. On May 13 demonstrations began among the students of the university, a group made rebellious by their long experience of uninspired instruction, police despotism, and unmentionable living conditions. A throng marched to the *Landhaus,* where the Estates of Lower Austria were meeting and, after some preliminary harangues, stormed the building. By midafternoon fighting had started in the inner city between detachments of the local garrison and the students, who had now been joined by workingmen from the suburbs.

The first reaction of the court was stupefaction; and the Emperor Ferdinand is reported to have gasped, when news of the fighting arrived, *"Ja, derfin s'denn das?"* ("But are they allowed to do that?"). As the situation deteriorated, this mood was replaced by one of panic; and, at nine in the evening, fearing that the mob might actually break into the imperial palace, the royal family abandoned Metternich as abruptly as Louis Philippe had dropped Guizot, announcing that the man who had held office uninterruptedly for thirty-nine years had resigned. Metternich himself took this quietly and even philosophically and made a dignified departure to London, the end station for all dismissed monarchs and oligarchs, leaving behind him a Vienna enraptured by the thought that the very symbol of despotism had been overthrown.

If Kossuth's speech had played an important part in precipitating these events in Vienna, the fall of the chancellor now gave new impetus to the revolutionary currents running in Hungary. On March 15 the Hungarian Diet gave a precise and dramatic formulation to ambitions held by Magyar patriots for a generation. It promulgated a new Hungarian constitution, which provided for a national diet to be elected by all Hungarians owning property worth one hundred and fifty dollars, established civil and religious liberty for all subjects and freedom for the press, and abolished the traditional privileges of the feudal nobility. Hungary was to remain within the empire but to have its own ministries of war, finance, and foreign affairs; and, to all intents and purposes, the Hungarians would henceforth enjoy complete autonomy.

On March 31 the government in Vienna was forced to agree to these sweeping reforms, which had been gained without loss of blood or even the exertion of physical force.

Where the Hungarians led, the leaders of the Czech national movement followed. In March they sent deputations to Vienna to demand the convocation of a Bohemian diet elected by democratic franchise, basic civil and religious freedoms, and, especially, the equality of the Czech and German language in schools and government services. On April 8 the emperor granted most of these demands, thus, giving Bohemia the same degree of local autonomy as that already won by Hungary.

The emperor was compelled to accept these demands—and, in Austria proper, to open the National Guard to the middle classes and to summon a united diet for the purpose of drawing up a new constitution—because he had no armed force capable of controlling the situation. This weakness was caused by the development of affairs in the Austrian provinces of Italy. In a violent insurrection that lasted for five days, the city of Milan arose and expelled the Austrian troops; and on March 22, Daniele Manin, a lawyer and politician of Jewish heritage, led a swift and entirely successful revolt in Venice and proclaimed the republic. Taking advantage of this situation, Charles Albert of Piedmont, an ambitious if emotionally unbalanced ruler, threw in his lot with the rebels of Lombardy and Venetia and sent his armies to help them forge Italian freedom. These sudden blows sent the Austrian forces commanded by Radetzky reeling back into the so-called Quadrilateral, four strong fortresses on the Adige and Mincio. The eighty-two-year-old field marshal, who, despite his years, had lost neither his interest in women nor his vigor in war, was not alarmed by these setbacks; but he saw that, unless put right, they might lead to the total collapse of the Hapsburg Empire. He insisted, therefore, that—even at the cost of temporary concessions at home—reinforcements must be sent to him, and he had his way.

This meant, however, that the emperor had to accept the reforms in Hungary and Bohemia, and, in Austria proper, to dismiss other unpopular ministers (like the police chief Sedlnitzky) and to agree to a whole series of further reforms. These included a reduction of the sales tax on food, the abolition of the censorship, and a general political amnesty; but the most notable of them was the imperial manifesto of April 11 which promised to free the peasants from all services and duties incumbent on the land. This new freedom was to be inaugurated on January 1, 1849, after the Diet had framed the necessary legislation, but it could be effected earlier by private arrangement, provided proprietors received suitable compensation.

The April decree was probably the most important positive action of the whole Austrian revolution, and, even before it was confirmed by the Austrian Parliament in September, it was exercizing a moderating influence upon the course of events. It was greeted with enthusiasm by the peasants and had the almost immediate effect of transforming them into a conservative force, more interested in law and order than in revolutionary agitation. As in France, the peasantry now grew critical of continued disorders in the capital. Their attitude was shared by the wealthier middle class in Vienna, who were satisfied with the gains made already and were increasingly fearful of the excesses of the students and the workers.

Thus, as early as April, the unity of the revolutionary movement was beginning to split. Nor was this caused only by economic and social differences. Nationality also played a part, as Austrian Germans came to resent the gains made by the Czechs and Hungarians, and Magyars to fear the growing ambitions of their Slav neighbors, who aspired to the same kind of privileges won by the followers of Kossuth. The imperial house, still impotent in April and May, was going to win its ultimate victory over the revolution by exploiting those widening social and national divisions.

The Revolution in Prussia and the German States / The Russian exile Alexander Herzen, who made a lifetime career of revolutionary agitation, was bitterly scornful of the risings in Germany in 1848. The Germans were not, he wrote in his memoirs, serious about revolution at all; they were merely enjoying themselves by imitating France in the days of the Terror.

> There was not a town . . . where . . . there was not an attempt at a "committee of public safety" with all its principal characters: with a frigid youth as Saint-Just, with gloomy terrorists, and a military genius representing Carnot. I knew two or three Robespierres personally; they always put on clean shirts, washed their hands and had clean nails. . . . If there happened to be a man . . . fonder of beer than the rest and more openly given to dangling after *Stubenmädchen*—he was the Danton.

This was written after the failure of the revolution and reflects the bitterness induced by that failure (if not by the additional fact that, in his retreat in London, Herzen had to put up with the eccentricities of German exiles for years after 1848—and actually lost the affections of his wife to one of them). But this statement hardly does justice to the idealistic drive of the German revolution or to the force that enabled it to humble the monarchy of the most militaristic power in Europe, the kingdom of Prussia. The mood of the German revolution is better described by the distinguished emigrant to the United States, Carl Schurz, who tells in his memoirs of how the news of the fall of Louis Philippe came to him when he was a student at Bonn and how it affected the academic youth of the day, who saw suddenly opening before them the chance not only to attain the civil liberties and the constitutional form of government so long denied them but also to realize the dream of German unity. "The word democracy," he writes, "was on all tongues and many thought it a matter of course that, if the princes should try to withhold from the people the rights and liberties demanded, force would take the place of mere petition."

In general, the petty princes did not relish the latter possibility and tumbled over themselves in an effort to grant concessions to their subjects before it was too late. In Baden and Württemberg, in Hesse-Darmstadt and Bavaria, in Saxony and Hanover, the rulers called to their side moderate liberals whom they have formerly ignored or persecuted and made promises of constitutional charters and other reforms.

In Prussia, however, the concessions came too late. Frederick William IV's attitude toward constitutional reform had not softened since 1847; and, now, with economic depression gripping much of this country, with artisans' riots breaking out in provincial cities like Cologne and Breslau, and with agitators beginning to address excited crowds in the Berlin Tiergarten, he still stubbornly refused to consider concessions and relied upon his troops to break up demonstrations, with a not inconsiderable number of resultant casualties. It was not until he heard the shattering news of Metternich's fall that the king turned from his military to his civilian advisors and, at their bidding, on the night of March 17, drafted a manifesto to his people in which he promised to convoke the Prussian diet at the beginning of April, to grant a constitution and sponsor a program of internal reform, and to use Prussian influence to promote a constitutional reorganization of the Germanic Confederation.

These promises, which, despite their lateness, appealed to moderate reformers and to advocates of national unity, were announced to the people of Berlin on the morning of the 18th. There then followed one of those unhappy accidents which always seem to occur in revolutionary situations. At noon a large throng, composed of both well-to-do citizens and common working people, crowded into the palace square, presumably to cheer the king for his concessions. Fearing for the king's safety, the commander of the royal cavalry guard sent a detachment to clear the area. Remembering the bloodshed of recent days, the crowd was first stubborn and then angry. More troops had to be put in to support their fellows; and, in the resultant scuffling—much as in Paris—someone fired two shots, and the troops responded with a volley into the crowd. With a cry of treason, the demonstrators fled from the palace; and, within an hour, barricades had been built across all the thoroughfares leading to the *Schloss* and fighting was in progress.

The Prussian army had not been engaged in battle since Waterloo, and it had never fought in cobbled streets against adversaries who sniped from rooftops or dropped chimney pots or boiling water from attic windows. When it took a barricade by frontal assault, it was apt to find that its defenders had escaped down side lanes or through corner houses, and new barricades were constantly springing up behind it. It was discouraging work; by nightfall the troops were spent; by morning they were demoralized, and their commander was urging the king to authorize their withdrawal from the city so that they could encircle and bombard it from outside. The king was aghast at the idea of his city being leveled by artillery, and rejected the idea. But he ordered the troops to leave Berlin, although refusing to go with them, preferring to put his trust in his "dear Berliners."

This was a gallant action and, from the long-range point of view, probably a wise one, but for the time being it left Frederick William a captive of the revolution—a "king of the pavement" as the tsar of Russia said savagely at this time. Like his brother sovereigns in Vienna and the lesser German capitals, he had to call liberal business and professional men to office and to promise speedy convocation of a National Prussian Assembly. Later in his life, he was ashamed of the speed with which his regime had capitulated, and said ruefully, "At that time we were all on our bellies."

The Frankfurt Parliament / The events in Prussia seemed to complete and make definitive the collapse of absolutism; and the time seemed to have come now to exploit this opportunity to satisfy the yearnings of generations of Germans and to transform the rickety old Germanic Confederation into an effective organization of national unity. Since the first days of March leaders of the constitutional movement in southern Germany had been consulting among themselves about the tasks of national reconstruction. At the end of the month, they joined with liberal leaders from other states to draw up a tentative program of action, and persuaded the Diet to invite the governments of all German states, including Austria and Prussia, to elect delegates to a National Parliament which would then proceed to transform Germany into a federal union with a liberal constitution. The individual states, now under liberal ministries, accepted the invitations; elections were held in the course of April; and on May 18, the first National Parliament in German history was solemnly convened in St. Paul's Church in Frankfurt on the Main.

The Frankfurt parliament has often been described as a gathering of impractical intellectuals who debated theoretical questions to the exclusion of the practical issues which demanded immediate attention. It is true that the percentage of highly educated people among its members was very large; out of a total of 586 members there were 95 lawyers, 104 professors, 124 bureaucrats, and 100 judicial officials. Moreover, from May until December, they did spend a lot of time talking about abstract questions, for this was the period in which they drafted the Fundamental Rights of the German People. Yet surely, after a past of unrelieved absolutism, it was important to have such things clearly defined. When it was completed, the Declaration of Fundamental Rights was an eloquent expression of middle-class liberal philosophy, which established freedom of speech and religion and equality before the law as basic rights of all Germans, asserted the sanctity of private property, and laid down rules for representative government and ministerial responsibility in the individual states.

It was hoped that this constitution would be put into effect in a Germany that was a federal union, presided over by a hereditary emperor, but with a strong parliament representing the educated and propertied classes and a ministry that was responsible to it. The exact composition of the empire and the role of Austria in it was the subject of long debate between two schools of thought. The Great German (*Grossdeutsch*) party believed that the empire must embrace all German states, including the German provinces of Austria, a solution that implied that there would be a Hapsburg emperor; whereas the Small German (*Kleindeutsch*) party insisted that all of Austria must be excluded. Eventually, the majority agreed on the latter solution, while advocating a close future connection between the new German Reich and the Hapsburg; and they concluded also—as we shall see—that the king of Prussia must be invited to preside over the new Germany.

Before the time-consuming debates on these matters were finished, events had taken a turn that made it unlikely that the conclusions reached in them would be accepted by the German states. This was not, as is sometimes argued, the fault of the longwindedness of the Frankfurt parliamentarians. Considering the complicated issues with which they had to deal, they did their job with dispatch. But, while their deliberations continued, the unity of purpose that had made the March revolution successful began to break down, and suspicion and ill feeling began to arise among the different classes and nationalities. The forces of reaction now showed an ability to exploit these divisions in such a way as to nullify the work accomplished at Frankfurt and the gains of the revolution in general.

It was not only in Germany that this reaction occurred. Like the revolution, it was European in scope; and, like the revolution, it had its first significant success in France.

THE FAILURE OF THE REVOLUTION

The June Days in France / The majority of the members of the newly elected French National Assembly came to Paris at the beginning of May

1848 with a strong desire to prevent new revolutionary experiments or disorders. They revealed the nature of their thinking by refusing to give Lamartine's ministry a vote of confidence until he had dropped from it not only the workingman Albert but also Louis Blanc, who was distrusted in the provinces because of his socialist views. Their attitude hardened further when an excited mob broke into the Assembly on May 15, in a pointless demonstration which working-class leaders like Blanqui had vainly sought to stop because they feared that it would invite reprisals. It did exactly that, by encouraging the Assembly to strike out at what they considered the root of all the disorder in Paris, the national workshops.

On May 24 an executive commission of the Assembly ordered Emile Thomas to begin the dissolution of the workshops by enlisting its younger members in the army, paying its rural members to return to their homes, and forcing others either to enter private industry or to undertake public works outside of Paris. Thomas tried to delay, recognizing that the members would resent being forced into private employment at reduced wages or into tasks for which they had no stomach; but he had no success, and by mid-June it was clear that the Assembly would soon act to dissolve the workshops completely. This prompted counteraction on the part of national workshop leaders and other workers groups; on June 18, some of them issued a call for a democratic and social republic; and on June 23, the day army enlistments were supposed to start in the workshops, a great throng of workers met at the Place de la Bastille, pledged themselves to fight for their rights, and began to build barricades.

With the issue thus forced, the Assembly acted with merciless efficiency. The national guard was mobilized immediately, and its majority rallied to the Assembly's cause. Calls were sent out to other towns for reinforcements and were answered promptly, 3000 national guards from Amiens arriving in Paris on June 23, and 1500 traveling 200 miles from Brittany some days later. Provincial France seemed all too ready to settle with radical Paris.

Even before the 23d was over, the Assembly had enough troops to proceed against the barricades and, in General Cavaignac, the new minister of war, it had a commander who was ruthless and uncompromising. In the circumstances, despite the valor shown by the workers and the ingenuity they displayed in the construction of defensive works, they had no chance. It took four days for Cavaignac's forces to put down the insurrection and, before the fighting ended, some 1460 lives had been lost; but the victory secured was definitive and left the working class with no will to further resistance. The cost of this bloody restoration of order, however, was a legacy of class hatred which was to become a permanent feature of French life in the second half of the century.

"The Judgment of Paris."
A British comment on the French presidential elections. The figures are Lamartine, Cavaignac, Louis Napoleon, and "Young Paris." From *Punch*, Oct. 28, 1848.

After the June Days, the desire for order and stability was unmistakeable and encouraged the Assembly to push ahead its plans for a new constitution. This was completed and accepted in October and provided that the Republic would have a president to be elected for a four-year term by universal manhood suffrage. When the presidential elections were held in December, the real beneficiary of the June Days was revealed. He was Prince Louis Napoleon, who had returned to France after the March revolution, had been elected to the Assembly in June, and who now appealed equally to the wealthy bourgeoisie, the conservative peasants, the Catholic Church, the nationalists, and even some workers and socialists who found him preferable to his opponents, Cavaignac and Lamartine. Napoleon's election, by 5,434,266 votes to 1,448,107 for Cavaignac and a mere 17,910 for Lamartine, was the end of the French revolution of 1848 and the prelude to the establishment of a new authoritarian regime.

The Recovery of Royal Power in Prussia / The failure of the revolution in Prussia can be attributed, like the corresponding failure in France, to increasing disunity and suspicion among the different classes of society; but two other factors played a part. The first was the stubbornness with which the king opposed basic reform of the Prussian state, and the second was the failure of the Prussian Assembly to fathom his intentions and to impose its will upon him. After his apparent submission to the people in March, Frederick William IV showed remarkable resilience. Once the first shock of revolution had passed, he persisted in acting as if his powers were, and would remain, undiminished; and, although he acquiesced in the appointment of a new liberal ministry, he steadfastly resisted their efforts to do what they wanted to do—namely, to arrogate to themselves the kind of powers possessed by cabinet ministers in England.

The king's opposition might have been fruitless if parliamentary action had been effective. A National Assembly, the first in Prussia's history, was elected by universal manhood suffrage in May 1848 and settled down to the task of writing a new constitution for the Prussian kingdom. But it showed no urgency in its work; it failed to assure its control over the real sources of power in Prussia, the army and the police; and it exhausted time and energy in interminable debates between liberal reformers, who wanted to devise constitutional restrictions for royal power while retaining monarchical institutions, and radicals, who were hoping to establish a republic. The incessant wrangling prevented any direct attack upon the royal prerogative, irritated moderate opinion and tended to arouse sympathy for the sovereign. This last tendency was strengthened by the new government's inability to prevent disorders in Berlin, where a sudden outbreak of mob violence on June 14, during which the armory was attacked and its stores of weapons and ammunition plundered, struck fear into the hearts of respectable burghers.

All of this played directly into the king's hands and, before the year was over, he calculated that the Assembly had been so discredited that he could risk a blow against it. Consequently, in November, he announced that its meetings would be suspended pending its removal to another place of meeting outside of Berlin and, simultaneously, he ordered the army under General von Wrangel to return to the barracks in the capital that they had been forced to evacuate in March. The king's order caused a momentary flare-up of revolutionary zeal. Attempts were made to raise a defensive force in the city, and one group of diehards captured Wrangel's wife and sent a message to the general, warning that they would hang her unless he stopped his advance toward the city. Wrangel did not allow himself to be influenced by this. As he led his grenadiers toward the capital he was heard to mutter, "I wonder if they have really hanged her? I hardly believe so!"; and the event proved him right.

The army's entrance into Berlin brought an end to the revolution in Prussia; but it did not usher in a period of black reaction, as some people had feared it might. To the dismay of his most conservative advisers, the king—unpredictable as ever—now decided to grant a constitution to his people of his own accord. The document that was issued by royal decree at the end of 1848, and was revised in 1850, laid down safeguards for the liberties of Prussian subjects and assured the country of a bicameral legislature that would meet annually. There was, to be sure, little likelihood that the new parliament would ever become a radical body. Its upper house was to be composed of hereditary members (princes of the royal house and the heads of certain noble families) and a smaller number of persons appointed by the king for life. The lower house was elected by universal manhood suffrage, but in a curiously complicated way. In each electoral district throughout the land, voters were divided into three groups, according to the amount of taxes they paid; and each group, voting separately, elected an equal number of delegates to a district convention which then proceeded to elect the district's parliamentary deputies. In practice, this meant that the two wealthier groups, comprising at most about 15 percent of the population, effectively controlled two thirds of the seats in the lower house of parliament. It is not difficult to see that this system, which was to last until 1918, would serve as a barrier to democratic reform and social legislation in behalf of the masses. On the other hand, it was better than what had preceded it. Prussia could at least be described now as a constitutional parliamentary state.

The restoration of royal power in Prussia had marked effects throughout Germany, especially in Frankfurt. In that capital, the National Assembly had now completed drafting its Fundamental Rights (which, incidentally, went further than Frederick William's *charte* in guaranteeing basic liberties) and had defined the geographical limits of the united German empire that they had their hearts set on. It remained now to choose a hereditary ruler for their creation and, in March 1849, they did so, by sending a delegation to Berlin to offer the crown to Frederick William IV.

Once more secure in his power, the Prussian king turned the offer aside with contumely. He may have been influenced by the knowledge that to accept a crown that had been worn by the Hapsburgs would be to invite certain Austrian hostility. He may also have been alienated by claims by Frankfurt parliamentarians that, in their new Reich, Prussia would lose her separate identity and be "merged" with the rest of Germany; and it is not unlikely that he had dreams of Prussia's uniting Germany by conquest. However that may be, in public he argued that a Prussian king could not take a crown from the hands of intellectuals and tradesmen who claimed to be representatives of the people. "If the thousand-year-old crown of the German nation, in abeyance now these forty-two years,[1] is again to be given away," he said proudly, "it is I and my likes who will give it." He was deaf to all appeals made by the delegation, whose members had to return dejectedly to Frankfurt.

The disappointing news they took with them had the effect of dividing the Frankfurt parliament hopelessly into factions. While some of the delegates, in discouragement, wanted to give up the fight for unity and freedom, and others hoped, by diplomacy and patience, to persuade the Prussian ruler to change his mind, a group of extremists advocated resort to armed insurrection as the most effective way of gaining the parliament's objectives. These hotheads were encouraged by the effect of the king's refusal throughout Germany, and especially in Saxony, the Rhine Palatinate, and Baden, where outbreaks of mob violence paralyzed government and seemed to presage a new wave of revolutionary action.

But Frederick William IV, having restored order in his own realm, was in no mood to tolerate agitation in the territory of his neighbors. In May 1849 Prussian troops were dispatched to Dresden where they suppressed the rebellion and restored the king of Saxony to his throne. The troubles in Baden and the Palatinate were more serious, for a revolutionary army of thirty to forty thousand men had been raised under the command of the Polish refugee Mieroslawski and an exotic group of poets, publicists, professional revolutionaries, and foreign adventurers. Before this "people's army" was routed and order restored, two Prussian army corps, under the command of the king's brother, the future King-Emperor William I, had to be put into the field, and the fortress of Rastadt had to be bombarded into submission. Later generations of Germans were to recall this fighting with pride—as did the first president of the Federal Republic of Germany, Theodor Heuss, whose grandfather led a company of volunteers against the Prussians—and to argue that it proved that a genuine democratic spirit was strong in 1849, especially in southern Germany. In its own time, it is likely that the rising in Baden further alarmed middle-class opinion and made it welcome both the Prussian victory and, a few months later, the dissolution of the Frankfurt parliament which that victory made inevitable.

Even after the failure of the Frankfurt parliament, the desire for unification of the long-fragmented German lands was still strong enough to persuade the king of Prussia to try, in his own way, to make some progress toward that goal. His scheme, which was devised under the influence of Josef Maria von Radowitz, a Catholic nobleman who had become the king's closest confidant, called for an agreement by the German princes to join their territories in a union that would be led by Prussia and would exclude Austria, although, for purposes of foreign

[1] That is, since Napoleon Bonaparte had abolished the Holy Roman Empire in 1806.

and economic affairs, it would be bound in perpetual alliance with the Hapsburg state. This was obviously a plan that could be effected, if at all, only by lengthy and laborious negotiations; and such negotiations did, indeed, fill the rest of 1849 and the first months of the new year. But these consultations never gave much reality to the Prussian union; and, before it was much more than an idea, the Austrians completed their recovery from the revolution and intervened to break up Frederick William's ambitious plans.

The Recovery of Austria / The Austrian crown took longer than either the French or the Prussians to put its house in order largely because it could not concentrate upon the situation in the imperial capital but had to think also of the revolutionary movements which had taken place in Bohemia, Hungary, and Italy. Yet it did master the situation in time, thanks to the social and national prejudices that came to divide the rebels and the vigor of the Austrian army and its commanders Radetzky, Windischgrätz, and Jellachich.

The tide began to turn in June 1848 in Bohemia, where the German and Czech wings of the revolutionary movement had become hopelessly estranged after their common victory in March. Led by men like František Palacký (1798–1876), the Bohemian historian, the Czechs had begun to dream of a nation of their own. They opposed sending a delegation to the Frankfurt Assembly and took a leading part in the calling of a Pan-Slav Congress which met in Prague early in June and issued a ringing call for the conversion of the Hapsburg empire into "a federation of nations all enjoying equal rights." This inflamed the feelings of the German population; brawling between Czechs and Germans led to more serious disorders; and, by mid-June, barricades were being built and mobs of Czech students were marching through the streets, smashing store fronts as they searched for arms. This violence, engendered by nationalistic passions, had a bloody sequel, for—after some days of negotiation for the purpose of restoring order—the imperial military commandant of Prague, General Windischgrätz, withdrew his troops from the city and then proceeded to bombard it with artillery with a ruthlessness that was perhaps influenced by the fact that his wife had been fatally wounded by a stray bullet a few days before. Helpless before this kind of force, the Czech students capitulated on June 17; the political liberties won in March were abrogated; and supporters of royal authority all over the empire had reason to feel that the situation was not as hopeless as it had seemed earlier.

This feeling was strengthened by events in Italy. In the first victories against the Austrians, the rebels of Lombardy had been supported by the army of the king of Piedmont and by detachments from Rome, Tuscany, and Naples. But by the middle of the year these last units were recalled to deal with troubles in their own states; and a waning of enthusiasm had begun to affect the Piedmontese and the Lombards. It was in these circumstances that Radetzky emerged from the Quadrilateral and over-whelmed the Piedmontese at Custozza on July 24. Within two weeks Lombardy had been rewon. The restoration of order in Tuscany had to wait until the spring of 1849 (as did that in Rome, where French troops put down a republic and restored papal authority in June); and Radetzky was not able to subdue Venice until August 1849.[2] But Custozza was, in a sense, a promise that those things were coming. Thousands of people now quoted Grillparzer's ode to Radetzky:

> Here's to my general! Now strike home;
> Not only fame for thy fee!
> Thy camp encloses Austria,
> Her separate members are we.
>
> By foolishness and vanity
> Came our collapse and fall,
> But when thou leadest men to war
> The old fire glows in all.[3]

The Italian victories produced a degree of enthusiasm for army and emperor that boded ill for the cause of revolution.

The next victory was in Vienna itself, although it was made possible by the course of events in Hungary. In that country, the victory won for autonomy by the Magyars in March was now challenged by the non-Magyar elements—notably the Croats, the Serbs, and the Rumanians, who demanded recognition of their separate identity and their right to conduct their affairs in their own language and under leaders of their own choice. These demands the Magyars, intent on a policy of centraliza-tion and cultural uniformity, refused; and this uncompromising attitude led to an explosion of indignation on the part of the other national groups. The Vienna government aggravated these passions by appointing an inveterate anti-Magyar, Colonel Jellachich, as governor of Croatia, from which position he did everything possible to defy the Magyar

---

[2] For a fuller account of events in Italy in 1848–1849, see below, pp. 202–204.
[3] *Glück auf, mein Feldherr, führe den Streich!*
Nicht bloss um des Ruhmes Schimmer,
In deinem Lager ist Oesterreich,
Wir andern sind einzelne Trümmer.

Aus Thorheit und aus Eitelkeit
Sind wir in uns zerfallen;
In denen, die du führst zum Streit,
Lebt noch Ein Geist in Allen.

authorities. Jellachich's policy culminated finally in open revolution against the Hungarian government, an action which in its turn brought the radical anti-Slav, anti-Austrian party of Kossuth to power in Budapest and made any political compromise impossible. That the Austrian crown welcomed this situation was indicated by the alacrity with which the emperor now dissolved the Hungarian Diet and gave Jellachich command of all imperial forces in Hungary.

These provocative actions were almost disastrous, for they inspired a wave of sympathy for the Magyars which touched off a new and bloody rising in Vienna, during which the minister of war, Count Latour, was murdered by the mob. Powerless to preserve order, the court and the government fled the city on October 7, leaving it in the hands of the students, the artisans and shopkeepers, and the proletarian masses. It was, however, a rising doomed to failure, for its leaders were bereft of political talent and its violence alienated not only the bulk of the middle class but also the peasants, who refused to give any support to the rebels in the capital, who arrested emissaries sent out to appeal to them, and who took advantage of the plight of the democrats in Vienna to exact exorbitant prices for the food they supplied. Meanwhile, the government showed that it had not forgotten the lesson of Prague. On October 15, at Olmütz, the emperor gave full powers to Windischgrätz to end "the reign of terror" in Vienna; on October 23, the "Bombardment Prince," as he was called by the Viennese democrats, gave the city forty-eight hours to surrender; on October 28 his troops, after an artillery barrage, began the assault on the city. Recognizing his debt to the Viennese rebels, Kossuth sent a Hungarian force of 25,000 men to their aid, but they were beaten off by Jellachich's Croats on October 30. Windischgrätz overcame the resistance of the last extremists on the following day, and imposed martial law over the city.

The capture of the capital brought a significant change in the government. Earlier in the month, Windischgrätz's brother-in-law, Prince Felix Schwarzenberg (1800–1852) had been authorized to form a government. He did so now, filling it with men who, like himself, were opposed to all reforms except those granted from above and whose first objective was the restoration of the imperial power. At the beginning of December, they persuaded the foolish and ineffective sovereign, Ferdinand, to abdicate in favor of his nephew Francis Joseph. This eighteen-year-old boy, who accepted his office with the rueful words "Farewell youth!," had a strong sense of responsibility and a willingness to work hard; but the circumstances of his accession to the throne, and the tutelage of Schwarzenberg, prejudiced him against the desires of his subject nationalities and the very idea of liberal reform, gave him an exaggerated regard for his own prerogatives, and induced in him an excessive reliance upon soldiers and bureaucrats. This was hardly the best preparation for a reign which was to last until 1916.

The eyes of the new emperor and his ministers turned naturally, in the first months of their power, to the situation in Hungary. Not for a moment did they contemplate a compromise with the Magyars. The concessions which had been made to them in March by Ferdinand were now abrogated, and war was declared. It was not a glorious war for the Austrians, whose commanders showed greater success against open cities and peasant villages than against the Hungarian forces. These last had been molded into a spirited and effective army by Arthur Görgey, an almost unknown officer who had so distinguished himself in fighting against Jellachich's Croats that Kossuth had made him a general. In the first months of 1849, in an astonishing series of victories, Görgey sent the Austrian forces of Windischgrätz reeling back to the frontiers of their own country. Inspired by these victories, the Hungarian Diet formally declared its independence of Austria, and Kossuth became the president of the new state.

But Francis Joseph and Schwarzenberg were willing to go to any length to suppress the rebels. They appealed now to the tsar of Russia for aid, and Nicholas, who prided himself on being the archfoe of revolution, responded by sending 140,000 troops against the Hungarians. Even Görgey's undoubted strategical gifts were not enough to overcome this addition to his enemy's strength; and on August 13, at Világos, his armies surrendered to the Russians. Kossuth and his cabinet fled, with several thousand soldiers, to Turkish soil, thus avoiding the fate of many of their companions, who died in the wave of hangings, shootings, and public floggings with which the Austrians celebrated their victory, to the accompaniment of shocked protests from the British and American governments and even the Russian field commanders.

Schwarzenberg, the real director of Austrian policy in these years, was impervious to these complaints. A cold and ruthless nature, scornful of the idealism which had motivated many of the forty-eighters, regarding power as the only thing that deserved respect, provided it was energetically employed ("Bayonets" he had warned Francis Joseph, "are good for everything except sitting upon"), he was determined to show the world that Austria's recovery from the revolution was complete. Simultaneously with the destruction of Hungarian liberties, Radetzky's armies had completed the reconquest of northern Italy. The only remaining threat to Austria's position was in the German states, which Frederick William IV had been seeking to form into a union under Prussian leadership. Schwarzenberg was now prepared to deal with that.

Since the middle of 1849, he had done everything possible to sabotage Prussian efforts by diplomatic means. Now, he resorted to menaces, and, in the course of 1850, made it clear to the Prussians that they would have to choose between abandonment of their project or war. As tension mounted between the two great German powers and Austrian troops were put in readiness for war, Prussian conservatives urged their king to give in, arguing that Russia would certainly support Austria and that the resultant conflict would help no one but the advocates of revolution. The king's friend Radowitz and his brother Prince William pleaded that Prussian honor forbade capitulation, but they were overborne. In November 1850, at Olmütz, Prussian ministers signed a convention— later called "the humiliation of Olmütz" by nationalists—by which they gave up the king's plan for the reorganization of Germany and agreed to the re-establishment of the old German Confederation which had been superseded by the Frankfurt parliament two years before.

This action completed Austria's recovery from the revolution that had come upon her in March 1848. While Schwarzenberg had been dealing with the Hungarian, Italian, and Prussian challenges to imperial authority, he had summarily disposed of one other source of irritation. This was the Austrian Constitutional Assembly, which was first elected in 1848 and, after the rising in Vienna in October, had removed to Kremsier in Bohemia, where its members had been patiently working on a constitution for the whole empire. At the beginning of 1849, they had actually put the finishing touches to a document which later generations of Austrians were to feel might have spared the empire many troubles. For the so-called Kremsier constitution sought to solve the nationalities problem by providing for extensive provincial autonomy, while at the same time granting local self-government to towns and villages, so that a German village in Bohemia, for instance, would be assured of minority rights. This was certainly a more rational arrangement than any tried in the subsequent period; but Schwarzenberg, who was opposed to decentralization of any kind, would have none of it. In March 1849 he confiscated all copies of the draft constitution and dissolved the Assembly. Some time later the emperor himself granted a charter to his subjects, which had none of the liberal features of the Kremsier constitution and was in any case abrogated in 1852.

CONCLUSION

By 1850 the fires of revolution had burned themselves out, and the victories of March 1848 seemed a remote and unreal memory. After all the rhetoric and the resolutions and the bravery on the barricades and in the field, the continent of Europe seemed to be, on the whole, unchanged. The attempt to liberalize and federalize the Hapsburg empire had failed as ignominiously as the movement to unify Germany; both Kremsier and Frankfurt were might-have-beens. The Bourbons were back in Naples and the pope was back in Rome. Austria was supreme in northern Italy; her influence in Germany was restored; and, if her serfs had been freed, her other subjects had not. The governmental methods of the Hapsburg state were still as autocratic as those of Russia, and this could almost be said of Prussia too, for despite their new constitutional system, the Prussians returned after Olmütz to their old association with the Eastern Powers and aped their ways. The only nation whose governmental structure had undergone marked change was France, but there was little reason in 1850 to put much faith in the durability of her republican institutions in view of the tactics of her president.

The psychological effects of the collapse of all the high hopes of March were profound and affected every aspect of European thought and activity after 1850. This was most immediately evident in the field of foreign affairs, where the principles and the tactics of those who guided the fortunes of the great powers were determined by their memory of the revolutions and where the nature of their objectives soon destroyed the European system that still seemed intact in 1850. These psychological and diplomatic effects of the revolutionary years are the subject of the pages that follow.

PART TWO

1850

1871

GENERAL OBSERVATIONS

The climate of opinion that prevailed after 1850 was marked by disillusionment with the values and methods of the past, distaste for ideals and abstractions, and exaggerated veneration of concreteness and tangibility. The new generation prided itself on its *realism*.

This was encouraged and reinforced by the contrast between the failure of political idealism in 1848 and the triumphs of science and industry in the years that followed. The European public could hardly fail to be impressed by *scientific progress*, because they saw its utility demonstrated daily in fields like metallurgy, where chemists discovered how to remove phosphorus from iron ore, and medicine, where Lister's germ theory decreased the incidence of death by blood poisoning, or embodied in such convenient by-products of scientific investigation as linoleum (1860), celluloid (1863), cement (1850), and vulcanized rubber (1869).

Their respect for these achievements tended to make them receptive to the generalizations that scientists now began to offer about human life and the universe. To a disillusioned generation seeking comfort in tangible things, the concept of the indestructibility of matter made a direct appeal; it was easy to be so impressed by it that one began to regard it as the ultimate reality, in terms of which all things had to be explained. Similarly, the formulation by Charles Darwin (1809–1882) of the theory of the origin of the species, with its emphasis upon the survival of those species which are selected by nature because of their ability to adjust themselves to the conditions of the continuing struggle for existence, was so seductive that those who accepted it were apt to apply it not only to the sphere of biology but also to sociology and politics, economic activity and international diplomacy. One of the outstanding characteristics of this period and the one that succeeded it was, thus, a *deepening materialism* which, as we shall see, assumed some dangerous forms.

This materialism was encouraged by the almost uninterrupted *economic expansion* of the period, as the indices of production, trade,

Charles Darwin, 1809–1882
(BRITISH INFORMATION SERVICES)

Louis Pasteur, 1822–1895
(FRENCH EMBASSY PRESS & INFOR-
MATION DIVISION)

and finance showed steady acceleration. In agriculture, the increase of yield was largely due to the use of artificial fertilizers, made possible by the chemical researches of Liebig, Chevreul, and Dumas, by the importation of Chilean nitrates and guano, which increased rapidly in the 1850s, and by the discovery of European deposits of phosphates. All of this made possible intensive cultivation, which increased grain production in Great Britain by 20 percent in ten years and in France by 10 percent in the same period and which, together with the beginning of the importation of American and Australian grains, freed Europe from the threat of famine which had been constantly present in the past. The growth of truck farming and cattle breeding was equally impressive, while the studies of fermentation made at the end of the 1850s by Louis Pasteur (1822–1895) facilitated the improvement and the profitable expansion of dairy farming, wine culture, and the brewing of beer.

More spectacular was the progress of industrial production, as can be seen from even the briefest consideration of progress in textiles and the heavy industries. The textile industry in these years was characterized by increasing mechanization; and the introduction of such devices as the sewing machine (first used successfully in the United States in the 1840s but widely adopted in Europe in the following decade) enabled the production of cotton goods to increase by 25 percent between 1850 and 1860. Simultaneously, the application of machinery to coal mining, in the form of improved drills, water and ventilation pumps, and hydraulic extraction devices, doubled French coal production and tripled that of Germany in the ten years after the revolution, and similar gains were registered in other industrial countries. This expansion in turn had an immediate effect upon metallurgy which, by the end of the period, had become almost exclusively dependent upon coal and coke rather than on wood. The superiority of the new furnaces and the general introduction of the Bessemer process (1856), which removed carbon and other impurities by blowing air through the molten iron, and the Siemens-Martin open-hearth process (1865), which did this more effectively and allowed the use of scrap iron and low-grade ores, was reflected in the doubling of European iron and steel production in the twenty years after 1860.

These advances were facilitated by the changes that were taking place in this period in the field of transportation. Oceanic transport was revolutionized by the increased use of steel and steam, by the introduction of the screw propeller in the 1850s and the compound engine in the 1860s, and by the shortening of well-traveled routes by such notable achievements as the opening of the Suez Canal in 1869; and the new British, French, German, and American lines founded in the 1840s and 1850s carried a mounting volume of trade. The world freight total in 1840 was about 10 million tons; in 1870 it was 25 million tons. The progress of railway transportation was no less remarkable, the European network alone growing from about 14,000 miles of track in 1850 to about 32,000 miles in 1860 and 78,000 miles in 1870. As a result of improvements in rolling stock, standardization of the gauge in all European countries except Russia and Spain, the growing adoption of the steel rail and the introduction of new signaling and braking devices, the safety, speed, and volume of railway travel grew throughout the period. The part this played in stimulating industrial and agricultural production is obvious.

Two other factors helped this ballooning production and exchange of goods: the expansion of the money economy resulting from the discovery of deposits in California and Australia, which doubled the stock of monetary gold during this twenty-year period, and the introduction of credit devices and new legislation that lent more flexibility to the fiscal system. No single innovation or reform was more important in this latter respect than the general adoption of the principle of limited liability. Employed first in the charters of railway companies, this principle made it safe for individuals to invest without risking the loss of their total resources in case the company failed; and its extension to other forms of legitimate speculation enormously expanded corporate investment. This in turn encouraged the establishment of investment banks, like the French *Crédit Mobilier* (1852) and the *Berliner Handelsgesellschaft*

(1856), which sold stock to private investors and used the proceeds to found new companies by the extension of long-term loans. Short-term credit was simultaneously expanded by the founding of new deposit and discount banks, which helped the movement of raw materials, the expansion of plant facilities, and the increase of variety and volume of production.

In face of all of this activity and the undeniable achievements of technical and economic progress, it is not surprising that the new generation should have been impressed and that its goals and its values should have been changed. Werner Sombart once wrote that, after the disappointment of 1848, young Germans turned more readily to business than to politics when they chose their careers, for the adventure promised to be as exciting and the rewards more sure. Nor was German youth alone in this. In all countries young men read, and were stirred by, the enormously popular book *Self Help* (1859), in which Samuel Smiles held before their eyes dozens of examples of men who had risen from rags to riches by making the most of their talents in the exciting and opportunity-laden world of business enterprise.[1] In an earlier period they might, like Stendhal's heroes, have dreamed of emulating Napoleon; now, like the protagonist of Gustav Freytag's novel *Debit and Credit* (1855), they were more likely to think of mercantile triumphs.

The Freytag book, with its detailed descriptions of commercial activity, illustrates the pronounced change that was taking place in *literature and the arts* in these years. If romanticism was not dead, it was no longer fashionable. The emphasis was now on the kind of realism that portrayed life, not as it might or should be, but as it was. In the novels of Gustave Flaubert, the fidelity to detail in description and characterization is impressive; and the characters who fail to recognize the facts of life, or who revolt against them, either undergo a painful conversion to reality, as did Frédéric Moreau in the *Sentimental Education* (1870), or are broken by it, like Emma in *Madame Bovary* (1856). The new realism characterized the works of Turgenev, George Eliot and Émile Zola, whose first masterpieces, *Thérèse Raquin* and *Les Rougon Macquart*, appeared in the closing years of our period; in the last novels of George Sand, it eclipsed the buoyant idealism of her earlier works and was combined with social criticism and reforming zeal; and this was also true of Charles Dickens' last great novels: *Bleak House, Hard Times, Little Dorrit, Great Expectations*, and *Our Mutual Friend*, all written between 1852 and 1865. In the works of the Russian novelists Dostoevsky and Tolstoy some of the older themes of romanticism persisted—the problem

---

[1] So, apparently, did their sons. The protagonist in George Orwell's *Coming Up for Air* (1939) says: "Father had never read a book in his life, except the Bible and Smiles' *Self Help*."

Charles Dickens, 1812–1870   Feodor Dostoevsky, 1821–1881

of the isolation of the individual from society, for instance, and the tendency to idealize the rebel—and, indeed, in the later works of both authors, the emphasis on the irrational was to be heightened; but few would question the mastery of realistic detail shown in *War and Peace* (1869) or deny that Dostoevsky, particularly in *Crime and Punishment* (1866), ranks with Dickens and Balzac in ability to give a truly naturalistic representation of the modern metropolis.

The transition from romanticism to realism was less pronounced in drama, poetry, and music, although it should be noted that the plays ground out by the enormously popular French dramatists, Dumas and Augier, proclaimed the optimism and materialism of the middle classes who flocked to see them and emphasized the values and the institutions that made for the kind of social stability desired by the bourgeoisie. Among the poets, Tennyson and Heine might make an occasional cut at the prevailing materialism, but they—and poets like Swinburne, Baudelaire, Verlaine, Mallarmé, Moerike, and Conrad Ferdinand Meyer—generally cultivated detachment from contemporary problems and remained true to an older lyrical tradition. Something of the sort was true also in music, where the brilliant harmonies of Berlioz and the tumultuous crescendos of Rossini continued to resound throughout the 1860s; where essentially romantic themes appealed both to Gounod (*Faust,* 1859;

Romeo et Juliette, 1867) and to Verdi (*Aida,* 1869); and where Wagner's poetic dramas (*Tristan und Isolde,* 1865; *Die Meistersinger von Nürnberg,* 1868; *Das Rheingold,* 1869; *Die Walküre,* 1870) shocked and entranced audiences. In the visual arts, however, the changed mode was made apparent by the almost brutal directness of Gustave Courbet (whose *Burial at Ornans,* 1850, first prompted the use of the word "realism" to describe a style of painting) and by its refinement and illumination in the works of the impressionist school, which had its beginnings in the 1860s with such paintings as Manet's *Dejeuner champêtre* (1863) and *Olympia* (1865), which scandalized the public of their time but are accepted today as among the finest achievements of modern art.

In three fields of human activity—religion, social relations, and international politics—the deepening materialism and increasing emphasis upon realism had pronounced, and generally unhappy, effects. These were years in which *the established churches* lost strength and prestige. This was due in part to the increasing drift of the working population toward the cities, where living and working conditions were hardly conducive to the retention or practice of faith; but it was attributable also to the fact that the literate classes of society were affected by the rationalism that marked the works of contemporary philosophers, historians, and popularizers of science. The scientific writers, in particular, showed a delight in making frontal assaults upon religious dogma, claiming that discoveries in astronomy, geology, physics, and biology invalidated theological explanations of human existence. The very intemperance of these attacks might have been self-defeating had it not been for the correspondingly passionate reaction of leading churchmen. All too often prominent divines elected to plunge into controversy for which they were inadequately prepared and to reveal publicly what appeared to be a stubborn resistance, not only to change, but even to common sense. There was no reason why the emendation and new interpretations proposed by the scientific biblical critics of the 1860s could not have been accepted in the spirit with which they have since been accepted. Instead, Protestant leaders often fought bitterly against any but the most literal interpretation of the sacred writings; and this attitude explains the astonishing vehemence of their resistance to Darwin's theory of evolution, which hurt rather than helped the cause they served.

Simultaneously, the hold of the Roman Church upon the intelligent sections of society was jeopardized by Pope Pius IX's systematic attack upon the major intellectual tendencies of the age in the encyclical *Quanta cura* of September 1864 and its accompanying *Syllabus,* in which such things as rationalism, indifferentism in religion, the idea that salvation was attainable outside the Roman faith, the principle of lay education, separation of church and state, political liberalism, and the idea of progress were castigated as errors to be shunned by the faithful. Liberal Catholic theologians, like Bishops Döllinger and Ketteler in Germany, were disturbed by the radical comprehensiveness of this condemnation, as they were six years later by the proclamation of the doctrine of papal infallibility, which claimed that, when speaking on matters of faith and doctrine, the pope's word was final. The resistance of these critics was, on the whole, ineffective, but their instinct was sound, for the papal policy seemed to many to be a vain attempt to resist the march of the intellect and, because it did so, it alienated the European intelligentsia.

These controversies and internal storms absorbed most of the energies of the established churches and weakened their ability to play a reforming or mediatory role in the social life of the times. This was regrettable, since the *relations between classes* were increasingly affected by materialistic and evolutionary theories that promised to subvert social peace. Classical economists like John Stuart Mill (1806–1873), venerators of science like Herbert Spencer (1820–1903), and followers of Karl Marx were all materialists at heart, believing that the phenomena they studied were subject to natural laws (supply and demand, struggle for existence, the inevitable movement from capitalism to proletarian society) that were not amenable to human control. With these leaders to supply them with arguments, it was not difficult for the middle class that dominated western society to disclaim social responsibility, for the mill owner to act toward his laborers with the callousness of Mr. Bounderby in Dickens' *Hard Times*, and for organizers of working-class movements to think in terms of inevitable class struggle. Both the capitalist and the socialist theorists of this period assumed that man was motivated primarily by the acquisitive instinct, an idea that would in other times have been rejected as ignoble and as a denial of history; and this kind of thinking led to an acceptance of the legitimacy of the use of violence in the solution of social and economic problems that was to find frightening expression in the last years of the century.

The stratification of most of the European societies in this period was different in marked respects from the period preceding it. Whereas the nobility might still occupy the social positions of greatest prestige, some of their prerogatives had been swept away by the revolution of 1848. East of the Elbe, in Hungary and in Russia, the nobility still combined the possession of great landed estates with judicial and other rights over the workers of those lands (although the emancipation of the serfs in Russia, in 1861, sensibly diminished noble privileges); and in other countries as well aristocrats had a virtual monopoly of positions in certain branches of the army. In general, however, politics fell increasingly under the control of those who dominated the economic life of Europe, the wealthier middle class, and political philosophy and state policy came increasingly to mirror their views. A striking characteristic of this period was the growing distinction between the upper and lower middle class, first made dramatically clear in the collapse of the 1848 revolutions, and the expansion in size of the latter. The petty bourgeoisie, composed of lesser officials, small business men, and what we have come to call white-collar workers, benefited from the democratic reforms in Great Britain in the 1860s; but in other countries it became a volatile and disorganized class, craving security and leadership, an important and potentially dangerous political force. At the base of the social pyramid were the agricultural and industrial workers, the former of whom were decreasing in number throughout this period (60 percent of the population of Europe in 1860, they were to comprise less than half twenty years later). To the swelling numbers of industrial workers, trade unionism and socialism promised protection against the wrongs they felt implicit in capitalism; and the working-class movement made its first significant advances in this period.

The period that opened with hopes of international solidarity and harmony and which, indeed, through the mouths of apostles of free trade like Richard Cobden, preached that the extension of the laissez-faire principle in international economics could not help but promote universal peace, ended nevertheless in a series of violent conflicts. These were prepared by statesmen who brought into *international politics* the same values that impregnated so many other aspects of European society at this time: realism, willingness to consider morals as irrelevant, refusal to consider any criterion for judging action except expediency, insistence that politics was an unremitting struggle in which only the facts of power counted. In these years also nationalism lost the idealism of the ingenuous pre-March days and often degenerated into jingoism, while the relationship between national aspiration and liberal ambition tended to change. The Mazzinian nationalists had fought for the unity and greatness of their country in order that it might be in the van of constitutional progress, human rights, and universal freedom; the liberal of the 1860s, especially in Italy and Germany, was not disinclined to jettison his constitutional and humanitarian ambitions so that his country might be able to demonstrate its greatness to others.

It is easy for us, looking back to the period 1850–1871, to see tendencies at work within the system that were to cause disaster and suffering later on. The gift of prescience was not given to contemporaries, and they did not believe that the realism of which they were so proud and the material progress that was so obvious could produce other than good. They can hardly be blamed for being impressed by the tremendous triumphs of their day: by engineering feats like the building of the Suez Canal and the piercing of the Alps by tunnel and the laying of the trans-Atlantic cable; by the penetration of European trade into every port of the known world and the establishment of European entrepôts in the Far East; and by the carrying of European ideas and institutions to the United States, Canada, Australia, New Zealand, and Latin America by the 200,000–300,000 emigrants who left Europe yearly in this period. European culture appeared to be attaining its finest flower, and there seemed every reason to believe that, by trade and emigration, the benefits of that culture would be shared to the universal advantage.

6

The Breakdown of the Concert and the Crimean War

THE WEAKENING OF THE CONCERT OF EUROPE

The Revolutionary Period / One of the most remarkable aspects of the revolutions of 1848 was the fact that the disorders they caused precipitated no war between major powers. That no great state was led by ambition or fear to take action that invited retaliation by another was a tribute in the first place to the habits of cooperation and restraint that had grown up between the powers in the years since 1815. But the maintenance of international peace during these difficult times was due also to the careful diplomacy of the two powers not affected by revolution at home, Great Britain and Russia.

At the very beginning of the disorders in Vienna and Berlin, Tsar Nicholas had written to the British queen and urged that an intimate union between their countries would be advisable if general disaster was to be averted; and, although Lord Palmerston was not willing to admit the necessity of a formal tie between the two countries, he wrote: "Our feelings and sentiments towards Russia are exactly similar to those [they express] towards England. We are at present the only two Powers in Europe . . . that remain standing upright, and we ought to look with confidence to each other." The basis of this mutual confidence was the desire of the two countries to prevent local disorders from leading to anything that might upset the arrangements of 1815; and, while it cannot be said that they worked together intimately in averting such situations, at least they understood and trusted each other's intentions and exercised mutual forbearance as they took the action they considered necessary.

The British were primarily concerned, at the beginning of the revolutionary disturbances, with two possibilities: namely, that the French republicans might be inspired by the traditions of 1792 to attempt to support the cause of revolution in Italy; and that the Prussian liberals, flushed with their initial victory in Berlin, might seek to liberate Poland, deliberately courting a war with Russia in order to arouse national sentiment and hasten the unification of Germany. In March 1848 the latter scheme was within the realm of practical politics, and Prussian envoys were actually seeking French support for a blow in behalf of the Poles. Nothing came of this, probably because of a stern dispatch from Lord Palmerston to the Prussian government, urging it "to abstain from any proceeding which could be considered by Russia as aggressive"—a warning that stiffened Frederick William IV's resistance to his ministers' designs and doubtless had a restraining effect in Paris also.

The danger of large-scale French intervention in Italy, either in 1848 or in 1849, was also averted in large part by Palmerston's diplomacy. In the first phase of the Italian disorders, when Radetzky lost Venetia and Lombardy, the British foreign secretary sought to remove the temptation to intervene by persuading the Austrians to acquiesce in the loss of those provinces. When the Austrians refused, and when the tide turned in their favor with their victories over the Piedmontese at Custozza in July 1848 and at Novara when the war was renewed in the spring of 1849, Palmerston restrained the French by the simple expedient of asking them to associate with him in urging the Austrians to show a decent leniency toward their rebellious subjects. Although the French came dangerously close to intervening by force of arms in support of Piedmont, they never quite did so; and major war was avoided in the Italian peninsula.[1]

In pursuing his policy, Palmerston was concerned solely with the requirements of the balance of power, and had scant regard for the aspirations of Italian nationalists. This was true also of his attitude in Hungarian affairs where, despite his private sympathies for the rebels, he

---

[1] The French did intervene in Rome in 1849 on behalf of the papacy and suppressed the republic. But this was the kind of intervention of which the Austrians would approve. See below, Chapters 7 and 8.

took the line that he had "no knowledge of Hungary except as one of the component parts of the Austrian Empire." He rejected all the requests for aid that came to him from Kossuth's supporters; and when the Russians intervened to suppress the Hungarian revolution, he told the Russian ambassador that he approved of the step but hoped they would "finish as quickly as possible." With this encouragement, the tsar assumed the role of guardian of the balance of power in Eastern and Central Europe, a part he also played, as we have seen, by assuming a threatening position behind the scenes in the days when the Austro-Prussian conflict came to a head in 1850. One of the most important causes of Frederick William's collapse before Olmütz and his willingness to give up his cherished plan of Prussian union was a blunt warning from the tsar that he would consider changes in European treaties that were made without the approval of the cosignatories as acts of aggression.

The British played no part in that affair, although they doubtless approved of the Russian attitude. Certainly they copied it in their intervention in one final dispute during the revolutionary years. This was the situation created by the revolt of the duchies of Schleswig and Holstein against the Danish crown, and the intervention of troops from Prussia and the German states in their behalf. With the tacit support of the Russians, Palmerston sought to have the *status quo* restored, lest the balance in the Baltic Sea be disturbed and friction created between Russia and Prussia; and, after two years of effort, he succeeded in arranging a settlement in that sense which, in 1852, was approved by all the Great Powers sitting in concert.

If the revolutions of 1848 did not, therefore, lead to international war, it was largely because the efforts of Britain and Russia and the acquiescence of the other powers maintained the diplomatic principles of the previous period.

After the Revolution / But those principles were not to remain unchallenged much longer, nor was the territorial settlement they protected. As has been indicated above, the revolutions had the effect of shaking the validity of all of the values of the past, and this was as true in the field of diplomacy as in any other.

For one thing, the revolutions marked the entrance into politics of a generation of European statesmen who were much less responsive to arguments in favor of restraint and compromise than their successors and who were more ruthless in their methods. If the new diplomatic style was created by Schwarzenberg, with his preference for solutions by force and his contemptuous disregard for the rules of private morality in the conduct of politics, he had many followers. The most gifted of them were Count Camillo di Cavour of Piedmont (1810–1861) and Otto von Bismarck of Prussia (1815–1898), who entered politics during the years of revolution and rose to prominence in the decade that followed. Their single-minded devotion to the interest of their countries and their willingness to use any means, including violent and cynical repudiation of the public law, in order to advance it came to be known as *Realpolitik*. Cavour once unconsciously defined this when he said; "If we did for ourselves what we do for Italy, we would be great rascals." The rise of these men was a clear threat to the existing treaty structure, for the simple reason that existing treaties blocked the attainment of their desire to increase the power and territory of their countries. This was true also of the man who made himself emperor of the French in 1852, Louis Napoleon, whose very name was a challenge to the territorial balance arranged in 1815.

In addition to this, the revolutions had left a legacy of distrust and suspicion between the powers that was to make concerted action by them much harder than it had been in the past. Tsar Nicholas of Russia could hardly be expected to put much confidence in a France that seemed to be repeating the pattern of the years 1789–1815; and Great Britain was also disturbed by the French transition from republic to empire. The Austrians resented the fact that they had had to rely upon Russian aid in the liquidation of their Hungarian troubles; and Schwarzenberg was reported to have said, "We shall astonish the world with our ingratitude." The Prussians might have reconciled themselves to their setback at Olmütz if it had not been for the imperious manner with which the Austrians treated them in the Diet of the Germanic Confederation in the years that followed. Before 1848 Austria and Prussia had tacitly agreed to submit no issue to the Diet to which either took exception; in amicable consultation, they always decided what should and should not be placed before the representatives of the lesser German states. After the Confederation was re-established in 1850, this cooperation disappeared. Increasingly, the Austrians sought to isolate the Prussians or overrule them by majority votes; increasingly, the Prussians resorted to sabotage and other blocking tactics in self-defense. This imposed a continued strain upon Austro-Prussian relations, and convinced the Prussian delegate to the Diet, Bismarck, that war with Austria was, sooner or later, inevitable.

The new international atmosphere affected even the two powers that had managed to escape revolution in 1848 and whose long-distance collaboration had prevented the out-break of major war between that date and 1850. It was the deterioration of relations between Great Britain and Russia that led to the Crimean War, the first conflict between major powers since 1815; and the war, in its turn, further increased tension among the powers and opened up new opportunities for the *Realpolitiker.*

THE CRIMEAN WAR

The Causes of the War / The Crimean War had its origins in what will appear to modern readers to be a trifling dispute between Christians of different sects over their rights in the Holy Land. Its essential causes, however, were two in number: the tactics employed by Russia in the dispute, which were high-handed and adopted without a clear appreciation of the effect they would have in the west; and the inability of the British government, as the dispute reached a critical stage, to follow a consistent course or to withstand the pressure of an excited public opinion.

In 1852, under French pressure, the Turkish government gave rights in certain sanctuaries in the Holy Land to Roman Catholic religious orders. The grant seemed to infringe rights previously recognized as belonging to Greek Orthodox orders, and the Russian government intervened in their behalf. In doing so, however, it demanded not only that the Turkish government revise its earlier decision with respect to the sanctuaries but that it give formal recognition to Russia's right to protect Greek Orthodox believers throughout the length and breadth of Turkish dominions. This demand seemed as potentially menacing as it was vague in its formulation; and the Turkish government refused to comply with it. Feeling that his personal prestige was at stake, the tsar, in June 1853, ordered Russian troops to cross the Pruth River into the Danubian principalities, with the intention of holding this Turkish territory as a pledge until the Turks gave in.

In taking this injudicious step, Tsar Nicholas seems to have been convinced that he was doing nothing more than protecting rights that had been properly his since the eighteenth century. He failed to see that his bullying intervention in the Holy Land dispute would be interpreted in the west as the first move in an attempt to destroy and dominate the Turkish Empire. He made the mistake of believing that the men whom he had visited during his English tour in 1844 would understand that, however much he might favor the breakup of the Turkish Empire, he would never seek to effect it unilaterally, but only in collaboration with the other powers. He unwisely believed that his friend Lord Aberdeen, now prime minister of England, would not only appreciate this but would be able to persuade the other members of the government that this was true.

But Lord Aberdeen was in no position to do this. As a consequence of the confusion introduced into British politics by the split of the Tory party over the Corn Law issue in 1846 (see pp. 118–120), the British cabinet in 1853 was a coalition ministry with no unified leadership. With respect to foreign affairs, two schools of thought were represented in it. One of them, led by Aberdeen and his foreign secretary, Lord Clarendon, believed in secret diplomacy, collaboration with other powers, and the settlement of disputes as quickly and quietly as possible. The other was led by the former foreign secretary, now home secretary, Lord Palmerston, always an impulsive man and now increasingly given to irresponsibility, a believer in a forceful foreign policy, and always more inclined to bully than to parley. Aberdeen wanted to solve the eastern dispute by having the European concert of powers arrange a settlement and impose it on the Turks, for whom he had no great regard. Palmerston apparently suspected Russian intentions and believed that the tsar would observe the integrity of the Turkish Empire only when convinced, by a forceful demonstration, that he must. He wished therefore to solve the dispute by giving open and undeviating support to Constantinople.

If either course had been followed consistently, war might have been avoided. As it was, a badly split cabinet vacillated between the two. Aberdeen and Clarendon suspected that their ambassador in Constantinople, Stratford Canning (Lord Stratford de Redcliffe), was not acting in the sense of the instructions that they were sending him; and the foreign secretary actually wrote at this time:

> It is a misfortune and a complication that we cannot feel sure of Stratford acting with us for a peaceful solution. He pretends to do so . . . and appears to carry out his instructions; but it is impossible to believe, if he put his heart into it and set about work *as he knows how to do there*, that everything should fail as it does. . . . He is *bent on war*, and on playing the first part in settling the great Eastern Question. . . . He seems just as wild as the Turks themselves, and together they may and will defeat every combination coming from the west, however well devised it may be.

But Clarendon made no attempt to withdraw Stratford, perhaps because Aberdeen and he feared that the ambassador might form an alliance with Palmerston and stampede the country into war. The result of this temporizing was to obscure British intentions. The tsar was encouraged by the diplomatic behavior of Aberdeen and Clarendon to believe that they sympathized with him; whereas the Turks were led, by Stratford's attitude and by British fleet movements in the vicinity of the Dardanelles, to assume that the British (and the French, who had dispatched a fleet to Salamis even before the Russians crossed the Pruth) were on their side.

Attempts were made by representatives of the Great Powers sitting at Vienna to find a formula that would guarantee the tsar's interests in the Turkish Empire and his right to protect his co-religionists, while at the same time safeguarding the actual and potential integrity of the Turkish realm. The solutions that the diplomats devised always failed because of the inflexible opposition of the Turks or because of declarations in St. Petersburg that cast doubt on Russian good faith. Thus, affairs were allowed to drift until October 1853, when the Turks demanded the immediate withdrawal of Russian troops from the Danubian principalities and, receiving no reply, declared war upon the tsar. A month later they opened hostilities by sending a fleet of seven frigates, three corvettes, and two steam gunboats into the Black Sea to shell the Russian coast. Off Sinope, this force was intercepted by a Russian squadron of equal strength under Admiral Nekhimov. In four hours of fighting, the Russians sank all but one of the Turkish naval units, with a loss to the Turks of 4000 men.

The tsar seemed sobered, rather than exhilarated, by this victory over Turkey; for he now proposed that he try to draft the terms of settlement of the Russo-Turkish dispute, which could then be amended by the other powers. Once they had persuaded the Turkish government to agree to it, he would withdraw his army from the principalities, and the British and French would withdraw their fleets from the straits. This seems, in retrospect, to have been a not unreasonable proposal. Yet when, in February 1854, the tsar submitted his draft settlement to the representatives of the powers at Vienna, it was rejected without having been given careful consideration; and Great Britain and France immediately declared war on Russia.

The French, who had displayed little initiative since the first phase of the long dispute, apparently took this step because the British were bent on action, and they did not want to be left out. Alliance with England was always Louis Napoleon's dearest wish. It is more difficult to explain the British declaration of war. There were neither convincing strategic nor plausible economic reasons for it, and one is led to the conclusion that the government was swept into war by the pressure of public opinion.

Ever since 1848, the English public had been in an exalted frame of mind. The revolutions that had toppled so many thrones in Europe increased their pride in their own institutions and their contempt for the foreigner. Believing in the natural superiority of the British nation, it was easy for them to believe that Britain had a moral duty to interfere in all European disputes. Combined with this superiority complex and this distorted sense of moral responsibility, there was a curious kind of romantic nationalism at work in England in 1853. This was perhaps a kind

of protest against the dull and pacific decorum of mid-century liberalism
which did little to satisfy what seemed to be a new craving for excitement. Tennyson expressed this amalgam of confused feeling excellently
when he wrote, as the war approached:

> it lighten'd my despair
> When I thought that a war would rise in defence
>   of the right,
> That an iron tyranny now should bend or cease,
> The glory of mankind stand on his ancient height,
> Nor Britain's one sole God be the millionaire:
> No more shall commerce be all in all, and Peace
> Pipe on her pastoral hillock a languid note . . .
> For the peace, that I deem'd no peace, is over and
>   done
> And now by the side of the Black and Baltic deep,
> And deathful-grinning mouths of the fortress, flames
> The blood-red blossom of war with a heart of fire.

The quarrel in the Holy Land had meant little to the English people
until Russian troops marched into the Danubian principalities; after that,
the vast majority were pro-Turk and anti-Russian. The spontaneous
affection for Turkey was remarkable. Richard Cobden, one of the few
men in public life who had some knowledge of the Near East, tried to
tell audiences some of the less palatable truths about the Turkish Empire—about its inefficiency, the corruption of its government, and its
imperviousness to reform. He was howled down by people who preferred
to regard Turkey as a weak liberal nation being attacked by a strong
autocratic one.

These feelings were encouraged by the newspaper press, which
was predominantly anti-Russian and which vilified all attempts at
moderation and sane diplomacy. The more sensational papers portrayed
Palmerston as fighting a lone fight against colleagues who wanted to
cede Constantinople to the tsar, while even ordinarily respectable
journals wrote of "the senile hesitations" of Aberdeen and Clarendon.
After the Turks declared war on Russia, pro-Turkish sentiment was transformed into prowar sentiment; and, when the Russians won their victory
at Sinope, this perfectly legitimate act of war was labeled "the massacre
of Sinope." By this time public opinion was so rabid that people could
seriously believe that the Prince Consort was working in the Russian
interest and could applaud newspaper statements like the one that said:
"Better that a few drops of guilty blood be shed on a scaffold on Tower
Hill than that the country should be balked of its desire for war."

The Crimean War came as a result of Turkish intransigence and inept
diplomacy and incautious military moves on the part of Russia and the

Western Powers. It would appear also, however, that there is much justification for the diary notation made by Thomas Carlyle after the outbreak of war: "It is the idle population of editors etc. that have done all this in England. One perceives clearly that the Ministers go forward in it against their will. . . . Poor Souls! What could the Ministry *do* after all?"

The Conduct of the War / The two things that are most frequently remembered about the Crimean War are, first, that a heroic British nurse named Florence Nightingale organized field hospitals for cholera-stricken British troops and, second (and this because of Lord Tennyson's poem), that a brigade of British light cavalry was sent, because of a badly drafted and wrongly interpreted order, against impregnable Russian gun positions and was almost completely destroyed. It is understandable that popular recollection goes no further. Disease bulked larger in the war than military action, which was on the whole undistinguished; no belligerent emerged from the conflict with laurels; and the military reputation of the Russians and the British in particular was seriously diminished.

It is significant of the failure of the western allies to make careful plans for war before precipitating it that, although Britain and France declared war on Russia in March 1854, their troops made no contact with the enemy until late September. The intervening six months was filled with negotiations designed to persuade Austria to join their alliance. The presence of Russian troops in the principalities, where they threatened Austrian economic interests on the Danube, gave a plausible pretext for Austrian intervention in the eyes of some civilian statesmen in Vienna; but the soldiers firmly opposed the idea, fearing that it would bring the whole weight of the war against the Austrian borders. In any case, the Russians, in August, withdrew the pretext by evacuating the principalities, and the Austrians decided, for the time being, to remain neutral.

The Prussians chose neutrality for reasons much like the Austrian; and the Swedes refused to be tempted into coming into the war by promises of the acquisition of Finland. The allies were finding it difficult to come to grips with their foe, and were embarrassed at having to cheat their public of the promised victories. They decided, therefore, to strike at the most important Russian naval base on the Black Sea, the port of Sebastopol; and in mid-September they landed 50,000 troops on the Crimean peninsula. Except for some confused and unrewarding naval maneuvers far to the north in the Aaland islands, the military action of the war was confined to the Crimea. Direct and determined action immediately after the landing would probably have enabled the allies to take Sebastopol at once, for they broke the initial Russian resistance at the battle of the

Alma River. But they preferred to rely on elaborate maneuvers, and this gave their opponent time to fortify the base and forced the western armies into siege warfare that lasted until June 1855. The Russians, on their side, tried to mount a counteroffensive that would clear the peninsula, but they failed at Balaklava (where the unfortunate charge of the Light Brigade took place) in October 1854 and again at Inkerman in November. After that, the conflict degenerated into a weary war of attrition broken by sporadic raids, while the troops suffered fearfully from cold, dysentery, and cholera.

In the accounts written of the war by *The Times's* correspondent W. H. Russell, one can sense the gradual dissipation of the romantic aura that surrounded its opening campaigns and the dawning of a sense of the pointless brutality of the last battles. During the allied advance towards the Russian positions overlooking the Alma River, Russell was impressed by the gallantry and color of the battle array; he wrote gaily:

> The troops steadily advanced in grand lines like the waves of the ocean, with our left frittered away as it were into a foam of skirmishers under Colonel Lawrence and Major Norcott, of the Rifle Brigade, 2nd battalion, covered by squadrons of the 11th and 8th Hussars, and portions of the 4th, 13th Light Dragoons, and 17th Lancers. This was a sight of inexpressible grandeur, and for the first time one was struck with the splendid appearance of our Infantry in line. Red is the colour, after all, and the white slashings of the breast of the coat and the cross belts, though rendering a man conspicuous enough, give him an appearance of size which other uniforms do not produce. The dark French columns on our right looked very small compared to our battalions, though we knew they were quite as strong; but the marching of our allies, laden as they were with all their packs, &, was wonderful—the pace at which they went was really "killing." It was observable, too, that our staff was more conspicuous and more numerous than the staff of our brave friends. Nothing strikes the eye like a cocked hat and a bunch of white cock's feathers. . . .

Russell's account of the dogged seesaw fighting at Inkerman, on the other hand, was in a different vein, emphasizing the fortuitousness and the planlessness of the struggle.

> Who was in command whilst the battle—a continuous series of detached combats and isolated engagements—was consuming the weary, dismal, anxious hours? No one in particular, I think! No one could judge of the progress of the fight, least of all those who were in the midst of it, and perhaps it was as well that "giving orders" was not much indulged in. Every one was fighting for his own hand where he stood. Wherever a grey cloud of Russians emerged in whirling columns from the mist, and became visible to any body of our infantry in valley, ravine, or hill, it was assailed by fire—fiercely resisted!—aye! charged with the bayonet! Every foot of ground was disputed by handfuls of men led by the officer of the moment,

The siege of Sebastopol, 1854. This contemporary drawing shows the allied sea blockade of the Russian port and, in the foreground, the allied positions for the bombardment of the base. From *Illustrated London News*, Nov. 18, 1854.

the accidental chief who became master of some vital spot, unknown perhaps to him in its relation to the safety of our whole position, but which was held with bulldog tenacity till death or numbers asserted their power. And so it was that mere subordinate personalities, inspiring the obdurate and resolute handfuls with their own power and resolution, without orders of general direction, carried out the great purpose or resistance, and as rocks meet the onset of the angry sea, broke the rush of the waves of Muscovites as they rolled on from the void.

As in later wars, the Russians seemed to have inexhaustible supplies of manpower, and it began to dawn upon the weary allies that even the capture of Sebastopol might not induce them to surrender. This consideration, and increasing criticism at home of the way in which they were conducting the war, convinced the western governments that something must be done to impress the tsar and to induce him to yield. One possible way of doing this was by widening their coalition. In January 1855, they had made a start toward this by winning the alliance of Piedmont, whose chief minister Cavour hoped that intervention might safeguard his country's interests in Italy by winning the sympathy of Britain and France. But this meant an addition of only 17,000 troops to the allied war effort, and it did not and could not open another front against Russia. It was clear that only Austrian intervention would contribute significantly to western strength.

In December 1854, under strong western pressure, the Austrian government signed an engagement which seemed to assure such intervention. The basis of this was a statement of war aims called the Four Points of Vienna, which called for the renunciation by Russia of her preponderant influence in the principalities, a similar renunciation of Russia's claim to protect Turkish subjects of Greek Orthodox faith, an international guarantee of free navigation at the mouth of the Danube, and a revision of the Straits Convention of 1841 "in the interests of the balance of power in Europe." If Russia did not agree to these points within two months, Austria agreed to enter the war, and the Western Powers agreed to guarantee her against any revolutionary troubles in Italy while the fighting continued.

The agreement of December 1854, which caused premature rejoicing in the west, remained a dead letter. In negotiating it, Britain and France had yielded to the Austrian argument that the Hapsburg empire could raise the necessary troops only if supported by the German Confederation; and this had been made a condition of the alliance. But the smaller German states had no stomach for dangerous adventures, and Bismarck, the Prussian envoy to the Confederation, had no desire to help the Austrians drag all Germany into a war from which the Hapsburg would derive whatever benefits accrued from victory. Bismarck's arguments and their own fears persuaded the members of the Diet to turn down the Austrian request for support.

The western governments were infuriated by this check, which meant further prolongation of the miserable campaign in the Crimea. They went on trying to win Austria's help; but it was not until Sebastopol had fallen in September 1855 and they had resorted to naked blackmail that they broke down her neutrality. Declarations to Cavour that they were now prepared to offer their "good offices" in Italian affairs, and threatening intimations to Vienna that continued neutrality might lead them to support a new Piedmontese drive, persuaded the Vienna cabinet, in December 1855, to send an ultimatum to St. Petersburg. This would probably merely have stiffened the resistance of Tsar Nicholas I, who bitterly resented Francis Joseph's failure to repay the service he had done him in 1849. But Nicholas had died in March (in that month, in London, Alexander Herzen, who had fled from the tsar's secret police, heard newsboys laughing and shouting: "Impernickle is dead!") and his successor Alexander II was ready for peace. On receipt of the Austrian ultimatum he declared his willingness to accept the Four Points; and the war was effectively over, having cost the lives of half a million men, two thirds of whom died, not of wounds, but of disease.

THE AFTERMATH

The Peace of Paris / The settlement of the issues that had caused war was already forecast in the Four Points and was now made more precise in the peace negotiations that took place in Paris between February and April 1856. For the Russians, the price of defeat was not exorbitant, but it was certainly humiliating. The tsar was now formerly deprived of the rights for which he had contested so stubbornly. The treaty placed the Danubian principalities of Moldavia and Wallachia outside the Russian sphere of influence; and it also denied Russian claims to a protectorate over the Sultan's Greek Orthodox subjects by affirming the complete independence of the Ottoman Empire. In addition, the tsar was forced to agree to leave the Aaland Islands, in the Gulf of Finland, unfortified, to return the fortress of Kars, which his armies had captured from Turkey in the last months of the war, to give up control of the mouths of the Danube by ceding the Bessarabian territory on both sides of the river to Turkey, and to acknowledge the authority of two international commissions which were appointed to deal with navigation rights on the important waterway.

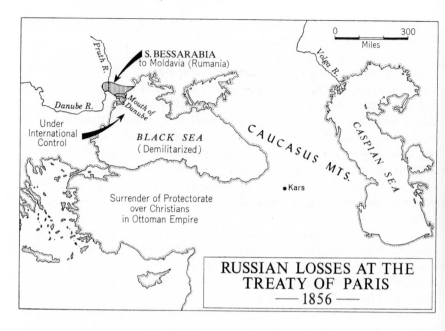

RUSSIAN LOSSES AT THE
TREATY OF PARIS
—— 1856 ——

At the same time, the Straits Convention of 1841 was revised. The sultan of Turkey undertook "to maintain the principle invariably established as the ancient rule of the Empire," prohibiting the entrance of war vessels into the Dardanelles and the Bosphorus, and the powers agreed to observe this rule. The Black Sea was neutralized; all arsenals and fortifications on its shores were forbidden; and freedom of trade was established in its waters. These provisions affected the Turks as much as the Russians, but they were clearly directed against the latter and designed to erect a barrier to Russian expansion to the south and west.

Probably the most important single action of the delegates to the Paris Conference was their regulation of the situation of the Danubian principalities. By abrogating the rights of interference that the tsar had possessed since the treaty of Adrianople in 1829 (see pp. 27–28), they took the first step toward creating a new European state, that of Rumania. Although the principalities were left under Turkish sovereignty, they really became wards of the powers, who promised them an "independent and national administration" within the Turkish realm; and, before the decade was over, that promise had been more than realized, and the principalities were united under a ruler of their own choice and had begun a career of political independence that was to last until 1941.

Another result of the conference's work was to be remembered by future generations, and especially by neutral nations in time of war. This was the so-called Declaration of Paris, by which the powers sought to codify the rules governing commerce during maritime wars. This laid down the principle that free ships make free goods and that noncontraband neutral property must be respected even on enemy ships. It forbade neutrals to issue letters of marque to privateers in wartime. It denied the validity of "paper blockades" by stating that the right to impose a blockade could be claimed only if it were established with adequate force to make it respected.

Finally, the conference brought Turkey into the Concert of Europe, and the signatory powers guaranteed the independence and territorial integrity of the Ottoman Empire and promised to settle individual disputes with the Turkish government by consultation with each other. The treaty specifically mentioned a recent Turkish announcement of prospective concessions to the Empire's Christian subjects and commended it. If this was an indication that the powers hoped, by exerting delicate pressure and encouragement, to lead the Turks into the paths of progressive internal reform, it failed in the result. Until the end of the century, Turkish reforms were largely on paper, and their insensitivity to the grievances of their subject peoples was the cause of much trouble for the powers.

The Future of the Concert / The conference in Paris seemed to be an impressive reaffirmation of the principle of collective responsibility and action by the Great Powers, and the delegates acted as if they fully believed that the European Concert would be effective in the years that followed. They showed this by the solemnity with which they declared that the Ottoman Empire would henceforth "participate in the benefits of the public laws of Europe and of the European Concert"; and they showed it also by the specific rights and responsibilities they claimed for "Europe." The peace treaty gave to the powers acting in concert a general right of intervention in international disputes and a number of specific mandates: to mediate when necessary between the Turkish Empire and any other state, to protect the privileges of the Danubian principalities and to watch over the autonomous rights of Serbia, to guarantee the Ionian Isles, and to define and regulate the free navigation of the Danube River. Moreover, by permitting Cavour to bring the Italian question before the conference in its last sessions, to criticize conditions in Naples and the Papal States, and to attack Austrian policy in the peninsula, the conferees seemed to imply that the future of Italy—and, indeed, all problems of similar international scope and importance—would have to be solved by the Concert of Europe and by it alone.

These apparent signs of a hopeful future for the principle of collective action in the interest of peace were misleading. The Italian question was not going to be solved by collaborative effort on the part of the powers;

and the Concert was to prove generally ineffective in the next twenty years.

This was almost inevitable, for the war had strengthened the suspicions and resentments that the revolutions of 1848 had sown among the powers, while at the same time it gravely weakened their commitment to the existing territorial and legal organization of Europe. Napoleon III had been in favor of thoroughgoing revision of the Vienna settlement even before he went to war in the Crimea, and his desire to advance that end, and to win glory and perhaps territory for his country, had been heightened by his military success. Nor was he alone in preferring change to the sanctity of the written law. There were signs that the Prussians were discontented with their present condition. The Prussian government had been angered and frightened by what had appeared to be an Austrian attempt to drag them into the war; and the reluctance with which the other powers extended an invitation to them to participate in the peace conference made Prussian statesmen fear that the Great Power status of their country was endangered. That fear soon led to the reorganization and strengthening of the Prussian army and the inauguration of an aggressive and expansionist foreign policy. Finally, Russia was transformed by the war from the strongest supporter of the treaty structure to a bitterly revisionist power. It could no longer be counted on to come to the defense of the European balance when it was threatened. This was partly because the damage wrought by the war necessitated a temporary withdrawal from the sphere of foreign politics (as Prince Gorchakov, the new Russian foreign minister, said at this time: "*La Russie ne boude pas; la Russie se recueille*") but more because Russia's principal aim in foreign policy now was to regain its military rights on the Black Sea, and it was thought possible that trouble elsewhere might advance that end. This is what Gorchakov meant in May 1856 when he wrote to his ambassador in Paris: "I am looking for a man who will annul the clauses of the treaty of Paris. . . . I am looking for him and I shall find him."

Austria and Great Britain could, it is true, still be described as supporters of the existing balance, but was it likely that they could, or would, withstand adventures by ambitious powers? Although it had not become an active belligerent in the war, Austria had been weakened by heavy expenditures for weapons that were never used, and it had lost even more heavily in reputation. Prussia resented its wartime behavior for reasons already discussed; Russia, because it smacked of rank ingratitude; Britain and France, because it had consisted of military commitments and promises never fulfilled. Isolated by this general dislike, and threatened in Italy, Austria hardly promised to be an effective bulwark of peace and the existing order.

As for Great Britain, doubt was thrown on its ability to withstand attacks on the public law by the disappointing performance of its forces in the Crimea. Its army had gone into the war without a field commissariat, an effective system of supply, a corps of service troops, or an ambulance corps or medical service (after the battle of the Alma it was discovered that there were no splints or bandages on hand), without any experience in the combined use of cavalry, infantry, and artillery, and without any generals who knew the duties of their rank. The military talents of the supreme commander, Lord Raglan, were exiguous; those of his chief subordinates, Lords Lucan and Cardigan, nonexistent. A junior officer wrote of this pair: "Without mincing matters, two such fools could hardly be picked out of the British Army. And they take command. But they are Earls!" The effect of all this on Britain's military reputation was shattering. When the war was over, Alexis de Tocqueville wrote to an English friend:

> The heroic courage of your soldiers was everywhere and unreservedly praised, but I found also a general belief that the importance of England as a military power had been greatly exaggerated, that she is utterly devoid of military talent, which is shown as much in administration as in fighting, and that, even in the most pressing circumstances, she cannot raise a large army.

Apart from this, it became increasingly clear in the years after 1856 that the British people wanted to be involved in no new European troubles. The war had had a sobering effect in England and had bred a desire for peace and a reluctance to make any commitments that might jeopardize it. This was known on the continent; and subsequently, whenever British statesmen and diplomats talked about the possibility of active intervention in European disputes, the other powers were less impressed than they might have been if the popular mood in England (and her military reputation) had been what they were before the fighting in the Crimea. Indeed, in 1864, Benjamin Disraeli was to say angrily in the House of Commons: "Within twelve months we have been twice repulsed at St. Petersburg. Twice we have supplicated in vain at Paris. We have menaced Austria, and Austria has allowed our menaces to pass her like the idle wind. We have threatened Prussia, and Prussia has defied us."

Because of the mutual distrust of the powers, the new ambitions of certain of their number, and the new weakness of others, the future of Europe was to be determined, not by the Concert of Europe, but by the actions of individual adventurers. Of these, the one who seemed most impressive and formidable in 1856 was Louis Napoleon, emperor of the French.

7

France: The Second Empire

FROM REPUBLIC TO EMPIRE

In January 1853, in one of his many savage attacks upon Louis Napoleon, the poet Hugo wrote:

> *O deuil! par un bandit féroce*
> *L'avenir est mort poignardé!*[1]

Hugo was thinking of the *coup d'état* by which the prince president had overcome the republic, stealing power by an act of violence that caused considerable loss of life. Yet even in the light of that event, it is hard to think of Louis Napoleon as a "ferocious bandit," just as it is difficult to agree with those more recent writers who have described him as the prototype of modern totalitarianism, the forerunner of the Mussolinis and Hitlers of the twentieth century. That he was a political adventurer, bent on securing power and willing to resort to force to attain it, is perfectly obvious; but he was no lover of violence and no believer in power for power's sake. On the contrary, at the height of his influence he showed himself capable of sacrificing his personal prerogatives in the interest of liberal political reform, and in both domestic and foreign policy his

[1] O sorrow! By a ferocious bandit
The future has been stabbed to death!

egotism was offset by genuinely humanitarian aspirations. It is the tragedy of his career that the deviousness that characterized his methods, and was perhaps derived from his conspiratorial past, often made even his most enlightened ideas suspect, while his desire to placate public opinion involved him in fatal contradictions in foreign affairs. But the debacle that ended his regime should not make us forget that he governed France well; and, far from killing her future, as Hugo thought he had done, he left her stronger than he found her.

The Prince President and the Assembly / The man who had been carried to political prominence by the revival of the Napoleonic legend in the 1840s (see p. 88) and elected, on the strength of his name, to the position of president of the French Republic in December 1848 (see p. 141) was not, at first sight, a commanding figure. Short in stature and already given to corpulence, he had a sallow complexion and a somewhat melancholy cast of features that led the governor-general of Paris, General Changarnier, to describe him, in an irreverent moment, as a "depressed parrot." When the Prussian soldier Moltke met him for the first time, he was struck by the immobility of his features and "the almost extinct look of his eyes," as well as his "friendly and good-natured smile which has nothing Napoleonic about it. He mostly sits quietly with his head on one side."

The appearance was misleading. Behind the pleasant, if enigmatic, mask, a keen political intelligence was making an estimate of the balance of political forces in France. Although his first action was to take an oath "to remain faithful to the democratic republic," and although he had declared that he would "regard as enemies of the country all those who endeavor to change by illegal means that which France has established," Louis Napoleon did not regard himself as committed to the republic. He seems, indeed, to have regarded the tremendous vote that elected him to the presidency as a sign of general dissatisfaction with the existing regime; and he might have acted immediately to overthrow it, as some of his intimates wished him to do, if he had not considered it wiser to wait until he was sure of the strength of his popular support.

In May 1849, elections were held for the Legislative Assembly, and the results showed a serious diminution of national support for the republic. Out of 750 deputies, only a third could be described as republicans: 75 followers of Lamartine and 180 democrats and socialists. Moreover, even this remnant seemed determined to destroy itself and, only a month after the elections, came pretty close to doing so in an ill-considered gesture against the prince president.

This came as a result of certain events that were transpiring in Rome, where the pope had been forced to flee from the city during the revolutionary disturbances of 1848, and a Roman Republic had been established under Giuseppe Mazzini. A French military expedition led by General Oudinot had been dispatched to Italy with the vague mission of effecting a reconciliation between the pope and his people; but at the end of April 1849 it had become involved in fighting around Rome and Louis Napoleon ordered Oudinot to begin an all-out offensive against the rebels in the city (see pp. 203–204). In France, the republican leaders in the Assembly immediately accused the president of exceeding his authority and violating the constitution of 1848, which stipulated that France "should never turn her arms against the liberty of any nation." Their declaration that they would defend the constitution, if necessary, "by force of arms" touched off demonstrations and riots in Paris on June 13 and in Toulouse, Perpignan, Strasbourg, and Lyons in the days that followed. Except in Lyons, however, where barricades had to be reduced by artillery bombardment, these *émeutes* were at best halfhearted and were easily suppressed. Their real importance was that they made it easy for the Right to take positive action against French republicanism.

Thus, the Assembly, whose majority was now strongly monarchist, ordered the arrest of thirty-three republican deputies, enacted legislation closing the political clubs that had been their centers of agitation and propaganda, and passed a new press law against "the spirit of revolt and disorder." Having dispersed the leaders of the opposition and silenced their newspapers, they pushed their advantage further; and, in the months that followed, revised the franchise by introducing property and residence requirements, and thus deprived three million workingmen of the vote. Finally, striking out at republican influence in the schools, they passed the so-called Falloux Law, which largely subjected the educational system of the country to church control, while reserving supervisory rights to the state.

While the monarchists in the Assembly were thus destroying the republican movement and earning the hatred of the working classes and the intellectuals in the process, Louis Napoleon held himself aloof. He sensed that, sooner or later, conflict would arise between the Assembly and himself, and he concentrated his efforts upon strengthening his own position in preparation for that. His first step in this direction was to secure unchallenged control of the executive branch of the government. The members of his first cabinet of ministers were elder statesmen who seemed to regard their duty as consisting mainly of curbing his independence and preventing indiscretions on his part. In October 1849, Louis Napoleon abruptly dismissed them, informing the Assembly that he had decided that the ministers should be of his own choosing and should, in general, share his views. As for the policy of the new cabinet, he said blandly:

The name of Napoleon is in itself a whole program. It means order, authority, religion, popular welfare at home; national dignity abroad. This policy, inaugurated by my election, I hope to make triumph with the support of the Assembly and that of the people.

The Assembly responded to this gesture of independence with irritation and with some petty reprisals in the form of limitations on the president's official expenditures. This did not worry him. He had embarked now on a campaign to appeal directly to the people of France; and, wherever bridges were to be opened or new railroad spurs dedicated or harvest festivals held, Louis Napoleon was almost certain to appear. In these continual junketings, he made himself known to millions of Frenchmen and developed a knack of saying precisely what they wanted to hear—telling businessmen about the necessity of civil peace and commercial prosperity, discussing agricultural problems with peasants, showing an interest in local problems, appealing to local patriotism. Before long, people were shouting *"Vive Napoléon!"* and *"Vive l'Empereur!"* at his meetings.

Meanwhile, he was also taking care to ingratiate himself with the army. His name commended him to the rank and file; his office gave him the right of appointment, enabling him to place his supporters in the upper echelons of the command; and he had long made a point of getting to know younger officers, especially those who had commanded troops in Algeria and were, in consequence, men of action rather than desk officers. Many of these *beaux sabreurs* distrusted politicians in principle and were, therefore, ideal allies against the Assembly. On the other hand, there were senior officers who disapproved of, and sought to check, the increasingly frequent army demonstrations which took place when Louis Napoleon appeared at parades. One of these was Changarnier, the governor-general of Paris, who was regarded by the members of the Assembly as their protector against the President's ambitions. But, in January 1851, Louis Napoleon—long wearied by Changarnier's vanity and his ill-concealed lack of respect for his own person—compelled his ministers to concur in the dismissal of the general, a stroke which deprived the Assembly of its hope of retaining the support of the Paris garrison in the case of a serious dispute with the prince president.

That was now not very far away. The road was prepared for it by a quarrel over Article 45 of the constitution, which forbade the re-election of the president after the expiration of his four-year term. Louis Napoleon had no desire to retire in 1852, and he could claim that the country did not want this either, since 79 out of 86 departments had petitioned for revision. When the Assembly refused to consider changing the constitution, the president resolved to destroy its power by force, and, to lay the basis for this, he began a systematic attack upon the

Assembly's franchise law, insisting that France must return to universal suffrage. Meanwhile, with his half-brother, the Duke of Morny, a daring and steel-nerved gambler, whether in the Bourse or in the world of politics, and with men like Persigny, the companion of his Strasbourg and Boulogne expeditions, Maupas, the chief of police, and Saint-Arnaud, the most dashing of "the Africans," who had become minister of war in August 1851, Louis Napoleon drew up a precise plan of action.

The Coup d'État and After / During the night of December 1–2, 1851, Paris was silently occupied by troops;[2] and police agents quietly and efficiently arrested seventy-eight persons, including most of the leaders of the Assembly and such opposition-minded notables as Cavaignac and Thiers. In the gray hours before dawn placards were plastered on walls and kiosks announcing, in the name of the president, that the Assembly had been dissolved, and that the franchise law was abrogated and universal suffrage restored. The people of France, it was stated, would be asked to vote on a new constitution, which would give the country a bicameral legislature, a council of state to frame necessary legislation, and a chief who would rule for ten years. In proposing this return to the pattern of his uncle's Consulate, Louis Napoleon nevertheless claimed to be the savior of the republic and called upon the army to respect "the first law of the land—the sovereignty of the people."

[2] In his poem "Cette nuit-là," Hugo described the operation:

Paris dormait, hélas! et bientôt, sur les places,
Sur les quais, les soldats, dociles populaces,
Janissaires conduits par Raybell et Sauboul,
Payés comme à Byzance, ivres comme à Stamboul,
Ceux de Dulac, et ceux de Kort et d'Espinasse,
La cartouchière au flanc et dans l'oeil la menace,
Vinrent, le régiment après le régiment,
Et le long des maisons ils passaient lentement,
A pas sourds, comme on voit les tigres dans les jongles
Qui rampent sur le ventre en allongeant leurs ongles;
Et la nuit était morne, et Paris sommeillait
Comme un aigle endormi pris sous un noir filet.

Les chefs attendaient l'aube en fumant leurs cigares.

[Paris, alas!, was sleeping; and soon, across the squares and along the quays, came the soldiers, an obedient breed—the janissaries of Raybell and Sauboul, mercenaries like those of Byzantium, drunk like those of Istanbul—the troops of Dulac and Kort and d'Espinasse, with their cartridge cases on their hips and their menacing eyes. Regiment after regiment they came, passing quietly beside the houses, with silent tread like the tigers one sees in the jungle, creeping on their bellies and extending their claws. And the night was gloomy, and Paris slumbered, like a sleeping eagle caught in a black snare. Their commanders waited for the dawn, smoking their cigars.]

Morny, who had planned the details of the *coup*, had said that "intelligent arrests may prevent civil war." They almost did. Deprived of their leaders, the deputies of the Assembly lacked plan and determination. A group of them assembled at the *mairie* of the Tenth *Arrondissement* at noon on December 2 but were arrested by troops before they could decide on a course of action (and then released singly). Meanwhile, the President installed Morny, Saint-Arnaud, Persigny, and others as ministers, with apparent confidence that there would be no further resistance.

He was wrong. On December 3 deputies of the left republican faction succeeded in organizing disorders in the working-class district in the Faubourg Saint-Antoine, and, when local troop detachments failed to put these down, the troubles spread. With icy self-control, Morny proclaimed a state of siege, but ordered General Magnan, commander of the troops in Paris, to withhold action until the rebellion had come to a head. This was done; and there was no interference as the insurrectionists erected their barricade and concentrated their operations. It was not until the afternoon of the 4th that Magnan made a three-pronged attack upon the center of these activities. A column under General Canrobert was blocked by a small barricade across the Boulevard de Montmartre near the Saint-Denis Gate and, under the insults of the mob, gave way to panic or rage and opened indiscriminate fire with small arms and guns upon the fleeing citizens and the shops and cafés in the vicinity. Some two hundred people lost their lives in this senseless *mêlée*; and Louis Napoleon, who had wanted to take power without the shedding of blood, was never to be wholly forgiven for the massacre of December 4.

The shooting, nevertheless, assured the success of the *coup d'état*. Terrified by the brutal efficiency of the army, Paris was not to rise again until 1871, and then in quite different circumstances. Apart from this, the troop action in Paris strengthened Louis Napoleon's support outside the capital, for the provinces regarded the insurrectionists as foes of order and property who ought to be put down ruthlessly. On December 21, 1851, the country was asked to vote *Yea* or *Nay* on the motion: "The French people desire the maintenance of the authority of Louis Napoleon Bonaparte and delegate to him the powers necessary for the establishment of the constitution on the foundation proposed by the proclamation." In Paris, out of 300,000 registered voters, only 133,000 voted for the motion, 80,000 voting *Nay* and the same number abstaining. But in the country at large the president's majority was overwhelming, 7,500,000 *Yeas* to 640,000 *Nays*.

In the months that followed, the new constitution was proclaimed and elaborated. The president's tenure of power was now extended to ten years, and he was given very extensive powers: to declare war and command the armies of France, to make treaties, to appoint ministers and ambassadors, to initiate all legislation and frame all laws, and, in the execution of all this, to be responsible "to the French people." In the machinery of government he was the motive force, for, although France was to have a bicameral legislature, composed of a Senate of life members appointed by the president and a Legislative Body (*Corps Législatif*) of 250 members elected for terms of six years by universal manhood suffrage, its operation always depended on impulse from above. The president proposed the laws, and they were then drawn up by a Council of State appointed by him, and sent on to a commission of the *Corps Législatif*, where they were explained and defended, if necessary, by members of the Council. Any amendments proposed had to be approved by the Council of State before the law was presented to the *Corps Législatif* as a whole. That body, whose presiding officers were appointed by the government, had virtually no powers of debate and was expected to pass what was submitted to it. As for the Senate, it merely examined what the Legislative Body approved, to see that it was not unconstitutional or prejudicial to religion or morality, although it might occasionally promulgate *senatus consulta* or constitutional rulings, which had to be approved by the president.

An important feature of the new system was the use of the plebescite. Since the people were sovereign, the president reserved the right to appeal directly to them over the heads of their representatives. This was a practice that he intended to use only sparingly, for, as he said on one occasion, "I don't mind being baptised with the water of universal suffrage, but I refuse to live with my feet in it." Nevertheless, the plebescite was conceived of, and used, as a means of supporting the president's authority.

His power was maintained also by the administrative system imposed upon the country as a whole. The government extended its appointive powers into the smallest communes of the nation, making the mayors appointive servants of the national government. At the same time, in the departments, measures were taken to root out oppositional officials and, especially, to see to it that the prefects performed their duties with undeviating obedience to the policies which the government laid down for them.

This was the system of government by which France was to be governed until 1860. The only significant change in it before then was one that had been forecast by the vote of December 1851. Increasingly after that time—sometimes spontaneously, sometimes by careful arrangement—crowds greeted the president with cries of "*Vive Napoléon III!*"; and, although Louis Napoleon hesitated for almost a year, he finally took the plunge in November 1852. In that month, the French people were asked whether they desired "the restoration of the imperial dignity" and answered affirmatively by 7,800,000 votes to 250,000. On December 2, Louis Napoleon was proclaimed emperor of the French.

THE DOMESTIC POLITICS OF THE SECOND EMPIRE

In a famous speech at Bordeaux on September 2, 1852, Louis Napoleon had said:

> We have immense territories to cultivate, roads to open, canals to dig, rivers to render navigable, railways to complete. . . . That is how I interpret the Empire, if the Empire is to be restored. Such are the conquests I contemplate; and you, all of you who surround me, you who wish our country's good, you are my soldiers.

This was not mere platform rhetoric. Ever since his imprisonment in the fortress at Ham, where he had passed the time by writing pamphlets on such themes as the extinction of poverty, the cultivation of the sugar beet, and the benefits to be derived from a trans-Isthmian canal in Central America, Napoleon's mind had teemed with schemes for the material betterment of his country. Those who have called him a "Saint-Simon on Horseback" have been close to the mark, for, like the Saint-Simonians (see p. 86), he believed that society ought to organize all its resources scientifically for the benefit of all its members. Once he had consolidated his power, he turned his mind from politics to his plans for society; and France's economy was soon showing the beneficial effects of his enthusiasm.

Economic Policies / Napoleon wanted to make France a prosperous country by encouraging industry, building railroads, expanding commerce, supporting agriculture, and inaugurating an expansive program of public works to reduce unemployment. The key to this comprehensive program lay in the expansion of credit; and from the beginning the emperor did everything possible to stimulate new investment.

Up to this time, the credit resources of the country had been controlled by a few great bankers who profited from their monopoly. One of the emperor's greatest personal contributions to the economic boom that was to begin during his regime was his use of public bond issues for the sake of raising funds that could be used for business expansion. Always oversubscribed, these bond issues helped the state to intervene in every sector of the economy, priming the pump in such a way as to encourage private investment. The combined use of public patronage and private investment under the guarantee of the state had particularly striking results in railroad construction. In 1848, there were only about 2000 miles of track in all France; in 1864, the historian Taine noted that 2000 miles of rail had been laid in the previous year alone; in 1870, France had 11,000 miles of railroad open to traffic, in a well-articulated network with Paris as its hub and with connections with the rail systems of Italy, Germany, and the Low Countries.

The government further promoted economic expansion by authorizing the establishment of a number of semipublic banking corporations, the most important of which were the *Crédit mobilier* and the *Crédit foncier.* The first of these was designed to promote industrial joint-stock enterprises and to open up new fields of business. Founded in 1852, it was particularly successful in financing railroad and harbor construction, public utilities, and shipping companies; and, although it failed in 1867, it did a great deal to demonstrate the advantages that accrued from the close association of industry and banking. The *Crédit foncier,* also founded in 1852, was a national mortgage bank, advancing funds to peasants and town dwellers on the security of their property. It has survived to our own time, as have other organizations like it which were established later in the Second Empire to encourage industry and commerce.

The emperor was an enthusiastic advocate of free trade and lost no time in attacking the protective tariffs left over from the July Monarchy. There is no doubt that he was motivated in part by political considerations, hoping to ingratiate his regime with the greatest free-trading nation of this time, Great Britain. But free trade also accorded with the vision of a Europe of free nationalities living in interdependence; and, apart from that, he hoped it would bring solid advantages to the French people: cheaper food for the poor, cheaper thread for the textile firms, cheaper rails for the railroads, and wider markets for French wines, silks, and *articles de Paris.* Even established industries would benefit, despite the loss of protection, if they adjusted their methods and products to the change. Between 1853 and 1855, therefore, Napoleon effected reductions in the duties on iron, steel, coal, and certain other raw materials and food stuffs; and in 1860, after much secret negotiation, he approved the so-called Cobden-Chevalier Treaty, which appreciably lowered duties on English goods entering France and opened the English market to French manufactures and wines and spirits. This Anglo-French treaty had, indeed, a wider importance, for it supplied a model that encouraged the general tendency of Europe toward a free-trade economy. From a strictly national point of view, there is no doubt that French commerce benefited from this treaty (as it did from the treaties concluded between 1860 and 1866 with Belgium, Turkey, the *Zollverein*, Italy, Sweden, the Low

Countries, and Austria); and the industries that suffered were helped by subventions from the state.

The emperor was always more interested in industry than in agriculture, but he did not neglect a way of life that still claimed the energies of most Frenchmen. He encouraged scientific farming and selective breeding; he organized agricultural societies, fairs, and model farms; he personally authorized projects which reclaimed waste land, drained swamps, preserved forests, and otherwise aided rural districts. Public works of this kind served the double purpose of improving the land and supporting the rural and the urban unemployed; and the importance which Napoleon attributed to the social good performed by public works gave substance to his claim that he was not a Bonapartist ("Only Persigny is a Bonapartist," he said once, "and he's crazy!") but a socialist.

The most impressive of Napoleon's public works were those performed in the cities. Albert Guérard has written that Marseille "owes more to the eighteen years of Napoleon III than to the preceding twenty-five hundred," and something of the same sort might be said of Paris. The imagination and daring of Napoleon and his prefect of the Seine, Baron Haussmann, completely transformed the capital, destroying the narrow winding streets of the medieval city and constructing wide boulevards and broad *places* with radiating avenues, like the Place de l'Étoile and the Place de la République, rebuilding the central markets (according to a design inspired by Napoleon himself), constructing a new opera house, and giving the city a modern water supply, a new sewage system, and several new parks. The vigor with which the emperor pushed the reconstruction of Paris has often been ascribed to a desire to make barricade building difficult and give imperial troops a clear field of fire in case of a repetition of December 4, 1851. Napoleon was always a man of mixed motives, and it would be idle to deny that strategical considerations played their part here. But certainly he was equally moved by the desire to provide for the increasing traffic of Paris, to improve the living conditions and recreational opportunities of the poor, and to make his capital a more beautiful city. All of these objectives he attained, while at the same time giving employment to thousands of skilled and unskilled laborers while the city was remade.

During the Second Empire, France had her moments of economic distress, especially in the 1850s, when the country suffered crop failures, a cholera epidemic, floods, and diseases of the silk worm and the vines, and during the American Civil War, when the interruption of shipments of raw cotton disrupted the textile industry of Normandy and other departments. The losses occasioned by these events, however, were made good; and, when Napoleon fell from power, France was basically prosperous and healthy. This she owned to Napoleon III, who had the imagination

The reconstruction of Paris by Napoleon III: The new Opera House. Designed by a young architect named Charles Garnier, who was selected after a public competition, the house took more than a decade to build. Work began in 1861 and the south front was finished in time for the Universal Exposition of 1867. The other façades were not uncovered until 1869, and the interior was not completed until 1874. This contemporary drawing shows the house from the Rue Meyerbeer. From *L'Illustration*, Oct. 7, 1871.

to see how the financial resources of the state could be used to stimulate private enterprise and lead it in new directions, while at the same time ameliorating the lot of the poor.

Toward Political Liberalism / During the 1850s the French people were almost completely deprived of the kind of political discussion and controversy that was so much a part of their past. The constitution of 1852 gave parliament virtually no power of debate; and, in any case, the electoral procedure, which was manipulated by the prefects so as to give maximum advantage to government-approved candidates, and the almost complete disappearance of organized political parties made the formation of an opposition in the *Corps Législatif* difficult, if not impossible. Newspapers were kept under constant surveillance, and political criticism was answered with suspension or loss of license, a situation which led to the almost complete disappearance of the provincial political press and the survival only of the hardiest Parisian journals, most of which found it expedient to be noncommittal if they did not support the regime. Even the universities were quiet, perhaps because their boards of direction were closely supervised by the state.

It cannot be said that, during this decade, there were many apparent signs of discontent with this authoritarian and bureaucratic regime. Most Frenchmen seemed perfectly content to let the emperor rule France and to turn their attention to economic or other activities. In the parliamentary elections of June 1857, the first held since 1852, government candidates polled 5,500,000 votes, opposition candidates only 665,000; and these figures seemed to indicate the general satisfaction of the country. It was not until 1860 that this mood began to change and, when it did, the emperor seemed to be ready to change with it.

By a decree of November 24, 1860, Napoleon granted both to the *Corps Législatif* and the Senate the right to respond to the speech from the throne, which meant, in effect, the right to hold an annual debate on the state of the nation. It has often been said that his step was prompted by the desire to strengthen the popularity of his regime with the middle classes, at a time when industrialists were criticizing the Cobden-Chevalier Treaty and the clerical vote was hostile to France's policy in Italy (see pp. 208–214); and this was probably true. But there is some indication that Napoleon, who had written in his youth of the strong hand that would dare bring liberty out of order, would have experimented with the relaxation of authority in any case.

As it turned out, the decree of November 1860 was the first step in a progressive liberalization of the regime. Publication of parliamentary discussion was authorized in 1860; and restrictions on press and public debate were slowly relaxed in the years that followed. The surveillance and intimidation that characterized elections in the early years were lightened, and the last elections of the empire were generally admitted to be free. Moreover, parliament's power was widened step by step. In November 1861, the *Corps Législatif* received broader rights over the imperial budget; in January 1862, it was announced that henceforth three ministers without portfolio would represent the government and defend its policies before the two legislative bodies. This first step toward ministerial responsibility was followed in 1863 by the decision to have the president of the Council of State, Rouher, sit regularly in the *Corps Législatif* and the Senate.

Napoleon's relaxation of controls was not confined solely to the political sphere. In 1865–1866, he instituted a comprehensive educational reform which pleased liberals by the way in which it diminished clerical control over secondary education. In May 1864, he allowed his long-held sympathy for the working classes to overcome his suspicion of combinations of workers by legalizing trade unions and the right to strike.

This whole line of imperial policy culminated in the years 1867–1869 when, in order to divert popular attention from setbacks abroad, freedom of the press and assembly was confirmed in law, parliament's power further widened, and Rouher and other unpopular ministers sacrificed to the now sizable opposition in the *Corps Législatif*. When, finally, in January 1870, Émile Ollivier, one of the famous Five, the leaders of the republican opposition since 1857, was asked to form a cabinet that would be (except for its military and naval members) independent of the emperor, the liberalization of the Empire seemed to be complete and a new period of genuine parliamentary government about to dawn.

As has been indicated, the emperor's course along the liberal road had been accelerated by growing criticism of his policies, especially with respect to foreign affairs. This was reflected in election returns. If only 600,000 opposition votes were cast in the parliamentary elections of 1852 and only 665,000 in 1857, the parliamentary elections of 1863 saw the negative ballots mount to 2,000,000; in the elections of 1869, all the large cities voted against government candidates, and the regime triumphed only by a vote of 4,438,000 to 3,355,000. It should be remembered, however, that these were parliamentary elections in which the emperor was not himself a candidate. There is every reason to believe that he was always more popular than his candidates and that he remained so, with the great majority of Frenchmen, until his defeat in battle.

This would seem to be proved by the great plebescite of May 1870 when the French people were asked whether they wished to approve "the liberal reforms introduced by the Emperor since 1870." Every Frenchman knew that he was really being asked whether he wanted Napoleon III to remain on the throne, and he voted accordingly. When the votes were counted, the Emperor had been endorsed by 7,336,000 citizens, with 1,572,000 against him. After twenty-one years of power, this was an impressive vote of confidence.

The Arts under the Empire / Even in the most authoritarian period of the Empire, it does not appear that arts and letters suffered seriously from government policy. France's most distinguished literary figure, Victor Hugo, was, it is true, in exile on the island of Jersey, whence he launched bitter verse attacks upon the man he called "*Napoléon le petit.*" The historian Michelet lost his professorship in 1851; Renan lost his in 1863 after his *Vie de Jésus* had earned the implacable hostility of the clergy; Flaubert was prosecuted in 1857 for publishing *Madame Bovary*; and there were other cases of injustice to individuals. But there was no systematic policy of repression and nothing faintly resembling persecution of literature; and Saint-Beuve could write sincerely in 1865: "I owe it to the Emperor that I have been able to work for fifteen years in peace and security under a regime that allows everyone to exercize his talents and spend his leisure on whatever work he finds useful or congenial."

The artistic achievement of the period was impressive, although this cannot in any way be credited to imperial patronage, since the literary tastes of Napoleon and the Empress Eugénie were pedestrian (as is shown by their preferring Mérimée to Flaubert). The luster of this period rests rather on the fact that, during it, Flaubert and Baudelaire did their major work and Zola and Verlaine had their beginnings, while such secondary figures as the brothers Goncourt (*Germinie Lacerteux, Reneé Mauperin*), Alphonse Daudet, Gautier, Leconte de Lisle, and Stéphane Mallarmé contributed to the variety and excitement of the literary scene.

The allied arts were scarcely less distinguished. The musical style of the Empire was, to be sure, that of Offenbach; and the greatest achievement of the French theater was the operetta (Meilhac and Halévy's *La belle Hélène,* with music by Jacques Offenbach, and the fabulous success of the Paris exposition year 1867, *La grande Duchesse de Gerolstein,* enchanted audiences), and Augier's and Dumas' plays on moral conflict and family problems. But the pictorial arts saw both the realism of Courbet and Daumier and the beginnings of impressionism; Manet, Renoir, Degas, and Cézanne all began their careers under Napoleon; and the great sculptor Carpeaux demonstrated his talent in busts of all the great figures of the imperial court. As for architecture, it was almost an official art, patronized by the emperor and Baron Haussmann; and its achievements can still be judged by any visitor to Paris.

COLONIAL AND FOREIGN POLICY

French Activities beyond the Seas / During the years of the Empire, France was remarkably active in many areas outside the continent, and the *tricouleur* was planted in farflung places whose names must have mystified French peasants when they heard them for the first time. In these activities, as in so many others that took place in his reign, the emperor took a leading part.

He took a personal interest, for instance, in the affairs of Algeria, a French colony since the crushing of Abd el Kader in the 1840s (see pp. 78, 88); and it was largely under his inspiration that a remarkable program of public works, port and railroad construction, and sanitary engineering was carried through in that colony. He was less successful with his plans to make an equitable land settlement between the natives and the French settlers (*colons*), to bring all the tribes within the same legal system, and to extend the full rights of French citizenship to them. His famous decree of 1865, declaring full equality of rights between the Arabs and the *colons*, remained largely a dead letter; and the administrative and social problems of Algeria remained alive to vex Napoleon's successors.

At the other end of the Mediterranean, Napoleon intervened, as we have seen, to protect the rights of Roman Christians in the Holy Places (see pp. 165ff.)—a dispute which helped bring on the Crimean War— and in 1860 he acted, for much the same reason, in Syria. With this Turkish province, France had historical and sentimental ties—Napoleon III's own mother had written a song "*Partant pour la Syrie*," which was a kind of unofficial anthem during the Second Empire—and the French church had a close association with the Maronite sect of Christians in Lebanon. In the spring of 1860, the warlike tribe of Druses attacked and massacred thousands of the Maronites and some Jesuits working among them. The French government immediately notified the other powers of its intention to intervene to restore order and, despite momentary opposition on the part of the British, received their approval and landed six thousand troops in Lebanon, where they remained for a year.

An infinitely more significant example of French initiative was provided in this same decade in Egypt. Since the 1830s French engineers and traders had been interested in the possibility of constructing a canal across the isthmus of Suez between the Mediterranean and the Red Sea. In 1854 Ferdinand de Lesseps, a former vice-consul of France at Alexandria, persuaded the khedive of Egypt to grant him a concession to build one. Strictly speaking, the construction of the canal was a private undertaking; but, if it had not been for pressure by the French government at Constantinople, the sultan would probably have refused to approve the khedive's concession (as the British were seeking to make him do), and, if it had not been for French investors, who supplied the greater part of the capital needed, the canal could not have been built. When the first ship passed through this vital waterway in November 1869, it was wholly fitting, therefore, that the empress should have been her most honored passenger.

In other parts of the world also French influence was felt. Settlements were established on the west coast of Africa, and, between 1854 and 1864, General Faidherbe created the port of Dakar and laid the basis for the flourishing colony of Senegal. In Somaliland, Obok became a French base in 1862; and in the same year the naval captain Dupré negotiated a treaty of friendship and commerce with the king of Madagascar. In the Far East, the French government cooperated with the British in a joint diplomatic—and finally military—operation which forced the Chinese government, in the Treaty of Peking (October 1860), to open eleven new ports to European traders, to allow traffic on the Yangtse-Kiang, and to permit European traders to go into the interior; and French troops aided those of the Chinese government in putting down the Taiping Rebellion in 1864. In China proper, French influence remained greatly inferior to that of Britain; but in southeast Asia it grew rapidly. In 1859 Napoleon authorized a naval demonstration and landing at Saigon, and the following year he sent the troops that had been co-operating with the British in the north into Cochinchina. By the end of the decade all Indochina was under French control, the emperor was protector of Cambodia, and French traders were opening up the routes into South China.

To balance these not inconsiderable successes, there was one very considerable failure. In 1861 Napoleon decided to take advantage of the American Civil War and to send a military expedition into Mexico to overthrow the revolutionary government of Benito Jaurez (1806–1872) and establish a monarchy, in the person of the Archduke Maximilian of Austria. His motivation in transforming what had started as a joint Anglo-Franco-Spanish diplomatic campaign to force the Mexicans to respect foreign property rights into a unilateral imperialist adventure is somewhat obscure. He probably wished to persuade zealous Catholics to forgive his Italian policy by attacking a Mexican regime that was notorious for its anticlericalism; and he may have wished to win favor in Vienna by giving a throne to Maximilian. The part played by financiers with Mexican interests in shaping his decisions was probably less than it appeared to some contemporaries; but certainly economic considerations played a large part in this venture, for Napoleon had been interested in the economic potential of central America since the 1840s. Whatever his reasons, he set out to win Mexico, and suffered a spectacular defeat.

Considerable time passed before this became apparent. French troops took Puebla and Mexico City in the middle of 1863; an assembly of notables was convoked; and this body offered the crown to Maximilian, who accepted it with the sincere belief that it was his duty to do so and the hope that he could bring good government and prosperity to the Mexican people. For two years, Maximilian tried to rule the country. But he developed no popular backing; the *Juaristas* remained in control of the northern and southern districts of the country; and it was clear that only the French garrison prevented them from overthrowing the new ruler. That bulwark was not to last, for, when the American Civil War came to an end, the United States government invoked the Monroe Doctrine and demanded the withdrawal of the French troops. Not wishing war with the United States, Napoleon complied; and the completion of the evacuation in 1867 was followed swiftly by the execution of Maximilian by a firing squad at Queretaro. Napoleon's most daring overseas adventure had been a fiasco, which seriously impaired the emperor's personal prestige while, at the same time, by tying up a large body of French troops in Mexico, it weakened France's position in Europe.

The Dilemmas of Continental Policy / The main reason for the failure of the July Monarchy, Napoleon III was convinced, was the ineffectiveness of its foreign policy. Louis Philippe had done nothing to restore France to her rightful position of continental leadership and, by maladroitness and lack of energy, had allowed her to be isolated and humiliated by the other powers. Napoleon was determined that the French people would not one day make the same reproaches of his own conduct of foreign affairs, and he set out deliberately to make France's voice heard in the councils of Europe.

As he did so, however, he was conscious of the suspicions aroused by his name and by his assumption of the imperial title and of the danger of diplomatic isolation. In his first years, therefore, he sedulously sought the friendship of Great Britain; and his desire for the British alliance was probably the chief reason for his violating his own promise that *"l'Empire c'est la paix"* by taking France into the Crimean War.

The war achieved Napoleon's original foreign policy objectives. It demonstrated that France was a considerable military power (at least, in comparison with the British and Russian commands, the French showed something resembling military talent); it wiped out the memory of the setback in Egypt in 1840–1841; and, in the disorganized situation created by the war, it left France in an apparently dominant position. Certainly Paris now became the diplomatic capital of Europe; both the Russians and the British found French friendship valuable, and the emperor's advice was sought by lesser powers.

He could now look ahead toward the realization of greater ambitions. He had long believed that the most striking demonstration of France's recovery, and the most gratifying to French esteem, would be a thoroughgoing revision of the settlement that had been imposed on France at Vienna in 1815. In thinking of this, he does not seem to have envisaged any significant acquisitions of territory for France; it would be enough for Frenchmen to know that the new order came into being under her aegis. For the new Europe would be one based on "completed nationalities and satisfied general interests"; and the drawing of boundaries according to the principle of national self-determination would bring such harmony and prosperity to the continent that the country that inspired the transformation would be held in universal respect. This noble dream of international amity Napoleon had nurtured since his youth, when he had written that, if "the nationalities [were granted] the institutions they demand, . . . then all nations [would] be brothers, and they [would] embrace one another in the presence of tyranny dethroned, of a world refreshed and consoled, and of a contented humanity." Like the most fervent Mazzinian or Saint-Simonian, he still believed in it and thought it might be realized. Indeed, when in 1858 the principalities of Moldavia and Wallachia, with Napoleon's encouragement, united under one ruler and under common institutions and thus laid the foundations of modern Rumania, it appeared that the process of transformation might be beginning.

But there were dilemmas to be faced. Was it reasonable to suppose that Russia's new friendship with France, which began in 1856, would withstand the strain of an attempt to apply the principle of national self-determination to Poland, or that Prussia and Austria, who also had

The attempted assassination of the Emperor and Empress by Felice Orsini, January 14, 1858. This artist's reconstruction shows the scene in front of the old opera house on the Rue Le Peletier as the bombs exploded, killing or wounding several members of the imperial escort and injuring many in the crowd. From *L'Illustration*, Jan. 23, 1858.

Polish provinces, would tolerate any such proposal? Or—to bring things closer home—was it reasonable to suppose that the French people themselves would favor a transformation of Europe which would create a united Italy and a united Germany on France's flanks? Even if they acquiesced in the destruction of the pope's temporal power, which would follow Italian unification, would they accept the shift in the balance of power caused by the creation of two new and vigorous rivals without demanding territorial compensation for France; and, if Napoleon yielded to such demands, would he not confirm the old suspicions of the British, destroy the tie with London, compromise his principles, and become involved in a maze of contradictions?

Questions like these might have made another man hesitate. But in foreign policy Napoleon was always less responsive to doubts than to appeals to his faith in his grand design; and he was given a reminder of this kind in 1858. On the evening of January 14, as the imperial carriage drew up before the old Opera House, bringing Napoleon and Empress Eugénie to hear a performance of *William Tell*, there were three loud explosions; and the windows and gas lamps in the entrance way were shattered to bits, wounding 150 persons with flying glass and killing eight persons. The imperial carriage was virtually demolished, but Napoleon and his wife escaped serious harm and insisted upon entering the theater and showing themselves to the audience. Before the night was over, the police had rounded up the perpetrators of the attempted assassination. They were four Italian patriots who had been living in exile in London and had planned the *attentat* to call attention to the plight of their country. Their leader, Felice Orsini, who had spent his life fighting for Italian freedom and had made a dramatic escape some years before from the dreadful Austrian prison called the Spielberg, was condemned to death after a dramatic trial, in the course of which his counsel read a letter from him to the emperor. Orsini wrote,

> Upon your will hangs the fate of my country for good or ill. I adjure your Majesty to return to Italy the independence her children lost in 1849 through the fault of France. . . . As long as Italy is not independent, the peace of Europe and of Your Majesty will be but a will o' the wisp. Let not Your Majesty deny the last prayer of a patriot on the steps of the scaffold, but deliver my country, and the blessings of five-and-twenty millions of citizens will follow you down the ages.

This appeal could not but affect a man who had himself conspired against Austria in Italy and whose dream was of a Europe of free nationalities. Before the year was out, Napoleon's plans for Italy had taken shape and, with their execution in 1859, he became involved in the foreign complications that were in the end to bring his downfall.

8

The Unification of Italy

In 1858, when Orsini and his accomplices threw their homemade bombs at Napoleon's carriage, their own country was still what Metternich had once called it, "a geographical expression." Politically, there was no Italy, for the peninsula that bore that name was divided into a number of separate states: the Bourbon kingdom of Naples and Sicily in the south; the Papal States, which straddled the Apennine range and extended from the Roman Campagna north through Umbria and the Romagna to the Adriatic coast; the Grand Duchy of Tuscany, with its capital of Florence, and its two small neighbors to the north, the duchies of Modena and Parma, all three under rulers who were members of the Hapsburg family; Lombardy and Venetia, provinces directly under Austrian administration and legally part of the Austrian Empire; and, in the northwest corner, bordering on France, the state of Piedmont, ruled by the house of Savoy, which also had title to the island of Sardinia. Between these separate states there were only the most tenuous connections. The condition of transportation was still so primitive that there was no real economic bond between north and south; and, in a country where a native of the Romagna could understand the language neither of a peasant of Sicily nor of townsmen of Milan or Turin, it was impossible to talk of even cultural unity.

The economic and cultural divisions of Italy were to continue and to present problems for a long time; indeed, they have not yet been entirely overcome. This was not true of the political divisions, most of which were swept aside by the dramatic events that filled the three years that followed Orsini's *attentat*.

THE NATIONAL MOVEMENT TO 1859

The Growth of National Feeling / Among the intelligentsia and the progressive middle class there was, after 1815, a growing interest in the prospects of national unification. This feeling was inspired and strengthened by a number of things. The fact that northern Italy had been under French control in the days of the great Napoleon was of particular significance, for memories of the efficiency of French administration and the liberalism of French legal codes made men dissatisfied with the feudal and reactionary practices that were restored in most Italian states in 1815 and made them believe that unification would sweep these away and bring an enlightened and efficient regime. At the same time, the mercantile classes became increasingly interested in unification because it promised to bring solid economic advantages: the removal of customs barriers between the Italian states; a wider Italian market; the construction of an Italian rail net; and improvement of port facilities so that Italy could play a major role in the expansion of the Mediterranean trade promised by the advent of steam. There were visionaries who thought of Italy as the future main route between England and India, once a canal had been built at Suez and there was a railroad from Turin or Milan to the heel of the Italian boot.

The interest in and desire for unity was inspired also by a growing hatred of Austria, whose armies, based on the four great fortresses of Verona, Mantua, Peschiera, and Legnano (the Quadrilateral), not only secured Austrian possession of Lombardy and Venetia but dominated the whole peninsula and supported reactionary regimes in all states. The presence of the Austrians was in itself enough to be a perpetual reminder to a historically minded people of the reduced state to which they had fallen; and this sense of humiliation rings through many of the odes of the greatest Italian poet of this period, Giacomo Leopardi (1798–1837).

> O my country, I see the walls and the arches
> And the columns and the images and the solitary
> Towers of our Roman forbears—
> But I do not see the glory.[1]

[1] O patria mia, vedo le muri et gli archi
E le colonne e i simulacri et l'erme
Torri degli avi nostri,
Ma la gloria non vedo.—*All' Italia*.

Moreover, the ruthlessness with which the Austrians suppressed liberal movements like the risings of 1820 and 1821 and the brutal persecution they visited upon everyone suspected of subversive activity made the term *tedeschi* one of opprobrium throughout Italy and led thousands of young Italians to regard the expulsion of Austria as a mission calling for the full expenditure of their talents. This feeling was fed by books like Silvio Pellico's *My Prisons* (*Le Miei Prigioni*, 1832), a meticulous description of the author's ten years in the Austrian prison of the Spielberg in Moravia, where political prisoners were kept in close confinement, chained to their benches or the walls of their cells when they were not working, and where they often died of fatigue, ill-treatment, scurvy, or plain starvation. The tremendous popularity of Alessandro Manzoni's *The Betrothed* (*I Promessi Sposi*, 1827) was also partly due to anti-Austrian feeling, for this sentimental novel of life in the seventeenth century, when the Duchy of Milan was under Spanish rule, was filled with sketches of Spanish officialdom which could be interpreted as hidden attacks upon Austrian bureaucracy.[2]

Mazzini and Young Italy / For twenty years after the Congress of Vienna had confirmed Austrian domination in Italy, the most significant movement of resistance was the *Carboneria* or Society of Charcoal Burners. A secret revolutionary society, devoted to the expulsion of Austria from Italy, it had been active in the revolutions in Naples and Piedmont in 1820 and 1821 (see pp. 22–23) and in Modena and the Papal States in 1831. The failure of those risings demonstrated the weaknesses of the *Carboneria*: its loose regional organization tended to break down in times of crisis, while its failure to define its aims clearly meant that its membership was heterogeneous and incapable of uniting on tactics.

In 1831 a young Genoan, Guiseppe Mazzini (1805–1872), founded a new society that was intended to correct the weaknesses of the Charcoal Burners. It was called Young Italy; and it was designed as a national rather than a regional movement and one which, while necessarily secret with respect to its plans and tactics, was open with respect to its aims. Whereas the *Carbonari* had sought on occasion to win the sympathy and support of local rulers, Young Italy was opposed to cooperation with them. It was to be a people's movement, guided by a national directorate under Mazzini's leadership and dedicated to the establishment of a free, independent, and republican Italian nation.

An English contemporary once described Mazzini as having the greatest fascination of manner he had ever encountered; and this feeling

---

[2] The popularity of this novel, and the fact that the author, in the second edition, corrected the style to conform to the Tuscan dialect, helped confirm the primacy of Tuscan as the language of literature and to this extent also contributed to the unity movement.

Guiseppe Mazzini,
1805–1872
(THE BETTMANN ARCHIVE)

was shared by the great majority of those Italians who came to know him. The attractiveness of his personality was the result of his striking physical beauty, his indomitable courage, his infectious enthusiasm, his complete optimism, and, not least important, the essential idealism of his thinking about Italy's future. If Mazzini worked for national unity, it was not because he thought in terms of potential material or military strength or because he wanted his country to have the prestige of other great powers. His patriotism had none of the narrowness that was to characterize the nationalism of Bismarck, or even of Cavour, to say nothing of that of the patrioteers of the 1870s and 1880s. It was rather a genuine cosmopolitan philosophy. As Mazzini said in his essay on "The Duties of Man":

In laboring according to true principles for our Country we are laboring for Humanity; our Country is the fulcrum of the lever which we have to wield for the common good. . . . Humanity is a great army moving to the conquest of unknown lands, against powerful and wary enemies. The peoples are the different corps and divisions of that army. Each has a post entrusted to it; each a special operation to perform; and the common victory depends on the exactness with which the different operations are carried out. . . . Your Country is the token of the mission which God has given you to fulfil in Humanity. . . . [It is] a fellowship of free and equal men bound together in a brotherly concord of labor towards a single end.

Italy must, in short, be united so that she could play an effective part in leading the world to a better future, which—as Mazzini made clear else-where—would be one of mutual interdependence of nations, universal peace, and republican freedom.

This noble dream, which Mazzini believed could be achieved by democratic revolution against all existing authorities, was bound to have only a limited appeal. The rural masses were generally unmoved by it, bound as they were for the most part by old institutions and ways of thought; the middle classes, even when sympathetic to the idea of unity, were too property-conscious to welcome the kind of revolution that threatened to overthrow the social as well as the political structure. The philosophy of Young Italy had its greatest effect upon the radical in-telligentsia and upon inexperienced youth; and, as the years passed and Mazzini's faith in armed insurrection proved as barren of practical re-sults as the tactics of the *Carbonari* before him, the movement lost strength even among these groups.

It would nevertheless be difficult to overestimate the importance of Mazzini's role in forging Italian unity. He was without doubt the most eloquent and effective prophet of the *risorgimento*; and the generation that succeeded in uniting Italy was one that had been inspired, in its youth, by the articles, manifestoes, and pamphlets that poured from his pen. Even after his influence had begun to wane, it was strong enough, as we shall see, to act as a goad to Cavour, whose policy in the 1850s might have developed more slowly had he not been afraid of losing the initiative to the leader of Young Italy; and the Mazzinian faith in libera-tion by popular insurrection had its greatest triumph in southern Italy in 1860. For the unification of Italy, therefore, Mazzini must be given much of the credit, despite the fact that, when he died in 1872, he died a disappointed man who regarded the new Italian nation as a betrayal of his principles of republicanism and humanitarian nationalism.

The Neo-Guelf Movement / A second school of unitarian thought was the Neo-Guelf movement, which took its name from that of the medieval papal party. The idea that the papacy was the best instrument for unit-ing the Italian states and modernizing political institutions had always had supporters in Italy; and the belief in organized religion as the re-generating force in Italian life had been one of the themes in Manzoni's famous novel. In 1843 it was given new strength by the publication of a 700-page volume by V. Gioberti (1801–1852), *The Civil and Moral Primacy of the Italians,* in which the author called for a federation of all Italian states under the papacy, with executive power being wielded by a college of princes.

This work was widely read and loudly praised, although there were sceptics who pointed out that, for two problems, Gioberti's treatise had no answer. It neither offered a program for freeing Italy from the Austrians nor explained how an Italy federated under the papacy would escape the corruption and reactionary methods that characterized the administration of the Papal States. But these embarrassing questions did not immediately slow the momentum of the Neo-Guelf movement, for in 1846 a new pope was elected whose talents seemed admirably suited to the task of national leadership.

Giovanni Mastai Ferretti (1792–1878), who became Pope Pius IX in 1846, began his long tenure of office with the reputation of being a liberal and seemed bent upon proving that it was genuine. In his first two years, he issued political amnesties, allowed exiles to come back to Rome in freedom, granted limited freedom of speech and the press, and—at the beginning of 1848—agreed to the establishment of a council of elected deputies to share in the government of Rome. There was nothing very radical about any of these measures. The most that can be said of them was that they were more progressive than anything that had been experienced in the Papal States since 1815. But they annoyed the Austrians, who actually occupied the town of Ferrara with troops in August 1847 in protest against the direction of papal policy.

This in itself was enough to encourage many people who were devoted to the cause of unity, but were too moderate to follow Mazzini, to put their faith in Pius IX.

The Roman Republic and Garibaldi / The Neo-Guelf movement was not, however, to retain this initial strength, for in 1848 Italy was caught up in the tide of revolution; and, before it had ebbed, faith in papal leadership of the unity movement had been weakened even more seriously than confidence in the efficacy of Mazzinian methods.

The revolution in Palermo in January 1848, the granting of constitutional charters in Sardinia and Tuscany in the same month, and the rising of Milan against Austrian rule caused tremendous excitement in Rome; and the Neo-Guelfs were confident that Pius IX would lend his support to the revolutionary cause. When the war in Lombardy began, papal troops were actually dispatched to the north, presumably to cooperate with the armies of Sardinia. But the enthusiasm engendered by this action disappeared completely on April 29, 1848, when the pope announced that he was opposed to an offensive war against Austria and would not permit his troops to fight against fellow Catholics. With that statement Pius IX lost the support of all liberals.

He also lost control of his capital city, for his action discredited the moderates in Rome and stimulated a radical republican movement which grew rapidly during the summer months. By autumn, disorders were so great that the papal bureaucracy was helpless to control them. The Austrian victory in Lombardy in August merely aggravated the pope's troubles, for many of the soldiers of the defeated armies flocked to Rome to take up the fight there. On November 15 the Pope's chief minister, Pellegrino Rossi, was stabbed to death by Lombard Volunteers as he was entering the Palazzo dell Cancelliera for the new session of the Council of Deputies; and on the following day the mob demonstrated before the Quirinal and fired upon the pope's Swiss Guards. After trying vainly to ride out the storm, Pius IX fled the city on November 24, disguised as a simple priest. This action handed the city over to the republicans. A provisional government governed the city until a constituent assembly could be elected, and in February 1849 this latter body proclaimed Rome a republic and called Mazzini to the capital to head its first government.

The expulsion of the pope aroused the whole of the Catholic world; and the governments of Spain, Naples, and Austria indicated their intention of coming to his aid. As we have seen (see p. 180), they were anticipated by France. There, the Constituent Assembly voted funds in March 1849 for a military expedition whose mission would be to effect a reconciliation between the pope and his rebellious subjects. A French army of eight to ten thousand troops commanded by General Oudinot was, therefore, landed at Cività Vecchia in April. When its first advances toward Rome were repulsed by the rebels, however, Oudinot—acting on orders from the prince president, Louis Napoleon—abandoned his ill-defined mission of mediation and began operations that were designed to force the surrender of the republican government inside the city.

The defense of Rome was conducted by Giuseppe Garibaldi (1807–1882), whose life from this moment onward was inextricably entwined with the history of Italian unification. Born in Nice, Garibaldi spent his early years as a sailor, winning his master's certificate in 1832. In 1833 he met Mazzini and became a member of Young Italy, taking a solemn oath (to which he remained true) to fight against injustice, oppression, and tyranny and to make Italy a united nation. In 1834 he was expelled from the kingdom of Sardinia for revolutionary activity and, for the next thirteen years, lived as an exile and a soldier of fortune in Latin America, where he fought vainly against Brazil for the independence of the province of Rio Grande and, later, commanded the Uruguayan fleet and an Italian Legion in the service of Uruguay in war against Argentina. Thanks to this apprenticeship, he became a soldier of great talent, particularly skilled in the leadership of irregular forces and the conduct of guerrilla warfare. His political gifts were less noticeable, for he was an essentially simple man who thought in stereotypes and was irritated by those whose approach to the complications of Italian politics was more sophisticated. But his candor and forthrightness added to the impression made by the nobility of his bearing and the leonine cast of his features. Tennyson was not sneering when he wrote that Garibaldi had "the divine stupidity of a hero." His heroic qualities he certainly displayed in 1848, when he sped back to Italy at the first news of the revolution and led a legion of volunteers in the fight against Radetzky's troops in Lombardy. When the fortunes of war turned against Piedmont, he recruited another force, hoping to make his way to Venice to fight for the republic established by Manin in March (see p. 135); but the news of the murder of Rossi made him turn instead to Rome, where he placed his troops at Mazzini's disposal.

There was little likelihood that this motley group of adventurers, clad in red shirts and Calabrian hats and indifferently armed, and the other volunteers raised by Mazzini, could successfully withstand an assault upon Rome by a force of French professionals. Garibaldi would have preferred to remain in the mountains, conducting guerrilla operations and keeping the revolution alive. Mazzini, however, resolved on a defense of the capital, knowing that it would probably fail, in order, as he said, "to attract the eyes and reverence of my country towards [Rome] . . . to place her again at the summit, so that the Italians might again learn to regard her as the temple of their common country." His decision probably did have the long-term result that the European Powers came to believe that Rome would have to belong sooner or later to a united Italy; but, immediately, it doomed the city to a protracted siege in which prodigies of valor were performed by Garibaldi's legion but which was marked also by great destruction and loss of life.

Garibaldi defended the city against the pounding of Oudinot's army from the end of April to the end of June. When further resistance was hopeless, he was given permission to break out of the city and make his way north. He did so, hoping to arouse the countryside to new efforts; but the Italian people were unresponsive to his appeals, and his volunteers melted away. Hounded by Austrian detachments, he managed to reach San Marino, where he disbanded his army and slipped, with his wife Anita and a small number of followers, through the Austrian lines to the Adriatic Sea. Here his wife, who had been his loyal comrade in arms since he had wooed her in Brazil in 1839, died of exhaustion; and, crushed by this final disaster, Garibaldi went once more into exile.

Piedmont and the Policy of Cavour / When the revolution was finally liquidated in Rome and the rest of Italy, it was clear that the Neo-Guelf movement was dead, while the failure of any truly popular unitary movement to materialize had seriously weakened confidence in Mazzinian tactics. In the circumstances, those who continued to work for Italian unity turned increasingly for leadership to the Kingdom of Piedmont-Sardinia.

This was understandable. Of all the established regimes in Italy, the House of Savoy had been the only one to fight wholeheartedly for freedom from Austria. In March 1848 King Charles Albert had brought his army into the war in Lombardy and, although his conduct of the campaign was ineffective and had led to his crushing defeat at Custozza and his withdrawal from the war in August, he had reopened hostilities in the spring of 1849. This time his defeat had been even more disastrous (Novara, March 23, 1849), and the unfortunate king abdicated in favor of his son and went into exile, where he shortly died. When he did so, however, he was regarded by many as a martyr to the cause of Italian unity, and these same people looked to his successor to complete his work.

The new ruler, Victor Emmanuel II, was indeed to become the first king of united Italy. This was not, to be sure, because of any conspicuous political talent of his own. A rude, almost primitive man, Victor Emmanuel preferred the joys of the chase and the ballet to the labors of politics. His greatest contribution to the cause of Italian unity was the popularity he won for himself and the dynasty by his bluff manners and his almost excessive virility. But it may be noted in addition that he possessed a native shrewdness that also served Italy well, for it prevented him from indulging his own political preferences and made him accept the advice of a minister whom he personally detested, Count Camillo di Cavour (1810–1861).

Cavour became a member of the Piedmontese cabinet in 1850, after years of experience as a soldier, farmer, industrialist, and banker. Starting as minister for agriculture, industry, and commerce, he soon took over the portfolio for naval affairs as well and, by the time of the Crimean War, dominated the council of ministers. A round-faced, rather rumpled man, he bore a vague resemblance to Mr. Pickwick, but was considerably less ingenuous than that gentleman. The basic ingredient of his political genius was a strong sense of practicality—the ability to recognize the prerequisites of political success and the will to set about acquiring them before committing himself to a dangerous course of action.

It is this pragmatic approach to politics that explains Cavour's views on the national question. He was a Piedmontese patriot, whose greatest ambition was to increase the material and political strength of his country. As for unification in a wider sense, he was willing to consider it as a possibility but not to regard it as an end to which everything else must be sacrificed. After 1848, Cavour had no illusions about Italy "making herself" by a spontaneous mass movement of the kind imagined by the Mazzinians, and he was convinced that further attempts at popular

Count Camillo di Cavour,
1810–1861
(THE BETTMANN ARCHIVE)

insurrection would only delay Italian unity. If Italy were ever to be one, this would come only after Piedmont had expelled the Austrians from northern Italy and absorbed Lombardy and Venetia; and Custozza and Novara had shown that even this first step could not be achieved by Italians alone. The aid of a foreign power would be essential.

And how was one to win such aid? Surely the first step would be to dispel the idea that Italians were a volatile and irresponsible people, given to pointless political frenzies but incapable of considered action. What Italy needed was a period of domestic peace and progress that might help her accumulate political credit abroad; and Piedmont must set the example.

It was thoughts like these that determined Cavour's domestic policy in his own country in the 1850s. A convinced believer in the principles of English liberalism, he sought to make over Piedmont on the English model, and he came close to doing so. By a skillful amalgamation of the middle-of-the-road political groups (the so-called *connubio* or "marriage"), he forged a cohesive liberal-conservative alliance that was capable of controlling the parliamentary situation and of keeping the extremists to the left and right powerless. It was this bloc that carried through the great program of domestic reform that made Piedmont easily the most progressive of the states of Southern Europe—a program that included the stabilization of the currency, a reformation of the tax and tariff structure, the funding of the national debt, the improvement of the railway net and the establishment of a trans-Atlantic steamship system, the encouragement of new private enterprise, and numerous other projects that aroused interest throughout Italy and Europe.

If the *connubio* and the domestic program helped win the approval of the powers, and particularly of Great Britain and France, Piedmont's intervention in the Crimean War won their friendship. As has been pointed out, Cavour's action in this respect was planned at a time when it seemed certain that Austria would be an active ally of the west against Russia and was conceived of as a defensive measure. But Austria's failure in the end to enter the war enhanced the value of Piedmont's contribution; and the British and French governments showed their gratitude by allowing Cavour to deliver a scathing indictment of Austria's Italian policy during the peace negotiations in Paris.

Cavour believed that this gesture was an indication that Britain and France would support his country in the event that it went to war again against Austria. This was not immediately true; and, in conferences in London and Paris after the Peace Conference, he was advised not to force the pace in Italy and warned that he would have to pay the penalty for any irresponsible action. In other circumstances, Cavour might have accepted that advice; he could not now. The sentiment for national unity had received new impetus from Piedmont's role in the war and at the Paris conference, and it would not be denied. As Cavour wrote later:

> If we had dropped the flag that we waved at Paris, Mazzinianism would have recovered and the moral influence of the revolutionary party would have reached complete ascendancy.

If that happened, all his work would be undone. Realizing this, Cavour saw that he had to push ahead with his anti-Austrian program, while simultaneously seeking foreign support for the inevitable conflict.

To maintain Piedmont's ascendancy in the national movement, Cavour followed a deliberately provocative, and very well-advertised, program of anti-Austrian speeches in the Chamber, contrived diplomatic incidents, and various types of subversion. Simultaneously, he gave secret support to the National Society, an organization founded in 1856 by Daniele Manin, Giorgio Pallavicino, and the Sicilian La Farina for the purpose of uniting monarchists, federalists, and even republicans behind a movement to make Victor Emmanuel king of Italy. Cavour thought the ends of this society somewhat utopian, but he found it useful in spreading anti-Austrian propaganda and encouraging disaffection in Lombardy and Venetia.

For foreign support he turned back to Paris and, in the end, found Napoleon III—perhaps partly because of the shock caused by Orsini's bombs—willing to give him a sympathetic hearing.

THE FIRST STEPS TOWARD UNITY

The Plombières Agreement / On July 20, 1858 Cavour and Napoleon met and talked for five hours at Plombières les Bains. The meeting had been preceded by an elaborate correspondence during which the emperor's readiness to do something for Italy had become clear; and the details were now worked out without great difficulty. The emperor agreed that, if Piedmont found herself at war with Austria, she would receive the support of the armies of France. In the event of victory, Piedmont would be allowed to annex Lombardy and Venetia, Parma and Modena, and part of the Papal States. The rest of Italy would be constituted as a federation under the presidency of the pope, which would include this new Piedmontese Kingdom, as well as a Tuscan state enlarged by the acquisition of Papal Umbria and the Marches, a greatly reduced Roman state, and an unchanged Naples. France would receive Nice and Savoy, and the bargain would be sealed by the marriage of Victor Emmanuel's fifteen-year-old daughter Clotilde to Napoleon's cousin Jerome, a man rich in years and bad habits.

In the history of international affairs in the nineteenth century, Plombières represented a new departure. It was less a concerting of defensive measures against an expected attack than a deliberate attempt to manufacture a war. However one may judge the motives of the participants, their agreement was clearly aggressive in nature. In a letter to Victor Emmanuel Cavour described the way in which Napoleon and he spent the latter part of their conference poring over a map in a search for a place where an incident might be created that would provoke the Austrians to action and how, in the end, they decided that troubles deliberately incited in the Duchy of Modena might serve that purpose.

Yet, if Plombières stands as a classic example of the new *Realpolitik*, it must nevertheless be noted that the subsequent course of events was far different from what Cavour imagined it would be. Indeed, Cavour would probably not have gotten the war he wanted so badly at all, if it had not been for the unparalleled ineptitude of the Austrians. In the first place, they supplied him with a much better opportunity for spreading anti-Austrian sentiment than he would have found in Modena. This they did at the end of 1858 by imposing military conscription upon Lombardy and Venetia, which proved to be so unpopular that hundreds of draft-evaders fled to Piedmont, and Austrian demands for their extradition and Piedmontese refusals to comply led to mutual recrimination and mounting tension, especially in the frontier areas. This gave Cavour an excuse for beginning military preparations, which he did by floating an issue of war bonds in February, securing legislation for the creation of a body of volunteers, and persuading the king in March to call up the army reserves.

Cavour's road to war might still have been blocked by the Great Powers if it had not been for a second Austrian blunder. In March and April 1859, it appeared likely that international pressure upon Napoleon III was going to force him to withdraw from the engagement he had taken at Plombières. On April 18, indeed, the French emperor actually asked Cavour to agree to the beginning of demobilization in order to prepare the way for an international conference on Italian and related problems. But, at the very moment when Cavour was yielding, with a heavy heart and a feeling that all his cleverness had been to no purpose, Emperor Francis Joseph saved the day for him. On the advice of his military entourage, and apparently without the full knowledge of his civilian ministers, the Austrian monarch sent an ultimatum to the Piedmontese government, offering it the choice between immediate disarmament and war. Victor Emmanuel's government could not give way in face of threats, and war followed between the Hapsburg monarchy and the partners of Plombières.

Even so, the pattern of subsequent events bore little resemblance to the expectations that Cavour and Napoleon had when they made their pact.

The War of 1859 and the Armistice of Villafranca / The war began in late April and was conducted with a lack of decisiveness on both sides. The Austrian army possessed able commanders, like Benedek, and competent strategists, like Hess, who had planned the campaigns of 1848 and 1849; but Emperor Francis Joseph preferred to rely for military advice upon his adjutant general, Count Grünne, a courtier-soldier who had no combat experience; and Grünne's choice for supreme command in Italy was a general named Gyulai whose only talent was the ability to appreciate his own deficiencies. Gyulai sought so strenuously to avoid being appointed that Grünne had to write to him: "What is the matter with you? What an old ass like Radetzky could manage at the age of eighty you will surely be able to pull off." Grünne was wrong. Gyulai's timid conduct of operations allowed the French to make a juncture with the armies of their ally, and the result was the serious Austrian defeats at Magenta (June 4) and Solferino (June 24), the conquest of all Lombardy by the allies, and the occupation of Milan.

Determined action on the part of Napoleon III might at this point have led to the liberation of Venetia as well. But the French emperor, who had taken to the field with his armies, was shaken by the heavy losses at Solferino; he was discovering that the war was not popular at home, especially among loyal Catholics; and he was afraid that the Prussian army, already in the first stages of mobilization, might enter the war at any moment. Without consulting his ally, then, Napoleon began secret negotiations with the emperor of Austria and, finding him as eager to abandon the war as he had been to bolt into it, concluded an armistice with him at Villafranca on July 11. The terms agreed upon provided for the transfer of Lombardy to Piedmont; but, for the rest, they foresaw the restoration of the Grand Duke of Tuscany and the Duke of Modena to the thrones from which they had been driven during the war, and the establishment, under papal leadership, of an Italian confederation in which Austria, by virtue of her retention of Venetia, would be a member. These last provisions seemed to negate the purposes of the war and to confirm Austrian domination of Italy.

When Cavour heard of Villafranca from his king, he raved like a maniac, becoming so violent that Victor Emmanuel had to leave the room. Rather than approve this termination of the war he had planned, the Piedmontese statesman resigned his office. He might have spared himself the trouble, for here again the actual course of events defied his expectations.

Villafranca was, in fact, unenforceable. In Tuscany and Modena, and in Parma and the Romagna, where the governing authorities had been expelled during the fighting, it proved impossible to turn back the clock. Thanks to skillful propaganda and leadership by agents of the National Society, revolutionary assemblies in these states met in August 1859 and voted in favor of union with Piedmont; and, in the months that followed, it was clear that only the use of military force could make them change their decision. It was most unlikely that Napoleon could condone this and, if he did, it was clear that he would arouse the opposition of Great Britain, where a strong liberal government had come into power and was openly sympathetic to the aspirations of the people of central Italy. In January 1860, indeed, the British government let it be known that it favored "freedom from foreign interference by force of arms in the internal concerns of the people of Italy."

The return of Cavour to power in the same month facilitated a solution of this problem, for he now bluntly asked Napoleon's price for annexation. The emperor answered by giving him a choice. He would agree to

Piedmont's annexation of Parma and Modena, provided Tuscany and the Romagna were given separate administrations, with nominal papal authority retained in the latter; and for this he would ask no compensation. If, however, Piedmont insisted on the annexation of Tuscany and the Romagna as well, thus creating a powerful state on France's flank, he would have to be compensated by the cession of Nice and Savoy. Cavour and his king did not hesitate. They chose the latter alternative; and later, when he defended the cession of Nice and Savoy to France before the Piedmontese parliament, Cavour never even mentioned that it had not been strictly necessary.

In March 1860, plebiscites in the four areas of central Italy confirmed the popular desire for annexation to Piedmont; and in April they passed under Victor Emmanuel's rule. Cavour had won rather more than he had bargained for at Plombières. His accomplice, Napoleon III, had not been so fortunate. He had performed undeniable services for Italy, but Villafranca had diminished the gratitude he might have expected in return, while the papal losses of territory had alienated the French Catholics, and the acquisition of Nice and Savoy had seriously weakened his good relations with Great Britain, without having the compensating effect of allaying the misgivings of nationalists in his own country.

Garibaldi's Conquest of Naples / The momentum of the revolution was still by no means spent. The success of the national movement in central Italy was an encouragement to its supporters in the south; and, in the spring of 1860, disorders began to occur on the island of Sicily. These gave Garibaldi an opportunity to come again to the center of the political stage.

He had not, to be sure, been far from it during the past year. The outbreak of hostilities in 1859 had brought him back from his solitary home on the island of Caprera, and he had commanded a body of irregulars in the Lombard hills in the neighborhood of Como and Varese. Later, when the revolutionary governments of central Italy formed a military league, he commanded part of their forces. He proved to be a temperamental and unreliable subordinate, for he was impatient with the delays imposed by diplomacy, wanted to invade the other papal provinces without delay, and resented the refusal of the political authorities to agree. In the spring of 1860, he began to build up a personal army of his own, and there were fears in Piedmont that he might use this to attack Venetia or Rome, with unforeseen results. Instead, the Sicilian disorders, and the news that the people of that island were expecting his support, drew him to the south. In May, with a tiny force of 1000 red-shirted volunteers packed aboard two leaky steamers, he slipped through a screen of Neapolitan gunboats, landed at Marsala, and declared himself dictator of Sicily.

The king of Naples had 20,000 troops on the island of Sicily, which should have been more than enough to defeat Garibaldi's collection of poets, students, and soldiers of fortune. But the Neapolitans were divided among the coastal garrisons and allowed themselves to be outmaneuvered and defeated piecemeal. After an initial victory over 3000 Neapolitan troops at Calatafimi, Garibaldi's army won thousands of local recruits; a rising in Palermo helped open the road to that city; and within six weeks Garibaldi was living in the royal palace there. By mid-July the rest of the island was under his control, and his army—now 10,000 strong—was poised for the leap to the mainland.

Cavour had watched Garibaldi's actions with suspicion and misgivings. The whole expedition of the Thousand he regarded as Mazzinian enterprise, and he had no faith in Garibaldi's strong monarchical feelings and his sincere desire to unite Italy under Victor Emmanuel. He had done everything in his power to prevent Garibaldi's going to Sicily (although he tried to pretend later that he had aided the expedition), for he was sure that the adventure would either fail miserably or succeed so well that Garibaldi would be encouraged to try an assault on Rome, and, in either case, there would be international complications. A gradualist and a believer in diplomacy, Cavour had no sympathy for Garibaldi's precipitate tactics and, even when Sicily had fallen, he was opposed to a Garibaldian attempt against Naples itself. He was, indeed, actually in diplomatic communication with the Bourbon government of Naples, doubtless feeling that circumstances might arise that would make a deal between Piedmont and Naples expedient.

Garibaldi had now, however, aroused such a tide of popular enthusiasm that neither warnings nor diplomatic considerations could influence him. During the night of August 18 he crossed the Strait of Messina with a small advance force of 3500 men and within two days had forced the capitulation of the Neapolitan garrison at Reggio. Panic now affected the Bourbon armies, and they dispersed or capitulated at the very appearance of detachments of red shirts. Their resistance was so negligible that Garibaldi threw caution to the winds and, outpacing his own army, raced ahead to the city of Naples, which he entered with half a dozen companions on September 7.

To have conquered a country of eleven million people in less than five months was a remarkable achievement, but Garibaldi was never one to rest on his laurels, and he did not allow the rapturous acclamations of the citizens of Naples to divert him from his most cherished objective. He remembered his Mazzinian oath to devote his life to freeing all of Italy, and he doubtless also remembered his own defeat in the Holy City in 1849; and he began to plan an invasion of the Papal Marches. He was apparently being encouraged secretly by King Victor Emmanuel, who

The Right Leg in the Boot
at Last!
Garibaldi: "If it won't go
on, Sire, try a little more
powder!"

From *Punch,* Nov. 17, 1860.

seems to have felt that Garibaldi might free him from his dependence
upon Cavour and to have believed further that he had nothing to lose in
urging Garibaldi forward, since he could always disavow him in case of
failure.

Cavour may not have known of the irresponsible conduct of his sovereign (although he doubtless suspected it), but he was fully conscious
of Garibaldi's military preparations and aware that an attack on the
Marches would almost certainly lead to trouble at Rome, where—as he
never forgot—there was still a French garrison protecting the pope. He
therefore decided to forestall this danger by action of his own. After
preparing the way by convincing Napoleon III that it was necessary to
block the further progress of Garibaldi's adventurers and after assuring
him also that the position of Rome itself need not be affected, he threw
the bulk of the Piedmontese army into the Papal States. On September 18
they overwhelmed the pope's forces at Castelfidardo; they then crossed
into the state of Naples, defeated the Neapolitans at Capria, and bottled
up the last of the Bourbon forces in the fortress of Gaeta.

This forthright military action was not, in fact, necessary to block
Garibaldi, for in his northward drive he had become involved in a series
of dogged engagements with a large enemy force posted along the

Volturno River; and it was not until October that he had eked out a victory. But the Piedmontese invasion restored the initiative in the campaign for national unity to Cavour's hands, and he made the most of this. Even before the military issue had been decided, he had secured parliamentary consent for the annexation of southern Italy, provided it was approved by plebescite in the districts concerned; and in October plebescites in Naples, Sicily, the Marches, and Umbria voted overwhelmingly for union with Piedmont. In the face of this, Garibaldi surrendered his conquests to Victor Emmanuel and sailed off alone to his obscure island home. In February, after the end of Neapolitan resistance at Gaeta, the city of Turin witnessed the assembling of a new Italian parliament, representing the whole of the peninsula except Rome and Venetia, and Victor Emmanuel II was declared king of Italy. Shortly thereafter, the national government took up new headquarters in Florence, which was to be Italy's capital city until 1870.

THE COMPLETION OF ITALIAN UNITY, 1860–1871

Cavour's Work in Retrospect / The crowning of the achievements of 1859 and 1860 by the addition of Venetia and Rome to the united realm was to take another decade, and Cavour did not live to see it realized. Worn out by the pressures and anxieties of the period that opened at Plombières, he fell seriously ill in the spring of 1861 and died, at the age of fifty-one, in June of that year. In his relatively short career in public life he had displayed political gifts of the highest order and diplomatic adroitness unequaled by any other statesman in the long history of the Italian states. Even so, while granting this and his other great talents—his foresight in economic matters, for instance, and his contribution to the strengthening of parliamentary institutions in Italy—it is worth noting that, seen from the vantage point of the twentieth century, Cavour's contribution to the territorial and administrative unification of Italy seems somewhat less impressive, and his diplomatic methods seem considerably more questionable, than they were to contemporaries.

With respect to the latter point, it need only be said that Cavour's diplomacy was founded upon calculated duplicity and flagrant disregard for inherited values and the stipulations of the public law, and that its very success had the unfortunate effect of encouraging imitation. With respect to the former, it should be noted that, once the plebescites had been held, the Piedmontese government showed scant respect for the wishes or the traditional usages of their southern provinces, preferring to impose a rigidly centralized administrative system on the country as a whole. Had Cavour taken the trouble to visit the south in 1860, he might have sensed the opposition which centralization would surely arouse; but he refused even to go to Naples at the time of Victor Emmanuel's triumphal entry into that city, writing to a friend: "I am ready to sacrifice for the King my life and everything I own; but as a man I ask of him but one favor, to remain as far away from his person as possible."

This pettiness made impossible the accumulation of information that would have avoided trouble. As a result, the Piedmontese treated the kingdom of Naples almost as if it were an African colony; local customs and codes were ruthlessly stamped out; there were numerous and flagrant incidents of economic spoliation and exploitation by northern administrators; and, as a result, the popularity which Victor Emmanuel possessed when he rode into Naples in November had almost completely evaporated by January. Pro-Bourbon agitation was common in the 1860s; there were open brushes between Piedmontese troops and peasant bands; and the south started off its new life in the united Italy with a feeling of resentment against the foreigners of the north that is not entirely dead even today.

Venetia and Rome / The primary objective of the new Italy's policy in the 1860s was the acquisition of Venetia; and Cavour's successors took a leaf out of the master's book in pursuing this, for they relied entirely upon the expedients of diplomacy. Since even the most skillful diplomacy in the world could not persuade the Austrians voluntarily to abandon their last Italian possession, the Italian government had to take advantage of the growing friction between Prussia and Austria and to sell their services to the former before Venetia was acquired. Italy's participation in the German war of 1866 was inglorious. Her armies were soundly defeated by the Austrians, and her fleet was destroyed in the disastrous battle off Lissa; but Venetia was nevertheless granted to Italy when the Austrians surrendered to their German rival.

Rome was a more difficult problem. Thanks to Mazzini's decision in 1848 to fight for the city and thanks to Cavour's last political act, the securing of a parliamentary declaration that Rome should be the capital of Italy, most Italians regarded unification incomplete as long as the city remained independent. Yet Pope Pius IX steadfastly refused to compromise in any way with the new Italy, protesting formally against Victor Emmanuel's assumption of the Italian crown; and Pius was still protected by a French garrison. There was reason to believe that Napoleon III was willing to terminate the military situation he had created in sending Oudinot's army to Rome in 1849—and as the emperor's political troubles multiplied in the late 1860s he became more so—but he was always restrained by the fear of alienating Catholic votes at home.

On two occasions, in 1862 and in 1867, Garibaldi, with oddly assorted and ill-equipped bands, tried to reach the Holy City. In the first attempt he was stopped by royal troops; and in 1867 his forces came under the merciless fire of the new French rifle—the chassepot—and ran away, in Garibaldi's own words, "like cowardly rabbits." This latter expedition had been secretly encouraged by Victor Emmanuel, although he denied it. Its only result was to cause parliamentary storms in Piedmont and to confirm French protection of Rome.

In the end, Rome was occupied by royal troops when there was no one to challenge their entrance into the city—during the Franco-Prussian war, when French armies were otherwise engaged. The royal government immediately transferred its capital to the Holy City, while the pope, withdrawing behind the walls of the Vatican, continued his steadfast opposition to the regime that now controlled the whole peninsula.

9

The German Question, 1850-1866

The events that had taken place in Italy in 1859 and 1860 had their counterpart in Germany in the decade that followed. There too the leadership in the movement toward national unification was taken by the strongest and economically most progressive of the interested states. There too the process was achieved by war and by the subsequent absorption of some of the lesser states by the victor and the imposition of his control over the others. And there too the victim was Austria, whose position in Germany was destroyed as completely as her position in Italy had been, with serious resultant repercussions on the internal structure of the Hapsburg Empire.

THE EVOLUTION OF PRUSSIAN POLICY

Prussia after 1850 / To the ordinary observer of German affairs in 1850 it would not have appeared likely that Prussia would extend her hegemony over Germany in the foreseeable future. It was true that the Prussian government had shown more imagination in economic affairs than other governments and had maintained the primacy Prussia had won in commercial matters when the *Zollverein* was founded earlier in the century (see pp. 49–50); and it was true that great economic progress had been made in the Prussian kingdom. Berlin had grown in two decades from a provincial capital to a thriving commercial center of 450,000 inhabitants, and Cologne, Magdeburg, and Breslau were growing fast. By 1860 the kingdom would have 3750 miles of all-season roads, a ninefold increase since 1815, and a railway net that was developing as quickly as any in Europe. Industrial production was expanding rapidly and becoming increasingly mechanized, the number of steam engines employed growing almost six times in the decade following the revolutions of 1848. The textile and clothing industry was still the most important single industry, but the iron, steel, and machine works of the Rhineland and Silesia were now beginning a period of marked growth, and smaller industries—brick kilns, breweries, saw mills, distilleries, refineries, and the like—were moving out into the rural areas and changing the predominantly agricultural character of the kingdom. All of this vitality and development was in sharp contrast to conditions in other German states and particularly in Austria, where industrial growth was slow, communications backward, and government encouragement of economic progress virtually nonexistent.

Leaving economic progress aside, however, there were few other obvious indications of progress in the Prussia of the 1850s and none of the kind of political enlightenment that would, presumably, be required if Prussia was to become the acknowledged leader of the movement for national unification.

For a decade after the revolutions of 1848, Prussian policy, both domestic and foreign, was completely negative in character. Despite Prussia's transformation into a constitutional state, and despite the marked growth of the middle class as a result of the economic growth of the country, political power was still in the hands of the aristocracy and the large landholders, who were entrenched in key positions at court, in the state administration and the army command, and in the upper house of parliament. This ruling caste devoted its energies to guarding against the possibility of any recurrence of revolutionary agitation, by persecuting persons who were suspected of harboring democratic or socialist ideas and by suppressing newspapers, books, and plays that expressed progressive sentiments. In foreign affairs it had no interest and made no attempt to pursue an independent policy, preferring rather to follow the advice of Austria and, whenever possible, Russia. In effect, this meant acquiescing in the dominance in German affairs that Austria had won at Olmütz. Not all Prussians, to be sure, liked this policy of playing second fiddle to Vienna, and some argued that Prussia should take advantage of Austria's foreign difficulties to extend her influence and territory in Germany; but even in 1859, when

Austria was at war with France and Piedmont, the Prussian government made no attempt to experiment with this kind of realism and, if the war had lasted a few weeks longer, Prussia would probably have intervened on Austria's side.

The possibility of Prussia's playing an independent hand in German affairs and making any significant contribution to the cause of national unification seemed to be even further reduced after Frederick William IV yielded the throne to his brother William, who became regent in 1858 and king in January 1861. The accession of this ruler was hailed as the beginning of a "New Era"; but William was already sixty-one years old when he became regent and was, if anything, more conservative than his brother. In any case, his coming to power was followed by a domestic conflict that threatened to make Prussia a complete nullity in foreign and German affairs.

The Constitutional Conflict / The reasons for this were rooted in the character of William I. A soldier by profession, he had long been critical of certain aspects of Prussian military organization and particularly of two things: the restriction of the term of active service, in most cases, to two years, and the heavy reliance placed upon a civilian militia (*Landwehr*) which elected its own officers and was largely independent of the regular army. In February 1860, on the basis of plans drawn up by his war minister, Albrecht von Roon (1803–1879), William laid an army reorganization bill before the Prussian parliament. It called for a marked increase in the annual number of conscripts to provide for a regular army double its present size; it lengthened the term of service to three years, with corresponding adjustments for special services and the reserve; it sharply diminished the role and the independence of the *Landwehr*; and it asked for a greatly expanded military budget to pay for the new regiments envisaged, as well as for barracks, schools, and training grounds.

This bill aroused the immediate opposition of the Prussian middle class, which was generally liberal in its views and suspicious of the military establishment on economic and political grounds; and its representatives—who, thanks to the franchise provisions of the constitution (see p. 143), now controlled the majority of seats in the Prussian Chamber of Deputies—attacked the proposed reform. Some of them objected to the cost of the reorganization. Others, mindful of the role played by the *Landwehr* in the fight against Napoleon, protested that the reform would destroy the "citizen-soldier" tradition. Some suggested that the lengthening of the term of service was designed to "militarize" the conscripts and turn them against liberal and civilian values. Finally, many noted that, since Prussia had no foreign policy, she had no need of a larger military force; and they went on to charge that the new units would be employed only as a police force to subvert popular liberties. When the bill went to committee, so many amendments were proposed that the government withdrew the proposed legislation from consideration.

In doing so, it asked for an extraordinary sum of 9,000,000 thaler to strengthen existing units of the army; and this the Chamber of Deputies granted on the understanding that the sum would not be used to make departures from the existing law. Once he had this money in his possession, however, William proceeded to use it to effect the changes for which he had not been able to win approval. Not unnaturally the liberal majority protested, and throughout 1861 they demanded that their ruler submit a comprehensive military reform bill for their approval. When the king did so at the beginning of 1862, laying before them proposals virtually identical with those of 1860, they defeated them out of hand and refused to make any further grant of funds to the government unless the recent military innovations were withdrawn, the two-year service term restored, the *Landwehr's* position protected, and the military budget completely itemized. The king's answer to this was to dissolve the Chamber. When new elections were held in May, however, the liberal majority was strengthened, rather than weakened, as he had hoped.

What followed was a complete and dangerous deadlock. Emboldened by their electoral success and led now by the new Progressive party, which had emerged in 1861, the liberal opposition became more ambitious, seeing in the crisis an opportunity to gain control not only over the army but over all aspects of the state administration, and more intransigent, abandoning their earlier willingness to compromise. On the other hand, the conservative forces, confronted by what seemed to them to be a revival of the spirit of 1848, became equally inflexible and increasingly inclined to listen to those reactionaries who argued that force alone would solve the parliamentary problem. In the immediate entourage of the king, men like Edwin von Manteuffel, chief of William's military cabinet, actually urged that the crisis be exploited in such a way as to force a liberal insurrection, or agitations that could be described as such, which could then be put down by military means and punished by the revocation of the constitution and a return to absolute government. One shrewd observer wrote at the time: "The military are panting after riots like the hart after the waterbrooks."

The king resisted the advice of his more reactionary advisers, for he had sworn to uphold the constitution and he took his oath seriously. But he resented the pretensions of the parliamentarians and refused either to yield to their desires or to undo the military reforms already instituted. Since the Chamber simultaneously held to its refusal to vote any funds for the conduct of state affairs unless it had its way, Prussian government was threatened with complete paralysis, and the king, in despair, seriously considered giving up his throne. When he had got to the point of drafting an abdication note, however, his war minister urged him to see whether a new chief minister might not be able to break the impasse and persuaded him, in September 1862, to appoint Otto von Bismarck (1815–1898) as his minister president.

Bismarck's Political Ideas / Because it was known that he had been an outspoken foe of the revolution of March 1848 and had violently opposed all royal concessions made at that time, Bismarck was generally considered to be a reactionary; and his appointment was greeted with satisfaction by those who hoped to crush liberalism once and for all. In reality, although he was himself an East Elbian landholder, the new minister president had none of the provincialism of his fellow *Junkers* nor was he, like them, preoccupied only with the domestic issues involved in the constitutional conflict. Since 1850, he had been serving his country as a diplomat, first in the Diet of the Germanic Confederation at Frankfurt, later in St. Petersburg and Paris; and this experience had broadened his vision and his ambitions for Prussia. Far from sharing the sentimental attachment to Austria that Prussian conservatives generally favored, he had become convinced that it was Prussia's destiny to extend her power in Germany, and that this could be accomplished only at the expense of Austria. As early as 1856 Bismarck had written: "Germany is clearly too small for us both. . . . In the not too distant future, we shall have to fight for our existence against Austria . . . since the course of events in Germany has no other solution."

Bismarck's views on the German question necessarily influenced his attitude toward the conflict with parliament. He fully agreed with the king's desire to reform the army, which would, after all, be the instrument that assured Prussian growth; and, as a supporter of the monarchical principle, he was opposed to any increase in parliamentary powers. On the other hand, he knew that, in the eventual struggle with Austria, Prussia would need the intelligence and industry of the midde classes just as much as the valor of the army and that the liberal opposition, for economic and other reasons, would be more sympathetic to his German plans than his fellow *Junkers*. He had no desire to turn the clock back by smashing the constitutional regime, for this would merely confirm Prussia's servitude to Austria.

After an initial attempt to persuade the parliamentary opposition to compromise, which was unsuccessful, Bismarck did not therefore go over to the camp of the extreme absolutists but struck out on a completely novel line. He decided to ignore the Chamber's failure to support the

Bismarck at the time of the Prussian constitutional conflict. From *Illustrated London News*, Sept. 29, 1866.

government's policy. If the Chamber of Deputies would not vote the budget, he said, "we will take the money where we find it." He ordered the civil service to carry out their duties—including those of recruiting troops and collecting the taxes needed to support government activities—with no regard for the speeches in parliament; and he punished or dismissed national, provincial, or city officials who had any qualms about this or who associated with the Progressive party in any way.

These tactics kept the government going. They did not weaken the parliamentary opposition, which increased its strength in the elections of 1863; but this was an illusory gain. Bismarck was by now looking beyond the walls of parliament to the world of foreign affairs. It was his belief that an active and successful foreign policy, which demonstrated the need for an effective army, would break the opposition and swing many of the liberals to his side; and he was determined to act upon this principle.

His first sally into foreign politics did not justify his hopes, although it was successful to a degree not realized at the time. In 1863, when the Poles rose against their Russian overlord (see p. 238), Bismarck concluded a secret convention with the Russian government providing for collaboration in suppressing the revolt. He did this out of fear that the tsar might otherwise defer to the pressure of the western powers and free Poland, in which case Prussia could expect serious trouble in her own Polish districts. Bismarck's action paid unexpected dividends. It not only encouraged the tsar to stand firm, but it helped persuade him to reorient his foreign policy, breaking off the cordial relations that he had had since the Crimean War with France (who had been overzealous in her support of the Poles) and inaugurating a friendship with Prussia that was going to last for almost thirty years.

Bismarck's convention with Russia was not of any immediate use in solving his domestic troubles, for it was roundly attacked by the liberals. Their opposition was to be far less united, however, to the minister president's next move in the foreign field.

FROM DÜPPEL TO KÖNIGGRÄTZ

Schleswig and Holstein / In the last months of 1863 a new chapter opened in the tangled history of Schleswig and Holstein.[1] Those provinces, thanks to the historical accident that one of their dukes had become king of Denmark, had for years been among the personal possessions of the Danish sovereign, without actually being part of the Danish kingdom. A further complication arose from the fact that Holstein, whose population was almost entirely German, was a member of the Germanic Confederation, while Schleswig was not, although its German citizens, comprising two thirds of its population, wished it to become so. This last wish was violently opposed by the Danish minority which wanted Schleswig to be absorbed by Denmark; and, in November 1863, the wishes of these nationalists were gratified by the promulgation of a new Danish constitution, which declared Schleswig an integral part of the kingdom.

This action was resisted in both Schleswig and Holstein and it touched off a wave of nationalistic indignation in Germany, where the Federal Diet immediately protested and, when its protest was unavailing, ordered a federal army to prevent the execution of the terms of Denmark's new constitution. Throughout Germany there was a vocal desire for the severance of all ties between Denmark and the two duchies, and the establishment of the latter as independent members of the Confederation.

Bismarck's conduct in the subsequent course of this dispute was so devious that one cannot, with any confidence, say what his thoughts and

[1] Lord Palmerston once said that only three men had ever fully understood the complications of the Schleswig-Holstein question and that unfortunately one (the Prince Consort) was dead, one (a former Foreign Office clerk) had gone mad, and he himself, the third, had forgotten them.

intentions were at any given moment. It seems clear, however, that he was always opposed to a solution that would have turned the duchies, which were of great potential strategic importance to Prussia, into independent federal states; and he probably thought from the beginning in terms of eventual Prussian annexation. He did not, in any case, publish his true views but instead—when the crisis broke out—stood forward as a defender of the treaty of 1852, by which the European concert had assured the king of Denmark possession of the duchies, provided their autonomous position was left unchanged (see p. 163). He urged the Austrian government to join Prussia in upholding international law, and the Vienna government, doubtless feeling that it might be awkward to do anything else, agreed. Disregarding the action of the Germanic Confederation, therefore, the two powers sent an ultimatum to the Danes, demanding that the new constitution be revoked; and, when the Danes refused (as Bismarck had calculated they would), they declared war.

The Danish war is important, principally, for three reasons. In the first place, it provided a baptism of fire, and a completely gratifying one, for the new Prussian army. It was in the campaign in Jutland that the field commanders who were later to defeat Austrian and French armies were tested, and it was here that the architect of those later victories, Chief of the General Staff Helmuth von Moltke (1800–1891), won the confidence of the king. And it was in this war, and particularly in the successful assault of the formidable Danish strongpoint of Düppel, that the army as a whole called itself to the attention of Europe. The victory at Düppel was described by the historian Droysen as "one of the events that mark an epoch in a nation's history"; and this is just, for it aroused a degree of patriotic pride that simultaneously weakened liberal opposition to the much-contested army reform and strengthened the tendency of German nationalists to look to Prussia for leadership.

Aside from this, the Danish war demonstrated the inadequacy of the European Concert in this new age, for, when the European powers, midway in the war, held a conference on the Schleswig-Holstein question, they were unable to agree on a settlement that would satisfy all parties and were powerless to prevent the resumption of hostilities, which continued until Denmark was defeated by the German powers and deprived of the duchies.

Austro-Prussian Friction / The comradeship in arms against the Danes had temporarily relieved a deterioration of Austro-Prussian relations that had continued since 1859 and had been marked, on each side, by economic maneuvering and attempts to reform the machinery of the Germanic Confederation to its own advantage. The rapprochement effected by the war was, however, quickly broken down by the failure of the allies to agree on the disposition of the spoils. Denmark, in defeat, had been forced to hand Schleswig and Holstein over to the victors; and it was up to them to decide their future. The Austrian government advocated the establishment of a separate Schleswig-Holstein state; Bismarck, with annexation in the back of his mind, took the position that this could be permitted only on condition that far-reaching military and commercial rights be granted to Prussia—that Kiel, for instance, be made a Prussian naval base. To this the Austrians, not unnaturally, refused to agree.

This Austrian opposition had the effect of causing a fundamental change in the attitude of the Prussian court, and of Prussian conservatives in general, toward the Hapsburg monarchy. The king, who was proud of his army's performance in the recent war, gradually, unconsciously, but nonetheless firmly, began to regard the duchies as having been won by Prussia alone and to view Austria's policy as an attempt to deprive Prussian troops of their legitimate reward; and, like him, the traditionally pro-Austrian conservative circles showed increasing irritation over Austrian tactics. It is significant that, in May 1865, a Prussian crown council could actually discuss the advisability of forcing war upon Austria if her government did not change its position.

The Prussian government did not force the issue in 1865, primarily because it realized that the power that took the initiative in precipitating a territorial dispute would find German public opinion solidly against it. Instead, after much involved haggling, the two disputants concluded the so-called Convention of Gastein (August 1865) by which they divided the duchies between them—Austria taking over the administration of Holstein and Prussia that of Schleswig. It is difficult to understand why the Austrians agreed to this arrangement, or why they insisted it be a temporary rather than a definitive one, for this meant that Prussia reserved her rights in Holstein and could protest against anything that happened there that was not to her liking. This blunder played into Bismarck's hands and enabled him to create incidents that, he hoped, would further alienate his sovereign's sympathies from Vienna and might even goad the Austrians into injudicious action that would give Prussia an excuse for war.

Meanwhile, the minister president took the political steps that he felt, would assure success if the Austrians were persuaded to force the issue. In the first place, he made his diplomatic preparations for war. He was reasonably sure that neither Great Britain nor Russia would intervene in the event of war; but France's attitude was doubtful and, like Cavour before him, Bismarck found it expedient to have discussions with Napoleon III. These took place at Biarritz in October 1865, and, while no written agreement was made, there seems to have been an understanding that France would remain neutral in the case of a German war, although she might receive some territorial compensation along the Rhine if a successful Prussia felt called upon to make extensive annexations in Germany. The vagueness of this agreement, if it may be called that, was probably due to Napoleon's belief that a German war would be a protracted struggle with results far different from those imagined by Bismarck and that his own role and compensation would be best determined during the hostilities. But the Biarritz meeting gave Bismarck a reasonable assurance against interference by France; and he strengthened it, and created military complications for his opponents, by concluding an alliance with the government of Italy in April 1866, by which Italy agreed to fight on Prussia's side if war came within the next three months, and Prussia agreed to reward her with the province of Venetia. This pact with Italy was a violation of Prussia's obligation to the Germanic Confederation, which bound her not to make alliances against fellow members; but Bismarck was too much the *Realpolitiker* to be deterred by that.

Simultaneously, Bismarck made his bid for the support of German public opinion by proposing a thoroughgoing reform of the Germanic Confederation, to be effected by adding to that body a national assembly elected by universal suffrage in all the German states. This revolutionary proposal, which summoned up memories of the Frankfurt Assembly and which could not, by any stretch of the imagination, be accepted by the Austrian government, bewildered but impressed liberal opinion throughout Germany, which had long been drawn to Prussia by her economic and political vigor but repelled by her reputation for reactionary government and militarism. To the extent that it did so, it prepared the way for the radical revision of the tenets of German liberalism that was soon to come.

Bismarck's tactics in Holstein and in the Diet at Frankfurt were in the end successful. As early as April 1866 the Austrians had convinced themselves that war was inevitable—"How can one avoid war," Francis Joseph was reported to have said, "when the other side wants it?"—and, after that, they neither tried very hard to avoid it nor guarded against measures that might seem to indicate that they were responsible for causing it. They actually resigned themselves to the loss of Venetia, promising Napoleon III (who was by now negotiating with both sides) that they would cede it to him for transfer to Italy if he would maintain a benevolent neutrality in case of war. One might have thought that the knowledge that Venetia was lost to them regardless of the fortunes of war would have persuaded the Vienna cabinet to grasp at any straw to avoid a conflict. Instead, it was Austria that first began the mobilization of troops; and, when Napoleon III suggested an international conference of the powers to consider the whole German question, it was Austria's objections and conditions that made the meeting impossible.

After that events moved swiftly. On June 1, 1866, Austria brought the Schleswig-Holstein question before the Diet of the Germanic Confederation, a move of questionable legality which Bismarck immediately declared a violation of the Gastein Convention. The Prussians immediately moved into Holstein. The Austrian government countered with a demand for military action by the Confederation against Prussia, and the Diet voted in favor of this on June 14. The Prussian government had warned that this would be considered as a declaration of war. They now declared the Confederation dissolved and threw their armies into the field.

The Seven Weeks' War / The war between Austria and Prussia lasted a scant seven weeks and ended with the overwhelming defeat of Austria. The Austrian debacle was the result of a number of factors. The army, for one thing, had not kept abreast of the latest military advances. Its administration and its intelligence and staff work were lamentably deficient in comparison with the Prussian army's General Staff system, which was unrivaled for efficiency in Europe. Its commanding generals, including Benedek, the commander-in-chief on the Bohemian front, lacked confidence and—thanks to the role played by imperial favoritism in the upper echelons of the army—had insufficient control over their subordinates. The troops were willing and brave, but they were trained in outmoded shock tactics in a day when battles were won by superior firepower; and they found it virtually impossible to come to grips with the Prussian infantry, who were armed with the new Dreyse "needle-gun," a breech-loading rifle that fired farther and more rapidly than their own hand weapons.

In addition, Italy's intervention in the war forced Austria to fight on two fronts and made impossible a concentration of all forces against Prussia. This need not have been as serious as it turned out to be, for, as early as June 24, the Austrians virtually knocked Italy out of the war by a crushing victory at Custozza, which should have freed troops for transfer to the Bohemian front.

But the truly decisive factor in the war proved to be Austria's deficiency in railroads. This not only made the movement of troops from the Italian front difficult but reduced Austrian mobility and paralyzed Austrian energies generally. The fact that there was only one main line running north from Vienna to Olmütz meant that the route to the main theater of war was clogged. It was this that prevented Austrian troops, despite a head start in mobilization, from effecting a juncture with their

Cavalry fight at Nachod. On June 27, 1866, in the first serious clash of the German war, General von Steinmetz won a brilliant victory over the Austrians at Nachod in the Bohemian plain. The Dreyse "needle gun" gave the Prussian superior fire power (their casualties numbered only 2100 compared to the Austrians' 5700). From *Illustrierte Zeitung*, August 1866.

German allies and deprived Benedek of the reinforcements he wanted when he took his stand on the Bohemian plain.

In contrast, the Prussians had a highly developed rail net that enabled the chief of staff, Moltke, to deploy his troops along an arc 600 miles wide, from the Elbe to the Neisse, to overrun the middle states and defeat the army of Hanover, and then to concentrate his forces against Benedek. The decisive battle of the war was fought on July 4, 1866, at Königgrätz, and it was an almost perfect illustration of the way in which Moltke's principle of "dispersed advance but concentration on the battle-field" could be applied to encircle and defeat an enemy. The trap did not quite close, and some of Benedek's army escaped; but the defeat was, nonetheless, a shattering one and decided the result of the war.

For the student of the political aspects of military affairs the war between Austria and Prussia has a special interest, for it illustrates the sharp conflict between civilian and military authority that became commonplace as techniques of warfare expanded in scope and in technical complexity. After Königgrätz Bismarck had serious difficulties with the Prussian High Command which, now that it smelled victory, wished to make it as big as possible, with heavy annexations of Austrian territory and a triumphal march into the Austrian capital. Bismarck opposed this because it would needlessly protract the war, thus increasing the risk of intervention by the other powers. During July, through his ambassador in Paris, he was carrying on delicate negotiations with Napoleon III, seeking to win his permission to organize all north Germany into a new confederation under Prussian leadership and, simultaneously, to make very extensive annexations. He was afraid that the policy favored by the soldiers and the king would make those negotiations fail and bring Napoleon to Austria's side. Moreover, he saw no point in inflicting needless punishment upon Austria, for it would only serve as a barrier to future friendship.

After the great victory in Bohemia, then, Bismarck boldly opposed all military plans for new advances to the southeast, and by doing so he earned the dislike of Moltke and the circle of young General Staff Officers called "The Demigods," who resented a civilian intervening in what they considered a strictly military sphere. Four years later, during the war against France, they showed that their resentment was still alive, by seeking to exclude Bismarck from all strategical conferences, even when political issues were at stake. In 1870 as in 1866, however, Bismarck had his way, pointing out that as long as he was responsible for policy, he could not cede his powers to soldiers simply because there happened to be a war on, and that, in any case, wars were fought for political objectives and should stop when those objectives were achieved. In 1866, he was aided in winning his point by Napoleon III's agreement that Prussia could have the annexations she desired in north Germany and could organize Germany north of the Main into a confederation, provided the southern states of Baden, Württemberg, and Bavaria remained independent and Saxony was not wholly destroyed. Even so, to make King William, who was more belligerent than his most belligerent soldiers, agree to make peace on these handsome terms was not easy; and Bismarck had to enlist the support of the Crown Prince and to threaten resignation before William was won over.

Peace terms were drawn up at Nikolsburg in July and confirmed and completed by the Peace of Prague a month later. Austria was forced to recognize its permanent separation from Germany, to pay a small indemnity, and to cede Venetia to Italy. Otherwise it lost nothing. Its German allies were less fortunate. The kingdom of Hanover, the duchies of Nassau and Hesse-Cassel, and the free city of Frankfurt were annexed by Prussia, whose territory was now united by the absorption of all the states between her eastern and western provinces and increased by 1300 square miles and four and a half million new subjects. All north Germany was under Prussian control, and even the independence of the southern states, upon which Napoleon III had insisted, was compromised, for, immediately after the re-establishment of peace, Bismarck negotiated offensive and defensive military alliances with all of them.

THE CONSEQUENCES OF THE WAR

Dualism in the Austrian Empire / Austria's defeat and its subsequent exclusion from Germany made it imperative for the Hapsburg monarchy to hasten the execution of plans which transformed the internal structure of the empire but which, as events were to prove, aggravated rather than alleviated its most pressing internal problems. To understand this change it is necessary to return, very briefly, to the events of 1848–1849.

The revolutions of those years had shaken the empire to its foundations and had revealed grave dissatisfaction, on the part of Austria's subject nationalities, with a form of government that did not recognize their historical rights or give scope to their cultural differences. They seemed to indicate further that a federal structure—similar to that proposed in the constitution drawn up at Kremsier (see pp. 149–150)—would have the best chance of holding the multinational empire together. These things, however, were completely disregarded by Francis Joseph and the Schwarzenberg government, who, after the revolutions had been suppressed, made absolutism and centralization their guiding principles. In the ten years that followed, local diets were abolished and the ancient constitution of Hungary was declared in abeyance; and the empire was ruled by an elaborately bureaucratic machine. This was directed by the minister of the interior, Alexander Bach, who sent his civil servants into every nook and cranny of the empire to supervise recruiting, collect taxes, and exercise judicial and administrative functions, and was supported, whenever local disaffection occurred, by the secret police and the army.

This system was unpopular throughout the empire, and most of all in Hungary, where resentment over the suppression of ancient rights took active forms and was one of the reasons for the uncertainty and vacillation of Francis Joseph's foreign policy during the Crimean War. But it was not until 1859, when the defeat in Italy shook the prestige of the monarchy, that the government became seriously concerned about the opposition to the Bach system and began to consider reforms.

In 1860 and 1861 the provincial diets were revived; the competence of the Imperial Council (*Reichsrat*) was broadened to give it the appearance of a consultative chamber; and a whole series of imperial declarations were issued, asserting the government's intention of recognizing the rights of all its subject peoples and of moving toward a constitutional system. To give a detailed description of these plans and declarations, and the subsequent ones that filled the years before 1866, would be otiose. The important thing about them all is that they were vitiated by the emperor's reluctance to countenance anything resembling genuine federalism or to abandon the bureaucratic methods to which he was accustomed. Thus, in 1860, while claiming to re-establish Hungary's political institutions in their full vigor, Francis Joseph sought to restrict the competence of the Hungarian Diet by reserving certain important matters for the exclusive deliberation of the *Reichsrat*, which was dominated by aristocratic and German elements who could be expected to follow the imperial desires. Thus again, in 1861, when a two-chamber parliament was established for the whole empire, the electoral procedure was such as to assure German majorities in the delegations sent to this parliament from the various regions of the realm.

These practices not only caused protests, and sometimes boycott of the imperial parliament by the provincial diets, but also had the effect of stimulating cultural movements that emphasized resistance to German domination. The establishment of a national theater in Prague and the organization throughout Bohemia of gymnastic and patriotic societies called *sokols*, the foundation of a society for the propagation of national culture by the Rumanians of Transylvania, and the beginning of a national political press in Croatia were all symptoms of growing dissatisfaction with the governmental principles of the Hapsburg monarchy.

Most implacable in their resistance were the Magyars of Hungary, who found a leader in Francis Déak (1803–1876), a superb tactician who exploited all the weaknesses of the imperial government. Déak was no extremist; he set his face against the ambitions of exiles like Kossuth, who dreamed of Hungarian independence, because he did not believe that Hungary could stand alone. But he insisted that agreement with the Vienna government was possible only on the basis of the complete return to Hungary of all the liberties she had won in 1848 (see p. 134); and, until these were granted, he advocated a policy of noncollaboration on Hungary's part—which meant refusal to participate in meetings of the Imperial Diet, or to pay taxes or to participate in other imperial activities.

The opposition of the subject nationalities made the efficient operation of the imperial system impossible, and, as Francis Joseph's ministers became convinced that war with Prussia was unavoidable, they were oppressed with visions of strikes and military desertions like those that had occurred during the war of 1859. They decided, therefore, to temporize and entered into negotiations with the most formidable of the dissidents, the Magyars. These discussions were interrupted by the outbreak of the war with Prussia, and it is impossible to say what their result would have been had that war been won. The fact that it was not won, however, made it inevitable that an arrangement would be reached on Hungary's terms, for her cooperation was needed, if not to prevent the complete dissolution of the empire, then at least to make Austria's recovery as a Great Power possible.

The negotiations terminated in 1867 with the conclusion of the so-called Compromise or *Ausgleich*, which transformed the Hapsburg Empire into a dual monarchy, comprising two independent and equal states with one ruler (who would be emperor of Austria and king of Hungary), one Imperial and Royal Army, and a joint ministry with responsibility for foreign policy, military affairs and financial matters. Each half of this new Austria-Hungary, as it was henceforth to be called, would have its own parliament, its separate cabinet of ministers, and its own civil service and administrative system. To supervise the work of the joint departments of foreign affairs, war, and finance, the two national parliaments chose committees or "delegations," which met in Vienna and Budapest, communicating with each other in writing and, very rarely, by means of joint sessions.

The Compromise restored reasonable efficiency to the governmental operations of the empire, permitted the Hapsburg monarchy to play an important role in international affairs, and even had beneficial economic results, by making possible an effective customs union and creating a great market in which the industrial and agricultural districts complemented each other to mutual advantage. But it did nothing to solve the nationalities problem, and did not try to do so. It may truly be described as a "deal" beween the German minority in the western half of the empire and the Magyar minority in the eastern at the expense of all of the other peoples—the Czechs, the Slovaks, the Croats, the Serbs, and the Rumanians. The true character of the arrangement was shown by the laws that implemented it in the two halves of the empire. By a series of decrees in the latter part of 1867, parliamentary government was established in Austria with a bicameral legislature chosen by the diets of the seventeen provinces west of the Leitha River; but the realm was gerrymandered so that German domination was assured and the system was run by bureaucrats in such a way as to make any truly liberal development impossible. In Hungary the constitution of 1848 was restored, but the suffrage was so limited that three fourths of the adult male population had no political power, a fact that facilitated the policy of Magyarization followed by the government.

The Compromise had the long-run effect of transforming the desire of the subject nationalities for autonomy within the empire into a desire for independence from the empire. As early as 1867, for instance, Czech leaders went to Moscow to attend a Pan-Slav congress; and in July 1868 the celebration in Prague of the anniversary of the birth of John Huss was so obviously an anti-Hapsburg demonstration that the city had to be placed under martial law. This was a sign of things to come. In short, the defeat in Germany, which might have led to the kind of reform of the imperial structure that would encourage internal harmony and peaceful development, brought instead an exacerbation of the national differences that were to pull the empire to pieces.

The Surrender of Prussian Liberalism / When the Prussian army smashed Benedek's forces at Königgrätz, it simultaneously inflicted a decisive defeat upon the liberal opposition in the Chamber of Deputies. The vigor and enthusiasm with which the liberals had opposed the royal military reforms in 1862 and 1863 had begun to wane during the campaign against Denmark and had been further attenuated when Bismarck announced, in April 1866, that he favored a basic reform of the Germanic Confederation and the creation of a national assembly elected by universal manhood suffrage. It disappeared almost completely as the war with Austria approached, for even the diehards of the Progressive party began to see that their opposition was losing them the support not only of the masses, who were filled with patriotic spirit, but also of the middle classes who had formerly supported them in their fight against Bismarck but who were now becoming convinced that his policies promised to create the national unity that they had always advocated.

This belated realization of the popularity of the government's policy was confirmed by the elections to the Chamber of Deputies which were held after the war had started, for these were an unmistakable defeat for the liberal forces. While the conservatives increased their representation from 38 to 142 deputies, the Progressive party received the smallest vote it had had since the beginning of its existence and was left so weak that even in combination with the moderates, it was still in the minority in the Chamber.

In viewing these results, Bismarck remained true to the ideas that had guided him in 1862. He was gratified by the liberals' defeat but was not anxious to see it go further, for he felt that he would need their support in the further elaboration of his German program. Therefore, he took advantage of the electoral victory to give the liberals a chance to end their opposition without completely losing face. He let it be known that the government was prepared to admit that it had acted in violation of the constitution by operating without a budget since 1862, if, in return, the Chamber would legitimize all past expenditures by an act of indemnity. The liberals seized this opportunity to escape from their predicament—indeed, it was easier to persuade them to agree to the arrangement than it was to win the approval of the king—and, in September 1866, after listening to a royal address that admitted the unconstitutionality, but emphasized the necessity, of the government's actions, the Chamber voted the indemnity bill by a large majority.

It cannot be denied that this was a capitulation on the part of the Prussian liberals. The socialist leader Wilhelm Liebknecht said scornfully: "Blood appears to be a special elixir, for the angel of darkness [Bismarck] has become the angel of light. . . . The stigma of violation of the constitution has been washed from his brow, and in its place the halo of glory rings his laurelled head." The liberals' change of front, their acceptance of the actions they had once condemned, and their significant silence about the military reforms during the indemnity debate, could not be explained on the grounds of political expediency alone; for many of them had voted for the indemnity with enthusiasm and now showed a distressing eagerness to declare themselves followers of Bismarck and believers in his principles and methods.

Thus, in October 1866, the Progressive party split in two. One group announced their complete acceptance of Bismarck's foreign policy, adding, almost as an afterthought, that in domestic affairs they would carry out "the duties of a vigilant and loyal opposition." This marked the birth of the National Liberal party, which was to be the chief spokesman of the middle classes in the next generation; but the gulf that separated its principles from those of the liberalism of 1848 and 1862 may be seen in the words of one of its members, who said: "The time of ideals is past. . . . Politicians must ask themselves today less what is desirable than what is attainable." Middle-class liberals had become somewhat ashamed of their earlier history and seemed determined to demonstrate that they were as realistic and as capable of appreciating the importance of facts as anyone else. All of this showed how effective Bismarck had been in debauching the values of his opponents so that they could now forget their former desire for freedom in face of the seductive attractions of force and its achievements.

Two other points may be made in this connection. In the first place, the Prussian victory over Austria, soon to be followed by an even more glorious victory over France, weakened the self-confidence of the middle classes when they compared themselves to the aristocracy. There had been a time when their own economic triumphs and their virtual monopoly of both wealth and culture had made them think of themselves as the future ruling class of Germany and encouraged them to regard the aristocracy with condescension, as a class of titled boobies, penniless backwoodsmen, and boorish brass hats. But the victories on the battle field, and their own political failure, had transformed this picture. The prestige of the officer corps, and the nobility that supplied it with candidates, rose to an all-time high, and their social and political position was made virtually impregnable. The upper middle class tended

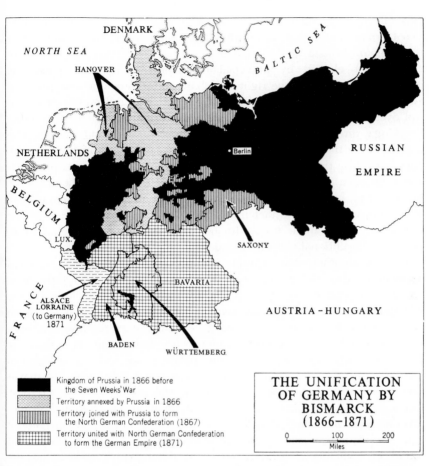

THE UNIFICATION
OF GERMANY BY
BISMARCK
(1866–1871)

Kingdom of Prussia in 1866 before
the Seven Weeks' War

Territory annexed by Prussia in 1866

Territory joined with Prussia to form
the North German Confederation (1867)

Territory united with North German Confederation
to form the German Empire (1871)

0   100   200
Miles

henceforth to accept this situation, while at the same time seeking to associate themselves with this now respected and glamorous upper social stratum by a sedulous aping of its manners, its pastimes, and even its vices. Thus, one of the long-term results of the wars of unification was a kind of feudalization of the upper middle class.

Another result, which stemmed from the sharp contrast between military and diplomatic success on the one hand and parliamentary ineffectiveness on the other, was to confirm many Germans in the belief, already widespread after 1848, that nothing much could be expected from parliaments and politicians. This was to impede Germany's progress toward democracy.

The North German Confederation / The war with Austria had destroyed the old Germanic Confederation, and Prussia now gave to the part of the nation that she controlled a new one. In July 1867, after months of planning, drafting, and debate, the constitution of this new body came into effect. The North German Confederation comprised the twenty-two German states that lay north of the Main River. Its president was the king of Prussia, and it had a bicameral legislature: a parliament (Reichstag) elected by universal manhood suffrage and possessing budgetary powers and the right to debate and approve or disapprove of all laws, but with no rights of legislative initiative and no effective control over ministers or over foreign and military policy, which were under the king's direction; and a Federal Council (Bundesrat) of delegates appointed by the princes of the separate federal states, which could veto laws passed by the Reichstag and had to approve amendments proposed there. Prussian preponderance was assured by the king's right to choose his ministers, by their immunity to Reichstag control, by Prussian control of the army, and by the fact that Prussia had 17 of the 43 seats in the Bundestag, which made it easy for her, by a minimum of negotiation, to get enough additional votes for a majority.

There was nothing about this organization to prevent its being widened to include other states, and it was, of course, the hope of those who voted for it that it would in fact be expanded soon to include Baden, Württemberg, Bavaria, and the part of Hesse-Darmstadt that lay south of the Main. It was true that the governing classes of those southern states did not look forward to union with enthusiasm, and that the Catholic clergy and many Catholic believers as well as democrats, socialists, and professional anti-militarists opposed it bitterly; but it was also undeniable that strong segments of the populations of all these states were eager to join the northern confederation. The National Society (Nationalverein), which had been working for a united Germany under Prussian leadership since 1859, had branches in all these states and found no difficulty in making converts. Even people who hated the thought of being under Prussian leadership had to admit that there was no very attractive alternative. The southern states could not join Austria, for she was permanently excluded from Germany; if they formed a union of their own, it would be dominated by Bavaria, a prospect that did not seem desirable to the citizens of Baden and Württemberg; and, if they remained as they were, their economic and political position in a troubled Europe would be precarious. Slowly, therefore, the sentiment for fusion with the north grew.

The state of southern opinion was one of Bismarck's main concerns after 1866, for, although he was determined to complete the unification of the German nation, he did not want to move in this direction until he was reasonably sure that a majority of the populations of the southern states would support him. But this was not, of course, his only concern. France was also interested in the fate of southern Germany, and Bismarck's policy had to be determined with Napoleon III in mind.

10

The Reorganization of Europe, 1866-1871

While these tremendous events were taking place in Central Europe, the rest of the continent and its neighboring islands remained uninvolved. Only the French government seriously considered intervening in the armed rivalry of the German powers, and, in the end, Napoleon III decided that neutrality offered more tangible advantages—an expectation that was not, as we shall see, fulfilled in the sequel. The attention of the other great powers was absorbed by pressing domestic problems, and the lesser states had neither the interest nor the power to be other than neutral.

GREAT BRITAIN FROM PALMERSTON TO GLADSTONE

Nonintervention and Colonial Problems / The English appetite for foreign involvements had been thoroughly sated by the unhappy experience of the Crimean War. In the years that followed that conflict, Britain was considerably less active in continental affairs than she had been at any time since 1815. The desire for peace was so strong in both political parties that, when British governments wished to take a stand or express an opinion on foreign problems, they could never be sure of parliamentary or popular support. During the Polish revolt of 1863, the Palmerston-Russell government made statements that came close to being promises of assistance to the rebels; and, during the early stages of the dispute over Schleswig and Holstein, the same government warned the German powers that an attack on Denmark might have serious consequences. But when the tsar refused to be cowed in the first case and Austria and Prussia disregarded the veiled threat in the second, the British government acquiesced in the result, sensing that the country would condone no positive resistance. The *Pall Mall Gazette* was probably speaking for most Englishmen when it said, rather brutally, in 1863: "Englishmen know that most of the Poles they have seen are dirty and that a good many that they have not seen are oppressed; but to go to war for a distant race of unwashed martyrs seems a desperate remedy." If the government was criticized, it was because it had been interested enough in continental events to express any opinion on them at all; and, in a debate in Commons in July 1864, speakers on both sides of the House called for an end of the "policy of meddle and muddle" and a return to the principle of nonintervention—by which was meant, apparently, a policy of leaving Europe strictly alone. In any case, that is the policy that was followed by all parties after 1864; and Britain had nothing to say about the great decisions of 1866 and 1870.

It was, of course, not only the reaction to the debacle in the Crimea that produced this result. Unlike the states in Central Europe, Britain possessed important territories and interests overseas, and these were constantly demanding attention. In the years of European transformation, problems arose in India, in the Far East, in the southwestern Pacific, and in North America; and these absorbed some of the interest and energy that might in other times have been turned across the Channel.

The year that followed the end of hostilities in the Crimea, for instance, witnessed a bloody rising against British power in India. Changes in the conditions of service in the Bengal army had for some time been causing discontent among the native troops of the British East India Company; and this was fanned by Indian civilians whose position had been weakened by British reforms and by Brahmin priests who objected to certain administrative decrees that affected religious practices and Hindu custom. Disorders were touched off when the rumor spread among sepoy regiments that the cartridges used in the new Enfield rifle, which had to be bitten before they were inserted in the breach, were greased with the fat of cows and swine and, thus, would pollute Hindus and Moslems who used them. British officers were dilatory in taking measures to reassure the troops and, when three regiments near Calcutta mutinied in

January 1857, showed insufficient energy in their attempts to restore order. After killing their officers, the mutineers advanced on Delhi and, took and sacked the citadel and the European quarters. The Calcutta mutiny inspired risings and the murder of European men, women and children elsewhere, until about a third of India's total area was under the control of the rebels.

The mutiny, however, had no clearly formulated aims, no central direction, and few talented leaders; and, after the initial shock had passed, the British put down the disorders with firmness and speed, repeatedly demonstrating, as they did so, that numbers were of no avail against good organization and modern weapons. In the last stages of the fighting, for instance, Sir Hugh Rose, with 3000 European troops and somewhat fewer native auxiliaries, captured the town of Jhansi, which had a garrison of 12,000, losing only 345 men in doing so, as against enemy casualties in the thousands; and, during the siege, he detached 2000 of his troops and with them defeated another native army of 22,000.

British authority in India was restored by January 1858, although mopping-up operations continued for some months. The most important result of the mutiny was a deepening of the gulf between the British and their native subjects, which was—as Sir Llewellyn Woodward has written—shown in a tendency on the part of the former to rely more on efficient administration than on the hope that India could be "westernized" and freed of superstition and prejudice by the introduction of social or political reforms. In the interest of efficiency, the last remnants of the authority of the East India Company were now assumed by the British crown, which took over the company's property and troops and henceforth governed India through a secretary of state and a council of fifteen members.

During the same years, British troops were engaged in the Far East, where Lord Palmerston, as a result of a series of brushes with Chinese authorities, demanded clear recognition of European diplomatic and commercial rights in China and, in conjunction with the French, resorted to force in order to secure compliance with his demands. In 1858, a joint force captured the Taku forts at the mouth of the Peiho River. When the Chinese continued to equivocate, another expedition advanced to Peking, capturing it in 1860 and burning down the emperor's Summer Palace in retaliation for a Chinese breach of truce. Under this pressure, the imperial government had to yield to the desires of the western nations and opened Tientsin and a number of other ports to their trade, simultaneously granting residence in Peking to their diplomatic representatives.

Far to the south in the Pacific, both Australia and New Zealand were in these years demanding attention from British legislators. Thanks to the discovery of gold in Victoria and New South Wales in the early 1850s, the population of Australia increased almost threefold between 1850 and 1860, and this growth brought political and administrative problems in its wake. These were solved, for the most part, by the willingness of the home government to grant a large degree of self-government to the colonists, approving locally drafted constitutions for the separate areas until such time as the country should be sufficiently developed for federation. In New Zealand, which had been a crown colony since 1840, the rapid increase of European population in this period (it doubled between 1847 and 1860) led to difficulties with the indigenous Maori people. Disputes over land titles and a general fear on the part of the Maoris that their civilization and tribal organization were threatened by European encroachments led to the outbreak of a war in 1860 that lasted for ten years. The fact that the expenses of the war had to be borne, for the most part, by the home government enabled it to bring pressure to bear upon colonial authorities to ameliorate their native policies, particularly with respect to land ownership. Eventually this led to a reconciliation and, by the middle of the 1870s, to Maori participation in the government of the country.

Finally, through much of this period, British attention was diverted from Europe to North America, especially after the outbreak of the Civil War in the United States. This conflict aroused much deeper passions in the British Isles than any of the wars that took place in Europe, partly because it had a direct impact upon the British economy by sharply reducing the imports of raw cotton to the mills of Lancashire and Yorkshire and thus affecting the livelihood of mill operatives in those districts, and partly because it raised political, ideological, and moral issues of the gravest importance. The question of the advisability of recognizing the Confederacy as a nation divided the government and the country. A man's stand upon it was apt to be determined as much by his views on the relative merits of aristocratic and democratic forms of government or the moral justification of slavery as it was by his calculation of the political results of recognition.

In the end, the government followed what it believed to be the will of the people, which was predominately pro-Northern in sympathy, particularly (and this defied all theories of economic determination) in those areas hit hardest by the cotton shortage. Even so, there were sharp crises between Great Britain and the Union government—over the boarding of a British ship by a Union commander (the famous Trent affair of 1861), over the depredations of commerce raiders built in British yards and sold to the Confederacy, and over other issues—and sometimes war between the two countries seemed not very far away. The British government was well aware that such a conflict would almost certainly lead to an American attack upon Canada. Concern for Canada continued, indeed, even after the American Civil War came to an end. In May 1866 a band of Irish nationalists, most of whom had fought in the Union army and were now organized in a society known as the Fenian Brotherhood, attempted a raid across the Canadian border. It was easily broken up, but it appeared to indicate that Canadian security could not simply be taken for granted.

All of these events across the seas are important in helping to explain Britain's relative abstention from European complications after 1856. But they do not stand alone. There was much going on in England itself in these years.

Party Politics / In the field of politics the most important single event, and the one that aroused the greatest amount of popular passion, was the passage of the second Reform Bill of 1867. But this was preceded, and in an important sense made possible, by a change in the nature and leadership of the political parties.

For some years after the end of the Crimean War, the confusion that had been introduced into British politics by the debate over the repeal of the Corn Laws in the 1840s was perpetuated. The parties had become loose coalitions without internal cohesion and with a continually shifting membership. On the one side, the aristocratic Whigs and the Manchester radicals made very strange bedfellows; on the other, the Tories had not made up their quarrel with the followers of Peel, who wavered between the two groupings. It has been said that it was impossible until the first parliamentary vote after a general election to tell what the exact state of the parties was. In the circumstances, it is apparent that they would not have sharply differentiated programs. Indeed, one can almost say that they had no programs at all and did not feel any need for them. Constant legislative activity was not yet considered a necessary or desirable aspect of governing the country. The leader of the Tories, Lord Derby, was more interested in racing and Homer than in political issues; and Lord Palmerston, the Whig chieftain, devoted himself to foreign policy almost to the exclusion of everything else.

This situation began to change in the 1860s, largely as a result of the rise and acceptance of new leaders. The emergence of a modern Conservative party that would appeal to urban voters as well as to the agricultural interest became possible only after the Tory party had accepted Benjamin Disraeli (1804–1881) as Derby's successor. This brilliant but flamboyant figure, the descendant of Spanish Jews who had come to England in 1748, had first made his mark in politics by leading the attack on Peel in 1846; but he was long viewed with suspicion by his colleagues as opportunistic, un-English, and unreliable. Yet, as his political novels show, Disraeli had reflected more deeply than any of his critics on the nature of parties and the character and traditions of British conservatism. Since the early 1850s he had urged Derby to turn his mind to issues that would win the support of the country and had founded a newspaper to spread party ideas; and his effective leadership of the party in the House of Commons gradually overcame opposition and led to his acceptance as Derby's successor in 1868. It was not, however, until the next decade that he was able to show the country what his idea of a Conservative program was.

The transformation of the old Whig-Liberal coalition into the modern Liberal party was largely the result of the efforts of two men, John Bright and William Ewart Gladstone (1809–1898). Bright, a cotton manufacturer and a Quaker, had, with Cobden, led the fight for the repeal of the Corn Laws. After 1847, he was member of Parliament for Manchester and the foremost leader of the so-called Manchester School, which stood for the extension of the principle of free trade, the reduction of taxation a cheaper foreign policy, and the extension of the suffrage to give greater representation to the populous districts of the country as opposed to the rural areas. One of England's greatest orators, he distinguished himself by his opposition to the Crimean War and his spirited advocacy of the Union cause during the American Civil War, which did much to assure Britain's neutrality. Perhaps his greatest service to modern British liberalism was the way in which he combatted Palmerston's prejudice against adding to the statute book by arguing the moral necessity of political and social reform and transforming an essentially negative laissez-faire philosophy into a positive creed of improvement.

For all his great gifts, Bright was not the man to lead a modern political party; he held extreme views on too many subjects for that, and his doctrinaire pacifism alone made him seem, to many people, to be impractical. The man who became the first leader of the new Liberal party and who continued in that position until almost the end of the century was Gladstone, who possessed as much eloquence as Bright on the hustings and in Parliament and as highly developed a sense of responsibility and passion for improvement, but was generally considered to be steadier and more reliable. The son of a Liverpool merchant, Gladstone, after a brilliant scholastic record at Oxford, had considered taking holy orders but had turned instead to politics where he became a follower of Sir Robert Peel and served in that stateman's last ministry as president of the Board of Trade and, later, as secretary for war and the colonies. In the governments of Aberdeen (1852–1855) and Palmerston and Russell (1859–1866), he was appointed chancellor of the exchecquer and distinguished himself by carrying forward the free trade policy, by abolishing the excise on paper—which helped increase the size of the reading public by reducing the price of books and news-papers—by devising an effective postal savings and insurance system that was much used by the working class, and by systematically reducing both direct and indirect taxation. His prestige and popularity were so great by this time that there was little question that he would become leader of the party after Palmerston and Russell had passed from the scene.

The Reform Act of 1867 / The new spirit which Gladstone and Bright brought to the Liberal coalition was shown in the campaign that culminated in the passing of the Reform Act of 1867. That there was need for a new law governing the franchise and the allocation of Parliamentary seats had been painfully clear for years. In the 1860s, only one adult male out of six had the vote and, although population distribution had profoundly altered since 1832, seats in Parliament had not been redistributed, leaving the metropolitan areas greatly underrepresented. On several occasions proposals for reform had been introduced in Parliament but had died there because of the lack of interest of the older party leaders and their deference to the fear on both sides of the House that to widen the suffrage appreciably would be to invite mob rule and raids on the treasury by an uncultivated and irresponsible electorate.

By the middle of the 1860s the country was in no mood to tolerate this situation any longer. It is probably true that the victory of the North in the American Civil War contributed to the growth of reform sentiment, for it was widely interpreted as a demonstration of the strength and effectiveness of democratic government. But even without this, it is unlikely that the limited suffrage could have been maintained. Gladstone seems to have realized this in May 1864 when, in a famous speech in Commons, he expressed the belief that "every man who is not presumably incapacitated by some consideration of personal unfitness or of political danger is morally entitled to come within the pale of the constitution." Bright had always favored the wider distribution of political power, and he now became the most impassioned pleader for change, calling upon the English people to repudiate those politicians "who, in every speech they utter, insult the workingmen, describing them as a multitude given up to ignorance and vice," and encouraging them to demonstrate actively for parliamentary action.

The issue was joined in June 1866 when Gladstone, as leader in the House of Commons in the Russell cabinet, introduced a reform bill which was promptly defeated by the combined efforts of the Conservatives and dissident Liberals led by Robert Lowe, who believed that suffrage extension would be a national disaster. This setback caused the fall of the Russell government but actually made the victory of the reform

The disorders in Hyde Park, London, in July 1866, during the agitation for parliamentary reform. The interest these outbreaks aroused in Europe is shown by this French drawing from *L'Illustration*, July 1866.

movement inevitable. It angered the Liberal reformers and increased their fervor; and it led to popular disturbances, like one in July 1866, when a reform demonstration that was barred from Hyde Park got out of hand and tore down 1400 yards of park railings. The effective leader of the Conservative government that had replaced the Liberals was Disraeli, and that wily politician decided that it was better to accede to the popular demand, and gain whatever political credit was to be derived from doing so, than to oppose it fruitlessly. It was Disraeli therefore who, in a masterly demonstration of parliamentary skill, introduced the Reform Bill of 1867 and secured its passage.

But the real authors of the bill—which started Britain on the road to democracy by doubling the electorate[1]—were Gladstone and Bright. Their efforts inspired the popular demonstrations which persuaded Par-

---

[1] The Reform Act of 1867 gave the vote, in the boroughs, to all householders, whatever the value of their houses, and to all lodgers who occupied quarters for which they paid at least £10 a year. In counties it gave the vote to everyone owning property which yield £5 income a year and to all tenants paying £12 a year. It added 938,000 voters to the existing English and Welsh electorate of 1,056,000. It was followed by an act redistributing Parliamentary representation.

liament that further delay would be unwise; and the details of the bill passed were based on features of Gladstone's earlier schemes. The new electorate seemed to realize this, for, in the elections of 1868, it returned the Liberals to power with a commanding majority; and Gladstone, for the first time, became prime minister.

Gladstone's Reforms / Gladstone's first term of office, the so-called Great Ministry, lasted from 1868 to 1874 and was characterized by a burst of legislative activity. This was least notable in the area of factory regulation and labor relations, for government intervention in this field was contrary to liberal principles and working-class organizations were not, in these years, actively pushing for reform in any case.[2] But elsewhere the government tried earnestly to supply needs and correct grievances. It passed basic reforms in the fields of civil administration, education, and Irish affairs; it finally satisfied the old Chartist demand for the secret ballot with the Ballot Act of 1872; and it made the first basic changes in the administration of the army since Waterloo (see p. 321).

Two measures that were typical of the Liberal spirit of reform were the civil service reform of 1870 and the Education Act of the same year. The first of these, by order of council, made appointments to most positions in the civil service dependent upon open competitive examinations. The second gave a tremendous stimulus to popular education, although it did not provide the kind of free, compulsory elementary education already available in some continental countries. The voluntary principle was so strong and the fear of state dictation so much a part of the liberal tradition that the Education Act was a tissue of ingenious compromises. It divided the country into school districts, which were considered separately. In those in which adequate elementary-school facilities existed, no change was made, except that existing schools had to submit to government inspection and could apply for parliamentary aid. Districts without schools were provided with local school boards which organized and supervised new schools and levied local taxes to support them. In districts where there was exceptional poverty, the school boards could set up free schools or pay fees for poor students; but, in general, it was expected that parents would pay for their children's tuition. Elementary education was not to become free until 1891.

If the Education Act of 1870 showed the old Liberal faith in private enterprise and the traditional distrust of extending government power, it was also characterized by the suspicion of established religion that was a part of the philosophy of liberalism. Although religious instruction was

---

[2] For labor conditions and trade-union activity in these years, see below, pp. 291–293.

to be permitted in both voluntary and board schools, in the latter it was to be undenominational; and, in either case, parents could request that their children be excused from religious instruction on grounds of conscience. Another victory over denominationalism was recorded in 1870, when the English universities were made truly national for the first time by the abolition of the religious tests that reserved them for members of the Church of England.

Gladstone and Ireland / The energies of the first Gladstone ministry were concentrated primarily, however, on the problems of Ireland. That unhappy country's grievances against England were religious, political, and economic. Predominantly Catholic, the Irish objected to having to pay tithes to the Anglican Church in Ireland and resented the fact that there was no Catholic university in the country that was qualified to grant degrees. Politically, they opposed the Act of Union of 1800 and were not at all grateful for the belated Act of Emancipation of 1829 which had given Ireland Parliamentary representation by permitting Catholics to sit in the House of Commons. Economically, they were the victims of a situation in which there was not enough land to support a rapidly growing population and no appreciable industrial development to absorb excess population. Those Irish who did not seek escape by emigration subsisted on the yield of miniscule subdivisions leased to them by tenants of English landlords. Most of them lived on one crop, the potato; and, when that failed, as it did in 1845 and 1846, their plight was pitiful in the extreme and deaths from starvation staggering in number. These economic ills could not be fairly laid at the doors of the English, but they were, simply because the English held most of the land; and these grievances were aggravated by others, such as the fact that most tenants had no security of tenure and could be evicted at a moment's notice without any compensation for improvements made during their possession. From the landlord's point of view, the right of eviction without compensation protected him from seeing his land subdivided indefinitely and covered with hovels for which he had to assume ultimate responsibility; but the Irish could not be expected to see things in the same way.

When Gladstone came to office in 1868, he had said, "My mission is to pacify Ireland!"; and his first step in this direction was to call for the disestablishment and disendowment of the Anglican Church in Ireland. In winning support for this, the widening of the franchise in 1867 was important, for a good proportion of the new electorate was Nonconformist and not disinclined to measures calculated to weaken the established church. The supporters of the church were wise enough to realize this and, although they fought for generous compensation for the property lost by the Irish Church, they permitted the passage of the Disestablishment Act in 1869.

The prime minister turned immediately to the more difficult question of land tenure and, in 1870, secured Parliamentary approval for an act designed to give justice to the Irish tenants. The Land Act of 1870 protected them from arbitrary eviction by providing for payment of damages to the tenant in all cases of eviction except when it was the result of nonpayment of rent and by stipulating that compensation must be paid for all improvements. This effected some improvement in the Irish situation, although loopholes and inequities were soon discovered in the working of the act. At the same time, the act did not go to the root of the Irish difficulty. The tenants wanted security of tenure and fair rents. Gladstone did not satisfy these demands and could not have done so without interfering with the rights of property, which the Liberal party would not have condoned.

Neither these reforms nor Gladstone's avowed intention of giving adequate facilities to Ireland for higher education,[3] therefore, appeased the Irish people; and their agitations continued to be a source of concern to British governments until World War I.

RUSSIA UNDER ALEXANDER II

Nonintervention and Imperial Expansion / The course of Russian history in these years bore a marked similarity with that of British history. Russia's abstention from European affairs was also determined by reaction to the Crimean adventure, by colonial concerns, and by the urgency of domestic affairs. As we have noted (see p. 176), both her losses in the war and her resentment over the Black Sea clauses of the Treaty of Paris inclined Russia to a policy of watchful neutrality as the duel for supremacy in Central Europe proceeded.

As in the case of Britain, this abstention was accompanied, and to some extent caused, by a shift of interest to areas far from the European center. Russian governments were discovering the Pacific area in these years and beginning to realize the potential significance of expansion in that direction. Even before the Crimean War, Russian traders had begun to make inroads into Chinese territory in the valley of the Amur River; in 1854 an expedition led by Nicholas Muravev, the governor-general of Eastern Siberia, founded the city of Khabarovsk on that river. During

[3] A bill for this purpose was introduced by Gladstone in February 1873 and was defeated by Parliament.

the Chinese difficulties with the British and French in the late 1850s (see p. 239), Muravev extended his holdings; other expeditions established coastal settlements and founded the city of Vladivostok in 1860; and the Russian government forced the Chinese government to recognize these holdings and to accord to Russia the privileges given the other powers in the treaties of Tientsin and Peking. In the decade that followed, the Russians also occupied the province of Kuldja in Chinese Turkestan and began their settlement of Sakhalin Island, which was confirmed by treaty with Japan in 1875.

As this new interest in expansion in the Chinese mainland was pursued, the Russian government, for economic and political reasons, decided to liquidate its holdings in North America. Thus, in March 1867, Russian rights and properties in what is now Alaska were transferred by treaty to the United States for a sum of $7,200,000. In the light of Alaska's present strategic and economic importance, it is interesting to note that the purchase was unpopular in the United States and the sale unregretted in Russia.

Along the southern borders of the Russian empire, the outward thrust continued in these years also. By 1864, Russian troops had put down the stout resistance of the Caucasian and Circassian tribes and made good their claim to all of the western shore of the Caspian Sea north of Persia. In the same year a major drive was begun against the Moslem khanates of Kokand, Khiva, and Bokhara; and, under Generals Cherniaev, Kaufman, and Skobelev, they were finally subjugated and annexed, although the process was not complete until the middle 1870s.

The economic promises sometimes made to justify this expansion were never fully realized. Even so, expansion in Central Asia, like that in the Far East, was popular in court circles, among the military (for obvious reasons) and among the informed public, to many of whom it appeared to offset the humiliation caused by the Crimean defeat. Its very popularity reinforced the tendency of the country to remain aloof from European affairs.

The Great Reforms / While these important territorial conquests were being made, the social and political structure of Russia was being profoundly affected by a series of reforms ever more comprehensive than those introduced in England. The Crimean War had brought a new tsar to the throne; and, while he can hardly be described as a liberal or a believer in reform for reform's sake, Alexander II (1855–1881) was shrewd enough to realize that there are times when change is imperative. He knew that the imperial regime had lost prestige as a result of the recent military defeat; and he feared that this might encourage groups with grievances to think that the time had come for them to take matters into their own hands and seek redress by revolutionary means. In particular, he seems to have feared that this might be the attitude of the peasants, and it was his hope that action by them might be forestalled if the government took the initiative in reforming the conditions of their life.

The great mass of the Russian peasantry were still, to all intents and purposes, slaves. They belonged to landowners who could dictate the most intimate details of their personal life, inflict corporal punishment upon them, even sell them or raise money by mortgaging them (in ways described in detail in Gogol's masterpiece *Dead Souls*). The peasants worked the landlord's soil for him with their own tools and performed other services in return for a living that was never much more than bare subsistence; and they had no authority to whom they could appeal against the landlord's decrees. Their resentment against these conditions flared up sporadically in the form of peasant risings; and the increasing frequency of these gave some substance to Alexander's fears. In any case, serfdom as an institution could hardly be defended on moral grounds, and there was increasing reason to suppose that it was not even defensible on economic ones. At a time when conditions abroad favored Russia's developing an export trade in wheat, the transition to large-scale grain farming was held back by a system in which the majority of the landlords knew nothing themselves about farming and the majority of the serfs employed traditional and uneconomic methods.

In March 1856 Alexander announced to an assembly of nobles in Moscow that "the existing order of serfdom cannot remain unchanged." "It is better," he continued, "to abolish bondage from above than to wait for the time when it will begin to abolish itself from below." These words inaugurated five years of investigation, negotiation, and formulation, during which the nobility, predominantly opposed to the projected change, slowly yielded to imperial pressure while at the same time fighting for the highest possible compensation for the rights they were going to relinquish. Plans were worked out on the local level and filtered through an elaborate committee framework until finally, in March 1861, the coordinated plan was promulgated by decree.

The emancipation edicts ended the personal dependence of the serf upon the landlord and made him, legally at least, a person who could move about freely, enter contractual relations, change his occupation, and enjoy other freedoms. These liberties, however, were restricted by the fact that the greatest number of serfs, after 1861 as before, lived in village communes which exercised considerable power over them. What land they received they held through the commune, which assumed a collective responsibility for seeing that redemption payments were made to the nobility ad taxes to the government. The commune carefully supervised the activities of the individual householder, restricting not only his freedom to dispose of the produce of his land as he saw fit but even his personal mobility. In comparison with other members of society, therefore, the peasant remained subject to significant disabilities for some years.

A basic assumption of the reform was that the liberated peasants (with the exception of those who had been household servants) would be given land to support them, but that, in order not to impoverish the nobility, they should pay for it over a period of years. In general, the nobility received more equitable treatment than the peasants. It is true that peasants who lived on estates of the imperial family or on state domains received generous allotments with moderate charges. Elsewhere, however, it has been estimated that close to half of the peasant allotments were too small to provide subsistence living, and in many cases the loss of the use of woods and pastures caused additional hardships. It should also be noted that most of the peasants regarded the necessity of making any payment for their allotments unjust; and it is indicative of the disillusionment which followed promulgation of the decrees that peasant disturbances were resumed within a very short period.

The emancipation of the peasants brought other reforms in its train. For one thing, the loss of police powers on the part of the landowning nobility necessitated some adjustment in the administration of rural affairs, for the nobility expected to receive a more extensive share in local government as compensation. This demand was satisfied in January 1864 when a new statute on local government was issued. This established assemblies called *zemstvos* in all counties and provinces of the empire. County zemstvos were elected by propertyholders of three categories: proprietors, townsmen, and peasants; provincial zemstvos were elected by county zemstvos. The amount of peasant participation, thanks to the ignorance of the peasant mass and the elaborateness of the electoral procedure, was not great.

The zemstvos were supposed to concern themselves with local affairs like the upkeep of roads and bridges, health and sanitation, maintenance of public institutions, promotion of trade and agriculture, education and relief of poverty, and the like. They were always kept on a very tight financial rein by the imperial government and could not, therefore, fulfill all of their assigned functions adequately. But, in a country in which centralized and bureaucratic methods had long been normal government procedure, the institution of these local and provincial assemblies was a first step toward representative government; the zemstvos built up public services to a height previously unknown in Russia; and, despite their inadequacies and the aristocratic preponderance in their deliberations, they were popular.

The third significant reform carried through in the early years of Alexander II affected the judicial system of the country. The disorder, inefficiency, and corruption of Russia's courts had long been known and, during the reign of Nicholas I, a committee had been set up to study the need for reform and draft appropriate legislation. New impetus was given to this committee's efforts by the Alexander II; in 1862 its basic ideas were widely publicized and discussed; and in November 1864 they were incorporated into statute form.

The principles underlying the reform were those long honored in western countries: equality before the law, trial by jury, uniformity of procedure, irremovability of judges (except for misconduct in office), and the like. These were announced in ringing tones to a country long used to executive trials and star-chamber methods. At the same time, a rigorous and systematic simplification of the court system was announced, with minor cases to be tried by justices of the peace and more important ones in a hierarchy of courts.

The promise inherent in all this was never fully kept. For one thing, the simplification of the court system was handicapped by the continued existence of military, ecclesiastical, and (for peasant affairs) township courts. For another, the individual legal rights so proudly announced were vitiated to some extent by the crown's retention of the right not only to pardon but to increase sentences and to take executive action to prevent crime or illegal activities. Finally, the system was operated by ministers of justice who were opposed to the spirit that animated the reform and who had no great respect for the principle of independence of judges. Despite these faults, however, the new system was immeasurably superior to the old.

THE SHOWDOWN BETWEEN FRANCE AND GERMANY

Napoleon III and the German Question / While the two great powers on the periphery of Europe busied themselves with domestic reforms, and the Austrian Empire underwent a fundamental reorganization as a result of the defeat suffered in 1866, relations between France and Prussia deteriorated rapidly. This was understandable. The Prussian victory over Austria and the subsequent establishment of the North German Confederation had simultaneously electrified advocates of German unification and dismayed French patriots who regarded a united Germany as contrary to the interest of their country. It was unlikely that Prussia would refrain from attempting, sooner or later, to complete the process so far advanced in 1866; it was inevitable that French public opinion would oppose further increases of Prussian strength.

In the years after 1866, Napoleon III seems to have tried to appease French patriots without seriously violating his professed faith in the principle of nationalities. He attempted to do this by seeking to persuade the Prussians to promise him compensation for any advance beyond the Main River, in the form of territorial grants in areas to which France had some historical claims, such as the Saarland, the Grand Duchy of Luxembourg, and even Belgium. These efforts were productive of nothing but bad feeling. In April 1867, for instance, after elaborate and protracted negotiations, Bismarck informed the French government that German public opinion would not tolerate France's acquisition of Luxemburg, and there was an ugly crisis in which serious consequences were averted only by an international conference that neutralized the disputed area.

After this rude blow, Napoleon's opposition to further Prussian growth hardened, and he sought to devise effective barriers to check it. His diplomats redoubled their activities at the courts of the German states south of the Main, seeking to inflame the traditional southern prejudice against Prussia. Simultaneously, conversations were begun with the Austrian and Italian governments with the intention of creating a triple alliance that might restrain Prussia's ambition or, failing that, defeat her in war.

Like so many of the schemes of Napoleon's declining years, these came to nothing. Some antipathy to Prussia still existed in Baden, Württemberg, and especially Bavaria, but it was not strong enough to serve French interests and, in 1870, it was to be swept away by patriotic enthusiasm. As for the negotiations in Vienna and Florence, they were—despite the sympathy for France that existed in those capitals—doomed from the start. Even if the Austrian Germans were willing to contemplate a new war against Prussia to regain the position lost in 1866 (and this was doubtful), the Hungarians were inflexibly opposed to it, for the simple reason that, if successful, it might lead to the loss of the powers gained by the Magyars by the Compromise of 1867 (see p. 232). And even though many Italians were grateful to Napoleon for his services to their country, they were unwilling to commit themselves to go to war for a government whose troops still denied them the possession of Rome. Since Napoleon dared not alienate Catholic opinion in France by withdrawing the garrison which had protected the pope since 1849, the Italian alliance, like the Austrian one, went aglimmering.

Meanwhile, in Prussia, Bismarck had watched the French negotiations and had insured himself against the unlikely chance of their succeeding by making a secret agreement with Russia. In return for a promise of Prussian support in the event of any Austro-Hungarian threat to Russian interests in southeastern Europe, the Russian government promised, in

March 1868, to concentrate enough troops in Galicia to keep the Austrians neutral in a Franco-Prussian war.

This does not mean that Bismarck was planning either a move south or a war against France at this time. For one thing, he was still too uncertain of the state of South German opinion to force the pace of German unification. For another, he had some hopes, as he saw the French government being liberalized, that the new ministers in Paris would eventually reconcile themselves to the inevitable and greet German unification with no more than verbal protests—again, provided he did not force the pace unduly.

Bismarck's willingness to wait, however, was shaken by the French plebiscite of May 1870 (p. 190). This gave the emperor such a resounding majority that the North German chancellor feared the results might encourage the imperial regime to be more, rather than less, intransigent. If this were so, nothing was to be gained by a policy of patience. Bismarck decided to go on the offensive.

The Hohenzollern Candidature / Since 1868, when a revolution in Spain had deposed Queen Isabella II, a provisional government in Madrid had been searching for a successor to the throne. The candidate most favored by the government was Prince Leopold of Hohenzollern, a distant relative of King William I of Prussia; but Bismarck, out of deference to French feeling, had discouraged the first offers to the prince, and he continued to oppose the project as long as he thought there was a possibility of a conciliatory French attitude in German affairs. When the results of the French plebiscite of May 1870 made this appear unlikely, the chancellor revived the succession question; and, on July 2, 1870, it was announced that Prince Leopold had accepted the Spanish throne.

Firm but prudent diplomacy on the part of France might have turned this stroke of the chancellor's against him, and for a moment it looked as if this was going to be the result. The French foreign minister, the Duke of Gramont, announced to the Chamber on July 6 that the presence of a German prince "on the throne of Charles V" would constitute an intolerable derangement of the European balance; and a few days later Benedetti, the French ambassador to Prussia, talked with the Prussian king at Ems and remonstrated so eloquently that William insisted that Leopold renounce the intention of going to Spain as king. But Gramont was not content with this substantial success; he wanted—as he admitted to the Austrian ambassador—"a political triumph that will efface the memory of previous retreats"; he now insisted that King William give assurances that Leopold's candidacy would not be renewed in the future.

In a further interview with Benedetti at Ems, the king refused, firmly but courteously, to give such promises. He then telegraphed a description of the conversation to Bismarck, who released the telegram to the press, after first abbreviating its text in such a way as to make his monarch's language much curter and Benedetti's rebuff much sharper than they had, in fact, been. The publication of this Ems dispatch and the resultant elaboration upon it in sensational newspapers on both sides of the border created an atmosphere in which reason and compromise were impossible. Under the pressure of inflamed Parisian mobs and a belligerent Chamber, the French government declared war on Prussia on July 19.

The Franco-Prussian War / In his memoirs Bismarck claims that he had always believed "that a Franco-German war must take place before the construction of a united Germany could be realized." If he had in fact believed this—and one cannot always trust the veracity of Bismarck's recollections—he was proved right even before the firing began, for the first result of the French declaration was the decision of the South German states to throw their lot in with Prussia and to send troops against France.

Thanks to this and to superior efficiency in mobilization, the German armies at the outset of the war outnumbered the French nearly two to one. They also had the advantage of a better supply system, which provided the troops with the means to fight, which was not always true on the French side, as well as a superior staff system, and a high command whose war plan had long been in readiness and was now put into effect with speed and efficiency. Napoleon, in the last week before the fighting began, improvised a plan for diversionary amphibious operations in the Baltic and an offensive of massed armies against southern Germany. Before the widely dispersed French reserves could be concentrated for any such operations, however, the Prussians rammed their way through the Lorraine gap and, after some hard-fought battles in which they suffered greater casualties than the French, got between Paris and the two main French armies, those of Marshals Bazaine and MacMahon. Bazaine was forced back eastward and bottled up in the fortress of Metz. When MacMahon's army, which had now been joined by the emperor, tried to come to his aid, it was surrounded at Sedan on the Belgian frontier and hammered by artillery fire until it surrendered.

The news that Napoleon III and over 100,000 troops were in Prussian hands brought the imperial regime crashing to the ground. In Paris a republican regime was organized with General Trochu as president; and, under the leadership of Léon Gambetta (1838–1882), who made his way from Paris to the provinces by balloon, new armies were raised along the Loire and an attempt was made to prosecute the war. These raw levies fought valiantly throughout the autumn and early winter months, but the heart of their resistance was broken when Bazaine surrendered his still very substantial forces at Metz in October. When Paris, besieged since September, finally capitulated in January—after every scrap of food in the city, including the animals in the zoo and the rats in the garrets, had been eaten, and the trees in the Champs Élysées and the Bois de Boulogne had been cut down for fuel—the armies in the provinces gave up too.

Before peace could be concluded, the Germans insisted that France be represented by a government that could speak for the whole nation; and, in February 1871, elections were held for a National Assembly which then elected Adolphe Thiers as chief of the executive power and authorized him to negotiate with the enemy. Thiers discovered that the Germans were in no mood for bargaining. He was forced to agree to the payment within three years of a war indemnity of five billion francs and to accept a German army of occupation until the sum was paid. In addition, his country had to cede to the victor all of Alsace and most of Lorraine with their potentially rich deposits of iron ore and their flourishing textile industry. Thiers' diplomatic skill was able to ameliorate these terms in some details—he saved the fortress of Belfort for France —but the Treaty of Frankfurt of May 1871 was, even so, a heavy burden on France and one whose memory was to plague the peace of Europe for two generations.

The Reorganization of Central Europe / The battles in France settled more than the fate of the Bonaparte dynasty; they completed the unification of both Germany and Italy. The fellowship in arms between the northern and southern German states was given political substance in January 1871 when the king of Bavaria was persuaded by Bismarck to urge the king of Prussia to revive the German empire and assume its crown. King William, Prussian to the very marrow, acted as if he resented the suggestion and was conspicuously cool for some time toward its real author; but he gave way and, on January 18 in the Hall of Mirrors in the Palace of Versailles, was proclaimed emperor of a Germany that now stretched from the Baltic to the Inn.

Meanwhile, the Italian government had taken advantage of the war to send their troops into Rome. It was not the most impressive way to secure a national capital; and the poet Carducci was later to write a scornful poem in which the geese on Capitoline Hill were heard to say

> Hush! Hush! Who goes there in the light
> of the moon?

and were answered

> Geese of the Capitol, be silent!
> It is I, Italy, the grand and united!

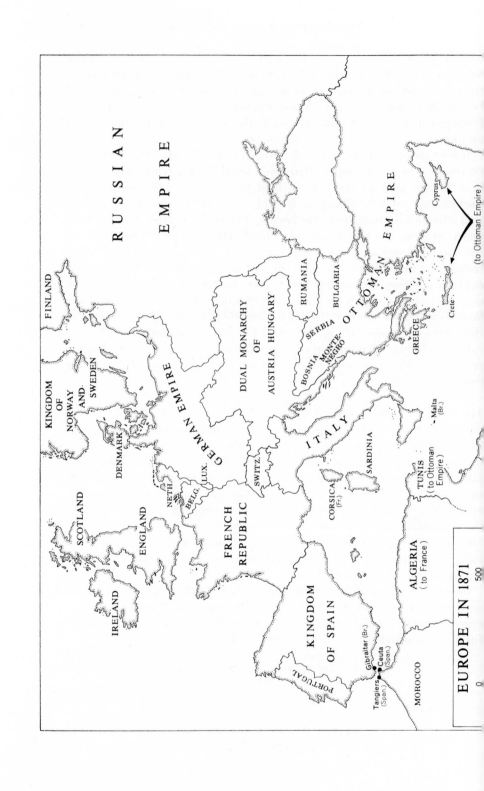

EUROPE IN 1871

0   500

The pope, who retired behind the walls of the Vatican, refused to recognize the pretensions of the Italian government, which meant that in the subsequent period Italy had to contend with the hostility of ardent Catholics at home and abroad as well as with all its other problems.

Back in the days when he first came to power, Napoleon III had dreamed of redrawing the map of Europe on national lines. That had now been done; but, although he had contributed strongly to the final result, he had gained none of the profit he thought would accrue from this accomplishment, and had instead lost his throne. The new Europe was in any case different from the one he had imagined. Its reorganization on national lines had not increased the interdependence and harmony of nations, as Mazzini and other nationalists of an earlier age had believed. The methods used to effect the changes in the map had left a heritage of bitterness between the continental states, while simultaneously showing the inadequacy of the European Concert and throwing doubt on the validity of international treaties and public law. Nothing better demonstrated the disrespect with which international obligations were now held than the unilateral abrogation of the Black Sea clauses of the Treaty of 1856 by the Russian government, an action taken in the middle of the Franco-Prussian war and accepted by the other powers because they were powerless, or disinclined, to forbid it.

PART THREE

1871

1914

GENERAL OBSERVATIONS

Perhaps the most striking aspect of the period that opened in 1871 was that, at its beginning, *liberalism* was in the ascendancy whereas, at its end, it was in full retreat. In the 1870s the most widely accepted economic and political ideas were those that had been elaborated by representatives of the middle class like Richard Cobden, John Stuart Mill, Benjamin Constant, Wilhelm von Humboldt. The prevailing economic philosophy was that of free trade, and, since 1860, most countries had been following the British and French example and scaling down their tariff schedules. The strongest political parties in Great Britain, Germany, Belgium, Italy, Switzerland, and Spain and strong ones in the Netherlands, Denmark, and Sweden either called themselves Liberal or held to such traditionally liberal tenets as constitutional parliamentary government based on limited suffrage, freedom of opportunity, and protection of individual liberties against arbitrary power, religious toleration, laissez-faire economics, national self-determination, and, in general, the solution of problems by rational and orderly means. Even in France, which had a republican government based on universal suffrage, the largest organized political grouping was a moderate middle-class party which held to most of these same beliefs; and we have already seen that Tsarist Russia was by no means impervious to their influence either.

By the end of the period, this situation was greatly changed. Nations that had subscribed to the free-trade policy in the 1850s and 1860s reversed themselves in the 1880s and 1890s, and tariff protectionism had once more become the order of the day. The great Liberal parties had either fallen to pieces—as was true in Germany—or lost strength in comparison to the conservative and the new working-class parties. And, most important of all, as a philosophy, liberalism had lost its cohesiveness and much of its relevance to the problems of the age.

This last point requires some elucidation. Back in the 1850s, and even in the 1870s, it was possible for an intelligent man to subscribe to all the reeds of liberalism—individualism, competition, *laissez faire*, suspicion of big government, and the like—without feeling any inconsistency. By he 1880s this was no longer easy. The prevailing economic tendencies eemed to favor, not individualism and competition, but combination, for his was the age of trusts, monopolies, and cartels. Industrialists who, in an earlier age, would have insisted that the government stay out of business now argued that it was the duty of government to support it by ariffs, subventions, convenient corporation laws, the acquisition of new narkets in colonial areas, and the like. They not infrequently sought political support for their new ideas from parties of the Right which, because they had traditionally believed in a strong active government, vere more open to these ideas than the Liberal parties; and this explains both the transformation of the Conservative parties into parties of big business (or, as in Germany, into allies of heavy industry) and the waning in strength of Liberal parties.

Simultaneously, men whose liberalism centered around a sincere belief in the necessity of protecting the individual from arbitrary power and vho, for that very reason, believed in *laissez faire* and opposed the growth of government functions began to suspect that the real threat to he individual was the tendency toward combination in business and that only the government could protect the individual, by regulating the operations of the great economic combines. These men, when their new belief proved unpopular with their former political associates, were apt to turn to the new labor parties which *did* believe in government regulation, with another resultant loss to the Liberal center. This latter tendency s shown clearly in the career of John Stuart Mill; in his classic *Essay on Liberty* (1859) he still regarded strong government as a threat to the free individual, but by the end of his life he was drifting rapidly in the direction of socialism.

The economic tendencies of the time, then, by forcing men to revise their views on the role of government, inevitably weakened the persuasiveness of the creeds of liberalism and the strength of Liberal parties. This in turn encouraged two things: on the one hand, a polarization of politics, a division into extremes, which was the inevitable result of the decline of the moderate parties of the middle, and was to reach its most dangerous form in the twentieth century; and, on the other, a growing acceptance of big government, the welfare state, and collectivism in general.

Another development that should be noted in this period was the *weakening of the liberal* attitude *in politics*, which may be defined as a belief in the efficiency of human reason to solve all of man's problems. The rational approach to politics was in opposition to the major intellectual tendencies of the age, which either deified violence or emphasized the irrational factors in human motivation. The acceptance of Social Darwinism, with its attempt to justify international war, colonial competition, and domestic conflict as natural manifestations of the struggle for existence, the spread of Marxism and anarchism with their emphasis on class struggle and (in the case of the anarchists) the use of violence for violence's sake, the growth of the behavioral sciences (sociology, anthropology, and the like) which tended to regard man as a statistic or as a being capable only of acting as a member of a class or group or other category, and, in the latter part of the period, the vogue of Bergsonian philosophy with its emphasis upon the *élan vital* and the beginning of Freudian psychology with its insistence that man is moved not by reason but by dark internal forces that he is powerless to control—all of these wore away the old liberal conviction, expressed in the writings of both Mill and Samuel Smiles, that man is a responsible being capable of improving himself by his own efforts and solving his difficulties with his own mind.

At a time when difficult new social problems were being created by the ballooning of European population (which increased by more than 30 percent between 1870 and 1900), by the continued drift to the cities (the majority of the British nation were born in cities after 1871 and the number of German cities with more than 100,000 inhabitants increased from eight in 1870 to forty-one in 1900) and by not infrequent crises of unemployment resulting from business depressions, the weakening of reliance upon reason was not a hopeful sign. For if reason could not be applied to these problems, how could they be solved? The answer that was given in more than one country was violence, applied either at those points where social distress led to agitation or at more remote points, outside the country or in distant colonial areas, where it might divert the attention of the masses from the troubles that beset them.

In these circumstances, the domestic politics of the European nations came to be marked by an increasing amount of class conflict and the relations between them by a degree of insecurity unknown in the past. In international affairs, these were, for the most part, years that were free from war, but they could hardly be described as years of peace. The mutual suspicions left over from the wars of the 1860s were heightened now by the *increased interstate friction* that resulted from the return from free trade to protection and from the resultant tariff wars and competition for markets overseas. They could hardly help but be increased further by the tendency just alluded to, that of seeking to solve domestic discontent by a search for impressive triumphs in the foreign field.

Other characteristic features of this period contributed to the uneasiness of the powers in their relations with each other. The new custom of forming permanent alliances in peacetime—a practice begun in the 1870s

—had the effect, in the end, of splitting Europe up into two great leagues held in an uneasy balance that was always threatening to, and finally did, break down. And equally important in increasing tension and insecurity were the important *changes in military administration* that occurred in his period.

With the exception of Great Britain, all of the major European states adopted universal military service after 1871, and military expenditures and the numbers in the standing army and reserves soon dwarfed the figures of the earlier period. In the conditions of competition that ensued, the lengthening by one nation of its term of service, with an implied increase in its number of effectives, became a matter of international importance, and the addition of a battalion to each regiment in Germany could cause consternation and debate in France. Moreover, all nations now copied the German general staff system, which had proven its worth in 1870–1871, and the continent was soon crowded with pseudo-Moltkes and latter-day Scharnhorsts. The chief occupation of such staffs was the scientific preparation of war plans for all possible eventualities, a task that required the combined efforts of thousands of specialists in intelligence, topography, communications, ordnance, transportation, and logistics, to say nothing of the labors of the military attachés abroad and the agents they employed to detect the plans of other powers. Once these formidable machines were put in motion, it was inevitable that they would arrogate to themselves policy-making functions. In all countries, the leaders of the armed forces were consulted when difficult decisions of foreign policy had to be made; in some countries, they tended to make decisions themselves of which the Foreign Office and government were only dimly aware but which had the effect of destroying their freedom of action in moments of crisis. Questions of peace or war tended thus to be settled on the basis of military expediency.

None of this would have mattered if there had existed other means or other organizations to check the destructive forces of the age, but there were not. The Liberal parties were not the only things weakened in this age; no organized political or social or religious organization proved capable in 1914 of asserting the claims of reason against the drift into chaos. For that matter, the most important religion of this age—stronger than liberalism, stronger than the varieties of socialism that will be described below, stronger even than organized Christianity—was *nationalism*, a blatant, uncritical, assertive nationalism that was propagated in the public schools, in the yellow journals which invented jingoism for the new and credulous reading public produced by those schools, and even in the lectures of university professors. Popular tribunes like Heinrich von Treitschke, Maurice Barrès, and Charles Maurras preached that the end of all state action should be "the exclusive pursuit of national policies, the absolute maintenance of national integrity, and the steady increase of national power"; and their eloquence persuaded countless numbers of otherwise reasonable people to regard foreigners as dangerous and untrustworthy enemies against whom stringent action was necessary and commendable. The existence of a new literate but gullible reading public, capable of being played upon by apostles of integral nationalism, was one of the complications of the age. Statesmen who sincerely wanted to preserve peace had to spend unceasing effort to inform and direct this impressionable public opinion. Politicians interested only in holding their jobs would be tempted to tickle the ears of the groundlings, thus aiding and abetting the ugly nationalism of the age.

That the period which extended from 1871 to 1914 was one filled with impressive achievements in many fields cannot be denied. One need only think of the tremendous improvement in the material conditions of living, the achievement in most countries of systems of free compulsory elementary education, the steady *progress of science* which was marked by such notable triumphs as the promulgation of the electron theory and the discovery of radioactivity, or the great increases in medical knowledge which found immediate reflection in longer life and the decline of infant mortality.

In the field of *the arts*, the accomplishments of this period were hardly less distinguished. The least cultivated elements of the vastly expanded reading public doubtless found their artistic tastes satisfied by the popular newspapers (like *Le Petit Journal* of Paris and *The Daily Mail* of London, which consistently sold more than a million copies daily by providing a varied literary fare for its subscribers) or by family journals with names like *Tit Bits* and *Gartenlaube*. But more serious readers could choose from a literature varied enough to suit every taste. This included the work of such masters of psychological realism as Tolstoy, Zola, Thomas Hardy, the Berlin novelist Theodor Fontane, and the Norwegian Björnson; the historical romances of Robert Louis Stevenson, Conrad Ferdinand Meyer, and Henryk Sienkiewicz, and tales of adventure in exotic lands by Rudyard Kipling, H. Rider Haggard, and Pierre Loti; H. G. Wells' stories of science and future worlds, and A. Conan Doyle's reports on the exploits of Sherlock Holmes (who became a European figure in the 1880s); the elaborately stylized novels of George Meredith, Henry James, and George Moore; and the first works of such writers of the postwar period as John Galsworthy, Thomas Mann, and Marcel Proust. In the field of the drama, the most popular productions continued to be of the type made fashionable by Dumas, but at the beginning of the 1880s naturalism began to conquer the stage. The most profound influence in this respect was that wielded by the Norwegian Henrik Ibsen, whose attacks upon the conventions of the romantic drama affected the

Luncheon of the Boating Party, 1881, by Pierre Auguste Renoir. The Phillips Collection, Washington, D.C.

work of a whole generation and were reflected in the plays of Hauptmann and Sudermann in Germany, Chekhov in Russia, Schnitzler in Austria, and, above all, Ibsen's truest follower, George Bernard Shaw, whose assaults upon bourgeois morality, romantic idealism, and the heroic and the sublime equaled those of his master in vigor.

In painting and in poetry the most significant movement was that of impressionism, which Arnold Hauser has suggested was an artistic reflection of the new dynamism and new feeling for speed and change that was introduced into European life by modern technology. In painting impressionism was characterized by an attempt to portray reality not as something existing but as something in the process of becoming or ceasing to be; and every impressionistic picture, whether it was painted by Degas or by Toulouse-Lautrec, was the portrayal of a moment in time in such a way that it enabled the observer to sense the unceasing processes of growth and decline. The poets of impressionism sought equally to express reality in terms of fleeting sensations, momentary moods, vague perceptions; and this made it more difficult for the general reader to understand the poetry of Verlaine and Mallarmé, or Detlev von Liliencron and Rilke, than it had been to understand that of Lamartine or Eichendorff.

Impressionism affected the philosophy as well as the art of the last years of this period. Both Freud's psychoanalysis and Bergson's philosophy of vitalism are intimately connected with it, for the Viennese doctor's notions would be incomprehensible without impressionism's view of reality as composed of constantly changing moods, impressions, and ideas, and Bergson's emphasis upon the spiritual as opposed to the mechanical forces in life was informed by impressionism's implicit denial of materialism as a philosophy. With respect to this last point, it may be noted that Bergson's philosophy had great influence (although perhaps not always for the good) on the writers of the years immediately preceding the outbreak of World War I, leading some of them, like Alain-Fournier and Francis Jammes, André Gide and Stefan George, Charles Péguy and Gabriele d'Annunzio, to abandon the passive art-for-art's sake attitude of earlier impressionist poets and turn to a new activism which sought to change society.

In music the giants of the period were still Wagner, Gounoud, and Verdi, whose work had begun before 1870. But Tchaikovsky, Moussorgsky, Rimsky-Korsakov, Smetana, and Dvorak were making the folk music of Eastern Europe known to the whole continent; Saint-Saëns, Massenet, Grieg, and Richard Strauss were at their height; Puccini's *La Bohême* was arousing lachrymose enthusiasm all over Europe; and Gilbert and Sullivan were delighting English audiences with operettas whose charm and wit are still undimmed.

These triumphs were so notable that one wonders what might have been achieved in Europe had not so much of the energy of these years been devoted to activities that were essentially destructive.

11

The Great Powers and the Balance of Power, 1871-1890

After a great storm, the sea is likely to work for some time. So, after all the conflicts of the 1860s and the culminating war of 1870, it was not surprising that the international climate should have been turbulent for a period. What was alarming, however, was that the atmosphere did not, with the passing of time, improve.

The great powers of Europe, in their dealings with each other, were never after 1871 able to re-establish that sense of interdependence and mutual confidence that had enabled the European Concert to work so effectively and with so little formal machinery in the first part of the nineteenth century. The Concert of Europe was, on occasion, called into existence and on one notable occasion, at Berlin in 1878, it acted with the authority and efficiency of an earlier age. For the rest, however, its infrequent meetings were for the purpose of dealing with matters that were not of vital interest to the powers, such as colonial affairs, rights of international navigation, and the like. For the protection of their essential interests, on the other hand, the powers preferred to rely on their own resources and efforts or—increasingly in the years after 1880—to find security in permanent secret alliances with states they felt they could trust against others whom they were sure they could not. Once this latter tendency had set in, it inevitably came to embrace all the large states of Europe so that they were arrayed against each other in armed coalitions.

To be sure, this created a kind of balance of power, but one which had none of the free play which characterized the equilibrium of forces that had maintained the peace in the first half of the century. Woodrow Wilson once said that the secret alliances were the principal cause of World War I. To the extent that they increased the distrust of the powers while at the same time limiting their freedom of maneuver, he was right.

Insecurity after 1871 / The overwhelming German victory over France and the resultant reorganization of Europe left all states feeling insecure and distrustful of their neighbors. Even the ordinarily phlegmatic British were dismayed by the completeness of the German victory. Gladstone felt that it would "lead from bad to worse and . . . be the beginning of a new series of European complications"; and, speaking in the House of Commons, Sir Robert Peel (the younger) said, "I must say that I look on the unification of Germany as a great peril to Europe. . . . It cannot be for the good of Europe that there should be a great military despotism in Germany built on the ruin and destruction of France." Other British leaders foresaw the possibility of German attacks upon the Low Countries; and there were some who actually feared a German invasion of England at a convenient moment.

This particular English fear was alleviated to some extent in the years that followed, for Bismarck's Germany took care not to threaten any of England's vital interests. But the marked increase in German population and power continued to worry the British and probably had something to do with their affirmative response to Disraeli's insistence, in a speech of 1872, that they must stop thinking in continental and begin to think in world terms, building up their imperial strength lest they suffer the fate of those whose horizons were limited to Europe (doubtless an oblique reference to Germany's recent victims). And, when the British people began to put a higher valuation upon their empire than they had formerly done, they became prey to suspicions of all powers which could jeopardize their lines of communication with the empire, especially the Russians, whose activities in the Middle East, the Persian Gulf, and Central Asia began seriously to worry Whitehall in the middle 1870s.

The Russians reciprocated these feelings, for the British were the main obstacle to their ambitions at Constantinople and along the northwestern frontier of India. But they were even more suspicious of the Austrians who, barred from Germany in 1866, had, under Hungarian influence, become increasingly interested in the opportunities for the economic exploitation of the Balkan areas. That great agglomeration of Slavic peoples the Russians regarded as an area to be liberated from Turkish rule by Russian initiative when the right occasion arose, and the thought of being anticipated by the Austrians was insupportable. Unless the proper countermeasures were prepared it might well be—as one Russian diplomat said in the 1880s,—that "Austria [would] girdle the Balkan Peninsula with railways, encircle Montenegro with fortresses, subject the Serbs and Bulgarians economically, and flood Bulgaria, Serbia, and Macedonia with Jesuit missions, with educational institutions, with Catholic propaganda, and, finally, with German colonists."

Austria's ambitions were not, perhaps, as extensive as the Russians thought, but there was no doubt that the Austro-Hungarian government was interested in the Balkans in general and was opposed to any pronounced extension of Russian influence there, or any liberation movement inspired by Russia that might affect the security of its own Slavic provinces. Thus, even in the early 1870s, it was possible to discern the outlines of future Austro-Russian conflict in this important area. Nor was the Austro-Hungarian government concerned only with the potential Russian threat to imperial unity. The newly united Italy also represented a danger, since the most ardent Italian patriots regarded the Austrian Brenner provinces (the so-called Trentino) and the port of Trieste as legitimate territorial objectives, because they were peopled largely by Italian-speaking inhabitants. The question of this "unredeemed Italy" was therefore a barrier to complete understanding between Austria and its southern neighbor.

Italy was the most recently recognized great power and the one whose status was most in question as a result of her unhappy military past. The desire to make other peoples forget that record often seemed to be a determinant of Italian policy, giving it an active character which aroused the irritation and suspicion of other powers. The sporadic agitations for the Trentino and Trieste are to be explained by this; and so are the repeated campaigns against the papacy, which had lost its temporal power as a result of Italy's unification but had steadfastly refused to recognize the government that has dispossessed it. The anti-Vatican demonstrations, which were as often as not supported by the government, made difficult Italy's relations with the governments of all other Catholic countries and especially, in the first years after 1871, with France.

France, as the one republican government in Europe, was regarded with wariness by all the powers. In return, its governments treated Great Britain, Austria-Hungary, and Russia with formal correctness, Italy with irritated condescension, and Germany with cold hostility. The results of the war of 1870 would have made relations between France and its eastern neighbor difficult in any case; but the necessity of ceding Alsace and Lorraine to Germany made them doubly so. "The surrender of Alsace-Lorraine," one French deputy wrote, "means an endless war behind the mask of peace."

In such conditions of insecurity the possibility of war was never absent from the minds of European statesmen in the decade after 1870.

The War Scare of 1875 / Momentarily, in the year 1875, it seemed as if their worst fears might be realized. French-German relations deteriorated steadily in the first years after the restoration of peace. This was partly due, as we have already seen, to the nature of the peace terms, but there were other reasons as well. The chief of them was the remarkable speed with which the French nation recovered from its defeat. The German terms had been conceived as a means of delaying the material and political recovery of France until its traditional rival had attained a position of unassailable superiority; and it had been assumed that the French would be unable to pay off the war indemnity on the date set in the treaty, March 2, 1874, and that in consequence German troops would continue to occupy France for perhaps a decade. To everyone's surprise, the French government fulfilled its obligations six months before the legal date. Moreover, in a gesture apparently designed to advertise France's return to great-power status, the government proceeded with the reconstitution of the French army. A law of 1872 made military service obligatory for all males (although with liberal provision for exemptions) and set the term of service at five years in the line army, and a cadre law of 1875 increased the number of battalions and indicated an intention of expanding the officer and noncommissioned officer corps.

All of this was profoundly disturbing to the Germans, who were under no illusions about French feelings. Among German soldiers the argument began to be heard that it was better to deal with France now, before she became too strong; and this preventive-war psychology seems to have affected even the chief of the General Staff, Helmuth von Moltke, despite the fact or, perhaps, because of the fact that the recent war had imbued him with considerable respect for French military prowess. Nor was this feeling confined to the soldiers. A high-ranking German diplomat admitted in the presence of his French counterpart that a preventive war would be considered justifiable by Germans; and a part of the German press took the position that war was inevitable.

It is still impossible to say with complete certainty what Bismarck's views were in this situation. He always claimed that he was opposed to preventive war on religious as well as political grounds, and once said that such a war was like committing suicide because you were afraid to die. Believing that Germany was now, in Metternich's phrase, a "saturated power," he was aware that the advantages which even successful war could bring to it were not very tangible and the dangers involved in resorting to such conflict almost overwhelming. He was nevertheless alarmed by the speed with which France was recovering

and was irritated by the protests made by French churchmε
recent measures that the Prussian government had taken aʲ
Catholic Church.[1] He seems to have encouraged both the
statements made by his diplomats and the menacing tone of tʰ
press; and one may conclude from this that, at the very least, he was
intent on intimidating the French government, perhaps in the hope of
making it renounce its recent military legislation.

If this was his intention, he made the mistake of giving too much
encouragement to the advocates of war. This had the effect of alarming
other powers besides France, and the French government was able to
play upon this fear. In response to its solicitation, both the British
government and the Russian government intervened in Berlin; and the
tsar of Russia paid a special visit to the German capital, presumably to
remonstrate with his brother sovereign. Bismarck found it expedient to
protest that Germany's intentions were entirely peaceful and that the
crisis was an imaginary one; but there were many who agreed with
Disraeli's foreign secretary, Lord Derby, who said tartly: "It is really imposing on our supposed credulity to tell us now that our ears have
deceived us and that nothing was said or meant against France."

For France this affair of 1875 was a minor triumph, proving that she
could, in certain circumstances, count upon the sympathy of other
powers. For Bismarck it was a decided setback, not only because he was
powerless now to impede French rearmament but because his tactics
had weakened Germany's position in other ways. Certainly all the powers
who had earlier regarded Germany's acquisition of Alsace-Lorraine as a
violation of the principle of nationalities and a sign that Germany might
have wider territorial ambitions had been given additional reason for
their suspicions. Moreover, even Germany's friends had shown no disposition to support her in this affair. In 1872 Germany, Austria-Hungary
and Russia had concluded a loose agreement calling for mutual consultation and support in matters of international importance. This so-
called Three Emperors' League had now proved to be without real
meaning, for the Russians had seen fit to support France in the crisis of
1875. All in all, Bismarck was led to believe that his country was in a
state bordering on isolation and this, unless corrected, might be dangerous.

Balkan Troubles, 1875–1877 / While the German chancellor was
reflecting on these things, a new series of Balkan complications began.
In August 1875, in Bosnia and Herzegovina, an area lying to the northwest of Serbia, an insurrection began against Turkish rule. The causes

---

[1] On these measures, which were part of the so-called *Kulturkampf*, see below,
pp. 377–379.

of this were mixed. The provinces in question were Southern Slav in nationality and predominantly Christian in religion and, for both reasons, were unhappy about their political condition. Their national self-consciousness had been encouraged by Serbian propaganda, for the Serbs had dreams of acquiring this sizable territory; and it had been influenced further by crop failures, which reduced much of the peasantry to penury, and by unemployment among the artisan class which seems to have been caused by Turkish trade practices.

Once agitation began in Bosnia and Herzegovina, it spread rapidly to other Turkish parts of the Balkans. This was particularly true of Bulgaria, where the ground had been carefully prepared by the Bulgarian church (which had been given a large measure of autonomy by the sultan in 1870 and had immediately become a focal point of nationalistic agitation), by schoolteachers and intellectuals, and, not least, by Russian agents, who were beginning to show great interest in Bulgaria.

If proof were needed of the inadequacy of the European Concert in the period after 1870 it would be easy to find it in the long series of Balkan crises. In this one, there can be no doubt that peace could have been restored if Russia, Great Britain, and Austria-Hungary had worked together to that end. But the Disraeli government in England was suspicious of Russian intentions at the Straits and was consequently reluctant to join in any pressure upon the Turkish government that might lead to territorial losses by that government. Simultaneously, the Russian government was split between those who favored working with the other powers for the maintenance of the *status quo* in the Balkans and the influential Pan-Slav group who believed that Russia must take advantage of the Balkan troubles to free the Slavic peoples of the yoke of foreign bondage and mold them into a great federation under Russian patronage. At the onset of the Balkan risings, Prince Gorchakov worked energetically for Austro-Russian collaboration; by 1876, as the agitations continued and as the principalities of Serbia and Montenegro declared war against the Turks, Russian foreign policy fell increasingly under the influence of the Pan-Slavs, who argued that Russia must go her own way.

The disharmony of the powers was seen most clearly at the end of 1876. Despite the inefficiency of Turkish government in general the sultan was fortunate in possessing able military commanders, and one of these, Osman Pasha, imposed such crushing defeats upon the Serbian forces in September and October that they appealed to the powers for protection. Under international pressure, the Turkish government was forced to agree to a conference which met at Constantinople in December and drafted a general settlement. But the British government—deluded perhaps by the promulgation of a new and supposedly "liberal" constitution by the new sultan, Abdul Hamid II—secretly encouraged that

In the Russian trenches during the siege of Plevna, 1877. From *Illustrated London News*, Nov. 10, 1877.

unscrupulous ruler to defy the conference, which he proceeded to do in January 1877.

This action exhausted Russian patience. In April 1877, when its military preparations were complete, the Russian government announced that it could no longer tolerate Turkish atrocities against its fellow religionists; and, in June, Russian forces crossed the Danube and began to move swiftly toward Constantinople, with every prospect of reaching it within a month. What the future history of Europe might have been like if they had succeeded is impossible to guess; it is difficult to see how the Russians could have been dislodged from the Straits if they had once been permitted to capture them. But it never came to that. In the middle of July a Turkish force of 12,000 men under Osman Pasha moved into the Bulgarian town of Plevna on the Russian flank and began swiftly to entrench themselves and to build redoubts for reinforcements that were on their way. The Russians did not dare proceed without removing this threat to their line of communication, and they turned their forces against Plevna. Despite prodigies of heroism and incredible losses, they were, however, unable to break the Turkish resistance until December 1877.

The battle of Plevna proved that, after the swift wars of movement of the 1860s, the power of the defense in warfare had revived and that—although professional soldiers were slow to realize this—the vast improvement in fire power made possible by the magazine rifle (and, in the not-too-distant future, the machine gun) would call into question all plans based on shock tactics alone. The political results of Plevna were more immediate. The protracted Turkish defense at Plevna transformed the anti-Turkish sentiment in the west into something bordering on sympathy, if not enthusiasm, while at the same time allowing suspicion of Russia's intentions to grow and preparations to block its ambitions to take form. When the Russians resumed their push toward the Straits, they found the international climate had cooled significantly; and, when Turkish resistance collapsed and the Russian government imposed terms, they discovered that Great Britain and Austria-Hungary were prepared to oppose them.

This is understandable, for the Peace of San Stefano of March 1878, negotiated by the Russian ambassador at Constantinople, an ardent Pan-Slav named Ignatiev, threatened to make Russian influence paramount from the straits to the Adriatic. It called for the cession to Russia of Kars, Ardahan, and Bayazid, and of Batum on the eastern shores of the Black Sea, as well as the area known as the Dobrudja. More significantly, it provided for the creation of a large Bulgarian state, which would stretch from Macedonia to Salonika on the Aegean and which would be occupied by Russian troops for a period of two years. The additional provisions of the treaty, for an increase of Serbian and Montegrin territory and for the creation of an autonomous Bosnia-Herzegovina under Austro-Russian supervision were hardly calculated to allay Austro-Hungarian fears (the more so because the Russians conveniently forgot that they had previously promised that, in the event of Balkan charges, they would support the Austrian acquisition of Bosnia); and the treaty as a whole was considered completely inadmissible by Great Britain. Indeed, even before its signature, the British government had ordered the fleet to proceed to the Straits, and British public opinion was in an excitable state. The modern term jingoism, meaning belligerence, stems from these tense moments of 1878, when British music-hall audiences were chanting

> We don't want to fight
> But, by jingo!, if we do
> We've got the ships, we've got the men,
> We've got the money too!

Throughout these complications, Prince Bismarck, to the irritation of those powers which wanted his advice or support, had remained elaborately disinterested; it was, indeed, during this tangled affair that he made his famous remark about the Balkans not being worth the bones of a Pomeranian grenadier. The German chancellor was, however, aware that he would be in an awkward position if war actually broke out, especially if Austria-Hungary and Russia were on opposite sides, for each would expect Germany's support, and refusal to give it might have unhappy political results, (as Austria had proved during the Crimean War). Aside from this, any major war would have incalculable results in the present state of Europe. Bismarck, therefore, assumed the task of mediation and offered the hospitality of Berlin for an international congress that might draw up a general settlement for eastern affairs.

The Congress of Berlin / The Russians accepted the offer primarily because their armies were exhausted by the unexpected rigors of the Turkish war and were not enthusiastic about a test against Great Britain, aided perhaps by Austria. The other powers fell in line, and the congress assembled in the German capital in June 1878. Including among its delegates such ornaments of the diplomatic art as Bismarck himself, Disraeli and Salisbury of Great Britain, Gorchakov and Shuvalov of Russia, Andrassy of Hungary, Waddington of France, and Corti of Italy, in addition to the representatives of Turkey and the observers of the Balkan states, the Congress of Berlin was easily the most distinguished diplomatic gathering between the Vienna Congress of 1814–1815 and the Paris Peace Conference of 1919. The results of its labors were not, however, as brilliant as its cast of characters.

It was probably inevitable that more people would be disappointed than pleased by a settlement of any kind, for almost all the Balkan peoples had been led by the events of the previous three years to entertain unreasonable expectations. Some of their aspirations were certainly realized. Rumania now completed the process begun in 1856 by becoming an independent sovereign state, as did Serbia and Montenegro; and Bulgaria was made an autonomous principality that was, to all intents and purposes, free from any further Turkish interference. On the other hand, when the terms of the Berlin Treaty were complete, in July 1878, the Serbs, who had hoped to acquire Bosnia and Herzegovina, found that these provinces were to pass under Austrian administration. The Rumanians were asked, in return for the Dobrudja, to cede to Russia those Bessarabian provinces that they had gained in 1856, although this meant that many of their co-nationals must now live under alien rule. The Bulgars, after all the high hopes of 1877, found that their country was going to be much smaller than they had expected and that the Serbs were to be compensated with districts they felt should rightly belong to them. The Greeks, who had expected a complete Turkish collapse that would bring them Epirus and Crete, received neither and were further outraged to see a restored and guaranteed Turkey cede Cyprus to Great Britain. Almost every territorial decision made at Berlin contained disappointment and the seeds of future Balkan revisionism and war.

Of the hopes of the Russian Pan-Slavs, very little was left; and because of this Russia was probably the most aggrieved member of the Congress (except perhaps Turkey, who lost half of its European territory and population). Despite their heavy expenditure of money and men in the recent hostilities, the Russians had little to show. The Bulgaria that was to have been the springboard of further Russian expansion was a mere shadow of what had been hoped; and Russian acquisition of Bessarabia, Kars, Batum, and Ardahan was hardly impressive, especially when one considered that, without the loss of a man, Great Britain had acquired Cyprus and strengthened its position at the Straits, Austria-Hungary had gained Bosnia, and the French had been encouraged to move into Tunis whenever they saw fit. The Russians were mortified with these results, and they tended to blame them on the man who, in their opinion, had refused to repay their former services to him in 1866 and 1870 and had invited them to Berlin only to be despoiled—Prince Bismarck.

Bismarck's Alliance System / The German chancellor was fully aware of Russian feelings and sufficiently impressed by them to feel that some urgent action on his part was necessary. Russian resentment might conceivably lead, he feared, to a *rapprochement* between St. Petersburg and Paris, which would place the German empire in a dangerously exposed position. In the past Bismarck had been willing to pursue his policies unencumbered by any but the most casual of engagements with other powers. Now, however, he felt it expedient to have some more formal assurances of aid in the event of trouble; and, in 1879, he turned to Vienna and concluded the famous Dual Alliance with the Hapsburg empire.

Because of his emperor's strong predilection for Russia, Bismarck hoped to make this a general treaty, calling for mutual assistance if either partner were attacked by a third power. The Austro-Hungarian foreign minister, Count Andrassy, felt that this might be interpreted as anti-French and, his own relations with Paris being good, insisted that the new treaty mention Russia explicitly. It is a measure of Bismarck's feeling of insecurity that he gave way, agreeing to a treaty which called for mutual assistance if either signatory were attacked by Russia and for benevolent neutrality if either were attacked by another power. The completed treaty (which Bismarck persuaded his sovereign to ratify only by threatening to resign if he refused to do so) was a landmark in European history. While previous treaties had usually been concluded during or on the eve of wars, or for specific purposes and restricted duration, this was a peacetime treaty and, as it turned out, a permanent one, for it did not lapse until 1918. It was, moreover, the first of the secret treaties, whose contents were never fully known but always suspected and which encouraged other powers to negotiate similar treaties in self-defense, until all Europe was divided into league and counterleague.

With these long-term results Bismarck could not be expected to be concerned. He had sought this treaty in order to attain a greater degree of security than he had felt since 1871, and it more than fulfilled his expectations. The Russian government proved to be far less interested in the friendship of France than Bismarck had feared in 1878; and the treaty of 1879, for from driving them toward Paris, turned them back to Berlin. Doubtless calculating that Austro-German collaboration might be turned against Russia in the Balkans, the Russians in 1880 asked for what amounted to a renewal of the Three Emperors' League of 1872 and, although the Austrians were less enthusiastic about this than Bismarck was, an alliance was signed in June 1881 that pledged the three partners to neutrality in the event of a war between one of their number and a fourth European power and provided for mutual consultation in Balkan affairs.

The renewal of the *Dreikaiserbündnis* gave Bismarck reason to hope that he might be able to avoid future troubles between Austria and Russia in Southeast Europe. From a more general point of view it gratified him because it gave him a measure of control over all European politics. As he said on one occasion, one must not lose sight of

the importance of being one of three on the European chess-board. That is the invariable objective of all cabinets and of mine above all others. Nobody wishes to be in a minority. All politics reduce themselves to this formula: to try to be one of three, so long as the world is governed by an unstable equilibrium of five Great Powers.

Aside from this, the alliance of 1881 effectively isolated France. There was always a possibility, of course, that it might become allied either with Italy or with Great Britain, but this was remote. The French seizure of Tunis in 1881—a belated consequence of the deliberations at Berlin in 1878—made the Italians fearful that this was the beginning of a policy which would eventuate in French control of all North Africa. To secure some assurance that they would not be excluded from an area where their economic interests were slowly growing, they consulted Bismarck about the possibility of an alliance but were told by him that they must first negotiate with the Austrians. This meant an end to any immediate hope of winning the Trentino or Trieste, but the Italians felt they had no choice. In May 1882 they joined with Germany and Austria in the so-called Triple Alliance which assured them of aid in the event of a French attack on Italy but obliged them to go to war if Germany were attacked by France or either Germany or Austria were attacked by two or more powers.

The Italian gains from this engagement were illusory, and French resentment at Italy's association with her enemy eventually took the form of a tariff war which had ruinous effects in Italy (see p. 341). For Bismarck the Triple Alliance had the advantage of eliminating one more potential ally of France. Almost simultaneously, the chances of any Anglo-French agreement were reduced to a nullity. In July 1882 a British fleet bombarded Alexandria and British forces occupied Egypt, and this action, in a country in which France had been active for almost a century, aroused a hostility against Britain that prevented any real understanding until the beginning of the new century.

Thanks to his decision to turn to Austria in 1879, to his subsequent negotiations, to the apprehensions of other powers, and to several unforeseen and unforeseeable occurrences, Bismarck had been able to improve Germany's position immeasurably by 1882. But even at this date the system he had elaborated to give Germany security was a very complicated one, and in its complications were the germs of future trouble.

The Bulgarian Crisis / In the middle 1880s, Bismarck's security system was strained to the utmost by new Balkan complications, this time in the state of Bulgaria. These arose from the fact that Russia, having fought for Bulgarian freedom and, in the first years after the Congress of Berlin, helped the fledgling state organize its political and military institutions, expected Bulgaria to repay these services, not only with gratitude but with deference to Russian advice. The majority of literate

Bulgarians, however, were imbued with national pride and had no desire to be particularly deferential to anyone. This difference of view was given specific point by the policies of Prince Alexander of Battenberg, a nephew of the tsar who had been elected to the Bulgarian throne in 1879 with Russian approval. An energetic but ambitious ruler, without judgment or balance, Alexander first annoyed the Russians by becoming involved in disputes with Russian officials who occupied high positions in his administration; he then infuriated them by giving preference to Austrian interests which were working for the construction of a Bulgarian link that would complete the projected Orient Railways, designed to run from Austria, across Serbia and Bulgaria, to Adrianople and Constantinople. To the Russians, already alarmed by Austrian political and commercial treaties with Serbia (1881) and Rumania (1883), it seemed essential to block the construction of the Bulgarian part of this rail system; Alexander's refusal to fall in with their plans was intolerable.

The prince's open brushes with the Russians nevertheless made him popular with the Bulgarian assembly and with those sections of the population who had learned to hate the highhandedness of Russian officials; and this made it impossible for him to change his course. His self-assurance was increased, moreover, by two events in 1885: his successful annexation of the Turkish province of Eastern Roumelia, after a revolution in its capital Philippopolis; and a brilliant military campaign against the Serbs, who were ill-advised enough to seek compensation for the Roumelian annexation by military means and were soundly beaten within four weeks.

After this had happened, the Russians were afraid that they might lose all control over the Bulgarian state. To prevent this, they fomented a conspiracy within the Bulgarian army that succeeded, in August 1886, in deposing Alexander and forcing him to leave the country. This patently contrived affair aroused and alarmed the other Great Powers, and so did the Russian government's high-handed attempts in subsequent months to reduce the Bulgarian state to the position of a satellite with a ruler chosen by itself. Against these tactics the Bulgarian assembly stood firm, eventually (in July 1887) choosing a new prince, Ferdinand of Saxe-Coburg, whose views were even more pronouncedly Austrian than his predecessor's. Before this had happened, however, Bulgarian affairs had embroiled all the Great Powers and come close to destroying Bismarck's alliance system.

Certainly the reconstituted Three Emperors League of 1881 was brought to the verge of collapse by these events, for the Russians, even in 1886, seemed on the point of employing force to subdue Bulgaria, and the Austrians had begun to make military preparations to counter Russian moves. If a military clash came between his two allies, Bismarck knew that he would have to support Austria-Hungary. He dared not suggest this to the Russians, however, because he feared that, even if such a warning temporarily deferred a Balkan war, it might prepare the way for a bigger conflict by driving the Russians into the arms of France. The Pan-Slav press was already openly discussing the possibility of a Franco-Russian alliance. Such an alliance was of special concern to the German chancellor at this moment because of an ugly turn in French politics. In the fall of 1886, there seemed to be a strong possibility that the Third Republic would be replaced by a dictatorship of the war minister, General Boulanger, who was currently the idol of French nationalists and who had made some menacing speeches about the necessity of regaining the lost provinces.[2] An alliance between a Boulangist France and a Pan-Slav Russia might confront Germany with a two-front war in the near future.

Or so Bismarck thought. And because he felt this way he believed it necessary, ostensibly at least, to support the tsar's Bulgarian ambitions. On the other hand, since their fulfillment might force Austria to go to war, he had, at the same time, to see that they were not realized! This was a difficult assignment, requiring skill and guile if it were to be effected.

These were qualities, however, with which the chancellor had always been richly endowed. To meet the French threat, he called for an increase in the German standing army from 427,000 to 468,000 men and, when the Reichstag refused to approve it, dissolved that assembly and conducted a tub-thumping electoral campaign that got him the majority he needed for passing his bill. This dramatized Germany's armed might and her willingness to use it, and had a sensibly sobering effect in Paris. So did the news, in February 1887, that Germany had renewed the Triple Alliance with Austria and Italy. This announcement led the French government to suspect that plans for concerted action against France may have been worked out in the secret discussions.[3]

If these events dimmed French ardor for any anti-German action, they did not deter the Russian push toward Bulgaria. But an Italian admission, during the alliance talks, that Italy was interested in the Balkans and would not welcome Russian domination of that area gave Bismarck an opportunity to suggest that Italy might find support for its Balkan views in London and Vienna. In March 1887 this suggestion blossomed into the so-called Mediterranean Agreement between Italy, Austria-Hungary, and Great Britain, which provided for mutual support in the case of differences with a fourth power; the agreement was clearly oriented against Russia. The Conservative prime minister in Great Britain, Lord Salisbury,

---

[2] On the Boulanger crisis, see below, pp. 361–363.
[3] In order to win Italy's renewal, the German government had, in fact, promised to support the Italians if they felt compelled to use military means against any French move in Tripoli or Morocco.

welcomed this engagement because he was firmly opposed to the growth of Russian influence in the Balkans and felt, as he said, that "it is well that the Tsar should know it." Salisbury hoped, moreover, that cooperation with the Triple Alliance in the Balkans might be repaid by support for Britain's new position in Egypt in case of strong French or Franco-Russian pressure there. These considerations led him to fall in with Bismarck's plans, and the resultant Mediterranean Agreement helped deter the tsar from aggressive action in Bulgaria without directly involving Bismarck.

These complicated maneuvers were followed by others even more so. To make quite certain that Russia would not, even at this date, turn to France, Bismarck negotiated a new alliance with Russia. The Reinsurance Treaty of June 1887 pledged each of the partners to benevolent neutrality in the event that the other was attacked by a third power. From a strictly legal point of view, it was not incompatible with Germany's alliance of 1879 with Austria, which was, after all, a defensive engagement. From a moral standpoint, it is harder to justify. By its secret clauses Germany promised to support Russian interests in Bulgaria and at the Straits; but, before the year was over, Bismarck was encouraging the three Mediterranean powers to conclude a supplementary agreement by which they declared themselves defenders of the existing status in the Balkans and provided for concerted action in case it were threatened. Before this clear warning the Russian government was forced to abandon its intentions of asserting its control of Bulgaria, not without some bitter reflections about the disadvantages of having an ally who took away with his left hand what he had given with his right. Relative peace now descended on the Balkans.

Economic and Military Influence in Diplomacy / Brief mention may be made here of two interesting aspects of this tangled Bulgarian problem. The first is the importance of economic factors, not only in the inception but also in the solution of the crisis. It had, after all, been economic ambition on the part of Austria and economic fears on the part of Russia that had supplied the context in which Alexander of Battenberg's policies were inaugurated. Moreover, this was only the first of a number of Balkan and Middle Eastern complications in which railroad building would play an important part. Finally, among the weapons used by Bismarck to control the Russians at the height of the Bulgarian crisis, financial manipulation was not the least important. The most dramatic instance of this came in November 1887, when the German government forbade the Reichsbank to accept Russian securities as collateral for loans. This move was regarded by investors as a sign of lack of confidence in Russian credit, and the resultant sales of Russian holdings led to a precipitous fall in prices and seriously handicapped Russian financial operations. The

German government's action was, in part, a retaliation against certain discriminatory Russian practices, but there is little doubt that Bismarck's primary motive was to create one more obstacle to effective Russian military action in the Balkans. His stroke doubtless had some effect on the solution of the crisis. It also had a more far-reaching result. It induced the Russian government in subsequent years to turn toward the French financial market and thus helped pave the way for the very Franco-Russian political *rapprochement* that Bismarck feared.

The Bulgarian crisis also showed a marked increase in the influence of the military in diplomacy. Leaving aside the dangers created by the eruption of General Boulanger in French politics, the most striking manifestation of this came in the development of Austro-German relations in 1887. As the Bulgarian affair reached its most dangerous state, Bismarck learned that the German military attaché in Vienna, apparently with the backing of the Great General Staff in Berlin, was encouraging Emperor Francis Joseph and the Austrian command to believe that Germany would support an Austrian war against Russia. The chancellor reacted swiftly to this recurrence of the preventive-war psychology of 1875. In a masterly instruction to his ambassador in Vienna, he pointed out that, under the Dual Alliance of 1879, Germany was obliged to support its ally only if it were attacked, and he urged him to remind the emperor of this. Simultaneously, Bismarck remonstrated with the military chiefs in Berlin and threatened to wash his hands of responsibility in case of further incursions into foreign policy by the soldiers. This was enough to stop military meddling on this occasion, but there were to be many instances of this sort of thing in the future. In 1909, for instance, another German chief of staff was to assure the Austrians of German support if they felt called upon to take the initiative in a war with Russia and, on that occasion, no German statesman was strong enough to maintain civilian supremacy in the sphere of foreign policy by protesting against this significant expansion of Germany's obligations under the treaty of 1879.

But all that lay far in the future and could not be foreseen in 1888. By the beginning of that year the troublesome Bulgarian crisis had finally been liquidated, and international tension had been relaxed. Bismarck could take satisfaction in the fact that his network of alliances was still in good repair and, indeed, had been strengthened by Great Britain's association with the junior members of the Triple Alliance. There was no immediate prospect of new troubles in Europe. The warmongers in France and the Pan-Slavs in Russian were in eclipse, and the attention of all powers was becoming increasingly absorbed by problems of territorial expansion and colonial exploitation in areas far from the European center.

12

The Evolution of Capitalism and the Spread of Socialism, 1871-1914

ECONOMIC DEVELOPMENTS

The Progress of Industrialization / It has become fashionable among economic historians to use the term "the take-off" to describe that decisive period during which a society abandons its traditional, static, agricultural economy and commits itself to a future of industrialism. When this transformation succeeds, economic growth becomes largely automatic. But in order to be successful, take-off requires, as W. W. Rostow has written, "a massive set of preconditions going to the heart of a society's economic organization and its effective scale of values." The parochialism and regionalism characteristic of an agricultural society must give way to a habit of thinking in national and international terms. A new elite must arise that believes in productive change and formulates methods of attaining it. The income of society above minimum levels of consumption must begin to be invested, not in the external adornments of a traditional leisure class, but in those things that will make sustained economic growth possible—roads, railways, schools, factories, and other forms of social capital; and the rate of such investment will have to reach a level at which the increase of output exceeds the increase of population.

In the history of Europe, the precise nature of the psychological and sociological reorientation that preceded take-off and the length of time needed to create the institutions and accumulate the capital necessary for the transition to modern industrialism differed from country to country. Great Britain led the way at the very beginning of the nineteenth century, and she was most closely followed by Belgium, where investment capital and technological skill were supplemented by English loans and assistance. In the years that stretched between 1830 and 1870 these trail-blazers were followed by France, whose take-off was presided over by Louis Philippe, and Germany, where the nationalism of the rising middle class and such tangible manifestations of it as the Prussian Customs Union and the railroad building of the 1850s and 1860s were the preconditions for the surge of industrial activity that was to take place after the unification of the country (see pp. 385–387).

The period that began in 1871 and ended with the outbreak of war in 1914 saw the other European nations enter the industrial age. The opening of British and French markets to Swedish timber, after the tariff reductions of the 1860s, stimulated the modernization of the timber industry and the building of railroads, and these, in turn, made possible the capital accumulation that prepared the way for Sweden's take-off in the early 1870s. Denmark and the Low Countries were further behind, largely because of the lack of mineral deposits of their own, but by the middle of the period, with the aid of imported machinery, they were applying modern industrial techniques to the production of glass and porcelain and of comestibles like sugar, cocoa and alcoholic beverages.

As one moved south or east in Europe, progress was still slower. Italian industry received a pronounced impetus from the completion of national unity, but its initial progress was slowed by the ruinous effects of the tariff war with France in the late 1880s and by the failure to modernize methods of agricultural production in such a way as to increase capital for investment. The traditional agricultural system and the social institutions that went with it had a persistence in Italy that was matched only in Spain.

In the Austro-Hungarian Empire, the picture was mixed. Austria itself and Bohemia had become industrial centers of importance even before 1870, but Hungary remained a rural-based traditional society, and, as late as 1914, the empire as a whole still lacked either the kind of social capital mentioned above, or a strong class committed to the idea of modernization. In consequence, it still suffered from the growing pains of the pre-take-off stage.

The progress made by Russia was more noticeable than that of her sister empire to the west. The abolition of serfdom was the first definite move away from the traditional system, although it took another generation before its effects in creating a new balance between urban and

ural population were felt and a middle class arose that was large enough
and energetic enough to have an effect on policy. The railroad building
of the 1880s and the efforts of Count Witte, communications and finance
minister between 1892 and 1902, to increase investment opportunities
and attract capital to industrial ventures were the prelude to Russia's
take-off, and the last years before the war saw the creation of an industrial system mature enough to serve as a foundation for the later Soviet
five-year plans.

Dynamic Capitalism / The economic growth that took place in the
years following take-off tended to be irregular and was generally accompanied by marked fluctuations and periodic crises. Some of the most
spectacular of the crashes can be traced to the excessive enthusiasm of
investors or lack of experience on the part of company directors; and, in
the case of the precipitous fall of English railway stock in the 1860s and
the collapse of the German building boom in 1873, the damage could
probably have been ameliorated to some extent by private circumspection
or government regulation.

It could hardly, however, have been avoided entirely. Schumpeter has
written that the outstanding characteristic of mature capitalism is that
it is engaged perpetually in a process of creative destruction, in which it
uses up and abandons its old forms and creates new ones. This process
is effected by recurring surges of productive energy, interspersed with
periods of recoil and apparent collapse. Each surge forward is marked
by a great increase in activity in certain sectors of the economy. In time,
investment in these sectors becomes excessive and leads to some form of
setback or depression. This provides an opportunity for a regrouping of
the economic resources of society and their allocation, in a renewed
burst of creative energy, to new forms or areas of production.

The history of the period after 1871 is rich in examples of this kind
of development. Sweden's entrance into the company of the industrial
states was, for example, based on the activity of its timber export industry
and its railway construction. This first period of productive activity came
to an end in the 1890s with a depression that destroyed the country's
export markets. Sweden responded by abandoning its former reliance
on timber exports in favor of diversified production. There was a greater
concentration on wood pulp. Modern extractive methods were employed
to exploit local ores, and mining activity led successfully to the production of pig iron and fine steel, and the creation and expansion of a
modern engineering industry. Simultaneously, the development of hydro-
electric sources of power made possible the establishment of an electrical
machinery industry that was later to revolutionize methods in all of
Sweden's basic industries.

What happened in Sweden happened also among its capitalistic neighbors, as will become apparent in the chapters that follow. The rise and fall of industrial activity that accompanied this recurrent rejuvenation of the productive apparatus was inevitably accompanied by a high degree of social hardship. But the constantly accelerating expansion of industrial production also progressively raised the standard of living of the masses and brought material comforts within their grasp.

Government and Capitalism: Subventions and Tariffs / As industrial capitalism extended its domain in the years after 1871, it began, in certain respects, to change its character. The rugged individualism and the unalloyed competitive spirit that marked the entrepreneurs of the early stages of capitalism disappeared; and their successors relied increasingly on government aid and on forms of combination intended to reduce the rigors and inconveniences of competition.

A much-read spokesman for classical liberalism, the English publicist Herbert Spencer (1820–1903), commenting on the relationship of government to business, once wrote: "Perpetually governments have thwarted and deranged growth, but have in no way furthered it, save by partially discharging their proper function and maintaining social order." The most striking thing about this dogmatic utterance is its remoteness from truth. As we have seen, economic growth is dependent in the first instance upon the creation of an efficient transportation system and other forms of social capital. During this phase, the government is generally called upon to play a most important part, since projects that do not promise a quick return on investment often find it difficult to obtain financial support. Students of American history are well aware of the role of federal-government subsidies during the construction of the transcontinental railway systems. The same sort of thing occurred in many European countries in the years when they were beginning their economic growth. Napoleon III's use of public bond issues to encourage railroad construction in France has already been mentioned (p. 185), and other forms of pump-priming were noticeable in European countries after 1871.

Indeed, even after the initial fund of social capital (roads, canals, railways) had been accumulated, there were other kinds of aid that the government could give, and soon came to be expected to give, to business. It could facilitate investment by progressive liberalization of laws of incorporation. Thus, one of the important factors in Germany's industrial growth was the general company law of 1870–1872, which ameliorated existing restrictions on corporate growth and extended the principle of limited liability so successfully that joint-stock companies increased in number from 2100 in the early 1880s to 5400 in 1912, and associations with limited liability from 200 to 16,000 in the same period.

The government could also open up new opportunities for investment and for the sale of the products of industry by paying the costs and assuming the risks of acquiring overseas colonies, a development the universality of which in this period will be discussed below (pp. 439–463). Finally, in time of war, it could protect those industries that were considered vitally important to the war effort from the normal risks of the market, a practice that was common to many European countries during World War I.

One of the most widespread forms of government assistance to private enterprise was the protective tariff. After a period of virtual free trade which had been inaugurated by the repeal of the British Corn Laws in 1846 (pp. 118–120) and confirmed by the Cobden-Chevalier Treaty of 1860 (p. 186), most European countries turned back to protectionism in the late 1870s. There were a number of reasons for this.

In the first place, in countries where the take-off point was reached after 1871, industrialists were likely to be vulnerable to the competition of those neighbors who had progressed further than they had themselves. German producers, for instance, were particularly sensitive to the impact of cheap English imports on the domestic market and were insistent that, without protection, they could not survive. The dumping of English goods at ridiculously low prices in continental markets during the first years of the depression that began in 1873 gave point to these claims, which were made by others besides the Germans.

In the second place, the industrial advocates of protection found supporters among the agricultural interest. Hitherto, European farmers had been reasonably content with the free-trade economy, since prices in the 1850s and 1860s had remained high. But before the latter decade was over, signs of change were apparent. The tremendous growth of railroads in the United States—an increase of 300 percent in the twenty years after 1860—the simultaneous lowering of freight rates, and the improvement of agricultural machinery caused a boom in American grain production at the very moment when the introduction of new marine engines and the decrease of shipping costs made it possible to deliver this grain (and later that of Canada, Argentina, and Australia) cheaply and speedily to European markets. These things (and some others, like the perfection of mechanical refrigeration to a point where frozen meats could be shipped across the ocean as well) caused a crisis in the agriculture of Western Europe in the 1870s. Farmers in Central Europe were simultaneously feeling the pinch because rail-transported grains from Rumania and Russia were forcing their prices down. It is not surprising that agricultural pressure groups soon came into existence and began to collaborate with others who were seeking government protective action. The alliance between grain and heavy industry became a common phenomenon in European politics.

This coalition was apt to find additional support among groups whose interests were not primarily economic. The wars of the 1860s had, as we have seen, left the European states mutually suspicious and ready to assume that new conflicts were coming soon. After 1871, a good many people were concluding from their reading (or misreading) of the works of Charles Darwin that war was inevitable among the different branches of the human species and that, this being so, reliance on free trade was dangerous, since it encouraged dependence upon imports that might be cut off in time of war. Even at the cost of economic disadvantage, self-sufficiency seemed to these people to be a desirable goal; and they called for tariffs as a means of protecting and promoting the production of critical goods and strategic materials at home.

Under the pressure of these political forces, European governments began to turn away from free trade. Perhaps the decisive push came with the passage of the German tariffs of 1879, although the new direction had already been indicated by upward revision of tariff schedules in Russia, Spain, and Italy in the three preceding years. But the German legislation, which was the result of joint agitation by agricultural and industrial groups, was bound, in view of Germany's leading position on the continent, to have wider effects than action by other countries. The tariff laws of 1879, which placed specific duties on grain, textiles, timber, meat, and iron, were imitated in France, Austria, Sweden, and Switzerland and encouraged Russia, Italy, and other countries to elaborate existing protective systems. When France passed the tariff of 1892, which increased agricultural duties about 25 percent while at the same time giving protection to native industries like silk, Jules Méline, who piloted the bill through the Assembly, cited the successful German and Austrian experience with tariffs in the last decade as an argument for France's following their example. He added:

> If we look over the table of our importations of the last fifteen years we find them perceptibly increasing in proportion as the principal countries of Europe raise their tariff barriers. If we do not give heed to this, we shall end by becoming the drain of the whole of Europe. Is it right, is it wise, to persist in keeping our doors open when all others are proceeding to close theirs?

His auditors did not think so; nor did legislators in most other countries. As a result, by the middle 1890s, only Great Britain, Belgium, and Holland could still be considered free-trading countries; and they were all countries, it should be noted, in which commerce was more important than agriculture, and industry was so far advanced that protection was difficult to justify.

Some of the results of this swing back to a protectionist economy have already been mentioned (see pp. 260–262). The old liberal idea of international peace based on the economic interdependence of nations seemed, under these new conditions, to lose all hope of realization, for once the administration of commercial relations became a governmental rather than a private matter, the area of potential friction between nations was greatly expanded. Moreover, once governments began to employ tariffs for economic reasons, they discovered that tariffs could be used politically also, and economic pressure became a feature of some of the uglier diplomatic crises of the years before World War I.

For our present purpose, however, it is enough to note that the return to protectionism strengthened the change that had been taking place in the relations between private businessmen and governments. To the extent that tariffs came to be considered indispensable aids to agriculture and industry, the principle of free private enterprise—no matter how often invoked in discussion—had been attenuated in practice.

The Movement toward Combination: Trusts and Cartels / The private-enterprise system suffered another change as the years passed. Industrial and banking firms that survived the bruising competition of the early stages of capitalism and expanded their operations from a local to a national, and even an international, level seemed to lose their enthusiasm for competition somewhere along the way. As business enterprises got bigger, they tended to collaborate with other large firms in their own field of activity, for the purpose of avoiding duplication of effort, lowering costs of production, dividing markets, or protecting prices from the fluctuations that unrestrained competition might cause.

Various forms of combination were popular. In England and the United States, the preferred arrangements were amalgamation, in which one firm absorbed competitors by purchase or by stock manipulation, and the trust or combine, in which plants that were engaged in the production of the same or allied products united under a joint directorate and pooled their administrative and sales forces. These arrangements made possible a degree of commercial and technical progress that was unlikely in situations where a great number of competing units existed side by side; and it frequently enabled the resulting combination to enjoy monopoly conditions. This was true of such trusts as Standard Oil in the United States, and Bryant and May (the match trust) and the Imperial Tobacco Company in England.

The German form of combination, which was also popular in other continental countries, was looser in form but no less effective. This was the cartel, an arrangement between all the enterprises in a given branch of industrial production which regulated their production, purchase of materials, areas of exploitation, sales procedures, and prices. These combinations could cross national frontiers; and, before World War I, there were marketing, production, and price agreements between German cartels and foreign trusts. The Allgemeine Elektrizitäts Gesellschaft (AEG) had such an arrangement with the General Electric Company of the United States, and German manufacturers of steel rails had cartel arrangements with their counterparts in Great Britain, France, Belgium, and the United States and, in collaboration with them, effectively controlled the world market.

Of special interest in this connection was the tendency of banking concerns to combine. In England the last years of the century saw a steady decline in the total number of banking concerns. There had been 600 banking houses in England in 1824. By 1914 there were only fifty-five, and this shrinkage was to continue into the postwar period, so that there were only eleven banking houses in 1937, and five sixths of the country's banking business was handled by the "Big Five": the Midland Bank, the Westmoreland Bank, Barclay's, Lloyd's, and the National Provincial. In Germany the financial business of the country in the years after 1871 came increasingly under the domination of the four so-called "D Banks" —the Disconto Gesellschaft of Stuttgart (founded in 1851), the Deutsche Bank (1870), the Darmstädter Bank (1870), and the Dresdener Bank (1872). The D Banks were specifically commissioned "to foster commercial relations between Germany and other countries" and were active in the Far East, Latin America, Eastern Europe, and the Middle East. At home, their role in the direction of business was very great, and they generally promoted ever greater degrees of business amalgamation.

In the expansion of the European economy in the last decades of the nineteenth century, these monopolistic practices played a positive role, for they made possible the introduction of new techniques and eliminated much inefficiency and duplicated effort in the productive process. These contributions were not easily perceived by contemporaries. Business combinations were unpopular because they were connected in the national memory with historical cases of exploitation, because the process of amalgamation often caused tragedy in individual cases, and because the misuse of power gained by combination often hurt consumers. Thus, they were a primary target for socialist critics of the capitalistic system.

THE LABOR MOVEMENT: TRADE UNIONS

One of the incidental effects of the large-scale combination of business was the unwitting encouragement it gave to similar combination on the part of labor. During the first part of the century, European businessmen and governments had successfully opposed this, arguing that laboring men should rely on individualism and self-help rather than on collective action. These arguments were still used, but after 1871 they rather lacked conviction; and honest businessmen were forced to agree with the Scottish-American industrialist and philanthropist Andrew Carnegie (1835–1919), who wrote: "The right of the workingman to combine is no less sacred than the right of the manufacturer to enter into associations and conferences with his fellows, and it must sooner or later be conceded."

This change of view, which was shared by national parliaments, gave a new legal standing to trade unions. These bodies, which had existed in England, Belgium, France, and other continental countries since the first decades of the century, had always been subject to crippling restrictions. In England, for instance, while given legal status by Parliamentary acts of 1824–1825, they were forbidden to "molest" or "obstruct" employers or to do anything that could be construed as encouraging breach of contract and, in the circumstances, found it difficult to bargain effectively for improved wages or working conditions and virtually impossible to strike without being subject to legal action (see p. 115). Conditions in other countries had, if anything, been even less favorable for union development. Now they were universally ameliorated. In England the Gladstone government made a start in 1871 toward regularizing the position of unions; and, in 1875, the Disraeli ministry widened their freedom of action by legalizing peaceful picketing and making it clear that combined action in the furtherance of a trade dispute could not punished as a conspiracy. In France the rights of unions were progressively widened between 1864 and 1884; in Austria they received legal status in 1870; and in other countries their position received similar clarification.

While these gains were being made, most existing unions were essentially benevolent and protective societies, small in membership and representing only the better-educated, better-paid workers of the skilled trades. They existed primarily for the purpose of extending assistance to their members in the form of unemployment and accident insurance and death benefits. They were cautious with their funds and, because of this, not very aggressive, using the strike weapon rarely. In the late 1880s and the 1890s, however, union membership began to grow significantly, and these characteristics gave way to others. The great increase in membership took place among the unskilled workers and was promoted by labor leaders who believed in more militant tactics than those employed in the past. Dramatic evidence was given of the change in a series of strikes: at Charleroi in Belgium, where there was bitter fighting between glass and mine workers and the police in 1886; at London in 1889, where the dock workers won an increase in wages by an impressive demonstration of discipline and patience; at Hamburg in 1896, where harbor workers sought to duplicate the English success and were stubbornly opposed by employers' associations.

The new unions were often strongly influenced by the doctrines of Marxian socialism and were allied with Marxian parties. This was true in Germany, for instance, where the fortunes of the Independent Unions varied with those of the Social Democratic party, so that they almost disappeared during the years of Bismarck's antisocialist legislation (see p. 381) and revived when it was repealed in 1890. There were other unions in Germany—the Hirsch-Duncker Unions, founded in the 1860s and modeled on the older English craft unions, and the Christian Trade Unions, which came into existence in the 1890s and kept their strength and vitality until 1933. But the Independent Unions always represented the majority of the organized labor force in Germany, and their politics remained socialist. In Austria, Italy, the Scandinavian countries, Holland, and Spain, Marxian socialists also directed the union movement; in England the unions were closely allied with the new Labor party which, while not Marxian, was socialist in philosophy (see p. 316). France represented a somewhat special case, for the union movement there was strongly influenced by the doctrines of syndicalism that are discussed below.

Despite its association with philosophies that called for the destruction of the existing order, the attitude of the union movement as a whole toward the idea of revolution was always ambiguous. As they grew in strength, unions continued in many cases to pay lip service to it, but they also acquired funds and property that made them feel a certain commitment to the capitalistic system. Moreover, even if their tactics had changed with the rise of industrial as opposed to craft unions, their basic purposes remained what they had always been: to improve the lot of the working classes and to raise their standard of living. When opportunities to do this appeared, they were inclined to grasp them, without troubling their minds too much about whether this would hasten or delay the coming of the revolution. They had no hesitation about making collective-bargaining agreements with capitalist employers, and the Independent Unions of Germany were particularly successful in concluding "gentlemen's agreements" with their class enemies. Thus, in general, unions tended to become a moderate force within the socialist movement; and union leaders were apt to be found supporting the revisionist movement that is discussed below.

The point has often been made that organized labor represented only a fraction of the total labor force of Europe at this time, and this is undoubtedly true. In the year 1900, total trade-union membership in Great Britain stood at two million, in Germany at 850,000, in France at 250,000; and the numbers in other countries were much smaller. Yet the unions' success in improving the wages and the working conditions of the urban proletariat was felt beyond the confines of their own organizations, and their work in general helped, however slowly, to communicate to the mass of the labor force some idea of their social rights. Oswald Schumann, who first organized the Berlin transport workers and draymen's union, once wrote of conditions in the German cities in the early days of his work (in the 1890s), when there were thousands of workers who

> had no understanding of what it was that inspired us, but lived the lives of beasts of burden, working fourteen, sixteen, twenty hours a day the whole year round, with the exception of Sunday, when they only had time to sleep off the weekly drunk with which they tried to make themselves forget all the misery, so as to be able to report again with their teams at three o'clock on Monday mornings to offer their *corvée* to the overseers. Among these people the union accomplished cultural work in the most eminent sense of the word.

A PHILOSOPHY FOR LABOR: KARL MARX

His Life and Influence / The second notable kind of labor combination in this period was the formation of working-class political parties. The most important of these took their inspiration from the writings of Karl Marx.

Marx was born in 1818 at Trier in the Rhineland. On both sides his parents were Jewish and on both sides descended from rabbis, a fact not without influence on Marx's view of history, which was unrelievedly apocalyptic. He went to local schools and then studied at the universities of Bonn and Berlin, where his original interest shifted, under the influence of the philosopher Hegel, from jurisprudence to philosophy. He received his degree in 1841 and might have embarked on an academic career had a university opening materialized. When it did not, he began to write philosophical articles for a newspaper called the *Rheinische Zeitung* and, in 1843, became its editor. The ferment of the times made it impossible for a mind so energetic to remain wholly sunk in philosophical speculation. The young Marx became interested in questions of the day and, particularly, in the doctrines of French socialism, which he studied critically and with a dawning conviction that, if the times were out of joint, they were not going to be improved by the prescriptions of people like Fourier and Louis Blanc.

Karl Marx, 1818–1883.
(CULVER SERVICE)

Before the year was over, the *Rheinische Zeitung* was banned by the government for being too outspoken on social questions, and Marx moved on to Paris. Here he met Friedrich Engels (1820–1895), the son of a Rhineland industrialist with manufacturing interests in England. The two men became collaborators, and Marx found in Engels, not only a lifelong friend who came to his aid at his not infrequent moments of dire want, but also an associate with an intimate practical knowledge of the working of the industrial system, which Marx himself lacked, as well as other gifts, including a keen insight into military matters, which in later years earned him the party nickname of "The General." Engels, on his side, never stopped admiring Marx's powers of analysis and conceptualization and said on one occasion, "Marx was a genius; we others at best were talented."

Along with others who were suspected of being dangerous radicals, Marx was expelled from France in 1847 and went to Brussels, where he and Engels were asked by a group of German socialists to draw up a program for them. The result was *The Communist Manifesto*, an eloquent and powerful denunciation of the existing social order, written on the very eve of the revolutions of 1848, although it was read only by a relatively small number of people during the next thirty years. During that time, Marx, after being declared *persona non grata* in Belgium, found asylum in Great Britain and spent his life working in the British Museum on the researches for his *Critique of Political Economy* (1859) and his monumental work *Capital* (1867), writing analyses of current events for newspapers, and—from the late 1860s until his death in 1883—playing a dominant role in the European socialist movement.

This prominence among socialists was largely the result of the increasing respect felt for *The Communist Manifesto*. As Harold Laski once wrote, this was rather belatedly seen to be the first document of its kind to give a direction and a philosophy to what had before been little more than an inchoate protest against injustice; and in a very real sense it can be said to have created the modern socialist movement. Some sense of why the *Manifesto* was able to do this may be acquired from a brief consideration of what it had to say about history, the nature and weaknesses of the capitalistic system, and the role and destiny of the Socialist party.

History, Capitalism, the Party / Marx's views on history were influenced by his study of Hegel, who had believed that history is a logical process in which change is effected by the opposition of antagonistic elements and the resolution of this antagonism in new forms. This idea—sometimes called the dialectic—Marx borrowed; but, whereas Hegel had believed that the key to change was ideological (since all history, to his mind, was a perpetual unfolding of the Absolute Idea), Marx held that the basis of history and the key to historical change was materialistic. In any society, he insisted, "the mode of production in material life determines the general character of the social, political and spiritual processes of life" and, when change takes place, it does so not because of the antagonism of competing ideas but because of the clash of competing economic groupings. As Engels once wrote, "the whole history of mankind . . . has been a history of class struggles, contests between exploiting and exploited, ruling and oppressed classes." The capitalistic society of Marx's day was the net result of a long series of such clashes, ending with the victory of the bourgeoisie over the formerly dominant feudal classes. But this victory was not final. The process of historical change would continue until a great revolutionary event smashed the existing order and ended class conflict by abolishing class differences.

The outlines of that happy event were already looming on the horizon, Marx argued, because the nature of the capitalistic system tended to speed up the process of change by intensifying and simplifying the antagonisms that caused it. In modern capitalistic society, human exploitation had been carried to the most extreme degree, and hatred between classes was greater than ever before. At the same time, the class struggle had been simplified to a sharp confrontation between a small plutocracy and a multiplying and ever more resentful proletariat, which must in time rise and destroy its oppressors and clear the way for the classless society.

Why this was inevitable Marx set out to prove by an analysis of certain features of the capitalistic order. His principal argument was that the labor force was being victimized by what amounted to an organized system of robbery. Like others before him, Marx professed the belief that the value of any commodity is properly measured by the labor expended to produce it; and, upon this law, he erected the proposition that, in an equitable society, workingmen would receive in payment for their labor its equivalent in goods, comforts, and services. Under capitalism this was not true, for the tendency of capitalist employers was to keep wages low and working hours long, with the result that their workers were creating by their daily labor goods whose value greatly exceeded that of what they received in return, and this surplus value was going directly into the pockets of the employers as profits. This was an injustice, and apprehension of this fact by the working classes could not help but feed the flames of revolution.

Revolution is all the more imminent because of another characteristic of capitalism. As the productive process becomes more complicated, it requires techniques and equipment beyond the understanding and the means of smaller entrepreneurs, who are therefore ruined and forced into the wage-earning class. By an inexorable process of concentration, the ownership and control of the economic system falls into fewer and fewer hands. This concentration and the simultaneous ballooning of the proletariat simplifies the class struggle, and the social suffering caused by it intensifies the resentment of the lower classes.

The proletariat is offered ever more numerous opportunities to express its feelings in revolutionary action, for the capitalists have proved to be incapable of controlling their own system. Marx wrote:

> Modern bourgeois society is like the sorcerer who is no longer able to control the powers of the nether world whom he has called up by his spells. . . . It is enough to mention the commercial crises that by their periodical return put the existence of the entire bourgeois society on its trial, each time more threateningly. . . . And how does the bourgeoisie get over these crises? On the one hand, by the enforced destruction of a mass of productive forces; on the other, by a conquest of new markets and by the more thorough exploitation of old ones. That is to say, by paving the way for more extensive and more destructive crises and by diminishing the means whereby crises are prevented.

In short, destructive economic crises will increase in frequency and scope. Nothing can prevent this, because capitalism is incapable of correcting its own faults. By its very nature, it rests upon contradictions. Its objective is not service or development but gain and accumulation. "Modern society, which soon after its birth pulled Plutus by the hair of his head from the bowels of the earth," Marx wrote in *Capital*, "greets gold as its Holy Grail, as the glittering incarnation of its very principle of life"; and this ideal, far from inspiring attempts to prevent depressions, can only encourage more unbridled competition and more destructive collisions. Again, although capitalistic production, with mechanization, becomes an increasingly technical effort of collaboration in which the worker plays an essential role, the capitalist entrepreneur either is incapable of seeing this truth or pursues his course of selfish exploitation in willful defiance of it. His obtuseness must eventually invite the system's destruction. Finally, however much he may rationalize and coordinate the operations of his own business, the capitalist will not recognize any restraint in his competition for markets with other producers. This state of anarchy encourages the boom-bust tendencies inherent in the system and hastens the coming of the final debacle.

Marx believed that the destruction of the capitalist system and the ushering in of a new age could be effected only by conscious and violent intervention by the workers themselves. The proletariat must seize the propitious moment for revolution and, until it arrived, must prepare for it. To show it how to do so, to unite working-class organizations into a common front, to carry out general tasks of education for effective political action, and to create the organization that would supply leadership when the time came was the first duty of the Socialist party. Its second task was to consolidate the revolution when the existing regime had been toppled. Marx foresaw a violent revolution in which the party-led workers would seize the centers of bourgeois power and the means of production, followed by a transitional period of indefinite duration called "the dictatorship of the proletariat." During this transitional stage, the party would systematically destroy the vestiges of bourgeois institutions and eradicate the remains of class prejudice, and, by educating the masses to their new opportunities and responsibilities, would lay the basis for the classless society of the future in which the state withered away and all men were permitted to live in conditions of justice and liberty.

Marx's picture of that ultimate stage in human development was confessedly vague, for he was more intent upon analyzing the ills of contemporary society and delineating the forces that would overcome it than he was in drawing blueprints for the remote future. But that future *would* come; the logic of history made this a certainty. The question of *when* it would come would depend upon the speed with which the capitalistic system disintegrated and the efficiency of the Socialist party in exploiting its disintegration.

Upon this last point, Marx put considerable emphasis. Both he and Engels were scornful of all socialist movements before their time. This was doubtless due in part to Marx's temperament. He was never kindly disposed to movements or ideas that differed from his own. The German-American writer and statesman Carl Schurz wrote that he had never in his life met a man "of such wounding, intolerable arrogance of behavior" as Marx, adding that he was perpetually denouncing those who dared oppose his views as "bourgeois"—"that is, as an unmistakeable example of deep spiritual and ethical degradation."

But Marx's feelings about such predecessors as Owen, Fourier, and Saint-Simon were not wholly the result of spleen. He believed that these men were not class-conscious enough and that they had deluded themselves and their followers by believing that socialism could be imposed from above by the disinterested action of benevolent members of the possessing classes. They were blind to history's revelation of the irreconcilable conflict between classes, and their trusting utopianism made them grateful for piddling concessions and surface reforms that left society essentially unchanged.

Marx chose the name "communist" for his famous manifesto partly to distinguish himself and his brand of socialism from the utopians who had gone before; his followers were to call his socialism "scientific socialism" for the same reason. Behind the semantic difference was a more essential one. Marx was calling for a socialist movement that would base its theories upon the materialistic view of history and society, upon the inevitability of the class struggle, and upon the clear recognition that the victory of the proletariat must be ushered in by violence.

Scientist or Prophet? / In the strict meaning of the word, Marx's socialism was no more "scientific" than any other social theory. Consider, for instance, his belief that "the mode of production in material life determines the general character of the social, political and spiritual processes of life." Marx did not, of course, mean by this that economics and economics alone would determine every aspect of our daily life and action, for he always admitted that other factors had a part to play in the drama of history and the life of man. But he did believe that, if there were such other factors, they were either themselves rooted in economics or were, in their totality, of less weight in any given situation than the economic factors; and it is precisely here that we must question the realism of his views. One need only think of the interplay of such things as human ambition and human fallibility, developments in domestic politics, climatic conditions and configurations of geography, economic distress, religious faith, national exaltation or irritation, technological progress or lack of progress, administrative efficiency, military genius, and sheer accident in the events that led to the revolution in Paris in 1848 or the outbreak of the Crimean War to realize that the question of causation is too complicated to permit us to claim that any single factor is always more important than others in determining the course of history. And this is what Marx was inclined to do.

At the same time, it should be noted that Marx's view of history left little or no place for human volition or initiative. Yet the very modes of production to which he gave such emphasis had come into existence, not by spontaneous generation, but by human decision and action. The system of production in use at any time was not a uniform or monolithic thing, as Marx often seemed to believe, but a composite of many ideas and institutions constantly being changed, corrected, and adapted to new circumstances by human beings. It would appear to be less scientific to talk of man as the tool of the prevailing mode of production than as its author.

In the same way, it is rather less than sound to assume, as Marx did, that individuals will tend to act socially in accordance with their class allegiance, or even that they will always recognize their membership in a given class. History is filled with examples of individuals and groups refusing to act in the way that their economic circumstances would seem to require, because they considered other things—status, social aspiration, tradition, or prestige—more important. An impoverished entrepreneur is likely to resist recognizing himself as a new proletarian and refuse to act like one, as is demonstrated by the fact that, throughout recent history, such new proletarians have turned more frequently to rightist political parties than to socialist or labor movements. For Marx, moreover, to believe that, as he once said, "the proletarians in all countries [had] one and the same interest, one and the same enemy" and that they were "in the great mass by nature without national prejudice" was to ignore the experience of the revolutionary movements and the impact of nationalistic fervor on all classes in the Europe of his time.

If Marx's historical views were less scientific than his followers were likely to claim, so were his economic theories. His theory of surplus value, for instance, had limited application to the realities of the age of high capitalism, for it made no allowance for the hidden costs of production—administration, advertising, interest payments, amortization of new building, and other things—that absorbed much of the profit that Marx claimed went into the employers' pockets; nor did it take account of the special skills of employers or their willingness to assume risks, although these things obviously helped assure employment for workers. Marx's statements concerning concentration of capital and periodicity of economic depressions bore a closer resemblance to the economic tendencies of his day, as a comparison of his views with the facts stated in the first section of the present chapter will make clear; but on the other hand there was evidence, even in Marx's time, that capitalist entrepreneurs were both more enlightened than he was willing to admit and more prepared to make economic sacrifices, if necessary, in order to correct palpable weaknesses in their operations. Recognition of the social character of their enterprises and acquiescence in controls designed to avoid economic trouble did not, in the long run, prove to be impossible for them.

Yet to say all this is in no way to depreciate the importance of Marx's work either as historian or as economist. To historians he brought a necessary corrective to the tendency to give undue weight to purely political factors and to write what has been called "drum and trumpet history"; and historians after his time were persuaded by his influence to devote more thought to the social and economic aspects of human evolution. To economic thought he brought an emphasis upon class structure and attitude that was new and provocative, as well as a more sharply defined conceptualization of capitalist economy which stimulated further study and analysis.

Aside from this, the question as to whether Marx's socialism was scientific or not is probably less important than he himself thought it was. Marx wanted to be thought of as rigorously objective, free from prejudice, completely analytical. He was, of course, nothing of the sort, and he should properly be considered as an angry prophet, denouncing an economic system that he loathed personally and predicting its imminent destruction and the coming of the millenium. It is, perhaps, precisely here that we can see the reason for the remarkable spread and acceptance of his teachings.

Karl Loewith has written that it is no accident that the last great battle between the bourgeoisie and the proletariat of which Marx writes so fervently reminds one of the apocalypses of the Old Testament and of the Book of Revelation. It is not by chance, Loewith continues,

> that the task of the proletariat corresponds to the world-historical mission of the chosen people, that the redemptive and universal function of the most degraded class is conceived on the religious pattern of Cross and Resurrection, that the ultimate transformation of the realm of necessity into a realm of freedom corresponds to the transformation of the *civitas terrena* into a *civitas Dei*, and that the whole process of history as outlined in *The Communist Manifesto* corresponds to the general scheme of the Jewish-Christian interpretation of history as a providential advance toward a final goal which is meaningful. Historical materialism is essentially, though secretly, a history of fulfillment and salvation in terms of social economy.[1]

Marxism was a promise of sure salvation, and it was this aura of inevitability rather than the logic of its propositions that explained its tremendous appeal. The miserable and the underprivileged wanted to be

[1] Karl Loewith, *The Meaning of History* (Chicago, 1949), pp. 44–45.

told that they would triumph in the end, and found it easy to turn to a creed that assured them that history was working toward that ultimate objective and could not be stayed. So did the guilty and the insecure. In the continental countries, in particular, bad conscience often led members of the possessing class to embrace Marxism as the surest means of correcting the injustice that they felt their class had caused, while intellectual insecurity and craving after ideological certainty led other representatives of the same class to follow their example.

Nor were the appeals of Marxism restricted to these groups. They were felt also by those whose main motivation was to correct injustices they thought had been done to them—individuals who blamed their loss of economic or social status upon "the system" or who resented the failure of society to appreciate their talents—and those who yearned for personal power and hoped to gain it if the existing system were destroyed.

To the suffering, the deprived, the unappreciated, and the ambitious, Marx held out the promise of a Golden Age, in which "in place of the old bourgeois society with its classes and class antagonisms [would] come an association in which the free development of each individual [would] be the condition for the free development of all." Yet the means he advocated were hardly likely to produce such millenial freedom. This was because Marx belonged to that group of nineteenth-century thinkers who made a cult out of violence, habituated society to accepting it as a legitimate tool of politics, and, by doing so, weakened the ideas of law, equity, compromise, and adjustment that were the hallmarks of nineteenth-century liberalism and had been in the past the best assurance of progress toward freedom.

THE DEVELOPMENT OF SOCIALISM

Marx and Bakunin: The Challenge of Anarchism / The spread of Marx's influence among the working classes was very slow. The first parties that accepted his doctrines did not come into existence until the end of the 1860s, and their progress was most uncertain for at least another decade. In the first international organization of labor, the International Workingmen's Association, which was founded in London in 1864 and lasted until 1876, Marx played a prominent role—actually delivering the inaugural address and declaration of principles—but hardly a dominant one. Indeed, the short history of the First International was marked by a bitter conflict between his philosophy and the competing doctrine of anarchism.

Anarchism has been called the *reductio ad absurdum* of nineteenth-century romanticism because of its fervent insistence that man was essentially good but had been corrupted by institutions. The anarchist conceived of his goal as one of restoring mankind to its state of primitive virtue by destroying the instruments of corruption—the established churches, the great agglomerations of economic power, and, above all, the modern centralized state. In contrast to Marxists, who wished to take over the existing state and the means of production by revolution, anarchists wished to destroy these things and to reorganize society on a voluntary basis.

The father of anarchism had been Proudhon, with his avowed hatred of the state, his belief that private property was theft, and his proposal that society should be decentralized on the basis of small cooperative producing societies (see p. 87). Its most sophisticated modern publicist was Prince Alexander Kropotkin (1842–1921), a Russian nobleman who wrote idealized portraits of voluntary societies in which free men labored for other than financial reward and lived without the necessity of organized government. But the man who made anarchism an important working-class movement and was responsible for its continuing influence in Europe was Michael Bakunin (1814–1876).

This remarkable figure had been born, like Kropotkin, a member of the Russian aristocracy. Destined for a military career, he abandoned it in favor of the study of philosophy, became interested in the sufferings of subject nationalities like the Poles and the Italians, and ended by becoming a professional revolutionist. He participated in the February revolution in Paris in 1848 and the rising in Prague later in that year, and was arrested by Prussian troops during the fighting in Dresden in 1849. Shipped back to his own country, he spent eight years in prison and four more in enforced exile in Siberia. He then escaped and made his way back to Western Europe by way of Yokahama, San Francisco, and New York, and plunged immediately back into revolutionary activity. In the 1860s he organized anarchist cells in Switzerland, Spain, and Italy and founded a Social Democratic Alliance with secret statutes and a program calling for "universal revolution." He was an ardent supporter of the Poles during the rising of 1863, was involved in 1869 with Nechaev's Society of the Ax in Russia (see p. 426), and organized a commune in Lyon during the revolutionary disturbances in France in 1871. He died in 1876 at the age of 62, with his body wasted by imprisonment and irregular living but his brain still teeming with revolutionary plans and his heart with hope.

It was during the 1860s, when the national states were taking their modern form and capitalism reaching its full development in the west, that Bakunin formulated his anarchist creed. He wrote,

Michael Bakunin, 1814–
1876, in 1869.
(BROWN BROTHERS)

The State was born historically . . . of the marriage of violence, rapine, pillage. . . . It has been from its origin . . . the divine sanction of brutal force and triumphant inequality. . . . Even when it commands what is good, it hinders and spoils it just because it commands it . . . because the good, from the moment it is commanded, becomes evil from the point of view of true morality . . . and from the point of view of human respect and liberty.

Capitalism was just as bad in its effects upon those whose lives it commanded. So was organized religion, and so was that idol of nineteenth-century intellectuals, modern science, with its presumptuous attempt to regulate life by defining its laws. Bakunin declared war on all institutions, all laws, all abstract principles that regulated—and, by doing so, hampered—human growth.

Bakunin was not a systematic thinker. He was vague about what would replace the things he detested, although he seemed to incline to Proudhon's preference for a society of small voluntary communities in which all decisions would be made by unanimous consent and no one compelled to do anything except by his own will. He did not attempt to spell out the details, preferring to believe that men would solve their own problems once they were free. The act of becoming free would have a regenerating force; and Bakunin went considerably further than Marx in deifying violence as the instrument by which this regeneration would be effected. Alexander Herzen, the dean of the Russian political exiles in London, once described Bakunin's philosophy as "a blind stumbling after the unknown god of destruction," and there is much to be said for this, for Bakunin dreamed of gigantic conflagrations that would accomplish what reason could not define. "Unchain the popular anarchy in country and town," he wrote. "Magnify it, till it rolls like a raging avalanche, devouring and destroying." "The tempest and life, that is what we need. A new world without laws, and consequently free." He called for "a phalanx 40,000 strong of young folk of the educated classes" to lead the masses in daring acts of terrorism and spontaneous risings against authority until the goal of universal revolution had been attained.

The French writer Albert Camus once pointed out that Bakunin's emphasis on the necessity of a revolutionary elite bore some similarity to Marx's insistence on the creation of a disciplined party, and that Lenin, who later elaborated this idea, owed as much to the anarchist as he did to the author of *The Communist Manifesto*. This is probably true but, if so, it is one of the few bonds between Marx and Bakunin, who detested each other personally and disapproved of each other's ideas. Bakunin hated Marx's authoritarianism and saw clearly that a successful Marxist revolution would leave the political and economic institutions that he reprobated untouched, even if they were controlled by other hands. He believed that the dictatorship of the proletariat would be fully as destructive of freedom as the bourgeois order and that, despite Marx's professions, the state would never wither away. Marx, in his turn, was contemptuous of the lack of system and general wooliness of Bakunin's declarations and had a genuine horror of the ill-prepared acts of individual terrorism that the anarchists admired. When Bakunin's eloquence began to win a wide following within the International Workingmen's Association, Marx preferred to force the expulsion of Bakunin's group from that organization in 1873 rather than allow the International to become a sounding board for ideas he considered dangerous, even though the departure of the anarchists so weakened the International that it collapsed three years later.

On the whole, Marx's apprehensions proved to be groundless, and his doctrines, in the long run, won many more converts than those of his rival. Yet Bakunin's influence continued, too. In France it appealed to many who were dissatisfied with the caution and moderation of French socialism after 1871; and there were anarchist-inspired attacks upon church buildings in the Haute-Loire, political assassinations in Paris, Lyons, and other cities (including the murder of the president of the Republic in 1894), a bomb plot inside the Chamber of Deputies, and other acts of terror. In Italy and Spain, where the rural classes were the most depressed and backward in Western Europe and were virtually immune to the logical and systematic creed of Marxism, anarchism was particularly successful. Under the influence of Bakunin's follower Malatesta, peasant disorders were fomented in the southern provinces of Italy throughout the last decade of the century, while in Spain anarchism spread rapidly among the landless peasantry of Andalusia and the industrial workers of Catalonia, who were recruited from the most depressed rural areas. By 1882 anarchist organizations in Spain totalled about 50,000 members and by 1900 anarchism was on its way to becoming the strongest wing of the Spanish working-class movement.

Syndicalism / In the period after 1900, an offshoot of anarchism also threatened the position of orthodox socialism. Syndicalism (which took its name from the French word for labor union, *syndicat*) was a protest against the prevailing socialist emphasis upon political action and the growing tendency toward moderation in the European Socialist parties after 1900 (which will be discussed in the section on revisionism that follows). The syndicalists argued that the emancipation of the workers would be won not in parliaments but in the economic field, and not by majority votes but by "direct action." Such action should be exercised through trade-union organizations and should take the form of sabotage, "conscious withholding of efficiency," and, above all, the strike. To enhance the effectiveness of such tactics, the syndicalists called for increased effort to unionize the unskilled workers, the organization of new unions for industrial combat rather than benevolent and fraternal purposes, the widest possible federation of such unions, and a general agreement that contractual agreements with employers need not be honored. Direct action would, it was believed, maintain the class consciousness and militancy of the labor movement while weakening the capitalist system and preparing the way for the "general strike" that would one day paralyze it and inaugurate the revolution.

Syndicalism had its most conspicuous success in France, which also produced its most brilliant exponent, Georges Sorel (1847–1922). The *Confédération Générale du Travail* (CGT), which was founded by an anarchist named Fernand Pelloutier, was syndicalist from the beginning. This federation of small aggressive unions set its face against such typical trade-union activities as the accumulation of funds for insurance purposes and devoted its energies to direct action, which it adopted formally as its policy in the so-called Charter of Amiens of 1906. Before World War I, the CGT was active in inspiring strikes among civil servants and railway workers and encouraging disaffection inside the army.

In other countries syndicalist successes were less impressive. The cult of direct action won a not inconsiderable number of recruits in English unions, however, and there was a wave of syndicalist activity in Ireland on the eve of the war. In Italy Filippo Corridoni was the leader of a strong anarcho-syndicalist movement in the same years. His teachings— and those of Sorel—influenced a young socialist named Benito Mussolini, who wrote in 1909, "Syndicalism restores to its place in history the creative value of man, man who determines and is determined, who can leave the imprint of his force upon things and institutions." After the war, Mussolini's new Fascist party was clearly influenced by the syndicalist emphasis upon applied violence.

In Spain, a federation of syndicalist industrial unions, the *Confederación Nacional del Trabajo* (CNT) was founded in 1910, and a similar agricultural federation, the *Federación Nacional de Agricultores Españoles* (FNAE), in 1913; and, after the war, when the older anarchist organizations called upon their members to enter syndicalist unions, over a million workers of one kind or another could be described as anarcho-syndicalists. As in Italy, the anarcho-syndicalist idealization of violence influenced rightist groups as well as labor organizations. By the 1930s, reactionary army officers were forming *sindicats* for action against the workers, and José Antonio Primo de Rivera had formed an association of ultra-conservative groups called the *Juntas de Ofensiva Nacional-Sindicalista* (JONS). It is no exaggeration to say, therefore, that when the Spanish civil war broke out in 1936, there were followers of Bakunin and Sorel on both sides. But that takes us rather far from the labor movement of the period presently under discussion.

Revisionism / Despite the anarcho-syndicalist preference for direct economic action as opposed to political maneuver, the main tendency in European socialism was political and, by the 1890s, Socialist parties had been organized in most countries, were vying for popular support in national and local elections, and—as subsequent chapters will show— were having considerable success. Most of these parties were Marxist in inspiration and doctrine, although the English movement looked back to the older socialism of Owen and the Chartists (see p. 113). Even when the Marxist label was present, it did not, of course, mean that the parties bearing it were always united and harmonious, for they often developed splinter groups and dissident minorities and were subject to doctrinal and tactical disagreements. During their lifetimes, Marx and Engels were often able to exert their authority so as to adjudicate these disputes; but even before Engels' death in 1895 a profound division was looming up that would probably have been beyond their powers of conciliation.

This split, which was to have profound and lasting effects wherever socialism developed, came to a head during the so-called revisionist controversy. For some time there had been unease among leading socialist and trade-union leaders about the gap between Marx's predictions and the realities of European economic development. Prominent among these was the German Social Democrat Eduard Bernstein (1850–1932), who, after years of study, summed up his views in the terse comment, "Peasants do not sink; middle class does not disappear; crises do not grow ever longer; misery and serfdom do not increase." If this was true—and Bernstein became sure it was as he carried his studies further—then the collapse of the capitalist system was not imminent, and the Socialist parties must change their tactics, if not their goals. Their logical course must be to exploit all the opportunities they could find for gradual reform in the interest of the working classes, even if this meant departing from the aloof, noncooperative attitude they had hitherto maintained toward the bourgeois political parties. They must, in a word, adopt the evolutionary tactics favored by the Fabian Society in Great Britain (see p. 316), with whom Bernstein had worked while in England; they must, as Bernard Shaw once wrote, rescue socialism from the barricades and made it a practical philosophy of social regeneration by democratic rather than revolutionary means.

Bernstein's views, published in articles and book form between 1896 and 1899, had European repercussions. They appealed to those members of Socialist parties who felt that the negative parliamentary tactics of the past doomed socialism to a permanently sterile opposition. They appealed even more directly to the trade-union wing of the socialist movement, whose leaders had long been irritated by the fact that collective-bargaining agreements, union-sponsored unemployment insurance schemes, and other things of which the union rank and file approved were always opposed by party doctrinaires on the grounds that they would weaken revolutionary fervor or dull the edge of the class struggle. Since Bernstein's strictures on Marx seemed to find verification in the rising level of real wages and the general prosperity of Europe in the years before World War I, they won wide acceptance in most countries with strong Socialist parties; and even many of the Socialist leaders who stoutly insisted that they were orthodox Marxists began in fact, in their day-by-day parliamentary work, to act in the spirit of revisionism.

This was true of the great French Socialist leader, Jean Jaurès (1859–1914), who—before his career was terminated by an assassin's bullet —had made it quite clear that he found in revisionism nothing alien to the spirit of Marx's teaching, "since Marxism itself contains the means by which it can be supplemented and revised." Like Bernstein, Jaurès rejected both the rigidity of Marx's economic theories and his emphasis on revolution. The victory of the proletariat would certainly come in due course, he believed, but by gradual degrees rather than by a sudden catastrophic event. Socialists should spend less time dwelling on that ultimate goal than on the positive tasks that must and could be carried out in the present. The important thing was "to live always in a socialist state of grace, working each hour, each minute" through the party, the trade unions, consumers' cooperative associations, and whatever other means came to hand to remake the world in accordance with socialist ideals.

The revisionist point of view was bitterly assailed by all those who held to the revolutionary doctrine of the founder of scientific socialism; and in 1902 they found their most effective spokesman in V. I. Lenin, whose pamphlet, *What Is to Be Done?* castigated the followers of Bernstein for their evident intention of bourgeoisifying the socialist movement. Lenin argued that victory could never be won for the proletariat by gradualist "bread and butter" socialism and that, rather than becoming bodies of parliamentarians and logrollers, the Socialist parties must be disciplined elites of professional revolutionaries, working incessantly to give the workers not what they thought they wanted but what they *should* want, and striving to replace the "trade-union mentality" with a revived faith in the class struggle.

By 1914, revisionism represented the majority view of most of the organized Socialist parties, if we can judge by their stand on major issues; and this result had been achieved by the way in which expanding capitalism had confounded the predictions of Karl Marx. In Lenin's protest against this victory of reformism, however, we can see a program and a rallying cry for all those who, during and after World War I, were to break away and form independent revolutionary parties, thus completing the division of the working-class movement into a democratic Socialist wing and a new Communist movement.

The Second International / Despite these doctrinal differences, the various Socialist and labor parties found it possible before 1914 to unite in an international organization that was designed to replace the one that had broken down during the conflict between Marx and Bakunin. In 1889, in Paris, the Second International came into existence, and, at this first meeting, delegations were present from France, Germany, Britain, Belgium, Austria, Russia, Holland, Denmark, Sweden, Norway, Switzerland, Poland, Rumania, Italy, Hungary, Spain, Portugal, Bohemia, and Bulgaria, as well as observers from the United States, Argentina, and Finland. The purpose of the new organization was to facilitate contacts and the exchange of information between the various Socialist parties, to provide, whenever possible, for mutual support, and, on great issues, to speak for socialism as a whole. In 1900 the International set up an

International Socialist Bureau with headquarters at Brussels, with sub-committees to coordinate the action of national parliamentary parties and to act for the whole International when it was not in session.

One aspect of the work of the International was to create a socialist public opinion on matters affecting the peace of Europe. The constituent parties were antimilitarist and, in the recurrent diplomatic crises of the period 1900–1914, they sought to mobilize world sentiment against the drift to war. The International had no common policy, however, with respect to means of preventing conflict if it should actually materialize; and, when the great crisis of 1914 came, although the International Socialist Bureau sought to coordinate the tactics to be followed by the national parties, its efforts were defeated by the forces of patriotism, which proved as seductive to socialists as to the bourgeoisie. The International did not survive the war that followed.

13

From Liberalism to Democracy: Political Progress in Western Europe, 1871-1914

From what has been said in the previous chapter, it will be easy to guess that the political history of the countries of Western Europe was far from placid in the years after 1871. The governing classes were under steady pressure to extend political freedom to the masses and to alleviate the social conditions in which they lived and labored; and in most countries, although sometimes only after protracted political struggles, they acknowledged this and instituted measures of political and economic democracy before 1914. The country that made the most conspicuous progress in this respect was, indubitably, Great Britain; but several of the lesser nations showed an equal ability to adjust their policies and institutions to the changing conditions of the times. Unfortunately, others—and their number included Italy and Spain—showed a greater willingness to imitate the forms than to be inspired by the realities of British parliamentary and social institutions.

GREAT BRITAIN

The Broadening of the Franchise / As a result of the reforms of the 1860s (see pp. 243–246), Great Britain was already far advanced on the road to political democracy, and she now carried this to its logical con-clusion. The Reform Act of 1867 had given the franchise to nearly all the male urban population. In 1884 a new act, passed during Gladstone's second ministry (1880–1885), gave similar voting rights to those elements of the rural population who had not been enfranchised in 1867 (farm tenants and agricultural laborers) and made the franchise uniform throughout the United Kingdom. The new act was supplemented a year later by a Redistribution Act that increased the size of the House of Commons to 607 members, who were to be elected, with some exceptions, by single-member constituencies of roughly equal size.

The most important of the demands that the Chartists (see pp. 115–117) had made forty years before this time had now been achieved; and there was little more that an Englishman could ask for in the way of political democracy unless he believed in female suffrage, a cause for which there was already much agitation but which was not to triumph until World War I. Nevertheless, the right to express oneself politically by means of the ballot was meaningless unless the political parties and parliament itself were responsive to such expression; and some English-men in this period, worried by the failure to deal with the problems caused by the great depression, doubted whether those bodies were sufficiently aware of the needs and the desires of the English people.

The Depression, the Parties, and Parliament / Starting in 1873, for reasons already touched upon (see p. 287), the British economy was affected by a series of troubles that were to continue with occasional periods of improvement until the middle of the 1890s. Agriculture was hit particularly hard, as the effects of the revolution in transportation began to be felt in England. Wheat, which had sold for 77 shillings the bushel in 1855, never reached 50 shillings again after 1877 and, in the 1880s, had slipped to below 40. To producers who, unlike their French and German counterparts, were not protected by tariffs, the price drop was ruinous; and their losses were reflected in the abandonment of once-productive grain areas to grazing or dairy and truck farming, the de-population of numerous rural areas, an increased drift of agricultural laborers to the slums of the great cities, and the decline of the wages and working conditions of those who stayed on the soil. English agriculture never completely recovered from the blows of this period. Its troubles were henceforth chronic.

Simultaneously, industry was passing through one of those periods of adjustment which, however much they may contribute in the long run to progress, are apt to involve both employers and laborers in economic distress (see p. 285). The years from 1876 to 1879 were marked by a slump in iron and steel prices that rapidly became general. Although there was some recovery at the end of the decade, prices began to fall again in 1883 and a depression set in that continued until 1886. The late 1880s were once more marked by a cautious recovery, followed by another setback at the beginning of the next decade. Throughout all these fluctuations there never seems to have been any danger of a total collapse; the slumps were linked with the continental speculative crashes of 1873 and 1882, with periodic financial strain, with the effects of continental tariffs and increased foreign competition, and with a retrenchment psychology on the part of business. The wealth of the country as a whole increased during the troubles, as did that of certain individual enterprises; and the fundamental health of the economy was never in doubt. Indeed, the depression encouraged measures which in the long run strengthened England's productive capacity, such as the introduction of new labor-saving devices, electrification, rationalization of processes, and exploitation of new areas of production.

The fact remains, however, that for millions these were hard times. By the 1880s, the word unemployment had attained general currency, as the situation it described became, or appeared to become, a permanent feature of the social order. The continuing decline of agriculture and the industrial slumps reduced thousands to near starvation. In a famous study called *Life and Labour of the People in London,* published in 1892, Charles Booth stated that over 30 percent of the population of England's largest city were living in poverty. A few years before, the economist John Rae had written that government reports showed that "in the wealthiest nation in the world, almost every twentieth inhabitant [was] a pauper," that a fifth of the community was insufficiently fed, that one third or more of the families in rural areas lived in conditions destructive of health and morality, and that the great proportion of the population led "a life of monotonous and incessant toil, with no prospect in old age but penury and parochial support."

Upon the wealthier classes this sort of thing might make little impact. In December 1883, *Punch* pictured a young lady saying breathlessly: "Lord Archibald is taking us to a dear little slum he has found . . . such a fearful place! Fourteen poor things sleeping in one bed!" But Beatrice Webb, one of the founders of Fabianism, was to recall years later that, while working in a clothing factory in London's East End in 1888, she had been appalled to learn how many of her co-workers actually lived in similar conditions and what deplorable effects it had.

The major parties made some attempt to correct the most obvious of these ills. But their record of accomplishment was limited, partly because they were distracted by other issues and more, perhaps, because the majority of their members did not agree that the correction of these conditions was a legitimate concern of the government.

Overdoing It

"What? Going already? And in Mackintoshes? Surely you are not going to walk!"

"Oh, dear no! Lord Archibald is going to take us to a dear little slum he's found out near the Minories—such a fearful place! Fourteen poor things sleeping in one bed and no window!—and the Mackintoshes are to keep out infection, you know, and hide one's diamonds, and all that!"

From *Punch*, Dec. 22, 1883.

The most impressive record of social legislation made by any ministry in the early years of this period was that of Disraeli's Conservative government of 1874–1880. In the single year, 1875, existing laws regulating trade-union activities were liberalized (see p. 291), and a Sale of Food and Drugs Act, an Artisans Dwellings Act, and a Public Health Act were passed, the last two of which remained the backbone of government legislation on housing and sanitation until the 1920s. These reforms proved the genuineness of Disraeli's professions about Tory Democracy and his desire to make the Conservative party a party of social progress in the interests of the people. But Disraeli himself, in the last years of his ministry, was forced to devote his declining energies[1] to such things as the crisis in the Near East (see p. 271), the Irish problem (which will be discussed below), and wars against the Zulus in South Africa and the Afghans. After his death in 1881 his party drifted away from Tory Democracy completely.

[1] Poor health was one of the main reasons for his transference to the House of Lords as the Earl of Beaconsfield in 1876.

It is true that, in the 1880s, when the party founded the Primrose League in Disraeli's memory, the famous father of a famous son, Lord Randolph Churchill (1849–1895), declared one of its principal objects to be "the vigorous and earnest promotion of every social reform which can in any degree raise the character and condition of the English people." But Churchill's increasingly radical social views frightened the majority of his party colleagues and—although he had at one time been regarded as a future prime minister—isolated and deprived him of influence. Disraeli's successor as leader of the party, Robert Cecil, third Marquess of Salisbury (1830–1903), was interested almost exclusively in foreign affairs; and the Primrose League, far from becoming a center of reforming activity, developed into an organization largely devoted to attracting the upper-middle classes to the Conservative fold, thus helping the party replace the Liberals as the representative of British industrial and commercial interests. This and the party's success in making the cause of imperialism its own (see p. 446), doubtless explains why the Conservative party, in contrast to its rival, continued to grow in strength and why it still thrives as a major party; but these things did not lead to much positive action to improve the conditions caused by the long depression.

In the Liberal party, the majority had never freed themselves from their old faith in the laissez-faire principle. Gladstone's own zeal for reform in England seemed to come to an end with the passage of the Education Act of 1870 (p. 245); and, during his ministries of 1880–1885, 1886, and 1892–1895, he concentrated on the problems of Ireland. The Liberals did have a numerous Radical wing which showed an awareness of the need for social reform, and in Joseph Chamberlain (1836–1914) they possessed an energetic and gifted man who demonstrated what could be done in the way of practical alleviation of the lot of the poor. Chamberlain (another father of famous sons, one of whom was to help negotiate the Locarno treaties of 1925 [p. 551] and another to be prime minister of England from 1937 to 1940 [pp. 663, 697]) made a fortune in business as a young man and then, from the age of 37, devoted most of his time to politics. Elected mayor of Birmingham in 1873, he won an international reputation by his measures to improve housing, public health, and education. But his efforts, after he entered Parliament in 1876, to persuade his party to do similar work on a national scale—and especially his declaration in January 1885 that the main problem of the future was the promotion of the greater happiness of the masses and that Liberal policy should be "to lessen the evils which poverty brings in its train, to increase the rewards of labour, to bring hope to the miserable"—alarmed more people than it convinced. The majority of his colleagues were relieved when differences with Gladstone on Irish policy led him,

William Ewart Gladstone,
1809–1898. Pen and ink
drawing by Harry Furniss.
(MUSEUM OF FINE ARTS,
BOSTON)

in 1886, to withdraw and form a group called the Liberal Unionists, which henceforth cooperated with the Conservatives. This loss to the Liberal party was not balanced by any increase in Conservative social conscience as a result of Chamberlain's collaboration, for his energies were soon entirely absorbed by colonial and commercial questions. At the same time, his secession deprived the Liberal party of its strongest advocate of reforming activity, weakened its appeal to the masses, and strengthened a growing feeling that Liberalism was bankrupt.

These remarks about the two parties are not intended to suggest that they did nothing in Parliament. In fact, the amount of legislation passed between 1871 and the turn of the century which regulated business practices dangerous to the health or safety of workers, provided new social services and utilities, facilitated the creation of public parks and libraries, raised the level of literacy (by making elementary education compulsory [1880], making county and borough councils responsible for elementary, secondary, and technical schools, and increasing state subsidies to both private and board schools), and provided for the care of the mentally ill and the seriously disabled would have staggered the generation of 1830. But much of this was done reluctantly, by worried M.P.'s who feared that government intervention was becoming excessive and resisted more thoroughgoing measures to alleviate the continuing economic distress. Even the Radicals, who professed to believe in a redistribution of wealth by taxing the wealthy, shied away from any fundamental criticism of the prevailing economic system and opposed government intervention in the field of wages and prices. When the working classes began in the 1880s to agitate for basic reforms, they got little support from Parliament or the established parties.

Toward a Labor Party / Given the widening of the franchise and the continued economic distress, it was probably inevitable that a new political party would arise to represent the masses. In 1884 revived interest in socialism led to the foundation of the Social Democratic Federation (SDF), the first sizable socialist political body since Owen's day. Marxist in inspiration, it never received the formal blessing of Marx and Engels, largely because its founder, H. M. Hyndman, had not given Marx credit for the ideas he borrowed from him when he wrote his book *England For All* in 1881. Marx's approval would hardly have helped it much, for its emphasis on imminent revolution never attracted the support of the British common people, and by the late 1880s it was already a spent force. The Labor party of the twentieth century sprang not from it but from the Fabian Society, from Keir Hardie's Independent Labor party, and from the new trade unions.

The Fabians were a group of middle-class intellectuals who came together in 1883 to discuss social questions and developed into one of the most influential forces in British politics—a point illustrated by the fact that, in 1945, there were 230 Fabians in the House of Commons, most of them associated with the Labor party. In the first years the society included such people as Sidney Webb, its founder and driving force, and his wife Beatrice,[2] the dramatist George Bernard Shaw, Annie Besant, (whose organization of the London match girls in the 1880s was one of the first successes of the new unionism in England), the novelist H. G. Wells, the historian of socialism G. D. H. Cole, and the future prime minister Ramsay MacDonald. Claiming as their spiritual predecessors both Robert Owen and John Stuart Mill, they pledged themselves to the ideal of a reconstitution of society and embarked on a systematic study of every phase of the industrial system of their day. In 1889 they presented their first findings and the outlines of their philosophy in a collection called *Fabian Essays*.

The Fabians emphasized the necessity of a fundamental reorganization of British society and stated that this would imply two things: unlimited democracy in the political sphere and socialism in the economic sphere. They made it clear that the socialism they professed was a philosophy of

---

[2] This collaboration, according to Anne Fremantle, inspired the couplet:

The world is so full of a number of plebs
I am sure we should all be as happy as Webbs.

economic equality to be accomplished by democratic means. They were not revolutionaries, but gradualists, believing that the country had long been moving in the direction of collectivism, and that the process must now be speeded up and the government induced to abolish the profit motive, nationalize the land and all key industries—public utilities, coal, electricity, railroads and other means of transport, communications, medical services, banks, and the like—grant free higher education to the masses, and otherwise promote a collective life of well-being for all citizens.

This philosophy was summed up succinctly by Bernard Shaw (1856–1950) when he wrote in 1896 that the Fabians aimed

> to persuade the English people to make their political constitution thoroughly democratic and so to socialize their industries as to make the livelihood of the people entirely independent of private Capitalism. . . . Socialism, as understood by the Fabian Society, means the organization and conduct of the necessary industries of the country, and the appropriation of all forms of economic rent of land and capital by the nation as a whole, through the most suitable public authorities, parochial, municipal, provincial or central.

The differences between these doctrines and those of Karl Marx will be obvious. Yet there is some truth in the remark made by Harold Laski, an outstanding twentieth-century Fabian and member of the British Labor party. Speaking of Marxists who had charged him with inadequate comprehension of their master's views, Laski said: "They understand Marx in their way; I understand him in *his*." It is undeniable that the Fabians appreciated one aspect of Marx's thought more clearly than some of his followers—namely, the strong practical sense that emphasized immediate rather than remote tasks. Fabians like Laski were convinced that, if Marx had lived longer, he might have agreed with them, even to the point of relegating the revolution to the remote future and becoming "gas and water socialists" like themselves.

Fabianism was not originally designed as a working-class philosophy. The Fabians hoped to "permeate" the middle classes and the parties and Parliament with the conviction that competitive capitalism had outlived its usefulness and that a careful, gradual transition to socialism was both necessary and practical. Despite their enthusiasm and propagandistic zeal (3339 public lectures were given by their members during 1891–1892 alone), they did not, however, win over the older parties and they turned their attention to organized labor. In 1893, disgusted with the Liberal party's disinclination to follow their advice about necessary reform, the Fabian Society sanctioned the publication in *The Fortnightly Review* of an article by Shaw and Sidney Webb, in which they called upon the working classes "to abandon Liberalism, to form a Trade

Union party of their own, to raise £30,000 and finance fifty candidates for Parliament."

In this same year, James Keir Hardie (1856–1915), a miner who had organized one of the first effective unions in Scotland, called a conference of labor leaders at Bradford and founded an organization with the purpose of sponsoring independent candidates for Parliament who would work for "the collective ownership and control of production, distribution and exchange." The establishment of branches of this Independent Labor party (ILP) in other parts of the country was begun with enthusiasm, although their success in their main purpose was delayed by the distrust with which the older unions viewed political activity in general and socialism in particular. But the rapid extension of unionism to the unskilled, encouraged by the success of the dockers strike of 1889 (see p. 292), soon overcame this obstacle. The militant spirit of the new unions was responsible for a Trades Union Congress resolution in 1899 which authorized a conference to investigate the question of labor's Parliamentary representation. In February 1900, union delegations met with representatives of the Fabian Society, the ILP, and the SDF, and founded a Labor Representation Committee (soon to be called the Labor party) under the secretaryship of J. Ramsay MacDonald (1866–1937), which would henceforth present a slate of candidates when Parliamentary elections were held.

In the decade that followed, the new party won increasing support from the rank and file of labor because of two incidents that seemed to represent government attempts to smash the unions. In 1900 railwaymen working for the Taff Vale Railway Company in South Wales struck for higher pay, without the prior approval of their union. The union nevertheless supported them, but was promptly sued by the company for the losses incurred in the strike and lost the case, having to pay damages in excess of £23,000. The Taff Vale verdict seemed to wipe out all the gains made by Disraeli's legislation of 1875 and to make the strike weapon wholly ineffective; and this made union members believe that it was important to support candidates of the Labor Representation Committee, who might remedy the situation in Parliament. Twenty nine such candidates won Parliamentary seats in the elections of 1906.

The Taff Vale decision was effectively revoked by a new Trade Disputes Act in 1906, but this did not end the threats to the organization of labor. In 1909, the House of Lords, acting as a judicial body, handed down the Osborne Judgment, which declared it illegal for any trade union to spend money in electing members of Parliament or in any other political activities. At a time when members of Parliament were still unpaid, this threatened to make a genuine labor representation impossible, and it was resented by the Labor party and the unions alike.

By borrowing and cheese-paring the party managed to get through the two elections of 1910, emerging with 42 seats in the second of them, a growth of 13 since 1906. A year later it was able to win the passage of a law stipulating that members of Parliament would be paid £400 a year; and in 1913 Parliament legalized political action by the unions, although certain annoying restrictions remained. The Liberal party's delay in passing this legislation (it had been in office since 1906) did not ingratiate it with the unions and helped strengthen their tendency to vote for Labor candidates.

On the eve of the war, then, a strong and growing Labor party had come into existence, supported by the new unionism and preaching a native British socialism brought up to date by the Fabian Society, many of whose members were Labor M. P.'s. An additional element of its strength lay in the fact that it appealed to religious Nonconformity. Among the leaders of the labor movement in the 1880s and the 1890s, there was a good number of Methodist ministers and chapel members, a fact that may explain something of the moral fervor of the movement and the religious intensity with which its members sang songs like William Blake's moving hymn:

> Bring me my Bow of burning gold:
> Bring me my Arrows of desire:
> Bring me my Spear: O clouds unfold!
> Bring me my Chariot of fire.
>
> I will not cease from Mental Fight,
> Nor shall my Sword sleep in my hand,
> Till we have built Jerusalem
> In England's green and pleasant land.

The Revival and Relapse of Liberalism / Confronted on the one hand with the defection of many of its former supporters to the Conservative party, and with the rise of a labor movement that attracted much of its Radical wing, the Liberal party seemed to face the prospect of a rapid decline. Before anything of the sort set in, however, it had one more great victory and one outburst of reforming activity.

Of the last twenty-five years of the nineteenth century, all but nine were years of Conservative (or Unionist, as the party came to be called at the time) government; and, after the Liberal ministry of 1892–1895, which saw Gladstone's farewell to politics, the Conservatives seemed prepared to govern indefinitely. They presided over the Diamond Jubilee of Queen Victoria in 1897; they survived the disastrous war with the Boers which followed quickly upon that celebration (p. 460); when the old queen died in January 1901, they made the preparations for the coronation of her son Edward VII (1901–1910); and they held on while the Russo-Japanese War and the first Moroccan crisis showed a dangerous deterioration of the international situation (see p. 470). But by 1905 their popularity in the country was beginning to wane rapidly. The Boer War and the new continental troubles ended the appeal of imperialism and inspired demands for an overhaul of the country's foreign policy. The passage of the Education Act of 1902, which provided for state aid to Anglican and Roman Catholic schools as well as to undenominational ones, aroused the Nonconformist churches, led to tax strikes and imprisonments for failures to pay rates, and caused strong defections from the Unionist fold. Finally, in 1903, Joseph Chamberlain began his campaign for imperial preferential tariffs, arguing that this was the only way to prevent disaster to England's already diminished foreign trade; this split the party into warring sects and led to its near collapse. In the elections of January 1906, the Liberals won 377 seats in Commons, a majority of 84 over all other parties combined. The Unionists received only 157; the Irish Nationalists, of whom something will be said below, 83; and the new Labor party, 29, although they received the additional support of 24 independent trade-union members.

The new Liberal cabinet was headed by Henry Campbell-Bannerman, a wise and unemotional Scot with long Parliamentary experience, who was, however, to die after only two years in office. His cabinet included such Liberal veterans as Lord Morley and Lord Bryce, at the India Office and the Irish secretaryship respectively; but its leading luminaries were H. H. Asquith (1852–1928) who became chancellor of the exchequer (and in 1908 prime minister), Sir Edward Grey (1862–1933), at the Foreign Office, R. B. Haldane (1856–1928), who became minister of war, David Lloyd George (1863–1945), who was at the Board of Trade, and Winston Churchill (1874–   ), who succeeded him there when he went to the Exchequer in 1908.

This combination buckled down to business with an enthusiasm that had been unknown for years. The prime minister's principal accomplishment in his brief term was an honorable and statesmanlike liquidation of the South African situation, which was accomplished by conceding self-government to the Transvaal and laying the basis for the new constitution of the Union of South Africa, which was ratified in 1909. Meanwhile, Lloyd George, who was known to the country only as a Welsh radical and an uncompromising opponent of the Boer War and the Education Act of 1902, showed that he was capable of constructive statesmanship by proposing and securing the passage of the Merchant Shipping Act of 1906, which prescribed standards of food and accomodations designed to stop the deterioration of conditions in the fo'c'sles of British ships a new Patents Act (1907) to remedy deficiencies in the existing law, and n act setting up a Port of London Authority to amalgamate existing dock uthorities and make possible rational development of the port's facilities.

Simultaneously, highly important reforms were carried out in the rmed services. There had been some scepticism when R. B. Haldane, a ultivated and urbane gentleman-scholar with a predilection for philo-ophical speculation, had become minister of war; and Campbell-Ban-erman had wondered publicly what Schopenhauer would accomplish n the barracks. But Haldane brought a critical and inquiring mind, ed by reflection upon German and French military theory, to his task; nd he had the good fortune to be supported strongly, in this area where oyal influence counted for much, by the king.

Nothing had been done to improve the administration or the organiza-ion of the British army since the first Gladstone ministry. At that time, he secretary of war, Edward Cardwell, reformed the army's disciplinary :ode, reduced the length of service from twelve to six years, placing ;reater reliance on an able reserve, rearmed the infantry with the Martini-Henry breech-loading rifle, divided Great Britain and Ireland nto new regimental districts, and fitted existing line regiments to them :o as to make an organic link between regular and auxiliary forces, and—nost important—abolished the system by which commissions and promotions in the army were secured by purchase. These reforms had :orrected important abuses; but, since then, continental armies had noved forward with new techniques and systems of organization, while the British army had been content to rest on Cardwell's work. The Boer War had demonstrated shocking confusion in all units, an awkward dispersal of forces around the globe that made effective union for war difficult, and inefficient administrative practices in the War Office itself.

Haldane corrected this situation and allayed some of the concern caused by ugly tendencies on the continent by recasting the whole structure of the army. He introduced divisions of the continental type, established an Expeditionary Force of six infantry divisions and one cavalry division, with supporting artillery, transport, and medical units and adequate reserves, and a Territorial Force that comprised all exist-ing militia units, and devised a speedy and practical mobilization schedule. He established officer training corps at all public and secondary schools, an institution that proved its worth in the war. Finally, he gave the British army its first permanent general staff and saw to it that able men like Sir William Robertson, Henry Wilson, and Douglas Haig were appointed to it. While doing all this, Haldane actually reduced the army budget, thus minimizing the complaints of the Radical wing of the party, which opposed excessive military expenditure.

The Radicals were less happy about the navy reforms that were simul-tanously being made by the first sea lord, Admiral Sir John Fisher. This

energetic and brilliant sailor advocated the disarming of all superannuated fleet units and the inauguration of a building program that
would concentrate on the new dreadnought type of battleship. His arguments were given point by the program of fleet construction currently
under way in Germany. Progress in that country was so marked that
Fisher was reported, in conversation with the king, to have suggested the
advisability of Copenhagening the German navy before it began to cause
real trouble;[3] and in 1909 British public opinion became so aroused
over the German threat that naval estimates had to be revised. This cost
money that might otherwise have been expended on social improvements
and was resented by many Liberals.

But military expenditures were not the chief obstacle to the most
cherished wishes of the more radical Liberals. More serious was the
opposition of the House of Lords, which had long been a Conservative
stronghold and which now, under the injudicious influence of Conservative leaders like A. J. Balfour and Lord Lansdowne, sought to block what
they seemed to consider to be dangerous leveling tendencies on the part
of the government.

In 1906 Lansdowne quite properly stated that the House of Lords had
the legal right "to arrest the progress of measures whenever they believe they have been insufficiently considered, and are not in accord
with the deliberate judgment of the country." The question, however,
was how competent this body of hereditary peers was to judge the
popular temper. It was not, after all, subject to election, and there was
some evidence that it was being rapidly plutocracized by that movement
of economic forces which Élie Halévy once described in the words:
"While business men were becoming peers, peers were becoming business men, so that when the new rich reached the Upper House they
found themselves on familiar ground."

Liberals argued that a hereditary body with large powers was an
anomaly in a progressive state, that the House of Lords was a stronghold
of privilege, and that it was flagrantly misusing its powers. The first
arguments were perhaps matters of opinion. For the third, there seemed
to be substantial grounds. In the years 1888–1892 not a single Conservative measure had been defeated in Lords. In the Liberal ministry of
1892–1895, on the other hand, nearly every measure of social reform
proposed had been vetoed and, since the Liberals had returned to power
in 1906, this had been happening again. In 1906 Lords vetoed a new
education bill and a plural-voting bill; in 1907 they mutilated four land-
reform bills; in 1908 they threw out a liquor-licensing bill; and in 1909
they actually rejected the government's budget.

---

[3] In April 1801, Admiral Lord Nelson sailed into Copenhagen harbor without any
declaration of war and destroyed the Danish fleet, thus effectively eliminating the
possibility of effective naval action by the League of Armed Neutrality.

Rich Fare

*The Giant Lloyd-
Gorgibuster:*
"Fee, fi, fo, fat,
I smell the blood of a
plutocrat;
Be he alive or be he dead,
I'll grind his bones to make
my bread."

From *Punch,* April 28, 1909.

Considering the fact that a civil war had been fought in the
seventeenth century to secure the House of Commons's control of the
purse, this was a provocative gesture. Those who advocated it took the
position that this budget was not a normal money bill but a deliberate
attempt to socialize England. It is not hard to understand their position.
The author of the budget was David Lloyd George, a curious amalgam
of political genius and irresponsibility, now taking the first spectacular
steps in a career that would bring him to the most cherished position in
British politics. Born in the humblest of circumstances in a mining district of Wales, he had a deep resentment of those with inherited wealth
and position and was opportunistic enough to see what could be accomplished by attacking them. "When you find the House of Commons is
lifeless and apathetic," he wrote, "You must stir public opinion by violent
means, so that the public will react upon legislation." The budget that he
drafted upon becoming chancellor of the exchequer in 1908 was designed
to do that.

Dubbed by its author the People's Budget, it raised the income tax,
especially on unearned incomes, increased death duties, put new taxes
on tobacco, spirits, and (now that the motor car had arrived) vehicles
and petrol, and imposed four new land taxes, the most important of
which was a tax on unearned increment—that is to say, on the increased
value of such things as building sites in the vicinity of the Port of London

which had skyrocketed not through the efforts of their owners but because of the growth of the port. There is some evidence that Lloyd George understood only imperfectly the economics of his proposals, and it is also true that his land taxes, in the end, never did produce much revenue. But he was more interested in their propaganda effects than in their economic soundness. He introduced his budget as "a War Budget . . . to wage implacable warfare against poverty and squalidness." He hoped the Lords would defeat it, so that he could make them the symbol of the victimization of the poor; and, in November 1909 they obliged him.

Neither the defeat of the budget nor the subsequent all-out campaign against the Lords and the landed interest, in which the Heavenly Twins, as Lloyd George and his stanchest supporter Winston Churchill were called, reached new heights of political invective, had quite the political effects expected. In the general elections of January 1910, the Liberal party lost the commanding majority it had enjoyed since 1906 and, when the country went to the polls once more, after the death in May of Edward VII and the accession of George V (1910–1936), it did not improve its strength, and henceforth had to depend on Labor votes for a safe margin in the House. But this did not prevent the Liberals from picking up the gauntlet that had been thrown down by the Lords, and they now carried through a constitutional change of the first importance.

In February 1910 the government had introduced in Commons a bill that excluded the House of Lords from interfering with any money bill whatsoever; gave Commons the right to pass any measure into law, despite the Lords' veto, by passing it in three successive parliamentary sessions, provided at least two years had elapsed since its introduction; and reduced the length of Parliaments from seven to five years. The elections and the preparations for the coronation of George V delayed decisive action on this bill until June 1911; but by that time the prime minister, Asquith, was ready to act. He had secured a promise from the new sovereign that, if the Lords refused to pass the Parliament Bill without amendment, he would create enough new peers to secure its passage; under this threat the Lords collapsed, although only after scenes of unparalleled disorder in both houses of Parliament.

The Parliament Bill of 1911 reduced the role of the Lords to that of a purely advisory body and placed full political power in the hands of the elected representatives of the people sitting in Commons. It also cleared the way for that program of basic social reform about which the Liberals had said so much during the days of the upper chamber's obstructionism. Their new freedom seems, however, to have embarrassed them.

Lloyd George once said to a friend, "I don't know exactly what I am, but I'm sure I'm not a Liberal. They have no sympathy with the people. . . . As long as I was settling disputes with their workers . . . these great Business Men said I was the greatest Board President of modern times. When I tried to do something for the welfare of their workmen, they denounced me as a Welsh thief." This is typical George-ian hyperbole. It would be more accurate to say that Lloyd George's colleagues were made restless by the violence of his denunciations of privilege and the sweeping nature of his proclamations of the welfare state; they were willing to be Benthamites but not socialists; and they became increasingly cautious and compromising in spirit after the battle with the Lords was won. The only great measure of social reform passed by them in the years before the war was the National Insurance Act of 1911, which insured workers against accident, sickness, and unemployment. This was an undeniably important piece of legislation, but nevertheless, like Bismarck's social insurance laws of the 1880s (see p. 381), an essentially conservative one, since it was supported, not by general taxation, but by contributions from employers and employees, with a relatively small additional state subsidy. What other legislation reached the statute books was purely regulatory, like the Coal Mines Regulations Act of 1911, which improved safety provisions in the mines.

In justice to the Liberals, it should be noted that their energies were now diverted to other things and especially to the intricacies of the Irish question. Even so, in their prewar hesitations we can see the reasons for their supersession in the 1920s by the Labor and Conservative parties, which had more resolution and less respect for compromise.

The Irish Question from Gladstone to World War I / The Irish unrest that had marked Gladstone's first ministry was aggravated in the years that followed. The coming of the agricultural depression to Ireland and the precipitous fall of agricultural prices destroyed most of the good effects of Gladstone's land bill (see p. 247) and led to widespread misery, 2110 families being evicted for failure to pay rent in the year 1880 alone. This led to renewed agitation in favor of comprehensive reform to provide not merely fixed peasant tenure but actual peasant ownership of the land. This was the objective, for instance, of the National Land League, which was founded in 1879 by Michael Davitt, a former peasant himself. Supplied with money by Irish immigrants to the United States and Australia, the Land League inspired and coordinated peasant unrest. Against unpopular landlords, it encouraged the use of those tactics of intimidation, denial of service, property damage, and general ostracism that came to be called boycotting, after a Captain Boycott who, in 1880, was their first victim. Not infrequently, more violent weapons were used by angry tenant farmers: ricks were burned, cattle injured, individuals assaulted.

The activities of the Land League gave added effect to the fight for home rule for Ireland, which was kept up throughout this whole period by the Irish members in the House of Commons. Their leader, Charles Stewart Parnell (1846–1891), was hardly the epitome of those qualities one would expect to find in an Irish nationalist leader, since he was aristocratic in appearance, cold and aloof in manner, and Protestant in religion; but he became the idol of millions in his lifetime, and his name, even after his death, was capable of arousing transports of emotion, like those described in the early chapters of Joyce's *Portrait of the Artist as a Young Man*. A superb orator and a shrewd tactician, Parnell, after his election to the House of Commons in 1875, organized the Irish members into an obstructionist bloc that developed the filibuster to a fine art, kept attention focused on Ireland's grievances, and sought to wear down Parliamentary resistance to Irish freedom.

Successive British governments sought to meet these tactics by a combination of reform and coercion. In 1881–1882, the second Gladstone ministry gave Ireland a new Land Reform Act, which assured Irish tenants of fixity of tenure, fair rents, and free sale (the so-called three F's), and also passed an Arrears Act, which helped defaulting tenants regain their land. The good effects of this legislation were offset to a large extent by the coercion employed by the British government in Ireland against boycotters and other agitators. This merely called forth more extreme forms of protest: in 1882 there were twenty-six murders and fifty-eight attempted murders in Ireland, including the slaying in Phoenix Park, Dublin, of the two principal secretaries to the viceroy.

The prevalence of these conditions finally persuaded Gladstone that some form of home rule was inevitable and, when he formed his third ministry in 1886, he brought in a bill that provided for an Irish parliament and executive in Dublin, with authority over all but military, foreign, and fiscal policy, and trade, coinage, and customs. It was this conversion of the prime minister that led Joseph Chamberlain to secede from the Liberal party; and it was his opposition, as much as anything else, that defeated the bill. But the defeat was not decisive, and in the next few years the cause of home rule seemed to be winning new supporters in England. But in 1890, when victory seemed possible, Parnell was named as corespondent in a divorce suit brought by a Captain O'Shea against his wife, and the resultant scandal ruined the Irish leader and his cause. The Conservative party, whose only Irish policy was coercion, gained strength from the disclosure of its enemy as an adulterer; Gladstone, whose private negotiations with Parnell had seemed on the point of success, felt compelled to break with him; and Parnell's own party split, partly because of the position taken by the Irish church.

Despite this disappointment, Gladstone persisted in his efforts—in 1893 his second Home Rule Bill actually passed in Commons, only to be defeated by the House of Lords—and his unflagging zeal convinced many

)eople that home rule was inevitable. When his party returned to power
n 1906, therefore, it was logical that it should have taken up the issue
gain. Superficially, conditions now seemed more favorable, for the Glad-
tone land reforms and the introduction of a degree of self-government
n local affairs in Ireland had greatly reduced the violence and terrorism
hat had necessitated earlier coercion laws. Unfortunately, during this
ame period, the Protestant districts of northeast Ulster had been grow-
ng in economic strength and self-consciousness, and they now showed
hemselves to be inflexibly opposed to any form of home rule that would
ubordinate them to the Catholic south. When talk of home rule was
enewed, indeed, they began to raise volunteer forces to withstand it.

This resistance, which was encouraged by the Conservative party,
night have been checked in its early stages, either by a professed willing-
less to exclude the northern districts from any home rule proposal or by
firmness. But the Liberal government could not expect to persuade
southern Ireland to accept the idea of partition, while, on the other hand,
they postponed action against Ulster until the agitation there could no
longer be controlled without a major show of force. The upshot of all this
was that, when a home-rule bill modeled on Gladstone's earlier ones was
passed by Parliament in 1914, Ulster refused to submit to it, and officers
of the British army units that were ordered to Ulster to guard against an
explosion declared that they would not obey these orders. The government, with a European war breaking around its ears, decided to postpone the application of home rule until after general peace was restored,
a decision that was understandable in the circumstances but which, by
frustrating the cause of Irish freedom once more, encouraged a revival
of extremism in the south and prepared the way for the Easter revolt of
1916 in Dublin and the time of troubles that followed the world conflict.

British Democracy in 1914 / In the years since 1867, Great Britain had
moved from the philosophy and institutions of liberalism to an increasingly great degree of political and economic democracy. The extension
of the suffrage had made possible a high degree of popular participation
in Parliamentary elections, and the ability of the House of Lords to balk
the popular will as expressed by their representatives had been destroyed.
Local government had simultaneously been transformed by the substitution of elected county, district, parish, and borough councils for the older
aristocratic system of government by closed corporations or by justices of
peace at quarter sessions. Social services had been expanded, in the form
of medical care, health insurance, recreational facilities, sanitation, transportation, and public education, and the government had recognized its
duty to protect its citizens by regulating certain aspects of their lives and
their employment—all of which forecast the coming of the welfare state

proclaimed by the Fabians. To the central government there had been added new Boards of Works (1851), Local Government (1871) Agriculture (1886), and Education (1899); and these agencies permitted the handling of vital problems efficiently and from a truly national point of view. Finally, the liberties and social gains that had been won at home had been extended, through grants of self-government and dominion status, to Canada (1867), Australia (1900), New Zealand (1907), and the Union of South Africa (1909).

These changes, with all their merits, were accompanied by an increase in the size, functions, and cost of government and an acceleration of the tendency toward the bureaucratization of society that would have been deplored by the Liberals of the mid-century. Nor was this their most unfortunate effect. As liberalism gave way to democracy, some of the values for which it had stood fell into disrepute. In the last years before World War I, this was demonstrated by the way in which organized groups in society deliberately abandoned that reliance upon law and reason and compromise that had been the heart of the liberal philosophy. When members of the House of Commons howled down the prime minister as he introduced the Parliament Bill in 1911, when army officers refused to go to Ulster as ordered, when British workers in the years 1912–1914 gave their ears to syndicalist leaders and participated in the bitterest wave of strikes to affect the country since the 1880s, and when the Women's Suffrage Movement indulged in a frenzy of vandalism, personal assault, and exhibitionism in 1913 and 1914 (with their leader remarking that "the broken window pane is the most valuable argument in modern politics" and their most ardent agitator committing suicide by throwing herself under the hooves of the king's horse as it thundered into the stretch in the 1913 Derby), they were all testifying to the decline of the liberal attitude in politics. As Winston Churchill said in 1914, "the civil and parliamentary systems under which [Englishmen] have dwelt so long [seemed] to be brought to the rude challenge of force [and] to be exposed to menace and brutality."

Whether this tendency would have continued is impossible to say, for these manifestations of a new spirit of violence in politics were soon submerged in the greater violence of the World War.

BELGIUM, THE NETHERLANDS, AND SWITZERLAND

The Belgian Democracy / The country whose development most closely paralleled that of Great Britain was Belgium. Like Britain, Belgium was a constitutional monarchy and was fortunate in being ruled by able and conscientious sovereigns whose reigns were long enough to enable them to master their trade and, within the limits of their authority, to contribute to the continuity and stability of national policy, particularly in the area of foreign and colonial affairs.

Belgium's first king, Leopold I (1830–1865), helped consolidate the neutral position in which his country had been placed by the great powers in 1831 (see p. 31), by cultivating good relations with his royal neighbors, and even by giving them the benefit of his advice when they desired it (and sometimes, as the young Queen Victoria had often complained, when they did not). This mentor of Europe was succeeded by Leopold II (1865–1909), who threw his abundant energies into economic enterprise and was the founder of Belgium's rich colonial empire (see p. 448). Albert I (1909–1934), perhaps the best loved of Belgian sovereigns, was the soldier king who tried vainly to stem the German invasion of his country in 1914.

Like Britain, Belgium moved from liberalism to democracy during the period under review. The original constitution of the country had placed political power in the hands of what has been described as a bourgeois oligarchy supported by a very limited franchise based on tax payments. The evolution of the industrial system—until 1870 Belgium was the only continental country to keep pace with the industrial expansion of Great Britain—led to the organization of the working classes for political action. Trade unions and socialists pressed for suffrage reform so successfully that in 1893 the constitution was amended to give the vote to all male citizens who had reached the age of twenty-five, supplementary votes being given to the most highly educated and taxed classes.

Of the two traditional parties, the Catholic party retained its preponderance in the country, but before 1914 the Liberals had become inferior in strength to the rising Socialist party and were able to maintain their position largely because of the introduction of proportional representation. This measure, passed in 1899, was designed to advance the cause of democratic government by assuring the representation of all shades of opinion.

Of democratic intent also was the law of 1898, which gave the Flemish language, widely used in the northern districts, equality with French, which was spoken by the majority of the country.

Finally, as in the case of Great Britain, Belgium experienced the first significant measures of economic democracy with the extension of elementary education to the masses in the 1880s, the beginning of factory regulation after 1890, and the institution of old-age pensions (1900), workmen's compensation for accidents (1903), and improvements in housing and public services for the working classes.

The Dutch Netherlands / Perhaps because its economy remained predominantly agricultural and commercial rather than industrial, as in the case of Belgium, or because, in contrast to Great Britain, its prosperity was more continuous throughout these years, Holland's progress toward democracy was slower than that of the two countries discussed above. The country did not have a constitution until 1849; and, during most of the long reign of William III (1849–1890), the sovereign retained a considerable amount of political power, including the right to veto legislation passed by the parliament. The suffrage was severely limited, and, even after reforms of 1887 and 1896, only 14 percent of the population had the vote. Universal manhood suffrage was legalized only in 1917.

The chief issue in Dutch politics until the end of the nineteenth century was, not economic policy or social reform, but education. As was true in other countries, the Liberal party advocated a system of free public elementary schooling without religious instruction of any kind. The Protestant Conservative and Catholic parties contended for, and in 1889 secured, state aid for their denominational schools. To contest the predominance of these older parties, which cut across class lines, there was no Labor or Socialist party of any importance before World War I.

Switzerland / At the other political extreme from this essentially conservative state stood the Swiss Federation, a flourishing center of political freedom, proud of its federal form and its institutions of direct democracy, as well as of the refuge it offered to political exiles from other lands.

The great German-Swiss writer and patriot Gottfried Keller (1819–1890) once wrote that, in contrast to other lands whose national self-consciousness was based on race or language or history, Switzerland based its nationality upon the idea of liberty. He wrote:

> Similar inclinations in a beautiful country, many neighborly contacts, and a common tough determination to maintain independence, have produced in Switzerland a common federal life distinguished from any other national life. This . . . has produced a far-reaching similarity of attitudes and character. In our common nationality we feel protected against the confusion which surrounds us on all sides.

During the first half of the nineteenth century, this independent spirit was so uncompromising as to make it unlikely that the Swiss could form an effective national unit. The federation was a mere collection of independent cantons that differed in language, religion, administrative forms, and educational institutions, and even pursued separate commercial policies and entered into private arrangements with foreign powers. Two things, however, corrected this situation. The first was the growth of a strong democratic movement in most cantons in the two decades before 1848, which demanded and secured extension of popular liberties, widening of the franchise, and the reform of local justice. Once entrenched conservatism and parochialism had been weakened by the reforms of this "era of regeneration" as the Swiss call it, it was inevitable that there should be a growing demand for a stronger central government.

This second demand precipitated a conflict between the democratic majority of the cantons, and a league (the *Sonderbund*) which was formed by the Catholic cantons, who resisted the increase of federal power. The issue was settled in 1847 by a short war, which was followed by a dissolution of the Catholic League and a thoroughgoing revision of the national constitution. Henceforward, Switzerland was to possess a bicameral legislature similar to that of the United States (one house in which the people were represented on the basis of population, the other in which the cantons had equal representation) and a Federal Tribunal and a Federal Council elected by the legislature. The cantons reserved great powers, especially in regard to education, public health, religion, crime; but the central government controlled foreign and military affairs, commercial policy, post and coinage, and fiscal policy.

Switzerland thus became a strong federal union, and one in which democracy took more advanced forms than in any of the countries of continental Europe. For one thing, the practice of direct democracy—that is, of decisions being taken by the vote of *all* the affected citizens—continued to be practiced in several of the smaller Swiss cantons. For another, in cantons whose area and population forbade this, laws passed on stipulated subjects by cantonal legislatures had to be referred to the people for their formal assent, and other laws could be referred to them on demand; and there was provision also for the submission of laws to the legislature by the initiative of a certain number of voters.

In 1874, when the federal constitution was revised, enlarging the powers of central government and authorizing it, among other things, to provide for free elementary education, provision was made for popular referendum on the national as well as the cantonal level and, in 1891, the initiative became part of federal law also. As a kind of corollary to these institutions, which made the Swiss people the absolute masters of their government, the government in 1874 underlined the individual's responsibility for protecting Swiss democracy by authorizing a system of compulsory military service. In keeping with the country's neutral position (established as a result of a decision taken by the Great Powers at Vienna in 1815), the military force subsequently raised was a strictly defensive one. But its organization, discipline, and efficiency were favorably commented on abroad, where the Swiss militia was often held up as the model of the kind of army which (in contrast to some of those in larger countries) neither jeopardized domestic liberty nor threatened the general peace by arousing the fear of neighboring countries. The growth of Swiss industry in the period after 1870 was notable, especially in textiles, watchmaking, luxury goods, and confections; and this led to the establishment of trade unions and the rise of an active socialist movement. This last was encouraged also by the permissiveness of the political climate, which, in the last quarter of the nineteenth century, made Switzerland the refuge for political exiles from other countries. In the 1870s the anarchist movement had headquarters here; later, the German Social Democrats, whose press was destroyed by Bismarck's persecutions (see p. 381), published their newspapers in Basel and smuggled them across the border; and, at the beginning of the new century, a group of left-wing socialists led by Lenin sat at sidewalk cafés in Bern and Geneva and dreamed of the time when they might be able to return to their native Russia.

Besides being a kind of headquarters for refugees, Switzerland, by virtue of its neutral position, was also considered an ideal place for the establishment of organizations like the International Red Cross, the International Postal Union, and the International Telegraph Union.

NORTHERN EUROPE

Denmark / In the course of the nineteenth century, the kingdom of Denmark had the misfortune to be deprived of much of its national domain by action of the Great Powers. At Vienna in 1815, the Danes were punished for their loyalty to Napoleon by being forced to cede Norway to Sweden; and, in 1864, as we have seen (p. 225), they were despoiled by the German powers of the provinces of Schleswig and Holstein. In the reduced realm, progress toward liberalism and democracy was delayed by the fact that the greater part of the population consisted of peasants with little interest in politics and by the resistance of King Christian IX (1863–1906) to anything resembling genuine parliamentary government. During his reign, Denmark was the scene of a constitutional conflict similar to that which took place in Prussia in the 1860s and concerned with the same issues, army reform and control of budget; and, as in Prussia, the king had his way by disregarding the constitutional desires and defying the opposition of the lower house.

By the turn of the century, however, demands for reform were being advanced, not only by the urban middle classes, but by the Social

The father of existentialism:
Sören Kirkegaard, 1813–1855.
(BROWN BROTHERS)

Democrats, who had been active since the 1870s, the youth movement, inspired and led by Denmark's most distinguished man of letters, Georg Brandes (1842–1927), and the more prosperous farmers. Even so, what appeared to be a victory for responsible parliamentary government in 1901 merely touched off new dissensions, and it was not until 1915 that the reform movement succeeded in winning a new constitution. This provided for an extension of the suffrage to all men and most women, the widening of the competence of the lower house of parliament, and—by measures not unlike those taken in England in 1911—the effective abolition of the veto of the upper house, which had in the past buttressed royal power. Thus, belatedly, Denmark entered a new period of democracy.

Norway and Sweden / In 1814 Sweden had voluntarily relinquished Finland to Russia on the understanding that Norway would be ceded to her. The Swedish regent, Marshal Bernadotte, had, however, to take Norway by conquest, for there was strong opposition to union in that country; and, if he was in the end successful, he found it advisable to recognize the Fundamental Law which the Norwegian Storting had accepted in May 1814 and which was based on the liberal Spanish constitution of 1812.

With this beginning, the history of the union of Norway and Sweden was bound to be a stormy one. Norway, already far advanced toward

democracy, began her new career with claims that she was "free
indivisible, and independent" even though united with Sweden, and
with parliamentary institutions which sought to give actuality to those
claims. On the other hand, Sweden was a country whose government
was aristocratic and feudal and whose rulers showed a stubborn attachment to royal prerogatives. They were particularly insistent on their right
to dictate the foreign and military policy of the two countries, and this
led to differences, notably in 1864, when the king wished to give aid to
the Danes and was opposed by the Norwegian Storting. Apart from this
the two countries had no real community of economic interests, Sweden
as we have seen (p. 285), moving rapidly after 1870 toward industrial
maturity and Norway remaining a predominantly agricultural and commercial state. It was indeed this last fact that led to the final rupture of
the union, for as the Norwegian carrying trade grew, the Norwegian
parliament began to insist on a separate consular service to protect it
and the Swedish government resisted this as destructive of the union
After a dozen years of bitter conflict in which the Norwegian universities
and intellectuals like the poet and dramatist Björnstjerne Björnson (1832–
1910) played a prominent part, the Norwegian parliament declared
unanimously on June 7, 1905, that the union with Sweden was dissolved
a decision subsequently confirmed by plebescite. Although there was
momentarily some talk of war, the Swedish government acquiesced in
this decision; and Norway became an independent, constitutional monarchy, inviting the younger son of the king of Denmark to assume the
throne with the title Haakon VII. The royal office was largely honorific
and the royal veto, at first provided for, was abolished in 1915.

Norway's democratic tendencies were encouraged by the separation
In 1907 it was the first sovereign state to give the vote to women, and
subsequently compulsory education and various forms of social insurance
were instituted.

In Sweden itself, the royal absolution of Bernadotte, who had ruled as
Charles XIV from 1818 until 1844, had given way gradually to a moderate
liberalism under his successors Oskar I (1844–1859), Charles XV (1859–
1872), and Oskar II (1872–1907). The constitutional laws of 1864 abolished the old estates and set up a bicameral legislature with considerable
power, although the deputies of the lower house were elected exclusively
by the propertied classes. In 1909, during the reign of Gustavus V (1907–
1950), universal manhood suffrage was introduced in elections for the
lower house and the property qualification for election to the upper
house was reduced; and in subsequent years, voting rights were extended
to women and proportional representation was introduced in elections
for both houses of parliament. This last innovation was of advantage to

The founder of the modern
drama:
Henrik Ibsen, 1828–1906.
(NORWEGIAN INFORMATION
SERVICE)

he socialist movement, which was a natural outgrowth of Sweden's
ndustrial progress.

SOUTHERN EUROPE

In most of the countries discussed in this chapter, substantial progress
oward democracy had been registered by 1914 and, even where there
vas a tendency toward an increased use of violence in politics, it
vas not so marked as to threaten the existing political regimes, most of
vhich had shown the ability to adjust themselves successfully to changed
eeds and new problems. None of this was true of the states of Southern
Lurope, where progress toward democracy was minimal, violence un-
ontrolled, and the stability of established government always in question.

pain / Gerald Brenan has concisely described the history of Spain in
he first seventy years of the nineteenth century by writing: "The glorious
ational rising against Napoleon had been followed by twenty-six years
f savage reaction and civil war: this had been succeeded by the anarchic
ule of the generals which, under a delightful but scandalously unchaste

queen, in a Ruritanian atmosphere of railway speculation and uniforms, had lasted for another twenty-eight." The queen in question was Isabella II, who was deposed in 1868, when her use of the methods that had made her father, Ferdinand VII (see p. 22), odious finally proved too much even for the generals who served her.

Isabella's fall was engineered by General Prim and Marshal Serrano, who also undertook to make arrangements for her successor. Their first attempt, when they offered the vacant throne to Prince Leopold of Hohenzollern, was unsuccessful and had the unforeseen effect, as we have seen (p. 253), of providing the incident that precipitated the outbreak of hostilities between France and Prussia in 1870. Their second was no more fortunate. In November 1870, Serrano's provisional government, with the authorization of the Cortes elected in 1869, invited Amadeo, the second son of the king of Italy, to become king of Spain. When this unhappy prince did so, he found himself opposed by the legitimists, who sought the throne for Isabella's son Alfonso, the Carlists, who were working for the heir of Ferdinand VII's brother, Don Carlos, the Catholic Church, which wanted no king of the dynasty that had robbed the pope of his temporal power, and the republicans, who wanted no king at all. After two years of frustration, while ministries were set up and fell again like ninepins, Amadeo turned his office back to the Cortes with the words: "My good intentions have been in vain. . . . Spain still lives in continual strife, departing day by day more widely from that era of peace and prosperity for which I have so ardently yearned."

There followed a brief republican interval (February 1873–December 1874), but the results were so lamentable that the European powers felt compelled to withhold their recognition of the regime. While monarchists and clericals alike boycotted the new government, the Carlists raised an army of 75,000 men and started operations designed to overthrow it, while in the south other irregular forces burned and looted in the name of federal liberty. Once more the military felt compelled to intervene, and, on Christmas Eve 1874, they declared in favor of Alfonso, the son of Isabella II and overthrew the republic.

This time at least some superficial stability resulted from the political change. The leading figure in the monarchical restoration and the author of the new constitution was Don Antonio Cánovas del Castillo, a conservative politician, a patriot, and an admirer of the English constitutional system as he understood it (which was, as things turned out, far from perfectly). In the constitution of 1876, Cánovas imitated the forms of English political life, to the extent of establishing a responsible ministry and a parliament of two chambers; and in the deliberations of the lower house in subsequent years members of Cánovas' Conservative party delivered Disraelian philippics and were answered by Gladstonian rotundities from the opposition benches, where the Liberal party of Práxedes Sagasta sat. All of this was artificial. The greatest part of the population was excluded not only from the actual exercise of political power, for only the propertied classes were given the vote, but even from the thoughts of the politicians who were supposed to represent them. No real principles divided the Conservatives and the Liberals; they vied only for power and had no intention of improving the lot of the common people or the general state of law in a country notorious for social injustice. Cánovas gave stability to Spain only by permitting the politicians, the clergy, and the army to enrich themselves at the expense of the nation; and this had the effect of creating a hopeless division between the governed and the governing class.

Alfonso XII died in 1885 and his wife reigned as regent until his son assumed power in 1902. The regency and the first decade of the reign of Alfonso XIII were marked by a series of crises which strained the resources of the regime to the utmost. The first of these had to do with the colonial empire, already greatly reduced in size by the secession of the Latin American colonies in the 1820s (see p. 22). Spain had retained possession of the rich island of Cuba, but persistent maladministration and exploitation had turned that colony into a center of continuous disaffection and caused an insurrection in 1868 that took ten years to liquidate. In 1895, disappointed by the nonfulfillment of promises of self-government, Cuba erupted again and this time the brutalities of the repressive methods employed by Spanish garrison troops led to intervention by the United States and, in 1898, to a war in which Spain lost both Cuba and the Philippines and was left with a depleted treasury, a shattered military establishment (200,000 Spaniards are said to have died of wounds and disease in Cuba), and, of her once expansive overseas empire, only a few small holdings in Morocco and West Africa.

These events coincided with growing dissatisfaction on the part of the peasantry and the industrial masses, which was shown (as has been indicated above, p. 305) by the growth of Marxist socialism and syndicalism in the industrial cities and the spread of anarchism among the peasantry of the south and the working classes of Barcelona. Nor was this all. The ineffectiveness and corruption of the regime led to a resurgence of Carlism and to the growth of separatist feeling among the Basques and Catalans, some of whom supported Carlist reaction, while others followed extremists of the Left. As a result of all this, the resort to violence became increasingly marked in Spanish politics: assassinations and terrorism became almost commonplace; there were attempts on the king's life in 1906 and 1912; and in 1909, when the government called up army reserves in Catalonia to avenge an ambush of Spanish troops in Morocco, the city of Barcelona rose in revolt, and there were five days of mob rule during which twenty-two churches and thirty-four convents were burned[4] before the troops restored order by shooting 175 workers in the street and subsequently executing many more.

To bring social peace to the country, the leader of the Liberal party José Canalejas, tried to form a working coalition with the Republicans and Socialists on the basis of a program of anticlericalism. This traditional Liberal policy may have seemed particularly appropriate in the circumstances, for the Spanish church had persistently chosen to ally itself with the forces of wealth and reaction and to rely upon repression rather than persuasion and understanding to combat the growth of socialism. It has been said that by 1910 Spain was ceasing to be a Catholic country, as anarchism grew among the peasants, scepticism among the middle classes, and naked hostility to church censorship among the intellectuals. Civil marriages were becoming common; church membership was falling off; a large percentage of children born in Barcelona, Valencia, and Madrid were never baptized.

Even so, an anticlerical policy was not enough to weld the atomized forces of the Left and Center into an effective political bloc. Its only tangible results were the murder of Canalejas himself in 1912 and a deepening of the political confusion of the country.

Portugal / The pattern of Portuguese political history was different from that of its neighbor, although the degree of violence that marked it was almost equally great. The first half of the nineteenth century was characterized by continuous wars between rival claimants to the throne and frequent insurrections. During the reigns of Pedro V (1853–1861) and Louis I (1861–1889) the country seemed to be moving toward liberal parliamentary government. This progress was interrupted, however, by the accession of Carlos I (1889–1908), a man whose absolutist temperament and unbridled lust for personal gratification led to financial mismanagement, frequent misuse of the royal prerogative, violation of parliamentary procedure, and, as a result of all these, the growth of internecine strife. On February 1, 1908, this model of self-indulgence and his eldest son were killed in the streets of Lisbon; and when the king's second son took the throne, he was able to hold it only until October 1910, when a revolution in Lisbon proclaimed the republic.

On the outbreak of the war of 1914, Portugal was nominally at least a democratic state. The constitution was modeled on that of the Third French Republic, as was the policy of anticlericalism that the republican government elected to pursue (see p. 368), more successfully, as i

---

[4] The troops had been ambushed on their way to occupy certain iron mines beyond Melilla. Army service had been unpopular since 1898; the conscripts proved receptive to the suggestion that the mines in question were owned by the Jesuits.

urned out, than the short-lived Canalejas government in Spain. Church
and state were formally separated in 1911; religious instruction was
barred from schools; and church schools were deprived of all state aid.
But an antireligious policy is not enough in itself to create political
stability; and Portugal, like Spain, suffered from a large debt and an
unstable fiscal system, an economy handicapped by a high degree of
illiteracy (elementary education was made compulsory only in 1911),
a lack of public services, and the usual quota of quarrelsome political
parties more intent on planning revolts than on devising constructive
policies.

Italy / By all odds the most melancholy spectacle presented by the
states of Southern Europe was that on display in Italy, where all of the
high hopes of the *Risorgimento* were confounded and all of the superficial forms of progress belied by the realities behind them.

The Italian political system after 1870 was, like that devised by
Cánovas in Spain, modeled on the English and bore just as little real
similarity to it. The monarchy was a constitutional one, governing
through a ministry responsible to parliament. This was composed of two
houses, a Senate of hereditary and life members appointed by the crown
and a Chamber of Deputies elected for terms of five years by the
propertied and educated classes. Effective power lay in the Chamber, the
Senate only rarely exercising its suspensive veto of legislation; and
politics in the Chamber was in the hands of two coalitions of parties,
the Right (*Destra*) and the Left (*Sinistra*). The flaw in the system was
that there was no essential difference between these groupings and no
possibility of constructive debate or alternation of power.

This does not mean merely that the vast majority of deputies were
middle class in origin and philosophy, rationalist in sentiment, anticlerical in matters touching on religion, and in favor of centralization of
government and laissez-faire economics, although this is true. It means
rather that a distressingly large number of them came to be so avid for
political office that they avoided issues that might force a clear-cut
division of opinion. This tendency, indeed, became so noticeable a
characteristic of the system that it was given a name—*trasformismo* or
transformism.

Trasformismo was the method by which a chief of ministry could
prolong the life of parliament and his own hold on power by disregarding
party labels, making bargains with deputies on the Left or the Right for
whatever votes they could command, and thus piecing together parliamentary majorities. In the hands of such gifted practitioners as Agostino
Depretis (1813–1887), who dominated Italian politics from 1876 to 1887,
and Francesco Crispi (1819–1901), who was supreme in the Chamber from

1887 to 1896, *trasformismo* gradually atomized existing political groups and turned parliament into an amorphous mass of deputies led by a ministry whose members changed so constantly (between 1871 and 1914, Italy had thirty-one different ministers of finance alone) that coherence and continuity of policy were impossible.

This system could only be made to work by an avoidance of the big questions about which differences of opinion were inevitable. There were lots of these. The united nation had inherited, in Naples and Sicily, backward areas that were gravely in need of irrigation and improved communications and were burdened with an inequitable system of land ownership that seemed to cry for rectification. It was seeking to push industrialization without possessing the resources of coal and iron that would make this easily practicable, and this raised some delicate questions of commercial policy. In an age in which economic development depended to an important degree upon the creation of a literate working class, Italy's percentage of literacy was almost the lowest in Western Europe. Her rate of population increase, on the other hand, was the highest in Europe, far in excess of job opportunities, and this led to the emigration of the most enterprising elements of the labor force (350,000 emigrated in 1900; 530,000 in 1910) and to a high degree of social distress and unrest among those who remained.

The viability of Italy as a nation depended on the solution of these problems; but they received very little attention while *trasformismo* was the order of the day. When any one of them became so pressing as to cause a dangerous rise in the popular temper, the tendency of the majority-mongers was to divert public opinion to issues capable of producing excitement and distraction. Anticlericalism was such an issue. The refusal of Pope Pius IX to accept the guarantees and the subsidies offered in 1871 by the Italian government in return for recognition, and his insistence on referring to himself as a prisoner and calling upon other governments to rescue him, annoyed Italian patriots. This annoyance could be played upon; and Crispi, for one, had a way of using antipapal demonstrations to bolster his own popularity. Equally useful were attacks on foreign powers, either in the form of irredentism—that is, the demand for the cession by the Austrian government of the predominantly Italian parts of the Hapsburg empire (especially the Trentino and Trieste)—or in the form of attacks upon France, a practice in which Crispi, as a loyal Garibaldian, frequently indulged. Finally, between 1871 and 1914, governments were repeatedly tempted to use colonial adventures to divert thought from domestic problems. Depretis and Crispi both sought glory in Abyssinia (and both failed disastrously to find it), while Giolitti was impelled to find a refuge from domestic complications in Tripoli.

These tactics caused pressing social and economic problems to go unsolved and made them more serious. The attacks on the church angered all Catholic countries, and left them disinclined to give any form of assistance to Italy, which sometimes was badly in need of economic or diplomatic aid; and the attacks on France invited French retaliation. When it became known in 1887 that Italy, a member of the Triple Alliance since 1882, had renewed that treaty in circumstances which indicated that its anti-French provisions had been strengthened, the French broke off long-pending commercial negotiations and instituted a tariff war whose effects were felt for almost ten years. As a result of the break, Italian exports dropped 40 percent; the curtailment of French credit caused financial stringency and the stopping of public-works projects and railway building; unemployment rose sharply; and the prevalence of social distress led to the rapid increase of emigration.

It was reflected also in widespread popular disaffection. In the south, where the wine trade had been particularly hard hit by the cessation of trade with France and where there had long been strong resentment against absentee ownership, feudal taxes, and other abuses, the year 1893 was marked by attacks on manor houses and police posts, often resulting in bloodshed. In the silk-producing areas of the north, also hurt by the tariff war, similar troubles broke out and continued throughout the decade. If Crispi fell from office in 1896 as a result of the disastrous Italian defeat at Adowa in Abyssinia (see p. 458), the prevalent economic distress of this decade was certainly a contributory factor. In 1898 popular resentment boiled over in a series of bloody riots in all major Italian cities, which culminated in the "Deeds of May" in Milan in which tram cars were upset to form barricades and resultant street battles cost the lives of two policemen and eighty civilians, while 450 were injured. This led to the imposition of martial law and, in the next two years, to a degree of royal and military intervention in politics that threatened the very existence of parliamentary institutions. In June 1899, for instance, General Pelloux, who had been appointed prime minister by the king without any attempt to consult parliament, announced that he would rule by royal decrees that would automatically give his projects the force of law without the necessity of parliamentary discussion or criticism.

This alarming turn of events brought the parliamentarians to their senses, at least momentarily. A new coalition was formed from the so-called Radical Left (a reform party inspired by the doctrines of Auguste Comte, Herbert Spencer, and the Italian sociologist Cesare Lombroso, which put its faith in positivism and experimental science), the Republicans (a small group of devoted Mazzinians), and the new Socialist party founded in 1892 by Filippo Turati (1857–1932). This union fought

342 / Political Progress in Western Europe, 1871-1914

Pelloux with the tactics made famous in the House of Commons by the Irish Nationalists, namely, obstructionism and sensation, and, in the end, with the additional support of the more moderate constitutional Left, forced the resignation of Pelloux in June 1900. This event coincided with the murder of King Humbert by an anarchist in revenge for those who were killed by the police in Milan. The dead ruler had been a ruler of dangerously absolutist tendencies. His successor, Victor Emmanuel III (1900–1946), was supposed to be more sensitive to the needs of the time.

The new era was hailed as the "liberal spring" of Italy; and, indeed there were some hopeful signs of political regeneration. On the one hand, there was, under the veteran Giuseppe Zanardelli (1826–1903) and the rising star of Italian politics, Giovanni Giolitti (1842–1928), an attempt to mold the different sections of the old *Estrema* into an effective democratic-liberal party. In 1900, Giolitti announced: "The country is sick politically and morally, but the principal cause of its sickness is that the classes in power have been spending enormous sums on themselves and their own interests, and have obtained the money almost entirely from the poorer sections of society." He called for "a policy that is frankly democratic" and talked of a revision of tax schedules, a reform of the law codes, and measures of agricultural reform.

Simultaneously, there was some indication that part of the revolutionary Left might adopt a more constructive policy than it had professed in the past and might even be willing to collaborate in social reform. Anarchism continued to have its effect in rural districts, to be sure, and Sorel's syndicalist doctrines became influential after the publication of the Italian edition of his book in 1903. But revisionism was making inroads among the Marxist socialists, and leaders like Turati, Bissolati, and Bonomi seemed prepared for parliamentary collaboration on key issues.

Finally, the Right seemed not entirely impervious to the new spirit. In 1902, Sidney Sonnino (1847–1922) and Antonio Salandra (1853–1931) began to try to stimulate a new patriotic conservatism, based on the belief in a strong monarchy and a strong centralized government and willing to correct social injustices while opposing the policies of the extreme Left.

Had these three political groups consolidated themselves, there is every likelihood that Italian parliamentary life would have revived, that there would have been a healthy alternation of parties in power, that the most crying of national abuses would have been corrected, and that the country as a whole would have benefited. Instead of this, Italy soon relapsed into the empty acrobatics of *trasformismo*. The three potentially strong coalitions dissolved into quarreling groups, and parliament again became an amorphous mass of deputies, manipulated now by Giolitti

That politician's democratic pretensions were, it is true, given some substance in 1911–1912 by the extension of the suffrage to all males over thirty years of age. But Giolitti proceeded to demonstrate that the new electorate could be manipulated by fraud and violence, a demonstration that was facilitated by the fact that there was no educational qualification for voting.

From 1903 to 1915 Giolitti was the unquestioned master of Italian politics. It may be admitted that he used his power to carry out some measure of necessary reform. The years of his parliamentary dictatorship saw the passage of factory laws, the nationalization of insurance companies and railways, the legalization of trade unions, state aid for agriculture cooperatives, and the encouragement of collective bargaining. The country benefited also from an economic upswing after 1900, although this was due less to the government's economic policy as such than to the end of the tariff war with France.

But, despite all this, Giolitti's unsavory methods in electoral campaigns and in the chamber finally undid the effects of Cavour's *connubio* of the 1850s. They brought the parties of the liberal center into disrepute and dissolved the parliamentary system, while giving a new lease on life to the extremist parties which now—thanks to Giolitti's franchise legislation—had the opportunity to win mass support.

Of the growth of a new extremism, there was lots of evidence in the last years before 1914. At the Socialist Party Congress at Reggio in July 1912, the left wing, led by Costantino Lazzari, Ettore Cicotti, and Benito Mussolini (the last two of whom were later to be fascists), revolted against the revisionism of Bissolati and Bonomi and declared that democracy was a bourgeois experiment and that socialism must return to the orthodox insistence that it be destroyed. The victory of these extremists was aided by the transformation of the party since 1900 into a mass party; and they were to dominate the party until its dissolution twelve years later.

Among the intellectuals on the extreme Right there was a growing interest in the theories of Vilfredo Pareto (1848–1923) and Gaetano Mosca (1858–1941), who mercilessly exposed the inadequacies and the shams of Giolittianism and, in something of the spirit of Sorel, called for a new elite, versed in the ways of power, who would lead society out of its present materialistic swamp. This coincided with the formation, in 1910, of a new Nationalist party which was frankly monarchist, antiparliamentarian, and imperialistic. Its most outspoken leader, Enrico Corradini (1865–1931) announced in his speeches the themes elaborated on by the fascist movement after the war: the heroic qualities of combat, the insignificance of individual life when the cause of the nation was at stake, modern Italy's legacy from ancient Rome, the necessity of subordinating the concepts of liberty and equality to those of discipline and obedience, and the moral satisfaction that came from living dangerously.

The fact that the youth of Italy in particular should have turned to this kind of thing shows how far Giolitti's cynicism had succeeded in draining the idealism out of Italian politics. This also explains the remarkable vogue of the poet Gabriele d'Annunzio (1863–1938), who in 1900 had foresworn the politics of the extreme Right to join the forces fighting General Pelloux, announcing grandiloquently that "as a man of intellect, I shall move toward life." By 1909, in poetry whose content was increasingly empty but whose rhetoric increasingly exhilarating, he was calling on young Italy to seek life, not in politics, but in violent action that would make an end of the dullness and mediocrity of the existing regime. On the eve of the war, therefore, the confident voices in Italian politics, and the ones listened to most eagerly by youth, were those of extremists of the Right and Left, all proclaiming the imminent destruction of a regime that had been unable to make any genuine progress toward a viable democracy and whose political processes seemed now to be affected by creeping paralysis.

14

France: The Divided Republic, 1871-1914

If the excesses of Italian political behavior seemed sometimes to be attributable to that nation's having too little history, certain aspects of French politics after 1871 are perhaps to be explained by the circumstance that France had too much. Past glories were always being used to belittle, or past failures to denigrate, the efforts of her ministries; and the fact that, since 1789, the country had experienced virtually every possible form of government gave an unhealthy relativism to the French political process. In time of difficulty or crisis, there were always partisans of old regimes ready to call for radical change, and this confirmed a national habit of political instability.

The Third French Republic was to last for seventy years. Had they been told that this would be true, the generation of 1870 would have found it difficult to believe. For the Republic was born in military defeat and civil war, and its adolescence and early maturity were years of almost constant conflict.

THE AFTERMATH OF DEFEAT, 1870-1878

The War's End and the Commune / When it became apparent that victory over the Germans was no longer possible, the French people, as we have seen (p. 255), elected a National Assembly and implicitly authorized it to treat for terms. This Assembly, acting through its elected chief of the executive power, Adolphe Thiers, carried out its assigned duty and then turned to the problem of restoring order in the country and getting its administrative machinery back into operation. Immediately, it came into bitter conflict with Paris.

There were several reasons for this. The people of Paris, who had fought against Germany until they were starved into submission, felt more sensitive about the defeat than they suspected the provinces did, and they were humiliated by the government's accession to the German demand for a triumphal entrance into the city. In the second place, as early as September 1870, Paris had proclaimed the republic; the National Assembly had not done so and, in view of its composition, which was overwhelmingly monarchist, did not seem disposed to do so. The tension caused by this was heightened by other provocative actions on the part of the Assembly. In March 1871 it made its headquarters in Versailles rather than in Paris, a decision that seemed a gratuitous insult to a gallant people, as well as a deliberate blow to their financial interests. Worse were the Assembly's abrupt termination of the moratorium on rents, debts, and promissory notes that had been in force during the siege, its demand that all arrears be made up within forty-eight hours, and its decision to cut off all payments to members of the National Guard. This last stroke was a grievous blow to the majority of workers in Paris who, as a result of the siege and the continuing dislocation of economic activity, had no occupation and depended on their Guard pay for sustenance.

These things encouraged the belief in Paris that the city must itself take the initiative in rallying the nation to the cause of liberty and the republic. This idea was encouraged by activists of various creeds, Jacobins, utopian socialists, and followers of Proudhon, who, working through political clubs organized during the winter of the siege, had become the leaders of the working classes. On March 18, 1871 the Assembly played into their hands by sending a troop of cavalry to remove the guns from the National Guard munitions park on the Butte Montmartre. Violence immediately exploded in Paris; the troops were repulsed and their commanders slain; the National Guard marched on the center of the city and seized the Hôtel de Ville; the government forces left the city; and the tragic episode of the Commune began.

Since Karl Marx, in one of his most brilliant pamphlets (*The Civil War in France*), was to make a legend of the Commune, it is important to note that it had very little in common with the kind of proletarian revolution that he predicted in *The Communist Manifesto*. There was nothing socialistic about its policies or its tactics. Its leaders—a General Council of 90 members, elected on March 26 to direct the Commune's activities—possessed no unifying philosophy and had neither a coherent plan of action nor a sense that one was needed. Bedazzled by their easy acquisition of power, they neglected to take the kind of steps that might have consolidated it, wasting their time instead in paying elaborate obeisance to history. Having taken the name of that Commune of Paris that had overthrown Louis XVI, they seemed to feel it necessary to carry imitation further—adopting the calendar of the Revolution, instituting a regime of virtue *à la* Robespierre (which necessitated raids upon cafés frequented by the higher class *cocottes* and arresting their patrons, who generally turned out to be British journalists) and indulging in floods of neo-Jacobin eloquence. Much of their legislative activity was, in the circumstances in which Paris found itself, plainly irrelevant—laws calling for the separation of church and state, for instance, and for the abolition of the regular army. Their only economic action of any significance was the restoration of the moratorium on rents and debt payments, and their only social legislation was the abolition of night work in bakeries. They never—as Engels regretfully noted later—seemed to have thought of seizing the Bank of France or to realize that their very existence depended upon striking Versailles while the National Assembly was still bereft of impressive military power.

Thus, Thiers was given time to rally his shaken forces and to supplement them with prisoners of war released by Bismarck and internees returned from Switzerland. By the beginning of April he had 150,000 men under arms and immediately went over to the offensive. Even this failed to arouse the Commune to effective action. For the next two months, indeed, while government forces closed in around the city, it fell into increasing disarray. The leadership of its defense forces was entrusted to a series of colorful but irresponsible leaders: Flourens, an adventurer with a great but unconfirmed military reputation who, during a sally against the Versaillese, lost contact with his own forces and was captured and shot; Cluseret, a soldier of fortune who had served with McClellan in the American Civil War, but was so lazy that he made no attempt to improve the city's defenses; Rigault, a doctrinaire anticlerical, probably insane, who was more interested in setting up a revolutionary tribunal to deal with traitors and spies than in the urgent military problem. Thanks to their failures, Thiers' siege operation found no real opposition, and on May 16 his troops stormed into Paris through an undefended section of the city's walls.

It was at this point, however, that the real resistance began. True to their revolutionary tradition, the workers fell back upon their own quarters, fighting doggedly with gun and torch. In a week of bloody fighting, thousands died on improvised barricades, and the flames took

Paris in the last days of the Commune: The burning of the General Accounting Office and the Headquarters of the Legion of Honor. From *L'Illustration*, June 3, 1871.

the Porte Saint-Martin, the Church of Saint-Eustache, the Tuileries, the Palais Royal, the Hôtel de Ville, most of the Rue Royale and the Rue de Rivoli, and much else. Not until May 28 did organized resistance end, when the last defiant Communards—having shot their own hostages, including the archbishop of Paris—died under government guns in the cemetery of Père Lachaise.

The revenge of the government was ruthless, despite an earlier promise by Thiers that only the law would punish. Any man wearing a National Guard uniform, or army boots, or a coat with a discolored shoulder was arrested and shot without trial, as were people even faintly resembling Communard leaders. These summary executions were followed by mass trials and deportations. At a conservative estimate, twenty thousand men died in the week following the end of the fighting. Nearly ten thousand more were punished by law, thousands being deported to New Caledonia. It was not until 1879 that an amnesty finally laid the ghost of the Commune and freed those imprisoned for their share in it.

The excesses of the Commune and its liquidation shocked all of Europe. On the whole, middle-class opinion tended to believe the theory spread by Thiers' propagandists—that the events in Paris were due to a conspiracy directed by the International Workingmen's Association (see p. 301)—and this helps to explain the virulence of the opposition in many countries to socialism and to other forms of working-class organization. In France itself, the development of both trade unionism and an effective socialist party was delayed at least a decade by the Commune, which also left a heritage of distrust between classes that was one of France's weaknesses in years to come.

Thiers as President / In 1871 Thiers was rounding out a varied and controversial career which had begun in the political excitement that preceded the revolution of 1830. He had never been widely liked, and his enemies accused him of excessive ambition and a high degree of disingenuousness; but no one had ever doubted his intelligence and his energy. Now, these qualities were tested to the utmost. As chief of the executive power,[1] he was called on to devise policy for a country shaken by the war and the disorders in Paris, with its economy at a standstill and its institutions in a state of total confusion. In the two years of his power he accomplished much.

Perhaps his greatest service to the country was his avoidance of the issue best calculated to cause new divisions among Frenchmen: the question of a definitive form of government for France. Thiers quite rightly felt that there were more pressing problems, and his prestige was great enough to convince the majority of the Assembly that he was right. Thus, instead of relapsing into new ideological conflict, the nation concentrated upon the task of freeing itself of German occupation troops, who were authorized by treaty to remain in France until the war indemnity of five billion francs had been paid. Thiers paid the entire sum off by September 1873, six months before the final installment was due, by floating two great government bond issues, both of which were oversubscribed by the French people.

The departure of German troops from its soil restored France to a position of equality among the powers, and this had a heartening and unifying effect. Another measure which worked in the same direction was the law of July 1872, which reorganized the military system of the country. This made all French males liable for five years of military service, with partial or total exemptions for university graduates, teachers, priests, ministers, and the like. It also revolutionized the army general staff, adopting certain features of the Prussian system, and in other respects modernized army methods and inspired that quick military recovery that caused so much concern in Berlin in 1874 and 1875 (see p. 270).

While these problems were being dealt with, it became apparent, from certain local elections, that republicanism had not died with the Commune but was on the upswing. To the monarchist majority in the

---

[1] In August 1871 this title was changed to president of the French Republic.

Adolphe Thiers, 1797–
1877.
After a caricature by
Gill in *L'Eclipse,* June
14, 1874.

National Assembly, this meant that further postponement of the question of the nature of the regime was inadvisable; and, since Thiers himself was now openly republican in view (believing, as he said, that the republic was the form that divided Frenchmen least), it meant that Thiers must go. In May 1873, the Assembly withdrew its support from the president and he resigned. As his successor, the Assembly elected Marshal MacMahon, who had contributed to Napoleon III's downfall by losing the battle of Sedan but was apparently expected to atone for this by bringing a new sovereign to France's empty throne.

The Failure of Royalism / French monarchists, however, were confronted with the Ancient Pistol's challenging question: "Under *which* King, Bezonian?" There were three claimants of the throne: the legitimist or Bourbon claimant, the Count of Chambord, grandson of Charles X; the Orleanist candidate, the Count of Paris, grandson of Louis Philippe; and the Bonapartist candidate, the son of the late emperor. Within the Assembly there was no apparent sympathy for the third of these; but the royal claims of the other two claimants had caused protracted and exasperating negotiations ever since peace had been restored. In the course of 1873, an arrangement was finally worked out. The Count of Chambord received the united support of the monarchists and, since he had no heirs, the Count of Paris was promised the succession after his death. There seemed to be no real obstacle now to the accession of the pretender, who let it be known that he would assume the title Henry V.

Unfortunately for the monarchist cause, however, he almost immediately revealed that he had none of his great forbear's ability to adjust to circumstances. Henry of Navarre had been willing to change his religion to assure himself of power; Henry V would not even change his flag. Under his rule, he announced, the banner of France would not be the *tricouleur*, with all its revolutionary associations, but the lily flag of the Bourbon dynasty. The most intransigent royalist could see the folly of this. As MacMahon said at the time, the repudiation of the flag that had waved over the fields of Marengo, Austerlitz, Sebastopol, and Solferino would cause "the chassepots [to] go off by themselves."

The flag issue killed the hopes of a royal restoration in 1873. The pretender was immune to logic and impervious to argument; his supporters were forced to abandon their plans to have him summoned to the throne. The most that they could hope for was that time would bring them to their desired goal; and they decided that it would be wise to keep MacMahon in power, so that he could act when the right moment came— when and if, for instance, the Count of Chambord died, leaving the way clear for his Orleanist rival. Therefore, before the year was over, the Assembly passed the Septennate Law which, for the first time, set a definite limit to the president's term and assured MacMahon of seven years of power.

In reality, the opportunity lost in 1873 was not to recur. The country was tired of provisional governments and of an Assembly that had been elected to draw up a constitution but had now postponed doing so for five years. Unmistakeable signs of popular dissatisfaction in the provinces and the growth of both republican and Bonapartist sentiment finally persuaded the Assembly to complete its work. In the course of the year 1875 it passed a series of basic constitutional laws.

These provided that France would henceforth be governed by a legislature of two houses: a Senate of 300 members, a fourth of whom were to be appointed by the present Assembly for a life term and the rest to be elected by departmental electoral colleges for a period of nine years[2]; and a Chamber of Deputies, elected by universal manhood suffrage for four years. By parliamentary procedure like that of England, the Chamber would control the ministry and, through it, the policy of the country. Joint sessions of Chamber and Senate could be called to amend the constitution when necessary and, at seven-year intervals, would convene in order to elect a president. This official was given the right to initiate

[2] In 1884 the life term was abolished and all senators came to be elected for nine years.

legislation and to promulgate laws when they were enacted, to grant pardons, to direct the military establishment, to make appointments to civil and military positions, and, with the consent of the Senate, to dissolve the Chamber and order new elections. These powers were, as it turned out, less real than they appeared.

The only reference in these laws to the republican form of government came in the title of the chief executive, who was called "the president of the Republic," and even this had been opposed by most of the monarchists and accepted by the barest of majorities. Yet whatever the constitutional texts might say, France was now predominantly republican. When the National Assembly finally dissolved itself in December 1875, and elections were held for the new Chamber and Senate, avowed republicans won a large majority in the former and narrowly missed dominating the Senate as well. In the next two years, this partial victory became definitive, although only after a major constitutional crisis, which tested the relative power of the president and the Chamber of Deputies.

This crisis was caused, essentially, by Marshal MacMahon's deepening conviction, in which he was encouraged by the monarchists and the higher clergy, that republicanism would be the ruination of France. His fears in this regard made him amenable in the spring of 1877 to suggestions that he use his power to block the potential republican conquest of the Senate by manipulating the elections to the departmental electoral colleges which selected senators. Since this would be impossible if his present cabinet, a determinedly republican one, was in office, MacMahon, on May 16, 1877, forced it to resign, despite the fact that it had the support of the Chamber. He then appointed a monarchist cabinet under the Duke of Broglie and called upon the Senate to agree to the dissolution of the Chamber, which it did.

MacMahon's intention was, of course, to secure a popular mandate for his assertion of presidential authority over the Chamber; and he was confident that he would secure it. So was Broglie, who undertook to influence election results by the persecution of the republican press, the dismissal of republican mayors, municipal councilors, civil servants, and election officials, the breaking up of republican clubs, and a powerful propaganda campaign in favor of monarchist and clerical candidates. After all this ("The silence of the country is terrifying," Broglie said) MacMahon and he expected victory. They failed, however, to make allowance for the powers of Leon Gambetta.

André Siegfried tells of an old man who said to him, "You see this hand? Gambetta shook it. I have not washed it since." There were many who felt that way about Léon Gambetta, remembering his great services in 1870, when he had been the soul of the resistance to the Germans and, by raising provincial levies, had made possible the renewal of the war

Léon Gambetta, 1838–1882.
From *Illustrated London News*, Oct. 15, 1870.

and the salvation of France's honor after the defeat of Sedan. Among the working and lower-middle classes he was loved for his warm impulsive nature, his splendid gifts of oratory, in which he has been called the equal of Mirabeau and Danton, and his known determination to work implacably for the restoration of the lost provinces. Gambetta believed in a democratic republic that would be founded on the support of the common people of France, peasants, workers, and lower-middle class; and, because of the affection he was able to inspire among them, he generated enough enthusiasm for this ideal to defeat the hopes of the Right entirely. He threw himself into the campaign of 1877 with enthusiasm, traveling and speaking incessantly, calling for the creation of one united republican bloc that would embrace the followers of Thiers as well as those of Hugo and Blanc, hurling memorable phrases at his opponents. Some of these were so barbed that he was sentenced to three months' imprisonment for attacks on the president; but this merely spread his message further. When the elections were finally held in October 1877, the results of all this were made clear, for, despite rightist obstructionism, a solid republican majority was returned to the Chamber; and MacMahon had to accept a ministry just as republican as the one he had dismissed.

A year later, the new Senate elections gave the republicans a majority in that Chamber also. This completed MacMahon's discomfiture and rendered his position untenable. For the Chamber now pushed measures that they knew he must oppose, until the president faced the inevitable and, in January 1879, resigned his office. He was succeeded by Jules

Grévy, a sincere republican who, it was felt, would indulge in none of the tactics of his predecessor.

THE REPUBLIC: BASIC PROBLEMS

Years of Accomplishment, 1879–1885 / Republicanism was now in the ascendant, and its supporters celebrated their triumph by moving the capital back to Paris in 1880 and accepting July 14, the day of the storming of the Bastille, as the national holiday and the *Marseillaise* as the national anthem. These measures were perhaps of a purely symbolical importance; but they were followed by more significant legislation, which safeguarded the civil liberties of the individual, protected the right of assembly, lifted restrictions upon the press, removed local government from the strict control of the central government, and permitted the formation of trade unions.

Like their Liberal colleagues in Belgium and England and Germany, the republicans tended to be strongly anticlerical; and this feeling had been strengthened by the political campaign conducted in behalf of MacMahon by French bishops and clergy. In May 1877, Gambetta had cried "*Le cléricalisme, voilà l'ennemi!*" It was in this spirit that the Chamber struck out in two areas in which church control had always seemed to them to be unjustifiable. In 1885 they restored provisions for divorce to the Civil Code, despite outspoken church opposition; and between 1881 and 1885, they carried through a comprehensive reform of education, designed to diminish the influence that the church had enjoyed under Napoleon III.

The man who inspired this legislation and piloted it through the Chamber was Jules Ferry (1832–1893), an able and tenacious statesman who was deeply convinced that the minds of the young, especially of the young bourgeoisie who would be the backbone of the republic in the next years, must be protected from clerical influence. Ferry began his campaign with a gambit that had, through its repeated use in the modern period, become the classic means of initiating anticlerical movements and uniting the Church's enemies: he demanded the expulsion of the Society of Jesus. Having secured this, in 1880, he pressed on with measures that struck at Catholic schools and teaching orders. Henceforth, no teaching order that was unauthorized by the state could maintain a school, and no one could teach in a state school without a state teacher's certificate. This last measure was designed to reduce the large number of nuns and teaching brothers in local schools (some 10,000 brothers and

40,000 nuns in 1877); and it was supplemented by the creation of two new higher normal schools to supply teachers for the departmental normal schools which, in their turn, trained teachers for elementary education.

The most important of the educational laws were those that made primary education in state schools free (1881) and an elementary education in *some* kind of school compulsory (1882). These laws greatly expanded the school population (and reduced illiteracy to less than 10 percent of the population); they also made it tempting for parents who could afford to pay fees for church schools to send their children to state schools instead. Both tendencies reduced church control of the minds of the literate population.

Laws were passed also which improved standards in state secondary schools and technical schools; and the first steps were taken toward the fundamental reform of university education that was to be carried through in the mid-1890s and was, among other things, to restore to the Sorbonne, after centuries of neglect, the position it had held in the world of learning in the Middle Ages.

The educational reforms were perhaps the most enduring of the achievements of the first phase of the Republic's history; but they should not be allowed completely to overshadow other constructive activity. In the field of transportation, for instance, the work of Charles de Freycinet deserves brief attention. Freycinet (1828–1893), known as "the white mouse" because of his shy, deferential manner and a general inoffensiveness that won him many cabinet posts in the course of his career, was a brilliant engineer and administrator, who had helped Gambetta raise and organize the army of resistance in 1870. In 1878, as minister of public works, he came forward with a gigantic scheme for what he called the completion of "the national equipment." This involved improvement of existing railways, canals, roads, and harbors, and new building in all categories. Freycinet's comprehensive and systematic program was supported by parliament and, although at the cost of some elaborate financial arrangements between the government and the larger railroad companies, started the process that doubled France's rail net before 1914. It led also the standardization of France's canal system so as to facilitate through communication without transshipment and the improvement of rivers as commercial arteries. These works led to an increase of metric tonnage carried by internal waterways from 21,000,000 in 1886 to 42,000,000 in 1913.

These were years also of Republican triumphs overseas, where the foundations of France's new colonial empire were laid. The guiding spirit in this French imperialism was, again, Jules Ferry. It was he who persuaded the Chamber to grant credits to support a campaign which secured Tunis before the end of 1881. The following year the government

The Eiffel Tower being built for the International Exposition of 1889. In this drawing, the tower, viewed from the Trocadero Palace, is in the final stages of construction in October 1888. From *L'Illustration*, Nov. 10, 1888

had a setback when disorders in Egypt, where French interests had been strong for a century, led the British to intervene unilaterally and to impose what came to be a protectorate over the country (see p. 278). This loss was offset by the gains made under Ferry's leadership in the years 1883–1885, during which France not only penetrated into Indochina, conquering Tonkin and extending a protectorate over Laos and Cambodia, but concluded a treaty with the government of Madagascar that was the first step toward outright annexation and improved the port of Dakar and established French Equatorial Africa. These adventures were not universally popular; military setbacks in Tonkin caused the repudiation and fall of Ferry as prime minister in 1885; but, as in other countries, even the masses became increasingly interested in empire as the years passed; and France's colonial activity was not perceptibly slowed down before the turn of the century.

While these undoubted successes were being registered, the Republic gained in stature and confidence. The new spirit was typified by the condition of Paris, which, in the mid-1880s, left the shadow of the Commune behind it and became, in the eyes of many, the intellectual and artistic capital and the greatest playground of the world. It was in this period that Paris was described as the place to which good Americans went when they died; but thousands were refusing to wait until then, and, with hordes of other tourists, were trooping yearly to the spirited and elegant city on the Seine, to marvel at the newly built Eiffel Tower, to visit the new opera house and hear Gounod's *Faust* or, perhaps, Bizet's *Carmen,* to eat *fraises de bois* in charming restaurants along the Boulevard Montparnasse, to shop on the Rue de Rivoli, to gape at the sinful night life of Montmartre, to watch the racing at Longchamps. More serious visitors came to work at the École des Beaux Arts, or to study medicine under Charcot and Becquerel, or to hear Bergson lecture at the Collège de France, or to learn to write in a city whose literary vitality had never been greater—where French poetry (and not French poetry alone) was being revolutionized by the influence of Baudelaire's followers Rimbaud, Tristan Corbière, Verlaine, and Mallarmé, where fierce battles raged between naturalists like Zola and de Maupassant and their detractors, and where every year saw a new sensation or a new movement, like the neo-romantic decadence that became fashionable with the publication of J. K. Huysmans' *À Rebours* in 1884.

Some Basic Problems / Yet, despite the creative legislative activity of the early 1880s and the vigor of the arts and sciences, all was not well in France. The rate of economic progress was slower than in either Britain or Germany, and the very fact that so high a percentage of French savings (a third to a half) was invested abroad was both a sign of and a reason for a lack of vitality and progress in the economy. France's industrial development was not, after 1870, impressive in relative terms; the average industrial enterprise was small; and there were few great industrial concentrations until the decade before the war, when the output of wrought iron and cast steel shot upward, and the Comité des Forges and the Comptoir Métallurgique de Longwy were established. Some basic industries had been dislocated by the war of 1870 and were hurt in the subsequent period by foreign competition. This was true, for instance, of French cotton spinning, which did not recover until it received a strong measure of protection from the Méline tariffs of the 1890s. The silk industry remained prosperous by changing its basis from home production of silk to importation of raw silk, cocoons, and thrown silk and by introducing power looms; but the linen industry declined steadily after 1870 because of backward techniques and Irish competition. In both chemical and electrical industries France lagged behind her neighbors.

France's economy remained predominantly agricultural throughout most of the period, more than half of the population living in rural areas as late as 1914. The prevalence of small subsistence farms reduced the effects of the agricultural malaise common to all Western European countries in these years; but the large grain producers were not immune to foreign competition and falling prices, nor were their laborers. The largest agricultural industry aside from wheat also suffered a grievous blow in this period, when the vines were attacked in the 1870s by phylloxera, a plant louse. Until the turn of the century, when American grafts improved the stock, the French wine industry was fighting for its very existence, not only against the blight that had hit it but against Italian, and (after the beginning of the Franco-Italian tariff war) Spanish, competition.

Economic troubles breed critics of any regime; and France was no exception here. But it was not only in the economic area that the Republic was criticized. The longer the Republic lasted, the less inspired did its political behavior seem to become; and, after the middle 1880s, it betrayed troubling signs of stagnation and lack of direction. French parliamentary life was characterized by a pervasive anarchy in which both forcible leaders and attempts to enforce party discipline were viewed with grave suspicion. It is significant that the two strongest men in the first twenty years of the Republic's life experienced revolts by the Chamber against their authority and were denied the ultimate position for which their talents commended them. The "great ministry" of Gambetta lasted only three months in 1881; and Ferry fell in 1885, ostensibly because of a setback in the Far East but really because there were too many who feared his ability. In the question of the presidency of the Republic, the deputies showed an almost pathological distrust of strong individuals, and, after MacMahon, France's presidents were generally respectable but innocuous men who were considered to be safe.

Meanwhile, the parties proved incapable of exercising control over their members, or, indeed, of holding their members, for a steady process of fragmentation of parties continued throughout these years. The republican center which Gambetta had sought to wield into a permanent bloc split up into a number of splinter groups; and these fissiparous tendencies were also to be the fate of socialism when it became a political force in the 1880s. More and more, the individual deputy tended to become a law unto himself, which made reasoned political action or systematic attacks upon political and social problems almost as difficult as in Italy.

Aside from this, as has already been indicated, France suffered from history. The artist Forain had once drawn a cartoon entitled "How fine the Republic was—under the Empire." The longer the Republic lasted, the more attractive did other regimes appear, especially to certain more or less organized groups in society.

There was no dearth of critics or, indeed, open enemies of the regime. There were, in the first place, the inveterate antirepublicans: aristocrats, clergy, upper civil service, army. These were generally monarchist in sympathy and opposed to all the prevailing tendencies in the Republic: especially its attacks upon the church, its apparent susceptibility to Jewish and Masonic influence (the Masonry of the Grand Orient did, in fact, have considerable power in French politics, and in the Chamber, in the 1880s), and its failure to give due attention to France's military power. The clerical wing of this group had many spokesmen, including such unregenerate and uncompromising ones as Louis Veuillot, the editor of the Catholic organ *L'Univers*, who rejected the Republic as both un-Christian and un-French, and Edouard Drumont, who published his *La France Juive* in 1886 and made anti-Semitism a force to be reckoned with.

The social center of this extreme right wing opposition lay in certain salons in the Faubourg St. Germain. It is doubtful whether the Faubourg by itself could have exercised much influence in French politics; but, by the curious operation of those forces which Proust's Baron Charlus described as "aristocratic prestige and middle-class cowardice," it served as a magnet that attracted socially ambitious members of the upper-middle class, as well as those who feared the rise of the working classes. In the long run, that merging of the ideas and the resources of the aristocratic Guermantes and the middle-class Verdurins, which is the basic theme of Proust's great work, *Remembrance of Things Past*, proved dangerous to the Republic.

Allied to the rightist opposition, but not entirely enclosed within it, was the nationalist opposition, composed of all of those who believed that France's main objective should be revenge for the defeat of 1870 and the loss of Alsace and Lorraine. The most frenetic of the patrioteers—the members of Paul Déroulède's League of Patriots, for instance—took the line that failure to push consistently for *revanche,* or diversion of the national effort into other lines, was treason to the true France. Déroulède opposed Ferry's policy of imperialism with the words, "I have lost two children and you offer me twenty servants."

Most of the members of Déroulède's society would, of course, have been enemies of the Republic even without the issue of *revanche,* but not all. There were many in France who were not by political orientation or social inclination enemies of the Republic but who nevertheless felt that what they regarded as lack of patriotic spirit in the government reflected an encroaching materialism and relativism that would be the ruin of France. These people were troubled and moved by Maurice Barrès' fulminations against the decadence of his generation (in his famous novel *Les Déracinés* in 1897, for instance) and by the appeal to French youth with which Paul Bourget prefaced his novel *Le Disciple* in 1889. "Our generation," Bourget wrote, "could never consider that the peace of 1871 was established for all time. How I would like to know if you think as we did! How I would like to be sure that you are not ready to renounce what was the secret dream and the consoling hope of each one of us, even of those who never mentioned it!" The fear that under republicanism France might cease to be herself made potential antirepublicans of many who had no use for the cheap jingoism of Déroulède, the anti-Semitism of Drumont, or the clerical absolutism of Veuillot.

Whether the working classes could be considered enemies or supporters of the middle-class Republic was still problematical in the 1880s. But the wounds of the Commune were not yet healed, despite the return of the proscribed Communards in 1880; and dissatisfaction with working conditions, long hours, and low wages was causing an increasing degree of labor violence. In 1884 there was a violent strike in the Valenciennes coal fields, which inspired Zola to write his best novel, *Germinal;* in 1886 there were others at Decazeville and Vierzon; and after 1890 the number of work stoppages mounted sharply. Finally, at the end of the 1870s, the influence of Marxist socialism began to spread among the more educated working classes; Marx's son-in-law, Paul Laforgue, and others encouraged it by translating basic works of Marx and Engels; and in 1879, Jules Guesde, "a Torquemada with a pince-nez," founded a new "Workers party" which proclaimed itself to be Marxist, revolutionary, and self-sufficient (that is, opposed to any cooperation with existing bourgeois parties). If this became an effective political party, it appeared likely that the weight of the organized working class would be thrown against a Republic already harassed by other foes.

THREE CRISES

The Boulanger Case / The last fifteen years of the century saw the Republic tested by three great crises in which the enemies enumerated above sought to overthrow the regime. The first of these was the result of accumulating exasperation with the economic troubles, the lack of leadership in government, the bickering of the parties, and some colonial setbacks that seemed more serious than they actually were. It took the form of a demand for a strong man who would clean up the mess at home and lead France in a victorious war against Germany.

The man who appeared capable of filling this role was General Georges Boulanger (1837–1891), who as minister of war in 1886 won popularity with the army by some improvement of conditions in the barracks and with the Paris mobs by his dashing appearance and the beauty of his black horse Tunis. General Boulanger did not repulse those who began to urge him to overthrow the Republic; and it is possible that, if his intelligence and courage had matched his ambition, and if he had had a sense of political timing, he might have succeeded in doing so. Certainly he was given an opportunity in 1887, when it was discovered that President Grévy's son-in-law, a certain Daniel Wilson, was using his position to influence elections to the Legion of Honor for his private profit, a revelation that forced the president's resignation in December. A coup at any time in the months that followed might have succeeded, but Boulanger seemed to prefer the road Hitler chose years later, the conquest of power by legal means. Throughout 1888, with invariable success, he contested parliamentary vacancies, but this merely gave the republican center time to put an end to its customary dissensions and take action against him. In the spring of 1889, the cabinet summoned Boulanger to appear before the Senate on charges of conspiracy against the state; and the general lost his nerve and fled to Belgium, where he committed suicide two years later. His movement fell to pieces as rapidly as it had formed.

The failure of *Boulangisme* strengthened the Republic by discrediting its enemies and rallying its friends. It also showed that the political parties that claimed to speak for the working classes were not as revolutionary and as opposed to compromise with the bourgeois regime as Guesde claimed. As in other countries, an important section of the

Boulanger's last victory was in the elections of January 1889, which were held to fill a parliamentary vacancy for Paris. After that his star quickly faded. Above are some election posters used during the heated campaign in Paris in the winter of 1888. From *L'Illustration*, Jan. 26, 1889.

socialist movement thought in moderate evolutionary terms rather than in the strictest Marxian ones; and, to many French socialists, heirs of an older tradition, Marxism was too Germanic to be completely palatable and Guesde too authoritarian to be entirely acceptable as a leader. Under the leadership of Paul Brousse, Joffrin, and Benoit Malon, a "Federation of Labor Socialists of France" had been founded to promote practical possible reforms. During the Boulanger agitation, these Possibilists or Opportunists, as they came to be called, formed an alliance with the republican center and declared: "We workers are ready to forget the sixteen years during which the bourgeoisie has betrayed the hopes of the people. We are ready to defend and conserve by all means the weak germ of our republican institutions against military threats. Long live the social Republic!"

Panama / If the Republic seemed to come out of the Boulanger case with renewed strength, its gains were largely dissipated four years later by a scandal worse than the Wilson affair. Since the late 1870s Ferdinand de Lesseps (1805–1894), the builder of the Suez Canal, had been engaged in a project to build a canal across the Isthmus of Panama. The work had been slowed by the unwise choice of a site, by unrealistic engineering, and by the terrible incidence of yellow fever, for which science had as yet found no answer. To prevent loss of faith in the scheme, with resultant drying up of credit and loss of original investment, the canal promoters resorted to bribery of the press and the politicians. But the truth could not be hidden forever, and its disclosure was bound to expose the corrupt attempts to hide it. That is precisely what happened in 1892, when a series of articles called "The Inside Story of Panama" appeared in Edouard Drumont's paper *La Libre Parole.*

The resultant washing of dirty linen could not help but convince many Frenchmen that parliamentary government was rotten to the core and that all politicians were crooks. This and the fact that many of the company manipulators were Jews were exploited to the full by Drumont, and his articles enabled the extreme Right to equate the Republic with corruption, inefficiency, and control by international Jewry. All of this was to affect the war of opinion during the Dreyfus case.

The French people seemed less concerned than many thought they should be by the scandal, and nothing catastrophic happened in the elections of 1893. But Panama perhaps contributed, in an indirect way, to the further development of French socialism in an evolutionary direction. The elections brought an increase in Socialist representation in the Chamber of 50 seats and brought to Parliament two men whose reputations very quickly eclipsed those of Guesde and Brousse. These were Jean Jaurès and Alexandre Millerand, both exponents of social reform by parliamentary means. Under their leadership socialism was to become a potent force in French politics.

The Dreyfus Affair / In October 1894 a cleaning woman working in the office of the German military attaché in Paris extracted a torn and crumpled piece of paper from a wastebasket and sent it to the Counter Espionage Section (or *Deuxième Bureau*) of the French General Staff. Examined there, it appeared to be a list of items of information about the French army which its unknown author was prepared to sell to the Germans, and it horrified the officers of the *Deuxième Bureau*. They decided that the author of the list (or, as it came to be known around the world, the *bordereau*) must be a French General-Staff officer, an artillerist, and one who had had a recent opportunity to inspect a number of France's military installations. This description, they further decided, fitted Captain Alfred Dreyfus. They asked Dr. Alphonse Bertillon, the well-known inventor of the fingerprint system and more recently an expert on graphology, to compare this officer's handwriting with that of the *bordereau*, and on the basis of his affirmative findings had the suspect arrested.

There was no apparent reason why Dreyfus should be a spy. A brilliant officer with a good record, the first officer of Jewish faith ever to be admitted to the French General Staff, he was happily married, had independent financial means, and was known to be a fervent patriot. He was nevertheless charged and, after a trial marked by considerable irregularity in the form of admission of unsupported testimony and reliance on documents which the defense was not allowed to see, was found guilty, sentenced to military degradation, loss of rank, and life imprisonment in a fortified place, and transported to Devil's Island in French Guiana.

Almost two years later, the *Deuxième Bureau* received a new chief, Colonel Georges Picquart, and Picquart, already puzzled as to why Dreyfus should have betrayed his country, discovered that the sale of secrets to the German embassy was still going on. This led him to embark on an investigation that convinced him that the true author of the *bordereau* was a Commandant Esterhazy, an officer with a known fondness for expensive pleasures and suspicious acquaintances, whose handwriting, moreover, matched that of the *bordereau* much more closely than did that of Dreyfus. Picquart immediately asked his superiors to arrest Esterhazy and make retribution to Dreyfus. To his stupefaction, he was informed that this would be impossible and, when he insisted, was transferred to a post in Algeria.

Before he left, Picquart saw to it that some of his evidence reached the hands of republican deputies of known integrity. Their interest and help gave new hope to the campaign for revision which the Dreyfus family had been doggedly pursuing since 1894. To work for Dreyfus was never easy. At the beginning one had to fight the forces of army evasion, bureaucratic obstructionism, and public indifference; later one had to be prepared to withstand the incredible violence the case released. Luckily for Dreyfus, a small band of deputies, newspaper-men, and intellectuals—men like Georges Clemenceau (1841–1929) and the novelist Anatole France (1844–1924)—were prepared to brave these things; and, thanks to their efforts, public interest and concern grew.

The case for revision was given new strength by a series of dramatic events at the beginning of 1898. On January 11, the army, in a gesture that was patently designed to allay any doubts about the merits of the original verdict, arraigned Esterhazy before a packed court martial, swiftly acquitted him of all suspicion, and publicly congratulated him. The next day Picquart was arrested on charges of calumniating Esterhazy's name and was imprisoned. It was these events that led Émile Zola (1840–1902), to release on open letter to the press entitled *J'accuse*, in which the novelist declared Dreyfus innocent and described the army's conduct as corrupt and dangerous to the Republic. The government immediately brought charges against Zola, and he found it expedient to leave the country; but his action had turned the Dreyfus case into an issue of national and international concern.

The resistance of the army hierarchy to a reopening of the case, and their subsequent resort to falsification of documents and forgery of new evidence in order to prevent it, can be explained in part by an unwillingness to admit error and an attempt to rationalize this by arguing that such an admission would be detrimental to the army's prestige in a time of international tension. The republican poet and moralist Charles Péguy (1873–1914), a revisionist himself, put it this way:

> The true position of the people who opposed us was, for a long time, not to say and believe Dreyfus guilty, but to say that innocent or guilty, the life and salvation of a people, the enormous salvation of a people, could not be troubled, could not be upset, could not be *compromised*, could not be risked for one man, for a single man. . . . From this point of view it was evident that Dreyfus should be sacrificed for France; not only for the peace of France, but for the salvation itself of France, which he imperilled.

This attitude was inexplicable to anyone who believed in law and morality. Convinced supporters of Dreyfus felt that the acceptance of an injustice of this kind, on any pretext, would not only place the army above the law but would dishonor France by acting—again in Péguy's words—like "a touch of gangrene that corrupts the whole body."

But, apart from this, the supporters of Dreyfus found it significant that the most vociferous defenders of the army's refusal to reopen the case were also those who had shown themselves, during the Boulanger and Panama affairs, to be the most notorious enemies of the Republic: the royalists, the inhabitants of the Faubourg, the upper clergy, the anti-Semites. Oblivious to any reasoned argument, these groups insisted that Dreyfus was a traitor and that his guilt was another sign of the rottenness of the Republic. Within the Chamber of Deputies, their representatives used obstructionist tactics whenever the case was discussed and disrupted proceedings sufficiently to bring new discredit on parliamentary government. Outside parliament, their tactics were even more dangerous. Paul Déroulède, for instance, was openly calling in September 1898 for an army revolt against the Republic.

This apparent threat had one profound political effect, for it persuaded the Socialist wing led by Jaurès and Millerand that an attitude of political neutrality in this crisis would be unwise. In June 1899 this led to an unprecedented example of collaboration, when the parliamentary Socialists declared their support of a new Radical Republican ministry headed by René Waldeck-Rousseau, and when Millerand actually accepted the post of minister of commerce—the first Socialist to serve in a bourgeois government.

This was not immediately successful in securing justice for Dreyfus. When, as a result of the confession and suicide of one of the chief witnesses against Dreyfus and the subsequent flight of Esterhazy to England, the Court of Cassation annulled Dreyfus' original court-martial and ordered a new trial, the judges again made a travesty of justice by excluding evidence that was clearly in Dreyfus' favor and once more finding him guilty, although this time, wholly illogically, "with extenuating circumstances." The trial and Dreyfus' subsequent sentence to ten years imprisonment caused a new outburst of passion throughout the country, and this was not allayed when the president of the Republic pardoned the long-maligned officer. His supporters declared that they would be content with nothing less than full exoneration, but this they did not attain until 1906, when the government declared Dreyfus completely innocent, restored him to the army, and made him a member of the Legion of Honor.

"The Affair" has fascinated dozens of great French writers and has received fictional treatment in Anatole France's *Penguin Island*, Proust's *Jean Santeuil* and *Remembrance of Things Past*, and Roger Martin Du Gard's *Jean Barois*, to mention only a few major works. This is not surprising, for it dramatized cleavages in French society and opposition to republican institutions that were to continue long after Dreyfus had been given the right once more to wear the uniform of his country. This division of France continued partly, perhaps, because the violence with which the anti-Dreyfusards had fought against exoneration elicited violent reaction on the part of Dreyfus' supporters after their cause had won.

THE PREWAR YEARS

Army Reform / It was only natural that the aroused republican forces, strengthened by the elections of 1902 and the continued collaboration of the Socialists, should want to strike out at the chief persecutors of Dreyfus, the reactionary officers in the army. Those whose names had figured prominently during the Affair were almost immediately purged, and a known reputation for monarchical or clerical sympathies became a grave handicap for an officer and often cost him his career. Some of the methods used by republican ministers of war were questionable; and it is hard to believe that encouragement of civil authorities in garrison towns to report on the behavior of suspected officers helped the morale of the officer corps or reconciled talented soldiers of rightist views who remained in the service (like the later Marshal Pétain and General Weygand) to the Republic they were supposed to serve.

A more profound military result of the Dreyfus case was a change in the system of recruitment. The law of 1872 had made all Frenchmen liable for five years of active service but had allowed liberal exemptions. A law of 1889 had lowered the length of service to three years and radically reduced the inequalities of the previous law, so that no able male could hope completely to escape service, although, depending on education and career, he might have to serve only one year. Now the republican bloc insisted on further reduction and perfect equality of service; and in 1905 a new recruitment law stipulated two-year service with virtually no exemptions.

This reduction of the period of active training and the simultaneous liberalization of the disciplinary code of the army was intended to diminish the control of the professionals over French youth and prevent the subversion of their values by reactionary officers. One supporter of the law of 1905 actually said that it would open for the army "an era which I will dare to call . . . the era of civilianism." The eruption of the sharp crisis over Morocco in this same year (see p. 470), however, and other signs of mounting international tension threw some doubt on the validity of the basic premise of the new law. At a time when French population was decreasing in relation to that of Germany and when the number of men in annual contingents could be expected to decrease also, was it wise to reduce the length of service? At a time when the German army was known to be basing its plans on a lightning war (*attaque brusque*) by highly trained forces, was it wise to make national security dependent upon a strictly defensive strategy conducted by hastily mobilized reserves? More and more people came to believe that it was not; and as international relations continued to deteriorate after the second Moroccan crisis (see p. 480), the Chamber in 1913 restored the three-year term of service on the grounds that it was necessary to provide the training that would make possible offensive operations. This was far from a unanimous decision, however, and there were many Frenchmen who, thanks to their memories of the Dreyfus case, continued, until the war came, to regard their army with grave suspicion.

Separation of Church and State / At the beginning of the 1890s, Pope Leo XIII had sought to dissociate the Catholic Church from its royalist ties and, through France's most eminent churchman, Cardinal Lavigerie, had called for the acceptance of the Republic by the faithful. This so-called *Ralliement* was wrecked on the shoals of the Dreyfus case; and, in the years that followed it, the church had to pay for the prominent role played by some of its leading dignitaries in the antirevisionist cause. Waldeck-Rousseau, prime minister of the Radical Republican and Socialist coalition in 1899, believed, as firmly as Gambetta had, that clericalism was the Republic's real enemy; and his successor Émile Combes said in 1902, "Clericalism is to be found at the bottom of every agitation and every intrigue from which Republican France has suffered during the last thirty-five years."

These sentiments led to a new spate of anticlerical legislation. In 1901 an Associations Law provided that no religious association could exist in France without specific government authorization. The Assumptionist Order, whose superior had been the most intransigent foe of Dreyfus, was immediately expelled, and others suffered the same fate, so that thousands of nuns and priests had to leave France. More serious was Combes' attempt to give the state a monopoly of education by rigorous execution of a new law of 1904 which stipulated that all teaching by religious orders must be terminated within ten years.

Ever since the Concordat of 1802 between Napoleon and the Vatican, church and state had been intimately associated in France, the state appointing archbishops and bishops with the pope's consent, the bishops appointing the priests with the state's assent, the state paying the salaries of the clergy and permitting it the use of the extensive church property to which it held title. In 1905 the Concordat was abrogated. The state's right to make appointments and its obligation to pay salaries were declared at an end; church property remained at the disposal of the clergy but was to be administered henceforth by elected parish religious corporations (*associations culturelles*). The refusal of Pope Pius X to allow churchmen to obey this legislation or accept the authority of the *associations* did not shake the government's determination to have its way. A new law of 1907 revoked the privileges offered two years before, reduced the amount of property to be used by the clergy, and stipulated that church buildings might be used without charge for purposes of worship on the basis of local arrangements between priests and the civil authorities. In all other respects, the church and the state were now separated.

Politics in the Last Years of Peace / Politically, the Republic was more stable in the decade after 1905 than it had been at any time since 1871. The Dreyfus affair had strengthened the middle-of-the-road republican parties and brought them into fruitful contact with the Socialists. It is true that, officially, this tie was terminated in 1905, when—largely as a result of pressure exerted by the 1904 Congress of the Second International—the different French Socialist parties came together in one, the French Section of the Workers International (or SFIO), and declared themselves to be "a class and revolutionary party" rather than a revisionist one, and specifically repudiated the policy of collaboration with bourgeois governments. Temperamentally, however, the French Socialists remained for the most part revisionists and supporters of the Republic in time of crisis (as the war was to show); and, if Socialists could not sit in bourgeois cabinets, *former* Socialists could. The republican parties were to acquire talented leaders by conversion. It was thus, for example, that Aristide Briand (1862–1932), who started in politics as a revolutionary, made his way to that middle position which he was to occupy when he was France's long-term foreign minister after the war.

The new vitality of the republican center was shown by the emergence of other leaders besides those brought over from Socialist ranks. Clemenceau's reputation had grown during the Affair; Joseph Caillaux succeeded Waldeck-Rousseau and Combes as the chief of the Radical Republicans; and the Right Center found a dynamic new leader in Raymond Poincaré (1860–1934), who was to be president of the Republic in 1912 and then, after the war, to go back to the Chamber as leader of the Right.

The strengthening of the Center did not mean that the Republic's enemies had been eliminated. To the left of the Socialists, the Syndicalists carried on their agitations through the smaller and more militant trades union, and their greatest ideologue, Georges Sorel, preached the uses of direct action. On the extreme Right, the forces of reaction sought a new rallying point and found it in the movement known as the *Action Française*, which had grown out of the Affair and had found its leader in Charles Maurras (1868–1952). A powerful and eloquent publicist, Maurras fulminated against the Republic as a hotbed of freemasonry, Jewry, Protestants, and foreigners (*Métèques*) and called for the restoration of a king who would make France great once more and put an end to the sad comedy of democracy. Maurras drew to his cause all of those foes of the Republic who had been discomfited by the exoneration of Dreyfus; and the *Action Française* held them together until the ills of the 1930s brought them new recruits and new opportunities.

Like Sorel, Maurras placed great emphasis upon action and vitality; and it was probably this, as much as his literary grace, that attracted the youth of France. It has been said that the young intellectuals who did not turn to syndicalism or revolutionary socialism before the war joined the *Action Française*. This is an exaggeration, but there is enough truth in it to show that France was not entirely free of that weakness from which Italy suffered—a tendency of the young to be bored with the system and to want to change it. A good deal of the idealism that had been generated during the fight for Dreyfus, and which had led Péguy in his memoir, *Notre Jeunesse*, to describe that struggle as a period of heroism and spiritual regeneration, had evaporated during the exploitation of the victory by Waldeck-Rousseau and Combes; and the disillusioned intellectuals who felt that attacks on the church and the army cheapened their fight for abstract justice either withdrew from politics or sought new creeds.

Aside from this, in the popularity of Maurras and Sorel, as in the vogue of Bergsonian philosophy, we can see further evidence of that cult of violence which we have noted in other countries in this period.

15

The German Empire: Pseudo-Constitutional Absolutism, 1871-1914

In a letter to the Munich economist Lujo Brentano, the great historian of Rome, Theodor Mommsen, spoke bitterly of the "pseudo-constitutional absolutism under which we live and which our spineless people has inwardly accepted." As a capsule description of the German empire this could hardly be improved upon. The Reich that Bismarck had created possessed all the trappings of constitutional government and yearly went through the motions of meaningful parliamentary activity. But, in a Europe that was moving toward democracy, Germany remained a state in which decisions affecting the lives and liberties of its citizens remained in the hands of persons and agencies not subject to parliamentary or popular control. Nor did the great majority of the people object to this state of affairs. Until disastrous defeat opened their eyes in 1918, they seemed to prefer the satisfactions that came from being commanded by a regime of material splendor and military might to the labors that political responsibility entailed.

BISMARCKIAN GERMANY, 1871–1890

The Constitutional Structure / By almost any standards, the imperial constitution, promulgated in April 1871, was a clumsy and illogical document. It created an imperial government without sufficient administrative agencies to give it much meaning, a federal state that was prevented from being truly federal by the special position of one of its members, and a parliamentary system based on universal suffrage that was rendered ineffective by limitations placed on its responsibility.

After 1871 the empire embraced Prussia, the kingdoms of Bavaria, Saxony, and Württenberg, eighteen lesser states, three free cities, and the so-called Reichsland, Alsace-Lorraine. Sovereignty was vested by the constitution in the Reich, but most of the matters that affected the daily lives of Germany's citizens were reserved to the individual states. Thus, education, police, the courts, most fiscal affairs, and much else were matters administered by agencies of the separate states, whereas the imperial government had administrative organs only for naval affairs, foreign affairs, posts and telegraphs, customs, and, after the turn of the century, colonies. Even in foreign affairs the South German kingdoms reserved at least a ceremonial independence, and they also had armies of their own, with officers appointed by their kings, although these passed under Prussian command in time of war. There was, it should be noted in this connection, no imperial army; the national army was, and remained, the Prussian one.

Despite the rights reserved to the federal states, there was no equality among them, for they were all, in one way or another, subject to Prussia. The hereditary leadership of the Empire was vested in the king of Prussia, with the title German emperor. He appointed the imperial chancellor and other imperial officials; he directed Germany's foreign affairs and, through his chancellor, took the initiative in all domestic legislation; he commanded its armed establishment in time of war; he made war and peace; he convoked and adjourned the two legislative bodies.

It was in the upper of these two chambers, the so-called Bundesrat, that the superiority of Prussia over the other states was most clearly demonstrated. The Bundesrat represented the federal states and was composed of delegates appointed by their governments. The size of the various delegations was determined by their relative extent and power; thus, Prussia had seventeen votes out of a total of fifty-eight,[1] Bavaria six, Saxony and Württemberg four each, and the other states even fewer. From these figures alone, it will be clear that, in all of the Bundesrat's business, Prussian influence would be great; and Bundesrat business included all legislation affecting the Reich, which was not legal until its affirmative vote had been secured. But, Prussian influence was even more extensive than that, for it was stipulated that no change

[1] In 1911 Alsace-Lorraine was admitted, raising the total to sixty-one.

in military matters or customs and excise duties could be taken without Prussian assent, and no amendment to the constitution could be accepted if fourteen votes were cast against it in the Bundesrat. This meant, in effect, that Prussia alone could block constitutional change.

The lower house of the imperial parliament, the Reichstag, represented the people and was elected by universal manhood suffrage, the legal voting age being twenty-five years. It had far less power than its sister chambers in Britain and France. Its right to initiate legislation was limited, and it acted, for the most part, on matters submitted to it by the government. It had little control over the chancellor and his secretaries of state, for in the German system the chancellor was responsible only to the emperor and the subordinate ministers responsible only to the chancellor, and if he or they were criticized or defeated in the Reichstag they did not lose their positions, as they were apt to do in other countries.

The Reichstag was often criticized for these weaknesses, and Helmut von Gerlach once wrote: "The people call the Reichstag a talk-shop (*Schwatzbude*), because they know that German policy is not made there but in a quite different place." This should not lead us to conclude, however, that it was either an innocuous or an unimportant body. It was a national political body composed of popularly elected representatives and, therefore, was watched with critical interest by the German people. It was an excellent sounding board for ideas and propaganda; and Bismarck found it useful, when he wished to impress foreign opinion, as a place in which to advertise German strength and intentions. It was an indispensable link in the legislative process, and reviewed, debated, and sometimes amended or defeated legislation. And, because it possessed powers of obstruction and control of the national purse (it had to vote the budget), it was, theoretically at least, capable of extending its powers, and, indeed, made sporadic attempts to do so. The very fact that reactionaries were constantly agitating for a reduction of the Reichstag's powers shows that its authority was not negligible.

Certainly Bismarck did not believe so. He valued if for its uses in foreign affairs, and he believed also that, as a kind of symbol of national unity, the Reichstag could be used in domestic affairs as a counter-weapon against the forces of particularism in the country. If he had ever heard the statement of Gerlach quoted above, he might have answered that, even if policy was not made in the Reichstag, the details of administrative, economic, and judicial projects were often elaborated and improved in the course of Reichstag debates and committee hearings.

In addition, Bismarck had personal reasons for valuing the Reichstag. Since it had power to obstruct and defeat the government's legislative program, the imperial chancellor had to be someone who could control and manipulate it so as to obtain safe parliamentary majorities. As long as Bismarck could do this better than anyone else, he felt safe from the secret attacks of courtiers and soldiers close to the emperor who wished to displace him. The Reichstag was, thus, a kind of insurance policy for Bismarck. He could use it to demonstrate his indispensability, as he did, for instance, during the debate over the military budget in 1874, in which the government's case was presented, during Bismarck's absence from Berlin, by other royal counselors, with results that would have been disastrous if he had not returned at the last moment and pieced together a parliamentary majority.

Bismarck was, of course, opposed to anything approaching a genuine parliamentary system like those of Britain and France, or to the introduction of ministerial responsibility in the chamber, or to an extension of parliamentary powers in the field of foreign or military policy; and, in resisting these things, he and his successors were aided by another peculiarity of the constitutional system, which should be mentioned here. As long as Prussia bulked so large in the empire, through the prerogatives of its king, its weight in the Bundesrat, and the virtual monopoly of force exercised by its army, imperial policy was inevitably determined largely by what Prussia's governing class desired. That class had retained its feudal-conservative character, thanks to the nature of the Prussian constitution of 1850, which was still in force, and of the three-class system of suffrage which was used in elections to the Prussian diet (see p. 143) and which assured a conservative majority. This being so, the imperial chancellor (who was also minister president of Prussia) could resist pressure for liberal constitutional reform from parties in the Reichstag in the sure knowledge that he would be supported by the Prussian diet and the Prussian delegation to the Bundesrat.

Because of this circumstance, the key to all constitutional reform in Germany lay in Prussia; and, before the coming of the war, the democratization of the Prussian franchise had become the primary goal of all German reformers.

The Parties / From the 1870s right down to the outbreak of war organized political activity in Germany centered in six main political parties, plus a number of splinter groups. It may be convenient here to note their differences in program and social composition.

On the extreme Right was the German Conservative party, the party of Prussianism, aristocracy, and landed property, with its main support in the districts east of the Elbe River. This party had its roots in the romantic feudalism of the early nineteenth century. Ideologically it was averse to liberalism and democratic reform, placing a high valuation on loyalty to the monarch and service to the state. Economically, it had no sympathy for, and little understanding of, industry; and although it originally believed in free trade, it came, after the beginning of foreign competition in grain, to be fervently protectionist, taking its economic ideas largely from the Association of Landlords (*Bund der Landwirte*) with which it became closely associated in the 1890s. It was less susceptible to issues affecting the Reich as a whole than other parties, for its horizons tended to be limited to Prussia, and it was in the Prussian diet, rather than the Reichstag, that the real strength of the party lay. It was a Protestant party which put great emphasis on the necessity of maintaining the Christian foundations of the state. This, at its best, led Conservatives to take a genuine interest in social reform; at its worst, it led to outbursts of anti-Semitism, as in the 1880s when the party supported the Christian Social movement of Adolf Stoecker, whose labors for social reform were marred by virulent attacks upon the Jews who, in his view, were responsible for all the evils of laissez-faire capitalism.

An offshoot of the Conservatives was the so-called *Reichspartei* (in Prussia called the Free Conservatives), which, by combining landlords and industrialists in its membership, typified the union of rye and steel that was to be so important in German history. Sometimes called the party of Bismarck *sans phrase,* because of its undeviating support of the chancellor's national policies, the *Reichspartei* sent many of its members into his ministries and his foreign service. The party never attained a mass following and eventually merged once more with the Conservatives, helping as it did so to broaden that party's social and political views.

Infinitely more important was the party which repeatedly, from 1870 until the advent of Adolf Hitler in 1933, played the decisive role at crucial moments in German history. This was the Catholic Center party, which from the date of its founding in 1870 enjoyed mass support, although it was most heavily concentrated in Bavaria and the Rhineland. An avowedly confessional party, the Center always embraced individuals and groups of varied political and social views. This meant that, unless the autonomy of the Catholic Church in Germany, or the question of freedom of religious education, or the defense of states rights was at stake, the party was apt to show a greater freedom of action than others; and it was consequently often accused of opportunism. But there was an inner consistency in its attitude. In general, it was conservative in its defense of tradition, of the prerogatives of the crown, and of the hierarchical structure of society, as well as in all matters affecting the morals of society. On the other hand, it was consistently favorable to constitutional government, in which it saw a means of protecting minority groups against the excessive centralization of government; and it was progressive in matters of social reform.

With respect to this last point, the party had been profoundly influenced by the doctrines of Adolf Kolping, who in the 1840s had founded Catholic journeymen's associations to give free vocational training to workingmen, and by those of Bishop Wilhelm Emmanuel von Ketteler, who from 1850 until his death in 1877 preached the necessity of combating the evils of capitalism by setting up workers' cooperatives, establishing Christian trade unions, and otherwise helping the poor to raise their standards of living. Ketteler, whose work had a profound influence upon Pope Leo XIII and served as a basis for his encyclical *De Rerum Novarum* in 1891, established a tradition of German Social Catholicism that was always strong in the Center party. The Center not only supported and expanded the program of vocational instruction that Kolping had started and encouraged the Catholic union movement, but also used its influence in behalf of legislation for the improvement of working conditions, the reduction of the working day, factory inspection, child-labor laws, and arbitration between labor and management.

There were two liberal parties. The National Liberals, who had the greatest parliamentary strength in the first decade of the empire, had seceded from the old Progressive party, which had fought against Bismarck in the constitutional conflict of the 1860s (see p. 220), and had given their support to the chancellor. Representing the educated and wealthy middle class and the upper bureaucrats, they shared many of the characteristics of Liberals in other lands, being supporters of centralization, laissez-faire economics, secularization of national life, constitutional government, and material progress.

The Left liberals, who still called themselves the Progressive party, although the name would change several times before 1914, shared some of these views (*laissez faire* and opposition to socialism, in particular) but were pronouncedly antimilitarist and antistate and were also much more vigorous in their demands for an extension of parliamentary government. Their leader in the early years of the Reich was Eugen Richter, an able critic but an essentially uncreative mind, whose great gift was the ability to infuriate Bismarck. After his death, he was succeeded by Friedrich Naumann, who sought to revitalize liberalism by promoting a merger with socialism. This did not succeed, and the Progressives remained a dwindling party whose strength came predominantly from urban centers and particularly from the lower-middle class and the lesser officials.

Finally, starting its remarkable growth in the 1870s and becoming before 1914 the strongest party in Germany and the largest and most disciplined labor party in Europe, there was the Social Democratic party. Its nature and activities will be discussed below.

The National Liberal Period and the *Kulturkampf* / In the first years of the new empire Bismarck's objective was to complete the process of unification by giving the Reich the institutions that would make it a homogeneous and effective nation. As far as possible, he wished to reduce institutional diversity and parochialism, at least in so far as they might weaken the political and economic efficiency of the empire. Since this involved legislation, the chancellor found it expedient to work with the party that commanded a majority in the Reichstag and had the greatest sympathy for the principle of centralization. This was the National Liberal party, and it responded to Bismarck's overtures with enthusiasm. In the decade of the 1870s, National Liberal votes were primarily responsible for the great program of constructive legislation that gave Germany its new imperial administrative agencies, a uniform coinage and a commercial code for trade and industry, a national civil and criminal court procedure, an imperial bank, and an imperial bureau of railroads.

Out of the collaboration between the National Liberals and the chancellor there grew, however, an ill-fated campaign against the Catholic Church that disrupted German political life until the mid-1880s. After what has been said above about anticlericalism in other countries, it should not be surprising that the National Liberals were interested in reducing the influence of the Catholic Church in education and in other aspects of German life. European liberals of all shades had been aroused by Pope Pius IX's *Syllabus of Errors* (1864), in which he had condemned "the errors of liberalism"; and German liberals in particular, including many loyal Catholics, had been incensed by the doctrine of papal infallibility in matters of faith and morals, which had been proclaimed in July 1870 during the war against France. Now that that conflict was over, they were eager to retaliate.

Bismarck's motives were more complex. He was annoyed by the growth of the Center party, which promised to be less amenable to national appeals than to those that emanated from the Vatican. He seems honestly to have believed that the church was fomenting resistance to the imperial government among Germany's Polish minority, which was largely Catholic. And, as usual, his views were influenced by considerations of foreign policy. If Germany went on the offensive against the Vatican, it might win the sympathy of other liberal anticlerical powers and seal the isolation of the papacy's strongest supporter, France.[2] This seemed doubly necessary since Bismarck, without much evidence, seems to have believed that the papacy was attempting to inspire a Catholic coalition directed against Germany.

Worn out by the labors of the last ten years and suffering from bad health, Bismarck may not have been thinking very clearly in these years.

[2] At this time, the French government was still monarchist and clerical in sympathy.

Certainly he was both intemperate and incautious in his tactics. In 1872 he launched an attack on the church in the imperial Reichstag and the Prussian legislature. As in other countries, the starting gun for the campaign was the expulsion of the Jesuits. There followed, in 1873 and the next two years, a series of laws passed by the Prussian legislature—depriving bishops of their disciplinary powers, placing clerical education under the control of the state, making civil marriage mandatory, abolishing church rights of self-government, dissolving religious orders, and much else.

As was to be expected, the papacy struck back by severing diplomatic relations with Prussia, and German bishops in convocation declared that Catholics could not obey these laws without violating their faith. Subsequently, criticism of the antichurch measures from Belgian and French pulpits led, as we have seen (p. 271), to German threats against France and to a minor war scare in 1875. But Bismarck's attack on the church—which the Liberals grandiloquently called "the battle for civilization" (*Kulturkampf*)—had two additional results that Bismarck could hardly have foreseen. It aroused Protestants almost as much as it did Catholics, and induced the Conservative party to throw its not inconsiderable influence at court against a policy that seemed capable of developing into an attack on all organized religion. At the same time, instead of weakening the Center party, the *Kulturkampf* seemed to strengthen the loyalty of its supporters, so that the Center improved its position in the Reichstag in the elections of 1877.

This last result, after four years of effort, would probably have been enough in itself to convince Bismarck that the anti-Catholic crusade was a mistake. But he had another reason for jettisoning the policy. He had decided to end his collaboration with the National Liberals, which meant that he needed Conservative, and even Center, support.

During the course of 1877, the National Liberals had intimated to Bismarck that their future cooperation would be dependent upon concessions on his part, in the form of ministerial appointments, recognition of the party's voice in policy determination, and other things. This convinced Bismarck that it was necessary for him to find wider parliamentary support than he presently possessed, and helped persuade him also to give way to the forces in the country that were demanding the substitution of a protectionist commercial policy in place of free trade. He hoped that, if he came out for new tariffs, he would ingratiate himself with the landlords of the Conservative party and the industrialists in the Free Conservative party, while simultaneously splitting the National Liberals, some of whom were losing their zeal for Manchesterian economics. He began secret negotiations with representatives of the two conservative parties with the objective of gaining pledges for the future; and his decision to abandon the fight against the Catholic Church was designed to facilitate collaboration with them.

The death of Pius IX and the accession of Pope Leo XIII in 1878 made it easier for Bismarck to change his direction. The new pope was far less intransigent than his predecessor, and he inaugurated his pontificate by sending a letter to Emperor William I, expressing the hope that an accommodation could be reached. Negotiations were begun; and, in 1879, in return for a promise that the government would receive prior notification of all papal appointments and that the German clergy would desist from attacks on the government, Bismarck began the process of revoking the anticlerical legislation. This took ten years and never completely restored the pre-*Kulturkampf* situation, for civil marriage and state inspection of church schools remained in force; but the great bulk of the legislation of 1873–1875 was suspended and later repealed, and the religious orders, with the exception of the Jesuits, were allowed to return to Germany. Moreover, the new spirit was felt almost at once, and church-state relations could be described as normal again as early as 1881.

Bismarck and Socialism / Once Bismarck had decided to break with the National Liberals, he did everything in his power to reduce that party's representation in the Reichstag. One of the weapons he used was the argument that the National Liberals were protecting the rapidly growing Socialist party, which was, by its own admission, a revolutionary and international party and thus was working against Germany's interests.

The German Social Democratic party had its origins in the activities of Ferdinand Lassalle in the early 1860s; and, even after it came to declare itself a Marxian party, it never escaped from his influence. This flamboyant and ambitious tribune of the people, the son of a Jewish merchant in Breslau, had become famous (or notorious, according to one's point of view) by his spectacular efforts in behalf of a Countess von Hatzfeldt, whose attempt to secure a divorce from her husband was blocked by an unjust and antiquated legal system. Lassalle's protracted and eventually successful labors in her behalf, his dramatic court appearances, and his imprisonment for revolutionary agitation before the case was terminated gave him a national reputation, and this led a group of workers in Leipzig, who were founding a political union in 1863, to ask him to help them by giving a systematic exposition of his social views.

His response supplied the new German socialist movement with a working program and made him its leader, although not for long. In the summer of 1864 Lassalle and Fraülein von Dönniges, the daughter of a Bavarian diplomat, decided to marry; but parental pressure broke the match, and Fraülein von Donniges became affianced, against her will, to a Rumanian nobleman. In a characteristically romantic gesture,

Lassalle challenged his rival to a duel and, in August 1864, was fatally wounded.

His legacy to the working-class movement was his "Open Letter" to the Leipzig group. In essence, this argued that economic pressure and trade-union activity alone were pointless, that concessions from employers were always vitiated by the operation of the iron law of wages, which kept labor at a bare subsistence level, and that only organized mass political action aimed at the conquest of state power would save the working class from capitalistic exploitation. It would do so because it would assure state aid for producers' cooperatives and other enterprises in the worker's interest. Lassalle's long-run economic objectives were never precisely defined and are not particularly important. His contribution to German socialism was his insistence upon political action.

Lassalle's spirited activities in the last year of his life succeeded, as his critic Karl Marx admitted, in arousing a labor movement that had been asleep since the revolution of 1848. Even so, the German Workingmen's Association that he helped found grew very slowly; and, after 1869, its progress was impeded by the opposition of a new Social Democratic Labor party founded by two followers of Marx, August Bebel (1840–1913) and Wilhelm Liebknecht (1826–1900). It was only after the two parties came together that the growth of German socialism became impressive. This union was effected in 1875 at Gotha, where the participants agreed on a statement of theory and a program of action that combined the two strains of influence, being Marxist in its criticism of capitalist society and its proclamation of the international character of the movement, but Lassallean in its emphasis upon political action to secure such practical objectives as equal and universal manhood suffrage in local and state elections as well as national ones, payment of deputies, abolition of inequalities of class and property, abolition of the standing army, separation of church and state, free compulsory education, progressive income tax, state credit for producers' cooperatives, and the like.

Even before the union, the Socialist vote had begun to grow: 124,000 in the Reichstag elections of 1871, 352,000 in 1874. In 1877, the united party polled 452,000 votes and sent twelve deputies into the Reichstag. This was a matter of concern to Bismarck, who was never able to regard the Socialists as just another political party but thought of them as enemies of his way of life and of the security of his state and, hence, as outlaws against whom the most ruthless of means could be used. In 1877 he began to seek means of taking legal action against them; and, in May of the following year, when a demented tinker named Hödel tried to kill the emperor, he introduced a bill into the Reichstag that embodied a number of anti-Socialist measures. This was heavily defeated, the bulk of the National Liberals remaining true to their avowed belief in political freedom.

A month later, there was a second attempt on the emperor's life, which seriously wounded him. Bismarck immediately dissolved the Reichstag and called for new elections. During the campaign, the government press attributed the assassination attempts to Socialist policy and delivered scathing attacks upon the National Liberals and the Progressives for their failure to vote for a bill that would have prevented the wounding of the emperor. Bismarck was deliberately seeking to turn the middle-class electorate away from the liberal parties and, in particular, to hurt his old ally, the National Liberals. To a large extent, he succeeded. In the elections of 1878, the Progressives lost thirteen seats and the National Liberals twenty-nine. The Progressives did not allow the results to alter their views, but the chastened National Liberals now yielded principle and, when a new anti-Socialist bill was brought in in October 1878, added their votes to the majority that made it law.

The Anti-Socialist Law forbade all associations and publications that sought to subvert the existing social order or showed "socialist tendencies." It gave the police such large powers of interrogation, arrest, and expulsion that suspected Socialists lost the customary protection of the law, while their party was forced to become a clandestine organization. Simultaneously, the law struck a crippling blow at the Independent Trade Unions, which were closely associated with the Social Democratic party, for unions cannot go underground and remain effective.

In 1866 Bismarck had embraced the cause of universal manhood suffrage in the belief that the masses could always be counted on to be loyal to the throne. The Anti-Socialist Law was a public admission that he no longer felt this way but believed that royal authority must be maintained by restricting freedom of political choice. Every attempt was made to destroy the Socialist party utterly. Many of the party's leaders were forced to leave the country, and others were arrested; the party press was reduced to a few newspapers which were printed abroad and smuggled across the borders; Socialist leaders enjoyed immunity in the Reichstag, but could not speak or campaign in public; party congresses had to be held in Switzerland or Holland.

Bismarck rarely committed himself to a single line of policy in either foreign or domestic affairs; and his offensive against the Socialists was no exception. It has been described as a policy of *Zuckerbrot und Peitsche* (the sugar plum and the whip), for the repressive measures were accompanied by tangible benefits designed to make the working classes forget their resentment over the repression of their organizations. Starting in 1881 the chancellor inaugurated a program of social-insurance legislation that was intended to prove to the unpropertied classes that "the State is not merely a necessary but a benevolent institution." In 1883 the Reichstag passed a Sickness Insurance Law which was to be financed by contributions from the employee and the employer in the ratio of 2:1; the following year, another law obliged employers to insure their workers against accident; and in 1889 provision was made for old-age and disability insurance to be supported by contributions from employee, employer, and the government. These laws were revolutionary and aroused interest throughout the western world. They were the model for Lloyd George's National Insurance Act of 1911 and for similar legislation in other countries.

Bismarck's crusade against socialism was no more successful than his fight against Catholicism. After initial losses, the Social Democratic party adjusted itself to the new conditions in which it had to work and steadily increased its strength. In the period of the Anti-Socialist Law (1878–1890), the party's national vote increased from 437,158 to 1,427,298 and its representation in the Reichstag from nine to thirty-five. And in the next dozen years, it raised its totals to 4,250,401 votes and 110 seats.

It is sometimes argued that, while the whip failed, the sugar plum worked, and there is perhaps some truth in this. In the years of repression, the Social Democratic party seemed to grow increasingly militant. In 1891, at Erfurt, it adopted an unrelievedly Marxist program, which outlined the evils of capitalism and called for its destruction by revolutionary action. Almost immediately, however, as we have seen (p. 306), opposition to these principles grew in the form of revisionism; and, in the first decade of the new century, the powerful Independent Trade Unions, now federated in a General Commission of Trade Unions under the leadership of Carl Legien, threw their influence behind the revisionist opposition, criticizing the Marxist party ideologues as doctrinaire and unrealistic and calling for a policy aimed at tangible objectives. It would be difficult to determine what influence Bismarck's social insurance had in turning the eyes of the working classes to such objectives and convincing them that they had too great a stake in the existing regime to wish to destroy it. Doubtless Bismarck's social policies had some effect, although it is well to remember that revisionism was a European phenomenon and would probably have been felt in Germany even if Bismarck had never existed.

Bismarck's Fall and His Legacy / In 1881, the Berlin novelist and critic, Theodor Fontane, wrote:

> Gradually a storm is brewing in the people against Bismarck. . . . He deludes himself as to the measure of his popularity. It was once colossal, but this is no longer true. . . . For his genius everyone still has a tremendous respect, even his enemies. . . . But the respect for his character is in a marked decline. Men are saying: "He is a great genius but a small man."

As the 1880s proceeded, this appraisal seemed to be true. In the Reichstag Bismarck had increasing difficulty in constructing parlia-

The gigantic statue of Bismarck at the head of the Reeperbahn in Hamburg. Fashioned from 3350 tons of granite by the sculptor Lederer and the architect Schaudt, it was unveiled in 1906. (STAATSARCHIV HAMBURG)

mentary majorities to support his policies. His break with the National Liberals had split that party, but more of its members were driven into opposition than into dependence on him. The Center was still unreconciled, and its support, sometimes granted, could not be counted on; the Socialists grew steadily in strength and voted against all government measures. In 1887, in order to get necessary legislation passed, Bismarck had to use the scare tactics he had used in 1878—this time seeking a parliamentary majority by exploiting the Boulanger agitation in France and alluding to the possibility of a French attack. This sort of thing could not be repeated often; and, as the Reichstag became more difficult to control, it was perhaps only natural that Bismarck should have dreamed of radical solutions to his problem. In his last years of office, he became increasingly enamored of the possibility of revising the constitution, perhaps by a special convocation of the princes of the realm, and of abolishing universal suffrage, which was proving so unmanageable. This strain of Bismarck's thought certainly played a part in his fall from office in 1890. In 1888, Emperor William I died and was succeeded by his son, who took the title Frederick III. This ruler, who had endeared himself to his subjects by his military exploits in the wars of 1866 and 1870, had been expected to open a new era of liberalism, but at the time of his accession he was suffering from cancer. Within three months he was dead and his son William was on the throne. An inexperienced and impetuous youth, who longed to make his mark in the world, William II had little patience with the policies of the past and no desire to be kept on leading strings by Bismarck, of whom he was reported to have said, "I shall let the old man snuffle on for six months, then I shall rule myself." He became critical of Bismarck's foreign policy, on the grounds that Germany's alliances had become too complicated; and he allowed himself to be persuaded that Bismarck had underestimated the Russian threat to German interests and was keeping information from the emperor's eyes. Moreover, since he wanted to be popular, he wished to abandon the anti-Socialist legislation and inaugurate a program of social reform—factory inspection, guaranteed wages, a shorter working day, and the like. He was appalled to discover that Bismarck not only intended to continue the campaign against Socialism but was thinking in terms of a constitutional coup that might lead to popular resistance and the use of military force. When he heard that the chancellor was negotiating with the parties for support with which to override his own objections, William's patience was exhausted. There was a stormy interview between him and the chancellor on March 15, 1890, and three days later the world learned that Bismarck had been dropped from office.

Under his leadership Germany had become the most powerful of the European states, but he had bequeathed to her some things that militated against that surface strength. His devotion to his country had always been accompanied by the conviction that it could remain great only if the monarchical tradition were protected against the subversive tendencies of the times. In the name of national security he had used parliamentary tactics that contributed to the atomization of the liberal forces in the Reichstag and legal methods that alienated many Germans permanently from the regime. His concern for his country had led him also, in the 1880s, to carry out a purge of progressive elements in the Prussian civil service, which seriously weakened the traditional independence of the Prussian bureaucracy and placed a premium on political conformity.

Bismarck had condoned a similar policy in the military establishment. The officer corps of the Prussian army had long been an aristocratic preserve but, in an age in which the size of armies was increasing rapidly, there were now an insufficient number of aristocrats to man the new units. With Bismarck's encouragement the army followed a deliberate policy of filling its needs exclusively from candidates from the upper middle class who were Christian in religion, conservative in politics, and socially as feudal-minded as the *Junkers* themselves. Since membership in the officer corps brought certain desirable social advantages, Bismarck's acceptance of this selection procedure, like his policies with respect to the civil service, encouraged what has been called a "feudalization of the upper middle class," which deprived that class of its independence and its rightful political role, the leadership of the bulk of the middle class. This, in turn, abandoned the lower middle class to a marginal political existence, caught between the organized working class and the new feudal plutocracy, resenting both and susceptible to the blandishments of demagogues who knew how to exploit resentment. These social tendencies were to be noted in other countries besides Germany, and they should not be attributed to Bismarck alone; but they were aided by his social policies.

Bismarck's greatest achievements were in the field of foreign affairs, where his great diplomatic gifts served his country well and, in the twenty years after 1870, helped preserve the European peace. Even here, however, his legacy to his country was an equivocal one. His successors were inclined to overlook the passionate devotion to the nation's interest, the strong sense of responsibility, and the admirable sense of perspective that made Bismarck a great diplomat. Their idea of Bismarckian statecraft was "realism," which they seemed to equate with brutality and bad manners. The very magnitude of Bismarck's achievements made them desire to emulate them and led them to embark on a fateful search for dazzling coups and stupendous triumphs.

WILHELMINE GERMANY, 1890–1914

Material and Intellectual Progress / At the time of Bismarck's fall, Germany was midway in one of the most rapid economic transformations in modern times. Still primarily agrarian in occupation and population distribution in the year 1871, she was to become one of the world's three greatest industrial nations by 1914, with 60 percent of her population living in urban centers.

This remarkable industrial development had been both galvanized and disrupted by the victory over France. On the one hand, the acquisition of Alsace-Lorraine strengthened Germany's textile industry by doubling the number of mechanical looms operating in the country,

The Krupp works at Essen in the Ruhr shortly before World War I. (BROWN BROTHERS)

brought into its possession the Lorraine iron deposits (which became enormously valuable once the Thomas-Gilchrist method of purifying phosphoric ores came into general use), and gave it a vital monopoly of the European potash industry by bringing it the unexploited Alsatian deposits. On the other hand, the speed with which the French war indemnity was paid touched off an inflationary spiral and a flood of dangerous speculation that contributed to the magnitude of the crash which came to Germany at the time of the world economic crisis in 1873. The years from 1873 to 1877 were years of depression; but the recovery thereafter was steady and, except for slight setbacks in 1900–1901 and 1907, uninterrupted.

This development can be illustrated by a very few examples. Thanks to mineral wealth (supplemented by conquest), rich coal deposits, and a good transportation system, Germany soon possessed the most powerful iron and steel industry in Europe. Pig-iron production increased from 1,500,000 tons in 1871 to almost 15,000,000 tons in 1910, while steel production in 1900 stood at 7,000,000 tons and was exceeding that of Great Britain by 1,500,000 tons. The development of heavy industry, in turn, enabled Germany to increase its domestic rail net 3½ times between 1871 and 1914; to build one of the greatest merchant fleets in the world, gross tonnage increasing from 82,000 to 4,500,000 between 1871 and 1913; to expand the machine industry into one of its largest export resources; and to build up that armaments industry which made the name of Krupp of Essen known the world over.

Germany's electrical and chemical industries also ranked among the world leaders in these fields. The Berlin firm of Siemens and Halske, founded by Werner von Siemens in 1847, gave Germany its first telegraph net, its first electric railway, and its extensive trolley system. At the same time, Emil von Rathenau, who secured the German rights to Thomas Edison's electric lamps in 1881, established the Allgemeine Elektrizitäts Gesellschaft (AEG) and rapidly built up a mass demand for electrical products. The expansion of the German electrical industry (it employed 26,000 people in 1895 and 107,000 in 1906) is a good illustration of those creative surges in new sectors of the economy which have been mentioned above as characteristic of mature capitalism (p. 285); and it made a large contribution to the prosperity of the prewar years. So did the progress of the chemical industries, which was marked by the greatly increased production of potash, sulphuric acid, potassium salts, and ammonia and by phenomenal developments in the field of synthetic dyes, photographic supplies, and pharmaceuticals, where the names Bayer, Agfa, and I. G. Farben became as well known as Krupp.

The spectacular increase of foreign trade was perhaps the best indication of Germany's economic power. The value of German exports increased fourfold between 1871 and 1914, from a figure of 2½ billion RM to 10 billion RM; and the value of imports shot up from 3½ billion RM to 11 billion RM. At the same time, German capital investment abroad was increasing as a result of the activities, mentioned above (p. 290), of the so-called D-Banks, which also, of course, promoted trade.

These tremendous results were not achieved at the cost of agriculture, which also showed progress. Despite the increase of the proportion of town dwellers to rural inhabitants, the agricultural population remained constant; and, thanks to tariff protection on the one hand and new agricultural techniques on the other, production increased and prices remained stable. Agricultural prosperity did, it is true, tend to be uneven, some of the larger estates being burdened with indebtedness; and it was always dependent upon artificial stimulation.

This economic vigor was matched by the intellectual and artistic vitality of Germany in these years. No country in the world matched its prowess in the natural sciences, and these years saw the pioneering researches in chemistry of August Kekulé, the invention of the opthalmoscope by Ludwig Helmholtz and the spectroscope by Gustav Robert Kirchhoff, the discovery of x-rays by Wilhelm Konrad Roentgen and the formulation of the quantum theory by Max Planck, Einstein's first studies on relativity, and the significant medical researches of Robert Koch (tuberculosis, cholera, sleeping sickness), Paul Ehrlich (syphilis), and

Rudolph Virchow (pathology). The great achievements of these men drew students from all over the world to German universities, as did the lectures of historians like Theodor Mommsen and Heinrich von Treitschke, philosophers like Wilhelm Dilthey, sociologists like Ferdinand Tönnies, Georg Simmel, and Max Weber, and economists like Adolf Wagner, Lujo Brentano, and Werner Sombart. The work of these scholars and the methods (particularly the seminar) they used to convey their teaching had great influence on the university life of other countries, perhaps most particularly in the United States.

In the rapidly growing German cities there was a vigorous intellectual atmosphere. This was particularly true of Berlin, whose population grew from 774,498 in 1870 to over two million in 1910. The national capital was, of course, the center of Germany's political activity and of the liveliest and most variegated journalistic life in Germany, some aspects of which were to be described in Heinrich Mann's novel *In the Land of Cockaigne*. But Berlin was also one of the musical centers of Europe; and, in the 1880s and 1890s as many as three hundred concerts were presented each year. One might hear Johannes Brahms as soloist with the Meininger Orchestra, under the direction of the great conductor Hans von Bülow, or Richard Strauss conducting his own first works with the Berlin Philharmonic. In the field of literature, it was the city where the major work of the sociological realists Spielhagen, Fontane, and Sudermann was accomplished and where a new era in the theater was inaugurated with the founding, in 1889, of *Die Freie Bühne*, dedicated to the cause of modernity and presenting the works of Ibsen, Strindberg, Björnson, and Hofmannsthal as well as the new German dramatists—Gerhart Hauptmann, whose *Vor Sonnenaufgang* created a sensation in 1889, and Frank Wedekind, the forerunner of expressionism.

German cultural life was not concentrated to the same extent as in France in one city. The other large urban centers—Hamburg, with almost a million inhabitants in 1914, Cologne, Leipzig, Frankfurt—had flourishing theaters and opera houses and were proud of their museums and their universities. As for the third city in the empire, Munich, with 650,000 inhabitants in 1914, it was, as Thomas Mann wrote in his story *Gladius Dei*, a radiant city of gay squares and broad avenues, of baroque churches and leaping fountains, a city dedicated to the arts, where line, decoration, and form had become a cult.

Yet these evidences of culture were perhaps less impressive than they seemed. Stefan George, the greatest German poet of this period with the exception of Rilke, called Berlin "the cold city of military and commercial serfs"; and Friedrich Nietzsche wrote scornfully of the culture of the great cities (*Grosstadt-Bildung*) and pointed out, with perhaps an ironic allusion to Munich, "how much *beer* there is in the German intelligence!"

With the eloquence of an Old Testament prophet, Nietzsche excoriated what he considered to be the true characteristics of the age—mediocrity, vulgarity, materialism, love of power—and was unimpressed by Germany's economic prosperity, which he felt sapped the people's will, or by the achievements of its universities, where what he called "the despiritualizing influence of our current science-industry" prevailed. "Power," he wrote in *The Twilight of the Idols* (1888), "*makes stupid.*"

> Even a rapid estimate shows that it is not only obvious that German culture is declining but that there is sufficient reason for that. In the end, no one can spend more than he has: that is true of the individual, it is true of a people. If one spends oneself for power, for power politics, for economics, world trade, parliamentarianism and military interests—if one spends in this direction the quantum of understanding, seriousness, will, and self-overcoming which one represents, then it will be lacking for the other direction.

If this seemed an unnecessarily harsh judgment of Bismarck's Germany, it was less so of William II's. The prevailing style of the Wilhelmine epoch was one of garish display and vulgar ostentation, manifest equally in such architectural monstrosities as the *Siegesallee* in Berlin, where grandiose statues of the rulers of Brandenburg-Prussia stood in uncomfortable marble attitudes, looking as if they were on their way to a fancy-dress ball; in the novels of Gustav Frenssen, Hermann Löns, and Hans Friedrich Blunck (infinitely more popular than the social criticism of Fontane, Hauptmann, and Sudermann), which glorified German power and the superiority of the German soul; in the parvenuism and servility of the once self-reliant middle class, which is admirably portrayed in Heinrich Mann's best novel, *The Patrioteer* (*Der Untertan*); and, finally, in the domestic and foreign politics of the Wilhelmine Reich.

Politics under William II / Typical of the spirit of the age was the emperor himself, of whom a member of one of Prussia's oldest families said icily: "He is and remains a parvenu." William II had attractive qualities and a quick intelligence. But he was ill-educated and fundamentally lacking in culture; his preferred companions were bankers and soldiers and his favorite amusements extensive junkets in luxurious yachts and rowdy parties in which broad practical jokes were considered high art. He cultivated a military bearing and a manly forthrightness of speech, which in practice degenerated into a shrill boasting about Germany's power and an overwhelming arrogance in his dealings with lesser nations. He had a jealous and demanding conception of the prerogatives of his office, and sought to assert himself in every aspect of his country's policy. He was the despair of his ministers; and his court chamberlain once said: "We all suffer from the Kaiser; he is the cross laid on us all."

One of the many comments on the military posturing of William II which appeared in the pages of the Munich satirical magazine *Simplicissimus*. In this caricature by O. Gulbransson in 1909, the emperor is shown at maneuvers with the king of Bavaria.

In the first years after Bismarck's fall, William hoped, as we have noted, to check the rise of socialism by a broad program of social legislation. Taking a phrase from Frederick the Great, he saw himself as a *roi des gueux*, a king of the poor, and, in 1891, with that cloudy moralizing about the *Volksgeist* which was so fashionable at the time, he wrote to his old tutor:

> The so-called reformation of the 16th century was nothing more than the first independent step taken by the German spirit in the world of the Idea, the first independent action of the German intellectual will, and it required great energy as well as a high degree of independence of thought and character to break through the strong tradition of centuries in order to take this step. . . . Now the solution of the so-called social question, it is my conviction, will be the second action of the German spirit in the world of the Idea. It will require the same high independence of thought and will. I believe that the new German Empire was made for this purpose, only for this and for no other.

The establishment of arbitration boards to help adjudicate labor disputes, the legal provision for health regulations and safety precautions in factories, laws restricting child labor, the establishment of a bureau of

abor statistics, and other legislation passed between 1891 and 1894 did
not, however, reduce the popular support given to the Socialist party; and
he emperor soon became discouraged. Perhaps the Reich had been made
or other things after all, he decided, and with some public references
to the Socialists as a "treasonable horde" and "a pack of men unworthy
to bear the name of Germans," and a good deal of talk, in the late 1890s,
about reverting to some form of anti-Socialist legislation, he turned most
of his attention permanently to what he now considered the empire's
proper concern—the search for more power, to be accomplished by an
enhanced armaments program, including the creation of a high-seas fleet,
the acquisition of a colonial empire, and a vigorous foreign policy in
every part of the globe.

These policies were embarked upon in the 1890s, at a time when
Germany's international position was strong and its relations with other
powers good. By 1907, all this had changed for the worse, and Germany's
new course had aroused the gravest suspicions. This was due partly, as
we shall see (p. 466), to the manner in which it was carried out, which
was usually a combination of abrupt forcing plays, attempts at blackmail, and the use of threats. It was due also to the essential inconsistency
of the various lines of policy pursued. One would have supposed, for
instance, that it was to Germany's interest to retain the friendship of
Great Britain, which, thanks to the Mediterranean agreements of Bismarck's last years (see p. 280), had cooperated with the Triple Alliance
and whose assistance would be useful if, at this late date, Germany was
to acquire a colonial empire. Yet the German government deliberately
alienated Great Britain by building a battle fleet that seemed to threaten
its interests. Nor was this the only case where love of display and a predilection for the violent gesture militated against German security by
turning its neighbors against it.

Absolutism and the Failure of Parliament / All this was much worse than
it might have been had there been any effective restraint upon the imperial will. Bismarck had had his difficulties with William I, but always
in the end he had kept control of policy in his own hands, thus assuring
its consistency and coherence. None of William II's prewar chancellors
was capable of this kind of firmness. General Count Leo von Caprivi
(1890–1894) tried and failed. The Bavarian Prince Chlodwig zu Hohen-
lohe-Schillingsfürst (1894–1900) had been in politics since the 1860s and
no longer had the energy to control the ebullience of the emperor. Bern-
hard von Bülow (1900–1909), the ablest of these ministers in terms of
natural ability, was as Wilhelmine in style as the emperor himself. To him
politics was a continual dramatic performance in which he had a leading
role, and he delighted in the bombast and fustian and the artful postur-

ings that imperialism and navalism made possible. His method of handling the emperor was to flatter him, which merely confirmed William in his worst habits. Finally, Theobald von Bethmann-Hollweg (1909–1917), a conscientious man with great administrative ability, had too little experience in the field of foreign affairs to feel confident about taking a firm line with the emperor.

One of the gravest difficulties confronting all these ministers was the way in which policy was fragmented, so that vital decisions were sometimes taken by totally irresponsible agencies. The military services, in particular, were able on occasion to make decisions that reversed the policy of the chancellor and the Foreign Office or committed them, without their knowledge, to courses of action that they would ordinarily have rejected. The naval staff consistently opposed Bethmann-Hollweg's attempts to reach a naval accommodation with the British and were backed up by the emperor. The general staff of the army not only made plans for the invasion of Belgium in the event of a war with France (leaving the chancellor inadequately informed about them) but also, in 1909, on its own authority, made commitments to Austria which fundamentally changed the defensive character of the Dual Alliance of 1879 (see p. 282) by promising aid in virtually any contingency.

The army and navy staffs were not alone in dabbling in the policy-making process without the perfect knowledge of the responsible minister. The emperor placed much reliance upon his personal adjutants, upon the heads of his civil and military cabinets, upon his traveling companions, and upon other secret camarillas, and they in turn encouraged him to adopt unexpected courses or to change policies agreed upon with his chancellor. It is impossible to give too much weight to the influence of these forces in German politics under William II. One need remember only that Caprivi fell from power in 1894 largely as a result of carefully contrived plots against him and that the dismissal of Bethmann-Hollweg in 1917 was prepared much the same way.

Why then did the parliamentary bodies of the realm not attempt to interfere, especially when it was clear that the policies of William II were to the disadvantage of the state? Part of the answer is that both the Prussian Landtag and the Reichstag had become so accustomed under Bismarck to leaving foreign affairs in the hands of the chancellor that they were incapable of consistent and vigilant criticism of the conduct of this aspect of policy by his successors. It was, moreover, never easy to persuade a majority of the Reichstag to criticize the government's policy of imperialism and navalism, because powerful interests with strong representation in that body had an economic stake in the policy. The same alliance of rye and steel that had secured the passage of the protective tariff of 1879 saw to it that the naval bills of 1898 and 1900 became law.

Heavy industry supported these bills for obvious reasons; the agrarians supported them because, in return, they got industrial votes for higher tariffs on foreign grains—which, incidentally, alienated the Russians as completely as the naval bills antagonized the British.

Again, it should be remembered that no representative body finds it easy to oppose public opinion, and popular opinion in Wilhelmine Germany was proud of Germany's power, wholly in favor of expressing it in the building of a fleet and the acquisition of a world empire, and unconscious of the dangers involved in these policies. The Center party, the Progressives, and the Socialists might on occasion unite to vote down a government request for funds to be used in colonial enterprise, as they did in 1906; but the fact of the matter was that in all of these parties, even the Social Democratic party, there was a sizable number of members who supported imperialism and believed it would benefit Germany —as, for example, the revisionist Eduard Bernstein did.

Finally, the assertion of control over the emperor would have required a willingness on the part of parliament to assume future responsibility for all aspects of policy. There is no indication that the members of the Reichstag—even some of those who talked loudly of parliamentary rights and ministerial responsibility—wanted anything of the sort. This at least seems to be the lesson of two incidents that occurred in the last years before the war.

In October 1908, the London *Daily Telegraph* printed an interview which one of its reporters had had with William II, in which the emperor had apparently made some gratuitously offensive statements about foreign powers, as well as claiming credit for devising the war plan used by the British in the Boer War (see p. 460). The storm of protest inside Germany was, for the moment, almost as great as that in England. There were demands for the imposition of restraints upon the emperor's prerogatives in foreign affairs, and one Berlin newspaper declared that to have the operations of government dependent upon the will of a single individual was "unbearable for a self-conscious nation." Here, apparently, was an opportunity for the Reichstag to make some progress toward real parliamentary government. Yet nothing was done. As Theodor Eschenburg has written,

> The lack of discipline and solidarity, the uncomprehending indignation and the tendency toward oratorical exaggeration which was characteristic of the whole Wilhelmine era, and the lack of any concrete political objective, caused the debate in the Reichstag . . . to blow itself out without result.

Another opportunity for the Reichstag to demonstrate its determination came in 1913, when troops in the village of Zabern in Alsace became involved in a series of incidents with civilians that led finally to the assumption of police powers by the military authorities and the wholesale arrest of civilians in defiance of normal process of law. When the matter was raised in the Reichstag, the minister of war supported the action taken in Zabern and was in turn backed up by the chancellor, Bethmann-Hollweg. The Reichstag immediately passed a vote of no confidence in Bethmann by a vote of 293 to 55. This did not lead to his resignation, however; and, when the Socialists suggested that it should, their view was rejected with indignation by the other parties. Like the *Daily Telegraph* affair, the Zabern case resulted in some rhetorical pyrotechnics and nothing more.

The French socialist Jean Jaurès, addressing the German Socialists at an international conference in 1904, told them: "Even when you attain the majority in the Reichstag you are the only country where you cannot become master. Your parliament is only a demi-parliament." In 1914 Germany was still an absolute state, despite its constitutional forms. It remained so, as the statement by Mommsen quoted at the beginning of this chapter indicates, and as the two incidents just cited would seem to confirm, because the majority of the German people were too satisfied with the *status quo* to have any strong impulsion to change it. It was not until the dangerous tendencies of Wilhelmine policy had helped bring war and defeat to Germany that that mood of self-satisfaction was to change.

16

Austria-Hungary, the Balkan States, and Turkey, 1871-1914

THE DUAL MONARCHY

Kakania / In his remarkable book, *The Man Without Qualities* (1930ff.), the Austrian writer Robert Musil has painted an affectionate portrait of his country, which he calls Kakania because its ruler was *Kaiser* (emperor) in part of his realm and *König* (king) in the rest and its institutions were all labeled *k. k.* or *k. & k.*

On paper it called itself the Austro-Hungarian Monarchy; in speaking, however, one referred to it as Austria; that is to say, it was known by a name that it had, as a State, solemnly renounced by oath, while preserving it in all matters of sentiment, as a sign that feelings are just as important as constitutional law. . . . The system of government was clerical, but the general attitude to life was liberal. Before the law all citizens were equal, but not everyone, of course, was a citizen. There was a parliament that made such vigorous use of its liberty that it was usually kept shut; but there was also an emergency powers act by means of which it was possible to manage without parliament and whenever everyone was beginning to rejoice in absolutism, the Crown decreed that there must be a return to parliamentary government. Many such things happened in this State, and among them

were those national struggles that justifiably aroused Europe's curiosity. . . .
They were so violent that they several times a year caused the machinery
of State to jam and come to a full stop. But between whiles, in breathing-
spaces between government and government, everyone got on excellently
with everyone else and behaved as if nothing had ever been the matter.

When disastrous things occurred—and they frequently did in Austria—
people said:

Es ist passiert, "it just sort of happened." . . . It was a peculiar phrase,
not known in this sense to the Germans, and with no equivalent in other
languages, the very breath of it transforming facts and the bludgeonings of
fate into something light as eiderdown, as thought itself.

Yes, Musil concludes, Kakania was a home for people with a genius for
taking things lightly, "and that, probably, was the ruin of it."
    This, of course, is satire, but, like all true satire, its core is truth. The
Austro-Hungarian Empire had many problems. Some of them, at least,
might have been solved if it had not also had so many people, especially
among the ruling elite, who confronted difficult questions with levity or
lack of energy or failure of imagination. One can surely find part of the
reason for the decline of the Hapsburg monarchy in the attitude of such
members of its governing class as that nameless staff officer who, in 1854,
when the Prussian military attaché described to him the *Kriegsspiel*
(war game) that was used in training Prussian commanding officers,
asked how one won money at it and lost interest when told that it was
not a game of chance; or in the behavior of the foreign minister Berchtold, who, at the height of the crisis of 1914, is reported to have stuck a
note from the British government between the pages of his racing program and forgotten all about it. As long as one lives in an organized
community, politics is a serious business; and political problems, even
when they cannot be solved, must be tackled vigorously and with intelligence. This, all too often, was not true in Austria-Hungary.
    In large part, the trouble stemmed from the very center and source of
political power. The emperor himself might have inspired and led a
constructive attack upon the problems of his realm. But, as another gifted
Austrian writer, Karl Kraus, wrote after Francis Joseph's death, it was
easier to believe that he was dead than that he had ever really lived. As
one of the characters in Kraus's *The Last Days of Mankind* says, "Never
before in world history had a stronger Un-Personality ever placed his
stamp on all things and institutions . . . Our destiny was decided by a
Daemon of mediocrity." In an empire of diverse peoples, the Emperor
lacked the resources of will and character to embody for them the idea
of a united State. He had neither strong convictions about the policy

hat should be followed nor firmness of will in pursuing what he decided in the end should be done. And, consciously or subconsciously, he avoided strong subordinates, showing—as the distinguished Austrian critic Hermann Bahr once wrote—"an almost touching weakness for untalented people."

This failure of leadership meant that the most serious of the problems confronting the monarchy, the problem of the nationalities, was never really faced. The nature and limitations of the Compromise of 1867, which created the Dual Monarchy by placing Hungary on an equal footing with Austria, have been described above (p. 232). As early as the 1870s, there was much evidence to indicate that if it remained unchanged, the non-German and non-Magyar majority of the Hapsburg peoples would be progressively alienated from their loyalty to the crown. If the ruling class of the Empire was aware of this danger, they made no strenuous attempts to avert it; and, in the last decade before the outbreak of the World War, as we shall see, the emperor himself advertized his lack of interest in any real change by abandoning suffrage reform in Hungary.

Politics and Economics in Austria / The government of the Hapsburg monarchy after 1867 was conducted on three separate levels: the intergovernmental, the Austrian, and the Hungarian. Certain matters of concern to the whole realm—notably foreign affairs, defense matters, and imperial finance—were conducted by a joint ministry appointed by the monarch and supervised in a vague sort of way by Austrian and Hungarian delegations. The internal affairs of Austria and Hungary were in the hands of autonomous and distinct governments, which were so different in structure and practice that they must be discussed separately.

The seventeen provinces that made up the Austrian part of the realm possessed individual diets that administered local affairs and were represented in an imperial parliament that met in Vienna. This latter body had two chambers, an upper one composed of dynastic aristocrats, leading churchmen, and other dignitaries appointed by the emperor, and a lower house whose members were originally selected by the local diets but, after 1873, were elected by a clumsy and indirect system that gave preference to property and education. Parliament as a whole had the right to approve or reject important items of state business; the budget and bills fixing the annual contingent for the armed forces had to originate in the lower house, which also had the right to question and to impeach ministers.

Ministers were appointed by the emperor and, although constitutionally responsible to the lower house, were in fact dependent on the monarch for continuance in power. The emperor also had the right to dissolve or suspend the parliament in accordance with rules defined in the constitution and possessed authority, under Article 14 of the constitution, to issue decrees that had the full force of law when parliament was not in session, provided they did not modify fundamental laws and were approved by parliament at its next session. These powers made it possible for the emperor to impose his will upon a refractory parliament, and he was not loath to use them. On the other hand, he preferred to work in harmony with the legislature whenever possible and sought ministers who could create parliamentary majorities. This explains Musil's reference to alternation between absolutism and parliamentarism in Austrian affairs.

In one marked respect, the course of politics in Austria paralleled that in Germany. Throughout the first decade of its new existence, the dominant force was a strong Liberal party which represented the views of the wealthy German middle class that was being created by the rapid industrialization of Austria and Bohemia. Like its German counterpart, this party was strongly in favor of constitutionalism, centralization, and administrative efficiency in the interests of commercial progress, and in addition shared the usual Liberal prejudice against clerical influence. During the 1870s, when it was grappling with the problems created by the reorganization of the realm and the economic difficulties caused by the crash of 1873, the crown found it expedient to rely on Liberals for parliamentary support. The legislative results of this collaboration were an improvement of judicial procedure, the liberalization of the press laws, the abolition of laws restricting the rights of the Jews, the revision of the disciplinary code and administrative procedures of the army, and a series of laws designed to promote economic growth and regulate the finances of the state. Simultaneously, the schools were removed from church control and religious instruction became voluntary; all Christian creeds were placed on a footing of equality; and civil marriage was authorized. In 1869, a new law had made elementary education free and compulsory for all children, but its administration was left to the provincial diets, which did little to implement it during the 1870s. Despite this, the amount of progressive legislation passed with the support of the Liberals was impressive to foreign observers.

The Liberal era ended abruptly, however, at about the same time and for much the same reason as it had ended in Germany. The emperor became annoyed at Liberal criticism of the results of the Congress of Berlin of 1878 and, specifically, of the assumption by Austria of administrative control over Bosnia and Herzegovina (see p. 275), which the Liberals believed was an unwise extension of Austrian responsibilities; and he decided to seek a different kind of parliamentary support. Like Bismarck, Francis Joseph seemed to feel that the Liberals were bent on increasing parliamentary rights at the expense of royal power, and that

NATIONALITIES
IN
AUSTRIA-HUNGARY

t would be wiser to rely upon the support of German conservatives and
upon the Slavs.

There was, of course, good reason for the government to turn its attention to the non-German peoples of Austria, who resented German
dominance and hoped to win rights similar to those granted to the
Magyars in 1867. The Poles of Galicia, the Slovenes and the Serbs in the
south all shared this feeling, but it was felt most strongly, perhaps, by
the Czechs of Bohemia, who were proud of their long history, of their
national heroes from Huss to Palacký, of the achievements of their culture, and of the rapid economic growth of their land.

The relationship between the Czech and the German peoples has been
called "a neuralgic point of the future of Europe and the maintenance
of the peace of the world," a statement that will assume greater meaning
when we consider Czechoslovakia's role in the postwar world. It is certainly true that in the history of the Dual Monarchy, the Czech problem
was crucial; and failure to solve it was one of the most important reasons
for the Empire's collapse. On only one occasion did Francis Joseph ever
come close to grappling with it. In 1871, he promised to elevate Bohemia
to the same autonomous position enjoyed by Austria and Hungary,
and prepared to go to Prague to be crowned as king of Bohemia. This

plan to convert the Empire into a triple monarchy was blocked, howeve1 by the intransigence of the Austrian Germans, who feared the loss o1 their preferred position, and the Magyars, who were afraid that libera1 tion of the Czechs would stimulate a demand for similar rights on th1 part of their own subject nationalities. The emperor capitulated t1 German and Hungarian objections; and the Czechs never forgave him Their immediate response was to boycott the imperial parliament an1 to pretend that its transactions were of no interest to them.

In 1879, when the emperor broke with the Liberals, he sought simul taneously to appease the Czechs and the other subject nationalities. Th1 man he chose to do this was a friend of his youth, Count Edward Taaff1 a man who hid behind a veil of levity and cynicism great political gifts which enabled him to remain as the emperor's chief minister from 187! until 1893. The political combination he created to replace the Liberal was known as "the Iron Ring" and was composed of clericals, Germa1 Conservatives, Slavs, Poles, and Czechs, whom Taaffe persuaded to giv1 up their policy of parliamentary abstention. A deputy from one of th1 Italian districts once called the Taaffe government a *luogo di traffico* (1 place for making deals), a not inaccurate description, for the ill-suitec partners were kept together by concessions to their special interests. I1 Galicia, for example, the Poles were permitted to win special privilege1 over the Ruthenians; and in Carniola, the Slovenes were allowed t1 oppress other nationalities. As for the Czechs, they were granted a ne1 electoral law that gave them a majority in the Bohemian diet, as wel as stronger representation in the imperial parliament; the University o1 Prague was divided into two universities, one of which was hencefort1 Czech; and a new ordinance required all civil servants in Bohemia anc Moravia henceforth to render judgments in the language of th1 petitioner. This last provision dethroned German as the sole officia1 language, and operated to the disadvantage of German officials, who now had to learn Czech, and it increased the number of Czechs in the civi1 service.

In the long run, the Taaffe policy of appeasement succeeded only i1 increasing the opposition of the Slavs and arousing the fury of th1 Germans, thus exacerbating the nationalities problem almost beyonc control. The concessions to Czech nationalism, for instance, failed to clo1 the appetite they fed. On the contrary, the moderate Czechs who hac cooperated with Taaffe were supplanted by a new Young Czech party whose spirit was shown by a speech made by one of their leaders Edward Grégr, in the imperial parliament in 1891:

> Bohemia is being sucked dry by Austria. . . . The majority of the Czec1 population is utterly wretched in the midst of this alien empire. . . . Thei1 nationality is oppressed and persecuted in this Austrian state, which is 1

state of violence and tyranny to all Slav races. The Bohemian people are made to hate this state—I repeat—hate this state, and, mark my words, the day of reckoning will come.

The other Slav peoples of the Empire also grew more outspoken in their demands and, at the same time, there was an intensification of the Pan-Slav ideas that had been so prevalent among the subject nationalities in 1848. Indeed, the older idea of the cultural community of all Slavs began now, in some quarters, to be superseded or supplemented by a new political Pan-Slavism that thought in terms of a federation of Slavic peoples free from Austro-Hungarian control. Those who were beginning to think in these new terms looked to Russia for assistance and were encouraged by the writings of Russian Pan-Slav theorists like R. A. Fadeyev and N. Y. Danilevsky, who talked of a future emancipation of the Slavs by that country.

These tendencies should not, of course, be attributed entirely to Taaffe's appeasement policy, for their origins lay farther back, in the Austrian government's persistent refusal to alter the constitution of the Dual Monarchy. In 1865 the great Czech leader Palacký had said:

> The day that Dualism is proclaimed will become, with irresistible natural necessity, the birthday of Pan-Slavism in its least gladdening form. The leaders of Dualism will be its sponsors. The result can be imagined. We Slavs will await it with justified pain, yet without fear. Before Austria was, we were; and after Austria we shall also be.

Taaffe's policies also aroused the Germans in Bohemia, with resultant disorders that forced the government to place Prague under martial law and, eventually, compelled Taaffe's retirement. German opposition to his policies was reflected also in the rise of a new Pan-German movement, led by Georg von Schönerer, which preached the racial superiority of the Germans over the Slavs and called for a union of Austria's German provinces with the Hohenzollern Reich.

Throughout the Taaffe period, the opposition to his coalition had been the old Liberal party, still the strongest single political grouping in Austria. But the Liberals never recovered the position they had enjoyed before 1879 and, like Liberal parties in other countries, they now entered a period of decline. In the confused political period that followed Taaffe's fall their strength was sapped by the movement of economic forces and by the government's decision to attempt to check the agitation of the nationalities by extending the suffrage to classes more interested in social problems than in nationality—a policy that culminated in 1907 with the establishment of universal manhood suffrage in Austria. These things led to the emergence of two parties that supplanted liberalism and played an important role in Austrian politics until the fall of the independent Austrian republic in 1938.

The first of these was the Christian Socialist party, a curiously ambivalent group that managed to combine within its membership some of the most progressive social thinkers and some of the most fanatical bigots in Austria. A Catholic party, appealing particularly to the urban petty bourgeoisie, the Christian Socialists placed great emphasis upon democracy, social reform, and an enlightened nationalities problem. Under their greatest leader, Karl Lueger, who served as mayor of Vienna from 1897 until his death in 1907, they strongly supported the successful movement to legalize trade unions and to grant accident and sickness insurance to workers (Lueger said in 1886: "A state that has no social insurance laws should be barred from all intercourse with other states!") and, in Vienna itself, carried through a program of municipal socialism which equaled that of Joseph Chamberlain in Birmingham (see p. 314).

But, as was true of the comparable movement led by Adolf Stoecker in Germany (see p. 375)—and of Schönerer's Pan-German movement, many of whose members shifted their allegiance to Lueger's party—the force that gave Christian Socialism its original mass support and always remained an important factor in its policies was anti-Semitism. One of the first effects of industrialism in Austria was to ruin a number of small concerns and to cause general depression among the independent artisan class, especially in Vienna where they had to compete with the new factories. It was easy for this class to blame their troubles upon the Jews, especially in view of the important role Jews played in financing Austrian industry. Even without that encouragement, they would probably have made the Jews their scapegoat, for in the western parts of the Empire migrants from the ghettoes of Galicia and Rumania had long been objects of suspicion and dislike. Admirers of Karl Lueger have always insisted that he was not an anti-Semite at heart. This is quite possibly true, but he identified himself so closely with anti-Jewish feeling that, in 1895, when the possibility of his becoming mayor first arose, the Liberal *Neue Freie Presse* lamented that, if this happened, "Vienna will be the only great city in the world whose administration is in the hands of anti-Semitic fanatics (*Hetzer*)." It may be noted also that one of Lueger's admirers was a young man from Linz who was going to make anti-Semitism his ladder to power, Adolf Hitler.

After the suffrage reform of 1907, the Christian Socialist movement turned to the Right, merging with the Conservatives. Meanwhile, the enfranchisement of the working class facilitated the growth of the Social Democratic party which had been organized earlier by Viktor Adler. The Socialists gradually took over the dominant position once held in Vienna by the Christian Socialists, whose strength was now in rural Austria and, while the Empire lasted, in Galicia. Marxist in inspiration, the Socialist party maintained close relations with the Socialist parties in neighboring countries. Like them, and perhaps to an even greater degree, it was affected by revisionism and advocated moderate social change to be achieved by parliamentary means. It supported the imperial tie and advocated a liberal policy of concessions to the nationalities.

The introduction of universal manhood suffrage did not check the agitation of the nationality groups in parliament, which continued to be paralyzed periodically by their demonstrations and their tendency to indulge in orgies of fisticuffs and chair-breaking. Its persistent failure to reform the settlement of 1867 forced the government to rely on frequent resort to emergency powers.

The Kingdom of Hungary / Political life in the Hungarian part of the Empire also centered in parliament, which was composed of a House of Magnates and a House of Deputies, the latter of which controlled the ministers and exercised the initiative in legislation. The House of Deputies was in no sense a popular assembly reflecting the wishes of the mass of the population, for the franchise was an extremely restricted one, only about 25 percent of the male population possessing the vote.

Out of Hungary's population of fifteen million, the Magyars constituted less than a half, yet they held a monopoly of political power and, through the central parliament and local institutions, not only dominated the subject nationalities but sought to assimilate them. The only exceptions to this were the Croats in the southwestern part of the kingdom, whose services to the Empire in 1848 were remembered and who were permitted to have their own diet, courts, schools, and police and to send a separate bloc of forty members to the central House of Deputies. Yet even the Croats found their rights being whittled away as the years passed; and the other subject nationalities—the Rumanians of Transylvania and the Slovaks and Serbs—were subject to an unremitting policy of Magyarization. Bismarck once said that all Magyars were either hussars or lawyers. Certainly it was by a blend of force and legalism that the government sought to wipe out national differences and to suppress newspapers, schools and other agencies that might keep the languages, arts, and customs of the other nationalities alive. Magyar was made compulsory in parliament, the administrative agencies of central and local government, the courts, the schools—even in the railways where no signs were permitted in any other language. The law of 1868, which had been drafted by the great Hungarian liberal Francis Deák and which guaranteed equal rights to all nationalities, was simply ignored.

The right to subjugate the nationalities—which dissolved the bonds of loyalty to the crown and had fateful results during World War I—was implicit in the Compromise of 1867 and may be described as the price paid to the Magyars for their continued support of imperial policies and institutions. As the years passed, however, the Magyars themselves succumbed to chauvinism and actually began to agitate for virtual independence from Austria. The leader of the movement in this direction was Francis Kossuth, the son of the hero of 1848, who formed an Independence party and demanded that Hungary be able to direct her own tariff and foreign policies and, more immediately, that Magyar become the language used in the Hungarian regiments of the imperial and royal army.

A concession of this nature would, of course, dissolve the unity of the military establishment, and Francis Joseph, who had watched the oppression of the Hungarian minorities with no great concern, reacted swiftly to this threat. The first years of the new century were marked by a series of crises between the crown and the independence movement. The struggle reached its point of greatest intensity in 1905 when a coalition led by Kossuth won such an overwhelming victory in parliamentary elections that it seemed capable of putting its plans into effect. At this point the emperor appointed an emergency government which threatened to introduce universal manhood suffrage in place of the restricted franchise that was the bulwark of Magyar power.

Had this plan been carried through, the subject nationalities might belatedly have received a measure of justice. But in 1906 the coalition leaders, terrified at the prospect of a new franchise law, agreed to assume office without insisting on the army reform; and Francis Joseph allowed the scheme for universal suffrage to be forgotten. Politics in Hungary became less stormy and, in the election of 1910, a new party founded by Stephen Tisza (1861–1918) and dedicated to maintaining the Compromise of 1867, smashed the Kossuth movement. Tisza, who was to be supreme in Hungarian politics until 1917, put an end to attacks on the emperor's military prerogative, and to the parliamentary obstructionism that accompanied them, by carrying through a radical reform of parliamentary procedure in 1912.

While this was going on, however, the subject nationalities had been forgotten again. By abandoning suffrage reform, the emperor had thrown away his last chance of breaking the power of the Magyar oligarchy, and that failure made the dissolution of his empire inevitable.

Splendor and Decline / This was not immediately perceptible, of course; and the casual observer of Austrian affairs was apt to see not the hidden weaknesses but the surface splendors of the Hapsburg realm. This was particularly true if he visited the imperial capital, for Vienna was never lovelier or more stimulating and gay than it was in the last years before World War I. Since the 1860s, its beauties had been enhanced by the razing of what was left of the medieval wall around the inner city and the construction in its place of the majestic Ringstrasse, one of the most beautiful avenues in the world, by the building of new bridges across the Danube, and by a series of architectural triumphs: the Rathaus, designed by Fredrick Schmidt; the new opera house; Theophil Hansen's Austrian parliament building; Karl Hasenauer's Burgtheater; and many more. Housed so nobly, arts and letters flourished in Vienna: music perhaps most of all, with composers like Bruckner, Mahler, Brahms (who spent most of his productive years in Vienna), Hugo Wolf, the greatest composer of songs since Schubert, and Richard Strauss, whose opera *Der Rosencavalier*, with lyrics by Austria's first poet, Hugo von Hofmannsthal, had its triumphant premiere in 1911. As for light opera, it was widely considered to be a Viennese speciality, thanks to the achievements of Johann Strauss, Karl Millöcker (*The Student Beggar and Gasparone*) and Franz Lehar (*The Merry Widow*).

The most popular painters of this period were men like Hans Makart, whose reputations did not long survive their deaths; and among prose writers, no one equalled the earlier achievement of Adalbert Stifter (1805–1868) whose *Nachsommer* (1857) was to remain one of the greatest German *Bildungsromane*. But in the field of drama Vienna produced three outstanding artists in Ludwig Anzengruber (1839–1889), who dealt seriously with the religious and social problems of his time, Arthur Schnitzler (1862–1931), whose mixture of scepticism and sentimentality captivated generations and still wins audiences in cities far removed from his own, and Hugo von Hofmannsthal (1874–1929), whose mystical dramas (*The Fool and Death*, 1893; *Elektra*, 1904; *Everyman*, 1911) were admired all over Europe for their lyrical beauty and whose last play (*The Tower*, 1925) looked with chilling foresight into problems that have since come to plague our world.

The University of Vienna was renowned the world over, especially for its work in medicine, which was distinguished by Theodor Billroth's pioneer work in antiseptic surgery and Theodor Meynert's in brain surgery. The other faculties were hardly less outstanding, with philosophers of the stature of Ernst Mach, economists like Carl Menger, and the historian of the war of 1866, Heinrich Friedjung. Other Viennese scholars of widespread reputation were Rudolf von Ihering and Joseph Unger in legal studies, Rudolf Pöch in anthropology, and the man who probably had a greater effect upon European thought than any of the others mentioned here, the psychiatrist Sigmund Freud (1856–1939).

In the middle of this illustrious city stood the Belvedere Palace, where the aging emperor presided over what was still one of the most glittering

Two gentlemen of Vienna: (left) Emperor Francis Joseph I, 1830–1916, and (right) Sigmund Freud, 1856–1939. (Both photos: THE BETTMANN ARCHIVE)

court societies in Europe and, despite his years, paid meticulous attention to the administration of the higher echelons of the imperial civil
service and of the army. It was here, at the heart and motive center of
the empire, that realities most clearly belied appearances, for beneath
the surface splendor were palpable evidences of declining vitality and
efficiency. Sentimental Viennese might attribute to Francis Joseph those
qualities of wisdom that are supposed to accompany age. He did not,
as his record on the nationalities question showed, possess them; and
there was not much evidence that they would be supplied by the
dynasty after his death. The emperor's only son, Rudolf, had become
involved in an extramarital love affair and had finally killed himself
and his mistress at Meyerling in 1889—a tragic event that has been the
subject of countless sensational books and several lachrymose motion
pictures. Rudolf's successor as heir apparent was the emperor's nephew
the Archduke Franz Ferdinand. He was an able soldier, with a good
tactical sense and great administrative gifts, but his political capacities
were untested. He has often been described as possessing the desire and
the will to reform the imperial structure in the interest of the nationalities
but, as his most recent biographer has pointed out, he progressively
lost faith in the minority groups and, by 1914, could be considered
essentially as a defender of the Compromise of 1867. He was, in any
case, too ambiguous a figure to restore the confidence of the minorities in

the crown; and, even if he had escaped the death that came
Sarajevo in 1914, it is unlikely that he could have checked the d
of the Empire.

Nor were the two services upon which the Empire relied
blance of unity as healthy as they might appear. The bureaucracy was
sometimes called the best bureaucracy in Europe, but—as Robert Musil
wrote—"it could not help regarding genius and enterprise of genius
in private persons, unless privileged by high birth or State appointment,
as ostentation, indeed presumption." As for the army, upon which
Francis Joseph had lavished such care and to which he had given so
much political latitude—a tendency that had been dangerous in the 1860s
when his favorite Count Grünne was alive (see p. 209), and was doubly
so after 1906, when Conrad von Hötzendorff, chief of staff of the army,
was openly advocating a preventive war against Serbia as a means of
solving the South Slav problem—there was some reason to doubt its
efficiency and even its reliability. The long dispute over the possible use
of the Magyar language in Hungarian regiments had weakened internal
unity and morale and given rise to doubts about the loyalty of some of
the national contingents in time of war. Much more damaging was the
revelation by the newspapers in May 1913 that Colonel Alfred Redl,
chief of staff of the Prague corps of the imperial and royal army, and
formerly for six years deputy chief of the army's Intelligence Bureau,
had been serving as a spy for the Russians for over ten years. Perhaps
more than any single event in the last decade before the war, the Redl
case shook public confidence in the governmental structure of the Austro-
Hungarian Empire, while at the same time weakening its reputation
among its allies.

Austria and the Balkans / All of the internal problems of Austria-
Hungary were complicated by the relations of the Empire with the
lesser states of southeastern Europe, with the Turkish Empire, which
still had nominal rights of suzerainty in some of those states, and with
Imperial Russia. The Hapsburg monarchy was drawn into this area by
strategical and economic factors affecting the security and well-being
of the whole Empire. Its dependence upon the Danube as a trade route
meant inevitably that it would be interested in the politics of Serbia,
Bulgaria, and Rumania, along whose borders or through whose territory
it passed. Aside from the Danube, the Empire's access to the sea
depended upon its continued possession of the Istrian Peninsula at the
head of the Adriatic, with its three important ports Trieste, Pola (now
Pula), and Fiume (now Ryeka), and of the Dalmatian coast with its
ancient port of Ragusa (now Dubrovnik). But these possessions would
be natural objectives of any expansionist movement that developed

in the Kingdom of Serbia, as would the provinces of Bosnia and Herzegovina which—still nominally Turkish—had been under Austrian administration since the Congress of Berlin (see p. 275). Because of this, the Hapsburg monarchy felt compelled to block any Yugoslav movement that would threaten the economic and (given the importance of the Dalmatian coast in a contest with Italy) the strategic interests of the Empire.

Until 1903, while Austro-Serbian relations were cordial, there was a school of thought in Austria that held that this could be done by the union of all the Serbs and Croats in Serbia, Montenegro, Dalmatia, Istria, Bosnia, Herzegovina, and the Hungarian province of Croatia-Slavonia in a Yugoslav state *within* the Hapsburg monarchy, a state that would, in every way, be on the same footing as Austria and the kingdom of Hungary. These "trialists" agreed that this would do away with the increasingly dangerous disaffection among the Empire's Croats and the growing nationalism of Serbia and would give Austria the dominance of the western Balkans. This plan—like the plan to raise the position of the Czechs in the Empire—was bitterly opposed by the Magyars and would probably have foundered on that rock alone, even if the change of dynasty in Belgrade in 1903 had not given rise to a sharp increase in Serbian chauvinism and Serbian intrigues inside Bosnia. As relations between Vienna and Belgrade deteriorated in the years that followed, all thought of winning the Serbs by kindness vanished, and the Hapsburg monarchy sought more aggressive means of solving the South Slav question. This contributed to the coming of that dangerous clash between Austria and Russia in 1908, which will be discussed below (p. 477), and which set in train the events that were to lead to the World War and the collapse of the Austrian-Hungarian Empire.

Before proceeding with the story of those events, however, it will be necessary to look briefly at the progress and problems of the Balkan countries since the Congress of Berlin and—in the next chapter—the condition and policies of Austria's great rival in this area, Imperial Russia.

THE STATES OF SOUTHEASTERN EUROPE

Rumania / Modern Rumania was largely the creation of the Crimean War, for the Congress of Paris at the end of that conflict had abolished the former Russian protectorate over the Turkish provinces of Moldavia and Wallachia and simultaneously made them virtually independent of the Porte. Within three years, these principalities were united under the leadership of an energetic native prince, Colonel Alexander Cuza, who ruled the new autonomous principality until 1866. In that year Cuza was deposed by the legislative chambers, which then offered the throne to Prince Carol of Hohenzollern-Sigmaringen, a cousin of Emperor William I of Germany. None of the powers objected (not even the French, who were to raise such strong objections to a similar arrangement in Spain four years later); and Carol himself was intrigued enough by the offer to accept. He is reported to have looked into an atlas and, discovering that Bucharest was on a straight line drawn between London and Bombay, to have exclaimed, "That is a country with a future."

During his long reign (1866–1914), Carol strove to lay the basis for that future. At the very outset, he convoked an assembly that drafted a liberal constitution on the western model, with royal powers limited by ministerial responsibility to the legislature and with a bicameral parliament elected by limited suffrage based upon the Prussian three-class system. Until 1878, the fiction of Turkish overlordship was maintained, but in 1877 Rumania declared herself entirely independent, and the sultan and the other powers acquiesced at the Berlin Congress, on condition that the legal equality of all citizens be recognized by the new state. This provision, designed to protect the Jews, was unfortunately always more honored in the breach than in the observance. In 1881, the Rumanian government proclaimed that the state would henceforth be known as the Kingdom of Rumania, and the prince as King Carol I.

A predominantly agricultural country, Rumania suffered from the social troubles incidental to inequitable land distribution, and in 1907 there was a major peasant revolt that required the use of 140,000 troops to restore order and forced the government to institute a series of reforms. Aside from this, there were many signs of progress. Exports of cereals and oil increased throughout Carol's reign, the first threefold, the second much more than that, since the importance of the Ploesti fields was just beginning to be discovered at the turn of the century. In 1866 Rumania had no railways at all; in 1914 it had almost 2500 miles of railway. Generally speaking, it was the most important of the Balkan countries commercially, and by 1914 was growing rapidly in industry as well.

Much of the revenue that this growth brought to the government was, unfortunately, spent on the army and navy, both of which were excessively large for a country Rumania's size. But Rumania was an ambitious state and one, moreover, with a grievance. Its armies had fought side by side with the Russians in 1877 and had helped break the Turkish resistance at Plevna; but Russia had not seen fit to repay it for this aid by ceding Bessarabia, which Rumanians considered, on ethnic grounds, to be rightfully theirs. Rumania had a vital interest, also, in the future of those Rumanian subjects of the Hapsburg monarchy who lived in Transylvania and Bukovina, and sporadically expressed sympathy for pockets of Rumanians in Macedonia, which Turkey still ruled. The possibility of a territorial dispute with one or more of its neighbors was always present, and, this being so, Rumania maintained a large military establishment, contributing its share to the raising of the general Balkan temperature.

Bulgaria / Because its people had been compelled, to free themselves from the rule of the Ottoman Empire and, then, almost immediately, to resist being forced into the position of being a mere satellite of Russia, Bulgaria's political history had been a stormy one. The critical events of the years 1885–1888, which saw the rapid growth of anti-Russian feeling in Bulgaria, as well as Prince Alexander of Battenberg's acquisition of Eastern Rumelia, his military victory over the Serbs, and his deposition by a Russian *coup de main*, came close to making Bulgaria the center of a major European war (see p. 279); and, although this was averted, the internal affairs of the country remained confused for some years.

Bulgaria was fortunate, nevertheless, in possessing a statesman of courage and determination in the first years after Alexander's fall. This was Stephen Stambulov, the son of an innkeeper, who had been educated in Russia and had returned to his country to enter politics. As president of the national assembly (*Sobranje*), he had played a prominent part in the union with Eastern Rumelia, had headed the provisional government after Alexander's abdication, and had been the leading spirit in the election of Prince Ferdinand of Saxe-Coburg-Gotha as his successor. In the first years of Ferdinand's reign, Stambulov was virtually dictator of Bulgaria. He used his authority to extirpate remnants of Russian and Turkish influence in the country and to encourage railroad building, increase commerce, stimulate the beginnings of industry, modernize the Bulgarian army, and beautify the national capital at Sofia. In a country that lagged far behind the west in educational and other kinds of progress, this program could be achieved only by authoritarian means; Stambulov's lack of scruples and his willingness to resort to brutal compulsion in order to force the pace of reform earned him a host of enemies, and cost him his position in 1894 and his life, by assassination, a year later.

The progress made under his direction, however, was so notable that it was recognized by the powers, who finally, in 1896, recognized Prince Ferdinand's title (which they had hesitated to do at the time of his election). Twelve years later, in 1908, they acknowledged his final severance of legal ties to Turkey and his assumption of the title tsar of Bulgaria.

Bulgaria's conflict with Russia in the late 1880s threw it, perforce, into the arms of Austria-Hungary, with whom, in any case, it had close economic ties and, after Ferdinand's accession, dynastic ones as well, since the new prince had served in the army of Francis Joseph and felt a bond of loyalty to that ruler. At the same time, Bulgaria's memories of the war with Serbia in 1885 and the fact that its territorial claims in Macedonia conflicted with those of that country, made relations between Sofia and Belgrade uncomfortable; and, after 1903, the government of Austria-Hungary recognized this and followed a deliberate plan of playing Bulgaria off against Serbia, encouraging its claims, when occasion arose, to block Serbian growth. This was a dangerous policy and, in the end, involved Bulgaria in a great-power struggle even more dangerous than that which had threatened it in 1887.

Serbia / An autonomous principality since the first part of the nineteenth century, Serbia had become wholly independent of Turkey at the Congress of Berlin in 1878 and, four years later, proclaimed itself a kingdom. This growth in international stature, if it can be described as such, was not accompanied by any clear evidences of internal strength and vitality. The reign of King Milan Obrenovitch was characterized by domestic disaffection, administrative incompetence, and financial mismanagement, all thrown into greater relief by the personal life of the ruler, who preferred to spend as much time as possible away from his capital, pursuing fashionable vice in Vienna and Abbazia (now Opatija.) It was probably to check the swift decline of this popularity, and as a reaction to an attempt on his life, that Milan made the mistake of going to war against the Bulgars in 1885. That short and inglorious campaign completed the bankruptcy of his reputation and, although he held on for four years, he was forced to abdicate in 1889.

This action did not save the dynasty or make for orderly government in Serbia. The new ruler, Alexander I, was only thirteen at the time of his accession and, during the necessary regency, disorder and factionalism increased in the country. They received additional encouragement when Alexander assumed power in his own right in 1893, for he proved to be an impulsive youth with a penchant for authoritarian gestures, and with little tact or political judgment. In 1900 he insisted upon marrying one of his mother's ladies-in-waiting, brushing aside as inconsequential the fact that his wife had already divorced one husband and that, for physical reasons, she could not perform the most essential task of queens in countries characterized by dynastic instability: that is, provide Alexander with an heir. The impolitic and unpopular union had a sequel not uncommon in the Balkans. In 1903, Alexander, his wife, and several of her relatives were brutally murdered at Belgrade, and their mutilated bodies thrown from the windows of the royal palace.

This action was of revolutionary importance in the history of southeastern Europe. Up till this time, relations between Serbia and the Austro-Hungarian Empire had been friendly, despite certain territorial differences. It had been Austrian intervention that had prevented the utter destruction of the Serbian army after the battle of Slivnitza in 1885; commercial relations between the two countries had been cordial and profitable; the ruling houses had been amicable. Now, however, the murder at Belgrade brought the Karageorgevitch dynasty to the throne in the person of Peter I, and Serbian policy immediately assumed an anti-Austrian character. This was not as clearly attributable to King Peter, whose energies were almost completely absorbed in correcting the internal conditions of his country, to its very great advantage, as to his son, the future King Alexander of Yugoslavia. This able and intelligent young man, a soldier and a patriot, believed that Serbia was destined to be the Piedmont of the Balkans and that her first task was to free Bosnia and Herzegovina from Austrian control and join them to Serbia and her second, to emancipate the Serbs and Croats who were subjects of the Hapsburg monarchy. Although we lack detailed knowledge of the extent of royal complicity in Serbian nationalist agitations in those years, there are strong indications that Prince Alexander gave his support to the secret patriotic societies (the Black Hand and others) that were working for those objectives through agents inside Bosnia and Austria, and that he encouraged high ranking civil servants and army officers to join these organizations. This new policy orientation had results felt throughout Europe in the years 1908–1914 (see p. 486).

In the pursuit of their foreign-policy objectives, especially in opposition to Austria, the Serbs could usually count on the support of the tiny Kingdom of Montenegro on the Adriatic coast, a country peopled by Serbs of pure blood with a highly developed feeling of Slav nationality, who were destined to become part of Yugoslavia after 1919.

Greece / The southernmost of the Balkan countries, the Kingdom of Greece, also presented a picture of internal confusion, discontent, and growing ambition for expansion. After its successful fight for freedom, Greece had been presented with a ruler by the Great Powers (see p. 28). The appointed sovereign, a younger son of the king of Bavaria, ruled Greece as King Otto I from 1832 to 1862. For the first ten years, his reign was marked by an attempt to impose centralized government and Germanic institutions upon a people who were temperamentally democrats and who, even under the Turks, had enjoyed extensive rights of local self-government. They resisted Otto's attempt to bureaucratize the country, eventually showing the seriousness of their protest by resorting, in 1843, to armed insurrection. Brought to his senses, the king authorized an extensive constitutional reform that worked no better than the system it supplanted, since it was elaborately liberal and parliamentary in the western sense but had no more meaning in a Greek context than the Cánovas constitution had in Spain (see p. 336). It enabled politicians to mimic the procedures of the west but failed utterly to deal with the serious problems of the country: economic backwardness, financial instability, domestic disorder, and brigandage.

In 1833, the great powers had drawn the country's borders in such a way as to leave large numbers of Greeks in Thessaly, Epirus, and Macedonia under Turkish rule. Otto's government had no success in securing any amendment of frontiers by negotiation, and an attempt to take advantage of the distraction of the powers during the Crimean War and correct the borders by force was a fiasco. The loss of prestige and the economic repercussions consequent upon this finished what was left of Otto's popularity and, in 1862, confronted with new insurrections, he felt compelled to seek safety abroad.

After some difficulty, a new ruler was found, Prince William George of Denmark, who came to the Greeks bearing gifts, since the British government (perhaps hoping to enhance his chances of survival in an unstable land) decided to accompany his nomination with the cession to Greece of the Ionian Islands (Corfu, Zante, Paxo, Ithaca, Cephalonia, Santa Maura, and Cerigo) which had been under British protection since 1815. The new reign began with a constitutional revision that introduced universal manhood suffrage and made the king's ministers responsible to a single chamber of paid deputies serving for four years. It cannot be said that this shift from a liberal to a democratic constitution made for greater stability. In the reign of George I (1863–1913), there were more than fifty different ministries, a fact that militated against continuity of policy. The state's troubles were enhanced by financial difficulties that were the result of the introduction of new social services (which accomplished a sensible improvement of educational standards), a perhaps too ambitious program of public works (with emphasis upon railroad and canal construction), and the burden of military expenses.

As in the case of other Balkan countries, the military budget was high because Greece's territorial aims were high. The country was not content with the cession of the Ionian Islands nor with the acquisition in 1881— as a result of Great Power pressure in Constantinople—of a third of Epirus and the greater part of Thessaly. The rest of those provinces, as well as Macedonia and the island of Crete, were the objectives of all Greek patriots and especially of the *Ethniké Hetaireia* (National

Society), a secret society formed in 1894 to encourage the government to break the restraints imposed by the great powers, to build up the national military establishment, and to promote union movements in the desired territories.

In 1885 and 1886, when Bulgaria was acquiring Eastern Rumelia and defeating Serbia at war and when great Balkan changes seemed in view, the Greek government mobilized its armed forces and seemed on the point of attacking Turkey, but was checked by a great-power blockade. Ten years later, when the Christians on Crete rose in revolt against Turkish administration and declared their union with Greece, Greek naval forces came to the aid of the insurgents, and Greek irregular forces poured into Thessaly bent on liberating its Turkish districts. In April 1897 the sultan declared war on Greece and, within thirty days, routed its land forces and threatened to take Athens. This debacle led to a precipitous decline of Greece's international reputation, and the hope of winning Crete had to be delayed for another fifteen years and part of Thessaly had to be receded to the victorious Sultan.

It cannot be said, however, that this defeat led to any diminution in nationalist agitation in Greece. The *Ethniké Hetaireia* remained alive and the fate of ministries often depended upon their ability to pursue policies favored by it. The Greek cause on Crete was pushed implacably by a gifted lawyer who was to become Greece's greatest modern statesman, Eleutherios Venizelos. And in Macedonia Greek agents anxiously watched the maneuvers of their rivals, the Bulgars and the Serbs.

Turkey and the Balkans / In the course of the nineteenth century, the Ottoman Empire had been forced, step by step, to yield to the claims of its national minorities and to give up territories that had once made it an unrecognized but very real European power. In the first half of the century Serbia and Montenegro had won their autonomy and Greece its independence; even before the Crimean War Turkish control over Rumania was slight and, after it, it was virtually nonexistent; the Balkan insurrections of the 1870s and the war with Russia had detached Bulgaria from the Empire, while snapping the last legal ties with Serbia; and the 1880s had been marked by forced cessions to Greece and the loss of Eastern Rumelia to the Bulgarian state. By the end of the century, Turkish possessions in Europe comprised only a belt of territory that extended from the Straits of the Bosphorus and the Dardanelles westward, over Thrace, what was left of Rumelia, and Macedonia, to Albania and the Epirus and the waters of the Adriatic Sea. In addition, the Turkish government held legal title to the provinces of Bosnia and Herzegovina which had passed under Austrian administration in 1878.

There was every expectation that these territories would not long remain Turkish. The Turkish government had for generations been characterized by administrative inefficiency and corruption and had been entirely unresponsive to the admonitions of the great powers and their insistence upon reform. Even its staunchest supporters among those powers were losing heart; and Lord Salisbury intimated in the 1890s that Great Britain had for years been putting its money on the wrong horse in supporting the Ottoman Empire. On the other hand, the number of those who coveted the Turkish possessions in Europe was uncomfortably large, including not only Greece, Bulgaria, and Serbia but Austria, who had an interest in Macedonian railway routes; and it could not be assumed that Rumania and Russia would remain disinterested in the case of changes either. The knowledge that a partition of Turkey's remaining possessions would be complicated and dangerous, therefore, counseled caution, and most statesmen preferred to play a waiting game.

In 1908, however, to the consternation of Balkan, Hapsburg, and Russian statesmen, there came evidence that Turkey might be on the point of becoming not a declining but a reviving power, not a passive but an active participant in the politics of southeastern Europe. In July of that year, a revolutionary party calling themselves the Young Turks seized control of the government in Constantinople, having first managed to detach the army from the side of the despotic Sultan Abdul

Hamid II. The Sultan was forced to agree to elections for a national parliament and to constitutional changes that promised to transform Turkey into a liberal state.

The enthusiasm with which this revolution was greeted in the Sultan's dominions and the energies it released were in sharp contrast to the spiritless inactivity of the Turkish government in the last quarter of a century. They seemed to herald a tightening up of the administration of the Empire, a more vigorous assertion of Turkish rights (in Bosnia, for example), and perhaps even a campaign to recover lost rights and territory. The very possibility of this aroused the apprehension of the Balkan states and those great powers with vital interests in southeastern Europe and tempted them to take action to forestall disappointment. Thus, the victory of the Young Turks had effects as revolutionary as the Serbian upheaval of 1903. But the events it precipitated will be discussed appropriately in the context of great-power politics in the decade before World War I.

17

Imperial Russia, 1871-1914

In Anton Chekhov's *The Cherry Orchard*, the "perpetual student" Trofimov has a speech at the end of the second act that must have profoundly moved the audience when the play was first performed in Moscow in January 1904.

> We are at least two hundred years behind, we have really gained nothing yet, we have no definite attitude to the past, we do nothing but theorise or complain of depression or drink vodka. It is clear that to begin to live in the present we must first expiate our past, we must break with it; and we can expiate it only by suffering, by extraordinary unceasing labor.

Ever since the 1860s speeches like this had been made by Russian intellectuals. The fact that Russia lagged behind the major nations of the western world in material progress and in the evolution of its political institutions was obvious to anyone whose view extended beyond the confines of his own country. Awareness of it governed the thinking of the majority of Russians who were politically conscious, making them dissatisfied with the *status quo*. There was no unity of view among them, however, concerning the nature of desirable change or the means of effecting it, although, generally speaking, the advocates of reform divided into three main groupings. The first were those who wanted economic and social improvements granted from above—that is, by imperial ukase or administrative action—without fundamental alteration of the political or social system. This group included Tsar Alexander II in his earlier years and a long line of bureaucratic reformers from Miliutin to Stolypin. The second group, which was composed of university professors, civil servants, members of the professions, and representatives of the growing capitalist class, believed that Russia must seek to emulate the liberal countries of Western Europe, attaining gradual reform by the progressive extension of political rights. The third, and least homogeneous, group was composed of revolutionaries of various types and with various programs, most of whom, however, were agreed that the break with the past must be a violent one.

Opposed to these apostles of change were those members of the governing class, at the court, in the higher civil service and the armed forces, in the church and among the landed gentry, who consciously opposed change for ideological or material reasons, and the inert mass of the population, which was sunk in ignorance and traditionalism. The political influence of organized reaction and the unresponsiveness of the masses helped to defeat or delay the kinds of reform advocated by the first two groups mentioned above and, in the end, to discredit those who favored them; and this meant that, as the years passed, more and more people came to believe in the inevitability of a truly radical reformation of conditions in Russia, including the actual overthrow of the dynasty.

ECONOMIC CONDITIONS

The Agrarian Problem / Nothing better illustrates the backwardness of Russian by western standards than the lagging pace of Russian agriculture through the period under discussion. Basically, the problem here was one of rural overpopulation, but this was aggravated by other things. The land would have supported many more people than it did if, after the emancipation edict, the traditional communal organization of agriculture had not been maintained (see p. 249). The system of land distribution commonly used by the communes necessitated a reliance upon the three-field system as the only practical method of rotation, and this meant that a third of communal lands were always producing nothing. The productive capacity of the soil was handicapped also by a lack of technical knowledge among the peasantry and by the failure of the government to provide information about methods of intensive cultivation or enough credit to bring machinery and fertilizer within the grasp of the small landholder. While the population increased, therefore, the yield remained stationary. Even so, the pressure upon the soil might have been relieved if the government had not been opposed to having its subjects move about at will. Without papers, which the authorities were reluctant to give, the rural masses had to remain stationary and, in hard years, to starve.

It was possible, of course, for individual peasants to increase their holdings by purchasing or leasing land from noble landlords. To purchase land, however, required funds which very few peasants possessed and the government was slow to extend credit facilities. Even when a Peasants Land Bank was founded in 1883, its terms were such that it could be resorted to only by the wealthier peasantry. Leasing took many forms and, for the most vulnerable peasantry, it became a kind of sharecropping that was accompanied by special dues and corvées which were not essentially different from those exacted before the emancipation edict. In whatever form, leasing, too, was an option that was open to a very small minority; and the great mass of the peasantry continued to live in the communes in conditions of deepening poverty. It is not surprising that the memory of the exciting promise of the days of emancipation should gradually have been transformed into a legend that the tsar's wishes and the peasants' hopes had been betrayed by evil forces, and that some day justice would be done and another greater sharing out of land, by an expropriation of the proprietors, would take place. In hard times, the willingness to wait wore thin; in 1902, for instance, there were serious peasant uprisings in some parts of European Russia.

The government was always aware of the misery of the rural masses and made sporadic efforts to relieve it, by reduction of land and poll taxes, occasional moratoriums on redemption payments, and the like. But until Stolypin's time, the reforms were palliative rather than basic, partly because the government was afraid of alienating the noble land-owning class by being too generous with the peasantry. The government always seemed to be saying what Alexander II had said in 1861 to a delegation of peasants from Tula: "There will be no emancipation except the one I have granted you. Obey the law and the statutes. Work and toil! Be obedient to the authorities and to noble landowners!"

Industry and Labor / In contrast to agriculture, Russian industry showed decided signs of growth in this period, although it did not reach a magnitude capable of relieving the agricultural overpopulation. The most marked gains were made by the textile and metallurgical industries. The growth of the metal industries received its impetus from the rapid railway building of the 1870s, which continued, although at a slower rate, through the 1880s and accelerated in the next decade, when the government became concerned with the deficiencies of its strategical rail net, and especially of facilities for westward troop movement and the supply of the new defensive works built during the 1890s. Between 1889 and 1902, total rail mileage doubled. The demand for steel rails and iron wheels was one of the principal reasons for the development of the great new coal and iron industry in the Donetz Basin and the rise of such new industrial centers as Ekaterinoslav and Rostov-on-Don. Another industrial area of growing importance was that around Baku in the oil fields of the Caucasus.

The government was less hesitant in extending assistance to industry than it sometimes seemed to be in dealing with agricultural problems. It promoted the building of railways by subventions of various kinds to private firms (and, at a later date, bought them out on terms favorable to the owners). It aided the metallurgical industry by granting state contracts and imposing heavy duties upon the goods of foreign competitors. From the late 1870s on, Russian tariffs showed a general increase, textiles benefiting from protection as much as the metal goods. Finally, industry in general benefited from the policies of Count S. Y. Witte (1849–1915), who, as minister of finance from 1892 to 1903, set out systematically to attract capital to Russia in order to encourage industrial expansion. His method of doing this was to use tariffs to increase state revenues and create a gold reserve sufficiently large to enable Russia to adopt the gold standard, thus enhancing its international fiscal standing. Witte accomplished his primary goal in 1897; and foreign capital began almost immediately to come into the country. By 1900, there were 269 foreign firms operating in Russia, helping to exploit her mineral and oil deposits and to stimulate such new industries as electrical and chemical engineering.

This progress was purchased at the cost of new social and political problems. As in other countries, the prevailing tendency in industrial organization was toward large-scale capitalist enterprises, and the appearance of such establishments, armed with all the advantages that mechanization and superior capital resources can bring, made inevitable the decline of craft industries, which also contributed to the complications of the agrarian probem in those areas where handicrafts had supplemented peasant incomes.

At the same time, conditions in the new capitalist enterprises resembled those that prevailed in England in the 1820s and France in the 1840s (see pp. 99 and 73). Pent up in squalid tenement slums or in miserable company barracks, the factory workers had to work 14 to 16 hours a day for wages so trifling that the pay of the head of the family was not sufficient to support its other members, so that women and children also had to labor in the foundries and the mines. Factory inspection, sanitary laws, and safety precautions were, until very late in the century, nonexistent.

Against these conditions and against the steady decline of their real income, the workers had no means of protection. They were caught in an economic squeeze caused by the fact that the growth of industry was not rapid enough to keep pace with the numbers of landless and job-hungry peasants; and, as long as the labor supply exceeded demand, the factory and mine owners could keep their workers at the barest subsistence level. Until the 1880s, the government took only a theoretical interest in labor grievances; and, even when regulation began, its first effect was further to hurt workers' income. The law forbidding the employment of children under 12 (1882), legislation later in the decade prohibiting night work for women and adolescents in certain industries, and the laws of the Witte period, which regulated the working day of all workers, were estimable reforms, long needed; but, at a time when hourly real wages were very low, they must have been regarded as a dubious gain by many workers.

The right to form protective organizations of their own was denied to Russian workers. In 1874, while English trade unions were being given a new charter of liberty by the Disraeli government (see p. 291), the Russian penal code laid down a scale of heavy punishments for anyone engaged in organizing societies that were likely to encourage hatred between employers and employees. The definition of such societies was sufficiently broad to include even purely benevolent societies, to say nothing of those that were designed to improve the lot of the workers by exerting economic pressure upon proprietors. Although certain branches of the state service, notably the Ministry of Finance, believed that a more enlightened policy would make for labor peace and greater production, the government in general cooperated with anti-union employers, on the theory that unions represented a political threat to the regime. Troops were often placed at the disposal of employers to put down unrest; and agents were put in factories to spy out attempts at illegal organization or to identify agitators. In 1901 the Ministry of the Interior tried another tack in its fight against unions. It established a workers' society under police patronage, the main purpose of which was to organize patriotic demonstrations, which, it was apparently hoped, would satisfy the workers' desire for direct action. The society was not successful and was disbanded when it was discovered that it supplied a useful cover for the spread of socialist propaganda.

Neither the government's repressive and diversionary tactics nor its cautious reforms prevented labor unrest. Despite the lack of legal organization, strikes were not infrequent from the 1870s on. A serious strike in the Moscow textile industry in 1885 persuaded the government to pass legislation limiting the employers' use of monetary fines for breaches of discipline; and new stoppages in the same industry in 1896 and 1897 prompted Witte's labor legislation. Two years later, Russia entered a general economic depression which was felt particularly heavily in the metal and oil industries and from which the country had not completely recovered when the war with Japan began. The effect of this was both to increase the number of strikes and to change their character. After 1900 the objectives of the workers always included political demands, and their strikes were often short and designed not to win economic concessions but to serve as demonstrations against the regime. Sympathy strikes also made their appearance. In November 1902 a general strike was declared in Rostov-on-Don and had to be put down by government troops; and in the following years a strike at Baku set off a chain reaction of labor walkouts and demonstrations in other industrial towns.

Foreign Trade / Russia's share in the world's trade did not exceed 4 percent, which was not markedly higher than it had been in the first half of the nineteenth century. The most striking development in the structure of trade was the steady growth of grain exports, from a yearly average of about 1,120,000 tons in 1860 to about 6,945,000 tons in 1897. Grain represented only 15 percent of the total value of Russian exports in 1836–1840, but about 50 percent after 1871; and this heavy reliance on the grain trade, had effects outside the purely economic sphere, notably in the area of foreign affairs. At the turn of the century, in a period of acute economic depression in Russia, the German government, under pressure from its own agriculturists, passed a tariff law that virtually excluded Russian grain from the German market (see p. 393). This action reinforced anti-German feeling among the Russian governing class (many members of which were hurt financially by the new tariffs) and strengthened the Franco-Russian alliance that had been concluded in 1894 (see p. 465).

POLITICAL DEVELOPMENTS

The Last Years of Alexander II / On April 4, 1866, a young man named D. V. Karakozov tried unsuccessfully to assassinate Alexander II. His shot was a kind of signal for the government to reverse its gears and turn away from the liberalism that had guided official policy since the end of the Crimean War and produced the emancipation edict, the establishment of the zemstvos, and the reorganization of the judicial system (see

p. 248). There was still some reforming activity. In the 1870s, the minister of war, D. A. Miliutin, completed a fundamental shake-up of the whole military system that brought a reduction of the top-heavy army bureaucracy, a new regional organization, the appointment for the first time of a chief of the general staff, and, in 1874, the introduction of compulsory military service for all able males. These reforms, which laid the basis for the modern Russian army, were accompanied by disciplinary changes that somewhat reduced the brutal treatment formerly meted out to the ranks; and, generally, they can be described as progressive in temper.

The military reforms, however, were an exception forced on the government by the unmistakeable superiority of western armies in the wars in the Crimea and in central Europe. In matters less obviously vital to the security of the state, an increasingly reactionary tendency was apparent. This was true, for instance, in the field of education where, under the inspiration of Count Dimitri Tolstoy, minister of education from 1866 until 1880, academic freedom in the universities was virtually extinguished, the faculties being commanded to make reports to the police about student opinion and all student activities being prohibited. Simultaneously, Tolstoy declared war on natural science, reducing the time allotted to it in secondary school curricula and enforcing a much greater emphasis upon classical and modern languages, literature, history, geography, religion, and other subjects that he appeared to regard as politically and morally innocuous.

These measures were regarded as an attempt to shelter Russian youth from modern knowledge and were widely resented. From a practical point of view, they neither protected students from subversive influences nor provided a very effective education, since Russia did not have enough competent classicists to make the reforms work. At a time when the country was producing scientists of world reputation—D. I. Mendeleev (1843–1901) in chemistry, I. I. Mechnikov (1845–1916) in biology, I. P. Pavlov (1849–1936) in physiology—they made it difficult for those great scholars to find and train students. In a curious way, this probably aided rather than hurt the future of Russian science, although not without doing a disservice to other disciplines. Hugh Seton-Watson has written that Tolstoy's policy confirmed Russian intellectuals in their naive belief that only scientific education is progressive and in their equally naive contempt for the humanities and for all disinterested learning. This had far-reaching repercussions, not least of all in the intellectual life of the Soviet Union.

Tolstoy's measures were strongly supported by the tsar, who in his later years, fell more and more under the influence of the ultra-conservatives. Prominent among those was the Moscow journalist M. N. Katkov

An illustration for Leo Tolstoy's *Resurrection* (1898) by the Russian artist, Leonid Pasternak, 1862–1945. His son Boris (see photo opposite) was the Russian novelist and poet.

(1818–1887), who had the distinction of having first published Leo N. Tolstoy's great novels *War and Peace* (1869) and *Anna Karenina* (1877), but probably considered his work in behalf of a conservative domestic policy and a nationalistic foreign policy as infinitely more important. There is no doubt that Katkov helped convince Alexander II that "destructive notions" were rife among the youth of the land and that a revolutionary movement of real importance threatened the regime.

When one considers the disharmony of opinion and the lack of organization that prevailed among critics of the regime in the 1860s and 1870s, this can be seen to have been an exaggeration. Katkov himself was shocked and revolted by the rise of the attitude that Turgenev, in his famous novel *Fathers and Sons* (1861), called nihilism—an exaggerated realism that rejected all traditional values, turned its back on the past, and insisted upon the rights of individuality and the human reason. That there was much talk along these lines among the progressive intelligentsia there can be no doubt; but nihilism could hardly be considered as a force capable of jeopardizing political stability.

More important was the doctrine of populism which in general held

Boris Pasternak, 1890–1960. Pasternak won the Nobel Prize for Literature in 1958 for his novel about the Russian Revolution, *Dr. Zhivago.* He was compelled by government pressure to renounce the honor. (PANTHEON BOOKS)

that social revolution was necessary, that it need not wait upon the achievement of a capitalism as mature as that of Western Europe but could be achieved on the basis of Russia's system of communal land tenure, and that the peasantry would be the driving force behind the revolutionary upheaval. Yet there was little agreement among the early populists about tactics and program, and in the 1860s and early 1870s populism tended to be a formless, idealistic, and highly unrealistic force. In the year 1873, when the remarkable movement "to the people" inspired thousands of young men and women of the educated class to go as missionaries to the peasants to preach the cause of revolution, they found little response, having much the same experience as Bazarov in *Fathers and Sons* who, as Turgenev tells us, prided himself on being able to talk to the peasants, but never suspected "that in their eyes he was all the while something of the nature of a buffooning-clown." The populist movement of this period made the mistake of idealizing the peasant and expecting wonders from him, ignoring the fact that he was too illiterate and brutalized to comprehend its message.

If the government had let matters take their course, this movement might have died a-borning. But police persecution and mass trials of agitators not only kept it alive but improved its efficiency. After the failure of the movement to the people and the arrests and trials that followed it, populist leaders began to use methods advocated earlier by Serge Nechaev and Peter Tchakev. Nechaev, a former follower of Bakunin, and the leader of a short-lived secret society in the 1860s, had emphasized the uses of terror as a means of promoting revolutionary objectives and had finally given a dramatic demonstration of the meaning of revolutionary discipline by cold-bloodedly murdering an associate suspected of what has come in our own time to be called deviationism. (This murder supplied the theme of Dostoevsky's novel *The Demons*.) Tchakev, who has been considered a forerunner of Lenin, taught that successful revolutions depended less upon the action of the masses than upon the vision and determination of a revolutionary elite. In the late 1870s, the populists accepted secrecy and terrorism as their methods, and, in particular, advocated the use of political assassination as the effective method of advertising the need for revolution and attracting mass support to the cause. While almost any high-ranking official was considered worth killing, the tsar himself became the most desirable target; and the society "The People's Will," led by Andrew Zheleabov and Sophie Perovsky, seems to have made Alexander's death their *raison d'être* and to have organized at least seven attempts on his life. In March 1881, they finally succeeded. As Alexander II was returning from a military review in St. Petersburg, a bomb was thrown at his carriage, wrecking it without harming him. A few moments later, as he stood beside it, a second bomb exploded at his feet, and he died within hours.

Full Reaction, 1881–1905 / The perpetrators of this deed were hunted down and hanged; their organizations were smashed; and the revolutionary movement was made ineffective for a generation. The years that followed the death of the tsar-liberator were years of full reaction, in which progressive views of any kind rendered their possessor suspect. In Dostoevsky's *The Demons*, Captain Lebiatkyn says:

> If I were to try to bequeath my skin for a drum to, let us say, the Akmolinsky infantry regiment, in which I had the honor of starting my service, with the proviso that the Russian national anthem might be beaten on it every day in front of the drawn-up regiment, they would consider it a liberal idea and forbid my skin to be used for that purpose.

This, as well as anything, describes the atmosphere that prevailed under Alexander III (1881–1894).

The new tsar was an unsophisticated, conscientious ruler with a firm will and unrelievedly conservative views. His political principles are usually summed up in the words Orthodoxy, Autocracy, and Nationalism. This description is just, for he was personally devout and regarded the Greek Orthodox Church as a bulwark against subversive influences and the spread of free thinking, was uncompromising in his defense of the prerogatives of the crown, and was a firm advocate of a policy of Russification at home, with respect to subject nationalities, and Pan-Slavism abroad.

Of Alexander III's chosen ministers only three need be mentioned. The most important personality in this reign and the first part of the succeeding one was Konstantine Pobedonostsev (1827–1907), procurator of the Holy Synod, that is to say, lay chairman of the governing body of the Russian Orthodox Church. An opponent of all western ideas, he was particularly vehement in his belief that a free press was the root of all evil and that parliaments served only the interests of their members. His ideal government was one of rigidly centralized autocracy, and it was largely due to his influence that a plan for a national legislative council with limited powers, which was being considered by Alexander II before his death, was jettisoned, and that the new tsar also curtailed the rights of the zemstvos and the town councils established in the 1860s.

Pobedonostsev's policies were ably seconded by the former minister of education, Tolstoy, who became minister of the interior in 1882 and immediately launched a program that tightened the already formidable censorship of the press, reduced the autonomy of the universities and destroyed the remnants of academic freedom, and placed libraries and reading rooms under stringent observation, removing books which—in official language—"do not correspond to the level of intellectual development and understanding of the simple people." This library policy was merely a reflection of the general educational policy inaugurated in the previous reign by Tolstoy and now administered by Count Delianov, minister of education from 1882 to 1897. The principles guiding elementary education in particular were designed to prevent social mobility and to make the lower orders content with their place in society. How greatly the government feared what education might do to the minds of the working class is perhaps illustrated by how little they accomplished in the field of elementary education. At the end of Alexander III's reign, only 21 percent of the population of Russia could read and write; and no appreciable change was to be made here until free compulsory education was instituted in 1908.

When Alexander III died of nephritis in October 1894, his passing brought no alleviation of this atmosphere of persecution and thought control. The new sovereign, Nicholas II (1894–1917), possessed a political philosophy that was not markedly different from that of his father, although it was not accompanied by the steadfastness and resolution characteristic of that ruler. Nicholas was always a tool in the hands of stronger individuals: Pobedonostsev in the first ten years of his reign, as well as certain of his military advisers, active and retired, like Bezobrazov, General Kuropatkin, and Admiral Alekseev, who advocated a dynamic foreign policy and were behind the disastrous adventure in the Far East; in later years, his wife and her favorites, especially the monk Gregory Rasputin, who won royal favor by supposedly saving the heir apparent, a victim of hemophilia, from death by bleeding. One thing in common all those who exerted influence on Nicholas possessed: the desire that he should do nothing to relax the prevailing absolutism; and the tsar was led by them to try to outdo his father in autocratic inflexibility. Since Nicholas II had no conspicuous talents of his own, it is perhaps not surprising that his reign, which had a tragic beginning, when 1300 people were trampled to death because of police inefficiency during the accession celebration, should have been marked by progressively greater tragedies until its denouement in war, revolution, and the end of the Romanov dynasty.

Reformers and Revolutionaries / The accession of the new tsar brought a revival of political activity not only on the part of advocates of revolution but among moderate liberal groups who had been relatively quiet since the death of Alexander II. In the zemstvos particularly there was an upsurge of hope in liberal reform, and leaders in these organs of local government began to call for a widening of their competence and for the creation of some kind of central zemstvo organization that could play a role in the national government. These proposals received short shrift from the emperor, and when zemstvo leaders tried on their own to establish a continuing national organization, its meetings were forbidden by the police. The zemstvos nevertheless continued to serve as forums for liberal opinion, and the frequent resolutions that they passed on matters beyond their jurisdiction made it clear to the government that such opinion existed.

The revolutionary opposition, which also revived during the first years of Nicholas' reign, was composed of two main organizations, the first of which was the Russian Social Democratic Labor party. The origins of this party lay back in the 1880s when George Plekhanov (1857–1918), a former populist, emigrated to Switzerland and founded a socialist organization called Liberation of Labor. After his break with populism, Plekhanov adopted the main tenets of Marxism and insisted that Russia must follow the pattern set in the west and pass through capitalism before it could hope for a transition to socialism. He rejected the faith in the peasant masses that had been characteristic of populism and called for the creation of a disciplined working-class party. Plekhanov's literary gifts and analytical power contributed to the wide dissemination of Marxist thought in his own country (Lenin once said that he had managed singlehanded to "rear a whole generation of Russian Marxists"), and by the mid-1890s there were twenty Marxist groups in St. Petersburg alone. Since they had to operate clandestinely, they were not very effective. When their first congress convened at Minsk in 1898 to discuss the organization of a nation-wide party, it was poorly attended, and several of the delegates and two members of the central committee elected by the congress were arrested almost immediately by the police. After this, leadership of Russian socialism necessarily shifted to the "League of Russian Social Democrats Abroad," which was located in Switzerland. It was among these exiles that the significant doctrinal developments took place in the next years and plans were made for the second party congress that met in Brussels (and London) in 1903.

This conference is remembered today primarily because, during its debates, a conflict of view—and one that had important results in the history of world socialism—developed between a group of delegates headed by one of Plekhanov's older associates, Y. O. Martov, and a second led by the most brilliant of the younger leaders, Lenin (1870–1924).

The second son of a school inspector in Simbirsk on the Volga, Lenin, whose real name was Vladimir Ilyich Ulyanov, had become a hardened enemy of the imperial regime in 1887, while still a schoolboy, when his older brother was arrested and hanged for complicity in an assassination plot against the emperor. Participation in a student protest at the University of Kazan a few years later led to the termination of his own formal education, the memory of his brother's crime hardening official minds against him. He nevertheless persisted in his studies and passed his law examinations without the benefit of university training. But he then fell under the influence of Plekhanov's writings and turned his attention completely to the study of Marxism and to practical work in a reading circle in St. Petersburg that was intended to indoctrinate the working classes. This eventually led to trouble with the police and to a term of imprisonment and three years of exile in Siberia, which Lenin employed in further theoretical studies. After his release, he managed to make his way abroad; he became one of the first editors of the party newspaper *Iskra* ("The Spark"); and his writings soon won him recognition as a theorist whose stature was comparable with that of Plekhanov himself.

During the dispute with Martov at the 1903 congress, which turned largely on matters of party organization, a momentary voting edge gave Lenin the opportunity to name his faction the Bolsheviks (or majority-ites), his opponents automatically becoming the Mensheviks (or minorityites). The names stuck, even during times when Lenin's group was no longer a true majority, and as years passed the momentary differences of 1903 hardened into differences of principle. Both sects continued to hold to the basic tenets of Marxism; both continued to be dedicated to the overthrow of tsardom; and both, following Plekhanov, believed that the fall of the imperial regime would be followed by a period of bourgeois democratic government before socialism could become effective. But, whereas Lenin and the Bolsheviks held that this period of bourgeois rule must be regarded as a purely transitional one during which the party pushed the proletariat and the peasantry on to the final revolutionary effort, the Mensheviks were inclined to regard it as a period that would presumably last a long time and during which genuine cooperation would take place between bourgeois and socialist parties. The Mensheviks were, thus, closer to the revisionist parties of Western Europe than they themselves admitted.

A second important difference had to do with party organization. As he had written in his brilliant pamphlet *What Is to Be Done?* in 1902, Lenin believed that the socialist movement must be led by an elite of professional revolutionaries, since the mass of the workers, without the discipline that such leaders provided, would lose their revolutionary *élan* and sink into the swamp of reformism. Translated into terms of organization, this implied a small party with a centralized and disciplined structure and with no members who did not have definite tasks assigned to them which they were bound to carry out in accordance with a line determined by the party directorate. At Brussels, Martov protested that he did not want a party whose members "abdicated their right to think"; and the Mensheviks always argued for a more comprehensive party, open not only to professional revolutionaries but to all workers and intellectuals who believed in its goals. But in the long run it was Lenin's view rather than theirs that triumphed, although not without proving that their worst fears were justified.

The victory of Bolshevism was still, however, far in the future; and in the revived revolutionary movement of Nicholas II's first years, Marxism did not have the authority it was to achieve later. It still had a powerful competitor in populism, which won many new converts in Russia and among the exiles in the 1890s, and which inspired the founding of the Socialist Revolutionary party in the first five years of the new century.

The Socialist Revolutionaries had many beliefs in common with the Social Democrats. Their principal differences lay in the importance they attributed to the peasantry (considered by both Bolsheviks and Mensheviks as a potentially negligible revolutionary force), their readiness to believe that socialism would follow directly upon the fall of the monarchy, and their greater belief in the efficacy of political terrorism. Although Lenin denied that the Social Democrats ever "rejected terror on principle," both he and most of his colleagues felt that its employment distracted revolutionaries from more important tasks of propaganda and organization. The Socialist Revolutionaries, on the other hand, not only approved daring acts of violence but actually had a terroristic organization which, under orders from the party's central committee, planned and executed political murders.

The Revolution of 1905 / As we have noted above, Russian industry experienced a protracted slump in the years 1899–1903, in which factory shutdowns caused great suffering among the working classes. Before the country had fully recovered from the effects of the depression, the reckless policy of the government in the Far East had led to war with Japan (see p. 462), and this necessitated a calling up of reserves from the rural districts that disrupted agricultural production and distribution sufficiently to cause serious shortages and new curtailment of industrial employment. The news from the fighting fronts was uniformly bad, a fact that contributed further to general dissatisfaction with the state of things, the more so because the government (as if trying to prove the truth of Captain Lebiatkyn's melancholy prophecy) repressed all patriotic movements in support of the war for fear that they might be a front for revolutionary activity. This was the fate, for instance, of a zemstvo organization to aid the wounded, which was made ineffective by restrictions imposed by the minister of the interior, V. K. Plehve.

In these years of growing discontent all of the opposition groups became furiously active. This was most spectacularly true of the Socialist Revolutionaries, who carried out a program of terror which, between 1901 and 1904, killed two provincial governors, a minister of education, and two ministers of the interior, the second being the much hated Plehve who was blown to pieces by a bomb in July 1904. The Social Democrats confined themselves, for the most part, to propaganda among factory workers, the effectiveness of which was shown in the St. Petersburg strike of January 1905. As for the liberal movement, which had been centered in the zemstvos, it tended to become broader in membership and acquired a foreign organization, the "League for Liberation," and a journal, edited by P. N. Miliukov and a former Social Democrat named Struve, which boldly called for the end of autocracy and the introduction of constitutional monarchy. By the fall of 1904, the liberals were holding banquets in St. Petersburg and Moscow similar to those in Paris in February 1848 (see p. 129), and something of the same atmosphere reigned in the country as a whole. "We have been talking and talking for fifty years and reading pamphlets," Chekhov's Uncle Vanya had said in 1899. "It's about time to leave off." This seemed to represent the national mood at the end of 1904.

The accumulated tension exploded at the beginning of the new year. In January 1905 a strike broke out in St. Petersburg and tied up several factories employing thousands of workers; and on Sunday, January 9, many of these joined in a protest march to the Winter Palace. They were organized and led by an Orthodox priest named Gapon, an equivocal figure who had organized the "Assembly of Russian Workers," a patriotic union approved by the police, who was later a Socialist Revolutionary, then once more a police agent (or collaborator), and who was finally "executed" by the Socialist Revolutionaries in 1906. Whatever his ultimate motives, Gapon seems in January to have been sincerely desirous of having the tsar consider the grievances of the workers, and his march was organized with that in view. As usual, the government acted suspiciously and in a spirit of panic. Troops blocked the march and then opened fire on its columns, killing and wounding hundreds of people and causing the day to be commemorated as Bloody Sunday.

Immediately, a general strike gripped the capital, and spread rapidly to Moscow, Saratov, Ekaterinoslav, and the principal towns of Poland and the Baltic provinces. A new wave of terrorism cost the life of the tsar's uncle, the Grand Duke Serge. Peasant revolts began in February in the province of Kursk and spread rapidly in subsequent months; and a Peasant Union was founded in June. Both the workers and the urban professional men formed new organizations. The armed services were shaken by reverses in the war (Port Arthur had fallen in December 1904; the Russian army had been routed at Mukden in February; and Admiral Rozhdestvensky's Baltic fleet had been virtually wiped out in the Straits of Tsushima at the end of May) (see p. 462); they also fell under the revolutionary spell. In June the crew of the battleship *Potiemkin* mutinied at Odessa—an event that must have sent a thrill of terror through court circles.

With his world apparently falling to pieces around him, the tsar acted hesitantly and without determination, asserting his intention of summoning a consultative assembly "of the most worthy people," but making it clear, by certain decrees of August, that the franchise would be such as to exclude the greater part of the intellectuals and workers. This attitude encouraged new agrarian and urban disturbances, as well as railway and university strikes and another general strike in the capital; and, in October, the first Soviet of Workers Delegates was formed in St. Petersburg and began to agitate for municipal self-government. In face of this accumulation of woes, the tsar seriously considered attempting to rule by military dictatorship but was finally persuaded by his advisers to issue the so-called October Manifesto instead. This document provided for a broadening of fundamental liberties (including the guarantee of press freedom and freedom of speech and assembly), announced the calling of a national legislative assembly or Duma, which would be elected by a franchise much wider than that provided for in August, and reorganized the Council of Ministers on western lines.

With this decree, which apparently marked the transformation of autocratic Russia into a constitutional monarchy, the unity of the revolutionary movement dissolved and its fire subsided. There were some attempts by radical elements in the zemstvo organization and the organized workers groups to push for greater demands, but the moderates professed to be satisfied, and public opinion was beginning to swing against the radicals. This was shown by the support given by the lower-middle class and unskilled workers to the "black hundreds," gangs of hooligans organized by the reactionary agrarian elements and the church and used to attack opponents of the government. When the police dared break up the St. Petersburg Soviet in December, it was a sign that the regime was recovering its confidence. The police action touched off sympathy strikes and large-scale fighting in Rostov and Moscow, but this was the last gasp of the revolution of 1905.

The Constitutional Experiment / Once relative order had been restored, it soon became clear that nothing very much had been won by the revolution after all, and that it was impossible, for the moment at least, to do anything about it. In the years from 1906 to 1914, the great mass of the Russian people seemed to sink back into apathy; and among the politically active elements in the nation, all the strength and unity of will seemed to lie on the side of reaction rather than on that of progress. The Left was hopelessly split. The liberal forces were divided among the Constitutional Democrats or Cadets, who wanted a greater degree of parliamentary power, and the Octobrists, who were content with the tsar's Manifesto. The Social Democrats were embroiled in intestine feuds; and the Socialist Revolutionaries were entirely absorbed in new plots against individuals. On the other side, the nobility, the landlords, the church, the bureaucrats, the soldiers, and the Pan-Slav patriots organized a "Union of the Russian People" to encourage the tsar to resist further concessions and to regain the ground he had ceded in October.

The tsar was readily amenable to this kind of prompting and, within three years, had deprived most of his promises of meaning. Before the first Duma met he had constituted a second parliamentary body by decree—a Council of the Empire that was largely appointive and whose assent was required to all laws before they went to the tsar for approval. When the Duma assembled, with the Cadets in large majority, it was

Tsar Nicholas II addressing the First Duma. The tsarina is standing beside him. (THE BETTMANN ARCHIVE)

confronted with an imperial announcement excluding certain "organic laws" from its consideration, stipulating that the military prerogatives of the sovereign were inviolate, and even limiting the parliamentary power of the purse by authorizing the government to operate, if necessary, without a budget. After this scarcely encouraging introduction, the Duma engaged in oratorical exercises for two months. The Cadets' attempt to force a real measure of ministerial responsibility was inflexibly opposed by the tsar, who finally dissolved the Duma and stated that he was "cruelly disappointed" that its members had "strayed into spheres beyond their competence."

A protest signed by 230 members of the Duma was ineffective, leading merely to the unseating of most of the signatories. The tsar's course was set and could no longer be diverted. During the meeting of the second Duma, from March to June 1907, the government actually arrested sixteen members for revolutionary activity, a palpable breach of parliamentary rights. After this inconclusive session, moreover, the franchise was drastically curtailed by decree (although electoral laws were supposed to be invalid without the Duma's assent) and was henceforth based on a system somewhat similar to that used in Prussia, so that the landlord class was given a preponderance of power. Thus, the Duma became a purely consultative body, without any real influence upon the actions of the ministers.

This might not have been disastrous if the tsar had chosen able ministers and given them the authority to remedy the worst of the administrative and economic abuses of the state. But these were precisely the years when the influence of Rasputin over the empress's mind began to grow, and people who could win or purchase the monk's favor were apt to be appointed to high office without regard to their qualifications. This sort of thing, and the tsar's personal lack of resolution when it came to key appointments, weakened the efficiency of all branches of the imperial administration, while discouraging attempts at reform. This was true, for instance, of the armed services, whose deficiencies had been made obvious by the Japanese war. Their correction, however, was entrusted to General Sukhomlinov, war minister from 1909 to 1914, who spent so much time combating intrigues against himself and conducting intrigues of his own that he found little time to improve the staff and communications system or to raise the level of officer education before Russia became involved in another and greater war.

The ablest of Nicholas' ministers in this period was P. A. Stolypin, prime minister from 1906 until 1911. He owed his position to his suppression of peasant risings in Saratov, where he was provincial governor in 1905, and to his known reputation for nationalism and conservatism; but he was no blind reactionary and showed himself capable of cooperating with liberal elements in the Duma whenever there was an opportunity to do so. Stolypin's first year as a prime minister was largely devoted to hunting down terrorists and breaking up revolutionary cells, an occupation in which he showed a ruthlessness that probably derived from the fact that, in August 1906, Socialist Revolutionaries had blown up his summer residence, killing thirty-two people and wounding twenty-two more, including Stolypin's son and daughter. Thereafter, he devoted his energies to agricultural reform, seeking to improve the efficiency of Russian agriculture by opening the way to modern methods of production. Specifically, he sought, by a series of laws passed in 1906, to reduce the restrictions that the village communes imposed on the individual peasants, which often destroyed their initiative (see p. 249), to help them secede from communes, and to promote communal redistribution of land so as to consolidate scattered holdings. Thanks to this legislation, about one tenth of the holdings in European Russia were consolidated by 1915 with resultant increases in production, and two and a half million households had broken away from the communes to become individual farmers. Russian agriculture was still backward in 1914, from the standpoint of the tenure of the mass of the peasantry and the methods they employed; but Stolypin's reforms had marked the first significant step forward since the emancipation edict.

It was characteristic of the regime that Stolypin suffered the same treatment meted out to Witte earlier, being attacked by reactionaries as a liberal and progressively losing the favor of the tsar as his personal stature grew. It was widely rumored in 1911 that he would soon be dismissed. Instead, while attending a theater performance in Kiev in September of that year, he was shot and killed by Dimitry Bogrov, a man who had been both a Socialist Revolutionary and a police spy, and who possessed a police pass at the time of his attack on the minister.

After this the government made few attempts to alleviate existing abuses. In an atmosphere of unrelieved reaction, Russia once more began to indulge in foreign adventures of the kind that had nearly proved disastrous in 1905 and were to prove so in 1917, when military defeat led to a greater revolution than that of 1905.

THE SUBJECT NATIONALITIES

Russification / Russia had as many subject nationalities as the Austro-Hungarian Empire and treated them no better. Besides those who could call themselves Russians, there were Ukrainians and White Russians, Poles, Germans, Lithuanians, Letts and Estonians, Rumanians, Armenians, various Turkish and Mongol peoples, some five million Jews, who were set apart and treated as an alien people, and Finns, who occupied a somewhat different position than the others.

The prevailing policy with respect to the nationalities, especially after the death of Alexander II, who had shown some respect for their separate cultures and customs, was designed to stamp out differences and to impose Russian modes of thought and speech upon them. Under Alexander III, for instance, a deliberate policy of Russification was directed against the Germans in the Baltic provinces, which included the introduction of Russian municipal institutions, the use of Russian as the language of instruction in the schools, the supersession of the German University of Dorpat by a Russian institution, and an attempt to weaken, and even destroy, the Lutheran religion by making the construction of new Lutheran churches dependent upon permission of the Holy Synod of the Orthodox Church. Similar policies were followed in this and the following reign in the case of the Armenians, the Tartars of the Volga, the Georgians, and other nationalities, and—as a general rule—Russification was always intensified in those areas where nationalist or revolutionary parties appeared.

The Jews were the conspicuous exception to this tendency, for every effort was made to make impossible any real assimilation of this people.

They had long been kept within a special Jewish Pale, comprising Poland and Lithuania, and, although Alexander II issued a series of decrees lightening this restriction and making greater freedom of movement possible for certain categories of Jews, this was reversed by his successor. The death of the tsar-liberator was attributed to them and resulted in fearful pogroms, encouraged by the police, in which thousands died. For the tsarist regime, as for tyrannical regimes elsewhere, victimization of the Jews became a safety valve for popular passions and a means of distracting the masses from other grievances. At the same time, extreme limitation of the number of Jews permitted to attend institutions of higher learning and other humiliating restrictions revealed the government's fixed intention of keeping the Jews in a state of permanent inferiority, and this explains the rapid increase in Jewish emigration, especially to the United States, in the 1890s.

Poland / After the suppression of the revolt of 1863 (see pp. 222 and 238), Russian policy in Poland was designed to break up centers of revolution and to weaken potentially dissident groups. Alexander II's government sought to promote these ends by suppressing the University of Warsaw and Russifying the schools, the courts, the railways, and the banks, and also by giving a more liberal interpretation of the emancipation edict than was employed in Russia proper in the hope of weakening the nationalist Polish landlord class. The nobility did tend to play a reduced role in Polish affairs in the subsequent period, but the nationalism they had represented was now preached by middle-class groups which grew up with the rapid development of Polish industry in this period. The National Democratic party became the most important of these, and in Roman Dmowski it had a leader whose teaching profoundly influenced those who forged Polish liberty in the war years. Nor was nationalism confined to this social group. The Polish Socialist party, founded in Paris in 1892, had a strong internationalist wing, headed by Rosa Luxemburg, who considered Polish independence as chimerical; but just as strong were those socialists who took their lead from Joseph Pilsudski (1867–1935), whose socialism was a thin veneer over a burning desire for freedom and who, one day, was to be dictator of a free Polish state (see p. 645).

During the revolution of 1905, there were serious disorders in Poland, and, in the first Russian Duma, Dmowski, who led the Polish delegation, tried to win support for Polish autonomy within the empire. This did not succeed, although the Duma approved some temporary relaxation of the Russification policy in Polish schools. These gains were wiped out in the Stolypin period, for that statesman was an ardent nationalist whose first action with respect to Poland was to withdraw the permission, granted in 1906, to establish private schools in which instruction in Polish would be allowed. Simultaneously, the electoral reform of 1907 greatly reduced Polish representation in the Duma, an action that increased resentment in Poland and encouraged the growth of a desire for a break with Russia.

Finland / Finland had been acquired by Russia in 1809; but until the end of the reign of Alexander II the connection had been a tenuous one, the state being constituted as a Grand Duchy with the emperor as grand duke, but having its own constitution and parliament and its own army, currency, and postal service. With the coming of reaction to Russia in 1883 and the growth of specific Russian nationalism, these rights were placed in jeopardy; and Alexander III took the first steps toward the Russification of Finnish institutions. The real turning point in Russo-Finnish relations, however, came in 1899 when an imperial decree stipulated that henceforth laws affecting both Finland and the rest of the empire would be within the jurisdiction of the Russian State Council, and the Finnish Diet would have only advisory powers with respect to them. This was followed by the absorption of the Finnish postal system by the Russian, the disbanding of the Finnish army, and a decree making Finns liable for service in the Russian armed services.

The Finnish people resisted these blows at their autonomy by a highly effective policy of passive resistance; and this, and the troubles attendant on the revolution of 1905, forced the revocation of the offensive decrees. This was only a temporary respite, however. As in the case of Poland, the policy of Russification was resumed under Stolypin, and there was a series of clashes between the Finnish Diet and the tsar's governor-general. By 1914, it was clear that the Russian government intended to wipe out Finnish autonomy, and recognition of this determined Finland's conduct in the last stages of the world war.

18

Imperial Expansion, 1871-1914

THE AGE OF IMPERIALISM

The Motive Factors / During the first three quarters of the nineteenth century few of the European states showed much interest in acquiring territory outside of Europe proper; and, in cases where new holdings were established in Africa or Asia (see p. 9), this was not always the result of conscious policy and was rarely accorded much popular support. This was true even in Great Britain, which had emerged from the wars of the eighteenth century and the conflict with Napoleon with the greatest accumulation of dependencies the world had ever seen. Englishmen who gave any thought to these areas were apt to be fretful about the military and administrative costs of possessing them and pessimistic about the possibility of holding them long enough to make good these expenditures. The experience of the American Revolution seemed to prove that colonies could not be made to pay and should not therefore be objectives of governmental policy. As for the other European states, their energies were for the most part absorbed by domestic problems and friction with their immediate neighbors, and the problem of expansion outside of Europe was too remote to arouse much interest.

All of this began to change in the late 1870s, and the 1880s and 1890s were years in which the European powers not only consolidated their existing non-European possessions but sought feverishly to add to them, with little regard for expense or for the political dangers involved. This was a period of imperialism, if we may use a much-abused word—that is, one in which empire-building became the accepted policy of all major powers and was supported by public opinion with a fervor that cut across class and economic lines.

How is one to account for the virtually unanimous pursuit of imperialistic policy by the governments of this period and for the enthusiasm with which it was supported even by those groups in society that received the least tangible advantage from it? The answer seems to lie in the economic and political conditions of this period and in its psychological atmosphere.

There is no doubt that economic factors played an important role in the growth of imperialistic activity. The growing maturity of European industry, the increase in productive capacity, and the accumulation of excess capital created groups of people inside all of the big nations who believed in the necessity of finding new markets, new sources of raw materials, and new areas for capital investment. These groups of individuals were inclined to support colonial policies and, in so far as they had political influence, to promote them, as were other people who, consciously or subconsciously, derived an economic advantage from national colonial enterprise: professional soldiers, shipping magnates, manufacturers of munitions or solar topees or mosquito netting, and the like. The hard times of the 1870s and 1880s helped to intensify their feelings and to persuade other groups to revise their views about the importance of colonies. In 1870, for instance, a delegation of workingmen presented a petition to Queen Victoria in which they argued that Britain's overseas possessions might help to reduce local distress if the government paid for the emigration of the unemployed; and this idea, which recurred frequently in different forms and under different auspices in the years that followed, indicated a growing belief that colonies need not be a liability after all. Finally, the general return to economic nationalism in the form of protectionism, which has been touched upon above (p. 287), aroused the fear, especially in countries which remained committed to free trade, that the area in which they could trade profitably would be steadily diminished unless they protected themselves by something like the British concept of "imperial federation"—which called for the creation, out of Britain's existing dependencies, of a great customs union in which British goods would receive preferential treatment—or by acquiring the richest of the remaining free areas of the world before the protectionist powers did.

The fact that such groups of interested parties existed and such ideas and apprehensions filled the minds of a good many people in most countries does not, of course, prove that economic factors "caused" imperialism. To assert, as the British liberal J. A. Hobson did in a famous study that appeared in 1902, that international finance was the directing force in imperialistic foreign policy, manipulating other influential groups through its control of the press and by more direct pressures, was to oversimplify and distort history, as Hobson himself admitted ruefully years later. To argue, as Lenin did in his brilliant essay *Imperialism, The Highest Stage of Capitalism* (1917), that capitalist states must become imperialistic in their policies simply because they are capitalistic was to give a predominance to the economic factor in policy formulation that was impossible to justify on the basis of concrete evidence.

If one insists upon thinking in terms of pressure groups, it is probably safe to say that missionary societies often played no less an important role than banking interests. One of the strongest determinants of both British and French policy in tropical Africa, for instance, was the anti-slavery movement. This cause was dramatized by the heroic work of Dr. David Livingstone, who walked the bush tracks of Africa for nearly twenty years accumulating evidence of the activities of Arab slavers, and by the devoted work of small mission communities in Nigeria and Nyasaland, which tried, often with arms in hand, to stem the tide of that shameful trade. It was publicized by eminent church leaders like Cardinal Lavigerie of France (see p. 368), founder of the *Société des missions africaines* in 1873 and the *Société anti-esclavagiste* in 1888, and was strongly supported by both Protestant and Catholic congregations, who often insisted on increased colonial responsibilities and could not be lightly disregarded by their governments.

Even when governments used economic arguments to justify their actions in colonial areas, they sometimes did so only because it seemed easier to win support this way than by speaking frankly of the political and strategical reasons for action. One might suppose, from the elaborate British explanations of their occupation of Egypt in 1882, that economic interests had brought them in. It is probably more accurate to say that their intervention was basically the result of the prevalent unrest in a country that lay athwart Britain's line of communication with India. In the case of the extension of British control over Nyasaland, Lord Salisbury, who had strong political reasons for desiring it, deliberately delayed action until he could arouse the interest of British business circles, which he did by inspiring articles in *The Times* about commercial advantage. Far from exercising a controlling influence over the diplomacy of imperialism, business interests often had to be cajoled or—as in the case of the German bankers who reluctantly supported the Berlin-Bagdad railway scheme—dragooned into supporting government policy.

Indeed, the more closely one studies the imperialism of this period, the more clearly it appears that the statesmen who directed the policies of the Great Powers embarked on imperialism with only an incidental consideration of economic factors. They were influenced much more directly by mutual suspicion and fear of future disaster, feelings that were encouraged by the psychological atmosphere of the years that followed the Franco-Prussian War. In the wake of that conflict, the significance of power had dawned upon the world, and the idea had taken root that great states possessed the respect of their neighbors only when they acted like great states and gave visible evidence of their power resources. Nations that had lost reputation either by military defeat or by inactivity were anxious now to demonstrate that they were not declining powers; and the most dramatic way of doing this was to increase the overseas territory under their control. Once they had embarked on this course they found it easy to convince themselves that failure to expand beyond the European area was the mark of decadence.

This note was struck first of all by Disraeli who, in a famous speech at the Crystal Palace in 1872, cried:

> I appeal to the sublime instinct of an ancient people. . . . The issue is not a mean one. It is whether you will be content to be a comfortable England, modelled and moulded upon Continental principles and meeting in due course an inevitable fate, or whether you will be a great country, an imperial country, a country where your sons, when they rise, rise to paramount positions and obtain not merely the esteem of their countrymen but command the respect of the world.

The same argument, presented with an almost equal grandiloquence, was used by John Ruskin in his lectures at Oxford University.

> This is what England must do or perish. She must found colonies as fast and as far as she is able, formed of her most energetic and worthiest men, seizing every piece of fruitful waste ground she can set her foot on, and there teaching her colonists that their chief virtue is to be fidelity to their country, and that their first aim is to be to advance the power of England on land and sea.

In 1883, when Sir John Seeley published his enormously popular book *The Expansion of England,* he pointed to the growth of Russia and the United States and warned that, inside of fifty years, they would have completely dwarfed states like France and Germany and would do the same to Great Britain if its people continued to regard it as "simply a European state." A similar argument had already been made in France by Leroy-Beaulieu, who stated that colonial expansion was for his country "a matter of life and death" and that, if France did not become a great African power, it was only a question of time before it was depressed to the position of Greece or Rumania. The same thoughts were expressed in Germany, where advocates of colonial activity pleaded for a German "place in the sun" and where—according to Peter Rassow— men like Chief of Staff Schlieffen and the influential foreign office counselor, Holstein, were convinced of the necessity of Germany's breaking out of its continental strait jacket and, in 1905, during the Moroccan crisis, actually desired war against France as the first step toward an effective imperial policy (see p. 471).

These fears for the future were shared by most powers, and this increased the speed and the indiscriminateness of the process of acquisition. Doubts might arise from time to time about the advisability of acquiring territories that seemed to have no great strategic or economic importance and promised to be difficult to defend. Was it to the interest of a maritime nation like Great Britain to acquire tracts of territory which stretched thousands of miles into the interior of Africa or Asia? There were reasons to doubt this, yet the spectacle of other powers vying for those very territories was generally enough to set doubts aside. After all, as the Liberal prime minister Lord Rosebery once asked, who could say how valuable these territories might one day become? The world was not elastic. "We have to consider not what we want now, but what we shall want in the future." Moreover, the governments of Europe could not always control their own agents, who were often, in Lord Salisbury's words, "men of energy and strong will, but probably not distinguished by any great restraint over their feelings . . . trying to establish by means which must constantly degenerate into violence the supremacy of that nation for which they were passionately contending."

These words well describe the breed of men who were the trail blazers of imperialism: men like the German explorer Carl Peters, who in the 1880s, while still in his twenties, explored and acquired, by treaty with native chiefs, a domain of 60,000 square miles in East Africa, or like that strange blend of patriot, visionary, and businessman, Cecil Rhodes (1853–1902). A clergyman's son, sent to Africa for his health, Rhodes made a fortune in the Kimberley diamond fields. Returning to England, he studied for a time at Oxford, where he heard and was fascinated by Ruskin's lectures. For the rest of his life he strove to "advance the power of England" in Africa. Like Peters, Rhodes not infrequently believed that he knew better than the British government what his country's interests really were, and he was not disinclined to force its hand. Like Peters also, he was not fastidious in the choice of methods to accomplish his objectives. His services to his country were great, but mixed in nature, and he must bear a large share of the responsibility for the Boer War.

The Popularity of Imperialism / Imperialistic policies were strongly supported by public opinion and were as popular among the working classes as they were among those economic groups which stood to profit more directly from them. This may suggest that there is truth in the theory, held by Schumpeter and others, that imperialism had an atavistic power that appealed to hidden instincts within all human beings—to lusts for conflict and domination that survived in the blood. More simply, this mass popularity may have been merely the result of the intrusion of something that was exciting and emotionally satisfying into lives that were confined in the drab ugliness of industrial cities and were yet unable to take advantage of such future anodynes as motion pictures, radio, and television. To read or hear about colonial victories at once relieved the tedium of the daily round and made it possible for the individual to share in the victory and the gained prestige by a simple process of identification.

Aside from that, was it really true, as the critics of imperialism claimed, that the working classes had nothing to gain from imperialism and that the money spent on colonial expeditions might better be devoted to social reform at home? The trade unions apparently did not believe so, inclining rather to the view that imperialism would help trade and industry and, by a trickle-down effect, benefit the whole economy and those employed in it. Taking their key from the unions, the revisionist wing of the Socialist party were generally supporters of imperialism. This was true of Bernstein (see p. 307), for instance, who stressed the humanitarian aspects of colonialism—the material improvements brought to native populations—but also admitted that the proletariat, as the future heirs of the bourgeoisie, "have an interest in a rational geographic expansion of the nation." At the meeting of the International at Stuttgart in 1907, Bernstein agreed that even Marx had admitted that possession of colonies was of advantage to the European economy and went on to say: "The colonies are there—one ought to occupy them—and I estimate that a certain tutelage of the civilized peoples over the uncivilized is a necessity."

The acknowledged leader of the German Social Democratic party, August Bebel, while criticizing German tactics during the Moroccan crisis of 1905, added: "It goes without saying that the interests of Germany's foreign trade should be protected"; and, during the second Moroccan crisis of 1911, he was actually heard to say that "the greatest guarantee of peace is the spread of international investments."

The discovery that the masses were emotionally susceptible to the appeals of imperialism and capable of being persuaded that imperialism was of economic advantage to them supplied certain governments with one more motive for embarking on imperialistic policies. In nations where the possibility of socialist revolution was real, the governing class was inclined to look on a dynamic colonial policy as a possibly effective diversionary tactic. The founder of the modern German navy, Grand

Admiral Tirpitz, advocated imperialism because he believed that "in this new national undertaking and the economic gains that will accrue from it lies a strong palliative against trained and potential Social Democrats." In Italy the same motive was at work in the launching of the Tripolitanian War in 1911. Official propaganda took the line that Italy was a proletarian nation that deserved its share of the spoils, and the war was described as an undertaking which would bring new land to the peasants of Italy's southern provinces.

This evidence of popular enthusiasm for imperialism and the fact that the sensational press encouraged it by describing the goriest details of colonial wars worried moralists and made them increasingly critical of governmental colonial policies. In 1906 the Center party bitterly attacked German policy in South West Africa because of the brutality and violation of fundamental decencies that had characterized operations against the Herreros. In England, in 1902, G. P. Gooch claimed that imperialism was debasing the moral currency by spreading the belief that ordinary standards of morality did not apply to the expansion of the dominant races, by narrowing the conception of God to that of a tribal God, by increasing international animosity, by exploiting native populations, and by glorifying war. He wrote:

> When we read on the bills, "Boers sabred by moonlight," we are supplied by a novel and striking image, which for a time relieves the monotony of life. The Romans clamored for *panem et circenses*. We have changed our religion and two thousand years have slipped by; but the cry is the same today. . . .

Imperialism was, indeed, open to many of these criticisms, and in the long run it grievously exacerbated suspicion and friction among the Great Powers. But, while the accusations of promoting brutality and exploitation cannot be dismissed, they must be balanced by the memory of the thousands of devoted missionaries and colonial administrators who strove to combat those abuses and to bring good government, education, material improvement, and the benefits of religion to native masses. The sense of mission that drove these men forward has often been made the object of cynical mirth; but, without it and the benefits it brought, the peoples of Africa and Asia would not have been able to rise, as they have in our day, to the position of self-governing nations.

THE COURSE OF IMPERIALISM

Africa / One of the keys to the understanding of the problems of the new African nations of the twentieth century is the briefness of the period which intervened between the end of their isolation from the modern world and their admission to statehood. As late as the 1880s, most of Africa was still uncharted and free from alien penetration. Then, with a rush that is still astonishing to recall, the white men arrived and within twenty years had carved all of Africa into dependencies of their home governments. The traumatic effects of the impact of an advanced industrial civilization upon a primitive tribal society are still having repercussions today—as, indeed, are other aspects of African imperialism: for example, the fine disregard which the empire-builders sometimes showed for tribal boundaries when they drew their own.

At the beginning of the 1870s, knowledge of Africa was largely restricted to the northern fringe, which was still, with the exception of French Algeria, nominally part of the Ottoman Empire, and to the tablelands of what is now the Union of South Africa, where the British had holdings and where communities of Dutch farmers (the Boers) were established in the Transvaal. In addition, there were various coastal settlements, particularly in West Africa where the British and French were established in Senegal and on the Niger River, and where there were also small Spanish holdings; in East Africa and its adjacent islands, where Moslem Arabs had trading settlements under the loose sovereignty of the sultan of Muscat; and in Mozambique and Angola, where Portuguese traders had been active for centuries. Of the interior, however, knowledge was scant and imprecise. The British explorer Speke had discovered Lake Victoria in 1858; Baker, another Englishman, had reached Lake Albert in 1864; and Livingstone, in his wanderings, had traced the course of the Zambezi River and the region around Lakes Nyasa and Tanganyika. But no one had yet reached the sources of the Nile; it was only in 1878 that Henry M. Stanley completed his investigation of the Congo River system; and vast areas of the sub-Sahara Africa were simply *terrae incognitae.*

An increase in the tempo of expansion, however, was already discernible in the 1870s. True to the principles enunciated in his Crystal Palace address, Disraeli advanced Britain's position in Africa during his term as prime minister. In Egypt, whose ruler, the Khedive Ismail, was the fourth successor to that Mehemet Ali who engaged our attention earlier (p. 33) and was as profligate as that sovereign had been energetic, Disraeli succeeded in 1875 in purchasing the Khedive's Suez Canal Company shares and also began the negotiations which led in 1879 to Anglo-French supervision of Egyptian finances. These steps were indications of the importance of the Egyptian route to India, and they led inevitably to the action taken reluctantly by Gladstone in 1882, when a native movement under Arabi Pasha and with the slogan "Egypt for Egyptians!" revolted against the khedive and seized Alexandria. The

British immediately bombarded that port, landed troops under General Wolseley which defeated Arabi Pasha at Tel-el-Kebir and captured Cairo, and imposed upon the khedive a British adviser, whose "advice" concerning necessary reforms was, as it soon became evident, mandatory.

In South Africa, also, Disraeli was active. Here he fought a war with the Zulus in order to stop the incursions of that proud and energetic nation and its gifted ruler Cetewayo (whose downfall is sympathetically commemorated in the works of H. Rider Haggard, especially the novels *Marie, Child of Storm,* and *Finished,* and the history *Cetewayo and His White Neighbours*).[1] He also announced the formal annexation of the Republic of the Transvaal (1877), but with less success, for the Boers resisted this decision and, four years later, defeated a British force at Majuba Hill so decisively that Gladstone made peace, with a somewhat ambiguous acknowledgement of the Transvaal's independence.

If the steps that Disraeli took had far-reaching consequences, so did one other event of the 1870s. In 1876 King Leopold II of Belgium convoked a conference of the powers to discuss African problems, with particular reference to "means of opening up the interior of the continent to the commerce, industry, and scientific enterprise of the civilized world." All of the major European powers participated; and the conference established an International African Association that would use funds subscribed by its members to promote the exploration and civilization of Africa. This international association was, to be sure, never very effective, but its establishment served as a signal for the outburst of imperialistic energy that followed on the part of all powers.

The pace was set by the king of Belgium, who now financed a series of expeditions by Henry Stanley into the Congo Basin where he began to conclude treaties with native chiefs for the exploitation of their territories. Stanley was allegedly acting for the Association, but he was generally regarded as an agent of Leopold, and his successes stimulated the competition of other powers. The French had already been caught by the imperialist fever and under the vigorous leadership of Jules Ferry (see p. 354) had launched an invasion of Tunis in 1881 (see p. 278). Now they became active also on the north bank of the Congo and in the basin of the Ubangui River, the area soon to be known as French Equatorial Africa. The Italians, impressed by the general activity, and bitterly offended by the French action in Tunis, where there were many Italian colonists, occupied Assab on the Red Sea coast in 1882 and Massawa in the same area three years later, thus laying the foundations of Italian East Africa. Finally, in 1884, Germany entered the race for territory and within twelve months proclaimed protectorates over South West

---

[1] It was during the conflict with Cetewayo in 1879 that the prince imperial, Napoleon III's heir, was killed.

Africa, Togoland, and the Cameroons, and the territories in East Africa where Carl Peters had been negotiating with local chieftains.

As early as 1884, less than ten years after the assembling of Leopold's conference, the competition between the powers had become so intense that it was considered expedient to call an international conference on African problems. This gathering, which met in Berlin from November 1884 to February 1885, had first to adjudicate the tangle of conflicting claims in the Congo Basin, where Stanley's treaties were contested by the Portuguese and the British. In the end, the International Association was given title to the greatest part of the Congo Basin on condition that it be organized as a free and neutral state, which allowed free trade and prohibited slavery. Since Leopold II paid the Association's bills, this made him sovereign of one of the richest areas of the world, for he gave little attention to the international character bestowed on the Congo, regarding it as a personal possession and declaring, in 1889, that, when he died, he intended to will it to the Kingdom of Belgium.

The Berlin Congress further stimulated European activity in Africa by facilitating trade on the Congo and Niger rivers, by reducing international law as it applied to Africa to the convenient formula that any power could acquire territory by occupying it and notifying its fellow powers, and most of all, perhaps, by giving further publicity to the opportunities that lay within the Dark Continent. As a result, the next ten years saw the almost complete division of Africa among the European powers.

Between 1885 and 1894, the British pushed their control of Nigeria into the interior and simultaneously, from the Cape of Good Hope, advanced northward over Bechuanaland, Rhodesia, and Nyasaland to the borders of the Congo. In 1890, by treaty with the Caprivi government in Germany, they adjudicated rival claims in East Africa and secured Zanzibar and other territories, in return for the cession to Germany of the North Sea island of Helgoland, long coveted by the German navy. Caprivi had no great interest in Africa, being in this respect much like his predecessor, Bismarck, who had once complained that the German consul at Zanzibar had written more dispatches and caused more trouble than all the rest of the foreign service combined; but it is indicative of the strength of imperialistic feeling in Germany that the 1890 treaty was bitterly attacked by the press and that Emperor William II soon decided that a more active African policy was necessary.

The hope of the British colonial enthusiasts, that their country would one day control a solid strip of territory from the Cape of Good Hope to the mouth of the Nile, was, at least momentarily, dashed by the 1890 treaty, which created a common boundary between the Belgian Congo and German East Africa and thus interposed a barrier to further British

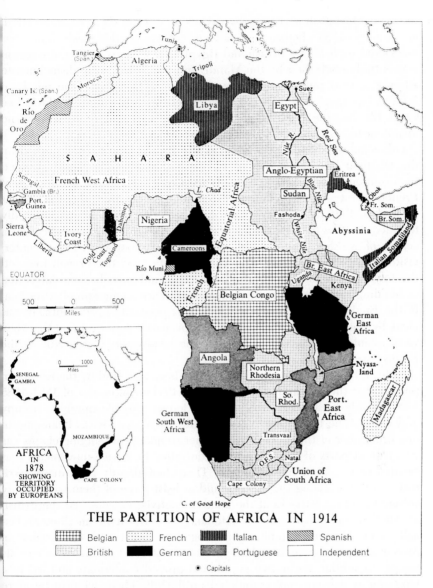

THE PARTITION OF AFRICA IN 1914

	Belgian		French		Italian		Spanish
	British		German		Portuguese		Independent

● Capitals

AFRICA IN 1878 SHOWING TERRITORY OCCUPIED BY EUROPEANS

progress northward. A second obstacle lay in the fact that the British did not control the Sudan. Since the 1880s, that great block of territory, which lay across the headwaters of the Nile, had been in the hands of a native revolutionary army led by a religious prophet who was known as the Mahdi. In 1884, the Gladstone government sent General "Chinese" Gordon, a quixotic and idealistic soldier who had proved in the Far East his knack for winning the confidence of native leaders, into the Sudan to evacuate English garrisons there. Gordon was cut off at Khartoum and, in January 1885, before a relieving column could reach him, was massacred with 11,000 British and Egyptian troops. After that, the region was entirely controlled by the Mahdi, and the British were disinclined to attempt a new push against him. Even so, especially in the minds of soldiers like the future Field Marshal Kitchener and empire-builders like Cecil Rhodes, the hope of an all-red Cape to Cairo route was by no means dead, as the sequel was to show.

Other nations were as energetic as the British. The French pushed up the Ubangui into the region of Lake Chad and simultaneously welded their settlements in Senegal, the Ivory Coast, and Guinea into a great French West African empire, extending as far into the interior as Timbuktu, that fabled town on the upper Niger, which was reputedly founded in the twelfth century, was for three centuries thereafter a center of Moslem culture, and was still an important trading center, visited yearly by great caravans of camels. In 1888 the French founded the town of Djibouti on the Red Sea coast and soon became interested in building rail routes into the independent native kingdom of Abyssinia. If the English direction of expansion was primarily north-south, it was clear by the 1890s that the French was primarily east-west and that they were as interested in the Sudan and the headwaters of the Nile as the English were.

Indeed, by 1894, so much of Africa had been acquired by the European powers that the free and easy rules of the Berlin conference of 1884–1885 were already breaking down. It was no longer possible simply to occupy and notify. The territories that were still not recognized as belonging to one or another of the powers were either subject to conflicting claims (as was true of parts of the Congo) or controlled by native movements that resisted loss of their independence. There had already been many territorial disputes among the powers; and at least three of them had already suffered military setbacks at the hands of nativist movements: the British at Majuba and Khartoum; the Italians, as a result of an ill-conceived sally into Abyssinian politics, at Dogali in 1887; and the French in Madagascar, the great island off the southeast coast of Africa, where attempts to subdue the native population proved inadequate and led to a long war which was not completed until 1896. There were to be more serious incidents of this kind in the future.

The Pacific and Asia / Collecting Pacific islands became as favored an occupation of the powers as annexing African colonies. The initiative was taken, as in Africa, sometimes by traders or missionaries and sometimes by governments themselves, for the islands often had more value as coaling stations and strategical strong points than as trading posts, as

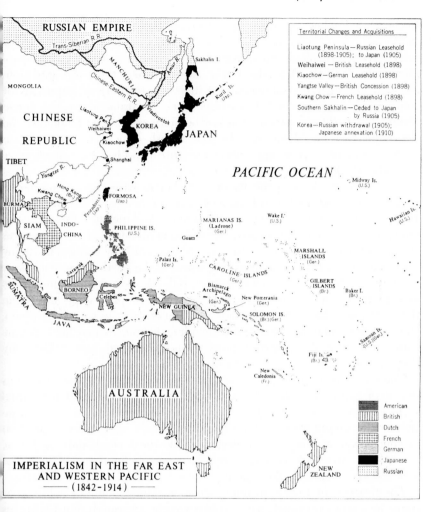

IMPERIALISM IN THE FAR EAST
AND WESTERN PACIFIC
——— (1842-1914) ———

Territorial Changes and Acquisitions

Liaotung Peninsula — Russian Leasehold (1898-1905); to Japan (1905)
Weihaiwei — British Leasehold (1898)
Kiaochow — German Leasehold (1898)
Yangtse Valley — British Concession (1898)
Kwang Chow — French Leasehold (1898)
Southern Sakhalin — Ceded to Japan by Russia (1905)
Korea — Russian withdrawal (1905); Japanese annexation (1910)

American
British
Dutch
French
German
Japanese
Russian

the course of World War II was to show. Of the powers that had Pacific possessions during the first part of the century, Great Britain, Holland, and France showed that their appetites were still good, but Spain showed so little energy that by the end of the century she had lost all of her holdings. The most active of the newcomers were Germany and the United States of America.

With a sound strategical sense, the British were primarily interested in those areas that were the natural approaches to Australia: New Guinea on the one hand and the Solomon Islands on the other; and they were also interested in the naval possibilities of the Fijis. The acquisition of the latter group of islands was one of Disraeli's first imperialistic coups. New Guinea, on the other hand, proved to be attractive to the Dutch, who wished to add it to their already extensive possessions in Borneo, the Celebes and Molucca Islands, as well as to the Germans, who were aggressive competitors of the British all over the Southwest Pacific. In 1885 this big island was subjected to a three-way partition: Holland getting the western half; Britain, the territory of Papua in the southeastern corner, which faces Cape York, Australia, across the Torres Strait; and Germany getting the northeastern coast. The Solomons and the Gilberts were taken over by the British somewhat later, as was Sarawak in Northern Borneo, where the British had had settlements since the early 1880s.

French imperialism in the Pacific had begun with Ferry's annexation of Tahiti in 1880, and in subsequent years France occupied the Society Islands, the Marquesas, and the Tuamotu Archipelago. French gains were, however, more spectacular on the Asian mainland. The reverse was true in Germany's case. In addition to her share of New Guinea, Germany acquired the Bismarck Archipelago, which included the islands of New Ireland and New Britain (whose port Rabaul was, as a Japanese base in 1943, to be pounded to helplessness by American planes operating from the Solomons), the Marshall Islands, and later, by purchase from Spain, the Carolines and the Marianas, including Guam, Saipan, and Tinian. Finally, after a dangerous dispute with the United States, Germany divided the Samoan Islands with that power.

These German purchases were largely the result of the disastrous defeat of Spain in 1898 in the war with the United States that resulted from its troubles in Cuba. That defeat was followed also by the annexation by the United States of the Philippine Islands. The earlier acquisition of the Hawaiian Islands had already made the United States a Pacific power; this now confirmed it, bringing the once-isolated American nation into the very heart of Asian politics.

The progress of European imperialism on the mainland of Asia was as impetuous and as competitive as it was among the islands, but the stakes were higher and the dangers greater. British policy, for instance, was determined to a large extent by the desire to protect India from possible assault by other powers, notably by Russia, whose swift advances in Turkestan and Baluchistan in the 1860s (see p. 248) aroused fears for the security of India's northwest front. The tightening up of India's administrative and military services during Disraeli's government and the passage of the Royal Titles Act of 1876, by which Queen Victoria received the resounding title Empress of India, were partly caused by these apprehensions, although the Titles Act appealed also to Disraeli's romantic nature and his taste for Oriental splendor. A more direct reaction to the fear of Russia was Disraeli's attempt to form a protective glacis in front of the supposedly menaced frontier, which he sought to do by using force to impose a protectorate upon the reluctant emir of Afghanistan in 1879. This led to a series of Afghan wars, and to a serious crisis in 1884 when Russian horsemen appeared in the Pamirs and on the ridge of Hindukush and, in March 1885, occupied the oasis of Pendjeh, near the pass that leads into the plateau of Afghanistan. Momentarily, an Anglo-Russian war seemed possible, but it was staved off by negotiations, which left Pendjeh in Russian hands while setting a momentary limit to their forward progress. Anglo-Russian rivalry for predominance in Afghan affairs was to continue, however, until 1907 and after (see p. 474).

To the east of India, British expansion was dictated by French advances in what is now Indochina. The French gains in Tonkin and Annam, as a result of their war with China in 1884–1885 (see p. 357), their penetration into what is now Laos, and the consolidation of their control of Cambodia and Cochin-China, where they had been established since the 1860s, were countered by a steady British advance into Burma. Between these two growing blocks of European territory lay the independent kingdom of Siam; and in 1893, the French seemed bent on forcing this state into a subordinate position, actually sending naval units to Bangkok to force concessions along the Mekong River. The British reacted strongly, and the French, while insisting on Siamese recognition of their protectorate over Laos, decided against pushing further. Three years later, an Anglo-French agreement defined the disposition of certain petty principalities on the upper Mekong, drew a common boundary between Burma and Tonkin in that area, and stipulated that nonintervention would be the rule in the valley of the Menam River to the south and in Siamese affairs generally. Simultaneously, British advances north from Singapore to the federated Malay states were halted and the southern boundary of Siam defined.

While these events were taking place, the second stage of Europe's penetration of the sprawling, disorganized, but enormously rich empire of China got under way. During the years between 1830 and 1860, Great Britain had taken the lead in breaking the isolation of China, waging two wars against the imperial government in 1839–1841 and 1857–1858, and forcing the Chinese to pay for defeat by opening their coastal ports to European traders and ceding Hong Kong and part of the Kowloon peninsula to the British crown. In the same years the Russians had advanced over the Amur River to the Pacific Coast and persuaded the Chinese government in 1860 to cede them the territory that became Russia's Maritime Province, with its ice-free port of Vladivostok.

For the next thirty years, complications in Europe and the Near East absorbed too much of the attention of the Great Powers to encourage new advances at the expense of China. This period of quiescence came to an end in the mid 1890s, and the powers that took the initiative in the new wave of imperialism were Russia and Japan.

Until the middle of the nineteenth century, the islands of Japan had been as isolated from the influences of the western world as the interior of Africa, although their level of culture was infinitely higher. The arrival in Japanese waters of an American fleet under the command of Commodore Perry in 1853 and the subsequent opening of Japanese ports to American ships and traders a year later marked the beginning of Japanese relations with and emulation of the countries of the western world. Within twenty years the feudal structure of the state had been smashed, and a political and social transformation of the country had taken place, and there had been widespread adoption of European institutions. The progress made in this respect was remarkable, Japan was soon endowed with such modern benefits as railroads, public education, modern health standards, popular newspapers, the European calendar, codes of law and judicial procedure, and, in 1889, a constitution modeled on western charters of liberties and providing for a bicameral legislature. Unfortunately, Japan also copied some less estimable European practices, chief among which were militarism and imperialism. No nation was more profoundly impressed by the Prussian successes of 1866 and 1870 than Japan or quicker to copy the Prussian system of universal military service, the Prussian staff system, and the Prussian tactical organization. And the establishment of a modern army was balanced by the development of a modern navy, in the rapid evolution of which expert British and American aid was solicited.

Imperialism became a prevalent ideology in Japan perhaps less because it was fashionable in the west (although the writings of western empire-builders did not go unnoticed in Tokyo) than because Japan was a small country with a very large population. Territorial expansion seemed not only desirable but necessary to Japanese leaders, and this could be effected only on the mainland. The closest desirable area was Korea, a country ridden with factionalism and internal disorder, in which both China and Japan claimed rights of political overlordship.

In 1893 an explosion of internal unrest in Korea prompted a joint Sino-Japanese intervention that degenerated into an interallied conflict and, finally, into a war. In this conflict the Chinese army acted, as the British statesman Curzon said scornfully, "like an undisciplined rabble of tramps." The Japanese invaded Manchuria and the Liaotung peninsula, stormed Port Arthur, captured Weihaiwei, smashed the Chinese fleet in the battle of the Yalu River, and threatened to advance on their capital of Peking. Utterly demoralized, the Chinese surrendered. The terms included a large war indemnity, the cession to Japan of the islands of Formosa and the Pescadores and the Liaotung peninsula, with its strongpoint Port Arthur, and the acknowledgement of the independence of Korea (which was tantamount to opening it to Japanese domination).

It was these terms that brought Russia into the picture and, by doing so, opened the second phase of European imperialism in China. In official circles in St. Petersburg there had always been a school of thought which, in contrast to the Pan-Slavs, felt that Russia's true interest lay in expansion in the Far East. In the 1890s this group was represented by such influential advisers of Nicholas II as War Minister Kuropatkin and Admiral Alekseev. These men could not be expected to view with equanimity Japan's winning a preponderance in Korea, which was dangerously near Russia's base at Vladivostok, or securing a foothold on the Liaotung peninsula, which would open the way into the province of Manchuria. In 1891, the Russians had begun to construct a trans-Siberian railroad to Vladivostok, and they hoped to persuade the Chinese to grant them permission to cross Manchurian territory, if not to cede the province to them entirely. This would be impossible once Japan was established there.

The Russian government decided, then, to intervene in the negotiations between China and Japan, with a view to reducing Japanese terms. With the backing of their new ally France[2] and of Germany, they insisted that the cession of the Liaotung peninsula to Japan would perpetually menace the peace of China, while rendering illusory Korean independence, and that it must be set aside. The Japanese, with suppressed indignation, complied.

All of the powers that had intervened now claimed their reward from China, Russia leading the way. By an elaborate series of cessions and financial arrangements in 1895–1896, Russia received the right to build railway lines not only across northern Manchuria to Vladivostok but also from Harbin, on the spur, south into that very Liaotung Peninsula from which the Japanese had just been ousted, with the additional privilege of patrolling such lines with troops of its own. In return for underwriting the Chinese war indemnity, the Russians also received supervisory powers with respect to Chinese finances and the right to establish a commission house, the Russo-Chinese Bank, which gave them a preferred position in the economic development of Manchuria.

France was compensated by permission to run a rail line northward from Annam into China and by the cession of valuable mining concessions in the provinces of Yunnan, Kwangsi, and Kwantung. Germany's compensation was delayed, but the murder of two missionaries in Shantung province in 1897 gave William II a pretext for sending naval units into Chinese waters, a show of force that persuaded the Chinese govern-

---

[2] On the Franco-Russian alliance see below, p. 465.

ment to grant his subsequent demand for a ninety-nine-year lease of the harbor of Kiaochow and a virtual protectorate over the entire Shantung peninsula. This, in turn, persuaded the Russians to take another step forward, which they did in March 1898, by pressuring the Chinese into leasing Port Arthur to them for a period of twenty-five years. This completed the Russian stranglehold over Manchuria, while at the same time placing Korea between Russian pincers at Port Arthur and Vladivostok.

The rapid growth of Russian influence infuriated the Japanese and increased their desire to protect their own interests in Korea before it was too late. It alarmed the British, who saw the Russians encroaching steadily upon what they had considered their own preserve. British apprehension was in no wise relieved by the fact that they themselves were permitted to lease the port of Weihaiwei in 1898. Russian expansion also prompted the United States government to try to defend the fast-weakening independence and integrity of the Chinese Empire by circulating to the powers the so-called Open Door Note, which asked them to admit that they possessed no exclusive rights, economic or other, in the areas in which their influence was predominant—a note that was, incidentally, answered evasively by the Russians. And, finally, it stimulated a rising tide of patriotism among Chinese intellectuals who saw their country being split up into spheres of foreign influence and felt that this process must be resisted by force. In short, everything was shaping up for a major explosion of one kind or another in China as the century reached its close.

The Near East / A word should be said, finally, of imperialism in the Near East, with particular reference to Germany's attempt to secure a predominant economic position in the Turkish Empire and adjoining areas.

Ever since the 1850s and 1860s, German missionaries and teachers had been active in Anatolia and Mesopotamia; and since the 1870s German banking and commercial interests had also had agents within the Turkish Empire. All of these people were impressed by the wealth of Turkey, and some of them were doing their best to tap it. The Deutsche Bank and the Württenbergische Vereinsbank of Stuttgart were extending loans to the Sultan in the 1880s and, in the same decade, a syndicate was formed by the Siemens banking group to construct railroads for the more efficient exploitation of the area. This group envisioned the possible linkage of these roads to the Austro-German system across the Bosphorus, so that eventually something in the nature of a Berlin-Constantinople-Baghdad system could be established, with branches running to Aleppo, Damascus, Smyrna, and eventually to Persia, Arabia, and Egypt.

It was not originally believed that this penetration should be exclusively German, and the railroad planners seemed to have hoped to invite the bankers of other countries to participate in their scheme. But all of this changed when William II threw off the restraints of his first chancellors and became an avowed imperialist. In 1898 the emperor paid a visit to the sultan in Constantinople. There he made several speeches which indicated that he believed Germany particularly suited to take the Moslem peoples under its protection. In the period that followed, the government urged German bankers to go on with their railroad planning but to drop their ideas of an international consortium. William, indeed, took to referring to the projected system as "my railroad" and one of his advisers was reported to have said, "With a bow to the British lion and a curtsey to the Russian bear, we will worm our way, little by little, down to the Persian Gulf."

To the British and the Russians, who were rivals for a preferred position in Persia, such avowed intentions were disturbing. So was the rapidity with which the Germans, under government direction, ingratiated themselves with the Turkish government and won a commanding position in Turkish finance, economic life, and even in the development and training of the Turkish military establishment. This concern on the part of the other powers was not without significance. German imperialism in the Near East had profound effects on the diplomatic alignments of Europe.

THE CLIMAX OF IMPERIALISM

European Defeats: Spain / Between 1895 and 1905 enthusiasm for imperialistic expansion reached its climax and began its decline. As the tide of expansion swept forward, it had become increasingly competitive; the clashes between the rival Great Powers had become more frequent and more dangerous; and the imperialistic governments had become incautious and inclined to overreach themselves. Now, within a period of ten years, there came a series of sharp crises, and the European nations that had succumbed to the imperialistic fever suffered setbacks that had sobering effects upon public opinion. Mention has been made above of what happened to Spain in 1898—a rather special case, it must be admitted, for Spain's troubles were caused not by policies inaugurated since the 1870s, but rather by its inability to give efficient administration to possessions inherited from a more remote past. Even so, the desperate losses inflicted on Spanish garrisons in both Cuba and the Philippines by native insurrectionary movements and the eventual loss of these territories as a result of the war with the United States were hardly designed to support any enthusiasm for imperialism among the Spanish people, as the subsequent liquidation of what was left of Spain's Pacific island empire soon showed. And Spain was not alone in suffering this experience; for similar shocks came to Italy, France, Great Britain, Russia, and Germany.

The Italian Defeat at Adowa / The man who dominated Italian politics for the ten years following 1887 was Francesco Crispi, who set his heart upon avenging the Italian defeat at Dogali in Abyssinia in that year. From the beginning of his period of office, he dabbled in the confused politics of the Abyssinian empire and, when the Negus John was killed by dervishes in 1889, had the good fortune to back the successful claimant to the throne, a tribal chieftain called Menelik of Shoa, who has the distinction of having once employed the French poet Rimbaud as a gun runner. The Italians persuaded Menelik to sign the Treaty of Uccialli as a reward for their support, and Crispi subsequently claimed that it gave Italy a protectorate over Abyssinia. He ordered Italian troops to occupy territories inland from Massawa and, in 1890, proclaimed a new Italian Red Sea colony called Eritrea.

Neither Menelik, who soon rejected the Italian interpretation of the treaty, nor the coastal chiefs were willing to tolerate these Italian pretensions. The years 1893–1895 were filled with skirmishes between Italian units and local bands, and negotiations between Menelik and the dervishes of the Sudan, who had been aroused by Italian incursions into their domain. On his side, Crispi seems to have concluded that the time had come to conquer all of Ethiopia, and he neither listened to the warnings of his soldiers nor heeded their requests for more men, ammunition, and supplies. When they hesitated to advance into the interior, he accused them of insubordination and cowardice. His irrational behavior finally produced a debacle.

In March 1896, General Baratieri, goaded beyond endurance by Crispi's taunts, marched with four columns of troops, totaling six thousand men, from his base at Massawa into the interior, seeking conquest and glory. The march was badly planned, without proper communications, supplies, or intelligence of the enemy and with no clear objectives. At a place called Adowa the Italians were surrounded by a much superior force of Abyssinians and dervishes and were literally cut to ribbons, the few survivors being led away into slavery. Thus, Italian imperialism in East Africa came to a shocking denouement with the loss in one day of more men than had died in the wars of 1859 and 1860.

The Anglo-French Showdown / Adowa produced a kind of chain reaction. The Italian defeat left a raging and exultant army of dervishes and Abyssinians in the Sudan, the existence of which seemed infinitely more menacing to the British in Egypt than it had at any time since the death of Gordon in 1885. In any event, the Salisbury government resolved to remove this threat and Sir Herbert Kitchener was ordered to proceed up the Nile with an Anglo-Egyptian force of 20,000 men to smash the dervish power. In a fierce action at the confluence of the Nile and the Atbara, Kitchener destroyed one dervish army and proceeded toward the dervish capital at Khartoum, 200 miles to the south. Before starting, his forces were joined by the 21st Lancers, among whom was a young sub-lieutenant named Winston Churchill, who later described the march south, the halt at Omdurman where the Mahdi's tomb was located, and the decisive defeat of the dervish army, 60,000 strong, by the crack British units.

> The result was not surprising. As the successors of the Saracens descended the long smooth slopes which led to the river and their enemy, they encountered the rifle fire of two and a half divisions of trained infantry, drawn up two deep and in close order and supported by at least 70 guns on the river bank and in the gun boats, all firing with undisturbed efficiency. Under this fire the whole attack withered. . . .

So did a second desperate dervish assault.

> Discipline and machinery triumphed over the most desperate valour, and after an enormous carnage, certainly exceeding 20,000 men, who strewed the ground in heaps and swathes "like snowdrifts," the whole mass of the Dervishes dissolved into fragments and into particles and streamed away into the fantastic mirages of the desert.

The British were now, for the first time, able to proceed, without fear of native attack, toward the headwaters of the Nile. But that objective was one shared with the French, still resentful of the British occupation of Egypt and hopeful that, if they could secure possession of Nilotic Sudan, they might be able to compel their rivals to reopen the Egyptian question. Long before Kitchener had received his orders to liquidate the dervish problem, the French government had ordered an expedition under Captain Marchand to proceed from the French Congo to the upper Nile and another, under Captain Clochette, to march from East Africa and join him there. Clochette died en route and his expedition turned back, but Marchand, with 150 men, reached the Nile and planted the French flag at Fashoda in late September 1898. A few days later Kitchener's victorious columns arrived from the north; and their commander, politely but firmly, requested immediate French evacuation from what was, he claimed, an acknowledged British sphere of influence.

The French had no real alternative to surrender, and this was recognized by their new foreign minister, Théophile Delcassé, a realist who saw that a conflict with Great Britain would serve no useful purpose except to gratify the Germans. He was, Delcassé confessed, "too much of a Gambettist to forget the wound of Strasbourg under the scratch of Fashoda." Even so, Marchand's enforced withdrawal, with its implied recognition of British claims that the French had contested since 1882, was a humiliation. It was bitterly resented in Paris, where anti-British feeling was undiminished in intensity for almost a decade.

The Boer War / The Fashoda affair left the British in a bumptious and exalted mood, and, a year later, this led them into difficulties in South Africa that proved, in the end, to be more humiliating than the French experience. To explain the incident, one must recall Britain's attempt to assert control over the Boers in the Transvaal in 1877 and its setback at Majuba Hill. That earlier conflict had been terminated by an agreement which, as was intimated earlier, was ambiguous in wording and meaning, being interpreted by the Boers as a grant of independence but by the British as an understanding that the Transvaal was part of the British empire and subject to British supervision in foreign and other affairs.

In the late 1880s, gold was discovered in the Transvaal, and it was soon apparent that the deposits were among the richest in the world. The discovery led to a tremendous rush of foreigners, especially Englishmen from the Cape, into the area, and these foreigners, or *Uitlanders* as the Boers called them, soon outnumbered the Boers themselves. The Boer government, which was led by an energetic and imperious statesman called Paul Kruger, felt compelled to impose political disabilities upon these latecomers, lest they dominate local politics. Simultaneously, they sought to escape economic and financial control by the Cape Colony, which owned all rail outlets from the Transvaal, by constructing railroads of their own to Lorenzo Marques in Portuguese Mozambique, and by giving valuable economic concessions to the traders of other European nations, notably Germany.

This was galling to Cape politicians and especially to Cecil Rhodes. To him and others the behavior of the Boer government seemed provocative, and their treatment of British subjects in the Transvaal intolerable; and they resolved on reprisals. These took the form of a romantic but badly conceived enterprise led by a Dr. Leander Starr Jameson, who invaded the Transvaal in 1895 with a small band of adventurers based on Bechuanaland. They were quickly surrounded and captured by a superior force of Boer troops.

This affair, promptly disavowed by the British government, caused a world-wide sensation and elicited a personal telegram of encouragement to the Boer government from Emperor William II of Germany. The emperor's message was greatly resented in Great Britain, but it confirmed the Boers in their discriminatory policy with respect to the *Uitlanders*. Again the British government was annoyed, claiming that the Boers were intent on expelling the British from South Africa entirely and establishing a great Boer state. In negotiations in 1899, the British demanded that the grievances of their subjects be satisfied and that the right of suffrage be accorded them. The Boers refused and, after further inconclusive talks and a number of incidents, war broke out in October 1899 between the British on the one hand and the Transvaal and their sister republic, the Orange Free State, on the other.

It was a conflict in which the British won no reputation and which led the British poet Kipling to write later:

> Let us admit it fairly as business people should
> We have had no end of a lesson, it will do us
>   no end of good.

To defeat the sixty thousand men whom the Boers put into the field, the British had to employ 350,000 and to fight until 1902, suffering heavy casualties and heavier monetary expenditures. In the end, they were successful and were wise enough to put their victory to good use—treating the defeated with leniency, granting extensive measures of self-government to the Boer governments, and, thus, making possible the act of September 1909 that combined the Transvaal, the Orange Free State, Natal province, and the Cape province into the South African Union. But, in the course of all this, a good many illusions had been dissipated, and the popularity of imperialism in Great Britain had been dimmed.

The Russo-Japanese War / Before the end of the South African war, the long-accumulating tension in the Far East exploded into violence. Resentment against European encroachments had led to the growth of certain nationalist societies in China, which came to be known as the Boxers (from their adopted name, which was loosely translated as the Righteous Harmonious Fists). The Boxers were dedicated to the expulsion of foreigners from China and, in the spring and summer of 1900, they inaugurated a program of terrorism directed against European missionaries and their Chinese converts and members of the consulate staffs and trading communities. Scores of Europeans were killed, and the legations at Peking were besieged for two months before a relief expedition of Japanese, Russian, German, French, British, and American troops arrived and restored peace.

During the course of the Boxer Rebellion, thousands of Russian troops had poured into Manchuria, and in the period that followed they showed a stubborn reluctance to leave. Expostulations by the Chinese government were met by evasions which seemed to indicate that Russia was intent on transforming Manchuria into another Bokhara, a course which General Kuropatkin had recommended to the tsar as being desirable This prospect not only worried the Chinese but was also a matter of concern to Great Britain and Japan.

Because of African complications, the British were in no position to take decisive action against Russia in the Far East, but they did wish at least to persuade the Russians (and Russia's ally, France) that any incursions into the British sphere of influence would be resisted. They sought to do this by a diplomatic gesture. In 1902, after a series of involved negotiations, they concluded an alliance with Japan, providing for mutual aid in the event that either partner became involved in a war with two other powers. Significant because it represented a break with Britain's long tradition of freedom from alliances in peacetime, the agreement had a more fateful consequence in Far Eastern politics. It gave the Japanese reasonable assurance that, if they went to war against Russia, they would be protected from the intervention of other powers; and this encouraged them to insist that Russia recognize the integrity of China by evacuating Manchuria. Throughout 1903, the request was made repeatedly and as repeatedly declined by the Russians. But the Japanese were, meanwhile, making military preparations and, when these were ready, they struck.

On the night of February 8, 1904, Japanese torpedo boats sank part of the Russian Far Eastern squadron in the harbor of Port Arthur; on the following morning Japanese armies invaded Korea and the Liaotung peninsula. The Russian army, riddled with personal jealousies on the command level and with disaffection among the troops, was in no way prepared for a war against well-equipped and inspired forces. It was rolled back and badly beaten in a series of battles around Mukden, in which more troops were engaged and heavier casualties suffered than in any fighting since the Franco-Prussian War. By the beginning of 1905, the Russian armies had been expelled from Manchuria, their fleet had been rendered ineffective, and Port Arthur, after a long siege, had been forced to surrender. A desperate attempt by the Russians to relieve that base by sending another fleet to the Far East failed disastrously; after painfully making its way from Reval around Europe, Africa, and Southeast Asia, this force of superannuated ships, commanded by Admiral Rozhdestvensky, was annihilated by Admiral Togo in a brilliant sea fight in the straits of Tsushima in May 1905.

Tsushima marked an inglorious end to Tsarist Russia's imperialistic career in the Far East. In the peace negotiations, held under the good offices of President Theodore Roosevelt of the United States, Russia ceded her lease of Port Arthur and the Liaotung peninsula to Japan, agreed to the evacuation of Manchuria, and admitted the primacy of Japanese influence in Korea.

The Return to Europe / Germany did not experience anything like the stunning setbacks suffered by Great Britain and Russia in these climactic years of European imperialism, but she was far from unscathed, as was shown by her unsuccessful attempt to compete with France in Moroccan affairs in 1905, which will be discussed in the next chapter. Apart from that, the bullying tactics and the not infrequent attempts to blackmail other powers into colonial concessions that had been characteristic of William II's policy in Africa and the Far East aroused the indignation of the other powers and influenced their future diplomatic conduct, to Germany's disadvantage. William II's telegram of encouragement to President Kruger of the Transvaal at the time of the Jameson raid was never wholly forgiven by the British; and German gains in the Near East were resented by the Russians, the more so because they were accomplished while Russia's energies were being fruitlessly expended in the Far East.

By 1905 the great age of imperialism was over. Vast tracts of the world's surface and millions of new subjects had been acquired by the European powers during the years since Disraeli had made his ringing challenge at the Crystal Palace. There were few more great acquisitions to be made. The colonial powers were now to learn how onerous the burdens of empire could be, how hard it was to hold the territories won, and (and this was a post-World War II discovery) how many difficulties arose when the decision was made to let them go.

But these discoveries lay in the future. In 1905 the European governments had more immediate problems. During the years of imperialism, and partly because of events in the colonial areas, the great European security system created by Bismarck had broken down, and the balance of power had become so precarious that any diplomatic incident was capable of touching off a major conflagration. Unfortunately for Europe and the world, there was no dearth of such incidents.

19

International Politics and the Coming of War, 1890-1914

THE DIPLOMATIC REVOLUTION, 1890–1907

The Franco-Russian Alliance / The fragility of the European balance alluded to at the end of the last chapter was the result of a diplomatic revolution which freed France from the isolation that Bismarck had managed to impose on it and divided the European states into two great coalitions.

This revolution had its origins in Bismarck's dismissal in 1890 and in the dramatic decision of the German government in that same year to repudiate a basic feature of his diplomatic system: the close tie with Russia that had been maintained, except for brief intervals, since 1813, and had been most recently confirmed by the Reinsurance Treaty of June 1887. In 1890, the Russians were told that that treaty could not be renewed.

As in the case of many of the diplomatic decisions of post-Bismarckian German governments, the motives for this move were mixed. The emperor and his inexperienced new chancellor and foreign minister, Caprivi and Marschall, were genuinely concerned about the complexity of Bismarck's diplomatic system, desired to clarify Germany's commitments, and wanted to eliminate the apparent incompatibility between their treaty obligations to Austria-Hungary and to Russia. At the same time, 1890 was the high-tide of Anglo-German cooperation—the Zanzibar-Helgoland exchange was effected in July 1890 (see p. 448)—and there were people in the German Foreign Office who felt that the exchange and the future benefits it might bring would be seriously jeopardized if the British government, which was firmly anti-Russian in its views, should learn about the Reinsurance Treaty. Personal motives were doubtless also a part of the decision. The emperor and Baron Holstein, the most influential of the Foreign Office counselors, were clearly anxious to demonstrate their independence from Bismarckian ideas by striking out on a new course. Finally, Holstein's views were clearly influenced by his strong antipathy to Russia and his intimacy with those army circles which had desired war with Russia in 1887.

The Russian government was shocked by the German decision and did its best to persuade the Caprivi government to change its mind. When it failed, it took the logical course and turned toward France. The Germans had made the mistake of believing that absolutism and republicanism were irreconcilable; the absolutists and republicans now disproved this. In the summer of 1891, the French and Russian governments exchanged notes in which they decided upon mutual consultation in the event of a threat to the peace and the concerting of measures to deal with it. A year later, upon French insistence, this agreement was supplemented by a military convention which called for common mobilization in the event that either party became involved in a war with a member of the Triple Alliance and mutual aid in the event that either was attacked by Germany. The explosion of the Panama affair in France (see p. 363) delayed ratification of these engagements by strengthening the hand of conservative anti-French circles in Russia. After another year had passed, however, the Russians took up the negotiations again; a Russian naval squadron paid a ceremonial visit to the French port of Toulon, returning an earlier French naval visit to Kronstadt; and, on January 4, 1894, the ratifications were finally completed, and France and Russia became allies.

The alliance was not, of course, necessarily final. In both Germany and Russia there were important groups who believed that the tie between their two countries must be restored. It is probably safe to say that the break was not regarded as definitive until later, after the Germanophils in Russia had been alienated by the exclusive German tariffs against Russian grain (see p. 393), the incursions in the neighborhood of the Persian Gulf (see p. 457), and the ultimatum of 1909 (see p. 480). It is nevertheless significant that, as early as 1892, one important agency seemed to conclude that the Franco-Russian tie was permanent. German war plans had always been based on the assumption that, if a major war came, it would probably become a two-front war, but that Germany would strike first toward the east. When Count Schlieffen became chief of the German General Staff in 1892, he reversed the order of attack in the German war plans, on the apparent assumption that France was now so closely tied to Russia that *any* war in Eastern Europe must involve France too and must begin with its elimination. To German soldiers after 1892, the Franco-Russian alliance was a fact of life, and their plans to deal with it threatened to turn even minor skirmishes between powers into a major European war.

The End of British Isolation / As we have seen, one of Germany's reasons for abandoning the Reinsurance Treaty had been the desire to avoid weakening what appeared to be a promising Anglo-German entente. In both countries there were influential people who regarded England and Germany as natural allies. This was the belief of Lord Salisbury, the Conservative prime minister (a realist who saw the advantages of having a continental supporter to deflect French ambitions from Egypt); it was an article of faith of Joseph Chamberlain, and continued to be as long as he lived; and it exercised so powerful an attraction upon Cecil Rhodes that, when he set up the Rhodes scholarships, he made it clear that they would be devoted to the idea of training young men in the British colonies, the United States, and Germany to carry on this natural alliance. On the German side, the desire to collaborate with the British was equally strong in many parts of society—some of which are well described in Fontane's greatest novel *Der Stechlin*—and in the government and the court. But the German attitude toward Britain was always ambiguous. William II, for instance, who had an English mother and an English grandmother (Queen Victoria), admired the British and was proud to have his portrait painted in the uniform of a British admiral; but, at the same time, he suffered from what appeared to be an uncontrollable inferiority complex that made him want to "show them" that Germany was in no way inferior to them. The emperor's equivocal attitude was reflected in German foreign policy in general and had unfortunate results.

Paul Hatzfeldt, the German ambassador in London in the 1890s, tried to convince the Foreign Office that, if it was truly the desire of the German government to have a working entente with the British, this would require a certain regard for British interests and desires wherever the two countries came into contact. This was a lesson that the German government never seemed to take to heart. While continuing to profess a desire to convert the British from an associate to an actual member of the Triple Alliance, the German government, in colonial affairs, seemed to believe that it could win territory by a not very subtle policy of blackmail. The British, long accustomed to finding the French in their way, began to discover in the 1890s that, whenever they hoped to extend their possessions in Africa or the Pacific, the Germans were likely to appear and demand compensation. After one such abrupt intervention in 1894, Lord Salisbury commented coldly that the Germans had used language in communicating with Her Majesty's government that they "might properly have used in addressing the State of Monaco," adding that he considered this attitude insufferable.

The gratuitous German intervention into South African affairs at the time of the Jameson raid (see p. 460) was even more impolitic. It appears to have been the result of one of those "incessant hysterical vacillations of William II" which Hatzfeldt predicted in 1901 would destroy Germany; its rationale was murky and its expected results unclear; and it succeeded only in infuriating the British. So did German policy during the Boer War. Their expressions of sympathy with the embattled Boers were so cordial that there seemed reason for Whitehall to believe that the Germans might actually be contemplating some form of intervention. The simultaneous launching of the Baghdad railway scheme was also annoying to London, where the feeling was beginning to grow that Germany was bent on opposing British interests in every part of the globe.

By all odds the most alarming German action and the one most calculated to make a working agreement with the British impossible was the decision to build a battle fleet. In 1896, in a speech delivered before the Colonial Society, William II announced that "the future of Germany [was] on the sea." By laws of April 1898 and June 1900 the government began a program of accelerated construction. Grand Admiral Tirpitz, the moving spirit behind the program, stated that it was necessary to create "a fleet capable of action between Helgoland and the English coast," and made it known that his objective was an armored fleet perhaps two thirds the size of the British fleet and certainly so large that its very existence would, in wartime, make the British attempts to destroy it potentially too costly to risk.

There was, of course, no reason why Germany should not build a fleet if it wished to do so. It was unreasonable, however, for the power with the greatest land army in Europe to begin serious competition with Britain on the seas and still, at the same time, expect Britain to conclude some form of alliance with it. But men like Holstein seem to have believed that Britain was a declining power (and that this was proven by the performance of its troops in the Boer War), that it was confronted with a real possibility of a war with Russia, that it needed allies more than it ever had in its long existence, that its only possible alliance was with Germany, and that, if Germany kept the pressure up, it would be willing to pay dearly for an agreement. This explains why British feelers for an alliance, made by Joseph Chamberlain and the Earl of Lansdowne between 1899 and 1902, were always evaded adroitly by the Germans. The chancellor by this time was that monument of super-ficiality, Prince Bülow, who agreed with Holstein that the longer the British were kept waiting the more eager they would become. When his ambassador in London suggested in 1903 that the British might try to make an accommodation with the French and the Russians, Bülow waved this aside airily. "In my opinion," he wrote, "we need not worry about such remote possibilities."

The Germans were right in only one respect: the British were con-cerned about the drift of world events and were prepared to modify their past isolation by diplomatic agreements. But they had a wider range of choice than was believed in Berlin. After Fashoda had elim-inated the Egyptian question as an active issue, there was no real con-flict of interest anywhere in the world between France and Great Britain; and, despite the continued antipathy between the two peoples, there were certain issues on which they were beginning to see eye to eye. Although for different reasons, the French were beginning to be as wor-ried about Russia's Far Eastern policy as the British. The British were afraid of Russian encroachments upon their sphere of influence in China. The French had two fears: first, that Russian absorption in Far Eastern affairs would deprive France of Russian support in areas closer to home (where were the Russians, for instance, when France was forced to back down at Fashoda?) and, second, that there would be an Anglo-Russian war in the Far East and that Russia would expect French aid there. This latter fear was enhanced by the conclusion, in 1902, of the alliance between Great Britain and Japan (see p. 462).

Delcassé and the Anglo-French Settlement / In Paris the man most awake to the dangers which the Russian course held for France was Théophile Delcassé, who had assumed office as foreign minister in 1898. As we have seen (p. 460), Delcassé believed that the principal concern of any French statesman must be France's relations with Germany and that the most desirable objective of French policy must be the recovery of Alsace and Lorraine. He had set himself the task of strengthening France's position *vis-à-vis* Germany, and he had no intention of diverting the energies of his country into useless wars in far-off places.

In the building up of France's diplomatic position, Delcassé had already had one significant success. When he came to power he had inherited, among other things, a tariff war with Italy that had been going on since 1887 (see p. 341). Delcassé showed himself amenable to the Italian desire for a commercial agreement that would terminate this ruinous conflict. In 1898 he granted it. In return, however, he received an explicit recognition of the primacy of French influence in Morocco (Delcassé assuring his opposite number that France would refrain from meddling in Tripoli, which the Italians coveted), as well as some important assurances with respect to Italy's membership in that obviously anti-French combination, the Triple Alliance. The Italians were anxious to count on the continued support of Paris banking circles, for they were embarking on a complicated refunding of their national debt, and they had no hesitation in giving Delcassé what he wanted. In a series of notes between 1900, when the Triple Alliance was renewed, and 1902, they declared that nothing in the wording of the alliance bound Italy to take any aggressive action against France and that Italy would remain neutral if France became "the object of direct or indirect aggression" or even if France "as the result of direct provocation, should find herself compelled in defense of her honor and security to take the initiative of a declaration of war." If these secret declarations meant anything—and they were made with every evidence of good faith—they indicated that Italy's enthusiasm for the Triple Alliance had reached the vanishing point and that, in the event of a war with Germany, France need have no fear of an attack on its flank.

This was heartening to Delcassé, but the threat in the Far East remained. If Russia continued to pursue its dangerous policy there, France might, against its will, find itself involved in the war it had avoided at Fashoda. The best way of avoiding this, he thought, would be to turn directly to Britain. A *rapprochement* between London and Paris would, Delcassé hoped, not only avoid the danger of French involvement in a Far Eastern war; it might even eliminate the possibility of such a war by promoting agreement between France's ally, Russia, and Britain's new ally, Japan.

In any event, Delcassé made soundings in London and found a cordial response in the government and at court. Indeed, England's new sovereign, King Edward VII, was so enthusiastic over the prospect of Anglo-French reconciliation that he volunteered to go to Paris on an extraordinary state visit designed to prepare public opinion for an agreement. As an example of personal diplomacy, the king's visit in May 1903 was an unparalleled success. Upon his arrival, he was met by hostile crowds who cheered for Marchand, Kruger, and, indeed, anyone but the royal visitor. The king's good-humored acceptance of this treatment, however, soon turned the popular temper in his favor and, when he left the city to return home, the cheers were for him. A subsequent visit to London by the president of the Republic in July went off well; and the diplomats were encouraged to believe that there was no longer any reason to fear public opinion. They accordingly got down to work and, between July 1903 and April 1904, agreed on the details of a comprehensive settlement of differences.

The agreement of 1904 settled certain disputes in Siam and Newfoundland and made boundary adjustments in West Africa, but its most important clauses had to do with Egypt and Morocco. Belatedly, the French government recognized the British protectorate at Cairo and declared that they would not obstruct British work in Egypt "by asking that a time limit be fixed for the British occupation or in any other manner." On their part, the British government recognized Morocco as a French sphere of influence, adding that it was for France alone to provide order in that enormously rich North African province and to suggest reforms to its sultan. The British agreed further, in secret articles, that they would raise no objections to any action that the French might consider appropriate in the event of a collapse of the sultan's authority, provided that northern Morocco with its Atlantic coastline should go, not to France, but to Spain. This last stipulation was dictated by considerations of strategy.

The broader significance of this agreement was that it marked the beginning of Anglo-French collaboration on other questions and the first step toward the alliance between the two Western Powers in World War I.

The First Moroccan Crisis / This was not immediately recognized by the people who were to suffer most from the new entente: namely, the Germans. They were still mesmerized by the vision of an Anglo-Russian war that would involve France also; and, to do them justice, it must be admitted that such a war seemed to be a real possibility in 1904. On a dark October night of that year, when Admiral Rozhdestvensky's Baltic fleet started its long journey toward its sad destiny in the straits of Tsushima (see p. 462), it mistook some British trawlers off the Dogger Bank for Japanese gunboats and blew them out of the water. For some weeks British retaliation seemed probable, but it was averted, partly because of the good offices of the French. As events took their course in the Far East, the possibility of an Anglo-Russian conflict vanished. As it did, the Germans seem to have decided that they would have to give more serious attention to the new Anglo-French combination.

Field Marshal von Moltke once said that the trouble with the Russians as allies in wartime was that they always came too late and then were too strong. The same might be said of Germany's diplomatic tactics in 1905. After having waited a full year, the German government decided to protest against the Anglo-French agreement as it pertained to Morocco, and did so in the most violent way possible. On March 31, 1905, William II landed at Tangier and, riding through enthusiastic native crowds, hailed the sultan as an independent ruler. Simultaneously, complaining that it had not been informed of the Moroccan agreement, the German government demanded, in menacing tones, that it be set aside.

Here again it is difficult to understand what exactly the Germans hoped to gain from intervention; it may well be that they didn't know themselves. Certainly there was no real unity of view among the leading figures in the German government. The chief of the German General Staff, Count Schlieffen, felt that Germany's power position was slowly being altered for the worse and he would have welcomed an opportunity to stop its decline by a victorious war against France. The year 1905 was ideal for this purpose: Schlieffen had just finished the final revision of his war plan, which now called for a great wheeling movement through Belgium and across northeastern France that would encircle Paris and then inexorably drive the reeling French armies south and east toward the Swiss frontier; and Russia, prostrated by her defeat in the Far East, was in no position to come to her ally's aid. In the Foreign Office, Holstein shared Schlieffen's fears for the future and would also have welcomed a trial by arms. He had been an advocate of preventive war in 1887, and there is good evidence that he was thinking along the same lines in 1905: that he planned a forcing play in Morocco which would either compel the French to give in to the most humiliating terms (leaving England's faith in France shattered and the new entente useless) or would goad it into a war in which it would be smashed in accordance with Schlieffen's prescription.

If this was Holstein's secret purpose, he either did not wish or did not dare to open his mind to the chancellor, Prince Bülow, who regarded the Moroccan policy as purely a matter of bluff and blackmail for what Germany might get out of it, or the emperor who was nervous about the whole business, had never wanted to go to Tangier in the first place, and had—as he informed a group of German officers at the height of the crisis—no intention of "fighting a war for Morocco." Given the profound differences of view between Holstein, Bülow, and William II, it is understandable that German policy would be incoherent and that at decisive moments it would lack determination. This proved to be true.

At the outset, the vigor of the German intervention shocked and frightened the French government and, although Delcassé pleaded that any willingness to grant concessions under duress would alienate the British, he was unable to convince the majority of his colleagues and, in June 1905, he resigned from office. The Germans had long wanted to revenge themselves on the man who had "debauched Italy" in 1902, and Delcassé's fall was a stunning victory for them. It seemed quite possible that the French would now give them anything they asked.

But the lack of coherence in German policy robbed them of their triumph. At the time of the original intervention, the German government had insisted that its object was to have the Moroccan question referred to an international conference. It could not renege on that now. But before a conference met at Algeciras in 1906, the attitude of the French government had stiffened, and a change of British government had brought the Liberals to power and Sir Edward Grey to the Foreign Office. Grey was a man who felt, much more strongly than his predecessor, that the Germans were attempting to dominate Europe and that it was important to prevent this by strengthening the tie with France. Certainly, he insisted, care must be taken not to leave France in the lurch. Thanks to his attitude, therefore, the French and the British went into the Algeciras conference determined to hold to their original Moroccan agreement. The Germans, with much of the steam gone from their drive, ruined what was left of their case by blustering tactics in the conference itself and found, in the first decisive conference vote, that they were virtually isolated, only Austria-Hungary and Morocco voting with them. No essential change was made in the original Moroccan settlement; and what had started out as a German diplomatic victory ended as a defeat. It is significant that both Schlieffen and Holstein retired from office at the beginning of 1906. This was just, and underlined the fact that the Anglo-French connection they had hoped to smash had been strengthened by their tactics. It is no coincidence that 1905 marked the beginning of staff talks between British and French soldiers and that these soon led to joint staff planning.

The Formation of the Triple Entente / The Anglo-French entente soon received an accretion of strength by the conclusion of an agreement between Great Britain and Russia. To bring Russia into this company was, as he admitted in 1904, Delcassé's dearest dream; but it had remained a political impossibility until after his fall from office. The event that cleared the way for an Anglo-Russian agreement was Russia's defeat in the Far East, and this was true for a number of reasons. In the first place, Russia wanted to save as much as possible of its Far Eastern position and was anxious for help in negotiations with Japan on this point. Britain was Japan's ally, and it seemed logical to suppose that an agreement with it might be advantageous. Britain was also intimate with France, which—at a time when Russia needed French financial aid more than ever before—seemed an additional reason for a new approach to the British. In the third place, the Russian government was already contemplating a renewal of its forward policy in the Balkans, in order to divert public opinion from internal grievances; and it had no desire to encounter the kind of opposition it had met in 1887. Finally, the Russians were more anxious than ever before to cooperate with powers bent on

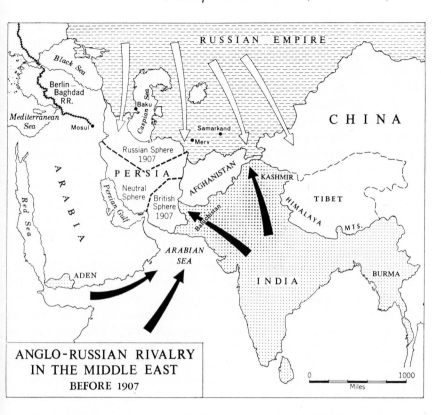

ANGLO-RUSSIAN RIVALRY
IN THE MIDDLE EAST
BEFORE 1907

baulking German ambitions, for they resented the fact that while Russia had been engaged in war with Japan, the Germans had been active in an area dangerously close to Russian interests on the Persian Gulf.

For all these reasons, the Russians were willing and anxious to attain more amicable relations with the British, and this desire was reciprocated. The procedure followed was similar to that used in negotiating the Anglo-French entente. In the course of 1906, the British sent to St. Petersburg one of their most experienced diplomats, Sir Arthur Nicolson. Working directly with the Russian foreign minister, Izvolsky, Nicolson applied himself to the three areas of the world where Anglo-Russian friction had been most dangerous: Afghanistan and Tibet, both of which represented threats to British security in India, and Persia, then as now an area of critical strategical importance. Nicolson showed great skill in winning the confidence of the Russian negotiator, but there is no doubt that he was aided in his task by Russian Far Eastern needs and by the fact that the spread of German influence in the vicinity of Persia gave the two powers a common interest.

In August 1907 the agreement was finally ratified. Both powers agreed to stay out of Tibet; and, while Russia agreed to regard Afghanistan as a British sphere of influence, the British in their turn agreed to do nothing to change the existing political situation there. As for Persia, while emphasizing their intention of preserving that country's independence and assuring other nations that their commercial rights would be respected, they proceeded to divide it into three zones. The British were acknowledged to have a virtual protectorate over the southernmost of these, which dominated the entrance to the Persian Gulf and included the province of Seistan, which gave access to Afghanistan and India. The northern zone, which included Ispahan and Teheran, fell to the Russians as their sphere of influence; and a large neutral zone was left between it and the British sphere to the south. Each power agreed not to seek economic concessions in the area allotted to the other; and together they tacitly agreed to bar Germany from Persia as a whole.

The Anglo-Russian agreement was one more example of the high-handedness of the imperialistic powers when dealing with backward countries. Its wider importance was that, even though it was popular in neither England nor Russia and by no means ended the mutual suspicion and dislike of the two governments, it did bring advantages to each party that were important enough to convince them of the necessity of remaining in contact. Even before the ratification of the agreement with Britain, Russia, in a secret agreement with Japan, got a sphere of influence in Manchuria, and its financial requests in Paris were received more cordially than they might have been had the peace with the British not been made. As for the British, they were assured of a diminution of the friction with Russia that had been so constant a preoccupation in the past and could count on Russian cooperation in placing obstacles in front of Germany's Baghdad Railway scheme.

Aside from this, the Anglo-Russian agreement laid the foundation for consistent diplomatic cooperation between Britain, France, and Russia. The diplomatic revolution that had begun when the Germans allowed the Reinsurance Treaty to lapse in 1890 was now complete, and the Triple Entente had come into existence to balance the Triple Alliance.

THE ROAD TO WAR, 1907-1914

New Tendencies / The reduction of European politics to this crude dualism was accompanied by three dangerous tendencies.

In the first place, it seemed much more important than it had ever been before to possess allies and much more damaging to lose them. Every government now suffered from recurrent nightmares in which it saw itself abandoned by its friends and encircled by a host of enemies; and every government, in its waking moments, strove to strengthen the loyalties of its allies and avoid even the suggestion of defection. Intent upon this objective, the powers not unnaturally lost some of their freedom of action. Their ability to cooperate in dangerous crises with members of the opposing coalition was limited by their estimate of how their own friends might react, and fear of offending allies was sometimes enough to prevent disinterested action in behalf of the general peace. By the same token, the ability of the coalition to restrain or discipline its own members by withholding support from moves that did not appear to be in the common interest was rendered imperfect by the fear of defection. A premium was placed upon what William II, in an unhappy moment, called *Nibelungen* loyalty; and this meant that, in the long run, both coalitions tended to fall under the control of their most irresponsible members.

In the second place, there was a general increase in armaments which, of course, merely fed the fears that produced it. Between 1900 and 1910 there had already been a significant rise in the army and naval estimates of the European powers, despite the fact that it was precisely in these years that there was considerable popular interest in arms reduction and two international peace conferences had met at The Hague (1899 and 1907) to discuss the possibility of submitting armaments to international control. These conferences had accomplished some useful work—defining the rules of war, outlawing certain inhumane weapons, extending the Geneva Red Cross Convention to naval warfare, establishing an international prize court and a permanent court of international justice—but they made no progress toward their main objective. Indeed, in the decade that saw these gatherings, the German government increased its army budget by a fifth, Russia by two thirds, Italy by a half, France by a third, Austria-Hungary by a quarter, and Great Britain by a third, while German naval estimates increased threefold and British naval estimates by more than a third. But this was nothing to the increases in the four years between 1910 and 1914, during which German and Austrian army expenditures doubled again and all other countries invested heavily in new ships, new guns, and new battalions. Some idea of this expanding investment in the tools of war is shown in the following table which presents in approximate figures the per capita expenditure of the great powers for armaments in the period we have covered in the last few chapters.

	1870	1880	1890	1900	1910	1914
Great Britain	$3.54	$3.46	$3.84	$12.60*	$7.29	$8.23
France	2.92	4.02	4.66	5.21	6.47	7.07
Russia	1.28	1.50	1.26	1.44	2.32	3.44
Germany	1.28	2.16	2.80	3.48	4.06	8.19
Austria-Hungary	1.08	1.70	1.50	1.46	1.68	3.10
Italy	1.38	1.74	2.52	2.34	3.36	3.16

* This figure represents the costs of the Boer War to the British taxpayer.

A third tendency, closely related to this last one, was the increase of military influence upon policy determination. In all countries military and naval officers were consulted more frequently by the political leadership and listened to more thoughtfully; and sometimes strong military personalities had a tendency to supersede the civilian authorities in certain areas of policy. Austria's policy in the Balkans was always more aggressive when Conrad von Hötzendorff was in office as chief of staff than when he was not; and Grand Admiral Alfred von Tirpitz succeeded in defeating all Foreign Office proposals for a naval accommodation with Great Britain in these critical years.

In the case of both Triple Alliance and Triple Entente, the soldiers of associated states held staff talks, exchanged technical information, and, in some cases, made arrangements of convenience. Theoretically, these had no binding force upon their governments. Yet, after British soldiers had been admitted to the secrets of the French General Staff in their continued consultations after 1905, it was difficult to deny that there was at least a presumption that, if France were attacked, Britain would help it. Between German and Austrian soldiers, commitments were even more explicit. In 1909, Conrad von Hötzendorff asked the German General Staff whether he could count on its support if Austria became involved in war as a result of an Austrian attack on Serbia. He was answered in the affirmative, although this reply represented a commitment which, in effect, removed the restrictions placed upon Austrian action by Bismarck's Dual Alliance of 1879 (see p. 277).

Given the mobility of modern war and the vast numbers employed in it, it was necessary for all general staffs to make detailed plans for the wars that might come, and it was only natural that they should have lavished most care upon the plan devised for the war that they considered most likely. In the elaboration of this plan, the soldiers were apt to allow technical advantage to take precedence over political considerations and to succumb in the end to the belief that any deviation from the projected operations would be disastrous. How destructive of a government's freedom of action this could be is illustrated by the Schlieffen plan. When the world was poised on the brink of war in 1914, a report came to Berlin that Britain might remain neutral if Germany did not attack France. The emperor suggested to his chief of staff that it might be well for Germany, therefore, to strike against Russia. He was informed that such a move was impossible, and that to depart from the plan of an initial assault against France at this late date would be disastrous. Germany's war plan had become so inflexible that the government was virtually incapable of acting in any but the prescribed way. They were even bound by their soldiers to start the war by violating Belgian territory, an act which was bound to alienate neutral sympathy but which the soldiers again said was imperative.

Finally, of course, soldiers who spent their lives studying the shifting power relationships of Europe were likely to press for action at moments when they thought their plans and their strength superior to that of any possible enemy combination. Mention has already been made of Schlieffen's fear that Germany's relative strength would decline with the years unless it took radical action against its rivals. He was not alone in this, and similar fears were felt by other soldiers in other countries. One of the most dangerous features of the crises of 1907–1914 was the fact that there were always influential soldiers who believed that this might be the last favorable moment for military action by their country and that it should not be allowed to slip.

The fearful dependence of the powers upon their alliances, their tendency to defer to their more irresponsible partners, the constantly accelerating armaments race, and the excessive military influence in policy determination were doubly dangerous because public opinion was largely unaware of their implications and, even when aware, powerless to do anything about them. Absorbed for the most part in domestic questions and well satisfied with the material comforts created by what appeared to be a century of progress, the great majority of citizens knew little of the way in which their country's foreign policy was made and nothing of the details of the secret agreements that bound it to others. Only when a new series of sharp crises broke out did they become aware that all was not well, and then they were not organized to correct the situation. In the years from 1907 to 1914, as the diplomatic machinery broke down, all of the organized groups of civilized society—churches, trade unions, political parties—proved just as ineffective as the diplomats themselves.

The Bosnian Crisis / The series of crises which led inexorably to the world war had its origins in a meeting that took place in a country estate at Buchlau, in Styria, between the Austrian foreign minister, Count Aehrenthal, and the Russian foreign minister, Alexander Izvolsky.

Despite the passage of the years, we still possess no completely reliable account of what these two ambitious and devious statesmen had to say to each other, but it is possible to reconstruct the substance, if not the nuances, of their talk. Izvolsky, who had lately concluded the negotiation of the Anglo-Russian agreement, burned for new triumphs and, in particular, was desirous, as he had told Aehrenthal in 1907, of having the Straits of the Bosphorus and Dardanelles opened to Russian warships, so that the Black Seas fleet could enter the Mediterranean. Aehrenthal was, as Izvolsky knew, anxious to annex the Turkish provinces of Bosnia and Herzegovina, which had been administered by Austria since 1878; and he regarded this annexation (although Izvolsky was surely not privy to *this* secret) as the first and necessary step in a policy which would encircle and destroy Serbia (see p. 408). The recent revolution in Turkey, which brought a militant and patriotic Young Turk party to power, served as a goad to both men, for it threatened to baulk their designs; this change in the political climate at Constantinople was the principal reason for the Buchlau meeting.

In their talk, the two foreign ministers agreed to support each other's plans, apparently assuming that if their governments announced their intention of changing the status of Bosnia and the Straits, there would be no serious objection by other powers, despite the infringement of treaty obligations such action would entail. They agreed, tacitly, that their announcements should be made at the same time. Yet Izvolsky did not apparently ask when that time was to be; in that lapse was the seed of much future trouble.

Leaving Buchlau, Izvolsky pursued a leisurely course westward to prepare the other capitals for the impending announcement. When he reached Paris on October 3, however, he was disagreeably surprised to receive a telegram from Aehrenthal saying that circumstances necessitated Austria's acting without further delay, and three days later the annexation of Bosnia was announced in Vienna.

This would not have mattered had Izvolsky been able to make his announcement too. But he was not. The adverse international reaction to the Austrian announcement indicated that there would be strong objection to any new violation of treaty law, which Russia was not prepared to brave. A change at the Straits with the consent of the other powers was also out of the question, as Izvolsky learned when he took the matter up in London. Lord Grey was disgusted with the Austrian action and implacably opposed to any new change that would weaken or offend the Turks, toward whom Grey's Liberal party was strongly sympathetic.

Under the impact of these unpleasant shocks, and the further discovery that Austria's annexation of Bosnia was as bitterly resented in Russia as in Serbia, Izvolsky, who had not informed his colleagues of his actions at Buchlau, lost his head. He denied that he had consented to the annexation, insisting that Buchlau had represented a mere exchange of views; he described Austria's action as a flagrant breach of written engagements; and he asked that an international conference meet to undo its action.

This irrational behavior was the reason for the crisis of 1908. The Serbs, already infuriated by the loss of provinces they had long considered their own, were encouraged by Pan-Slav agitations in Russia and by Izvolsky's lack of moderation to believe that Russia would support them, and they began to prepare for action. The Austrians responded with a partial mobilization and moved troops toward the Serb border. Both Conrad and Aehrenthal seemed delighted with the prospect of a war that would finally eliminate the Serbian irritation, and they were not much worried about what Russia might do. In his airy way, Aehrenthal told the British ambassador in Vienna that he knew Russia "like his own pocket" and was sure that she was in no position to go to war.

For the sake of the internal morale of the Triple Entente, the British decided that they must come to Izvolsky's aid. "It is evident," the permanent under secretary for foreign affairs said, "that we must do our best to support Izvolsky, such as he is." With that genius for devising compromises that is characteristic of British diplomacy, they tried to make an arrangement that would fob off the Serbs with monetary compensation and give Austria what it had taken, after certain ceremonial rituals had been performed to save Izvolsky's face.

This might have worked had not the Germans felt just as strongly about standing by their ally as the British. It was true that they were no more enthusiastic about Aehrenthal than the British about Izvolsky, for the Austrian foreign minister had not consulted them and his annexation of Bosnia had outraged the Turks, whom the Germans were bent on cultivating. Even so, the Germans felt compelled to act, for reasons which Bülow spelled out in words that tell much about the way in which alliance loyalty overruled prudence in the years before 1914:

> Our position would indeed be dangerous if Austria lost confidence in us and turned away. So long as we stand together, we form a bloc which no one will lightly attack. In eastern questions above all, we cannot place ourselves in opposition to Austria, who has nearer and greater interests in the Balkan peninsula than ourselves. A refusal or a grudging attitude in the question of the annexation of Bosnia and Herzegovina would not be forgiven. The old Emperor and official Austria see in the possession of these provinces a compensation for the loss of Italy and Germany.

In March 1909, Bülow proposed a solution of the Bosnian affair that dispensed with any idea of an international conference and supported the Austrian case. When Izvolsky hesitated to give in, Bülow reverted to the brutal directness that characterized so much of the diplomacy of William II. "We expect a precise answer, Yes or No," he said. "Any evasive, complicated or ambiguous reply will be regarded as a refusal. In that event we should withdraw and allow matters to take their course." In face of this scarcely veiled threat, Izvolsky caved in, and the crisis came to an end.

It nevertheless had serious consequences. It rendered Austrian policy suspect through all Europe and gave the impression that Germany was more interested in demonstrating its power than in serving the cause of peace. It strengthened the Triple Entente indirectly by making the Russian government more dependent upon it. Most serious of all, it opened the way for an era of Balkan wars. Izvolsky now devoted himself with a molelike persistence to revenging himself on Austria. He encouraged the Serbs to regard the loss of Bosnia as a merely temporary setback, and he provided funds for the continuation of Great-Serb propaganda work in Bosnia and Austria. He carried Delcassé's work in Italy one step further by making a secret agreement with the Italians at Racconigi in October 1909 that provided for consultation in Balkan affairs, for Italian support of Russia's plans at the Straits, and for Russian support of Italy's policy in Tripoli and Cyrenaica, if and when it decided to act in those regions. Finally, Izvolsky bent all his not inconsiderable diplomatic skill to the task of reconciling the long hostile Serbs and Bulgars in the interests of a new Pan-Slav program that would give him the triumph denied him by Aehrenthal. In view of these policies and their results, there was some justification for his boast in 1914: "This is *my* war, *my* war!"

Agadir / It has been argued persuasively that one of the most important contributory causes of the war was the failure of the designated leaders of the German government—that is, the emperor and the chancellor—either to direct or control German policy in the last prewar years. After the *Daily Telegraph* affair of 1908 (see p. 393), the emperor seemed in a chastened and submissive mood, and tended henceforth to defer to his military chiefs. After Bülow's fall in 1909, the chancellorship also seemed to lose some of its authority. In foreign affairs particularly, the new Chancellor Theobald von Bethmann-Hollweg had no experience and found it difficult to control those who had, or claimed to have: the realist and pro-Austrian school in the Foreign Office, the military staffs, and the military and naval attachés at foreign posts, all of whom favored a more aggressive policy than he thought safe.

Probably this explains the inexplicable and ill-conceived intervention of Germany in Moroccan affairs in 1911. This was largely the brainchild of the new Foreign Minister Alfred von Kiderlen-Wächter, a self-styled *Kerl* ("tough guy"), who had drafted for Bülow the ultimatum of 1909 to Russia and whose willfulness always terrified the chancellor. In April 1911, he demonstrated just how far he could carry that characteristic. As a result of disorders in Morocco, the French had sent troops into Fez, presumably to protect foreign residents. This exceeded France's legal rights as defined at Algeciras, but the government had argued that the need was great and that even the Germans would see no reason to object, since their economic interests had been protected by a separate Franco-German agreement of 1909. The French were wrong. In July 1911, without warning, Kiderlen dispatched the German gunboat *Panther* to the Moroccan port of Agadir.

This menacing action—it could hardly be regarded as anything else—shocked and puzzled Europe. What exactly did the Germans want? It is likely that the Germans did not know themselves. Kiderlen seems to have believed that a show of truculence would frighten the French into making some kind of offer. When it did not do so, he was embarrassed and perplexed; but, since he had to do something, he demanded that France cede all of the French Congo to Germany as compensation for its real and projected gains in Morocco.

To the Western Powers, this claim seemed so fantastic that the French considered it as a mere pretext for military action, while the British concluded that the Germans must really be after something else—perhaps a naval base on Morocco's Atlantic coast. Grey hinted delicately to the German ambassador that, whatever happened from now on, Britain would expect to be consulted. Kiderlen was obtuse enough to try to evade this, which further alarmed the British and finally led to Grey's authorizing a speech by the chancellor of the exchequer, David Lloyd George, which was almost as menacing as the *"Panther's* spring." With all the passion that he could command, Lloyd George accused Germany of seeking to disregard Great Britain in a matter affecting its interests, adding that, if peace could be preserved only

> by the surrender of the great and beneficent position Britain has won by centuries of heroism and achievement, by allowing Britain to be treated, where her interests were vitally affected, as if she were of no account in the Cabinet of Nations, then I say emphatically that peace at that price would be a humiliation intolerable for a great country like ours to endure. National honor is no party question.

The injection of national honor into this muddled dispute raised it to the level of a real threat to the peace. Encouraged by the British attitude, the French hardened to the point of obduracy in the matter of possible concessions; and the Germans were too far committed to back down without something to show for their efforts. In the end, it took all Grey's skill, and some special pleading in Paris by the Russians, to effect a settlement. The French got a free hand in Morocco; the Germans received some thousands of acres of African wastes; and the fragile peace was put together again.

The Consolidation of the Alliances / The narrowness with which war seemed to have been averted in 1911 shocked moderate opinion in both Britain and Germany and led some men of influence to criticize the bases of past policy and to call for a reappraisal. In England there was growing unease over what appeared to be incessant involvement in crises precipitated by French and Russian indiscretions; in Germany, there were increasing complaints over the political effects of the naval program, which Tirpitz now once more wished to expand in scope. Would it not be wise, men in both countries asked, to attempt an Anglo-German accommodation?

It was soon demonstrated that such an arrangement was unlikely. In February 1912, Lord Haldane, the British minister of war, a man who had studied at German universities and loved the country and its people, went to Berlin to discover whether any agreement was possible. The nub of the matter, it was soon apparent, was the projected German naval bill. Tirpitz, who appeared to be the dominant personality in Berlin during Haldane's visit, made it clear that this could not be sacrificed and that even modifications would depend upon Britain's willingness to agree to neutrality in the event of a French attack upon Germany. To the British Foreign Office, well aware of the difficulties of defining aggression, a binding promise of neutrality seemed unwise, especially since, the more Tirpitz' proposed modifications were studied, the less conciliatory they appeared to be. Fitful negotiations continued for some weeks after Haldane's return to London, but reached no conclusion. Meanwhile, Tirpitz had his way in Berlin; and his bill was passed in its original form by the Reichstag. When this happened, the best chance of an Anglo-German detente was lost.

Instead, both countries turned back to their allies and further strengthened their ties with them—Germany by increasing the intimacy of staff talks with the Austrians, Britain by moving closer to an alliance with France. Lord Grey had always opposed French requests for a formal alliance, for constitutional and political reasons and because he believed Britain must retain as much freedom of action as possible; but he could not avoid taking steps which gave the French a moral right to call for British aid in time of war. In November 1912, in order to persuade the French to move their Atlantic fleet to the Mediterranean to protect

British interests there while the British fleet was concentrated in the North Sea, Grey not only specifically authorized a continuation of the Anglo-French staff talks but gave the French the assurance that "if either Government had grave reason to expect an unprovoked attack by a third Power, it should immediately discuss with the other whether both Governments should act together." It is difficult to avoid the conclusion that this declaration and the fleet transfer that followed it imposed a moral obligation upon Britain to fight with France if Germany attacked.

It is safe to say that there was some continued concern in official circles in both Germany and England over these tendencies, but the surge of dangerous events in Eastern Europe now made loyalty to one's allies seem the highest form of political wisdom.

Tripoli and the Balkan Wars / One of the most fateful results of the Agadir crisis was that it aroused the fear in Italy that France might soon, despite all its assurances to the contrary, move into Tripoli, unless it was anticipated there. Before the dust had settled in Morocco, therefore, the Italian government informed the Turkish government that it intended to extend its "protection" over Tripoli and, when the Turks rejected this communication, declared war and invaded Tripoli in September 1911.

The Italian action, in turn, led the Balkan countries to fear that Austria might take advantage of Turkey's embarrassment to seize what was left of its European possessions, and they hastened to complete the work that Izvolsky had projected and which had been promoted by Hartwig and Nekliudov, the Russian ambassadors in Belgrade and Sofia. In March 1912, Bulgaria and Serbia concluded an alliance promising to aid each other in case of attack, to cooperate in repelling attempts by Great Powers to acquire Balkan territory, and to follow a common policy *vis-à-vis* Turkey, recognizing each other's natural interests if it should become necessary to go to war against her. Within a few months, both Greece and Montenegro had adhered to these articles, and the Balkan League had been formed.

To expect it to remain a league of peace at a time when so many enticing prospects were opening before the eyes of its members would have been unreasonable. In October 1912, the four Balkan powers launched a concerted attack upon Turkish forces in Europe and, within a few months, had swept them back to the Straits. They then turned to the pleasant task of dividing the spoils.

This turned out to be rather more difficult than had been imagined in the talks that preceded the war. For one thing, the two Great Powers most interested in the Balkans intervened: Austria, to prevent the acquisition by Serbia of access to the Adriatic Sea; Russia, to insist that Serbia and Montenegro be granted such access. This and other explosive territorial questions had to be submitted to an international conference at London, which solved the Adriatic problem by creating an independent Albania and compensating Serbia with territory in the interior. Peace was restored in May 1913 and lasted exactly one month, at the end of which time territorial disputes among the members of the Balkan League touched off a second war, during which Bulgaria was attacked and despoiled of its recent gains by its late friends with the additional aid of Rumania and Turkey.

In both of these conflicts, peace was maintained among the Great Powers by the cooperation of Great Britain and Germany. Grey and Bethmann-Hollweg sponsored the London Conference and devised the Adriatic compromise that was the key to the settlement of the first Balkan war. The English restrained the Russians during both conflicts, and, in the second, when there was a real possibility of Austria intervening by force of arms on the side of Bulgaria, Bethmann persuaded its government not to do so. The success of joint Anglo-German efforts in behalf of peace in 1912 and 1913 seemed to indicate that those who encouraged Haldane to go to Berlin had reason on their side.

Even so, this fruitful cooperation was not destined to continue. At the end of the Balkan wars, the Austrians were critical of Germany's failure to support them and open in their accusations that Germany was responsible for dangerous accretions to Serbian strength. In much the same way, the Russians blamed the British for the creation of Albania, which blocked Serbia from the sea, and were critical of France for having done nothing to defeat this unfortunate arrangement. The bitter complaints of these powers made their diplomatic partners uneasy and unwilling to try their patience with new disappointments. German soldiers, prompted by Conrad's reproaches, warned of the serious consequences of future lack of support. Sir Arthur Nicolson, now permanent under secretary for foreign affairs in Great Britain, confessed that he was haunted by the fear that "Russia should become tired of us and strike a bargain with Germany"; and the French felt even more strongly that Russia must be handled delicately from now on.

This reluctance to continue to restrain the most irresponsible members of the family of nations was doubly ominous in view of two related facts. The first was that both the Austrian and Russian governments were now dominated by men who felt that the moment of decision could not be long delayed—that it must be made clear once and for all whether Austrian or Russian influence was to be predominant in the Balkans. The second was that the Serbian government was not content with its sizable gains during the Balkan wars. Its premier had said bluntly, after the

Archduke Francis Ferdinand of Austria and his consort in Sarajevo one hour before their assassination. (THE BETTMANN ARCHIVE)

cessation of hostilities in August 1913, "The first round is won; now we must prepare for the second, against Austria."

The Final Crisis   /   Throughout the spring of 1914 all nations accelerated their military preparations and persuaded their parliaments to vote new funds for expansion. This activity moved Europe one more step toward the brink, for it led to the kind of elaborate calculations which soldiers indulge in and which have not been unknown in our time. The experts of the Central Powers, viewing the projected Russian and French programs, were now more than ever convinced that the balance was turning against them. "For us in the Triple Alliance," Field Marshal Conrad remarked to the German military attaché, "there are only two alternatives, either to strike at once or to strengthen our armaments correspondingly, and of the two the former is by far the more correct from a military point of view." The only thing that seemed to be holding Conrad back was concern over the length of time Austria might have to stand alone against Russia before Germany came to its aid. In May, however, he learned, first, that the German chief of staff, the younger Moltke, was sympathetic to his view that further postponement of a conflict that appeared inevitable would be fatal, and, second, that Moltke's plans, based on those of Schlieffen, called for a thrust westward that would knock France out within six weeks, followed by the diversion of

Germany's full strength to the drive against Russia. Moltke apparently believed that Britain would intervene on France's side, but that her intervention would be ineffective and would not disrupt the schedule.

Conrad was heartened by these intimations, and it would be interesting to know how he would have acted upon them if the Serbs had not relieved him of the necessity of action. But on June 28, 1914, in the Bosnian town of Sarajevo, a young Serbian patriot named Gavrilo Princip shot and killed the Austrian heir apparent, Archduke Franz Ferdinand, and his consort; and Conrad and those who thought like him did not have to exercise their powers of invention. There was every reason to suspect that the assassination was not a private act; and, indeed, it was later proved that Princip and his fellow assassins were the idealistic tools of a Colonel Dragutin Dimitrijevic, chief of the Intelligence Department of the Serbian General Staff and leading spirit in the patriotic Black Hand Society, who had coldbloodedly planned the deed. Although this and the degree to which the Serbian government was aware of the planned assassination were not fully known in Vienna, the government there had the excuse it had long wanted for action against Belgrade.

It was not until July 23, however, that Europe learned how drastic that action would be. The initial shock of the coup at Sarajevo had diminished and Europe was beginning to relax again, when on July 23 the Austrian government sent an ultimatum to Belgrade, charging the Serbian government with complicity in the deed and laying down a series of demands which, if fully met, would virtually have deprived Serbia of independence. Lord Grey was shocked when he saw them and told the Austrian ambassador that he had never before seen one government send another "a document of so formidable a character." The Russian foreign minister, Sazonov, who had been counseling the Serbs to do everything in their power to appease the Austrians, was aghast and blurted out to the Austrian ambassador: "This means a European war. You are setting Europe alight!"

The harshness of the Austrian terms was no inadvertence. Vienna was resolved on the extermination of Serbia and was confident that Germany would back her all the way. On July 5, 1914, a Crown Council in Berlin had agreed that Austria must be encouraged to liquidate the Serbian problem and that Germany must support Austria in the event of Russian intervention. The Austrians had been informed of this and, when the Serbian government answered their ultimatum with promises of far-reaching concessions to its demands, declared this answer unsatisfactory and, on July 28, declared war. The ultimate crisis had arrived.

It is difficult to avoid the conclusion that, when it did so, the diplomats, as if worn out by the long series of crises that had begun in 1908, succumbed to defeatism. It is true that they did go through the motions of trying to save the peace, but their hearts were no longer in it. The men of energy and will in August 1914 were the soldiers. It was they, for instance, who overcame the doubts of the tsar and some of his advisers by insisting that Russia must not abandon the Serbs. The news on July 29 that the Russians had ordered partial mobilization shocked Bethmann in Berlin, and he sought feebly and belatedly to hold the Austrians back. For the German soldiers, however, there was no turning back: and on July 30, Moltke, without informing either the emperor or the chancellor, sent a telegram to Conrad in Vienna, urging him to start mobilization against Russia immediately and to reject compromise solutions that were currently being made by Lord Grey. War, he added, was now a condition of Austria's survival. "Germany will go along with her unconditionally." When Conrad informed Foreign Minister Berchtold of this telegram, Berchtold, who had been listening to Bethmann's pleas, said inelegantly, "That's something! Who's ruling in Berlin?"

The answer was that the soldiers were. On the same day (July 31) that Austria followed their advice and mobilized against Russia, the German government sent an ultimatum to St. Petersburg, demanding hands off in the Balkans, and when it received no reply, declared war on August 1. The rigidity of Germany's war plan now required the speediest possible inception of hostilities and in the west of Europe rather than in the Balkans. Dismissing the emperor's suggestion that operations might at least temporarily be confined to the Russian front, Moltke secured the dispatch of an ultimatum to France and a note to Belgium demanding free passage of German troops. When these were refused, the German declaration of war followed automatically on August 3, and the invasion of Belgium began. This action relieved Lord Grey of the necessity of explaining the extent of his diplomatic commitments to France and allowed him to base his demand for English intervention upon the protection of England's traditional interests. On August 4, Britain and Germany were at war.

Responsibility / If the last few pages have seemed to stress the responsibility of Austria-Hungary and Germany for driving Europe into war, it should not be forgotten that the other powers shared the blame. The incident that brought the final crisis was the result of a crime planned by official agents of the Serbian government; the aggressive policy of the Serbs was at least in part the result of Russian encouragement; the foolhardiness of the Russians in promoting a provocative policy on the part of the Serbs was in part the result of the failure of the British and French governments to impose adequate restraints upon them; and this failure was caused by the fact that Britain and France suffered from the same fears that dimmed the judgment of the German and Austrian governments. Whatever one may decide about the relative guilt of the powers—and this is something on which historians still differ widely—it is clear that no power bears the full responsibility for the war and none is completely guiltless.

Seen in a wider setting, the coming of the war may be regarded as a reflection of tendencies that we have noted in the domestic history of the European states in the years after 1871. The division of Europe into two armed camps after 1907 corresponded roughly to the process of polarization which was taking place in internal politics and was dividing country after country into two extreme factions. The erosion of the moderate position, the abandonment of the liberal attitude, the flight from the reasonable solution and, indeed, from the very use of the human reason to reach solutions—these tendencies, which we have noted in the domestic history of Europe, had their counterparts in its diplomatic history. And now in 1914 that progressive acceptance of violence which characterized so many areas of European thought and activity became complete, and Europe ended its century of progress in an orgy of violence from which it never recovered.

PART FOUR

1914
1945

GENERAL OBSERVATIONS

When war burst upon the world in August 1914, a great number of people in every country of Europe comforted themselves with two thoughts. The first was that their country would be victorious in very short order and at very little cost and that life would return to normal very soon. The second was that, by some magic process, the war would solve all outstanding political, economic, social, and even moral problems and purge Europe of its accumulated ills. As one of the characters in Ernst Gläser's war novel *Class of 1902* said:

> At last life had regained an ideal significance. The great virtues of humanity . . . fidelity, patriotism, readiness to die for an ideal . . . were triumphing now over the trading and shopkeeping spirit. . . . This was the providential lightning flash that would clear the air. . . . He could see a new world, ruled and directed by a race of aristocrats who would root out all signs of degeneracy and lead humanity back to the deserted peaks of the eternal ideals. . . . The war would cleanse mankind from all its impurities.

This was, as the English writer C. E. Montague commented sardonically, a "happy vision, beautiful dream!—like Thackeray's reverie about having a very old and rich aunt. But the dreamer awakes among the snows of the Mont Cenis with a horrid smell in the corridor and the hot-water pipes out of order." Some such rude awakening awaited all the participants in World War I. For that conflict was not short, as we shall see in the next chapter; the enemy was not beaten easily and cheaply; and, after five years of desperate fighting in which a generation of young men was destroyed, it was very difficult to differentiate in any meaningful way between the condition of the victors and that of the vanquished.

Moreover, the war seemed to create far more problems than it solved. Friction between nations was so bitter and so continuous after 1919 that the widows of the first world holocaust were soon contemplating the fearful probability that their sons would die in a second. Meanwhile, within the different European countries, conflict between parties and social classes assumed an intensity of violence unknown before 1914. Even in a country like England, with a strong tradition of orderly change and respect for law, nothing is more striking in the speeches of government officials, representatives of employers' groups, and labor leaders and in newspaper articles and editorials during the 1920s than the frank recognition that industrial relations had become a running class war. In England, after the general strike of 1926 (see p. 658) had brought the country to its senses, there was a marked diminution in the virulence of this social strife. Other countries, however, were less fortunate; and in many intestine conflict made orderly government impossible and eventually dissolved the social fabric.

The details of these troubles will fill the chapters that follow. In the appropriate place, it will be seen how they all, in one way or another, stemmed from the losses of the war and the decisions of the Peace Conference, how they were affected by the crippling or actual destruction of the old political hierarchies, how they were influenced by economic dislocations set in train during the long conflict and aggravated by the subsequent depressions and the shrinking role of Europe in the world economy, and, finally, how they were heightened by the rise of totalitarian ideologies with strong national bases.

So much will be said, indeed, in the pages which follow, about the more violent aspects of this quarter of a century that it would be well at the very outset to note that there were other things going on in these years besides external and internal war. The ingenuity of European minds was not directed solely to devising more diabolical weapons or new ways of overthrowing regimes; and it would be a mistake, even in an account that is predominantly concerned with political and social history, to pass over the achievements of Europe's scientists and engineers, its scholars and artists, its writers and musicians. If this was—as it has often been called—an age of conflict, it was nevertheless an age of creative accomplishment as well. How true this is becomes apparent if we think of how greatly our view of the world and the universe of which it is a part has changed as a result of the theory of relativity and the development of atomic research, both essentially products of this period; or of what tremendous advances in medicine, physiology, and surgery have been made possible by the contributions of biophysics and biochemistry to genetics, germ-cell and gland research, and particularly by the discovery of vitamins, of insulin (1922) and cortisone (1936), and of such enemies of the virus diseases as penicillin (1929), sulpha pyridine (applied in 1938 in the treatment of pneumonia), and the now familiar and readily available antibiotics, streptomycin and aureomycin; or of how our ability to treat mental disease and to attack certain forms

Albert Einstein, 1879–
1955.
(CULVER SERVICE)

of antisocial behavior has been improved by the development and refinement of clinical neurology and psychiatry; or of how our schools on the one hand and our prisons on the other have benefited from advances in psychology and sociology; or of how many aspects of life, including the political, have been revolutionized by the invention and perfection of such things as the automobile, the aeroplane, motion pictures, radio, and television.

Not all of these things were, strictly speaking, European in origin; but the part played by European brains and energy in these achievements of pure and applied science was very great. The new physics, which sensibly departed from nineteenth-century concepts of energy and mass, received its initial impulse from the German Max Planck's quantum theory of 1900 and found its most comprehensive exposition in the Special and General Theories of Relativity formulated in 1905 and 1915 by Planck's countryman Albert Einstein, who reconciled the apparent contradictions between Newtonian assumptions and the electromagnetic theory of Clerk Maxwell (1873) in a new form of field physics. The development of atomic research began essentially in 1911 with the New

Zealander Rutherford's deduction from his studies of radioactivity that the atom, far from being solid, as had been believed since the time of Democritus, was largely an empty structure comprising a minute nucleus (or proton) with a positive electrical charge, surrounded by a shell of negatively charged electrons—in a word, a kind of miniature solar system. With the aid of this explanation and Planck's quantum theory, the Dane Niels Bohr formulated his general theory of atomic structure in 1913; and upon this basis the later work of such distinguished European physicists as Werner Heisenberg of Germany and Erwin Schrödinger of Austria, Enrico Fermi of Italy, and the Englishmen Cockcroft, Walton, and Chadwick was accomplished.

In other sciences, both pure and behavioral, the European contribution was correspondingly great. In clinical and social psychiatry, for instance, the great names were those of the Austrian Sigmund Freud and the Swiss Carl Jung; while in sociology the German Max Weber and the Italians Vilfredo Pareto and Gaetano Mosca devised methods of diagnosis that completely superseded the techniques of the older sociology, while their studies of such things as bureaucratic behavior and the role of elites in history made possible a more realistic appreciation of the way society works.

All in all, it must be said that, at a time when Europe's financial and industrial superiority was being lost to the New World, when markets that had once been the preserve of European traders were being invaded by American, Indian, and Japanese goods, and when, despite appearances, Europe's political primacy was already a thing of the past, it retained the scientific leadership of the world throughout most of this period. It was only after 1933, when Hitler's persecution of the Jews and his war against independence of thought led many of Europe's finest scientific minds to go into exile, that the balance began to shift toward the United States and Russia, a development confirmed by World War II, which left those two countries the best fitted, in financial and other ways, to promote scientific research and development.

In the field of the arts, the same vitality and high achievement were to be noted, although these qualities should perhaps be emphasized less than the spirit of rebellion against the forms and values of the past that characterized them. In architecture, the break with tradition was seen in a marked emphasis upon functionalism—that is, upon the use of new materials and techniques of construction to make the appearance of buildings conform to their use. In cities like Berlin, Vienna, Stockholm, and Helsinki, the new style produced buildings that were perhaps startling to the eyes of those who were accustomed to regard massiveness and external decoration as the hallmarks of architectural style but combined beauty with a cleanness and directness of design that was

The new architecture: The Machine Shop, the Bauhaus, Dessau. (PHOTO SIGFRIED GIEDION)

singularly appropriate to urban industrial society. A fine example was the famous Bauhaus at Dessau, built in 1925 by Germany's leading representative of the new architecture, Walter Gropius. Less interested in function than in the poetic use of form was the French-Swiss architect, Le Corbusier, whose work showed a close affinity with the abstract painting of the period.

Much of the painting and sculpture of these years was more difficult to enjoy or even to understand, for here the break with the past took the form of a deliberate repudiation of any kind of naturalism. Arnold Hauser has written that the idea that art was supposed to be faithful to nature had never been seriously questioned in principle since the Middle Ages and had remained an article of faith with the impressionist school of the nineteenth century. Post-impressionist art, however, renounced all illusion of reality and set out to "express its outlook on life by the deliberate deformation of natural objects." The expressionist paintings of Chagall, the works of Picasso's cubist period, the surrealist painting of Chirico and Dali, the sculpture of Epstein and Henry Moore possessed undeniable power; but, in most cases, they portrayed worlds or fragments of worlds not easily recognizable or accessible to the viewer. In some cases, indeed, the artist seemed uninterested in communicating with any audience outside himself, refusing to use accepted methods of communication and inventing a language of his own. This tendency was not confined to painting and sculpture, although it was perhaps most marked there. It also appeared in much of the music of the period and in some of the literature. The road from Stravinsky to Schoenberg was most easily traveled by trained musicians, or mathematicians; the lover of Dickens could find his way through the denser passages of *Finnegans Wake* only with guidebook in hand.

This was a period of literary distinction, and a list of its greatest figures would compare favorably with those of any previous period discussed in this book. It would include, in the field of the novel, Thomas Mann, Hermann Hesse, Alfred Döblin, Marcel Proust, André Gide, Franz Kafka, D. H. Lawrence, and James Joyce; in poetry, A. E. Housman, William Butler Yeats, T. S. Eliot, W. H. Auden, Paul Valéry, Georg Trakl; in the drama, George Bernard Shaw, Paul Claudel, Luigi Pirandello, Bertolt Brecht; in the film, Sergei Eisenstein, René Clair, and Fritz Lang.

In common with the painters and sculptors, most of these men were in revolt against the past, and they showed this sometimes by the choice of radically unconventional style or organization—as in the case of the expressionist dramas and films of the first postwar years (the German film *The Cabinet of Dr. Caligari* would be a good example) and Joyce's *Ulysses* (1922) and *Finnegans Wake* (1939)—and sometimes by a deliberate rejection of commonly accepted values and institutions. The latter tendency took various forms and was to be found in the Fabian frivolities of Shaw, the militant reformism of plays like Ernst Toller's *Mass Man* (1920) and *The Machine-Breakers* (1922), the cynicism of Brecht's *Threepenny Opera* (1928), and the pronounced pessimism of Housman's poetry and novels like Hermann Broch's *The Sleep-Walkers* (1929) and Kafka's *The Trial* (1920) and *The Castle* (1926). As in the case of the painters also, the writers sought in some cases to withdraw completely from contemporary realities, seeking new inspiration or new values in non-European climes and cultures. Gide looked for inspiration to Africa, and Hesse, who wrote in his sensational novel *Demian* in 1919 that Europe had "fallen finally into a deep spiritual devastation," turned to the East.

In much of the literature of these years, emphasis was placed either upon the inadequacy of reason to control life or upon the necessity of transcending the limitations of reason in order to attain greater freedom. The latter idea, which was influenced by the Freudian theory that man can be free if he will loose himself from old burdens and repressions, was seen in much of the work of the expressionist school and was reflected in the widespread popularity, among the postwar youth of Europe, of writers like Dostoevsky and the theologian Sören Kierkegaard, who had emphasized the irrational as a regenerative force and exalted faith over logic. On the other hand, the belief that man's life was determined by dark instinctual forces and by external compulsions over which he had no control colored the work of Proust, Joyce, Thomas Mann (especially in works like *Death in Venice* and *The Magic Mountain*) and Alfred

Döblin (particularly in his great novel *Berlin Alexanderplatz*, which appeared in 1930).

The continued vogue of Bergson, the interest in Ludwig Wittgenstein's systematic denial of the possibility of a rational metaphysics, and the development of an increasingly radical empiricism showed that the same reaction against rationalism was important among the philosophers of this period; and, during and after World War II, the growth of existentialism, which stemmed essentially from Nietzsche and Kierkegaard, was to confirm this tendency. This was offset to some extent by the strong revival of Aquinian rationalism, and, under the influence of Étienne Gilson and Jacques Maritain, the scholastic philosophy made a considerable number of converts in this period. In the area of philosophy of history, the work that attracted most attention was Oswald Spengler's *The Decline of the West* (1918), a massive and pedantic book which sought, by biological analogy, to demonstrate that cultures pass through stages from birth to death like living organisms but seemed bent on persuading western civilization to avoid its inevitable fate. More people quoted *The Decline* than read it; and, on the whole, it probably had less influence than Spengler's much shorter essay *Prussianism and Socialism* (1919), which, with its argument that the ideals of Frederick the Great were the real alternative to Marxism, had a profound effect upon the revival of neo-conservatism in Germany.

The progress of urbanization, the success of secular religions, and the victory in some countries, particularly the Soviet Union, of governments that were opposed in principle to formal religion raised serious problems for the established churches but at the same time stimulated religious thinkers to rise to the challenge of the times. The tendency of church leaders to adjust themselves to the prevailing materialism and to compromise with popular philosophies of science and the like, which had been reflected before 1914 in the spread of reformism and the avoidance of dogma in Protestantism and Judaism, now gave way to a more stubborn and convincing defense of the elements of religious faith. Roman Catholicism, always less responsive to the forces of appeasement than other religions, had two determined and eloquent spokesmen in these years, Pope Pius XI (1922–1939) and his successor Eugenio Pacelli, who took the title Pope Pius XII (1939–1958). In the person of Karl Barth, Protestantism found its most persuasive enemy of watered-down and rationalistic theology; and, under his leadership and the influence of writers like Albert Schweitzer and Emil Brunner, there was a marked revival of elements in Christianity that had their origin in the teaching of the apostle Paul.

This cursory sketch of the intellectual and artistic tendencies of this quarter of a century may, if it does nothing else, leave an impression

of the vitality and the diversity of European thought. The years after
1919 were difficult and perplexing ones, and there was much truth in the
words which Paul Valéry addressed to a French audience shortly after
the war:

> All the fundamentals of our life have been affected by the war and some-
> thing deeper has been worn away than the renewable parts of the machine.
> You know how greatly the general economic situation has been disturbed,
> and the polity of states and the very life of the individual; you are familiar
> with the universal discomfort, hesitation, apprehension. But among these
> injured things is the Mind. The Mind has indeed been cruelly wounded; its
> complaint is heard in the hearts of intellectual man; it passes a mournful
> judgment on itself. It doubts itself profoundly.

It is true that the confidence that had characterized European thought
in the nineteenth century had been weakened by the war; and, when
the threat of a new conflict became very real in the late 1930s, that loss
made itself felt. But, as we look at the period as a whole, we are apt to
be impressed less by the presence of defeatism (that came very late)
than by the evidence of a critical testing of old values and an earnest
search for new ones. Even in this period when Europe's role in the world
was in rapid decline, its spirit was alive and its contributions to the
civilization of the western world very great.

20

War and European Society, 1914-1918

The onset of hostilities in August 1914 was greeted in many of the cities of the larger countries with an almost carnival gaiety. In London, the mood was one of excitement and enthusiasm; in German towns, reservists on their way to mustering centers were pelted with flowers; in Vienna, crowds promenaded along the Ringstrasse, shouting "Down with Serbia!" with every evidence of happiness. These raptures were, of course, the result of ignorance. No one in 1914 had the slightest idea of what the war was to be like; on this score, the generals and the statesmen were no wiser than those who bawled out their enthusiasm in the streets. The operational plans that had been devised by the different general staffs showed that the soldiers believed in a short and mobile war, not essentially different from the brisk conflicts of the 1860s; and the fact that their governments agreed with them was demonstrated by the almost total absence of plans for financing a long war, for producing the munitions or acquiring the strategical materials to support it, or for organizing society in such a way as to prevent the breakdown of normal production and services. No one dreamed that the conflict would last for more than four years and that it would kill two million young Germans, more than a million Frenchmen, almost as many Englishmen and Austrians, half a million Italians, and an unknown number of Russians.

Nor did any of those who shouted in the streets in 1914 realize that the war they were greeting so lightheartedly would destroy the Europe they had known and leave them with sadly depleted physical and psychological resources to face a forbidding future.

THE COURSE OF THE WAR, 1914–1916

The Western Front from Liège to the Marne / From the very beginning the war confounded expectations. The Germans, for instance, whose war plans had been reviewed and amended yearly since the days of Schlieffen, had confidently expected that, by seizing the initiative, they would be able to win a quick and decisive victory in the west that would enable them subsequently to devote their full energies to the slower task of defeating Russia. As it turned out, their most devastating victories in the first months of the war were won in the east, while their western plan came to nothing.

This was partly the result of a German underestimation of their opponents, particularly of the Belgians and the British. The German plan called for a sweep through Belgium, which they did not expect to be opposed, since it was known that the outbreak of war had caught the Belgian army in the middle of a basic reorganization. But the Belgians did fight, gallantly and with such effect that the ring of fortresses around Liège stalled the German columns for four days. When this initial resistance was broken and the Belgian army had been thrown back on Antwerp, the German drive picked up speed, and the great wheeling movement began that was meant to envelop the now uncovered left of General Lanrezac's Fifth French Army, which was holding grimly on the Sambre River. The Germans, however, had forgotten the British or, rather, had supposed that what help the British could send would be late and would arrive at ports remote from the decisive area of operations. Unknown to them, the British had landed one cavalry division and four infantry divisions under Sir John French at Le Havre, Rouen, and Boulogne while the Germans were still being held at Liège. These "Old Contemptibles" were now rushed forward to Mons, where, on August 21, they fell in on the French left and prevented them from being outflanked and overrun.

The battle on the Sambre and the stubborn resistance put up by the British and French armies as they fell back upon Paris slowed the momentum of the German drive, and casualties from battle and fatigue were so heavy that Kluck, the commander of the German First Army, began to doubt the feasibility of enveloping Paris in accordance with the Schlieffen plan. After another hard fight with the British at Le Cateau

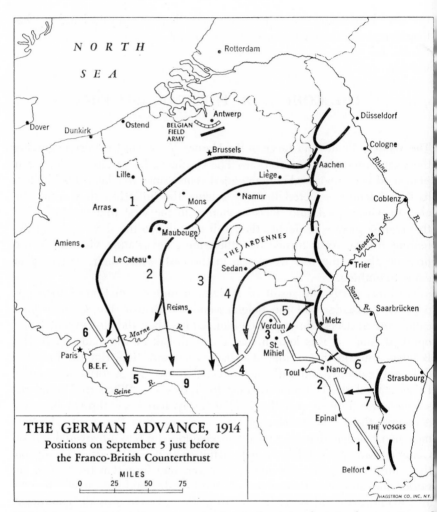

THE GERMAN ADVANCE, 1914

Positions on September 5 just before
the Franco-British Counterthrust

This adaptation of a German map shows the imperfect implementation of Schlieffen's great plan.

(August 26), therefore, he wheeled his forces to the east, rather than the west, of Paris. His intention was, once more, to smash Lanrezac's army, now engaged in bitter fighting with the German Second Army near Guise; but it was a fatal maneuver. The French commander-in-chief, Joffre, a sensible if not brilliant soldier, had been holding his reserves at Paris; and, as Kluck wheeled, he threw them against his rear. Thus began the battle of the Marne, which put the Germans on the defensive for the first time. The situation might have been retrieved if the German chief of staff, Moltke, had not at this juncture made the mistake of committing his left wing to an offensive against Nancy. The result was that the Germans found themselves engaged in two violent and uncoordinated battles, on the Marne and in Lorraine, a situation that proved too much for Moltke's weak nerves and induced him to leave one of the most crucial decisions of the war to a subordinate, Lt. Col. Hentsch. This officer, sent to Kluck's front on September 9 to review the situation, ordered him to break off hostilities and to withdraw behind the Aisne River. The retreat represented a psychological blow from which the German armies never completely recovered.

The War in the Trenches / This was not only because it was a clear defeat and one that marked the definitive failure of the Schlieffen plan, but also because it turned the war in the west into a kind of struggle for which the German officer corps, raised in the tradition of lightning, mobile, destructive war, was not prepared. Even after Moltke was retired on September 14 and replaced by a more confident and energetic chief of staff, Erich von Falkenhayn, a resumption of the German offensive proved impossible. The Germans dug in along the line Noyon-Rheims-Verdun; their opponents followed their example; and the two great armies faced each other in a double line of trenches, each protected by dense barbed-wire entanglements and cunningly disposed machine-gun nests and mortar batteries, and backed by a support line and, further back, by heavy artillery. This elaborate underground system soon extended all the way from the Channel ports to the frontiers of Switzerland.

It was to be four years before the deadlock thus created was broken and mobility of operations restored. In the meantime, the youth of England, France, and Germany was squandered on futile assaults upon each other's fixed positions. In this fantastic new form of warfare, men lived like foxes and moles, in burrows that were sometimes only a score of yards from those of their adversaries. By day, they exchanged desultory rifle fire over the parapets, or lobbed grenades into the enemy's trenches, or laid down a systematic pattern of mortar or artillery fire upon his supply lines. At night, small parties crept out into the no-man's land between the lines, their faces blackened so that they would not show in the glare of Véry rockets, and cut their way through the wire, seeking prisoners who might divulge information about the enemy's plans. Periodically, the high command, with an enthusiasm and optimism that never seemed to dim, ordered a general offensive in this or that sector of the front. These big pushes were preceded by a protracted artillery barrage that was intended to flatten the enemy's wire, destroy as many of his strong points as possible, and leave his troops cowering in their trenches in a state of shock. The barrage was frequently preceded by elaborate engineering operations, which dug beneath the enemy's

"Well, if you knows of a better 'ole, go to it!"

This cartoon by Bruce Bairnsfather, which originally appeared in *The Bystander* (London), appealed to fighting men of all nations and won world fame. © *The Tatler & Bystander*.

trenches and mined them with explosive charges; and it was sometimes accompanied by the release of chlorine gas, one of the more horrible innovations of the war. When these preparatory steps were complete, the infantry began to go over the top of their parapets in waves and, with fixed bayonets and, under a rolling barrage, to walk toward the enemy trenches. All too often it was discovered at this point that the barrage had not been long enough to do what it was expected to do, or that the enemy had withdrawn from the shelled lines and was now fighting back from intact ones, or that the bombardment had turned the battlefield into a swamp that made movement impossible, or that the wind had shifted and was blowing the gas the wrong way, or that some other miscalculation had been made. As a result, the gains were always infinitesimal and the losses tremendous.

During all of 1915, for instance, despite repeated attacks, the British and French did not gain more than three miles at any one point; but the French suffered 1,430,000 casualties. Falkenhayn hammered at Verdun for ten months in 1916 and did not take it, but lost 336,000 men.

In the battle of the Somme in the same year, the Allies lost 614,000 men and the Germans 650,000, without any appreciable gain on either side. In the third battle of Ypres in 1917, the British fought for five months and, with casualties of 450,000, advanced less than five miles on a nine-mile front.

The Eastern Front from Tannenberg to Gorlice / In contrast to this situation, the war in the east was marked with great mobility and with considerable gain and loss of territory. The pace was set here at the outset by the Russians, who surprised both the Germans and the Austrians by accelerating their mobilization and throwing two armies into East Prussia and four against the Austrian lines in Galicia.

The advance in East Prussia was in response to the urgent plea of Russia's ally France; and it suffered from overhasty preparation, from grave defects of logistical support, and from lack of coordination at the command level. Since the war against Japan, there had been bad blood between Rennenkampf, the commander of the Russian First Army, and his opposite number in the Second Army, Samsonov; and this and their temperaments (Samsonov was impetuous; Rennenkampf, cautious and slow) made it difficult for them to work together. Their advance into East Prussia had the initial effect of panicking the German corps under Mackensen and making the commander-in-chief in East Prussia, Prittwitz, telephone to Moltke for aid. Cooler heads among the Germans noticed, however, that there was a wide and inviting gap between the two Russian armies; and even before help arrived in the form of a retired general named Paul von Hindenburg, who replaced Prittwitz, and a younger major general named Erich Ludendorff, who had distinguished himself only days before at Liège, plans had been drawn up to exploit the separation. While a single cavalry division was left to face Rennenkampf, a German corps under François moved by rail from Königsberg around Samsonov's flank to Tannenberg, where it detrained and held his army until two other German corps enveloped it from the rear. The bewildered Russians reeled into the trap, 90,000 of them surrendering before the fighting stopped on August 30. Their unhappy commander shot himself.

This stunning German success was followed by Hindenburg's victory over Rennenkampf's now isolated force in the battle of the Masurian Lakes. By September 15, East Prussia was freed of Russians, and a legend had been born that was to have profound effects upon Germany's internal politics: that of the military genius and invincibility of the Hindenburg-Ludendorff team.

To place too much emphasis upon the battles of Tannenberg and the Masurian Lakes would be to belittle the important contribution made by the Russians to the Allied cause in the first period of the war. While

Rennenkampf and Samsonov were being encircled in East Prussia, four Russian armies under General Ivanov had advanced into Galicia and, between August 23 and the middle of September, a series of hard battles was fought between them and the bulk of the Austrian army. Under Conrad von Hötzendorff's gifted direction, the Austrians had initial success at Krasnick and Komarow, but numbers soon began to tell against them; by September 10, with the two forces locked in conflict all along the line, the Russian Fifth Army under Plehve began to creep around Conrad's rear, and a major envelopment seemed in progress. The Russian habit of sending operational orders by wireless without taking the trouble to encode them, however, warned the Austrian chief of staff in time to extricate his forces; but he had to withdraw his badly mauled armies to a line 140 miles west of Lemberg, abandoning Galicia to the enemy.

Meanwhile, the Austrians were having trouble in another sector. It will be recalled that the first declaration of war in 1914 had been that of Austria against Serbia, and the Austrians had expected the chastisement of the Serbs to be quick and easy. But the Russian advance into Galicia had forced Conrad to withdraw half of the strength of the Austrian Second Army that was poised on the Save west of Belgrade, and this forced a major alteration of plans for the Serbian campaign. When the Austrian attack began on August 12, it was made by two smaller armies facing east on the Drina, and, to everyone's astonishment, they were promptly thrown back across the river by the aroused Serbians. Dogged seesaw fighting, marked by great atrocities on both sides, followed on the Save, the Drina, and in Bosnia, until both armies had literally marched and countermarched themselves into a state of exhaustion. In December, the Austrians limped back across the Danube, having inflicted 170,000 casualties on the enemy but having themselves suffered 227,000 out of a total force of 450,000 engaged.

By the end of 1914, Austria's losses had been so heavy and its setbacks so marked that the morale of its armies was severely shaken. Since Russian pressure was maintained along the whole eastern front, the Germans felt it necessary not only to bolster the Austrian lines but, in effect, to take over the management of all fronts. The favorite German means of doing this was to organize new armies composed of eight German and three Austrian divisions under higher German command.

If the Austrians found German command humiliating they at least had the satisfaction of seeing a great success in 1915 achieved on the basis of the plans of their own chief of staff. Although Hindenburg and Ludendorff had drafted a plan for relieving Russian pressure by launching an offensive from East Prussia, the German chief of staff Falkenhayn, with his emperor's approval, opted for a plan drafted by Conrad, which called for a combined thrust in the neighborhood of Gorlice and Tarnow in

Galicia. Launched on May 2, 1915, this drive hit the Russians at a moment when they were short of shells, guns, and food, and what started as a Russian setback developed into a rout. The disorganized armies fell back beyond Przemysl, Lemberg, Warsaw, and Brest Litovsk until, after six months of desperate rear-guard fighting, they had been pushed behind a line that ran from Riga on the Baltic to the eastern end of the Carpathians. They were 300 miles east of the positions they had held in August 1914, and they had lost 300,000 men and 3000 guns to the enemy. If the pursuing forces had not had to stop from sheer fatigue, the fate of the Russian empire might have been decided in 1915. So tremendous were its losses that it remains a marvel that it could still, in 1916, mount a new offensive strong enough to help relieve the German pressure on Verdun.

The Intervention of Japan, Turkey, and Italy / While these campaigns were being fought, the warring coalitions were making every effort to win new allies. At the very outset, the Triple Entente registered a success when the Japanese government declared war upon Germany. This brought little advantage to the Allies in the theaters in which they were most hotly engaged, for the Japanese were interested primarily in divesting the Germans of their possessions in areas which they coveted themselves, like the Shantung peninsula and the islands in the central Pacific which Germany had acquired at the end of the nineteenth century; and they devoted most of their energies to this end.

More important for the conduct of the European war was the position of Turkey and Italy, and in Constantinople and Rome the diplomats of both sides strove to persuade the governments to declare for them or—that failing—to remain neutral. Given the intimacy between the Turks and the Germans in the immediate prewar years, the Turkish decision was almost a foregone conclusion. After some preliminary diplomatic sparring, the Turkish government in October sent a fleet into the Black Sea to harry the Russian coastal trade; and, at the beginning of November, the Entente powers responded by declaring war.

The clarification of Italy's position took somewhat longer. When war broke out, the government in power, which was headed by Salandra, announced that, since Austria's action against Serbia was not defensive in nature, Italy could not consider itself bound by the provisions of the Triple Alliance and that she would consequently maintain a position of neutrality. There seems little doubt that this decision was popular in the country as a whole, and it certainly represented the position of the bulk of the Socialist party, the parliamentary Center, which regarded Giolitti as its leader, and the Italian high clergy, whose acceptance of neutrality was in part dictated by fear that its alternative would be war against that pillar of the church, Austria. The position of the neutralists was complicated by the belief of many of them that Italy should be paid for its neutrality by Austria's surrender of the Trentino and Trieste and perhaps its acquiescence in Italy's acquisition of Albania, but this was not an essential article of their faith.

From the very outset, there was a strong countermovement that favored intervention on the side of the Entente powers. Liberal idealists and republicans who clung to the principles of Mazzini and Garibaldi felt that the cause of England and France was the cause of civilization and that Italy must not be absent from the ranks of its defenders. Intervention was supported also by the Nationalist party, who frankly expected greater gains from it than could be won by remaining neutral; by the Masonic lodges, which were as anti-Austrian as they were anti-clerical and had great influence in the political parties, the army, and the press; by influential circles around the king, who was firmly pro-English; and by numerous opportunists, who saw a chance for personal aggrandizement. These last included the Socialist editor Benito Mussolini, who had vigorously opposed the Tripolitanian war but now swung over (some said because of French subventions for his new newspaper *Popolo d'Italia*) and, more important at the time, the poet Gabriele D'Annunzio, who appealed to all those who were disillusioned or discontented with the Italian political system. D'Annunzio carried on a remarkable campaign in which he preached that Italy would rise regenerated from war; and his carefully contrived mass demonstrations (from which the Fascists later borrowed many ideas) began to swing Italian public opinion over to war in the spring of 1915.

The Salandra government was meanwhile coldbloodedly bargaining with both the Entente and the Central Powers and was discovering that the Entente was ready to make the more tempting offers. Indeed, any hesitation they may have had was removed by the Entente's promise that, if Italy fought against Austria, it would, at the war's end, receive the Austrian Tyrol as far north as the Brenner Pass, Trieste, part of Albania and other territory at the head of the Adriatic, part of Turkey, and a share in the general war indemnity that would be levied on the beaten foe. These terms were embodied in a secret treaty and signed in London in April 1915.

A last-ditch stand against intervention was made by the man who had been the strongest force in Italian politics since 1903 and who still had the votes to defeat any proposal for intervention that was submitted to parliament. When Giolitti sought to bring parliamentary pressure to bear on the government and the king, however, he had no success. By mid-May excited crowds were prowling the streets of Rome shouting "Death to Giolitti!" and breaking the windows of the Chamber of

Deputies; noninterventionists were being beaten up by nationalist mobs; and news from other cities and from the rural villages indicated that the war spirit was strong there also. In face of the violence of this emotion, the Socialist party and the church remained immobile, and parliament allowed itself to be intimidated. On May 18, when Salandra laid a war resolution before the Chamber, it was approved by all but a handful of Giolitti's loyal supporters.

Diplomacy and War in the Balkans / In return for a treaty that was to cause difficulties at the Peace Conference in 1919, the Entente powers had won an important victory, for Italian adhesion to their cause significantly increased the pressure upon Austria. They were less successful in attaining their diplomatic objectives in the Balkans.

In this area, they were forced, by Turkey's entrance into the war on Germany's side, to try, somehow or other, to prevent her from establishing direct contact with the Central Powers. The best way of doing this was to win the support of the Balkan states that lay between. The key to the situation was Bulgaria, which, because of past Austrian favors, dynastic ties with the German royal family, and enmity for Serbia, did not promise to be won easily. At the beginning of 1915, Entente diplomats tried to impress the Serbs with the importance of appeasing the Bulgars by restoring to them some of the lands seized during the Balkan wars. The Serbs, already infuriated by what they had managed to learn about Allied concessions to Italy, refused.

Aware that the Central Powers were prepared to promise the Bulgars gains in Thrace and Macedonia if they would enter the war, the Entente governments tried a different tack. They sought the alliance of Greece and Rumania, hoping that this would frighten the Bulgars into continued neutrality. But the Rumanians also wanted territory that the Entente could not promise them, since it, too, belonged to the Serbs; and in Athens German agents had ingratiated themselves with King Constantine, who was consequently unresponsive to Entente offers.

The attitude of the Rumanian and Greek governments and the whole complexion of the political struggle in the Balkans was determined, in large part, by the most ambitious, and, in the end, most unsuccessful, of the military operations tried by the British in 1915. This was the Gallipoli campaign.

In January 1915 the Russians asked the British to stage some kind of demonstration at the Straits of the Dardanelles that would draw Turkish forces away from the Caucasus, where they were pressing upon the Russian lines. The idea was taken up enthusiastically in London by the first lord of the Admiralty, Winston Churchill, who was an opponent of the one-front complex of many British soldiers, which, as far as he could see, meant only a continued blood bath in Western Europe. Churchill wanted a more open war, with as many fronts as possible; and with respect to the Straits, he had visions of seizing Constantinople and, with one blow, winning the support of all the doubtful Balkan states. After hard fights with the service chiefs, Admiral Lord Fisher being in particular vehemently opposed to risking ships on this enterprise, Churchill won his point.

The Dardanelles campaign was a long series of missed opportunities. In March 1915 the Straits were almost forced by a mixed Anglo-French naval force, but an undiscovered mine field sank three old battleships and disabled three cruisers; and the admiral in command lost heart, and, despite the pleading of his junior officers, called off the attempt. The decision was next made to land the two divisions of the ANZAC Corps (Australians and New Zealanders), with supporting French and British divisions, at two points on the Gallipoli peninsula and to advance over-land to positions that would dominate the Straits. Lack of appreciation of what a successful amphibious operation entailed, muddled command relationships, and bad intelligence defeated these plans when the original landings were made in April and again in August, when another attempt was made at Suvla Bay. On both occasions, although landings were made successfully, the British failed to get off the beach and seize the high ground behind it when it was open to them; and on both occasions also, the opportunity they lost was exploited to the full by a young Turkish soldier named Mustafa Kemal, who was destined to be the postwar leader of his country. In face of the initiative shown by Kemal and his superior, the German Liman von Sanders, the prodigies of valor shown by the invaders did them no good. In December 1915 and January 1916, after months of being raked by Turkish guns, their forces were evacuated, after suffering 252,000 casualties.

Even before the final evacuation, the Balkan countries had seen that the enterprise was bound to fail; and the Greeks and Rumanians had been confirmed in their neutrality. And this, of course, relieved the Bulgars of any further hesitation. In October 1915, they came into the war on the side of the Central Powers and, in conjunction with Austrian divisions, invaded Serbia and, despite stubborn resistance, overran that country before the end of the year.

By the end of 1915, therefore, the Central Powers dominated the Balkans and had a solid connection with the Turks on their southern flank. This did not prevent Allied diplomats from persisting in their efforts in this area. In 1916, indeed, they had two qualified successes. During the great German offensive at Verdun, when there was danger that this hinge of the western front would be broken, the Entente powers appealed to Russia for a new offensive and simultaneously bought Rumanian aid with the territorial offers they could not make while Serbia was still in the war. The great Brusilov offensive of June–July 1916 and the subsequent Rumanian entrance into the war probably contributed to the German failure at Verdun, by drawing troops away from that point. It did not, however, permanently alter the Balkan situation, since Rumania lasted only a month as a belligerent before being overwhelmed by German armies.

In the course of 1916, also, the Allies won a somewhat tenuous position in Greece by the use of what today would be called subversive tactics. At the end of the previous year, in the hope of saving Serbia, the Allies had landed troops at Salonika, disregarding Greek protests against violation of their soil. This force did nothing of military importance for the next three years, but its commander, the French general Sarrail, carried on elaborate and not unsuccessful political intrigues designed to arouse opposition to King Constantine's policy of neutrality. These seem to have influenced the thinking of Eleutherios Venizelos, always a Westerner in sympathy and now anxious to create a Greater Greece at the expense of Bulgaria and Turkey. In August 1916, when an antiroyalist revolt broke out in Salonika, Venizelos joined it, formed a provisional government, and was immediately recognized by the Entente powers. He could not, however, claim to rule the country as a whole. That was not to come until mid-1917, when Allied pressure finally proved too much for Constantine and led him to abdicate in favor of his son Alexander. That act was followed by Venizelos' appointment as prime minister and by a formal declaration of war on the Central Powers.

Mesopotamia, the Arab Lands, and Africa / It was not only at the Straits that the British and the Turks clashed in these years. In 1915 a British force under General Townshend advanced from the head of the Persian Gulf up the Tigris towards Baghdad, only to be stopped at Ctesiphon and forced back to Kut el-Amara where it was surrounded and eventually forced to surrender in April 1916. This victory, however, and their exertions at Gallipoli seem to have overstrained Turkish resources, and from this point on their troubles multiplied. While the Russians captured large areas of Turkish Armenia in the first months of 1916, the British resumed offensive operations in Mesopotamia, which were finally crowned with success in the recapture of Kut in February 1917. Meanwhile, by pledging support to the cause of Arab independence (the so-called McMahon pledge of October 1915, confirmed and made more precise by the Sykes-Picot Agreement of 1916), the British won the support of the Arabs of the Hejaz, who revolted against the Sultan in June 1916 and subsequently played an important role in the British campaign of 1917 in Palestine.

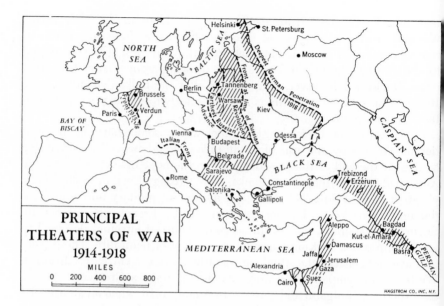

PRINCIPAL
THEATERS OF WAR
1914-1918

MILES
0   200   400   600   800

In Africa, a force of South Africans under Botha, using tactics learned
in the Boer War, invaded and conquered German South West Africa in
a vigorous campaign in the late spring of 1915. Togoland and the
Cameroons fell to French and British troops in the same year. The conquest of German East Africa, on the other hand, proved much more
difficult. Here a brilliant soldier, Lieutenant Colonel von Lettow-Vorbeck,
severely trounced a mixed Indian-British force when it sought to land at
Tanga in 1915 and, throughout 1916, outfought an army composed of
South African, Indian, British, Belgian-Congolese, and Portuguese detachments, commanded by General Jan Smuts. Indeed, Lettow remained at
large through most of the war, although his area of operations was steadily whittled away.

The War at Sea / More decisive, as far as the final result of the war
was concerned, were the operations on the high seas, where each side
sought to weaken his antagonist by destroying his shipping and, whenever encountered, the naval forces that protected it. In this struggle, the
British succeeded during the first year of the war in attaining supremacy, at least on the ocean's surface. The Germans had one spectacular
success in November 1914, when their China squadron under Admiral
Graf Spee sank two British armored cruisers off Coronel; but, a month
later, Spee's force was destroyed in the battle of the Falkland Islands,
and by the spring of 1915 there were no German fleet units or merchantmen at large. The High Seas Fleet of which William II was so proud had
a brush with the British off the Dogger Banks in January 1915 and then

remained at its home bases until May of the following year, when it emerged to fight an indecisive battle at Jutland. In this encounter, the Germans under Scheer sank three British battle cruisers, three cruisers, and eight destroyers at the cost of one battleship, one battle cruiser, four light cruisers, and five destroyers; but these figures are less significant than the fact that the German fleet never dared sally forth from its bases again. Jutland thus confirmed British control of the seas.

The lack of any surface shipping of their own forced the Germans to rely upon neutral ships for their imports, and this in turn led the British and the French, in the interests of imposing an effective economic blockade on Germany, to claim the right to inspect and divert traffic in any goods that might conceivably help the German war effort. This interference elicited strong complaints from neutral countries and most particularly from the government of the United States. Despite his personal sympathy for the Allied cause, President Woodrow Wilson regarded the British behavior as high-handed in the extreme and, with that jealous regard for the interests of his country that was characteristic of him, protested so vigorously on occasion that it was feared that relations between the British and American governments would be broken off.

That matters never got to that point was due in large part to the fact that the Germans were guilty of conduct even more offensive to American feelings. Their inability to match Britain on the surface led them to concentrate on the use of the submarine, which most people considered an even more barbarous weapon than poison gas. American opinion was revolted in particular by the practice of submarine commanders of torpedoing vessels without warning and without any attempt to help survivors; and it was unimpressed by the argument that submarines were frail craft, that many merchantmen were known to be armed, that to surface was always dangerous, and that to remain long on the surface was suicidal.

In February 1915, when the German government announced in a note to the United States government that, within a defined "war zone" which included the British and French coasts, its U-boats would sink Allied ships and ships flying neutral flags that were suspected to be Allied ships, the American attitude was made crystal clear. President Wilson answered with a grave warning that he would hold the Germans to a "strict accountability" for the loss of American ships and American lives. The subsequent sinking of several British ships with American passengers or crew aboard and, especially, the torpedoing of the Cunard liner *Lusitania* on May 7, 1915, with a loss of 1198 lives, including 139 Americans, aroused a storm of indignation in the United States, and the first serious stirrings of an interventionist spirit became apparent.

The intensity of American feeling impressed the Germans; and the fact that they did not, in any case, have enough submarines to be really effective induced them to make concessions to it. The German ambassador informed the American secretary of state that there would be no further attacks on ships like the *Lusitania*. This reassurance and the sharp falling off of submarine attacks of any kind in the fall of 1915 reduced tension.

In the course of 1916, however, the Germans built up their U-boat force swiftly; by January 1917, the naval staff was confident that, if they were allowed to employ them without restrictions, they could starve Britain into submission within five months. At a Crown Council at Pless in January 1917, the sailors and the army high command overbore the doubtful emperor and his chancellor Bethmann. No concern need be felt, they argued, about that "disorganized and undisciplined [country across the seas] which was presided over by a professional crank." Even if the United States should seek to intervene in the war, the chief of the Naval Staff said flatly, "I give Your Majesty my word as an officer that not one American will land on the continent." In face of this military self-assurance, the civilians gave way, and the decision to resume unrestricted submarine warfare was taken.

By this step, the German government went a long way toward nullifying all of the setbacks it had imposed upon its opponents in the eastern and western theaters of operations and in the diplomatic competition in the Balkans. It strengthened the hands of all those Americans who, because of descent, regard for tradition, economic interest, anxiety about America's future strategical position, respect for public law, or other reasons, wanted to enter the war on the side of England and France. The German decision went into effect on February 1; on April 6, the United States declared war on Germany.

THE HOME FRONT

Total War / On February 10, 1916, a panic broke out along the east coast of England because of a rumor that a German Zeppelin had appeared over the resort town of Scarborough; and public indignation over this outrage was so great in the weeks that followed that the government found it expedient to appease it by creating ten home-defense squadrons of the Royal Flying Corps.

The incident is worth mentioning because it illustrates the fact that World War I was the first total war in modern history, in the sense that its rigors were apt to be visited upon all citizens of the participating powers, however remote they might be from the battle area. In earlier wars—even in the protracted and enormously destructive wars against Napoleon—it was only occasionally that the average citizen at home felt the war's effects, and, for long periods of time, it was quite possible for him to forget that there was fighting in progress. In the war of 1914–1918 this kind of detachment was impossible. Citizens of northeast France or Belgium or Poland, whose countries were overrun, whose homes were commandeered as billets, and whose friends and relatives were sometimes held by the occupying forces as hostages to assure the maintenance of local order, knew the war as intimately as the troops who passed through their streets. But they were by no means alone. Crofters in the Scottish highlands, businessmen in Leipzig, Russian farmers in the Volga lands were all brushed by the touch of war, even when they did not attract a visit from a Zeppelin or were well out of range of guns like that notorious Big Bertha which the Germans used to shell Paris. The fortunes of war influenced or determined their freedom of action, their employment, their diet, and even what they were allowed to think and to say. It subjected every aspect of their lives to an increasing degree of control and regimentation. And the fact that it did so had effects which persisted even after the war was over.

Only three aspects of this total war need concern us here: the progressive centralization of political authority, even in countries where political centralization had long been suspect; the economic regimentation practiced by all governments; and the tendency toward thought control and restriction of civil liberties.

Political Centralization / In all of the countries that participated in the war, the beginning of the fighting elicited a wave of patriotism and a closing of ranks. Even political parties and organizations that had been the bitterest opponents of governments six months before the war rallied to the national cause in August 1914. In France, the anarchist Gustave Hervé, who had been the defendant in a sensational trial in 1912 in which he was accused of encouraging mutiny in the French army, now became the most ardent of patriots; and his attitude was symptomatic of the general attitude of French socialism and French labor. In the French Chamber there was a party truce and the creation of what was called a *Union sacrée*, and this situation had its counterpart in Germany, where the parliamentary factions buried their differences and listened with sincere emotion to the emperor's words: "I recognize parties no more. I recognize only Germans!" In Great Britain, although Ramsay MacDonald resigned the leadership of the Labor party rather than support a war for which he believed Great Britain shared much of the responsibility, his action was repudiated indignantly by the majority of his party and by the trade-union movement as well. Similar evidence of political union was manifest in other countries.

This recognition of the overriding importance of the national interest freed governments from the criticism to which a vigilant opposition normally subjected them and enabled them to indulge in practices and to make claims to authority that would never have been tolerated in time of peace. The result was an increasing centralization of power which, by the end of war, had assumed the appearance of government dictatorship in more than one of the great European states; it is not too much to say that no country was entirely exempt from this drift toward totalitarian political methods.

It is, of course, not surprising that this sort of thing should have happened in Russia, Austria, and Germany, where the tradition of parliamentary government was weak; and it was, of course, in those countries that the tendency was most marked and most disastrous in its results. In Russia, what progress had been made toward the separation of political power and the sharing of political responsibility came to an end during the war. This was unfortunate, because the vigorous and useful criticisms of the weaknesses of the Russian war machine came from the Duma and from the zemstvos. But, in September 1915, the tsar, who had already assumed over-all command of the armed forces in a quixotic gesture in August, suspended the Duma for the duration. In effect, then, the affairs of a great country were left in the hands of the empress, her favorite Rasputin, and whatever bureaucrats were willing to be their pliable tools.

In Austria and in Germany, centralization was marked by a diminution of parliament's role and an increase of that of the military. Until the death of Emperor Francis Joseph in November 1916, after which time the fabric of the Empire began rapidly to dissolve, Austria was held together by the authority of bureaucrats and soldiers. This was even more marked in Germany. At the outset of the war, the new tone was set when the local army commands were given the right to intervene in certain aspects of local government and, in some cases, to supersede local-government authorities entirely. On the national level, military influence was pronounced in 1914 and predominant from September 1916, when Hindenburg became chief of staff, until the end of the war. The team Hindenburg-Ludendorff and their Political Bureau in the General Staff not only made military decisions but laid down the main lines of economic and diplomatic policy. Backed by a popular support that amounted to adulation, they arrogated to themselves authority that properly belonged to the emperor and the chancellor and, when crossed, won their point by threatening to resign. It was they who were responsible for the decision to resume submarine warfare; it was they who forced the resignation of Chancellor Bethmann-Hollweg in July 1917, because he had permitted the Reichstag to debate and pass a vague resolution expressing interest in the possibility of a negotiated peace; it was they who dictated the terms of the treaty of Brest Litovsk, which did so much political disservice to their country. Until the armies collapsed in the summer of 1918, their dictatorship was virtually free of any control.

This degree of centralization was never reached in the countries of the west. It is worth noting, however, that even England was not free from either concentration of power in few hands or the growth of excessive military influence. England started the war governed by a loose coalition government and ended with a small, tight war cabinet dominated by Lloyd George, with powers infinitely greater than those enjoyed by any peacetime government. Moreover, Britain's soldiers, usually silent in peacetime, were far from being so during the war, and some of them showed a dangerous contempt for the "frocks" and seemed to believe that military men could do a better job of directing the war.

In France, the government started the war by declaring a state of siege and, during the first year of hostilities, the major decisions were made by the High Command and put into effect by presidential decree. This was perhaps understandable, given the extent of the threat to France in the first months of the war; but, even after the danger of defeat had receded, the High Command was reluctant to give up the position it had won. Not until November 1917, when Clemenceau became premier, was it reduced to its proper role, for Clemenceau was a man who believed that even war, let alone politics, "was too important a matter to be left to the generals." It should be noted, however, that if Clemenceau restored civilian authority in France, his government, by normal standards, was dictatorial in its own right.

In neither England nor France did parliament, in any sense, abdicate. For reasons of security or efficiency, however, certain areas of action commonly subject to parliamentary decision or review were now handled by administrative or executive agencies. The growth of executive authority and the expansion of government powers in areas formerly considered private did not go as far as it did in the countries of Eastern Europe and was not as disastrous in its results; but it was, nonetheless, marked.

Economic Regimentation / Two stories are often told to illustrate the naive attitude of European governments toward economic matters at the beginning of the war. The first is that the French government permitted the Renault motor works to cease production at the beginning of hostilities because it could foresee no military use for its products. The second is that when the German industrialist Arthur Dix sent a memorandum to Chief of Staff Moltke outlining the need of an economic general staff, he received the answer: "Don't bother me with economics. I am busy conducting the war."

It did not take many months of war to show how unrealistic these attitudes were. One of the rudest awakenings—and it was experienced by all countries—was the discovery that there were not enough shells to keep the war going and no present means of producing enough to keep up with the demand. In September 1914 Joffre informed the French government that he needed a minimum of 70,000 shells per day and that his batteries had less than a month's reserve. At the same time, the British commander, Sir John French, was pleading with his government for more ammunition, and soon ugly hints were appearing in English newspapers about troops having to go over the top with inadequate artillery preparation and being slaughtered as a result. In Russia in 1914 factories were producing only a third of the shells needed at the front, and infantry was forced to rely wholly on night bayonet attacks because the armies had neither artillery shells nor rifle ammunition. In Germany, where the army had been confident that its preparations were sound, experts were appalled at the rate at which ammunition reserves melted away in modern war.

The shell shortage in France was caused by the fact that the enemy's swift advance had robbed the country of its richest industrial areas; in other countries, it was the result of a feckless mobilization policy, which sent skilled workers in industries soon to be discovered as crucial to the front, and by a general failure of imagination. The crisis was too critical to be solved by normal methods. Instead, governments appointed what might be called munitions tsars—the Socialist engineer Albert Thomas in France, David Lloyd George in Britain, men of similar energy in other countries—with extensive control over all branches of production of munitions and related articles, with authority to grant or deny government contracts to private firms, with adjudicative powers in labor-management disputes, and with the right to exempt skilled metal workers from military service and return them to bench and lathe. From this beginning, the European governments gradually extended their authority over all aspects of their countries' economic activity.

In Germany, for instance, Walther Rathenau, the son of the founder of the Allgemeine-Elektrizitäts-Gesellschaft, persuaded Moltke's successor Falkenhayn that an inventory of Germany's material resources was a prerequisite of any effective war planning. With government authorization, Rathenau established a War Raw Materials Department (*Kriegsrohstoffabteilung*, or KRA), which conducted an extensive survey and determined that Germany's stocks of essential raw materials would last less than a year and that it was, therefore, necessary to impound and control existing stocks, to eliminate luxury production, to requisition strategically important materials in occupied areas and purchase them from contiguous neutral states, to develop new production techniques, and to encourage the introduction of substitutes and synthetics. Starting with a miniscule staff, the KRA developed into a mammoth organization with subdivisions in all vital industries, each with authority to apportion raw materials to manufacturers with war contracts.

Simultaneously, the German government set up bureaus to control the import and export trade, the most important being the Central Purchasing Company (*Zentral-Einkaufs-Gesellschaft* or ZEG), which had a monopoly of all purchasing abroad, and a War Foodstuffs Office, with subsidiary agencies, to control food supplies, regulate rationing, and encourage the use of substitutes. In November 1916, in order to solve the problems created by a growing labor shortage which had not been alleviated by extensive use of women, children, and foreign laborers (French prisoners, Belgians, and Poles), a Central War Office (*Kriegsamt*) was established under the direction of General Wilhelm Groener, with wide powers to adjudicate between management and labor. A month later, with the inauguration of the so-called Hindenburg Program, a National Service Law came into effect that provided for compulsory employment of all noncombatant Germans between the ages of seventeen and sixty-one, made arbitration of labor disputes compulsory, and made change of employment subject to the approval of boards under the chairmanship of a representative of the local army command.

In the other belligerent nations, similar steps were taken to mobilize economic resources, efficiently in Britain and France, less so in Austria, Italy, and Russia. In most cases, manpower laws were passed and normal labor activity was restricted. In England, for instance, the trade unions agreed in March 1915 that there should be no strikes for the duration of the war, that contracts should be relaxed to permit longer hours, speeding up of production, and the employment of women and unskilled labor in the interests of the war effort. The government assured the unions that these concessions would not hurt their postwar position and that the old conditions would be restored with the peace. Even so, as the war proceeded, there was growing suspicion in labor ranks that the concessions had been a mistake and that the workingmen were being asked to make sacrifices not borne by the employers or other classes of society. Something of the same feeling began to permeate labor ranks in Germany and other countries in the last years of the war and was reflected in a rise in the number of strikes, although most of these were unofficial.

Thought Control / The regulation of economic life placed restrictions upon the freedom of citizens to sell their labor or services as they wished and to spend their wages as they would normally have done. But the war placed more serious limitations upon their liberty than these, affecting their rights of assembly and speech, and even their freedom of thought. In all belligerent countries, special laws were passed for the internment of people suspected of being enemy agents or sympathizers, for the prevention of the dissemination of information that might be useful to the enemy, and for the prohibition of activities that threatened to spread defeatism among the population; and, since these laws were administered by tribunals that were not immune to the influence of local hysterias and often openly encouraged tale bearers and self-appointed guardians of the national security, injustice was often committed in the name of the law. The democratic nations were no more enlightened in this matter than the absolute monarchies. In England, the Defense of the Realm Act gave the government the right to do anything it pleased with citizens suspected of sins against the war effort. Houses were searched without warrant; the possession of any literature considered by some overzealous magistrate to be subversive made a person liable to legal action; despite habeas corpus, deportation and internment were not unknown; public meetings were prohibited by the police without right of appeal; and speeches held to be unpatriotic were punished by prison sentences.

Newspapers were subject everywhere to a rigorous censorship. Items which might give aid or comfort to the enemy or weaken the population's determination to fight to total victory were deleted. Some of the censorship was private (when Lord Lansdowne sent a letter to *The Times* in 1917 urging the necessity of seeking peace by negotiation, the editors refused to print it), but generally it was imposed by the government, which inserted into the spaces created by its deletions official propaganda that often baldly misrepresented the facts, magnified national successes and depreciated those of the enemy, and recounted atrocity stories designed to arouse hatred of the foe.

Since these practices deprived the reader of any objective presentation of fact, they denied him true freedom of thought and imposed distortions and myths upon his mind. In some cases, official propaganda bred a confidence in victory that was disastrous in its result. The discovery that they were not, after all, going to win the war came with such a shock to the German people that they succumbed to despair and let the tide of revolution sweep over them. In other countries, there can be little doubt that wartime propaganda played a large part in creating the hatreds and the illusions that made the job of arranging a just peace so difficult.

THE COURSE OF THE WAR, 1917–1918

Western Setbacks / For the Western Powers, the year 1917 began with two exhilarating events. The first was the overthrow of the auto-

cratic regime in Russia and the coming to power of a democratic government (thus removing the ideological division within the alliance), which
was determined to pursue the war energetically and efficiently. The
second was the United States' entrance into the war.

It was not long, however, before it was seen that the latter event did
not mean that strong American armies would be landing in Europe in the
near future. Until the United States had time to conscript and train an
expeditionary force, the brunt of the fighting would still have to be
borne by Britain and France and Italy. Moreover, since it was soon
apparent that the events in Russia heralded not a regeneration but a
collapse, the burden of the war promised to be heavier.

Events soon proved that more troubles were in store for the Allies
than they dreamed even in their most pessimistic moments. The year
1917 was a long series of defeats. In April the Allies launched one more
of those big pushes to end the war that have been described above. In
the Arras theater the British Third Army under Allenby dented the
Hindenburg line, as the German defenses were called, and the Canadians
took Vimy Ridge in one of the most brilliant assaults in the war. But to
the south, the French offensive in Lorraine under General Nivelle was
an unmitigated disaster, with losses in the neighborhood of 200,000 men;
and it was followed by a wave of mutinies in the French army that made
any offensive action impossible for months, until Nivelle's successor,
Pétain, and his chief of staff, Foch, had taken action to improve front-
line conditions, increase leaves, and restore morale.

In July, the British commander Haig launched his long-planned drive
in Flanders, against the better judgment of Lloyd George, who called it
a "wild military speculation," an "insane enterprise," a "muddy and
muddle-headed enterprise." Haig was a stubborn man, and he continued
his push until November 20; but, for fifty square miles of wire and mud,
he lost 150,000 dead and almost 300,000 wounded or captured. The third
battle of Ypres was, like the Somme a year before, a patent revelation of
the stupidity of all the talk about "wearing the enemy down," for British
losses were almost twice those of the Germans. A brilliant British success
at Cambrai in November 1917, when tanks were used for the first time
in strength, showed that there was an alternative to this ghastly strategy
of attrition; but the soldiers were not yet ready to consider it.

In October it was Italy's turn. In a carefully planned thrust, the Central Powers threw six German and nine Austrian divisions at Caporetto on
the Isonzo River and smashed the whole Italian position. The rout that
followed has been brilliantly described in Hemingway's *Farewell to Arms*.
In the course of it, two Italian armies were swept all the way back to
the Piave River, losing six thousand square miles of territory and 600,000
men. British and French divisions had to be rushed to the Italian front

to stave off complete collapse and to effect a reorganization of Italy's defenses and command.

Finally, to complete the dark catalogue, November brought news of the second revolution in Russia, the seizure of power by the Soviets of Soldiers, Peasants and Workers, the elevation of the Bolshevik leaders Lenin and Trotsky to executive authority, their appeal to the belligerents for an immediate peace without annexations and indemnities, and, in December at Brest Litovsk, their conclusion of an armistice with the Germans. These events promised that the Germans would soon be able to throw their full weight against a west seriously weakened by the bloodletting of 1917.

The Weakening of the German Coalition / All was not well, however, with Germany and its allies. The waning of Turkish strength, which has been mentioned above, was far advanced by the end of 1917. In the course of the year, the British General Allenby, fresh from Arras, put new life in the Egyptian Expeditionary Army and smashed his way into Jerusalem, after chewing up the Seventh Turkish Army under Mustafa Kemal. He was now preparing to thrust his way into Syria, while simultaneously other Allied forces were pushing toward Mosul in Mesopotamia and threatening Turkish lines in Macedonia. The Turkish enthusiasm for the German cause, still strong in leaders like Enver Pasha, was no longer shared by the war-weary armies or the people as a whole. Across the straits, Bulgaria was feeling the same pinch. Its armies had, after all, been fighting since the first Balkan war; the constant pressure upon their lines in the Salonika sector was rapidly wearing them down; and German and Austrian support troops had been sharply reduced in the course of 1917. Meanwhile, the country was at the end of its economic tether, for there had been bad harvests. Both army and populace were fast approaching a state of demoralization.

Even more serious was the situation in Austria-Hungary, where any semblance of cooperation between the Magyar oligarchs and the government in Vienna had broken down, and where serious defections were apparent among the subject nationalities. At a meeting of the Austrian Reichsrat in May 1917, both the Czech and the South Slav representatives had demanded far-reaching rights of autonomy; and it was evident that their military contingents were no longer reliable. In the first months of 1918, the disaffection of the subject nationalities was sharply increased by two things. The first was a series of speeches by the President of the United States, culminating in his address to Congress on January 8, 1918, in which he laid down, in the soon famous Fourteen Points, the principles that he felt should guide a peace settlement, including a promise that the peoples of Austria-Hungary would be assured an autonomous development. The second—in sharp contrast to the Wilson offer—was the nature of the treaties which the Central Powers concluded with Russia at Brest Litovsk and with Rumania at Bucharest (March–May 1918). These treaties, which demanded huge territorial and monetary concessions from the defeated states, made it all too clear that a victory for the Central Powers would mean continued Teutonic domination of Eastern Europe, with no autonomous development for the subject peoples at all. Nothing had more success in sharpening the desire for freedom at the cost of the defeat of Germany and Austria than these punitive settlements.

Germany itself, despite its apparent successes, was at the end of 1917 feeling further from victory than ever before. The promises made by the naval staff in February, about the imminent strangulation of Great Britain by submarine, had come to nothing. It was true that great losses had been inflicted upon Allied and neutral shipping: 2122 ships had been sunk in the Atlantic in 1917 and 844 in the Mediterranean. But their losses had not made the British falter, and now the losses were decreasing and the mortality of submarines mounting fast. What was saving the British was a World War I innovation second only in importance to the tank: the convoy system, in which supply ships moved to their destination in large numbers under the protection of submarines, surface vessels, and aircraft. The convoy was making nonsense of all of the German calculations at a time when the British blockade was bearing more and more heavily upon the German economy, and when murmurs of disaffection and wildcat strikes were making the first cracks in the nation's solidarity. In July 1917 the passage by the Reichstag of a resolution inviting the government to consider peace by negotiation was, to many Germans, a warning of rapidly weakening will to resistance.

The High Command answered these signs of weakness, however, not by any spirit of concession but by calling for a grand offensive that would end the war in victory in the spring of 1918.

The Collapse / After the war was over, much was written about the criminal stupidity of Hindenburg and Ludendorff's pledging the whole security of their nation on one desperate gamble, when they might have exploited their position of apparent strength to win moderate terms by negotiation. Aside from the fact that there is no assurance that the Allies would have responded to any offer of negotiation, this argument overlooks the fact that neither the High Command nor the economic interests that supported them could afford to accept moderate terms. The most palpable fear in their minds was that of a victory of democracy in Germany, and it was their belief that only a total victory with rich annexations in Eastern and Western Europe would divert the German people from their desire for self-government. Their objective, as one of their number admitted, was to escape "the democratic swamp into which we should be drawn undoubtedly after a lukewarm peace." The High Command, therefore, suppressed all talk of negotiation, planned its great offensive, and used all of the resources of its propaganda to assure the Germans that it could not fail.

On March 21, 1918, Ludendorff's spring offensive opened with a crash of guns and with the might of the whole German army thrown upon the British front between St. Quentin and Arras. The British Third Army was thrust aside and Gough's Fifth overrun; Bapaume, Peronne, the line of the Upper Somme were lost; and the hinge between the British and French armies threatened to snap and open the way to Paris. But Ludendorff's momentum was slowed down by the lack of fuel for his motorized units and by other logistical faults, and he lacked the reserves to keep up the pressure. When the expected gap did not appear between the Allies (and it was at this time that the British, French, and Americans lessened the likelihood of its doing so by taking the long delayed step of creating a Supreme Command under Foch to coordinate their operations), Ludendorff allowed himself to be diverted from his key objective and shifted his attack to points where it seemed easier to break through. In April, he rolled over the Portuguese in Flanders and retook all of the ground lost to Haig in 1917. But the British held at Ypres, and Ludendorff changed direction again, developing a series of attacks between Soissons and Rheims in May and crossing the Marne in the first week of June. The German thrusts were becoming weaker now and increasingly disarticulated. Within sight of the positions held in September 1914, the great offensive in July began slowly to grind to a halt.

Then, on August 8, General Rawlinson's Fourth Army, supported by French units, struck with dramatic suddenness east of Amiens, and masses of Allied tanks tore the German lines to shreds. This was "the black day of the German army," and it recoiled, never to seize the initiative again. By the beginning of September, the Allied armies were sweeping forward in every sector: the British were through the Somme and hammering at the Hindenburg line; the French were pushing forward in the Champagne; and the Americans, whom the German navy had vowed to keep out of Europe, had won their first fight at St. Mihiel and were advancing in the Meuse-Argonne.

And now, at the other end of Europe, the process of dissolution began. In mid-September, the French commander at Salonika, Franchet d'Esperey (known to all British troops as "Desperate Frankie"), attacked and smashed the Bulgarian lines and began a headlong advance into Serbia. The Bulgars immediately sued for armistice terms and signed them on September 29. Turkey was left at the mercy of converging

Allied armies, and its government hastened to follow the Bulgarian example. Even before these events had taken place, the Austrians had informed their ally that they could fight no longer and had begun diplomatic exchanges with the Allies.

Even the indomitable Ludendorff could not stem this rush of events. On October 3, his strong nerves snapped, and he frantically informed his government that it must sue for peace. Prince Max von Baden, just appointed chancellor by the emperor, had, like most parliamentarians and the majority of the German people, believed as late as September that victory was certain. He was incredulous at the message from the High Command. He had no alternative, however, to obedience and appealed to President Wilson for terms.

This maneuver the American President defeated neatly by informing the Germans that he would not even consult his allies until he was assured that the Germans were prepared to lay down their arms, thus rendering resumption of hostilities impossible, and to accept the Fourteen Points as the basis of the peace, and until he was certain, moreover, that the German government truly represented the German people. This last point convinced a lot of Germans that they would secure better terms if they got rid of the emperor and their military masters, and it was from this point on that revolutionary agitation began to mount in Germany. Meanwhile, Prince Max did his best to satisfy Wilson of German compliance with his wishes; Wilson referred the request to his allies; and the armistice negotiations began. By the time the terms were ready, revolution had gripped Berlin, Munich, Hamburg, and other cities and the emperor had laid down his title and fled across the border into Holland. With their proud empire in ruins, the German representatives signed the armistice terms on November 11, 1918, and the long war came to an end.

CONCLUSION

Some Social Effects / The effect of the war upon the territorial organization of Europe, its economic prospects, and its political future will be best discussed in the next chapter, in connection with the decisions of the Peace Conference. In view of what has been said above, however, about the behavior of governments during the war, two observations are appropriate here.

The first has to do with something we have noticed in several connections in the chapters above: the decline of liberalism and of the liberal attitude in politics and economics. There is no doubt that this decline was greatly advanced by the war. Governments expanded their size and their functions, and people became so accustomed to seeing them do things previously performed by private agencies that they did not protest very loudly when governments continued to do them after the war. *Étatisme* had become not only normal but desirable to many people.

In some cases, when governments relinquished powers or gave up functions with the restoration of peace, their doing so was not greeted with universal approbation. During the war, for example, governments had encouraged industrial expansion, while at the same time protecting the enterprises affected from the normal risks of such expansion. Nothing could have done more to weaken the competitive spirit and the willingness to accept risk that had been characteristic of liberal capitalism. It is small wonder that, when economic storms began to blow in the 1920s, many European businessmen yearned for the security of the war years, when they were partners of government, protected against bankruptcy if they overextended themselves, assured of big profits, and—not least important—supplied with a docile labor force. Part of the reason why so many industrialists supported men like Mussolini and Hitler was that those political dictators promised to restore the wartime economic relationships.

Finally, in connection with the waning of the liberal attitude in European politics, it should be noted that the war accustomed governments to working in a crisis atmosphere and gave them the dangerous idea that, when things were going to pieces around them, action was always to be preferred to inaction. As Mendelssohn Bartholdy has written, this amounted to

> a new philosophy of public morals called decisionism. It denounced caution as unmanly. It upheld the virtue of courage in the taking of the responsibility for the rights and wrongs of an ill-considered decision on the grounds that actually *taking* it . . . even if it proved wrong or unnecessarily expensive, is always better than shrinking from responsibilities and losing fortune's fleeting moment.

In postwar Europe, in both the democratic and the totalitarian states, this attitude was productive of much harm.

Lost Generations / The character of postwar politics might have been different and the leadership of the democratic states in particular might have been stronger if it had not been for the terrific losses suffered by all nations during the war of 1914–1918. Europe was to pay dearly for the generation of young men who died in Flanders and Poland and Greece and Palestine.

But it should be noted that the war had made another lost generation. This was composed of all of those veterans who found, when the fighting was over, that they could no longer adjust themselves to the requirements of civilian society. Sometimes this attitude was the result of disenchantment on the part of men who had gone off to war in the hope that they were creating a better world and had come back to find that those who had remained at home had not shared their dreams. These men felt like the returned soldier in Erich Maria Remarque's fine novel *The Road Back*, who says to a friend:

> Ludwig, what are we doing here? Look about you: look how flat and comfortless it all is. We are a burden to ourselves and others. Our ideals are bankrupt, our dreams are *Kaputt*, and we wander around in this world of rotten opportunists and speculators like Don Quixotes in a foreign land.

In many cases this kind of disillusionment was overcome or suppressed, but all too often it hardened into a fixed resentment against civilian society and a longing for the comradeship and the sense of shared sacrifice that had been present in the war. Those who felt this way came to idealize the war, to see values in it that might yet save Europe from materialism, and to believe that the soldier—the true soldier, not the brass hat, or *Bürogeneral*, or staff officer at the rear, but the *Frontkämpfer*, the man in the trenches—might lead the way to Europe's regeneration. Ernst Jünger, a front-line soldier himself, wrote in 1920, in a widely read book called *Battle as an Inner Experience*:

> There is the new man, the storm fighter, the elite of Europe. An entirely new race, smart, strong, full of will. What has been revealed here in battle will tomorrow be the axis around which life revolves, more and more swiftly. . . . This war is not the end, but the chord that heralds new power. It is the anvil on which the world will be hammered into new boundaries and new communities. New forms will be filled with blood, and might will be hammered into them with a hard fist. War is a great school, and the new man will be of our cut.

Here is the authentic voice of the revolution of the right, of the *squadristi* of Mussolini, of Hitler's brown shirts, who rose from the ranks of those whom World War I left disenchanted and alienated, with the war still in their bones.

21

The Peace Treaties and the Search for Collective Security

In 1919 there were a good many people in the world who seemed to believe that peace was something you could declare, in the same way that you declared war. They soon discovered that this was not true. In number and complexity, the problems facing the peacemakers of 1919 greatly exceeded those that the negotiators at Vienna had had to deal with in 1814 and 1815, and their deliberations lasted longer than was desired by electorates anxious to return to normal conditions. World War I ended formally in November 1918, so abruptly that the victorious powers found themselves without any clear idea of how to go about making peace. It was four months before serious negotiations got under way, and it was not until June 1919 that the terms of a treaty with Germany, the Treaty of Versailles, had been worked out, submitted to the former enemy, and accepted. This treaty had to be followed by other laborious negotiations and other peace treaties: the Treaty of St. Germain-en-Laye with Austria, September 10, 1919; the Treaty of Neuilly with Bulgaria, November 27, 1919; the Treaty of Trianon with Hungary, June 4, 1920; and the Treaty of Sèvres with Turkey, August 10, 1920.

Long before this last date, the statesmen and the peoples of Europe had learned that the transition from war to peace was not going to be easy. Even in the first phase of the peace negotiations—when Woodrow Wilson, Lloyd George, Georges Clemenceau, and Vittorio Orlando were directing the proceedings in Paris (January–June 1919)—the possibility of new wars was being made evident by Poland's incursions into the territory of its neighbors, by the activities of German freebooters in the Baltic countries, by the establishment of a Soviet in Budapest under Béla Kun, and by serious differences between Italy and Yugoslavia over the possession of the port of Fiume. Moreover, almost as soon as the various peace treaties were completed, they were challenged in whole or in part by states which felt that they had been unjustly treated; and these challenges were sometimes made with arms in hand. Meanwhile, the machinery that had been devised to meet problems of this nature, the League of Nations, started its existence with the defection of the country under whose aegis it had been founded and with the two other principal Allied powers hopelessly split on the question of how it should be used, as well as on other fundamental problems.

In the circumstances, anything resembling peace was slow in coming to Europe, and it was not until 1925 that there was a general detente and relaxation of tension.

THE PEACE TREATIES

The Paris Peace Conference / The assembly of nations that convened in Paris in January 1919 to begin the task of arranging a general peace settlement was the greatest gathering of its kind since the Congress of Vienna (see pp. 12–19), and its very membership reflected all of the changes that had taken place in the territorial balance of Europe and the world in the intervening century. Of the five Great Powers that had dominated the proceedings at Vienna, only two were present here: Great Britain, represented by her great war premier, Lloyd George, the foreign secretary Arthur Balfour, and a host of able subordinates; and France, whose delegation was headed by Georges Clemenceau and included, among others, the head of the united command that had won the war, Marshal Foch. Of the other Vienna powers, two were excluded from the deliberations because, as defeated powers, they were to be the recipients of the decisions made, and the third, Russia, was absent because its new government was the object of universal detestation on the part of the victors, as a result of the separate peace it had concluded with Germany at Brest Litovsk and also, of course, because of its ideological beliefs.

On the other hand, the membership of the conference was swollen by representatives of states whose independence had not been recognized in 1815 or whose potentiality for political growth might have been denied at that time. Chief among these were Italy, which, in the person of its prime minister Vittorio Orlando, occupied a place in the directorate of the conference; Belgium, accorded universal respect for its sufferings during the war; Greece, who, thanks to the political acrobatics of Venizelos (see pp. 414 and 652), had ingratiated itself with the French and British governments; Poland, now resuming independence after more than a century of oppression; the brand-new state of Czechoslovakia, still more a concept than a reality when the conference began its sessions.

The most startling difference from the Vienna Congress was the important role played at Paris by non-European states, a sign that the age had passed when it could be claimed—in Mazzini's words—that Europe was "the lever that moved the world" and an intimation that the time had come when Europe could not even solve its own problems without external help. The British dominions were represented by the prime ministers of Canada, Australia, New Zealand, and Newfoundland and Generals Botha and Smuts of South Africa. Marquis Saionji of Japan was not only present but a member of the Council of Ten that directed the conference in its first stages, an honor granted in recognition of Japan's contribution to victory by its naval operations in the Pacific and the Mediterranean. And finally, the center of all attention as the conference opened and, more than any other single individual, its guiding spirit, was the President of the United States, Woodrow Wilson, who had broken precedent by deciding to come to the negotiations in person.

Procedural Questions / From the standpoint of intellectual grasp and general ability, the leading statesmen at Paris were in no way inferior to their predecessors at Vienna. They soon demonstrated, however, that they were somewhat less competent in matters of organization and procedure.

When the war came to an end, the Allied and Associated Powers had reached no agreement concerning their war aims or the procedures to be followed in realizing them. They had all made the mistake that they were to repeat in World War II, of believing that political plans could and should wait until the fight was over; and they had reacted with irritation to suggestions that this might have awkward results. The sudden collapse of the enemy, therefore, found them in possession of neither a philosophy nor a strategy for peace; and, although President Wilson persuaded them, at the time of the German request for an armistice, to accept the Fourteen Points[1] as the basis of their future deliberations, this was hardly a sufficient preparation for the tasks that lay before them.

It seems clear that, with the possible exception of the French, the leaders of the Allied nations did not appreciate the importance of procedural questions. They might have learned much from a study of the way in which the Congress of Vienna had gone about its business, but Lloyd George was too indifferent to history to bother to read the excellent handbook on Vienna and other conferences prepared for him by the Foreign Office, and President Wilson bridled at the very suggestion that a democratic statesman should consult Metternich and Castlereagh. In consequence, they made some unfortunate mistakes.

In particular, they allowed the full conference to convene before the principal Allies had clarified or coordinated their views about the general nature of the settlement to come, or devoted any systematic thought to the machinery of negotiation, or even prepared a tentative agenda. They began their work with no agreement as to how many treaties they were going to write or with whom. They did not even have a clear understanding on the vital point of whether their decisions at Paris were to be final or tentative. There was a vague idea, to which the representatives of the leading powers referred frequently, that the present meeting was merely a preliminary conference, to be followed by a more definitive one to which the enemy states would be invited, with powers to negotiate. But this was never made explicit and precise.

In due course, by a process of trial and error, the conference found a procedure and a workable machinery of negotiation. The organ originally

[1] See above, p. 520. President Woodrow Wilson's address to Congress on January 8, 1918 enumerated a peace program based on Fourteen Points, as follows: (1) Open covenants openly arrived at; (2) absolute freedom of navigation alike in peace and war, except as the seas might be closed by international action to enforce international covenants; (3) the removal, as far as possible, of all economic barriers; (4) adequate guaranties that armaments would be reduced to the lowest point consistent with domestic safety; (5) an impartial adjustment of all colonial claims on the principle that the interests of the population must have equal weight with the claims of the government; (6) the evacuation of all Russian territory and the free determination of its own political and national policy; (7) evacuation and restoration of Belgium; (8) evacuation and restoration of French territory and righting of the wrong done to France in the matter of Alsace-Lorraine; (9) readjustment of the frontiers of Italy along clearly recognizable lines of nationality; (10) opportunity for autonomous development for the peoples of Austria-Hungary; (11) evacuation and restoration of Rumanian, Serbian, and Montenegrin territory, together with access to the sea for Serbia; (12) the Turkish parts of the Ottoman Empire to be given a secure sovereignty, but the other nationalities to be given an opportunity for autonomous development, and the Dardanelles to be permanently opened to the ships of all nations under international guaranties; (13) an independent Poland, to include territories indisputably Polish, with free and secure access to the sea; (14) a general association of nations to be formed to afford mutual guarantees of political independence and territorial integrity to great and small states alike.

The Big Four at Versailles. From left to right: Lloyd George, Orlando, Clemenceau, and Wilson. (BROWN BROTHERS)

established to direct and coordinate the conference's work—a Council of Ten composed of two representatives of each of the principal Allies (the United States, Great Britain, France, Italy, and Japan) was found to be too rigid and unwieldy and was replaced by a more flexible system. This had two principal organs: a Council of Four (Wilson, Lloyd George, Clemenceau, and Orlando) with powers of over-all direction and ultimate decision; and a Council of Five (composed of the foreign ministers of the five principal Allied Powers) which dealt with special problems assigned to it, especially economic questions rising out of the blockade of Germany, and was the recognized organ for handling the reports of the Territorial Committees. These committees, originally appointed by the Council of Ten, were made up of experts who were given the duty of assigning frontiers to new states like Poland and Czechoslovakia and performing related tasks, in the execution of which they were, unfortunately, handicapped by the lack of clear instructions or, until very late, of a central coordinating agency. Finally, there was a Plenary Conference, on which the lesser states were represented, which dealt with the questions of war guilt, reparations, the League of Nations, international labor legislation, and ports, waterways, and railways.

Once this organization had been devised (in mid-March), and it had been agreed that individual treaties should be concluded with all of the former enemy powers, much of the confusion of the first weeks was cleared up and the negotiations fell into a coherent pattern. Unfortunately, by this time there had been so much delay that any thought of making a preliminary settlement with Germany in preparation for more comprehensive negotiations later on was abandoned. This had one deplorable effect. Decisions made by the Territorial Committees in the belief that they were tentative and would be revised now became definitive and were written into the treaties, with much resultant injustice.

One other procedural mistake may be mentioned here, if only because it was repeated in World War II. The Allies made no attempt to make sure that they retained enough military strength to enable them, if necessary, to impose their will upon recalcitrant enemies or friends. The pressure of public opinion at home led to a precipitous demobilization of American and British troops, beginning almost immediately after the armistice. Demobilization weakened the ability of the Allies to impress people like the Poles, when they began to violate the territory of their neighbors; and it probably contributed to their decision to continue the blockade of Germany, as the most expeditious means of preventing any serious German resistance, until that country accepted the peace terms. This failure to provide for contingencies that would require the use of force, combined with the delay caused by the procedural errors mentioned above, contributed to the progressive political and economic disintegration of Central and Eastern Europe.

The German Settlement / In the pre-armistice negotiations between the Germans and the Allies, the German government had been given to understand that the future peace would be made on the basis of President Wilson's Fourteen Points, with two reservations: first, that the Allies retained full discretion concerning the freedom of the seas (which meant that the British would refuse to give up their doctrine of the blockade) and, second, that it was to be understood that "compensation will be made by Germany for all damage done to the civilian population of the Allies and their property by the aggression of Germany by land, by sea and from the air." Unfortunately, the Germans were not informed of other more informal concessions made by the Americans to avert their allies' objections to the Fourteen Points; and this put them in the position of being able, in 1919 and for years thereafter, to charge the Allies with bad faith.

It must be admitted that the Germans had a case. Since they were excluded from the negotiations at Paris, Wilson's first point, calling for "open covenants openly arrived at," was certainly rendered meaningless as far as they were concerned. Point Two, calling for freedom of the seas, had been eliminated by prior agreement. Point Five, which had talked of an "impartial adjustment of all colonial claims," was passed over silently at Paris, and all of Germany's former colonies, disguised as mandated territories, were parceled out among Japan, Great Britain and the Dominions, and France. Point Thirteen, which had stipulated that the future independent Poland would be composed of territory inhabited by indisputably Polish populations, was interpreted in such a way as to hand large numbers of Germans over to Polish control. Nor did this exhaust the list of decisions that could be called, and were called by the Germans and others, flagrant violations of Wilson's charter of principles.

This is not, however, a black and white matter. It is true that the colonial question was handled in a manner that flatly contradicted Wilson's principles, because the President, here as on many other points at issue in Paris, felt that he had to satisfy the territorial desires of Japan and the British Dominions in order to make sure of their support of the League of Nations (see p. 542). But other violations were unavoidable. In the Polish question, for instance, it was virtually impossible to give the new Polish state access to the sea without including some Germans in the corridor created, unless one resorted to forcible evacuation; and the population of the territory affected was so mixed that it was difficult, even by a process of elaborate fragmentation, to create districts that were "indisputably" either Polish or German.

As far as the territorial settlement was concerned, the final treaty—apart from the colonial clauses—must have contained few surprises for the Germans. Once the war was lost, they knew that they would have to renounce their grandiose plans for the Baltic regions and the Ukraine, the gains they had exacted from the Russians and the Rumanians at Brest Litovsk and Bucharest (see pp. 521 and 563), and their hold over Poland; and it should have been no secret to them that they would also lose Alsace-Lorraine, which they had taken after the Franco-Prussian War, to France. These territorial changes were stipulated in the treaty. In addition, Germany had to cede the towns of Eupen and Malmédy to Belgium, to place the Baltic port of Memel in Allied hands for future disposal (in 1923 it was taken by Lithuania), to cede the province of Posen and a strip of territory running through West Prussia to Poland, and to allow plebescites to determine the future possession of Schleswig, which had been seized by Prussia after the Danish war of 1864 (see p. 224), and certain districts of East Prussia and Silesia, which had large Polish populations. These provisions could all be justified by the principle of national self-determination, which the Peace Conference had accepted from President Wilson as one of its guiding principles in territorial adjustment. In some cases German protests were honored and ad-

justments made in their favor; and, in general, the plebescites (by which
Germany eventually lost Northern Schleswig and part of Upper Silesia)
were fair and conducted under impartial auspices.

There were two final territorial clauses that could hardly have been
foreseen and were less easily justified. The first was the transformation
of the German Baltic port of Danzig into an internationalized free city;
the second was the transfer of the Saar coal region to the administration
of the League of Nations and the economic control of France for a period
of fifteen years, after which time its future would be determined by
plebescite.

This last provision was one of several that aggravated the problems
created for Germany by the reparations clauses of the treaty, which were
the harshest and the most unrealistic part of the German settlement. During the pre-armistice negotiations, the principle that Germany must pay
for damage to the civilian populations of her enemies had been established and accepted by the Germans themselves. What had not been
made clear was that such damage would later, at Britain's request, be
made to include not only shipping and property losses but service pensions and allowances as well, an addition that more than doubled the
German liability. Nor was it foreseen that Germany's means to pay would
be seriously weakened by its forced loss of territory and population,
colonies and natural resources, and by the confiscation of practically its
whole merchant fleet. Even during the peace conference, this last point
was not clear to those charged with formulating the reparations terms,
for—and here we come back to the procedural weaknesses of the conference—they worked without any knowledge of the decisions that were
being made concurrently with respect to cessions of territory and
resources.

The victors decided in the end not to set a total figure for reparations
until a later date. In a meeting of the Council of Four, Lloyd George
said frankly: "If figures were given now, they would frighten rather than
reassure the Germans. Any figure that would not frighten them would be
below the figure with which he and M. Clemenceau could face their
peoples in the present state of public opinion." Thus, the German people
had to wait until 1921 to learn that, in addition to the down payment of
five billion dollars, the cessions of shipping and territory, and the coal
deliveries to neighboring countries that were required by the treaty, they
would be expected to pay thirty-two billion dollars to their former
enemies.

The figure was perhaps not in itself important, for long before 1921
the very idea of reparations was anathema in Germany, even to people
who might otherwise have admitted the justice of Germany's paying a
war indemnity. This was because the reparations clauses of the treaty

were prefaced by an article (Article 231) that stated that "the Allied and Associated Governments affirm and Germany accepts the responsibility of Germany and her allies for causing all the loss and damage to which [they] and their nationals have been subjected as a consequence of the war imposed upon them by the aggression of Germany and her allies." Drafted by the young American expert and future secretary of state, John Foster Dulles, the clause was intended as a concession to the British and French, who had been persuaded by the Americans not to ask for even larger reparations, but who insisted on some formula that would clearly state their *right* to ask for more even if they did not use it. Unfortunately, it was interpreted by the Germans as an attempt to make them solely responsible for having caused the war; and, as Dulles himself wrote later, "it was the revulsion of the German people from this article of the treaty which, above all else, laid the foundation for the Germany" of Hitler.

Equally humiliating to many Germans was the demand that the emperor of Germany be tried, by an international court, for his offenses against international morality. This forecast of the elaborate trials of war criminals after World War II came to nothing. On November 10, 1918, William II had left his country and taken refuge in Doorn, Holland, where he spent the rest of his life. An attempt by the Allies in 1920 to persuade Holland to surrender him for trial was declined politely but firmly, the Netherlands government expressing doubts about the legality of the proposed procedure and a disinclination to withdraw their protection from one who had freely sought it.

As was to be expected, the Allies spent much time and effort in drafting the military sections of the treaty, and they imposed heavy restrictions upon Germany's future freedom of action in military affairs. In order to deprive it of the means to disturb the peace of the world a second time, they stipulated that the future German army be limited to a force of 100,000 officers and men, without the right to possess military aircraft, tanks, or other offensive weapons, that the General Staff, the War Academy, and the cadet schools, which were supposed to be the breeding places of Prussian militarism, be dissolved, and that the future navy be limited to a token force with no vessels exceeding 10,000 tons and no submarines. Until these provisions were carried out, and the Allies were, in addition, satisfied that all production of war material had been made impossible, the Rhineland was to be occupied by Allied troops, and it was to be permanently demilitarized, together with a strip fifty kilometers wide to the east of the Rhine.

Leaving aside the practical difficulties of enforcing these provisions (and more is known today about the problems of arms control and inspection than was known in 1919), these military clauses turned out to have two weaknesses. The first lay in the Allied insistence that the future German army be made up entirely of long-term volunteers, the officers serving for twenty-five years, other ranks for twelve. The French had been willing to tolerate a larger army based on short-term conscription, but they had given in to the insistence of Wilson and Lloyd George, leaders of countries in which conscription had always been unpopular. Their victory meant that Germany would have an army that was, by its very terms of service, sealed off from civilian life and values and would, moreover, be likely to appeal to those elements which were most devoted to the Germany of the past and least tolerant of progress toward democracy. In the second place, in another example of textual clumsiness, the Allies prefaced the military clauses with a statement expressing the hope that German disarmament would be followed by general disarmament. This unnecessary clause was to be interpreted by Adolf Hitler and others as an Allied pledge to disarm, the nonfulfillment of which justified German violation of the treaty terms.

The Versailles Treaty, which embodied all the terms of the German settlement, might have been an even more severe document than it was if it had not been for Woodrow Wilson's spirited and successful opposition to French desires to detach the whole of the Rhineland from Germany. Even so, when seen in its totality, it was harsh enough to cause misgivings to those who had worked on its separate parts. The terms were the result, however, of so many delicate compromises between the Allies that any serious revision promised to open up innumerable questions and prolong the peacemaking process indefinitely. When the treaty was presented to the Germans in May 1919, therefore, the Allies made few concessions to the objections and the lists of proposed amendments that came back from Berlin. Instead, they made it clear that, unless the treaty were accepted in its entirety by June 23, hostilities would be resumed. Allied firmness was doubtless hardened by German success on June 21 in scuttling their High Seas Fleet, which had been interned at Scapa Flow. Infuriated by what must have seemed a proof that the Germans were unregenerate, they brushed aside the last notes from Berlin and ordered Foch to prepare to begin his advance at 7 P.M. on the 23d. The Germans gave way and, five days later, in the Hall of Mirrors in Versailles, signed the treaty.

The Settlement in Eastern Europe / The conferees at Paris were now confronted with what Lord Balfour called "the immense operation of liquidating the Austrian Empire." This had been forecast by the rapid dissolution of imperial unity under the stress of war, a process that had been accelerated on the one hand by the terms of the treaties of Brest Litovsk and Bucharest, and on the other by the encouragement given to

EUROPE AFTER
WORLD WAR I

World War I Losses

by Germany
by Austria Hungary
by Bulgaria
by Russia

0   500
Miles

the subject nationalities in President Wilson's Fourteen Points address and other wartime speeches (see p. 520). It proved to be an enormously complicated operation that was not complete until three more treaties had been written and signed by former enemy states, and a large number of territorial, commercial, and military conventions concluded with the states that were the beneficiaries of the dissolution of the Hapsburg monarchy.

The main outlines of an Austrian settlement had taken shape before the Council of Four turned the bulk of the peacemaking work over to subordinates and held its last meeting on June 28, 1919, and it was rapidly concluded in the weeks that followed. The resultant treaty was, in the first instance, a recognition of events that had taken place inside the Hapsburg Empire since October 1918. In that month, Thomas Masaryk and Eduard Beneš, who had worked tirelessly throughout the war years to win Allied sympathy for the cause of Czech independence, proclaimed the deposition of the young Emperor Charles and the creation of an independent Czechoslovakian republic. In the same month, the Poles of Galicia seceded from the Empire, and a diet in Croatia proclaimed the secession of Croatia and Dalmatia from Hungary, thus preparing the way for the fusion of these and other Southern Slav provinces of the Empire, including Bosnia and Herzegovina, with the Kingdom of Serbia a month later. On October 24 also, a liberal government under Count Michael Karolyi had seized power in Budapest, and two weeks later it proclaimed Hungary to be an independent republic. Now, the Treaty of St. Germain of September 1919 required Austria—which had itself become a republic by revolution and the abdication of Emperor Charles on November 11, 1918—to accept all of these losses and to recognize the independence of Czechoslovakia, Poland, Yugoslavia, and Hungary.

Whether what was left of Austria—a trifling territory with a population of six and a half million, a third of whom lived in Vienna—could become a viable state does not seem to have concerned the peacemakers at Paris to any great degree. It was a question that worried the Austrians themselves. On November 12, 1918, when they set up their new regime, they had specifically declared that Austria would be "a component part of the German Republic." This the Allies refused to countenance, and the Austrian Republic was forced to begin a career of reluctant independence, clouded in advance by the prospect of grave economic troubles. This outlook was made more forbidding by the loss of any access to the sea, by the cession of part of the German-speaking Tyrol to Italy, and by the treaty's stipulation that Austria would be required to pay an undisclosed amount of reparations. In the circumstances, the provision that the Austrian army must be restricted to 30,000 officers and men was not regarded unfavorably in the republic.

Hungary was treated with even greater severity and suffered in particular from the fact that its new boundaries were drawn by a number of committees (on Czech claims, on Rumanian claims, and so forth) which operated independently and made no attempt to inform each other of their prospective exactions. As a result, the former Magyar kingdom, in the name of national self-determination, lost three fourths of its area— its South Slav lands to Yugoslavia, Slovakia to the new state created by Masaryk and Beneš, and Transylvania to Rumania. The Treaty of Trianon also provided for stringent limitations on Hungary's military establishment.

Peace was made with Bulgaria by the Treaty of Neuilly. The only enemy state whose dynasty survived the war, Bulgaria received treatment no better and no worse than that accorded those who had embraced democracy at the war's end. Its main territorial losses were the cession of its Thracian outlet to the Aegean Sea to Greece, and the transfer of its holdings in Macedonia to Yugoslavia.

What these countries lost was won by the states who had contributed to the victory of the Allies. Nor were their gains made only at the expense of their enemies. Rumania, for example, which acquired former Bulgarian and Hungarian territory, also took Bessarabian districts from its former ally, Russia, a step hardly calculated to make for good relations with that power. Poland, not content with what could be gained in Paris, quarreled with the Czechs over the duchy of Teschen (and eventually gained part of it by Allied award in 1920) and resorted to military means to seize territory from Russia (see p. 567) and to wrest the city of Vilna from Lithuania.

The settlement of the South Slav question was also marked by a dispute between Allies, which began during the peace conference and was prolonged until 1924. Not satisfied with the territories promised them by secret treaty when Italy came into the war in 1915, the Italians insisted that their new possessions on the Istrian and Dalmatian coast should include the port of Fiume. Woodrow Wilson's resistance to this, on the grounds that the Yugoslavs had a better claim on ethnic grounds and his attempt to appeal to the Italian people over the heads of their government caused a major crisis in Paris, marked by temporary Italian withdrawal from meetings of the Council of Four. The unresolved dispute was aggravated when Gabriele D'Annunzio, at the head of an expedition of black-shirted patriots, seized the port in September 1919. His subsequent antics in the town proved as embarrassing to the Italian government as they were instructive to Italy's future dictator, Mussolini, already resolved to out-D'Annunzio the poet-politician; and in the end the Italians found it expedient to strike a compromise. By the treaty of Rapallo (November 1920) they surrendered to Yugoslavia the whole Dalmatian coast south of Fiume with the single exception of the town of Zara (Zadar). Italy retained most of Istria and four of the Dalmatian islands. Fiume was left as a free city until 1924, when a new agreement ceded most of the port to Italy and its suburbs to Yugoslavia.

Seen in its totality, the settlement of Eastern Europe was rather sounder than its critics were willing to admit. By 1919 it was too late to stop the disintegration of the Hapsburg Empire. The most equitable guiding principle for the inevitable territorial readjustment was the principle of nationality, and this was followed. Given the mixed state of the populations of Eastern Europe, it was obviously impossible to redraw the map in such a way as to eliminate national minorities. All of the new countries had such minorities; and the new Czechoslovakia was made up of peoples with no ethnic ties, Czechs, Slovaks, Germans, Poles, Hungarians, and Ruthenians—a mixture that spelled future trouble. But, granted the inevitability of minorities, it says something for the peacemakers at Paris that on the whole the boundaries they drew stood the test of time.

The principal weaknesses of the Eastern settlement were two. The increased political diversity of the area was destined to cause a high degree of economic instability. This might have been avoided if the succession states had adopted economic policies that reproduced the conditions of interdependence and collaboration that had existed inside the Austrian-Hungarian Empire. But the nationalism engendered by their new independence and the suspicions that those who had gained territory entertained toward those from whom they had acquired it prevented this kind of mutual support and led to wasteful economic competition and military spending, which contributed to the general instability of the area. It is difficult to see how this could have been entirely avoided by anything within the power of the peacemakers at Paris.

In the second place, the whole Eastern settlement suffered from the failure of the conferees in Paris to come to grips with the Russian problem. The opposition of the Allies to the Bolshevik regime, which was to lead in 1919 to actual intervention in the civil war and to toleration of the Polish invasion of the Ukraine (see p. 567), permitted them to believe that they could exclude Russia from European affairs, at the same time as they were excluding Germany from the European system by the imposed limitations on its freedom of action and exclusion from the League of Nations. But Russia and Germany were too large and potentially powerful to become political nullities; and events were to prove that the failure of the peacemakers in Paris to integrate at least one of them into the new European system was to render tentative all of their decisions in Eastern Europe.

The Near Eastern Settlement / During the war promises of Turkish territory as compensation for aid to the Allied cause had been made to a number of states and national groups, and an attempt was now made to sort them out and resolve their inconsistencies. This was not easy, but it was attempted by the Treaty of Sèvres, which gave Palestine, Mesopotamia, and Transjordan as mandates of Great Britain, and Syria as a mandate to France, made the Arab state of Hejaz independent, granted Smyrna, Thrace, Adrianople, and Gallipoli to Greece, gave large spheres of influence to France and Italy, and internationalized the Straits. The execution of this treaty was delayed in the hope that the United States might be prepared to accept a mandate over either Armenia or Constanti-

BULGARIA
BLACK SEA
Constantinople
SOVIET
UNION
CASPIAN SEA
Ankara Erzerum Baku
Smyrna T U R K E Y
Tabriz
Rhodes
(Italy)
Mosul
Cyprus SYRIA
(Br.) LEBANON French Tehran
MEDITERRANEAN SEA Beirut Mandate
Damascus
British British Baghdad
Mandate Amman Mandate I R A N
Alexandria TRANS-JORDAN I R A Q
Cairo Suez British
Canal Mandate
Basra
E G Y P T KUWAIT
PERSIAN GULF Bander Abbas
Bahrein QATAR
S A U D I TRUCIAL Muscat
Medina NAJD Riyadh OMAN
HEJAZ OMAN
A R A B I A
Jidda
Mecca
RED SEA
A N G L O- ASIR
E G Y P T I A N
S U D A N
YEMEN A D E N
ERITREA Sana (British)
0 500
THE PARTITION OF Miles
TURKEY
AFTER Aden
WORLD WAR I Jibuti

nople itself; and, by the time this hope had proven to be illusory, a revolutionary nationalist movement, headed by the hero of the Gallipoli
campaign, Mustafa Kemal, had risen to contest the moribund Sultanate
and had declared its inflexible opposition to the Sèvres terms.

Kemal was encouraged by the diplomatic recognition and support
accorded him by the Bolshevik regime in Russia, and he was greatly
aided by deep dissension among the Allies. The French and the Italians,
resentful of the gains made by Britain and Greece, soon expressed the
belief that the Treaty of Sèvres should be revised, and began secretly to
supply the Nationalists with arms and ammunition. The Lloyd George
government in England completely misread the situation, and the prime

minister himself—a great believer in personal diplomacy—encouraged the Greeks to embark on a fatal attempt to suppress the Kemalist movement and enforce the treaty from which they had gained so much. In September 1922, the Greek armies were routed and driven into the sea at Smyrna; and Kemal's armies threatened the small Allied forces upon the Asiatic shores of the Straits. At this juncture the French and Italians withdrew, leaving the British to find their way out of an apparently hopeless situation in which one false step might mean a major war. The British, however, held their ground; and Kemal, displaying great qualities of statesmanship, elected to negotiate. Talks at Mudania in October 1922 laid the basis for a new conference at Lausanne in the early summer of 1923, where the Sèvres Treaty was completely rewritten.

Turkish interests were ably defended at Lausanne by Ismet Pasha, a future president of his country; British claims were skillfully presented by the foreign secretary of the new Conservative government, the Earl of Curzon. Britain retained most of the territorial gains made at Sèvres, as did France and the Hejaz. Greece lost to Turkey virtually everything that had been granted it, and even had to turn the Dodecanese Islands, which it had acquired from Italy in 1919 with Turkish assent, back to Italy. Ismet's diplomacy established Turkey's rights over Anatolia, Cilicia, Adalia, Smyrna, eastern Thrace, and Constantinople and complete independence in directing its internal affairs. Freedom of navigation was established in the Straits, and they were demilitarized.

Turkey was thus the first successful revisionist power; but it had accomplished its revision without touching off a major war, and the settlement gained was sounder than the one it replaced.

In the lands that it took from Turkey, the British government tried patiently but with eventual failure to reconcile the promises made during the war to the Arabs and the Jews. The original pledge of support for Arab independence made in 1915 (see p. 509) had, in Arab eyes, been attenuated by the Sykes-Picot agreement of 1916 which provided, it is true, for an independent Arab state or a confederation of states, but also made it clear that there would be large British and French spheres of influence and that Palestine and the Holy Places would be given a special status. Uneasiness over these provisions ripened into indignation when Lord Balfour declared in November 1917 that "His Majesty's Government view with favour the establishment in Palestine of a national home for the Jewish people." Made in an effort to gain the sympathy and financial support of world Jewry for the Allied cause, and also because of the admiration that the British government had come to feel for the work of Dr. Chaim Weizmann, the president of the World Zionist Organization, the Balfour Declaration was regarded by the Arabs as a violation of the spirit of pledges made to them and an attempt to give political control of Palestine to the Jews in defiance of their own historical rights and their services to the Allied cause.

To conciliate Arab nationalism, the British assigned their mandates in the Near East to Arab rulers who would work under their supervision. Thus, Prince Faisal, son of the ruler of the newly independent Hejaz, King Hussein, was installed in Mesopotamia with the title king of Iraq and another of Hussein's sons became the ruler of Transjordan. Agitation for self-government began almost immediately in these territories, as it did in Syria and Lebanon, which passed under French control in accordance with the Sykes-Picot arrangement. Meanwhile, the heavy Jewish immigration into Palestine, while of inestimable value to that land, further incensed the Arabs and led to frequent and bloody clashes between the two contending populations in the postwar period.

Machinery for Revision / Any final judgment of the great peace settlement that followed World War I must take into consideration the fact that the peacemakers created machinery designed to complete the organization of the peace, to carry out special tasks made necessary by the treaties (the administration of plebescites in disputed areas, for instance, the protection of minorities in countries like Poland and Czechoslovakia, and the supervision of mandates), and to perform whatever tasks of adjustment, revision, and compromise might prove necessary for the preservation of international order and harmony. In his Fourteen Points address, President Wilson had declared that: "A general association of nations must be formed under specific covenants for the purpose of affording guarantees of political independence"; and, when he came to Paris, the President insisted that this be given top priority among the subjects to be discussed there. So great was the importance that he attributed to this concept that he did not scruple to assent to decisions of the Council of Four of which he personally disapproved, when he felt that this was necessary in order to assure the establishment of the new world organization. It was his fixed belief that the organization would correct any mistakes made and injustices done at Paris.

Largely as a result of the President's insistence, a special covenant was inserted into the major peace treaties that provided for a League of Nations, to which all Allied and Associated Powers, and such other states as were invited, would belong. It would be composed of an Assembly in which all members would be represented, a Council in which the Great Powers would have permanent seats and four seats would be assigned for shorter periods to other states, and a Secretariat, composed of international civil servants whose first loyalty was to the League. Provision was also made for the establishment by the Council of an International

Court of Justice and for an International Labor Office to further the improvement of conditions of labor by international action.

The organization of these bodies got under way immediately; the British diplomat, Sir Eric Drummond, was made the first secretary general of the League and charged with the task of arranging for its first meetings; and there was general hope that once established, the League and its sister bodies would make possible the achievement of peace and security through collective action.

FROM VERSAILLES TO LOCARNO

The Weaknesses of the League / The first Assembly of the League of Nations gathered in Geneva in November 1920. The British delegation, headed by Lord Balfour, took up its quarters in the Hotel Beau Rivage, where they discovered that the management had installed a shiny new slot machine in the lobby for the diversion of the delegates. This device fascinated Balfour, and he rarely passed it without feeding coins into it. One day, however, in an excess of enthusiasm, he pulled the handle too hard; and the machine, after vomiting coins all over the lobby, broke down. The management removed it.

On anyone sensitive to portents, this incident, carefully recorded by Balfour's biographer, must have made a foreboding impression. For the League of Nations was also a shiny new machine, and who could tell how much strain it would be capable of withstanding? Considering the tasks which it was created to perform, it began its existence with certain grave weaknesses.

In the first place, although the original membership list was impressive, it was marked by some notable omissions. The annex to the Covenant listed thirty-one Allied and Associated states which had signed the treaties as the original members and thirteen neutral states which had been asked to accede to the Covenant. All of the European Allies, the British Dominions, the succession states of Eastern Europe, Japan, China, and Siam in the Far East, all of the Latin American states, and Persia, the Hejaz, and Liberia had been asked to send representatives. But none of the former enemy states was included in the original list and, although Austria and Bulgaria were admitted after the first meeting of the Assembly, Hungary was not a member until 1922, Germany until 1926, and Turkey until 1932. Just as important as the absence of Germany was that of the Soviet Union, which continued until the early 1930s to attack the League as a front for capitalistic imperialism and tried to organize a countersociety of underdeveloped or anticolonial states.

More shattering in its effect upon the mood in which the League began its work was the decision of the United States government not to be represented in the organization for which Woodrow Wilson had fought so hard. This disappointing decision was partly due to domestic political factors and to tactical mistakes made by the President himself during and after the Peace Conference; but its primary cause was certainly a marked change in American public opinion in the months after the end of hostilities. The American people had gone to war in a spirit of idealism and reforming zeal, but this faltered and died in the face of the expenditure of life and resources required by the struggle, the unexpected length of the peace negotiations, the discrepancies between the final peace terms and the original Fourteen Points, the postwar revelations of the secret treaties concluded before and during the war, and, above all, the discovery that "to make the world safe for democracy" would demand continued effort and sacrifice on the part of the United States. By the end of 1919, there were fewer citizens of the United States who desired membership in the League than there were Americans who feared that it would seriously impair American sovereignty, or believed that the United States should return to a policy of isolationism, or had simply stopped thinking about the problem at all. The United States Senate, under the circumstances, blocked ratification of the Covenant until the Presidential elections of November 1920, in which the Democratic candidate, who had campaigned on Wilson's program, was overwhelmingly defeated. After that, the League was a dead issue in the United States; and the government decided against ratifying any of the treaties, making separate peace arrangements with the former enemy powers in 1922.

The effect of the American decision upon the authority and the morale of the League in its first days need not be dwelt on here, but mention may be made of another of its consequences. In some ways, the most serious result of American abstention was that it left Great Britain and France face to face in the League with no power of equal stature to mediate between them and adjust their views. This vacuum was unfortunate because these two countries had sharply opposed conceptions of what the League should be, and their differences had consequences as serious as the American decision.

Anglo-French Differences / Once the war was over, the British people, in a movement of opinion somewhat akin to that in the United States, reverted to their traditional aversion to continental entanglements. This change of attitude was reflected in the behavior of their government, as was shown by a significant action taken at the end of 1919. During the meetings of the Council of Four in Paris, Woodrow Wilson had persuaded Clemenceau to give up the French demand for cession of the German Rhineland; in return for France's surrender of these claims, the British and American governments had promised to guarantee France against any future German attack. When the United States Senate refused to ratify the Versailles Treaty, it repudiated this pledge too, and the British government decided to follow suit.

This action threw a shadow over relations between Britain and France for at least a decade. Arnold Toynbee, indeed, has written recently that

> This was, in effect, a dissolution of the Anglo-French Entente of 1904, after the necessity of the Entente for the survival of Great Britain, as well as France, had been demonstrated, in the first World War, by a terrifying practical experience of Germany's military strength. . . . The non-ratification of the post-war British guarantee to France dealt a blow to Franco-British relations from which these never recovered; and, from that time onwards, the two former partners . . . fell farther and farther out of step with one another till the eventual tragic parting of their ways in June 1940.

In 1919, the British were not, of course, looking that far ahead. Rather, they were thinking of avoiding undue risks and entanglements in Europe at a time when they had to concern themselves with pressing problems among their own dependencies and along the lifelines of their empire (see p. 664). Moreover, their reluctance to assume responsibilities on the continent was endorsed by the Dominions who, having fought one major war rising out of European complications, did not want to become involved in another. Since the Dominions now claimed, and received, a voice in the determination of imperial foreign policy, the home government no longer possessed the freedom of action in European affairs that it had had before 1914.

These factors determined Great Britain's attitude toward the League. In that organization's early days, Lord Balfour always seemed to be remembering the slot machine. He insisted that the League's true purpose was to promote international cooperation and that it should avoid assuming tasks which exceeded its powers. It was better designed to serve as a meeting place in which delegates could learn to know and understand each other's points of view than as an organ for taking executive action. Above all, it should avoid being placed in the position of applying, to either members or nonmembers, those military and economic sanctions mentioned in the Covenant as the means to be employed against refractory and aggressive states.

The French, for geographical and historical reasons, took an entirely different view. They were not protected by water from the possibility of invasion, and they had had German troops on their soil twice within half a century. They were aware that their recent victory had been won only with the aid of half the world and that, with a population that was now only two thirds that of Germany, and falling relatively, they would have to supplement their own defensive resources with those of other powers. They had thought that such aid was assured by the Rhineland pledge of the United States and Great Britain; once that evaporated, they had to find a substitute, and they could not regard the League, in its present form, as an effective one. As they read the Covenant, they were, in contrast to the British, particularly interested in the provisions for collective action against aggressors: in Article X, in which the members undertook to "respect and preserve against external aggression the territorial integrity and existing political independence" of all other members; in Article XI, which declared that "any war or threat of war [is] a matter of concern to the whole League" and "the League shall take any action that may be deemed wise and effectual to safeguard the peace of nations"; in Article XVI, which mentioned the economic, financial, and military means which League members might severally employ in case of an act of war. Their principal criticism was that the obligations implicit in these provisions were not binding upon all members and that the actions designed to check aggression would not come automatically into play when the aggression was committed. In their view, steps must be taken immediately to put teeth into the Covenant so that it would become a terror to wrongdoers.

In the first years of the League's operation, the French government sponsored two plans for strengthening the League. The first was the Draft Treaty of Mutual Assistance of 1923, which proposed that, once the Council had declared that a member state was the object of aggression, all other members would be obliged to come to its assistance. The second and more carefully devised proposal was the Geneva Protocol of 1924, which provided for the submission of all international disputes either to the International Court of Justice or to the League Council and declared that refusal to submit would automatically constitute an act of aggression, which each member of the League would be obliged to resist "in the degree which its geographical situation, and its particular situation as regards armaments, allows."

Both of these proposals, and the Geneva Protocol especially, received wide backing among League members. Both failed as a result of the opposition of the British government and the Dominions. In one respect, the British were admittedly in a difficult position, for they had been warned by the American secretary of state, Charles Evans Hughes, that, if they signed the Geneva Protocol and if the United States then became involved in a dispute with a League member and was branded as an aggressor, they might be required to go to war against the United States.

But this possibility could have been removed by an amendment to the protocol, if it had been the only thing that stood in the way of its acceptance. The real reason for British opposition was their disinclination to accept automatic obligations in Eastern Europe and other areas in which they had no vital interests—or thought they had none. Besides, as Sir Austen Chamberlain told the League Assembly, the protocol was too logical an arrangement. The British had always distrusted logic in politics and had generally been right!

The French Search for Security / Even before the defeat of their efforts to reform the League had been made definitive, the French had been pursuing other lines of policy that were designed to give them the security they desired. For one thing, they had begun to build up a network of military alliances outside the League of Nations.

In 1920, for instance, the French government concluded a defensive alliance with Belgium and immediately inaugurated staff talks with the object of devising joint plans to make any future German invasion through Belgium impossible. The agreement was a source of satisfaction to French soldiers who remembered how nearly Schlieffen's plan had come to winning the war in 1914; but it was not in itself sufficient. Germany must be made to realize that, in any future war, it would have to fight on two fronts again; and this realization would be forced on it only if France could find allies in Eastern Europe to take the place occupied by Russia after 1891.

France therefore turned to Poland, which seemed potentially the strongest military state in the east and the one least likely to become friendly with the Germans. An opportunity of winning Polish gratitude was found in 1920 when the Poles overreached themselves in an attempt to seize the Ukraine and were pushed back to the outskirts of Warsaw, which seemed in imminent danger of capture by units of the Red Army commanded by Marshal Tukhachevsky (see p. 567). The French helped organize the successful defense of the capital and the subsequent Polish advance that retrieved some of the lost territory. This collaboration led to the conclusion of a formal treaty in February 1921, in which the two powers agreed to "consult each other in all questions of foreign policy so far as those questions affect the settlement of international relations in the spirit of the Treaties" and, in the event of unprovoked aggression upon the territory of either, "to take concerted measures for the defense of their territories and the protection of their legitimate interests."

The first alliance led to others. From a strategical point of view, Czechoslovakia was as useful an ally against Germany—and from a political point of view as natural a one—as Poland. In 1924 France concluded a military alliance with it and, in subsequent years, sent French engineers to construct its defensive rampart in Bohemia. But Poland was already allied with Rumania, out of common fear of the Soviet Union; and Czechoslovakia had joined with Rumania and Yugoslavia to form the combination that came to be called the Little Entente and was designed as a means of common defense against a resurgent Hungary. It seemed logical for France to combine with the friends of its friends and, by 1927, it had forged military ties with them as well.

The French alliance system always seemed stronger than it actually was, and the future was to show that the French people were not willing to make the financial and military commitments necessary to hold it together when it was actually needed against Germany in the 1930s. It seems clear in retrospect that Eastern Europe could have been made a bulwark of collective security only by a joint Anglo-French commitment in that area. This was always an unlikely possibility, but it was made more so by France's unilateral policy of alliance building, which annoyed the British and made Anglo-French cooperation, in Eastern Europe, in the League, and elsewhere, more difficult than before.

Aside from this, it can be argued that the French alliance policy contributed both to the weakening of the League in its formative years and to the general insecurity of the continent. France's alliance ties sometimes placed it in a position in which it felt justified in bypassing the League. Thus, in 1923, when Poland attacked Lithuania for possession of Vilna, the French government blocked League mediation and arranged a Great Power award of the disputed area to their ally. This sort of thing is likely to invite emulation. In the same year as the Vilna dispute, Italy's new dictator, Mussolini, refused to allow League interference in his dispute with Greece over Corfu and was allowed to have his way (see p. 597). Nor was this the end of Mussolini's experiments in imitation. In Eastern Europe, he sought to compete with France for allies, turning his attention particularly to Austria, Hungary, and Bulgaria; and this increased the general unease of the area.

Finally, the new search for allies inaugurated by France contributed to the failure to implement Article VIII of the League Covenant, which provided for the formulation of plans for "the reduction of national armaments to the lowest point consistent with national safety." In the ten years that followed World War I, the only progress made toward such reduction was in naval armaments, and that was not impressive. The Washington Conference of 1921–1922 provided that the United States, Great Britain, Japan, France, and Italy should observe a ratio of 5:5:3:1.67:1.67 in capital ships for a period of ten years; but it was unable to establish any effective limits on cruisers or submarines. Nor were the Geneva Naval Conference of 1927 and the London Conference of 1930 successful in this regard. As for land armaments, there was a good deal of discussion of limitations but nothing in the way of results. By 1929 all powers were arming on a scale exceeding that of the prewar period, with the exception of the former enemy powers, whose efforts in this field were limited by treaty. Even in their case, it was known that illegal arming was going on in Austria and Hungary; and there were secret agreements between the Red Army and that of the German Republic which enabled German soldiers to receive training in weapons denied them by the Versailles Treaty (see p. 609).

Britain, France, and the German Question / Meanwhile, the differences between Britain and France that had begun with the repudiation of the Rhineland pledge and had been aggravated by their failure to agree about the League, their diverse policies in face of Kemal's national revolution in Turkey (see p. 540), and France's alliance policy in Eastern Europe were being made more serious by France's German policy.

In large part, this centered on the reparations problem. The French persisted in believing that the Germans should pay on the scale envisaged during the Peace Conference. The British very rapidly came to doubt whether this was possible or even desirable and to suspect that the French were actuated by political rather than economic motives—that their insistence on complete payment was, in fact, merely another aspect of their security policy, designed to keep Germany permanently impoverished.

As if ashamed of his having yielded to popular passions during the Paris Conference, Lloyd George undertook the job of persuading the French that it would be to Europe's interest and their own to lighten the burden imposed upon the Germans. His efforts were rendered ineffective by maladroitness on the part of the people he was trying to help. When the British prime minister persuaded the French to allow the Germans to appear at a conference at Spa in July 1920 to suggest how, and how much, they could pay in reparations, the German government sent a delegation that included General von Seeckt, who wore his uniform, complete with iron cross, and the industrialist Hugo Stinnes, who made incoherent speeches in which he accused the French of being "afflicted with the disease of victory" and of wishing to use black troops to oppress Germany and threatened them with a stoppage of all coal shipments. These provocations hardened the French in their attitude. Two years later, when Lloyd George organized a general economic conference at Genoa, which might have done something to alleviate the German economic position, the German delegation, headed by Foreign Minister Walther Rathenau (see p. 516), became nervous because they were excluded from private conferences in Lloyd George's villa. They allowed the Soviet delegation to talk them into a special pact of friendship and collaboration, the Treaty of Rapallo, the announcement of which had the effect of a bombshell, blowing up the Genoa Conference before any consideration was given to Germany's economic difficulties.

The Rapallo Treaty made the British government more eager to secure some reduction of Germany's burdens, lest she slip completely into the Soviet camp. In France, it had the opposite effect, strengthening the resolve to insist upon complete fulfillment of the reparations obligation. Thus, there was a direct causal relationship between Rathenau's action at Rapallo and the French invasion of the Ruhr in January 1923. The author of this fateful action was the French prime minister, Raymond Poincaré, an inveterate opponent of any concessions to France's former enemy. Taking advantage of a German failure to make certain timber shipments to France in accordance with an agreed schedule of payments in kind, Poincaré insisted that the Reparations Commission declare Germany in violation of its legal obligations. When this was done, over the opposition of the British representative, he announced that France must seek redress and dispatched French troops into the Ruhr, one of the most valuable of Germany's remaining mining and industrial areas.

As a means of attaining security for France—which is doubtless how Poincaré regarded his stroke—this was a drastic blunder. For one thing, as will be indicated below (p. 614), it seriously weakened the prospects of democracy in Germany and strengthened the forces of reaction. The social effects of the inflation brought to a head by the French action were disastrous and permanent, and it is no mere coincidence that Adolf Hitler made his first bid for power during the political confusion incidental to the Ruhr invasion. But even immediately the invasion backfired. When the tottering German economy collapsed under this new blow, it became impossible for the Germans to make any reparations payments; and, when the default occurred, there were serious repercussions abroad, not least of all in France.

The Dawes Plan, Locarno, and After / The critical situation created by these events did, however, elicit an effective response on the part of the Western powers and did something to resolve the Anglo-French differences on German policy. In 1924, under the leadership of the American banker Charles Dawes, an international commission of economic experts worked out a new long-term schedule of reparations payments for Germany, while at the same time laying a basis for foreign loans to that country which would enable it to resume reparations payments during the period when its own currency was being reformed. The easing of the economic situation encouraged the ablest German statesman of the interwar years, Gustav Stresemann, to seek a political agreement that would place Germany's relations with the Western powers, and particu-

Into the Light
A 1925 commentary on Locarno by the American cartoonist
Rollin Kirby.

larly with France, on an entirely new basis. Stresemann informed London
and Paris that, in the interests of a general detente and in the hope that it
might facilitate the evacuation of German soil by Allied troops, the
German government was prepared to recognize the permanence of
Germany's present boundaries with France and Belgium and to have
them placed under international guarantee. Pushed enthusiastically by
the British, this proposal led to negotiations between Stresemann, Sir
Austen Chamberlain, Aristide Briand (Poincaré's successor, a man
infinitely more receptive to the idea of Franco-German collaboration in
the interest of general appeasement), and other interested parties at
Locarno, Switzerland. The negotiations eventuated in a number of
treaties and agreements. Germany, France, and Belgium agreed to
respect their common frontiers and to forswear the use of war against
each other except in self-defense or in accordance with the League
Covenant; Great Britain and Italy agreed to guarantee this so-called
Rhineland Pact; Germany agreed to seek admission to the League of

Nations, on condition that it receive a permanent seat on the Council and (in view of its inferiority in armaments) that it be exempted from certain of the military obligations of the Covenant; Germany also agreed to submit any disputes that it might have with its neighbors to arbitration or conciliation and, while not accepting its eastern frontiers, to seek their modification only by peaceful means. A covering protocol declared that in concluding these agreements the powers were seeking "by common agreement means of preserving their respective nations from the scourge of war and for providing for the peaceful settlement of disputes."

To a Europe tired of the tension and quarrels of the last six years, Locarno seemed to be a hopeful sign that those goals might be attained. The collaboration of Stresemann, Briand, and Chamberlain aroused great enthusiasm in the continent, which saw resulting from it the beginning of a genuine Franco-German rapprochement, and a reinvigoration of the League of Nations and the principle of collective security in general.

These hopes were not wholly groundless. The entrance of Germany into the League in 1926 did bring new prestige and authority to that organization; and, thanks to the earnest efforts of Briand and Stresemann, relations between their countries improved sufficiently to make possible a relaxation of the controls placed upon Germany in 1919, the evacuation of German soil by Allied troops (completed in 1930), and the scaling down of the reparations burden by the Young Plan of 1929—all measures designed further to contribute to the relaxation of European tension.[2]

Nevertheless, with the benefit of hindsight, we can see that the enthusiasm engendered by Locarno was excessive and, in some cases, dangerous.

If the League gained strength from Germany's adhesion, it was nevertheless not the kind of strength that might have been derived from the passage earlier of the Draft Treaty of Mutual Assistance or the Geneva Protocol. In a sense, the enthusiasm aroused by Locarno tended to make people forget the justice of the French argument that the enforcing machinery of the League and the provisions for action against aggressors were still too weak to be effective in a major crisis.

In the second place, what security the new treaties brought to Europe was rather one-sided and would not be complete until the Rhineland Pact was supplemented by some kind of eastern Locarno. Despite French efforts, this proved to be unattainable, among other things because of British opposition. Although it was not generally appreciated at the time, Great Britain's signature of the Rhineland Pact was not evidence of a new

[2] Another measure that served the same purpose was the Pact of Paris (Kellog-Briand Pact) of August 1928 by which some 23 nations, including the European great powers and the United States, renounced the use of aggressive war. The pact made no provision for sanctions.

willingness to accept European responsibilities. It was rather a final answer to the Geneva Protocol. In guaranteeing the Rhine boundaries, Britain was expressing its inflexible opposition to commitment on the Vistula, and this meant that an Eastern security pact would be impossible.

Finally, Locarno did not, as some enthusiasts thought, assure lasting friendship and cooperation between its signatories. Germany followed its ratification of the Rhineland and the other treaties by concluding a new treaty of friendship (the Treaty of Berlin, 1926) with the Soviet Union, a power that had done its utmost to prevent the Germans from going to Locarno and was a declared foe of the League system. Italy, despite its collaboration in the work at Locarno, plunged into a new and dangerous rivalry with France in the Danubian area; and Great Britain remained vaguely suspicious and generally opposed to the main line of French policy.

Locarno, in short, was important only as a beginning to the solution of European tensions. It bore some good fruit in the five years that followed. But, because it induced a general euphoria, it tended to make the European peoples relax and prevented them from urging their governments on to new efforts in the interests of collective security.

22

The Russian Revolution and the West, 1917-1933

In a letter written in March 1868, Feodor Dostoevsky predicted that within a hundred years the whole world would be regenerated by Russian thought. That prophecy has not been fulfilled in the sense that the great novelist meant it; but it is undeniable that the political, economic, and social thinking, and in some cases the system of government and the institutional framework, of many countries all over the globe have been profoundly influenced by Russian ideas, Russian examples, and, in recent years, Russian conquests.

It is hardly likely that this would have been true, or true to the same extent, if Tsarist Russia had survived. The impact of Russian thought upon the rest of the world began to become impressive only with the victory of communism in the land of the tsars.

THE RUSSIAN REVOLUTION

The End of Tsardom / How long the tsarist regime might have lasted if there had been no world war it is, of course, impossible to say. Considering its inherent weaknesses and its failures of omission and commission after 1905 (see pp. 433–436), it is difficult to believe that its life could have been much prolonged. However that may be, the war threw a glaring light upon its inadequacies, while at the same time exposing the Russian people to hardships and suffering that made them increasingly intolerant of their lot.

Russia was unprepared agriculturally, industrially, or financially to fight a long war. Even after Stolypin's agrarian reforms (see p. 435), Russian agriculture lagged far behind the countries of the west in efficiency, and, once the war deprived it of the manpower upon which it depended in lieu of machines, production fell off precipitously. Russian industry was too backward either to remedy this situation by producing more farm implements or to supply the military needs of the state. In the course of three years of war, it produced hardly more than a third as many rifles as there were men mobilized. These deficiencies were reflected in food shortages that sapped civilian morale and in military weaknesses that made Russian casualties in the field higher than they would have been if the troops had been adequately armed. In the campaigns of 1915, in which the Russian armies were driven out of Galicia and Poland (see p. 505), Russian casualties have been conservatively estimated at more than two million; and in Brusilov's great push in 1916 (see p. 509) his forces lost close to a million men and were left in a state of near-demoralization.

By the end of 1916, these disasters had exhausted the patience even of former supporters of the regime. In November, when the Duma reconvened, Paul Miliukov, the leader of the Constitutional Democratic (or Cadet) party, delivered a furious attack upon the inadequacies of the government's policy and did not hesitate to extend his criticism to the throne itself by intimating that the empress shared the responsibility for them. In December these protests took a more tangible form, when a group of noblemen led by Prince Yusupov invited the empress' favorite, Rasputin (see p. 428), to a private dinner party, fed him cakes and wine liberally dosed with cyanide of potassium, and, when the wine had no perceptible effect, shot him and threw his body into the freezing waters of the Neva. Neither these events, however, nor the reports of bread riots in his principal cities had any effect upon Nicholas II, who, as the crisis of his regime approached, proved his intellectual immaturity by immersing himself in trivialities, relying upon his police and his home garrisons to put down disorders.

But it was now too late for that. At the beginning of March, a series of strikes broke out in the national capital of Petrograd,[1] and on March

---

[1] St. Petersburg was renamed Petrograd during the war.

Revolution in St. Petersburg, July 1917: The police of the Kerensky government firing on a workers' demonstration. (SOVFOTO)

8, International Women's Day, demonstrations of housewives touched off attacks on bakeries and other disorders. These became so serious that by March 10 all factories and industrial establishments in the city were closed down and, on Sunday, March 11, troops had to be called out to disperse the crowds, some of which were filled with people carrying banners and signs reading "Down with the German woman!," a reference to the empress. The troops did their duty, so effectively that some sixty people were killed in one of these affrays, but there were some fateful signs of fraternization between the troops and the demonstrators.

On March 12 it became clear that the situation had deteriorated too seriously to be corrected and that the collapse of the regime could not be prevented. On that day, the local garrisons, led by the Volinsk Regiment, arrested their officers and joined the revolutionary cause. Simultaneously, factory strike committees met with representatives of the different socialist factions and, as in 1905 (see p. 432), organized a Soviet of Workers Deputies. By the following morning, the Soviet had been recognized by the mutinous garrisons, had taken over direction of all vital public services, and was in complete control of the city.

The authority of the Soviet did not extend beyond local affairs, but its creation jolted the Duma into taking more extensive action. Strictly speaking, this national legislative body had no legal standing, for the tsar had declared it prorogued on March 11. But it defied that order and established a provisional committee "to restore order and deal with institutions and individuals." This group was presided over by Prince Lvov and included members of the non-socialist parties from Cadets to Progressive Nationalists, as well as one Socialist Revolutionary, Alexander Kerensky, serving in his own right rather than as a representative of his party. On March 14, the committee constituted itself as a provisional government and, in the hope of restoring order to the country, sent representatives to the tsar to urge him to abdicate. On March 15, Nicholas II did so, in favor of his brother Michael, who declined the honor, leaving the succession open and making Russia a *de facto* republic. There is no evidence that the loss of his power caused Nicholas II any sorrow or soul searching. His rule had shown him to be a strangely insensitive person with a warped perspective; and he was able to write in his diary on the day after the loss of his throne: "I had a long and sound sleep. Woke up beyond Dvinsk. Sunshine and frost. . . . I read much of Julius Caesar." He seemed perfectly happy with the prospect of being able to devote himself entirely to his family. This, however, he was not to be permitted to do. After months of detention, first at Tsarskoe Selo and then in Siberia, Nicholas and his family were murdered by the Communists in July 1918.

From March to November / The abdication of the tsar left a confused situation in the country, with political authority divided between the provisional government of Prince Lvov and the soviets that had been organized in Petrograd and other cities. On the face of it, these bodies appeared to be natural enemies, since the provisional government, if it represented anyone, represented the middle and aristocratic classes, who had abandoned the monarchy reluctantly and could be counted on to oppose radical social change, whereas the soviets spoke in the name of the toiling and oppressed masses and the soldiers who had made the revolution and would presumably want to carry it further. That there was no open clash between them in the first months was due largely to the fact that the provisional government was uncertain of the resources at its disposal, while the leaders of the soviets, to the growing disgust of their rank and file, were reluctant to claim power for themselves.

The hesitation of the soviet chiefs to assume political responsibility was due largely to the fact that most of them were socialists who desired to make the revolution that had burst upon them accord with their theoretical preconceptions. Aware that Russia was a backward country, they were inclined to believe that the present revolution was the long-awaited bourgeois revolution designed to free it from the bonds of feudalism, and that logically it should be directed by bourgeois leaders (*i.e.,* the provisional government). A proletarian revolution would doubtless come some day, but only after a bourgeois regime had created the conditions for it. This kind of doctrinal rigidity produced what Isaac Deutscher has called "the honeymoon" of the March republic, in which Mensheviks, Socialist Revolutionaries, and for a time even the Bolsheviks agreed to tolerate the Lvov government. Moreover, they carried their toleration to the point of supporting the war, which they had once denounced as a reactionary and imperialist venture, on the theory that it had now become a revolutionary crusade which would achieve a democratic peace without annexations and indemnities. They were also hesitant about the advisability of extensive changes in the ownership of land until the war was over.

The end of the honeymoon and of the relative unity of the socialist groups was not, however, long delayed. It came in April 1917 with Lenin's return to Russia from his exile in Switzerland. The acknowledged leader of the Bolsheviks owed his return to Petrograd to the German government, which supplied the famous "sealed train" to carry him across Europe in the hope that his agitations would disrupt the Russian war effort. This hope was fulfilled, for Lenin used his influence to persuade the socialists to terminate their support of the war. In his so-called April Theses, he pointed out that the war was still an imperialistic one and that neither it nor the groups profiting from it deserved any assistance from representatives of the people. It was doubtless true, he argued, that the Russian revolution was a bourgeois-democratic one, but it would soon pass on to its next phase, the socialist phase, a transition to be aided by revolutions in Central and Western European countries. In Russia the socialist phase would be ushered in by the conquest of full political power by the soviets. This should be the objective of Bolshevik policy, Lenin insisted, and to promote it the Bolsheviks should not only strive to gain a majority in the soviets but do everything in their power to transform the imperialist war into a civil war, encouraging the expropriation of the landlords by the peasantry and the assumption of control of the factories by the workers.

Lenin's demand for a more militant program was greeted with misgivings by some of the other Bolshevik leaders, but they were unable to withstand the force of Lenin's personality. His views were accepted as the new party line, and the Bolsheviks began a propaganda campaign designed to discredit the provisional government and weaken its authority. From the beginning the campaign was enormously successful with the city masses, partly because of the efficiency of the party organization and the polemical skill of the Bolshevik leaders, but more perhaps because of the essential attractiveness of the picture of the Russia of the future that they held up before the people. In Lenin's own words:

All power in the state, from top to bottom, from the remotest village to the last street in the city of Petrograd, must belong to the Soviets of Workers', Soldiers' and Peasants' Deputies. . . . There must be no police, no bureaucrats who have no responsibility to the people, who stand above the people, no standing army, only the people universally armed, united in the Soviets—it is they who must run the state.

The masses could hardly foresee that this idyllic future would not be realized in Lenin's time and would recede almost completely from view in Stalin's. They responded to Bolshevik slogans with enthusiasm, so much so that they became impatient for their realization and, in July, attempted a rising in Petrograd which was put down by front-line troops summoned to the capital by the provisional government. That body, under fire because of heavy losses suffered in a new Galician offensive that had been ordered by its war minister Kerensky, took advantage of the abortive July rising to blame its defeat in Galicia upon Bolshevik agitators and accuse Lenin of being an agent of the German General Staff. Bolshevik headquarters were raided by government police and rightist vigilantes; Trotsky and Kamenev were arrested; and Lenin and Zinoviev had to go into hiding—Lenin fleeing to Finland.

This did not affect the steady growth of Bolshevik support in Petrograd and in Moscow; and, in any case, Kerensky found that he could not afford to do without Bolshevik aid. This flamboyant and eloquent figure, whom the Bolsheviks accused of regarding himself as the Bonaparte of the Russian revolution, had become prime minister and minister of war in a coalition government formed in July, when the government of Prince Lvov resigned. Between Kerensky and the commander-in-chief of the army, General L. G. Kornilov, there was much bad blood, and the ambitious general made no secret of his lack of faith in the war minister. In September he went further. News of the loss of Riga to the Germans in that month led to charges and countercharges of treason and subversion, and Kornilov withdrew his support from the government and sent troops to take Petrograd. In self-defense, Kerensky freed his Bolshevik captives and urged them to help in suppressing the mutiny, which they did by mobilizing their Red Guards and by sending agitators who succeeded in persuading Kornilov's forces to abandon him. The general's defeat brought little credit to the provisional government, which now underwent another of those reorganizations that were signs of weakness rather than strength—Kerensky now becoming the chief of a five-man Directorate. The Bolsheviks, on the other hand, gained prestige and, more important, won a clear majority in the Petrograd and Moscow soviets and in the provincial soviets as well. That was the beginning of the end for Kerensky.

The Bolshevik Revolution / Lenin was still in hiding in Finland, but he was able to judge the significance of the shift of power within the soviets. He reacted by sending a message to the Central Committee of his party in which he argued that the time for armed insurrection had come. On October 23, he slipped into the country to urge this in person, and a protracted debate ensued in which he pointed out that revolution by violence was the logical conclusion of the tactics followed since April. His arguments failed to convince Zinoviev and Kamenev, but all of the other party leaders, including Trotsky, Stalin, and Dzerzhinsky, were won over. Thus, in these weeks when Kerensky was trying to maintain order in the face of renewed strikes in the cities, heightened peasant violence, and mass desertions from the army, and was discovering that his new government commanded no more support than the ones that had preceded it, the Bolsheviks were methodically making plans for their *coup d'état*.

The master-mind of the operation was Leon Trotsky (1879–1940), who now demonstrated for the first time the strategical gifts and the tactical virtuosity that were to serve the Bolshevik cause so well during the civil war. Born Lev Davidovich Bronstein, the son of a well-to-do Jewish farmer in a province of Kherson in the Ukraine, the future war commissar became a convert of Marxism and entered revolutionary politics before he was twenty, was arrested by the tsarist police in 1898, and, after two years imprisonment in Odessa, was exiled to Siberia. He managed to escape and to make his way out of the country with a forged passport in the name of the chief jailer at Odessa, Trotsky, a name which he used for the rest of his life. Already known for his propaganda work, he became one of Lenin's associates on the editorial board of *Iskra* in London (see p. 429). During the revolution of 1905 he returned to Russia and was the outstanding figure in the Petrograd Soviet, over which he was presiding at the time of the police raid that resulted in the arrest of its entire executive committee (see p. 433). Exiled once more to Siberia, he again escaped to the west, where he worked with socialist groups in Vienna and Paris and—after his expulsion in 1917 by the French government for spreading antiwar propaganda—in New York, where he edited the newspaper *New World*. After the abdication of Nicholas II, he returned to Russia once more and, for the first time, joined the Bolshevik party, having previously been associated with the Menshevik wing of the old Social Democratic party. His prestige within the party is shown by the fact that when the first Politburo of the Bolshevik Central Committee was appointed—at the same meeting in October 1917 at which it was decided to organize an armed insurrection—he was made a member along with Lenin, Zinoviev, Kamenev, G. Y. Sokolnikov, A. S. Bubnov, and the man who was to become his most hated enemy, Joseph Stalin.

It was Trotsky who pointed out that a rising against the provisional government would have a greater chance of success if it were made under the auspices of a soviet and in the guise of a defensive action against a counterrevolutionary plot, than if it were undertaken openly in the name of the Bolshevik party. His advice was followed. Working through the Revolutionary Military Committee of the Petrograd Soviet, the Bolsheviks deliberately challenged Kerensky's right to order troop movements in and around the capital. When, as was expected, the premier reacted with a ringing denunciation of their tactics and an ineffectual attempt to arrest their leaders once more, they accused him of treason to the revolution and struck back with deadly efficiency. On the night of November 6–7, the Soviet's Red Guards, supported by regular army units, seized every key point in the city and surrounded the Winter Palace, the seat of the provisional government. In a matter of hours, the operation was complete, and the city woke to find the Bolsheviks in control. The coup had been timed to coincide with the opening of the Second All-Russian Congress of the Soviets;[2] and, on the evening of November 7, when that body convened, Lenin appeared before it as the effective ruler of the capital.

The Bolsheviks had a majority in the Congress when it assembled, and it became overwhelming when the Mensheviks and the right wing of the Socialist Revolutionary party walked out in protest against the insurrection. Those who remained approved the formation of an all-Bolshevik government—the Council of Peoples' Commissars, with Lenin as its head, Trotsky as commissar for foreign affairs, and Stalin as commissar for nationalities—and elected a new Central Executive Committee composed of 62 Bolsheviks and 29 left-wing Socialist Revolutionaries. They also passed two decrees laid before them by Lenin: one proposing the immediate conclusion of a peace without annexations and indemnities, and one abolishing private property in land and transferring all private and church lands to land committees and soviets of peasant deputies for later distribution.

Meanwhile, Kerensky had fled to the provinces, where he sought to rally the army against the insurgents in Petrograd. His efforts failed miserably, and he was forced to seek refuge abroad. There was, indeed, little resistance at this stage to the Bolshevik expansion of the authority they had taken in Petrograd. Moscow fell to them after a week's fighting, and, within a month, most of the cities of Russia were in their hands. Their consolidation of power was enormously facilitated by the apparent failure of the other parties to comprehend what the consequences of a Bolshevik dictatorship would be. The parties that might have challenged the Bol-

[2] A First All-Russian Congress had met in June.

sheviks effectively, the Mensheviks and the Socialist Revolutionaries, showed a disinclination to think in terms of power that played directly into the hands of Lenin and his followers. Thus, when elections were held in late November for that Constituent Assembly which the Russian Left had made the object of their hopes for generations and which was expected to make constitutional arrangements for the new Russia, Lenin interfered openly in the electoral procedures, arrested some of those who were elected, outlawed the Cadet party. In January, when the Assembly finally met, Lenin had it dissolved by Bolshevik guards after one session. No one was in a position to protest effectively against these measures, because the Bolsheviks by this time had a monopoly of force in the country.

First Decrees and the Peace of Brest Litovsk / The dissolution of the Constituent Assembly was part of a deliberate Bolshevik policy of smashing all institutions that might serve as a rallying point for opposition. The members of the old provisional government were deported; the municipal councils of Petrograd and Moscow, which were anti-Bolshevik, were dissolved; in December, the Imperial Senate was abolished; and, a month later, a Bolshevik decree did away with the zemstvos (see p. 428), which, in the last years before the war, had been centers of liberalism and agitation for moderate constitutional reform. Meanwhile, a series of decrees ordering the election of all officers in the army, changing the rank system, and speeding up demobilization removed the threat of military opposition by causing the army literally to disappear. In February 1918, complete separation of church and state was announced and although no attempt was made to abolish the Russian Orthodox Church, its power and authority were seriously weakened by expropriation of its lands, repeal of the old marriage and divorce laws, and withholding official recognition from any but civil marriage. A potential threat to complete Bolshevik control of the peasantry was removed in December 1917 when clever tactics by Lenin forced a split in a Congress of Peasant Deputies meeting in Petrograd and created an opportunity for effecting a fusion of the Peasant Soviets with the Workers and Soldiers Soviets, thus breaking the Socialist Revolutionary party's power in its last remaining stronghold.

Meanwhile, the sharing out of the great landed estates, which proved to be the measure that generated most popular support for the new regime, was carried out and other steps were taken to transform the national economy. In November, workers' committees were authorized to supervise factory production, and the eight-hour day became universal. In subsequent months, the government created a Supreme Economic Council, nationalized the banks, and, in a step productive of many future complications, canceled the debts of the tsarist regime.

While all this was going on, the national domain was being seriously diminished. Poland's independence had been recognized by the provisional government before its demise; Finland demanded independence immediately after the Bolshevik take-over, and, in a unique example of voluntary surrender of territory by the Soviet regime, this was recognized, in the name of national self-determination, by the commissar of nationalities, Stalin. Between December 1917 and the following February, Lithuania, Latvia, and Estonia all declared their independence and, although the Bolsheviks resisted, they had their way in the end.

The implementation of Lenin's Decree of Peace led to additional losses. Despite the daring improvisations and the skillful tactics of delay employed by Trotsky in the negotiations with the Germans at Brest Litovsk, the German General Hoffmann insisted on sizable annexations and, when these were refused, ordered a new advance which the Bolsheviks were powerless to oppose. Some members of the party's Central Committee believed that a revolutionary war should be resorted to, but Lenin insisted that the Germans' terms be met and threatened to resign if they were not. He was supported by the narrowest of margins, and the Bolshevik regime accepted the peace of Brest Litovsk in March 1918.

By its terms, Russia was forced to accept the loss of Poland, the Baltic states, Finland, large areas of Byelorussia and the Ukraine, and part of Transcaucasia: a total of 1,300,000 square miles and 62 million people, not counting the loss of Bessarabia to Rumania, which was stipulated in Germany's Treaty of Bucharest with that country. The losses were so great in extent that Petrograd was considered too close to the new border to be safe, and the center of government was shifted to Moscow.

The Civil War / The conclusion of the peace of Brest Litovsk was considered an act of betrayal by the Allied governments who were still locked in conflict with Germany. It threatened to release an untold number of German troops for action against the weary Allied armies on the western front and to enable the Germans also to lay their hands on the vast quantities of stores and ammunition that the Allies had been sending to Russia as late as October 1917.

To prevent the latter of these possibilities from being realized, the British landed naval units at Murmansk in March 1918; and other landings and occupations followed, made from more obscure motives. The Japanese sent strong forces into Vladivostok, which were followed by British and American units, presumably designed to watch over them. The British occupied Archangel, Batum, and the Baku oil fields. A mixed force under French command took Odessa, and a comprehensive blockade of Russian waters was established.

Leon Trotsky, 1879–1940, in 1919. (CULVER SERVICE)

The broader significance of these military moves was that they gave encouragement and material assistance to anti-Bolshevik and counterrevolutionary movements. Local Allied commands did not hesitate to recognize and supply White governments which grew up in the districts under their authority, and before long there were a score of these dotted around the boundaries of Bolshevik authority from Siberia to the Ukraine. Along the southern borders of the country between the Black and Caspian seas, the leaders of the Don and Kuban Cossacks were opposed to the regime. This area was the base for a White Army commanded first by General Kornilov, who had managed to escape from the detention into which he had been placed after the failure of his coup, and later, after Kornilov's death in fighting around Ekaterinodar, by General Anton Denikin. In south central Russia, from Samara on the Volga to Omsk and Tomsk in central Siberia, a second anti-Bolshevik front was created by the revolt of the Czech Legion. This force, which had fought beside the Russians during the last year of the war, was left without occupation by Brest Litovsk. It was given permission by the Bolshevik government to leave the country by way of the Trans-Siberian railway, with the idea that it might go around the world and reappear on the western front. Difficulties with Bolshevik officials en route led it to break with the government and to seize a chain of strong points along the railroad.

The Czech success not only heartened Denikin in the south and encouraged the Allies to increase the scope of their intervention but soon led to a fusion of all anti-Bolshevik groups in Siberia. This was effected in September 1918 at Ufa, where a national government called the Directory was set up with headquarters at Omsk and with the mission of directing the anti-Bolshevik crusade. The effective functioning of this government was hampered by difficulties between the partners, the most troublesome of whom were the Socialist Revolutionaries, whose right wing, it will be remembered, had broken with Bolshevism after Lenin's armed insurrection and whose left wing had been expelled after it reverted to terrorism in protest against the treaty of Brest Litovsk. The trouble with the Socialist Revolutionaries in Siberia was that they hated the bourgeois groups with which they had to cooperate almost as much as they did Lenin's party. In November the conservatives at Omsk tired of their tactics, arrested their leaders, and handed supreme power over to the former commander of the Black Seas Fleet, Admiral Alexander Kolchak.

At the beginning of 1919, the tsarist general, E. K. Miller, took over power at Archangel from a local Socialist Revolutionary group and placed himself and his forces at Kolchak's disposal, and at the same time a North Western White Army was assembled in Estonia by General Yudenich and supplemented by the Iron Division of Count von der Goltz, a force made up of volunteers from the former German occupation army, *Frontkämpfer* who preferred adventure to the uncertainties of civilian life in a now defeated Germany. Thus, the Bolsheviks were confronted with four sizeable armies of great initial strength.

If the Whites had had the forces in 1918 that they had a year later, they might have destroyed Bolshevism. Their initial weakness gave Leon Trotsky the opportunity to do his greatest service for the state that finally rejected and killed him. In March 1918, Trotsky became war commissar and began to build up the force that became the Red Army. In April 1918 compulsory military service was decreed for all workers and peasants. Rejecting the early revolutionary notion that an army can be run by political committees, Trotsky returned to a more traditional system of discipline and openly relied upon the only trained officers he could find, former commanders in the imperial army. During the civil war, almost fifty thousand former tsarist officers served with the Red Army, some rising to the highest ranks, like the young Michael N. Tukhachevsky, who in 1917 escaped from a German prison camp (where one of his fellow prisoners was a French captain named Charles de Gaulle), made his way home and volunteered for the Red Army, and by 1920 was commander-in-chief of all Red forces on the western front.

To watch over the officers and to carry out essential propaganda tasks, Trotsky appointed political commissars, who were not, however, supposed to interfere with command decisions. Once the army had taken to the field desertion and failure were punished with death; success, with new opportunities to serve the state. The war commissar himself appeared on every front, hectoring, bullying, inspiring men who only months before thought they had thrown away their rifles for the last time. But they fought and fought well, and with their successes came a pride and *élan* that the Whites could not match.

There were moments in 1919 when the fate of Bolshevism trembled in the balance. The White commanders slowly tightened their ring around the Bolshevik center. In October Denikin was in Kiev and Orel, and Yudenich was on the outskirts of Petrograd. But in the end both those drives failed; and, even before they had reached their point of greatest promise, Kolchak had been checked at Glazov by a Red Army under Michael Frunze (whose name today graces the Soviet War Academy) and had been slowly pushed back into Siberia. The Whites suffered from deficiencies that they were incapable of correcting. Their military leadership was, on the whole, of inferior quality. Not until Baron P. N. Wrangel succeeded Denikin in April 1920 did they find a commander of truly outstanding ability, and then it was too late. They received inadequate aid from the Allied governments, who never fully committed themselves to the war against Bolshevism. The various White forces generally failed to coordinate their drives and thus frittered away great opportunities and were defeated piecemeal. Their rule of the areas they controlled was weakened by party squabbling; and they failed to impress local populations with the sincerity of their democratic professions. Finally, the fact that they gave protection to former landlords seeking to regain their estates deprived them of the support of a peasantry that was determined not to allow the old agrarian system to return.

For all of these reasons, the Whites were beaten. Yudenich was driven back into Estonia in November 1919, where his army dissolved; Kolchak was captured by the Reds at Irkutsk in January and shot; Miller was overthrown at Archangel and made his way abroad, where he played a part in refugee politics until September 1937 when he was kidnapped by Soviet agents in Paris and never seen again; Denikin was isolated at Novorossiisk in March and evacuated by the British. Wrangel, after playing a part in the Polish war described below, fell back to the Crimea, where he held out until the end of 1920, when his force was evacuated by the Allies to Gallipoli and a year later to Yugoslavia and Bulgaria. By that time, Russian soil was free of Allied and White troops, with the exception of part of the Maritime Province, which was not evacuated by the Japanese until October 1922.

The Polish War / In the first months of 1920, when the White threat in the north and east was abating, the Bolshevik regime was threatened

1914 — **1921**
THE WESTERN BORDER OF RUSSIA

by a vigorous offensive on the part of the Poles, in conjunction with the Ukrainian nationalists led by Petlyura and the White Army of Wrangel, advancing from the south. The Poles had great initial successes and took Kiev and other centers, but they were soon in difficulties. Their aggression aroused a wave of genuine patriotic enthusiasm in Russia, which gave weight to a powerful counterthrust by the Red Army. In June Kiev was retaken, and the Poles began a general retirement. In July Soviet forces under Tukhachevsky advanced to the very walls of Warsaw, and communism seemed about to burst into Europe. But at this point Colonel Aleksander Yegorov, commanding the forces on Tukhachevsky's left flank, decided—perhaps on the advice of his political commissar, Stalin— to march on L'vov instead of backing the main drive against Warsaw. Before the gap created by this decision could be closed, the Polish commander, Joseph Pilsudski, acting in consultation with the French general, Maxime Weygand, struck at the exposed flank and the Red Army broke and retreated.

Both armies were wearied and, when the Bolsheviks sued for peace, negotiations were begun and concluded at Riga in October 1920. The

Poles benefited from the mistake in front of Warsaw. They received a boundary well to the east of the ethnic frontier, the so-called Curzon Line laid down by the Allied Supreme Council in December 1919, and with it acquired a Russian minority of four million persons.

THE TOTALITARIAN STATE

The Organs of Power / The Soviet Union, or Union of Soviet Socialist Republics, was formally established in January 1924 when the constitution of July 1918 was replaced by a new one that adopted this name rather than the previous title of the Russian Socialist Federated Soviet Republic (RSFSR). According to the constitution of 1924, the USSR comprised seven republics: the RSFSR, the Ukraine, White Russia, the Transcaucasian Federation (Azerbaijan, Armenia, and Georgia), Turkmen, Uzbek, and Tajik. By the constitution of 1936, the number was increased to eleven, Azerbaijan, Armenia, and Georgia being given equal standing with the others, and Kazak and Kirghiz being added.

Within this vast and variegated realm, power was wielded by four main agencies: the soviets, the party, the secret police, and the military establishment. In all three of the constitutions, pride of place was given to the soviets, as if Lenin's demand that all power be vested in the soviets had become a reality, which was not the case. Even so, the soviets remained of undeniable importance, for they were the link between the new rulers of Russia and the masses; and they were, as Lenin said, "the vanguard and the school of the whole gigantic mass of the oppressed classes which till now have stood outside all political life and all history."

The soviet system was a great pyramidal structure with its base resting on the villages, each of which had a soviet of its own, which elected delegates to the territorial soviets, which in turn sent representatives to provincial soviets, which in their turn elected the soviets of the republics, which finally elected the All-Union Congress of Soviets. All citizens over eighteen were entitled to participate in elections on the local level, provided they did not belong to one of many categories specifically excluded from political life: criminals, mental defectives, priests, members of forbidden parties, officials of the old regime, and whatever other groups were proscribed at any given moment.

The All-Union Congress was composed of about two thousand members, too unwieldy for any real business. In reality, it met only at two-year intervals to hear progress reports from the real rulers of the country and to elect a Central Executive, the name of which was changed in 1936 to the Supreme Soviet and was described then as "the highest organ of state power." The Supreme Soviet was composed of a Council of the Union, representing the nation as a whole, and a Council of the Nationalities, representing the constituent republics. Nine members elected by each of these bodies and nine by the two of them acting jointly constituted the Presidium of the Supreme Soviet, whose functions, however, were largely ceremonial. The actual business of the State was in the hands of a ministry called the Council of People's Commissars, which was appointed by the Central Executive Committee and presided over by Lenin from 1917 until 1924.

This system was both logical and impressive, but it obscured the real source of power in the country, which lay in a body not mentioned in the constitutions of 1918 and 1924.[3] This was the party, which in the writings of Marx and Engels had been assigned the role of directing the revolution and ruling during the presumably transitional dictatorship of the proletariat and which had been described repeatedly by Lenin as a body of trained and dedicated professional revolutionaries. The party, which in 1918 took the name the Russian Communist party (Bolsheviks), was obviously designed as an elite, and one without competition, since all other parties were abolished. In 1921 it had 730,000 members, of whom a third were purged before the end of the year; in 1929 it had more than one million members; and in 1939, it had a million and a half. Even if one added to this total the members of the youth groups, who numbered up to five million at the latter date, this was a small percentage of the national population. It was kept deliberately so.

The structure of the party was similar to that of the soviets. There were local cells, urban, provincial, and republican conferences, and, above these, a 3000-member Party Congress that met at Moscow at stated intervals. Each Congress elected a small Central Committee of the party which remained in permanent session and was composed of a Secretariat, an Organization Bureau, and a Political Bureau or Politburo. From the very beginning of the revolution, this last body had been the actual governing body of the country and during the civil war it had been composed of five men: Lenin, Trotsky, Stalin, Kamenev, and Bukharin, to whom Zinoviev and Tomsky were later added. The agenda for the Politburo was prepared by the Secretariat of the Central Committee, whose general secretary after 1922, Stalin, made it an increasingly important post. Without going into details about the complicated shifting relationship between the soviet and party structures, it can be said simply that power decisions made in the higher organs of the latter were automatically carried out by the supreme agencies of the former.

[3] It was formally recognized in the constitution of 1936.

Lenin and Stalin, photographed near Moscow in 1922. (SOVFOTO)

Exercising increasing power in the state after the first years, although doing so under the direction of the party chiefs, was the secret police, which had its origin in the Extraordinary Commission for Struggle with Counterrevolution and Sabotage (Cheka). This body was established in December 1917 and is believed to have liquidated as many as fifty thousand persons between that date and the end of 1922, most of them in the terror that followed the assassination of its chief Uritsky and the serious wounding of Lenin by Socialist Revolutionary terrorists in August 1918. In February 1922 the Cheka was abolished, but replaced by an even more formidable body, the GPU (later the OGPU) or Unified State Political Administration. Ostensibly, this organization was under the direction of the Ministry of the Interior, but its leader Dzerzhinsky and his successor Menzhinsky were always close to Stalin and followed his orders. Like the Cheka, the OGPU was used to track down counter-revolutionaries, a term that proved in time to be very elastic; and its duties also included the apprehension of "exploiters" and "wreckers" and the operation of various concentration camps, including those for nonpolitical prisoners. In the trials of the Stalin period, it played a key role, especially after 1936, when (now under the name Peoples Commissariat of Internal Affairs, or NKVD) it was directed by N. I. Yezhov, for a time the most feared man in Russia.

Finally, there was the army. In the first years after the civil war, it was able to maintain a large degree of independence from the party organization. This was gradually whittled away by the elimination of most of the ex-tsarist officers, by careful indoctrination of new officers and recruits, and, finally, as will be noted below, by the great purge of the mid-1930s. At the cost of some military efficiency, the party assured itself of the political reliability of the army; and this, and the control of its secret police, made it reasonably safe against the internal explosion that refugees and foreign anti-Communists kept hoping would occur in Russia.

From Lenin to Stalin / The first leader of the Russian revolution suffered a stroke in May 1922 and a second one in November of the same year. After that it was clear that the country was going to be caught up in a succession struggle of heroic proportions between his two strongest associates, Trotsky and Stalin. Lenin himself seems to have been disturbed by the prospect of such a conflict and even to have feared what he must have guessed would be its outcome. In a postscript to his political testament, written in January 1923, he expressed strong criticism of Stalin and proposed that the party should remove him from his post of general secretary and appoint a man "more patient, more loyal, more polite and more attentive to comrades, less capricious, etc." Lenin would probably have sought to effect this change by arguing for it personally at the Party Congress of 1923, but he suffered his third stroke before it met and was inactive politically from then until his death in January 1924.

The target of Lenin's suspicion had been born, as Joseph Vissarionovich Dzugashvily, near Tiflis in Georgia in 1879. His parents had hoped that he might become a priest, but he was forced to leave the Tiflis Seminary either because of health (as his mother later told newspaper reporters) or because he propagated Marxist doctrines among his fellow students (as he himself insisted was true). He became involved in socialist politics, adhering to the Bolshevik wing after the party division in 1903, and acquiring a reputation for resolution and energy during the revolution of 1905, when he was an agitator in the Baku oil fields. He preferred underground work in Russia to prolonged exile abroad, and carried on a duel with the tsarist police that was marked by frequent arrests and escapes until 1913, when he was exiled to Siberia. He returned in 1917 to play a prominent role in the revolution and the civil war. Scorned by Trotsky as "the outstanding mediocrity of the party," Stalin (as he had called himself since the days in Baku) possessed gifts of bureaucratic finesse and political manipulation that enabled him to defeat and exile his more brilliant rival, and to secure a position in which he could indulge what was clearly his strongest motivation, a lust for untrammeled personal power.

Once Lenin's strong hand had been weakened by illness, his authority came to be wielded by a triumvirate within the Politburo, composed of

Zinoviev, Kamenev, and Stalin, all of whom were enemies of Trotsky. Their tactics were to weaken the war commissar's position by transferring his closest associates to jobs remote from the center of power, while simultaneously giving encouragement and influence to the many enemies whom he had made in the party organization during his meteoric career. Since brilliance is rarely popular, they succeeded, and, by the time of Lenin's death in 1924, Trotsky's power was in decline, and he was being criticized for "factionalism," a dangerous charge in a party already tending toward monolithic unity. In January 1925, his enemies persuaded the Central Committee to dismiss him from the War Commissariat, and, although some of his supporters expected him to resist by calling on the Red Army to support him, he refused to do so. He was too loyal to the party to attempt a coup against it, and his concurrence in his dismissal marked the end of his power. Within two years he had been expelled from the Central Committee and, as a result of street demonstrations in his favor in November 1927 (he was always more popular with the masses than with the party hierarchs), from the party. In 1929 the Politburo authorized his expulsion from the Soviet Union, and the creator of the Red Army was forced to begin that troubled odyssey from one foreign refuge to another which ended in 1940 when he was assassinated in Mexico.

Even before Trotsky's fall was complete, Stalin had freed himself from the embrace of the other original triumvirs by using his authority as general secretary to build up his power at their expense, by using divisive tactics in the Politburo, and by accusing his former partners of deviation from Lenin's views (a useful argument, since Stalin, alone among the Old Bolsheviks, had never opposed Lenin on a serious issue and could claim to be the best judge of orthodoxy). Zinoviev and Kamenev were both expelled from the party in 1927 for association with Trotsky's ideas and, although they were later readmitted, their power was now spent. Similar tactics proved effective against the other Old Bolsheviks in the Politburo—Bukharin, Tomsky, and Rykov. By the end of 1930 they had been forced out of the Politburo, which thus came to be composed exclusively of Stalin's followers, as did the party organizations of the large cities and organs of central government like the Council of People's Commissars, whose chairman, another loyal Stalin man, Vyacheslav Molotov, had once answered one of Trotsky's gibes by saying, "We can't all be geniuses, Comrade Trotsky, but we'll see who lasts longer."

Economic Regimentation / The ascendancy of Stalin and Russia's progress toward totalitarianism were both advanced by events in the economic sphere. Whatever ideas Lenin and his associates had had about socializing the economic system of Russia had been rendered unrealistic by the chaos caused by the civil war and by the great drought in the grain areas of the Volga and the Don during 1920. By 1921 industry was at a standstill and a fifth of Russia's population was in the grip of famine and cholera. Lenin was hard-headed enough to see that production was more important than theory, no matter how much departure from Marxist orthodoxy might aggrieve the party ideologues. Over the opposition of people like Trotsky, Lenin carried a series of resolutions through the Party Congress in 1921 which laid the foundations for what came to be called the New Economic Policy (NEP). In effect, NEP allowed what Lenin admitted was "a partial return to capitalism" by permitting the revival of private industry and authorizing the peasants to produce and trade for profit. At the cost of tolerating the rise of a new bourgeoisie, the Soviet regime was able to repair the ravages of its first years, and by 1927 industry, with some exceptions, was producing at 1913 levels and agriculture was prosperous once more.

The old dream of effecting the utter destruction of capitalism by transforming the economy remained, and Stalin made it his own with the promulgation of the first Five-Year Plan in 1928. It is likely, nevertheless, that he was less interested in the economic aspects of this plan, which put an abrupt end to NEP and placed the accent once more on orthodox socialist economics, than he was in the political advantages that he suspected would accrue from it. For the successful imposition of a socialized economy upon Russia promised to make the state machine, of which he was now virtually the master, supreme by weakening all the other loyalties that diverted the minds of the masses—loyalty to the soil, to the trade union, to the family—and by giving the state an argument for liquidating those who persisted in holding older values.

The first Five-Year Plan went into effect in October 1928. It set norms for production in all basic industries, calling for increases that ranged from 200 to 400 percent. In agriculture, an increase of 150 percent was demanded, to be accomplished by a policy of collectivizing the peasant farms. Stalin expected some popular resistance to the new policy and the sacrifices it demanded of the workers and peasants, and he was prepared to meet it. Resistance to collectivization by the peasantry was put down with complete ruthlessness, OGPU agents and army units surrounding villages, shooting indiscriminately into crowds, burning down houses, transporting trainloads of men, women, and children to Siberia. Since the troops called upon to do these tasks were often drawn from the peasantry themselves, serious morale problems arose in army units; but no relaxation of the terror was allowed. The desperate peasants fought back by burning their crops and destroying their livestock, with the result that by 1933 there were less than half as many houses in the Soviet Union as there had been in 1928, and it was not until 1937 that over-all production regained the 1928 level. The number of people who died in the collectivization struggle and the famine of 1932–1933 to which it contributed exceeded five million. As against these losses, however, Stalin had succeeded in breaking the will of the peasantry and making it subservient to the totalitarian state.

In the industrial sector also, events encouraged the drift toward totalitarianism. In order to dramatize the economic drive and stimulate effort to meet the assigned goals, a series of sensational state trials were held of people charged with being wreckers, saboteurs, foreign agents, and the like. In these trials, the effects of what has come to be called brainwashing were first revealed to the world, for a high percentage of those tried confessed to an astonishing variety of unlikely crimes and often implicated other people in their confessed conspiracies against the state. The trials created an atmosphere of fear and suspicion in the factories and discouraged the expression of any opinions except those that reflected loyalty and devotion to the regime. This was another gain for totalitarianism.

The objectives of the first Five-Year Plan were not met, partly because the industrial goals had been set too high. The state, out of sheer necessity, had to accept a version of agricultural collectivization less extreme than that originally envisaged, and to embark on another Five-Year Plan to stimulate sectors of the economy that had not responded to the first. Even so, the gains were not negligible. It was obvious that Russia was on its way to becoming an industrial power of the first magnitude; and foreign observers, imperfectly informed of the human cost, were impressed by what could be accomplished in a relatively backward country by state planning on a massive scale. Indirectly, therefore, the Five-Year Plans made the capitalist countries, who were about to encounter serious economic difficulties of their own, more amenable to the idea of a planned economy than they had previously been.

The most important result of the Russian "Second Revolution," however, was internal, and it was not economic. It tightened the state's grip on the peoples of the Soviet Union and diminished even further their liberties.

The Great Purges / Stalin's personal autocracy was consolidated and given an almost oriental character in the mid-1930s, when the instruments of terror that had been used against the masses were turned against the Communist elite itself. The violence and waste of the years 1928–1933 had caused growing opposition in the upper hierarchy of the party and in certain of the army commands (Marshal Blücher, for instance, had successfully blocked collectivization in eastern Siberia by warning bluntly that otherwise the area could not be held against possible attacks from the Japanese in Manchuria); and it appears that at least one serious conspiracy was being hatched with the objective of forcing Stalin's downfall. Other evidence indicates that Stalin, while not actually aware of any plots against himself, had decided that the time had come to make a palace revolution impossible by inventing conspiracies and culprits and liquidating them *pour encourager les autres*; and it has been further suggested that he had a shrewd suspicion that totalitarian regimes can only be made to work by terror and fear and that it was up to him to supply these things.

We shall probably never know the whole truth about the party purges of 1936–1938, or even about the event that touched them off: the assassination in December 1934 of Sergei Kirov, Zinoviev's successor as head of the party in Leningrad and, in the opinion of some, Stalin's chosen heir. Kirov's death was blamed on a gigantic conspiracy planned by men like Zinoviev and Trotsky, and arrests of supporters of these former titans began immediately and continued through 1935. These were followed by the arrest and trial of Zinoviev and Kamenev, of lesser lights like Karl Radek, of the most respected generals of the Red Army, among them the hero of the civil war, Tukhachevsky, and, finally, of Bukharin, Rakovsky, and the former police chief Yagoda. Thousands died without the benefit of trial, including the man who carried out most of the arrests and executions of the first two years of the purges, Yagoda's successor, Yezhov. The total number of victims is unknown, but it has been estimated in millions. The Soviet Union's ruling elite suffered incredible losses. In a recent tabulation, Geoffrey Bailey has written that 800,000 party members were killed, including six of the thirteen members of the Politburo, ninety-eight of the 138 members of the Central Committee, fourteen of the eighteen members of the Council of People's Commissars, and nearly all the premiers and peoples commissars of the federated republics, while, in the army, the dead included three of the five marshals, thirteen of the fifteen army commanders, fifty-seven of the eighty-five corps commanders, 110 of the 195 brigade commanders.

This was social prophylaxis on a grand scale, something unheard of in the age that preceded this, boldly undertaken despite the weaknesses it imposed on the state in a time of growing foreign peril, in order to eliminate the possibility of an alternate government. With the purges Stalin's totalitarianism was complete.

SOVIET FOREIGN POLICY, 1917–1933

World Revolution as an Objective / The Bolshevik regime began its life by repudiating the traditional framework and standards of international relations and pledging itself to the overthrow of capitalist regimes everywhere. During the war, Lenin had said that, when his party came to power, they would

> systematically start to incite rebellion among all the peoples now oppressed . . . all the colonies and dependent countries of Asia (India, China, Persia, and others). And we would also raise the socialist proletariat of Europe in rebellion against their governments. . . . There is no doubt that the victory of the proletariat in Russia would create very favorable conditions for the development of the revolution in Asia and Europe.

Once he had assumed power, Lenin put that master strategy into effect, beginning with the Proclamation of Peace, the first formal act of his regime, which called on the masses everywhere to rise against their rulers. Throughout the whole of 1918, the Bolsheviks did what they could to exploit the unrest caused by the war in Eastern Europe, in the Middle East, and elsewhere; and, in March 1919, with the formation of the Comintern, they institutionalized revolutionary agitation as a permanent feature of Soviet foreign relations. The Comintern, or Third (Communist) International, was an agency for world revolution. It was designed to be a central directorate for Communist parties in other countries; and its executive, which was headed by Zinoviev and dominated by other Bolshevik leaders, had the mission of instructing the leadership of those parties in the tactics of subversion, infiltration, and propaganda best designed to promote revolution in their countries. In Bolshevik eyes, the Comintern, rather than traditional diplomacy, would be the chief instrument for carrying out the Soviet Union's foreign objectives in their countries. They placed so much importance on the idea of world revolution that they saw no reason for any other foreign policy and no use for any diplomatic machinery other than that provided by the Comintern's network of agents.

The Bolshevik hope that Europe would succumb to revolution, once the process had started in Russia, was not fulfilled. There were revolutions in 1918 in both Germany and Austria, but they merely brought to power moderate Socialist parties with pronounced bourgeois predispositions. In 1918 and early 1919, Soviets were established in Bavaria and Hungary but failed to receive mass support and were quickly suppressed. As for Britain and France, their governments not only refused to collapse but took the offensive against Bolshevism by intervening in the civil war and helping check the Red Army's drive on Warsaw. The capitalist states were, in short, showing surprising resources of strength, while the Bolshevik regime, on the other hand, was weakened by the rigors of the civil war and subsequent economic troubles. In the circumstances, while not entirely abandoning their belief in the efficacy of the Comintern, the Bolshevik leaders acknowledged that new tools of foreign policy would have to be devised to deal with the capitalist states and prevent them from new assaults against Russia. This meant a reluctant return to traditional diplomacy.

The Uses of Diplomacy / The man who directed this new effort was Georgei Chicherin, a former archivist in the Tsarist Foreign Office, who had been a Menshevik before the war, had joined the Bolshevik party in 1917, and, in the following year, when Trotsky moved from the Commissariat of Foreign Affairs to the War Commissariat, had succeeded him. By temperament a realist, Chicherin was conscious of his country's weakness and felt that the best protection against foreign exploitation was a truce with the capitalist world. If the countries of the west, in particular, could be persuaded to recognize the new Russia as a member of the family of nations and to conclude political and economic agreements with it, the risk of a new attack would be minimized.

The fear of new pressure from the capitalist world was not imaginary. In the years 1920–1922, there was a good deal of discussion in the west of the possibility of arranging an international consortium to exploit Russia's known economic distress in such a way as to compel the Communist regime to repay the tsarist debts that had been repudiated, restore confiscated European property, and even submit to a series of capitulations that would permit European traders to do their business in Russia under the protection of extraterritorial rights. This possibility was eagerly canvassed on the eve of the European economic conference which Lloyd George convened at Genoa in 1922.

It was at Genoa that Chicherin showed what diplomacy could accomplish for his country. Invited to bring a delegation to the Italian city, he made the most of the opportunity to ingratiate himself with the representatives of the smaller powers in the assembly and to exploit their jealousy of the greater ones. The consortium idea he sidetracked by insisting that his country was ready to make arrangements with foreign traders on an individual basis, and by portraying the advantages of trade under Russia's New Economic Policy in such a way as to stimulate the competitive instincts of the other powers. He raised issues that were not on the agenda—the need for universal disarmament and for a planned global redistribution of natural resources—which appealed to liberal groups in all countries but which merely served, at the moment, to confuse the Genoa discussions. And, finally, by his sensational coup at Rapallo, where he persuaded the German foreign minister to conclude a treaty forging political and economic ties between Germany and his own country (see p. 550), he caused the Genoa conference to break up in confusion and was able to return home with credit for the only triumph registered there: the termination of his country's diplomatic isolation.

In the years that followed, Chicherin exploited his gains. In the Lausanne conference of 1923 (see p. 541), he won the sympathy of several small nations by championing the cause of Turkey and simultaneously protected Russian interests in the Near East. In the same year, he undermined a recently concluded treaty that promised to subordinate Persia to a large degree of British control, and helped alleviate the distress caused in Germany by the Ruhr invasion (see pp. 550 and 612) by sending grain into that country. These evidences of Russian vigor and friendship for weak nations appealed to important groups within many European states and had the result of further relieving the Soviet Union of its former isolation. In 1924, when Left governments came to power in both Britain and France, they sought normal relations with the Soviet Union. Indeed, 1924 came to be known as "the year of recognitions," because, during its course, the Soviet Union was formally recognized by Great Britain, France, Italy, Norway, Sweden, Denmark, Austria, Hungary, Greece, Mexico, and the Chinese Republic, with Japan joining the impressive list in January 1925.

New Setbacks, 1924–1927 / These gains were not permanent. The Old Bolsheviks still retained their preference for revolutionary methods and their contempt for traditional diplomacy; and even in the period of Chicherin's greatest success, his delicate maneuvers were handicapped by startling reversions to the early policy. In 1923, for instance, the Comintern inspired unsuccessful revolutions in Bulgaria and Germany, which forced the foreign minister to exhaust all of his inventive powers in devising proof that the Soviet Union had not been involved in them. And, after 1924, during the confused power struggle that followed Lenin's death, the coordination between various branches of the Soviet government broke down, and the Comintern became as active in foreign politics as it had in 1919 and 1920, with unfortunate results for the Soviet Union's foreign position.

In October 1924, the British Foreign Office came into possession of a letter allegedly sent by Zinoviev to the Communist party of Great Britain, urging increased agitation and the formation of cells within army and navy units. The question of this letter's authenticity has long been debated and is probably not important. Its text was in line with Zinoviev's known ideas; it was widely believed to be genuine when it was published in the press; and it helped bring the defeat of the first Labor government and a perceptible cooling of Anglo-Soviet relations. In December 1924, Zinoviev inspired an attack by a group of Russian officers, supported by a few hundred Estonian Communists, upon the

Estonian port of Reval. It was a miserable failure, and it was publicized all over Europe and lowered Soviet stock even further. Finally, in April 1925, the Comintern was widely believed to have instigated a renewal of revolutionary ardor on the part of the Bulgarian Communist party, the first result of which was the explosion of a time bomb in the Svetya Nedelya Cathedral in Sofia, which killed 128 persons.

From these three events can be dated the Soviet Union's swift decline from the position of relative strength gained for it by Chicherin. Signs of this were immediately apparent. No overtures of any kind were made to the Soviet Union during the Locarno negotiations of 1925 (see p. 551); and these talks were, after all, of vital importance to Russia, since they threatened to detach Germany from the Rapallo line by inclining it to the west and bringing it into the League of Nations.

Against this drift of Germany and against the strengthening of the League, which was always an object of special detestation to the Soviet Union in the 1920s, Chicherin fought a spirited but losing fight. He managed to persuade Germany to balance its western commitments by concluding a new treaty, the Treaty of Berlin (1926), with the Soviet Union, but his efforts to build up a rival League under Soviet sponsorship attracted favorable response only from Lithuania, Turkey, Afghanistan, and Persia. The fact of the matter was that all the old distrust of the Soviet Union had been reawakened, and it was now deepened by other Soviet actions that countered Chicherin's efforts.

Since 1923, the Soviet Union had maintained formal relations with the Kuomintang, the Chinese nationalist party founded by Sun Yat-sen and led now by Chiang Kai-shek, which controlled south China and was seeking to do the same in the north. They were also on good terms with the Japanese government, which, as before the war, had interests in Manchuria and in Korea. Now, in 1925 and 1926, at a moment when its European contacts were being jeopardized, the Soviet government indulged in tactics that were bound to weaken its position in the Far East as well. Comintern agents became active in all major Chinese cities, as well as in Korea and Japan, and the Soviet government sought simultaneously to play politics inside the Kuomintang, supporting the left wing against the authority of Chiang Kai-shek.

These activities brought the indignation of the powers to a boiling point, and in 1927 disaster fell on Russia from every side. In the spring of that year, Chiang Kai-shek liquidated the Kuomintang's left wing and instituted the anti-Communist policy that he was to follow for the rest of his life. Simultaneously, in Japan, the government was taken over by forces that favored an active Manchurian, and hence anti-Soviet, policy. In May, the British police raided the headquarters of the Soviet trade mission in London and seized its files. On the basis of evidence of anti-

British propaganda and subversive activities found in them, the British government severed diplomatic relations. In June there was a flare-up of anti-Soviet feeling in Poland, and the Soviet ambassador in Warsaw was murdered. In October, the French government demanded the recall of the Soviet ambassador. In Germany, evidence of Soviet subversion caused enthusiasm for the Rapallo-Berlin line to wane. In Persia and Afghanistan, Great Britain won back ground that had been lost earlier to Russia. By the end of the year Russia was as isolated as she had been in 1917.

The Soviets and the West after 1927 / These setbacks helped discredit Zinoviev and his methods, and probably contributed indirectly to Stalin's rise to complete authority by demonstrating the dangers of the policy of world revolution preached by some of his chief rivals and the advantages of his own policy of "socialism in one country." Under Stalin, Comintern adventures went out of fashion, and Russian diplomats were instructed to sell the Soviet Union as a peaceful and cooperative nation. Especially after the threat of National Socialism became apparent, a policy of ingratiation with the west was followed that was to culminate in Russia's entrance into the League in 1934.

To repeat the work that Chicherin had done was not easy, and it was never completely successful. Despite the admiration that existed in western countries for the economic and technological gains of the Soviet Union, accumulating evidence of the internal conditions of that country appalled large sections of the western populations and even dimmed the former enthusiasm of their left-wing and labor parties. At the same time, the Soviet government's tendency to slip from the ways of peaceful diplomacy into the intrigue and violence of revolution was not forgotten in the west. Its bland assurances that the Comintern was an independent organization and that the Soviet Union had not been involved in its activities convinced nobody and deepened the feeling that any real cooperation between the Soviet Union and the west was impossible.

Even when the threat of Hitler became more immediate than that of communism, the western countries would find it difficult to make common cause with the great revolutionary power in the east.

23

The Rise of Italian Fascism

The victory of communism in Russia and the known desire of Russia's leaders to spread its doctrines to the rest of the world had one effect that was not dwelt upon in the previous chapter. Especially in countries that seemed potentially vulnerable to Communist subversion, it encouraged the rise of totalitarian movements of the Right headed by strong men who promised to keep their countries free from Marxist infection. This was the case in Italy, which surrendered itself to the dictatorship of the Fascist party in the first decade after the war.

It would nevertheless be a mistake to regard the emergence of communism as the sole, or even the most important, reason for the victory of fascism in Italy. Fascism was the result of many things, among which the economic and psychological dislocations caused by the war, the resentment of returning veterans over the lack of recognition for their services, the frustrated ambitions of Italian nationalists, and the failure of the Italian party system were fully as important as the fear of Communist infiltration.

THE VICTORY OF FASCISM

The Results of the War / The results of World War I in Italy justified all of the doubts and hesitations expressed by those who had resisted intervention in 1915. There were no outstanding victories in the field to look back on, and the clumsy greediness of Italy's negotiators at Paris had left its allies annoyed and its own liberals so ashamed that one of them, G. A. Borgese, wrote that his country had forfeited the opportunity for a future of spiritual greatness and social progress. The most valuable of the territorial gains made as a result of the war—those at the head of the Adriatic and along the northern frontier—would probably have come to Italy even if it had remained neutral, and, in any case, it was doubtful that they were worth the loss of 500,000 men. Aside from this, the war left the country in a state of economic chaos.

All told, the long conflict had cost a sum about twice as large as the total of all government expenditure between 1861 and 1913, and the government had been able to withstand this burden only because of the unlimited credit extended by the Allied governments. As soon as hostilities were terminated, that economic aid came to an end, and Italy found itself with a staggering debt, a great imbalance in foreign trade (imports far exceeding exports), and an inflation that was threatening to get seriously out of hand. This last danger was increased by the continuation of subsidies to grain farmers and to the industries that had converted their production to meet war needs and now expected to be reconverted at government expense.

Meanwhile, other wartime chickens were coming home to roost. To maintain the will to victory, the government had promised that peace would bring a more equitable distribution of land in the interests of the peasants, as well as any number of benefits for the industrial masses. The potential recipients of these promises decided not to wait for their fulfillment; and the result was a number of violent strikes in industry and, in rural areas, a series of spontaneous risings—admirably described in Panzini's novel, *Il padrone sono me* (*The Boss Is Me*)—in which the peasants simply took matters into their own hands and seized their landlords' fields. The resultant confusion and dislocation of the economic system was further deepened by the existence of thousands of army deserters, who took to brigandage in order to support themselves, and by the demobilization of those who had fought until the end of the war, which immediately created a serious unemployment problem.

The Failure of the Parties / This situation called for vigorous action by the political parties. Their response was wholly ineffective. In the parliament elected in 1919, the three largest parties were the Socialists, the Catholic Popular party, and the Liberals who recognized Giovanni Giolitti as their leader. The Socialists were both disunited and irresponsible. Their tendency to split into factions was increased by the events in Russia, which caused violent doctrinal debates and, in 1920, led to the secession of the party's left wing, which constituted itself as the Italian Communist party. Those who did not secede seemed more desirous of persuading the departed brethren that they were true Marxists than of playing an effective role in Italian politics, for they refused to collaborate with the parties to the right of them in any program to check social deterioration and went on mouthing revolutionary slogans in which they did not believe. The Catholic Popular party, led by the Sicilian priest Don Luigi Sturzo and some gifted younger men, including a future prime minister (Alcide de Gasperi), also lacked internal cohesion. Although its leaders professed some useful ideas of social reform, the party as a whole was united only on opposition to anticlericalism, and since the majority of its members were suspicious of both liberals and socialists and opposed to collaborating with them, the role of the *popolari* was necessarily a negative one. As for the Liberals, they were characteristically opposed to government action in the economic sphere, and their leader Giolitti had, in any case, always believed that problems solved themselves if you were wise enough to leave them alone.

In addition, all three of these political groups had been predominately anti-interventionist in 1915, when Italy had been jockeyed into war by the maneuvers of D'Annunzio and others (see p. 506). They all suffered from an understandable craving to have their prescience acknowledged by those who had overborne them, and they indulged this weakness to a dangerous degree. In parliamentary debates, they spent more time recalling the past than grappling with the present, and they recognized current social problems only to prove that they were the inevitable result of the victory of their enemies in 1915. There were times, indeed, when it seemed that they actually welcomed every new disaster that befell their country, because it strengthened their case against the interventionists.

In these circumstances, the first postwar governments, loose coalitions of various liberal and Right groups with intermittent participation by the *popolari,* headed first by a former professor of political science named Francesco Nitti and then by the venerable Giolitti, accomplished little. They had no constructive policy for checking the runaway inflation or for reducing the government's debts. In face of continued lawlessness in the countryside and the towns, they recognized no responsibility for government action. Nitti found it expedient to give retroactive sanction to land seizures by the peasants; and, in September 1920, when industrial workers in northern Italy responded to employers' lockouts by seizing several large factories, the Giolitti government followed a policy of strict nonintervention.

The behavior of the government had the result of alienating three important groups in the country. In the first place, the wealthy landowners and the industrialists whose economic interests were threatened by the continuation of strikes and expropriations began to cast about for a leadership that would be more responsive to their plight than those of the older parties. In the second place, the nationalist groups that had pressed for intervention in 1915 and still believed that it was Italy's mission to become a great Mediterranean and Balkan power not only resented the drumfire of criticism that the Socialists and Liberals directed against them in parliament but were bitter about what they considered to be the government's blindness to Italy's vital interests. Unlike the Liberals, who felt that Italy had asked for too much at the Peace Conference, these groups thought that Italy had received far less than it deserved. They were unconvinced by the argument that Italy's safety was assured by the breakup of the Austro-Hungarian Empire, and they regarded the constitution of a large Yugoslavia with a coastline on the Adriatic as an Allied plot against Italy. They were enthusiastic about the expedition which D'Annunzio led against Fiume in September 1919 and his subsequent establishment of a "Regency of Carnaro" there which claimed to be an independent state and sent manifestoes to other governments; and they were furious when the Giolitti government signed the death warrant of that adventure by concluding the Treaty of Rapallo in November 1920 with the Yugoslav government and by recognizing Yugoslavia's rights on the Dalmatian coast and in the area surrounding Fiume (see p. 538). These actions and Italy's evacuation of Albania in 1920 seemed to the nationalists to savor of cowardice. When D'Annunzio, now nearing sixty and worn out by his political and amorous activities, failed them by abandoning his regency at Fiume, they began to look around for a stronger man to represent their cause.

Finally, there were the veterans of the war. Considering the state of Italy's armaments in 1915, which was described by the journalist Prezzolini as "prehistoric," they had fought bravely, if not brilliantly; and their gallant stand on the Piave had done much to repair the earlier collapse at Caporetto. They came home expecting to find some sign of gratitude for their service and some evidence that their sacrifices had helped to produce a better Italy. They found neither. Their reward was often the discovery that their former jobs were gone and that to appear in the streets dressed in uniform was to court abuse and assault, since Socialist antiwar propaganda took violent forms. At the same time, as one of their number, Riccardo Bacchelli, was later to write:

> The ex-service men . . . found faction and demagogy presenting the war to the people as a monstrous and bloody deception, and the educated classes, with the characteristic insouciance of decadence, using an illusory prosperity to amuse themselves and, one may even say, making it a point of good breeding and *savoir faire* not to play the returned hero.

This was not the Italy they had fought to protect; and some of them—the black-shirted shock troops or *arditi*, in particular, and the younger officers —wanted to do something to change it and were anxious to find leaders who would show them how to do so.

All of these critics of prevailing tendencies in Italian politics found a way of expressing their protests in fascism and in the leadership of Benito Mussolini.

Mussolini and the Fascist Movement / When Mussolini's long-suffering wife was informed in October 1922 that her husband had just been made prime minister of Italy, her first remark is said to have been: "What a character!" There was probably as much astonishment as admiration in those words and, if so, it must have been an astonishment shared by others who had known Mussolini as long as Donna Rachele, and who knew how fluid his principles were and how frequent his fundamental shifts of political position.

Benito Mussolini was born in 1883, the son of a blacksmith, who was an ardent socialist, and a schoolmistress. Like Stalin (and this was the only thing he shared with his fellow dictator), he was educated at a Catholic seminary and expelled from it, apparently for stabbing a fellow student. He taught school for some time but abandoned this career, allegedly because he could not maintain discipline among his students. In 1902 he went to Switzerland in order to escape being drafted for service in the Italian army. After living from hand to mouth for two years, he returned home, performed his military service, and then turned to journalism, the career for which he was best suited temperamentally and which made a decisive impression upon his later political style. In 1909 he was expelled from the then Austrian district of Trent (Trentino) for his violent and subversive articles in the Socialist press, and in 1911 he was jailed by the Italian government for his attacks upon government policy in North Africa. His journalistic prowess brought him considerable reputation in Socialist circles, and in 1912 he became editor of the chief party paper, the *Avanti* of Milan. Yet he was never an entirely orthodox socialist, being given to the expression of views that bordered on anarchism or seemed to indicate that he was interested in power for its own sake; and there was always more than a suspicion that he was concerned primarily with personal advancement rather than with the causes he advocated.

Having been the most impassioned opponent of the adventure in Tripoli in 1911 and having played a leading role in the excommunication of those party members who had dared support it, Mussolini changed his bearings completely after the beginning of World War I and became an interventionist hardly less insistent than D'Annunzio (see p. 506). This finished his career as a Socialist and left him, when the war was over, with a clouded future. For a time, he considered attempting to outbid the official Socialist party for the support of the working classes, an experiment which, as the elections of 1919 were to show, had no prospects of success; but he soon discovered, through his journalistic activity, that there were better opportunities for personal aggrandizement in other directions. At a time when so many people were saying that the war had been a mistake, Mussolini was perverse enough to say that the war had been one of the finest chapters in Italian history, that Italy had been cheated of the gains won by the blood of its sons, and that those who tolerated the peace of renunciation and traduced the heroism of Italy's dead youth must be driven from power. He was not original in this, but he said what he had to say eloquently and often, and his writings became popular with discontented officers, with perfervid D'Annunzians, and with a younger generation brought up on tales of Garibaldian adventure, baulked of the chance of serving their country by accident of age and disgusted by the flat spiritlessness of their times. It was people like them who joined with Mussolini in the first *Fascio di combattimento,* or fighting group, which he founded in Milan in March 1919 and which was the nucleus of the Fascist party of the future.

About the growth of the Fascist movement there was something adventitious, and there were times in the early days when it threatened to get out of Mussolini's control completely. It started as a loose league of local organizations, some formed in imitation of the Milan *Fascio,* some (associations of veterans, anti-Bolshevik unions, youth leagues, societies for an Italian Dalmatia, and the like) converted from their original purposes. It was aided by the collapse of D'Annunzio's Fiume adventure, for most of the poet's legionnaires became Fascists; but it was also weakened, and even threatened with disintegration, by the individualism of these recruits and of some of its local leaders. Men like Dino Grandi in Bologna, Italo Balbo in Ferrara, and Robert Farinacci in Cremona resisted centralized direction of party activities, partly because they discovered that they could make private profit by hiring their squads out to local businessmen as strikebreakers or to landlords as protectors of property. These *ras* (as the local party chieftains were named, after the tribal chiefs of Abyssinia) were not only capable of resentment of Mussolini's pretensions to over-all leadership but, at times, overruled his views and threatened to repudiate his leadership entirely. It seems clear that it was their influence that made fascism a definitely antisocialist movement, for as late as November 1921, when Mussolini was still thinking of the possibility of a pact between the Fascists and the non-Communist Left, the local party chiefs forced him to abandon this idea in favor of continued support of conservative business interests.

On the other hand, Mussolini was indispensable to the local chiefs and, despite their irritation at his radical changes of opinion and his timidity at moments when daring was called for (for the future Duce was never the hero that legend made him), they admitted their dependence on him and, in the end, their subordination. Mussolini had a charismatic authority that none of them possessed; he wielded the pen that won them new converts; and he possessed the ability to speak to the Italian people in ways that could flatter, amuse, and move them. Grandi and Balbo and Farinacci and their like were successful local bosses, but their abilities did not go beyond that; Mussolini made fascism a party with national support.

The Surrender of Italian Liberalism / It is nevertheless doubtful whether the Fascists would ever have come into power if it had not been for the failure of Italian liberalism to carry out its political responsibilities and to remain true to its principles. It was the refusal of Giolitti's Liberal government of 1920–1921 to interfere in the serious industrial and agrarian disorders that gave the Fascists the chance to pose as the guardians of public order against Communist attack; and it was the willingness of distinguished Liberal institutions like the great Milan newspaper *Corriere della Sera* to condone the violence and the terroristic methods used by Grandi's thugs and Farinacci's goon squads that gave fascism an aura of respectability, won it a position in parliament, and commended it to the middle class as their natural protector.

By November 1921, when the Fascist party was formally established, it had only thirty-five seats in the Chamber of Deputies, but it had a national membership of close to 300,000 and its ambitions had grown commensurately with its numbers. It had learned, during the elections of May 1921, that neither the government's prefects nor the police would interfere if its *Squadristi* used force to intimidate voters. It had learned that Socialist clubs and trade unions would not even unite to resist attacks upon their headquarters, a sign that they were incapable of action for other purposes. It had learned that parliamentary parties of the Center and Left found it difficult to cooperate on any issue and that the formation of a vigorous ministry with strong parliamentary support was unlikely. It had detected sympathy for fascism both in the army command and at the royal court. In view of these discoveries, there was every reason to believe that an all-out drive for power would be successful. Mussolini openly hinted to parliament that this was now his intention when he said, in the spring of 1922, that he would start a full-scale revolt if any prime minister were appointed who stood for "anti-Fascist reaction."

Even this threat did not convince the Liberal and Socialist parties to join forces against what was clearly an imminent revolution of the Right. The Socialists instead indulged in a wholly suicidal maneuver by declaring a general strike in August 1922. The strike was so badly prepared that it was bound to fail, as it did. But the very fact that it was tried exasperated the general public, which was tired of strikes and agitations, and gave the Fascists an excuse to declare open war on socialism, to destroy all Socialist and union headquarters in Leghorn, Genoa, and other key cities, to smash the presses and burn the building of Mussolini's old paper, *Avanti,* in Milan, and actually to depose the Socialist government of that city. When the public did nothing about this and the conservative and liberal press commended the action, the Fascists were emboldened to go further and, in the weeks that followed, they took over the town councils of Ferrara, Cremona, Parma, Ravenna, and Leghorn as well.

This last step was a necessary preliminary to the national coup that was now in preparation. In September and October delicate negotiations were entered into with royalist and church circles, designed to avert possible interference from either direction. Meanwhile, Mussolini appointed a small general staff to make an operational plan for the seizure of power, and, on October 27, 1922, he ordered the mobilization of his Black Shirts and the beginning of a general advance on Rome. He was not entirely sanguine about the results of the projected coup and stayed carefully in the vicinity of the Swiss border, lest he find it advisable to flee. That necessity never arose. The one possibility of resistance evaporated when King Victor Emmanuel III refused to sign a declaration of martial law demanded by the current prime minister, Luigi Facta. A Fascist mission headed by Grandi then persuaded the king that Mussolini was the only possible premier, and the king agreed to appoint him. Once that decision had been made, Mussolini felt it safe to make his personal March on Rome, arriving by sleeping car from Milan on the morning of October 30, looking a not very martial figure in morning coat and white spats.

The Consolidation of the Revolution / In his first major address to the Chamber, Mussolini told the curious deputies that he had refused to "overdo the victory."

> With 300,000 youths, fully armed, fully determined, and almost mystically ready to act at my command, I could have chastised all those who have defamed and tried to injure Fascism. I could have made of this sordid, gray assembly hall a bivouac for *Squadristi,* I could have kicked out parliament and constructed a government exclusively of *Fascisti.* I could have done so, but I did not want to, at least not for the present.

This speech had the effect of lulling its auditors into the drowsy assumption that the new premier would be no different from those of the past and that, if he became fractious, they could always get rid of him later on. They were reassured also by his willingness to head a twelve-man ministry that had only three Fascist members; and they had no objections whatsoever to conferring "full powers" on him for the period of one year.

Mussolini took advantage of this mood to take over the administration of the state by slow degrees. During his first year of power, the prefectures, the offices of police, and the key positions in the national bureaucracy were filled with new Fascist appointees, and simultaneously the appointment of a large number of new Fascist senators gave the party the control of the upper house. More daring strokes followed. The first, and the one that opened many eyes to Mussolini's real intentions, was the transformation of his *Squadristi* into a national party militia paid by the state and the simultaneous abolition of the Royal Guards (a supplementary police force created by Nitti), which were now declared to be superfluous. The second was the proposal at the end of 1923 of the so-called Acerbo electoral bill.

This proposal stipulated that in national elections the party or coalition winning the largest number of votes, provided it received at least 25 percent of the total votes cast, would automatically receive two thirds of the seats in the Chamber. One might have thought that memory of Fascist tactics in the elections of May 1921 would have been enough to warn the other parties of the probable consequences of the passage of such a measure. There was, indeed, opposition on the part of the *popolari*, the reformist Socialists, and the Left Liberals, but the Center and Right, including such dignitaries as Giolitti, Orlando, and Salandra, voted for the bill and assured the consolidation of the Fascist dictatorship.

In the elections of April 1924, there were, despite Fascist violence at the polls, two and a half million votes cast for non-Fascist parties. But Mussolini's party got four and a half million and received two thirds of the seats in the Chamber. Immediately, it began to bring pressure to bear upon the opposition parties and the press, and the drift toward totalitarianism became evident. The clearest sign of this was the liquidation of the new regime's most dangerous foes, which began with the brutal murder, in June 1924, of Giacomo Matteotti, a leader of the moderate Socialists and an unflinching critic of Mussolini's policies.

The news that this courageous and widely admired man had been kidnapped and left dead in a ditch caused a national revulsion so strong that the whole Fascist organization was shaken, and Mussolini felt it necessary to dismiss his chief of police and make other concessions to the national temper. It is barely possible that the Liberal and Socialist parties might have taken advantage of this popular mood to curb Mussolini before it was too late, but this possibility was never tested. After waiting in vain for the king to discipline his new premier's party, the opposition deputies made a tactical mistake of the first order, taking their key from Filippo Turati's speech in memory of Matteotti, in which he referred to the last stand of Caius Gracchus and his followers on the Aventine Hill and said:

> The only real representatives of the people are those who now stand on the Aventine of their own conscience, whence no wiles shall move them until the rule of law is given back and the representation of the people ceases to be the ghastly jest to which it has been reduced.

In this spirit, they absented themselves from the Chamber of Deputies. This "Aventine secession" meant, in reality, that the opposition had abandoned the only arena in which they might have fought fascism before the eyes of the whole nation. They had surrendered the field to their enemy.

Mussolini himself realized this, and he recovered from his momentary loss of nerve. In January 1925, in a dramatic speech in the Chamber, he declared: "I alone accept the political, moral and historical responsibility for everything that has happened." Simultaneously, he ordered new attacks upon the opposition, which wilted before them. In the course of 1925, the non-Fascist members in the ministry lost their posts; all other parties were dissolved; censorship of the press was tightened, and owners of newspapers like *Corriere della Sera* were persuaded to dismiss independent-minded editors; the Fascist-ization of the bureaucracy and local government was completed; and a secret police (OVRA) was established. Italy had become a totalitarian state.

THE INSTITUTIONS OF FASCISM

The Machinery of Government / No immediate attempt was made by the Fascists to do away with the governmental machinery that they had inherited. Mussolini had at one time flirted with republicanism, as with every other shade of political thought, but he saw no advantage to making Italy a republic in a formal sense. Victor Emmanuel III remained on the throne, although it must have been difficult at times in the years of Mussolini's glory for the Italian people to remember that they had a king. The bicameral legislature was permitted to continue to function also, although it too had suffered a sea change, for both houses became exclusively Fascist, and neither had much contact any longer with the Italian people. After 1928, the election of the Chamber was carried out on the basis of an approved party list of candidates for which the voters could vote either yes or no—a method which eliminated both campaigning and free choice. The powers of the Chamber were nominal and limited for the most part to hearing and obeying. The prime minister (Mussolini) was given the right to initiate all legislation and to govern, when he wished, by decree. He had extensive rights of appointment, and all appointees were responsible to his person, including the other department heads and ministers of state.

As in the Soviet Union, the party was the source of real power in the country. Small in relation to total population (it came to number about a million members or 2.5 percent of the population), it was the guardian of the regime throughout the country. It was organized on a local basis and was ultimately composed of about 10,000 *Fasci*, grouped into provincial federations. At the head of the party pyramid was the Fascist Grand Council, a body of about twenty men that included the leaders of the March on Rome and several other officials. The Grand Council was supposed to rule the party and shape its policy and to be consulted in all constitutional matters, changes in the royal succession or in the powers of the prime minister, and other important issues. In reality, it never seems to have had much to do—at least not until 1943 when, to everyone's surprise, it deposed Mussolini—and real authority was wielded by its chairman (Mussolini) and the party's secretary general.

Party membership was a prerequisite for a political career, and it brought certain advantages in other forms of employment as well. It was therefore—at least until the depression years, when there were more party members than jobs—eagerly sought, and the party was able to be selective and to insist that candidates meet certain standards. After 1927, for instance, no one could hope for admission who had not passed through the graded youth organizations of the party: the *Balilla*, the *Avanguardia*, the *Giovani Fascisti*.

The party controlled the other agencies of power within the state by infiltration and parallelism. That is to say, there were many devoted Fascists within the hierarchy of the regular army and the national and local police organizations; but the party also maintained a police force of its own and, as a possible check on the regular military establishment, a large and well-armed party militia.

With one other powerful institution, the Fascists found it expedient to make a truce. In 1929, after prolonged negotiations between Mussolini and Pope Pius XI, the Treaty of the Lateran brought to an end the long feud between the Vatican and the Kingdom of Italy (see p. 340). The Italian government now recognized papal sovereignty within Vatican

An American artist's view of Fascist Italy: *The Eternal City,* 1937, by Petei Blume (1906–   ). Collection Museum of Modern Art, Mrs. Simon Guggen heim Fund.

City and St. Peter's in return for papal recognition of the Kingdom of Italy and renunciation of claims to former papal estates. Supplementary agreements provided for a financial settlement and gave the pope the right to appoint all bishops in Italy after consulting the Italian govern ment to see whether there were any political objections. The state con tinued to pay the salaries of churchmen and exacted an oath of loyalty from them. These agreements removed a perennial source of friction between church and state and diminished the possibility of church opposition to Fascist policies.

The Corporative State / One of the most advertised aspects of Fascist rule was corporativism, which was designed ostensibly to do away with the harsh individualism of the liberal state, to promote mutual under standing between capital and labor, and to eliminate class conflict These purposes were sought by the dissolution of the older trade union

and the abolition of strikes and lockouts, and the subsequent organization of a good part of the population into syndicates or corporations of
employers, employees, and professional men, under whose joint auspices
labor courts were established to deal with disputes. This system was
supplemented by codes of fair practice, guaranteeing working conditions
and providing social insurance. In time, the various corporations were
given the right to suggest to the Fascist Grand Council the names of
people who should be parliamentary candidates and, as the system
became more involved, to send delegates to a National Council which
was meant to advise parliament on economic matters. In 1939 it was
announced that a Chamber of Fasci and Corporations would actually
supersede the Chamber of Deputies, but the war made this final elaboration unrealistic.

The corporative system aroused much interest abroad, and the English
conservative John Buchan (Lord Tweedsmuir) was probably thinking
of it when he said, rather incautiously, in 1929, that "but for the bold
experiment of Fascism, the decade [had] not been fruitful in constructive
statesmanship." In reality, corporativism was a fraud, which never
worked in practice as it seemed to do on paper. For the Fascists, it served
three purposes. It drew a veil over the harsh outlines of their totalitarianism and permitted foreigners to think that Italy was devising a new and
more equitable social system which gave full expression to the people's
will. In the second place, it satisfied the most important supporters of the
Fascist movement, the industrialists and landlords, by eliminating the
possibility of effective labor organization. In the third place, it supplied
a great number of jobs for party members.

Wiser than Lord Tweedsmuir, the London *Economist* pointed out in
1935 that

> the new corporative state only amounts to the establishment of a new and
> costly bureaucracy, from which those industrialists who can spend the neces-
> sary amount can obtain almost anything they want and put into practice the
> worst kind of monopolistic practices at the expense of the little fellow who
> is squeezed out in the process.

Economic and Social Policy / The institutions of corporativism helped
eliminate the social disorder that had characterized the years immediately
before the march on Rome, but they did very little to improve the
working of the Italian economy or the conditions in which the Italian
people lived. It has indeed been argued that what prosperity Italy had
in the 1920s was due to the governments of the pre-Fascist period, and
that it was shortened in duration and Italy made more vulnerable than
it might have been to the shock of the world depression by Mussolini's
policies.

Possessing no coherent economic ideas of his own, Mussolini was fascinated by the spectacular and the unattainable. He weakened the financial structure of the state by elaborate public-works programs and overambitious transportation schemes (which did, nevertheless, as was always pointed out by his admirers, make the trains run on time and give Italy some of the best roads in Europe) and by the establishment of an army, navy, and air force that far exceeded Italy's needs and in the end proved to be luxuries, better designed for show than for use. More dangerous was his insistence that Italy follow the road of autarchy, which, given its resources and geographical position, was illogical and imposed a heavy strain on all aspects of its economy. Mussolini's desire to make Italy self-sufficient led him to inaugurate a "battle of wheat," which succeeded in producing large quantities of that commodity at uneconomic prices and at the cost of taking land away from olive culture, pasturage, and fruits, with resultant disruption of the economy. It led him to indulge in grandiose but impractical schemes like the one that was supposed to make the country self-sufficient in oil and gasoline by 1938. It persuaded him, in a much-publicized "battle for births," to subsidize matrimony and award procreation with medals and prizes, and to announce that his goal was to increase the population of the country to sixty million.

What this would have done to the standard of living in Italy if Mussolini had succeeded is not difficult to predict. Already in 1930, a report of the International Labor Office pointed out that real wages in Italy were lower than in any country of Western Europe, including Spain. This did not seem to bother Mussolini, who said publicly in 1936 that the goal of fascism was *not* to restore prosperity and that Italy was probably moving to a permanently lower standard of living, which would nevertheless be healthier morally and physically for all.

In the field of popular education, fascism registered some progress, at least in increasing attendance and reducing illiteracy. The problem here was a formidable one, for as Ignazio Silone pointed out in the introduction to the English edition of his brilliant anti-Fascist novel *Fontamara*, there were villages in which the peasants did not even *speak* Italian, let alone read or write it, and the gulf between them and organized society was complete. The Fascists increased attendance in elementary schools from three million to four and a half million in the first decade of their power and reduced illiteracy to about 20 percent of the national population.

On the other hand, the content of elementary education left much to be desired, since much time was devoted to inculcating military virtues and "Fascist culture" that might better have been spent on basic disciplines. The mind did not, after all, derive much sustenance from pablum like the following excerpt, which Denis Mack Smith has culled from a Fascist text for eight-year-olds.

> A child who, even while not refusing to obey, asks "Why?," is like a bayonet made of milk. . . . "You must obey because you must," said Mussolini, when explaining the reasons for obedience.

Fascist Doctrine / The official doctrine of the Fascist movement was as fraudulent as the concept of corporativism and as disorganized as the mind of its leader. Mussolini, as we have noted, had no firm principles of his own, and, at the beginning of his career in power, was given to boasting that fascism needed none either, that the Fascists were "the gypsies of politics," and that action was more important than philosophy. It was only when the world began to take an interest in his movement and when foreign pundits began to write pieces about its philosophical foundations that he thought it necessary to oblige them with doctrinal statements of his own.

Since he was always against more things than he was for, these were rich in negatives. Fascism was always declared to be the antithesis of liberalism and democracy and socialism, but anyone who desired to know why this should be considered a recommendation, or what fascism gave to the individual that these philosophies did not, found it very difficult to get a straight answer, either from Mussolini or from the man officially appointed to explain fascism in philosophical terms, Giovanni Gentile. In general, the line taken was that those older philosophies sacrificed the ideal of the community and the nation to a false conception of freedom and destroyed man's essential nobility by promoting individualism, materialism, and cold-blooded rationalism. Fascism, on the other hand, brought freedom through authoritarianism, and heroism and nobility through discipline and sacrifice. This could not be proved; it had to be felt. As Gentile wrote:

> We all participate in a sort of mystic sentiment, [in which] we do not form clear and distinct ideas, nor can we put into precise words the things we believe in, but it is in those mystic moments when our soul is enveloped in the penumbra of a new world being born that creative faith germinates in our hearts. . . . The fascist spirit is will, not intellect.

Intellect failing, it was necessary to fall back on incantation. The doctrinal statements of Fascist leaders are for the most part rhapsodic and incoherent glorifications of the state and the heroic virtues, in which the words "power," "courage," "blood," "sacrifice," "discipline," "victory," and especially "will" appear and reappear with monotonous regularity, as if the authors hoped by incessant iteration to give them reality.

If this was their hope, it was not fulfilled. The most striking thing about what passed for Fascist philosophy was that the values it invoked were not very evident in the actual practice of fascism or in the lives and behavior of Fascists. In the remarkable pictures of Fascist reality that we find in the novels of Alberto Moravia (especially *The Indifferent Ones*), there is precious little power or courage or heroism, and, after the devastating record of graft and corruption that Mussolini's police chief Senise has left to the world in his memoirs, all the proud talk of sacrifice and discipline sounds ludicrous.

The Cult of the Leader / If the corporative state and the philosophy of fascism were taken more seriously than they deserved to be, this was largely due to the respect and fear in which the leader of the party came to be held in Italy and in the rest of the world. The Duce's imposing stature was in large part the creation of his controlled press. This is not to say that he did not possess natural talents. He had an animal vitality that impressed both men and women, a bluff and bullying manner that overbore people weaker than he, an incurable habit of self-dramatization that helped him dominate any situation, a flair for the sensational that came from his journalistic past, a not inconsiderable fund of peasant shrewdness, and oratorical gifts of the first order. But he was also timid, ill-educated, ignorant of foreign affairs, bereft of administrative ability, and too self-indulgent to repair his deficiencies, and it is a pity that Italy and the world did not appreciate these weaknesses sooner than they did.

Instead, thanks to Fascist censorship and control of the means of mass communication, Mussolini was presented to his people and the world as the *Übermensch* for whom they had long been waiting—the man of inflexible resolution, the soldier of experience and genius (he had, like Hitler, been a corporal, but without Hitler's long front-line service), the devoted public servant who labored day and night for his people, the man of strong passions but ascetic discipline, and the political genius whose predictions had an uncanny accuracy. The countryside was filled with signs reminding his subjects that "*Mussolini ha sempre ragione*" ("Mussolini is always right!") and gigantic pictures showing him in commanding poses—the calm and confident leader, sure of his course and its ultimate success.

It is perhaps understandable that the unlettered peasants and workers of Italy should have been taken in by this, but it is still hard to believe that so many Italian intellectuals and foreign statesmen were impressed by qualities that the Duce did not really possess. The acceptance of the legend of Mussolini by people like Austen and Neville Chamberlain, and their willingness to take his boasts and his threats at face value, had the long-run effect of convincing Mussolini himself that he possessed the

qualities and the power they thought he had. And this had tragic results
for Italy and for the world.

THE EARLY FOREIGN POLICY OF FASCISM

First Steps: Corfu / During the years before the March on Rome,
Mussolini had repeatedly attacked the "peace of renunciation" and
insisted that Italy under Fascist leadership would refuse to be bound
by its terms. Over and over again he asserted that Italy must be an
expanding power and that "imperialism is the basis of life for every
people which tends to expand economically and spiritually." To the
extent that the peace treaties stood in the way of Italian expansion, they
must be revised; and Italy would not be baulked of its just deserts either
by the letter of the law or by the procedures of the new League of
Nations. For this organization Mussolini professed to have the greatest
scorn. "Fascism," he said in 1921, "does not believe in the vitality and the
principles of the so-called League of Nations. It is a kind of Holy
Alliance of the plutocratic nations of the Franco-Anglo-Saxon group, to
guarantee to themselves the exploitation of the greater part of the
world."

Once he had come to power, the Duce seemed to have felt it necessary
to demonstrate that these were not idle boasts. In his first speech to
parliament, he sternly warned Europe that Italy had no intention of
maintaining the *status quo* just for the sake of peace, although he rather
weakened the effect of this by intimating that he could be bribed into
remaining quiet.

> We cannot afford the luxury of a policy of foolish altruism or of acting en-
> tirely in the interests of others. . . . My formula is simple: *Niente per
> niente*. Those who wish to have concrete proofs of friendship from us must
> give us concrete proofs of friendship in return.

When no one rose to this suggestion, Mussolini undertook to prove
it was dangerous to disregard him. In August 1923 an Italian general
and his staff were killed on the Greco-Albanian border, probably by
Albanian bandits. Without waiting to discover who was responsible for
the deed, or even on whose soil it was committed, Mussolini sent an
ultimatum to the Greek government, demanding any number of apologies
and compensations and, when they were not immediately forthcoming,
bombarded and occupied the Greek island of Corfu. When Greece
appealed to the League of Nations, the Duce was contemptuous. "In case

the Council of the League declares itself competent in this matter," he said loftily, "the question whether to remain or resign from the League arises for Italy. I have already voted for the second alternative." The western powers were not particularly impressed by this, but they decided not to force the issue and referred the dispute to the Council of Ambassadors in Paris, who arranged the return of Corfu to Greece in return for the payment of damages to Italy. Thus, Mussolini won a cheap triumph and aroused the first serious doubts about the efficacy of the collective security system.

Corfu, however, seems to have exhausted his inventiveness, and his energies were in any case absorbed for the next two years by pressing domestic problems. He was content to leave the management of foreign affairs for the most part in the hands of professionals, who toned down ideological matters and sought to win the confidence of Italy's traditional friends and to contribute to the general appeasement of Europe. Under their direction, Italy, as we have seen (pp. 538, 551), not only adjusted its relations with Yugoslavia but also participated in the negotiations at Locarno and guaranteed the Rhineland Pact which was concluded there.

Toward Revisionism and Imperialism / Mussolini was not incapable of being flattered by opportunities to play the guardian of order and public law and, as Stuart Hughes has pointed out, he was never able to refrain from putting his signature on any treaty placed before him. Even so, a conciliatory foreign policy was not congenial to him and seemed contrary to the "Fascist style" which he was always talking about and which he equated with courage, resolution, action, forcefulness, and dynamism. The satisfactions to be gained from collaborative diplomacy did not seem to him to be worthy of Fascist Italy, which must dazzle the world with spectacular triumphs of its own.

His prejudices in this regard were shown clearly in the policy he followed in the late 1920s in the Danubian area. Here real statesmanship might have garnered economic advantage and personal prestige, while at the same time contributing to the general security of Eastern Europe. Mussolini seemed less interested in these things than in carrying on a pointless competition with France in that area, seeking first to detach the Little Entente powers from its security system and, when that failed, to build up a rival bloc under Italian leadership. In pursuance of this second objective he made secret agreements with Austria, Hungary, and Bulgaria and had no hesitation about violating the military clauses of the Versailles Treaty when this promised to serve his purposes. In January 1928, Italian agents were caught red-handed shipping five carloads of machine guns into Hungary, and a little later the Italian government was involved in a scheme to send large numbers of rifles and machine guns to fascist elements in Austria. These actions could not help but awaken lively fears in the other Balkan nations, and the resultant insecurity weakened the cause of peace.

This was a matter of no very great concern to the Duce. The deterioration of economic conditions at the end of the 1920s and the consequent disruption of European power relationships opened new vistas to his eyes and made him impatient of old restraints. In 1930 he appointed his son-in-law Galeazzo Ciano as his foreign minister, a sign that the reign of the professionals was over and that the *tono fascista* would be stamped on all future foreign policy. Simultaneously, he announced a large increase in the Italian navy and gave the first intimation of the future program of imperialism by announcing that Italians would not remain prisoners in the Roman sea. "Words are very fine things," he told his Black Shirts in the same year, "but rifles, machine-guns, warships, airplanes, and cannon are still finer things. They are finer because right without might is an empty word."

Unprincipled opportunist that he was, he was still uncertain as to his future course, but he sensed that something would turn up. He had predicted some years earlier that Europe would pass through a major crisis between 1935 and 1940 and that Fascist Italy must be prepared to act then. Now, in 1930, he announced that "in 1950 Europe will be wrinkled and decrepit. The sole country of young men will be Italy. . . . Either we or they! Either our ideas or theirs! Either our State or theirs!"

24

The Republican Experiment in Germany

While totalitarian regimes were consolidating their power in Russia and in Italy, an experiment was being conducted in Germany to determine whether a democratic republic could be made to work in that country. After fifteen years of trial and crisis it failed, and the ultimate consequences of that failure were a second world war and the death of millions of men, women, and children.

If some benevolent spirit had granted the peoples of Germany and the neighboring European states even a fragmentary glimpse of what lay in store for them in the 1940s, it is impossible to believe that they would not have made every possible sacrifice to maintain the Weimar Republic against its enemies. But that kind of foresight is not given in this world, and the German republic always lacked friends and supporters when it needed them most.

THE FOUNDING OF THE REPUBLIC

The Revolution / The German revolution of 1918 was not the result of planning but the offspring of confusion. The abrupt announcement that the military effort had collapsed and that the government was requesting an armistice stunned public opinion, paralyzed the wills and energies of the governing class, and created a situation in which war-weariness, fear, hunger, disillusionment, and social resentment exploded into violence, which spread with frightening rapidity from one locality to another. At the end of October, the rumor spread in the naval base at Kiel that the German High Seas Fleet was going to be ordered to take to sea to make a last stand against the British. Protests by the men against this suicidal gesture led to arrests, which resulted in further demonstrations, until finally, on November 4, workers in the town established a Workers and Soldiers Council on the Soviet model. The Kiel example was imitated in other coastal towns—Lübeck, Hamburg, Bremen; and the movement then spread rapidly to Hanover, Magdeburg, Braunschweig, Oldenburg, Schwerin, Rostock, Cologne, Dresden, and Leipzig.

In all cases, the councils seized control of the local government but confined their efforts for the most part to formulating demands for an end to the war and for the abdication of Emperor William II, whose continued rule seemed to them to jeopardize the chances of peace. In South Germany, however, events took a more serious turn. On November 8, a Constituent Soldiers, Workers, and Peasants Council was established in Munich under the leadership of the Independent Socialist Kurt Eisner, and it immediately proclaimed the establishment of a Bavarian Democratic and Social Republic. It was this action—which seemed to forecast the imminent dissolution of the Bismarckian Reich—that finally sealed the doom of the monarchy by forcing the national government in Berlin, against its will, to take the republican road.

On the morning of November 9, Prince Max von Baden, who had been made chancellor by the emperor at the end of September and had been engaged in armistice negotiations ever since, laid down his seals of office. In doing so, he declared that it was the intention of William II and the crown prince to relinquish their rights to the German and Prussian thrones, and that he himself was turning his office over to Friedrich Ebert, the head of the Majority Socialist party, who would serve as "Reich chancellor." Ebert immediately announced that the new government would be "a people's government" and that its goal would be "to bring peace to the German people as soon as possible, and to establish firmly the freedom which it has achieved."

He said nothing, however, about a republic; and, had he had a free hand, he would certainly have left the decision as to whether Germany should change its basic form of government to a later date and to a constituent assembly representing the whole of the German people. But Eisner's action in Munich was now known in Berlin, and the tide seemed to be running so heavily in the direction of republicanism that

Ebert's colleagues felt it necessary to make that cause their own, lest they be anticipated by parties to the left of them. Thus, at 2 P.M. on November 9, 1918, Philipp Scheidemann ended a speech to a mass demonstration in front of the Reichstag building by shouting: "The Hohenzollerns have abdicated. Long live the great German Republic!"

Throughout the country, this announcement was accepted calmly. There were no anguished protests and no signs of a Vendée-an rising by embittered royalists. The monarchical system and the political and military hierarchy that supported it had been so completely discredited by the war that no one was prepared to fight for them. And this very fact might, if conditions had been different, have eased the transition from the old to the new and facilitated the laying of solid foundations for a democratic Germany.

What prevented this was the disunity of the Socialist party. The greater part of this—the Majority Socialists, led by men like Ebert and Scheidemann—were revisionists (see p. 306), who had long since given up any belief in the necessity of violent revolution and, now that power seemed within their grasp, wished to proceed by orderly methods towards the consolidation of democracy and the inauguration of a program of social development. They were disinclined to attempt too much in the way of social reform until certain urgent tasks—the restoration of normal food supplies to the population, for instance—had been carried out. Ebert himself, a patriot and a realist, was aware that an excess of revolutionary zeal might promote social disintegration and make the country vulnerable to separatist ambition and the depredations of the Poles and others. His desire was to restore order and then to proceed as quickly as possible to elections for a national assembly which would draw up a new constitution for the country, give it a government with a clear mandate, and make orderly progress possible. He fully agreed with Friedrich Stampfer, the editor of the Socialist newspaper *Vorwärts*, who wrote at this time: "Socialism is organization. Disorganization is the worst enemy of socialism."

The views of the Majority Socialists were contested by two groups. The first of these, led by Karl Liebknecht, the son of the founder of the Social Democratic party, and by the gifted Polish Jewess, Rosa Luxemburg, called itself the Spartacist Union and (after January 1919) the German Communist party. It was an internationalist party, seeking to emulate the success of the Bolsheviks in Russia. Luxemburg held that "the role of the working class is to be realized only through the path of an armed workers' revolution"; her associates agreed that a National Assembly would be a bourgeois and counter-revolutionary body; and their objective was to prevent the meeting of that body by seizing power in the state before it could convene.

The Spartacists were too few in number to take effective action by themselves, but they were always able to count on considerable support from the third socialist group, the Independent Socialist party, which had broken away from the majority in 1916 in protest against further support of the war effort. A heterogeneous and disorganized group, which nevertheless had considerable popular backing, the Independents were never as radical in their views as the Spartacists; but, like the Socialists in Italy (see p. 583), they seemed in their dealings with the Communists to have an inferiority complex and to feel the necessity of proving their common Marxist faith. Thus, in effect, in most disputes with the Majority Socialists, they lent their support to the radical wing.

The Days of Spartacus / These Socialist divisions had two results. In the first place, they threatened to defeat Ebert's efforts to restore public order. The Majority Socialist leader had sought to promote this by establishing a provisional government of three Majority Socialists and three Independent Socialists with authority to conduct necessary state business; but the effectiveness of this body was hampered by attempts of the Independents and Spartacists to subordinate it to control by the Workers and Soldiers Councils, as well as by continual strikes, demonstrations, and armed *Putsches* openly encouraged by the Spartacists. In the second place, they led Ebert, because of his concern for public order and his justifiable fear that the Spartacists would attempt a major rising in the near future, to look for aid to groups to which he might not have turned in other circumstances. As early as November 9, for instance, he felt it necessary to conclude a gentlemen's agreement with General Wilhelm Groener, Ludendorff's successor at the Supreme Army Command, which called for a policy of mutual support against the danger of Bolshevism. Later, as the threat of a Spartacist insurrection became more palpable, he authorized his Majority Socialist colleague Gustav Noske to build up volunteer forces to protect the state in an emergency; and Noske, finding little enthusiasm for such service among members of the Socialist party or the trade unions, was forced to rely upon bands of ex-soldiers which had been forming in various parts of Germany in response to appeals from their former officers. These free corps, as they were called, were much like the original *Squadristi* in Italy (see p. 586). Some had come into existence to cope with local disorder; others had been formed to fight communism or to guard the eastern frontiers; some had been fighting the Reds in the Baltic lands, like Goltz's Iron Division (see p. 565), and had just got home. They were all composed of trained soldiers—*Frontkämpfer* of the most hard-bitten variety—and for Noske's purposes they were ideal. Their political convictions, however, left much to be desired, and it was not hard to imagine them being as willing to fight against democracy as against Bolshevism.

Ebert's arrangement with Groener robbed him of much of his future freedom of action in military affairs, and his reliance upon the free corps in 1919 made it difficult for him to disband them later on, even when they had revealed their basic antirepublicanism. The Reich chancellor's justification for assuming these liabilities was that his fears of new attacks upon the shaky republican state were well-founded. In January 1919, the Spartacists did attempt an armed insurrection in Berlin and for four days Ebert and his colleagues were isolated in a city that, for all intents and purposes, had fallen to communism. But Noske's work had been well done, and, on January 10, the free corps began their advance into the city. The Reinhard Brigade (named after its commander) drove the Spartacists out of the munitions plant at Spandau; and Stephani's Free Corps, using flame-throwers, machine guns, mortars, and artillery, attacked the Belle-Alliance Platz and forced the Spartacists in the *Vorwärts* building to capitulate. Other bands sought out and liquidated the remaining centers of resistance. By January 15 the action was complete; Rosa Luxemburg and Liebknecht had been brutally murdered, and Berlin was free of Reds. The government was firmly in control.

Spartacist week ended the possibility of a Bolshevik revolution in Germany. The government, still relying on the free corps, built their strength up rapidly. By the end of January, they were strong enough to begin operations against the provincial centers, and a systematic elimination of subversive elements in all the former revolutionary centers began. In February, Bremen, Wilhelmshaven, Halle, and other towns were pacified; in March, a second Spartacist rising in Berlin was crushed, with 1500 deaths; in April and May, Magdeburg, Dresden, and Leipzig were purged of Spartacists; and in June order was restored in Munich, where conditions had steadily deteriorated since February, when Kurt Eisner had been murdered and where, in recent weeks, Comintern agents had been active. The violent phase of the German revolution was now over.

The National Assembly / The removal of the threat to the government's authority in Berlin had meanwhile enabled Ebert to attain his most cherished objective: the calling of a National Assembly. Elections for this body were held on January 19, 1919, and, on February 6, the deputies gathered in Weimar. The composition of the Assembly showed that the non-Socialist forces in the country had recovered from the paralysis that seemed to affect them in November and December, for, of the 423 deputies, only 187 were Socialists (165 Majority; 22 Independents). On the other hand, the Catholic Center party had won 91 seats; the new

Democratic party (which took over from the prewar Progressives) had won 75; 44 deputies described themselves as Nationalists; a new People's Party (which inherited the remains of the National Liberal cause) had 19; and there was a smattering of others. It was apparent that, in the future, the Socialists could not expect simply to have their own way.

The National Assembly had three tasks to perform. It had to establish a legal government, to conclude peace with the Allies, and to write a constitution for the new republic. It completed the first of these with dispatch. When Friedrich Ebert surrendered the powers of his government to the Assembly, it elected him to the post of Reich president and authorized his party to set about forming a new cabinet, which, in view of the election returns, would necessarily be a coalition cabinet if it were to expect majority support. After trying to persuade the Independent Socialists to collaborate (an effort that failed because of their resentment over Ebert's use of the free corps against fellow Marxists), Philipp Scheidemann formed a coalition cabinet in which half of the ministers were Majority Socialists and the other half were drawn from the Center and Democratic parties. This was the original Weimar coalition, and its members were to prove to be the most loyal supporters of the Republic throughout its career.

The task of concluding peace was more difficult, and, indeed, subjected the new governmental machinery to an almost intolerable strain. The first reaction to the peace terms that were forwarded to Berlin in mid-May (see p. 535) was one of incredulity, and this was succeeded by an indignation shared by all parties. "What hand would not wither that would sign such a treaty!," cried Scheidemann passionately. It was nevertheless soon apparent that blind rage would serve no useful purpose. The Allies made it clear that they would renew hostilities if the terms were not accepted; and no responsible German statesman could permit that to happen. Yet it was not easy to accept the inevitable, for it was precisely at this juncture that Germany had its first taste of the irrationalism of the Right from which it was to suffer so grievously later on. In mid-June, the war minister Reinhardt called a meeting of leading generals at Weimar, informing General Groener beforehand that the meeting was intended as a council of war and that, if the cabinet decided to accept the peace terms, he intended to repudiate the action and lead an insurrectionary movement in eastern Germany, regardless of Allied action.

Nothing came of his fantastic scheme. The enthusiasm of the generals evaporated when Groener demonstrated to them that neither troops nor munitions would be available for a new war and that no support could be expected from the civilian population of the East Elbian districts. A memorandum spelling out these military realities, which he prepared at Ebert's request, succeeded also in persuading the majority of the National

Assembly to drink the bitter draught prepared in Paris. During the impassioned debate that raged over the peace terms, the Scheidemann government had resigned; but a new one was formed under the Socialist Gustav Bauer, and, on June 28, two of its members signed the treaty.

The crisis over the peace terms had ominous results. The memories of the extreme conservatives and the superpatriots were notoriously short. They had already forgotten how decisively Germany had lost the war; and it was in these very months that the *Dolchstoss* legend was being born—the myth that the invincible German armies had been defeated, not by the enemy, but by "a stab in the back" inflicted by pacifists, socialists, and defeatists on the home front. They found it equally easy to forget that a renewal of hostilities was completely beyond Germany's capacities in 1919; and they were to claim repeatedly in the years that followed that the Socialists and other supporters of the Republic had willingly accepted a shameful peace, when they might have resisted it successfully with arms in hand.

The third order of business for the National Assembly was the drafting of the constitution, and this occupied the delegates until August 14, 1919, when the new charter was proclaimed to the German people. The constitution that resulted represented an impressive attempt to do what the members of the Frankfurt Assembly had sought to do in 1848: to reconcile liberty with national unity and strength.

The first article stated: "The German Reich is a republic. Political authority derives from the people"; and the powers and rights of the people were stressed throughout the document. While executive authority was vested in a Reich president with broad prerogatives, serving for seven years, that officer was to be elected by secret, direct, and universal suffrage. The constitution provided for a bicameral legislature, but the upper chamber or Reichsrat, which represented the member states, had only nominal powers; all real authority was centered in the Reichstag, the members of which were elected by popular vote with proportional representation. In this people's chamber all legislation originated, and before its members the chancellor and the other cabinet ministers had to defend their policies. Besides providing in this way for the expression of popular sovereignty, the Weimar constitution guaranteed to all Germans such fundamental rights as equality before the law, freedom of speech and association, and freedom of belief. Church and state were separated, and the education of the young was placed under the supervision of the state.

One of the most striking features of the Weimar constitution was the attempt made in it to correct some of the weaknesses of the Bismarckian Reich. The central government was no longer made dependent upon the financial contributions of the separate states but was granted the right of direct taxation, which the imperial government had never possessed. The national government was given exclusive jurisdiction over foreign and colonial affairs, citizenship, travel and residence, national defense, currency, customs duties, posts, and telegraphs and telephones, and it assumed ownership of the railway system. Its laws were given priority in matters in which the separate states had the right of concurrent legislation—civil and criminal law, judicial procedure, social welfare and insurance, expropriation and socialization, press laws, and the like. The national government also claimed the right to lay down normative regulations concerning religion, education, and housing.

If the drafters of the constitution had had their way, centralization would have been carried even further; but the Assembly yielded to the strong protests of southern Germany and left extensive rights of local government to the separate states. It was stipulated nevertheless that they must all recognize republican principles and use universal suffrage and proportional representation in their elections; and, in general, the diminution of their authority greatly reduced the forces of particularism in the country.

In two respects the enthusiasm for the utmost in democratic method shown by the framers of this constitution caused future trouble. Proportional representation is doubtless the best method ever devised for seeing that all shades of opinion are represented, but it works best in times of political and social peace and in situations in which there is a general acceptance of certain basic values. Neither of these conditions obtained in postwar Germany, and the use of proportional representation in Reichstag elections complicated the legislative process by increasing the number of parties, thus making it difficult for any single one to get a majority. This made coalition government inevitable and also jeopardized the security of the Republic by giving representation (and an opportunity for publicity and growth) to antirepublican splinter groups that might otherwise have died from lack of attention.

Another evidence of the anxious deference paid to popular sovereignty was the provision made for initiative and referendum. Perhaps because this was not accompanied by adequate safeguards against misuse, it too had unfortunate results. The conditions for making a referendum necessary on any public issue were so easy to fulfill that enemies of the Republic used it as a means of obstructionism, as they did, for instance, during the debate over the Young Plan in 1929.

Finally, events were to prove that the extensive powers granted to the Reich president could be misused. The president was given the right to command the armed forces, to appoint and dismiss the chancellor, to call for a national plebescite in certain contingencies, and, in time of emergency, to suspend the constitution. This last right was laid down in

Article 48, which read: "Should public order and safety be seriously disturbed or threatened, the President may take the necessary measures to restore public order and safety; in case of need, he may use armed force . . . and he may, for the time being, declare the fundamental rights of the citizen wholly or partly in abeyance." This was the article that, in the last stages of the Republic, was to be used to undermine its foundations. Its authors were doubtless intent upon giving the government sufficient power to deal with renewed Communist disorders; and, given the state of Germany while they were completing their work, they can perhaps be forgiven for failing to foresee that the real danger was to come from a president under reactionary influence.

Antirepublican Forces / The Weimar constitution did everything that a piece of paper could do to create the conditions in which a democratic republic could grow and attain strength. What the Republic really needed now, however, was time and friends—a period free of crisis in which to consolidate itself and a large group of dedicated republicans in parliament, the civil service, and the general public. It got neither. The four years that followed the promulgation of the Weimar constitution were years of continual crisis, caused for the most part by external events and pressures; and, even after the dangers of the year 1923 were passed, the public was allowed no real alleviation of the tensions that plagued it.

At the same time, there were always fewer devoted friends of the Republic than there were enemies and neutrals. At both extremes of the political spectrum stood inveterate foes, who would do everything in their power to destroy the republican experiment. On the Left were the Communists, supplemented by the left wing of the Independent Socialists, who believed that the Majority Socialists had betrayed the revolution. On the Right were the Nationalists, for the most part unregenerate monarchists and landowners and industrialists who regarded the Majority Socialists as being as dangerous as the Bolsheviks; and, even further to the Right, the welter of anti-Semitic, anti-Bolshevik, antidemocratic splinter groups that would eventually coalesce and form the National Socialist party. In the political groups nearer the Center, open opponents of the Republic were rarer, but there were many in the People's party and even in the right wing of the Center who maintained a studious neutrality toward the regime and who could not be counted on to support the new system in a real crisis.

This was true also of departments of the public service upon which any regime must depend for support of one kind or another: the universities and schools, the bureaucracy, the courts, the police, the army. The revolution of 1918 had not been carried to the point of driving all public servants whose democratic sentiments were not unimpeachable from their jobs. To have attempted to do this would, for a period at least, have invited chaos. All branches of the public service, therefore, were staffed for the most part with their prewar incumbents. All too often their attitude toward the new regime was one of tolerance, broken not infrequently by revelations of latent or open hostility. There were many different manifestations of this. It was to be found in the way in which schoolteachers glorified the past. It was seen in the contrast between the "boys-will-be-boys" attitude taken by the police toward the hooliganism of nationalist thugs and the stern treatment which they meted out for violations of the law by socialist organizations. Similarly, it was evident in the light sentences that magistrates imposed upon men charged with desecration of the symbols of the republican regime or even with the murder of its leading statesmen.

A crucial question throughout the history of the Weimar Republic was that of the reliability of the army. Here again the natural unwillingness of the Ebert government of 1918 to court chaos had prevented the raising of a truly republican force; and the 100,000 man *Reichswehr* authorized by treaty (see p. 534) came to be filled with royalist officers and former members of free corps, who were not sympathetic to the Republic, and with long-term volunteers who could hardly expect to learn devotion to the Republic from these leaders. About the patriotism of the upper hierarchy of the army, there was never a suggestion of a doubt, but their allegiance was paid to the German Reich rather than to any particular government or regime, and they had a tendency to arrogate to themselves the right to determine what was the best interest of the Reich they served. This meant that in any crisis their attitude was ambiguous, and there was always a real possibility of their withdrawing their support from any government whose policies did not accord with their views.

To a much greater extent than was true in imperial Germany, the army became a state within the state. Claiming to be the best judges of what was good for Germany, its leaders had no hesitation about inaugurating policies of which the government was either ignorant or imperfectly informed. Thus, General Hans von Seeckt, chief of the Army Command from 1920 to 1926, entered into secret agreements with the Red Army, providing for technical assistance to that force and for German use of Soviet tank and air facilities for training purposes; and he also made other financial and administrative arrangements designed to strengthen the German army in defiance of the military clauses of the Versailles Treaty. Seeckt felt justified, again on grounds of national interest, in carrying on a subterranean campaign of opposition to Stresemann's Locarno policy; and he found nothing unseemly about giving information to the Russians which he hoped would help them defeat it. Seeckt finally lost his job in 1926, partly because Stresemann and other republican leaders could no longer tolerate his political pretensions, but his fall did not make the army an entirely reliable body in the hands of the Republic, and during the final crisis of the Weimar regime, his successors gave aid and comfort to its enemies.

THE CRISIS YEARS, 1919–1923

The Kapp *Putsch* / Nothing did more to harden the opposition of the Republic's enemies and increase their number than the efforts made by its leaders to carry out the terms of the Versailles Treaty. These also led to the first serious attempt to overthrow the Republic from the Right: the so-called Kapp *Putsch* of March 1920.

This affair arose out of the Allied demand that the German army be reduced to 100,000 officers and men and that no supplementary forces be allowed to exist. In accordance with this, the German government felt compelled to begin the dissolution of those free corps that had fought the Spartacists in 1919, as well as those that had returned from the Baltic lands. This led to resentment, secret conferences between the officers affected, and the elaboration of a plot against the regime. In March 1920, when the government ordered the demobilization of the Marine Brigade of Captain Hermann Ehrhardt and the Baltikum Brigade of the Iron Division (both back from the Baltic lands and both stationed outside Berlin), the commandant of Berlin, General Walther Lüttwitz, defied the government and ordered Ehrhardt's brigade to advance on the capital. At 6 a.m. on the morning of March 13, the troops entered the city and were met by Lüttwitz, General Ludendorff, and a not very distinguished East Prussian politician named Dr. Wolfgang Kapp. They immediately proclaimed a new government under Kapp's leadership.

The Kapp *Putsch* illustrated the ambiguous attitude of the army toward the Republic. When an agitated cabinet met with President Ebert on the night of March 12 to decide what should be done about the threat to Berlin, Defense Minister Noske and War Minister Reinhardt both argued for military resistance to Ehrhardt's advance. They were baulked by the then chief of staff, Seeckt, the most influential of the army's commanders, who icily pointed out that "troops do not fire on troops. . . . When *Reichswehr* fires on *Reichswehr*, then all comradeship within the officer corps has vanished."

Since Seeckt's attitude made it clear that support of the local garrison could not be counted on, the government had to flee the city, and the Kapp *Putsch* was put down not by the action of a local army but by the

Kapp's Menagerie

A contemporary comment (1921) by the German artist George Grosz. From George Grosz, *Das Gesicht der herrschenden Klasse,* Berlin: Malik-Verlag, 1921.

crippling effects of a general strike called by the Socialist party and the trade unions. This paralyzed the Kapp "government" in Berlin, which did not, in any case, possess a very clear idea of what it intended to do with the power it had seized. On March 17, Lüttwitz and Kapp fled the city, and the Ehrhardt Brigade—after firing one sullen volley into the crowd that came to watch its departure—withdrew also.

The republican government might very well have visited pains and penalties upon the army that had failed them, if the Kapp *Putsch* had not had an awkward sequel. The general strike gave new life to the Communists, who operated under its cover to start disorders in Berlin and Münster, and especially in the Ruhr, where a "Red Army" whose strength was put as high as 50,000 men captured several industrial towns and dominated the whole area around Düsseldorf by the end of March. In face of this new threat from the Left, Ebert and his colleagues gave up any plans they may have had to punish the army and authorized Seeckt, now raised to the position of chief of the Army Command, to restore order in the Ruhr. This he did with severity, using some of the same free corps whose insubordination had caused the Kapp *Putsch*.

The Inflation / These scenes of violence were trifling in comparison with those that were to come as the republican government wrestled with the probem of reparations. The main outlines of this question have been given above (pp. 533–534), where it was pointed out that the failure of the powers to agree at an early date on a sum to be paid by the Germans that would satisfy the Allies but also be within Germany's capacity to pay was due to Anglo-French differences of view and German lack of tact at the Spa Conference of 1920. The total German liability was set by the Allies in May 1921 at the sum of 132 billion gold marks (roughly 32 billion dollars). The German government (still a coalition of the Weimar parties and now headed by a Center deputy named Joseph Wirth) announced that it would follow a "policy of fulfillment," and this policy was loyally followed by the governments that succeeded Wirth's until the beginning of 1923. But they did not have the political courage to attempt to raise the sums due to the Allies by taxation. They knew that such taxation would be resented by all classes and would force a reduction of social services that would cost them the support of their own followers. This perhaps understandable reluctance to invite new social and political troubles led them to rely upon borrowing and upon the printing of new money.

This process started a disastrous inflationary spiral. Foreigners lost confidence in German currency, and the mark, which had stood at 4.2 to the dollar in 1914 and 8.9 in 1919, began to depreciate in value on the international exchange. This had immediate repercussions at home, where people began to try to turn their money into goods. Prices began to rise and soon were rising faster than the exchange rate was declining, since owners of goods were reluctant to exchange them for currency of dubious value, and more money was printed to take up the slack. Continued differences between the English and the French prevented timely foreign intervention in the form of a reparations moratorium; and the French seizure of the Ruhr in January 1923 (see p. 550) turned the steady decline of values into a raging avalanche. It did so because the German government answered the French action with a policy of passive resistance that was enormously expensive and had to be financed by more printing. By the end of 1923, 133 printing offices with 1783 presses were turning out currency at top speed; the mark stood at 25 billion to the dollar; and one German statesman pointed out that the annual profit of the Darmstädter Bank would now be insufficient to buy a tramway ticket.

In the midst of the resultant chaos, there were some Germans who profited, for the inflation provided many opportunities for gifted speculators. Exporting industries, whose expenses were paid in depreciated

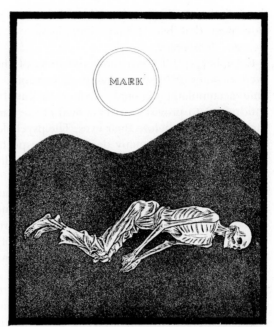

The New Currency comes—
too late.

The revaluation of the currency at the end of 1923 was powerless to help many whose resources had long been exhausted. From *Simplicissimus*, Oct. 29, 1923.

currency while their income was in stable monies, made great profits, and by creating subsidiaries abroad they were able to manipulate fluctuations to their advantage. Some of the largest of Germany's industries became larger as a result of the inflation, by absorbing competitors with fewer reserves than their own and taking advantage of the decline of labor costs to enter upon ambitious programs of construction and plant expansion. Some of the objections raised by industrial magnates to the government's termination of the policy of passive resistance to France in the Ruhr were due less to outraged patriotism than to the realization that the action forecast the end of the conditions which had brought them so many profits.

To the working classes, on the other hand, the inflation meant lower wages, longer working hours, and a decline in real income that brought hunger and sickness to their families. The chief mayor of Berlin reported in 1923 that 22 percent of the boys and 25 percent of the girls in elementary schools were below normal with respect to height and weight, and that 31 percent were incapable of doing their assigned work for reasons of health. The plight of the working classes was aggravated by the fact that the inflation wiped out the reserves of the Independent Trade Unions, making it impossible for them to pay benefits to their members or to pay their employees. Because of this and the fact that wage agreements negotiated by the unions became meaningless during the inflation, millions of workers left their unions, thus weakening a movement that had been potentially one of the strongest bulwarks of German democracy.

Even harder hit were those members of the middle classes who had fixed incomes or lived on savings or pensions. Men who had spent a lifetime accumulating enough savings to pay for the education of their children or to provide for their own old age now saw the result of their thrift melt away before their eyes. The psychological effect was shattering and explains why so many decent and respectable people turned for salvation to demagogues whom they would ordinarily have shunned.

The Culmination of Violence / These economic conditions weakened the authority of the government and threatened to cause the overthrow of the Republic. All of the ills of the time were blamed by the extremists of the Right on the Republic's acceptance of the peace treaty and the inauguration of the policy of fulfillment. Fanatical rightists regarded it as an honor to belong to organizations whose purpose was to murder the persons responsible for what they considered to be treason to the Reich. In August 1921, Matthias Erzberger, the outstanding leader of the Center party and one of the signatories of the armistice of November 1918, was murdered while walking in the Black Forest; and in June 1922 a band of young men shot and killed Walther Rathenau as he drove to work one morning, because this brilliant man—who had been the author of Germany's wartime plan for economic mobilization (see p. 516) and who, as foreign minister, had concluded that Treaty of Rapallo which rescued Germany from complete diplomatic isolation (see p. 549)—was considered by them to be the embodiment of the policy of fulfillment. Other republican leaders were targets of attacks and murder attempts, and the government seemed powerless, and the courts unwilling, to check the progressive breakdown of law and order.

The year 1923 brought attacks not only on individuals but against the very structure of the state. One of the effects of the French invasion of the Ruhr was to stimulate attempts by groups of separatists in Düsseldorf and Aachen to set up an independent "Republic of the Rhineland." This movement was soon discredited by the known fact that it was encouraged by the French, but more serious troubles arose in the east and the south. In Saxony and Thuringia, for instance, there was a marked resurgence of communism, and a "united front" of Communists and Left Socialists took over the state government at the beginning of October. Using tactics that have since become familiar, the Communists attempted to get control of the police and, when this was resisted by their Socialist partners, tried a *coup de main* in Saxony that failed but caused a deterioration of the public order. The coup and disorder gave the Berlin government an excuse to intervene; Saxony and Thuringia were placed under martial law; and *Reichswehr* units deposed the government that had caused all the trouble.

The government found it much less easy to deal with the dangerous situation in Bavaria. The state government there had been dominated since 1920 by Gustav von Kahr, a man of inflexibly reactionary views who made himself the head of an antirepublican conspiracy that included Bavarian separatists, supporters of both the Hohenzollern and Wittelsbach dynasties, anti-Semites, and men who wanted to do to Germany what Mussolini was beginning to do to Italy. Kahr had attracted General Ludendorff to his side, a dubious advantage, since the wartime hero's megalomania was now approaching madness; he had won the confidence of General von Lossow, commander of the *Reichswehr* units stationed in Bavaria; and he had entered relations with a young man named Adolf Hitler.

Born in Austria in 1889 and still a citizen of that country, Hitler had come to Munich from Vienna in 1913. He served in a Bavarian unit of the army during the war, attaining the rank of corporal, being twice wounded, and winning the Iron Cross First Class, a distinction rarely bestowed on common soldiers. He had returned to Munich when peace was restored and joined a small racist, militarist group founded by Anton Drexler and called the German Workers party. He soon showed that he possessed remarkable talents as an orator, and his fulminations against the Versailles Treaty, the crimes of the Republic, the evils of Marxism, the unwholesome influence of the Jews, and the necessity of a national regeneration won a wide following in Munich and rural Bavaria. The party's membership increased rapidly; its name was changed in 1920 to the National Socialist German Workers party (NSDAP); and in 1921 Hitler was given unlimited powers as its leader or Fuehrer—a party decision that gave birth to "the leadership principle," about which Nazi propagandists later on had so much to say. At about the same time Hitler created a private army called the *Sturmabteilung* (storm troopers) or S.A. —a body of brown-shirted thugs who were used to protect the Fuehrer at his own meetings and then, as their numbers and discipline grew, to prevent (and these are Hitler's own words) "all meetings or lectures that are likely to distract the minds of our fellow countrymen." It was the support of this body that Kahr was seeking when he approached Hitler.

The precise objectives of the Kahr movement were not known, but its preparations were ominous enough to indicate that it was probably going to attempt a major blow against the Reich government. That government, however, showed none of the determination it had displayed in dealing with the situation in Saxony and Thuringia. This was partly because it was always more difficult in the Weimar period to win popular support for a blow against "national elements" than it was to take action against threats from the extreme Left. It was also the result, once more, of the position taken by the chief of the Army Command, General von Seeckt. Since the commander of the Bavarian army group was one of Kahr's allies, action to nip Kahr's plot in the bud might cause a situation in which *Reichswehr* would have to fire on *Reichswehr*. Seeckt was so opposed to this that he actually suggested to President Ebert that the time had come for "a reconciliation with the Right" and intimated that the present government was losing the confidence of the army.

The situation was saved for the Berlin government, however, by Hitler. On the evening of November 8, 1923, when Kahr was holding a meeting of his supporters in the Bürgerbräukeller, the Fuehrer broke into the hall at the head of a detachment of his storm troopers, climbed on a table, and fired a shot into the ceiling, declaring that both the Reich and Bavarian governments were desposed and that the "National Revolution" had begun. He herded Kahr, Lossow, and their associates into a side room and made them pledge their support for his government, granting them offices in his cabinet in return.

This demonstration of the art of political hijacking was too much for the Bavarian leaders. During the night, while Hitler planned his campaign against Berlin, they publicly repudiated their agreement with him and declared that they would defend the constitutional order against his attack. In response, Hitler decided to rally the city to his defense by a show of force. On the morning of November 9, the storm troopers, led by the Fuehrer and by General Ludendorff, marched from the Bürgerbräukeller across the river into the heart of the city. At the opening to the Odeonsplatz they were met by a force of police and army troops. There was an order to halt, a sharp fusillade, and a confused melée. Ludendorff was captured; Hitler and his chief lieutenants fled (to be apprehended two days later and jailed); and fourteen storm troopers were killed. They were the first Nazi martyrs, and from 1933 to 1945 a plaque to their memory was fastened to the wall of the Feldherrnhalle where they fell, guarded by two burly sentries who made passers-by lift their arms reverently in the Nazi salute.

The Beer Hall *Putsch* of Adolf Hitler completely destroyed the Kahr conspiracy and eliminated the last serious threat to republican authority and Reich unity. It was now possible for the Berlin government to breathe more easily and to push ahead its plans for recovery.

THE STRESEMANN ERA, 1923–1929

Toward Financial Security / The first steps toward recovery had already been taken before matters in Bavaria came to a head, and the man who had had the courage to take them was Gustav Stresemann who, in August 1923, had become chancellor of a coalition of all the moderate parties from the Socialists to his own People's party.

Stresemann, the wisest and most courageous statesman during the whole Weimar period, had been in German politics since 1907, when he became a member of the National Liberal party and, shortly thereafter, one of its most prominent spokesmen in the Reichstag. In the years before the war, he had been known for his extreme nationalism, his uncritical support of imperial foreign policy, and his advocacy of imperialism and navalism. During the war he had been an uncompromising supporter of the military and an opponent of all suggestions of negotiations with the enemy. In a speech in 1917 that is reminiscent of one of Bismarck's most famous speeches, he had declared that the war would be won "not by the speeches of statesmen, not by diplomatic negotiations, not by diplomatic notes, not by Reichstag resolutions, but by Ludendorff's hammer, the strength of our army, the power of our might." He wrote later; "Until 1 October 1918 I believed Germany invincible." The discovery that it was not was a blow from which he recovered painfully and which forced a reorientation of his ideas.

Although many National Liberals entered the Democratic party after the war, Stresemann refused to do so and was one of the leading spirits in the formation of the German People's party which, he hoped, would become the true middle party, attracting the liberal middle classes who were repelled by communism and socialism on the one hand and by reactionary nationalism on the other. Although he remained a monarchist at heart and believed that monarchy was the form of government best suited to the German people, he set his face against attempts to restore it by illegal *Putsches* and persuaded his party—which he hoped would be a bridge between the old Germany and the new—to accept the Republic as the legitimate form of government.

Stresemann's nationalism had remained undimmed by the defeat of his country, and it was his ambition to restore Germany to its place among the leading nations of the world. Unlike the reactionaries, however, he knew that this could not be accomplished by defying the Allies or making threats that could not be carried out. The Nationalists, he once said, would "not learn that you can get nowhere by saber-rattling, especially when you have no saber in your scabbard." He was realistic enough to see that Germany's recovery would necessitate sacrifice and even surrender, and he was willing to take responsibility for what he knew was sure to be labeled by the Right as cowardly behavior.

When Stresemann took office, the policy of passive resistance to the French invasion of the Ruhr, which had led to a complete work stoppage in the area, was depriving the government of desperately needed revenues while at the same time costing it 350 million gold marks a week in subsidies to the resisters. In what was one of the most courageous decisions of his career, Stresemann terminated the policy, although he was violently denounced for it. It was quite clearly a surrender to the French; but it strengthened the hands of those abroad who wished to persuade them to temper their German policy, and it was, in any case, the only step that could avert a total economic collapse in Germany. Once this plunge had been taken, Stresemann went to the Reichstag and asked for a grant of plenary powers to take any and all measures considered necessary in the financial, economic, and social sphere. This law, passed over the objections of the Nationalists and the extreme Left, gave the government the authority to pass a series of drastic measures designed to stop the inflation.

These were worked out under the supervision of Hjalmar Schacht, the president of the Reichsbank, and Hans Luther, the minister of finance. They included a cessation of all note printing, the withdrawal of the old currency and the issuance of a new one, the so-called *Rentenmark*, and a number of innovations (new taxes and reductions of state expenditures) that were designed to balance the budget. The new currency had no gold basis and was not convertible, being issued, in theory, against a mortgage on all the land and real estate in the country. In reality, of course, the basis of the currency was the confidence of the German people in it, the result of the vigor and resolution with which the government attacked the economic problem.

While terminating the policy of the passive resistance, Stresemann had appealed to the western powers for a new approach to the reparations problem and had won the support of the British and the United States governments. When France finally agreed, two committees of experts began to meet in Paris. One of them, under the chairmanship of the American banker, Charles G. Dawes, formulated the plan that was to regulate German reparations payments for the next five years. Germany undertook to make annual payments, beginning at 250 million dollars and rising over a four-year period to a standard annuity of 625 million dollars. Variations from this payment would thereafter be determined by the index of German prosperity. Foreign credits were advanced to speed German recovery and make possible speedy resumption of payments—and in the end a total of 25 billion marks was pumped into Germany in foreign loans, largely from the United States.

The introduction of the Dawes Plan was attacked by the Nationalists in the Reichstag as a surrender to foreign domination and as acceptance of what Hitler called "interest slavery." Ludendorff shouted from his seat in the Chamber: "It is a shame for Germany. Ten years ago I won the battle of Tannenberg. Today you have made a Jewish Tannenberg." In reality, the plan was the necessary foundation for recovery, and it made possible the remarkable progress of German industry and commerce and the steady rise of living standards and real wages that took place between 1924 and 1929. In 1928 Germany's national income was 50 percent greater than it had been in 1913, and per capita income had increased by the same proportion. The recovery was almost as spectacular as that which followed World War II and which then gained for the Bonn Republic the name of "the economic wonder."

Stresemann's Foreign Policy / Stresemann's chancellorship lasted only one hundred days, and he fell from office when the Socialists withdrew their support from his cabinet in protest against the difference of treatment accorded by his government to Saxony and Thuringia on the one hand and Bavaria on the other. He was never to be chancellor again; but, in every succeeding cabinet from the time of his fall until his death in 1929, he occupied the post of minister for foreign affairs. It was here that he accomplished his greatest work and, in the words of the British ambassador in Berlin, "raised Germany from the position of a stricken and disarmed foe into that of a diplomatic equal."

The first stage in that accomplishment—the negotiation of the Locarno treaties and the admission of Germany into the League of Nations—has already been described (p. 551); but two additional points may be made with respect to it. First, while proposing and accepting a guarantee of Germany's western frontiers, Stresemann refused to make any pledges concerning the boundaries in the east, which he hoped one day to be able to change in Germany's favor, although by peaceful means. Secondly, he refused to be deterred from concluding the Rhineland Pact and entering the League by the formidable campaign of threats and blandishments waged against him by the Soviet Union. Stresemann understood the advantages of Germany's ties with the Soviet Union; and in 1926 he was willing to conclude a new pact of friendship, the Treaty of Berlin, with Moscow. But he distrusted the motives of the Soviet government and, basically, his orientation was always toward the west.

Once Locarno was concluded, Stresemann's main objectives were to secure the removal of Allied missions and troop contingents from German soil and to win a further reduction of the reparations burden. His first victory in this respect came in 1927 when the Inter-Allied Control Commission, which had been sent to Germany in 1919 to supervise the reduction of the army to the treaty limit and the elimination of war industries, was finally withdrawn. He found it harder to persuade the Allies to evacuate their troops from the Rhineland. Despite his excellent relations with Aristide Briand, Stresemann could not convince the French statesman that speedy evacuation might accomplish more than the policy of cautious delay that Briand favored. Briand was impressed by the presence in Germany of private armies like Hitler's Brownshirts, disciplined veterans organizations like the *Stahlhelm*, and other irregular forces, and insisted that France must not withdraw its troops until they were dissolved. Stresemann argued—wholly sincerely, since he was no admirer of the forces in question and their *Maulheldenthum* (mouth-heroism)—that their growth was encouraged by the continued presence of the Allied troops. It is impossible, in retrospect, to tell which of the two views was correct. The British thought that Stresemann's was, and they applied all possible pressure on the French to make them agree.

The question was finally resolved at the Hague Conference of 1929. At this meeting, the powers drew up the so-called Young Plan, a new arrangement for alleviating the pressure on the German economy by scaling down the schedule of payments set by the Dawes Plan five years earlier. Stresemann's success in persuading the powers that this new adjustment would benefit the European economy in general was in itself a major diplomatic success. But he also convinced them that any agreement on reparations—even one which lightened past burdens—would be unpopular in Germany and that national support for the Young Plan would be easier to attain if a simultaneous announcement were made that Allied evacuation of the Rhineland would be completed by 1930. The French remained doubtful but finally gave way under British pressure. Thus, when Stresemann died in October 1929, he knew that his dearest desire was going to be accomplished and his country was going finally to be freed of foreign occupation.

After Stresemann's death, the French writer Jacques Bainville said that his diplomatic achievement had been greater than that by which Bismarck had brought Prussia from Olmütz to Sedan, for, unlike Bismarck, Stresemann did not have great military power at his disposal. Stresemann's own estimate of his performance was more modest. In an interview with the British publicist Bruce Lockhart shortly before his death, he talked, indeed, as if his work had been a failure, noting that the benefits which might have been gained by a more conciliatory Allied attitude on reparations and evacuation could hardly be gained at this late date and that the mood of reconciliation prevailing at the time of Locarno had been dissipated by the long delay in exploiting it.

Signs of Continued Weakness / The years in which Stresemann pursued his diplomatic effort to restore Germany's full sovereignty and position in the world were good years for the German people economically and were filled with impressive achievements by German writers, artists, and scholars. There is no room here for an intellectual history of these years, and it will perhaps be enough to note that a period which saw the best work of men like Thomas Mann, Albert Einstein, Paul Hindemith, Oskar Kokoschka, Max Weber, Friedrich Meinecke hardly deserves the label of decadence that was fastened upon it later by the Nazis.

But if there were many signs of intellectual vigor, there were few of political vitality—or, at least, the vital political forces were not on the side of the democratic Republic. Although the Socialists possessed many able theorists and publicists, they produced few who aroused much interest or enthusiasm among the rising generation. This was true also of the other republican parties. In contrast, neo-conservatives like Spengler, who scoffed at the revolution of 1918 and preached that the true socialism was Prussian (see p. 496), Arthur Moeller van der Bruck, whose book *The Third Reich* proclaimed a new and better order, and Ernest Jünger (see p. 525), who called for a return to the heroic virtues of the war years, were read eagerly by young Germans, who also displayed a not inconsiderable interest in the preachments of the German Communist party. One of the most disturbing signs of political weakness in the Republic was that the republican parties did not make an effective appeal to the postwar generation, that the median age in the membership of the Socialist party, for instance, crept gradually upward, and that German youth, as the crisis of Weimar democracy approached, seemed disposed to obey the command of the young conservative newspaperman Hans Zehrer—"*Draussenbleiben!*," which may be translated as, "Remain uncommitted!"

Stresemann's impressive diplomatic achievements brought little prestige or domestic strength to the Republic. One sign of this, perhaps, was the fact that in 1925, when Friedrich Ebert died, the man who was elected to succeed him as Reich president was not a known republican but Field Marshal von Hindenburg, despite the fact that he was already 77 years old and the additional fact that he had displayed little political wisdom during the war. Another disturbing omen was that every diplomatic success won by Stresemann had to be followed by a bitter domestic struggle before it was approved by the parties and the public. This was true of the Dawes Plan and also of the Young Plan which, thanks to the Nationalists, became the subject of a public referendum that was held among scenes of violence and hooliganism.

One of the greatest sources of weakness in the Republic was the operation of the party system. It has been noted that the use of proportional representation multiplied the number of national parties and made coalition government necessary. The effectiveness of coalition ministries, however, was always hampered by another feature of the system: Reichstag deputies were not elected from single-member constituencies but on the basis of party lists drawn up by the party organization. Thus, if a party's national vote entitled it to thirty seats in the Reichstag, the top thirty men on the list became deputies automatically. This system not only prevented the emergence of deputies with strong local roots but it tended to make a fetish of party discipline and to stifle individual initiative.

These weaknesses had unfortunate effects on the working of government. The parties participating in any given government never allowed the ministry to forget that its existence depended on their forbearance. They kept their own representatives within the ministry on the tightest possible rein, and had no hesitation about commanding them to resign, or to threaten to resign, on questions of no more than tactical importance. Keeping a coalition intact was always difficult, and keeping it intact and working was often impossible. Thus between February 1919 and January 1933 there were twenty-one different Reich cabinets, and there was a growing interest in the possibility of establishing a cabinet of "experts" who would stand above the existing parties and not be controlled by them—an experiment tried with unfortunate results in 1930, when the Bruening government was formed (see p. 624).

In view of the existence and growth of extremist parties dedicated to the destruction of the republican regime, the parliamentary habits of the moderate parties bordered on irresponsibility. Throughout his career, Stresemann devoted the portion of his time and energy that was not absorbed by foreign affairs to the task, first, of convincing the parties to show more understanding of the requirements of coalition government and, second, of creating a "great coalition" of the moderate parties which would resemble Cavour's *connubio* (see p. 206) and serve the same purpose of containing and defeating extremism. Such a coalition had existed during Stresemann's 100 days in 1923 and had been broken up by the doctrinaire tactics of the Socialists. In 1928, Stresemann's efforts helped piece together a new one, combining ministers of the Socialists, the Democrats, the Center, and his own People's party.

Old habits, however, die hard. Stresemann's own party had never been willing to accept his views about ministerial autonomy, and its members were, moreover, becoming increasingly conservative in their views about social and economic policy. On their side, the Socialists were no less uncompromising on matters of economic principle than they had been in 1923. Even in the best of circumstances, cooperation between these partners would have been difficult. As it was, the formation of the great coalition anticipated the onset of the world depression by only a few months, and, when that set in, the differences between the parties became irremediable and the coalition collapsed.

This manifestation of the basic weakness of the party system was a clear sign of the impending end of the German democracy. As the depression deepened and the extremist parties grew in strength and militancy, the republican forces presented to the country an uninspiring picture of confusion and disunity.

25

The Crisis of Democracy: Central and Eastern Europe

On Wednesday, October 23, 1929, after a month of nervous fluctuations, the stock market in New York suddenly collapsed. When trading began next morning, it did so in panic conditions and, before "Black Thursday" was over, 12,894,650 shares of stock had been sold and values had tumbled to levels so low that some of the most respected banking houses in the city were forced to close their doors and tens of thousands of small investors were wiped out. Desperate attempts were made in the days that followed to shore up the market, and state and national officials tried to rally public confidence by statements that were, unfortunately, robbed of conviction by their frantic optimism. None of this helped. By the end of the first week of November, the holocaust was complete. As prices continued to fall, markets shriveled and disappeared, production faltered and stopped, manual laborers, salesmen, clerks, technicians, and junior executives began to receive notices of dismissal, breadlines started to form, and the United States entered the greatest economic depression in its history.

The causes of the stock-market crash of 1929 have long been the subject of heated debate, and they need not concern us here. It is more important to consider its consequences. Thanks to the spread of industrialism and capitalism, the world had become so integrated in an economic sense that the collapse of what had become in 1919 the financial capital of the world inevitably had profound repercussions in every part of the globe. This was particularly true in Europe, where many important national industries had an intimate connection with American firms and where, in addition, a great amount of American capital was invested. One of the first effects of the New York crash was the calling in of short-term loans and the virtually complete halt in new lending; this had a depressing effect on the economy of European countries, especially in Central Europe which had depended so heavily on American credit. Throughout 1930, governments in this area sought strenuously to stave off trouble by programs of retrenchment and fiscal stringency; but trade and production declined with ominous steadiness and, even before the end of the year, thousands of people in Germany and Austria were feeling the pinch of hunger. The first six months of 1931 saw the failure of both the great Viennese bank, the *Creditanstalt für Handel und Gewerbe*, and one of Germany's three largest joint-stock banks, the *Darmstädter und Nationalbank*. The shock caused by these crashes not only deepened the distress of Central Europe but was communicated to Great Britain and to France, the last remaining stronghold of prosperity. The depression now became general.

The depression subjected democratic institutions, wherever they existed, to a rigorous trial. In some countries, notably the United States and Great Britain, they survived the test and, indeed, were strengthened by the revelation of weaknesses that could be corrected. But this was not true of Central and Eastern Europe, where democracy's roots were not deep enough to survive a storm of this magnitude and where one country after another sought security in dictatorship.

The most important country in this part of the world was Germany, and it was here that the collapse of democracy was most complete and most tragic in its results.

THE VICTORY OF NATIONAL SOCIALISM IN GERMANY

The Bruening Government / At the end of 1929 the chancellor of Germany was the Social Democrat Hermann Mueller, presiding over that government of the great coalition which Stresemann had helped create the year before (see p. 622). One of the first effects of the coming of the depression to Germany was to destroy the internal cohesion of this government and, in March 1930, to force its resignation.

The question that broke the coalition up was whether the government,

with its already unbalanced budget, could afford to make the heavy out-
lays in unemployment insurance necessitated by the sharp increase in the
numbers of the jobless. As in Bismarck's days, unemployment insurance
was provided from funds to which labor, employers, and the state contributed, but the state's share was heavier than it had been under the
empire and, in the opinion of those parties representing the business community, would become insupportable in a long depression. Therefore, the
People's party, a member of the government coalition, demanded that
unemployment payments be reduced and in some cases (like domestic
and seasonal workers) eliminated entirely. Mueller's own party protested
that this would simply increase suffering and, while expressing a willingness to approve a slight increase in the assessments levied on employed
labor, refused to support any reduction of benefits. The issue was one on
which compromise should have been possible, but the worst features of
the German party system asserted themselves, and parochialism and intransigence brought the cabinet down. Many of those who contributed to
this result were later to curse their own shortsightedness, for their action
opened the door to those who were to destroy the Republic.

It was pushed open further by the army, which, from this point on,
played an unhappy role in German history. The defense minister in
Mueller's cabinet was Wilhelm Groener, the same general who had succeeded Ludendorff in 1918 and had made the bargain with Ebert in
November of that year (see p. 603). Groener had served the Republic
loyally since that time, but he was worried about the failure of the parties
to provide effective government, and he feared that, in depression times,
this would be dangerous to the national security. He was, therefore, responsive to a plan suggested by his most intimate advisor, General Kurt
von Schleicher. Schleicher's proposal envisaged the formation of a cabinet
composed of men who would be unhampered by any narrow conception
of party loyalty but would govern from the standpoint of the nation
alone, and in case they encountered parliamentary difficulties, would rely
upon the emergency powers of the Reich president. To head such a cabinet Groener and Schleicher favored the appointment of Dr. Heinrich
Bruening, a member of the Center party, whose distinguished war record
they felt would appeal to President von Hindenburg and whose sound
financial views would assure him of support from parties to the right of
his own. On the first score, at least, they were correct. The president
authorized Bruening to form a cabinet in March 1930.

The new chancellor proved to be a man of great energy, intellectual
power, and courage, but these qualities were offset by an arrogance that
made enemies and a willfulness that gave them opportunities to do harm.
To deal with the economic plight of the nation he had a program rigidly
deflationary in nature and emphatic on the score of government economy

and retrenchment; and he was unwilling to countenance either opposition or amendment to it. When he took office, he warned the Reichstag that his ministry represented "a last attempt to achieve a solution of the nation's pressing problems in conjunction with the people's legislature" and that, if the parties would not cooperate, he would look elsewhere for support. This was hardly language calculated to win supporters, and the Reichstag refused to accept his financial proposals. Bruening immediately appealed to the president and received authority to put them into effect by emergency decrees under Article 48 of the constitution. To Socialist charges that this represented a dangerous step toward dictatorship, the chancellor answered, quite sincerely, that, on the contrary, it was designed "for the education of the German people to political thinking." When the Reichstag expressed its dissatisfaction by passing a vote of no confidence in his policy, Bruening dissolved it and ordered new elections to be held on September 14, 1930.

The chancellor and his military backers were confident that this energetic behavior would impress the voters and create a workable Reichstag majority. They paid no attention to those people who warned that elections held during the depression could help no one but the parties on the extremes. But the warning voices were correct. When the vote was counted, Bruening's party had gained six seats, while the Socialists, the People's party, and the Nationalists had all declined in strength. But the Communists had increased their Reichstag representation from fifty-four to seventy-seven, and—most amazing of all—the National Socialists had increased theirs from twelve to one hundred seven and had become second only to the Social Democrats in strength.

The Growth of National Socialism / The Nazis had had some lean years following the debacle in Munich in 1923. While Adolf Hitler served his reduced sentence[1] in the fortress at Landberg-on-the-Lech, whiling away the time by dictating his book *Mein Kampf* to Rudolf Hess, his party had fallen to pieces, its leaders had scattered, and its members had drifted away to other messianic cults and sects of salvation. A new beginning had to be made, and Hitler was resolved to make it, but in a different way. While in prison, he told a friend:

> When I resume work, it will be necessary to pursue a new policy. Instead of working to achieve power by armed coup, we shall have to hold our noses and enter the Reichstag against the Catholic and Marxist deputies. If outvoting them takes longer than outshooting them, at least the result will be guaranteed by their own constitution. Any lawful process is slow. . . . Sooner or later we shall have a majority—and after that, Germany.

[1] After the Beer Hall *Putsch*, he had been sentenced to five years' detention but served less than a year.

Although forbidden by law to speak in public for two years after his release from prison in 1925, Hitler set about reconstructing his party with great energy. Through the pages of the *Völkischer Beobachter*, a newspaper acquired by the party in 1920, he carried his antirepublican, anti-Marxist, anti-Jewish views to the public and attracted new dues-paying members. Growth was slow but, even in these days of republican consolidation, steady; the party rolls swelled from 27,000 in 1925 to 178,000 in 1929. More important was the creation of an effective and surprisingly elaborate party structure. For electoral purposes, the country was divided into districts or *Gaue* that corresponded roughly with the Reichstag electoral districts, and each of these was divided into circles or *Kreise* and these, in turn, into local groups or *Ortsgruppen*. The leaders of these divisions—the *Gauleiter*, *Kreisleiter*, and *Gruppenleiter*—were the hard core of the party, and carried its message to the remotest corners of the country. *Gaue* were created also for Austria, Danzig, the Saar, and the Sudetenland of Czechoslavakia—a plain hint that Hitler was deadly serious about the views on foreign policy expressed in *Mein Kampf* (see p. 685).

In looking to the future, Hitler said later, he had realized that it was "not enough to overthrow the old State, but that the new State must previously have been built up and be practically ready to one's hand." Thus, the party structure included a number of organs that paralleled the ministries of the legitimate government. The party's Political Organization, for example, had departments of foreign affairs, labor relations, press affairs, agriculture, justice, and national economy. There was also a separate Propaganda Division, in which Hitler took a very direct interest, a *Wehrpolitisches Amt*, to study defense questions, and a Youth Organization with various divisions that was to be of great importance later on. The party's private army was composed of the *Sturmabteilung*, which was expanded in size and given a more effective organization by Ernst Roehm, a soldier of fortune who was one of the oldest members of the party and who, after a temporary break with Hitler and some years of freebooting in Bolivia, took over the direction of the S.A. in 1930. There was also a second elite force, which was destined to become the most fearsome organization in Germany, the *Schutzstaffel* or S.S. This body was designed originally as a personal bodyguard for Hitler and had various leaders until 1929, when it found its permanent chief in an unimpressive looking chicken farmer named Heinrich Himmler.

At the head of the elaborate party organization stood Hitler himself, with the title supreme leader of the party and the S.A., chairman of the National Socialist Labor Organization. His personal authority stemmed from a party decision of July 1921, but it was maintained essentially by the compulsive power of his personality and the shrewdness with which he handled his subordinates. His control over the organization enabled him to deal with potential rivals by appeasing them with new jobs or undermining their strength by a variety of means. While Hitler was in prison, Gregor Strasser, a former druggist who had joined the party in 1920 and was always very popular with the rank and file, had taken over the leadership of the party, made alliances with other nationalist groups, and collaborated with them in the Reichstag elections of 1924. Strasser, after all this, was reluctant to submit to "the Leader"; but Hitler reduced him to subordination, first, by seeming to give him a free hand in directing party affairs in northern Germany and, then, by rendering this meaningless by seducing to his own side and appointing to the post of *Gauleiter* in Berlin Strasser's chief aide, Paul Joseph Goebbels, a stunted little man with a club foot and a genius for propaganda.

In the last analysis, Hitler maintained his control over the motley assortment of nihilists, disinherited intellectuals, and *condottieri* by sheer strength of will. Men like Strasser and Roehm might complain bitterly to their own underlings about his decisions; but they rarely made the same complaints in Hitler's presence, and, when they did, they were either browbeaten or charmed into acquiescence with the Leader's point of view. Most of Hitler's closest associates—men like Hess, Goebbels, and the former war ace Hermann Goering, who had fled to Sweden after the *Putsch* of 1923 but returned to duty in 1927—regarded him with an attitude that bordered on reverence. This was true of lesser lights like Himmler, Alfred Rosenberg, the confused and turgid philosopher of Nordic supremacy, Walther Darré, the party's expert on agriculture, Hans Frank, the head of its legal division, and Baldur von Schirach, the Reich Youth Leader. The fact that Hitler was able to inspire and awe these often gifted but self-centered and cynical men, as well as men like the habitual drunkard Robert Ley, the future labor boss, and the perverts Roehm and Julius Streicher, *Gauleiter* of Nuremberg, helps to make less mysterious his later success in impressing the generals, the industrialists, and the press, as well as any number of foreign statesmen, including Lloyd George, Neville Chamberlain, Benito Mussolini, and Joseph Stalin.

If the party grew slowly during the years 1925–1929, its rate of growth in both membership and popular support after 1929 was tremendous. The reasons for this lay, of course, in the depression, which brought back to Germany all of the suffering of 1923. One index of the seriousness of the depression was unemployment, which increased sharply from 1,368,000 in 1929 to 3,144,000 in 1930 and then went on rising to 5,668,000 in 1931 and 6,014,000 in 1932. What this meant in human terms has been described by German novelists of this period: the plight of the white-collar worker most poignantly perhaps in Hans Fallada's *Little Man, What Now* (1932); and the collapse of normal values of political and social morality very effectively in Erich Kästner's *Fabian, the Story of a Moralist* (1932). In the foreword to a new edition (1950) of his novel, Kästner recalled the conditions that did so much to bring victory for National Socialism:

> The great unemployment, the spiritual depression that followed the economic one, the craving for oblivion, the activity of thoughtless parties, these were the storm signals of the coming crisis. Even the frightening calm before the storm was not absent—the laziness of the spirit that resembled an epidemic paralysis. Many were impelled to stand against the storm and the calm, but they were shoved aside. People preferred to listen to the circus barkers and the drummers who recommended their own mustard plasters and poisonous patent medicines. People ran after the pied pipers, down into the abyss where we now are, more dead than living. . . .

During the good years of the Republic, the NSDAP had been supported for the most part by superheated patriots, fanatical anti-Semites, and social misfits. Once the depression had set in train the progressive demoralization of society, the party appealed to a much wider audience; and Hitler saw to it that special messages and promises of salvation were carried to unemployed manual workers, to agricultural laborers and small farmers who had been hit hard by the fall of prices, to industrialists whose markets had disappeared, and to other special economic groups. The messages were sometimes carefully reasoned and based upon work done by the separate sections of the party's Political Organization, but party orators had no compunction about directing their appeal to the prejudices of their audiences or to the willingness to repudiate reason that often overcomes people in extremity. Peter Drucker has written of hearing a Nazi spokesman shout to a wildly cheering crowd of farmers: "We don't want higher bread prices! We don't want lower bread prices! We want *National Socialist* bread prices!" This sort of thing was especially popular with audiences of the lower-middle class—that sector of society whose security was always provisional, whose members were the first to be affected by depression and the least well prepared to resist it, since they had neither the reserves of the upper-middle class nor the organization of the working class, and which had been, throughout German history, a hotbed of social resentment. It was here that Hitler had least trouble in persuading audiences to believe that Jews, plutocrats, and socialists were the cause of all their woes and that only the destruction of the Republic by a Nazi party victorious at the polls would save them.

Bruening and his supporters failed either to pay sufficient attention to the strength of Hitler's party organization or to imagine how effective its propaganda might be in conditions approaching economic collapse. They were completely unprepared for Hitler's victory in the elections of September 1930, when six and a half million Germans voted for the NSDAP.

New Types: The Racial Man (or The Man of Breeding).

In July 1924, in *Simplicissimus*, Karl Arnold portrayed the anti-Semites who flocked to Hitler's support with this drawing, entitled ambiguously *Neue Typen: Der Rassemensch*.

Schleicher's Maneuvers and the Appointment of Hitler / Bruening's position after September 1930 was one of mounting difficulty. The Reichstag was more unmanageable than ever before, with the Communists and the Nazis indulging in continual obstructionism and disorder. Bruening was able to stave off votes of no confidence only by a slim majority that depended on the willingness of the Social Democrats to tolerate him because they feared what might happen if he fell. For the carrying out of his economic program—which was so Spartan in its character that it had earned him the name of the "Hunger Chancellor"—this was not enough, and he had to rely on the continued authority of the president exercized under Article 48.

It was the chancellor's hope that he would be able to strengthen his position by winning a resounding foreign success which would impress public opinion at home; and he set his mind on such things as a complete termination of reparations and the concession to Germany of equality of status in armaments. Throughout 1931 he sought to convince the other powers that it would be to their interest to make concessions to a democratic Germany rather than to have to deal with a Communist or Nazi one. The British proved amenable to this sort of argument, but Bruening's success in winning over his other neighbors was handicapped by a series of impolitic speeches by members of his government, in which they alluded to the necessity of correcting the eastern frontiers and talked querulously about the restrictions on Germany's freedom of action in the Rhineland. The Bruening government also hit on the idea of seeking to improve economic conditions in Central Europe by creating a customs union between Austria and Germany but, instead of consulting the other powers first, made the mistake in March 1931 of announcing the new *Zollverein* as a *fait accompli*. The results of this lack of tact were shattering. France, supported by Italy and the Little Entente, protested that the union was incompatible with the peace treaty and other agreements; the plan had to be submitted to the World Court at The Hague, which eventually set it aside; and what had seemed a promising gain for the Bruening government was transformed into a humiliating diplomatic defeat. Moreover, it had economic effects as well, for it was one of the reasons for French delay in accepting President Herbert Hoover's proposal, in June, for a one-year postponement of all intergovernmental debt payments. The French delay robbed the Hoover moratorium of much of its potential effect, and it had no success in checking the deepening depression in Germany.

As 1932 opened, Bruening had two new problems. Despite Hitler's decision to seek power by legal means, which he had declared publicly in a court trial in 1930, his Brownshirts were indulging in acts of violence and terrorism all over Germany. Several of the state governments wanted federal action against Nazism, and the Social Democratic party was intimating that, unless Bruening agreed, their support of him in the Reichstag would stop. In the second place, President von Hindenburg's term of office expired in the spring of 1932 and, unless the parties agreed to a prolongation, there would be elections that would almost certainly disrupt the economy and the public order. Bruening wished to avoid this and, because he hoped to persuade all the parties to agree, refrained from any action against the Nazis.

This did him no good. Hitler refused to assent to Bruening's plan for prolonging Hindenburg's term and put himself forward as a candidate. The elections were conducted in conditions that justified all the chancellor's fears. The first polling was indecisive, Hindenburg receiving 49.6 percent of the vote, Hitler 30.1 percent, the Communist candidate Thaelmann 13.2 percent, and the Nationalist candidate Duesterberg 6.8 percent. In the second poll, held on April 10, 1932, the old field marshal, thanks to Duesterberg's withdrawal from the race, received 53 percent of the vote to Hitler's 36.8 percent and Thaelmann's 10.2 percent and was declared elected.

On the eve of the first election, the S.A. had been mobilized and had thrown a cordon around Berlin. The purpose of this exercize was not clear, but it alarmed the government, as did materials discovered in police raids of Nazi centers, which seemed to indicate that a *Putsch* was being planned. On the advice of Defense Minister Groener, the chancellor decided to strike out at Hitler and, on April 14, decreed the suppression of the S.A. and the S.S.

What appeared for the moment as a sign of strength was soon revealed, however, to be the cause of Bruening's downfall. The agent of this was Groener's friend and subordinate, Schleicher, who had originally supported the ban on the S.A. but now reversed himself. In Schleicher's view, Bruening, who he had hoped would lead Germany out of the swamp of party politics, was now proving himself to be merely a pawn of the Socialists. It was time, he thought, to try a new political combination whose first order of business would be to reduce the Socialists to impotence, so that if it was necessary to use force against the Nazis later on, there would be no doubt that such action was taken in the national interest rather than for the benefit of the Left. Schleicher does not seem to have believed that a blow against the Nazis would be necessary. He hoped to persuade Hitler to accept political responsibility under conditions that would keep him under restraint or, failing that, to split his party and detach important groups from it.

Immediately after the promulgation of the ban on the S.A., therefore, Schleicher used his influence with the president's son, Oskar von Hindenburg, to persuade the old man that the decree had alarmed and offended the army. There was some truth in this. National Socialism was beginning to attract the junior officers of the *Reichswehr* and, even among senior officers who disliked Hitler and his opinions, there was admiration for the spirit and energy of the movement and respect for the military potential represented in it. Several retired generals wrote letters to the president expressing concern over this blow to Germany's military resources. Hindenburg was impressed by these complaints and felt he had been insufficiently informed by his chancellor; and, once the seeds of suspicion were planted, it was easy for Schleicher, Oskar von Hindenburg, and others in the president's entourage to nourish them. Although Groener tried to protect Bruening by attempting to assume responsibility for the ban and resigning as defense minister on May 13, the chancellor himself lasted only to the end of the month, when Hindenburg made it clear that he would no longer support him.

The politics of the next eight months were so complicated that it is impossible to give more than the barest outline of them in a brief account. They were dominated by the figures of three arch intriguers: Schleicher, who sought to carry out the policy sketched above; Baron Franz von Papen, former Guards officer, military attaché in Washington during World War I whence he was expelled for espionage, and now member of the Center party; and Hitler. Papen was the man selected, and sold

A prophetic cartoon printed in *Simplicissimus* (July 3, 1932) shortly after Heinrich Bruening's dismissal. Here the departing chancellor is saying to President von Hindenburg: "And sometime write me a post card from the Third Reich."

to the president by Schleicher, to replace Bruening and give Germany the authoritarian government that Bruening had failed to create. To give Papen a fair start, Schleicher made a secret agreement with Hitler in which the Fuehrer apparently promised to tolerate Papen in return for a promise that the ban on the S.A. would be lifted and new Reichstag elections would be held at the end of July. Armed with this equivocal pledge, Papen—at Schleicher's bidding—struck out at the main center of Socialist power in Germany, the Social Democratic government of Prussia. This he deposed, on grounds that it was falling under Communist influence and could not maintain public order, and replaced it with a Reich commissioner in his own person. The Socialist party and the trade unions, who had resisted the Kapp *Putsch* of 1920 by calling a general strike, did nothing of the sort in this instance, a demonstration of acquiescence that must have been noted with interest by Hitler.

Neither the Prussian coup nor Papen's energetic foreign policy—his success at a conference at Lausanne in freeing Germany from the reparations burden and his temporary withdrawal from the Geneva disarmament conference in protest against Germany's unequal status—won him any appreciable success with middle-class or conservative voters or had any effect on the Nazis at all. When Reichstag elections were held at the end of July, the only two parties that gave Papen any considerable support lost forty-four seats between them, whereas the Communists gained twelve seats and the Nazis doubled their representation, becoming the largest Reichstag party with 230 seats. To stave off a vote of no confidence supported by the two extremist parties, Papen had to dissolve the Reichstag immediately and call for new elections in November; but, when they were held, the results from his standpoint were even worse, 90 percent of the vote being clearly against the government.

At this juncture, Papen seems to have decided that, if a pledge of support could not be secured from the parties, the constitution must be dispensed with, the Reichstag, the parties, and the trade unions dissolved, and the cabinet, backed by the president and the army, must rule by decree. It says much for his powers of persuasion that he had the president convinced that all this was necessary when Schleicher intervened. The general pointed out that the result of Papen's projected action would be joint Nazi and Communist risings, complicated in all probability by border forays by the Poles. The army, he said, was not strong enough to maintain public order and national security in those circumstances. Considerably set back by this confession, Hindenburg had no recourse but to refuse Papen the dictatorial powers he had requested and to accept his resignation. He insisted, however, that Schleicher now assume responsibility for the government and appointed him chancellor on December 2, 1932.

Schleicher was not displeased by these events. To him the most interesting features of the November elections had been the sudden fall of Nazi strength—a loss of two million votes and thirty-four Reichstag seats. If the Nazis were now past their peak strength, if the public was beginning to be revolted by the rapine and plunder and political murder that had been practiced by the Brownshirts for the last year, then perhaps the time had come to force Hitler to compromise or to split his movement. Schleicher knew that Gregor Strasser was worried by the election returns and thought that he might be willing to enter a new government, bringing people like Roehm with him. It was, indeed, because he saw this possibility and because he felt that Strasser and Roehm would serve under him but not under Papen that Schleicher had brought the chancellor down by giving Hindenburg a deliberately pessimistic army report.

Alas for Schleicher's hopes! His estimate of the situation was right as far at it went. The Nazi party was in difficulties; it was short of funds; and several of its leaders wanted to take office before it was too late. But Schleicher had not counted on Hitler's political shrewdness or his ability to keep his lieutenants in line. Some secret sense told Hitler that to accept a share of political responsibility on Schleicher's terms would be disastrous. When Schleicher offered Strasser the post of vice chancellor in his cabinet and Strasser urged the party to consent to this, Hitler vetoed the suggestion. Strasser then resigned from the NSDAP, although he did not immediately attempt to start a defection toward Schleicher. In any case Hitler soon made a mass defection impossible by abolishing the Political Organization that Strasser had dominated and setting up a new central party organization under Rudolf Hess that assured him of the support of a united party.

This solution of the crisis in the Nazi party doomed Schleicher. He tried desperately to win' party support in the Reichstag, actually promising fundamental agrarian and social reforms in an attempt to win Socialist support, but the Socialists remembered his role in the dissolution of the Prussian government and were unsympathetic. He turned to the president and asked for the same dictatorial powers that Papen had requested, but the president, who was fond of Papen, remembered the arguments Schleicher had used against him and declined. Hindenburg's attitude was doubtless influenced by the alarm that Schleicher's talk of land reform had aroused in the agrarian circles in which he moved, and he let his chancellor know that, unless he could find a Reichstag majority, he would have to go.

There were now only two possible successors, Papen and Hitler. Out of resentment over Schleicher's tactics, Papen had been instrumental in easing Hitler's financial troubles by procuring support for him from some prominent Rhineland industrialists. He was now discussing the possibility of a new Papen-Hitler government with the Fuehrer, who, on his side, was holding out stubbornly for the position of chancellor in any such combination. It was rumored in Berlin that, if an attempt were made to make Hitler chancellor, the army would intervene to block it. In reality, there was no possibility of this. Schleicher, the man in the best position to call for army intervention, was more fearful of a Papen chancellorship than of a Hitler one. Moreover, there is reason to believe that, in the last days of January, when Berlin was filled with rumors of imminent *coups d'état*, Schleicher was secretly intimating to Hitler that the army would support him if its own interests were protected—that is, if he himself received the position of defense minister in Hitler's cabinet. The attempt of the army chiefs to cure Germany of the ills of parliamentary government, inaugurated with the appointment of Bruening in 1930, had thus been transformed by January 1933 into an attitude of resignation. A Hitler government seemed to them to offer better prospects of order than a return to Papen, and they stifled their doubts about the Austrian corporal by telling themselves that they would be able to control him.

Thus, the army remained neutral and, by its neutrality, assured Hitler's successful acquisition of power. On January 30, 1933, Papen's negotiations reached their conclusion. The president was persuaded to overcome his former antipathy to Hitler and accept him as chancellor of a coalition cabinet with Papen as vice chancellor, Hugenberg of the Nationalists as minister of economics, Seldte of the Stahlhelm as minister of labor, General von Blomberg (instead of Schleicher) as defense minister, the Nazi Frick as minister of interior, and Goering as minister without portfolio. Although there were only three NSDAP members in the predominantly Nationalist cabinet, the crowds of jubilant Nazis that swarmed through the streets of Berlin on the night of January 30 acted as if they were the new rulers of Germany. They were justified by the result.

The Consolidation of Nazi Power / For a few weeks at least, the new chancellor had to move with caution. The president had not given him emergency powers, and, even with the support of the Nationalists, he did not command a majority of the Reichstag. But new Reichstag elections were scheduled for March, and the Fuehrer was counting on the efforts of his lieutenants to make the most of them. Goering, whom he had appointed as minister of interior in Prussia, showed that his confidence was not misplaced. Goering used his position to legitimize assaults on the political meetings of other parties by supplementing the regular police with an auxiliary force of 50,000 men, four fifths of whom were recruited from the S.A. and the S.S. and spent most of their time hounding down enemies of the party. Men like Bruening and Stegerwald, the head of the Catholic Trade Unions, found it virtually impossible to make public speeches, and Communists did so at the peril of their lives.

This campaign of intimidation was not in itself enough. Hitler needed an event that would frighten the parties into giving him powers to deal with what he called "the Bolshevik menace." He got it on the night of February 27, 1933, when the Reichstag building was gutted by fire. A half-witted Dutch Communist named Marinus van der Lubbe was arrested in the building and confessed to the crime. The fire may have been planned and laid, if not actually ignited, by Nazi agents (Goering is reported to have boasted in 1942, "The only one who really knows about the Reichstag is I, because I set it on fire!"), although this has never been proved; but, however that may be, it was enough to give Hitler solid cabinet backing for a request for a presidential decree "for the protection of the people and the state." This document, signed by Hindenburg on February 28, suspended those sections of the constitution that guaranteed civil and individual liberties, and authorized the government to use any methods it desired, including house search and arrest, to guard against "Communist acts of violence endangering the state."

Armed with this decree, truckloads of storm troopers roared through the streets of Germany arresting Communist, Socialist, and liberal leaders, entering homes and carrying persons off to S.A. barracks, smashing newspaper presses, breaking up opposition meetings, and generally terrorizing the country. Meanwhile, the government radio poured out a constant stream of revelations about Communist conspiracies against the state. In face of all this, it is surprising that, when the elections were held on March 5, 1933, 56 percent of the voters still opposed Hitler, the Socialists holding their own, the Center increasing its strength, and even the Communists managing to poll 4,848,058 votes. The Nazis, with 288 seats, and the Nationalists, with fifty-two, had a bare majority in the Reichstag, but no more.

But Hitler still had the powers granted by the decree of February 28, which gave him the right to arrest enemies of the Reich at will; and by holding these over the head of the Reichstag he now got what he wanted. On March 23 he laid before the Reichstag the so-called Enabling Act, or "Law for Relieving the Distress of the People and the Reich." This gave the cabinet full legislative and budgetary powers, including the right to initiate constitutional amendments, for a period of four years, and thus called for a complete abdication of power by the Reichstag. In the tense debate in the Reichstag, only the Socialists spoke and voted against the bill. The Center party played the key role at this crucial moment in German history. In its caucus earlier its leader, Monsignor Kaas, argued that if Hitler didn't get full power this way, he would get it another. The Center decided to vote as a bloc for the bill but to seek assurances from Hitler that the president's right of veto would be observed and other constitutional safeguards provided. Such assurances were not received, but the Center voted for the bill anyway and—since there were no Communists present—their action was decisive. By a vote of 441 to 84, the Reichstag made Hitler a dictator.

Gleichschaltung / There followed the process called by the untranslatable German word *Gleichschaltung*—the systematic smashing, or taming, or "coordination" of all independent agencies or organizations. One of the first steps in this direction was the abolition, in March and April 1933, of the historic rights of the separate states of Germany, the dismissal of their governments, and the appointment of Reich governors, responsible to the chancellor, with extensive powers. The process thus begun was completed on the first anniversary of Hitler's assumption of power, by the Law for the Reconstruction of the Reich (January 30, 1934). The popular assemblies of all states were abolished, their sovereign powers were transferred to the Reich, their governors were put under the authority of the Reich Ministry of the Interior, and Germany was completely centralized for the first time in its history.

Long before this law had been promulgated, the parties that might have objected to it had all disappeared. The Communists had been outlawed in February; in June the minister of the interior declared that the Social Democratic party was subversive and must be dissolved; in

July the two Catholic parties, the Bavarian People's party and the Center party, announced their own dissolution; the Democrats and Stresemann's People's party yielded to pressure and did the same. Hitler's partners in the cabinet of January 30, 1933, the Nationalists, had seen the light even earlier, although only after their offices were occupied by the police and the S.A. and they had been invited to leave. The whole process was legitimized by a law of July 14, 1933, which declared that the NSDAP was the only political party in Germany and that attempts to found or maintain others would be punished by prison sentence.

The weakness revealed by the trade unions during Papen's coup in Prussia in July 1932 did not persuade Hitler that it was safe to leave them unreconstructed. As long as they existed independently, there was a possibility that they might become centers of subversion or conspiracy against the state; and Hitler was never one to take chances. On May 2, 1933, police and S.A. units raided the headquarters of all of the Independent Trade Unions, arrested their leaders and seized their funds, and ten days later all of their property was attached. On June 24 the Catholic Trade Unions were crushed in the same way. To replace the union structure, a Labor Front was created under the leadership of the perpetually intoxicated *Gauleiter* of Cologne, Robert Ley. This body, which eventually embraced all gainfully employed persons outside of the civil service, had no genuine political or economic functions and nothing to do with the regulation of wages or working conditions (which was left to specially appointed labor trustees, who were supposed to "regulate labor contracts" and "maintain labor peace"). The Labor Front administered the taxation of the working class and performed certain tasks of stewardship and definition of rules of labor, but its essential job was to keep labor in an atomized and powerless condition, with no leaders or representation of their own, and to extirpate from their minds the last traces of Marxism by an incessant process of indoctrination.

No one recognized better than Hitler that the permanent civil service could effectively sabotage the work of a regime, and he was determined that what had occurred under the Weimar regime would not be repeated under his own. Within two weeks of the passage of the Enabling Law, Hitler decreed a "law for the restoration of the professional civil service" (April 7, 1933), which called for the elimination from the service of all non-Aryans and people who were "no longer prepared to intercede at all times for the National Socialist State." This was soon extended to the judiciary and the universities. In a purge that in some ways resembled that of Bismarck in the 1880s (see p. 384), 28 percent of the higher members of the Prussian civil service, including all potential dissidents, were dismissed or demoted. A more thoroughgoing combing out was not necessary, for the psychological results of the first dismissals were pervasive.

Aside from applying the law of April 7, 1933 to the judiciary, no very energetic attempt was made to coordinate the majority of the German courts. But the decision of the *Reichsgericht* or Supreme Court to acquit three of the four defendants in the Reichstag fire trial led to the establishment of a new court, the People's Tribunal, to deal with cases of treason; and, after March 1933, cases of political crime were tried before the *Sondergericht* or Special Court, where defense attorneys had to be approved by Nazi officials. It is, moreover, impossible to appreciate the true nature of Nazi justice unless one realizes that Hitler and, for a time, Goering had the right to terminate criminal proceedings of which they did not approve and that Rudolf Hess, the Fuehrer's deputy, was authorized to take further action against defendants who in his opinion had been treated too lightly. Moreover, the Gestapo or Secret Police, established by Goering in April 1933, and the S.D. or Security Service of the S.S., did not hesitate to inflict arbitrary arrest, imprisonment in concentration camps, corporal punishment, and death upon thousands of Germans and, by the decree of February 1936, were declared to be above the law when carrying out "the will of the leadership."

Shortly after his appointment as chancellor, Hitler talked of his desire to maintain "a peaceful accord between church and state" and to improve relations with the Vatican. In July 1933, he actually concluded a concordat with the papacy that guaranteed the freedom of the Roman Catholic religion in Germany and the right of the church to regulate its own affairs. The ink was hardly dry upon this treaty when systematic attacks were launched against the Catholic Youth League and other church organizations, upon the Catholic press, and upon the persons of leading churchmen. These were intermittent, but, as the years passed, their number became too great to be ignored, and the church found it impossible to close its eyes any longer to other features of the Nazi system—its brutal persecution of minorities, its callous indifference to normal processes of law, its introduction of legislation calling for the sterilization of undesirables, and much more. In March 1937, Pope Pius XI, in the encyclical "With Burning Sorrow," protested eloquently against infringements of the concordat; and, if this had little effect upon the direction of Nazi policy, it influenced many Catholics to enter the resistance movement against what was clearly, as the pope noted, an attempt to exterminate their faith.

Meanwhile, the Lutheran and Reformed churches were being subjected to a state-backed campaign by a group called the "German Christians" who wanted to unite Protestantism in a Reich church, which would incorporate the Nazi racial doctrine and the leadership principle into its body of belief. Despite its long history of being more than eager to render unto Caesar what was Caesar's, German Protestantism found it difficult to agree that the Fuehrer should supplant Jesus Christ; and hundreds of pastors resisted and were sent to concentration camps for their resistance. As in the case of the Catholic Church, Hitler was able to break open opposition by force and to exact from churchmen an oath of allegiance as the price of keeping the churches open. But the ranks of the underground resistance were swelled by loyal Protestants who felt they could not tolerate the abuses of the regime.

Gleichschaltung did not stop with these organizations. It was extended to all agencies that could affect the minds of Germans for good or evil. The Reich Press Law of October 4, 1933, stipulated that all newspaper editors must be German citizens, Aryan, and not married to Jews, and laid down censorship laws of the utmost rigidity. In the years that followed, some of Germany's oldest and most respected journals—the *Vossische Zeitung*, for instance, which had been founded in 1704—were forced out of existence, and those that were kept for show were mere shadows of their former selves. The radio was already a state monopoly and had become a mere voice of the party, controlled by Joseph Goebbels. Goebbels' Propaganda Ministry also controlled all aspects of the film industry, including production. The most conspicuous result of this control of the means of mass communication was that their intellectual level fell to abysmal depths and their dullness became apparent even to the loyalest Nazi. What happened to German culture may be illustrated by an incident that occurred in 1943 when Germany's largest film company, UFA, celebrated its twenty-fifth birthday. Thanks to Goebbels' ministrations, UFA had so few talented artists by this time that, in making the commemorative film *Münchhausen*, it had to get government permission to employ Erich Kästner, whose books had been banned since 1933, as script writer, Hans Albers, a known opponent of the regime in the title role, the Hungarian Josef von Baky as director, and the Russian Irmen Tschet as camerman for special effects. Needless to say, only Albers' name appeared in the credits, and then only because he could not be hidden.

The flight of talent and its proscription for reasons of politics and race also affected the German educational system. All teachers at whatever level were subject to the racial laws and had to take an oath of allegiance to Hitler, and the subject and content of their courses and the books they could use were prescribed by people chosen for their political orthodoxy rather than their pedagogic skill. Thousands of great scholars and teachers lost or left their positions, and those who remained watched willingly or unwillingly, as learning was distorted to serve the ends of the Nazi state. Hitler boasted that his new Reich would "give its youth to no one, but itself take youth and give it its own education and its own upbringing." It succeeded perhaps in the task it considered most important—in making a large proportion of youth loyal Nazis,—but it did not give them a good education. By 1939 German industry was complaining of the shortage of well-trained chemists, engineers, and technicians, and both the economy and the state services were beginning to feel the effects of an educational system that regarded its chief aim as political and racial indoctrination.

The Subordination of the Party and the Armed Forces / By the methods described above, Hitler succeeded, in the words of Franz Neumann, in annihilating "every institution that under democracy preserves remnants of human spontaneity." His tyranny was not complete, however, until he had eliminated two possible threats to his power: that from his own party and that represented by the armed forces.

Hitler never felt the necessity of conducting a party purge on the scale of the purges of Joseph Stalin (see p. 574); but he nevertheless demonstrated, in June 1934, that he was capable of it, by eliminating some of his oldest comrades and most outspoken party critics. The essential reason for what came to be known as the Night of the Long Knives was the dissatisfaction felt by many of Hitler's followers at what they considered to be the conservative turn of his policy after March 1933. These people—many of them former followers of Gregor Strasser—had taken the Socialist part of their party's title seriously, and they expected the Enabling Act to lead to expropriation of the wealthy few and distribution of goods to the deserving many. Instead, they saw Hitler on the most cordial terms with the industrialists and the great landowners and the generals and the old elite. Criticism of Hitler was particularly vocal in the S.A., whose commander Ernst Roehm was a genuine revolutionary who wanted, as he said, "to lift the world off its hinges" and who thought of the S.A. as the true revolutionary army that would replace the old *Reichswehr*. Roehm's grumblings were reported to Hitler by malicious colleagues. They also came to the ears of the leaders of the army who, jealous of their own monopoly of power and fearful of a possible coup by the S.A., urged Hitler to deal with his unruly private army.

Whether the leaders of the S.A. were actually considering a blow against the Fuehrer is still not clear. Hitler, after long hesitation, decided to act as if they were and, with that shattering speed which always characterized his action once his mind was made up, struck in the pre-dawn hours of June 30, 1934. Detachments of S.S. troops and Gestapo agents snatched Roehm and other S.A. leaders from their beds and shot them without hearings of any kind. Meanwhile, other murder gangs took advantage of the occasion to dispose of prominent anti-Nazis and to pay off old grudges. General von Schleicher and his wife were shot down in their home; General Kurt von Bredow, an associate of Schleicher's, suffered the same fate; Gustav von Kahr, who had broken with Hitler in 1923, was hacked to death and thrown into a swamp near Dachau; two of Papen's closest aides were shot, as a warning to the vice chancellor. All told, hundreds of people met their death (at one of the postwar trials the number was set at more than a thousand), and the memory of this night of terror was enough to discourage serious dissension within the party until Hitler's death.

One of the reasons for Hitler's decision to act against the S.A. was his desire to please the army, and this stemmed from a special circum-stance. It was known in mid-1934 that Hindenburg's health was failing rapidly, and Hitler intended to take over the powers of his office when the President died. He wanted no interference from the army when that happened, and, as a result of his elimination of the army's chief rival he met none. When Hindenburg died on August 2, 1934, it was imme-diately announced that the offices of chancellor and president had been combined and that Hitler would rule as head of state (Fuehrer and Reich chancellor) and commander of the armed forces. All officers and men in those forces were required to take a special oath of allegiance to the Fuehrer, pledging unconditional obedience to him.

The acceptance of this oath by the armed forces—and there were no open objections to taking it—was the second step in the subjection of the army to Hitler's domination. The first, which had irretrievably weakened the army's moral position, had been its acquiescence in the murders of June 30 and its failure to protest against even the deaths of Generals von Schleicher and Bredow. Henceforth, the army's in-dependence would be progressively sapped.

The senior officers of the army might continue to delude themselves with the belief that, if necessary, they could control Hitler, or depose him; but, as the years passed, the likelihood of this tended to disappear. Especially after March 1935, when breakneck rearmament began (see p. 690), the army grew so enormously in size that the inner homogeneity of the officer corps dissolved, and the older more conservative officers could no longer speak for the whole. After 1936, the new officer candi-dates and the new conscripts tended to be boys who had already been indoctrinated in Nazi-controlled schools; and, even among more mature officers, old values began to disintegrate under the pressure of ambition jealousy, and opportunism in the expanding service. In the air force and the navy, loyalty to National Socialism paid dividends in the form of quick promotions; inevitably, junior officers in the army began to seek the same road to the top.

Hitler's respect for the senior army officers, which had been strong in the beginning, began to wane when he found them raising objections to the pace of the rearmament program and the adventurousness of his foreign policy (see p. 693). When the time came for him to launch his all-out drive to dominate Eastern Europe, he felt confident enough to "coordinate" the army as he had the trade unions. At the beginning of February 1938, taking advantage of a scandal arising from the second marriage of his defense minister, General von Blomberg, and professing to believe fabricated charges of moral turpitude on the part of the chief of Army Command, General von Fritsch, he dismissed both of those officers—and a number of others whose views he suspected—and re-organized the armed forces completely. Henceforth, all of the services were to be subordinate to a new Supreme Command of the Armed Forces (OKW), under Hitler's immediate command, with General Keitel, a complete admirer of Hitler, as his deputy. The army command and its famous and once all-powerful General Staff were thus demoted, having henceforth to submit its views to Hitler's personal military staff. This outraged the senior commanders but they did not resist; and the last limits to Hitler's absolute power in Germany were removed.

The War Economy / Under Hitler, Germany emerged from the de-pression with a speed that amazed the world. Unemployment sank from six million in 1932 to less than one million four years later; the gross national product doubled in the same period, as did the national income. Government pump-priming, expanded public-works programs, tax relief for industry, and financial juggling by the capable Dr. Schacht, now serving Hitler more loyally than he had the Republic, all played their part in this. Essentially, however, the stimulus to recovery came from the rearmament program, and the whole economy came to be a war economy, predicated on the assumption that war was coming and making the necessary preparations in advance. The Four-Year Plan inaugurated in September 1936 was designed to make Germany self-sufficient and hence invulnerable to a blockade like that of 1914–1918. Accumulation of strategic materials, development of synthetics, mobiliza-tion of war industries, all began under its aegis; and all made for em-ployment and prosperity.

To Germany's neighbors, who did not realize the end objective of Hitler's policy, this economic recovery was most impressive, and it helped to make totalitarianism seem attractive, and friendship and collaboration with Nazi Germany desirable.

This was particularly true in the countries to the east, where the trend to dictatorship had already been noticeable before Hitler came to power

THE RETREAT OF DEMOCRACY IN EASTERN EUROPE

Poland and the Baltic States / The postwar history of Poland afforded a good illustration of the difficulties of making democracy work in Eastern Europe. The Poles, whose qualities of courage and chivalry had always made them popular in the west, were treated generously at Paris, and the new Republic started its existence with geographical advantages and economic resources that were superior to those of its neighbors and with reasonable assurance of continued support by the Allied powers. These initial advantages were offset, however, by territorial ambitions that created difficulties that might have been avoided and by political practices that made the solution of internal problems virtually impossible, and consequently destroyed the people's confidence in democratic institutions.

Much of Poland's trouble stemmed from its attempt to expand its territory by assaults upon its neighbors in the immediate postwar years These aggressions have been described above, and it has been noted that they were not entirely unsuccessful (see p. 567). Even so, they left behind them a legacy of bitterness and tension, and gave Poland frontiers that were less secure than those originally authorized at the Peace Conference. The fear of future attack from neighbors they had despoiled and the knowledge that one of the results of their aggression was the acquisition of disaffected national minorities convinced all postwar Polish governments that a large military establishment was essential to national   security. In effect, despite French encouragement and aid Polish military expenditures were so heavy that they constituted a strain on the budget and contributed to the steady deterioration of the financial situation that took place in the postwar years. Thanks to the war against Russia, the budget deficit for 1920 was 50 billion zloty; and the zloty dropped from 120 to 500 to the American dollar in the course of the year By 1922 it was closer to 3000 to the dollar, and by 1923 inflation had gone so far that Poland had to go through an experience similar to that of Germany in the same year—abandoning the old currency and starting all over again on the basis of foreign loans.

Poland did not, however, have anything like the economic resurgence that took place in Germany after 1923. The key to economic growth in Poland was agrarian reform, and the need for expropriation and redis ribution of large estates and the modernization of agricultural methods had long been recognized. But, although the Polish parliament discussed and passed several partial reforms, the landlord class was always strong enough to prevent any fundamental change; and the country muddled on in the old way until it was engulfed in the world economic depression, which snuffed out what little economic progress had been made.

The failure to deal with basic economic problems was the result of the nature of Polish parliamentary practice. The Polish constitution, which had been accepted in March 1921, exalted the legislature at the expense of the executive. The powers of the president, who was elected by the two legislative houses (the Sejm and the Senate), were rigidly delimited; the two houses, which were elected by universal, direct, secret, and proportional vote, were not even restricted in their actions by the possibility of presidential veto. At the same time, they soon showed that they could make no effective use of their extensive powers, for they became battlegrounds for the too numerous parties and splinter groups that Polish individualism seemed to demand. Joseph Pilsudski (see p. 437) described the Sejm as "a sterile, jabbering, howling thing that engendered such boredom that the very flies on the walls died of sheer disgust"; and, by the mid-twenties, as one coalition government succeeded another without noticeable accomplishment (there were thirteen such governments between 1919 and 1926), many Poles agreed with him and urged him to change the situation.

In May 1926, Pilsudski yielded to their pleas. He marched upon Warsaw at the head of a mixed force of volunteers and mutinous government troops, and, at the end of three days fighting, forced the parliament to capitulate. Although he preserved the external forms of the republican government and even refused to accept the presidency, Pilsudski was from this time on the real force in Polish politics, and he and his "colonels" monopolized the premiership and other important offices and persistently reduced the powers of the legislature, having no compunction about arresting political opponents and trying them on charges of subversion and conspiracy.

This change to dictatorship did perhaps moderate the tendency to political anarchy that had at times seemed present in the activities of the Sejm, but it did not make the political system work effectively enough to improve the country's economic condition, to relieve the plight of the depressed working class and peasantry, or to satisfy the grievances of the national minorities. Pilsudski's financial reforms had only short-term effects and did not prepare the country to withstand the shock of the world depression, which greatly increased the already heavy incidence of unemployment and complicated other social problems.

Perhaps the most unfortunate result of Pilsudski's coup of 1926 was that it gave power to a military elite which carried its contempt for democracy over into foreign affairs and pursued a policy marked by such a degree of irresponsibility that the hope of an effective collective security system was weakened. Increasingly after 1926, the colonels were critical of the League of Nations, resenting that body's legitimate interest in the minorities question and the administration of the Polish Corridor. Increasingly, they showed a desire to assert their independence of France, and this led to a fatal strain of opportunism in their policy decisions. Thus, when Adolf Hitler took power in Germany, the Polish government gave him his first victory in foreign policy by concluding a pact of friendship with the Nazis in January 1934. It is clear that the colonels, already fascinated by the aberrant notion that Poland could be a great power in its own right, believed that, in the new and confused state of international affairs, they had a chance to play power politics on a grand scale and that the German pact gave them an advantage over both France and the Soviet Union. Time was to show that this was the purest dilettantism. In reality they had played into Hitler's hands by starting the dissolution of France's security system in Eastern Europe and leaving its members to be absorbed by Germany one by one.

The political evolution of the Baltic countries was much like that of Poland. Lithuania, Latvia, and Estonia started their existence with democratic institutions that proved to be ineffective because of the inexperience of those using them, the violence of factional strife, and—in the case of Lithuania, which quarreled incessantly with Poland over Vilna (see p. 548) and incurred lasting German enmity by seizing the former German area of Memel in 1923—the financial and political costs of overambitious foreign policy. In all three countries, strong men eventually took over. In the same year that Pilsudski marched on Warsaw, a group of army officers, industrialists, and landowners seized power in Lithuania and formed a one-party state with strong similarities to Mussolini's Italy, including the existence of a fascist militia called the Iron Wolf. Estonia and Latvia followed suit, as the progressive incompetence of democratic government was speeded up by the problems caused by the depression. Dictatorships were established in Estonia in 1934 and in Latvia in the following year.

Czechoslovakia / Events took a different course in the country that had been created as a result of the efforts of Thomas Masaryk and Eduard Beneš. Superficially, the Czech parliamentary system worked much like that of Poland's: there was the same multiplication of parties and the same swift succession of coalition governments. But, in contrast to its northern neighbor, Czechoslovakia's constitution had a better balance between the legislative and executive branches, and the country had the benefit of the continuity of policy made possible, first, by the continuous service of Masaryk (president, 1918 and 1920–1935) and Beneš (foreign minister, 1918–1935, and president, 1935–1939) and, second, by the inheritance from the Austrian Empire of a competent civil service. In contrast with Poland also, the Czech state did not handicap its future progress by an adventurous foreign policy and, although its military expenditures became heavy, especially after it began the construction of the so-called Little Maginot Line around its western borders, it paid its way by a careful financial policy based upon equitable but heavy taxation.

Economically, Czechoslovakia solved the problem that was never met in Poland by expropriating the former crown lands and the large private estates (the latter with compensation) and distributing them on easy terms to small holders. Agricultural production increased until the country was virtually self-sufficient in basic foodstuffs, although it had to import nonessentials and raw materials for industry. The general prosperity of the country depended essentially on its great industries: munitions, glass, porcelain, brewing, and the like. In general, its economy was better balanced than other countries of Eastern Europe, and it suffered less than they from the economic results of the breakup of the Hapsburg Empire. Like all Eastern European countries, however, it was less prosperous than it might have been if it had not been for the economic nationalism and protectionism that characterized the policies of the former Hapsburg states.

All of the conditions described helped make democracy a going concern in Czechoslovakia. Even so, it was never completely secure because of the minorities question. The country was, essentially, an artificial creation, composed of bits of other states; and in result it was filled with people who were never entirely satisfied with their new status. This was particularly true of the 747,000 Magyars in the eastern part of the country and the 3,123,000 Germans in the western fringe, called the Sudetenland; but germs of separation were present also in the minds of many of the 2,190,000 Slovaks, whose union with the Czechs had given the country its name.

Throughout the 1920s, the disaffection of the minorities was kept within bounds by the economic prosperity of the country and the liberal nationalities policy of the government, which permitted the different national groups to have their own schools and use their own language for official and legal business in areas where they predominated. This relative peace came to an end, however, with the coming of the world depression, which, because of the country's dependence on foreign trade, hit Czechoslovakia particularly hard, and with the rise of Adolf Hitler. The misery caused by the depression produced a desire for change;

National Socialism offered a means of effecting it. The Sudeten German were naturally the first to pin their hopes on Hitler, forming a National Socialist party of their own (the Sudeten German party of Konrad Henlein) and beginning a campaign for special privileges which, in reality, cloaked the intention of seeking fusion with Germany. But it did not take long for the other nationalities to begin to wonder whether they too might not gain a better status by appealing to Hitler to save them. These speculations led, as we shall see (see p. 701), to the destruction of the only country in Eastern Europe that remained true to democracy throughout the whole of the interwar period.

Austria / The destruction of democracy in Austria came sooner, as the result of a dramatic series of events in which the two most prominent European dictators both had parts to play. Austria, as we have seen, started its existence as a new state in highly unfavorable circumstances, deprived of most of the provinces that had assured its greatness in the past and doomed to a future of continual economic and political crisis. Kept afloat by League loans throughout the 1920s, the Austrian republic was denied an opportunity of improving its economic condition by the World Court's veto of the Customs Union Plan of 1931 (see p. 631). This setback completed the collapse of Austrian morale and made the impact of the world depression in Austria greater than in any part of the troubled continent.

Politically, the country was divided between the Social Democratic party, whose greatest strength was in Vienna, and the Christian Socialist party, which was supported by the majority of the rural population, although there was always a small but vigorous Nationalist party which advocated fusion with Germany. Throughout most of the 1920s, the Christian Socialists were the government party and were led by the able Catholic priest, Ignatius Seipel, who was chancellor from 1922 to 1924 and from 1926 to 1929. Seipel's government had a decided authoritarian cast, and this was even more true of that of his disciple and successor, Engelbert Dollfuss.

Dollfuss came to the fore at a time when the depression was destroying the last remnants of social stability, and political extremism was on the upgrade. Communism was exercizing a perceptible influence on the left wing of the Social Democratic party, while, on the other hand, the old Nationalist party had become National Socialist in sympathy and tactics and was not only obviously working for union with Germany but actually following orders laid down in Berlin. Dollfuss, a diminutive but energetic man, with a high regard for his own political wisdom (he was called "Millimetternich" and does not seem to have disliked the title), thought he could contain both movements and elected to do so by a policy of secret collaboration with Mussolini, which was intended to convert Austria into a fascist state on the Italian model.

Dollfuss's strong right arm inside Austria was Prince Starhemberg, the scion of a decayed Austrian family, who had been building up a private army of *Squadristi* called the Home Guard (*Heimwehr*). In these efforts he had, even in the 1920s, been aided by arms shipments from Italy, and, once Hitler came to power, they increased. Mussolini was worried by the possibility of an *Anschluss* of the two German states which would bring the Nazis to the Brenner Pass. He told Starhemberg on one occasion:

> Pan-Germanism is extending its tentacles toward the Adriatic. Italy has as little use for Pan-Germanism as it has for Pan-Slavism. That is why Austria is so important. If Austria ceases to exist, there can be no more order in Central Europe. Great dangers will then threaten Italy.

There was much truth in these words, and Mussolini would have been well advised to remember them in later years. But the force that the Duce helped to build up in Austria was not used primarily to guard against the dangers of a National Socialist conquest of the country. Dollfuss and Starhemberg were more immediately impressed by what they considered to be the danger on the Left and, with Mussolini's apparent approval, they proceeded to make the same mistake that Schleicher and Papen had made in July 1932: they set out deliberately to smash Austrian Social Democracy, the trade unions that supported it, and the defense force (*Schutzbund*) that it had built up to protect its meetings from *Heimwehr* attacks.

Throughout 1933, the strength of the *Heimwehr* was increased until, in the opinion of one competent observer, it had enough arms and munitions, including tanks and howitzers, to have equipped an army of 500,000 men for a campaign of moderate length. When these preparations were made, Dollfuss dissolved the parliament and announced, in September 1933, that it was his intention to form a new corporative state. These measures aroused the Socialists, and there was much talk of general strike and other forms of resistance. The chancellor was now, however, prepared to smash any opposition and, at the beginning of 1934, *Heimwehr* squads began to round up political opponents and to occupy Socialist and trade-union headquarters. Open fighting began in the provincial towns but was quickly suppressed and, on February 12, the *Heimwehr* advanced into the working districts of Vienna, using artillery against the great block of worker's tenements, the construction of which had been one of the triumphs of Austrian socialism, ruthlessly slaughtering knots of resistance and arresting the last of the Socialist leaders.

Once order was restored, Dollfuss promulgated his corporative constitution, convened the parliament for the last time so that it could note its own dissolution, and, with Starhemberg and Major Emil Fey (one of the *Heimwehr's* original founders) as his vice chancellor and minister of public security respectively, began to rule Austria as a dictator. His reign, however, was short. The Austrian Nazis had also been building up their strength, and on July 25 they tried a *Putsch* of their own, confidently expecting to be supported from Berlin. Their coup was a miserable failure and German aid never materialized, but for a few hours the rebels held the Chancellery and in that time they shot Dollfuss and allowed him to bleed to death.

In the days that followed, Mussolini mobilized four divisions of troops and stationed them near the Brenner Pass, announcing simultaneously that Italy would defend Austrian independence. Hitler disavowed any complicity in the rising (and saw to it that those German Nazis who had encouraged it disappeared from sight). Dollfuss's position was assumed by Kurt von Schuschnigg, a devoted follower of the dead chancellor and a supporter of his policies. But the July *Putsch* was a forecast of what was to come four years later. Schuschnigg was to discover then that the armed attack upon the working-class organization in February 1934, of which he had approved, had destroyed the only force capable of resisting National Socialism, for, as Germany became stronger and more popular, while Austria remained sunk in depression, the middle classes became increasingly receptive to the idea of *Anschluss*. The Dollfuss-Schuschnigg authoritarian state was thus a mere way station on the road to absorption by the more brutal totalitarianism of Germany.

The Middle Danube and the Balkans / The prevailing tendency toward dictatorship was apparent in all of the states of the middle Danube area and the Balkans, and was encouraged by the depression and by the apparent success of the Italian and German dictators. In the case of Hungary, democracy never had an opportunity to take root at all. After the suppression of the Soviet dictatorship of Béla Kun in November 1919 (see p. 527), the government had been organized as a kingdom without a king but with Admiral Horthy, the liberator of Budapest, as regent. From 1921 to 1931, the Hungarian premier was Count Bethlen, a complete reactionary who did everything in his power to restore the feudal rule of the Magyar notables, progressively restricting the suffrage and setting his face against agrarian or other reform. The world depression, a series of fiscal troubles, and a bad harvest finally brought Bethlen down in 1931; but he was succeeded by Julius Gömbös, an anti-Semite and fascist, who tightened the authoritarian regime further. When Hitler came to power in Germany, Gömbös was one of the first leaders of a oreign government to court his favor, and from 1933 on Hungary was a German client state responsive to suggestions from Berlin.

The other countries of this area were all subject to royalist dictatorship. In Yugoslavia, conflict between the Croats, who were Catholic in religion and federalist in politics, and the Serbs, who were of Orthodox faith and firm believers in centralized government, led to a wave of disorders and assassinations, and the establishment in 1929 of a dictatorship under King Alexander (see p. 412). Although this was modified in 1931, the king continued to command the state bureaucracy and the armed forces and, indirectly, to control elections to the Chamber of Deputies. In foreign politics, Alexander remained true to his tie with France; but, after his assassination at Marseilles in 1934, the regency that ruled during the minority of his son Peter II tended to flirt with both Mussolini and Hitler. At the time of the outbreak of war in 1939, the country was well on its way to being absorbed in the German economic system and seemed ripe for membership in Hitler's New Order.

Until 1930 Rumania maintained at least the appearance of parliamentary government; and, under the leadership of Maniu's Peasant party from 1917 to 1921 and from 1928 to 1930, and the Liberal party in the intervening years, accomplished a measure of agrarian reform and nationalization of natural resources. In 1930, however, Prince Carol, who had been forced to renounce the throne in favor of his son because of his liaison with a woman of unsavory reputation, deposed the young king and took the throne. Henceforward, as the depression deepened, as anti-Semitism grew, and as politics came to be dominated by fascist murder gangs like the Iron Guard, parliamentary institutions were increasingly restricted, until in 1938 a royal dictatorship was proclaimed. After this, the loyalty of Rumania to the Little Entente and the system of collective security was dubious.

In Bulgaria, the fortunes of democracy were affected by a high incidence of political assassination (which claimed among its victims the ablest of the country's postwar premiers, Alexander Stambulisky) and the active policy of the Bulgarian Communist party, whose outrages— notably the bombing in the Cathedral in Sofia in 1926 (see p. 579)— encouraged the rise of fascist fighting groups. There were rightist *Putsches* in 1934 and 1935, and in the latter year a royal dictatorship was established under Boris III. In Albania, democratic beginnings were snuffed out by an army *coup d'état* in 1925, the leader of which, Ahmed Zogu, was subsequently proclaimed king. Not even Greece, the ancient home of democracy, escaped the general trend. Although parliament expelled King George II at the end of 1923 and established a republic, the disorder that had accompanied Greek politics throughout the nineteenth century continued; and a seesaw struggle between royalist forces and groups supporting Venizelos (see p. 414) led to bloody fighting in 1935, the restoration of the king, and, in 1936, the establishment of a dictatorial regime headed by General Metaxas.

Even during the few years when democracy was the prevailing form of government in Eastern Europe, there had been few signs of cooperation among the various states to solve the common economic problems of the area; and the growth of dictatorship heightened the corrosive economic nationalism and promoted the political atomization of Eastern Europe. At the same time, the kind of opportunism that we have noted in the case of Poland came to characterize the foreign policies of all of these states, with the exception of Czechoslovakia and, perhaps, Greece. Thus, when Hitler came to power and began to menace the whole system of collective security, the majority of the Eastern European governments yielded to the temptation of seeking material advantage from collaboration with him. In the end, this cost their peoples the remnants of their freedom.

26

The Crisis of Democracy: Western Europe

To the prevailing tendency to prefer dictatorship to democracy, Western Europe was not, of course, immune. All of the forces that produced fascism in Italy and national socialism in Germany were present in the countries west of the Rhine in the postwar years: economic distress, parliamentary incompetence, heightened class conflict, middle-class fear of communism, and the existence of large numbers of unreconstructed war veterans, disenchanted intellectuals, and misfits who would rather parade in colored shirts than try to find a place in civilian society. Even a country like Great Britain, with a tradition of parliamentary government that was centuries old, experienced moments when the whole system of inherited law was subjected to serious challenge; and, while Britain survived these crises without sacrificing its democratic institutions, some of its closest neighbors were not so fortunate when their moments of testing came.

GREAT BRITAIN AND THE EMPIRE

Postwar Troubles / The poet Louis MacNeice once expressed the desires of what was probably a not inconsiderable number of war veterans and other Englishmen after 1918 in the words:

> All we want is a bank balance and a bit
> of skirt in a taxi

But he added sadly:

> It's no go, my honey love, it's no go, my poppet;
> Work your hands from day to day, the winds will
> blow the profit.
> The glass is falling hour by hour, the glass
> will fall forever,
> But if you break the bloody glass, you won't
> hold up the weather.

Certainly nothing seemed capable of holding up the foul economic storms that swept over England in this period. Everything seemed wrong in the economic sphere. The country's foreign trade had been ruined by the war, and when attempts were made to revive it, it was discovered that many of Britain's prewar markets had been taken over by the Americans or had simply disappeared because of the rise of new manufacturing in the British dependencies. The shipping industry was equally hard hit and was not helped by the confiscation of the German merchant marine, which merely denied contracts to British firms, so that, by 1921, two thirds of the men normally employed by British yards were out of work. The backbone of the British economy, the coal industry, was menaced by increasing continental competition (spurred on by German reparations payments in coal, which made it possible for France to sell German coal to former British customers like Italy and the Scandinavian countries), as well as by the increasing use of oil and electricity in place of coal power. The scientific techniques that made coal production profitable in the United States were virtually unknown in England; the organization of the industry was highly inefficient; and the resistance of the coal producers to basic reform kept the industry in a state of depression throughout the whole interwar period. In addition to all this, the economy of the country was strained by the loss of its prewar foreign investments, the fiscal dislocations caused by the war, and the large debt owed to the United States.

Although it was not immediately perceived, Britain's old supremacy as a manufacturing and commercial power had gone for good. There was a brief postwar boom, but it was an artificial one that stopped as soon as other countries resumed production and began to compete with British goods. After that, the long period of stagnation began and unemployment began to mount. At the end of 1920, 690,000 of those workers registered under the National Insurance Act of 1911 were unemployed; by June 1921, this number had increased to 2,171,000; and, although it sank in the following year, it varied between one and one and a half million for the rest of the decade and doubled as soon as the great depression of the 1930s arrived.

The first postwar government, that of Lloyd George, tried to deal with this problem by passing tariff and other measures to protect key industries from competition and by placing obstacles to prevent countries with depreciated currencies from invading British markets. It also increased the government's contribution to the national insurance funds and thus made possible small relief payments to those out of work. But these were palliatives rather than cures; and "the dole," as the relief payments came to be called, gave the jobless sustenance without hope and, when it became a permanent feature of English life, as it did, tended to kill the spirit. The novelist J. B. Priestley wrote angrily in the 1930s: "The dole is part of no plan; it is a mere declaration of intellectual bankruptcy. . . . Nobody is getting any substantial benefit, any reasonable satisfaction, out of it. . . . The Labour Exchanges stink of defeated humanity."

Rather than this sort of thing, what England needed was a thoroughgoing reorganization of its industrial plant. This was quite apparent to leading economists, who pointed out that the fundamental weakness of the British economy lay in the fact that productive capacity had fallen off as a result of worn-out techniques, reliance upon man power rather than machine power, duplication of services, and uneconomic competition in the domestic market. The cotton industry, for instance, quite apart from its technical backwardness, suffered from uneconomic competition. Some 700 spinning and 1200 weaving firms were competing with each other, oblivious to the fact that their failure to consolidate placed them at a marked disadvantage in comparison with more efficiently organized foreign industries. The same thing was true of the coal industry, where 1400 independent producers vied with each other, many working mines too poor for efficient production. Consolidation here might make possible lower production costs and the introduction of much needed machinery. Without those improvements, Britain's share in the world market promised to decline even further.

Instead of being willing to make basic changes, the industrialists generally preferred to rely on government subsidies and, for the rest, to keep wages as low as possible. This was perhaps understandable. Less so was the toleration of this attitude by Parliament, which did not speak well for the quality of political leadership in this period. Commenting on this in one of his most biting essays, George Orwell suggested that the British ruling class had begun to decay; that, living as they did on the profits of firms run for them and on the returns on investments made for them by specialists, its members had lost any real function in society; and that, realizing this in a vague sort of way but wishing to retain both their position and their self-esteem, they had taken refuge in stupidity. "They could keep society in its existing shape only by being *unable to* grasp that any improvement was possible." There may be truth in this, although it is probably safer to say merely that England was now beginning to suffer from the loss of almost a whole generation of talent at Ypres and on the Somme. But, whatever the reason, it is undeniable that the general level of political intelligence and behavior in the interwar Parliaments was far below that of Parliaments of the nineteenth century, and there were few leaders of outstanding quality.

The Course of Politics / The prime minister in 1918 was still David Lloyd George, a man who, in contrast to his successors, did possess qualities of political genius and deserves to be ranked as a war minister with Pitt and Churchill. But the "Welsh Wizard" had no spells with which to ward off Britain's postwar troubles. His economic program, as Sir Llewellyn Woodward has written, was "a handful of amateur notions picked up at random." He was responsible for the dole but, aside from that, had little constructive to offer. His attention was, in any case, largely engrossed by foreign affairs and by the political troubles that his conduct of them brought down upon his head. Lloyd George was originally a Liberal, but he no longer represented the majority of that party and he depended, as prime minister, upon the support of the Conservatives. By 1922 they had grown tired of his leadership and the crisis in the Near East (see p. 541), which they attributed to his alienation of the French and his irresponsible encouragement of the Greeks, exhausted what was left of their patience. At a meeting of the Conservative party, the majority of those present voted to break the connection with Lloyd George, after listening to a speech by Stanley Baldwin, in which he acknowledged that the prime minister was a dynamic force but added that "a dynamic force is a very terrible thing." Lloyd George resigned immediately, and never held office again.

In the elections of October 1922, the Conservatives won a clear majority and formed a government under the ailing Andrew Bonar Law. The most prominent member of the government, and the successor to the post of prime minister when Bonar Law retired in May 1923, was Stanley Baldwin, and he was to remain the leader of the Conservative party until 1937. An earnest and patriotic man, he possessed few of the qualities that one expected to find in a prime minister, for he had neither knowledge of nor interest in foreign affairs, and his economic and social ideas were even more rudimentary than those of Lloyd George. A modest man, he was always the first to admit his mistakes, and this endeared him to large sections of the British electorate, despite the fact that the faults confessed were sometimes very serious indeed, as was true, for instance, of his miscalculation of the rate of growth of Germany's air strength in 1935.

Lloyd George once said that Baldwin was "honest to the point of simplicity." The remark was unkind, but it has some relevance to his approach to the pressing problems that faced his government. He believed that economic recovery would be best promoted by a demonstration of Britain's reliability as a debtor. After some complicated talks in Washington at the beginning of 1923, he accepted terms for the payment of Britain's debt to the United States that his own colleagues thought could have been improved by shrewder negotiation and were certainly less generous than those that the United States government subsequently granted to France and Italy. As a means of restoring international confidence in Britain and attracting trade, this had little effect, and it imposed a considerable strain on Britain's fiscal position for the next ten years.

If the Conservative party had no formula for relieving economic distress except this, the Labor party was no better. It is true that when the first Labor government was formed, after the elections of November–December 1923, the party had only 192 seats in the House of Commons to 258 for the Conservatives and 158 for the Liberals. It had to rely on Liberal support, and the price of this was the abandonment of any attempt to realize a truly socialist program. Even if Labor had had a majority, however, it is doubtful whether the party would have adopted a radically new approach to the economic problem, for neither Ramsay MacDonald, the prime minister, nor his chancellor of the exchecquer, Philip Snowden, were socialists in any systematic sense, and they were quite happy to follow the economic policies of the previous government, even to the extent of supporting Baldwin's fiscal policy. This led some of their supporters to moan:

> Oh Ramsay dear, and did you hear
> The news that's going round?
> They're cutting down our wages
> For the saving of the pound.

It is not easy to understand why MacDonald, with his upper-class tastes and admiration for the aristocracy, his fundamental lack of sympathy for organized labor, and his preference for foreign affairs rather than domestic, retained the leadership of his party so long. He did so because he possessed the charismatic quality necessary to leadership, always looking and acting like a great man, even though he was not one, and because he was adroit in manipulating the rival groups within his own party. In addition, as D. C. Somervell has written, the emotional idealistic oratory for which he was known appealed to a people that had stopped going to church but still craved sermons. Read today, these speeches show a remarkable emptiness of content.

> My friends, I see no end of the journey. We have come, we shall journey, and we shall go on, and our children coming after us will go on with their journey, and their children will go on with theirs. But, my friends, what you and I have to take care of is that the journey is both onward and upward.

This sort of thing may have given little intellectual sustenance but, delivered with conviction by this strikingly handsome man, it at least left its hearers in a state of comfortable befuddlement and made many of them followers of MacDonald simply because he was so sincere.

The principal efforts of the first Labor government were in foreign policy, where the negotiations were inaugurated that eventuated in the Dawes Plan (see p. 550) and a treaty was concluded whereby Great Britain accorded recognition to the Soviet Union (see p. 578). Despite the fact that the Anglo-Soviet treaty was little more than a formalization of relations established in the field of foreign trade in 1921, it led to a withdrawal of Liberal support from the MacDonald government, which therefore appealed to the country in new elections. The publication of the so-called Zinoviev letter (see p. 578) in the middle of the campaign scored heavily against Labor, and the Conservatives came back to power with a commanding majority. Baldwin once more became prime minister and by resuming his policy of fiscal conservatism, he proceeded to demonstrate that his year out of office had brought him no new ideas.

Indeed, he and his chancellor of the exchecquer, Winston Churchill, accentuated it, for in 1925 they returned to the gold standard at the prewar parity of the pound to the dollar. The economist John Maynard Keynes immediately accused the government of subordinating the true interests of British industry to the desire of the Bank of England and the Treasury to restore the prestige of the City of London as a financial center. The pound, he argued, was overvalued by at least 10 percent, and revaluation meant an immediate rise in the price of British exports sold abroad. Unless they wished to lose their share of the foreign market, the export industries, already hard hit by the trade slump, would have to reduce their costs, and the only way they could do this was by driving down wages. Events soon proved that Keynes' argument was sound.

The General Strike / It was perhaps inevitable that the failure of the postwar governments to make a constructive attempt to deal with the continuing depression would lead, sooner or later, to some form of violent protest on the part of the working class, especially since the syndicalist philosophy of direct action (see p. 305) was still influential in many of the large unions. But the return to the gold standard was perhaps the chief reason for that protest taking the form it did. No industry was affected more deleteriously by this step than the coal industry which, after an artificial spurt in 1923, caused by the stoppage of coal production in the Ruhr during the French occupation (see p. 550), was now suffering from the effects of the resumption of German coal exports in 1924. The added shock of the revaluation of the pound led the mine owners to announce, in June 1925, that previous wage agreements must be terminated and that wages must be reduced and working hours lengthened immediately.

It was this decision that led, by slow degrees, to the general strike of 1926. The Miners Federation refused to accept the owners' proposals or even to discuss a new agreement until they were withdrawn, and in July 1925, with the backing of the General Council of the Trades Union Congress (TUC), they threatened comprehensive strike action. To avoid this, Mr. Baldwin persuaded the mine owners to postpone their intended changes, pending an investigation of the industry by a royal commission, and agreed to support them in the interim by renewed government subsidies.

This action was widely criticized by the Conservative and Liberal press as a capitulation to blackmail and Bolshevism, and one of Baldwin's ministerial colleagues warned that the nation would have to decide whether it was to be "governed by Parliament and the Cabinet or by a handful of trade union leaders." The union leaders would have been well advised to take note of the hardening of middle-class opinion after July 1925. They did not do so and, while their more irresponsible members alienated moderate opinion by making triumphant speeches about the imminence of the victory over capitalism, they adopted a position in the pending dispute that made a reasonable solution impossible.

This became clear when a commission, headed by Sir Herbert Samuel, was appointed to investigate the industry and made its report in March 1926. It recommended a basic reorganization, to start with the cessation of subsidies, the closing down of pits that could not pay their way, and a temporary reduction of wages until the effects of reorganization took hold. To people outside the industry these proposals made sense, and even some labor leaders—notably Ernest Bevin, the head of the Transport and General Workers Union—felt that the temporary sacrifices might be worth making to secure the long-needed reorganization. But the Miners Federation proved to be as opposed to basic change as the mine owners themselves. While the owners were reluctantly constrained to accept reorganization in principle, the miners refused to com-

The British general strike of 1926. Here London policemen rescue a food van after strikers had tampered with the engine. Many trucks were marked "food only" in the hope that they would not be attacked. (WIDE WORLD)

mit themselves to it unless they were assured in advance that there would be no departure from current rates of pay.

When matters came to a head at the end of April 1926, the government proved less than effective in mediating the dispute. The intransigent statements of the miners and the renewal of the strike threat convinced a sizable group in the Conservative party and the ministry that the time had come to put an end to union threats, and Baldwin did not dare defy this by taking any action that could be interpreted as another capitulation. On the other hand, the General Council of the TUC, while often irritated by the high-handedness of the miners, was too devoted to the principle of labor solidarity to break with or restrain them, and in any case felt that the government showed too little understanding of the merits of the miners' case. The leaders of the parliamentary Labor party played an ineffectual role throughout the last critical negotiations. Thus, the strike, which began on May 3, 1926, was the result of the rigidity and lack of statesmanship of all the interested parties.

The general strike of 1926 involved one sixth of the working population of England, Scotland, and Wales, including mining, all forms of transport, iron and steel, metals and heavy chemicals, building trades, and electric and gas power. Considering the prevalent unemployment, the risks taken by those who walked out in sympathy with the miners were great; and, as Alan Bullock has written, the response to the strike call was a remarkable demonstration of working-class unity. The strike was, nevertheless, ill-planned, and the leaders had not thought out the consequences of their action.

Since the previous fall, the government had had plans for the protection of necessary services and supplies, worked out by the able permanent under secretary in the Home Office, Sir John Anderson; and it had foreseen the necessity of using the Emergency Powers Act to take what other action was needed to protect the national interest. When the strike came, the flow of supplies was maintained; Hyde Park was closed and turned into a milk depot; volunteers were recruited to run trains and buses; and communications and public information were assured by the publication of a government broadsheet called the *British Gazette*, edited by Winston Churchill, and by the continued operation of the British Broadcasting Company, which was government-controlled. In contrast, the unions had no scheme of organization that provided liaison between headquarters and the local strike committees. Since they had called out the printers, they had no authoritative organ to keep their members informed and to counteract the influence of the Churchill sheet or the *Daily Mail*, which, printed in Paris and flown to England, was filled with articles purporting to prove that the strike was controlled by Soviet agents.

The union leaders were appalled by the discovery that, outside of the working class and Left intellectuals, there was virtually no sympathy for their cause. In their desire to demonstrate their power, they had failed to realize that their action would be interpreted by the great majority of the British people as an attempt to substitute direct action for parliamentary government. When this was brought home clearly to them, and when they saw, after the first week, that the government was not only determined to resist them to the end but, thanks to the volunteers, showed every indication of being able to succeed, their resolution began to wane. Strike funds were approaching exhaustion, and reports were beginning to trickle in of clashes between workers and the police that led them to fear that their members might get out of hand and provoke the government into using more forceful countermeasures. In consequence, the General Council of the TUC seized upon a new formula suggested by Sir Herbert Samuel, which called for the establishment of a National Mines Board to settle disputes and a general agreement that there would be no reduction of wages until measures of reorganization had been agreed upon. The TUC asked the miners to accept this as a new basis for negotiations. The Miners Federation, consistent to the last in its resistance to *any* wage cuts, refused; and the TUC called off the strike. The miners remained out for another six months but finally had to capitulate in December.

In a speech in Commons, the prime minister said that he would not countenance attempts to exploit the collapse of the strike in order to force down wages or destroy unionism. Thanks to this and a general feeling of relief that the strike had passed without a major explosion of violence, there were few reprisals. The miners were the hardest hit, having to go back to work at longer hours and lower pay in an industry which had, as a result of the long interruption of production, lost markets that it would never regain.

Perhaps the true importance of the general strike lies in the fact that it alleviated the tendency toward class conflict which had been growing in the first half of the decade. Thanks in part to the revolution in Russia, the middle classes had begun to be almost afraid of the common people; the uproar over the Zinoviev letter was a symptom of that fear. The strike helped put matters in their proper perspective and, once broken, left the middle classes less susceptible to the scare stories of the right-wing press than they had been earlier. Thus they never responded to the future growth of the labor movement with the exaggerated fear and resentment shown in other countries, including France.

The failure of the strike also contributed to a better relationship between the classes by discrediting Marxist and syndicalist theories about the inevitability of class conflict. Henceforth, wild talk about revolution was unpopular in labor circles; and, although the unions did not abandon the strike weapon, they kept it as a last resort and no longer thought in terms of concerted strike action, preferring to rely on other means, notably parliamentary ones, to gain their objectives. They therefore tended to follow the advice of their party rather than to dictate to it, and, since the Labor party always sought to widen its appeal beyond the working class, this too made for more understanding between the classes.

The Impact of the World Depression / All this was to the good, and it perhaps helps to illustrate the fundamental stability of Great Britain, which was able to withstand the fiercer storms that lay ahead during the world depression and the war.

It is nevertheless true that the failure of the general strike allowed the mine owners, other producers, and the government to relax, with the result that plans for basic industrial reorganization were dropped. In the long run, this obtuseness, and the parallel attempt of big business to seek protection by turning increasingly toward cartels and trusts, played into

he hands of the Labor party and helped it to persuade a growing
audience that productive inefficiency coupled with monopoly was not
o the public interest and must be corrected by nationalization of key
ndustries. But it was not until after 1945 that Labor had an opportunity
o realize its objective. Meanwhile the English economy continued to
stagnate until it was overwhelmed by the world depression.

Six months before the stock-market crash in New York, Parliament
reached its statutory term and new elections were held. The Labor party
eceived 290 seats, not a clear majority; the Conservatives, 260; and the
Liberals—the last time that this riven party appeared in significant
strength—60. MacDonald once more became prime minister and
Snowden, chancellor of the exchequer, with J. H. Thomas appointed to
deal with the problem of unemployment, a task in which he was aided
by Sir Oswald Mosley, one of the most brilliant of the younger men, who
was soon, however, to break away and set himself up as head of the
British Fascist party.

The efforts of the government to alleviate unemployment and other
problems proved ineffective in face of the avalanche that fell on them at
the end of 1929; and during the next two years matters deteriorated
steadily. By 1931, the Unemployment Insurance Fund was running in
debt at the rate of one million pounds a week. Destitution was widespread, especially in the so-called distressed areas in West Cumberland,
South Wales, and Tyneside, while the fiscal position of the country was
threatened by heavy withdrawals of gold from the Bank of England.
Snowden's answer to all this was a program calling for rigid economies
designed to balance the budget, and it was hinted that the sacrifices
called for might soon include a cut in the unemployment benefits.

These suggestions the bulk of the Labor party and the TUC rejected
angrily; and, on August 24, 1931, the government resigned. When King
George V asked MacDonald to head a new national, or nonparty, government, however, he agreed to do so, forming a ministry of four Laborites,
four Conservatives, and two Liberals. When it became clear that he
intended to carry out the kind of program that they had just repudiated,
the Labor party read him and the other Labor ministers (Snowden,
Thomas, and Lord Sankey) out of the party and went almost solidly into
opposition.

The National government came to be dominated by the Conservatives,
under the leadership of Baldwin and the rising man in Conservative
ranks, Neville Chamberlain. This was especially true after the elections
of 1931, in which 558 National Government candidates were elected
(471 Conservatives, thirty-five National Liberals, thirty-three Liberal free
traders, thirteen National Laborites) against an opposition of only fifty-
six Labor and five Lloyd George Liberals. Being a government of national

concentration, it gave a sense of purpose which helped bolster up confidence in the country, and it showed itself capable, at least sporadically, of determined action. Its first act was to correct the mistake that had been made in 1925 by abandoning the gold standard and allowing the pound to find its own level, which turned out to be 30 percent below parity. It also granted subsidies to shipping and tried to solve the problem of the distressed areas by relocating the unemployed; and in 1932 it brought eighty years of free trade to an end by going over to protectionism.

Even so, there was no large-scale comprehensive plan for recovery, nothing like the New Deal in the United States; unemployment remained high (2,000,000 in 1934 and 1,600,000 as late as 1936); and recovery did not get under way until the country began to rearm.

Ireland, the Near East, India, and the Commonwealth / Throughout this period, the British government was constantly preoccupied with imperial problems and with the rising tide of nationalism in certain of the British dependencies. Ireland was a center of particular unrest, for the decision to postpone the implementation of home rule (see p. 327) exacerbated anti-British feeling and led to the rise of extremist groups, notably the Sinn Fein ("Ourselves Alone") party. In Easter week of 1916, these groups staged a violent revolution, which was put down with much bloodshed and had tragic aftereffects. When elections for the British Parliament were held in Ireland in 1918, 75 percent of the constituencies elected Sinn Fein candidates. They immediately announced their refusal to go to Westminster and organized a separate parliament (the Dail Eireann) in Dublin, which proclaimed the Irish Republic, with Eamon De Valera as president.

The British government, not unnaturally, resisted; and there followed three years of violence, marked by outrages committed by the self-styled Irish Republican Army against police stations and military garrisons, and reprisals by a British auxiliary force, the "Black and Tans," recruited from former army officers. Lloyd George's plan to end these troubles by permitting the establishment of separate parliaments for Ulster and Southern Ireland was rejected outright by the Republicans, who aspired to a free and united country. But he persisted, and in December 1921, persuaded the southern leaders to sign a treaty that provided for an Irish Free State as a self-governing Dominion and left Ulster the option of belonging to the Free State or having a separate status. This was accepted by both Parliament and the Dail but was fought bitterly by the left wing of Sinn Fein under De Valera until the end of 1922, when William Cosgrave became president of the Free State. Under his quiet but capable leadership, the disorders came to an end, the boundary with Ulster, which had decided to remain apart, was defined, and the terms of the treaty of 1921, including those requiring allegiance to the king and granting naval and harbor facilities to Britain, were observed.

In 1932 De Valera was elected president and ended ten years of exile. His policy at first was one of whittling away the terms of the treaty without completely severing the tie with Great Britain; but, in May 1937, he piloted a new constitution through the Dail that made no reference to the treaty of 1921 or to the king and the Commonwealth. A year later, by concluding certain financial and tariff agreements and surrendering its port facilities, the British government recognized the independence of Southern Ireland. The North remained true to the Crown.

In several of its other dependencies, Great Britain had to make similar concessions to rampant nationalism. In Egypt, for instance, the movement for independence was so vigorous that it seemed expedient to yield to it and, in February 1922, the government announced that the protectorate was at an end and that Egypt was an independent sovereign state. To this grant there were reservations, for the British claimed the right to appoint a high commissioner to supervise the new Egyptian king's policy, to garrison the Suez Canal, to protect Egypt against foreign aggression, and to protect foreign interests and minorities. These limitations were unpopular with the Egyptian Nationalist party (Wafd), which became the majority party in Egypt in 1924 and carried on a constant campaign against the 1922 proclamation, using terrorism and political murder as its weapons. British patience and the threat posed for Egypt by Italy's invasion of Abyssinia in 1935 (see p. 691) tempered these excesses sufficiently to make possible an Anglo-Egyptian Treaty in August 1936, which gave Egypt complete independence on terms the British considered reasonable and gave Britain the right to station troops at the Canal and to use the naval base at Alexandria.

In the mandates taken over by Britain in 1919, there were also independence movements of varying strength (see p. 542). In 1930 the Labor government concluded a treaty with Iraq, recognizing its independence and agreeing to sponsor its admission into the League of Nations and to surrender its mandatory rights when this was effected. This promise was fulfilled by the National government, and the last British garrisons were withdawn from Iraq in 1935. Britain also extended limited self-government to Transjordan, while maintaining supervisory and military rights. The problems of these two countries paled into insignificance beside those of Palestine, where the British were engaged continually in efforts to keep the Arabs and the Jews from each others' throats and where their plans for a Palestinian parliament or, alternatively, for partition were rejected by both sides.

During the war, the secretary of state for India had announced that it was the intention of the British government in India to follow a policy of "increasing association of Indians in every branch of the administration and the gradual development of self-governing institutions with a view to the progressive realization of responsible government in India as an integral part of the British Empire." In the years that followed, however, progress toward the execution of this admirable program was too deliberate to please Indian nationalists, and the agitations of the All India Congress, the organization that had been working for self government since 1885, became increasingly radical throughout the 1920s.

The acknowledged leader of the Congress after 1921 was Mohanda Gandhi, a lawyer who had been educated in England and had worked for twenty years in South Africa, protecting the rights of Hindu immigrants. After his return to India in 1914, he had thrown himself into the fight for independence, urging his followers to rely upon the tactics of civil disobedience, passive resistance, nonviolent sabotage, and boycott of British goods. By sheer force of personality, Gandhi was able to create a movement that attracted world-wide attention and sympathy; but in India itself he was unable to overcome caste differences or the gulf between Hindu and Moslem, nor was he able to restrain those of his followers who periodically resorted to acts of terrorism against the British authorities.

Violence became the rule on both sides once the world depression began to be felt in India, for this led on the one hand to agrarian revolts and the murder of British officials and on the other to police brutality, the attempted suppression of all nationalist organizations, and the imprisonment of Congress members. The prospect of an indefinite continuation of these conditions was too much for Englishmen who remembered how ineffective repressive measures had been in Ireland; and, in 1935, despite the opposition of convinced imperialists like Winston Churchill, Parliament passed a new India Act that provided for a federation of all the provinces of British India and the Indian native states (that is, those ruled by Indian princes who had alliances with the British crown), with a constitution similar to those of the other British Dominions. Executive power was vested in a governor general appointed by the crown and responsible for national defense, external affairs, fiscal and tariff policy, and supervision of the civil service. The legislature was bicameral, and its members were appointed by the native princes or elected by indirect methods to represent communities. The provinces were granted rights of autonomous self-development and government but their governors were appointed by the crown. The franchise for provincial and national elections was restricted to about 14 percent of the population.

This constitution was more popular with the native princes, whose extensive powers were left undiminished, and with the Moslem League which believed in local autonomy and had always limited its end objective to Dominion status, than with the Congress, whose leaders now wanted outright independence. Gandhi's leading disciple, Pandit Jawaharlal Nehru, said of the new Act, "We will resist it, we will break it, we will tear it, and we will burn it!" Hindu agitation, therefore, continued to be a source of concern to the British government in the years before the war.

Among the other British Dominions, it was only in South Africa that there was serious trouble. Despite the statemanship of men like Botha and Smuts, Boer nationalism had continued to smolder and, in the 1920s, General Hertzog's Nationalist party, while denying any desire to break the connection with Britain, agitated for "sovereign independence." Elsewhere, the growth of nationalism strengthened rather than weakened the ties between Great Britain and the Dominions, while at the same time changing the nature of their relationship.

The nature of the change was defined when Parliament passed the Statute of Westminster in December 1931. This act recognized that Canada, Australia, New Zealand, South Africa, and the Irish Free State were independent states on a footing of legal equality with the mother country, and that, while freely united in common allegiance to the crown, they were subject only to those laws passed by the British Parliament to which they expressly assented, while their own laws could not be vetoed by the home government. By this act, the British Commonwealth of Nations came into being.

Britain and Europe / The gravity of economic problems at home and the complications of the Palestinian, Indian, and other colonial situations left the British Parliament with little energy or desire to concern itself with other foreign problems. This should be borne in mind when one considers the reluctance of the British government to intervene when Japan invaded Manchuria in 1931 or when Hitler and Mussolini began their depredations in 1935 (see p. 691).

Even if the governments of the early 1930s had shown a greater willingness to support collective security than they did, they would have had difficulty in persuading the public to give them the arms to make this possible. The general feeling in England throughout the postwar period was that money should not be spent on armaments when it could be devoted to the easing of social distress, and this belief was supported by a doctrinaire pacifism, which held that the best way to avoid war was to prevent the accumulation of new weapons. In the 1920s the army was cut to a level barely commensurate with Britain's imperial needs, and it was kept there. All branches of the service that were considered nonessential were cut to the bone or liquidated entirely. The tank corps was particularly hard hit, with the result that while the country possessed, in J. F. C. Fuller and Basil Liddell Hart, the most distinguished theorist of armored warfare in the world, it was the Germans rather than their own countrymen who studied their teachings and were ready to put them into effect in 1940. Similarly, the air arm was kept on such short ration that practically all experimentation stopped during the 1920s, and ardent pacifists went so far as to call for a boycott of the annual Hendon Air Show.

As long as there was any hope of general disarmament, this policy could perhaps be justified. After the virtual collapse of the Geneva Conference in 1933 (see p. 688), this was no longer true. Yet for some years it remained difficult to persuade the British people that the time had come to start building up their armed strength. "The whole country," Stanley Baldwin wrote to Conservative candidates in 1933, "irrespective of party, is solidly united in favor of peace and disarmament." In 1934 when the National government took the first hesitant steps toward increasing defense expenditures, it was attacked by Labor M.P.s who claimed that rearmament was "neither necessitated by any new commitment nor calculated to add to the security of the nation." (Neither they nor the ministers they were attacking had any way of knowing that two of the steps taken in 1934—the decision to double the armament of the new Hurricane and Spitfire fighter planes and the beginning of the construction of a radar warning system—would save the country from defeat in the Battle of Britain in 1940.) So heavy were the attacks on the government at the time that Baldwin, who was always responsive to the popular temper, postponed the bulk of his program, with the result that serious rearmament did not get under way until 1936 and did not become effective until 1939.

The policy of appeasement, which will be discussed in the next chapter and which contributed to the collapse of democracy in Europe, must be considered in connection with the relative weakness of Britain's armed strength. In the last analysis, this was the result of the economic troubles through which Britain had passed since 1919, troubles that had not succeeded in shaking the British people's faith in their own democracy but tended to make them inattentive to the threats to European democracy as a whole.

THE FRENCH REPUBLIC

Economic Recovery / The postwar history of France presents an interesting contrast with that of its neighbor across the Channel. In recovering from the physical damage wrought by the war, the country showed a remarkable resilience and achieved a degree of prosperity that could not be matched by Britain. Hidden beneath this surface well-being, however, were those serious social cleavages and political resentments that had never died since 1870 (see p. 369); and, when the storms of the 1930s swept over France, these proved to be strong enough to destroy the foundations of the French democracy.

No country had suffered more heavily during the war than France. Its casualties had been in the neighborhood of four million, of whom 1,300,000 had been killed and 120,000 permanently disabled; and its material losses had been greater even than those suffered by Belgium, Poland, and Russia, to say nothing of those belligerents whose soil had been spared the physical impact of the fighting. Battles like those for Verdun and the Somme had taken place in its most populous and industrialized departments, and the resultant damage to the nation's economic potential was enough to make the strongest heart quail.

Yet, within a few years, France had removed most of the ravages of the war and seemed in a fair way to complete recovery. The government threw all its resources into the task of clearing away the rubble that covered the northeastern part of France, restoring the five million acres of devastated farm lands to cultivation, rebuilding the 800,000 houses and farm buildings that had been destroyed, dredging the damaged canals, and repairing the 600 miles of railroad that had been made inoperable in the department of the Nord alone; and by 1926 it had completed a job of reconstruction that was described by D. W. Brogan as "the greatest economic achievement of postwar Europe."

The very necessity of reconstruction from the ground up brought unexpected advantages. In contrast to British industry, which resisted basic reorganization and modernization, French industry had no choice. It had to rebuild completely, and it did so with modern equipment and techniques, with the result that French textile mills, steel plants, and coal mines were soon operating on a level of technological skill unsurpassed by any of France's competitors. Industry was supplied, moreover, with important new resources. The reacquisition of Lorraine gave France one of the great iron fields of the world and enabled it to become a very considerable steel exporter; and the recovery of Alsace so strengthened the textile industry that France soon became the third largest of the world's producers of cotton goods. Since the markets of the world were also clamoring once more for French articles that defied competition—the wines of Burgundy and Beaune, and the products of Chanel and Mainbocher—French trade revived with gratifying swiftness.

The full effects of this recovery were not felt until an answer was found to the difficult financial troubles of the first postwar years. These stemmed from the aversion of the typical Frenchman to paying taxes and the tendency of French politicians to defer to this feeling. As a result France had entered the war with a heavy debt and had come out of it with a greater one, since no new taxes had been imposed during the conflict except a levy on excess profits and a tax on luxury goods, neither of which was very effective as a means of raising revenue. In 1918 the government had debts in the neighborhood of 150 billion francs, and these were increased rapidly by the costs of reconstruction. It had, of course, been expected that the Germans would pay all the costs of the war; but, before the first reparations installments had been received, the government had to borrow money for its ordinary, as well as its extraordinary, expenses. Moreover, since the Germans never lived up to the unreasonable expectations of their victors (and could not be compelled to do so by maneuvers like the invasion of the Ruhr [see p. 550]), it had to continue to borrow until investors began to show reluctance to lend, which did not take long. At the beginning of 1924, a government loan yielding 6.29 percent actually failed to find enough takers; after that the franc began to slip rapidly in the world market.

Parliament was slow in dealing with this problem and spent perhaps an excessive amount of energy in cabinet-making and cabinet-wrecking (there were six cabinets and seven different ministers of finance in the twelve months following June 1925), but in the end they did solve it. In July 1926 a cabinet of all the parties to the Right of the Socialists was formed under the leadership of Raymond Poincaré, whose extreme nationalism and rigid legalism had been responsible for the Ruhr debacle. His long experience in French politics and his always abundant energy served the country well at this critical juncture, for, within thirty-five days, he had carried through a program of basic reform that saved the nation from what had appeared for a time to be possible bankruptcy. He increased taxation of all kinds and improved the system of collection; he imposed a series of administrative economies; he did away with the former system of several different budgets and unified the accounting system; and he negotiated a new loan with the Bank of France that enabled him to balance the budget and drive the value of the franc up to about one fifth of its prewar value, where it was pegged by France's return to the gold standard in 1928. This amounted, in effect, to a capital levy on the rentier class, who were deprived of four fifths of their savings and, in a sense, made to pay for the war. But it relieved the government of most of its capital charges and enabled French industry, for a time, to undersell its competitors in foreign markets; and the very vigor of the government's actions bolstered confidence in the parliamentary system.

The five years that followed were years of solid prosperity. Industry and agriculture flourished; and small businesses and services profited from the yearly discovery, by thousands of happy and financially solvent tourists, of the delights of the Côte d'Azur, the rich beauties of Chartres, and the heady excitement of Paris. There was no unemployment problem and no other social problems serious enough to inflame political tempers; and the avowed enemies of the regime had few issues to exploit. There had been a Communist party in France since 1920, when the left wing of the United Socialist party seceded during the party conference at Tours; and in 1922 the *Confédération Générale du Travail* (see p. 305) had also suffered a split, which resulted in the founding of a Moscow-oriented *Confédération Générale du Travail Unitaire*. Neither of these organizations waxed fat in the years following Poincaré's reforms. Nor did the inveterate foes of the republic who stood on the Right. The *Action Française* (see p. 370) was still alive, but no one regarded it as a serious threat to French democracy.

The Colonial Empire / France's possessions, like Britain's, girdled the globe and, in addition to old settlements like St. Pierre and Miquelon in the Gulf of St. Lawrence, Martinique and Guadeloupe in the West Indies, the island of Réunion, and various stations in India, included Algeria, the protectorates of Tunis and Morocco, Equatorial and West Africa, Somaliland, Madagascar, New Caledonia and islands in the Pacific, and the greater part of Indochina. To these were added, at the war's finish, the mandates of Togo and Cameroon in Africa and Syria in the Near East.

During the war, nearly two million troops had been raised by the colonies, including 680,000 fighting men, and this aroused new hopes that union between the homeland and the colonies would be useful in maintaining France's postwar power position, while at the same time forming a great economic community, the parts of which would have specialized functions and would be mutually interdependent. In general, French imperial policy, especially in Africa, was well designed to produce the native confidence that was necessary for any such development. French investors, however, were slow to support the policies that would have given a real push toward modernization of the more backward colonies, and they were discouraged further by the heavy expenses of colonial administration in the more unsettled dependencies.

The showcase of French imperialism was Algeria, which had been French since 1830 and had gradually been made an integral part of the home country, so that it was now considered to form three departments of France and was entitled to send ten deputies to the Chamber. In 1919 native Algerians were offered citizenship, and two years later they were given a share of local government. Throughout the 1920s, this policy of integration showed every sign of working, and the country, despite some economic setbacks, was generally prosperous and satisfied. This was true also of the neighboring protectorate of Tunisia, thanks to careful concessions made by French officials to nationalist groups and the institution of collaborative economic enterprises. Morocco, on the other hand, despite the tremendous achievements of the great soldier-administrator Lyautey in pacifying the tribes, instituting basic agricultural reform, and transforming Casablanca into a modern port, continued to represent a heavy financial burden throughout the 1920s. This was largely due to the rising of the tribes in that part of Spanish Morocco called the Riff. Under a tough and tenacious leader, Abd-el-Krim, the Riffi drove the Spanish garrisons out of their own part of Morocco and then, growing more ambitious, extended their operations into French Morocco as well. The French phase of the Riff war consumed much of 1925 and 1926 before Abd-el-Krim was forced to surrender, and its costs hurt all of the other French colonies.

Morocco was not the only French dependency that was the scene of native war. In Syria, Arab nationalism was as potent as it was in neighboring Iraq, and none of the administrative schemes introduced by the French blunted it. In 1925 rioting in Damascus and a simultaneous revolt on the part of the Druses placed local French garrisons in serious jeopardy, and the danger was not relieved by the bombardment of Damascus by General Sarrail, which simply made the insurrection general. Sarrail was recalled and a new commissioner sent to the area, but it was not until 1927 that even relative calm was restored, and there were frequent clashes in the years that followed.

On the other side of the world, Indochina represented an enormously rich area where French colonial administrators had followed a policy of frank exploitation to a much greater degree than was true in colonies closer to home. This had unfortunate results. Throughout the postwar period, the younger generation in all parts of Indochina found inspiration in the Chinese revolution and in the teachings of communism, especially the propaganda beamed by the Soviet Union to the underdeveloped areas. Nationalism on an organized scale was slow to grow, but it was able to take advantage of peasant unrest when the world depression forced prices down in the early 1930s. In Annam, Tonkin, and Cambodia there were outbreaks of violence in the decade before World War II came to the area.

When the Popular Front government was formed in France in 1936, its leader Léon Blum warned that there would be more risings throughout the colonies unless positive steps were taken to conciliate nationalist feeling. By that date, however, Frenchmen were too preoccupied with troubles closer to Paris to give much of their minds to the colonies.

The Impact of the World Depression / It is perhaps a sign of the solidity of Poincaré's reforms that France was the last country in Europe to be affected by the storm that had started in New York in 1929. But the curtailment of the tourist trade, the cancellation of orders for luxury goods, and the tendency toward economic nationalism on the part of countries already suffering hard times eventually eroded the bases of French prosperity. Since France remained on the gold standard even after Great Britain and the United States had abandoned it, the prices of its goods were soon too high for effective competition and exports fell off rapidly. By 1932 the country was in the same desperate position as its neighbors. Unemployment and social distress made their appearance; and, as they did so, the people looked to their government for the kind of effective corrective action that had solved the crisis of 1926. When it was not forthcoming, their faith in parliamentary government began to weaken, and the extremists gained a new hearing.

The French Chamber proved incapable of taking determined action, largely because of unbridgeable differences of principle between the government parties. The elections of May 1932 resulted in a victory for the parties of the Left, the strongest of which were the Radical Socialists, led by Édouard Herriot, and the United Socialists, led by Léon Blum. Effective collaboration by these parties proved impossible because the United Socialists' prescription for the depression was a program that included nationalization of key industries and the Bank of France, increased taxation on the upper brackets, introduction of the forty-hour week as a means of reducing unemployment, and extensive government pump-priming in the form of public works. The Radicals, on the other hand, represented the interests of small businessmen, holders of government obligations, and middle-class farmers; and they considered all the above ideas reprehensible, preferring to rely upon a program of rigid governmental economy. This incompatibility led to a degree of ministerial instability (there were four ministries in little more than a year) that irritated the public and led to mounting criticism of the political system.

This was reflected in the rapid growth of communism but also, and more spectacularly, in the revivification of antirepublican organizations of the Right, which now took on a distinct fascist tinge. In addition to the old *Action Française*, which now spawned an auxiliary organization of young thugs called the *Camelots du Roi*, the most important of these was the *Croix de Feu*, which had been founded in 1927 as a society of war veterans but had now become, under the leadership of Colonel de la Rocque, a militant group of young conservatives. In addition, there were the *Jeunesses Patriotes*, which had been founded to carry on the tradition of Déroulède's League of Patriots (see p. 360) but bore a marked similarity to Mussolini's *Squadristi*; the *Solidarité Française*, founded by the perfume manufacturer Coty, which was violently anti-Semitic and professed a preference for government by dictatorship; the *Francistes*, who dressed like Hitler's S.A.; the Neo-Socialists of Marcel Déat, who were ideologically indistinguishable from the National Socialists; and others—all with not inconsiderable numbers of members.

Like the British Fascist party, to which fleeting reference has been made above (and which never attained any significant strength), the rise of these groups was stimulated by the contrast between the apparent inefficiency of parliamentarianism and what seemed to be the vigor and purposiveness of the totalitarian regimes of Italy and Germany. Their arguments appealed to many respectable and responsible Frenchmen who were concerned about the inadequacies of the present political system. But they also grew as a result of encouragement and support given them by selfish interests—by the heavy industries represented in the *Comité des Forges* and the banking groups represented in the Bank of France, who were alarmed by the strength shown by socialism in the elections of 1932 and by Blum's projected program of nationalization and heavy corporate taxation.

In 1934 the Republic experienced another of the scandals that seemed to stud its history, and it proved, before it was over, to be more serious than the Panama scandal of 1892 (see p. 363). A stock manipulator named Serge Stavisky was arrested for having issued some fraudulent bonds and committed suicide to escape imprisonment. It was soon discovered that he had been arrested for fraud in 1926 but had never been tried, thanks to repeated postponements of his case, which were due, it was alleged, to the intervention of republican politicians. The conservative press, financed by the same interests that supported the Fascist Leagues, began to trumpet that the government had been involved in a conspiracy with Stavisky and his kind to defraud the French people and that the police had "suicided" Stavisky in order to prevent his revealing the names of his accomplices. The failure of the government to investigate the matter promptly and to take vigorous action against people found guilty of laxity lent an air of veracity to the charges; and, since the economic slump had been in no wise relieved, popular indignation was intensified. On February 6, 1934, in response to a call for direct action issued by the whole of the rightist press, the Royalist and Fascist Leagues, supported by thousands of students and by some Communist groups, assembled in the Place de la Concorde and tried repeatedly to storm the Chamber of Deputies. They were dispersed with great difficulty and only after the police had used fire hoses and small arms against the crowd. The night's rioting caused twenty-one deaths and 1600 other casualties. More important, it led to the resignation of the cabinet then in power, despite

Léon Blum, 1872–1950.

the fact that it could claim the support of the majority of the Chamber. It appeared, in short, as if action on the street was on the point of supplanting rule by law and parliamentary procedure.

The Decline of the Republic / For the next two years—more precisely, until the elections of May 1936—French affairs were directed by a series of emergency cabinets, which did not represent the will of the people as it had been reflected in the last parliamentary poll of 1932 and which often included men who were, overtly or secretly, opponents of the republican form of government (like Pierre Laval and Philippe Pétain, to name only two). Whether their political sympathies had anything to do with their lack of vigor in pushing the French armament program and in showing resistance to the first aggressive moves of Hitler and Mussolini would be difficult to prove conclusively; and, in any case, there were other reasons for these deficiencies. The French people were as reluctant as the British to support heavy military expenditures in time of economic depression, and they were no more perceptive than other people when it came to discerning Hitler's true objectives. The fact remains, however, that the first significant victories of the dictators were won while France was ruled, as a result of the disorders of 1934, by stopgap governments.

During these two years, the Fascist Leagues grew in strength and activity, and their imitation of the street tactics of their German predecessors stimulated the growth of a militant countermovement of the Left, in the shape of the Popular Front, which was formed by the beginning of collaboration between the Radicals, the Socialists, and the Communists in 1935. In the 1936 elections, these parties won a great victory and formed a government under the leadership of the Socialist Léon Blum, one of the most courageous and capable republican figures of this period.

When Blum took office, the fiscal stability of the state was threatened by a flight of gold from the country, and industrial production was seriously handicapped by a wave of sit-down strikes. Blum sought to check the first of these dangers by reorganizing the Bank of France and bringing it under government control and by negotiating international agreements for monetary cooperation; he tried to cope with the second by introducing the forty-hour week, by establishing labor's right to use collective bargaining in making contracts, and by promising annual holidays with pay. These and other government measures—the nationalization of the arms industry, for example—further stimulated the suspicion and hatred of the Right and led it to accuse the Republic, not only of being corrupt, but of falling under the influence of communism.

Although Blum's opposition to fascism at home and abroad did not seem vigorous enough for his Communist partners, who soon withdrew their support from his government, it seemed dangerously impolitic to people who, as Hitler grew in strength, remembered the losses of the last war and feared the results of another. Blum's opponents exploited this fear too, arguing that his tactics would, unless checked, precipitate a conflict that would ruin France and benefit only Soviet Russia. The more reactionary newspapers began in 1936 to make a point of explaining the horrors of modern warfare and the inadequacy of French armaments to their readers, while repeating that the Soviet Union was seeking to involve France in wars for its own advantage. As the foundations of collective security were systematically undermined by the dictators, this argument was used against anyone who suggested resistance. "French intervention in the Spanish war," Le Candide explained, "would be the beginning of the European conflagration wanted by Moscow." "France's present condition, its prestige, its authority are not increasing in strength," argued the Revue de France in 1938, "the facts, alas, prove it," and hence opposition to the dictators would be foolhardy. During the Czechoslovakian crisis (see p. 703), the Action Française argued that any attempt to save the imperiled democracy would lead "to an absurd objective and a disastrous result."

Propaganda like this was the end result of the series of events set in train when the world depression destroyed the foundations of the economy, revealed old habits of parliamentary inefficiency, revived antirepublican hatreds, and led inexorably to a dangerous bipolarity of political life. In these circumstances, which encouraged the growth of defeatism, the possibility of French democracy withstanding an all-out offensive by the dictators was dubious.

THE LESSER STATES

The Low Countries and Switzerland / Despite economic troubles and some trying political disputes, neither Belgium nor the Netherlands showed any strong symptoms of political weakness in the period under review. Belgium came out of the war and the long German occupation with a problem of reconstruction and industrial reorganization similar to that of France but smaller in scope, and with troubles caused by the decline of Antwerp, which was suffering from the diminution of German trade and the transfer of the overseas trade of Alsace-Lorraine to French ports. Thanks to planning and hard work, however, recovery was steady; and the worst of the problems of adjustment to new conditions were eased by the passage of social-insurance legislation which was actively promoted by the growing labor movement. On the political side, the Belgian government had to deal with the old tension between the Flemings and the Walloons, which the Germans had made more serious by encouraging the hope of Flemish separation. In 1921 the country was divided along language lines into two administrative sections, and later laws divided the army in the same way and made other concessions to the Flemings, notably in the field of education.

Loyalty to the existing regime was assured by the popularity of the wartime king, Albert I, who continued on the throne until his death in 1934; and political extremism made little headway in the country. It was not, however, entirely without influence. In the 1930s a fascist movement, the Rexists, was organized by Léon Degrelle and received active support from Hitler and Mussolini; and, by working in cooperation with the extremist wing of the Flemish nationalists, it helped effect an important change in Belgium's foreign policy, one that was disadvantageous to the cause of democracy in Europe.

At the Peace Conference of 1919, Belgium had been freed of the restrictions placed upon it by the treaty of 1839 (see p. 31) and was allowed to pursue an independent foreign policy. The postwar governments elected to ally with France and, after 1920, to collaborate with it in a common defensive system (see p. 547). In 1936, after the German military occupation of the Rhineland, King Leopold III announced to his Council of Ministers that Belgium must follow an exclusively national policy and, the next year, both the British and French governments, acting presumably on Belgian insistence, released the country from its obligations under the Locarno Treaties (see p. 551). This retreat to neutrality, doubtless taken to still the nationalist anti-French agitations of the Flemings and the Rexists, did not protect Belgium in 1940.

The domestic politics of both Holland and Switzerland remained calm throughout the period. In Switzerland, the notable tendencies were an increase of the powers of the national government at the expense of the cantons, and a further extension of state socialism and government responsibility in the fields of agriculture and industry. The use of the instruments of direct democracy in politics was continued and widened. In Holland, politics had a more conservative cast. The most pressing problems for the Dutch government proved to be colonial rather than domestic ones. Throughout the 1920s, there was unrest in the Far Eastern dependencies, with riots in Java and Sumatra and, by the beginning of the next decade, a growing nationalist movement in all parts of Indonesia. In Europe, as the conflict between the democracies and the totalitarian states loomed up, both countries tried to preserve their traditional neutral position.

Northern Europe / In a period in which democracy was retreating in many parts of the continent, it made solid gains in the Scandinavian countries. The newest of these, Finland, started its life with a tumultuous period in which Red formations supported by the Bolshevik regime in Russia and White Guards led by General Mannerheim and backed by the German General von der Goltz's Iron Division fought for control of the country. By May 1918 the last Red units had been defeated and, after the armistice, the Germans were withdrawn; and the country could think about organizing itself. In the middle of 1919 a democratic constitution was adopted and the first president was elected. Finland had rich timber resources and a flourishing paper industry; and, thanks to agrarian reforms begun in 1922, one person in three owned his own land. The country prospered throughout the interwar period, and its economic and political health was shown by the pride the Finns took in their institutions and in their graceful capital, which has some of the finest public buildings in Europe. Its faith in democracy was shown also in the stern laws passed against political extremism (forbidding, among other things, the maintenance of political fighting groups) and the bravery with which its citizens defended their system when it was attacked in 1940 (see p. 717).

In the kingdoms of Denmark, Norway, and Sweden, prewar progress toward democracy was carried further in this period. A new Danish constitution of 1915 brought universal suffrage and liberal reform to that country; and here, and in the two neighboring states, there was a notable growth of Socialist and Labor parties that remained true to the revisionist ideal of peaceful evolution by parliamentary means. Communism made little headway in Scandinavia. In all three countries progress toward economic democracy was steady, and there were strong cooperative movements.

The Iberian Peninsula / The story in southwestern Europe was a less happy one. Portugal, weakened by a gallant but costly participation in the world war, was afflicted by grave economic dislocations that were in no way relieved by the incompetence and corruption of its politicians. In 1926 the government was overthrown by a military coup, and General Antonio Carmona became president and dictator, legitimizing his power in 1933 by promulgating a new constitution. In 1928, this strong man appointed Professor Antonio de Oliveira Salazar as his chief aide, investing him with greater and greater power as his administrative and financial gifts became apparent. In 1932 Salazar became prime minister and, in the following year, supervised the adoption of the new constitution. In subsequent years, he assumed dictatorial powers, and if he employed them for the material improvement of his country, it remains true that his regime was not characterized by respect for civil liberties. Free party development was not permitted in Portugal, and the government intervened with a stern hand when signs of opposition appeared.

Finally, in neighboring Spain, the first decade after the war saw the gathering of forces for what promised to be a great victory for democracy but led in the end to one of democracy's most dramatic and fateful defeats.

During World War I, Spain remained neutral, but its internal history continued to be plagued by the turbulence and the ministerial instability that marked the prewar period (see p. 335). Conditions deteriorated further as a result of colonial troubles; and the disastrous war in the Riff in particular seriously weakened public confidence in the monarchy, especially when it was discovered that King Alfonso XIII had taken a personal hand in planning the offensive that led to the battle of Anual (July 1921) in which 10,000 Spaniards were killed and 15,000 taken prisoner. To save his throne, the king connived in a plot by which the captain general of Catalonia, Don Miguel Primo de Rivera, seized power in September 1923. The regime that he proceeded to establish bore a marked similarity to the one currently being consolidated in Italy; and, indeed, both Alfonso and Primo de Rivera showed the utmost cordiality toward Mussolini. Inside Spain, opposition parties were banned, and the press and the universities were subjected to new controls. On the other hand, the government showed a new vigor in dealing with old problems. An extensive public-works program was instituted; the transportation net was modernized, with resultant benefits to the economy; and, in 1926, in collaboration with French forces, the army was able to end the war in Morocco.

Despite its initial successes, Primo de Rivera's dictatorship soon began to show signs of weakness. It never developed any mass support and never appealed, as Italian fascism did, to the intelligentsia or to the youth. Men like Miguel Unamuno and José Ortega y Gasset, who during the war years had called for a national regeneration, turned away in disgust from the brutalities, the thought control, and the crude materialism of Primo de Rivera's dictatorship; and even the army, which had put him in power, began to defect. The coming of the world depression exhausted what was left of his reputation, and the king hastened to disembarrass himself of his presence by asking him to resign in January 1930.

The sovereign had outlived his usefulness by this time also; and, as republican agitation grew in every part of the country during the next year and began to make inroads in the armed forces, Alfonso XIII decided to go into exile. On April 13, 1931, he fled, and the Republic was proclaimed, amid widespread jubilation during which 200 churches were burned to the ground.

The constitution of December 1931 declared that "Spain [was] a workers' republic" and sought to lay the foundations for economic as well as political democracy. Legislative power was vested in a single chamber or Córtes, to which the ministry was responsible. Alcalá Zamora was elected president, and the veteran republican leader Manuel Azaña became prime minister. The new government immediately launched a program that was designed to destroy the old ruling forces of the country: the church, the plutocracy, and the army. The Jesuit order was expelled, state schools were established to diminish the church's role in education, large estates were confiscated, and a beginning was made toward a more equitable distribution of arable land, railroads were nationalized, as was the Bank of Spain, the eight-hour day and social insurance were introduced, and, finally, the officer corps of the army was reduced by almost a half.

Some of these measures were clearly unworkable. The Jesuits had to be allowed to continue to run some schools, otherwise there would not have been enough teachers. The plans for industrial and agricultural reorganization had to be decelerated in order to prevent the total breakdown of the economy. Thus, the old governing forces were weakened but left with enough power to do something about their grievances, while the beneficiaries of the revolution began to feel that the pace of change was not fast enough.

The result was that the new republican regime was soon confronted with peasant rioting, military plots, anarchist outrages, monarchist agitations (encouraged by the elections of November 1933 in which the Left parties received severe setbacks), separatist movements, labor strikes, and the beginning of a new fascist movement, the Falange, led by one of Primo de Rivera's sons. In October 1934 a revolt of the miners of the Asturias all but destroyed the city of Oviedo and caused 3000 deaths before it was suppressed.

At the beginning of 1936, the moderate Republicans joined with the Socialists, the Catalan and Basque Nationalists, the Anarcho-Syndicalists, and the Communists to form a Popular Front on the French model and, in the elections of February, they won an impressive victory. A government was formed under Azaña, and the program of 1931 (which had been in abeyance since the elections of November 1933) was pushed ahead once more. The rightist parties began a bitter campaign in which they claimed that the government was directed from Moscow (although there were at this time no Communists in the cabinet, only fifteen in the Córtes, and only a few hundred in the country); and the Falange, in particular, resorted to acts of terrorism that soon provoked reprisals. On July 12, 1936, Falangists murdered a young lieutenant of the Republican Assault Guards. On the next day, Calvo Sotelo, finance minister during Primo de Rivera's dictatorship, was shot and killed in retaliation.

It was this last bloody act that served as a signal for the army coup that had long been in preparation. On July 18, 1936, General Francisco Franco flew from the Canary Islands to Morocco and raised the flag of revolt. Ten days later, using German planes, Moroccan troops began to cross to the mainland, and there now began the civil war that was to destroy Spanish liberty and bring the international conflict between democracy and dictatorship to a new pitch of intensity.

27

The Road to War, 1933-1939

Distracted by the rigors of the depression and the internal political problems caused by it, the democratic nations reacted slowly and with little urgency to the beginning of a new era of aggression by the totalitarian states. Their leaders were facile in inventing excuses both for the lawless acts committed and for their own disinclination to do anything about them, and they were supported for years by their peoples, who wanted to be assured that foreign affairs would not add to their troubles.

The first example of this blindness to reality came in 1931–1932, when the Japanese government, under the influence of its military leaders, created an incident in Manchuria and used it to begin the systematic conquest of that Chinese province, actually placing a puppet ruler on its throne in February 1932. Although the League of Nations appointed a commission to investigate, which subsequently recommended the censure of Japan, the democratic states failed to agree to apply sanctions against the aggressor or to try by any other means to make it withdraw from Manchuria. Their parliamentarians, and editorial writers in their newspapers, vied with each other in citing economic and military arguments to prove the inexpediency and probable ineffectiveness of sanctions, as well as elaborate proofs that forbearance and understanding would in time solve the dispute to everyone's satisfaction. The ordinary citizen, if he thought of the matter at all, accepted these arguments and took

Is It Beginning to Dawn upon the Diplomats? "Entirely between us, messieurs, a new peace should really be created; the old one doesn't seem to be capable of living." (The cross is labeled "Versailles.")

This pregnant comment by Karl Arnold appeared in *Simplicissimus* in the year (1932) that saw the collective security system gravely shaken by the Manchurian crisis.

comfort in the thought that what happened in a place as remote as Manchuria could not possibly affect him. This attitude merely encouraged more flagrant assaults on the public law so that, in the last analysis, the failure to stop Japan in Manchuria led inexorably to its attacks in 1940 and 1941 upon French, Dutch, and British possessions in the Far East.

It is perhaps not hard to understand the slowness of the democracies to appreciate what was at stake in the Far East in 1931; but it is more difficult to explain their fatal failure to respond to the danger posed by the rise of Adolf Hitler to power in 1933. The brutalities of his storm troopers in his first months of office might have been expected to warn the west that a regime whose domestic practices were so contemptuous of law would probably have a foreign policy with the same characteristics. But they did not see the connection between Hitler's foreign and domestic policies, nor did they for years understand the end objectives of his activity in the foreign sphere. Meanwhile, they deluded themselves with the notion that what Hitler really wanted was merely a revision of the Versailles Treaty and the restoration of Germany's 1914 boundaries, and that he would become a law-abiding citizen as soon as he was satisfied on these points. Their delusions helped make another war inevitable.

HITLER'S FOREIGN POLICY

Hitler's views on foreign policy were largely formulated under the shock of Germany's collapse in 1918. What thoughts he had had about the subject before that time were incoherent and disjointed. While he was a schoolboy in Linz, he seems to have become a Pan-German nationalist. This tendency was strengthened after 1909 when he lived in the slums of Vienna in close proximity to hundreds of rootless and impoverished wanderers from the Slav lands of the east, all of whom he came to detest and to regard as a potent threat to Germanic civilization which must be resisted. The war in its turn made him a convinced militarist with a preference, which never left him, for military solutions to political problems. But the basic ideas that guided his future foreign policy were not worked out systematically until 1918, when, in the face of a defeat that dumbfounded him, he began to analyze the reasons for it.

William II's foreign policy had ended in disaster, Hitler convinced himself, because both its objectives and its methods were mistaken and because inadequate efforts had been made to assure it of public support if and when it got into difficulties. The emperor had been an expansionist, but the expansion he sought had taken the form of foreign trade and colonial acquisition. Hitler was convinced that heavy reliance on trade was to the benefit only of the Jews who controlled it, and that annexation of areas like South West Africa brought no tangible national benefits but merely helped to disperse Germans and to divert their strength from greater aims. William II's tactics in pursuing these objectives were equally faulty and alienated all the powers with a reputation for strength and reliability, leaving Germany with only Turkey and the decaying "mummy state," Austria-Hungary, as allies. When Germany finally had to go to war, these countries were of little help to it. Germany was handicapped further by the fact that the government had not taken care to suppress or render harmless those elements within the country—moderates, internationalists, pacifists, Marxists, Jews—who could not be counted on to fight till the end. As a result, these groups stabbed the German army in the back and imposed upon their country a shameful peace.

From the beginning of his career as a popular tribune in the postwar years, Hitler made attacks upon the peace settlement a constant ingredient of his speeches and propaganda. Since this emphasis was later to confuse western statesmen, it is well to note that Hitler never regarded the Versailles Treaty as an unjust one. He wrote shortly after the war, "If I were a Frenchman, and if the greatness of France were as dear to me as that of Germany is . . . I would not act differently than Clemenceau did [in formulating the peace terms]." The settlement was a natural penalty of defeat; and Hitler fulminated against it not because it was unjust but because it was inconvenient. He was always infuriated by people in his audience who answered his attacks on Versailles by shouting "Brest Litovsk!," failing to see that Brest Litovsk (see p. 563) had been a "good" peace because it was to Germany's advantage, whereas Versailles was a "bad" peace because it prevented bigger and better Brest Litovsks. "One could," he wrote, "have crushed one's head against the wall in despair about such a people."

But even worse than these moralists were those Germans who seemed to believe that, because he attacked Versailles, Hitler was arguing for a restoration of the frontiers of 1914. When he wrote *Mein Kampf*, Hitler said (in one of those passages not read soon enough in London and Paris):

> The demand for the re-establishment of the frontiers of the year 1914 is political nonsense of such a degree and consequences as to look like a crime. Entirely aside from the fact that the frontiers of the Reich in the year 1914 were anything but logical, they were in reality neither complete with respect to the inclusion of people of German nationality, nor intelligent with respect to geo-military appropriateness. They were not the result of considered political action, but momentary frontiers of a political struggle in no way concluded.

Implicit in this cloudy statement was a rejection of mere treaty revision and the announcement of a future program of expansion that promised to be much more ambitious than anything dreamed of by William II. It would, moreover, involve a fundamental departure from the main line of imperial policy. Hitler wrote:

> A policy of land acquisition cannot be carried out in a place like the Cameroons, but is today almost exclusively possible only in Europe. [We must think in terms of] winning land which increases the area of the motherland itself and thereby not only keeps the new settlers in the most intimate community with the land of their origin but insures to the total area those advantages deriving from its united magnitude.

This meant that Germany must expand eastward, effectively removing the Slav threat by doing so, and bringing under control the most fertile and the strategically most secure land in Europe. In a significant passage in *Mein Kampf* Hitler wrote:

> We National Socialists consciously write FINIS under the aims of the foreign policy of our prewar period. We start where an end was made six hundred years ago. We stop the everlasting German movement toward the

south and west of Europe and turn our eyes towards the land in the east
. . . When in Europe today we speak of new territory, we cannot help
thinking in the first instance of Russia and the border states that are subject
to her.

If not in his speeches, then at least in *Mein Kampf*, Hitler made it clear
that, unless the other powers submitted cravenly to his will, German expansion could not be effected without a new war. The idea of war ran
like a red thread throughout the book, and its author constantly reiterated
the principle that all foreign policy must be predicated on the assumption
that war was coming. Indeed, William II's failure to act on that assumption was one more reason for his downfall.

In the post-Versailles world, Hitler believed that war was made inevitable by France, for no matter who ruled that country, "whether Bourbons
or Jacobins, Bonapartists or bourgeois democrats, clerical republicans or
red Bolshevists, . . . France relentlessly throttles us." The projected
Drang nach Osten could not begin until this threat was removed, and it
could in all probability be removed only by war.

To prepare for that, the mistakes made by William II must not be repeated. This time the home front must be prepared for war, and this
preparation would involve basic political changes. Instead of the welter
of parties that existed before and during World War I, all political parties
must be subordinated to, and coordinated by, the state—as must all other
independent organizations, whether political, economic, religious, or
purely social. All potential dissidents—especially Jews and Marxists—
must be liquidated; and, in accomplishing this task, "all humanitarian and
esthetic considerations become absolutely meaningless." Hitler admired
the way in which Mussolini had dealt with such groups and wrote of "the
great man south of the Alps who, in his hot love for his people, did not
make pacts with the domestic foes of Italy but strove to destroy them by
every means wherever he found them." Germany must act in the same
way so as to be able to pursue its foreign aims with a united will and
determination. The future *Gleichschaltung* (see p. 637), in short, was the
prerequisite of a successful expansionist policy that would probably have
to be effected by war. This was the connection between foreign and domestic policy that the western powers failed to perceive when the Nazi
domestic purges began in 1933.

The second step preparatory to war was the acquisition of more
efficient allies than "the putrid state corpses" with which Germany had
been allied in 1914. Fascist Italy would be one such ally. But more important, if its collaboration could be won, was Great Britain—the most
valuable of allies, Hitler wrote, "as long as its leaders and the spirit of
its masses permit us to expect that brutality and toughness" which had
characterized Britain's policy in the past. To gain an alliance with Great

Britain, Hitler was willing to make great sacrifices—the sacrifices that should have been made before 1914. He was willing to renounce colonies and sea power and even, apparently, industrial challenges in the markets of the world in order to bring Britain to his side and, thus, to isolate and make possible the destruction of France.

But the crushing of France was not to be regarded as an end in itself but rather as "a means of subsequently and finally giving our nation a chance to expand elsewhere." And that elsewhere, of course, was Eastern Europe.

These views, formulated immediately after 1918, elaborated in many speeches, and put down in cold print in *Mein Kampf* in 1924 for all the world to see determined the main line of Hitler's foreign policy after he came to power in 1933. But, as Hermann Rauschning warned, in a passage written in 1938 to people in the west who were belatedly beginning to take *Mein Kampf* seriously, Hitler was greater than his book, which must not therefore be taken as an exact blueprint. If Hitler followed the pattern laid down in *Mein Kampf*, he was not bound by the details and was perfectly willing to adjust them according to circumstances. It should be remembered also, Rauschning pointed out, that Hitler had "carried to a pitch of virtuosity the pursuit of tactical elasticity."

HITLER'S POLICY IN ACTION

The First Years, 1933–1935 / Tactical elasticity was the hallmark of Hitler's foreign policy in the first years of his power, when a misjudgment or a false step might have been fatal for him. He had three things that he wished to accomplish in this first phase. He wanted to complete domestic preparations for a dynamic foreign policy by *Gleichschaltung*, by ordering affairs in his own party, by beginning to build up his armed forces. He wanted to regain Germany's freedom of action in foreign affairs by withdrawing from engagements entered into by Stresemann and Bruening. And he wanted to test the other powers' will to resistance in order to calculate the speed with which he might move toward his objectives when he had accumulated appreciable armed strength. Hitler had his setbacks in these years, but he did not expose himself to any serious danger, and what he learned about the other powers encouraged him to believe that he would achieve all he desired.

Nothing better illustrates the technique with which Hitler advanced his objectives than his withdrawal from the Disarmament Conference and the League of Nations in 1933. Hitler had inherited the disarmament negotiations from his predecessors. In the negotiations that began in Geneva in 1932, German negotiators had already won a significant victory by persuading the other powers at long last to grant Germany equality of status in armaments. This concession did not particularly please Hitler; nor was he interested in obtaining other concessions, for these might deprive Germany of a grievance that he wanted to exploit. After all, if the Disarmament Conference should succeed in devising a new arms-control plan acceptable to all other powers, Germany would have no excuse for refusing to abide by it and would be subjected to continued controls. This Hitler was determined to avoid.

He did so by using tactics that foreshadowed those he would employ in the Sudeten affair of 1938: he made demands that he was reasonably sure the other powers could not accept. He insisted that equality of status was not enough but that, since the other powers were reluctant to reduce their forces to Germany's level, all controls on its military establishment must be lifted so that it could seek actual equality in its own way. Needless to say, the French government blocked all attempts to yield to this point of view. In October 1933, Hitler withdrew from the Disarmament Conference and, for good measure, from the League of Nations as well.

Before taking this daring step, Hitler appealed, in a number of effective speeches, to the guilt complex of all those in the west who felt that the Versailles Treaty had not treated Germany fairly and that France was stubborn in seeking to hold to the letter of a settlement which should have been revised long ago. He also stated repeatedly that Germany would adhere to any mutual agreements for total elimination of offensive weapons and was prepared to enter pacts of friendship with anyone who desired to conclude them. This left the other governments with the feeling that, if he were treated adroitly and not threatened with sanctions or reprisals, he would return of his own accord to the League and to the disarmament discussions. The persistence of this idea was remarkable, especially in England, where, as late as the spring of 1939, Neville Chamberlain told reporters that he thought there was still a good chance of a reopening of the disarmament conference, with German participation.

In reality, the Fuehrer had broken once and for all with disarmament talks and with all kinds of collective-security arrangements. He continued to affirm his faith in international collaboration; but, whenever a concrete proposal was made for realizing it, he sidestepped it or refused it by indirection, insisting that he was quite willing to enter agreements for the maintenance of peace, provided they were bilateral agreements. The other powers were so anxious to believe that Hitler was a man of peace that they dropped their more comprehensive projects and, in two notable cases, made the kind of agreement he preferred—forgetting that bilateral pacts could be broken whenever Hitler wished to break them.

Hitler's first success was his conclusion of a nonaggression pact with Poland in January 1934. The Fuehrer's withdrawal from the League and the Disarmament Conference had worried some of his advisers, for—coupled with the progressive cooling of relations with the Soviet Union and the breaking of the old tie between the *Reichswehr* and the Red Army—this seemed to indicate that Germany was headed for a dangerous isolation. The Polish pact, the possibility of which occurred to Hitler as early as April 1933, at least reduced the potential danger of trouble on Germany's eastern flank while simultaneously driving a wedge into the French security system in Eastern Europe (see p. 646).

What was gained here was lost almost immediately by the unfortunate impression created by the Blood Purge of June 1934 and, more important, by the Vienna *Putsch* of July 1934, in which Dollfuss was killed (see p. 650). Despite all of Hitler's disclaimers, it was well known that he had supplied arms to the Austrian Nazis, permitted them to broadcast their propaganda from a station in Munich, and allowed the formation on German soil of an Austrian Legion whose apparent mission was to invade Austria. Momentarily, it appeared that Italy, at least, might be ready to take military action against Germany; but the storm blew over, and the powers returned to their attempt to convince Hitler to collaborate with them in some form of collective security. The British and French governments, after consultation with the Italians, offered Germany what is today called a package deal. In return for a grant of complete equality in arms, Germany would adhere to certain armament-control conventions and would cooperate in new mutual-assistance pacts designed to give security to Eastern and Central Europe. They also expressed the hope that Germany would consider returning to the League.

This comprehensive set of proposals was drawn up in February 1935, and the British foreign secretary, Sir John Simon, and Anthony Eden made preparations to go to Berlin to discuss it in the first week of March. Hitler had other ideas. He contracted a diplomatic cold and asked that the British visit be postponed for three weeks. Then, on successive Saturdays, he made two announcements that made the Anglo-French proposals pointless. On March 8, 1935, he let it be known that Germany had a new military air force (it soon transpired that the air force was not, as a matter of fact, new but was already as large as Britain's). Then, on March 15, he announced that he no longer intended to abide by any of the military clauses of the Versailles Treaty and that he was expanding the German army from its legal size of 100,000 officers and men to a 36-division force of 550,000.

Prosit!
Herr Hitler: "The more
we arm together, the
peacefuller we'll be!"
Sir John Simon: "Well—
er—up to a certain point
—and in certain cases—
provisionally—perhaps."

From *Punch*, March 27,
1935. © *Punch*.

Hitler calculated that the very effrontery of these actions would confuse the other powers and make effective counteraction impossible; but, in order to make sure of this, he intimated to the British government that he was prepared to make a separate naval agreement with them. The British proved more receptive to this than to suggestions that Hitler be forced to withdraw his unilateral repudiation of the arms clauses of the treaty. Immediately after the announcement of March 15, the governments of Britain, France, and Italy sent representatives to a conference at Stresa to discuss countermeasures, and the western press talked of a "Stresa Front" that was preparing to take punitive action. But the essential artificiality of this "front" was shown in June, when the British, without consulting the other partners, concluded an agreement with the German government that gave Germany the right to build a fleet 35 percent as large as Britain's and also to construct as many submarines as it desired.

The motives of the British are still somewhat murky, although it is probably true—as Sir Samuel Hoare has written—that they saw in this arrangement a good bargain: a guaranteed superiority over the German fleet that was twice as great as the one they had had in 1914. But the solidity of this advantage depended, of course, on Hitler's good faith, which, even in 1935, there was plenty of reason to distrust. Aside from this, there was no avoiding the fact that the Anglo-German Naval Pact had, in a real sense, legitimized Hitler's repudiation of the arms clauses of the Versailles Treaty by being in itself a violation of those clauses.

Abyssinia and the Rhineland / What was left of the Stresa Front after this body blow disappeared in October 1935 when the Italian member of the combination invaded Abyssinia. Italy had long been interested in this sprawling semifeudal country and, on two occasions (see pp. 450 and 458), had paid for its interest with humiliating military defeats. Mussolini seems to have regarded the domination of Abyssinia as the first step toward the creation of a colonial empire that would make Italy the most powerful state in the Mediterranean and the Near East. Since the beginning of his term of power, he had engaged in negotiations with other Near Eastern powers and with local rulers to advance this end. He was no more successful than Crispi had been before him (see p. 458) in winning his way by diplomacy and treaty arrangements, and he decided that he could do so only by military means. He did not believe that the western powers would interfere with his plans, because they were distracted equally by the depression and by the problem of the new Germany. In any case, he seems to have received secret intimations from the French foreign minister, Pierre Laval, that France would give Italy a free hand in the area. Fortified by these assurances, the Duce seized upon an incident that took place in December 1934 at Walwal on the border between Abyssinia and Italian Somaliland, in which fighting between Ethiopian and Italian forces led to thirty Italian deaths. He charged Abyssinia with aggression and started preparations for war.

Under the energetic leadership of Haile Selassie I, who had ruled the country since 1917, Abyssinia had made a considerable amount of political and social progress, and, as early as 1923, it had been admitted to membership in the League of Nations. The League now used all its resources to adjudicate the dispute, in the hope of maintaining peace; and most of 1935 was given over to attempts to appease Italy by offering it territory and economic rights at Abyssinia's expense. All of these Mussolini rejected, meanwhile pushing ahead his military plans, and in October he inaugurated hostilities.

This action threatened to elicit more determined counteraction from the west than Mussolini had imagined. It is true that the French government was unenthusiastic about resistance to the Duce's plans, for they wished to reserve what energies the depression left them for opposing Hitler. The British people, on the other hand, were furious over Mussolini's callous indifference to the public law; a wave of genuine enthusiasm for the League was sweeping the country; and the government, in response to this, showed every indication of giving material support to Abyssinia, even at the risk of war with Italy. British fleet units were concentrated in the eastern Mediterranean; pledges of support in the event of an Italian attack upon these forces were solicited and received from Yugoslavia, Greece, Turkey, Czechoslovakia, Rumania, and—albeit reluctantly—France; and, on October 11, 1935, under British leadership, the League Assembly—in the first example of such action—voted economic sanctions against Italy. These went into force on November 18.

The crucial commodity in the conflict in Abyssinia, however, was oil and, unless this was cut off, Italy would not be seriously inconvenienced. To avoid so drastic a blow to Italy as would be represented by oil sanctions, Pierre Laval made one more attempt to find a compromise solution, and he persuaded the British government to cooperate. The proposal was worked out in December between Laval and Sir Samuel Hoare, the British foreign secretary; it was supposed to be secret, but someone leaked the details to the French press, which published them. The revelation that the two statesmen were apparently prepared to give Mussolini very extensive tracts of Abyssinia and virtual control over its trade and resources, caused a sensation. Alfred Duff Cooper wrote later: "During my experience of politics I have never witnessed so devastating a wave of public opinion." Hoare was forced to resign and the plan was jettisoned, but the incident had unfortunate effects. It compromised the western cause, at least in the eyes of the United States, whose cooperation in economic sanctions was vital if Italy were to be stopped; and it caused a period of mutual recrimination between London and Paris that necessarily postponed effective action.

All this worked to Mussolini's advantage. He proceeded with his campaign, inspiring his armies with a grandiloquent statement in which he attacked his western critics for their voting of sanctions. He said:

> The Italian people is capable of resisting a very long siege, especially when they are certain. . . . that right is on their side and wrong on the side of a Europe that does dishonor to itself. The war we have begun on the soil of Africa is a war of civilization and liberty. It is a war . . . of the poor, the disinherited, the proletariat. Against us is ranged the front of conservatism, selfishness and hypocrisy. . . . It is a trial . . . which is a test of our virility.

The references to civilization and liberty rang decidedly false in the ears of Europeans who noted with disgust that the Italians, whose troops outnumbered the Ethiopian forces and were vastly superior to them in the quality of their hand weapons and artillery, were not content with these obvious advantages but felt called upon to attack spear-bearing tribesmen with military aircraft and—despite international conventions forbidding its use—poison gas.

Even with these means, the war was not an easy one. There was bitter fighting throughout the winter months and, despite a series of Italian victories in the first months of 1936, the Abyssinian emperor still had a large undefeated army under his personal command. This heartened those in the west who continued to work for the imposition of more stringent economic limitations on Italy; and Anthony Eden carried on extensive negotiations with other League members with the objective of winning assent for oil sanctions against the aggressor. At the beginning of March it appeared as if these talks might have a fruitful result—but at the crucial moment this hope was dashed by the third of what came to be called Hitler's "Saturday Surprises." On March 7, 1936, Hitler marched troops into the Rhineland, simultaneously repudiating the Locarno Treaties and those clauses of the Versailles Treaty which stipulated that this area must be kept free of military garrisons or installations.

This was the most daring of Hitler's actions to date, and he had had difficulty in persuading his generals of its wisdom. The generals felt that the French would resist and that, if they did, they would have no difficulty in expelling the Germans, who were few in number (the troops which crossed the Rhine, for instance, being only in battalion and company strength). Reason was on the side of the generals; but Hitler, who relied not on logic but on what he called his *"schlafwandlerische Sicherheit"* (sleepwalker's assurance), proved more realistic than they. In France the Popular Front had not yet taken power and a stopgap government under Albert Sarraut had to deal with the crisis. Its members proved to be badly split on the question of what should be done, and Sarraut called in the soldiers to help clarify the situation. Sarraut wrote later that he was dismayed to find that they lacked "that *élan*, that tautening of the muscles, that combative feeling" which had always characterized the French army. The commanders seemed to have an inflated conception of German strength, to be unwilling to act without general mobilization, and to be unenthusiastic about action in any circumstances. This attitude had a dampening effect on the cabinet. They now put the thought of military action out of their minds—although, as Winston Churchill wrote later, a clear request for British military support of a Rhineland operation could hardly have been refused and although the Polish government had intimated its support of such an operation. They entered upon a fruitless exchange of diplomatic notes that let Hitler get away with his breach of treaty law.

It is impossible to overestimate the importance of the Rhineland coup. By virtually destroying the Locarno Treaties, it lowered the stock of all international conventions and brought further discredit on the Geneva system, which had been already seriously weakened by the Manchurian and Abyssinian crises. This increased general insecurity and led the smaller states to revise their commitments—Belgium, for instance, decided in the wake of the Rhineland coup to withdraw from the French security system (see p. 677). All of France's military alliances suffered from Hitler's action, and even the strength of its western border defenses, the much-advertised Maginot Line, seemed diminished now that German troops were once more poised west of the Rhine. The French themselves seemed to feel their stature had been reduced, and it is from this point that the defeatism which was to be so significant a force in 1938 and 1940 began to grow.

Finally, the Rhineland coup put an end to any serious attempt to apply oil sanctions against Italy. Mussolini was able to finish his military operations without interference and to announce in May, when his troops entered Addis Ababa, that "Ethiopia is Italian—Italian in fact, because occupied by our victorious armies, and Italian by right because, with the sword of Rome, civilization has triumphed over barbarism."

The Spanish War and the Axis / There had been moments during the Abyssinian war when Mussolini had fallen prey to doubts and hesitations; but, as his troops mopped up in Abyssinia, these fleeting apprehensions gave way to a new excess of confidence. The thought of making the Mediterranean a Roman lake appeared to him now to be within the range of possibility; and, when the Spanish Civil War erupted in July 1936, he saw in it an opportunity for promoting his ambition. He decided to intervene on the side of the rebels.

It was this decision that led him finally to make a deliberate attempt to seek closer relations with Hitler. Up to this time he had watched the rise of his fellow dictator with mixed feelings and, although he was one of the chief beneficiaries of Hitler's Rhineland stroke, he was reported to have been angered by it and to have sat at his desk furiously twisting and untwisting paper clips as the news of it was received. Now he felt it expedient to court Hitler's favor, and thus began that fateful series of events which led to his complete subordination to Hitler's will.

It is significant, for instance, that in the same month that marked the beginning of the Spanish war Mussolini advised the Austrian chancellor, Schuschnigg, to seek an improvement of Austro-German relations. This Schuschnigg did, signing an agreement which, although it was not widely realized at the time, significantly advanced the cause of *Anschluss*. For a cessation of German attacks upon his government and a spurious promise that Germany would not interfere in Austrian internal affairs, Schuschnigg engaged to follow a foreign policy that would "always be based on principles which correspond to the fact that

Austria acknowledges itself to be a German state." In a world in which Hitler claimed to be the judge of what was true German-ness, this was a perilous admission. Equally dangerous was the oral agreement by which Schuschnigg agreed to allow German social and cultural organizations to have branches in his country and to give a greater share of political responsibility to "representatives of national circles" (that is, Nazi sympathizers).

Despite his previous statements about the importance of Austrian independence, Mussolini not only approved of these terms but claimed, in conversation with German representatives, that he had inspired the Austrian request for an agreement with Germany. He used the Austrian agreement, in short, as a proof of his good intentions in his attempt to win German friendship. For his own reasons Hitler received these overtures graciously and, in October—in conversations with Mussolini's son-in-law and foreign minister, Count Ciano—agreed that Germany and Italy were natural allies against the democracies and that he was prepared to support Italy's policy in Spain. Mussolini was gratified and, on the afternoon of November 1, 1936, from a balcony in the Piazza del Duomo in Milan, announced that the Berlin conversations had resulted in a comprehensive understanding and created a new "Berlin-Rome line . . . not a diaphragm but an axis, around which can revolve all those European states with a will to collaboration and peace."

Meanwhile, the emphasis on peace in these words was being belied by his intervention in Spanish affairs. The background of the Civil War has been touched on above (p. 681). The point which must be made here is that, without foreign aid, the rebel cause might have collapsed before the end of 1936. Although part of the Spanish army went over to General Franco at the outset, he was unable to get control of either the navy or the air force, and this would have proved to be a serious deficiency had not Italy, and to a lesser extent Germany, come to his aid. In a conversation with Hitler in 1940, Ciano recalled that at the beginning of the war "Franco had declared . . . that, if he received 12 transport or bombing planes, he would win the war in a few days. Those 12 planes had grown into more than 1000 planes, 6000 dead, and 14 billion lire." In the battle of Brihuega in 1937, the Franco forces were supplemented with four full Italian divisions. The fighting quality of these "volunteers" was not always high, and there was occasional suspicion that Mussolini was attempting to solve his economic problems by sending his unemployed to Spain; but the total Italian contribution to the Franco cause was impressive, in size at least.

The German contribution was smaller but no less important. In addition to weapons shipments that were heavy enough to worry the army staffs at home, the Germans sent the Condor Legion, which comprised

Guernica, 1937, by Pablo Picasso (1881–   ). On loan to the Museum of Modern Art, New York, from the artist. The painting was inspired by the German Condor Legion's ruthless aerial bombardment of a defenseless town during the Spanish Civil War.

four fighter-bomber, four fighter, one reconnaissance, and two seaplane squadrons, all of which were detached from the new *Luftwaffe*; they were of inestimable value to Franco's operations. Germany also sent one tank battalion under General von Thoma, who used it for training purposes and, by skillful dilution of German personnel, created four tank battalions and thirty antitank companies for Franco before 1938. Some elements in the Nazi party advocated a greater commitment than this, but Hitler seems to have been more interested in seeing that the Spanish war was prolonged than in trying to end it, for its continuation was sure to keep Mussolini involved and might also create crises of which he could take advantage.

The Spanish Republic found it more difficult to get material aid, even though it was the legitimate government of Spain. Much was later made of the fact that it received assistance from the Soviet Union, which was held up by the Republic's enemies as proof that Spain was a potentially Communist state. Yet, as the Germans themselves admitted privately, the Russians intervened reluctantly and only because they dared not lose face with the Communist parties of the west; their help was limited to advisers, technicians, some aircraft, and supplies which had to be carried to Spain by merchant ships, and their aid was not continuous, stopping a full year before the end of the war. The Republican fighting forces, composed of loyal army and navy units, plus contingents from trade unions, universities, and the Catalan and Basque nationalists, were supplemented by brigades of international volunteers, among which were the Abraham Lincoln Brigade and the Thälmann Colonne, named after the German Communist leader. These brigades were not large and their equipment was sometimes scant. The Republican government had hoped for aid from the Popular Front government in France (see p. 676); but of the three government parties there, only the Communists advocated aid, and Blum, while sympathetic to the Republican cause, could overcome neither the opposition of the Radicals nor the pacifism that now became dominant in his own party. Moreover, after the Rhineland, France was more dependent than ever before on British backing for its policies, and the British government set its face against any intervention in Spain.

Throughout 1936 the British people were occupied with pressing domestic matters that made concentration on foreign affairs difficult. In January King George V died, and the subsequent months were given over to preparations for the coronation of his successor, the popular Edward VIII. Before the coronation, however, it was discovered that he desired to marry Mrs. Wallis Simpson, an American divorcée. When efforts to dissuade him failed, a constitutional crisis of first importance arose. It was settled in the end by the king's abdication and the accession of his brother as George VI, but not until the winter of the year, months after the onset of hostilities in Spain.

Through this crisis, which if badly handled might have destroyed the monarchy or seriously weakened the unity of the Commonwealth, the country had been piloted with skill and patience by Stanley Baldwin, who succeeded Ramsay MacDonald as head of the National Government in 1935. In 1937, he retired in favor of Neville Chamberlain and this event soon brought about an important change in foreign policy. Whereas Baldwin was frankly uninterested in foreign affairs, Chamberlain had decided opinions in this sphere. Specifically, he believed that the time had come for a new realism that would seek to stop the deterioration of international affairs not by repeating old shibboleths but by trying to discover the real grievances of the dictators, to correct them, and to attain a general appeasement. Enunciated by Chamberlain, a confident and forceful man, these views appealed to many people, who failed to note that collective security and support of the League were among the ideas that he considered outworn, and who also failed to reflect that, since the things which the dictators wanted all belonged to other nations, the appeasement policy could probably be made to work only at their expense.

The British had taken the initiative in September 1936 in organizing a Committee on Non-Intervention, with twenty-seven participating nations, including Germany, Italy, and the Soviet Union. The ostensible purpose of the committee was to prevent the shipment of men, war materials, and munitions to the belligerents in Spain and to withdraw any volunteers already there. The German delegate to the committee wrote home that, as far as he could see, the real purpose of the committee was the task "of pacifying the aroused feelings of the leftist parties in France and England by [its] very establishment" and that neither the British nor the French government would allow it to take any real action. This proved to be all too accurate a forecast. The Italians and the Germans not only continued their aid to Franco but advertised it. In August 1937, for instance, the news associations printed a telegram from Mussolini to Franco in which he openly mentioned the role of Italian troops in the battle of Santander and promised that "this brotherhood in arms, already close," would continue. The committee proved ineffective in stopping this sort of thing; and, when questions were raised in the House of Commons about similar incidents, government spokesmen took the line that even to try to prevent them might result in more serious conflict.

By the time Chamberlain became prime minister in May 1937, it was clear that the rebels would win the war in Spain if things continued as they were. The new prime minister was apparently willing to accept this outcome. He was anxious to inaugurate his appeasement policy by reaching a new understanding with Mussolini. He soon made it clear that it was time for Britain to recognize the Italian conquest of Abyssinia formally and to accept Mussolini's assurances that he would recognize British interests in the Mediterranean and would withdraw his volunteers from Spain *after* the Civil War was over. Mr. Chamberlain's foreign secretary, Anthony Eden, pointed out that this policy betrayed the principle of collective security and gave Franco and Mussolini a victory which might bring grave strategical disadvantage to Great Britain. But the prime minister had his way and, in February 1938, Eden resigned his office. After that, there was little possibility of any interference with the dictators' designs in Spain. Even those Englishmen who had advocated aid to the Republic earlier were distracted by a new eruption of violence in the Far East. In 1937 Japan inaugurated the second stage of its drive to dominate all Asia by launching a full-scale attack against China, which promised, before it was finished, to affect British Far Eastern interests; and in November, when the Japanese joined Germany and Italy in the so-called Anti-Comintern Pact, Mr. Chamberlain was given one more reason for wishing Spain out of the way so that he could concentrate on reaching an understanding with the head of that combination, Adolf Hitler. Finally, the attention of both the British and French peoples were soon completely absorbed in Central European affairs, so that the last stages of Franco's victory went almost unnoticed.

The war in Spain was fought with great bravery, much savagery, and tremendous destruction on both sides. By the spring of 1939, when Franco's armies finally broke Republican resistance in Catalonia and advanced on Madrid, Spain's condition was pitiable. One million persons had been killed, wounded, or exiled and every part of the country showed the wounds of war. The words of the poet Lorca, himself a victim of the first stages of the war (he was killed in 1936) seemed to have come true:

> *las lágrimas amordazan al viento,*
> *y no se oye otra cosa que el llanto.*[1]

The end of the war led to the establishment of a new one-party dictatorship in Spain, which immediately (in April 1939) adhered to the Anti-Comintern Pact and began a tub-thumping campaign for the return of Gibraltar to Spain. It weakened France's strategical position in any dispute with Germany by placing a potential enemy on its flank. It deepened the tendency toward defeatism in the democracies and carried the principle of collective security closer to bankruptcy. And it strengthened the suspicion that already existed between the western democracies and the Soviet Union. Stalin, a supporter of collective security at the beginning of the war, said at its close:

> Far be it for me to moralize on the policy of nonintervention, to talk of treason, treachery, and so . . . . It must be remarked, however, that the big and dangerous political game started by the supporters of the policy of nonintervention may end in a serious fiasco for them.

The Anschluss / On November 5, 1937, in a secret conversation with his service chiefs and his foreign minister, Adolf Hitler informed them that the time was coming for Germany to solve its problem of living space (*Lebensraum*). The first stages of the solution were to be the acquisition of Austria and Czechoslovakia. The exact date for the beginning of the drive would depend upon the political events in the next months and years (the state of relations between Italy and the western democracies being particularly important in this connection), but he made it clear that "if the Fuehrer was still living, it was his unalterable resolve to solve Germany's problem of space at the latest by 1943–1945." He urged the service chiefs to speed up their current programs but—in answer to a direct question from General von Fritsch—indicated that he still thought the time of action reasonably remote.

Two weeks later, however, the new British foreign secretary, Lord

---

[1] "Tears muffle the wind, and nothing else is heard but the weeping." "Casida del llanto" from *Diván del Tamarit* (1936).

Halifax, talked with Hitler, and the result of this visit was to make Hitler revise his timetable. According to Baron von Neurath,

> Halifax admitted of his own accord that certain changes in the European system could probably not be avoided in the long run. The British did not believe that the *status quo* had to be maintained under all circumstances. Among the questions in which changes would probably be made sooner or later were Danzig, Austria, and Czechoslovakia. England was only interested in seeing that such changes were brought about by peaceful means.

To make this kind of suggestion to Hitler was dangerous, for it seemed to indicate that the British were thinking purely in terms of form rather than of strategy and interest; and, if that were true, why should he wait any longer? France seemed paralyzed by internal troubles and would be incapable of independent action of any kind. The Fuehrer decided to liquidate Austria.

Before doing so, he carried through that basic reorganization of the armed forces which was designed to assure him of its absolute reliability (see p. 643). That done, he accused the Austrian government of violating the provisions of the Austro-German Pact of July 1936, started a violent press campaign against the Schuschnigg government, and in February 1938 summoned the Austrian chancellor to consultations at Berchtesgaden. By threatening to invade Austria in case of noncompliance, he browbeat Schuschnigg into agreeing to legalize the Austrian Nazi party, to fill the posts of minister of war, minister of finance, and minister of the interior with pro-Nazis, to establish closer relations between the Austrian and German armies, and to submit to preparations for "the assimilation of the Austrian into the German political system."

This was the real end of the Austrian Republic, although it still had four weeks to live. Hitler began immediately to protest against imaginary violations of the new agreement. Schuschnigg belatedly sought to rally his people behind him, but with little success, for the Socialists and trade unions had too lively a memory of the events of February 1934 (see p. 649) to give him enthusiastic support. On March 9 the chancellor announced that, a week hence, there would be a plebescite to determine whether the people desired to remain a "free, independent, social, Christian, and united Austria." This announcement infuriated Hitler, who let it be known that an attempt to hold the plebescite would result in immediate German invasion. Schuschnigg was also informed that Hitler would no longer tolerate him as chancellor, and, resigning himself to what appeared to be inevitable, he gave up his office. Some momentary resistance was put up by the Austrian president, Wilhelm Miklas, but it was overcome by a trick doubtless calculated to appeal to Chamberlain's respect for legality. The pro-Nazi minister of the interior, Dr.

Arthur von Seyss-Inquart, was instructed from Hermann Goering's office to assume Schuschnigg's functions and, immediately, to request that German troops be sent into Austria to help the government establish peace and public security, which were supposedly threatened by Red disorders. This was done; and in the course of the night of March 11 German troops invaded Austria, entering the capital the next day while Berlin newspapers carried the headline "German Austria Saved from Chaos." On March 13, Austria was made a province of the German Reich, and the process of *Gleichschaltung* got under way.

Hitler had been more worried about Italy's reaction to the *Anschluss* than about what other powers might do, and he was relieved when Mussolini, despite the strong anti-German reaction in Italy, gave him his blessing. "Please tell Mussolini," he said to Prince Philip of Hesse, "that I will never forget him for this. . . . I shall be ready to go with him through thick and thin—through anything." As for the western democracies, the Fuehrer was beginning to believe them incapable of action, either political or military. He would have been strengthened in this conviction had he known of Neville Chamberlain's response to a Soviet note of March 17, 1938. The note proposed a meeting of representatives of the American, British, French, and Soviet governments to discuss means of collective action against new aggression. Mr. Chamberlain, who had accepted the *Anschluss* with no apparent qualms, turned down the proposal on the grounds that Great Britain could not accept "mutual undertakings in advance to resist aggression" and that the results of such a meeting would be "to aggravate the tendency towards the establishment of exclusive groups of nations which must . . . be inimical to the prospects of European peace."

Munich and Prague / Hitler's next target was Czechoslovakia, and he saw no reason to delay moving against that state. The instrument he chose for this purpose was the German minority in the Sudeten district (see p. 648). In March 1938, the leader of the Sudeten German party, Konrad Henlein, visited Hitler at Berchtesgaden and was instructed to begin an intensive agitation for special privileges and rights of self-government, always placing his demands so high that the Czech government could not afford to meet them, but not making a premature demand for anything like independence, since that might cause international complications. Henlein obeyed and, in April, submitted the so-called Karlsbad Program to the Czech government, asking for what amounted to complete autonomy of the Sudeten area, the right of the German minority to adhere to the principles of national socialism, and a revision of Czech foreign policy—presumably in the direction of severance of treaty relations with France and the Soviet Union.

The knowledge that a German campaign against Czechoslovakia was shaping up worried the French government, which was conscious of its treaty obligation to defend that country but aware that it was unsupported by a similar British pledge. In April the new prime minister, Édouard Daladier and his foreign minister, Georges Bonnet, visited London and tried to persuade Chamberlain that an explicit British commitment was the best way to deter Hitler. Mr. Chamberlain refused to believe them. It would be a bluff that would not work, he said. Czechoslovakia was a bad risk; its other ally, the Soviet Union, had, thanks to the purges, neither the will nor the strength to support it, and Britain's military forces were incapable of doing so. He did not believe that Hitler wanted to destroy Czechoslovakia but, if he did, Chamberlain "did not see how this could be prevented." Someone said later that, if Chamberlain had been writing a letter to the Czechs, his message would have been:

> Dear Czechoslovakyer
> I don't think he's going to attack yer
> But even if he does
> I'm not going to back yer.

The only practical course, he insisted, was to persuade the Czech government to make satisfactory concessions to their German minority and, simultaneously, to sound out Hitler concerning his idea of a just settlement.

The French finally agreed and, in so doing, they tacitly admitted that they would not abide by their treaty. Henceforth, they engaged with the British in the hopeless task of persuading the Czechs to make concessions that would satisfy a minority which had been ordered by Hitler to set demands that could not be satisfied.

The urgency with which they pursued this task was increased in late May when the Czech government, alleging that it had received reports of German troop movements on the Bohemian border, called up their army reserves and manned their defensive rampart. In the sharp war scare that followed, the British and French governments made stiff representations in Berlin, warning Hitler of the grave consequences that would follow a German attack on Czechoslovakia. The German government protested its innocence and the crisis passed, but it left two results behind. The fact that the western press hailed the affair as a German setback infuriated Hitler and led him to order his army to be prepared to invade Czechoslovakia no later than October 1. At the same time, the war scare frightened the French (rightist newspapers in Paris were now carrying articles with headlines reading "Do you want to die for Czechoslovakia?") and made Chamberlain more determined than ever that the Czech business must be solved, in the words of his ambassador in Berlin, by giving "Prague a real turn of the screw." His pressure upon the Czech government was successful in one respect. It forced the Czechs, in the first week of September, to grant virtually all of the original Karlsbad Demands. To Henlein and Hitler this was embarrassing, for it forced them to come out into the open. Still, they had no intention of turning back now. On September 12 in an impassioned speech about the suffering of the German minority in Czechoslovakia, Hitler offered his support to "these tortured creatures." The following day, Henlein openly declared that the Sudetenland must be ceded to Germany.

Military experts have argued ever since 1938 about what might have happened if Czechoslovakia had been encouraged by Britain and France to resist and if war had come. It is, of course, impossible to answer this with any assurance. It should be noted, however, that German defenses in the west were unfinished and would not have withstood invasion, that Germany had insufficient troops to hold a western and an eastern front, that a Czech campaign would have been difficult in view of the size of the Czech army and the strength of its defenses, that even General Keitel believed (as he admitted during the Nuremberg trials) that "our means of attack against the frontier fortifications of Czechoslovakia were insufficient," and that other German generals were so sure of impending disaster that they were planning to attempt a *coup d'état* if Hitler insisted on war. Finally, despite Mr. Chamberlain's low opinion of Soviet strength and intentions, it seems likely that national interest would have dictated Soviet intervention on Czechoslovakia's behalf if the western powers had undertaken to fight for that country.

But none of these things has any relevance to the actual course of events. Chamberlain was already privately well disposed to the idea of separating the Sudeten area from Czechoslovakia. He now flew to Berchtesgaden to persuade Hitler to give him time to arrange the separation. When this was granted, President Beneš of Czechoslovakia was forced to accept the loss of the Sudetenland by a plain intimation that he would receive no support if he refused.

Even after this, Europe had a narrow escape from war. At a subsequent meeting with Chamberlain at Godesberg, Hitler declared that the mere cession of the Sudetenland was not enough, adding demands for a triumphant entrance of German forces and the humiliating withdrawal of all Czech troops, leaving their installations intact. When these terms were submitted to the Czechs, they refused them indignantly and, in a last flicker of French resistance to Hitler, they were backed by Paris. But, as the tension mounted in the European capitals, Hitler—perhaps because he suddenly sensed a total lack of enthusiasm for war in Germany—held his hand and, in a personal letter to Chamberlain,

Munich, 1938. From left: Chamberlain, Daladier, Hitler, Mussolini, and Coun
Galeazzo Ciano. (UNITED PRESS INTERNATIONAL)

promised to wait until a last effort was made to reach an agreement. The
British prime minister reverted to an idea that he had long toyed with—
that of a four-power conference to solve the Czech problem. He telephoned Paris and received eager approval; he telephoned Rome and
received equally enthusiastic support from the Italian government
which was at this moment as fearful of a major war as were statesmen
in London and Paris. The Duce undertook to make the proposal to
Hitler, who accepted on September 28. The next day Hitler, Mussolini,
Chamberlain, and Daladier gathered at Munich and, in short order,
gave Hitler everything he had demanded at Godesberg, depriving
Czechoslovakia of a third of its population, its most important industrial
areas, and its only means of self-defense.

Mr. Chamberlain was convinced that results would justify these concessions to Hitler and he reacted to criticisms of the Munich agreement with irritation. "A lot of people," he wrote in October, "seem to me
to be losing their heads, and talking and thinking as though Munich had
made war more, instead of less imminent." The very fact that Hitler
had been willing to sign a new declaration of friendship with Great
Britain, expressing the intention of avoiding the use of war in disputes
that might arise between them, indicated, in the prime minister's opinion,
that the appeasement policy had worked and that a new era of peace
was about to open.

His optimism was not justified. Both Hitler and Mussolini regarded the Sudeten settlement as a western capitulation and were encouraged to seek new conquests. After Munich the Italians began to plan the seizure of Albania, which was consummated in April, and by the beginning of the new year the Fascist press had started a shrill campaign demanding that France be forced to cede Nice, Savoy, Tunis, and Jibuti to the new Italian empire.

Hitler, in the meantime, proceeded with the liquidation of what was left of Czechoslovakia. He encouraged all the centrifugal and disruptive forces that the shock of Munich had released in Czechoslovakia, and gave financial support to Slovakian and Ruthenian separatist movements so that, even before the end of 1938, the rump state was virtually divided into three autonomous sections. Having got that far, the Fuehrer saw no reason to stop, and he returned to the tactics that had worked so well in the case of Austria. In January 1939 he summoned the Czech foreign minister and told him that the disorders in his country were a menace to German security and must be suppressed, ordering him at the same time to purge the Czech army of Jews and anti-Germans and to bring his country's foreign policy into conformity with Germany's. Two months later, as the Czech government tried vainly to restore some kind of order in a country torn by German conspiracies, he decided to strike. On March 14, Joachim von Ribbentrop, Hitler's foreign minister, informed the Italian ambassador that:

> Our patience is exhausted. Intrigues have been spun with our enemies in the west. An attempt has been made to make Czechia once more a pawn in the European game. The Fuehrer intends to lance the abscess. The liquidation of this problem is of interest not only to Germany but also to the Axis. The present event is a useful preparation for a contest in another direction which will be necessary sooner or later and for the tasks which this will bring to the Axis powers jointly.

On the same day Hitler peremptorily ordered the Czech President, Emil Hácha, to come to Berlin. When he arrived, Hácha was put through a grueling night session, in which Goering and Ribbentrop threatened to destroy his capital city immediately and literally forced him to sign an agreement "placing with entire confidence the destiny of the Czech people and the Czech country in the hands of the Fuehrer of the German Reich." On the following morning, German troops marched into Prague.

The Polish Pledge and the Duel for Russia / The Prague coup dispelled the illusions of all those who had persisted in believing that Hitler was interested only in reclaiming German territory for the Reich, and it marked the complete bankruptcy of the appeasement policy. Even Neville Chamberlain was disillusioned, horrified—as Rebecca West has

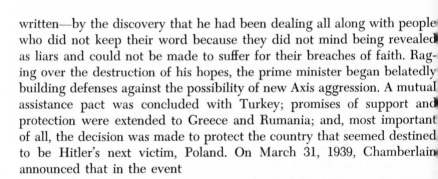

MILES
0   200   400

March 1939
Memel

DENMARK

SWEDEN

ESTONIA
LATVIA
LITHUANIA

Berlin
1936
Sept 1938
Mar. 1939

POLAND

BELGIUM
RHINELAND
NETHERLANDS

Prague
March 1939
SUDETENLAND
CZECHOSLOVAKIA

FRANCE
1936-1939

SWITZER-
LAND
AUSTRIA
Vienna
HUNGARY

RUMANIA

ATLANTIC OCEAN

ITALY

YUGOSLAVIA

S·P·A·I·N
1936-1939
Rome
April 1939

BULGARIA
ALBANIA

PORTUGAL

To Abyssinia
1935

GREECE

AXIS AGGRESSION
1935-1939

HAGSTROM CO., INC., N.Y.

written—by the discovery that he had been dealing all along with people who did not keep their word because they did not mind being revealed as liars and could not be made to suffer for their breaches of faith. Raging over the destruction of his hopes, the prime minister began belatedly building defenses against the possibility of new Axis aggression. A mutual assistance pact was concluded with Turkey; promises of support and protection were extended to Greece and Rumania; and, most important of all, the decision was made to protect the country that seemed destined to be Hitler's next victim, Poland. On March 31, 1939, Chamberlain announced that in the event

> of any action which clearly threatened Polish independence, and which the Polish government accordingly considered it vital to resist with their national forces, His Majesty's Government would feel themselves bound at once to lend the Polish government all the support in their power.

France, he added, had authorized him to say that it would do the same.
The question now was whether this would be enough to persuade Hitler to hold back and, if it were not enough, whether Britain and

France could do anything to defend Poland. It seemed clear to many, and was pointed out in the House of Commons by both David Lloyd George and Winston Churchill, that the democracies' ability to deter or oppose Hitler effectively would depend upon how close their cooperation was with the Soviet Union. It proved difficult, however, to convince Chamberlain of this.

The prime minister had once written:

> I must confess to the most profound distrust of Russia. I have no belief whatever in her ability to maintain an effective offensive even if she wanted to. And I distrust her motives which seem to me to have little connection with our ideas of liberty and to be concerned only with getting everyone else by the ears.

This fundamental suspicion of Soviet motives made it impossible for Chamberlain to admit that the Soviets and the west might have a community of interest in opposing Hitler. Thus, he had turned down the Soviet suggestion for a four-power meeting of the democratic states after Hitler's invasion of Austria, and had persistently slighted the Russians during the long Czechoslovakian crisis. Despite the fact that the Soviet Union was allied to France and to Czechoslovakia, its government was not consulted, nor was it invited to the Munich conference. The Russians, who had been loyal supporters of collective security, even if for reasons of self-interest, may be forgiven for being suspicious. Shortly after Munich, Stalin said: "One might think that the districts of Czechoslovakia were yielded to Germany as the prize for its undertaking to launch war on the Soviet Union."

Even after he had begun to build defenses against Hitler, Chamberlain was very hesitant about approaching the Russians. Not until mid-April did the British government suggest that the Soviet government might wish to cooperate in the defense of Eastern Europe by giving a unilateral guarantee of the western borders of Poland and Rumania. This idea the Soviets rejected.

The truth of the matter was that recent western policy had convinced the Russians, as they thought about the threat to Poland, that they must at least consider the advantages of a *rapprochement* with Germany. Immediately after Munich, a Russian Foreign Office official said to Robert Coulondre, the French ambassador: "My dear friend, what have you done? Don't you see that there is now no alternative to a fourth partition of Poland?" These words indicated that the idea of a German deal was already being canvassed. By the beginning of the new year, Stalin seems to have decided to make some soundings in Berlin, without, however, closing the door to an arrangement with the west. In the months that followed, the Soviet Union had a dual policy: on the one hand, delicately hinting in Berlin of the possibility of an agreement on Polish and other affairs (the first such hint seems to have been dropped in February 1939); on the other, warning the western powers that only a comprehensive eastern defensive league with specific military commitments by both the Soviet Union and the western powers would succeed in deterring Hitler. In rejecting the British suggestion for a unilateral Soviet guarantee, Stalin proposed the conclusion of actual military and political conventions between the Soviet Union and the west.

In considering the Soviet suggestion, the western powers immediately encountered some awkward questions. The Soviets insisted that no alliance system would be effective unless it provided for defense against indirect, as well as direct, aggression—the kind of subversion that had weakened Czechoslovakia before March 1939. They insisted also that they could not guarantee Poland and Rumania unless their troops were permitted to operate inside those countries if war came and unless joint staff talks began immediately. The British soon discovered that both the Poles and the Rumanians were opposed to having Red troops bivouacked among them even for purposes of defense. The British were disinclined to put pressure upon them, showing a greater sensitivity to the feelings of lesser states in this case than they had in the case of Czechoslovakia in the previous year. As a result of this, between April and August 1939, no real progress was made in bringing the Soviet Union and the west together. Innumerable conversations were held with the French and the other states and counterproposals were drafted and submitted to the Russians, but a defense system did not come any closer to actuality.

Meanwhile, the Russians stuck to their terms and pursued their tentative soundings in Berlin. It cannot be said that they did not warn the west of the dangers of delay. One such warning was the dropping of Maxim Litvinov from the post of people's commissar for foreign affairs. Litvinov's name had been intimately associated with the policy of collective security. Vyacheslav Molotov, his replacement, was a rigid nationalist. Nor were all the warnings from the Russian side. On April 28 Hitler denounced the Nazi-Polish Pact of January 1934 and the Anglo-German Naval Agreement of 1935 in a furious speech which, significantly, was absolutely silent with respect to the Soviet Union—a fact noted by the perceptive Coulondre, who sensed that Soviet-German talks must be getting under way. Also, on May 22, while the German press fulminated against Poland, Germany and Italy concluded a formal military alliance (the Pact of Steel), an indication that war might not be far away. On the following day, although this was not known outside Hitler's intimate circle, the Fuehrer announced to his chief advisers that Poland must be attacked "at the first suitable opportunity."

Chamberlain was not entirely unresponsive to these warnings. In June he decided to send a special emissary to Moscow to see if divergent points might be ironed out. But instead of choosing a man of undoubted stature (Eden volunteered to go), he sent the head of the Central Department of the Foreign Office, William Strang, a man with all of the necessary gifts except rank. This deficiency, as Molotov later admitted, offended the Russians and made them feel that the British were not serious. Strang was not successful in advancing the negotiations, and in July the Russians took another step toward Germany by agreeing to begin negotiations for a new economic agreement. They still did not close the door on the west. Indeed, in July they asked the British and French to send a military mission to Moscow to discuss the possibilities of defending Poland and the Baltic states. It is clear in retrospect, however, that Stalin was now pitting London against Berlin and that only quick and decisive action by the west had any chance of holding his support.

That decisiveness the western powers did not show. In August they appointed military missions to go to Moscow, but the British mission was composed of a retired admiral and two generals who had no connection with strategical questions and, as the German ambassador in London noted, the mission seemed designed to find out the fighting value of the Soviet army rather than to make any agreement. Moreover, the missions traveled to Moscow by the slowest possible route, going by ship to Leningrad and then by rail to Moscow, instead of flying, as Chamberlain had always done when consulting Hitler, although this was at a time when the Germans had made up their minds that a deal with Russia must be reached and were working at top speed to that end. Finally, when the mission arrived on August 11, and were informed by Marshal Voroshilov that he was empowered to sign a military convention and that the time had come to put all their cards on the table, it turned out that the head of the British mission had no power to conclude agreements. Indeed, his credentials did not arrive until August 21, and by that time they were useless. The Germans had acted too quickly. On August 14, Ribbentrop proposed by wire that he fly to Moscow "to set forth the Fuehrer's views to M. Stalin [and] . . . to lay the foundations for a final settlement of German-Russian relations." The Russians accepted on the following day, suggesting that the talks be concrete and center on the feasibility of a nonaggression pact. It took almost a week to settle the details, but, on August 21, the German radio was able to announce to a stupefied world that

The Reich government and the Soviet government have agreed to conclude a pact of nonaggression with each other. The Reich minister for foreign affairs will arrive in Moscow on Wednesday, August 23, for the conclusion of the negotiations.

Rendezvous (1939)

Appearing immediately after the conclusion of the Nazi-Soviet pact, this is one of the British cartoonist David Low's masterpieces. From *Low's Autobiography* (New York: Simon & Schuster, 1957).

The public announcement made no mention of the secret agreement which had been signed at the same time as the innocuous pledge of friendship. This defined the boundary between the Soviet and German spheres of influence in Eastern Europe "in the event of a territorial and political rearrangement." It assigned Finland, Esthonia, Latvia, and Bessarabia to the Soviet Union and Lithuania to Germany. In Poland, the boundary between the Soviet and German spheres was defined as the line of the Narew, Vistula, and San rivers. Questions of detail arising out of future political developments would be settled, the secret protocol said, "by means of a friendly agreement." To all intents and purposes this amounted to an alliance, and it removed any hesitations that Hitler might still have felt.

Three months before this time, in May 1939, an American newspaperman,[1] referring to the pending Soviet-Western negotiations, had written: "Consummate the alliance, say the Russians, and Mussolini would be negotiating in London and Paris within 24 hours. There would be peace. Fail to consummate the alliance, or water it down, or even parley too long and there will be war this year." It is, of course, possible that the Soviets would have turned to the Germans in any case, that their real desire was to remain at peace, and that they were finally convinced that even a Soviet-Western military alliance would not assure peace, especially since the British admitted in Moscow that they had only two divisions of troops to throw into action on the day of mobilization. Stalin said something of the sort to Churchill in August 1942. It remains difficult, however, to reject the thought that the long protracted negotiations and the deference to Polish and Rumanian feelings helped produce the debacle. The west had parleyed too long, and the Germans had won the Soviet Union for their own purposes.

The Coming of War / It is unnecessary to give a detailed account of the events of the week that followed the conclusion of the Nazi-Soviet Pact of Nonaggression. The important thing is that it convinced Hitler that he could now attack Poland without further hesitation. He may have felt that the British would now withdraw their pledge to Poland, enabling him to dispose of that country, and that he could then turn to his ultimate plans in Eastern Europe, after solving the French problem as the occasion seemed to require. If this was the line of his thinking, he was disagreeably surprised.

On September 1, 1939, the German armies invaded Poland. The British immediately informed the German government that they would uphold their obligation to Poland unless the action were called off. When they

[1] John W. Owens of the Baltimore *Sun.*

received no reply, the British government, early in the morning of September 3, informed the Germans, that, unless the Germans gave assurance by 11 A.M. that they would terminate hostilities forthwith, a state of war would exist between Germany and Britain as of that hour. Paul Schmidt, Hitler's interpreter, has written that, after he had translated the British ultimatum, "Hitler sat immobile, gazing before him. . . . After an interval which seemed an age, he turned to Ribbentrop, who had remained standing by the window. 'What now?' asked Hitler with a savage look."

It was too late now for questions of that nature. From the beginning, Hitler's foreign policy had been predicated on the assumption that it could probably be carried out successfully only by war. The Polish action had now touched off what was to be the greatest war the world had ever seen. Germany was better prepared for that conflict than any of the other European states, and its chances of attaining Hitler's most grandiose objectives were good. But the thought of what lay ahead momentarily daunted even so confident a man as Hitler, and there must have been many on September 3, 1939, as the British time limit ran out, who felt as Goering did when he said to a friend: "If we lose this war, then God have mercy on us!"

28

World War II

Before it was finished, the conflict that began when Hitler's columns sliced into Poland made even the war of 1914–1918 look like a small-time affair. In scope, it was much more truly a world war than the first contest, for, although Europe was, as in World War I, the major theater of operations, the importance of other areas and the magnitude of the battles fought in them was infinitely greater than in the earlier struggle, and the fate of Europe depended much more clearly upon the turn of events at places like El Alamein and Midway Island than it had ever done then. In another respect also its scope dwarfed that of World War I: namely, in the totality of effort and risk required of its participants. Something has been said above about the ways in which civilian populations were affected in that war (see p. 512). This time the mobilization of human resources and the controls placed upon the customary liberties of civilians were infinitely more rigorous, while the dangers to which they were exposed were proportionately greater. In the war of 1914 saturation bombing of cities and systematic extermination of whole populations were, after all, unknown, and nothing remotely like the holocaust of Hiroshima had ever been dreamed of.

In this great global conflict, the art of war was carried to its ultimate point of sophistication. To the armory of military combat World War I had introduced the submarine, the convoy system, the airplane, and the tank. The technique of using these weapons was vastly refined during the second war. The freeing of armor from the shackles that had bound it to the infantry in order to permit the full exploitation of its offensive capabilities, together with the development of close air support of ground troops, restored mobility to land warfare. The elaboration of strategic bombing techniques greatly enhanced the effects of the older naval blockade as a weapon of attrition. The war on the sea was revolutionized by the appearance of the aircraft carrier, the development of amphibious doctrine, the creation of specialized craft for ship-to-shore movement, and the use of electronic rays for the detection of submarines.

In no previous war had the resources of science been so completely engaged in devising new instruments of war or so productive in their results. A list of the discoveries and inventions of the war years would be long and would include, at the very minimum, such things as the various types of magnetic mines that were used by the opposing naval forces, as well as the different means devised to frustrate them (degaussing techniques and the creation of sound barriers, for example); the remarkable adaptation of radar to special uses, like the antisubmarine defenses made possible by the Braun scanning tube, which operated by means of high-frequency vibrations, and the equally remarkable evolution of the *Schnorkel* air mast, which enabled U-boats to recharge their batteries and replenish their air supply without surfacing for weeks on end; the Norden bombsight, which greatly improved the accuracy of high-level bombing, and the proximity fuse, a kind of electronic trigger which, when used in anti-aircraft fire, made defense against air attack more effective; and, coming late in the war and pointing to a grimmer future, the jet aircraft, the liquid fuel rocket (even in 1945 not susceptible to interception), and the atomic bomb.

Finally—and this was partly the result of the invention of these ingenious new tools of war—no conflict in human history had been as destructive to life and property as this turned out to be. At least 17,000,000 men died on the battlefields of this war, while 18,000,000 noncombatants were killed in one way or another. Among the great powers, Russia, forced for so long to bear the burdens of the war, suffered most heavily: 6,115,000 military deaths and 14,012,000 military casualties, and civilian deaths in the neighborhood of 10,000,000. The Germans, who inflicted most of these terrible losses, suffered grievously themselves, with over 6,000,000 military deaths, 7,250,000 other casualties, 1,300,000 missing, and very heavy civilian losses. Almost 2,000,000 Japanese troops died of wounds or disease, while 78,000 civilians died in the atom bombing of Hiroshima alone, and almost as many in that of Nagasaki. In general, the casualties of the other major participants were much lower (357,116 British troops were killed, 369,267 wounded, and 46,079 missing) but in all cases they represented a crippling loss.

Almost as staggering as these totals, which, in military casualties alone, were double those of World War I, were the financial and material costs of the war. Military expenditures alone totaled more than a trillion dollars, and property losses were incalculable. Some of the scars were ineradicable—as long as they stand, the cities of London and Hamburg will bear visible testimony to destructiveness of World War II—and much that was capable of repair could be put right only after years of effort. When hostilities ceased, the economic structure of Europe seemed completely shattered.

Less tangible but equally real was the political destruction wrought by the war. The strength of the European states was, indeed, so diminished that their future ability to assume the responsibilities that go with great-power status seemed questionable. This forecast a significant diminution of the once dominant role of Europe in world affairs.

THE INITIAL TRIUMPHS OF THE DICTATORS, 1939–1942

The Polish and Finnish Campaigns / The first revelation of the new mobility possible in war came in the Polish campaign. It took Hitler only a month to conquer Poland, and this was the result less of Germany's great superiority in numbers, firepower, air, and armor than of its co-ordinated tactics and the speed with which they were employed. The *Luftwaffe* led the way by systematically destroying the Polish air force on the ground and disrupting transportation facilities and communications. Divebombers were then directed against concentrations of Polish troops and against the towns and cities. As terror and disorder spread, German armored columns crossed the borders and cut their way into the interior, using the tactics of *Blitzkrieg*, which were later defined succinctly by one of Germany's most gifted commanders of armor, Erwin von Rommel, as "the art of concentrating strength at one point, forcing a breakthrough, rolling up and securing the flanks on either side, and then penetrating like lightning, before the enemy has time to react, deep into his rear." Into the gaping holes torn by these tank thrusts came the columns of motorized and nonmotorized infantry. There were no fronts in this kind of war—no main lines of resistance upon which the bewildered Poles could stand and fight and die. The enemy was on every side, and to stand meant to be encircled and strangled into submission, as 170,000 Polish troops learned at Kutno in the third week of the war. By September 21 western Poland had been completely overrun, and the only serious resistance was in Warsaw, which was holding on under

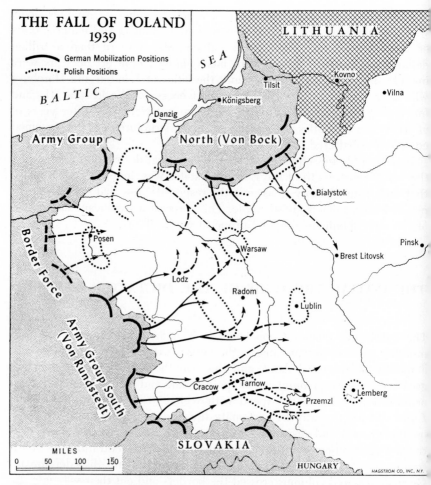

THE FALL OF POLAND
1939

━━━ German Mobilization Positions
••••••••• Polish Positions

Blitzkrieg I: Poland. This map, showing the weight and diversity of the German assault, is based on a German military map.

ceaseless aerial bombardment. Meanwhile, Russian troops had occupied the eastern part of the country and eliminated any possibility of effective resistance there. In Warsaw the Poles fought on courageously until September 27 and then had to give in.

On the following day, Ribbentrop met with his opposite number Molotov and completed the fourth partition of Poland of which Coulondre had been warned in October 1938 (see p. 707). The eastern half of the country, comprising some fourteen million people, was joined to the Soviet Union. The industrial areas of the west were absorbed by Germany, and the area around Cracow was established as a separate "protectorate," ruled over by the Nazi Hans Frank, who was sentenced to death at Nuremberg in October 1946 for the cruelties committed in his satrapy. Although thousands of Poland's bravest sons escaped to fight in the British and French armies and to help defeat the *Luftwaffe* in the skies over London and a Polish government in exile was established in the British capital, their country was now subjected to long years of terror and exploitation.

While the Germans regrouped their forces, the Russians took another step forward. Perhaps remembering Germany's expansion in the Baltic lands during World War I, the Russians extended their military control over Lithuania (defined as a Russian sphere in a recent revision of the secret agreement of August 23) and Esthonia and Latvia by demanding the right to garrison them and establish military and naval bases there. At the same time, they pushed forward negotiations with Finland for border changes on the Karelian isthmus and the cession to Russia of a group of islands in the Gulf of Finland that could be fortified to improve the defenses of Leningrad. Here again the motive was fear of a future German attack (Stalin admitted to the Finnish ambassador in October 1939 that the Nazi-Soviet Pact would probably not last forever), and the Soviet terms, at least originally, were regarded by Marshal Mannerheim as being in the main acceptable. But the majority of the Finnish government were unimpressed by the Soviet insistence and, backed by a public opinion which was emotional and in part chauvinistic, took a rigid and unyielding position. The Soviets responded by fomenting border incidents and used these to justify an invasion that began on November 30.

In the outside world, the Soviet attack on Finland aroused universal disgust which changed to satisfaction when the Finns fought the first five-pronged Russian assault to a standstill. In Geneva, the League of Nations brushed aside Soviet explanations and, on December 14, 1939, expelled the aggressor from its membership, the only time in its existence that it took such action. This gesture of sympathy did not, however, bring material aid to the Finns, whose resources were soon strained to their limits. At the turn of the year, Stalin shook up the command of the northern army, put some of his best units and his most modern equipment into the fight, and concentrated his attack upon the Mannerheim Line facing Leningrad, instead of persisting in his attacks in north and central Finland. After that, the result was inevitable; and, on March 12, 1940, after submitting for a month to a bombardment that at times reached the intensity of that against Verdun in 1916, the Finns capitulated. They were forced to accept the original Soviet demands and to cede, in addition, the city of Viborg and the whole of the Karelian peninsula.

The Phony War / The western powers had remained true to their pledge to Poland and, backed by the whole British Commonwealth, except Eire, had gone to war with Germany on September 3. The British sent all available trained combat troops to France (158,000 in the first five months of the war), instituted new training programs at home, began to assemble a large combat force in the Middle East, and appealed successfully to Australia and New Zealand to send troops into Egypt for the defense of the Canal.

On the other hand, despite the relative weakness of the German defenses in the west and the involvement of most of the Nazi forces in Poland, no truly offensive action was taken on the western front, the Allied armies making at most a few probing thrusts that lacked determination. The speed with which Poland was conquered and the curious lull that followed seemed to rob the conflict, if not of reality, then certainly of urgency. In French government circles, there was more enthusiasm for entering the war against the Soviet Union in Finland's behalf than for any action that might seriously annoy Hitler; and General Gamelin, the supreme French commander, neither pressed for more energetic action nor used the pause that followed the Polish campaign to give his conscripts combat training, allowing a degree of slackness in the armed forces that had fatal effects a few months later. In Great Britain, too, the war seemed remote. It is true that there was no disposition to consider making peace with Hitler—and the Fuehrer's hints that he might be induced to negotiate elicited no response—but it was also evident that the British people had not yet faced up to the full implications of being at war.

In the winter of 1939–1940, the war effort of the west was for the most part confined to occasional air raids for the purpose of dropping propaganda pamphlets. There was, however, more serious action on the seas. The first naval successes of the war were won by German submarines. Leaving aside the torpedoing of the passenger ship S.S. *Athena* off the northwest coast of Ireland on September 3, an exploit that brought no honor to German arms, the sinking of the aircraft carrier *Courageous* on September 16 was an undoubted German triumph, and this was excelled on the night of October 13–14 when Lieutenant Prien took the German U-47 through the harbor defenses of Scapa Flow and avenged the internment of the German fleet in that port in 1918 by sending six torpedoes into *Royal Oak*, sinking her with a loss of 800 men, and escaping into the open sea.

The Royal Navy got a bit of its own back in December, when the cruisers *Exeter*, *Achilles*, and *Ajax* intercepted the pocket battleship *Graf Spee* off the coast of Uruguay and, by attacking as if they were destroyers, offset their disadvantage in range and firepower and so badly damaged the finest of the German capital ships that she had to put in to Montevideo for repairs. There, two days later, her captain destroyed her rather than face a renewal of the battle.

Despite this success, the British found themselves threatened, as in World War I, with the possibility of economic strangulation effected by the submarine. Winston Churchill said later: "This was the only thing that ever really frightened me during the war." British success in defeating this danger was partly due to the fact that Germany had not produced as many submarines before the war as the Anglo-German Naval Agreement of 1935 (see p. 690) would have permitted it to do and had started the war with only fifty-seven U-boats, of which only twenty-two were equipped for Atlantic operations. Other factors were the aid given by the United States both before and after its formal entrance into the war, the successful use of statistical method and the principles of mathematical probability to reduce cargo-ship losses by the adjustment of the size and pattern of convoys, and—most important—the success of British scientists in devising tools of detection. Even so, it was not until the middle of 1943 that success seemed to be assured, and until then the economic pinch was severe.

The German Offensive in the West / The Nazi offensive had not yet made sufficient strides in the winter of 1939–1940, however, to awaken the peoples of Britain and France to the hard facts of war. Their enlightenment came in the spring, as a result of a series of German hammer blows in the west.

The first of these came in Scandinavia. In pursuance of their plans to impose a naval blockade upon Germany, the British and French had been concerned over the use of Norwegian territorial waters by German ships carrying Swedish steel from Narvik to home ports. They finally decided to stop German shipping and informed the Norwegian government on April 8, 1940, that they were sowing mines for this purpose. While they prepared to answer the expected Norwegian protests, Hitler gave them a tougher reply. On the morning of April 9, Nazi columns rolled across the undefended frontier of Denmark and seized the capital, German planes dropped parachute troops on the Norwegian towns of Oslo, Bergen, Trondheim, Stavanger, and Narvik, and German ships brought infantry into the more important Norwegian coastal towns. Unlike the Danes, the Norwegians fought back, and the coastal defense guns at Oslo sank the cruiser *Blücher* and damaged the pocket battleship *Deutschland*, the cruiser *Emden*, and a training ship. Nonetheless the Germans made good their landings, seizing the capital (King Haakon and the government escaped to England) and setting up a puppet government under a man whose name became a byword for traitor throughout the world, Vidkun Quisling.

Caught completely unaware by this stroke, the British tried to rally by landing troop units at Andalsnes and Namsos on the Norwegian coast, but the forces thrown into this desperate maneuver, without artillery or anti-aircraft defenses, were cut to ribbons and had to be withdrawn after a month's desperate fighting. The sole tangible result of the British campaign in Norway was that it awakened the British people with a start and, incidentally, at long last, brought down the government of Neville Chamberlain. His remark at the outset of Germany's Scandinavian thrust, "Hitler has missed the bus!", exhausted the patience of even his close supporters. In May his policies were subjected to a scathing review in the House of Commons by Leo Amery, who ended his speech with the words of Oliver Cromwell to the Long Parliament: "You have sat too long here for any good you are doing. Depart, I say, and let us have done with you. In the name of God, go!" Two days later, the once arrogant and self-confident prime minister obeyed. His place was filled by the man who, after years in the political wilderness, was now to bring his great talents to a great task and to become the indomitable voice of Britain's defiance of the dictators and the inspirer of its victory over them. This was Winston Churchill.

He entered upon his assigned role in the darkest of circumstances, for on the very day of his appointment, Hitler's armies struck with full force in the Low Countries, inaugurating the struggle that Hitler said in his order to his troops would "decide the fate of the German people for a thousand years."

Western strategists had long expected that, when Hitler attacked, he would violate the neutrality of Belgium and Holland, but this calculation did them no good. The two neutral governments persisted in hoping that they could dissuade Hitler from attacking them by avoiding joint military preparations. They had refused not only to cooperate with the British and French army commands but even to divulge their plans in the event that their hopes were disappointed. Already at a disadvantage in terms of numbers (Hitler had 140 divisions in the west, compared with their own 89), the British and French now had to count on moving fast enough, once hostilities started, to prop up the Belgian and Dutch defenses before they collapsed.

They proved incapable of doing so. The German *Blitz* was even more spectacular in Holland than in Poland. The *Wehrmacht* started its invasion shortly after midnight of May 9–10 and, by the use of parachute troops, seized every important airfield and most of the strategic bridges by dawn. Armored columns were across the Maas before the Dutch plans to flood the area had been executed. Within four days, the backbone of resistance had been snapped, and a savage air raid on Rotterdam, which caused 30,000 deaths, led to the capitulation of the army on May 14. The Nazis were frustrated in their hope of seizing Queen Wilhelmina and her government, who escaped to England; but the country was theirs.

The attack on Belgium had started at the same moment as the one on Holland and was equally successful, although it took eighteen days instead of four. On May 11, German glider troops knocked out Fort Eben Emael, the key to Belgian defenses. On the same day armored forces crossed the Albert Canal and, by turning the Belgian flank, forced the first of a series of retirements. The Belgians were supported by the British Second Corps on the Dyle River, by the French Seventh Army in the north, and by the French Cavalry Corps on the Meuse. The maneuverability of these forces disappeared on May 13–14 when General Ewald von Kleist crashed through the supposedly impassable Ardennes and threw two armored corps across the Meuse north of Sedan. Corap's Ninth French Army was overrun, and Guderian, with three German armored divisions, raced for the coast, closely supported by motorized infantry. He reached it on May 23, and the whole Belgian army and its supporting French and British units were caught in a girdle that now tightened remorselessly.

An Allied plan to effect a break-out by concerted attacks from inside and outside the ring was frustrated by German pressure and by lack of vigor in the French command, which was already showing signs of the indecision that foretold complete collapse. Inside the circle, the Allied forces were pushed slowly toward the coast. On May 27 the limit of Belgian resistance had been reached, and King Leopold II sued for an armistice and ordered a cessation of hostilities. For this he was bitterly criticized by his allies and by his own people, on the grounds that he had given insufficient warning to his allies. This is not wholly just. Communications were, at this time, far from perfect, as is shown by the fact that Leopold's allies had begun their evacuation before he approached the Germans and had not succeeded in consulting him before doing so. But the Belgian capitulation created a wide gap on the northeastern flank, and forced the British and French back upon the beaches of Dunkirk.

From this predicament 338,000 troops were extricated as a result of German mistakes and British valor. The "miracle of Dunkirk" was possible only because the Germans pressed their attack not with armor but with artillery and airpower and because the *Luftwaffe* made the fundamental error of concentrating on the beaches rather than upon the evacuation fleet. These errors permitted a miscellaneous armada of Royal Navy and private craft, including tugs, fire-floats, pleasure

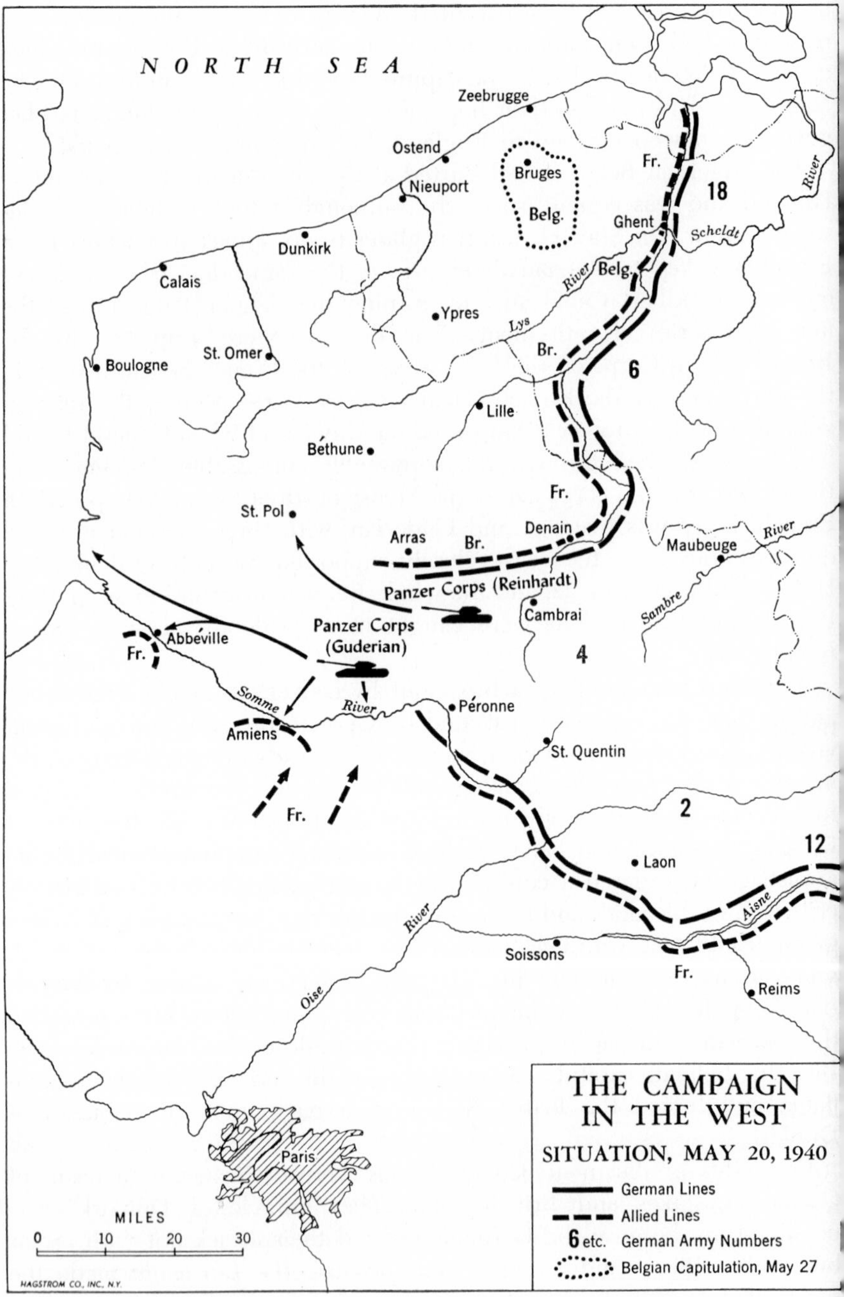

NORTH SEA

Zeebrugge
Ostend
Nieuport
Bruges
Belg.
Fr.
18
Ghent
Scheldt
Belg.
Dunkirk
Calais
River
Ypres
Lys
Br.
6
Boulogne
St. Omer
Lille
Béthune
Fr.
St. Pol
Arras
Br.
Denain
Maubeuge
River
Panzer Corps (Reinhardt)
Cambrai
Sambre
Panzer Corps
(Guderian)
4
Abbéville
Fr.
Somme
River
Amiens
Péronne
St. Quentin
Fr.
2
12
Laon
Aisne
River
Oise
Soissons
Fr.
Reims

THE CAMPAIGN
IN THE WEST

SITUATION, MAY 20, 1940

——— German Lines
━ ━ ━ Allied Lines
6 etc. German Army Numbers
⋯⋯⋯ Belgian Capitulation, May 27

Paris

MILES
0   10   20   30

HAGSTROM CO., INC., N.Y.

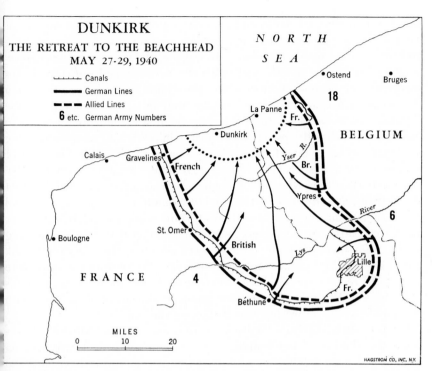

DUNKIRK

THE RETREAT TO THE BEACHHEAD
MAY 27-29, 1940

- ⌐⌐⌐⌐ Canals
- ▬▬▬ German Lines
- ▬ ▬ ▬ Allied Lines
- **6** etc. German Army Numbers

N O R T H

S E A

Blitzkrieg II: Dunkirk. A German portrayal of the remorseless pressure on the Allied lines.

cruisers, and sloops, to carry the bulk of the British forces and 139,000 French and Belgians to safety in England. Winston Churchill was doubtless right in warning the House of Commons that "we must be very careful not to assign to this deliverance the attributes of a victory. Wars are not won by evacuations." Even so, the importance of this remarkable operation should not be underestimated. By bringing back the core of a professional army, it facilitated military recovery and expansion and saved for the future British army a large number of commanders who had learned more in the brief and shattering campaign in Flanders than they could have learned in years at staff schools. It simultaneously awakened British pride in what they could accomplish even in defeat and gave them a new commitment to the struggle.

Unfortunately, it could do nothing to retrieve the situation in France, which now deteriorated swiftly. The French still had enough reserves to equal the enemy in numbers and as much armor and superior artillery; their only relative weakness was in the air. But French staff planners had never been able to think in terms of a truly mobile war; they had persisted in parceling out tanks and aircraft to ground formations instead of using them in concentration; their artillery was static rather than mobile; and they had no real battle plan. The speed of the German advance overwhelmed General Gamelin and, when he was relieved on May 19, his successor, the seventy-three-year-old Weygand, showed less vigor than the occasion warranted. Indeed, as the Somme front crumbled and the German armies wheeled to the south, the new commander tended to blame all his misfortunes on the British, while refusing to withdraw the unused divisions in the Maginot Line to bolster his defenses. The hope of making a stand was weakened by an incredible amount of administrative confusion. At a time when the French were insisting, unsuccessfully, that the British move the last of their fighter squadrons to France, they had 150 fighter planes in good condition at Tours while the pilots of Corap's army were sitting 30 kilometers away, complaining that they had nothing to fly. At a time when the French were pleading for British anti-tank guns, 520 new 20 mm antitank guns and 750 25 mm antitank guns were sitting in French depots, where the Germans found them when the fighting was over. With this sort of thing going on and the roads clogged with refugees, it is not surprising that the armies did not hold.

On June 10, the signs of collapse were so evident that Mussolini overcame the doubts of his generals and insisted upon declaring war on France. ("I need a few thousand dead," he is reported to have said, "so that I can attend the peace conference as a belligerent.") On June 14 the Germans entered Paris unopposed. Two days later they outflanked and breached the Maginot Line and pressed across the Loire.

The French Surrender and the Vichy Regime / The French government had meanwhile fled to Bordeaux. Viewing the rout, Prime Minister Paul Reynaud, backed by a solid majority of his colleagues, argued that the army should, if it were absolutely necessary, surrender, but that the government should go to North Africa and continue the war. General Weygand, on the other hand, declared that it would be dishonorable for the army to act in this way and insisted that the government must take the responsibility for seeking an armistice. He was unmoved by Reynaud's argument that this would violate an earlier pledge to the British not to seek a separate peace and unimpressed by pleas that Britain would fight on and win and that France must be at her side. He made it clear that he expected a British collapse almost immediately.

Reynaud, nevertheless, insisted on consulting the British. After some hesitation, they agreed on May 16 not to object if the French sounded out the Germans on terms, provided the French fleet were dispatched to British ports. Later in the day, the British government sought to recall that permission by proposing in its place that France and Britain unite

one nation, with joint citizenship and common policy and with joint
responsibility for repairing the ravages of the war once it had been won.
This revolutionary proposal had no result. In Bordeaux the supporters
of an appeal to the Germans had grown in numbers and determination;
the British declaration was regarded as an attempt to degrade France to
the position of a dominion; Reynaud resigned in despair; and all parties
turned to Marshal Pétain, the hero of Verdun, who now became head of
the government and, on June 17, asked the Germans for armistice terms.
    The agreement that the French were forced to sign was a harsh one.
German troops were to occupy more than half of France, including all of
the northern part of the country, Paris, and the whole Atlantic coast to
the Spanish border. Occupation costs were to be borne by the French,
who in the unoccupied zone were to maintain a regime friendly to
Germany. The terms included provisions for the immediate surrender of
German prisoners, the disbanding of the French army, and—and this was
to cause serious misunderstanding between France and Britain—the concentration and demobilization of all French fleet units in ports under
German or Italian control.
    The Pétain government accepted these terms in return for a pledge that
Germany would not use the fleet units in question. To make doubly sure,
Admiral Darlan, the French naval commander in chief, in a secret signal
on June 24, ordered his fleet commanders to scuttle their ships if the
enemy tried to seize them by force. Unfortunately, the British government was not kept fully informed of these orders and assurances and
regarded the possibility of German use of the French navy as a danger
that must be eliminated. Consequently, on the night of July 2, a British
naval force appeared off the roads of Mers-el-Kebir in Algeria, where
the French Atlantic squadron (four cruisers, six destroyers, one carrier,
four submarines, and smaller ships) was berthed, sealed off the harbor
with magnetic mines, and then invited the French commander to join
forces with them or take the consequences. The French commander,
Admiral Gensoul, refused but sought to explain the nature of Darlan's
order, adding personal assurances of his intention of obeying it. The
British commander was under too great pressure from London to be content with his explanation and proceeded to destroy the French fleet in a
bombardment that lasted only thirteen minutes and from which only one
cruiser and three destroyers escaped.
    Mers-el-Kebir caused a wave of anti-British feeling in Vichy, where
the Pétain government was now stationed, and brought further discredit
upon the Third Republic by making it possible to accuse it of having
based its foreign policy on an alliance with a power that would attack
defenseless French ships. This played into the hands of those who wished
to destroy the Republic and establish a totalitarian regime. Under the

cunning leadership of Pierre Laval, what was left of the old Frenc
parliament now voted the Republic out of existence and vested fu
powers in Marshal Pétain. This octogenarian had long believed that th
Republic was decadent and should be replaced and, with the help of a
entourage filled with members of the *Action Française* and similar group
he now established a regime that was strongly totalitarian in cast. Indeec
in the four years of its existence, the Vichy regime enacted some of th
most repressive laws that France had ever known, made all Frenchme
the subjects of possible administrative sanctions, and excluded certai
categories of Frenchmen (Freemasons and Jews, for example) from th
protection of the laws. The individual liberty of even the most di
tinguished citizens was subject to restriction: André Gide was forbidde
by the local head of the *Légion des Combattants* to deliver a lecture i
Nice, on the grounds that it would not be fitting for "the triumpha
champion of the spirit of pleasure" to speak in these times of sacrifice an
suffering. Humbler persons were apt to suffer from appalling injustic
Foreigners who had volunteered for service in the Foreign Legion durin
the campaign of France were penned up in concentration camps in Afric
and treated with a brutality that rivaled that of the Nazi camps at Dacha
and Auschwitz.

In foreign affairs, Pétain himself, whose most marked characteristi
was slyness, sought to keep wires open to both Berlin and London, so a
to secure France's future whatever happened in the war. On the othe
hand, Pierre Laval, always the strongest man in Vichy, although his rela
tions with the marshal were sometimes less than cordial, believed i
wholehearted collaboration with Germany and, had he had his way
would probably have gone to war against Britain. The line that wa
followed was an equivocal one. The Vichy regime was accorded diplc
matic recognition by the western powers because of the obvious advar
tages that such recognition brought, but it won no affection either abroa
or at home. The real France, to a growing number of Frenchmen, wa
represented by the resistance in the *Maquis* (or underbrush) and b
those who fled to England to join the Free French movement of Gener;
Charles de Gaulle.

The Battle of Britain / After the fall of France, as after the fall c
Poland, Hitler paused and put out feelers to the British; and once mor
he found no disposition to treat. He therefore began preparations for a
invasion of the British Isles—an operation that was given the code nam
Sea Lion. Throughout the summer and the early fall of 1940, a grea
invasion fleet of barges was assembled at the coastal ports, and troop
were trained for the amphibious operation. Many of Hitler's naval con
manders, in particular, viewed all these preparations with foreboding

They need not have worried. In the end, Sea Lion was abandoned, because the air battle that preceded it was lost.

After the war was over, some Russian officers asked the German general Gerd von Rundstedt what he thought had been the decisive battle of the war. Doubtless to their disappointment, he named the Battle of Britain, and there is much to be said for his answer. If the British had collapsed in 1940, the Germans would have been able to launch their Russian drive sooner and with stronger forces, and they might have taken Moscow in 1941. Moreover, a British collapse would have completed the deterioration of faith in democracy that had been growing ever since the mid-1930s and had by this time begun to make even some Americans believe that totalitarianism was the wave of the future.

The Battle of Britain was won by the RAF and by the people of London and the other industrial cities of Great Britain. They were helped, it is true, by German mistakes. When the *Luftwaffe* began its great assault in early August, its mission was to knock out the British air force and soften up England for the invasion. Despite the overconfidence of its commander Hermann Goering, it was neither trained for the kind of operations demanded of it nor supplied with a proper advance assessment of British strength or effective intelligence during the battle. Inconsistency of target selection and faulty coordination between the bombing and fighter arms were characteristic of German performance throughout the operation, and the *Luftwaffe's* best chances of success were lost by strategic errors, like the decision in early September to shift the attack from control stations and airfields to London and other cities—a decision made at the very moment when the airfield attacks seemed on the point of exhausting British resources.

On the other hand, the Battle of Britain deserves to be thought of in positive terms rather than as a victory by German default. It was won by the British, and won because of five things. The first was the possession of an effective radar net, which had been built up since 1934. The second was the heavy armament of Spitfires and Hurricanes, which bore the brunt of the fighting and outgunned the aircraft that they had to intercept (see p. 668). The third was the skill and the unpretentious gallantry of the British fighter pilots. The fourth was the fact that—thanks to Winston Churchill's refusal to commit the last of Britain's fighter planes to the battle of France in May—the RAF had enough planes to fight until the tide turned. The fifth was the spirit of the British people, who took the terrific pounding without panicking or calling for surrender.

Thanks to these things, Goering's offensive failed, at a cost from which the *Luftwaffe* never recovered. And when the failure was obvious, in the winter, Sea Lion was abandoned by its author. But the Battle of Britain accomplished more even than that. It put an end to doubts about

Britain's will to fight on and inspired resistance movements in the Low Countries, Norway, and France with new hope. It aroused new enthusiasm for the British cause in the United States and made it easier for the administration of Franklin D. Roosevelt to win support for measures of aid to Britain. In September 1940, the United States, in return for a lease of naval bases in the West Indies and Bermuda, transferred fifty over-age destroyers to the British navy, who put them to good use immediately. Simultaneously, the War Department released surplus material and weapons to the British army. Even more important than these measures of aid was the Lend-Lease Act of March 1941, by which Congress authorized the manufacture, sale, loan, lease, or transfer of war material to "the government of any country whose defense the President deems vital for the defense of the United States." The President was given discretion to make such arrangements without requiring repayment, if he so desired, and he proceeded to use his authority to bolster Britain's defenses.

Africa and the Mediterranean / The junior partner of the Axis had derived little personal satisfaction from his intervention in the last stages of the French campaign. Although collapsing everywhere else, the French had stood so firmly against Italian attacks on the southeastern front that, at one point, Mussolini had asked the Germans for transport planes to fly units over the line of resistance into the rear. The Germans had refused, and the campaign had ended with no laurels for Italy at all.

With Britain fully engaged in its fight for existence, however, Mussolini saw prospects of victory and spoils in Africa and, indeed, in the whole Mediterranean area. In August 1940, at the height of the Battle of Britain, he ordered the Duke of Aosta, with 200,000 Italian and native troops under his command, to advance from Eritrea and Italian Somaliland against British troops at the entrance of the Red Sea. Within two weeks, the British had been forced out of Somaliland. On September 14, the second stage of Mussolini's ambitious campaign opened. An army of 250,000 under Marshall Graziani moved from Libya eastward into Egypt and forced the ill-armed, vastly outnumbered troops of General Sir Archibald Wavell to fall back on Mersa Matruh, the railhead on the way to Alexandria.

All might have gone well if the British had been willing to admit the danger of their position in the Mediterranean and to withdraw their fleet units entirely from that sea. But, under the leadership of Admiral Sir Andrew Brown Cunningham, who has been called the greatest English sailor since Nelson, they not only refused to do this but proceeded to raise havoc with Graziani's supply lines. Nor were they content with that. On November 11, 1940, a British task force had the temerity to steam into the Italian base of Taranto, where, using torpedo planes, they sank or severely damaged three battleships, two cruisers, and two auxiliaries and left the harbor in flames.

While the Duce reflected on this humiliation, Wavell made what was supposed to be a raid in force from Mersa Matruh in December. It developed into an Italian rout. Hitting Graziani's forward forces at Sidi Barrani, the mixed British, Indian, and Anzac forces took the town and its whole garrison after two days' fighting and then rolled over Bardia in Libya to Tobruk, moved on to Derna, and in February actually reached and captured Benghazi. Within three months the British had knocked out ten Italian divisions, taken 113,000 prisoners, captured 1300 guns and hundreds of tanks, and eliminated the threat to Suez. And, as if that were not enough, in January 1941 British forces from the Sudan conquered Eritrea, and a column from Nairobi reconquered all of Somaliland. In May the Duke of Aosta was crushed at Amba Alagi, and Ethiopia was liberated. The Duce's African empire was in ruins; and his navy, hard hit at Taranto, had suffered another grievous beating in March, when Cunningham caught it off Cape Matapan and sank three cruisers and three destroyers and severely damaged a new battleship.

So desperate did the plight of his partner seem by now that Hitler intervened. In April General Erwin Rommel appeared in North Africa and immediately struck back at the British in Libya. Within a week he had bypassed Tobruk, stormed Bardia, and forced Wavell to withdraw into Egypt. The Desert Fox, as he was soon called, was no Graziani, and with his coming the threat to Suez became very real again.

Greece and Yugoslavia / It was not from his African plight alone that Mussolini needed to be extricated. He had become enmeshed in more serious troubles in Greece. The idea of launching an attack upon Greece from Albania had been on the Duce's mind for some time, and—perhaps because he was resentful about the number of times he had been surprised by his ally—he decided this time to strike without consulting Hitler. In October 1940, therefore, he dispatched an ultimatum to the Greek government, charging it with unneutral behavior and other crimes and demanding the right to occupy certain strategic areas in Greece for the duration of the war. Without giving the Greeks a chance to reply, the Italians crossed the Greco-Albanian border on October 28 with 200,000 troops.

The British immediately offered their aid to the Greeks and brought troops across from Africa, beginning a process of draining Wavell's strength that was soon to be exploited by Rommel. But the Greeks were already in command of the situation. Mountain troops trapped the overconfident Italian invaders in the narrow mountain valleys and began to

THE MEDITERRANEAN
THEATER OF WAR

MILES
0   100   200   300   400

pound them with artillery. In the first week of November, the 3d Italian Alpini division lost 5000 men in the Pindus gorges; a week later, the whole invading army was being pressed back to the Albanian border; a month after that, having suffered frightful losses, they had been expelled from Greece and were in danger of losing Albania as well.

If Mussolini was cast down by these setbacks, his fellow dictator was infuriated, and for good reason. Hitler had never lost sight of his main objective, which was expansion toward the east; and, even while he pursued his onslaught against Britain, he had been using the resources of diplomacy to extend German domination over the quarreling Balkan countries, so as to be in an advanced position when the break with Russia came. In the twelve months that followed the conclusion of the Nazi-Soviet Pact, he had succeeded—to the dismay of the Soviet Union—in winning paramount influence over the governments of Hungary, Bulgaria, and Rumania. This he had accomplished by supporting the territorial am-

bitions of the first two and by granting a guarantee to what was left of
Rumania after it had been forced, in July and August 1940, to cede a
large part of its territory to Hungary, Bulgaria, and Russia. Rumanian territorial losses caused the abdication of King Carol, and the new king,
Michael, was not only grateful for the guarantee of his fast-dwindling
realm but actually requested Germany to send troops to help restore
order. These forward strides, which brought the Germans an excellent
jumping-off place for any future operations, far exceeded Russian gains
in Rumania, from which they had exacted Bukovina and Bessarabia, and
in Finland.[1] But the Russians had not dared utter more than formal protests, preferring to indulge in an appeasement policy that yielded far
more territory to Hitler than Anglo-French appeasement had given him
between 1933 and 1939.

[1] Especially in view of the fact that the Germans sent troops into Finland presumably for protective purposes in September, 1940.

These gains were all jeopardized by Mussolini's action in Greece, which began at a time when Hitler was preoccupied with western rather than eastern problems. For some time he had been under pressure from Admiral Raeder, the navy's chief, and the naval staff to make up for the failure of Sea Lion by striking a blow in the western Mediterranean, capturing Gibraltar, and closing its straits. Raeder insisted that Britain, becoming stronger monthly as a result of American aid, must be subjected to new attacks and that the crucial strategical area for this was Africa and the Mediterranean. Hitler was sufficiently impressed by these arguments to meet with General Francisco Franco at Hendaye in October 1940 and to try to persuade him to agree to a joint Spanish-German campaign. He had no success. Indeed, he was so exhausted by the Caudillo's counterarguments in their long conversation that he said later that he would rather "have three or four teeth yanked out . . . than go through that again." It was not, however, Franco's verbal delaying action that put an end to the idea of a campaign against the straits of Gibraltar. It was the news, which came immediately after Hendaye, that Mussolini had invaded Greece and the subsequent disastrous development of that adventure. The British response especially worried Hitler, for their occupation of Crete and Lemnos and their troop landings on the mainland threatened the whole German position in the Balkans.

The Fuehrer, therefore, abandoned whatever plans he may have been considering for another blow in the west and prepared to liquidate the threat in Greece. At the beginning of the new year, he sent requests for troop transit to the governments of Bulgaria and Yugoslavia. On March 1, 1941, the Bulgarians signed a treaty of alliance and permitted German troops to enter Sofia and Varna. The regency in Yugoslavia, which had become increasingly pro-German in its views (see p. 651), indicated its intention of doing the same later in the month.

This was regarded, however, as a shameful capitulation by the people of Yugoslavia, who were by nature courageous, combative, and independently minded. On March 27, 1941, with every evidence of strong public support, an army revolt deposed the regent Paul and put the young King Peter II on the throne. He immediately appointed an anti-German cabinet and would probably have sought to give aid to the victorious but now tiring Greeks had he been given more time. But the infuriated Hitler was not generous with that commodity. In April 1941, his planes subjected Belgrade to one of the most terrific bombardments of the war; twenty divisions of his troops came tumbling through the mountains and seized all the principal cities of the country; the king and his government fled; the realm was divided into an independent Croatia, leaning toward Germany, and a Serbia under direct German military control; and the Nazi juggernaut rolled on toward Greece.

By this time, the British had put 56,657 trained desert troops, most of them Australians and New Zealanders, into the country. But they had to face an enemy of half a million men, who possessed, in addition, command of the skies and a great superiority in armor. The issue was decided in advance. The Germans moved with an incredible rapidity that made their containment impossible. The Greeks fought bravely but with far less spirit than they had shown against the Italians—perhaps because of weariness, perhaps because of the aura of invincibility that surrounded the gray columns which swept into their country. The British lost 15,000 troops trying to find a line that could be defended, and then were forced once more to retire by sea—this time to the island of Crete, whence they were expelled by bombing attacks and parachute drops in May.

The conquest of Crete gave Hitler an important base from which to harry Cunningham's fleet and Wavell's supply lines. It also gave him a jumping-off place for penetrating the oil-rich Middle East, an invasion which, if pushed in strength and in conjunction with increasing support for Rommel's operations in Africa, might have been disastrous for Britain. It is difficult to avoid the conclusion that Hitler's greatest strategical mistake was his failure to exploit these opportunities after the end of the Greek campaign. But once he had completed his domination of the Balkan area, Raeder's arguments meant little to him. His eyes and his mind were filled with visions of victory over Russia, and he now turned his armies to the east.

Hitler's Attack on Russia / The Fuehrer had, indeed, definitely decided on an invasion of Russia before his troops were actually committed in Greece. The directive for what was called Operation Barbarossa had been issued on December 18, 1940, and began with the words:

> The German Armed Forces must be prepared to crush Soviet Russia in a quick campaign even before the conclusion of the war against England. For this purpose the Army will have to employ all available units. . . .

Both Finland and Rumania were counted on as allies in this war, and both had already been transformed into German *places d'armes*. By February 1941 there were 680,000 well-equipped German troops in Rumania; and, during the preparations for the blow against Greece, they were increased in number, and units were sent to Bulgaria as well. This meant that German planes had command over the southwestern approaches to the Ukraine and the Caucasus, the richest agricultural and industrial areas in the Soviet Union. By May Hitler's preparations were well in hand, and the decision to attack waited only upon the end of operations in Greece and Crete. On June 22 the text of the declaration of war was handed to the Russians, and the German armies attacked

along the whole front from Finland to the Caucasus. To Mussolini, Hitler
wrote:

> Since I struggled through to this decision, I again feel spiritually free. The
> partnership with the Soviet Union, in spite of the complete sincerity of
> efforts to bring about a final conciliation, was nevertheless often very irksome
> to me, for in some way or other it seemed to me to be a break with my
> whole origin, my concepts and my former obligations. I am happy now to
> be relieved of these mental agonies.

It is not improbable that his sentiments were genuine.

Once more the world witnessed an impressive demonstration of
German power. Within ten days of the opening of hostilities, the *Luftwaffe* had won almost complete air supremacy, German armored columns
were piercing and encircling the dazed Russian defenders, and Nazi
legions had already captured 150,000 prisoners, 1200 tanks, and 600 big
guns. The main German objective was the line Leningrad-Moscow-lower
Volga, which would give Hitler control of the Ukrainian grain fields,
the Donets mineral deposits, Caucasian oil, and command of the Baltic
and Black seas. For a time it seemed that this line would be reached with
ease. General von Leeb's army group in the north occupied Riga in the
first week of fighting and, by September, were poised before Leningrad.
In the center, General von Bock's army advanced 500 miles in the first
month but was held up in front of Smolensk for almost three months by
the most desperate kind of resistance. It was then reinforced and rolled
on toward Moscow in October. In the south, Rundstedt's army group
encircled Kiev and rushed on to the line Taganrog-Kharkov-Kursk in the
same period, and in November Manstein invaded the Crimea and Kleist
took Rostov-on-Don.

All three of these massive thrusts failed, in the end, to reach their objectives, although Bock's forces could at one time actually see the spires
of the Kremlin outlined against the sky. The Russian winter, which had
defeated Napoleon, defeated Hitler too, by arriving three weeks early.
In late November the freezing cold immobilized German transport and
armor and caused frightful suffering among the invading armies, who
were ill-equipped for it and found it difficult to meet the counter-
attacks that Marshal Zhukhov now mounted north and south of Moscow.
German staff officers urged a general withdrawal to permit a regrouping
for a spring offensive. Hitler refused, and was probably right in doing so,
since a general withdrawal in these circumstances might have led to a
dissolution of the whole battle line. There were some local retirements
and then a general stabilization of the thousand-mile front.

The *Blitzkrieg* had failed, but not definitively. The Russians had lost
over a million troops in prisoners alone, as well as an enormous area of

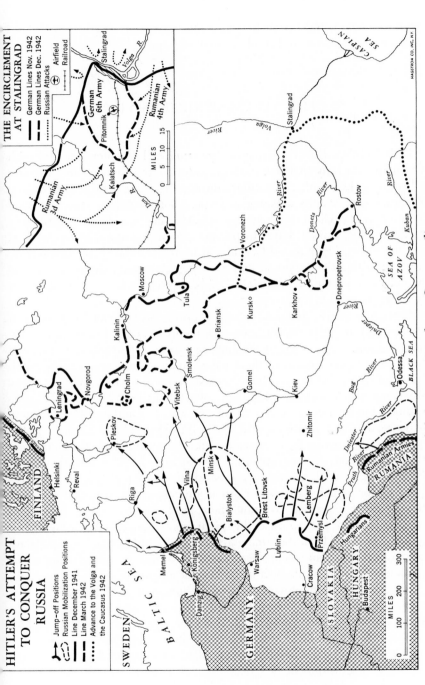

THE ENCIRCLEMENT AT STALINGRAD

━━━ German Lines Nov. 1942
┅┅┅ German Lines Dec. 1942
┉┉┉ Russian Attacks
⊕ Airfield
━━━ Railroad

German 6th Army
Stalingrad
Pitomnik
Kalatsch
Rumanian 4th Army
Rumanian 3d Army
Don R.

MILES
0 5 10 15

HAGSTROM CO. INC. N.Y.

HITLER'S ATTEMPT TO CONQUER RUSSIA

Jump-off Positions
Russian Mobilization Positions
Line December 1941
Line March 1942
Advance to the Volga and the Caucasus 1942

SWEDEN
FINLAND
Helsinki
Reval
Leningrad
Novgorod
Pleskov
Riga
Memel
Königsberg
Danzig
Vilna
Bialystok
Minsk
Brest Litovsk
Lemberg
Przemysl
Lublin
Warsaw
Cracow
GERMANY
SLOVAKIA
HUNGARY
Budapest
Hungarians
RUMANIA
Rumanian Armies
Odessa
BLACK SEA
BALTIC SEA
Cholm
Vitebsk
Smolensk
Gomel
Kiev
Zhitomir
Kalinin
Moscow
Tula
Briansk
Kursko
Karkhov
Dnepropetrovsk
Voronezh
Don River
Donets River
Rostov
Kuban River
SEA OF AZOV
Stalingrad
Volga River
CASPIAN SEA
Dnieper River
Bug River
Dniester River
Pruth River

MILES
0 100 200 300

The blitz that failed: Russia. Based on a German military map.

territory. Who could say that they would have the strength to withstand the new blows that would surely come in the spring?

THE JAPANESE OFFENSIVE

In September 1940 the Japanese government had entered a pact with Germany and Italy that bound the signatories "to assist one another with all political, economic and military means if one of the three Contracting Parties is attacked by a Power at present not involved in the European War or in the Chinese-Japanese conflict." This was designed primarily to induce the United States to be cautious in giving aid to the west. It did not oblige Japan to aid Germany if it attacked the Soviet Union, and, in April 1941, the Japanese and Soviet governments signed a pact by which each promised to maintain a benevolent neutrality if the other became involved in a war.

Japan, therefore, did not directly support the German drive when it started in June 1941. Nevertheless, six months later, it brought powerful aid, at least temporarily, to the German cause. By attacking the United States and Great Britain in the Pacific, Japan greatly reduced the possibility of these countries giving assistance to the Soviet Union, while weakening their resources for their own battles on other fronts.

Since the beginning of the European war, the ambitions of Japanese expansionists had grown rapidly. The fall of Holland and France and the absorption of Britain's energies in the European and Mediterranean theaters seemed an open invitation for Japan to lay its hands upon their Pacific possessions. As early as June 1940, the Tokyo government was pressing for special rights and bases in Indochina, and the Vichy authorities found it expedient to grant them air bases in Tonkin. These first concessions did not appease the Japanese but merely intensified their hunger. In July 1941 they moved troops into Indochina and Siam and began menacing motions in the direction of Burma, the Dutch possessions in Indonesia, and the British naval base at Singapore.

The United States government could not view with equanimity the further weakening of powers which it was supporting with economic aid and military supplies in Europe; and, in any case, Washington had opposed Japan's Asian ambitions ever since 1931 and had, since the opening of the Japanese offensive of 1937, been giving all possible aid to the Chinese government of Chiang Kai-shek. The Roosevelt administration did not respond to British suggestions that it send the American fleet to Singapore; nor did it, on the other hand, follow the advice of those of its own members who wanted a rigid economic strait jacket imposed on Japan as early as 1940. Either of these lines, it was felt by the President and his chief military advisers, might precipitate a major Pacific war, which would seriously reduce the possibility of a democratic victory in Europe. Throughout 1940 and 1941, therefore, the United States government relied upon diplomatic representations accompanied by a gradual tightening of economic pressure (freezing of assets, embargoes on certain products, and the like), while at the same time holding staff talks with the British and the Dutch.

This policy did at least prevent hostilities for a long time, but it neither impressed the Japanese sufficiently to make them give up their aggressive designs nor weakened their resources for a war in any significant way. By the fall of 1941, the diplomatic positions of both sides had become rigid: the Japanese demanding a withdrawal of all embargo measures and of all aid to Chiang Kai-shek as the price of agreement, the United States refusing to lift any restrictions until the prewar situation was restored. This deadlock was resolved on December 7, 1941, when the Japanese fleet, in accordance with a carefully worked-out plan and without any warning, struck at Pearl Harbor in Oahu, where the bulk of the United States fleet was assembled, sank the battleships *Arizona*, *West Virginia*, and *Oklahoma*, severely damaged five other battleships, killed 2343 men, wounded over 1200, and virtually destroyed the striking force of the United States in the Pacific.

To the astonishment and dread of the democratic world, this shattering victory was succeeded by a long string of others. Guam, Wake, and the Philippines were conquered by Japanese task forces by March. A belated British attempt to bolster the defenses of Singapore was frustrated when their new 35,000 ton battleship *Prince of Wales* and the 32,000 ton armored cruiser *Repulse* were caught 150 miles from the base and sunk by naval torpedoes on December 10, 1941. A month later, Japanese forces systematically conquered the Malayan peninsula and, taking Singapore from the rear, forced it to surrender on February 15 with 60,000 troops. Simultaneously, Japanese columns invaded the Kra Peninsula in Burma, captured Moulmein and Rangoon, cleared the country of British and Chinese troops, closed the great Burma Road (the main supply line to China), and installed a puppet government. Finally, in mid-February, in the battle of the Java Sea, the Japanese fleet destroyed a mixed Allied force of five cruisers, six destroyers, and a sloop under the command of the Dutch Admiral Helfrich and made possible the conquest of all of the Netherlands East Indies by March.

There was no reason to suppose at that time that further Japanese expansion could be checked. The confident aggressors were already looking toward Australia, and there were few barriers in their way. Moreover, a renewal of German activities could be expected as soon as spring came to Russia. All in all, the outlook for the democracies was distinctly unpromising.

THE TURN OF THE TIDE, 1942–1943

The Grand Alliance / As it happened, the aggressors had reached the peak of their power in the early spring of 1942, and they were never to be as strong and as close to victory again. Even before the end of 1942, there were signs that the democratic powers were regaining the initiative, and the year 1943 saw the definite beginning of a shift in the fortunes of this gigantic war.

The first order of business for the democratic powers, after the shock of Pearl Harbor had passed, was the creation of an effective coalition to combat the forces of totalitarianism. The basis for this had been laid by the cordial cooperation between Franklin Roosevelt and Winston Churchill even before the formal entrance of the United States into the war, and by the immediate decision made by these statesmen in June 1941 that, despite their ideological differences with the Soviet Union, they must do everything in their power to help the Russians withstand the German onslaught. This informal collaboration was given a more public and dramatic form in January 1942 when the three major powers, with twenty-three others, issued the Declaration of the United Nations, pledging common action against the aggressor powers and expressing their adhesion to the principles of the Atlantic Charter that had been formulated by Churchill and Roosevelt in a famous meeting on the high seas in August 1941. That charter had denied any desire for aggrandizement, territorial changes without the assent of interested populations, or infringements of sovereignty, and had expressed the intention of creating a world in which "all the men in all the lands may live out their lives in freedom from fear and want." The fact that these principles were not universally respected when the war was won is perhaps not as important as the fact that they helped to hearten men in the free world in 1942.

The coalition was not merely a matter of words. In the crucial period of the war, it provided for consultation and exchange of information between Hitler's chief adversaries; and it was always backed by the tremendous productive capacity of the United States, which had started, during its period of neutrality, to make itself the arsenal of democracy and was now tooled for the job.

To supply the fighting forces of this war was a difficult task; and a shortage of landing craft, to take only one example, could—and for a time did—mean that amphibious operations could not be conducted simultaneously in two theaters of war. But despite Hermann Goering's jeer that the United States "could make nothing except refrigerators and razor blades," these difficulties were overcome. American industry helped supply the force that finally broke Rommel's back in Africa and sent a constant stream of indispensable supplies to Russia. By the end of the war (according to Louis L. Snyder), the United States had produced 296,601 planes, 87,000 tanks, 2,434,553 trucks, 17,400,000 rifles, 315,000 pieces of field artillery, and 4,200,000 tons of artillery shells, among other necessities of war. Large amounts of these materials went to America's allies, under the aegis of Lend-Lease (which sent $4,750,000,000 of supplies to the Soviet Union alone in the course of the struggle); and all of it was used in the fight against the Axis powers.

The problem of maintaining supply lines was never easy. In the Atlantic, the effectiveness of the wolf-pack tactics of German submarines was finally overcome, as has already been indicated, by the refinement of convoy techniques and the perfection of underseas detection devices; and, in the Atlantic particularly, the security of shipping was attained by mid-1943. Supply routes in the Mediterranean were subject to heavy bombardment by land-based planes until the time of the Italian invasion, and this menace was even greater along the northern supply routes—the Murmansk run—to Russia. To circumvent the dangers of the northern route, the western Allies developed an alternate route through the Persian Gulf and across Iran. Before the southern route could be relied upon, however, British and Free French forces had to eliminate the threat posed by the collaboration of Vichy French authorities in Syria with the Nazis, as well by pro-Axis sympathies in Iraq and Iran. This was accomplished in mid-1941, and the Persian Gulf route was put into operation.

The Pacific War / Had Japanese aggression not been contained, it is possible that the Pacific war would, in time, have absorbed the greater part of the fighting energies of the United States, despite the general agreement of its staff planners that the main strategical effort should be in Europe. Even as it was, the heavy drain on American resources by Pacific needs severely limited possibilities of action in Europe.

Nevertheless, the helter-skelter retreat before Japanese might was checked in 1942 in three great battles. The first was a hard-fought engagement in the Coral Sea between Australia and the Solomon Islands, during which American carrier-based planes attacked a heavy Japanese fleet concentration, sank a carrier, four cruisers, and two destroyers, crippled seven other ships, and forced the enemy to retire northward. American losses in this battle were not inconsiderable—the carrier *Lexington*, a destroyer, and a tanker—but the action succeeded in checking a possible thrust against the southeast coast of Australia. Equally important was the defeat of a Japanese attempt to seize the island of Midway in the central Pacific, in order to secure their outer defensive perimeter (Kiska-Midway-Wake-the Marshalls-the Gilberts-Fiji) and to acquire a jumping-off point for future thrusts into the Hawaiian group. In May 1942, the Japanese assembled a fleet of 200 ships, including eleven battleships, eight carriers, twenty-two cruisers, sixty-five destroyers, and twenty-one submarines, together with 700 planes, and advanced toward Midway in five tactical forces, hoping to entice the remnants of the U.S. fleet into a hopeless battle. On June 4 they launched their attack with a seventy-plane strike on the island. Forty of these planes were shot down by U.S. marine and army interceptors, and those that returned to their carriers were never flown again. For the Japanese fleet was now hit by naval aviation from two American task forces lying northeast of Midway and, in a four-day inferno of fire, suffered the greatest defeat in the history of the Japanese navy, losing 5000 men, 322 planes, four carriers, and a heavy cruiser and having at least six other fleet units disabled.

These naval encounters slowed the momentum of the Japanese drive but did not stop it. The Japanese high command still looked toward Australia and planned a great pincers movement against the subcontinent, the arms of which would extend from Port Moresby in New Guinea on the one hand and the Solomons chain on the other. But Japan's strategy was too ambitious for its resources and, by attempting to gain both these widely separated areas, it won neither. Under the command of General Douglas MacArthur, who had been forced to flee from beleaguered Bataan in the Philippines, Australian and American forces defeated Japanese attempts to cross the mountains and seize Port Moresby. In August 1942, the U.S. marines anticipated the Japanese thrust toward the southern Solomons by making a daring landing on Guadalcanal and, through months of desperate fighting on the sea, in the air, and in the fever-infested jungles, made good their possession of this vital point.

These successes were the key to future victory. By the spring of 1943, MacArthur's forces were beginning to move northward through the coastal swamps of New Guinea toward Salamaua and Lae, while allied amphibious forces advanced up the Solomons chain and seized the Russell Islands and Bougainville. It was not long before the main Japanese base in the southwest Pacific, Rabaul on New Britain, was being pounded into helplessness. By the middle of 1943 the Japanese dream of Pacific-wide empire was fading fast: the Allies had reconquered the southwest Pacific and the beginning of their island-hopping advance was not far away.

Western Europe / Throughout 1942 operations in Western Europe were confined to a stepping-up of the Allied bombing offensive against German bases and installations in Norway and northern France and German industrial cities, and occasional raids to destroy or test defenses. The most daring of these last came early in March 1942 when a tiny British force carried by launches and torpedo boats crept into St.-Nazaire harbor on the Bay of Biscay, rammed HMS *Campbeltown* (one of the over-age destroyers given to Britain in 1940) against the main locks, and blew her and the dry docks up. This raid immobilized *Tirpitz*, (the last great German battleship after the torpedoing of *Bismarck* in May 1941) for, without an Atlantic port capable of servicing her, she did not dare leave Norwegian waters.

A second raid, less happy in its immediate results, was on Dieppe, staged by a force of 5000 troops, mostly Canadian, in August 1942. Western planners, thinking ahead to the future invasion to liberate Europe, felt it essential to try something on a scale sufficient to test landing equipment and techniques and throw light on what, in 1942, was considered the primary invasion problem—the seizure of a major port. The Dieppe raid, executed by a frontal assault on the port with infantry and tanks, combined with landings on the flanking beaches, was repulsed with heavy losses, more than a thousand men dying on the beaches and two thousand being captured by the Germans; but its long-run value was incalculable. It taught the Allies that the magnitude of the invasion task was much greater than they had thought and that attacks on open beaches were to be preferred to assaults on ports. Simultaneously, it deluded the Germans into believing that ports would be the primary Allied objectives, and this warped their defensive system to the Allied advantage.

North Africa: Crusader and El Alamein / The same months saw the rise and fall of Rommel's fortunes in Africa. The arrival of that energetic commander in April 1941 had retrieved sagging Axis fortunes, driven the British desert army back into Egypt, and isolated and bypassed the port of Tobruk, whose Australian garrison won the attention of the world by refusing to surrender despite a terrific and incessant bombardment from the air. Rommel was less concerned by the exertions of the "desert rats" in Tobruk than he was by the failure of Hitler and the OKW to give him the supplies he needed for a real offensive. It is generally believed, even by Rommel's foes, that if he had been given the three extra divisions of tanks that he kept asking for in 1941, he would have reached Cairo and the Suez Canal at the beginning of the next year and could then have rolled on to Basra and cut the flow of American supplies that were going to Russia by the Persian Gulf routes. The Allies were saved from that disaster by Hitler's preoccupation with the main offensive against Russia and by the failure of the supreme German staffs to take the African war seriously.

This is not all there is to it, however, for the British Eighth Army also played its part. In December 1941, Wavell's successor in the Middle East, General Auchinleck, launched a well-planned offensive against Rommel's lines and drove him all the way back to El Agheila, liberating Tobruk in the process. But Rommel, as Winston Churchill admitted in the House of Commons at the height of Auchinleck's "Crusader" operation, was "a daring and skillful opponent . . . a great general," and he not only escaped the snares set before him but kept the bulk of his armor intact. By the late spring, he was moving forward again and, in May, he began the great counterattack that finally took Tobruk and rolled on into Egypt, past Sidi Barrani and Mersa Matruh, until he had reached El Alamein, only 60 miles west of Alexandria.

During this advance, however, his stocks of fuel had been seriously depleted, and he could expect no reliable replenishment, since Malta-based planes and ships were now seriously hampering his supply lines. His tanks were being knocked out of action by combat fatigue and by the harassing tactics of RAF fighter bombers, now using American-made shells. His pleas for aid were disregarded or met with empty promises.

This was fatal, for, under the methodical supervision of Lieutenant General Bernard Law Montgomery, the British Eighth Army had been gathering every ounce of available power for a death thrust. In the bright moonlight of October 23, 1942, it opened a massive artillery barrage upon Rommel's lines. Four hours later came the assault by the hand-picked Commonwealth troops, and Rommel's columns were thrown into a retreat that did not stop until the last of the haggard *Afrika Korps* laid down their arms in Tunis months later.

As they staggered toward that inevitable end, pursued by furious demands from Hitler to stand and die in their places, a great Allied invasion fleet bore down upon the Moroccan coast and began, on November 8, to land British and American troops at Casablanca, Oran, and Algiers. This was the long-planned Operation Torch, which it was hoped, although in vain, would be unopposed by French garrisons. Unfortunately, the Americans did not make allowance for the sinuosities of Vichy politics and negotiated with the wrong people or put inadequate trust in the right ones to effect their purposes. There was, therefore, resistance at Casablanca, where thirteen French ships had to be sunk and 15,000 Americans and Frenchmen were killed, and at Oran, although not at Algiers, where pro-Allied conspirators seized the town. Hostilities were finally terminated on November 10 as a result of an arrangement made by the American commander, General Dwight D. Eisenhower, with Admiral

Jean François Darlan, commander of the French navy and former Vichy foreign minister. This decision was not popular in London and the United States, but it gave North Africa to the Allied cause and made any recovery by Rommel impossible.

In January 1943, at the Casablanca Conference attended by President Roosevelt, Winston Churchill, and Charles de Gaulle, the Allies announced to the world their intention of fighting on until the "unconditional surrender" of Germany, Italy, and Japan. Privately, they agreed to intensify their air offensive against Germany and to push on the preparations for a cross-Channel invasion of the continent, to sustain the Soviet Union by providing the greatest possible volume of supplies, to keep the pressure on Japan—but not at the risk of slowing European operations—and, immediately, to start planning an attack on Sicily for the summer of 1943. This last operation conformed more to Winston Churchill's preference for peripheral operations than to the views of the Clausewitzian Americans, who wanted to concentrate all forces for a punch across the Channel. It was decided, however, that the time had not come for the main drive, and that a thrust into Sicily would secure the Mediterranean supply routes, divert German pressure from the Russian front, and knock Italy out of the war.

Hitler meanwhile had been making frantic attempts to hold on to North Africa by pouring reinforcements and supplies into the ports of Tunis and Bizerte. What might have won Cairo in 1941 or saved Rommel in 1942 was not enough to retrieve Axis fortunes in 1943. Rommel's tired forces and the levies flown across to Tunisia managed to mount an offensive in February that hit the inexperienced Americans at the Kasserine Pass and inflicted heavy losses on them. But they recovered from this jab quickly and, in March and April, in conjunction with Montgomery's veterans, they drove Rommel's troops to the tip of Cape Bon peninsula, where a quarter of a million of them finally surrendered in May 1943.

The Fall of Italy / With hardly a pause, the plans laid at Casablanca were carried out. In June aerial and naval bombardment began to soften up Sicily; in July a fleet of 3000 vessels launched the first major amphibious assault on Axis-held territory. Montgomery's Eighth Army and Canadian forces landed on the east coast and took the port of Syracuse. George S. Patton, the most dashing of the American commanders, landed in the south, took Marsala and Palermo, and then linked up with the British and drove the three German divisions to the sea. Here—in an imitation of Dunkirk—they managed to evacuate 60,000 men to the mainland. But Sicily was in Allied hands, after only thirty-nine days of fighting.

These events and the beginning of serious bombing of the Italian mainland (Rome was bombed for the first time on July 19 by 700 Allied planes) brought an abrupt end to the career of the man who had aspired to make the Mediterranean a Roman lake. Mussolini's popularity had long since evaporated, and conspiracy was rife even among his closest supporters. On July 24, 1943, the Fascist Grand Council, which the Duce had easily dominated in the past and which had not even met since 1939, convened itself and demanded that Mussolini hand over command of the army to the king. The next day, the Duce was told by Victor Emmanuel that he no longer desired him as premier. As Mussolini left the palace, he was arrested and interned. Later in the year, he was rescued in a daring coup by German agents and installed as head of a puppet government in the north. But he never regained a popular following and, when the total collapse came, he was captured and brutally murdered by Italian partisans.

Speedy action by the Allies in the days following Mussolini's fall might have brought all Italy into Allied hands. The protracted armistice negotiations that took place between them and the new government of Marshal Pietro Badoglio gave the Germans an opportunity to build up their defenses. Thus, when an armistice was finally signed on September 3, it did nothing to facilitate the Allied landings that began on the same day. The Eighth Army found comparatively little resistance to their landings on the Calabrian coast; but the assault of the U.S. Fifth Army at Salerno in September was met by four days of counterattack, which at times seemed likely to turn the landing into a debacle. This did not happen, but it was clear that the advance northward was not going to be easy.

Stalingrad and the Recoil in Russia / Even before these reversals had taken place, the tide had begun to turn for Hitler in Russia also. In the spring of 1942 he had resumed offensive operations along the whole front and, although he had no success in taking Leningrad or Moscow, his armies had made impressive gains on the southern front. But Russian resistance was hardening daily, partly as a result of American supplies and partly as a result of German behavior toward the Russian people. Alexander Dallin has written that, in the early stages of the Russian war, Germany "had a rare opportunity to appeal to the population of the Soviet Union . . . [who were] potentially receptive to a skillful attempt to drive a wedge between the rulers and the people." Hitler failed utterly to take advantage of this. He is reported to have said in July 1941, "Russia is our Africa and the Russians are our Negroes," and he persisted in the years that followed in thinking of the Russian people as objects for enslavement or extermination. Russian prisoners of war, who might have been easily turned against their former masters, were treated with brutality or callous neglect and, by the Germans' own admission, the incredible number of 3,700,000 POWs died in German hands. Civilian populations were exploited or killed or turned over to the mercies of addlepates like Alfred Rosenberg or sadists like Erich Koch, the German commissar for the Ukraine, whom Stalin once described as "the chief of those blockheads in Berlin who reminded every man in the Soviet Union every day of what he had to fight against." German brutality, political obtuseness, and administrative inefficiency deprived them of the support of subject populations, the economic reserves that would have fed their war effort, and the aid of trained soldiers eager to change sides, and gave them, instead, the problem of coping with an aggressive and massive partisan movement that operated behind their lines.

As Hitler's difficulties in Russia mounted, he became increasingly suspicious of his generals, and his prejudice against operational flexibility and maneuver, his lack of sympathy for the troops, and his proneness to self-deception became dangerous. Nothing illustrates these qualities more strikingly than his conduct duing the battle of Stalingrad. In August 1942 the German Sixth Army under General von Paulus reached and invested this industrial center on the west bank of the Volga and proceeded to attempt to pound it into submission. Despite the difficulty of keeping the city supplied (all food, clothing, and munitions had to be ferried across the river under German bombardment), the Soviet troops and the citizens of the city held out in the rubble of their homes, and were still holding out at the end of the year.

By this time, Hitler had set his heart on the capture of the city. On November 9 he said publicly:

> I wanted to get to the Volga and to do so at a particular point where stands a certain town. By chance it bears the name of Stalin himself. I wanted to take the place and, do you know, we've pulled it off, we've got it really, except for a few enemy positions still holding out.

Ten days after this speech the Russians smashed the front held by Germany's Rumanian ally northwest of Stalingrad; on November 20 they launched a successful attack south of the city, and, two days later, they closed the pincers and encircled the German forces (see map, p. 735).

One of General von Paulus' subordinates wrote at this time: "To remain where we are deliberately is not only a crime from a military point of view, but it is a criminal act as regards our responsibility to the German nation." It was nevertheless a crime insisted upon by Hitler, who flatly refused to countenance a break-out (which would have involved leaving the Volga and the city bearing Stalin's name) and who entrusted Goering with the task of keeping the Sixth Army supplied. Goering expressed every confidence in the *Luftwaffe's* ability to fulfill this mission;

in fact, as any airman of competence could have seen, it was impossible. Yet, as his soldiers fought, and starved, and died, and as the Russian ring became so thick and strong that a break in or out of it was impossible, Hitler remained adamantly opposed to any withdrawal. But human resistance has limits. Paulus had begun the siege with 300,000 men. In the first days of February 1943, their ragged remnants, 123,000 officers and men, surrendered. Germany had suffered its greatest defeat as a result of the deliberate and callous indifference of its ruler to the fate of its sons.

In the same month in which the Sixth Army died, the Russians recaptured Rostov, Kursk, and Kharkov and, before their momentum slowed, they had won back 185,000 square miles of territory. The German offensive of 1943 was an attempt to regain this lost ground, and it failed badly. The fact was that the days of conquest in Russia were over. By the end of 1943 the Russians were back in Kiev (where the Germans had slaughtered the entire Jewish population before evacuation) and in Zhitomir, close to the old border of Poland.

THE ROAD TO VICTORY, 1943–1945

Problems of the Coalition / Once their armies had begun to press the Germans back, the Soviets became more difficult partners than they had been. Not that they had ever been the most comfortable of allies, for, conscious of the fact that their armies were carrying the brunt of the fighting on land, they had always been demanding in the matter of supplies and less than grateful when Allied seamen braved the perils of the Murmansk passage to bring them. Moreover, they had kept up a drumfire of criticism against Allied failure to provide a second front in Europe—exasperating Mr. Churchill on one occasion into asking where they had been when there *was* an Allied front bearing the full weight of German aggression in 1940.

The Allied statesmen were for the most part, however, patient in the face of these attacks and tried to explain their own difficulties and to show their gratitude by the volume of their supplies. There was never any disposition on their part to undervalue the Soviet contribution to the war or the indispensability of Soviet cooperation in rebuilding the international system when the war was over. On the whole, their tactics seemed to work. In October 1943 the British foreign secretary, Anthony Eden, and the United States secretary of state, Cordell Hull, traveled to Moscow to hold talks with their opposite number, Molotov. After meeting Stalin, Eden noted that there was no recrimination about the past and that Stalin seemed to understand that the Allies were bending all their efforts toward an invasion of the continent, adding that "the confidence he is placing in our word is most striking." The talks ended with a pledge of joint action to defeat, disarm, and control Germany, to free Italy of fascism, to liberate Austria from its forced union with Germany, and to punish all Germans guilty of atrocities. With respect to the long future, the foreign secretaries spoke of the possibility of establishing a world organization.

All these pledges were reaffirmed in December 1943 at Teheran, where Roosevelt, Churchill, and Stalin had their first joint meeting. There the determination to establish a world organization with membership from all nations dedicated to peace was expressed more emphatically. Indeed, in the following year, at Dumbarton Oaks, Virginia, representatives of the three Allied powers and China held talks in an attempt to make more precise the nature and purpose of what was eventually to become the United Nations.

The Soviet Union's collaboration in these talks was gratifying. Less so was its growing interest in the postwar disposition of European territory. As in World War I, the western powers had a tendency to wish to push political questions into the backs of their minds until the war was won. Not so the Russians, to whom war and peace were reverse sides of the same coin. As early as 1943, Stalin was evincing a desire to discuss the future eastern frontiers of Poland with some responsible Polish authority, an indication that he had his mind set on acquiring the eastern districts. And, as his troops advanced further, his interest in both the Baltic and those Balkan states that had fought on Hitler's side also began to awaken. There were obvious signs of future trouble here, although Allied statesmen tried very hard not to see them.

Italy from Salerno to the Fall of Rome / The year 1944 was one long slugging match in Italy with heavy Allied casualties. Attempts to restore the operational mobility that had been lost by the delay before Salerno were frustrated by the terrain and by the tenacity of the defense organized by the German supreme commander in Italy, Marshal Kesselring. Kesselring slowed the double-pronged advance of the British Eighth Army and the U.S. Fifth Army of General Mark Clark by building a strong defensive position called the Gustav Line, which had as its center the 1700-foot Monte Cassino, and which blocked the road through the Liri valley to Rome. To outflank the Gustav Line, the Allies on January 22, 1944, made another amphibious landing at Anzio on the coast 33 miles south of Rome. This met the most stubborn kind of German resistance, and the G.I.s were pinned to the beaches and the adjoining slopes for four months before a break-out was effected.

To reduce pressure upon them, Clark had launched an attack across the Rapido River in front of Cassino at the time of the original landing. This was nothing short of disastrous and temporarily destroyed the 36th (Texas) Division as a fighting force. In February, another attempt was made to draw the Germans away from Anzio, when Cassino was assaulted by the 2d New Zealand and the 4th Indian divisions. It was during this second battle that the decision was made to bomb the Benedictine abbey on Monte Cassino, a decision that was subsequently much criticized in Allied countries and was heavily exploited by German propaganda agencies. To the troops on the spot this controversy would have meant nothing. They were sure that the Germans were using the abbey for observation purposes and expected and wanted the bombardment to be made. Unfortunately, when it came, it was not coordinated with a ground attack and served no useful purpose.

Cassino finally fell in April in a battle that might have been a masterpiece. Planned by Field Marshal Alexander, the supreme Allied commander in Italy, it was designed to smother Cassino by numbers and, at the same time, to suck in, encircle, and destroy the bulk of the German forces in Italy. It was preceded by diversionary amphibious feints. It was then delivered with a massive force that effected its first objective and might have justified all the bloodshed and sacrifice that had gone before, if it had only been properly coordinated with the simultaneous breakout from Anzio. But at the very moment when Alexander's trap was closing on the out-generaled and broken Germans, General Clark detached his forces from the pursuit and sent them racing toward Rome. His desire to be first in the Eternal City prevented the destruction of the German Tenth Army.

This rather took the bloom off the triumphal entry into Rome in June, for it meant that fighting had to continue. When, a little later, seven Allied divisions were withdrawn from Italy to support the Normandy invasion by a landing in Southern France, the prospects of an early end to the Italian war vanished completely.

Cross-Channel Attack / In the first days of June 1944, the BBC transmitters beamed to the forces of the French resistance the prearranged signal that indicated the start of the long-awaited invasion of France. They had chosen for the purpose two lines from Verlaine's *Chanson d'Automne*:

> *Les sanglots longs des violons de l'automne*
> *Blessent mon coeur d'une langueur monotone.*

In view of the violence that was to follow, one can hardly imagine more inappropriate words.

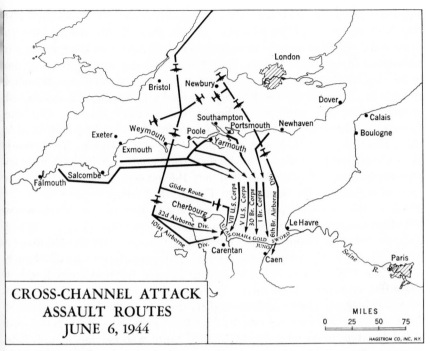

CROSS-CHANNEL ATTACK
ASSAULT ROUTES
JUNE 6, 1944

Based on a map prepared by the Office of the Chief of Military History, Department of the Army, U.S.A.

The preparations for Operation Overlord had been going on since 1942, and the forces that had been assembled constituted the greatest amphibious force in history. More than five thousand ships and landing craft were waiting to transport 150,000 trained men, 1500 tanks, and thousands of guns, vehicles, and supplies to the Normandy coast. They were supported by 12,000 planes, some of which had been systematically destroying bridges and access routes in order to seal off the invasion area from the interior, while others—transports and gliders—prepared to drop paratroopers and demolitions teams well behind the beaches in order to complete that job. To facilitate constant supply for this immense host until such time as a major port could be seized, artificial breakwaters and docks—the so-called Mulberries—had been built in England and were ready to be towed across the Channel and installed along the beaches. D-Day was June 6.

Throughout the spring months, Field Marshal Rommel, brought to the west from Italy, had been applying his energies to the gigantic task of preparing for the blow that he knew was coming. He was confronted with a hopeless task. Hitler, with complete scorn for strategical principles, was insisting that every foot of land be held—in Russia, in Italy, in

France—and his rigidity not only made tactical mobility impossible but deprived the western commanders of adequate forces with which to oppose the Allied thrust. As Rommel's chief of staff wrote later, the much advertized Atlantic Wall was "in its manning and armaments . . . no more than a thin line without depth or substantial reserves." Rommel did his best to improve the beach defenses by increasing the number of strong points and building elaborate underwater obstacles. But the Germans had no naval forces to help in repulsing a landing and, by this time, their air force had been shot out of the skies. And, as if this were not enough, the commanders in the west were constantly bedeviled by an incredible chain of command that left the power of decision, even in tactical matters, in the hands of the Fuehrer in Berlin.

All of these weaknesses played into the hands of the Allies when Overlord began and British and American forces poured onto the selected beaches between Caen and the Cherbourg peninsula on the Normandy coast. There was heavy initial resistance, especially on Omaha Beach where the U.S. 29th Division was pinned down by murderous fire, but there was no repetition of Anzio. Within five days the German defensive ring was broken. The Canadians and the British on the left were headed for Caen; the defenses on Omaha had been knocked out by aerial and naval bombardment, and the U.S. First Army was moving inland. The sixteen Allied divisions had established a beachhead eighty miles long and twenty miles deep. By D-Day plus twenty, a million men were ashore; more were pouring in over the Mulberries near the British beach at Arromanches; and the German garrison in the great port of Cherbourg was preparing to surrender.

The Plot against Hitler / On July 20, 1944, at approximately 12:30 in the afternoon, Colonel Count Claus Schenk von Stauffenberg entered Hitler's conference hall at Rastenburg, while the Fuehrer and his staff were listening to a situation report, slid his brief case under the table, and unobtrusively left the room. Five minutes later there was a terrific explosion. The windows of the wooden building were blown out, the roof partially collapsed, there was the sound of men screaming. Stauffenberg, standing at a safe distance outside, climbed quickly into a staff car and drove off to the airstrip, where a plane was waiting to take him to Berlin.

His action was the end result of years of planning and debate by a German underground that reached into every class of society and had as its leaders Prussian aristocrats, high-ranking civil servants, Socialist politicians and trade-union leaders, ministers of the Gospel, diplomats, university teachers, and soldiers. Some of them had already died because of their participation in the conspiracy; some had risked their lives in attempts on Hitler's life that had failed; all were, by the middle of 1944, in great danger, for the Gestapo was, at long last, closing in on them. But their plans were ready. Hitler was to be killed; military authorities in Berlin and Paris were to seize power, arrest the other Nazi notables, set up a provisional government with General Ludwig Beck as head of state, and open negotiations with the western Allies. Stauffenberg's bomb was the first step in the chain of events that was supposed to lead to liberation from both tyranny and war.

But the bomb did not kill Hitler, and the news that it had not done so, relayed quickly to Berlin, paralyzed the plotters with indecision and persuaded some of the troop commanders upon whom they had been counting to attempt to withdraw from the enterprise. These delays and hesitations were adroitly exploited by Joseph Goebbels in Berlin in such a way as to reassert Hitler's authority. The conspiracy collapsed; its leaders were arrested; and the immediate result was a series of ghastly public trials followed by the degradation and butchery of all who were suspected of complicity in the plot. July 20 had no effect on the course of the war. But it was a reminder that not all Germans were Nazis by conviction and that, in addition to the "other Germany" in exile, there had been an "inner emigration" into which those whose consciences had been revolted by Hitler's acts had withdrawn, not merely to ride out the storm but, in a great many cases, to risk their lives in making plans for the liberation of their country. The Bonn government annually commemorates this plot that failed, and it is just that it should do so.

The End of Nazi Germany / Speaking to his generals after the failure of the conspiracy, Hitler said:

> We'll fight until we get a peace that secures the life of the German nation for the next fifty or a hundred years. . . . If my life had been ended, I think I can say that for me personally it would only have been a release from worry, sleepless nights, and a great nervous suffering. . . . Just the same, I am grateful to destiny for letting me live, because I believe.

Uttered at a time when the Allied armies, spearheaded by Patton's tanks, were pouring through the gap at Avranches and beginning the sweep toward the Rhine, when the second Allied landing—this time on the southern coast of France between Toulon and Cannes—was only days away, when the RAF bomber command was dropping 25,000 tons of bombs nightly on German cities, and when Russian armies were pushing from Riga into East Prussia, encircling Warsaw, and approaching Bucharest, the Fuehrer's words might be taken only as a proof of deepening megalomania. What was there, after all, for him to believe in?

Hitler's conviction that he would win his war rested in part on faith in himself, in the belief that, somehow or other, like a second Frederick

The Grand Alliance: Churchill, Roosevelt, and Stalin at Yalta in the Crimea, February 1945. (UNITED PRESS INTERNATIONAL)

the Great, he would extricate himself from his difficulties by sheer force of will. But it is clear also that he was relying on two other things: upon new and more dreadful secret weapons and, most of all, upon a sudden dissolution of the coalition that opposed him. "Do you think," he said to his staff in January 1945, "that, deep down inside, the English are enthusiastic about all the Russian developments?"; and Goering answered comfortably, "They certainly didn't plan that we hold them off while the Russians conquer all of Germany. If this goes on, we will get a telegram in a few days."

Hitler's faith in this sort of resolution of his problem was disappointed. His scientists did invent wonder weapons, the most impressive of which was the V-2, a liquid-fuel rocket of about twelve tons take-off weight capable of carrying a one-ton warhead approximately 200 miles from its launching point. If the V-2 had been operational before D-Day, the Normandy invasion would have been infinitely more difficult. As it was, it came into use only in September 1944 and, although the Germans launched 1500 V-2s against England and 2100 against Antwerp, the swift advance of the Allies soon made it unusable. Other weapons—the jet plane, for instance—came too late to save Germany.

Nor was the dissolution of the enemy coalition to take place, at least until the war was over. At the very moment when Goering was talking about telegrams from London, the British and the Americans were preparing for their meeting with the Russians at Yalta in the Crimea, which took place in the first part of February 1945. Here Roosevelt, Churchill, and Stalin, in an atmosphere of cordiality, agreed upon the postwar control of Germany and the division of that potentially conquered country into zones of occupation. They also concluded agreements concerning the future world organization (setting April 25, 1945, as the date for a conference in San Francisco to begin the drafting of a charter), the postwar organization of Eastern Europe, and the common pursuit of the war against Japan. In the course of these discussions, it was apparent that there were deep differences of view between the Allies, especially with regard to the boundaries and the government of postwar Poland, but these were overcome by Allied concessions to the Soviet point of view, granted in order to secure Soviet participation in the war against Japan. Nothing that was done at Yalta brought any comfort or hope to Hitler.

Moreover, the will of the German soldier was now broken. On the eastern front, it had been worn down by time, weather, and the relentless pressure of the Russian armies. In the west, the last flicker of hope and combativeness was snuffed out by the failure of the German offensive in the Ardennes in January 1945. This battle—known best in the west as the Battle of the Bulge—was a last desperate throw by Hitler, an attempt to crack the American lines by surprise, which would permit the German armor to cross the Meuse between Liège and Namur and to drive toward Antwerp. If this was accomplished, the supply and communications lines of Allied forces in the Brussels-Antwerp area could be cut, twenty-five to thirty Allied divisions could be destroyed and an Allied offensive against the West Wall could be delayed indefinitely. These hopes were not realized, although, for some days during the dark December of 1944, it appeared that they might be. The brunt of this last German punch fell on a thinly held sector of the American lines, manned by green troops, at a time when the reserve and supply system was muddled and weather made air support impossible. The initial effect was shattering; confusion and panic reigned for days and as late as the beginning of January the issue was in doubt. In the battle around Bastogne, some battalions of the U.S. 17th Airborne Division suffered 40 percent casualties; and George Patton wrote, "We can still lose this war." But by the middle of the month, it was all over and the Germans never recovered. Now it was just a matter of time before the Allied victory was made final.

In March and April, Russian armies under Marshals Zhukhov and Konev took Danzig and Vienna, overran Czechoslovakia, and pressed on toward Berlin. On March 7, by a stroke of luck, American forces seized

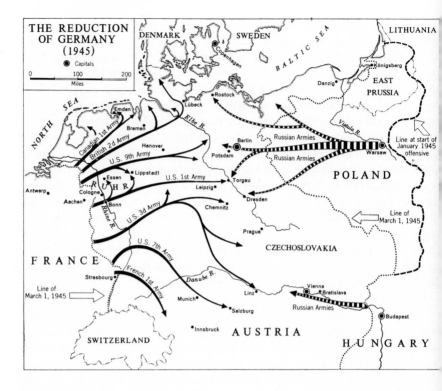

THE REDUCTION
OF GERMANY
(1945)

● Capitals

0 ——— 100 ——— 200
Miles

DENMARK SWEDEN *BALTIC SEA* LITHUANIA

Copenhagen

Königsberg

Danzig EAST
PRUSSIA

Rostock

Lübeck

NORTH SEA

Emden

Bremen *Elbe R.*

Hanover

Canadian 1st Army
British 2d Army

U.S. 9th Army

Berlin Russian Armies *Vistula R.* Line at start of
January 1945

Potsdam Russian Armies Warsaw offensive

Line of start of
January 1945

Essen Lippstadt U.S. 1st Army Torgau

Antwerp Cologne *RUHR* Leipzig POLAND

Aachen Bonn Dresden

Rhine R. U.S. 3d Army Chemnitz Line of
March 1, 1945

Prague

U.S. 7th Army CZECHOSLOVAKIA

F R A N C E

French 1st Army

Strasbourg *Danube R.*

Line of
March 1, 1945 Munich Linz Vienna Bratislava

Salzburg Russian Armies

Innsbruck A U S T R I A Budapest

SWITZERLAND H U N G A R Y

the bridge over the Rhine at Remagen before it could be destroyed and
upset the whole German defensive system along the river. In Italy, Allied
forces took Bologna and crossed the Po. Mussolini, fleeing for safety, was
caught and killed with his mistress on April 28 by Italian partisans. Hitler
shot himself and his bride of one day in a bunker in Berlin on April 30.
Three days earlier the western armies and the Russians had made their
first contact in Saxony. On May 2 Berlin fell to the Russians. On May 7,
the Third Reich, in the person of Admiral Karl Doenitz, surrendered unconditionally to the Grand Alliance.

The End of Japan / Victory over the remaining enemy was not long
delayed. Since the latter part of 1943, the Allies had tightened the ring
around Japan. The hard-fought victory of the U.S. marines at Tarawa
in November 1943, where, at a cost of 1100 dead and 2072 wounded, an
apparently impregnable island fortress had been taken in four days, was
the beginning of a long series of brilliant amphibious operations, which
were characterized by amazing coordination of ground, naval, and aerial
operations, as well as by the speed and economy of effort employed.
Here the war attained its greatest degree of mobility, as the U.S. navy
carried army and marine forces long distances, bypassing Japanese strong

points and allowing them to die of inactivity, hitting at places where attack was not expected, and advancing by tremendous strides toward the very heart of the Japanese empire. Kwajalein was seized in January 1944 and with it control over the Marshalls; Eniwetok fell in February; in the same month the great Japanese naval base at Truk was pounded into helplessness; in June and July, Saipan and Tinian fell to marine and army forces; in July, American troops landed on Guam; in September, Pelelieu was in American hands, eliminating a threat to General MacArthur's flank as he now crossed, after a remarkable advance up the coast of New Guinea, to Leyte in the Philippines; in October, the great naval battle of the Leyte Gulf finished what was left of the offensive capabilities of the Japanese navy; in January 1945, MacArthur invaded Luzon; in February, in an epic battle, the Marines took Iwo Jima and provided an essential refueling base for B-29s returning from bomb runs on Tokyo; in April, the great island of Okinawa was invaded and systematically conquered by U.S. army and marine troops. Only by tracing this progress of American arms on a map of the Pacific can one appreciate the magnitude of the accomplishment.

Plans were now made for the invasion of the Japanese homeland, which was thought of in terms of simultaneous landings on the island of Kyushu and on the Tokyo plain. Considering the fanatical resistance shown by Japanese fighting men on Saipan and Iwo Jima and the suicide missions of Japanese pilots at Okinawa, the bitterest kind of resistance was expected. Even the prospective entrance of the Soviet Union into the war, which, it was hoped, would bottle up Japan's Manchurian armies, would not prevent serious casualties to the invading forces, which were expected to run as high as half a million men.

It was this calculation that led to the hard decision to use against Japan the weapon that had been devised by American and European scientists working in the United States since 1942. This was the atomic bomb, first successfully tested at Alamogordo Flats, New Mexico, in July 1945. Convinced that no mere warning would be effective in persuading the Japanese government to surrender and fearing the effects of an announced demonstration that might fail, the U.S. government, (now headed by Harry S. Truman), backed by its Allies, decided that this terrible weapon must be used against Japanese cities. On August 6, 1945, two days before Russia declared war on Japan, the first atomic bomb was dropped on the city of Hiroshima, destroying the city and killing 78,000 people. On August 9 the second bomb was dropped, this time on Nagasaki in Kyushu, demolishing the torpedo yards and the great steel mill for which the town was noted, destroying the whole municipal area, and killing tens of thousands of people. On the following day, the Japanese government surrendered. The global war was over, although the formal armistice was not signed until September 2.

PART FIVE

Since
1945

GENERAL OBSERVATIONS

The most striking political developments of the period that began with the cessation of hostilities in 1945 were the division of Europe into two halves, separated by an institutional and ideological barrier; the development inside each of these two Europes of unitary tendencies that weakened old national and cultural frontiers; and, finally, the radical diminution of Europe's power and influence in world affairs.

The first of these, the imposition of a vast dualism upon the European continent, was the end result of that dissolution of the Allied wartime coalition for which Hitler had longed in vain. It took three years before western statesmen were forced to admit that the fellowship in arms was not going to be prolonged after the defeat of Germany and Japan and that, far from wishing to promote the economic and political recovery of the war-shattered European countries, the Soviet Union was hoping to exploit misery and want in order to spread communism to the west. The Truman Doctrine, the Marshall Plan, and the establishment of the North Atlantic Treaty Organization were successive responses to what had become an obvious threat to the political freedom of Europe; the Warsaw Pact was the Soviet rejoinder, which indicated that the Soviet Union had no intention of relinquishing the control that it had won over the states of Eastern Europe in the first postwar years, and which thus completed the establishment of what came to be known as the iron curtain, dividing the continent in two.

On the eastern side of this barrier, the presence of Soviet military power enforced ideological and institutional conformity and political and economic cooperation on the part of the lesser states. Yugoslavia alone succeeded in breaking away from the iron grip of this system and establishing an independent position, and this was largely due to accidents of geography. Hungary's attempt to imitate its southern neighbor was crushed by Soviet armor with a brutality that discouraged further imitation.

Examples of centralization and unity of policy accomplished by the use or threat of force have not been infrequent in history and are never particularly impressive. A more notable postwar political development was the voluntary movement toward unification on the western side of the curtain. This, as we shall see below (p. 798), took various forms and involved grappling with many difficult problems; but, in view of the historical disinclination of the European states to any sacrifice of their sovereignty, its results were impressive.

The third of these developments, the reduction of Europe's world stature, had begun during the war of 1914–1918 and had been accelerated by the economic ills of the interwar period. Yet, until the outbreak of the second global conflict, Europe remained the center of world politics, and the decisions of the European powers determined the course of events in far-flung regions of the world. The long hard years that stretched from the Nazi capture of Warsaw to Hitler's suicide amid the rubble of Berlin changed all this in a fundamental way. They inflicted upon all European powers material and psychological damage so great that the resources necessary for their full political recovery were eaten up and even their desire for such recovery was exhausted. When the war was over, there was a tendency for some Europeans to view the transfer of power and responsibility to the United States and the Soviet Union with a resignation that was tinged with fear but also with satisfaction. Thus, *Punch* wryly discussed the positive advantages that might accrue from becoming a state of second, or even third, rank.

The changed position of the European states in the world was thrown into sharper relief by the loss of their colonial empires as a result of nationalistic movements in the Orient, the Near East, and Africa. These movements too had existed before the war, but they had been greatly encouraged by that conflict's demonstration in its first stages that white nations are not necessarily superior in military skill to peoples of different pigmentation. Postwar illustrations of this same truth, in Korea and Indochina, stimulated opposition to colonialism and forced concessions to it in British, French, Dutch, and Belgian dependencies. Once the process of liberation had started, it proceeded with a rush that defied all wartime expectations. By the end of 1960, African and Asian nations, most of which had won their independence after 1945, made up almost half of the membership of the Assembly of the United Nations—an organization, incidentally, that the European nations had learned, because of their reduced strength in comparison with the United States and the Soviet Union and for other reasons, to take more seriously than they had taken the League of Nations.

In the economic field, the postwar period began with the most dismal prospects for Europe as a whole. Trade was at a standstill; industry was paralyzed by wartime destruction and shortages of raw materials and fuel; agriculture was suffering from the lack of machinery, seed, and fertilizer; transportation and communications systems had been disrupted and in some cases largely destroyed by bombing; markets and distribution systems were hopelessly confused by the destruction of the Nazi empire, which had embraced most of the continent for five years; currencies were depreciated and credit facilities uncertain; food and fuel stocks were inadequate and promised to become dangerously so in the near future; and all problems were made doubly difficult by the demobilization of the armies and by the existence of millions of displaced persons who lacked the very necessities of life.

The recovery from these conditions was slower in Eastern Europe than in the west, largely because the decision of the eastern countries to defer in all basic matters to the Soviet Union led them to deny themselves opportunities open to the western countries, and also because their patron, suffering terrible physical and economic damage from the war, was in no position in the first postwar years to extend material aid to them. The western countries, in contrast, were encouraged, psychologically as well as economically, by loans from the United States and by the aid advanced after the implementation of the Marshall Plan in 1948. Their recovery was steady and in some cases (notably that of West Germany) spectacular.

In the intellectual and spiritual sphere, it is difficult to make generalizations about the period after 1945. It must be noted, however, that the iron curtain was not merely of political and economic significance. It represented a barrier to the free exchange of ideas, to mutual stimulation, and to scholarly and scientific collaboration that was virtually insurmountable. Not since the religious wars of the sixteenth century had two parts of Europe been so effectively sealed off from each other, and it was impossible to calculate the extent to which this hampered Europe's spiritual recovery from the war.

29

The Reconstruction of Europe

THE FRAMEWORK OF PEACE

The United Nations / History may yet decide that the most important single result of World War II was the creation of the organization that, in 1945, replaced the old League of Nations, which had passed out of existence six years before. Discussion of the necessity of a new world organization had begun early in the war, and planning in detail began at Dumbarton Oaks in 1944 (see p. 747). Although there was considerable wrangling at the subsequent Big Three conferences at Yalta and Potsdam (see p. 765) over questions of voting procedure and membership, agreement on all contested points was finally reached. The San Francisco Conference, which met in April 1945, completed the task of drafting and adopting the Charter of the United Nations in June.

The new organization was not intended to be a world government, for it recognized the sovereign rights of its members and was specifically forbidden to "intervene in matters which [were] essentially within the domestic jurisdiction" of member states. Its declared purposes were rather to maintain peace and security, to develop good relations between nations, to promote the solution of economic, social, and other problems by international action, and to provide a forum at which the opposing views of its members might be reconciled.

To effect these purposes, the United Nations was provided with a number of different bodies of a representative, executive, and consultative nature. Like the League of Nations (see p. 542), it had an Assembly in which all its members had equal rights of representation and a Council (now called the Security Council) with more restricted and preferential membership. The General Assembly was given the authority to discuss all questions falling within the scope of the Charter, the right to appoint numerous standing and special committees, and the additional right to make recommendations to member states and to the Security Council. The Council, which was composed of five permanent members (the United States, the Soviet Union, China, Great Britain, France) and six others elected for two-year terms by the Assembly, was designed to give direction and leadership to the work of the organization as a whole and would have the authority to deal swiftly and effectively with threats to the general peace. Its decisions on procedural matters were made by simple majority vote, but in all other questions the majority had to include the five permanent members. In short, every permanent member had the right of veto on most important issues.

This provision was written into the Charter in order to protect the interests of the greater and more responsible powers, and it was not believed, by the western powers at least, that the veto right would be abused. When the coming of the cold war proved the frailty of this assumption of great-power cooperation, the work of the Security Council was hampered and at times paralyzed. As a result, the General Assembly achieved an importance that was probably not intended by the founders of the United Nations. In November 1950, the Assembly adopted a resolution stipulating that, when lack of unanimity made it impossible for the Council to meet a threat to the peace, an emergency meeting of the General Assembly could be called at the request of a majority of its own members or of seven members of the Security Council and could make recommendations for collective action in the cause of peace, even to the point of recommending the use of military force. This broadening of the Assembly's mandate proved to be productive of good, and, in general, the history of the U. N. saw a steady increase in the authority of the Assembly, with the approval of world public opinion.

Another body which gradually expanded its functions was the Secretariat, which was established to carry out administrative and technical tasks under the direction of a secretary general elected for a five-year term by the Assembly on the basis of recommendations made by the Security Council. In the late 1950s and the first year of the following decade, when the U. N. was called upon to send troops to preserve peace in the Near East and the strife-torn Congo, the secretary's tasks increased in number and variety, and he was frequently

UNESCO Headquarters, Paris. A general view of the Secretariat and Conference buildings. The statue in the piazza (foreground) is by Henry Moore. The buildings occupy a seven-and-a-half-acre site made available by the French government. Plans for the headquarters were prepared by Marcel Breuer (U.S.), Pier Luigi Nervi (Italy), and Bernard Zehrfuss (France), and were approved by a panel of noted architects consisting of Lucio Costa (Brazil), Walter Gropius (U.S.), Le Corbusier (France), Sven Markelius (Sweden), and Ernesto Rogers (Italy). Eero Saarinen (U.S.) was also consulted. (UNESCO/DOMINIQUE LAJOUX)

required to act more as a diplomat than as a mere administrator. His growth in stature also reflected and reinforced that of the General Assembly, which tended to regard him as its spokesman and leader.

A very important agency of the U. N. was the Economic and Social Council, whose mission was to contribute to the elimination and control of international friction by initiating studies in the area of social, health, and educational needs. This body, composed of eighteen members elected by the General Assembly without preferential treatment for great powers, had the right to appoint its own committees and worked through a network of such bodies, chosen for special tasks or work in specific areas. It maintained liaison with older organizations like the International Monetary Fund and the World Bank and supervised the establishment and functioning of new "specialized agencies," like the World Health Organization and the United Nations Educational, Scientific and Cultural Organization (UNESCO), to mention only two of the most important.

Other organs of the U. N. were the Trusteeship Council, which supervised the administration of territories whose peoples had not yet won full self-government (former mandated territories, former enemy colonies, territories handed over to the U. N. by their former administrators), and the International Court of Justice, which replaced the old Hague Court and was established in the same place. A special body set up in 1953 was the International Atomic Energy Agency (IAEA), which, despite its virtual autonomy, was required to report upon its activities to the U. N.

In the deliberations at San Francisco fifty states participated. The enemy powers were excluded, as were such neutrals as Spain, Portugal, Eire, Sweden, and Switzerland and one allied state, Poland, because it did not possess a government that was recognized by all the great powers.[1] Under pressure from the Latin American states, the United States government agreed to seek admission for Argentina (at that time, a country with a dictatorial regime), and succeeded in gaining it by promising the Soviet government to support the admission of two of Russia's provinces, the Ukraine and Byelorussia, as members with full rights and privileges. Membership was subsequently made available to other countries, provided they were "peace-loving states," recommended by the majority of the Security Council (with all permanent members either approving or abstaining) and backed by a two-thirds majority of the Assembly. The greatest changes in membership were those that followed the creation of the new independent states of Africa at the end of the 1950s.

The Peace Treaties / The transition from war to peace was even more difficult than it had proved to be after World War I and, as if recognizing that this would be true, the victorious powers made no attempt to hold a general peace conference. The territorial settlement was worked out on a piecemeal basis in many conferences and negotiations, some of which were successful in short order, while others finished their work, if they finished it at all, only after years of meetings. Fifteen years after the cessation of hostilities against the Axis powers, the boundaries of a large part of Europe were still, from a legal point of view, mere *ad hoc* arrangements, without treaty sanction.

This was true, for instance, of Germany. The general principles of a postwar settlement for Germany had been agreed upon by the Allies during the war, although they soon broke down in practice. With respect

[1] Poland was admitted to U. N. membership in October 1945.

to territory, it had been decided at Yalta in February 1945 (see p. 753) that Germany would be deprived of certain of its eastern provinces, which would go to the Soviet Union and to Poland; and, at the Potsdam Conference of July and August 1945, Stalin, President Truman of the United States, and the new British prime minister, Clement Attlee, had defined the Polish grant as comprising the lands east of the Oder and Neisse rivers, the southern part of East Prussia (the rest of which went to the Soviet Union), and the former free city of Danzig. But there were subsequent differences even on this aspect of the German settlement, for the western powers insisted that the grant was provisional and could not be considered otherwise until it was legitimized by a formal German treaty. The Poles, who regarded their gains as compensation for the provinces west of the old Curzon Line (see p. 568) that they had had to cede to the Soviet Union, took the Potsdam grant to be definitive and, with Soviet backing, proceeded to act accordingly.

The decision to punish the German leaders who were guilty of crimes of aggression and of crimes against humanity, which had led to the death of six million people in countries occupied by Germany, aroused no great conflicts of view. In November 1945, an Inter-Allied Tribunal began the trials of the major war criminals. These lasted for over a year and led to the conviction of twenty-two defendants and the sentencing of eleven to death: Goering (who escaped execution by committing suicide), Rosenberg, Ribbentrop, Streicher, Seyss-Inquart, Frick, Frank, Kaltenbrunner, Sauckel, and Generals Keitel and Jodl. Aside from this, however, the Allies were soon divided on all aspects of their German policy.

In accordance with decisions reached as early as 1943 and made more precise at Yalta, the conquered country was divided into four zones, to be occupied and administered by Great Britain, France, the Soviet Union, and the United States. Berlin, lying well within the Soviet zone, was also divided into four zones; and an Allied Control Council, composed of four military commanders-in-chief with supreme authority, was established to direct affairs in the almost demolished capital. The basic assumption was that the occupying powers would carry out a rigorous policy of de-Nazification, demilitarization, dismantling of war industries, and re-education; that reparations would be paid by Germany in the form of capital equipment and external assets; but that, after the process of expiation and rehabilitation was reasonably complete, Germany would be reunited and its rights of sovereignty restored.

This system of four-power control was put into effect, but difficulties arose almost immediately. They were caused in the first instance by Soviet insistence upon taking reparations out of current production rather than from assets. To the United States government, which had

Down Barriers in Germany (August 1, 1946)
A cartoon by David Low. From *Low's Cartoon History* (New York: Simon & Schuster, 1953).

by this time recovered from the romantic wartime notion that Germany could be forcibly transformed into a purely agrarian state, and to the other western powers, who had a more intimate knowledge of the interdependence of European national economics, Soviet policy seemed designed to prevent German recovery and, by spreading general economic depression, to promote communism. This impression was strengthened by the Soviet refusal to abide by its promise to share food stocks from its zone in return for reparations from the three others. Western protests were answered by Soviet demands for new rights—a share in the control of the Ruhr industrial area, for example—and conferences of the foreign ministers at Paris and Moscow in 1946 and 1947 proved powerless to solve the growing dispute.

By 1948 the pretense of following a common policy was abandoned. To check growing economic distress, the western powers introduced a currency reform in their zones that had the effect of creating two economic systems in the country. The Soviet government had already made it clear, however, that it would follow an independent economic line in its zone and, in June 1948, by cutting off access by land to the western sectors of Berlin, it showed that its ambitions went beyond the economic sphere. The Berlin blockade was defeated by an Anglo-American airlift that kept the western part of the city supplied until the Soviet Union lifted the restrictions in May 1949. Before that happened, the western powers decided to take steps to effect an economic and political fusion of their zones and to encourage the creation of an autonomous German government in the united territory, and the Soviet government had sponsored a People's Congress in Berlin to start the drafting of a constitution for eastern Germany. By the end of 1949, Hitler's Reich was divided into two Germanies, protected by rival power blocs, although the semblance of four-power control was maintained and a definitive German settlement continued to be a subject for negotiation.

Meanwhile, more progress had been made toward liquidating the state of war that existed between the Allies on the one hand and Italy and the other Axis satellite states on the other. Meetings of the foreign ministers in London and Paris in 1946 and 1947 laid the basis for a peace conference in the latter capital in July–September 1947, which succeeded in drawing up treaties with Italy, Bulgaria, Hungary, Rumania, and Finland. The treaty that posed most difficulties was the Italian one because of a long-standing Allied dispute over the future of Trieste and the thorny questions raised by the necessity of disposing of Mussolini's colonial empire. In the end, Italy was required to cede most of Venezia Giulia to Yugoslavia, including the scene of D'Annunzio's exploits, the port of Fiume (see p. 538). Trieste was made a free city under the supervision and guarantee of the U. N.'s Security Council until 1954, when a compromise was reached between Italy, which regained the port city, and Yugoslavia, which acquired the surrounding territory.

The settlement of 1947 required Italy to pay $360,000,000 in reparations, to surrender the remains of its navy to the Allies, and to cede some coastal islands in the Adriatic to Albania, the Dodecanese Islands to Greece, and some trifling areas along its western frontier to France. The empire of Abyssinia, reconquered from the Duce by British troops in 1941 (see p. 729), had its independence confirmed, while Libya, Eritrea, and Somaliland, after remaining for another year in the hands of their British conquerors, were handed over to U. N. supervision.

Finland, which had made itself useful to German aims during the war, now paid for that with the loss to the Soviet Union of the northernmost province of Petsamo, some territory on the central Finnish-Soviet border, most of the Karelian peninsula, including Viborg, and (by fifty-year lease) a naval base in the Gulf of Finland, which the Russians subsequently abandoned. The other Axis satellites suffered in various degrees. Hungary was forced to cede territory to Czechoslovakia and to surrender Northern Transylvania to Rumania, which, in turn, had (as in 1940) to hand Northern Bessarabia and Bukovina over to the Soviet Union and Southern Dobrudja over to Bulgaria. The last-named state had no territorial losses but, like its neighbors, had to pay reparations to the victorious powers[2] and to submit to the reduction and control of its armed forces. All of these states, including Italy, had to guarantee human rights and fundamental freedoms to their peoples, to bring war criminals to trial, and (most significant, since it provided an excuse for subsequent Soviet attacks upon independent governments in Eastern Europe) to agree to dissolve fascist organizations and to keep fascist elements out of public life.

Another significant feature of these treaties was that, while they provided for the withdrawal of Allied troops ninety days after they were ratified, the Soviet Union was given the right to maintain forces in Rumania and Hungary, on the grounds that they were necessary to make secure Soviet lines of communication to Austria, where the USSR had continued occupation duties. As in the case of the Polish acquisition of the Oder-Neisse lands, the Soviets came to regard the provisional grant as definitive and did not withdraw their troops after the end of the occupation of Austria.

The Allied foreign ministers had decided in their Moscow meeting of October 1943 that Austria should be restored as an independent state. The first of Hitler's victims had to wait until 1955, however, for the fulfillment of that promise. For a whole decade after the war, despite continuous negotiations, the former Allies were at odds on significant points, and Austria remained divided into four occupation zones, with its capital administered somewhat after the fashion of postwar Berlin.

In making a settlement with the last of the former enemy states, Japan, the European Allies left matters for the most part in the hands of the United States government. After a conference at Cairo in November 1943, President Roosevelt, Prime Minister Churchill, and Generalissimo Chiang Kai-shek had announced that Japan's conquests would be taken from it at the restoration of peace. The expectations of the Chinese government were doubtless modified by the subsequent decision of the Big Three at Yalta to restore to the Soviet Union the rights that Imperial Russia had enjoyed within the Chinese empire before 1905, including rights in Manchuria, joint operation with China of railroads in that area, and the lease of Port Arthur (see p. 456). The Soviet Union was further authorized to annex the southern part of Sakhalin Island and the Kuril Islands, and—at the subsequent conference at Potsdam—to occupy that

[2] Bulgaria had to pay $70,000,000; Finland, Hungary, and Rumania, $300,000,000 each; Italy, $360,000,000.

part of Korea lying above the 38th parallel of latitude, the United States exercising similar rights in the southern half of that traditionally troublesome but strategically important country. Time was to bring all of these concessions into question, and they doubtless facilitated Communist conquest of the mainland, although they were by no means the only, or even the most important, reason for that. But they had been made to assure the entrance of the Soviet Union into the war against Japan, which, at a time when the effectiveness of the atomic bomb was unknown, seemed essential.

After the Japanese surrender, while the Soviet Union busied itself on the mainland, United States troops occupied Japan and a policy of demilitarization and democratization was instituted under the authority of General Douglas MacArthur, the Supreme Allied Commander. In general, the evolution of western policy toward Japan was much like that of the policy followed with respect to western Germany. That is to say, as inter-Allied cooperation broke down and as communism conquered China, the United States pushed for a definitive settlement with Japan that would convert that country into a bastion against Communist influence. The American line was that the best way of effecting this result would be by concluding a separate treaty between Japan and the western powers. In September 1951, after many difficult negotiations, the United States and Great Britain concluded the treaty, in which Japan accepted the loss of the territories taken from it. The question of Japan's relations with the Communist Chinese government on the mainland and Chiang Kai-shek's regime on Formosa and the settlement of reparations payments to the various powers were left to later negotiations between Japan and the interested parties. By separate treaty between Japan and the United States, American troops were given the right to garrison bases in Japan for the purpose of protecting the country and contributing to the general security of the Far East.

The Soviet Union did not recognize these arrangements and did not end its state of war with Japan until 1956.

REBUILDING THE WEST

Socialist Britain / While these diplomatic arrangements were being made, the countries of Europe were once more making the painful effort to overcome the ravages of war. Once again the plight of the victors was almost as desperate as that of the vanquished. Great Britain, for example, had not only suffered far more physical damage than in the first world war but had also virtually exhausted its foreign assets and stretched its economic resources to the breaking point. One discouraged Englishman, writing in the magazine *Horizon* shortly after the end of the war, said gloomily:

> The advantages which position, coal, skill and enterprise won for us in the nineteenth century have been liquidated, and we go back to scratch—as a barren, humid, raw, but densely over-populated group of islands with an obsolete industrial plant, hideous but inadequate housing, a variety of un-healthy jungle possessions, vast international commitments, a falling birth-rate, and a large class of infertile rentiers or over-specialized middlemen and brokers as our main capital.

With these conditions, the British people proceeded to "cope"—a favorite British expression of the 1940s. Their first step toward coping was to retire Mr. Churchill from the prime ministership by bringing the Labor party to power in the elections of 1945. Churchill's defeat caused some consternation in the United States, where the behavior of the British electorate was considered to show a lack of gratitude to the great wartime leader. In reality, it had nothing to do with Mr. Churchill, whom the British people continued to hold in affection and admiration. The Labor party's victory of 1945, which gave it 390 out of 640 seats in the House of Commons, was a belated judgment on the ineffective social policy of the Conservative party during the 1930s and the expres-sion of a determination to make economic democracy work in Britain. That 50 percent of the electorate were prepared to face up to the prospect of radical reform (it may be noted in passing that the Labor party had never before polled more than 30 percent of the vote) was probably due to two things: the Labor party's success since 1926 in convincing the middle classes that it was not a band of wild-eyed visionaries or Bolshevik egalitarians (see p. 662) and the basing of American troops in England during the war. The presence of Americans in Britain kept the social question firmly before the British common people. They saw that their American counterparts were better paid and better provided for and that they bore visible signs of having social advantages superior to those enjoyed in England; and the British determined that they should receive some of the benefits which G.I.'s seemed to take for granted.

In their six years of office,[3] the Labor government sought to satisfy these desires by an elaborate program of social reform and industrial reorganization. In 1946 a National Insurance Act went far beyond the Act of 1911 (see p. 325) by providing for health, old-age, and unemploy-

---

[3] The Labor party was re-elected to office in February 1950 when they won 315 seats to the Conservative bloc's 297 and the Liberals' nine. In the elections of October 1951, however, the Conservatives returned to power with 321 seats to Labor's 295.

ment insurance to be supported by weekly contributions by employers, employees, and the state. It was supplemented by the Industrial Injuries Act and, two years later, by the National Assistance Act, which was designed to supply the needs of the indigent who were not covered by the Insurance Act. A more revolutionary piece of legislation was the National Health Services Act which gave free medical care (including hospital services, nursing care, and dental and other appliances) to all British subjects who registered for such coverage.

These benefits helped make up for the austerity of English life during the first postwar years, when financial stringency and an excess of imports over exports made it necessary for the government to prolong wartime rationing of food, fuel, and clothing and to restrict the amount of currency that British travelers could take out of the country. In time, the currency pinch was relieved by loans from the United States and the European Recovery Program, as well as by a new devaluation of the currency in September 1949. Despite the fact that relative prosperity returned to both trade and industry, the trade balance of the country remained unfavorable. Because of the exhaustion of its foreign assets by two world wars (between 1939 and 1945 Britain had to sell £1,118,000,000 of overseas investments), the country was forced to pay its way by exports, and only the virtual exclusion of consumers goods from the domestic market could have corrected the imbalance.

The Labor government sought with some success to ease this problem with the second part of their program, which was designed to increase production by effecting the basic reorganization and modernization of British industry that had not been carried out in the interwar period (see p. 655). This was set in train by a series of measures that nationalized key industries with compensation for their former owners: the Bank of England, the cable and wireless services, and civil aviation in 1946; the coal mines, the canals and docks, and the road transport system in 1947; the electrical supply and gas works in 1948; and the iron and steel industry in 1951.

After the return of the Conservatives—and Churchill—to power in 1951, part of this program was undone. Steel was denationalized and road transport turned back to private hands, although both were made subject to supervision by government boards. Yet, however much Conservative speakers fulminated against Labor on the hustings and in Parliament, they found it difficult and inexpedient to return to the old private-enterprise system. Whether they liked it or not, England had passed through a revolution—a cautious revolution perhaps, at least in its means, but one that nevertheless established the most fully elaborated social welfare state in the western world and opened to the British common people prospects that had been denied them in the past. Nor was this a one-party accomplishment. At least one important contribution had been made to it by the National Government before its demise in 1945. This was the Education Act of 1944 which raised the compulsory school age, made secondary education free, and provided free lunches to all children in primary and secondary schools. This basic law was supplemented after 1945 by an active program of school construction, by a state-supported program of adult education, and by increased attention to scholarship programs which provided equality of opportunity in higher education.

During the years of greatest austerity, there was no tendency in Great Britain to reject the political heritage of the past nor was there any significant increase in political extremism. The war years had allowed the constitutional crisis of 1936 (see p. 697) to recede into the back of people's minds, and the fact that King George VI and his queen had shared the rigors of the Blitz (and had even suffered a bombing of Buckingham Palace) had made the monarchy a more popular institution than it had been since the last years of Queen Victoria. When George VI died in February 1952, national mourning was sincere and deep, giving way very soon, however, to widespread rejoicing as the late king's daughter assumed the throne as Elizabeth II. In the trials that lay ahead for the country in its foreign and imperial relations (see pp. 808 and 814ff.), the queen was a symbol of the essential unity of the Commonwealth of Nations.

France: The Fourth and Fifth Republics / The first postwar government of France was organized by the Free French movement of General Charles de Gaulle, which, since 1940, had inspired resistance to the Axis both inside France and out. When the Allied landings were made in France in June 1944, what semblance of authority the Vichy regime (see p. 724) retained quickly crumbled. It is melancholy to observe that Vichy's leader, Marshal Pétain, now quite senile and apparently insensitive to the crimes committed under the shadow of his name (including political murders carried out even after the Allied landings), believed that he could still count on some form of Allied recognition. Indeed, he sent a message to General de Gaulle through a secret agent, informing him that he hoped to remain in power

> a few months with him in order to ensure the transition and consolidate the union which will come to birth through our mutual understanding. Then, as soon as possible, I want to go back and live in peace on my estate and finish my days in tranquillity.

The hero of Verdun was denied the fulfillment of these wishes. His overtures were received with bleak indifference at de Gaulle's headquarters. Then, to Pétain's intense indignation, he was forced by the Germans, in August 1944, to take up residence at Sigmaringen in the Black Forest. When this part of Germany was occupied by American forces, the marshal voluntarily surrendered to the French government, but he was tried for treason and condemned to death, this sentence then being commuted to life imprisonment on a lonely island in the Bay of Biscay. There Pétain died in July 1951.

Meanwhile, General de Gaulle had entered liberated Paris. In September 1944, he appointed a temporary government of the French Republic that governed France in collaboration with the Provisional Consultative Assembly, which had been organized in Algiers in November 1943 and had crossed to France at the time of the Allied invasion. These provisional agencies gave direction to French affairs while the country was passing through the turmoil and dislocation of the liberation period, and they instituted the program of nationalization of mines, basic industry, and credit that was to play an important part in the country's economic recovery.

At the end of 1945, when more orderly conditions at last prevailed, elections were held for a National Assembly whose mission was to draft a constitution for the state. The discussions of this body soon indicated that most of the deputies desired to revive the constitutional system of the Third Republic, centering power in the legislative body and keeping the executive power weak. De Gaulle, who had been elected provisional president by the Assembly, objected strenuously to this, and in January 1946 he resigned his office in order to carry on a campaign against the proposed constitution. He was not successful in effecting more than minor changes, and the constitution was accepted by popular plebescite in October 1946. It is worth noting, however, that, while nine and a quarter million people voted to approve the document, eight million voted no, and eight and a half million abstained, figures that gave few grounds for confidence in the longevity of the new regime.

The Fourth French Republic, which thus came into being, nevertheless lasted for twelve years and accomplished much for the country, especially in the economic sphere. Its success in this respect becomes very clear if we reflect that in 1947 the economy of the country was dislocated by a wave of strikes and social misery was so marked that the gloomier newspaper pundits of the west were predicting a Communist take-over by the end of the year. Ten years later, this threat had become very remote; the country was prosperous; and the minister of finance could boast, "In the domain of industry our country is holding a world record. It is in France that, from 1952 on, the most rapid rate of growth has taken place: 10 percent per year."

The reasons for French recovery were varied. Marshall Plan aid from the United States played its part, particularly in overcoming the crisis of 1947–1948. So did the nationalization decrees of the previous year. Much was accomplished by the systematic modernization of power resources, industrial equipment, and farm machinery, the last being particularly important, since at long last the old balance between agriculture and industry was beginning to break down, and there was a decided movement toward the urban centers, which the government, in the interest of industrial expansion, encouraged. Progress was accelerated also by state planning, the Monnet Plan of January 1947, for instance, setting production goals for the coal, power, steel, cement, agricultural machinery, and transport industries. Finally, the spirit with which the French people approached their job of rebuilding was one of confidence and energy, reflected, as Raymond Aron has written, in a substantial increase in the birth rate and in a positive desire for expansion that could be detected among the workers as well as among the entrepreneurs. Thanks to the operation of these forces, the gross national product increased by 49 percent between 1949 and 1957 and, in the same period, the population between the ages of 4 and 13 rose by 37 percent, agricultural production by 24 percent, production of industrial chemicals by 132 percent, the number of vehicles by 100 percent, the volume of investments of 142 percent, and so forth. This was perhaps inferior to progress made in the same period in West Germany, but it attested to the essential vitality of France.

Unfortunately, none of this admirable spirit and drive was to be detected in the working of France's political institutions. With parties on the Right and the Left that were enemies of the regime (de Gaulle's Reunion of the French People—RPF—on the one hand and the Communists on the other), government rested on uneasy combinations of Socialists, Radicals, members of the Catholic Popular Movement (MRP), and various kinds of conservatives. These coalitions were so frail that, in the twelve years of the Fourth Republic, there were nineteen separate governments. As Aron has written, the deputy's life seemed to center around three ceremonies that recurred at intervals of three, six, or twelve months: an execution (the overthrow of a cabinet), a *fête* (a ministerial crisis), and a distribution of prizes (the composition of a new cabinet). He was so exclusively concerned with these crises that he rarely turned his eyes outward to see what was really going on in France and the world. In popular parlance, the Assembly came to be known as "The House without Windows."

Preoccupation with the game of politics was accompanied by what can fairly be described as an essential unwillingness to accept responsibility or even to admit that there was such a thing as responsibility to be accepted. In this new "republic of pals," no one was ever blamed for anything, and it was tacitly assumed in time of unpleasantness—as it had been tacitly assumed in pre-1914 Austria (see p. 396)—that these things "just sort of happened." Responsibility for France's unsuccessful postwar colonial policy (see pp. 818ff.) was spread so thin that no one was thought of as being culpable in any way. When an occasional energetic minister arose who was willing to assume partial blame for a disaster—as René Pleven did in the case of the defeat at Dienbienphu in Indochina—or who sought to liquidate impossible situations and to impute responsibility for their existence—as Pierre Mendès-France did with respect to the Indochina war—he was considered by the ordinary parliamentarian to be violating the rules of "the system." This sort of thing, D. W. Brogan has written, doubtless "made for an amiable form of parliamentary life but destroyed the voter's sense that he was voting for anything or anybody in particular, or that his formal representatives, once they were elected, were responsible to him or to anybody." This led to a frustration of democracy and a gradual erosion of public confidence in the regime. It also caused behavior in foreign policy that exasperated France's allies (as in August 1954, when the Assembly, acting largely for reasons which had little to do with the issue at stake and out of a desire to overthrow one more government, destroyed years of inter-allied planning by voting against the European Defense Community [see p. 802]); and it led to fatal mismanagement of affairs in Africa and the Far East.

The mishandling of overseas affairs eventually aroused the opposition of a body that had refrained from intervention in politics since the Dreyfus case: the French army. It had fought bravely in Indochina, Tunis, and Morocco since 1945, with frightful losses—of its officers, the equivalent of a whole class of St. Cyr had died in Indochina—only to be forced in the end, by political decisions made in Paris, to withdraw from the contested ground. Its officers felt that this was a betrayal not only of the army but of the native levies that had fought with them. One lieutenant wrote:

> I thought of all those in Indochina who were massacred for having believed that France, having engaged them on its side, would not abandon them; of those in Tunisia, faithful to the end, but vanished without a trace since our departure; of those in Morocco. And once more I asked myself whether my comrades and I would not, one day, have on our consciences the deaths of all those whom we had rallied to our side and compromised forever.

The army officers feared another sell-out in Algeria, where civil war had been raging since 1954 (see p. 820). To prevent this, they seized power in Algeria in May 1958 and demanded that General de Gaulle be called to head the government.

The government in Paris gave way before the rapidly expanding revolt and entered into negotiations with de Gaulle, who proved to be willing to take political responsibility. He was empowered by the Assembly to submit a new constitutional reform to a popular referendum and, in September 1958, he did so. His draft constitution provided for a popularly elected Assembly and a Senate elected by indirect vote, but left their powers vague. Wide authority was vested in a president who would be elected for a seven-year term by an electoral college of more than 80,000 electors, or approximately one grand elector for each thousand inhabitants, representing all the peoples of the French Community. The constitution had a marked authoritarian tone; and the president was given much more power than that possessed by Clemenceau in 1917 or Poincaré in 1926, being rather comparable in authority to the prince president at the outset of the second Bonapartist regime (see p. 183). The ministers of state were still in theory responsible to the Assembly; in actuality, they became interpreters and agents of the will of the president. Even so, aside from the Communists and a small group around Mendès-France, there was no real opposition to this shift to the Right, primarily because everyone was heartily sick of the Fourth Republic. In May, when it was being overthrown by the military coup, a journalist spoke of "the prodigious lack of interest of an entire people"; in September, the plebescite on the constitution was approved in Metropolitan France by a majority of four to one and was subsequently approved by all members of the Community with the exception of Guinea, which, by its action, severed its connection with France.[4]

The Fifth Republic began its existence with an electoral reform that divided Metropolitan France into 465 single-member constituencies. In elections in November 1958, supporters of de Gaulle won a resounding victory, while the Communists, who had held about a third of the seats in the assembly since 1945, were reduced from 144 seats to ten, although their popular vote remained sizable. De Gaulle was elected president of the French Republic on December 21, 1958, by more than 62,000 of the electoral college votes, or 76 percent of the electoral college. He immediately buckled down to the task of seeking a solution for the troubled situation in Algeria, although, in the two years that followed, it continued to elude him. On the other hand, the economic progress of France continued; and, under de Gaulle's leadership, France won new

[4] The Community was defined as comprising thirteen states, which, in order of population, were: the French Republic (Metropolitan France, the Algerian and Saharan departments, the Overseas Departments, and the Overseas Territories), Malagasy Republic, Sudanese Republic, Republic of the Upper Volta, Republic of the Ivory Coast, Republic of Chad, Republic of the Niger, Republic of Senegal, Republic of Dahomey, Central African Republic, Republic of the Congo, Islamic Republic of Mauretania, and Gabon Republic.

prestige in Europe, where, among other things, it commenced fruitful collaboration with the Bonn Republic.

The Liberated States / Like France, the Low Countries, Luxembourg, Norway, and Denmark had suffered German occupation and the imposition of puppet regimes. In every case there were political and economic problems consequent upon the restoration of freedom and self-government. Belgium turned out to be the most fortunate of these states economically and the most troubled politically. Its economic recovery started almost immediately upon the arrival of Allied troops in the country in September 1944, for Antwerp became an important supply center for the last push against Germany. Economic progress was set back, at least temporarily, by the Battle of the Bulge (see p. 753) but was steady thereafter. Belgium was soon the most prosperous country in Western Europe and was able to demonstrate the fruits of its recovery in the Brussels Exposition of 1958. Progress was encouraged by modernization of its industrial plant and by tariff agreements with the governments of the Netherlands and the Grand Duchy of Luxembourg, which formed the basis of the so-called Benelux Union of January 1948, later elaborated as the Benelux Economic Union of February 1958. This organization eliminated tariff barriers between the three participants and provided a common trade policy toward the outside world as well as a single labor market with free movement of workers between the three nations.

Politically, the most serious issue in postwar Belgium was that of the status of the king, Leopold III. Because of his surrender to the Germans in 1940, his supposed predilection for authoritarian rule, and his marriage to a commoner after the death of his wife, the widely admired Queen Astrid, Leopold had lost the support of many of his subjects. The fact that his new wife was a Fleming helped assure him of the Catholic vote although it alienated those who resented the gains made by the Flemish movement during the German occupation. In 1950, a national referendum showed that 57 percent of the voters were prepared to tolerate Leopold's continued rule, but subsequent disorders encouraged by the Socialist opposition persuaded him to abdicate in favor of his son Baudouin, who ascended the throne in 1951. Belgian politics thereafter were relatively quiet until 1960, when the decision to grant independence to the Congo and the subsequent troubles of that vast country caused attacks on the government for its alleged mishandling of the situation (see p. 824).

The governments of Luxembourg and the Netherlands were restored without incident. In the latter country, Queen Wilhelmina, who had spent the war years in exile, was able to celebrate the fiftieth anniversary of her accession to the throne in her own capital, before abdicating in favor of her daughter Juliana. Parliamentary life was characterized in the Netherlands, as in Belgium, by the division of power between Catholic and Socialist parties, the latter showing a slight preponderance in the late 1950s. This was probably due in part to economic troubles rising out of the loss of Holland's empire in Indonesia (see p. 816).

Both Denmark and Norway recovered rapidly from the economic effects of German occupation. As in the case of the Benelux countries, there was a tendency toward regional economic collaboration, although its effects were slow in being realized. In 1957 a Committee on Economic Cooperation, founded by the governments of Norway, Denmark, Sweden, and Iceland[5] ten years earlier and joined by Finland in 1956, submitted to its member governments a draft convention for a Nordic Customs Union with common tariffs against outsiders, a common market, and a labor and credit pool for members.

In both Denmark and Norway, politics was dominated in the first postwar years by the liquidation of those who had collaborated with the Germans, and, until people like Quisling were hunted down, tried, and executed, life did not return to normal. There was no disposition to change the monarchical institutions of the past, despite Communist attempts to undermine the idea of monarchy. In Denmark, Christian X resumed his throne and, when he died in 1947, was succeeded by his son, Frederick IX, a tall handsome man with a military bearing, who won the respect and admiration of his subjects. Norway too had a peaceful change of reign, when, after ruling for fifty-two years, King Haakon VII died in 1957 and was succeeded by Olaf V. Predominantly an agrarian country, Denmark's strongest political parties were the Socialists and the Agrarians, which usually governed in coalition. The same political pattern was to be noted in Norway, although there, by the end of the 1950s, the Socialists held a clear majority of parliamentary seats. Under Socialist influence, prewar experiments in economic democracy, with special emphasis on social insurance, were carried further in both countries.

The Western Neutrals / Five states of Western Europe had remained neutral during World War II: Sweden, Switzerland, Eire (although thousands of Irishmen fought in British armies), Portugal, and Spain.

The first two of these neutral states profited greatly from the war, as a result of German orders and Allied pre-emptive buying programs that were designed to deny strategical materials to the enemy. The termination of hostilities gave rise to some fear that there would be grave economic dislocations. This was not borne out in fact, although wartime American generosity was replaced, in the case of Switzerland, by tariffs

---

[5] Iceland became independent of Denmark in 1944.

on certain products like watches and bicycles. Throughout most of the postwar period, Switzerland had full employment and, in addition, gave employment to foreign laborers, and, for the most part, it enjoyed export surpluses. In the case of Sweden, the loss of the important German market in the first years after 1945 was partly made up by a profitable economic agreement with the Soviet Union and, by the mid-1950s, the country's trading position was sound again.

The most important political development in Switzerland was the relaxation of wartime controls that had tended to increase the already strong tendency toward centralization of power in the hands of the federal government. In Sweden, as in other Scandinavian countries, politics centered around the expansion of social-insurance legislation at the insistence of the Socialist party. Sweden continued to be a monarchical country, Gustaf Adolf succeeding his father as King Gustaf VI in 1950.

Eire, which had long occupied an ambiguous position within the British Commonwealth (see p. 665), broke its last legal ties to Great Britain in 1949 and assumed the title of the Republic of Ireland. The country became a member of the U. N. in 1955; and, in the important meeting of the General Assembly in September and October 1960, it was an Irishman, Frederick H. Boland, who, as president of that body, sought, not without success, to control the ebullitions of Premier Nikita Khrushchev and the discourtesies of some of the other Soviet-bloc leaders—angrily terminating one session at which a Rumanian delegate included the Irish people among those oppressed colonial peoples who deserved, in his opinion, to be liberated.

From popular wartime literature and from the motion pictures, one gets the impression that the people of Lisbon could have lived comfortably during the war if they had had no other income than the tips left by Axis and Allied agents and counteragents working in that capital. This is doubtless an exaggeration, but it is true that Portugal benefited economically from its neutral position. With the end of the war, however, the country suffered an appreciable slump. The deterioration of economic conditions doubtless accounts for the unusual appearance of political opposition in the presidential elections that followed the death of Marshal Carmona (see p. 679) in 1951, as well as later in the decade. This was not strong enough to shake the regime, although the dictatorship of Salazar felt called upon to increase its vigilance with respect to subversion and to restrict individual political rights even further. Portugal became a member of the U. N. in 1955 but, in all essentials, remained an authoritarian state.

So did Spain, where Franco had managed to resist all of the threats and blandishments of the Fuehrer and to retain the position of neutrality that he had taken at Hendaye (see p. 732), although he had permitted

Spanish "volunteers" to fight on the Russian front in behalf of the Axis. This concession, and the memory of the Civil War, was enough to destroy any hope of reconciliation with the victor states in the immediate postwar years; and the nations meeting at San Francisco in 1945 banned Spain from membership in the U. N.[6] This vote became a bit of an embarrassment at a later date, when the cold war led western soldiers to ponder the importance of an Iberian redoubt and when the strongest of the NATO countries felt it necessary to have bases in Spain. If Spain remained for a time beyond the pale, there were lots of people willing to cross it in order to deal with its government, or, as was true of thousands of American tourists, to discover the bull rings and gypsy dances of Andalusia, the grandeur of the Basque provinces, and the primitive magnificence of the Costa Brava.

The money spent by these visitors and the American military assistance extended after 1953 helped to ease, but did not cure, the problems caused by the unhappy combination of a static economy and a rising birth rate. The discipline of dictatorship was also ineffective in coping with these. Politically, the regime remained much what it was at the end of the civil war, a fascist state that tolerated none of the institutions of democracy and in which there was no freedom of individual expression. By the law of 1947, Franco was chief of state for life. Upon his death a council of regency was to appoint his successor, who must acknowledge his loyalty to the principles of the Falange (see p. 681) and be accepted by the Córtes. It was generally believed that the monarchy would be restored when this happened, in the person of Alfonso XIII's grandson, Prince Juan Carlos.

Italy and Austria / In most of the countries of Western Europe, communism increased its strength as a result of the war[7]; but in none did it have as much chance actually to take over power as it did in postwar Italy. Here both economic and political conditions were suitable to its growth, for the country was prostrate economically as a result of the

---

[6] Spain was admitted in 1955.

[7] The strength did not last in most cases, as is shown by the following table of Communist parliamentary strength in the first postwar years, reproduced from Hugh Seton-Watson's *From Lenin to Khrushchev* (New York: Frederick A. Praeger, 1960), p. 304:

Britain: 1945, 2 seats out of 615; 1950, 1; 1951, none.
Belgium: 1946, 23 seats out of 202; 1949, 12; 1950, 7.
Holland: 1946, 10 seats out of 100; 1948, 8; 1952, 6.
Denmark: 1945, 18 seats out of 148; 1947, 9; 1950, 7.
Iceland: 1946, 10 seats out of 52; 1949, 7.
Norway: 1945, 11 seats out of 150; 1949, none.
Sweden: 1948, 8 seats out of 230; 1952, 5.

In France, as we have seen above, the Communists continued to receive one third of the vote and the seats until 1958.

fearful hammering it had received in the last stages of the war, and the collapse of fascism left a political vacuum into which the Communists (as the party least encumbered by a record of past mistakes of execution or omission) seemed likely to move. The Italian Communist party was a well-disciplined and organized body led by Palmiro Togliatti, who spent the war years in Moscow and returned to Italy in April 1944. In the first government of liberated Italy, Communists held the important ministries of Justice and Finance, and the party was supported by thousands of idealistic middle-class intellectuals who dreamed of a new *risorgimento* led by the only truly revolutionary party.

This mood did not last. In June 1946, when a national referendum decided that the country should be a republic rather than a monarchy and sent the House of Savoy into exile, the elections to the Constituent Assembly of the republic gave the Communists only 19 percent of the poll, the united Socialist groups 21 percent, and 35 percent to the Christian Democratic movement, which was headed by Italy's ablest postwar statesman, Alcide de Gasperi. The subsequent dissolution of Socialist unity brought new strength to the Communists, who became the undisputed leaders of the working class, but their gains were matched by those that de Gasperi made by piecing together coalitions of the moderate Left and Center. In the winter of 1947–1948, the Communists made their big bid for power by fomenting nation-wide strikes and demonstrations and by building mass organizations in factories and among the peasants. Nevertheless, in the April 1948 elections, the first held under the new democratic constitution, the Christian Democrats, supported by the Catholic Church and exploiting the promise of American economic aid, won 48 percent of the vote as compared to the 32 percent won by the Communists and the left-wing Socialists. This made it clear that the Communists would not take over in the near future. De Gasperi became prime minister, a post he held until 1953. Luigi Einaudi, a distinguished economist, was elected president of Italy, and served as such until he was succeeded in 1955 by the Christian Democrat, Giovanni Gronchi.

Communism retained the support of a majority of the Italian working class and could generally count on that of the left-wing Socialists led by Pietro Nenni. In their attacks upon the regime and its foreign policy, the Communists profited from the revival in the 1950s of neo-Fascist and monarchist groups. Nevertheless, a *connubio* of center parties grouped around the Christian Democrats continued to rule the country throughout the period. It had to grapple with serious economic problems—agricultural depression and unemployment, subnormal industrial production, inadequate housing, poor educational standards (reflected in inadequate popular understanding of scientific methods in agriculture and industry), heavy pressure for emigration (which could not be fulfilled), and others

—but in the fifteen years that followed the war it made considerable progress in solving them. Marshall Plan aid amounting to $1,303,000,000 helped spark an industrial surge that was, thanks to its low starting point and the large pool of unemployed labor, unaccompanied by inflation; and by 1960 industrial production was ahead of the prewar volume, and the country's gold and dollar reserves were better than those of Great Britain. Agriculture continued to impose an undue strain upon the national economy, but American technical advice induced the government to embark on a long-range program of reform designed to place greater emphasis upon livestock than upon unremunerative grain production and to fit Italy into the Common Market in the most profitable manner. Finally, income-tax reform had begun a redistribution of wealth that promised to have healthy political results.

In Austria, the economic difficulties were as great as those being grappled with in Italy, but communism was able to make less headway there. This was largely because the Austrian Socialist party—unlike its Italian counterpart, which showed all the fissiparous tendencies of the years 1890–1922 (see p. 342)—evinced a courage and discipline that retained the loyalty of the Austrian working class. In the provisional government that was set up in Austria in April 1945 by the Soviet authorities, Socialists, Communists, and the Catholic People's party participated under the leadership of the veteran Socialist Karl Renner, and with a Communist as minister of the interior. The hope that this might pave the way for Communist domination came to nothing; and, in the parliamentary elections of November 1945, the Communists won only four seats out of 163. Austrian politics, as before the war (see p. 648), was ruled by the Socialists and the old Christian Social party of Dollfuss, now purged of its authoritarian ideas and rechristened the People's party.

Although under four-power occupation, the Austrian government was recognized by the powers and permitted to conduct foreign affairs, which it did with vigor under the leadership of Renner (president after 1945) and Leopold Figl and Julius Raab (prime ministers from 1945 to 1953 and from 1953 on, respectively). Its initiative in talks with the Russians was probably responsible for the breaking of the diplomatic log jam that led to the conclusion of the Austrian State Treaty of May 1955. By this, Austria became an independent, sovereign state with the boundaries of 1937. It was pledged to neutrality and promised not to enter military alliances or to permit the establishment of foreign military bases on its soil. *Anschluss* with Germany was forbidden.

Divided Germany / The course of political events in Germany until the year 1949 has already been sketched above, in connection with the postwar peace treaties (pp. 764–767). Economically, those same years were years of steady disintegration and mounting misery. By the decisions of Yalta and Potsdam, Germany had lost to the Poles an area that had supplied 25 percent of its food supply as well as much of its industrial coal. From that area, over twelve million Germans had been evicted and were now forced to live and seek work in western Germany, where food stocks were limited. The results were grim to observe. In 1947 Germany's greatest modern novelist, Thomas Mann, in his last major work, *Dr. Faustus*, wrote a moving comparison of the Germany of Hitler's time with the broken country that had emerged from the war.

> At that time [he wrote] Germany, with her cheeks feverishly flushed, reeled drunkenly at the height of her empty triumphs. . . . Today, girt round with demons, a hand over one eye, but staring with the other into horrors, she plunges from despair to deeper despair. When will she reach the bottom of the abyss? When, out of the ultimate hopelessness, will the light of hope dawn, a wonder that passes all belief?

Although Mann could not know it, the light of hope was not far away and the wonder was soon to be born. The fusion of the western zones by the Allies, after they had realized that they could not count on Soviet cooperation in promoting German recovery, and currency reform in 1948 laid the basis for recovery. It was promoted, in the first instance, by Marshall Plan aid and, later, by the careful planning of German administrators, the austere taxation and subvention policy adopted by the West German government after its establishment, the thrift and industry of the average German, and—not least important—the fact that, unlike its neighbors, West Germany had no military expenses and was indeed forbidden to have any until 1955.

Progress, once under way, was remarkable. As early as 1953, West Germany held third rank, after the United States and Great Britain, among the nations participating in world trade. Five years later the country was exporting almost twice as much of its national product as Germany was in 1936 and importing two thirds as much as the United States. German industry was producing two and a half times as much as before the war; the country was enjoying full employment; prices were stable; and the country had come close to balance of payments equilibrium. Moreover, West Germany had thus far escaped the kind of inflationary spiral that occurred in other countries as a result of continued labor-management disputes. This was due in large part to German labor's traditional lack of enthusiasm for strikes, the strong tradition of effective collective bargaining, the sense of joint responsibility which resulted from the share granted to labor in the management of industry (the so-called *Mitbestimmungsrecht*), and the success of the government's effort to persuade people not to make excessive demands on the economy.

The political recovery of Germany was almost as spectacular as the economic. This was the result of the growing recognition by the western allies that they would need German military strength in any trial with the Soviet Union; and it was due further to the ability of Germany's outstanding postwar statesman, Konrad Adenauer.

Germany's political development began with Allied authorization of the revival on the local level of party organization and activity. As early as 1946, state constitutional conventions were held, legislatures were chosen, and the first regional political parties appeared: the Social Democrats, taking up where the old party of that name had left off in 1933; the Christian Democrats (in Bavaria, the Christian Social Union), a party designed to appeal to both religious faiths but predominantly Catholic, like the MRP in France, the People's party in Austria, and the party of de Gasperi in Italy; the Free Democratic party, a liberal-conservative party standing for free enterprise; and the Communists, who never represented more than 10 percent of the voters in the western zones but flourished in the Soviet zone, where, in 1946, they merged with the Socialists to form the Socialist Unity party (SED), which in time became wholly Communist.

The decision of the western Allies to unite their zones led to the convocation of a Parliamentary Council of delegates of the western state governments in Bonn in September 1948. This body proceeded to draft the Basic Law for the Federal Republic of Germany, which was ratified by the state governments and went into effect in May 1949. The Basic Law provided for a bicameral legislature composed of an upper chamber or Bundesrat of thirty-eight members, representing the state governments, and a lower chamber or Bundestag, elected by a combination of direct and proportional electoral procedures by all persons who had reached the age of 21. The Federal Republic had a president, elected for a term of five years by the lower house and representatives of the state governments, but he was given none of the prerogatives that had been misused by Field Marshal von Hindenburg in the 1930s. Real power was vested in the chancellor and the cabinet, who were freed from the perpetual insecurity of their Weimar predecessors (see p. 621) by a rule that prohibited the Bundestag from dismissing them unless it was prepared to elect their successors immediately—a stipulation that eliminated the lengthy cabinet crises of an earlier era.

The first Bundestag elections were held in August 1949 and led to the creation, by a narrow margin of votes, of a coalition government composed of Christian Democrats, Free Democrats, and the so-called German party (a conservative nationalist group), with Konrad Adenauer as chancellor. The Social Democrats, under their brilliant leader, Kurt Schumacher, formed the opposition, which was to be their role for the next decade.

The new chancellor had entered politics before World War I, had been chief mayor of Cologne from 1917 to 1933, when he was dismissed by the Nazis, and had been an unsuccessful candidate for the chancellorship in 1926. In 1944, when he was arrested by the Gestapo, the warden of Brauweiler prison had said to him: "Now, please do not commit suicide. You would cause me no end of trouble. You're sixty-eight years old, and your life is over anyway." That official would have been astonished to know that sixteen years later his prisoner would still be going strong and rounding out a chancellorship that promised to be at least as long as that of Adolf Hitler.

It was under Adenauer's leadership that West Germany was transformed from a beaten foe to a respected ally. The chancellor did not concentrate his energies on the pursuit of national unity and the liberation of the seventeen million Germans in the Soviet zone, for these things seemed remote and impossible of achievement. Instead, he bent his efforts to reducing the restrictions still imposed on West Germany by the Allies, and he went about this task with a blend of realism and idealism. In November 1949, he negotiated the Petersberg Agreement with the western powers, in accordance with which they put an end to the policy of dismantling German factories, and he accepted the Ruhr Statute of December 1948, which set up an international authority for that important industrial area. Although attacked at home for this concession, Adenauer believed that it was more than made up for by the termination of the ruinous dismantling policy and that this concession might, in any event, be productive of later advantage. In any case, he was no narrow nationalist, believing, indeed, that the time had come when Germany must rise above the nationalism of the past. The future lay, he believed, in collaboration between Germany and its neighbors, especially France, and the Ruhr Statute might be, as he said in a speech at Berne, "a promising starting point for general and comprehensive cooperation among the nations of Europe."[8]

In subsequent years, Adenauer always held before the eyes of his people the vision of a new Europe founded on such institutions as the Coal and Steel Community, the European Defense Community, the Common Market and Euratom (see p. 798). His devotion to these ideals not only won him continued support at home, as his electoral victories of 1953 and 1957 showed, but convinced the western powers of his reliability and helped persuade them that it was safe to relax the postwar controls on Germany. Their willingness to do so was prompted also by their desire, especially after 1950, for German military aid, and Adenauer shrewdly played to this by becoming an advocate of German rearmament within the western alliance system. Despite opposition by the Socialists, sections of the German church, and university youth, he won a series of parlia-

---

[8] The plan of internationalizing the Ruhr was not, in fact, implemented.

Four postwar statesmen. From top left: Charles de Gaulle, Nikita Khrushchev, Sir Anthony Eden, and Konrad Adenauer. (FRENCH EMBASSY PRESS & INFORMATION DIVISION; SOVFOTO; BRITISH INFORMATION SERVICES; GERMAN INFORMATION CENTER)

mentary battles on this issue, finally obtaining Bundestag assent for the Federal Republic's entrance into NATO. This was accompanied by West Germany's reacquisition of untrammeled sovereignty.

Adenauer's policy with respect to the reunification of Germany was based essentially on the theory that close association of the Bonn Repub-

Paul-Henri Spaak of Belgium,
secretary general of NATO
(BELGIAN GOVERNMENT INFORMATION
CENTER)

lic with the western powers and the common pursuit of a "policy of
strength" would persuade the Soviet Union to yield on contested points
and give up its control of East Germany. As the years passed, there was
little indication that this policy was going to succeed.

The Soviet Union had also sponsored a constitutional congress in its
zone, and the work of this body eventuated in the proclamation of the
German Democratic Republic in October 1949. This state had a president
(Wilhelm Pieck, head of the German Communist party), a prime minister
(Otto Grotewohl, head of the SED), and a popularly elected single cham-
ber, but power was concentrated for the most part in the hands of the
Politburo of the SED, which was directed by Walter Ulbricht. The
Democratic Republic was organized on Soviet lines, and the policy of
strict centralization eliminated all local agencies that might serve as
centers of resistance to state power. Internal repression was heightened
after the outbreak of riots against Soviet control in East Berlin and other
German cities in June 1953. In 1955, the republic was recognized by the
Soviet regime as a sovereign state, and thereafter the Moscow leaders
took the line that German reunification could come about only as a result
of negotiations between the two German governments. This was rejected
by the western powers, with a resultant stalemate. As it continued and
Germany remained divided, the economic strength and general stability
of the eastern regime undoubtedly increased.

A particularly dangerous issue in German affairs and in east-west relations generally was created by the anomalous position of Berlin. Situated
a hundred miles within the Soviet zone and recognized by both German

regimes as the natural capital of the country as a whole, Berlin continued to be split into a western sector, subsidized by West Germany and garrisoned by Allied troops, and an eastern sector under the control of the Democratic Republic and protected by Soviet arms. In November 1958, the Soviet Union announced that it intended to terminate the last vestiges of four-power control over the city and hand its rights over to the East German government. Since this would place the delicate matter of control of western access routes to Berlin in the hands of a government which they refused to recognize, this threat was repudiated by the western governments. But it was soon repeated, and the possibility of a Berlin crisis of major proportions remained real.

THE SOVIET ORBIT

The Soviet Union from Stalin to Khrushchev / If there were Russians who had believed, at the war's end, that the victory would lead to a new era in which the wartime collaboration with the western democracies would be perpetuated and the rigid domestic controls relaxed, they were soon disenchanted. The Soviet regime seemed to sense that any tendency in this direction could only weaken its authority over the Russian masses, a reflection that was probably strengthened by the fact that thousands of Soviet citizens and members of the armed forces had defected to the west during the war and that thousands more, whom the fortunes of war had brought under foreign control, had desperately resisted repatriation.

Stalin and his aides reverted, therefore, to the line of policy they had followed before World War II. They preached that the Soviet Union was ringed about by capitalist enemies, bent on the destruction of communism, and that they were being aided by unpatriotic Russians on the home front. In February 1946, Stalin restated the thesis that war was inevitable as long as capitalism existed; and simultaneously, under the direction of Andrei Zhdanov, who was now recognized as Stalin's probable successor, a virulent campaign began against those who had succumbed to the lure of bourgeois culture. Meanwhile, as part of the reindoctrination process to which Soviet society was subjected, the victory over Hitler was credited by the press solely to Soviet arms, and Soviet pre-eminence in every aspect of human activity became a matter of faith.

The ludicrous nature of some of these claims had the effect of making the outside world overlook or depreciate the real achievements of the

Soviet Union in the postwar period. These were notable. From the devastation wrought by the war and the staggering losses of population and resources, the country recovered with impressive speed. New five-year plans introduced in 1946 and 1951 gave direction and impetus to the drive for rehabilitation and growth, while the "Stalin Plan for the Transformation of Nature," inaugurated in 1948, set out to reforest the southern steppes, modernize the network of canals, and harness the rivers for the production of electric power. By disregarding what would be considered in the west as minimal consumers' needs, the state was able to launch a weapons and nuclear program that matched—and by the 1950s probably exceeded—that of the United States in magnitude and results, while at the same time it brought production of steel, coal, oil, and electrical power to levels that were sometimes twice what they had been in 1940. As for agriculture, the system of collectivization, which had in some respects been liberalized during the war, was tightened again and, in 1948 and 1949, was extended to the newly annexed provinces in the west. A new tendency toward the creation of larger collective units, urged particularly by Nikita Khrushchev, strengthened party control over agriculture, although its economic results were spotty. Indeed, the general rule seemed to be that the state's success in promoting peasant docility was made at the expense of agricultural efficiency, the peasant having few incentives to improve his performance.

In March 1953, Joseph Stalin died, presumably of a heart attack, although there were inevitable rumors of palace revolutions and assassinations. Zhdanov, his putative successor, had died the year before, and his position as chairman of the Council of Ministers was assumed by Georgi M. Malenkov, whose chief associates were Lavrenti Beria, Vyacheslav Molotov, and, as party secretary, a man still little known outside the Soviet Union, Nikita S. Khrushchev. The tendency of the new regime in internal affairs was toward a relaxation of the program of agricultural collectivization and a new emphasis on the production of consumers' goods. The Malenkov interregnum was, however, of short duration and was marked from the start by dissension within the hierarchy and friction between the Red Army and the secret police. This led to the arrest and execution of Beria in July 1953, and a purge of the Moscow, Leningrad, and provincial party organizations, carried out under the direction of the party secretary, whose star had started to rise. In December 1954, Khrushchev launched an attack in print upon Malenkov's industrial policy, and two months later the premier resigned.

Although he was succeeded by Nicholas A. Bulganin, the real power in Soviet affairs was now in Khrushchev's hand, and he dominated both domestic and foreign policy. He immediately repudiated Malenkov's new course in industry and embarked on a basic reorganization of the whole industrial bureaucracy as a means of increasing efficiency in all sectors, including consumers' goods. He also continued the policy of enforcing the large-scale organization of agriculture. Emphasis was placed upon "overtaking and surpassing" the United States in the economic sphere, and progress toward this was sufficiently great to make the sharp rise in Soviet economic growth a subject of concern and political debate in the United States in 1960.

In 1957 and 1958, Khrushchev consolidated his personal power by effecting the removal from the Presidium of the Party Malenkov, Kaganovitch, and Molotov, who were all considered to be his rivals, and by dismissing the most popular of the Red Army marshals, Zhukhov, from the same body and from the Central Committee. This last stroke eliminated the possibility of the army assuming a dominant role in politics, a possibility much speculated about at the time of Beria's death. Khrushchev now felt able to dispense with Bulganin, who was dismissed in March 1958, at which time Khrushchev combined the offices of prime minister and party secretary in his own person and showed that he had won that primacy over party and government that had been held by Stalin.

In 1956, in a famous unpublished speech at the Twentieth Party Congress, Khrushchev had attacked the excesses of Stalin's regime. The hopes expressed at the time that this might herald new intellectual and political freedom in the Soviet Union were not, however, fulfilled. It is almost certain that Khrushchev never meant them to be and that the true meaning of his speech was that such abuses as Stalin's were possible only because of the moral decline of the party, which could be corrected only by new loyalty to communism, new attention to orthodoxy, new discipline, and—in the continuing struggle with the capitalist world—new vigilance.

Eastern Europe / Between 1945 and 1948 almost a hundred million Eatern Europeans were brought under Communist rule, as "people's democracies" were established in Albania, Poland, Rumania, Bulgaria, Hungary, Czechoslovakia, East Germany, and Yugoslavia. This represented a tremendous victory for the Soviet Union and fundamentally altered the balance of world power.

A word must be said first about the two countries at the extreme ends of this great belt of territory, Finland and Greece, for here Soviet ambitions were not realized. In Finland, the prospects of communism seemed good in the immediate postwar years. In the first coalition governments formed after 1945, the Communists played an important part and controlled the Ministry of the Interior, a vital position from which, in other countries, they often succeeded in infiltrating the police forces. This did not take place in Finland; the Communist minister was forced out of office in 1948; and the Socialist and Agrarian parties soon sapped the strength of the Communists so effectively that none of the Finnish governments after 1948 included Communist members. Inroads into trade unions were also checked by the Socialists; and communism in general was reduced from a threat to a nuisance. The Soviet Union was willing to tolerate this setback because control of the country was not essential to Russia. Finland was bound by the terms of the Soviet-Finnish Mutual Aid Treaty of 1948 and by the limitations placed on its armed forces by the peace treaty (see p. 767). It did not lie athwart the main routes to the west. Any attempt to exert control over Finland would alarm Sweden and possibly drive it into the arms of NATO. All of these things counseled restraint.

A victory of communism was more nearly achieved in Greece, where, as early as 1941, the Communists had an effective underground, the Greek Liberation Front (EAM), and a fighting force, the Greek People's Liberation Army (ELAS). When the British landed in Greece after the German evacuation in October 1944, EAM-ELAS had a strong position throughout the country and could probably have consolidated its authority if it had seized Athens before the British were in effective control. Fighting between the British and the Communists broke out in December, but did not go well with the Communists, who found it expedient to agree to disarm ELAS and to promise to rely on legal parliamentary means of extending their influence. These promises they repudiated a year later, when they reopened the civil war and, thanks to Soviet and satellite aid, fought on for another three years. But American assistance to the non-Communist forces in Greece, and Yugoslavia's break with Moscow, which led to the closing of the Yugoslav-Greek frontier and prevented supplies being shipped to the rebels from that direction, finally broke the back of Communist resistance and saved Greece for democratic government.

Elsewhere, however, communism was successful, and its conquest of Eastern Europe followed a general pattern, although there were differences in detail from country to country. Its basis was generally a tacit or explicit agreement on the part of the west that the Soviets had a right to, or could be allowed, a commanding position in the country in question. Thus, in 1944, Winston Churchill, in return for a promise of Stalin's recognition of primary British interest in Greece and equality of interest in Yugoslavia, admitted on paper that the Soviets had a predominant interest in Rumania, Hungary, and Bulgaria. Thus, also, at Yalta, concessions were made to Soviet views on Polish affairs that were tantamount to acknowledging Soviet primacy of interest there, although

Soviet assurances were given that, in all eastern states, principles of democratic government would be observed. In some countries—notably Albania and Czechoslovakia—no western acquiescence was necessary, since the governments took the initiative in inviting the Soviet Union to assume an influential position in their affairs.

The next phase in the take over was one in which the Communists participated in the local political process and entered into governments in coalition with the other parties, gradually acquiring control of the governmental apparatus and infiltrating and splitting the other party organizations, until such time as they were able to dispense with their partners.

After that came the period of *Gleichschaltung* (see p. 637), during which the other parties were forced to fuse with the Communists (as was done in the case of the SED in East Germany), political opposition in parliament, the press, and public meetings was forbidden, political opponents and former political allies were liquidated, and a Soviet system was imposed on the country. In some cases (East Germany and Poland), these measures were facilitated by the menacing presence of Soviet troops; in others, they were promoted by more discreet means, like economic pressure and threats, such as those which compelled the Czechoslovakian government to withdraw from the Paris conference on the Marshall Plan in 1947 after it had accepted the invitation.

The first states to go Communist were Albania and Yugoslavia, both of which were conquered by Communist resistance movements that had arisen during the war. In Bulgaria and Rumania, it was not until mid-1945 that the leaders of the non-Communist parties were isolated and driven from power and the deposition of the reigning sovereigns, Simeon of Bulgaria and Michael of Rumania, was accomplished. In Poland, whose political future had been the subject of interminable inter-Allied discussions during the war and especially at Yalta and Potsdam, the Communists showed their hand clearly only in 1947. In June of the same year they took over completely in Hungary; and, in February 1948, in a series of events that shocked the western world into a new comprehension of the momentum of the Communist march, a Communist regime was established in Czechoslovakia.

The case of Czechoslovakia was, in one respect, special, for, of all the countries of Eastern Europe, it alone was predominantly industrial, with a social structure similar to that of the highly developed states of Western Europe and with strong middle-class democratic parties. That the Communists were able to take over here was due to their superior tactics, the mistakes of their opponents, and the traumatic experience of the years 1938–1945 which deprived the Czech people of any real will to resistance.

The Czechs began the postwar period filled with good will toward the Soviet Union, and leaders like President Eduard Beneš, still hoping to make their country a bridge between east and west, were anxious to do nothing that might offend their great eastern neighbor. Popular gratitude for the liberation of the country was reflected in the strength shown by communism in the elections of 1946 and the share given to the Communists in government. When the Communists proceeded to exploit the sectional differences which had always plagued Czechoslovakia, to infiltrate police and local administration, and to resort to open lawlessness, the democratic parties resisted, effectively for a time. In February 1948, however, they committed the grave tactical error of seeking to force the Communist minister of the interior out of office by withdrawing their representatives from the cabinet without first making sure that they had the support of the president, the Socialists, or anticommunist elements in the army and the police. The Communists persuaded President Beneš to accept the resignations, proceeded to foment agitations that threatened to make public order break down completely, and then, backed by armed factory workers and the presence of Soviet forces on the frontiers of the country, boldly seized power. In face of this, President Beneš and the democratic leaders simply gave in. Munich had left them with a fundamental distrust of the west, from which they now expected no assistance; and the country as a whole had had its powers of resistance exhausted during the war and was in no mood to support last-ditch stands.

Whatever may be said about the economic benefits that the extension of communism brought to the peoples of Eastern Europe (and to some sections of society, these were doubtless real), there is no doubt that the Soviet Union profited greatly from it. As early as 1947, the satellite states were taking more than half of the Soviet Union's exports and were supplying over a third of its imports, besides paying reparations in kind which the Soviets could re-export. Strategically, the forward march of communism gave to the Soviet Union that protective *glacis* that its foreign policy had striven to establish since the 1920s, and gave it, moreover, in a much more solid form than could have been attained by mere treaty arrangements.

It was impossible to hide from the rest of the world that this represented a new form of imperialism, which Soviet dialecticians had always maintained was a disease peculiar to capitalism. The imposition of Soviet economic and social forms upon captive peoples, with little regard for cultural or physical differences, and the systematic exploitation of their resources was clearly reminiscent of the worst abuses of European colonial expansion. As in the case of the older imperialisms, moreover, there now came disturbing "native risings" against the colonizers, although these proved to be less successful than some of those treated above (see p. 450). Even so, the demonstrations of 1953 in East Germany were so serious that Soviet tanks had to be brought in to put them down. Three years later in Poznan, Poland, armed clashes between factory workers and the police led to perhaps a hundred deaths and revealed widespread disaffection in that country; and, in a special visit to Warsaw, Khrushchev seems to have decided that it was wiser to make concessions to the demands of the Central Committee of the Polish Communist party for internal changes than risk a widespread armed insurrection.

The most serious of these risings was that in Hungary, which took place in October 1956 and assumed the dimensions of a full-scale revolution before it was finally suppressed. Starting as a movement of university students, it spread rapidly to the workers, the middle classes, and even the army and the police, and took the form of stormy demonstrations in favor of the withdrawal of Soviet troops, the reconstitution of the government, the guaranteeing of basic civil liberties, and widespread social reforms. When crowds were fired on by the Hungarian secret police, fighting broke out and spread throughout the country; workers' soviets began to be organized, this time against the regime; Russian troops had to retire from Budapest; and a popular government was formed under the leadership of Imre Nagy, who immediately appealed to the U. N. for assistance in defending Hungary's independence and neutrality.

At the U. N. the representative of the United States said to the Security Council: "We can truly say to the Hungarian people: 'By your sacrifice you have given the United Nations a brief moment in which to mobilize the conscience of the world on your behalf. We are seizing that moment, and we will not fail you.'" But the events in Hungary coincided with the crisis at Suez (see p. 808), and in the end the promises were unfulfilled. On November 4 Soviet armored columns entered Hungary and swept into the larger urban centers. In Budapest there was desperate resistance, but it was put down with brutal severity, and the gallant fight for freedom ended in a new wave of executions and proscriptions.

Order was quickly restored in Hungary. A new government was formed under an obedient satrap, Janos Kadar; and Nagy was seized in defiance of a safe conduct given him by the Yugoslav embassy and subsequently executed as an example to others whose loyalty to the Soviet Union might be wavering. Nevertheless, the Hungarian revolution left scars. Even within the Soviet Union, it shook the faith of many members of the party and seriously disturbed university youth, while in Communist parties in the west there were many defections. But this, of course, did not help the people of Hungary.

The only country in Eastern Europe that succeeded in establishing partial freedom from Soviet imperialism, aside from Finland and Greece, was Yugoslavia. Entering upon the postwar period with a strong native Communist movement that had already liquidated its domestic opponents and with the prestige that came from the exploits of its leader, Tito (Josif Broz), in the resistance against German occupation during the war, Yugoslavia proved unresponsive to Soviet desires for conformity of policy. Its increasingly open gestures of independence led to an open break with the Soviet Union in 1948, when Yugoslavia was expelled from the Soviet association of nations. Worse might have followed, for the Soviets had no hesitation about encouraging economic blockade and military depredations on the part of Yugoslavia's neighbors. But these measures, when tried, merely kindled the fires of Yugoslav patriotism and made it apparent that only a major military effort could hope to wipe out the Titoist defection, and that even this might not succeed, for Yugoslavia had a long coastline and the western powers were obviously prepared to supply the heretic with weapons and food supplies. American generosity, in particular, in providing both financial and military assistance, helped stiffen Tito's resistance and make it successful.

Yugoslavia's defection was one of degree. The country remained Communist, and restrictions on free thought and expression were hardly less stringent than in the Soviet Union. Institutionally, Tito favored a certain amount of decentralization in order to give authority to men who were in touch with local problems. Agriculture was decollectivized, and various experiments with profit sharing were made in order to stimulate industry and the social services. These were sufficiently successful to contribute to the stability of the regime. After 1955, the Russians recognized this and tried to reach a *modus vivendi* with the Yugoslavs. Their efforts had not, by the end of 1960, succeeded in bringing Yugoslavia back into the Soviet orbit, but neither had western aid succeeded in detaching Tito from the world of communism. Yugoslavia had become a neutral state but—as a U. N. observer noted—one of those "positive neutrals," whose neutrality seemed to operate against the west and in favor of its former friends and associates in Eastern Europe.

Science and Culture / Within the bloc, the intellectual and scientific progress made after 1945 was impressive. The governments of the Soviet Union and the satellite states lavished attention and support upon education, being particularly solicitous about the training of specialists who were needed in the economic, scientific, and engineering sectors of state activity. Soviet achievements in technical training certainly equaled those of the west in this period, and their effort in the field of foreign-language training, to take one example, dwarfed anything being done, or even contemplated, in the United States. Soviet accomplishments in missile and rocket research and in cognate fields were particularly notable, and the successful launching of the first earth satellites in 1957 had a stunning impact on world opinion, causing some pessimistic western observers to fear that supremacy in science had been lost irretrievably by the noncommunist world.

The political uses to which the Soviets put their success with the *Sputniki* illustrated an important truth about Communist support of research and development. Generally speaking, the Soviet and satellite governments gave their backing primarily to intellectual and scholarly activities that promised to increase state power or to advertize it. Thus, in addition to the obviously important or dramatic scientific activities, the performing arts were generously provided for, and those troupes from the Communist countries which were permitted to show themselves at the Brussels Exposition of 1958 and on similar occasions dazzled western audiences.

In the creative arts, on the other hand, results were not so happy. During the period when Zhdanov was acting as a kind of tsar of culture, he insisted that the role of the Soviet artist was to glorify the state and that failure to do so would not be tolerated. Among his victims were such outstanding figures as the musicians Prokofiev and Shostakovitch and the film director Eisenstein, who had to go to humiliating private Canossas in order to expiate their sins.

With the state thus reserving the right to decide what was good art or bad and, in many cases, dictating both theme and treatment to writers, painters, and musicians, the result was apt to be dreary, if not banal. Commenting on "socialist realism," a young Russian, who preferred to remain unnamed, wrote in 1959 that, since the theme of all Soviet novels was the Revolution, all of the endings had to be happy, although sometimes it was the technical processes rather than the human characters which survived.

> The reader gradually learns that, in spite of all break-downs, the machine-tool will be set to work, or that the kolkhoz "Victory," despite wet weather, is amassing a rich harvest of maize; and he closes the book with a sigh of relief, feeling that we have taken one more step toward communism.

To an even greater extent than was true in the Russia of Nicholas I, criticism of the regime, even if it were indirect or referred to superficial aspects of Soviet life or governmental practice, was subject to punishment. This was shown all too clearly by the treatment accorded Boris Pasternak's novel *Doctor Zhivago*, which had a merited success throughout the western world in 1957 and 1958 and won its author a Nobel prize but was banned in the Soviet Union, Pasternak being forced publicly to decline the honor paid him.

30

Europe and the World

THE DEFENSE OF WESTERN EUROPE

Challenge and Response / The western powers faced up to the threat of Soviet imperialism reluctantly and slowly, clinging to the hope of collaboration with Russia and deferring the sacrifices necessary for effective opposition as long as possible. Perceptive observers saw the danger early and dutifully reported it. George Kennan, the United States chargé d'affaires in Moscow, wrote home in February 1946, "We have here a political force committed fanatically to the belief that with [the West] there can be no permanent *modus vivendi*, that it is desirable and necessary that the internal harmony of our society be disrupted, our traditional way of life be destroyed, the international authority of our [states] be broken, if Soviet power is to be secure." It was not, however, until 1947, when the Soviet threat to Greece and Turkey became obvious and pressing that the western states prepared for a real defensive effort. The enunciation of the Truman Doctrine in March 1947, in which the United States government promised economic aid to Greece and Turkey and support to "all free peoples who are resisting attempted subjugation by armed minorities or by outside pressure," and the presentation of the Marshall Plan in June of the same year, promising American support for any European recovery effort that was undertaken by collaborative means, put an end to hesitation and to the mood of resignation that had reigned in more than one European capital since 1945 and stimulated a vigorous movement toward European integration.

This took several forms. On the political level, it led in 1949 to the establishment of the Council of Europe, a consultative body that eventually had sixteen members who found it a useful agency for the exchange of views and the establishment of common policy in areas of particular concern to the European states. On the economic level, it led, after the announcement of the Marshall Plan and the approval by the United States Congress of a total sum of financial aid to Europe, to the establishment of an Organization for European Economic Cooperation (OEEC) in April 1948. This body, which was designed to define the specific needs of the separate states requiring Marshall Plan aid and to draw up a long-term plan for European recovery, contributed greatly to the speed with which Europe got back on its feet. The OEEC also laid a foundation for other forms of economic cooperation; and, in the next decade, it was followed by such agencies as the European Coal and Steel Community (ECSC), formed to stimulate the production of coal and steel by reducing trade barriers, the European Atomic Energy Community (Euratom), set up in order to promote joint exploitation of the peaceful uses of atomic energy, and the European Economic Community (Common Market), which envisaged the elimination of all economic barriers between its members. The difficult problems that confronted these organizations were many, but the will to overcome them was strong, and their very creation showed a recognition of inter- dependence that had been lacking in Europe since the free-trade era of the 1860s.

The Birth of NATO and the Korean War / Significant as these things were, it was considered of greater urgency to erect some kind of military barrier against the possibility of a westward surge of Soviet imperialism. Recognition of this need was behind the conclusion in March 1948 of the Treaty of Brussels, by which Great Britain, France, Belgium, the Netherlands, and Luxembourg committed themselves to common defense in case of an attack upon the European territory of any of their number. But even when this step had been taken, it was realized that the states of Western Europe would not succeed in raising very impressive military forces, at least in the foreseeable future, unless they received American military assistance.

This, however, was not long delayed. In March 1948 President Harry S. Truman endorsed the purposes of the Brussels Treaty; and in June the United States Senate—acting during the Soviet blockade of Berlin— adopted the so-called Vandenberg Resolution which, while affirming

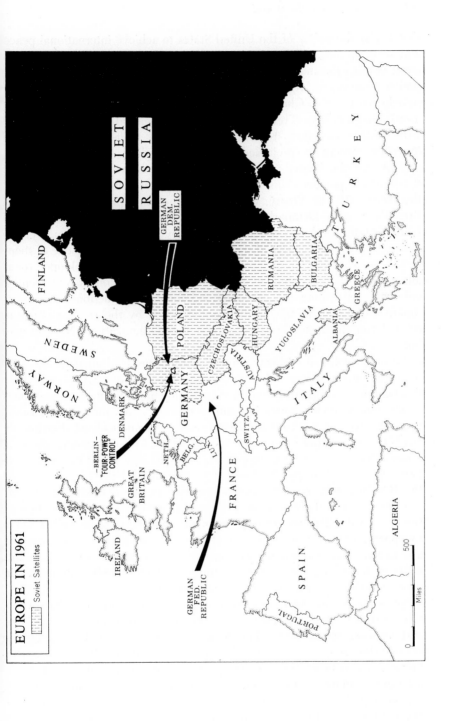

EUROPE IN 1961

▨ Soviet Satellites

that it was the policy of the United States to achieve international peace and security through the U. N., stated that the United States must also contribute to the maintenance of peace "by making clear its determination to exercise the right of individual and collective self defense under Article 51 [of the Charter] should any armed attack occur affecting its national security." This revolutionary identification of national security with collective action—revolutionary because it flew in the face of inherited American prejudice against entangling alliances—made it possible for the United States government to throw its support behind the Brussels powers. This assumed tangible form in the conclusion of the North Atlantic Treaty, which was signed in April 1949 by the five Brussels powers, Denmark, Norway, and Iceland, and Canada and the United States, and subsequently ratified by their governments. By this treaty, the signatories agreed that an armed attack upon any one of them in Europe or North America would be considered as an attack upon them all and would be resisted by all of them by such action as was deemed necessary, "including the use of armed force," such action being coordinated whenever possible with parallel action by the U. N. Upon this mutual guarantee, the North Atlantic Treaty Organization (NATO) was built.

Although political and economic functions were envisaged for the new organization, or at least alluded to in the basic treaty, NATO was from the beginning a primarily military body, intended by its very existence to deter new Soviet aggression and to resist it if it came. How feasible this was, at least for the time being, was problematical. At the time of NATO's organization, there were in all Western Europe only about a dozen divisions of ground troops (including what was left of the United States army in Europe) backed by a few hundred planes. In contrast, the Russians were reported to have at least twenty-five divisions in the satellite states and many more at home, as well as thousands of operational aircraft. The western governments, therefore, were called upon to enact the legislation and vote the funds that would make possible the raising of forces numerous and well-armed enough to deny to the superior Soviet numbers a quick and easy victory, while giving their own countries the time for full mobilization.

The drive toward this objective was given impetus in June 1950, when the North Korean Communists drove across the 38th parallel (see p. 769) and invaded South Korea. The background of this event lies properly beyond the scope of a book that is devoted primarily to European history. It was bound up with the postwar collapse of Chiang Kai-shek's attempts to maintain his government on the mainland of China, despite the great volume of American aid and advice that had been lavished upon him, and the systematic conquest of China by the Chinese

Communists under their leader Mao Tse-tung, which was completed in 1949 and restricted Chiang's power to Formosa and neighboring islands. These events gave confidence to communism elsewhere in the Far East, not least of all in North Korea, where Soviet agents had remained after the withdrawal of Russian troops at the war's end. There had been frequent conflict between the two Korean regimes and several border incidents, but what ensued now was full-scale war.

The United States government determined without hesitation to resist the breach of law and despatched troops and planes to Korea from General Douglas MacArthur's headquarters in Japan to reinforce the local garrisons and the South Korean army. It also sought the sanction of U. N. for its actions and, despite Soviet resistance to this (and in part because of a tactical error on the part of the Soviets in absenting themselves from the Security Council at the time of a crucial vote), received it. Thus, the war became an international effort with the objective of resisting the initial aggression and restoring the *status quo*, and British, Canadian, Australian, Turkish, and other U. N. troops participated in it before it was over, although the bulk of the U. N. force was supplied by the United States.

This, in itself, created some difficulties, for, if the great majority of those in the U. N. who had favored resistance regarded this as a limited war, many Americans were impatient with this idea and demanded, in the press, in Congress, and in public debate, that there should be a total solution. This insistence increased when the first overwhelming enemy drive was at last beaten to a standstill in the very outskirts of the southern port of Pusan, and when the counteroffensive began and—thanks to a brilliant amphibious operation at Inchon on the east coast, where MacArthur's forces and the U.S. Marines stormed ashore behind the enemy lines—drove the North Koreans back to the 38th parallel. General MacArthur shared the view that wars should end in total victory, and he ordered his armies to advance across the parallel and to move north to the Yalu River. This action brought Chinese Communist "volunteer forces" into the fight; and, striking hard at a gap that had appeared in the U. N. lines during the rapid advance, they routed American forward units and changed the whole complexion of the war. It now became a dogged seesaw conflict that went on until a truce was finally patched up in the summer of 1953 that restored the situation of 1950. By that time, the United States suffered about half as many casualities as it had in World War II.

The heated controversy that embittered American politics during the last years of this conflict, which led to charges of inefficiency and treason against the Democratic administration and compelled President Truman to dismiss General MacArthur for what amounted to insubordination, need not concern us here. It is important to note, however, that, in refusing to expand the war into an all-out conflict with China, as some of its critics seemed to desire, the Truman Administration was holding to the belief that the critical strategic area in the struggle against communism was Europe. It shared the fear of its European allies that an attack similar to that of the North Koreans might be launched at any moment from the eastern satellite states, where the Russians were known to be encouraging the raising of military forces.

These fears had a direct and important effect upon the development of NATO's strength and operational plans. The fear of imminent attack stimulated the efforts of the European states to increase their military strength quickly and persuaded the United States government to let Europe share the results of its own mobilization for the Korean war. It also made it seem necessary for NATO planners to think in terms of a "forward strategy," so that, if an attack from the Soviet orbit actually came, it would be checked as far to the east as possible, thus eliminating the dismal prospect of an easy Soviet conquest of Western Europe, followed, possibly, by a reliberation of the devastated continent by western armies. These considerations led in the last months of 1950 to a reorganization of the NATO forces (which, among other things, placed American and French troops in Germany under NATO), the creation of a Supreme Command under General Dwight D. Eisenhower, the sending of additional American forces to Europe (four new divisions in 1951), the admission of Greece and Turkey to NATO (although their memberships did not become effective until 1952), and—not least important—the decision, in principle, to authorize the rearmament of Germany.

This last proposal was one that, not unnaturally, raised grave doubts in many minds in countries that had suffered under Nazi invasion and occupation; but, especially after a NATO Council meeting in Lisbon in February 1952 had set the level of forces required for a forward strategy at ninety-eight divisions, to be available within thirty days of the outbreak of a war, a German contribution to European defense was seen to be inevitable for economic and other reasons. The French government, which had the greatest original hesitation about rearming the Germans, was forced to see the logic of this, but nevertheless proposed that, as a safeguard against danger, the European army should be organized as an integrated force, in which there were no national units of more than battalion strength. This was the famous project of a European Defense Community (EDC) which involved the NATO governments in laborious negotiations until August 1954, when the French Assembly, in a highly fractious mood, rejected it out of hand.

This caused a crisis of major proportions within the alliance, although it was finally overcome by patient diplomacy in which the British took the lead. In return for a British promise not to withdraw their forces from Europe without the concurrence of the Brussels powers, the French government agreed to amend the Brussels Pact, create out of it a Western European Union (WEU) with Germany and Italy as new members, and permit Germany to join NATO. By the London and Paris agreements of December 1954, ratified in the following spring, West Germany was admitted to NATO and authorized to raise an armed force of 500,000 officers and men as a contingent in the NATO line of battle.

The Soviet Union countered these moves in May 1955 by organizing its satellites in a military league known as the Warsaw Pact. It simultaneously began a skillful propaganda campaign that was designed to slow German rearmament by intimating that the Bonn government's membership in NATO would be a permanent barrier to German reunification. This was not without effect in West Germany, the Socialists in particular arguing that new negotiations with the Soviet Union on the German question should precede any implementation of the London and Paris agreements. Socialist opposition was not strong enough to block Bonn's adhesion to NATO, since there was a good deal of evidence that the German question was not negotiable. When it was actually discussed in 1955 at a summit meeting in Geneva that was attended by President Eisenhower, Prime Minister Eden of Great Britain, and the Soviet leaders Bulganin and Khrushchev, and at a subsequent meeting of Soviet and western foreign ministers, eastern and western views proved to be wholly irreconcilable, not because of the armaments issue but because the western governments wanted reunification of Germany by means of free elections, while the Soviet Union argued that the most expeditious means of approaching the problem would be by direct negotiations between the two German governments.

NATO'S Subsequent Development / In the years that followed, NATO was subjected to trials that left it weaker than it was in the period immediately after the outbreak of the Korean war. Stalin's death in 1953 led to a thaw in east-west relations that reached its height at the summit meeting of 1955, which produced a euphoria similar to the one that followed Locarno and led to as much talk about the "spirit of Geneva" as there once had been about the "Locarno spirit." The inevitable result of this was a relaxation on the part of the states of Western Europe, which now showed no urgency about meeting the force levels set at Lisbon. Their performance was, indeed, so disappointing that, in its meeting of December 1954, the NATO Council authorized its commands to plan their operations on the assumption that they would be free to use nuclear weapons supplied by the United States in the case of an attack. Tactical nuclear weapons were to make up for numerical deficiencies in the deterrent force. Since the Russians would presumably have nuclear weapons too, this rationale was not entirely convincing to some Western Europeans, who were further concerned over the probable effects of atomic bombardment in a highly urbanized area like their own. After the December decision, therefore, as NATO became increasingly dependent upon nuclear weapons, both tactical and strategical, there was mounting public criticism of its operational plans.

The strength of NATO forces was further weakened by France's Algerian troubles (see p. 820), which necessitated the withdrawal of all but two of France's divisions from the NATO battle line; and the organization's internal cohesion was threatened by two crises in the Near East. Troubles on the island of Cyprus in September 1955 led to sharp differences between the British and Greek governments on the one hand and the Greek and Turkish governments on the other (see p. 805), all of which made for disharmony in the alliance. More serious was the Suez crisis of November 1956 (see p. 808), which led to a situation in which the United States government associated with the Soviet government in censuring the actions of its British and French allies before the U. N. Security Council. This might have led to the total collapse of NATO had it not been for the subsequent Soviet threats to rocket-bomb London and Paris. These threats and the blood-letting in Hungary served as a healthy reminder to the NATO partners that the Soviet menace was still real and pressing, and at the Paris meeting of the NATO Council in December 1956 steps were taken to solve differences and strengthen the alliance.

In the subsequent period, Western Europe witnessed the opening of the Space Age, ushered in by the Soviet success in launching the first earth satellites (the *Sputniki*) in October 1957; it saw both the Soviet Union and the United States make great advances in the building of intercontinental missiles, which promised one day to eliminate the need for strategical bombers with human crews; and it suffered a continuing campaign of Soviet threats and blandishments designed to weaken the unity and will of the alliance. This last reached its height in the spring of 1960, when the capture of an American espionage plane (the U-2) inside Russian territory led the Soviet government to warn several NATO governments that future use of their bases for such purposes would invite the gravest kind of reprisals.

Despite all this and its own internal problems, NATO continued to hold to its purpose of giving to Western Europe a ground force that could deter aggression and, if war actually came, could provide a chance that it would be limited to something less than an exchange of thermonuclear strikes which would destroy western civilization. The NATO strategy remained a forward one, and, even if the Lisbon force levels were now discreetly forgotten, strength was being accumulated. By the autumn of 1960, West Germany had raised ten of its projected twelve divisions, and the NATO Supreme Command had as its objective a force of thirty fully mobilized divisions, armed with both conventional and nuclear weapons, standing in a state of constant readiness along the line that ran from the Baltic to the Alps, and backed by the tactical and strategical air power and missile forces of Great Britain and the United States.

EUROPE AND THE NEAR EAST

The European Stake / While the defenses of western Europe were being built up, great changes were taking place in the Near East. This was an area in which the European states had been interested throughout the whole period covered by this book, and during that time they had invested time, money, technological skill, and political effort in the lands at the eastern end of the Mediterranean. Whether the strategic importance of the Near East was as great to the western powers as it once had been was, in these days of long-range strategical bombers and intercontinental missiles, was at least debatable, although no NATO commander would have admitted for a moment that bases in Turkey were an insignificant contribution to western defense or that a growth of Soviet influence in the area would have negligible strategical results. As for its economic value to the west, there was no doubt whatsoever. Western European industry and transportation systems were heavily dependent upon the rich oil deposits of the area and would be exposed to danger if these were denied to the west.

The western powers were therefore anxious to retain their position in the Near East. Because of the explosive nationalism that affected the peoples of the area, however, and because of their own tactical mistakes and the ability of the Soviet Union to exploit them, they lost ground very perceptibly.

Greece and Turkey / Western European strength in the area was, for one thing, weakened by grave differences between Great Britain and Greece, despite the services of the former to the Greek cause during the war and the first years that followed it, and between Greece and Turkey, despite their mutual membership in NATO.

The Anglo-Greek conflict arose in the island of Cyprus, which had been acquired as a British base in 1878 by Disraeli, who thought of it as the "key to western Asia" (see p. 276). British government of the island, during its days as a protectorate and, after 1925, as a Crown Colony, was benevolent and efficient and probably satisfactory to most of its Greek and Turkish inhabitants. Nevertheless, Cyprus had long been an objective of Philhelline aspiration, and the Greek church and a significant number of educated Greeks on the island worked long and faithfully for *Enosis* (union of Cyprus with Greece). In the early 1930s an outburst of pro-union feeling led to so much disorder and material damage that the government had to arrest its leaders and send them into exile. In the 1950s a more systematic movement began under the leadership of Michael Mouskos, Archbishop Makarios III; and, starting in 1954, a guerrilla movement directed by George Grivas carried on a campaign of terrorism that was intended to win international sympathy and support for *Enosis*. It proved to be so bloodthirsty in its methods and so indiscriminate in its choice of victims that it had the opposite effect. In addition, it alienated the Turkish minority on the island, who took to anti-Greek terrorism on their own account; and this led to riots against the Greeks in Istanbul in September 1955 and to the bombing of the Turkish consulate in Salonika in reply.

British patience and the pressure of world opinion finally led to a provisional solution in 1959. Cyprus would achieve independent status, with the Greek and Turkish inhabitants administering their own affairs and with British strategical interests guaranteed, but with *Enosis* permanently denied. Cypriote independence brought some alleviation of tension, but relations between the three NATO partners could hardly be described as cordial at the end of the decade.

Turkey's strength as an ally was cast in some doubt by the occurrence of serious internal troubles in 1959 and 1960. The one-party system that had obtained in the country after Kemal's revolution (see p. 540) had begun to break down before World War II; and, in 1946, a new party, the Democratic party, was founded and, four years later, was swept into power by a large majority. Under the prime ministership of Adnan Menderes, this party played an active role in rebuilding an economy that had been badly shaken by the war, in modernizing the transportation network, and in increasing agricultural production. The regime nevertheless showed a growing inattention to the laws of sound finance and its mistaken belief that its deficits would be made good by the United States Treasury soon involved it in credit shortages, inflation and social distress. To still its critics, the Menderes government used increasingly authoritarian methods. Political opponents were jailed with little provocation, and, when student demonstrations took place in the spring of 1960, the police invaded university precincts without authorization, mishandled the rector when he protested, and acted with the utmost brutality against unarmed crowds of students.

By the early fall of 1960, a good part of the Turkish populace had had enough of Menderes, and a military coup led to the arrest of the prime minister and most of his cabinet. The officers who engineered this were loud in their protestations that the *Putsch* was intended to restore respect for law and would make no difference in Turkey's commitment to NATO. But there was no way of telling, at the end of 1960, how strong the new regime was and how reliable its promises.

The Problem of Israel / Ever since World War I, many of the political troubles of the Arab world had centered around the problem of the Jews in Palestine and the conflicting promises made to them and the Arabs by the western powers (see pp. 509 and 541). These assumed a new intensity after 1945. In that year the British announced that they planned to give up their mandate over Palestine and referred the long-vexed problem to the U. N. The U. N., responsive to the needs of homeless Jewish refugees in Central and Eastern Europe, accepted a plan in November 1947 for the partition of Palestine and the establishment there of a Jewish state, an Arab state, and an internationalized city of Jerusalem. Partition proved difficult to implement. While the Jews proceeded, in the spring of 1948, with the establishment of an independent republic in Palestine with its capital at Tel Aviv, they were attacked by military forces raised by the Arab League (Egypt, Syria, Lebanon, and Iraq), and disorderly fighting went on until the beginning of 1949. The Arab forces were ill-trained, badly led, and greatly inferior to their antagonists. When U. N. mediators, with great difficulty, finally arranged a truce, the new Israeli republic was given the greater part of Palestine.

Israel had made good its claim to statehood, was recognized by the U. N., and admitted to U. N. membership in May 1949. For the next seven years, under the leadership of its prime minister, David Ben Gurion, it concentrated on its domestic tasks. Its population grew threefold in this period, as refugees came to the homeland from all over Europe. These immigrants had to be trained in the skills that would make for survival in a hard land and to be given the tools with which to earn their livelihood. For this and for various cooperative enterprises, the Israelis depended upon foreign loans, German reparations, and collections among Jewish communities abroad; but the United States, in particular, was generous, and the new republic made remarkable progress.

It was a progress with which the mounting indignation of its Arab neighbors kept pace. The Arab League had not accepted its setback as definitive. It exploited the grievances of the Palestinian Arabs, who had fled into neighboring lands where they lived in squalor and penury, and it began to organize terrorist gangs from the more active elements of these dispossessed people and to encourage border affrays. The new Egyptian regime was particularly active in these enterprises. The

Israelis, scenting the imminence of another attack from that quarter, accelerated the training program of their armed forces, following procedures that later won the unstinted admiration of western military observers. One of them, S. L. A. Marshall, wrote later:

> Both in the reserve and in the active army, training is more rigorous, puts heavier emphasis on field combat exercises, and makes heavier demand on the physical powers of the individual than in the United States Army.

The results of this preparation were evident in the campaign in the Sinai desert in 1956.

Egypt and the Suez Crisis of 1956 / During the first postwar decade, Egyptian politics was marked by a frenetic nationalism that exceeded in violence even that of the years before 1936. This feeling, which was directed particularly at the remnants of British influence in Egypt, especially their rights in the Sudan and at the Suez Canal as defined in treaties of 1899 and 1936, became so virulent that in 1951 it defeated an Anglo-American plan for a Middle East Command based in Egypt and allied to NATO. When this proposal was submitted to the Egyptian government, they did not give it even the courtesy of careful study, replying obliquely by denouncing the two aforementioned treaties.

The importance of Egypt in any strategical plan for the defense of the Near East made the western governments persist in their efforts to reach an agreement with Cairo. The deterioration of Egypt's internal situation seemed to favor their cause, for, after a military revolt had overthrown King Farouk's government and replaced it with one led, first, by General Naguib and then, in 1954, by Colonel Gamal Abdel Nasser, who became president and prime minister, it appeared that a political-military arrangement would be possible. At this stage of his career, Nasser seemed to be pro-western in his views and was well regarded in Washington, whence he received substantial financial assistance and a promise to support the construction of a dam at Aswan, a project upon which the new dictator had set his heart. With Britain, Nasser concluded a new treaty in 1954, by which the British agreed to withdraw their troops from the Canal Zone within two years, on condition that they would have the right of re-entry in case of an external threat to Egypt's control of the Canal and that the Egyptian government would continue to respect the Convention of 1888, which guaranteed freedom of transit on this important international waterway. The Sudan question was also regulated, that country being given the choice of union with Egypt or independence, the second of which the Sudanese chose in 1955.

These signs of Egyptian friendship with the west were transitory. Nasser's insistent demands for military aid were refused by the west, which feared that any weapons sent him might be used against Israel. The Egyptian leader turned immediately to the Soviet bloc and, in September 1955, concluded an agreement for the delivery of arms, ostensibly with Czechoslovakia but in reality with the Soviet Union. The failure of the west to retaliate effectively encouraged him to go further. He began to stimulate anti-western propaganda in other Arab countries, to give aid to the rebels in Algeria (see p. 820), and to negotiate for the establishment of relations with Red China, while at the same time being exceedingly arrogant in his negotiations with the United States government for the financing of the High Dam at Aswan. Nasser's attitude irritated John Foster Dulles, the American secretary of state, who was already deeply concerned over the multiplying contacts between Nasser and the Soviet bloc. As he later said in a press conference, "The Egyptians, in a sense, forced upon us an issue to which I think there was only one proper response. That issue was, do nations which play both sides get better treatment than nations which are stalwart and work with us?" He decided that they should not and, in July 1956, announced that American aid for the dam would be withdrawn.

Nasser regarded this as an attempt to humiliate him and his country, and he retaliated by seizing the Suez Canal Company in defiance of international conventions and of his own recent assurances to the British.

At this point, all semblance of unity within the western alliance broke down. The British and French governments felt that firm action should be taken to make Nasser give up the Canal and that, if he would not recognize some form of international administration of the Canal, then the west must be ready to use military force to compel him to give way. Anthony Eden, foreign minister at the time, wrote to President Eisenhower:

> The seizure of the Suez Canal is, we are convinced, the opening gambit in a planned campaign designed by Nasser to expel all Western influence and interests from Arab countries. He believes that if he can get away with this, . . . his prestige in Arabia will be so great that he will be able to mount revolutions of young officers in Saudi Arabia, Jordan, Syria, and Iraq. (We know that he is already preparing a revolution in Iraq, which is most stable and progressive.) These new Governments will in effect be Egyptian satellites, if not Russian ones. They will have to place their united oil resources under the control of a united Arabia led by Egypt and under Russian influence. When that moment comes, Nasser can deny oil to Western Europe and we here shall all be at his mercy.

The United States government might have been more responsive to this appeal had it not been for the fact that the country was in the throes of a Presidential campaign in which the incumbent Administration was using the settlement of the Korean war as an argument for its return to office. It was definitely opposed to the use of force to solve the Egyptian problem and preferred to let matters drift rather than to take any course which might in the end make forceful intervention necessary. It did not, however, make its position entirely clear to its allies. Its statements were so ambiguous that the British and French began to suspect it of a deliberate lack of candor, if not of a desire to deceive. Since Soviet and Yugoslav votes in the Security Council made any useful action by the U. N. unlikely, the frustration of the two European powers mounted and finally led them to take rash and ill-considered action.

The occasion for this was presented in October 1956, when the steady increase in the number and intensity of incidents on the Arab-Israeli border and the growing evidence of Egyptian preparations for a full-scale war induced the Israeli government to anticipate danger by striking first. In what must be one of the shortest campaigns in history, lasting just about one hundred hours, the Israeli army invaded the Sinai peninsula, a fortified area about half the size of Nevada, held by an enemy who possessed superiority in numbers, equipment, and munitions, and proceeded to smash all its fighting units, capture all of its defensive positions, and force it to flee in wild and humiliating panic back across the Canal into Egypt.

While these brilliant operations were being fought, the British and French governments had decided to seize the Canal with their military forces. Their operation was not so brilliantly staged and ended in a damaging setback. Logistical difficulties, lack of complete determination, and political interference in tactical matters blunted the power and speed of a thrust that might otherwise have succeeded. The United States government separated itself from its allies and joined in a U. N. demand for a cease-fire. This pressure, combined with Liberal and leftist opposition at home, forced the British and French to call off the operation. The Soviet Union improved the occasion by sending ambiguous threats to the two Western European capitals but, although Moscow subsequently claimed—and, in some quarters, received—credit for having solved the Suez crisis, it was the split in the NATO alliance and the action of the U. N. that actually did so and saved Nasser from the consequences of his policies.

The Other Arab Lands / In the subsequent period, the fears expressed in Anthony Eden's letter to President Eisenhower seemed on the point of being realized. Nasser's influence was now at its height and was exercized in other capitals beside his own. It grew rapidly in Syria and made possible the fusion of that country with Egypt in a new United Arab Republic in February 1958. Five months later, it had even more dramatic

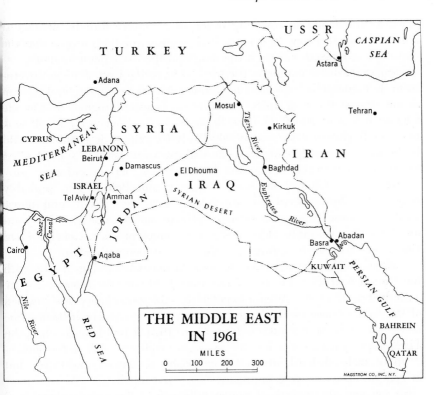

THE MIDDLE EAST
IN 1961

MILES
0   100   200   300

HAGSTROM CO. INC. N.Y.

effects in Iraq. This former British dependency had remained on good relations with Great Britain and, under its long-time prime minister, Nuri as-Said, had in 1955 joined the Baghdad Pact, a mutual defense arrangement of which Britain, Turkey, Pakistan, and Iran were also members and the United States a close associate. This tie, and Nuri as-Said's foreign policy in general, had been under bitter attack from Cairo since that time, and Nasser had done what he could to spread subversion inside Iraq. All of this came to a head on July 14, 1958, when a group of army officers led by General Karim el-Kassem suddenly seized power in Baghdad. King Faisal II and his brother were brutally slain; Nuri as-Said was hunted down and dispatched in the same manner; and a one-party dictatorial government, similar to that in Cairo, was set up. Iraq severed its ties with the Baghdad Pact.

The force of Arab nationalism was so great that, in neighboring Jordan, young King Hussein felt compelled to bow before it and to distance himself from the British, the traditional protectors of his territory. In 1955 Hussein refused to join the Baghdad association of powers, and in 1956 he dismissed his British military advisor, Sir John Glubb. After the Iraqi revolution, however, Hussein felt dangerously exposed and decided to call for British aid in restoring order in a country torn by nationalist plots. The British sent in a force from Cyprus for the purpose and the tension was relaxed, although the king's position remained insecure.

Despite its disinclination to use force at Suez, the United States government felt compelled to imitate Britain's Jordanian action in Lebanon during the summer of 1958. Here the pro-western regime of Camille Chamoun was under attack from Radio Cairo; and, when the revolt took place in Baghdad, it seemed highly likely that the little republic would be invaded by triumphant Arab nationalists. To forestall this, the United States, at Chamoun's request, sent a force of U.S. marines and some army paratroopers airlifted from West Germany into Beirut. This probably prevented a bloody civil war and prepared the way for a compromise solution. Chamoun gave up his hope of a second term as president, and the Lebanon Assembly elected the army chief of staff, General Fuad Chehab, to that position. American forces were then withdrawn.

Nasser's influence was strong enough to persuade Yemen to ally with the United Arab Republic in 1958, a result facilitated by Yemen's dispute with Britain over the Aden Protectorate; and it weakened the position of the ruling house in Saudi Arabia, forcing the government there to be more amenable to suggestions from Cairo than it had been in the past. The Egyptian leader was less successful in making inroads in the sheikh-doms of such oil-rich lands as Muscat, Bahrein, Kuwait, and Qatar; but in general his gains were impressive.

So too was the growth of Soviet influence in the area in the period following the arms deal of 1955 and the crisis at Suez. Soviet gains were not in any important sense due to the activities of local Communist parties, for Nasser did not take kindly to Communist activity in areas in which he was interested. In Egypt itself the strength of the Communist party was not great and its freedom was closely restricted. There was a much more powerful Communist movement in Syria, but, after the formation of the United Arab Republic, its leader, Khalid Bakdash, was forced to flee the country. In Iraq, the Communists supported Karim el-Kassem, but it was not clear that their influence approached predominance; and elsewhere they had little success in reaching the masses or in making their advice known.

Soviet influence grew nevertheless, independently of party organization. It resulted from the prestige that accrued to the Soviet Union because of its role in the Suez crisis; and it was maintained and expanded by the important part played by the Soviet Union in the Egyptian economy through its arms deliveries to Nasser and its subsequent decision to finance the High Dam, as well as through the activity of Soviet-bloc trade delegations and technicians in the Arab area. The western powers had interested themselves primarily in military-aid pacts with the Near

Eastern states—such things as the proposed mutual assistance pact of 1951 and the Baghdad Pact—and they were somewhat at a disadvantage when confronted with Soviet economic diplomacy, or, as one western scholar called it, "ruble diplomacy." As in other underdeveloped areas, so here the Soviets showed a greater readiness than the Western powers to advance economic aid and technical assistance with a minimum of conditions, and they won a reputation for generosity that was not always justified by the results of their assistance and barter deals. To a greater extent than was true of the western powers also, their effort was a collaborative one, with Czech engineers, East German soil experts, Polish construction men, and technicians from other satellite countries sharing in the projects that were negotiated, and this joint effort seemed to impress many people.

If the western position in the Near East was weakened by these events, its decline was not as disastrous as some observers feared. As Suez receded into the background, there were signs of tension and disunity between the Arab lands themselves (between Egypt and Syria, for instance) and some clear indications that Nasser did not want to become too dependent on his Soviet friends. A meeting at Brioni in 1958 laid the basis for a continuing association between Nasser and Tito of Yugoslavia, which was probably a sign of growing reserve. In the meeting of the U. N. General Assembly in New York in the autumn of 1960, Nasser did not act like a mere Soviet rubber stamp and showed marked cordiality toward the United States government.

At the same time, some of the western fences had been patched up in Iraq and Jordan and even in Syria; and it is perhaps worth noting that, in the U. N. debate on the Lebanon-Iraq crisis of 1958, the members of the Arab League (Iraq, Jordan, Lebanon, Libya, Sudan, UAR, Saudi Arabia, Yemen) agreed to refrain from interfering in each other's domestic affairs in the future and accepted an American proposal for a regional organization for the economic development of the whole area. Successful implementation of this suggestion could possibly do more to promote western security interests in this area than any number of military pacts.

Iran / A seesaw political battle between the Soviet Union and the west was waged in Iran in the postwar period. In the first years after the war, Soviet military incursions in Azerbaijan were terminated after firm intimations of reprisals on the part of the west. In the early 1950s, western interests within the country were severely shaken by the rise of a fanatical nationalist prime minister, Moses Mossadeq, who, by his nationalization of the British oil refineries and by other actions, reduced the administration and the economy of the country to a shambles and presented the powerful underground Communist party with an excellent opportunity for a coup. This they did not seize, perhaps because they had no instructions from Moscow, and in August 1953 Mossadeq was overthrown by General Zahedi.

After this, the Shah returned from abroad, established an authoritarian regime of his own, and purged the military and civil services of the large number of Communists who had managed to infiltrate them. Iran then moved into the western camp once more, joining the Baghdad Pact in 1955. The country still had grave economic and social problems, however, and the opportunities afforded communism were great.

THE PASSING OF THE EUROPEAN EMPIRES

India, Pakistan, and Burma / In these years that saw the retreat of the European powers from the great empires that they had built in the eighteenth and nineteenth centuries, perhaps the most impressive, because the most symbolical, of all the withdrawals was that of the British from India. In contrast to later examples of the relinquishment of colonial domains, this was marked for the most part by good sense and political intelligence, and in consequence much evil was avoided.

The decision to liquidate the British Raj was a direct result of the war, which deprived the British people of the means and the inclination to oppose what had come to be regarded even before 1939 as inevitable. The problem confronting the Labor government was how to withdraw without plunging the subcontinent into civil war. Internal dissension was complicated not only by the tension between the Indian Congress party and the Moslem League but also by the growth of communism, especially in the city of Calcutta but also in Kashmir and the far south. Moreover, a solution had to be found with speed, for the British government had decided during the war to stop recruiting for the Indian Civil Service, and, by 1947, it was clear that the reduced bureaucracy could not administer the country for many more months. In addition, the British people were firmly opposed to further military commitments in India.

The task of breaking the deadlock between the parties in India was entrusted to Lord Louis Mountbatten, who succeeded Lord Wavell as viceroy of India in February 1947. By a remarkable job of personal diplomacy, Mountbatten was able, within seventy-three days of his arrival in India, to persuade the leaders of the Congress party and the Moslem League to agree on a plan for the creation of two states, India and Pakistan, the partition of the Punjab and Bengal and the division of the Indian army between them, and the grant of Dominion status to both of

AFGHANISTAN

KASHMIR AND JAMMU

PAKISTAN

KARACHI

KUTCH

Saurashtra

PUNJAB

Himachal Pradesh

DELHI

RAJASTHAN

AJMER

UTTAR PRADESH

VINDHYA PRADESH

BHOPAL

MADHYA PRADESH

NEPAL

BIHAR

MADHYA PRADESH

WEST BENGAL

CALCUTTA

PAKISTAN

ORISSA

BHUTAN

ASSAM

Manipur

Tripura

BURMA

BOMBAY

BOMBAY

I N D I A

HYDERABAD

GOA (Port.)

COORG

MYSORE

MADRAS

PONDICHERRY

MADRAS

INDIA IN 1961

0   300

Miles

TRAVANCORE-COCHIN

CEYLON

COLOMBO

them in order to provide a maximum of administrative and constitutional continuity during the transfer of power.

This achievement, which was facilitated by the good sense shown by the Hindu leader Jawaharlal Nehru and the head of the Moslem League, Mohammed Ali Jinnah, was merely the beginning of Mountbatten's work. The administrative problems involved in implementing the plans were of staggering complexity. The partition of the Punjab and Bengal led to unrest and eventually to the migration of some nine million people, which was accomplished at a heavy human cost; among the Sikhs, who suffered most from partition, there were outbreaks of violence; there were difficulties among the Indian princely states, which were called upon to accede to India or to Pakistan; and, after Independence Day (August 15, 1947), there were serious differences between the Indian and Pakistani governments with respect to the eventual disposition of the important states of Junagadh, Kashmir, and Hyderabad. And always those who dealt with these problems and disputes were aware, as one of them wrote later,

that "the crust upholding order from the depths of chaos [was] dangerously thin" and that the forces of fanaticism might render all their efforts
meaningless.

Nevertheless, by the middle of 1948, when Mountbatten had completed his mission, most of the problems were in hand, the country was
calm, and the two new states were functioning effectively. One reason
for this, perhaps, was the assassination of Mohandas Ghandi by a young
provincial newspaperman in January 1948, a senseless act that shocked
the nation and sensibly diminished Hindu-Moslem strife.

In the ten years that followed, the Kashmir problem continued to be a
source of continued friction between India and Pakistan, both of which
maintained forces in this disputed area. In the late 1950s, however, India
had a more pressing concern, violations of its northeastern frontiers by
large bodies of Red Chinese troops; and Nehru's attempt to solve this
problem by patient negotiation did not succeed in persuading the in-
vader to give up what he had taken. Neither this incident nor his troubles
with communism in the southern state of Kerala weakened Nehru's
devotion to the policy of neutralism in the struggle between communism
and the democratic world. His maintenance of good relations with both
sides was instrumental in mediating the Korean war and the conflict in
Indochina.

Both India and Pakistan continued to belong to the Commonwealth
(formerly British Commonwealth) of Nations; and Pakistan, foreswear-
ing Nehru's brand of neutralism, became a member of the Baghdad Pact.

At the same time that the British effected their withdrawal from India,
they recognized the independence of Burma, whose freedom had been
proclaimed during the war by Japan, in an action the reversal of which
was considered to be impractical and undesirable. The grant of independence was made on January 4, 1948, and was accompanied by an
Anglo-Burmese treaty that gave Great Britain the right to maintain
military missions, but not bases, in the country.

Indonesia, Malaya, and Southeast Asia / Events soon showed that
Japan's wartime conquests of other colonial areas had destroyed the
prestige of the European powers and stimulated nationalist movements
that now successfully resisted their return. This was particularly true in
Indonesia, where the Dutch colonial empire had been overrun by the
Japanese in the first weeks after Pearl Harbor.

When the war was over, the British undertook the task of reoccupy-
ing the main Indonesian centers until such time as the Netherlands government had re-established itself and reorganized its colonial service.
Eventually, this led to an unfortunate difference of view between the
allies, for the British tended to cooperate with the Indonesia republic

that had been organized in August 1945 by the Javanese nationalist leader Achmed Sukarno, whereas the Dutch were opposed to all republican movements in their former domains and set out to destroy them. Despite British attempts to bring the two parties together, bitter fighting raged throughout 1947 as the Dutch sought to blockade republican centers and force their submission. U. N. intervention, although at first indignantly repudiated by the Dutch, succeeded in arranging a conference at The Hague in 1949, where it was decided to establish a United States of Indonesia as a sovereign state united in partnership with the Netherlands and recognizing the Dutch crown. This lasted, with much friction among the partners, until February 1956, when Indonesia unilaterally abrogated the treaty and elected to go its own way in what Sukarno called "guided democracy."

Communism had been a force in Indonesia since the 1920s, and Sukarno's attempt to collaborate with the Communists in his first government after 1956 aroused fears in the west of a general drift of this strategically important area into the Soviet bloc, a development that would represent a direct threat to the British position in Malaya and even to Australia. In general, Sukarno tended to follow a neutral line, seeking to propitiate the Left and the nationalists by nationalizing Dutch plantations and expelling Dutch colonists, but preferring not to alienate conservative elements by a decided Communist orientation. At the meeting of the U. N. Assembly in the autumn of 1960, Sukarno associated with the neutralist block composed of Nehru, Tito, Nasser, and Kwame Nkrumah of Ghana in urging new contact between the leaders of the United States and the Soviet Union.

In Malaya, the British avoided the fate of the Dutch by their customary patience and flexibility. After their return, their plan to create a Malayan Union with equal rights of citizenship for Malays, Chinese, and Indians and a reduction of the powers of the Malay sultans foundered on the opposition of the Malay population; and the British went over to a federal scheme that assured continued Malay supremacy. Communist insurrections began in 1948 and continued with great intensity for the next four years and at a lesser pitch thereafter. The British sought to combat this with military action on the one hand and, on the other, by encouraging a sense of Malayan nationalism so that the country might soon become independent. After 1955, they introduced a system of national elections for the legislative council and otherwise endeavored to encourage the spread of self-government.

The most disastrous retreat of a European colonial power in this area took place in Southeast Asia, and there, as in the Near East, the violence of nationalism, the tactical disarray of the western allies, and Communist skill in exploiting this all played their part.

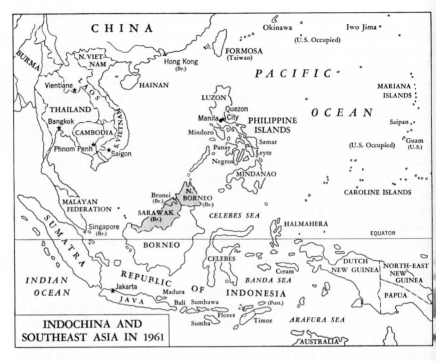

INDOCHINA AND
SOUTHEAST ASIA IN 1961

Once more the delayed influence of Japan's wartime successes was felt
here. The Japanese occupation authorities had encouraged the growth of
a native revolutionary movement; and in August 1945 this organization,
the Vietminh party, deposed the pro-French ruler of Annam, Bao Dai,
and established an independent republic, Vietnam, which embraced
northern Annam and Tonkin and was presided over by Ho Chi Minh.
Meanwhile, the French returned to the area, reasserted their authority in
Laos, Cambodia, and Cochin China, and organized these separate states
into a Federation of Indochina within the French Union. They sought
to induce Ho Chi Minh to join the federation and, had they been willing
to grant a large measure of self-government to Tonkin, Annam, and
Cochin China, they might have succeeded, for Ho Chi Minh, while a
Communist, was pro-French and anti-Chinese in his views. But the
French insisted that Cochin China, the wealthiest of the regions and the
one with the largest city, Saigon, remain separate and under their control. The negotiations broke down and war began between the French,
who sought, stubbornly and unrealistically, to put Bao Dai back on the
throne of a united Vietnam, and the Vietminh forces, supported by many
local patriots who were not Communists but had no place to turn.

This war reached its height after the outbreak of the conflict in Korea
had dramatized the struggle between communism and the democratic

world and had persuaded the United States Congress to extend economic
and military assistance to France and to the Bao Dai regime in Vietnam.
The local French commanders gradually made their way, against strong
guerrilla opposition, into Northern Vietnam; but, in 1954, they overextended their lines of communication and were trapped by superior
enemy forces at a place called Dienbienphu.

At this stage of affairs the French government, on April 23, 1954,
appealed to the United States for aid, apparently arguing that, unless it
was forthcoming immediately, all Indochina would fall. This sensibly
agitated Washington, where some unfortunate public statements were
made about the transcendent importance of Indochina to the free world
which made it seem as if the United States were prepared to intervene.
This was not strictly true. The United States government had already
decided against the commitment of any ground forces in Indochina. Admiral Bradford, the chairman of the Joint Chiefs of Staff, and Secretary
of State Dulles seem to have convinced themselves, however, that intervention by air power alone would save the situation, but they wanted
the collaboration of the RAF in any strikes planned. After much discussion, the British government decided that this was an irresponsible
plan that would not save the French situation at Dienbienphu and
might very well bring the Chinese Communists into the war, and they
declined to cooperate. No action was, therefore, taken, and Dienbienphu
fell, not without causing recriminations among the allies and leaving a
public impression of western disunity and unwillingness to make good
on threats delivered and promises made. The situation in Indochina was
regulated at a conference at Geneva whose meetings extended from
April until July 1954 and which finally divided Vietnam between French
and Vietminh forces at the 17th parallel. Although provisions were made
for elections for a united government, they were never held, and the
division still held at the end of the decade.

In the Republic of Vietnam south of the parallel, French influence
declined after 1954 and that of the United States increased. This was also
true in Cambodia and Laos, which had been recognized as independent
states within the French Union in 1949. That the stability of all these
states was questionable was illustrated by the fact that, at the end of
1960, pro-western, pro-Communist and neutralist forces were locked in
uncertain conflict in Laos.

North Africa / The French setback in Indochina had profound effects
upon France's empire on the other side of the world, particularly in
North Africa. In both Tunisia and Morocco nationalist movements had
been active since 1945, but they had been met by an inflexible policy of
repression. This became impossible after the blow given French prestige

in Southeast Asia, and the Mendès-France government, which had courageously faced up to the necessity of accepting defeat in the Far East, now took the initiative in North Africa as well.

The leader of the nationalist movement (*Néo-Destour*) in Tunisia was Habib Bourguiba, who had been in imposed exile from his country since the end of 1951. In July 1954 he was brought to France for consultation; and, in the same month, Mendès-France announced, in a speech at Tunis, that the protectorate would be given complete internal independence. Negotiations for this purpose continued after the Assembly had overthrown Mendès-France; and, in May 1955, a Franco-Tunisian agreement was signed, and Bourguiba was allowed to return to his country. His moderate policy after he had assumed the leadership of the Tunisian government invited new concessions. In March 1956 Tunisia became virtually independent by a new agreement which acknowledged its right to maintain its own armed forces and carry on its own foreign policy, while giving France certain military and naval rights in the country.

Similar concessions had to be made in Morocco. The French had been particularly high-handed in this protectorate in the first postwar years, as if believing that the Moroccans should be willing to forego political ambitions in view of the undeniable economic advantages that they derived from their association with France. During the period when General Juin was resident of Morocco in the late 1940s, the French not only sought to break up all independent political movements but, when the Sultan, Sidi Mohammed ben-Yusuf, showed his support of the objectives of the chief nationalist party, the *Istiqlal*, forced him in 1953 to hand his powers over to a joint Franco-Moroccan Council and deported him to Madagascar. This action was widely resented and united all sections of the Moroccan people against French rule, a fact which the French themselves were forced to admit after two years of terrorism and disorder. In November 1955, the government acknowledged that the deposed Sultan was the rightful ruler of Morocco; and, in the spring of 1956, negotiations were begun which eventuated in the grant of Morocco's independence later in the year.

These belated French concessions might have led to a fruitful and mutually advantageous cooperation between France and its former protectorates if it had not been for the continuation of the Algerian war which, not unnaturally, attracted the sympathies of Moroccans and Tunisians and led to French charges that the rebels were being supported from the soil of their neighbors.

The Algerian war began in November 1954 when the *Front de libération nationale* (FLN), a nationalist, terrorist organization richly supplied with leaders trained in Egypt and Iraq, began an armed insurrection that rapidly won support among the Algerian Moslems, although part of this, it must be admitted, was induced by fear of the consequences of loyalty to the French authorities. The European colonists (*colons*), on the other hand, had been established in Algeria for a longer time than in the neighboring protectorates; their economic stake was greater; and their resistance to concessions to the opposition was stronger. It was largely their fear of a governmental drift toward a Tunisian or Moroccan solution that prompted the May 1958 rising in Algiers, which was also supported, as we have seen (p. 775), by an army that felt that it had already been too frequently the victim of governmental concessions.

The fighting in Algeria was carried on with great savagery on both sides and, as the war continued, this aroused concern in France, where churchmen expressed horror at the inhumane methods used in the fighting, and student and trade union demonstrations called for a negotiated peace. President de Gaulle's own thinking ran in the same direction, to the indignation of the *colons* and many of his original supporters. His search for a moderate solution derived greater urgency from the fact that the rebels themselves leaned increasingly on aid from the Communist world. In October 1960, Ferhat Abbas, premier of the so-called Algerian Provisional Government, said in an interview in Tunis, "I was told in Peiping and Moscow a few days ago that Communist support will be greater this year than last, and still greater next year than this year." He went on to say: "They said also that, because we are fighting colonialism, there is no need to look for any other ideological bond. Our Chinese and Soviet friends recognize frankly that we are not Communists, and they ask no engagement whatsoever from us."

Sub-Sahara Africa / The retreat of the European powers from the holdings they had acquired in sub-Sahara Africa in the last years of the nineteenth century was general and, in some cases, precipitate, and was marked by the emergence of unprecedented problems. Only Portugal was virtually unaffected by nationalist movements, perhaps because of the poverty and backwardness of its colonies.

British policy varied from area to area. In West Africa, where there were no large non-African communities and where the social development of the Africans was well advanced, the British gradually yielded authority and broadened the basis of self-government. In both the Gold Coast and Nigeria, popularly elected assemblies were authorized by the early 1950s; in March 1957, after some tribal difficulties were overcome, independence was granted to the Gold Coast, which took the name Ghana; and, in the autumn of 1960, Nigeria became an independent nation as well. Both states became members of the U. N., where the Ghanaian leader, Kwame Nkrumah, became a prominent member of the neutralist bloc.

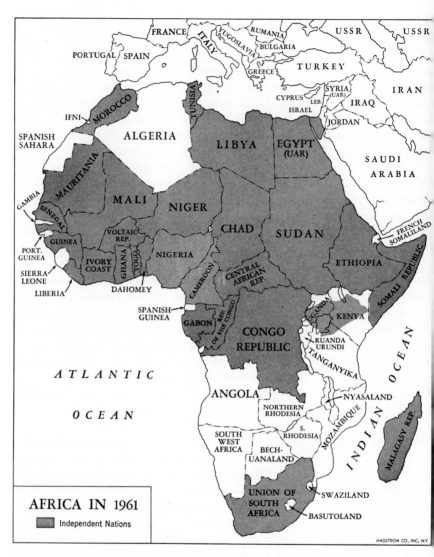

FRANCE
PORTUGAL / SPAIN
ITALY
YUGOSLAVIA
RUMANIA
BULGARIA
GREECE
USSR
USSR
TURKEY
CYPRUS
LEB.
ISRAEL
SYRIA
(UAR)
IRAQ
JORDAN
IRAN
IFNI
MOROCCO
TUNISIA
SPANISH
SAHARA
ALGERIA
LIBYA
EGYPT
(UAR)
SAUDI
ARABIA
GAMBIA
MAURITANIA
SENEGAL
GUINEA
MALI
NIGER
CHAD
SUDAN
FRENCH
SOMALILAND
PORT.
GUINEA
VOLTAIC
REP.
IVORY
COAST
GHANA
TOGO
NIGERIA
ETHIOPIA
SOMALI REPUBLIC
SIERRA
LEONE
LIBERIA
DAHOMEY
CAMEROON
CENTRAL
AFRICAN
REP.
SPANISH
GUINEA
GABON
REP. OF THE CONGO
UGANDA
KENYA
CONGO
REPUBLIC
RUANDA
URUNDI
TANGANYIKA
ATLANTIC
OCEAN
ANGOLA
NORTHERN
RHODESIA
NYASALAND
MOZAMBIQUE
INDIAN
OCEAN
SOUTH
WEST
AFRICA
S.
RHODESIA
BECH-
UANALAND
MALAGASY REP.
UNION OF
SOUTH
AFRICA
SWAZILAND
BASUTOLAND

AFRICA IN 1961
Independent Nations

HAGSTROM CO., INC., N.Y.

In African colonies where there were large white populations, the British were slower to make concessions, and this often alienated native intellectuals, drove them into extremist movements, or persuaded them to seek the aid of communism. In Kenya, this was true of the brilliant Jomo Kenyatta, a London-trained sociologist, who was alienated by the treatment he received in his own country from Europeans, turned to Moscow for aid and advice, and returned to Kenya in 1946 to become the leader of the Kenya Africa Association (KAU). This body worked for agricultural reform and was not ostensibly revolutionary; but Kenyatta was regarded by members of more militant native organizations as their natural leader. Other native intellectuals, including some of Kenyatta's associates, supplied leadership for the notorious Mau Mau movement, and it was due to their organizing abilities that the antiwhite rebellion started by it in 1952 resisted attempts at suppression by trained European troops for four years. This protracted struggle, which was marked by unparalleled savagery, made the European colonists more hostile to the independence movement, which has, nevertheless, under the leadership of Tom Mboya, continued its pressure for a majority democratic system of government.

In the Central African Federation (formed in 1953 from Northern Rhodesia, Southern Rhodesia, and Nyasaland), the policy followed by the government also showed hesitation about yielding to native demands. One writer described the predominant European view as an abstract willingness to give rights to civilized Africans, combined with a conviction that few would become civilized and that very few must be given the opportunity to do so. There were indications in the late 1950s that this attitude would be productive of trouble, especially in Nyasaland, where an overwhelmingly African population was held under control by drastic security laws.

The situation was even more critical in the Union of South Africa, where the resistance of the white population to concessions to the natives hardened and interracial tension mounted steadily in the postwar years. This was largely the result of the rise of a new Nationalist party that rejected the moderate conservatism of General Hertzog (see p. 667) and called for a definite breaking of the connection with Great Britain, the establishment of a republic, and a more radical approach to native problems. Under the leadership of Dr. Daniel Malan, this party won a majority in the elections of 1948, maintained and strengthened it during the next decade, and was strong enough by the autumn of 1960 to win parliamentary assent for the transformation of the country's status to that of a republic. On racial questions, the Nationalist party followed a policy of *apartheid*, which called for a rigid separation of the native and European cultures. Presented as a means of saving the Bantus from a false and corrupting Europeanization, *apartheid* was in sharp contrast to prevailing economic tendencies, for the growth of industrialism, upon which South Africa's future to a large extent depended, promoted the integration of Bantu and European. In practice, *apartheid* seemed to be little more than a doctrine of racial superiority that appealed to lower-class Afrikaners who were afraid that integration would force their already low standard of living even lower. Since it was an entirely negative system of policy, it could be made to work only by force; and by the 1960s clashes between the police and native demonstrators had become frequent and bloody.

In the colonies of West and Equatorial Africa, the French proved to be more foresighted than they had been in other parts of their empire. The new French constitution of 1958 recognized the political development of the colonies, which had been actively supported and encouraged by French administrators, and allowed the territories to choose between complete independence and membership in the French Community either individually or in federation. The greatest number voted for the second alternative (see p. 776), the significant exception being Guinea which, through its leader Sekou Touré, announced the intention of forming a union with Ghana as a nucleus of a future union of West Africa. Like Nkrumah, Touré became one of the new "positive neutrals" at the U. N. Assembly of 1960, tending in his sympathies toward the Soviet bloc.

The swift progress of the French colonies toward independence was probably the chief cause of the emergence in 1960 of the most explosive situation that had arisen in Africa since the Mau Mau troubles. This was the Congo problem. Until the end of the 1950s, this great Belgian possession was apparently quiet and prosperous, without a ripple of racial tension or a discernible sign of a nationalistic movement of any importance. In 1955, King Baudouin had spoken, during a trip to the Congo, of "leading the natives to lead themselves . . . though with the right of the colonizers to remain"; and in 1956 the Belgian Socialist party had formulated a long-term program for independence "in progressive stages." But even the warmest supporters of Congolese independence were thinking in terms of a thirty-year evolution.

The problem became immediate, however, as a result of two things: General de Gaulle's visit to Brazzaville, only three miles away from the Congolese capital, to offer a referendum on independence to the peoples of French Equatorial Africa; and the Brussels Exposition, in which some of the pavilions were manned by young Congolese who saw the outside world for the first time. By October 1958, under these influences, the Congo's first political parties had been born; and in January 1959 the first serious troubles erupted in the Congo, with four days of pillage, rape, and riot in Leopoldville.

This shocked the Belgian government, and the king announced on January 13, 1959, that the Congo would be given independence "without fatal delay . . . but without unconsidered haste." In view of the unrest in the country and the rapidly expanding ambitions and growing rivalry of native leaders, a clear statement of the government's intentions and its proposed procedure and timing would have been advisable; but the government could not agree on these vital matters. The result was that ambiguity led to increased Congolese importunity, and the latter to an ill-considered Belgian announcement that independence would be granted on June 30, 1960.

When that day came, it became immediately clear that the Congo had neither the trained leaders nor the unity of will to make independence effective. Almost immediately, the country was paralyzed by anti-Belgian demonstrations, rapine and pillage, tribal warfare, political dissension, and, inevitably, Communist subversion. By the end of 1960, the over-hasty withdrawal of the Belgians from their colonial empire had created one more major threat to world peace.

EUROPE IN THE NUCLEAR AGE

The Continuing Crisis / The forced retreat of the European powers from the far-flung regions that they had controlled when they were at their prime might have been tolerable if it had eliminated the necessity of their being concerned any longer over what happened in those areas. It has been said that the loss of the Congo meant nothing to the people of Belgium, because they had never wanted the area in the first place. This is possibly true; but it is also true that, even after they had lost it, the Belgians had to go on worrying about it, simply because what happened in the Congo might determine whether Belgians—and other Europeans—would be permitted to go on living or not. In an age in which distance had been abolished by the revolution in long-range communication, in which science had invented weapons of unimaginable destructiveness, which were also incapable of interception once launched, and in which, finally, every Indochinese or Algerian or Congolese crisis threatened to become a clash of ideological absolutes from which a universal holocaust might result, there was no real satisfaction to be gained from the relinquishment of the burdens of world responsibility.

In 1815, when this consideration of modern European history began, Europe was still the lever that moved the world, and the five great powers of Europe were still in effective control of world politics. In 1960, there were no European great powers any more, and Europeans often felt that their destinies were at the mercy of intractable problems and of superstates whose resources of military power sometimes seemed to exceed their political wisdom.

How to escape from this delicate balance of terror and how—despite their own diminished stature—to influence or control the political behavior of the world powers were matters that preoccupied all thoughtful Europeans. In general, their thinking proceeded along three different lines, although these were by no means mutually exclusive. There were, in the first place, those who continued to believe that the only security lay in impressive military power. This was equally the view of Charles de Gaulle, who strove to enhance France's authority and prestige by acquiring nuclear capabilities, and of the citizens of West Berlin who, in 1960, were visibly heartened by the news of the successful American testing of the Polaris missile, launched from the atomic-power-driven submarine. This represented the view also of the majority of the governments of Western Europe, which continued to support NATO.

The second group, which was very strong and vocal in the middle 1950s, were the supporters of disengagement. There were several variants of this philosophy, but the one most generally advocated called for the creation of a neutral area in central Europe consisting of Germany, or perhaps Germany, Poland, and Czechoslovakia, the withdrawal of foreign troops from the area defined, and the dissolution of the ties binding the states within the defined area to the NATO and Warsaw alliances. The difficulties involved in this scheme were obvious. It would necessitate the abandonment by Western Germany of its efforts in behalf of European integration and would call upon the Soviet Union to relinquish its control over Eastern Europe; it might create a military imbalance in favor of the Soviet Union, since a military disengagement in Western Europe would raise such difficulties that American forces might have to be withdrawn from Europe entirely; and it would require the discovery of an effective guarantee against the re-entry of Soviet forces into the areas evacuated by them once the American withdrawal had taken place. Disengagement had great emotional appeal, however, and it was probably supported by more people who did not, or who refused to, appreciate the difficulties of implementation than it was by people who sought to remove them.

Finally, there were those who placed their hopes not upon any single solution but upon patient and untiring exploitation of all the resources of diplomacy to find solutions to awkward problems, to bring the major antagonists face to face in as many contexts as possible, to encourage continuous negotiation on problems ranging from truce provisions in the Congo to arms control and inspection, and to use the agencies of the U. N. for purposes of warning, restraint, delay, mediation, and even, if need be, dispatch of troops when major crises arose. Their views were represented, for instance, by those small powers at the U. N. General Assembly meeting of 1960 who, despite the disappointing record of summit meetings (like the Geneva meeting of 1955 and the Paris fiasco of the spring of 1960, which was effectively torpedoed by the U-2 flight and was productive of no result), urged that a new meeting between the Soviet prime minister and the President of the United States be held in the near future. Their faith in U. N. mediation was justified by U. N.'s role in such crises as those in Israel, Indochina, and the Congo. Their faith in negotiation was given substance by the patent fact that, in the nuclear age, the classical alternative to diplomacy as a means of advancing state interest had become unusable except at the risk of eliminating the states whose interests it was intended to promote.

The Future / And what could one say of Europe's spirit as it faced the future? There could be little doubt that it was troubled. The changed fortunes of Europe, the shock and suffering caused by the last world war and still present to the sight and the memory, and, above all, the awareness of the possibilities of universal annihilation that had been opened up by the ingenuity of the western mind—these things involved Europe's intellectuals, especially those of the rising generation, in a major spiritual crisis. Many of them—how many it would be impossible to estimate—found their solution in a kind of intellectual disengagement, which was expressed, on its lowest level, by the cries of *"Ohne mich!"* ("Without me!") with which German youth responded to the NATO decision to permit the rearmament of Germany. The same attempt to withdraw from commitment, either political or intellectual, was seen in the philosophy and the art of many who now proudly described themselves as existentialists. Although Jean-Paul Sartre, one of France's leading existentialists, denied that this philosophy was one of quietism, since "it defines man in terms of action," most of its followers seemed to regard individual subjectivity as both the point of departure and the end objective of intellectual effort.

On the other hand, many of those who talked most passionately about man's forlornness, to employ a term much used by the German existentialist Heidegger, were capable of equal enthusiasm for projects of European integration, just as most of those who shouted *"Ohne mich!"* served willingly and cheerfully in the West German contingent to NATO when their names were called. The perils of the new age did not, in fact, make commitment impossible, otherwise one would have found it impossible to explain the spirit and variety of intellectual activity in the European universities, in the press, in the theater and the cinema, in the visual arts and literature and music. Even in an age of anxiety, the products of this ferment retained the power to astonish and delight non-Europeans, while making it impossible for them to believe that Europe would not rise to the challenge of the nuclear age as it had risen so often to challenges in the past. On the whole, Europeans still looked to the future with confidence, in something of the mood of the Nobel prize-winning poet Saint-John Perse, who ended his great poem *Chronique* with the lines:

> Summit of time, here are we!
> Measure the heart of man!

BIBLIOGRAPHY

BIBLIOGRAPHY

The lists that follow are intended to be suggestive rather than exhaustive and for that reason have been kept short. They can be supplemented from other sources, notably from the 1961 revision of the *Guide to Historical Literature*, prepared by specialists on various fields under the sponsorship of the American Historical Association, from such useful compilations as Lowell J. Ragatz, *A Bibliography for the Study of European History, 1815–1939* (1942; supplements 1943, 1945) and Alan Bullock and A. J. P. Taylor, *A Select List of Books on European History, 1815–1914* (1957), and from the excellent bibliographical essays in the volumes of the series *The Rise of Modern Europe*, edited by William L. Langer.

The selection of titles has been made with an eye to the needs and interests of undergraduate, rather than advanced, students. Emphasis has been placed upon recent historical literature, although not to the exclusion of older works that have stood the test of time. No attempt has been made to list individual works of art and music.

GENERAL WORKS

Among the many single-volume histories of the nineteenth century, Eduard Fueter's *World History, 1815–1920* (1920) and Benedetto Croce's *History of Europe in the Nineteenth Century* (1933) are provocative and well written, while C. E. Black and E. C. Helmreich's *Twentieth Century Europe: A History* (2d ed., 1959) is the most satisfactory comprehensive account of the recent period. Of the general works dealing with shorter periods, the three volumes of the *Cambridge Modern History* (1902–1912) that treat the years since Napoleon are out of date but include chapters on domestic history that have not been superseded. When the *New Cambridge Modern History* is complete, four of its volumes will be devoted to the nineteenth and twentieth centuries. Of these, *The Zenith of European Power, 1830–1870*, edited by J. P. T. Bury (1960), and *The Era of Violence, 1898–1945*, edited by David Thomson (1959), have appeared. Both include good chapters on intellectual history, science, and military affairs, in addition to their chapters on politics and economics. In the *Rise of Modern Europe* series, only three of the projected volumes on the modern period have been completed: F. B. Artz, *Reaction and Revolution, 1814–1832* (1934); R. C. Binkley, *Realism and Nationalism, 1852–1871* (1935), a brilliantly executed volume; and C. J. H. Hayes, *A Generation of Materialism, 1871–1900* (1941).

Among the general histories of economic development, S. H. Clough and C. W. Cole's *An Economic History of Europe* (1941) and Bowden, Karpovich, and Usher's *An Economic History of Europe since 1750* (1937) are outstanding. W. Ashworth, *A Short History of the International Economy, 1850–1950* (1952), is useful; A. Birnie, *An Economic History of Europe, 1760–1939* (rev. ed., 1951), includes good sections on unionism and social legislation; W. A. Lewis, *Economic Survey, 1919–1939* (1949), is an authoritative treatment by a brilliant scholar.

General accounts of foreign affairs include Sir Charles Petrie, *Diplomatic History, 1713–1933* (1947); R. W. Seton-Watson, *Britain in Europe, 1789–1914* (1937), which is more comprehensive than its title suggests; A. J. P. Taylor,

The Struggle for Mastery in Europe, 1848–1918 (1954), sometimes a bit sweeping in its judgments; R. J. Sontag, *European Diplomatic History, 1870–1932* (1933), a fine account whose later chapters are in need of revision; Hajo Holborn, *The Political Collapse of Europe* (1951), brief but illuminating; and L. C. B. Seaman, *From Vienna to Versailles* (1956), slapdash but occasionally rewarding.

The important part played by war in the history of the period is dealt with in E. L. Woodward, *War and Peace in Europe, 1815–1870* (1931). More detailed and comprehensive are Theodore Ropp, *War in the Modern World* (1959), which has excellent bibliographical notes; Gordon B. Turner, *A History of Military Affairs in Western Society since the Eighteenth Century* (1953), a collection of carefully selected readings; F. J. C. Fuller, *A Military History of the Western World*, vol. III (1956), by one of Britain's leading military experts; *Makers of Modern Strategy: Military Thought from Machiavelli to Hitler*, edited by Edward Mead Earle, Gordon A. Craig and Felix Gilbert (1943). Problems of civil-military relations are treated in Alfred Vagts, *A History of Militarism* (1937); Michael Howard, ed., *Soldiers and Governments* (1957); and Gordon A. Craig, *The Politics of the Prussian Army, 1640–1945* (1955).

National political histories are listed in the appropriate sections below. Of the general works dealing with political ideas and movements, C. J. H. Hayes, *The Historical Evolution of Modern Nationalism* (1931), treats one of the explosive forces of the age with brevity and authority. J. H. Hallowell's *Main Currents of Modern Political Thought* (1950) is a solid introduction, and M. Oakeshott's *Social and Political Doctrines of Contemporary Europe* (1939) a useful compilation of doctrinal statements. R. Kirk, *The Conservative Mind from Burke to Santayana* (1953), is well-written and illuminating. Peter Viereck, *Conservatism Re-Visited: The Revolt against Revolt* (1949), is essentially an attack on the philosophy of liberalism, which finds its classical exposition in Guido Ruggiero, *European Liberalism* (1927), a comparative study. H. Marcuse, *Reason and Revolution: Hegel and the Rise of Social Theory* (1941), is an indispensable volume, and H. W. Laidler, *Social-Economic Movements: An Historical and Comparative Survey of Socialism, Communism, Cooperation, Utopianism and Other Forces of Reform and Reconstruction* (1944), is a valuable reference work which includes succinct summaries of doctrine and of the contents of basic socialist texts. A challenging intellectual history of the recent past is H. Stuart Hughes, *Consciousness and Society: The Re-Orientation of European Social Thought, 1890–1930* (1958).

The whole range of intellectual activity is treated in J. T. Merz, *A History of European Thought in the Nineteenth Century* (4 vols., 1896–1914), which is particularly important for students interested in the development of science, as are Charles C. Gillispie's *Genesis and Geology* (1951) and *The Edge of Objectivity* (1960). For the spread of Darwin's influence, the most useful work is Loren C. Eiseley, *Darwin's Century* (1958), but see also Paul Sears, *Charles Darwin: The Naturalist as a Cultural Force* (1950), and Jacques Barzun, *Darwin, Marx and Wagner* (1941). The work of a great scientific mind is described in Fritz Wittels, *Freud and His Time* (1948), and in the now standard and justly admired work of Ernest Jones, *Sigmund Freud* (3 vols., 1953–1957). The best general works on medicine are Charles Singer, *A Short History of Medicine* (1941), and Richard Shryock, *The Development of Modern Medicine* (1947). James Conant's *On Understanding Science: An Historical Approach* (1947) is illuminating.

Élie Faure, *A History of Art*, vols. IV and V (1937), and Fernand Hazan, ed., *Dictionary of Modern Painting* (1956), are reliable guides. The second volume of Arnold Hauser's stimulating *Social History of Art* (1952) discusses, among other things, the role of the artist in society. Georg Brandes, *Main Currents in Nineteenth Century Literature* (6 vols., 1901–1906), is still an indispensable general guide. Irving Howe, *Politics and the Novel* (1957), examines the relationship between politics and literature with particular reference to Stendhal, Dostoevsky, Malraux, Orwell, and others. Edmund Wilson, *Axel's Castle: A Study in the Imaginative Literature, 1870–1930* (1931) deals with symbolism and its conflict and fusion with naturalism. Studies of national literatures include Martin Turnell, *The Novel in France* (1950) and *The Art of French Fiction* (1959); Victor Lange, *Modern German Literature, 1870–1940* (1945); Michael Hamburger, *Reason and Energy: Studies in German Literature* (1957), which includes a good treatment of the expressionists; and Ernest Simmons, *An Outline of Modern Russian Literature, 1880–1940* (1943). Ernst Kohn-Bramstedt's *Aristocracy and the Middle Classes in Germany* (1937) uses literary sources to illustrate problems of social stratification and change. Hugo Leichtentritt, *Music, History and Ideas* (1938), and Jacques Barzun, *Berlioz and His Century: An Introduction to the Age of Romanticism* (1956), place musical activities in their social context.

The best historical atlases are those of W. R. Shephard (8th ed., 1956), R. R. Palmer (1957), and E. W. Fox (1957).

Chapter 1 / The Great Powers and the Balance of Power, 1815–1848

C. K. Webster's *The Congress of Vienna* (1937) and Harold Nicolson's *The Congress of Vienna* (1945) are both sound accounts of the preliminaries and the actual negotiations. The personality and policies of the chief participants in the Congress are analyzed in C. K. Webster, *The Foreign Policy of Castlereagh, 1815–1822* (2d ed., 1937); A. Duff Cooper, *Talleyrand* (1932); G. Ferrero, *The Reconstruction of Europe: Talleyrand and the Congress of Vienna* (1941); A. A. Lobanov-Rostovsky, *Russia and Europe, 1789–1825* (1947), which deals with Alexander I and his advisers; and the biographies of Metternich by Algernon Cecil (1933) and H. du Coudray (1935). Metternich's approach to foreign affairs is also treated in E. L. Woodward, *Three Studies in European Conservatism* (1930), which includes studies of Guizot and the Roman Catholic Church as well; and, more recently, in Henry Kissinger, *A World Restored: Metternich, Castlereagh and the Problems of Peace, 1812–1822* (1957).

The problems of the Concert are discussed in W. A. Phillips, *The Confederation of Europe* (1914); H. G. Schenk, *The Aftermath of the Napoleonic Wars: The Concert of Europe—An Experiment* (1947); George Romani, *The Neapolitan Revolution, 1820–1821* (1950); and H. W. V. Temperley, *The Foreign Policy of Canning, 1822–1827* (1925). H. C. F. Bell's *Lord Palmerston* (2 vols., 1936) and C. K. Webster's *The Foreign Policy of Palmerston* (2 vols., 1951) have good accounts of Belgian affairs, and the latter contains a good analysis of the Egyptian crises. Near Eastern problems are treated generally in J. A. R. Marriott, *The Eastern Question* (4th ed., 1940), and W. Miller, *The Ottoman Empire* (4th ed., 1936), and more specifically in C. W. Crawley, *The Question of Greek Independence* (1931), M. L. Harvey, *The Development of Russian Commerce in the Black Sea* (1938), Philip E. Mosely, *Russian Diplomacy and the Opening of the Eastern Question in 1838 and 1839* (1934),

V. J. Puryear, *France and the Levant* (1941), and F. S. Rodkey, *The Turco-Egyptian Question in the Relations of England, France and Russia, 1832–1841* (1924).

Chapter 2 / The Eastern Powers: Absolutism and Its Critics

Among the many histories of Russia, S. Pares, *A History of Russia* (rev. ed., 1953), and R. D. Charques, *A Short History of Russia* (1956), are handy brief surveys, and M. T. Florinsky, *Russia: A History and Interpretation* (2 vols., 1953), a gracefully written longer account that includes comprehensive treatment of nonpolitical aspects. The Decembrist revolt has been described with psychological overtones in Mikhail Zetlin, *The Decembrists* (1958), and with greater circumstantial detail in A. G. Mazour, *The First Russian Revolution, 1825: The Decembrist Movement* (1937). N. V. Riasonovsky, *Nicholas I and Official Nationality in Russia, 1825–1881* (1959), and Constantin de Grunwald, *Tsar Nicholas I* (1955), are useful in offsetting the passionate denunciations of Nicholas in Alexander Herzen's *My Past and Thoughts* (6 vols., 1924–1928), the remarkable work of the dean of Russian exiles. For social and economic development, see the monumental study of Jerome Blum, *Lord and Peasant in Russia* (1961).

Readable texts on German history are Koppel S. Pinson, *Modern Germany: Its History and Civilization* (1954), R. Flenley, *Modern German History* (1953), and Veit Valentin, *The German People: Their History and Civilization* (1946). The economic aspects of the period are treated in the important work of J. H. Clapham, *The Economic Development of France and Germany, 1815–1914* (4th ed., 1936), and in T. S. Hamerow, *Restoration, Revolution, Reaction: Economics and Politics in Germany, 1815–1871* (1958). Hans Kohn's *The Mind of Germany* (1960) treats movements of thought, and Leonard Krieger's *The German Idea of Freedom* (1957) the role and dilemma of the intellectuals.

On Prussian history, see, in addition to books listed above, Walter Simon, *The Failure of the Prussian Reform Movement, 1807–1819* (1955), and Friedrich Meinecke, "Liberalism and Nationality in Germany," *Cambridge Modern History*, vol. XI. On Austria, see A. J. P. Taylor, *The Habsburg Monarchy, 1809–1918* (new ed., 1948); R. W. Seton-Watson, "Metternich and Internal Austrian Policy," in *The Making of Modern Europe*, edited by H. Ausubel, vol. II (1951); and Jerome Blum, *Noble Landowners and Agriculture in Austria* (1948).

Chapter 3 / France: The Restoration and the July Monarchy

The liveliest of the good one-volume histories is D. W. Brogan, *The French Nation, 1814–1940* (1957). Less impressionistic are J. P. T. Bury, *France, 1814–1940* (1949), and J. B. Wolf, *A History of France since 1814* (1940), the latter excellent on social organization. Basic to any understanding of socio-economic movements are Clapham's *Development of France and Germany* and S. H. Clough's *France: A History of National Economics, 1789–1939* (1939).

The domestic history of the period is treated in F. B. Artz, *France under the Bourbon Restoration, 1814–1830* (1931); J. Lucas Dubreton, *The Restoration and the July Monarchy* (1929); Gilbert Stenger, *The Return of Louis XVIII* (1909); J. M. S. Allison, *Thiers and the French Monarchy* (1926); Woodward, *Conservatism* (on Guizot); and R. Soltau, *French Political Thought in the*

Nineteenth Century (1931). C. S. Philips, *The Church in France, 1789–1907* (2 vols., 1929, 1936), and P. H. Spencer, *The Politics of Belief in Nineteenth Century France* (1954), throw light on religious developments and controversies. The literature on the political opposition and on reform movements is less rich in English than in French but includes J. Plamenetz, *The Revolutionary Movement in France, 1815–1871* (1952), Alan Spitzer, *The Revolutionary Theories of Louis Auguste Blanqui* (1957), F. E. Manuel, *The New World of Saint-Simon* (1956), and George G. Iggers, *The Cult of Authority: The Political Cult of the Saint-Simonians* (1958), which sees the seeds of modern totalitarianism in the movement.

On romanticism, see N. H. Clement, *Romanticism in France* (1939), A. J. George, *The Development of French Romanticism* (1955), and, for its social consequences, D. O. Evans, *Social Romanticism in France, 1830–1848* (1951). André Maurois's *Lélia: The Life of George Sand* (1953) and *Olympio: The Life of Victor Hugo* (1956) and Matthew Josephson's *Victor Hugo* (1946) describe the intellectual vigor of the period. Finally, Alexis de Tocqueville, *Recollections*, edited by J. P. Mayer (1949), should be read by every student of the period.

Chapter 4 / Great Britain: Social Unrest and Social Compromise, 1815–1848

For a general survey of the period, the most reliable guide is E. L. Woodward, *The Age of Reform* (1938), which includes an account of imperial developments; while the most comprehensive is the magnificent work of Élie Halevy, *A History of the English People in the Nineteenth Century* (vols. I–IV, 1927–1947). Economic developments are discussed in J. H. Clapham, *An Economic History of Modern Britain* (1938), and W. H. B. Court, *A Concise Economic History of Britain from 1750 to Recent Times* (1954); and their social consequences receive attention in G. D. H. Cole and R. Postgate, *The British Common People, 1748–1938* (1939), J. L. and B. Hammond, *The Village Labourer, 1760–1832* (new ed., 1948) and *The Town Labourer, 1760–1832* (1919), R. J. White, *Waterloo to Peterloo* (1957), and Donald Read, *Peterloo: The Massacre and Its Background* (1958).

Crane Brinton, *English Political Thought in the Nineteenth Century* (rev. ed., 1950), and S. Maccoby, *English Radicalism, 1786–1832* (1955), are good introductions to the political thinking of the age, while Élie Halevy, *The Growth of Philosophical Radicalism* (one-vol. ed., 1949), is deservedly considered to be the classic analysis of the doctrines of radicalism stimulated by Jeremy Bentham. On these, see also John Bowle, *Politics and Opinion in the Nineteenth Century* (1954), and M. S. J. Packe, *Life of John Stuart Mill* (1954). The movement for political and social reform is described in H. W. C. Davis, *The Age of Grey and Peel* (1929), J. R. M. Butler, *The Passing of the Great Reform Bill* (1914), J. L. and B. Hammond, *Lord Shaftesbury* (new ed., 1930), and Graham Wallas, *The Life of Francis Place* (new ed., 1925). Early socialism and unionism are treated in G. D. H. Cole, *Life of Robert Owen* (1930), and Max Beer, *A History of British Socialism* (2 vols., 1920); and Chartism in M. Hovell, *The Chartist Movement* (2d ed., 1925), still the best account, as well as in Julius West, *The History of the Chartist Movement* (1920), and A. R. Schoyen, *The Chartist Challenge: A Portrait of G. J. Harney* (1958). An illuminating account of the consequences of the Reform Bill and the growth of modern political organization is N. Gash, *Politics in the Age of Peel: A Study in the Technique of Parliamentary Representation* (1953).

Chapter 5 / The Revolutions of 1848

Priscilla Robertson, *The Revolutions of 1848* (1952), is well-written and detailed and covers the whole range of revolutionary disturbances. More entertaining but less thorough is R. Postgate, *The Story of a Year: 1848* (1955). Arnold Whitridge's *Men in Crisis: The Revolution of 1848* (1949) concentrates on the activities of Louis Philippe, Lamartine, Louis Napoleon, Mazzini, Garibaldi, Marx, Széchenyi, Kossuth, and Metternich. F. Fejtö, ed., *The Opening of an Era: 1848—An Historical Symposium* (1948), is interesting but uneven. Events in Germany are described in Veit Valentin, *1848: Chapters in German History* (1940), J. G. Legge, *Rhyme and Revolution in Germany* (1918), a highly original collection of historical material, and the brilliant essay by Sir Lewis Namier, *1848: The Revolution of the Intellectuals* (1945). Events in France are treated in R. Arnaud, *The Second Republic and Napoleon III* (1930), and Donald McKay, *The National Workshops: A Study in the French Revolution of 1848* (1933); Italian developments in A. J. P. Taylor, *The Italian Problem in European Diplomacy, 1847–49* (1934), and G. M. Trevelyan, *Garibaldi and the Defence of the Roman Republic* (1907) and *Manin and the Venetian Revolution of 1848* (1923); and aspects of the revolution in Hungary in C. Sproxton, *Palmerston and the Hungarian Revolution* (1919). Josef Redlich, *Emperor Francis Joseph* (1929), and R. John Rath, *The Viennese Revolution of 1848* (1957), should be consulted for events in Vienna and for the success of reaction.

Chapter 6 / The Breakdown of the Concert and the Crimean War

The effects of the revolutions of 1848 on the diplomatic temper of the age are discussed in Binkley's *Realism and Nationalism* and in Gordon A. Craig, "The System of Alliances and the Balance of Power," *New Cambridge Modern History*, vol. X. The background of the Crimean war is dealt with in V. J. Puryear, *International Economics and Diplomacy in the Near East: A Study of British Commercial Policy* (1935) and *England, Russia and the Straits Question, 1844–1856* (1931), and in H. W. V. Temperley's splendid *England and the Near East: The Crimea* (1936). Illuminating essays on the relations between the powers are to be found in G. B. Henderson, *Crimean War Diplomacy* (1947), while the role of public opinion in precipitating the conflict is discussed engagingly in B. Kingsley Martin, *The Triumph of Lord Palmerston* (1924). Among recent works that deal with the course of the war, see especially C. Woodham-Smith, *Florence Nightingale* (1951) and *The Reason Why* (1953), the latter a critical examination of the British performance. One of the positive results of the war is treated fully in T. W. Riker, *The Making of Rumania* (1931).

Chapter 7 / France: The Second Empire

F. A. Simpson, *The Rise of Louis Napoleon* (1909) and *Louis Napoleon and the Recovery of France, 1848–1856* (3d ed., 1951) are rich in detail and balanced in judgment; J. M. Thompson, *Louis Napoleon and the Second Empire* (1954), is less satisfactory on the nonpolitical aspects of the reign;

Philip Guedalla, *The Second Empire* (1922), is brilliantly written, entertaining, but often flippant in tone. A. Guérard's *Napoleon III: An Interpretation* (1943) sees Napoleon's "Caesarian democracy" as a forerunner of modern totalitarianism. T. Zeldin's *The Political System of Napoleon III* (1958) is a methodical and original study. F. C. Palm, *England and Napoleon III* (1949), explains the reasons for the lack of confidence between the Crimean allies. David S. Pinckney's *Napoleon III and the Reconstruction of Paris* (1958) is a fascinating study of how Paris was rebuilt and how it was paid for. The same subject is treated in J. M. and Brian Chapman, *The Life and Times of Baron Haussmann* (1958).

Chapter 8 / The Unification of Italy

The most satisfactory general histories are R. Albrecht-Carrié, *Italy from Napoleon to Mussolini* (1950), L. Salvatorelli, *A Concise History of Italy* (1940), and A. J. Whyte, *The Evolution of Modern Italy* (1950). A brilliant study of the relationship between economics and politics is K. Roberts Greenfield, *Economics and Liberalism in the Risorgimento: A Study of Nationalism in Lombardy, 1814–1848* (1934). Bolton King's *A History of Italian Unity* (2 vols., 1899) is still readable and sound, as is William Thayer's *The Life and Times of Cavour* (2 vols., 1914). Cavour's role is treated critically in Denis Mack Smith, *Cavour and Garibaldi in 1860* (1954), and admiringly in M. Paléologue, *Cavour* (1927), and A. J. Whyte, *The Political Life and Letters of Cavour* (1930).

There is no satisfactory life of Mazzini in English, but see Stringfellow Barr's *Mazzini: Portrait of an Exile* (1935). Garibaldi's contribution to unification is treated in brief in Denis Mack Smith, *Garibaldi* (1956), and with verve and rich detail in G. M. Trevelyan, *Garibaldi's Defence of the Roman Republic* (1907), *Garibaldi and the Thousand* (1911), and *Garibaldi and the Making of Italy* (1911). Special studies of importance are W. K. Hancock, *Ricasoli and the Risorgimento in Tuscany* (1926), C. S. Forester, *Victor Emmanuel II and the Union of Italy* (1922), and M. S. J. Packe, *Orsini: The Story of a Conspirator* (1957). On the Church, see S. W. Halperin, *The Separation of Church and State in Italian Thought from Cavour to Mussolini* (1937), and C. C. Eckhardt, *The Papacy in World Affairs* (1937).

Chapter 9 / The German Question

The general works cited for Chapter 2 and Craig, *Politics of the Prussian Army* have sections on Germany's progress toward unification. In addition, the reader should consult the classical account written in the 1890s by the Austrian historian Heinrich Friedjung, *The Struggle for Supremacy in Germany, 1859–1866* (abridged ed., 1935), and the special studies by C. W. Clark, *Franz Joseph and Bismarck: The Diplomacy of Austria before the War of 1866* (1934), L. Steefel, *The Schleswig-Holstein Question* (1932), and W. E. Mosse, *The European Powers and the German Question* (1958). The best separate account of the Prussian constitutional conflict in English is E. N. Anderson, *The Social and Political Conflict in Prussia, 1858–1864* (1954), which has much new material. The best biographies of Bismarck are those of C. Grant Robertson (1919) and A. J. P. Taylor (1955). Erich Eyck's *Bismarck and the German Empire* (1950) is an abbreviated version of the author's three-volume life. See also F. Darmstaedter, *Bismarck and the Creation of the*

Second Reich (1948). Bismarck's own memoirs are printed in English as *Bismarck, the Man and the Statesman* (2 vols., 1899) and *The Kaiser vs. Bismarck: New Chapters of Bismarck's Autobiography* (1921).

Chapter 10 / The Reorganization of Europe, 1866–1871

British imperial developments are described in Woodward's *Age of Reform* and, at greater length, in *The Cambridge History of the British Empire* (8 vols., 1929 ff.). The centenary of the Indian Mutiny brought a rash of books, including J. Leasor's *The Red Fort* (1957) and two Indian accounts, S. N. Sen, *Eighteen Fifty Seven* (1957), and H. Chattopadyaya, *The Sepoy Mutiny* (1957). See also such older accounts as T. R. Holmes, *A History of the Indian Mutiny* (1913), and George Dangerfield, *The Bengal Mutiny* (1933). For the war in China, see W. C. Costin's *Great Britain and China, 1833–1860* (1937).

G. M. Young's *Victorian England: Portrait of an Age* (2d ed., 1953) is a book of charm and wisdom. Asa Briggs, *Victorian People: A Reassessment of Persons and Themes, 1851–1867* (1954), includes fine essays on Samuel Smiles, Thomas Hughes, and John Bright, and a discussion of Disraeli's role in passing the Second Reform Bill. The basic work on that statesman is still W. F. Monypenny and G. Buckle, *Life of Disraeli, Earl of Beaconsfield* (6 vols., 1913 ff.), but André Maurois, *Disraeli: A Picture of the Victorian Age* (1936), is perceptive. Lord Morley, *Life of Gladstone* (3 vols., 1904), is still essential, despite the excellent qualities of Philip Magnus, *Gladstone: A Biography* (1954). W. D. Jones, *Lord Derby and Victorian Conservatism* (1956), is devoted to the "Rupert of debate" and his part in the reform of 1867. On the court, see Lytton Strachey's *Queen Victoria* (1921) and Frank Eyck's *The Prince Consort: A Political Biography* (1959). Among special political studies, H. J. Hanham, *Elections and Party Management: Politics in the Time of Disraeli and Gladstone* (1959), deserves special notice as an admirable supplement to Gash's study of the earlier period.

The reforms in Russia receive attention in Stephen Graham, *Tsar of Freedom: The Life and Reign of Alexander II* (1935), and W. E. Mosse, *Alexander II and the Modernization of Russia* (1958). On economic questions, P. I. Liashchenko, *History of the National Economy in Russia* (Eng. trans., 1949), is the work of a distinguished Russian economic historian. On the agrarian problem, see particularly G. T. Robinson, *Rural Russia under the Old Regime* (1932), and G. Pasvolsky, *Agricultural Russia on the Eve of the Revolution* (new ed., 1949).

The Franco-Prussian *dénouement* is treated in several of the works cited under Chapter 9. See also Hermann Oncken, *Napoleon III and the Rhine* (1928), which has a strong anti-French bias, Georges Bonnin, ed., *Bismarck and the Hohenzollern Candidature for the Spanish Throne* (1958), and R. H. Lord, *The Origins of the War of 1870* (1924), still the most satisfactory treatment. The many works on the war itself need not be cited here, but Melvin Kranzberg, *The Siege of Paris, 1870–1871* (1950), is a useful if not an original account.

Chapter 11 / The Great Powers and the Balance of Power, 1871–1890

The best of the general diplomatic histories of these two decades is W. L. Langer, *European Alliances and Alignments* (revised ed., 1950), which includes very thorough bibliographical sections at the end of the chapters. The Near Eastern crisis is treated in several of the works cited in Chapter 6; the Russo-Turkish war in an interesting short book by Rupert Furneaux, *The Breakfast War* (1958); and the Congress of Berlin in W. N. Medlicott, *The Congress of Berlin and After* (1938), and M. D. Stojanović, *The Great Powers and the Balkans, 1875–1878* (1939). German policy is surveyed in Malcolm Carroll, *Germany and the Great Powers* (1938). J. V. Fuller's *Bismarck's Diplomacy at Its Zenith* (1922) is a detailed account of the Chancellor's handling of the Bulgarian crisis, while Gordon A. Craig's *From Bismarck to Adenauer* (1958) has chapters on the principles guiding Bismarck's statecraft and his methods of foreign policy administration. R. J. Sontag, *Germany and England: The Background of Conflict, 1848–1894* (1938), and R. J. S. Hoffmann, *The Anglo-German Trade Rivalry, 1875–1914* (1933), deal with the growing friction between these powers. R. W. Seton-Watson's *Disraeli, Gladstone and the Eastern Question* (1935) and A. L. Kennedy's *Salisbury, 1830–1903* (1953) throw light on Britain's policy in the Balkans and at the Straits. In addition to B. H. Sumner, *Russia and the Balkans* (1937), itself an impressive work, three recent volumes are helpful on Russian policy: M. B. Petrovich, *The Emergence of Russian Pan Slavism, 1856–1870* (1956); Hans Kohn, *Pan Slavism* (1953); and Charles Jelavich, *Tsarist Russia and Balkan Nationalism: Russian Influence in the Internal Affairs of Bulgaria and Serbia* (1958). On economic influences, see, *inter alia*, L. C. Robbins, *The Economic Causes of War* (1939), and A. H. Imlah, *Economic Elements in the Pax Britannica* (1958). On military influence, see Alfred Vagts, *Defense and Diplomacy* (1956) and the books cited under *General Works*.

Chapter 12 / The Evolution of Capitalism and the Spread of Socialism, 1871–1914

On some characteristic features of late nineteenth-century capitalism, see Joseph A. Schumpeter, *Capitalism, Socialism and Democracy* (3d ed., 1950); Robert Liefmann, *International Cartels, Combines and Trusts* (1927); Jacob Riesser, *The German Great Banks* (1911); and G. W. Edwards, *The Evolution of Finance Capitalism* (1938). W. W. Rostow's *Stages of Economic Growth* (1960) is a challenging analysis of mature capitalism with the subtitle "A Non-Communist Manifesto."

In addition to works already cited, G. D. H. Cole's *A History of Socialist Thought* (3 vols., 1953 ff.) should be mentioned. Excerpts from basic works of Marxist literature will be found in Emile Burns, *Handbook of Marxism* (1935) and *Karl Marx and Friedrich Engels: Selected Works* (2 vols., 1951). The best biographies of Marx are those of Isaiah Berlin (1939), E. H. Carr (1934), and Franz Mehring (Eng. trans., 1936), and the most satisfactory analysis is M. Bober, *Karl Marx's Interpretation of History* (rev. ed., 1948). See also Edmund Wilson's *To the Finland Station* (new ed., 1953). On Engels, see G. Mayer, *Friedrich Engels* (abridged ed., 1936); on Bakunin, E. H. Carr, *Michael Bakunin* (1937), and E. Lampert, *Studies in Rebellion: Belinsky, Bakunin, Herzen* (1957); on revisionism, Peter Gay, *The Dilemma of Democratic Socialism: Eduard Bernstein's Challenge to Marx* (1952), a thoughtful volume; on syndicalism, R. Humphrey, *Georges Sorel: Prophet without Honor* (1951). On the international organization of socialism, G. M. Stekloff, *History of the First International* (1928), and James Joll, *The Second International, 1889–1914* (1955), are useful.

Chapter 13 / From Liberalism to Democracy: Political Progress in Western Europe, 1871-1914

R. C. K. Ensor's *England, 1870–1914* (1936) is a reliable and comprehensive survey. Helen Lynd's *England in the Eighteen Eighties: Toward a Social Basis for Freedom* (1945) is admirably executed. E. F. Benson, *As We Were: A Victorian Peep Show* (1930), is amusing and provocative. Conservative politics receive attention in R. B. McDowell, *British Conservatism* (1959), W. S. Churchill, *Lord Randolph Churchill* (1906), and J. L. Garvin, *Life of Joseph Chamberlain* (3 vols., 1932–1934). Gladstone's liveliest successor is treated at length in John Edwards, *David Lloyd George: The Man and the Statesman* (2 vols., 1929), and more informally in Frank Owen, *Tempestuous Journey: Lloyd George, His Life and Times* (1954). On Ireland, see J. L. Hammond, *Gladstone and the Irish Nation* (1938), John E. Pomfret, *The Struggle for Land in Ireland* (1930), and the studies of Parnell by R. Barry O'Brien (1899) and J. Haslip (1937). Fabianism is examined in E. R. Pease's history of the society (1916) and, in a lighter vein, in Anne Fremantle, *This Little Band of Prophets* (1960). A stimulating account of social unrest on the eve of war is George Dangerfield, *The Strange Death of Liberal England* (1936).

On the lesser states of Western Europe, Adrian Barnouw, *The Dutch: A Portrait Study* (1940), G. Edmundson, *History of Holland* (1922), Emile Cammaerts, *The Keystone of Europe: History of the Belgian Dynasty, 1830–1939* (1939), and Johannes Gous, ed., *Belgium* (1945), are all useful guides. William Rappard, *The Government of Switzerland* (1936), is written by an outstanding Swiss scholar; and E. Bonjour and others, *A Short History of Switzerland* (1952), is reliable but regrettably brief. Robert Bain's *Scandinavia: A Political History* (1905) has basic facts, but is less searching in its analysis of motive forces than R. E. Lindgren's *Norway-Sweden: Union, Disunion, and Scandinavian Integration* (1959). See also R. Svanström and C. F. Palmstierna, *Short History of Sweden* (1934), John Danstrup, *The History of Denmark* (1948), and O. J. Falnes, *National Romanticism in Norway* (1933).

H. V. Livermore's *History of Portugal* (1947) is a general survey, and V. de Bragança Cunha's *Revolutionary Portugal, 1910–1936* (1938) a more detailed account of political movements. The troubled history of Spain is treated with balance and perspective by Salvador de Madariaga, *Spain* (2d ed., 1946), and, with specific attention to revolutionary movements, by J. McCabe, *Spain in Revolt, 1814–1931* (1932). J. B. Trend, *Origins of Modern Spain* (1934) covers the period before 1914 in some detail. The religious question is the subject of Edgar Peers, *The Church in Spain, 1739–1937* (1938), and is handled somewhat differently in Gerald Brenan, *The Spanish Labyrinth* (1943), a work which also sheds light on the agrarian problem and on varieties of socialism. On cultural history, J. B. Trend's *The Civilization of Spain* (1944) and Jose Castillejo's *The War of Ideas in Spain* (1937) are important.

Benedetto Croce, *A History of Italy, 1871–1915* (1929), is a concise survey by one of Italy's greatest modern thinkers. Denis Mack Smith's *Italy: A Modern History* (1959) embodies the result of modern scholarship and is well-written. Cecil Sprigge, *The Development of Modern Italy* (1944), is a good short account which is perhaps too intent on showing roots of fascism, and M. Hentze, *Pre-Fascist Italy* (1939), suffers from the same fault but is equally useful. A. W. Salomone, *Italian Democracy in the Making* (1945), concentrates on the Giolitti period. Good histories of socialism are Richard Hostetter, *The Italian Socialist Movement*, vol. I, *Origins* (1958); H. L. Gualtieri, *The Labor*

Movement in Italy, 1848–1904 (1946); and W. Hilton Young, *The Italian Left* (1949).

Chaper 14 / France: The Divided Republic, 1871–1914

Reliable basic surveys are D. W. Brogan, *France under the Republic: The Development of Modern France, 1870–1939* (1940), and David Thomson, *Democracy in France: The Third Republic* (rev. ed., 1952), the latter somewhat more analytical. Articles on various political and social problems by outstanding students of French affairs are found in *Modern France*, edited by Edward Mead Earle (1951). C. J. H. Hayes, *France: A Nation of Patriots* (1931), includes a fascinating analysis of the teaching of history in elementary schools; and C. S. Philips, *Church in France*, vol. II gives the main outlines of the thorny religious question. The most balanced work on the Commune is E. S. Mason, *The Paris Commune* (1930); and, on the equally controversial Dreyfus case, A. Charpentier, *The Dreyfus Affair* (1935), and Guy Chapman, *The Dreyfus Case* (1955), are sane reconstructions. Good studies of individuals include Geoffrey Bruun, *Clemenceau* (1943); T. F. Power, *Jules Ferry and the Renaissance of French Imperialism* (1944), J. P. T. Bury, *Gambetta and the National Defence* (1936), J. Hampden Jackson, *Jean Jaurès, His Life and Work* (1943), and H. R. Weinstein, *Jean Jaurès* (1936), which emphasizes the Socialist leader's patriotism. Two recent studies of French nationalism are Michael Curtis, *Three Against the Third Republic: Sorel, Barres, and Maurras* (1959), and Eugen Weber, *The Nationalist Revival in France, 1905–1914* (1959). On colonial affairs, H. I. Priestley, *France Overseas, A Study of Modern Imperialism* (1938) is useful.

Chapter 15 / The German Empire: Pseudo-Constitutional Absolutism, 1871–1914

To general political histories already cited may be added W. S. Dawson, *The German Empire and the Unity Movement* (2 vols., 1919), still good on constitutional aspects, and, briefer but more suggestive, Arthur Rosenberg. *The Birth of the German Republic* (1931). Economic developments are treated well in G. Stolper, *German Economy, 1870–1940* (1940), and Werner Bruck, *Social and Economic History of Germany from William II to Hitler, 1888–1938* (1938). A study of the political influence of economic groups is Alexander Gershenkron, *Bread and Democracy in Germany* (1943). J. Alden Nichols, *Germany after Bismarck* (1958), gives a good picture of the competition of irresponsible agencies in the Caprivi era. On the rise of socialism, see Evelyn Anderson, *Hammer and Anvil: The Story of the German Working Class Movement* (1945); William Dawson, *German Socialism and Ferdinand Lassalle* (1899), and David Footman, *Ferdinand Lassalle: Romantic Revolutionary* (1947), and, especially, the treatment of Lassalle in Wilson, *To the Finland Station*. Carl W. Schorske, *German Social Democracy, 1905–1917* (1955), analyzes the divisive forces in the movement and gives a convincing portrait of Bebel as party leader. Andreas Dorpalen's *Heinrich von Treitschke* (1957) is a full-scale treatment of one of the leading voices of strident nationalism.

Chapter 16 / Austria-Hungary, the Balkans, and Turkey, 1871–1914

O. Jaszi, *The Dissolution of the Habsburg Monarchy* (1929), is still useful, but see A. J. May, *The Habsburg Monarchy, 1867–1914* (1951), and especially Robert Kann, *The Multinational Empire: Nationalism and National Reform in the Habsburg Monarchy, 1848–1918* (2 vols., 1950). D. C. Kosáry, *History of Hungary* (1941), and R. W. Seton-Watson, *Racial Problems in Hungary* (1908), are sound accounts, and the latter work is supplemented by the same author's authoritative *The Southern Slav Question and the Habsburg Monarchy* (1911), *The Rise of Nationality in the Balkans* (1917), and *History of the Czechs and Slovaks* (1943). The problems of Bohemia within the Empire are also discussed in S. Harrison Thomson, *Czechoslovakia in European History* (2d ed., 1953). Austrian politics in this period have attracted relatively little attention from western scholars, but see W. A. Jenks, *The Austrian Electoral Reform of 1907* (1950).

Notable works on the Balkan countries are C. E. Black, *The Establishment of Constitutional Government in Bulgaria* (1943), R. W. Seton-Watson, *History of the Roumanians* (1934), David Mitrany, *The Land and the Peasant in Rumania* (1930), E. S. Forster, *A Short History of Modern Greece* (1941), H. W. V. Temperley, *History of Serbia* (1917) and, also on Serbia and Montenegro, the beautifully written *Black Lamb and Grey Falcon* by Rebecca West (2 vols., 1941). Joan Haslip, *The Sultan: The Life of Abdul Hamid* (1958) is also eminently readable. On the background of the Turkish revolution of 1908, see E. E. Ramsaur, Jr., *The Young Turks* (1957).

Chapter 17 / Imperial Russia, 1871–1914

Hugh Seton-Watson's *The Decline of Imperial Russia* (1952) is a survey that gives satisfactory treatment of economic growth, labor policy, and local government problems in addition to the larger issues of foreign and domestic policy, and includes sections on Poland and Finland. Richard Charques, *The Twilight of Imperial Russia* (1959), is also notable. Intellectual movements are examined in S. R. Tompkins, *The Russian Intelligentsia* (1957), which covers the period between the Crimean War and the revolution, and Walter Bruford, *Chekhov and His Russia* (1948), a sociological study. For the revolutionary movement, see Avrahm Yarmolinsky, *Road to Revolution: A Century of Russian Radicalism* (1959), which deals with early underground movements; J. H. Billington, *Mikhailovsky and Russian Populism* (1958); L. H. Haimson, *The Russian Marxists and the Origins of Bolshevism* (1955); and the brilliantly-conceived work of B. Wolfe, *Three Who Ruled: A Biographical History* (1948), which treats the early careers of Lenin, Trotsky, and Stalin. John Curtiss, *Church and State in Russia, 1900–1917* (1940), is a good guide, and Alfred Levin, *The Second Duma* (1940), a useful special study.

O. Halecki, *Poland* (rev. ed., 1955), J. Hampden Jackson, *Finland* (2d ed., 1940) and *Estonia* (1941), J. H. Wuorinen, *Nationalism in Modern Finland* (1931), and L. S. Greenberg, *The Jews in Russia* (1944), all deal with the nationalities problem within the empire.

Chapter 18 / Imperial Expansion, 1871–1914

Two classical critiques of imperialism are J. A. Hobson, *Imperialism: A Study* (3d ed., 1938), and V. I. Lenin, *Imperialism, the Highest Stage of Capitalism* (1916). More recent analyses are E. M. Winslow, *The Pattern of Imperialism* (1948), and E. Staley, *War and the Private Investor* (1935). An account of British critics of colonial expansion is to be found in A. P. Thornton, *The Imperial Idea and Its Critics* (1959); and the reflections of one of the most outspoken anti-imperialists in W. S. Blunt, *My Diaries, 1888–1914* (one-vol. ed., 1932).

The spread and the consequences of imperial activity are described in W. L. Langer, *The Diplomacy of Imperialism* (2d ed., 1951), and in Herbert Feis, *Europe, The World's Banker, 1870–1914* (1930). Notable books on empire-builders are S. G. Millin, *Rhodes* (1933); Basil Williams, *Cecil Rhodes* (1938); Margery Perham, *Lugard; The Years of Adventure, 1858–1898* (1956) and her edition of *The Diaries of Lord Lugard* (3 vols., 1959), and Roland Oliver, *Sir Harry Johnston and the Scramble for Africa* (1958).

Accounts of national expansion are A. J. P. Taylor, *Germany's First Bid for Colonies, 1884–1885* (1938), W. O. Aydelotte, *Bismarck and British Colonial Policy* (1937), M. E. Townsend, *The Rise and Fall of Germany's Colonial Empire* (1930), D. J. Dallin, *The Rise of Russia in Asia* (1950), B. H. Sumner, *Tsardom and Imperialism in the Far East and Middle East* (1942), a series of excellent studies, and E. M. Earle, *Turkey, the Great Powers and the Bagdad Railway* (1923). W. S. Churchill, *A Roving Commission* (1930), tells the story of the defeat of the Dervishes. Edgar Holt, *The Boer War* (1958), and Rayne Kruger, *Goodbye Dolly Gray* (1960), tell of the war in South Africa; and the Frank Thiess, *The Voyage of Forgotten Men* (1937), gives a dramatic description of the Russian disaster at Tsuschima.

Chapter 19 / International Politics and the Coming of War, 1890–1914

The most recent full-scale account of the origins of the war is L. Albertini, *The Origins of the War of 1914* (3 vols., 1952 ff.), by a former Italian newspaperman. Earlier ones, and still standard, are S. B. Fay, *The Origins of the World War* (2 vols., 1930), and Bernadotte Schmitt, *The Coming of the War* (2 vols., 1930). Shorter accounts are Nicholas Mansergh, *The Coming of the First World War* (1949), which lacks balance, L. Reiners, *The Lamps Went Out in Europe* (1955), readable but over-simplified, and the very useful brief account by Bernadotte Schmitt, *Triple Alliance and Triple Entente* (1934). G. P. Gooch, *Before the War* (2 vols., 1936–1938) focuses on the leading statesmen of the great powers in separate essays and is particularly incisive on Delcassé, Bülow, Aehrenthal, and Izwolsky. E. Brandenburg, *From Bismarck to the World War* (1927), is a critical account of German policy by a German historian. Aspects of Anglo-German relations are discussed in P. R. Anderson, *The Background of Anti-English Feeling in Germany* (1939), E. L. Woodward, *Great Britain and the German Navy* (1935), and A. J. Marder, *The Anatomy of British Sea Power* (1940), as well as in Hoffmann's *Anglo-German Trade Rivalry*, cited in Chapter 11. Military influence is described in J. E. Tyler, *The British Army and the Continent, 1904–1914* (1938) and Craig, *Politics of the Prussian Army*. Compare Gerhard Ritter's *The Schlieffen Plan* (1958). Studies of single crises are E. N. Anderson, *The First Moroccan Crisis* (1930), and Irma Barlow, *The Agadir Crisis* (1940). Harold Nicolson's *Portrait of a Diplomatist* (1930) gives some intimate glimpses of the British Foreign Office on the eve of war.

Chapter 20 / War and European Society, 1914–1918

The most satisfactory single-volume histories of military operations are Sir James Edmonds, *A Short History of World War I* (1951), B. H. Liddell Hart, *The War in Outline, 1914–1918* (1936), and, most recently, Cyril Falls, *The Great War, 1914–1918* (1959). These can be supplemented by L. Stallings, ed., *The First World War: A Photographic History* (1933). The number of accounts of single campaigns and of biographies and memoirs is enormous. Some notable items are Alan Moorehead, *Gallipoli* (1956); Leon Wolff, *In Flanders Fields: The 1917 Campaign* (1958); A. Duff Cooper, *Haig* (1935); Karl Tschuppik, *Ludendorff: The Tragedy of a Military Mind* (1932); and J. W. Wheeler-Bennett, *Wooden Titan: Hindenburg* (1936). C. E. Montague, *Disenchantment* (1922), and Siegfried Sassoon, *Memoirs of an Infantry Officer* (1930), convey a sense of the excitement and the disillusionment felt by participants, and Ernst Jünger, *Storm of Steel* (1929) describes the *Frontkämpfer* mentality. T. E. Lawrence, *Seven Pillars of Wisdom* (1935), an account of the Arab revolt, has become a minor classic. The home front and the social changes effected by the war are treated in Frank Chambers, *The War Behind the War* (1939); A. Mendelssohn Bartholdy, *The War and German Society* (1938), W. Chamberlain, *Industrial Relations in War-Time Great Britain* (1940), Caroline Playne, *Society at War* (2 vols., 1934), and A. Fontaine, *French Industry During the War* (1927).

Chapter 21 / The Peace Treaties and the Search for Collective Security

H. W. V. Temperley, ed., *History of the Peace Conference* (6 vols., 1920–1924) is the standard work. Organization and procedure are described in F. S. Marston, *The Peace Conference of 1919* (1944); a short impressionistic view by a participant is given by Harold Nicolson in *Peacemaking 1919* (1939), and a balanced re-assessment by P. Birdsall in *Versailles Twenty Years After* (1941). An unfavorable view of the economic terms is J. M. Keynes, *The Economic Consequences of the Peace* (1920). Its conclusions have been attacked in E. Mantoux, *The Carthaginian Peace* (1952). Other problems rising out of the treaties are discussed in C. A. Macartney, *National States and National Minorities* (1934); Alfred Cobban, *National Self-Determination* (1944); Arnold Wolfers, *Britain and France between the Wars: Conflicting Strategies of Peace* (1940); the fine study of W. M. Jordan, *Great Britain, France and the German Problem, 1918–1939* (1943), which is particularly enlightening on disarmament and arms control; Harold Nicolson, *Curzon: The Last Phase* (1939), which has good accounts of some postwar conferences; and, from the voluminous Stresemann literature, Henry L. Bretton, *Stresemann and the Revision of Versailles* (1953). The story of the League and its troubles is told in F. P. Walters, *A History of the League of Nations* (2 vols., 1952); but see also Sir Alfred Zimmern, *The League of Nations and the Rule of Law* (1936), and Viscount Cecil, *A Great Experiment: An Autobiography* (1941). Good surveys of the postwar period are G. M. Gathorne-Hardy, *A Short History of International Affairs, 1920–1939* (2d rev. ed., 1942), and E. H. Carr, *The Twenty Years Crisis* (2d ed., 1956). The most thorough diplomatic history covering the whole period, based on available printed documentary series, is the symposium edited by Gordon A. Craig and Felix Gilbert, *The Diplomats, 1919–1939* (1953).

Chapter 22 / The Russian Revolution and the West, 1917–1933

Basic surveys are Donald Treadgold's *Twentieth Century Russia* (1959) and Hugh Seton-Watson's *From Lenin to Khrushchev* (2d ed., 1960). E. H. Carr, *The Bolshevik Revolution, 1917–1923* (3 vols., 1951–1953) is the standard work, but shorter accounts are numerous and include George Vernadsky, *The Russian Revolution, 1917–1921* (1932) and Alan Moorehead, *The Russian*

Revolution (1958), popular and oversimplified. N. N. Sukhanov, *The Russian Revolution, 1917: A Personal Record*, edited by Joel Carmichael (1953) is an abridgement of the seven-volume memoir by a leading nonparty theoretician who witnessed the revolution and participated in the government. Useful biographies are David Shub's *Lenin* (1948) and Isaac Deutscher's *Stalin: A Political Biography* (1949). On Trotsky, Deutscher has also written the most satisfactory biography in *The Prophet Armed: Trotsky, 1879–1921* (1954) and *The Prophet Unarmed: Trotsky 1921–1929* (1959). The former of these has much fascinating detail on the birth and growth of the Red Army, which is also treated in D. Fedotov White, *The Red Army* (1944). John S. Reshetar, Jr., *A Concise History of the Communist Party of the Soviet Union* (1960) is a useful guide; and the international activities of the party are analyzed in Franz Borkenau, *The Communist International* (1938), and S. T. Possony, *A Century of Conflict: Communist Techniques of World Revolution* (1953). The origins of Soviet diplomacy are treated in Arno J. Mayer, *Political Origins of the New Diplomacy, 1917–1918* (1959), and its course during the first decade in Louis Fischer, *The Soviets in World Affairs* (2 vols., 1930).

Chapter 23 / The Rise of Italian Fascism

Benito Mussolini, *My Autobiography* (1938), gives the dictator's approved version of what he stood for, and Luigi Villari, *The Awakening of Italy* (1924), is an account by an ardent admirer. More balanced and critical accounts are H. W. Schneider, *Making the Fascist State* (1928), and A. Rossi [Tasca], *The Rise of Italian Fascism, 1918–1922* (1938). G. A. Borgese, *Goliath: The March of Fascism* (1938), and G. Salvemini, *The Fascist Dictatorship in Italy* (vol. I, 1938), are openly hostile. Useful analyses of the practice of fascism are H. Finer, *Mussolini's Italy* (1935); M. T. Florinsky, *Fascism and National Socialism* (1935), W. Ebenstein, *Fascist Italy* (1939), and James Meenan, *The Italian Corporative System* (1945). P. Monelli's *Mussolini* (1953) is an intimate life that sees the Duce as a petty bourgeois.

Chapter 24 / The Republican Experiment in Germany

Good surveys of the period are to be found in R. T. Clark, *The Fall of the German Democracy* (1935), and S. W. Halperin, *Germany Tried Democracy* (1946). The background and events of the revolution are given in A. J. Berlau, *The German Social Democratic Party, 1914–1921* (1949), Hans Gatzke, *Germany's Drive to the West* (1950), a history of wartime politics which shows why an explosion was inevitable, Harry Rudin, *Armistice 1918* (1944), which gives the situation at the time of the military collapse, Eric Waldman, *The Spartacist Rising of 1919 and the Crisis of the German Socialist Movement* (1958), a sound account, and J. W. Wheeler-Bennett, *Wooden Titan* (1936) and *The Nemesis of Power: The German Army in Politics, 1918–1945* (1953), which discuss the important role of the army during the revolution. On the latter subject, see also Craig, *Politics of the Prussian Army* and H. J. Gordon, Jr., *The Reichswehr and the German Republic, 1919–1926* (1957). The early political history of the republic is discussed in A. Rosenberg, *History of the German Republic* (1936), Klaus Epstein, *Matthias Erzberger and the Dilemma of German Democracy* (1959), and Count Harry Kessler, *Walther Rathenau* (1928). On Stresemann, see Antonina Vallentin, *Stresemann* (1931), and Hans Gatzke, *Stresemann and the Rearmament of Germany* (1954). Rathenau, Stresemann and Bruening are discussed in Craig, *From Bismarck to*

Adenauer. M. J. Bonn, *Wandering Scholar* (1948), throws light upon the inflation years, P. Kosok, *Modern Germany* (1933), on problems of justice and education, Klemens von Klemperer, *Germany's New Conservatism* (1957), on the intellectuals of the right, and Robert Waite, *Vanguard of Nazism: The Free Corps Movement* (1952), on one of the most pressing threats to social peace. S. Kracauer's *From Caligari to Hitler* (1947) is a psychological history of the German film that is illuminating on social relationships. The republic's relations with the Soviet Union are discussed in Gerald Freund, *Unholy Alliance* (1957), E. H. Carr, *German-Soviet Relations between the Two World Wars* (1951), and Ruth Fischer, *Stalin and German Communism* (1948), by a former German Communist leader.

Chapter 25 / The Crisis of Democracy: Central and Eastern Europe

On the depression and its impact, see J. K. Galbraith, *The Great Crash, 1929* (1955), and Paul Einzig, *The World Economic Crisis, 1929–1932* (1932).

On the rise of National Socialism, Adolf Hitler, *Mein Kampf* (1939), gives the Fuehrer's own account, which is supplemented by *Hitler's Secret Conversations,* with an introduction by H. Trevor-Roper (1953), Hermann Rauschning, *Hitler Speaks* (1939), and *The Speeches of Adolf Hitler,* edited by Norman Baynes (2 vols., 1942). On Hitler, August Kubizek, *The Young Hitler I Knew* (1955), is a fascinating account by a friend of his youth; Konrad Heiden, *The Fuehrer: Hitler's Rise to Power* (1944), is dated but still useful; and Alan Bullock, *Hitler: A Study in Tyranny* (1954), is a masterly brief biography. William Shirer's *The Rise and Fall of the Third Reich* (1960) is strongest on foreign affairs after 1938. Franz Neumann, *Behemoth: The Structure and Practise of National Socialism* (1944), is especially informative on economic organization, on which see also Jürgen Kuczynski, *Germany: Economic and Labor Conditions under Fascism* (1945), C. W. Guillebaud, *The Social Policy of Nazi Germany* (1939), and Burton H. Klein, *Germany's Economic Preparations for War* (1959). The social origins of the ruling class are analyzed in Daniel Lerner *et al., The Nazi Elite* (1951), and party organization and structure in Sigmund Neumann, *Permanent Revolution: The Total State in a World at War* (1942). Nathaniel Micklem's *National Socialism and the Roman Catholic Church* (1939) is a basic study. The best account of the growth and activities of the S. S. is G. Reitlinger's *The S. S.: Alibi of a Nation, 1922–1945* (1957).

On the countries to the east, see Hugh Seton-Watson, *Eastern Europe between the Wars, 1918–1941* (1945). The political history of Austria is told in Julius Braunthal, *The Tragedy of Austria* (1948), which includes some correspondence between Mussolini and Dollfuss, Joseph Buttinger, *In the Twilight of Socialism* (1953), valuable for its insight into socialist disunity, Malcolm Bullock, *Austria 1918–1938: A Study in Failure* (1939), and Charles Gulick's lengthy and detailed *Austria from Habsburg to Hitler* (2 vols., 1948). C. E. R. Gedye, *Betrayal in Central Europe* (1939), is an account of the failure of democracy in Austria and Czechoslovakia by a perceptive British journalist.

Chapter 26 / The Crisis of Democracy: Western Europe

British politics in the postwar period are covered clearly and concisely in D. C. Somervell, *British Politics since 1900* (1950), and social history is treated informally, but with great insight, in Robert Graves and Alan Hodge, *The Long Weekend, 1918–1939* (1939). The problems of industry and labor are discussed in G. D. H. Cole, *A History of the Labour Party from 1914* (1948), and Alan Bullock, *The Life and Times of Ernest Bevin*, vol. I, *The Trade Union Leader, 1881–1940* (1960), which includes an excellent account of the general strike. On the crisis of the 1930s, see Harold Nicolson, *King George the Fifth: His Life and Reign* (1952); R. Bassett, *Nineteen Thirty One Political Crisis* (1958); Philip Viscount Snowden, *An Autobiography* (2 vols., 1934). Perceptive biographies are G. M. Young's *Stanley Baldwin* (1952) and Keith Feiling's *Life of Neville Chamberlain* (1946). Hugh Dalton's sparkling memoirs, *Call Back Yesterday, 1887–1931* (1953) and *The Fateful Years, 1931–1945* (1957) throw much new light on the politics of these years. England's failure to rearm is discussed in John F. Kennedy, *Why England Slept* (1940).

The problems of France are analyzed in the volumes by Brogan, in E. M. Earle, ed., *Modern France* (1951), and in Alexander Werth, *The Twilight of France, 1933–1940* (1942). See also John T. Marcus, *French Socialism in the Crisis Years, 1933–1936: Fascism and the French Left* (1958), and Charles A. Micaud, *The French Right and Nazi Germany, 1933–1939* (1943). R. D. Challener, *The French Theory of the Nation in Arms, 1866–1939* (1955) treats the military problem.

Events in the lesser states are covered in works cited earlier. The background of the Spanish civil war is treated in Frank E. Manuel, *The Politics of Modern Spain* (1938), E. A. Peers, *The Spanish Tragedy* (1936), and Brenan, *Spanish Labyrinth*. A general work of importance, with essays on France, Britain, Sweden and Spain, among others, is Adolf Sturmthal, *The Tragedy of European Labor, 1918–1939* (1943).

Chapter 27 / The Road to War, 1933–1939

In addition to works cited under Chapter 21, the following should be noted: L. B. Namier, *Diplomatic Prelude, 1938–1939* (1948) and *In the Nazi Era* (1952); Elizabeth Wiskemann, *The Rome-Berlin Axis* (1949); G. Salvemini, *Prelude to World War II* (1953), which emphasizes the role of Italy; John W. Wheeler-Bennett, *Munich: Prologue to Tragedy* (1948); Max Beloff, *The Foreign Policy of the Soviet Union* (2 vols., 1947).

Chapter 28 / World War II

The diplomatic history of the war is found in W. S. Churchill, *History of the Second World War* (6 vols., 1948–1953), W. L. Langer and E. Gleason, *The Challenge to Isolation* (1952) and *The Undeclared War* (1953), which emphasize the American side, Robert E. Sherwood, *Roosevelt and Hopkins: An Intimate History* (1948), the fine volumes of Herbert Feis, *Churchill, Roosevelt, Stalin: The War They Waged and the Peace They Sought* (1957) and *Between Peace and War: The Potsdam Conference* (1960), and others too numerous to cite.

The best single-volume histories of military operations are F. J. C. Fuller, *The Second World War: A Strategical and Tactical History* (1949), and Louis Snyder, *The War, 1939–1945: A Concise History* (1960), although Chester Wilmot, *Struggle for Europe* (1952) is also notable. Strategic planning is treated in John Ehrmann, *Grand Strategy*, in the British official history of the war, edited by J. R. M. Butler (1956 ff.), and in two volumes in the series *The United States Army in World War II*, prepared in the Office of the Chief of Military History, Department of the Army: M. Matloff and E. M. Snell, *Strategic Planning for Coalition Warfare, 1941–1942* (1953), and M. Matloff, *Strategic Planning for Coalition Warfare, 1943–1944* (1959). Two interesting books on the turning points in the war are *Command Decisions* (1959), prepared by the Office of the Chief of Military History, and *The Fatal Decisions* (1956), edited by S. Freidin and W. Richardson, a series of essays by German generals. Supplementing the latter volume is B. H. Liddell Hart, *The Other Side of the Hill* (new ed., 1951), which is based on interviews with captured officers. The early campaigns of the European war are well described in Telford Taylor, *Sword and Swastika* (1952) and *The March of Conquest* (1958); the fall of France by Major General Sir Edward Spears, *Assignment to Catastrophe* (2 vols., 1954), which treats political as well as military aspects, and Col. A. Goutard, *The Fall of France* (1959), a military critique. What followed in France is the subject of two excellent studies: Robert Aron, *The Vichy Regime* (1958), and Adrienne Hystier, *Two Years of French Foreign Policy, 1940–1942* (1958). Allied policy toward Vichy is treated delicately in W. L. Langer, *Our Vichy Gamble* (1947).

The battle of Britain is the subject of Walter Ansel, *Hitler Confronts England* (1960); Peter Fleming, *Operation Sea Lion* (1957), Constantine FitzGibbon, *The Blitz* (1957), and Drew Middleton, *The Sky Suspended* (1960), which deals with air operations. Books on the sea war and the Mediterranean theater are numerous and include *A Sailor's Odyssey: The Autobiography of Admiral Viscount Cunningham* (1951); Raymond de Belot, *The Struggle for the Mediterranean* (1951); *The Rommel Papers* (1953), edited by B. H. Liddell Hart; and Desmond Young, *Rommel: The Desert Fox* (1950).

Political and military aspects of the struggle in Russia are treated in G. L. Weinberg, *Germany and the Soviet Union, 1939–1941* (1954), Alexander Dallin, *German Rule in Russia, 1941–1945* (1957), G. Reitlinger, *House Built on Sand* (1960), on conflicts of German policy in the east, and, on the tragic conclusion of all this, Heinz Schröter, *Stalingrad* (1958).

Brilliant accounts of single battles or campaigns are to be found in David Divine, *The Nine Days of Dunkirk* (1959), Fred Majdalany, *The Battle of Cassino* (1957), Gordon A. Harrison, *Cross-Channel Attack* (1951), and the magnificent account of the Normandy invasion by Cornelius Ryan, *The Longest Day* (1959).

Two interesting strategical critiques are Samuel Eliot Morison, *Strategy and Compromise* (1958), and Trumbull Higgins, *Winston Churchill and the Second Front* (1957).

Memoirs are too numerous to list.

Chapter 29 / The Reconstruction of Europe

E. P. Chase, *The United Nations in Action* (1950), C. M. Eichelberger, *U. N.: The First Ten Years* (1955), and J. Maclaurin, *The United Nations and Power Politics* (1952), are all useful. Barbara Ward, *Faith and Freedom: A Study of Western Society* (1954), and T. H. White, *Fire in the Ashes: Europe in Mid-Century* (1953), are both critical appraisals of European recovery. On France, Gordon Wright, *The Re-Shaping of the French Democracy* (1948), is still useful, while Raymond Aron, *France: Constant and Changing* (1960), and E. S. Furniss, *France: Troubled Ally* (1960), consider the state of the country under De Gaulle. On Germany, J. F. Golay's *The Founding of the Federal Republic of Germany* (1958) is enormously useful. K. W. Deutsch and L. Edinger, *Germany Rejoins the Powers* (1957), is a study of mass opinion and elites, as is Hans Speier and W. P. Davison, *West German Leadership and Foreign Policy* (1957). Paul Weymar's *Adenauer* (1957) is an official biography; and W. P. Davison's *The Berlin Blockade* (1958) a study of the first crisis over that beleaguered capital.

On Eastern Europe and the Soviet Union, in addition to works already cited, see Josef Korbel, *The Communist Subversion of Czechoslovakia* (1959), and, especially, Robert Lee Wolff, *The Balkans in Our Time* (1956), an admirable detailed survey.

Chapter 30 / Europe and the World

On NATO and the defence of Western Europe, Lord Ismay, *NATO: The First Five Years, 1949–1954* (1955), is a useful guide to organization and functions, which should be supplemented by the essays in Klaus Knorr, ed., *NATO and American Security* (1959), and the fine essay by James E. King, "NATO: Genesis, Progress, Problems" in *National Security in the Nuclear Age* (1960), edited by Gordon B. Turner and R. D. Challener.

Two books by Hugh Seton-Watson are valuable guides to world politics in the most recent period: *From Lenin to Khrushchev: The History of World Communism* (1960) and *Neither War Nor Peace: The Struggle for Power in the Post-War World* (1960), which gives a useful chronological survey and analyzes the racial and colonial problems of our time. *The Politics of Developing Nations* (1960), edited by Gabriel A. Almond and James S. Coleman, should also be consulted.

The events that led to India's independence are described in Alan Campbell-Johnson, *Mission with Mountbatten* (1953). Lucian W. Pye, *Guerrilla Communism in Malaya* (1956), and R. H. Fifield, *The Diplomacy of South East Asia, 1945–1958* (1958), discuss some of the problems of the former colonial powers in one part of the world. John C. Campbell, *Defense of the Middle East: Problems of American Policy* (1960), gives a useful review of the main events in that area since the end of the war. The Indochina crisis of 1954 and the Suez crisis of 1956 are treated in *Full Circle: The Memoirs of Anthony Eden* (1960), with bitter criticism of United States policy; and the Israeli-Egyptian fighting of the latter in S. L. A. Marshall, *Sinai Victory* (1958). K. H. Karpat's *Turkey's Politics: The Transition to a Multi-Party System* (1959) is another recent work on significant changes in the Middle East. Most of the books on the new Africa are journalistic, but the pertinent sections in Hugh Seton-Watson, *Neither War Nor Peace* (1960), give some background to the problems of different areas.

Finally, the world's preoccupation with the dangers caused by the weapons revolution is reflected in Herman Kahn, *On Thermonuclear War* (1960), which includes brilliant and original reassessments of problems and performance in the wars of 1914–1918 and 1939–1945.

INDEX

INDEX

Aaland islands, 169, 173
Abd-el-Kader, 88, 191
Abd-el-Krun, 672
Abdul Hamid II, sultan of Turkey,
272f., 416f.
Aberdeen, Earl of (George Hamilton
Gordon), 165, 166, 168, 242
Abraham Lincoln Brigade, 697
absolutism, 38ff.
Abyssinia, 340, 450, 458, 586, 691,
698, 767
Abyssinian war (1935–1936), 693–
694
Action Française, 671, 673, 676, 726
Adenauer, Konrad, 784–788
Adler, Viktor, 402
Adowa, battle of, 341, 458
Aehrenthal, Count, 447f.
Afghan wars, 313
Afghanistan, 47, 127, 453, 473, 579,
580
Africa, 356; after 1845, 821ff. *See
also* imperialism, in Africa
Agrarian party (Denmark), 778
Agrarian party (Finland), 791
agriculture, 4, 40ff., 48, 54ff., 70f., 98,
119f., 129, 153, 159, 187, 246f.,
249, 286ff., 311, 326, 409, 418f.,
435, 594, 782
Aix-la-Chapelle, Congress of (1818),
21, 76
Alain-Fournier (Henri Alain Four-
nier), 266
Alaska, 248
Albania, 24, 484, 584, 651, 705, 729f.;
after 1945, 767, 792
Albers, Hans, 640
Albert, prince of Saxe-Coburg, 118,
167, 223n.
Albert I, king of Belgium, 329, 677
Alekseev, Admiral, 428, 455
Alexander, king of Yugoslavia, 412,
651
Alexander of Battenberg, Prince, 281,
410
Alexander I, king of Serbia, 411

Alexander I, tsar of Russia, 11, 13ff.,
19, 21, 22ff., 27, 29, 32, 42f., 51,
100
Alexander II, tsar of Russia, 173,
248ff., 418, 419, 422ff., 428
Alexander III, tsar of Russia, 426f.,
436, 438
Alexander, Field Marshal Sir Harold,
748
Alfonso XII, king of Spain, 336f.
Alfonso XIII, king of Spain, 337,
679f., 780
Algerciras conference (1906), 472
Algeria, 2, 24, 72, 78, 88, 181, 191,
446, 671, 776, 804; after 1945,
820f.
Ali Pashi of Janina, 24
Allenby, Edmund, Viscount, 519, 520
Allgemeine Elektrizitäls Gesellschaft
(AEG), 290, 387
alliances and agreements: Anglo-
French entente (1904), 469; Anglo-
French-Austrian (1815), 17; Anglo-
French-Russian (1927), 27; Anglo-
Japanese (1902), 468; Anglo-Rus-
sian (1907), 472f.; Austro-Prussian
(1864), 224; Dual Alliance (1879),
277, 281, 282, 392, 476; Franco-
Belgian (1920), 547; Franco-Polish
(1924), 547; Franco-Russian
(1894), 464ff.; Grand Alliance
(1813), 11, 13; Holy Alliance
(1815), 19ff., 23f., 27, 28, 29, 38;
Little Entente, 548; Mediterranean
Agreements (1887), 280, 391;
Prusso-Italian (1866), 226; Quad-
ruple Alliance (1815), 19ff.; Three
Emperors League (1872), 271;
Three Emperors League (1881),
277f., 279; Triple Alliance (1882),
278, 280, 341, 391, 466, 469, 485;
Triple Entente, 472ff.
Alma, battle of the (1854), 170
Alsace-Lorraine, 255, 269, 271, 360,
385, 468, 677
Altenstein, Karl, Baron von Stein zum,
52
amalgamations, *see* capitalism